Paperback Oxford
Large Print Thesaurus

OXFORD
UNIVERSITY PRESS

OXFORD

UNIVERSITY PRESS

Great Clarendon Street, Oxford OX2 6DP

Oxford University Press is a department of the University of Oxford.
It furthers the University's objective of excellence in research, scholarship,
and education by publishing worldwide in

Oxford New York

Auckland Bangkok Buenos Aires Cape Town Chennai
Dar es Salaam Delhi Hong Kong Istanbul Karachi Kolkata
Kuala Lumpur Madrid Melbourne Mexico City Mumbai
Nairobi São Paulo Shanghai Taipei Tokyo Toronto

Oxford is a registered trade mark of Oxford University Press
in the UK and in certain other countries

Published in the United States
by Oxford University Press Inc., New York

© Oxford University Press 2003, 2004

Database right Oxford University Press (maker)

First published as the Oxford Mini Thesaurus 2003
First published as the Oxford Large Print Thesaurus 2004

British Library Cataloguing in Publication Data

Data available

Library of Congress Cataloging in Publication Data

Data available

ISBN 0–19–860887–X (pbk)
ISBN 0–19–860886–1 (hbk)

1

Designed by George Hammond
Typeset in Stone Serif and Arial
by Morton Word Processing Ltd
Printed in Great Britain by Clays Ltd, Bungay

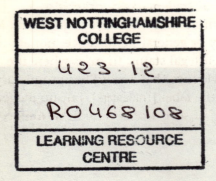

Contents

Note on trademarks and proprietary status

This thesaurus includes some words which have, or are asserted to have, proprietary status as trademarks or otherwise. Their inclusion does not imply that they have acquired for legal purposes a non-proprietary or general significance, nor any other judgement concerning their legal status. In cases where the editoral staff have some evidence that a word has proprietary status this is indicated by the label [Trademark], but no judgement concerning the legal status of such words is made or implied thereby.

Guide to the thesaurus

The *Paperback Oxford Large Print Thesaurus* is a compact and up-to-date thesaurus presented in a large, clear type. The text, which is based on that of the *Oxford Mini Thesaurus*, draws on extensive research into current English carried out by Oxford lexicographers.

Entries are divided into numbered sections according to sense. The first synonym in each section is the most useful and helps to identify its sense. Most of the synonyms given are part of standard English, but some have restricted use. These are placed at the end of each group and have the following labels in front of them:

[inf], e.g. *swig*: words normally only used in speech or informal writing.

[formal], e.g. *thereupon*: words normally only used in writing, such as official documents.

[technical], e.g. *admixture*. Words used in specific fields are labelled *Medicine, Nautical*, etc.

[poetic/literary], e.g. *plenteous*.

[dated], e.g. *rotter*.

[historical], e.g. *serfdom*: words only used today to refer to things that are no longer part of modern life.

[humorous], e.g. *posterior*.

[archaic], e.g. *aliment*: words not in use today except for old-fashioned effect.

Synonyms are also labelled if they are exclusively or mainly British, Scottish, North American, Australian, or New Zealand expressions.

The large type and generous spacing and margins make this an ideal thesaurus for adults and schoolchildren seeking a text that is clear and easy to read. It is especially suitable for people with sight problems.

In producing this thesaurus, the editors have worked closely with the Royal National Institute of the Blind in the UK, who have approved and made recommendations on all aspects of design and layout.

Abbreviations

ADJ	adjective
ADV	adverb
CONJ	conjunction
PL	plural
PREP	preposition
PRON	pronoun
Austral.	Australian
Brit.	British
N. Amer.	North American
NZ	New Zealand

Aa

abandon VERB **1** = **desert**, leave, forsake, depart from, leave behind, cast aside, jilt; [inf] run out on. **2** = **give up**, renounce, relinquish, dispense with, forgo, desist from; [formal] forswear. **3** = **yield**, surrender, give up, cede, relinquish, abdicate, deliver up, resign.
Opposites: keep.
▶ NOUN = **lack of restraint/inhibition**, wildness, impulse, impetuosity, immoderation, wantonness.
Opposites: self-control.

abandoned ADJ
1 = **deserted**, forsaken, cast aside. **2** = **reckless**, unrestrained, uninhibited, impetuous, wild, careless, wanton.

abashed ADJ
= **embarrassed**, ashamed, shamefaced, mortified, humiliated, taken aback, disconcerted, nonplussed, discomfited, discomposed, perturbed, confounded, dismayed, dumbfounded, confused, put out of countenance, discountenanced.

abbreviate VERB
= **shorten**, reduce, cut, cut short/down, contract, condense, compress, abridge, truncate, crop, shrink, constrict, summarize, abstract, precis, synopsize, digest.
Opposites: expand.

abdicate VERB **1** = **resign**, stand down, retire; [inf] quit. **2** = **give up**, renounce, relinquish, abjure, repudiate, reject, disown, waive, yield, forgo, refuse, abandon, surrender, cast aside.

abduct VERB = **kidnap**, carry off, run away/off

with, make off with, seize, hold as hostage, hold to ransom; [inf] snatch.

aberration NOUN = **deviation**, anomaly, abnormality, irregularity, variation, freak.

abhorrent ADJ = **detestable**, loathsome, hateful, hated, abominable, repellent, repugnant, repulsive, revolting, disgusting, distasteful, vile, horrible, horrid, heinous, obnoxious, odious, offensive, execrable; [inf] yucky.
Opposites: delightful, admirable.

abide VERB = **stand**, tolerate, bear, put up with, endure, accept, stomach; [formal] brook; [archaic] suffer.
■ **abide by** = **keep to**, comply with, observe, follow, obey, agree to, hold to, conform to, adhere to, stick to, stand by.

ability NOUN 1 = **talent**, competence, competency, proficiency, skill, expertise, expertness, adeptness, aptitude, dexterity, adroitness, qualification, cleverness, flair, gift, knack, savoir faire; [inf] know-how. 2 = **capacity**, capability, potential, potentiality, power, facility, faculty, propensity.
Opposites: inability.

ablaze ADJ 1 = **on fire**, burning, blazing, alight, flaming, aflame; [poetic/literary] afire. 2 = **lit up**, gleaming, glowing, aglow, illuminated, brilliant, radiant, shimmering, sparkling, flashing, incandescent.

able ADJ = **competent**, capable, talented, skilful, skilled, clever, intelligent, accomplished, gifted, proficient, fit, expert, adept, efficient, effective, qualified, adroit.
Opposites: incompetent.

abnormal ADJ = **unusual**, strange, odd, peculiar, uncommon, curious, queer, eccentric, extraordinary, unexpected, exceptional,

irregular, weird, unnatural, erratic, singular, atypical, anomalous, deviant, deviating, divergent, aberrant; [inf] oddball, off the wall, wacko.
Opposites: normal.

abolish VERB = **do away with**, put an end to, end, stop, terminate, axe, eliminate, eradicate, exterminate, destroy, annihilate, stamp out, obliterate, wipe out, extinguish, quash, expunge, extirpate, annul, cancel, invalidate, nullify, void, rescind, repeal, revoke, abrogate.
Opposites: retain.

abominable ADJ = **hateful**, loathsome, detestable, odious, obnoxious, base, despicable, contemptible, damnable, cursed, disgusting, revolting, repellent, repulsive, offensive, repugnant, abhorrent, foul, vile, wretched, horrible, nasty, disagreeable, unpleasant, execrable; [inf] yucky, god-awful.

Opposites: good, admirable.

aboriginal ADJ = **indigenous**, native, original, earliest, first, ancient, primitive, primeval, primordial, autochthonous.
Opposites: immigrant.

abortive ADJ = **failed**, unsuccessful, non-successful, vain, futile, useless, worthless, ineffective, ineffectual, fruitless, unproductive, unavailing.
Opposites: successful.

abound VERB = **be plentiful**, proliferate, teem, overflow, swarm, thrive, flourish; [inf] be two/ten a penny.

abrasive ADJ **1** = **erosive**, eroding, corrosive, chafing, rubbing, coarse, harsh. **2** = **caustic**, cutting, grating, biting, rough, harsh, irritating, sharp, nasty.
Opposites: smooth, kind, gentle.

abridge VERB = **shorten**, cut down, summarize, condense, precis, abstract, epitomize,

a

synopsize, digest,
contract, compress,
abbreviate, reduce,
decrease, diminish,
curtail, truncate, lessen,
trim.
Opposites: expand.

abridgement NOUN
1 = **summary**, synopsis,
precis, abstract, outline,
résumé, digest, cut-down
version. **2** = **shortening**,
cutting, condensation,
contraction, reduction,
summarization.
Opposites: expansion.

abrupt ADJ **1** = **sudden**,
quick, hurried, hasty,
swift, rapid, precipitate,
headlong, instantaneous,
surprising, unexpected,
unanticipated,
unforeseen. **2** = **curt**,
blunt, brusque, short,
terse, brisk, crisp, gruff,
unceremonious, rough,
rude; [inf] snappish.
Opposites: gradual,
gentle.

abscond VERB = **run away**,
bolt, clear out, flee, make
off, escape, take flight,
fly, decamp, slip/steal/
sneak away, take to one's
heels, run for it, make a
quick getaway, beat a
hasty retreat; [inf] show a
clean pair of heels,
skedaddle, skip; [Brit.
inf] do a bunk, do a
runner.

absent ADJ **1** = **away**, off,
out, gone, missing,
truant. **2** = **absent-
minded**, distracted,
preoccupied,
daydreaming, dreaming,
dreamy, faraway, blank,
empty, vacant,
inattentive, vague,
absorbed, abstracted,
musing, unheeding.
Opposites: present,
attentive.

absent-minded ADJ
= **distracted**, preoccupied,
absorbed, abstracted,
vague, inattentive,
forgetful, oblivious, in a
brown study, distrait;
[inf] scatterbrained.
Opposites: alert.

absolute ADJ
1 = **complete**, total, utter,
out-and-out, outright,
perfect, entire,
undivided, unqualified,
unadulterated, unalloyed,
downright, undiluted,
solid, consummate,

unmitigated. 2 = **fixed**, independent, non-relative, non-variable, rigid, established, set, definite. 3 = **unlimited**, unrestricted, unrestrained, unbounded, boundless, infinite, ultimate, total, supreme, unconditional, full, utter, sovereign, omnipotent.
Opposites: qualified.

absolve VERB = **forgive**, pardon, excuse, reprieve, give amnesty to, give dispensation/indulgence to, clear, set free, vindicate.

absorb VERB 1 = **soak up**, suck up, draw up/in, take up/in, blot up, mop, sponge up, sop up.
2 = **take in**, incorporate, assimilate, appropriate, co-opt. 3 = **occupy**, engage, preoccupy, captivate, engross, spellbind, rivet.

absorbent ADJ = **spongy**, sponge-like, porous, permeable, pervious, penetrable, absorptive, assimilative, receptive.
Opposites: impervious.

absorbing ADJ = **fascinating**, gripping, interesting, captivating, engrossing, riveting, spellbinding, intriguing.
Opposites: boring.

abstain VERB = **refrain**, decline, forbear, desist, hold back, keep from, refuse, renounce, avoid, shun, eschew.

abstemious ADJ = **moderate**, temperate, abstinent, self-denying, austere, sober, self-restrained, ascetic, puritanical.
Opposites: self-indulgent.

abstract ADJ 1 = **theoretical**, conceptual, notional, intellectual, metaphysical, philosophical. 2 = **non-representational**, non-realistic, unrealistic.
Opposites: actual, concrete
▶ VERB = **extract**, remove, take out/away, separate, detach, draw away, isolate.
▶ NOUN = **summary**, synopsis, precis, résumé, outline, abridgement,

condensation, digest.

abstruse ADJ = **obscure**, deep, profound, complex, hidden, esoteric, mysterious, incomprehensible, unfathomable, inscrutable, enigmatic, perplexing, puzzling, recondite, arcane, nebulous.
Opposites: comprehensible.

absurd ADJ = **ridiculous**, foolish, silly, idiotic, stupid, nonsensical, senseless, inane, crazy, ludicrous, funny, laughable, comical, preposterous, farcical, hare-brained, asinine; [Brit. inf] daft.
Opposites: sensible.

abundance NOUN = **plenty**, plentifulness, profusion, copiousness, amplitude, affluence, lavishness, bountifulness; [inf] heaps, bags, stacks, loads, tons, oodles.
Opposites: scarcity.

abundant ADJ = **plentiful**, large, great, huge, ample, well supplied, well provided, profuse, copious, lavish, bountiful, teeming, overflowing, galore.
Opposites: scarce.

abuse VERB 1 = **misuse**, misapply, misemploy, mishandle, exploit. 2 = **mistreat**, maltreat, ill-use, ill-treat, manhandle, injure, hurt, harm, beat, damage, wrong, oppress, torture. 3 = **insult**, swear at, curse, scold, rebuke, upbraid, reprove, inveigh against, revile, vilify, slander; [formal] castigate; [archaic] vituperate against.
▶ NOUN 1 = **misuse**, misapplication, misemployment, mishandling, exploitation. 2 = **mistreatment**, maltreatment, ill-use, ill-treatment, manhandling, injury, hurt, harm, beating, damage, wronging, oppression, torture. 3 = **swearing**, cursing, scolding, rebuke, upbraiding, reproval, invective, revilement, vilification, vituperation, defamation, slander,

insults, curses, expletives, swear words; [formal] castigation.

abusive ADJ = **insulting**, rude, offensive, disparaging, denigratory, derogatory, defamatory, derisive, scornful, vituperative, opprobrious, slanderous, libellous; [formal] castigating, calumniating.

abysmal ADJ = **very bad**, dreadful, awful, terrible, frightful, atrocious, deplorable, lamentable; [inf] rotten, appalling, pathetic, pitiful, woeful, lousy, dire; [Brit. inf] chronic.
Opposites: excellent.

abyss NOUN = **chasm**, gorge, ravine, canyon, crevasse, cavity, void, pit, bottomless pit, hole, gulf, depth.

academic ADJ
1 = **educational**, scholastic, instructional, pedagogical.
2 = **scholarly**, studious, literary, well read, intellectual, erudite, highbrow, learned, cultured, bookish, pedantic, donnish, cerebral; [inf] brainy.
3 = **theoretical**, hypothetical, abstract, conjectural, notional, impractical, unrealistic, speculative.
▸ NOUN = **scholar**, lecturer, don, teacher, tutor, professor, fellow.

accede
■ **accede to** = **agree to**, consent to, accept, assent to, acquiesce in, endorse, comply with, go along with, concur, grant, yield to.

accelerate VERB = **speed up**, go faster, pick up speed, hasten, hurry, quicken.
Opposites: decelerate.

accent NOUN
1 = **pronunciation**, intonation, enunciation, articulation, inflection, tone, modulation, utterance. 2 = **stress**, emphasis, accentuation, force, beat, prominence. 3 = **emphasis**, stress, prominence, importance, accentuation, priority, underlining,

underscoring.

accentuate VERB
= **emphasize**, stress, highlight, underline, draw attention to, give prominence to, heighten, point up, underscore, accent.

accept VERB 1 = **receive**, take, get, gain, obtain, acquire. 2 = **accede to**, agree to, consent to, acquiesce in, concur with, endorse, comply with, go along with, defer to, put up with, recognize, acknowledge, cooperate with, adopt, admit. 3 = **believe**, trust, credit, be convinced of, have faith in, count/rely on.
Opposites: reject.

acceptable ADJ
1 = **welcome**, agreeable, delightful, pleasing, desirable, satisfying, gratifying.
2 = **satisfactory**, good enough, adequate, passable, admissible, tolerable.
Opposites: unacceptable.

accepted ADJ
1 = **approved**, recognized, sanctioned, authorized, received, allowable, acceptable. 2 = **usual**, customary, normal, expected, standard, conventional, recognized, acknowledged, established, traditional.

access NOUN = **entry**, entrance, way in, means of entry/entrance, admittance, admission, approachability, accessibility, approach, means of approach.

accessible ADJ
1 = **attainable**, reachable, available, approachable, obtainable, achievable; [inf] get-at-able.
2 = **approachable**, available, easy-going, informal, friendly, pleasant, agreeable, obliging, congenial, affable, cordial.
Opposites: inaccessible.

accessory NOUN
1 = **attachment**, fitment, extra, addition, adjunct, appendage, supplement.
2 = **accomplice**, associate, confederate, abetter, helper, assistant, partner.

▸ ADJ = **additional**, extra, supplementary, contributory, subsidiary, ancillary, auxiliary, secondary.

accident NOUN **1** = **mishap**, misfortune, misadventure, injury, disaster, tragedy, blow, catastrophe, calamity. **2** = **crash**, smash, collision; [inf] pile-up; [Brit. inf] shunt. **3** = **chance**, mere chance, fluke, fate, twist of fate, fortune, good fortune, luck, good luck, fortuity, hazard.

accidental ADJ = **chance**, unintentional, unintended, inadvertent, unexpected, unforeseen, unlooked for, fortuitous, unanticipated, unplanned, uncalculated, unpremeditated, unwitting, adventitious. **Opposites:** intentional.

acclaim VERB = **applaud**, cheer, celebrate, salute, welcome, approve, honour, praise, commend, hail, extol, eulogize, exalt; [formal] laud.

▸ NOUN = **applause**, ovation, praise, commendation, approval, approbation, homage, tribute, extolment, cheers, congratulations, plaudits, bouquets, salutes, eulogies; [formal] laudation.

acclimatize VERB = **adjust**, adapt, accustom, get used, accommodate, become seasoned, familiarize oneself, become inured.

accommodate VERB **1** = **put up**, house, cater for, board, lodge, shelter, give someone a roof over their head, harbour, billet. **2** = **help**, assist, aid, oblige, meet the needs/ wants of, cater for, fit in with, satisfy.

accommodating ADJ = **obliging**, cooperative, helpful, considerate, amenable, unselfish, willing, polite, kindly, hospitable, kind, friendly, agreeable.

accommodation NOUN = **housing**, lodging, board, shelter, place of residence, house, billet,

lodgings, quarters;
[inf] digs, pad.

accompany VERB
1 = escort, go with, go along with, keep someone company, attend, usher, show, see, conduct, squire, chaperone, convoy.
2 = occur with, go with, go together with, go hand in hand with, coexist with, supplement.

accomplice NOUN
= partner in crime, associate, accessory, confederate, collaborator, abetter, henchman, fellow conspirator;
[inf] sidekick.

accomplish VERB
= achieve, carry out, fulfil, perform, attain, realize, succeed in, bring off, bring about, effect, execute;
[formal] effectuate.
Opposites: fail in.

accomplished ADJ
= skilled, skilful, expert, gifted, talented, proficient, adept, masterly, polished, practised, capable, able, competent, experienced, professional, deft, consummate.
Opposites: incompetent.

accomplishment NOUN
= talent, ability, skill, gift, attainment, achievement, capability, proficiency.

accord VERB **= agree**, concur, fit, correspond, tally, match, conform, harmonize, suit, be in tune.
Opposites: disagree, differ.
▶ NOUN **= agreement**, consensus, unanimity, harmony, rapport, unison, amity;
[formal] concord.
Opposites: disagreement.

account NOUN
1 = description, report, statement, record, narration, narrative, story, recital, explanation, tale, chronicle, history, relation, version.
2 = financial record, ledger, balance sheet, financial statement, books. **3 = bill**, invoice, reckoning, tally, charges, debts. **4 = importance**, consequence,

significance.

accumulate VERB
1 = **gather**, pile up, build up, collect, amass, increase, augment, cumulate, accrue.
2 = **amass**, gather, collect, stockpile, pile up, heap up, store, hoard.

accumulation NOUN
= **pile**, heap, build-up, mass, collection, store, supply, stockpile, hoard, stock, conglomeration, gathering, growth.

accurate ADJ = **correct**, right, true, exact, precise, authentic, factual, truthful, faultless, reliable, scrupulous, faithful, meticulous, careful, sound, sure, certain, strict; [Brit. inf] spot on, bang on; [formal] veracious.
Opposites: inaccurate.

accusation NOUN
= **charge**, allegation, indictment, complaint, summons, arraignment, citation, denunciation, imputation; [N. Amer.] impeachment.

accuse VERB **1** = **charge**, indict, bring/prefer charges against, make allegations against, arraign, prosecute, summons, cite; [N. Amer.] impeach.
2 = **blame**, hold responsible, denounce, censure, condemn, incriminate, tax; [inf] point the finger at.
Opposites: defend.

accustomed ADJ
1 = **usual**, customary, habitual, regular, established, normal, conventional, expected, routine, familiar, common, fixed, traditional, ordinary, set, prevailing; [poetic/literary] wonted. **2** = **used to**, familiar with, habituated, adapted.
■ **become/get accustomed** = see **adapt**.

ache NOUN = **pain**, soreness, discomfort, hurt, distress, throbbing, twinge, pang, suffering, anguish, smart.
▶ VERB = **hurt**, be sore, be painful, smart, sting, pound, throb, suffer.

a **achieve** VERB **1** = **succeed in**, accomplish, manage, do successfully, carry out, complete, attain, bring off, effect, perform, conclude, finish, discharge, fulfil, execute, engineer, consummate. **2** = **gain**, obtain, get, acquire, earn, reach, win, score, procure.

acid ADJ **1** = **sharp**, tart, sour, vinegary, tangy, stinging. **2** = **caustic**, acerbic, sharp, sardonic, scathing, trenchant, vitriolic.
Opposites: sweet, pleasant.

acknowledge VERB **1** = **admit**, concede, accept, agree, confirm, allow, confess, grant, own, affirm, profess. **2** = **greet**, salute, address, hail, say hello to. **3** = **answer**, reply to, respond to, react to, return.
Opposites: deny, ignore.

acquaint VERB = **familiarize**, make familiar, make aware of, inform of, advise of, notify of, apprise of, let know, get up to date, brief, prime; [inf] fill in on.

acquaintance NOUN **1** = **contact**, associate, colleague. **2** = **association**, relationship, contact. **3** = **familiarity**, awareness, knowledge, experience, understanding, grasp.

acquire VERB = **get**, obtain, buy, purchase, procure, come by, pick up, receive, earn, secure, appropriate; [inf] get hold of, get one's hands on.
Opposites: lose.

acquisition NOUN = **possession**, gain, purchase, property, prize, addition, accession; [inf] buy.
Opposites: loss.

acquit VERB = **clear**, find innocent, declare innocent, absolve, set free, free, release, liberate, discharge, reprieve, vindicate, exonerate; [inf] let off; [formal] exculpate.
Opposites: condemn.
■ **acquit oneself** = *see* **behave** (**1**).

a

acrid ADJ = **pungent**, sharp, bitter, harsh, acid, caustic.

acrimonious ADJ = **bitter**, angry, rancorous, caustic, acerbic, scathing, sarcastic, acid, harsh, sharp, cutting, virulent, spiteful, vicious, vitriolic, hostile, venomous, bad-tempered, ill-natured, malicious, waspish.
Opposites: good-natured.

act VERB 1 = **do something**, take action, move, react, take steps. 2 = **behave**, carry on, conduct oneself; [formal] comport oneself. 3 = **perform**, play, appear as, enact, portray, represent, assume the character of, overact; [inf] tread the boards. = *See also* **pretend** (1). 4 = **function**, work, operate, have an effect, take effect, serve.
▶ NOUN 1 = **deed**, action, feat, exploit, undertaking, effort, enterprise, achievement, step, move, operation, proceeding. 2 = **law**, statute, bill, decree, order, enactment, edict. 3 = **performance**, routine, number, turn, item, sketch.

acting ADJ = **temporary**, provisional, interim, stopgap, substitute, stand-in, fill-in, surrogate, deputy, pro tem.
Opposites: permanent.

action NOUN 1 = **deed**, act, feat, exploit, undertaking, process, enterprise, measure, step, effort, endeavour, proceeding, performance, work. 2 = **activity**, movement, motion, exertion, drama, liveliness, excitement, vigour, energy, vitality, initiative, exercise, enterprise. 3 = **story**, events, incidents, happenings. 4 = **mechanism**, works, operation, functioning, working.

activate VERB = **set off**, set in motion, operate, start, trigger, initiate, actuate, energize, trip.

active ADJ 1 = **energetic**, lively, sprightly, spry, mobile, vigorous, vital, dynamic, sporty, busy,

occupied; [inf] on the go, full of beans. **2** = **hard-working**, busy, industrious, diligent, tireless, effective, enterprising, involved, enthusiastic, keen, committed, devoted, zealous. **3** = **operative**, working, functioning, functional, operating, operational, in action, in operation, live; [inf] up and running.
Opposites: inactive.

activity NOUN
1 = **movement**, action, bustle, motion, excitement, liveliness, commotion, energy, industry, hurly-burly, animation, life, hustle, stir. **2** = **hobby**, pastime, interest, task, job, venture, project, occupation, undertaking, scheme, pursuit. = *See also* **work** NOUN.

actual ADJ = **real**, authentic, genuine, true, factual, verified, realistic, bona fide, definite, existing, current, legitimate, indisputable, unquestionable, tangible, certain, truthful, in existence, living, confirmed, corporeal.
Opposites: imaginary.

acute ADJ **1** = **serious**, urgent, pressing, grave, critical, crucial, precarious. **2** = **severe**, critical, intense. **3** = **sharp**, piercing, intense, severe, extreme, fierce, excruciating, cutting, sudden, violent, shooting, keen, exquisite, racking. **4** = **intelligent**, shrewd, sharp, quick, penetrating. = *See also* **clever** (**1**).
Opposites: mild, chronic, dull.

adapt VERB **1** = **get used**, adjust, get accustomed, habituate oneself, acclimatize, reconcile oneself, attune, accommodate, become hardened, become inured. **2** = **alter**, change, modify, adjust, convert, remodel, transform, rebuild, remake, refashion, reshape, reconstruct, tailor.

add VERB = **attach**, append, put on, affix, tack on,

include, combine.
Opposites: subtract.
■ **add to** = *see* **increase**
VERB (**2**).
■ **add up** = **total**, count,
reckon, tot up.

addict NOUN = **abuser**,
user; [inf] junkie, druggy,
— freak, —head.

addiction NOUN
= **dependency**, craving,
habit, compulsion,
obsession, enslavement,
dedication, devotion.

addition NOUN
1 = **increase**,
enlargement, expansion,
supplement, extension,
increment,
augmentation, gain,
adjunct, accessory,
addendum, appendage,
development, additive,
appendix, postscript,
afterthought,
attachment, annex,
amplification, accession;
[technical] admixture.
2 = **adding up**, counting,
totalling, calculation,
reckoning, computation;
[inf] totting up.
Opposites: reduction,
subtraction.

additional ADJ = **extra**,
more, further, added,
supplementary, other,
new, fresh, increased,
spare, supplemental.

address NOUN **1** = **location**,
whereabouts, place,
home, house, residence,
situation;
[formal] dwelling, abode,
domicile. **2** = **speech**,
talk, lecture, oration,
sermon, homily, diatribe,
discourse, disquisition,
harangue; [poetic/
literary] philippic.
▶ VERB **1** = **speak to**, talk to,
lecture, give a speech to,
declaim to, harangue,
preach to. **2** = **greet**, speak
to, talk to, engage in
conversation, approach,
accost, hail, salute;
[inf] buttonhole. **3** = **direct**,
label, inscribe,
superscribe.
■ **address oneself to**
= *see* **tackle** VERB (**1**).

adept ADJ = **expert**,
proficient, clever,
accomplished, talented,
gifted, practised,
masterly. = *See also*
skilful.
Opposites: inept.

a

adequate ADJ
1 = **tolerable**, passable, all right, average, satisfactory, competent, unexceptional, acceptable, unexceptionable, mediocre, good enough; [inf] OK, so-so.
2 = **competent**, up to, capable, able, qualified.
Opposites: inadequate.

adhere VERB = **stick**, cling, bond, attach, bind, fuse.

adherent NOUN
= **supporter**, follower, devotee, disciple, advocate, fan, upholder, defender, stalwart, partisan.

adjacent ADJ
= **neighbouring**, adjoining, bordering, next, close, next door, touching, attached, abutting, contiguous.

adjourn VERB = **break off**, interrupt, discontinue, postpone, put off, delay, defer, shelve, suspend, prorogue.

adjournment NOUN
= **interruption**, break, breaking off, postponement, pause, delay, deferral, deferment, recess, suspension, prorogation.

adjust ADJ 1 = **get used to**, become accustomed to, adapt, reconcile oneself, accommodate, acclimatize, habituate oneself, conform.
2 = **modify**, alter, adapt, fix, repair, regulate, put right, put in working order, rectify, change, arrange, amend, set to rights, tune, rearrange, tailor, balance, vary, position, set, refashion, remake, remodel, reorganize.

administer VERB
1 = **manage**, direct, run, administrate, control, organize, supervise, oversee, preside over, superintend, regulate, govern, conduct, rule, command. 2 = **give**, dispense, issue, provide, supply, treat with, hand out, deal out, distribute, measure out, dole out.
3 = **dispense**, provide, implement, carry out, mete out, distribute, disburse, bestow,

execute.

admirable ADJ
= **commendable**, worthy, praiseworthy, laudable, good, excellent, fine, exemplary, wonderful, great, marvellous, enjoyable, respectable, creditable, pleasing, meritorious, first-rate, first-class, masterly, awe-inspiring, deserving, estimable.
Opposites: deplorable.

admiration NOUN
= **approval**, regard, respect, praise, appreciation, commendation, approbation, esteem, awe, veneration, honour.
Opposites: contempt.

admire VERB = **approve of**, like, respect, appreciate, praise, have a high opinion of, look up to, think highly of, applaud, wonder at, esteem, value, commend, sing someone's praises, love, honour, idolize, revere, venerate, hero-worship, marvel at, be delighted by; [formal] laud. = *See also* **love** VERB (**1**).

Opposites: hate.

admissible ADJ
= **allowable**, allowed, accepted, permitted, permissible, tolerable, justifiable.

admission NOUN
1 = **admittance**, entry, entrance, access, entrée, ingress.
2 = **acknowledgement**, acceptance, confession, declaration, disclosure, profession, divulgence, utterance, avowal, revelation, affirmation.
Opposites: denial.

admit VERB 1 = **allow in**, let in, permit entry to, grant access to.
2 = **acknowledge**, confess, reveal, concede, own up to, declare, make known, accept, disclose, agree, profess, recognize, allow.
Opposites: exclude, deny.

admonish VERB = *see*
reprimand VERB.

adolescent ADJ
= **teenage**, youthful, pubescent, immature, childish, juvenile, puerile, girlish, boyish.
▶ NOUN = **teenager**, youth, youngster, young person,

juvenile.

adopt VERB 1 = **take in**, foster, take care of, take under one's wing.
2 = **accept**, endorse, approve, support, back, sanction, ratify.
3 = **embrace**, assume, take on, espouse, appropriate, affect.

adore VERB = **love**, worship, dote on, cherish, idolize, adulate, revere, venerate, honour, glorify. = *See also* **admire**.
Opposites: hate.

adorn VERB = **decorate**, embellish, ornament, enhance, beautify, grace, emblazon, bedeck, trim.

adrift ADJ 1 = **drifting**, unmoored, unanchored, floating. 2 = **unfastened**, untied, loose, detached.
3 = **wrong**, amiss, astray, awry, off course.

adult ADJ = **fully grown**, grown up, mature, fully developed, of age, nubile.
Opposites: immature.

adulterate VERB
= **contaminate**, make impure, taint, pollute, debase, degrade, doctor, corrupt, alloy, defile, dilute, thin, water down, weaken.

advance VERB 1 = **move forward**, move ahead, go forward, proceed, forge ahead, gain ground, make headway, approach, push forward, press on, press ahead, push on, bear down, make strides.
2 = **progress**, move forward, go ahead, improve, flourish, thrive, prosper. 3 = **speed up**, bring forward, accelerate, step up, expedite, forward, hurry, hasten.
4 = **put forward**, suggest, present, submit, propose, introduce, offer, proffer, adduce, furnish. 5 = **lend**, pay in advance, loan, provide, supply, proffer.
Opposites: retreat.
▸ NOUN = **development**, breakthrough, discovery, finding, progress, improvement, invention.

advanced ADJ
1 = **sophisticated**, modern, latest, up to date. 2 = **progressive**, innovative, original,

new, forward-looking, inventive, contemporary, revolutionary, experimental, novel, avant-garde, pioneering, trendsetting, ahead of the times; [inf] way-out. **3** = **higher-level**, complex, complicated, difficult, hard. **4** = **mature**, grown up, precocious, sophisticated, well developed.
Opposites: backward.

advantage NOUN
1 = **benefit**, good point, asset, gain, convenience, profit, use, boon, blessing. **2** = **superiority**, dominance, edge, upper hand, whip hand, trump card.
Opposites: disadvantage.
■ **take advantage of** = *see* **exploit** VERB (**2**).

advantageous ADJ
1 = **beneficial**, helpful, useful, of benefit, profitable, valuable, worthwhile.
2 = **favourable**, dominant, superior, powerful.

adventure NOUN
1 = **exploit**, deed, feat, experience, incident, escapade, venture, undertaking, operation. **2** = **excitement**, danger, hazard, risk, peril, precariousness.

adventurous ADJ
1 = **daring**, brave, bold, courageous, heroic, enterprising, intrepid, daredevil, valiant, venturesome, reckless, rash. **2** = **risky**, dangerous, exciting, hazardous, challenging, perilous, precarious.
Opposites: cautious, boring, uneventful.

adverse ADJ
1 = **unfavourable**, unfortunate, harmful, disadvantageous, inauspicious, unlucky, detrimental, untoward, prejudicial, unpropitious, uncongenial, deleterious, contrary. **2** = **hostile**, unfriendly, antagonistic, negative, disapproving, derogatory, attacking, uncomplimentary, opposing, unkind, unsympathetic, hurtful, unfavourable, censorious, inimical.
Opposites: favourable.

adversity NOUN
= **misfortune**, bad luck, trouble, disaster, sorrow, misery, hard times, tribulation, woe, affliction.

advertise VERB
= **publicize**, promote, market, display, tout, make known, call attention to, merchandise, flaunt, show off, announce, promulgate, proclaim; [inf] push, puff, plug, hype.

advertisement NOUN
= **commercial**, promotion, display, publicity, announcement, notice, circular, handout, small ad, leaflet, placard; [inf] ad, plug, puff, blurb; [Brit. inf] advert.

advice NOUN = **guidance**, help, counsel, suggestions, recommendations, hints, pointers, tips, ideas, views, warnings, caution, admonition.

advisable ADJ = **prudent**, recommended, sensible, appropriate, expedient, judicious, politic. = See also **wise** (2).
Opposites: inadvisable.

advise VERB = **give guidance**, guide, counsel, enjoin, offer suggestions, caution, instruct, urge, exhort, advocate, warn, encourage, commend, admonish.

■ **advise someone of** = see **inform** (1).

advocacy NOUN = **support**, backing, promotion, argument for, advising, recommendation.

advocate NOUN
= **supporter**, proponent, backer, spokesman, exponent, apologist.
▶ VERB = **advise**, recommend, support, back, argue for, urge, favour, endorse, champion.

aesthetic ADJ = **artistic**, tasteful, beautiful, sensitive, in good taste, cultivated.

affable ADJ = **friendly**, agreeable, pleasant, amiable, good-natured, civil, courteous.
Opposites: unfriendly.

affair NOUN 1 = **event**, occurrence, episode, incident, happening, circumstance, case, proceeding, occasion, matter, issue, subject, topic. 2 = **business**, concern, activity, responsibility, province, preserve, problem, worry; [Brit. inf] lookout. 3 = **relationship**, love affair, romance, involvement, liaison, intrigue, amour, attachment; [Brit. inf] carry-on.

affect¹ VERB 1 = **have an effect on**, influence, act on, change, have an impact on, modify, shape, transform. 2 = **move**, touch, upset, trouble, disturb, concern, perturb, stir, agitate, hit, grieve.

affect² VERB = **adopt**, assume, feign, sham, simulate; [inf] put on. = See also **pretend** (1).

affectation NOUN = **pretence**, affectedness, pretentiousness, pretension, posturing, artificiality. = See also pretence (3).

affected ADJ = **unnatural**, contrived, put on, artificial, mannered, insincere, studied. = See also **pretentious**. Opposites: natural.

affecting ADJ = **moving**, touching, heart-rending, poignant, upsetting, pathetic.

affection NOUN = **fondness**, liking, love, warmth, devotion, attachment, tenderness, friendship, partiality, amity, warm feelings; [inf] soft spot. = See also **love** NOUN (1). Opposites: dislike, hatred.

affectionate ADJ = **fond**, loving, caring, devoted, tender, doting, warm, friendly. = See also **loving**. Opposites: cold.

affinity NOUN 1 = **liking**, fondness, closeness, relationship, kinship, like-mindedness, rapport, empathy, understanding; [inf] chemistry. 2 = **likeness**, closeness, similarity, resemblance, correspondence, similitude.

affirm VERB = **state**, assert, declare, maintain, attest, avow, swear, pronounce, proclaim; [formal] aver.
Opposites: deny.

affirmation NOUN = **statement**, assertion, declaration, confirmation, proclamation, pronouncement, oath, attestation; [formal] averment.
Opposites: denial.

affirmative ADJ = **assenting**, agreeing, concurring, consenting, positive, approving.
Opposites: negative.

afflict VERB = **trouble**, burden, distress, affect, try, worry, bother, harm, oppress, pain, hurt, torture, plague, rack, torment, beset, harass, wound, bedevil, grieve, pester, annoy, vex.

affluence NOUN = **wealth**, prosperity, riches, fortune, substance, resources.
Opposites: poverty.

affluent ADJ = **rich**, wealthy, prosperous, well off, well-to-do, moneyed, opulent, comfortable; [inf] well heeled, loaded.
Opposites: poor.

afford VERB 1 = **pay for**, find enough for, have the means for, spare the price of, meet the expense of, run to, stretch to, spare. 2 = *See* **provide** (2).

afraid ADJ 1 = **frightened**, scared, terrified, fearful, apprehensive, terror-stricken, timid, intimidated, nervous, alarmed, anxious, trembling, cowardly, panicky, panic-stricken, uneasy, agitated, pusillanimous, faint-hearted, reluctant, craven, diffident, daunted, cowed, timorous; [inf] chicken, yellow, jittery; [Brit. inf] windy. 2 = **sorry**, apologetic, regretful, unhappy.
Opposites: brave, confident.

aftermath NOUN = **after-effects**, consequences, repercussions, results, outcome, end result, upshot.

afterwards ADV = **later**, subsequently, then, next, after; [formal] thereupon. **Opposites:** beforehand.

age NOUN **1** = **maturity**, old age, advancing years, seniority, elderliness; [Biology] senescence. **2** = **era**, epoch, period, time, generation. **3** = **a long time**, an eternity, aeons, hours, days, months, years; [Brit. inf] yonks.
▸ VERB = **grow old**, mature, grow up, ripen, develop, mellow, wither, fade.

aged ADJ = **old**, elderly, ancient, long in the tooth, superannuated; [Biology] senescent; [inf] getting on, over the hill. **Opposites:** young, youthful.

agent NOUN = **representative**, middleman, go-between, broker, negotiator, intermediary, mediator, emissary, envoy, proxy, factor, trustee, delegate, spokesperson, spokesman, spokeswoman, executor.

aggravate VERB **1** = **make worse**, worsen, exacerbate, intensify, inflame, exaggerate, make more serious, compound, increase, heighten, magnify, add to. **2** = *See* **annoy**. **Opposites:** alleviate, improve.

aggressive ADJ **1** = **hostile**, violent, belligerent, combative, attacking, destructive, quarrelsome, warlike, antagonistic, provocative, pugnacious, bellicose, bullying, contentious, jingoistic, militant. **2** = **assertive**, forceful, pushy, insistent, vigorous, dynamic, bold, enterprising, energetic, zealous, pushing; [inf] go-ahead. **Opposites:** peaceable, retiring.

aggrieved ADJ = **resentful**, affronted, indignant, angry, distressed, piqued, disturbed; [inf] peeved.

agile ADJ = **nimble**, lithe, fit, supple, sprightly, graceful, acrobatic, lively,

spry, adroit, deft, quick-moving, limber, in good condition; [inf] nippy.
Opposites: clumsy, stiff.

agitate VERB **1** = **upset**, worry, fluster, perturb, disturb, disconcert, trouble, alarm, work up, ruffle, disquiet, unsettle, unnerve, rouse, excite, discomfit, confuse, shake up; [inf] rattle. **2** = **stir**, whisk, beat, shake, toss, work, churn, froth up, ruffle, ferment.
Opposites: calm.

agitator NOUN = **troublemaker**, rabble-rouser, agent provocateur, instigator, firebrand, fomenter, revolutionary, demagogue.

agonizing ADJ = **excruciating**, painful, acute, harrowing, searing, unendurable, torturous.

agony NOUN = **suffering**, anguish, hurt, torment, torture, distress. = *See also* **pain**.

agree VERB **1** = **concur**, be of the same mind, comply, see eye to eye.

2 = **match**, correspond, accord, conform, coincide, fit, tally.
3 = **consent to**, accept, assent to, approve, allow, admit, acquiesce in.
Opposites: disagree.

agreeable ADJ = **pleasing**, enjoyable, nice, delightful, acceptable, likable, to one's liking, pleasurable. = *See also* **pleasant**.
Opposites: disagreeable.

agreement NOUN
1 = **accord**, concurrence, harmony, accordance, unity, assent; [formal] concord.
2 = **contract**, deal, compact, settlement, pact, bargain, treaty, covenant, concordat.
3 = **correspondence**, similarity, conformity, match, harmony, accordance, coincidence.
Opposites: disagreement.

agricultural ADJ
1 = **farming**, farm, agrarian, pastoral, rural.
2 = **farmed**, cultivated, planted, productive, tilled.
Opposites: urban.

agriculture NOUN
= **farming**, cultivation,
tillage, husbandry,
agronomy, agronomics,
agribusiness;
[Brit.] crofting.

aground ADV & ADJ
= **grounded**, beached,
ashore, shipwrecked, on
the bottom, stranded,
stuck, high and dry.
Opposites: afloat.

aid NOUN 1 = **help**,
assistance, support,
succour, encouragement,
a helping hand,
cooperation.
2 = **contribution**, gift,
donation, subsidy, loan,
debt remission, relief,
sponsorship, backing,
grant; [historical] alms.
Opposites: hindrance.
▶ VERB 1 = **help**, assist,
support, succour, lend a
hand, sustain, second.
2 = **facilitate**, speed up,
hasten, help, encourage,
expedite, promote,
contribute to, sustain.
Opposites: hinder.

ailing ADJ = **unwell**, sick,
poorly, sickly,
indisposed, infirm;
[inf] under the weather.

= See also **ill** ADJ (**1**).
Opposites: healthy.

ailment NOUN = **illness**,
disease, sickness,
disorder, complaint,
malady, infirmity,
affliction. = See also
illness.

aim VERB 1 = **point**, direct,
take aim, train, sight,
focus, address, zero in
on. 2 = **intend**, mean,
resolve, wish, aspire,
want, plan, propose,
seek, try, strive,
endeavour.
▶ NOUN = **ambition**,
objective, object, end,
goal, purpose, intention,
intent, plan, target,
hope, aspiration, desire,
wish, design, direction,
focus, dream,
destination.

aimless ADJ 1 = **pointless**,
purposeless, futile,
undirected, goalless,
objectless.
2 = **purposeless**, drifting,
wandering, undirected,
unambitious,
undisciplined, wayward.
Opposites: purposeful.

air NOUN 1 = **sky**,
atmosphere, airspace;

[poetic/literary] heavens, ether. **2 = oxygen**, breath of air, breeze, draught, puff of wind; [poetic/literary] zephyr.
3 = appearance, impression, look, mood, atmosphere, quality, feeling, ambience, character, flavour, demeanour, effect, manner, bearing, tone, aspect, mien.
4 = affectations, pretension, pretentiousness, affectedness, airs and graces, posing, posturing.
5 = melody, tune, song, theme, strain.
▶ VERB **1 = express**, make known, voice, publicize, broadcast, give vent to, publish, communicate, reveal, proclaim, divulge, circulate, disseminate, vent, disclose.
2 = ventilate, aerate, freshen, refresh.

airless ADJ **= stuffy**, close, stifling, suffocating, muggy, unventilated, oppressive, sultry.
Opposites: airy.

airy ADJ **1 = well ventilated**, fresh, spacious, uncluttered, light, bright.
2 = nonchalant, casual, light-hearted, breezy, cheerful, jaunty, flippant, blithe, insouciant; [dated] gay.
Opposites: stuffy, studied.

aisle NOUN **= passage**, passageway, gangway, walkway, corridor, lane, alley.

akin ADJ **= related to**, allied with, connected with, corresponding to, similar to.
Opposites: unrelated, different.

alacrity NOUN **= readiness**, promptness, eagerness, enthusiasm, willingness, haste, swiftness.
Opposites: reluctance, sluggishness.

alarm NOUN **1 = fear**, apprehension, anxiety, uneasiness, distress, consternation, panic, fright, trepidation, disquiet. = *See also* **fear** NOUN (**1**). **2 = warning sound**, siren, alert, alarm bell/signal, danger/distress signal;

[archaic] tocsin.
▶ VERB = **frighten**, scare, panic, terrify, unnerve, agitate, distress, disturb, startle, shock, upset, worry; [Brit. inf] put the wind up.
Opposites: reassure.

alcohol NOUN = **drink**, liquor, spirits; [inf] booze, hard stuff, the demon drink, the bottle, grog, tipple; [Brit. inf] bevvy.

alcoholic ADJ = **intoxicating**, strong, inebriating, hard; [formal] spirituous.
Opposites: soft.
▶ NOUN = **drunkard**, drunk, hard/heavy drinker, dipsomaniac, problem drinker, inebriate, tippler, sot, imbiber; [inf] boozer, lush, dipso, wino, alky.
Opposites: teetotaller.

alert ADJ 1 = **aware**, alive to, watchful, vigilant, observant, wary, wide awake, on one's guard, attentive, on the alert, sharp-eyed, heedful, circumspect, on the lookout, on one's toes.
2 = **sharp**, quick, bright, perceptive, keen, lively, wide awake; [inf] on the ball, quick off the mark.
Opposites: inattentive, slow, absent-minded.
▶ VERB = **warn**, make aware, caution, advise, forewarn, inform, apprise, notify; [inf] tip off.

alibi NOUN = **excuse**, defence, justification, explanation, pretext, plea, vindication.

alien ADJ = **foreign**, strange, unfamiliar, outlandish, remote, exotic, extraterrestrial.
Opposites: familiar.
▶ NOUN = **foreigner**, stranger, outsider, newcomer, extraterrestrial.
Opposites: native.

alight¹ VERB = **get off**, come down, get down, dismount, disembark, come to rest, land, descend, touch down, settle, perch.

alight² ADJ 1 = **on fire**, burning, ablaze, blazing, lighted, lit, aflame. 2 = **lit up**, shining, bright, illuminated, brilliant.

align VERB 1 = **line up**, arrange in line, put in order, straighten, rank, range. 2 = **ally**, associate, affiliate, cooperate, side, join, unite, combine, join forces.

alike ADJ = **similar**, like, resembling, indistinguishable, identical, interchangeable, corresponding, matching, the same, twin, uniform. Opposites: different.
► ADV = **similarly**, just the same, identically, in a like manner, in the same way. Opposites: differently.

alive ADJ 1 = **living**, breathing, live, animate; [inf] alive and kicking, in the land of the living; [archaic] quick. 2 = see **alert**. Opposites: dead.

allay VERB = **lessen**, diminish, reduce, alleviate, calm, assuage, ease, quell, relieve, appease, moderate, mitigate, check, lull, subdue, soothe.

Opposites: increase, stimulate.

allegation NOUN = **charge**, accusation, claim, assertion, statement, declaration, testimony, deposition, avowal.

allege VERB = **claim**, declare, state, profess, assert, maintain, affirm, avow, attest, contend, lay a charge; [formal] aver.

alleged ADJ = **supposed**, claimed, declared, so-called, professed, stated.

allegiance NOUN = **loyalty**, faithfulness, adherence, fidelity, devotion, duty, obedience; [historical] fealty.

allergic ADJ 1 = **hypersensitive**, sensitive, sensitized, susceptible. 2 = **averse**, opposed, antagonistic, disinclined, hostile, antipathetic, loath.

alleviate VERB = **reduce**, lessen, diminish, relieve, ease, allay, mitigate, assuage, abate, palliate, lighten, soothe, subdue, temper, ameliorate, check, quell, soften, make lighter.

Opposites: aggravate.

alliance NOUN
= **association**, union,
coalition, partnership,
affiliation, agreement,
league, confederation,
federation, relationship,
connection, pact, bond,
understanding, treaty,
marriage, compact,
concordat, syndicate,
cartel, consortium, bloc,
combination, covenant,
entente.

allot VERB = **allocate**,
assign, apportion,
distribute, give out, share
out, award, dispense,
deal out, ration, divide
up, mete out, dole out,
dish out.

allow VERB **1** = **permit**, let,
give permission to,
authorize, consent to,
sanction, approve,
license, enable; [inf] give
the go-ahead to, give the
green light to. **2** = **admit**,
acknowledge, concede,
recognize, grant, confess.
Opposites: forbid, deny.

allowance NOUN **1** = **quota**,
allocation, ration,
portion, share.
2 = **payment**, subsidy,

remittance, grant,
contribution. **3** = **rebate**,
discount, deduction,
concession, reduction.
■ **make allowances**
1 = **take into account**,
bear in mind, have
regard to. **2** = **excuse**,
make excuses, forgive,
pardon.

alloy NOUN = **mixture**,
blend, amalgam,
combination, compound,
composite;
[technical] admixture.

allude
■ **allude to** = **refer to**,
mention, speak of, touch
on, make an allusion to,
cite, suggest, hint at;
[formal] advert to.

allure VERB = **attract**,
fascinate, charm, seduce,
captivate, enchant,
bewitch, beguile, tempt,
magnetize, lure, entice,
cajole, draw, inveigle.

allusion NOUN = **reference**,
mention, suggestion,
citation, hint,
intimation.

ally NOUN = **associate**,
colleague, partner, friend,
supporter, collaborator,
confederate, accomplice,

abetter, accessory.
Opposites: enemy,
opponent.

▶ VERB = **join**, unite, join
forces, combine, merge,
go into partnership, band
together, form an
alliance, team up, link
up, affiliate, be in league,
cooperate, collaborate,
side.

almighty ADJ 1 = **all-
powerful**, supreme, most
high, omnipotent. 2 = *see*
huge, **loud (1)**.

almost ADV = **nearly**, just
about, close to, not
quite, practically,
virtually, as good as,
approaching, not far
from, verging on, well-
nigh.

alone ADJ & ADV = **by
oneself**, on one's own,
solitary, apart,
unaccompanied, isolated,
single, separate,
unassisted, solo, lonely,
friendless, forlorn,
deserted, desolate,
lonesome.
Opposites: accompanied.

aloof ADJ = **distant**,
unapproachable, remote,
stand-offish, unfriendly,

unsociable, reserved,
unresponsive, reticent,
supercilious, cold, chilly,
haughty, formal,
inaccessible, detached,
undemonstrative,
unsympathetic,
unforthcoming.
Opposites: familiar,
friendly.

aloud ADV = **out loud**,
clearly, audibly,
distinctly, plainly,
intelligibly.
Opposites: silently.

already ADV 1 = **by now**,
by this time, previously,
before, before now. 2 = **as
soon as this**, as early as
this, so soon, so early.

also ADV = **in addition**,
additionally, moreover,
besides, too, to boot, on
top of that.

alter VERB = **change**, make
different, adjust, adapt,
modify, convert, reshape,
remodel, remake, vary,
amend, revise, transform,
emend, edit.

alteration NOUN = **change**,
adjustment,
modification, adaptation,
revision, amendment,
transformation,

conversion, metamorphosis, reorganization, transfiguration.

alternate VERB = **take turns**, follow each other, rotate, interchange, substitute for each other, replace each other, oscillate, see-saw.

alternative NOUN **1** = **choice**, option, preference. **2** = **substitute**, back-up, replacement.

alternatively ADV = **on the other hand**, as an alternative, instead, otherwise, if not, or.

although CONJUNCTION = **though**, even though, even if, despite the fact that, whilst, albeit.

altogether ADV = **completely**, totally, entirely, thoroughly, fully, utterly, absolutely, perfectly, quite, wholly.

always ADV **1** = **every time**, on every occasion, invariably, consistently, repeatedly, unfailingly. **2** = **continually**, constantly, repeatedly, forever, perpetually, incessantly, eternally.

3 = **forever**, forever and ever, evermore, endlessly, everlastingly, eternally. Opposites: never.

amalgamate VERB = **combine**, merge, unite, join, blend, integrate, mingle, intermingle, mix, intermix, incorporate, fuse, come together, join forces, coalesce, associate, compound, link up. Opposites: split.

amass VERB = **collect**, gather, accumulate, pile up, assemble, store up, hoard.

amateur NOUN = **non-professional**, layman, dabbler, dilettante, enthusiast. ▸ ADJ = **unpaid**, inexperienced, lay, unqualified. Opposites: professional, expert.

amateurish ADJ = **unprofessional**, unskilful, untrained, unskilled, incompetent, inexpert, clumsy, crude, bungling, shoddy, unpolished, inept, second-rate, rough and

a

ready.
Opposites: skilled.

amaze VERB **= astonish**,
surprise, astound, startle,
dumbfound, rock, shock,
stagger, stun, bewilder,
stupefy, daze, disconcert,
confound, awe;
[inf] flabbergast, bowl
over.

amazement NOUN
= astonishment, surprise,
bewilderment, shock,
wonder, stupefaction.

amazing ADJ
= astonishing,
astounding, stunning,
staggering, surprising,
breathtaking,
extraordinary, incredible,
remarkable, sensational,
phenomenal, prodigious,
stupendous, exceptional;
[inf] mind-boggling.

ambassador NOUN
= envoy, consul,
diplomat, emissary,
representative,
plenipotentiary;
[archaic] legate.

ambiguous ADJ
1 = ambivalent, equivocal,
double-edged.
2 = obscure, cryptic,
vague, unclear,

uncertain, indefinite,
woolly, indeterminate,
confusing, puzzling,
perplexing, enigmatic.

ambition NOUN **1 = drive**,
enterprise, desire,
initiative, eagerness,
thrust, push, zeal,
pushiness, striving,
yearning, hankering;
[inf] get-up-and-go,
oomph. **2 = goal**, aim,
objective, desire, object,
intent, purpose, design,
target, wish, aspiration,
dream, hope, ideal.

ambitious ADJ
1 = forceful, enterprising,
purposeful, assertive,
pushy, aspiring, zealous,
enthusiastic, committed,
eager, energetic; [inf] go-
ahead, on the make.
2 = challenging,
formidable, demanding,
difficult, exacting, bold,
unrealistic.
Opposites: aimless,
apathetic, easy.

ambivalent ADJ
= equivocal, ambiguous,
uncertain, doubtful,
inconclusive, unclear,
unresolved, unsettled,
confusing, mixed,

conflicting, clashing, opposing, vacillating, two-faced.
Opposites: unequivocal.

ambush NOUN **= trap**, snare, surprise attack, pitfall, lure; [archaic] ambuscade.
▶ VERB **= lie in wait for**, lay a trap for, pounce on, entrap, ensnare, intercept, surprise, waylay, swoop on, decoy; [archaic] ambuscade.

amenable ADJ **= agreeable**, accommodating, persuadable, cooperative, tractable, compliant, responsive, willing, acquiescent, adaptable, open-minded, biddable, complaisant, submissive, deferential.
Opposites: uncooperative.

amend VERB **1 = alter**, change, revise, correct, modify, adjust, emend, reorganize, reshape, transform. **2 = improve**, remedy, fix, set right, repair, enhance, better, ameliorate, mend.

amenity NOUN **= facility**, service, convenience, resource, advantage.

amiable ADJ **= friendly**, agreeable, pleasant, charming, likeable, sociable, genial, amicable, congenial, good-natured, well disposed.
Opposites: unfriendly, disagreeable.

amnesty NOUN **= pardon**, general pardon, reprieve, forgiveness, absolution, dispensation, indulgence.

amorous ADJ **= loving**, passionate, sexual, sexy, erotic, carnal, lustful, affectionate, ardent, fond, enamoured, impassioned; [Brit. inf] randy.
Opposites: unloving, cold.

amorphous ADJ **= formless**, shapeless, structureless, unstructured, unformed, nebulous, vague, ill-organized, indeterminate.
Opposites: shaped, definite.

amount NOUN **= quantity**, number, total, aggregate, sum, volume, mass, weight, measure, bulk, extent, expanse.

amount to = add up to, total, come to, equal, make, correspond to, approximate to.

ample ADJ = **enough**, sufficient, plenty, more than enough, enough and to spare, abundant, considerable, copious, lavish, substantial, bountiful, profuse, liberal, generous, munificent, unstinting; [poetic/literary] plenteous.
Opposites: insufficient.

amplify VERB **1** = **boost**, increase, intensify, augment, heighten, magnify, supplement.
2 = **expand**, enlarge on, add to, expound on, go into detail about, elaborate on, fill out, make longer, flesh out, develop, extend, lengthen, broaden, explicate, expatiate on, dilate on, supplement.

amputate VERB = **cut off**, sever, chop off, saw off, remove, lop off, excise, dismember, truncate, dock, poll.

amuse VERB **1** = **entertain**, delight, enliven, gladden, cheer, make laugh, please, divert, beguile, regale with, raise a smile in. **2** = **occupy**, entertain, divert, interest, absorb, engross.

amusement NOUN **1** = **laughter**, mirth, hilarity, fun, gaiety, pleasure, delight, enjoyment, merriment.
2 = **entertainment**, interest, diversion, recreation, pastime, hobby, sport, game, pleasure.

amusing ADJ = *see* **funny (1)**, **enjoyable**.

anaemic ADJ = **pale**, colourless, pallid, ashen, sickly, unhealthy, wan, bloodless, weak, feeble, powerless, ineffective, ineffectual, impotent, vigourless.
Opposites: healthy, rosy, vigorous.

analogous ADJ = **similar**, comparable, parallel, corresponding, related, matching, equivalent, like, kindred, homologous.

analyse VERB **1** = **break down**, dissect, separate

out, anatomize,
fractionate, test, assay.
2 = **study**, examine,
investigate, review,
evaluate, interpret,
scrutinize, enquire into,
dissect.

analysis NOUN
1 = **breakdown**,
dissection,
anatomization,
fractionation, assay.
2 = **study**, examination,
investigation, enquiry,
review, evaluation,
interpretation.

analytical, **analytic** ADJ
= **investigative**,
inquisitive, critical,
diagnostic, interpretative,
enquiring, searching,
systematic, questioning,
rational, methodical, in
depth.

anarchy NOUN 1 = **absence
of government**,
lawlessness, nihilism,
misrule, misgovernment,
mobocracy, revolution.
2 = **disorder**, riot, chaos,
pandemonium, tumult,
mayhem, rebellion,
insurrection, mutiny.
Opposites: order, law.

ancestor NOUN = **forebear**,
forerunner, forefather,
progenitor, predecessor,
precursor, antecedent.
Opposites: descendant,
successor.

ancestry NOUN 1 = **lineage**,
descent, parentage,
extraction, origin,
genealogy, stock, blood,
pedigree, derivation.
2 = **antecedents**,
forebears, forefathers,
progenitors, family tree.

anchor NOUN = **mainstay**,
cornerstone, linchpin,
bulwark, support.
▶ VERB 1 = **moor**, berth,
make fast, tie up.
2 = **secure**, fasten, attach,
connect, bind.

ancient ADJ 1 = **early**,
earliest, prehistoric,
primeval, primordial,
immemorial, bygone.
2 = **very old**, time-worn,
age-old, antique, long-
lived, venerable, elderly.
3 = **old-fashioned**,
antiquated, out of date,
outmoded, obsolete,
archaic, superannuated,
antediluvian, atavistic.

ancillary ADJ
= **secondary**, auxiliary,

subsidiary, supplementary, additional, subordinate, extra.

angelic ADJ **1** = **heavenly**, seraphic, cherubic, ethereal, beatific, holy, divine, blessed. **2** = **innocent**, pure, virtuous, saintly, beautiful, adorable. = *See also* **good** ADJ (**1**).

anger NOUN = **rage**, fury, wrath, rancour, temper, annoyance, irritability, antagonism, vexation, exasperation, outrage, indignation, spleen, pique, passion, hostility, tantrum; [poetic/literary] ire, choler.
▶ VERB = **make angry**, infuriate, enrage, madden, incense, outrage, irritate, annoy, exasperate, provoke, antagonize, rile, vex, inflame, aggravate; [inf] make someone's blood boil, needle, bug, drive crazy.
Opposites: pacify, placate.

angle NOUN **1** = **bend**, corner, fork, nook, niche, recess, elbow. **2** = **point of view**, approach, viewpoint, standpoint, opinion, position, slant.
▶ VERB **1** = **tilt**, slant, slope, turn, bend. **2** = **slant**, distort, skew.

angry ADJ = **furious**, irate, enraged, incensed, maddened, outraged, wrathful, seething, raging, annoyed, irritated, exasperated, fuming, indignant, bitter, irascible, vexed, heated, provoked, raving, wild, fiery, apoplectic, hot-tempered, ill-humoured; [inf] hot under the collar, mad, up in arms; [Brit. inf] aerated.
Opposites: calm, pleased.

anguish NOUN = **agony**, suffering, pain, distress, torment, torture, misery, sorrow, grief, woe, heartache, tribulation.
Opposites: pleasure, happiness.

angular ADJ **1** = **bent**, crooked, jagged, zigzag, pointed, V-shaped, Y-shaped, forked, bifurcate. **2** = **bony**, gaunt, spare, scrawny, skinny, lean.
Opposites: rounded.

animal NOUN **1** = **creature**, beast, brute, organism, being. **2** = **brute**, beast, savage, fiend, barbarian, monster; [inf] swine.
▸ ADJ = **sensual**, carnal, physical, bodily, fleshly, brutish, bestial.

animate VERB = **enliven**, give life to, liven up, cheer up, gladden, brighten up, make lively, revitalize, perk up, inspire, excite, exhilarate, rouse, stir, stimulate, invigorate, fire, move, energize, rejuvenate, revive, encourage, galvanize, urge, arouse, activate, spark, kindle, incite; [inf] buck up, pep up.
▸ ADJ = **living**, alive, live, breathing, conscious, sentient.
Opposites: inanimate.

animated ADJ = **lively**, energetic, excited, enthusiastic, spirited, exuberant, vivacious, bubbling, vibrant, cheerful, bright, ebullient, dynamic, eager, zestful, busy, brisk, active, alive, sprightly, passionate, vigorous, quick.
Opposites: lethargic, lifeless.

animation NOUN = **liveliness**, energy, excitement, enthusiasm, passion, dynamism, vitality, vivacity, eagerness, ebullience, exhilaration, zest, exuberance, life, spirit, high spirits, verve, buoyancy, forcefulness, sparkle, briskness, activity, vigour, sprightliness; [inf] pep, zing.
Opposites: apathy, lethargy.

animosity NOUN = **dislike**, enmity, unfriendliness, hostility, resentment, antagonism, hate, hatred, loathing, antipathy, bitterness, spite, bad blood, rancour, venom, ill will, acrimony, vindictiveness, malice, animus, asperity, sourness, malignancy, malignity, odium, acerbity, virulence, sharpness.

Opposites: goodwill, friendliness.

annex VERB = **seize**, take over, conquer, appropriate, acquire, occupy, usurp.

annihilate VERB = **destroy**, wipe out, exterminate, obliterate, eliminate, eradicate, extirpate, erase, liquidate, raze, extinguish, slaughter, kill off, finish off.

annotate VERB = **comment on**, gloss, add notes to, explain, interpret, elucidate, explicate.

annotation NOUN = **note**, comment, gloss, footnote, commentary, explanation, interpretation, elucidation, observation.

announce VERB **1** = **make known**, make public, publish, put out, report, state, give out, reveal, declare, disclose, divulge, broadcast, proclaim, advertise, notify of, promulgate, propound, blazon, intimate. **2** = **introduce**, present, give someone's name, name, usher in, herald.

Opposites: suppress.

announcement NOUN **1** = **declaration**, reporting, proclamation, disclosure, publication, statement, promulgation, notification, advertisement, intimation, revelation. **2** = **statement**, report, bulletin, message, communiqué.

announcer NOUN = **presenter**, newsreader, broadcaster, newscaster, reporter, commentator, anchorman, anchor, herald, master of ceremonies, compère, MC.

annoy VERB **1** = **irritate**, exasperate, displease, infuriate, anger, madden, vex, provoke, upset, put out, try someone's patience, drive mad, antagonize, irk, gall, nettle, make cross, pique, jar; [Brit.] rub up the wrong way; [inf] get on someone's nerves, aggravate, bug, peeve, get to. **2** = **bother**, disturb, pester, harass, trouble, fret, worry, plague, harry, badger, molest; [inf] bug.

annoyance NOUN
1 = **irritation**,
exasperation, anger,
displeasure, vexation,
chagrin, pique; [poetic/
literary] ire. **2** = **nuisance**,
pest, bother, irritant,
trial, offence,
provocation; [inf] pain,
hassle, pain in the neck,
bind, bore.

annoyed ADJ = **irritated**,
exasperated, cross,
displeased, upset, vexed,
riled, put out; [inf] miffed,
peeved, huffy, in a huff;
[Brit. inf] shirty; [N. Amer.
inf] sore.
Opposites: pleased.

annoying ADJ = **irritating**,
infuriating, exasperating,
maddening, upsetting,
trying, galling, tiresome,
grating, troublesome,
worrying, vexing,
irksome, bothersome,
vexatious, wearisome;
[inf] aggravating,
pestilential.

annul VERB = **nullify**,
cancel, declare null and
void, invalidate, rescind,
revoke, repeal, quash,
void, negate, abrogate.

anoint VERB **1** = **oil**, apply
ointment to, spread over,
rub, smear, lubricate,
grease. **2** = **consecrate**,
bless, sanctify, ordain,
hallow.

anomalous ADJ
= **abnormal**, irregular,
atypical, aberrant,
deviant, exceptional,
unusual, odd, eccentric,
bizarre, peculiar.

anonymous ADJ
1 = **unnamed**,
unidentified, nameless,
unknown, unspecified,
incognito, uncredited,
unattributed, unsigned.
2 = **characterless**,
unremarkable,
impersonal, nondescript,
boring, dull,
uninteresting.
Opposites: named,
known.

answer NOUN **1** = **reply**,
response,
acknowledgement,
rejoinder, retort, riposte;
[inf] comeback.
2 = **solution**, explanation,
resolution. **3** = **defence**,
plea, refutation, rebuttal,
vindication.

▶ VERB 1 = **reply to**, respond to, acknowledge, react to, come back, retort, riposte, make a rejoinder, rejoin. 2 = **solve**, explain, resolve. 3 = **meet**, satisfy, fulfil, suit, measure up to, serve. 4 = **fit**, match, correspond to, be similar to, conform to, correlate to.

▪ **answer back** = **talk back**, argue with, be cheeky, contradict, be impertinent.

▪ **answer for** 1 = **pay for**, suffer for, be punished for, make amends for, atone for. 2 = **vouch for**, be accountable for, be responsible for, be liable for.

answerable ADJ = **responsible**, accountable, liable.

antagonism NOUN = **animosity**, hostility, enmity, antipathy, rancour, opposition, rivalry, friction, conflict, dissension.
Opposites: friendship.

antagonize VERB = **annoy**, anger, irritate, alienate, offend, provoke, put out, upset, make an enemy of, arouse hostility in.
Opposites: pacify.

anthem NOUN = **hymn**, psalm, song of praise, chorale, chant, canticle, paean.

anthology NOUN = **collection**, compilation, miscellany, selection, treasury, compendium, digest.

anticipate VERB 1 = **expect**, predict, forecast, foresee, await, prepare for, reckon on, look for, look forward to. 2 = **prevent**, intercept, forestall, pre-empt; [inf] beat to it, beat to the draw.

anticipation NOUN 1 = **expectation**, prediction, preparation, contemplation. 2 = **expectancy**, hopefulness, hope.

anticlimax NOUN = **disappointment**, let-down, disillusionment, comedown, bathos; [Brit.] damp squib.

antics PL NOUN = **pranks**, capers, escapades, tricks, romps, frolics, clowning, horseplay, skylarking; [inf] larking about.

antidote NOUN = **countermeasure**, antitoxin, neutralizing agent, cure, remedy, corrective.

antipathy NOUN = **dislike**, hostility, enmity, opposition, hatred, animosity, antagonism, loathing, repugnance, animus.
Opposites: liking, affinity.

antiquated ADJ = **old-fashioned**, out of date, outmoded, old, dated, outdated, ancient, aged, archaic, antique, obsolete, antediluvian, outworn, passé, medieval, primitive, primeval, quaint; [inf] prehistoric, past it, superannuated.

antique ADJ
1 = **antiquarian**, collectable, vintage, historic, traditional, veteran. 2 = *See* **antiquated**.
▶ NOUN = **collector's item**, heirloom, collectable, curiosity, curio, objet d'art, rarity, relic.

antiquity NOUN = **classical times**, former times, bygone age, the past, days gone by, olden days.

antiseptic ADJ
1 = **disinfected**, disinfectant, sterile, sterilized, sterilizing, hygienic, sanitized, germ-free, medicated, germicidal, bactericidal.
2 = **clinical**, characterless, anonymous, unexciting, undistinguished.

antisocial ADJ
1 = **unsociable**, unfriendly, uncommunicative, reserved, withdrawn, retiring, misanthropic, alienated. 2 = **disruptive**, disorderly, rude, unruly, nasty, undisciplined, offensive, obnoxious, rebellious, lawless, asocial.
Opposites: sociable.

antithesis NOUN = **opposite**, reverse, converse, inverse, other extreme.

anxiety NOUN 1 = **worry**, concern, apprehension, disquiet, uneasiness,

nervousness, dread, stress, tension, tenseness, strain, misgiving, foreboding, fear, uncertainty, fretfulness, distress, angst. **2 = desire**, eagerness, longing, keenness, enthusiasm, avidity.
Opposites: serenity.

anxious ADJ **1 = worried**, concerned, apprehensive, fearful, nervous, nervy, uneasy, disturbed, afraid, perturbed, agitated, alarmed, edgy, troubled, upset, tense, distraught, fraught, overwrought, fretful; [inf] jittery, on edge. **2 = eager**, keen, longing, desperate, yearning, impatient, intent, avid, desirous; [inf] dying, itching.
Opposites: unconcerned, nonchalant.

anyhow ADV **1 = in any case**, in any event, no matter what, at all events. **2 = haphazardly**, carelessly, heedlessly, negligently; [inf] all over the place.

apathetic ADJ
= uninterested,

indifferent, unenthusiastic, unconcerned, unmotivated, impassive, half-hearted, uncommitted, uninvolved, unresponsive, casual, cool, dispassionate, unfeeling, unemotional, emotionless, phlegmatic, unambitious.
Opposites: enthusiastic.

apathy NOUN
= indifference, lack of interest, lack of enthusiasm, unconcern, impassivity, unresponsiveness.
Opposites: enthusiasm, passion.

aperture NOUN **= opening**, gap, hole, crack, slit, window, orifice, fissure, breach, eye.

apex NOUN **1 = top**, peak, summit, tip, head, crest, crown, pinnacle, vertex. **2 = high point**, height, zenith, climax, culmination, apogee, acme.
Opposites: nadir.

apocryphal ADJ
= unverified,

unsubstantiated, debatable, questionable, dubious, spurious, mythical, fictitious, untrue, false; [inf] phoney. **Opposites:** authentic.

apologetic ADJ = **regretful**, sorry, remorseful, contrite, repentant, penitent, conscience-stricken, ashamed, rueful. **Opposites:** unrepentant, impenitent.

apologize VERB = **say sorry**, make an apology, express regret, ask forgiveness, ask for pardon, beg pardon, eat humble pie.

apology NOUN 1 = **regrets**, expression of regret. 2 = **mockery**, travesty, caricature, substitute, poor excuse.

apostle NOUN = **evangelist**, missionary, spreader of the word, preacher, crusader, teacher, supporter, advocate, propagandist.

appal VERB = **shock**, dismay, horrify, sicken, disgust, outrage, astound, alarm, nauseate, revolt.

appalling ADJ = **shocking**, horrifying, disgusting, dreadful, awful, frightful, ghastly, dire, hideous, harrowing. = See also **bad**.

apparatus NOUN = **device**, equipment, instrument, contraption, mechanism, appliance, machine, machinery, tackle, gadget, tool, plant; [inf] gear.

apparel NOUN = **clothing**, clothes, dress, garments, garb, attire, costume; [inf] gear.

apparent ADJ 1 = **obvious**, clear, plain, evident, recognizable, noticeable, perceptible, manifest, discernible, visible, unmistakable, patent, perceivable. 2 = **seeming**, ostensible, superficial, outward. **Opposites:** hidden.

apparition NOUN = **ghost**, phantom, spirit, presence, spectre, manifestation, vision, wraith, shade, chimera; [inf] spook; [poetic/ literary] phantasm.

a

appeal NOUN **1** = **request**, plea, call, application, entreaty, petition, prayer, solicitation, cri de cœur, supplication.
2 = **attraction**, interest, allure, charm, temptation, fascination, seductiveness.
▶ VERB **1** = **ask**, request, beg, plead, implore, entreat, solicit, call, petition; [poetic/literary] beseech.
2 = **interest**, tempt, fascinate, charm, engage, entice, enchant, beguile.

appear VERB **1** = **turn up**, come into view, come out, emerge, materialize, loom up, arrive, enter, surface, bob up; [inf] show up. **2** = **occur**, materialize, be revealed, be seen, arise, develop, originate, crop up, spring up.
3 = **seem**, look, give the impression of, have the appearance of.
4 = **perform**, act, take part, play, come on.
Opposites: disappear.

appearance NOUN
1 = **coming into view**, emergence, arrival, advent, materialization, surfacing. **2** = **look**, impression, air, manner, bearing, demeanour, aspect, expression, mien.
3 = **image**, impression, semblance, guise, pretence.
Opposites: disappearance.

appease VERB **1** = **placate**, pacify, conciliate, mollify, soothe, propitiate. **2** = **satisfy**, assuage, relieve, blunt, diminish, take the edge off.
Opposites: provoke.

appendage NOUN
1 = **addition**, attachment, addendum, adjunct, appurtenance, affix.
2 = **limb**, extremity, projection, protuberance.

appendix NOUN
= **supplement**, addition, addendum, postscript, adjunct, codicil, rider, epilogue, extension.

appetite NOUN **1** = **hunger**, taste, relish, desire, palate, stomach.
2 = **keenness**, eagerness, passion, desire, lust, hunger, thirst, yearning, longing, craving, zest, gusto, relish, zeal,

hankering, yen, predilection.

appetizing ADJ
1 = **delicious**, mouth-watering, tasty, succulent, palatable.
2 = **inviting**, tempting, appealing, enticing, alluring.
Opposites: unappetizing.

applaud VERB 1 = **clap**, cheer, give a standing ovation to; [inf] put one's hands together for, give someone a big hand, bring the house down.
2 = **praise**, admire, express approval of, commend, compliment on, congratulate, salute, acclaim, hail, extol.
Opposites: condemn, criticize.

applause NOUN
1 = **clapping**, ovation, cheering, bravos, encores, curtain calls.
2 = **praise**, acclaim, admiration, approval, commendation, approbation, accolades, plaudits.

appliance NOUN = **device**, gadget, instrument, apparatus, machine, mechanism, tool, implement, contraption.

applicable ADJ = **relevant**, appropriate, pertinent, apposite, apropos.
Opposites: inapplicable.

applicant NOUN
= **candidate**, interviewee, competitor, claimant, enquirer, petitioner, supplicant, suitor, postulant.

apply VERB 1 = **use**, employ, exercise, bring to bear, utilize, put into practice, bring into effect. 2 = **put on**, rub on/in, cover with, spread, smear, administer. 3 = **be relevant**, relate, have a bearing on, be germane, appertain. 4 = **enquire after**, put in for, request, try for, seek, appeal.
■ **apply oneself** = **make an effort**, be industrious, commit oneself, devote oneself, persevere, persist.

appoint VERB 1 = **set**, fix, arrange, decide on, establish, settle on, determine, ordain, designate. 2 = **select**, name, choose, designate, settle on, plump for, elect, assign, delegate, install as, vote for, co-opt.

appointment NOUN
1 = **meeting**, engagement, date, arrangement, interview, rendezvous, assignation, fixture; [poetic/literary] tryst.
2 = **selection**, choice, naming, nomination, commissioning, election.
3 = **job**, post, position, office, situation, place.

appreciable ADJ
= **considerable**, substantial, sizeable, significant, goodly.

appreciate VERB **1** = **be grateful for**, be thankful for, be appreciative of, be indebted for. **2** = **rate highly**, prize, value, enjoy, admire, approve of, respect, treasure, hold in high regard, think much of, esteem.
3 = **recognize**, realize, acknowledge, see, know, be aware of, understand, comprehend, perceive.
4 = **increase**, rise, grow, go up, gain, mount, soar,

escalate.
Opposites: disparage, ignore, depreciate.

appreciative ADJ
= **grateful**, thankful, obliged, indebted, beholden.
Opposites: ungrateful.

apprehensive ADJ
= **worried**, uneasy, nervous, frightened, afraid, alarmed, fearful, mistrustful, concerned, troubled; [inf] on edge, jittery.
Opposites: fearless, unconcerned.

apprentice NOUN
= **trainee**, learner, pupil, student, beginner, novice, probationer, neophyte, cub, tyro; [inf] rookie; [N. Amer. inf] greenhorn.

approach VERB **1** = **reach**, come/draw near, come/draw close, near, move/advance towards, bear down on. **2** = **appeal to**, make overtures to, proposition, solicit, sound out. **3** = **set about**, tackle, begin, start, make a start on, embark on, commence, undertake.

4 = **come near/close to**, compare with, be comparable with, approximate to.
Opposites: leave.
▶ NOUN **1** = **method**, procedure, way, style, attitude, manner, technique, means, mode, modus operandi.
2 = **appeal**, application, proposal, overture, proposition. **3** = **coming near**, advance, arrival, advent. **4** = **drive**, driveway, avenue, access road.

approachable ADJ
= **friendly**, open, affable, relaxed, accessible, sympathetic, well disposed.
Opposites: aloof.

appropriate ADJ
= **suitable**, fitting, right, apt, timely, applicable, seemly, proper, becoming, correct, well judged, relevant, germane, well suited, pertinent, apposite, opportune, apropos.
Opposites: inappropriate.
▶ VERB **1** = **take over**, take possession of, seize, confiscate, requisition, commandeer, annex, expropriate, arrogate.
2 = **steal**, embezzle, misappropriate, pilfer, purloin, pocket; [inf] filch, swipe; [Brit. inf] nick, pinch.

approval NOUN
1 = **admiration**, acceptance, praise, liking, support, favour, appreciation, respect, esteem, commendation, approbation.
2 = **acceptance**, agreement, endorsement, authorization, confirmation, assent, consent, ratification, sanction, blessing, permission, mandate, concurrence, acquiescence, licence, seal, validation, imprimatur; [inf] OK, thumbs up, go-ahead, green light.
Opposites: disapproval, rejection, refusal.

approve VERB **1** = **be pleased with**, think well of, like, look on with favour, give one's blessing to, hold in

regard/esteem, admire, respect, praise. **2 = agree to**, accept, consent to, permit, pass, allow, sanction, authorize, bless, support, back, uphold, endorse, ratify, validate, accede to, countenance; [inf] go along with, rubber-stamp.
Opposites: disapprove, condemn, refuse, veto.

approximate ADJ
= rough, estimated, near, close, inexact, imprecise, loose.
Opposites: exact.

■ **approximate to = be close/near to**, come near to, approach, border on, verge on, resemble, be similar to, roughly equal.

approximately ADV
= roughly, about, round about, around, just about, circa, more or less, nearly, close to, near to, in the region/ neighbourhood of, approaching, almost, not far off.
Opposites: precisely.

apt ADJ **1 = suitable**, appropriate, fitting, applicable, apposite, felicitous. **2 = likely**, inclined, prone, liable, given, disposed.
Opposites: inappropriate, unlikely.

aptitude NOUN **= talent**, ability, gift, skill, flair, knack, bent, capability, capacity, faculty.

arbiter NOUN **= judge**, authority, determiner, controller, director, governor, expert, master, pundit.

arbitrary ADJ
1 = capricious, unreasonable, whimsical, irrational, illogical, personal, subjective, random, chance, erratic, wilful, unreasoned, inconsistent, unpredictable, unplanned, unjustified.
2 = dictatorial, despotic, autocratic, absolute, tyrannical, imperious, domineering, high-handed.
Opposites: rational, reasoned.

arbitrate VERB
= adjudicate, judge, referee, sit in judgement,

mediate, umpire, settle, decide, determine, decide the outcome of.

arbitration NOUN
= **adjudication**, judgement, settlement, decision, determination, mediation, negotiation, good offices.

arbitrator NOUN
= **adjudicator**, judge, referee, umpire, arbiter, ombudsman, mediator, negotiator, intermediary, go-between, peacemaker.

arc NOUN = **curve**, bend, bow, crescent, semicircle, half-moon, arch, curvature.

arch¹ NOUN = **archway**, vault, span, bridge.
▶ VERB = **curve**, bend, bow, arc.

arch² ADJ = **playful**, mischievous, roguish, artful, sly, knowing.

archetype NOUN
= **prototype**, example, pattern, model, original, standard, ideal, paradigm, precursor.

architect NOUN
1 = **designer**, planner, building consultant, draughtsman. 2 = **creator**, author, engineer, originator, planner, deviser, instigator, founder, prime mover.

ardent ADJ = **passionate**, fervent, impassioned, eager, enthusiastic, intense, keen, zealous, vehement, fierce.
Opposites: apathetic.

arduous ADJ = **hard**, difficult, demanding, exhausting, laborious, strenuous, tiring, gruelling, punishing, tough, onerous, heavy, rigorous, back-breaking, taxing, Herculean.
Opposites: easy, effortless.

area NOUN 1 = **region**, district, environment, vicinity, locality, zone, territory, neighbourhood, environs, terrain, sector, quarter, province, precinct, realm, domain.
2 = **field**, subject, sphere, discipline, sector, realm.
3 = **size**, extent, expanse, measurement, space, compass, range, square footage, acreage, dimensions.

argue VERB 1 = **claim**, maintain, hold, reason,

insist, contend, declare,
assert, demonstrate,
make a case, plead,
suggest. **2 = quarrel**,
differ, disagree, fall out,
have an argument,
bicker, have words,
bandy words, fight,
squabble, debate,
dispute, answer back,
object, take exception,
wrangle, feud,
remonstrate; [inf] row.
3 = dispute, debate,
discuss.

argument NOUN
1 = disagreement, quarrel,
fight, squabble, dispute,
difference of opinion,
falling-out, altercation,
wrangle, conflict, clash,
feud, controversy,
remonstration; [inf] row,
tiff, set-to, dust-up.
2 = case, reasoning,
reasons, line of
reasoning, grounds,
logic, evidence, polemic,
argumentation.
3 = subject matter,
theme, topic, gist,
outline, storyline,
summary, synopsis,
abstract, precis.

argumentative ADJ
= quarrelsome,
contentious, combative,
belligerent, disputatious,
litigious.

arid ADJ **1 = dry**, dried up,
waterless, parched,
moistureless, scorched,
desiccated, barren,
infertile, desert, lifeless,
sterile. **2 = dull**, tedious,
dreary, dry, boring,
uninteresting,
monotonous, flat, vapid,
lifeless.
Opposites: wet, fertile,
interesting.

arise VERB **1 = come to
light**, turn/crop up,
emerge, occur, begin,
come into being. **=** *See
also* **appear**. **2 = result**, be
caused, originate, follow,
proceed, emanate, ensue.

aristocracy NOUN
= nobility, peerage, upper
class, gentry, high
society, elite, ruling class,
patriciate; [inf] upper
crust.

aristocratic ADJ
1 = noble, titled, high-
born, blue-blooded,
upper-class, patrician.
2 = well bred, dignified,

refined, courtly, elegant, gracious, haughty, proud.

arm¹ NOUN **1 = inlet**, creek, cove, fjord, bay, estuary, firth, sound. **2 = branch**, department, section, wing, division, sector, offshoot, extension.

arm² VERB **= equip**, supply, provide, issue, furnish.

armaments PL NOUN **= weapons**, guns, arms, firearms, weaponry, munitions, ordnance.

armistice NOUN **= ceasefire**, truce, peace, treaty, agreement, suspension of hostilities.

armoury NOUN **= arsenal**, arms depot, ammunition dump, magazine, ordnance depot.

army NOUN **1 = armed force**, troops, soldiers, infantry, land force, soldiery. **2 = crowd**, horde, throng, swarm, pack, host, multitude, mob.

aroma NOUN **= smell**, scent, odour, fragrance, perfume, bouquet, savour; [poetic/literary] redolence.

arouse VERB **1 = induce**, prompt, trigger, kindle, provoke, engender, stir up, spark off. **2 = wake**, wake up, awaken, rouse. **Opposites:** allay.

arrange VERB **1 = put in order**, set out, sort, lay out, organize, position, group, sift, align, tidy, file, rank, classify, categorize, array, systematize. **2 = fix**, settle on, set up, agree, determine, plan, organize, schedule, bring about, coordinate, make preparations for. **3 = score**, adapt, set, orchestrate, harmonize. **Opposites:** disturb, cancel.

arrangement NOUN **1 = order**, ordering, organization, positioning, grouping, distribution, disposition, system, alignment, filing, marshalling, ranging, spacing, tabulation. **2 = agreement**, plan, deal, contract, compact, bargain, pact, understanding, settlement, terms, preparations, provisions.

3 = **score**, orchestration, adaptation, instrumentation, setting, harmonization.

array NOUN
1 = **arrangement**, collection, line-up, formation, presentation, display, exhibition, show, parade, assemblage, muster.
2 = **dress**, attire, clothing, garments, garb, finery; [formal] apparel.
▶ VERB **1** = *See* **arrange** (**1**).
2 = **clothe**, dress, fit out, adorn, garb, rig out, deck, robe, accoutre.

arrest VERB **1** = **take into custody**, apprehend, take prisoner, capture, detain, seize, catch, lay hold of; [inf] pick up, pinch, collar, haul in, nab, bust, run in; [Brit. inf] nick.
2 = **stop**, halt, block, end, prevent, obstruct, hinder, impede, interrupt, delay, slow down, bring to a standstill, check, restrain, stem, retard, nip in the bud.
Opposites: release, start.
▶ NOUN = **apprehension**, capture, detention,

seizure, taking into custody.
Opposites: release.

arresting ADJ = **striking**, remarkable, extraordinary, impressive, outstanding, unusual, stunning, conspicuous, noticeable.
Opposites: inconspicuous.

arrival NOUN **1** = **coming**, appearance, approach, advent, entrance, entry, occurrence. **2** = **visitor**, incomer, guest, immigrant, newcomer, caller.
Opposites: departure, leaver.

arrive VERB **1** = **come**, appear, enter, get here/ there, turn up, get in, put in/make an appearance, drop by/in; [inf] show up, roll in/up, blow in. **2** = *See* **succeed** (**1**).
Opposites: leave, depart.

arrogant ADJ = **haughty**, proud, conceited, self-important, pompous, overbearing, patronizing, superior, high-handed, egotistical, condescending,

snobbish, disdainful, imperious, lordly, swaggering, presumptuous, cocky, boastful, supercilious, overweening, blustering, insolent; [inf] stuck up, high and mighty, snooty, uppity.
Opposites: modest, diffident.

art NOUN **1** = **painting**, drawing, fine art, design, visual art. **2** = **skill**, craft, talent, flair, aptitude, gift, knack, facility, technique, proficiency, expertise, ingenuity, skilfulness, mastery, dexterity, virtuosity, adroitness.

artful ADJ = **cunning**, sly, wily, clever, shrewd, canny, crafty, devious, tricky, subtle, ingenious, astute, scheming, designing; [inf] smart, foxy; [Brit. inf] fly.
Opposites: ingenuous.

article NOUN **1** = **thing**, object, item, commodity. **2** = **story**, piece, item, account, report, feature, column.

articulate ADJ = **fluent**, eloquent, lucid, expressive, clear, comprehensible, coherent, intelligible, understandable, glib, silver-tongued.
Opposites: inarticulate.
▶ VERB = **enunciate**, say, utter, express, pronounce, vocalize, voice.

articulated ADJ = **hinged**, jointed, segmented, flexible, bendy.

artifice NOUN = **trickery**, cunning, deceit, deception, craftiness, artfulness, slyness, duplicity, guile, chicanery.

artificial ADJ
1 = **manufactured**, man-made, fabricated, synthetic, imitation, simulated, ersatz.
2 = **false**, affected, fake, unnatural, insincere, forced, sham, contrived, pretended, assumed, put on, mock, unreal, feigned, bogus, pseudo, laboured, hollow, spurious, meretricious; [inf] phoney.

Opposites: natural, genuine.

artist NOUN **1** = **painter**, drawer, sculptor, old master. **2** = **craftsman**, craftswoman, expert, master, past master, genius, adept. **3** = *See* **performer**.

artistic ADJ **1** = **creative**, imaginative, talented, gifted, accomplished, sensitive, cultured, cultivated. **2** = **attractive**, tasteful, decorative, beautiful, stylish, elegant, graceful, aesthetic, ornamental, exquisite.
Opposites: ugly.

artistry NOUN = **skill**, art, talent, ability, flair, gift, expertise, creativity, proficiency, craftsmanship, workmanship, brilliance.

ascend VERB = **climb**, go/move up, rise, mount, soar, take off, lift off, fly up, levitate, scale.
Opposites: descend.

ascendancy NOUN = **domination**, dominance, control, authority, power, rule, command, supremacy, sway, mastery, sovereignty, the upper hand.

ascent NOUN = **climb**, rise, hill, slope, ascension, gradient, ramp.
Opposites: descent.

ascertain VERB = **find out**, establish, discover, learn, determine, decide, identify, confirm, make certain, get to know, verify, make sure/certain, settle, pin down.

ascribe VERB = **attribute**, put down, assign, impute, credit, accredit, chalk up, lay on, blame, charge with.

ashamed ADJ
1 = **embarrassed**, shamefaced, sorry, apologetic, sheepish, red-faced, blushing, humiliated, conscience-stricken, remorseful, mortified, crestfallen, discomfited, bashful, contrite, penitent, repentant, rueful, chagrined; [inf] with one's tail between one's legs.
2 = **reluctant**, loath, unwilling, indisposed.

Opposites: proud, shameless.

asinine ADJ = **idiotic**, stupid, foolish, nonsensical, ridiculous, half-witted, imbecilic, fatuous, moronic; [inf] batty, nutty, dumb, gormless; [Brit. inf] daft. **Opposites:** intelligent, sensible.

ask VERB **1** = **question**, inquire, query, quiz, put a question to, interrogate, cross-examine, give the third degree to; [inf] grill, pump. **2** = **request**, demand, appeal to, apply to, beg, solicit, implore, plead, seek, supplicate; [poetic/literary] beseech. **3** = **invite**, summon, bid. **Opposites:** answer.

asleep ADJ **1** = **sleeping**, fast/sound asleep, in a deep sleep, dozing, resting, slumbering, snoozing, napping, catnapping, reposing, comatose, unconscious, sedated, dormant; [inf] out like a light, dead to the world; [Brit. inf] kipping; [humorous] in the land of Nod. **2** = **numb**, without feeling, deadened. **Opposites:** awake.

aspect NOUN **1** = **feature**, viewpoint, facet, side, circumstance, angle, characteristic, element, light, standpoint, slant, attribute. **2** = **appearance**, look, expression, features, air, manner, demeanour, bearing, countenance, mien, visage. **3** = **direction**, outlook, prospect, orientation, view, exposure, situation, location, position.

asphyxiate VERB = **suffocate**, choke, smother, stifle, strangle, throttle, strangulate.

aspiration NOUN = **aim**, desire, objective, ambition, goal, wish, hope, dream, longing, yearning, craving, eagerness, enthusiasm.

aspire VERB = **desire**, hope to/for, long for/to, wish to/for, dream of, yearn for/to, seek, pursue, crave, hunger for.

aspiring ADJ = **would-be**, potential, hopeful,

expectant, ambitious, optimistic, wishful, striving.

assail VERB = **attack**, assault, set on/upon, fall on, rush, storm; [inf] lay into, tear into, pitch into.

assassin NOUN = **murderer**, killer, executioner, contract killer, liquidator; [inf] hit man; [poetic/literary] slayer.

assassinate VERB = **murder**, kill, execute, eliminate, liquidate; [inf] hit; [poetic/literary] slay.

assault VERB **1** = **attack**, charge, storm, rush at, set about/on, strike at. **2** = **strike**, hit, attack, beat up, aim blows at; [inf] lay into, pitch into, wade into, do over. **3** = **molest**, rape, sexually assault, interfere with.

assemble VERB **1** = **come together**, collect, gather, congregate, meet, convene, join up, flock together, converge, rally round, throng around. **2** = **bring/put together**, collect, gather, round up, summon, muster, mobilize, accumulate, marshal, rally, amass; [formal] convoke. **3** = **construct**, build, erect, put together, set up, piece together, fit together, fabricate, manufacture, connect, join.
Opposites: disperse, dismantle.

assembly NOUN = **gathering**, meeting, crowd, group, congregation, throng, rally, convention, conference, congress, conclave, synod; [inf] get-together. = *See also* **crowd**.

assent NOUN = **agreement**, consent, acceptance, approval, permission, sanction, acquiescence, compliance, accord, accordance, approbation.
Opposites: dissent.
▸ VERB = **agree**, accept, consent, be willing, comply, approve, acquiesce, concede, concur, give one's permission, submit, yield, accede.
Opposites: refuse.

assert VERB 1 = **declare**, state, maintain, proclaim, pronounce, emphasize, insist on, profess, claim, swear to, stress, affirm, avow; [formal] aver.
2 = **uphold**, insist on, stand up for, defend, press/push for, vindicate.

■ **assert oneself** = **behave confidently**, make one's presence felt, stand up for oneself, exert one's influence.

assertive ADJ = **confident**, self-assured, assured, forceful, pushy, strong-willed, positive, authoritative, dominant, domineering, strong, aggressive, decisive, firm, definite, emphatic, uncompromising, stubborn, opinionated; [inf] bossy.

assess VERB = **judge**, evaluate, estimate, gauge, appraise, weigh up, rate, determine, reckon, work out, assay, compute, calculate, fix; [inf] size up.

asset NOUN = **advantage**, benefit, strength, strong point, help, aid, resource, support, blessing, boon, godsend.

■ **assets** = **wealth**, money, resources, capital, means, property, possessions, belongings, holdings, goods, valuables, reserves, securities, estate, effects, chattels.

assiduous ADJ = **diligent**, industrious, hard-working, persistent, indefatigable, zealous, persevering, sedulous.

assign VERB 1 = **allocate**, allot, distribute, share out, give out, dispense, apportion, consign.
2 = **appoint**, select for, nominate, designate, name, install, delegate, commission. 3 = **ascribe**, put down, attribute, accredit, credit, chalk up.
4 = **transfer**, make over, convey.

assignation NOUN = **rendezvous**, date, meeting, appointment; [poetic/literary] tryst.

assignment NOUN 1 = **task**, job, duty, mission, responsibility, obligation, charge, commission.
2 = **allocation**, distribution, allotment,

apportionment, dispensation, consignment. **3 = transfer**, making over, handing down, consignment.

assimilate VERB
1 = absorb, take in, incorporate, ingest, digest. **2 = adapt**, adjust, accustom, become like, acclimatize, blend in, homogenize.

assist VERB **1 = help**, help out, aid, support, lend a hand, rally round, cooperate with, collaborate with, work with, play a part, abet, succour. **2 = facilitate**, make easier, boost, further, promote, expedite.
Opposites: impede, hinder.

assistance NOUN **= help**, aid, support, cooperation, collaboration, succour, à (helping) hand, encouragement, patronage, sponsorship, subsidy, contribution.
Opposites: hindrance, impedance.

assistant NOUN **1 = deputy**, subordinate, second-in-command, auxiliary, right-hand man/woman, man/girl Friday, henchman, minion. **2 = helper**, collaborator, associate, partner, colleague, mainstay, accessory, abetter. **3 = shop/sales assistant**, salesperson, salesman, saleswoman, checkout operator, server; [N. Amer.] clerk.

associate VERB **1 = link**, connect, identify, equate, bracket, relate. **2 = mix**, socialize, keep company, mingle, fraternize; [inf] hobnob, run/go around, hang out. **3 = affiliate**, connect, combine, join, attach, band together, team up, ally, incorporate, syndicate.
Opposites: dissociate.

association NOUN **= federation**, affiliation, alliance, partnership, union, confederation, syndicate, coalition, combination, league, fellowship, merger, cartel, consortium, club.

assorted ADJ = **mixed**, varied, various, diverse, miscellaneous, sundry, multifarious, manifold, motley, heterogeneous, variegated; [poetic/literary] divers.

assortment NOUN = **mixture**, selection, variety, collection, range, jumble, miscellany, medley, diversity, melange, farrago, potpourri, mishmash, hotchpotch.

assume VERB 1 = **suppose**, presume, think, presuppose, take for granted, believe, suspect, understand, expect, imagine, guess, gather, surmise, fancy. 2 = **take on**, adopt, take up, acquire, put on, affect, come to have, don. 3 = **undertake**, accept, take upon oneself, shoulder, embark on, enter upon. 4 = **seize**, take over, appropriate, commandeer, usurp, pre-empt.

assumption NOUN = **supposition**, presumption, belief, hypothesis, presupposition, theory, suspicion, guess, expectation, conjecture, surmise, premise.

assurance NOUN 1 = **self-confidence**, confidence, self-assurance, poise, nerve. 2 = **guarantee**, commitment, word, promise, undertaking, oath, pledge, affirmation.

assure VERB 1 = **declare**, give one's word, affirm, guarantee, promise, swear, pledge, certify, vow, attest. 2 = **ensure**, make sure/certain, guarantee, confirm, secure, clinch, seal.

assured ADJ = **confident**, self-confident, self-assured, self-reliant, poised, positive.

astonish VERB = **amaze**, astound, stagger, stun, surprise, dumbfound, leave speechless, take someone's breath away, take aback, startle, stupefy, daze, bewilder, dazzle; [inf] flabbergast, floor, wow.

astonishing ADJ
= **amazing**, astounding, staggering, surprising, breathtaking, striking, stunning, bewildering, impressive.
Opposites: unremarkable.

astound VERB = *see* **astonish**.

astray ADV & ADJ **1** = **off course**, lost, off the right track, adrift. **2** = **wrong**, into sin, into wrongdoing, into error; [inf] off the rails.

astute ADJ = **shrewd**, clever, quick, quick-witted, acute, cunning, intelligent, sly, artful, knowing, canny, ingenious, perceptive, observant, crafty, wily, calculating, perspicacious, sagacious; [inf] foxy; [Brit. inf] fly.
Opposites: stupid, dull.

asylum NOUN **1** = **refuge**, sanctuary, shelter, safety, protection, safe keeping, haven, retreat, harbour, port in a storm.
2 = **mental hospital**, psychiatric hospital, institution; [inf] loony bin, madhouse, funny farm.

asymmetrical ADJ
= **uneven**, irregular, crooked, distorted, lopsided, unbalanced, misshapen, malformed.
Opposites: symmetrical.

atheist NOUN = **unbeliever**, disbeliever, non-believer, sceptic, freethinker, heretic, heathen, pagan, infidel.
Opposites: believer.

athletic ADJ **1** = **muscular**, strong, well built, powerful, fit, active, energetic, sturdy, robust, strapping, wiry, hardy, vigorous, brawny.
2 = **sporting**, sports, gymnastics.
Opposites: puny.

atmosphere NOUN **1** = **air**, sky, aerospace, stratosphere; [poetic/literary] heavens, ether.
2 = **environment**, climate, mood, feeling, spirit, ambience, surroundings, setting, milieu, character, tone, quality, flavour, vibrations, aura, tenor; [inf] vibes.

atom NOUN = **bit**, particle, scrap, shred, speck, spot, fragment, jot, trace, iota, dot, crumb, grain, morsel; [inf] smidgen.

atone VERB = **make amends**, compensate, pay for, be punished, do penance, answer, pay the penalty/price, make reparations, redeem oneself, redress, expiate.

atrocious ADJ **1** = **wicked**, vicious, brutal, barbaric, evil, dreadful, horrific, horrifying, sickening, abominable, savage, cruel, murderous, frightful, revolting, villainous, heinous, ruthless, monstrous, inhuman, gruesome, hideous, fiendish, diabolical, outrageous, vile. **2** = **very bad**, terrible, appalling, dreadful.
Opposites: commendable, excellent.

atrocity NOUN = **outrage**, crime, offence, horror, abomination, monstrosity, violation, evil.

atrophy VERB = **waste away**, wither, shrivel, decay, wilt, deteriorate, decline, degenerate.

attach VERB **1** = **fasten**, stick, affix, join, connect, link, tie, couple, pin, hitch, bond, add, append, annex. **2** = **place**, put, ascribe, assign, attribute, lay, impute, invest with. **3** = **assign**, appoint, second, allocate, detail.
Opposites: detach.

attached ADJ **1** = **married**, engaged, spoken for, having a partner. **2** = **fond of**, devoted to, having a regard for.

attack VERB **1** = **assault**, set on/upon, beat up, strike, strike at, rush, storm, charge, pounce upon, beset, besiege, beleaguer; [inf] lay/wade into, let someone have it, do over. **2** = **criticize**, berate, reprove, censure, rebuke, find fault with, denounce, revile, blame, harangue, vilify, snipe at, fulminate against, impugn, malign, inveigh against, traduce. **3** = **begin**, set about, get/ go to work on, get started on, embark on, undertake.

attacker

Opposites: defend, praise.

▶ NOUN **1** = **assault**, offensive, raid, ambush, sortie, onslaught, charge, strike, invasion, rush, foray, incursion, battery, bombardment.
2 = **criticism**, abuse, censure, outburst, tirade, rebuke, reproval, vilification, diatribe, impugnment, invective.
3 = **fit**, seizure, bout, spasm, convulsion, paroxysm, stroke.

attacker NOUN = **assailant**, aggressor, assaulter, mugger, opponent, raider, critic, detractor, persecutor, slanderer.

attain VERB = **achieve**, accomplish, gain, obtain, get, win, earn, acquire, reach, realize, arrive at, fulfil, succeed in, bring off, grasp, secure, procure.

attempt VERB = **try**, strive, endeavour, tackle, seek, set out to, venture, aim, undertake, make an effort, bid; [inf] have a go/shot at, give something a whirl, have a crack at.

▶ NOUN = **try**, effort, endeavour, venture, undertaking; [inf] go, shot, crack.

attend VERB **1** = **be present**, be at, be there/here, appear, put in an appearance, turn up, visit, show, frequent, haunt; [inf] show up.
2 = **pay attention**, listen, concentrate, follow, heed, pay heed, take note, notice, mark, watch. **3** = **look after**, take care of, care for, nurse, tend, see to, mind, minister to. **4** = **escort**, accompany, guard, follow, chaperone, squire, usher, convoy.

attendant NOUN
1 = **steward**, waiter, waitress, porter, servant.
2 = **escort**, companion, retainer, aide, lady in waiting, equerry, chaperone.
▶ ADJ = **related**, accompanying, consequent, resulting, concomitant, accessory.

attention NOUN
1 = **concentration**, attentiveness, notice,

observation, scrutiny, heed, regard, diligence, thought, thinking, studying. **2** = **notice**, awareness, observation, recognition, regard, consciousness. **3** = **care**, treatment, therapy, ministration.
4 = **overtures**, approaches, suit, wooing, compliments, flattery; [dated] courting.

attentive ADJ **1** = **alert**, aware, watchful, awake, observant, wide awake, vigilant, intent, mindful, on guard, heedful.
2 = **considerate**, thoughtful, conscientious, polite, kind, obliging, accommodating, gallant.
Opposites: inattentive.

attire NOUN = **clothing**, dress, clothes, garments, garb, costume, outfit, wear, ensemble, accoutrements; [inf] gear, togs, glad rags, rig; [formal] apparel; [archaic] habit.
▶ VERB = *see* **dress** VERB (**1**).

attitude NOUN **1** = **view**, point of view, opinion, viewpoint, outlook, belief, standpoint, frame of mind, position, approach, perspective, reaction, stance, thoughts, ideas.
2 = **position**, pose, stance, bearing, carriage; [Brit.] deportment.

attract VERB **1** = **appeal to**, interest, fascinate, charm, entice, captivate, tempt, engage, bewitch, seduce, beguile, lure, allure, inveigle; [inf] turn on.
2 = **cause**, generate, encourage, provoke, incite, stir up. **3** = **draw**, pull, magnetize.
Opposites: repel.

attractive ADJ **1** = **good-looking**, beautiful, handsome, pretty, lovely, stunning, striking, gorgeous, irresistible, glamorous, desirable, appealing, captivating, fascinating, charming, adorable, enchanting, alluring, enticing, seductive, bewitching, fetching, prepossessing, winsome; [inf] tasty; [N. Amer. inf] cute; [archaic] comely.

2 = appealing, agreeable, interesting, tempting, pleasing, inviting. **Opposites:** ugly, uninviting.

attribute NOUN = **quality**, feature, characteristic, property, mark, sign, trait, indicator, distinction, idiosyncrasy.
▶ VERB = **ascribe**, assign, put down, accredit, credit, impute, chalk up, lay at the door of.

attrition NOUN
1 = weakening, wearing down, debilitation, sapping, enfeebling.
2 = abrasion, friction, rubbing, corrosion, corroding, erosion, wearing/eating away, grinding, scraping, excoriation.

attune VERB = **accustom**, adjust, familiarize, adapt, acclimatize.

audacious ADJ = **bold**, daring, fearless, brave, courageous, adventurous, intrepid, valiant, plucky, reckless, brazen, daredevil; [inf] gutsy. **Opposites:** timid.

audacity NOUN
1 = boldness, daring, fearlessness, bravery, courage, valour, pluck; [Brit. inf] guts. = *See also* **courage**. **2 = effrontery**, cheek, impudence, brazenness, impertinence, shamelessness, presumption; [inf] sauce. **Opposites:** timidity.

audible ADJ = **discernible**, perceptible, clear, distinct, recognizable, hearable, detectable. **Opposites:** inaudible, faint.

audience NOUN
1 = spectators,
= listeners, viewers, onlookers, crowd, gathering, assembly, house, turnout, congregation, gallery.
2 = interview, meeting, hearing, consultation, discussion, reception.

audit NOUN = **inspection**, examination, investigation, scrutiny, review, check.
▶ VERB = **inspect**, examine, review, check, scrutinize, investigate, go over/

through.

augment VERB = **increase**, enlarge, make larger/ greater, add to, expand, multiply, grow, extend, boost, enhance, raise, inflate, heighten, strengthen, intensify, amplify, swell, supplement, magnify. Opposites: decrease, diminish.

augur VERB = **be a sign of**, bode, foretell, predict, herald, prophesy, foreshadow, harbinger, portend, forecast, presage.

august ADJ = **dignified**, solemn, stately, majestic, noble, imposing, impressive, exalted, grand, illustrious. Opposites: obscure, insignificant.

auspicious ADJ = **favourable**, promising, hopeful, encouraging, bright, fortunate, propitious, timely, felicitous. Opposites: inauspicious.

austere ADJ **1** = **plain**, severe, simple, unadorned, unornamented, stark, subdued, sombre, unembellished. **2** = **stern**, formal, serious, solemn, severe, cold, distant, aloof, stiff, forbidding, unsmiling, unbending, unyielding, harsh, rigorous, stringent, unrelenting. **3** = **strict**, abstemious, disciplined, puritanical, spartan, frugal, ascetic, self-denying, restrained, chaste, celibate, abstinent. Opposites: elaborate, genial, immoderate.

authentic ADJ **1** = **genuine**, real, true, bona fide, actual, legitimate, valid, undisputed; [inf] the real McCoy. **2** = **true**, accurate, honest, credible, reliable, dependable; [inf] straight from the horse's mouth. Opposites: fake, unreliable.

authenticate VERB = **verify**, validate, confirm, substantiate, certify, guarantee, endorse, ratify.

author NOUN 1 = **writer**, composer, novelist, dramatist, playwright, poet, screenwriter, essayist, journalist, reporter, columnist. 2 = **creator**, originator, producer, designer, architect, planner, cause, prime mover, maker, initiator, inventor; [poetic/literary] begetter.

authoritarian ADJ = **dictatorial**, tyrannical, strict, domineering, despotic, autocratic, imperious, harsh, Draconian, disciplinarian, dogmatic; [inf] bossy.
Opposites: democratic, liberal.

authoritative ADJ 1 = **reliable**, accurate, authentic, sound, dependable, factual, definitive, valid, certified. 2 = **confident**, self-assured, assertive, commanding, masterful, imposing, arrogant, overbearing, imperious.
Opposites: unreliable, timid.

authority NOUN 1 = **right**, power, jurisdiction, authorization, influence, might, prerogative, rule, command, charge, dominion, sovereignty, supremacy, ascendancy; [inf] say-so. 2 = **permission**, authorization, consent, sanction, licence, mandate, warrant. 3 = **government**, administration, officialdom, management, establishment, bureaucracy; [inf] powers that be. 4 = **expert**, specialist, master, scholar, pundit, adept.

authorize VERB = **permit**, allow, agree to, give permission, consent to, approve, sanction, endorse, back, license, ratify, legalize, certify, countenance, give leave for, warrant, commission; [inf] give the go-ahead for, give the green light to.

authorized ADJ = see **official**.

automatic ADJ
1 = **automated**,
mechanical, mechanized,
electronic, self-
regulating, self-
activating, push-button,
programmable, robotic.
2 = **instinctive**,
spontaneous,
involuntary,
unconscious, reflex,
habitual, natural,
unintentional,
unthinking, mechanical,
conditioned.
3 = **inevitable**, routine,
certain, assured.
Opposites: manual,
deliberate.

autonomous ADJ
= **independent**, free, self-
governing, sovereign.

autonomy NOUN
= **independence**, self-
determination, self-
sufficiency,
individualism, autarchy.

auxiliary ADJ
= **secondary**, subsidiary,
subordinate, ancillary,
supporting, additional,
extra, reserve, back-up,
spare, supplementary,
substitute.

available ADJ = **free**,
untaken, obtainable, to
hand, handy, procurable,
unoccupied, vacant,
usable, ready,
convenient, accessible,
employable.
Opposites: unavailable,
inaccessible.

avarice NOUN = **greed**,
acquisitiveness,
covetousness,
materialism, meanness,
miserliness.
Opposites: generosity.

avaricious ADJ = **greedy**,
grasping, covetous,
acquisitive, miserly,
parsimonious; [inf] tight-
fisted, stingy.
Opposites: generous.

average ADJ 1 = **normal**,
typical, ordinary,
common, regular, usual,
commonplace, everyday,
widespread,
unexceptional, medium,
middling, moderate;
[inf] run-of-the-mill.
2 = **mediocre**,
unexceptional, moderate,
second-rate, pedestrian,
banal.
Opposites: exceptional,
outstanding.

▶ NOUN = **mean**, midpoint, median, centre, norm, standard, rule, yardstick.
▶ VERB = **even out**, equalize, normalize, standardize.

averse ADJ = **opposed**, hostile, antagonistic, unwilling, disinclined, reluctant, resistant, loath, ill-disposed.

aversion NOUN = **dislike**, distaste, hatred, repugnance, antipathy, reluctance, unwillingness, evasion, avoidance, shunning.
Opposites: liking, inclination.

avid ADJ = **keen**, eager, enthusiastic, fervent, dedicated, ardent, fanatical, zealous, passionate.
Opposites: apathetic, indifferent.

avoid VERB 1 = **evade**, elude, hide from, keep away from, keep clear of, shun, ignore, dodge, steer clear of, give a wide berth to, shirk, eschew; [inf] duck. 2 = **abstain from**, circumvent, refrain from, bypass; [Brit. inf] skive off.

Opposites: face, seek.

await VERB 1 = **anticipate**, expect, wait for, hope for, look out for. 2 = **be in store for**, wait for, be ready for, lie ahead for, lie in wait for, be round the corner.

awake ADJ 1 = **wakeful**, sleepless, wide awake, insomniac, open-eyed, restless, tossing and turning. 2 = **aware**, alert, conscious, attentive, vigilant.
Opposites: asleep, unaware.

awaken VERB 1 = **wake**, wake up, awake, waken, rouse, call, alert. 2 = **kindle**, arouse, stimulate, call forth, stir up, excite, revive.

award NOUN 1 = **prize**, reward, trophy, honour, decoration, medal, badge, cup, grant, scholarship. 2 = **gift**, grant, conferment, bestowal, presentation.
▶ VERB = **confer**, present, give, grant, accord, allot, assign, bestow, endow.

aware ADJ = **conscious**, alive to, informed,

knowledgeable, familiar, acquainted, mindful, heedful, sensitive, responsive, observant, attentive, sensible, conversant, cognizant, versed in.
Opposites: ignorant, insensitive.

awareness NOUN
= **consciousness**, perception, realization, knowledge, sense, feeling, understanding, sensitivity, perceptiveness.
Opposites: ignorance, insensitivity.

awe NOUN = **wonder**, amazement, admiration, reverence, veneration, respect, dread, fear.

awesome ADJ
= **breathtaking**, awe-inspiring, magnificent, stupendous, overwhelming, sublime, majestic, solemn, imposing, dramatic, grand, formidable, marvellous, amazing, staggering, stunning, fearful, impressive;
[inf] mind-blowing;
[poetic/literary] wondrous.

= See also **wonderful**.
Opposites: unimpressive.

awful ADJ **1** = see **bad**.
2 = See **awesome**.

awfully ADV **1** = **very**, extremely, intensely, deeply, exceedingly;
[inf] terribly, dreadfully;
[Brit. inf] ever so; [inf, dated] frightfully.
2 = **terribly**, badly, dreadfully, appallingly, atrociously, disgracefully, frightfully.

awkward ADJ
1 = **unwieldy**, cumbersome, unmanageable, inconvenient, bulky.
2 = **inconvenient**, difficult, troublesome, problematic, unhelpful, unsuitable. **3** = **tricky**, difficult, perplexing, taxing, puzzling, thorny, troublesome, trying, vexed. **4** = **uncooperative**, unhelpful, disobliging, contrary, obstructive, perverse, troublesome, trying, exasperating, obstinate, stubborn, refractory, intractable;
[Brit. inf] bloody-minded, bolshie; [N. Amer.] ornery.

a

5 = **clumsy**, blundering, bungling, ungainly, uncoordinated, inelegant, inexpert, clownish, inept, unskilled, maladroit, gawky, gauche, wooden; [inf] ham-fisted.

6 = **uncomfortable**, uneasy, strained, embarrassing, unnatural; [inf] edgy.

Opposites: convenient, handy, cooperative, graceful, skilful, relaxed.

Bb

babble VERB = **chatter**, prattle, burble, gabble, jabber, gibber, murmur, mutter; [inf] waffle; [Brit. inf] rabbit.
▶ NOUN = **chatter**, chat, gabble, prattling, murmur, clamour.

baby NOUN = **infant**, newborn, child; [poetic/literary] babe; [technical] neonate.
▶ ADJ = **tiny**, miniature, mini, little, dwarf, diminutive, minute.
▶ VERB = **cosset**, pamper, spoil, indulge, coddle, mollycoddle, pet.

babyish ADJ = **childish**, infantile, immature, juvenile, puerile, silly, inane.
Opposites: mature.

back NOUN 1 = **rear**, rear end, stern, tail end, hindquarters, posterior, end. 2 = **reverse**, reverse side, other side.
Opposites: front.
▶ ADJ 1 = **rear**, hind, end, hindmost, last. 2 = **dorsal**, spinal.
Opposites: front.
▶ VERB 1 = *See* **support** VERB (5), **uphold**. 2 = **reverse**, go backwards, move back, back away, back off, retreat, retire, recede, recoil, withdraw, backtrack.
■ **back down** = *see* **withdraw** (4).

backer NOUN = **supporter**, sponsor, promoter, patron, advocate, benefactor, champion, seconder; [inf] angel.

background NOUN 1 = **backdrop**, setting, surroundings, context, circumstances, conditions, framework, environment. 2 = **family**, origins, ancestry, upbringing, education, milieu, culture, training, tradition, experience, qualifications, credentials, history. **Opposites:** foreground.

backing NOUN **1** = **support**, encouragement, approval, endorsement, promotion, recommendation, assent, agreement, assistance, help, aid, sponsorship, funding, patronage, subsidy, funds, grant, loan. **2** = **accompaniment**, obbligato.

backlash NOUN = **reaction**, recoil, rebound, response, retaliation, counterblast, repercussion, reversal.

backward ADJ **1** = **reverse**, retreating, rearward, retrograde, regressive, retrogressive. **2** = **slow**, late-starting, behind, behindhand, retarded, undeveloped, unprogressive, underdeveloped, disadvantaged, handicapped; [dated] subnormal. **3** = **shy**, bashful, timid, diffident, hesitant, self-effacing,

reticent, unforthcoming, reserved, unassertive, modest, coy, inhibited. **Opposites:** forward, advanced, precocious, confident.

bad ADJ **1** = **poor**, inadequate, unsatisfactory, substandard, inferior, imperfect, defective, deficient, faulty, incompetent, inefficient, incorrect, unsound, useless, worthless, shoddy, abysmal, awful, appalling, disgraceful, atrocious, dreadful, frightful, hopeless, abominable; [inf] lousy, rotten, diabolical; [Brit. inf] grotty, ropy. **2** = **unsuitable**, unpropitious, unfavourable, inappropriate, adverse, unhelpful, inconvenient, unlucky, dangerous, harmful, deleterious, detrimental, damaging, unhealthy, risky, injurious, hurtful, destructive. **3** = **unpleasant**, disagreeable, nasty,

horrid, horrible, harsh,
unwelcome, gloomy,
distressing, dreadful,
awful, frightful, terrible,
foul, appalling, atrocious.
4 = **serious**, severe, grave,
dangerous, disastrous,
calamitous, terrible,
awful, dreadful, frightful,
critical, acute, dire,
hideous. **5** = **immoral**,
wicked, evil, wrong,
corrupt, sinful, vicious,
criminal, depraved,
villainous, vile, rotten,
delinquent, guilty,
blameworthy,
reprehensible, dishonest,
dishonourable, ignoble,
base, reprobate.
6 = **naughty**, mischievous,
unruly, wayward,
disobedient, disorderly.
7 = **rotten**, decayed,
mouldy, off, rancid,
tainted, spoiled, sour,
decomposing, putrid,
contaminated, foul,
polluted, mildewed,
diseased. **8** = *see* ill ADJ (**1**).
9 = **remorseful**, regretful,
ashamed, guilty, sorry,
unhappy, contrite,
apologetic, penitent.
Opposites: good,
favourable, fine, fresh.

badge NOUN = **emblem**,
pin, crest, insignia,
medal, token, sign, mark,
symbol, logo, device,
characteristic, trademark;
[N. Amer.] button.

bad-tempered ADJ
= **irritable**, short-
tempered, quick-
tempered, peevish,
touchy, prickly,
crotchety, irascible, cross,
angry, ill-humoured,
testy, quarrelsome,
truculent, grumpy,
acrimonious, querulous,
petulant, gruff, sullen,
moody, sulky,
disgruntled, grumbling,
scowling, churlish,
cantankerous, dyspeptic,
bilious, crabbed,
shrewish; [inf] snappy;
[Brit. inf] shirty.
Opposites: good-
humoured, affable.

baffle VERB **1** = **bewilder**,
bemuse, mystify, perplex,
puzzle, confuse,
confound, nonplus,
floor; [inf] flummox,
bamboozle, stump.
2 = **thwart**, foil, frustrate,
defeat, prevent, check,
hinder, block, obstruct.

bag NOUN = **handbag**, carrier bag, shoulder bag, case, grip, satchel, sack, holdall, rucksack, haversack, reticule.

▶ VERB 1 = **catch**, capture, shoot, kill, trap, snare, land. 2 = **get**, gain, acquire, obtain, reserve, secure, get hold of.

baggage NOUN = **luggage**, bags, cases, belongings, things, equipment, accoutrements, paraphernalia, impedimenta; [inf] gear.

bait NOUN = **lure**, attraction, enticement, temptation, incentive, inducement, bribe, decoy, carrot.

▶ VERB = **tease**, provoke, goad, pester, annoy, harass, plague, torment, persecute, taunt; [inf] needle; [Brit. inf] wind up.

balance NOUN 1 = **stability**, poise, steadiness, equilibrium. 2 = **correspondence**, equivalence, symmetry, equality, parity, equipoise, evenness, proportion. 3 = **remainder**, rest, difference, surplus, excess, residue. 4 = **scales**, weighing machine. **Opposites:** imbalance, instability.

▶ VERB 1 = **keep balanced**, poise, steady, stabilize, support. 2 = **offset**, cancel out, counterbalance, match, compensate for, even up, level, equalize, parallel, counterpoise, counteract, neutralize.

bald ADJ 1 = **hairless**, bare, smooth, bald-headed; [inf] thin on top. 2 = **blunt**, frank, plain, straightforward, forthright, direct, not beating about the bush, stark, uncompromising, downright, simple, unadorned, unembellished. **Opposites:** hairy.

ball NOUN = **sphere**, globe, orb, globule, spheroid.

ballot NOUN = **vote**, poll, election, referendum, plebiscite.

ban VERB = **prohibit**, forbid, veto, outlaw, put a ban on, proscribe, suppress,

disallow, interdict, bar, debar, prevent, restrict, exclude, banish, ostracize.
Opposites: authorize, permit, sanction.
▸ NOUN = **prohibition**, veto, embargo, boycott, bar, interdict, interdiction, proscription, restriction, taboo, suppression.

banal ADJ = **trite**, clichéd, hackneyed, commonplace, unoriginal, cliché-ridden, unimaginative, uninspired, stale, boring, dull, everyday, stock, stereotyped, platitudinous, obvious, predictable, tired, pedestrian, humdrum, prosaic, vapid, fatuous; [inf] corny, old hat.
Opposites: interesting, original.

band¹ NOUN 1 = **stripe**, strip, line, belt, bar, streak, border, swathe.
2 = **braid**, belt, fillet, sash, tie, ribbon, cord, loop, girdle.

band² NOUN 1 = **group**, troop, crowd, crew, gang, company, body, pack, mob, horde, flock, bunch, gathering, party, throng, society, club, clique, set, association.
2 = **ensemble**, group, orchestra; [inf] combo.

bandit NOUN = **brigand**, outlaw, robber, highwayman, footpad, marauder, desperado, gangster, gunman, pirate, buccaneer, hijacker, plunderer, thief.

bandy¹ ADJ = **bowed**, crooked, curved, bent, bow-legged, misshapen.

bandy² VERB 1 = **exchange**, swap, trade, pass, reciprocate. = See also **argue**. 2 = **spread**, circulate, pass on, disseminate.

bang NOUN 1 = **boom**, crash, thud, slam, knock, clash, clap, report, explosion.
2 = **blow**, bump, hit, knock, slap, punch, stroke, cuff, smack, rap; [inf] whack.
▸ ADV 1 = **with a bang**, crash, thump, thud, noisily, violently. 2 = **exactly**, precisely, absolutely, right; [inf] slap bang.

banish VERB **1** = **exile**, expel, exclude, deport, expatriate, ostracize, transport, eject, evict, outlaw, oust, throw out, proscribe. **2** = **dismiss**, drive away, dispel, shut out, eliminate, get rid of, dislodge, remove, bar, ban, suppress.

bank¹ NOUN **1** = **slope**, mound, embankment, hillock, incline, ridge, rise, rampart, ramp, dyke, pile, mass. **2** = **edge**, shore, brink, side, margin, embankment. **3** = **row**, array, collection, display, panel, rank, tier. ▶ VERB = **tilt**, lean, slope, slant, list, tip, incline.

bank² NOUN = **store**, reserve, supply, fund, stock, hoard, repository, pool, reservoir. ▶ VERB = **deposit**, save, put by, save up, keep, store, hoard. Opposites: withdraw. ■ **bank on** = *see* **rely on**.

bankrupt ADJ **1** = **insolvent**, ruined, failed, in liquidation, destitute, penniless; [inf] broke, bust.

2 = **morally bankrupt**, deficient, lacking, poor, impoverished, worthless. Opposites: solvent.

banner NOUN = **flag**, standard, pennant, pennon, colours, ensign, banderole, streamer.

banquet NOUN = **feast**, repast, dinner, meal, party; [inf] binge, blowout, spread.

banter NOUN = **repartee**, joking, badinage, persiflage, pleasantry, jesting, wordplay.

bar NOUN **1** = **beam**, rod, pole, shaft, stake, stick, spar, rail, batten, girder, crosspiece. **2** = **barrier**, obstacle, obstruction, impediment, hindrance, check, deterrent, drawback, prohibition, prevention, problem, difficulty. **3** = **band**, stripe, belt, strip, streak, line. **4** = **cake**, slab, chunk, block, piece, wedge, lump, hunk, nugget, ingot. **5** = **hostelry**, inn, tavern; [Brit.] pub, public house; [Brit. inf] local, boozer.

▶ VERB **1** = **exclude**, ban, banish, keep out, prohibit, forbid, preclude, outlaw, ostracize, proscribe.
2 = **block**, check, impede, obstruct, prevent, hinder, stop, halt, deter, restrain, arrest, thwart.

barbarian NOUN = **savage**, vandal, boor, yahoo, churl, brute, ruffian, hooligan, heathen, pagan, philistine, ignoramus; [Brit. inf] yob, yobbo.
▶ ADJ = *see* **barbaric**.

barbaric ADJ
1 = **uncivilized**, primitive, wild, savage, barbarian, uneducated, unsophisticated, crude, brutish. **2** = **cruel**, brutal, savage, bestial, barbarous, vicious, ferocious, inhuman.
= *See also* **cruel**.
Opposites: civilized.

bare ADJ **1** = **naked**, nude, undressed, unclad, uncovered, stripped, unclothed, exposed, denuded; [inf] in the buff, butt naked; [Brit. inf] starkers; [N. Amer. inf] buck naked.
2 = **empty**, unfurnished, undecorated, plain, austere, unadorned, vacant. **3** = **bleak**, barren, featureless, treeless, unsheltered, desolate, open. **4** = **plain**, simple, unadorned, unvarnished, unembellished, uncompromising, basic, essential, literal, straightforward, bald, stark, direct, uninterpreted, unelaborated. **5** = **mere**, basic, essential, minimum, minimal, least, smallest, meagre, scanty, inadequate.
▶ VERB = **reveal**, uncover, expose, lay bare, undress, unmask, unveil, show, disclose, make known, publish, betray.
Opposites: conceal.

barely ADV = **hardly**, scarcely, just, only just, by the skin of one's teeth, with difficulty.

bargain NOUN
1 = **agreement**, deal, pact, contract, arrangement, settlement, treaty, transaction,

understanding, promise,
pledge, compact,
covenant, concordat,
engagement, negotiation.
2 = good buy, good deal,
special offer, discount,
reduction; [inf] snip,
giveaway.

▶ VERB = **negotiate**, haggle,
barter, argue, discuss,
deal, trade, traffic,
compromise, agree,
settle, promise, pledge,
engage.

■ **bargain for = expect**,
allow for, anticipate, be
prepared for, take into
account.

■ **into the bargain** = see
moreover.

barrage NOUN
1 = broadside, gunfire,
bombardment, fusillade,
salvo, volley, battery,
shelling, cannonade.
2 = onslaught, deluge,
torrent, stream, hail,
storm, flood, mass,
avalanche, abundance,
plethora. **3** = See **barrier**
(**1**).

barrel NOUN = **cask**, keg,
vat, butt, tub, tank,
firkin, hogshead.

barren ADJ **1 = infertile**,
unproductive, unfruitful,
waste, desert, arid, bare,
bleak, desolate, lifeless,
empty. **2 = sterile**,
infertile, childless;
[technical] infecund.
Opposites: fertile.

barricade NOUN = see
barrier (**1**).
▶ VERB = **block off**, blockade,
bar, obstruct, close up,
fortify, defend.

barrier NOUN **1 = bar**, fence,
railing, barricade,
obstruction, blockade,
barrage, roadblock,
rampart, palisade,
bulwark, dam, stockade.
2 = obstacle, hindrance,
impediment, handicap,
difficulty, problem,
restriction, check, bar,
limitation, drawback,
stumbling block.

barter VERB = **bargain**,
trade, traffic, exchange,
swap, deal, haggle.

base¹ NOUN **1 = foundation**,
bed, foot, bottom, basis,
support, stand, rest,
pedestal, prop, plinth,
substructure. **2 = basis**,
core, fundamentals,
essence, essentials, root,

heart, source, origin, mainspring.
3 = **headquarters**, centre, camp, station, post, starting point, settlement, site.
▸ VERB **1** = **found**, build, settle, support, ground, rest, derive from, construct, establish.
2 = **locate**, station, centre, post, situate, place, install.

base² ADJ = **ignoble**, mean, low, sordid, contemptible, shameful, vulgar, shabby, despicable, unworthy, inferior, corrupt, depraved, vile, dishonourable, disreputable, unprincipled, immoral, evil, wicked, sinful, detestable, degrading.
Opposites: noble.

bashful ADJ = **shy**, diffident, timid, shrinking, backward, modest, self-effacing, retiring, nervous, self-conscious, reserved, inhibited, reticent, unforthcoming, hesitant, coy, demure,

shamefaced, abashed, sheepish, embarrassed, blushing, uneasy.
Opposites: confident.

basic ADJ **1** = **fundamental**, essential, intrinsic, underlying, primary, elementary, central, key, indispensable, vital, main, principal, chief, crucial, rudimentary.
2 = **plain**, simple, austere, spartan, unadorned, stark, minimal.
Opposites: luxurious.

basin NOUN = **bowl**, dish, pan, vessel, container, receptacle.

basis NOUN **1** = **foundation**, base, grounding, support, rest, stand, stay, infrastructure, bottom.
2 = **starting point**, source, origin, core, essence, beginning, impetus, impulse, material, ingredients, stimulus.

bask VERB **1** = **lie**, laze, relax, sunbathe, lounge, loll. **2** = **revel**, wallow, exult, delight, take pleasure, luxuriate, glory, rejoice, enjoy, relish, savour.

bastard NOUN
1 = **illegitimate child**; [dated] love child; [archaic] natural child.
2 = **scoundrel**, villain, brute, rogue; [inf] beast; [dated] cad, blackguard.

batch NOUN = **set**, group, lot, cluster, bunch, quantity, collection, accumulation, assemblage, pack, crowd, aggregate, conglomeration.

bathe VERB 1 = **wash**, clean, cleanse, rinse, soak, steep, moisten, wet, immerse. 2 = **swim**, go swimming, take a dip. 3 = **suffuse**, envelop, cover, soak.

baton NOUN = **stick**, wand, rod, bar, cane, staff, club, truncheon, mace.

batter VERB 1 = **beat**, hit, strike, bludgeon, assault, belabour; [inf] bash. = See also **hit** (1). 2 = **damage**, injure, hurt, harm, crush, shatter, exhaust, ruin, destroy, buffet, wear down, wear out, impair, squash, mar, spoil, demolish.

battle NOUN = **conflict**, fight, fighting, clash, engagement, skirmish, struggle, confrontation, combat, encounter, collision, campaign, war, tussle, scuffle, melee, action, strife, hostilities, fray, crusade; [inf] scrap.
▶ VERB = **struggle**, fight, contend, compete, contest, combat, feud, quarrel, wrangle, argue, war, cross swords.

battlefield NOUN = **battleground**, front, battle lines, combat zone, theatre of war, arena.

bawdy ADJ = **ribald**, lewd, indecent, salacious, earthy, broad, suggestive, indelicate, naughty, racy, risqué, off colour, obscene, dirty, filthy, smutty, erotic, prurient, pornographic, gross, coarse, titillating, licentious, lascivious, unseemly, vulgar, Rabelaisian; [inf] blue, raunchy.
Opposites: decent, proper.

bawl VERB 1 = **shout**, cry, yell, roar, bellow,

thunder, clamour, vociferate; [inf] holler.
2 = **sob**, wail, cry, roar, howl, weep, blubber, squall, snivel, grizzle.

bay¹ NOUN = **cove**, inlet, gulf, basin, harbour, indentation, sound, arm, bight, creek, firth, fjord, estuary.

bay² NOUN = **alcove**, recess, niche, opening, nook, booth.

bazaar NOUN 1 = **market**, mart, souk, exchange.
2 = **fête**, fair, sale; [Brit.] jumble sale, bring-and-buy (sale); [N. Amer.] rummage sale.

be VERB 1 = **exist**, live, be alive, breathe. 2 = **be situated**, be located, be positioned, stay, remain, continue, dwell, live, inhabit, be present, attend, persist, survive, endure, last. 3 = **take place**, occur, be due, be planned for, happen, come about, arise, transpire; [poetic/ literary] come to pass, befall.

beach NOUN = **shore**, seashore, sands, sand, seaside, coast, coastline, littoral, margin, foreshore, water's edge, waterfront; [poetic/ literary] strand.

beached ADJ = **stranded**, aground, grounded, ashore, high and dry, stuck, cast up, marooned, wrecked, abandoned.

bead NOUN = **ball**, pellet, pill, drop, globule.

beaker NOUN = **cup**, mug, glass, goblet, tumbler, tankard.

beam NOUN 1 = **bar**, spar, rafter, girder, support, boom, plank, board, joist, timber, stanchion, scantling. 2 = **ray**, shaft, bar, stream, streak, pencil, gleam, glimmer, glow, glint.
▶ VERB 1 = **emit**, radiate, shine, broadcast, transmit, direct, aim.
2 = **smile**, grin, laugh, be radiant.
Opposites: frown.

bear VERB 1 = **hold**, support, carry, uphold, sustain, prop up, shoulder, take. 2 = **bring**, carry, transport, convey, fetch, deliver, move,

take, transfer; [inf] tote.
3 = be marked with,
display, exhibit, show,
present. **4 = endure**,
tolerate, abide, accept,
stand, put up with,
submit to, suffer, sustain,
cope with, live with,
stomach, admit, allow,
resign oneself to;
[formal] brook.
5 = produce, yield, give,
give forth, supply,
provide. **6 = give birth to**,
produce, breed, generate;
[archaic] bring forth.
■ **bear out** = *see* **confirm**
(1), **support** VERB **(4)**.
■ **bear up** = **cope**, survive,
endure, manage, keep
on, hold out, keep going.
■ **bear with** = **be patient**
with, be tolerant towards,
make allowances for,
tolerate, suffer, indulge.

bearable ADJ = **endurable**,
tolerable, supportable,
sustainable, sufferable,
acceptable, admissible,
manageable.
Opposites: intolerable,
unbearable.

bearing NOUN **1 = carriage**,
posture, gait, demeanour,
air, aspect, behaviour,
manner, attitude, mien,
composure, stance, style;
[Brit.] deportment;
[formal] comportment.
2 = course, direction.
3 = relevance, pertinence,
connection, implication,
significance, relation,
relationship, application,
effect, consequence.

beast NOUN **1 = animal**,
creature, brute. **2 = brute**,
savage, monster, fiend,
devil, sadist, barbarian,
wretch;
[archaic] blackguard.

beat VERB **1 = hit**, strike,
batter, thrash, slap, whip,
lash, cuff, cudgel, buffet,
cane, scourge, smack,
thwack, thump, pound,
drub, hammer, flog,
chastise; [inf] bash, whack,
clout, wallop, lay into,
rough up, knock about,
tan, biff. **2 = pulsate**,
throb, pound, pulse,
palpitate, thump, vibrate.
3 = defeat, outdo,
conquer, surpass,
trounce, vanquish,
overcome, excel, subdue,
master, best, outclass,
outdistance, outpace,
outwit, quash, worst;

[inf] thrash, lick. **4 = whisk**, whip, stir, agitate, blend, mix. **5 = flap**, flutter, quiver, vibrate, tremble.
▸ NOUN **1 = pulse**, vibration, throb, throbbing, pounding, palpitation. **2 = rhythm**, stress, accent, pulse, tempo, metre, measure, time. **3 = round**, rounds, route, circuit, path, track, course, way, itinerary.

beautiful ADJ = **lovely**, attractive, pretty, gorgeous, ravishing, stunning, handsome, good-looking, elegant, exquisite, charming, delightful, pleasing, picturesque, decorative, scenic, spectacular, superb, fine, glamorous, graceful; [poetic/ literary] beauteous, pulchritudinous; [archaic] fair, comely; [Scottish & N. English] bonny.
Opposites: ugly.

beautify VERB = **adorn**, embellish, decorate, ornament, bedeck, enhance, improve, prettify, glamorize, smarten, gild; [inf] do up, doll up, titivate.
Opposites: spoil.

beauty NOUN = **attractiveness**, loveliness, prettiness, handsomeness, good looks, allure, appeal, charm, picturesqueness, glamour, elegance, grace, magnificence, radiance, splendour, artistry; [poetic/literary] pulchritude.
Opposites: ugliness.

because CONJUNCTION = **since**, as, for the reason that, in that, seeing that.
▪ **because of** = **on account of**, owing to, due to, as a result of, in view of, by reason of, by virtue of, thanks to.

beckon VERB **1 = gesture**, signal, motion, gesticulate, call, summon, bid, invite, encourage. **2 = attract**, tempt, pull, draw, allure, entice.

become VERB **1 = turn into**, turn out to be, change into, grow into, develop into, be transformed into, evolve into, metamorphose into.

2 = **suit**, flatter, look good on, sit well on, set off, enhance, go well with, grace.

becoming ADJ = **flattering**, pretty, attractive, elegant, stylish, chic.
Opposites: unflattering.

bed NOUN **1** = **couch**, cot, berth; [inf] the sack, the hay; [Brit. inf] one's pit.
2 = **base**, foundation, bottom, basis, support, substratum, substructure, layer.

bedraggled ADJ = **dishevelled**, untidy, unkempt, disordered, muddy, wet, soiled, drenched, soaked, stained, soaking, sodden, soggy, messy, dirty, muddied.
Opposites: neat, clean.

beef NOUN = **brawn**, muscle, strength, sinew, physique, bulk, burliness, robustness, muscularity.

befall VERB = **happen**, occur, happen to, take place, come about, chance, arise, ensue, follow, transpire; [poetic/literary] come to pass, betide.

before PREP **1** = **prior to**, ahead of, earlier than, sooner than. **2** = **in front of**, in the presence of, in the sight of.
Opposites: after.
▸ ADV = **earlier**, previously, beforehand, in advance, formerly, ahead.

befriend VERB **1** = **make friends with**. **2** = **take under one's protection**, protect, look after, take under one's wing, support, assist, succour.

beg VERB **1** = **ask for money**, solicit; [inf] scrounge, cadge.
2 = **plead**, entreat, ask, request, seek, crave, importune, implore, pray, supplicate, petition, cajole, wheedle; [poetic/literary] beseech.

beggar NOUN = **vagrant**, tramp, down-and-out, derelict, vagabond, mendicant; [inf] scrounger, sponger, cadger.

begin VERB **1** = **start**, commence, set about, start on, set in motion, set going, activate, spark off, embark on, initiate,

establish, institute, inaugurate, originate, found, pioneer, open, launch, give rise to, cause, instigate, be the source of. **2 = come into being**, start, commence, arise, emerge, appear, occur, happen, originate, materialize, dawn, spring up.
Opposites: finish, disappear.

beginner NOUN = **novice**, learner, trainee, apprentice, student, recruit, tyro, fledgling, neophyte, novitiate; [N. Amer.] tenderfoot; [inf] rookie; [N. Amer. inf] greenhorn.
Opposites: expert, veteran.

beginning NOUN **1 = start**, origin, opening, commencement, outset, dawn, birth, inception, starting point, source, emergence, onset, genesis, conception, germ, root, spring. **2 = establishment**, foundation, institution, inauguration, opening, creation, introduction.

3 = prelude, introduction, preface, opening.
Opposites: end, conclusion.

begrudge VERB = **grudge**, resent, give unwillingly, be jealous of, object to, envy, mind, be dissatisfied with.

beguile VERB **1 = charm**, attract, delight, enchant, allure, bewitch, please, entice, seduce, tempt. **2 = amuse**, absorb, engross, engage, divert, entertain, distract, occupy.

behalf
■ **on behalf of 1 = in the interests of**, for the sake of, in support of, for the good of, on account of. **2 = representing**, in the name of, in place of.

behave VERB **1 = act**, conduct oneself, perform, operate, function, acquit oneself; [formal] comport oneself. **2 = be good**, be polite, mind one's manners, be obedient; [inf] mind one's Ps and Qs.

behaviour NOUN = **conduct**, actions,

demeanour, manners, ways, activity, functioning, performance, operation; [N. Amer.] deportment; [formal] comportment.

being NOUN **1** = **creature**, living thing, entity, animal, person, individual, human, mortal. **2** = **existence**, life, living, animation, actuality, reality.

belated ADJ = **late**, overdue, delayed, unpunctual, tardy, behind time, behindhand.
Opposites: early.

belief NOUN **1** = **opinion**, judgement, view, thought, feeling, conviction, way of thinking, theory, notion, impression. **2** = **trust**, faith, credence, reliance, assurance, certainty, confidence, security, sureness. **3** = **faith**, creed, credo, doctrine, dogma, persuasion, conviction, tenet, teaching, ideology.
Opposites: doubt.

believe VERB **1** = **accept**, be convinced by, trust, subscribe to, rely on, swear to; [inf] swallow, buy, fall for, take as gospel. **2** = **think**, hold, suppose, reckon, be of the opinion, assume, presume, imagine, consider, conjecture, guess, hypothesize, theorize, maintain, understand, surmise, postulate.
Opposites: disbelieve.

believer NOUN = **adherent**, devotee, follower, supporter, disciple.
Opposites: sceptic.

belittle NOUN = **disparage**, decry, slight, depreciate, deprecate, make light of, underestimate, underrate, undervalue, detract from, denigrate, downgrade, minimize, criticize, scoff at, sneer at.
Opposites: praise.

belligerent ADJ
1 = **aggressive**, argumentative, pugnacious, combative, antagonistic, confrontational, disputatious, bellicose, provocative, militant, quarrelsome, hot-

tempered, quick-tempered, irascible, captious. **2 = warring**, at war, hostile, battling, combatant, contending, militant, warmongering, warlike, martial.
Opposites: peaceable.

belong VERB **1 = be owned by**, be the property of, be held by. **2 = be a member of**, be part of, be one of, be connected with, be associated with, be affiliated to, be allied to, be included in, be an adherent of. **3 = have a place**, be supposed to be. **4 = be at home**, be suited, be welcome, fit in, be accepted.

belongings PL NOUN **= property**, possessions, things, effects, goods, chattels, paraphernalia, appurtenances, accoutrements, impedimenta; [inf] stuff, gear, junk.

beloved ADJ **= loved**, adored, dear, dearest, cherished, worshipped, treasured, prized, precious, sweet, idolized, darling.

Opposites: hated.
▸ NOUN **= sweetheart**, lover, love, girlfriend, boyfriend, inamorata, inamorato; [archaic] paramour.

belt NOUN **1 = girdle**, sash, waistband, band, cummerbund, girth; [poetic/literary] cincture.
2 = strip, stretch, band, stripe, streak, bar, region, zone, area, district, tract, extent.
▸ VERB **= hit**, strike, beat, thump, cuff; [inf] whack, wallop. **=** *See also* **hit** (**1**).

bemused ADJ **= bewildered**, dazed, confused, stunned, muddled, puzzled, perplexed, baffled, befuddled, stupefied, amazed, astounded, astonished, overwhelmed, disconcerted.

bend VERB **1 = curve**, crook, make crooked, arch, bow, twist, flex, warp, fold, contort, mould, shape.
2 = turn, curve, twist, curl, veer, swerve, loop, diverge, deviate, wind, coil, spiral, incurvate.

3 = **stoop**, lean, crouch, bow, hunch, duck.
Opposites: straighten.

▶ NOUN = **curve**, corner, turn, twist, arc, angle, loop, coil, spiral, crook, swerve, deflection, deviation, zigzag, dog-leg.
Opposites: straight.

beneath PREP **1** = **below**, under, underneath, lower than. **2** = **inferior to**, lower than, subservient to, subordinate to, secondary to.
3 = **unworthy of**, not proper for, degrading to, undignified for, unsuitable for, inappropriate for, unbecoming for.
Opposites: above.

benefactor NOUN
= **helper**, supporter, sponsor, patron, backer, donor, promoter, subsidizer, subscriber, well-wisher, sympathizer, philanthropist, fairy godmother; [inf] angel.

beneficial ADJ
= **advantageous**, profitable, helpful, useful, worthwhile, valuable, gainful, healthy, rewarding, fruitful, productive, salutary, salubrious, wholesome, improving, serviceable, propitious, promising, favourable, obliging, accommodating, nutritious, nourishing, nurturing.
Opposites: disadvantageous.

beneficiary NOUN = **heir**, heiress, inheritor, recipient, legatee, payee, assignee, receiver, successor.

benefit NOUN
1 = **advantage**, asset, blessing, boon, plus, plus point; [inf] perk; [formal] perquisite.
2 = **good**, well-being, advantage, interest, profit, gain, welfare, convenience, prosperity, good fortune, aid, assistance, help, service, privilege, betterment.
3 = **aid**, allowance, subsidy, grant, payment, assistance; [Brit. inf] dole.
Opposites: disadvantage, detriment.

▶ VERB **1** = **help**, profit, be advantageous to, be good for, serve, aid, assist, advance, further, promote, advantage, forward, boost, avail, enhance, improve, better. **2** = **gain**, profit, do well, reap benefits/reward, prosper, put to good use, do well out of; [inf] cash in.
Opposites: damage, suffer.

benevolent ADJ = **kind**, kind-hearted, kindly, generous, warm-hearted, caring, benign, amiable, friendly, beneficent, liberal, magnanimous, bountiful, humane, humanitarian, altruistic, philanthropic, compassionate, sympathetic, considerate, thoughtful, obliging, well meaning, helpful.
Opposites: malicious, unkind.

benign ADJ **1** = **kindly**, benevolent, kind-hearted, kind, generous, cordial, genial, amiable, warm, gentle, tolerant, gracious, friendly, accommodating. **2** = **favourable**, auspicious, propitious, opportune, lucky, advantageous, helpful, providential, suitable, appropriate, healthy, wholesome, health-giving, salubrious, pleasant, refreshing, agreeable, mild, temperate, balmy. **3** = **non-malignant**, curable, treatable, remediable, innocent, harmless.
Opposites: unfriendly, unfavourable, malignant.

bent ADJ **1** = **curved**, crooked, twisted, angled, bowed, arched, warped, distorted, contorted, folded, coiled, buckled, hunched. **2** = **corrupt**, dishonest, fraudulent, criminal, untrustworthy, unprincipled, immoral; [inf] crooked.
Opposites: straight, honest.
▶ NOUN = **tendency**, inclination, predisposition, leaning, talent, gift, flair, ability, aptitude, penchant, predilection, propensity,

proclivity.

bequeath VERB = **leave (in one's will)**, will, make over, pass on, hand on/down, transfer, donate, give, bestow on, confer on, endow with.

bequest NOUN = **legacy**, inheritance, endowment, settlement, estate, heritage.

bereavement NOUN = **death in the family**, loss, passing (away), demise; [formal] decease.

berserk ADJ = **mad**, crazy, insane, out of one's mind, hysterical, frenzied, crazed, demented, maniacal, manic, frantic, raving, wild, amok, on the rampage; [inf] off the deep end, ape, bananas, bonkers; [Brit. inf] spare.

berth NOUN 1 = **bunk**, bed, cot, hammock.
2 = **mooring**, dock, quay, pier.
▸ VERB = **dock**, moor, land, tie up, make fast.

beseech VERB = **implore**, beg, entreat, plead with, appeal to, call on, supplicate, importune, pray to, ask, petition.

besiege VERB 1 = **lay siege to**, beleaguer, blockade.
2 = **surround**, mob, crowd round, swarm round, ring, encircle.

best ADJ = **finest**, greatest, top, foremost, leading, pre-eminent, premier, prime, first, supreme, of the highest quality, superlative, par excellence, unrivalled, second to none, without equal, nonpareil, unsurpassed, peerless, matchless, unparalleled, unbeatable, optimum, optimal, ultimate, ideal, perfect; [inf] star, number-one.
Opposites: worst.
▸ NOUN = **finest**, top, cream, choice, prime, elite, crème de la crème, flower, jewel in the crown; [inf] pick of the bunch.

bestial ADJ = **savage**, animal, brutish, brutal, barbaric, cruel, vicious, violent, inhuman, depraved, degenerate.
Opposites: civilized, humane.

bestow VERB = **confer**, grant, accord, afford, endow with, vest in, present, award.

bet VERB = **wager**, gamble, stake, risk, venture, hazard, chance, put/lay money, speculate; [Brit. inf] have a flutter, have a punt.
▶ NOUN = **wager**, gamble, stake, ante; [Brit. inf] flutter, punt.

betray VERB 1 = **break one's promise to**, be disloyal to, be unfaithful to, break faith with, play someone false, inform on/against, give away, denounce, sell out, stab in the back; [inf] split on, rat on, peach on, stitch up, do the dirty on, sell down the river, squeal on; [Brit. inf] grass on, shop, sneak on; [N. Amer. inf] finger. 2 = **reveal**, disclose, divulge, tell, give away, leak, let slip, let out, blurt out; [inf] blab, spill.

better ADJ 1 = **superior**, finer, of higher quality; [inf] a cut above, streets ahead, head and shoulders above. 2 = **well**, healthy, cured, healed, recovered, recovering, on the road to recovery; [inf] on the mend.
Opposites: worse, inferior.
▶ VERB = *see* **improve** (1).

beware VERB = **be on your guard**, watch out, look out, mind out, be alert, be on the lookout, keep your eyes open/peeled, keep an eye out, take care, be careful, be cautious, have a care, watch your step.

bewilder VERB = **baffle**, mystify, bemuse, perplex, puzzle, confuse, nonplus; [inf] flummox, stump, beat, fox, discombobulate.

bewitch VERB = **captivate**, enchant, entrance, cast/ put a spell on, enrapture, charm, beguile, fascinate, enthral.

bias NOUN = **prejudice**, partiality, partisanship, favouritism, unfairness, one-sidedness, tendency, inclination, predilection, bigotry, intolerance, discrimination.
Opposites: impartiality.

b

▶ VERB = **prejudice**, influence, colour, sway, predispose, distort, skew.

biased ADJ = **prejudiced**, partial, partisan, one-sided, blinkered, jaundiced, distorted, warped, twisted, skewed, bigoted, intolerant, discriminatory.
Opposites: impartial.

bid VERB = **offer**, put up, tender, proffer, propose.
▶ NOUN **1** = **offer**, tender, proposal. **2** = **attempt**, effort, endeavour, try; [inf] crack, go, shot, stab.
▪ **bid for** = **try to get**, go for, make a pitch for, make a bid for.

big ADJ = **large**, great, of considerable size, sizeable, substantial, goodly, tall, high, huge, immense, enormous, colossal, massive, mammoth, broad, vast, prodigious, gigantic, giant, monumental, stupendous, gargantuan, man-size, king-size, outsize, considerable; [inf] whopping, mega, astronomical, humongous; [Brit.

inf] ginormous.
Opposites: small.

bigot NOUN = **dogmatist**, partisan, sectarian, racist, sexist, chauvinist.

bigoted ADJ = **prejudiced**, biased, one-sided, sectarian, discriminatory, opinionated, dogmatic, intolerant, narrow-minded, blinkered, racist, sexist, chauvinistic, jingoistic.
Opposites: open-minded.

bill NOUN **1** = **invoice**, account, statement; [N. Amer.] check; [inf] tab. **2** = **draft law**, proposed legislation, measure.
▶ VERB = **invoice**, charge, debit, send a statement to.

billow VERB **1** = **puff up/out**, balloon (out), swell, fill (out), belly out. **2** = **swirl**, spiral, roll, undulate, eddy, pour, flow.

bind VERB **1** = **tie (up)**, fasten (together), hold together, secure, make fast, attach, rope, strap, lash, truss, tether. **2** = **bandage**, dress, cover, wrap, strap up, tape up. **3** = **unite**, join, bond,

knit.
Opposites: untie, separate.

binding ADJ = **irrevocable**, unalterable, inescapable, unbreakable, contractual, compulsory, obligatory, mandatory.

birth NOUN 1 = **childbirth**, delivery, nativity, birthing; [dated] confinement.
2 = **beginning(s)**, emergence, genesis, dawn, rise, start.
3 = **ancestry**, lineage, blood, descent, parentage, family, extraction, origin, genealogy, stock.
Opposites: death, demise, end.

■ **give birth to** = **have**, bear, produce, be delivered of, bring into the world; [N. Amer.] birth; [inf] drop.

bisect VERB = **cut in half**, halve, divide/cut/split in two, cross, intersect.

bit NOUN 1 = **piece**, portion, segment, section, part, fragment, scrap, shred, crumb, grain, speck, snippet, snatch, spot, drop, pinch, dash, soupçon, morsel, iota, jot, whit, atom, particle, trace, touch, suggestion, hint; [inf] smidgen, tad.
2 = **moment**, minute, second, (little) while; [inf] sec, jiffy; [Brit. inf] mo, tick.
Opposites: lot.

■ **bit by bit** = **gradually**, little by little, in stages, step by step, piecemeal, slowly.

bite VERB 1 = **sink one's teeth into**, chew, munch, nibble at, gnaw, crunch, champ, tear at. 2 = **grip**, hold, get a purchase.
3 = **take effect**, be effective, work, act, have results.
▶ NOUN 1 = **chew**, munch, nibble, gnaw, nip.
2 = **snack**, mouthful, refreshments; [inf] a little something. 3 = **piquancy**, pungency, spiciness, tang, zest, sharpness, tartness; [inf] kick, punch.

biting ADJ = *see* **cold** (1), **scathing**.

bitter ADJ 1 = **acrid**, tart, sour, sharp, acid, unsweetened, harsh, biting, acerbic,

astringent, pungent,
vinegary, acetous,
unpleasant. **2 = resentful**,
angry, sullen, embittered,
sour, sore, rancorous,
acerbic, acrimonious,
peevish, petulant,
spiteful, malicious,
vicious, sharp, waspish,
piqued, jaundiced,
jealous, envious,
indignant, morose,
begrudging, crabbed.
Opposites: sweet, happy.

bizarre ADJ
= **extraordinary**,
outlandish, eccentric,
fantastic, surreal,
freakish, grotesque,
peculiar, odd, strange,
curious, abnormal, weird,
unusual, uncommon,
outré, unconventional,
queer, aberrant, deviant,
ludicrous, droll;
[inf] offbeat, oddball,
way-out, wacky; [Brit. inf,
dated] rum.
Opposites: ordinary.

black ADJ = **jet**, ebony,
sable, inky, sooty, pitch-
black, pitch-dark, dark,
dusky, coal-black,
funereal, raven; [poetic/
literary] Stygian.

blacken VERB = **darken**,
make dark, dirty,
smudge, stain, soil,
begrime, befoul.

blame VERB **1** = **accuse**,
hold responsible,
condemn, find guilty,
find fault with, criticize,
censure, reprimand,
reproach, admonish,
reprove, reprehend,
scold, upbraid, chide,
berate, take to task.
2 = **attribute**, ascribe,
impute, pin on.
▶ NOUN **1** = **responsibility**,
accountability, guilt,
fault, culpability,
liability, onus.
2 = **criticism**,
condemnation, censure,
accusation,
incrimination, stricture,
reproach, reproof,
recrimination,
reprimand, indictment,
complaint, berating;
[inf] stick, rap;
[formal] castigation.

blameless ADJ
= **innocent**, faultless,
guiltless, in the clear,
irreproachable,
unimpeachable, above
reproach, upright, moral,

virtuous, unoffending, impeccable, stainless, unblemished.
Opposites: guilty.

bland ADJ 1 = **tasteless**, insipid, flavourless, mild.
2 = **dull**, boring, uninspired, uninspiring, unoriginal, unexciting, tedious, nondescript, trite, vapid, mediocre, humdrum, weak.
Opposites: tangy, interesting.

blank ADJ 1 = **bare**, plain, clean, unmarked, empty, vacant, clear, void, unfilled, spotless.
2 = **expressionless**, inscrutable, impassive, unresponsive, deadpan, poker-faced, indifferent, vacant, empty, uncomprehending, vacuous, glazed, emotionless, uninterested. 3 = **empty**, vacant, at a loss, nonplussed, confused, baffled, bewildered, lost, dumbfounded, uncomprehending, puzzled, perplexed.
Opposites: full, expressive.

▶ NOUN = **gap**, void, space, vacancy, emptiness, vacuum, nothingness, vacuity.

blasphemous ADJ = **profane**, sacrilegious, irreligious, impious, irreverent, ungodly, godless, sinful, disrespectful, unholy.
Opposites: reverent.

blasphemy NOUN 1 = **sacrilege**, profanity, impiety, impiousness, irreverence, irreligiousness, profaneness, ungodliness, desecration, unholiness, execration. 2 = **oath**, curse, swear word, profanity.

blast NOUN 1 = **gust**, draught, rush, gale, storm, squall, blow.
2 = **explosion**, detonation, blowing up, discharge, burst, bang, eruption.
▶ VERB 1 = **blow up**, blow to pieces, explode, shatter, demolish, burst, ruin.
2 = **boom**, roar, blare, screech, trumpet.

blatant ADJ = **flagrant**, glaring, obvious,

blaze

unconcealed,
undisguised, overt,
manifest, brazen,
shameless,
unembarrassed,
barefaced, naked, sheer,
conspicuous, prominent,
obtrusive, apparent,
stark, unmistakable,
unmitigated, outright,
out-and-out.
Opposites: discreet,
inconspicuous.

blaze NOUN **1** = **fire**,
conflagration, burning,
flame, inferno. **2** = **beam**,
gleam, glitter, shine,
radiance, dazzle,
brightness, brilliance,
flash, flare.
▶ VERB **1** = **burn**, be on fire,
be ablaze, flame, catch
fire, flare up, burst into
flame. **2** = **shine**, gleam,
glimmer, dazzle, beam,
flare, flash, glitter.

bleach VERB = **fade**,
blanch, discolour, turn
white/pale, etiolate,
decolorize, lighten,
whiten, peroxide.

bleak ADJ **1** = **desolate**,
bare, barren, forbidding,
exposed, cold,
unwelcoming,

unsheltered, waste,
desert, windswept,
windy, arid,
uncultivated, wild,
dreary, lonely, grim.
2 = **dismal**, dreary,
gloomy, depressing,
melancholy, wretched,
hopeless, sombre,
discouraging,
disheartening,
unpromising,
comfortless, miserable,
cheerless, joyless.
Opposites: lush,
promising.

bleary ADJ = **blurred**,
blurry, dim, unclear,
indistinct, fuzzy, cloudy,
clouded, foggy, misty,
hazy, filmy, smeary,
obscured, fogged, murky,
watery, rheumy.
Opposites: clear.

blemish NOUN = **defect**,
stain, flaw, fault,
disfigurement,
imperfection, deformity,
ugliness, blot, mark,
smear, blotch, crack,
chip, taint.
▶ VERB = **spoil**, mar,
damage, injure, flaw,
mark, stain, taint, impair,
disfigure, discolour,

tarnish, blot, deface, sully, besmirch.

blend VERB 1 = **mix**, combine, intermix, mingle, amalgamate, unite, commix, commingle, merge, compound, fuse, coalesce, integrate, homogenize, synthesize, meld, alloy; [technical] admix. 2 = **harmonize**, complement, fit, suit, go with.

▶ NOUN = **mixture**, mix, combination, amalgam, compound, fusion, union, amalgamation, synthesis, composite, alloy, melange, concoction.

bless VERB 1 = **sanctify**, consecrate, hallow, dedicate, anoint, make sacred. 2 = **glorify**, extol, praise, exalt, adore; [formal] laud.
Opposites: curse.

blessed ADJ 1 = **sacred**, holy, divine, venerated, consecrated, hallowed, sanctified, beatified, revered. 2 = **happy**, fortunate, blissful, lucky, favoured, joyful, joyous, glad, cheerful, contented; [poetic/literary] blithe. 3 = **wonderful**, marvellous, welcome, longed for.
Opposites: cursed, wretched.

blessing NOUN 1 = **benediction**, consecration, dedication, prayer, grace, thanksgiving, commendation, invocation. 2 = **approval**, permission, consent, sanction, backing, endorsement, assent, support, concurrence, agreement, encouragement, approbation; [inf] go-ahead, the green light. 3 = **godsend**, boon, gift, favour, benefit, advantage, asset, comfort, convenience, help, bit of luck.
Opposites: veto.

blight NOUN 1 = **disease**, plague, pestilence, fungus, infestation, canker, mildew. 2 = **affliction**, misfortune, plague, disaster, calamity, trouble, ruin, catastrophe, curse, bane, scourge, tribulation, woe.

▶ VERB = **ruin**, destroy, spoil, shrivel, wither, crush, blast, mar.

blind ADJ **1** = **sightless**, unseeing, visually impaired, visionless, partially sighted, purblind. **2** = **obtuse**, blinkered, imperceptive, unaware, insensible, insensitive, unseeing, heedless, careless, unobservant, oblivious, indifferent, neglectful, slow, slow-witted, dense, stupid. **3** = **uncritical**, unthinking, unreasoning, undiscerning, unreasoned, irrational, indiscriminate, injudicious, partial, prejudiced, biased.

▶ VERB **1** = **make blind**, deprive of sight, blinker, blindfold. **2** = **dazzle**, deceive, delude, beguile, infatuate, confuse, bewilder, hoodwink; [inf] pull the wool over someone's eyes.

▶ NOUN = **shutter**, shade, curtain, screen.

bliss NOUN = **joy**, ecstasy, delight, rapture, euphoria, elation, happiness, pleasure, gladness, blessedness, beatitude, heaven, paradise, seventh heaven. **Opposites:** misery.

bloated ADJ = **swollen**, distended, puffy, puffed up, inflated, enlarged, expanded, dilated.

blob NOUN = **drop**, droplet, globule, dollop, gobbet, bubble, ball, bead, daub, blotch, dab, spot, splash, blot, smudge, smear; [inf] glob.

block VERB **1** = **clog**, choke, jam, close, obstruct, constrict, stop up, plug, dam, bung up, barricade, bar. **2** = **hinder**, prevent, obstruct, hamper, impede, bar, frustrate, thwart, check, resist, deter, oppose, arrest, stop, halt, scotch, stonewall.

▶ NOUN **1** = **blockade**, barrier, barricade, obstacle, bar, hindrance, impediment, obstruction, deterrent, check, stumbling block, difficulty, drawback, hitch. **2** = **bar**, piece, chunk, hunk, cake, lump, mass, slab, ingot, brick. **3** = **group**, set, batch, section, quantity.

blockage NOUN = **obstruction**, congestion, constriction, stoppage, occlusion, block, impediment, jam, bottleneck.

blood NOUN **1** = **gore**, vital fluid; [poetic/literary] lifeblood, ichor. **2** = **ancestry**, lineage, family, descent, birth, extraction, pedigree, origin, genealogy, inheritance, stock, race, kinship.

blood-curdling ADJ = **terrifying**, horrifying, spine-chilling, chilling, frightening, fearful, dreadful, terrible, horrendous, horrific, appalling, frightful.

bloodshed NOUN = **killing**, carnage, slaughter, murder, massacre, butchery, bloodletting, bloodbath; [poetic/literary] slaying.

bloodthirsty ADJ = **savage**, cruel, murderous, ferocious, homicidal, vicious, brutal, ruthless, barbaric, barbarous, inhuman, sadistic, bloody, slaughterous, violent, warlike, bellicose; [archaic] sanguinary.

bloody ADJ **1** = **bleeding**, bloodstained, blood-soaked, blood-spattered, unstaunched, raw. **2** = **savage**, fierce, gory, cruel, slaughterous; [archaic] sanguinary.

bloom NOUN **1** = **blossom**, flower, floret. **2** = **freshness**, radiance, lustre, glow, sheen, flush, perfection, blush, beauty. **3** = **perfection**, prime, heyday, vigour, strength, flourishing. ▶ VERB **1** = **flower**, blossom, burgeon, bud. **2** = **flourish**, prosper, thrive, be healthy, be happy, do well.

blot NOUN **1** = **spot**, smudge, speck, blotch, stain, mark, dot, patch, blob, smear; [Brit. inf] splodge. **2** = **blemish**, imperfection, eyesore, defect, stain, fault, flaw, taint, ugliness.

▶ VERB = **mark**, stain, dot, speckle, smudge, spoil, blotch, spot, spatter, bespatter, disfigure; [poetic/literary] besmirch.

■ **blot out** = **obliterate**, erase, efface, wipe out, delete, expunge, destroy, obscure, conceal, darken, dim, shadow.

blotchy ADJ = **spotted**, speckled, blotted, discoloured, patchy, smudged, uneven, streaked, stained, blotched, spattered.

blow¹ NOUN = **wind**, gale, breeze, blast, gust, storm, tempest.

▶ VERB 1 = **puff**, blast, gust, flurry, bluster. 2 = **waft**, flutter, buffet, whirl, whisk, sweep, drive, carry, transport, convey. 3 = **breathe**, breathe out, exhale, puff, pant, gasp, whistle. 4 = **sound**, play, blare, toot, blast.

■ **blow over** = **subside**, die down, pass, cease, settle, end, vanish.

■ **blow up** 1 = **explode**, shatter, burst, detonate, go off, blast, erupt.

2 = **inflate**, pump up, expand, swell, distend, puff up. 3 = **enlarge**, magnify, heighten, exaggerate, overstate, embroider, colour, improve on. 4 = **lose one's temper**, rage, fume, erupt, go wild; [inf] blow one's top, hit the roof, fly off the handle.

blow² NOUN 1 = **hit**, bang, knock, stroke, slap, smack, punch, buffet, rap, impact, jolt; [inf] whack, wallop, clout, bash, belt, biff, thwack. 2 = **affliction**, misfortune, shock, upset, disaster, calamity, catastrophe, grief, disappointment, setback, reversal, bombshell.

blueprint NOUN = **design**, plan, draft, prototype, model, pattern, scheme, sketch, diagram, outline, layout, representation.

bluff¹ VERB = **trick**, deceive, mislead, hoodwink, hoax, take in, dupe, delude, fool, sham, feign, fake, lie; [poetic/literary] cozen.

▶ NOUN = **bluster**, deceit, deception, trickery, fraud, fake, front, facade, pretence, sham, subterfuge, humbug.

bluff² ADJ = **blunt**, straightforward, frank, candid, outspoken, direct, hearty, rough.

blunder VERB **1** = **make a mistake**, slip, err, be in error, miscalculate, misjudge, mismanage, bungle; [inf] slip up, screw up, botch, blow it, put one's foot in it.
2 = **stumble**, stagger, lurch, flounder, be clumsy.
▶ NOUN = **error**, fault, mistake, slip, miscalculation, misjudgement, false/ wrong move, faux pas, oversight, inaccuracy, gaffe; [inf] slip-up, boo-boo, howler, clanger; [Brit. inf] boob, cock-up.

blunt ADJ **1** = **dull**, edgeless, unsharpened, unpointed, rounded. **2** = **direct**, frank, straightforward, candid, forthright, bluff, outspoken, plain-spoken, unceremonious, undiplomatic, tactless, rude, brusque, curt, abrupt, insensitive; [inf] upfront.
Opposites: sharp.
▶ VERB = **dull**, take the edge off, deaden, weaken, dampen, allay, abate, lessen, appease, impair.

blur VERB = **smear**, besmear, smudge, mist, cloud, fog, befog, bedim, blear, becloud, obscure, mask.

blurred ADJ = **indistinct**, blurry, hazy, misty, cloudy, foggy, fuzzy, vague, unfocused, unclear, obscure, ill-defined, nebulous, dim, faint, smeary, smudged.
Opposites: clear.

blurt
▪ **blurt out** = **say**, utter, let slip, blab, disclose, reveal, let out, divulge, tell, babble, exclaim; [inf] spill the beans, let the cat out of the bag, give the game away.

blush VERB = **redden**, go red/pink, flush, colour, crimson, glow, be ashamed, be embarrassed.

bluster VERB 1 = **blow**, storm, rage, blast, gust, roar. 2 = **boast**, bluff, brag, swagger, show off, vaunt, lord it, hector, bully, domineer, threaten, rant, harangue, be overbearing; [inf] throw one's weight about.
▶ NOUN = **boasting**, bravado, bluff, bombast, bragging, braggadocio, hectoring, domineering, swagger.

blustery ADJ = **stormy**, windy, gusty, squally, wild, tempestuous, violent.
Opposites: calm.

board NOUN 1 = **plank**, beam, panel, slat, timber, sheet, block. 2 = **food**, meals, sustenance, provisions, keep. 3 = **panel**, committee, council, directorate.
▶ VERB 1 = **get on**, get aboard/on board, enter, embark, mount. 2 = **lodge**, stay, live, room, billet.

boast VERB 1 = **brag**, swank, crow, swagger, vaunt, show off, exaggerate, bluster, blow one's own trumpet, pat oneself on the back; [inf] talk big. 2 = **possess**, have, own, pride oneself on, take pride in, enjoy, benefit from, exhibit, display.
▶ NOUN 1 = **brag**, self-praise, vaunt, overstatement; [inf] swank. 2 = **pride**, treasure, joy, gem; [inf] pride and joy, apple of someone's eye.

boastful ADJ = **conceited**, bragging, vain, arrogant, cocky, egotistical, proud, swaggering, swollen-headed, blustering, vaunting, braggart, overbearing; [inf] swanky, big-headed; [poetic/literary] vainglorious.
Opposites: modest.

bob VERB = **bounce**, dip, jump, nod, leap, hop, jerk, jolt, quiver, wobble, toss, shake, oscillate.

bodily ADJ = **corporeal**, physical, carnal, corporal, fleshly, material, substantial, tangible, incarnate.

body NOUN 1 = **figure**, frame, form, physique, shape, build, anatomy, skeleton, trunk, torso.

2 = **corpse**, carcass, remains, relics, mummy; [Medicine] cadaver; [inf] stiff. **3** = **set**, group, band, party, company, crowd, number, assembly, association. **4** = **accumulation**, collection, quantity, mass, corpus.

bog NOUN = **marsh**, swamp, marshland, fen, quagmire, morass, mire, slough, mud.
■ **bog down** = **mire**, stick, hamper, hinder, obstruct, impede, delay, stall, detain, entangle, ensnare, embroil, swamp, overwhelm.

bogus ADJ = **counterfeit**, fake, sham, false, spurious, forged, fraudulent, artificial, pretended, pretend, pseudo, imitation, mock, inauthentic, supposititious, soi-disant; [inf] phoney.
Opposites: genuine.

boil VERB **1** = **bubble**, seethe, simmer, stew, heat, cook, effervesce, foam, fizz, steam.
2 = **rage**, fume, seethe, storm, rant, rave, fulminate, flare up.

boisterous ADJ **1** = **lively**, bouncy, playful, exuberant, frisky, romping, unruly, disorderly, rough, wild, irrepressible, undisciplined, spirited, animated, obstreperous, riotous, rollicking, uproarious, rowdy, noisy; [Brit. inf] rumbustious.
2 = **rough**, choppy, stormy, wild, squally, breezy, turbulent, tempestuous, raging, gusty, blustery.
Opposites: restrained, calm.

bold ADJ **1** = **daring**, brave, adventurous, dauntless, unafraid, courageous, plucky, intrepid, audacious, fearless, valiant, gallant, hardy, heroic, valorous, undaunted, confident, venturesome, enterprising, daredevil, reckless, resolute.
2 = **forward**, audacious, presumptuous, impudent, pert, impertinent, brazen,

shameless, immodest, insolent, brash, cheeky, rude, barefaced, blatant, unashamed; [inf] saucy. **3 = striking**, eye-catching, prominent, pronounced, conspicuous, noticeable, emphatic, obvious, vivid, bright, showy, flashy, strong, distinct, marked. **Opposites:** timid, modest, faint, subdued.

bolster NOUN **= cushion**, pillow, support, prop, stay, rest.
▸ VERB **= support**, prop up, shore up, hold up, reinforce, buttress, strengthen, boost, maintain, build up, aid, assist, augment.

bolt NOUN **1 = bar**, latch, lock, catch, fastening, pin, peg, rivet, rod. **2 = flash**, streak, flare, shaft, burst. **3 = arrow**, dart, missile, projectile, shaft. **4 = run**, dash, sprint, dart, rush, bound, escape.
▸ VERB **1 = bar**, lock, fasten, secure, rivet, pin, nail, clamp. **2 = run**, dash, sprint, dart, rush, hurtle, hurry, fly, flee, run for it,

escape, abscond; [Brit. inf] scarper, do a bunk. **3 = gobble**, guzzle, wolf, stuff, gulp, cram, devour.

bombard VERB **1 = shell**, bomb, blitz, strafe, blast, pound, fire at, attack, assault, assail, batter. **2 = badger**, pester, harass, bother, hound, plague, besiege, beset, assail, importune, belabour.

bombardment NOUN **= assault**, attack, bombing, shelling, strafing, blitz, air raid, cannonade, fusillade, barrage, broadside.

bombastic ADJ **= pompous**, pretentious, grandiose, grandiloquent, turgid, verbose, ranting, extravagant, magniloquent, blustering, ostentatious, affected, inflated, periphrastic.

bonanza NOUN **= windfall**, godsend, bonus, boom, plenty, cornucopia, surplus, amplitude, sufficiency.

bond NOUN **1 = chain**, fetter, rope, cord, shackle, manacle, tie, restraint,

restriction, limitation, harness, straitjacket.
2 = **link**, connection, tie, attachment, affinity, union, relation, relationship, closeness, intimacy, nexus, ligature.
▸ VERB = **unite**, join, bind, connect, link, attach, fasten, secure, stick, glue, fuse, weld, blend, merge.

bondage NOUN = **slavery**, servitude, enslavement, subjection, captivity, oppression; [historical] serfdom, vassalage, thraldom.
Opposites: freedom.

bonus NOUN **1** = **gain**, advantage, extra, plus, benefit, boon. **2** = **gift**, gratuity, tip, present, bounty, reward, commission, honorarium; [inf] perk.

bony ADJ = **thin**, skinny, scrawny, angular, lean, skeletal, emaciated, cadaverous, gaunt, raw-boned.
Opposites: plump.

book NOUN = **volume**, tome, work, title, publication, paperback, hardback, folio, edition, copy.
▸ VERB = **reserve**, engage, charter, secure, bag, order, sign up, arrange, organize, schedule, programme.

bookish ADJ = **studious**, scholarly, scholastic, learned, erudite, highbrow, bluestocking, intellectual, academic, literary, pedantic, impractical; [inf] brainy, egghead.

booklet NOUN = **leaflet**, pamphlet, brochure, notebook.

boom NOUN **1** = **crash**, bang, report, explosion, blast, rumble, roar, thunder, reverberation.
2 = **boost**, surge, increase, upturn, improvement, growth, expansion, spurt, upsurge, success, bonanza, prosperity, advance, popularity, development.
Opposites: decline.
▸ VERB = **resound**, reverberate, rumble, roar, thunder, bang, blast.

boorish ADJ = **rude**, crude, loutish, churlish, unrefined, coarse, ill-

mannered, impolite,
uncouth, gross, oafish,
uncultured, philistine,
unsophisticated, vulgar,
ignorant, indelicate,
insensitive; [Brit.
inf] yobbish.
Opposites: refined.

boost VERB **1** = **lift**, raise,
push, thrust, elevate,
support, hoist, heave,
shove. **2** = **encourage**,
support, uplift, increase,
raise, heighten, promote,
further, advance,
improve, foster, assist,
expand, enlarge, develop,
facilitate, sustain;
[inf] hike up, jack up.
▶ NOUN **1** = **push**, shove, lift,
thrust, helping hand.
2 = **impetus**, impulse,
encouragement, support,
increase, expansion, rise,
improvement, advance,
stimulus; [inf] shot in the
arm.

boot VERB = **kick**, knock,
punt.

booth NOUN **1** = **stall**, stand,
kiosk, counter.
2 = **cubicle**, compartment,
enclosure, hut, carrel.

booty NOUN = **loot**,
plunder, haul, spoils,
gains, prizes, profits,
takings, pickings,
winnings; [inf] swag,
boodle, the goods.

border NOUN **1** = **edge**,
perimeter, verge,
boundary, limit, margin,
periphery, brink, fringe,
hem, brim, rim, skirt,
surround. **2** = **frontier**,
boundary, borderline,
limit.
▶ VERB **1** = **be next/adjacent
to**, be close to,
neighbour, adjoin, abut,
touch, join, connect,
edge, skirt, bound.
2 = **edge**, fringe, hem,
trim, bind, decorate, rim.
▪ **border on** = **verge on**,
approach, come close to,
approximate, be near/
similar to, resemble.

bore¹ VERB = **pierce**,
penetrate, drill, puncture,
perforate, burrow, tap,
tunnel, mine, dig out,
sink.

bore² VERB = **be tedious to**,
weary, tire, fatigue,
exhaust, depress, jade,
pall on, send to sleep,
leave cold, bore to tears,
bore to death; [inf] turn
off.

Opposites: interest, amuse.

boring ADJ = **tedious**, dull, uninteresting, uninspiring, unexciting, unstimulating, monotonous, unvaried, repetitive, dreary, humdrum, commonplace, flat, lacklustre, dry, dry as dust, stale, soporific, dead, soul-destroying, tiring, tiresome, wearisome; [inf] deadly. **Opposites:** interesting, amusing.

borrow VERB **1** = **ask for the loan of**, beg, be lent, take as a loan, have temporarily, lease, hire; [inf] cadge, scrounge, bum; [N. Amer. inf] mooch. **2** = **copy**, plagiarize, take, imitate, adopt, appropriate, commandeer, steal, pirate, purloin, help oneself to; [inf] filch, grab; [Brit. inf] nick, pinch. **Opposites:** lend.

boss NOUN = **head**, chief, leader, supervisor, manager, director, employer, superintendent, foreman, overseer, controller, master; [inf] numero uno; [Brit. inf] gaffer, governor; [N. Amer. inf] head honcho.

▶ VERB = **order about/ around**, give orders/ commands to, control, bully, push around, domineer, dominate; [inf] throw one's weight about.

bossy ADJ = **domineering**, overbearing, dictatorial, high-handed, authoritarian, autocratic, tyrannical, despotic, assertive, pushy, imperious, oppressive, bullying, lordly, officious, hectoring. **Opposites:** submissive.

botch VERB = **bungle**, make a mess of, do badly, spoil, muff, mismanage, fumble; [inf] mess/screw up, make a hash of; [Brit. inf] cock up.

bother VERB **1** = **disturb**, trouble, worry, pester, harass, annoy, upset, irritate, vex, inconvenience, plague, torment, nag, molest; [inf] hassle, get in someone's hair.

2 = distress, worry, concern, trouble, perturb, disconcert.

▶ NOUN **1 = nuisance**, annoyance, irritation, pest, trouble, worry, vexation. **2 = trouble**, disturbance, commotion, disorder, uproar, fighting, violence, furore, brouhaha.

bottle NOUN **= flask**, container, carafe, pitcher, decanter, flagon, phial, magnum, jeroboam, carboy, demijohn.

■ **bottle up** = *see* **suppress** (**2**).

bottleneck NOUN **= narrowing**, constriction, obstruction, congestion, blockage, jam, hold-up.

bottom NOUN **1 = base**, foundation, basis, support, substructure, pedestal, substratum, underpinning. **2 = lowest point**, foot, base, nadir. **3 = underneath**, underside, lower side, belly. **4 = buttocks**, rear end, rear, seat, rump; [inf] backside, behind; [Brit. inf] bum, arse, jacksie; [N.

Amer. inf] butt, fanny; [humorous] posterior. **Opposites:** top, surface.

▶ ADJ **= lowest**, deepest, least, last, minimum.

bottomless ADJ **1 = deep**, immeasurable, fathomless, unfathomable, unplumbable. **2 = unlimited**, inexhaustible, infinite, boundless.

bounce VERB **= jump**, leap, spring, bob, rebound, skip, recoil, ricochet, jounce.

▶ NOUN **= springiness**, spring, elasticity, give, resilience.

bound¹ ADJ **1 = certain**, sure, definite, very likely, fated, predestined. **2 = obligated**, obliged, required, forced, compelled, constrained, duty-bound. **3 = tied**, tied up, roped, tethered, fettered, secured.

■ **bound for = going/ travelling towards**, going to, heading for, making for, off to.

bound² VERB **= leap**, jump, spring, skip, hop, vault

bounce, hurdle, bob, gambol, romp, prance, caper.

boundary NOUN = **frontier**, border, limit, edge, dividing line, perimeter, verge, margin, threshold, bounds, periphery, fringe, borderline, brink, extremity.

boundless ADJ = **limitless**, unlimited, infinite, endless, unbounded, unending, never-ending, without end, unrestricted, inexhaustible, immeasurable, incalculable, vast, great, immense.
Opposites: limited, restricted.

bountiful ADJ = **abundant**, plentiful, ample, superabundant, copious, lavish, profuse, princely; [poetic/literary] plenteous, bounteous.
Opposites: mean, meagre.

bounty NOUN 1 = **reward**, recompense, remuneration, gratuity, tip, premium, bonus.
2 = **generosity**, munificence, altruism, largesse, benevolence, kindness, philanthropy.

bouquet NOUN 1 = **bunch of flowers**, spray, posy, wreath, garland, nosegay, corsage, buttonhole.
2 = **smell**, aroma, odour, fragrance, scent, perfume; [poetic/literary] redolence.

bout NOUN 1 = **match**, contest, fight, engagement, round, competition, encounter, struggle; [inf] set-to.
2 = **attack**, spell, fit, period, paroxysm.

bow VERB = **incline the head/body**, curtsy, bob, stoop, make obeisance, genuflect, bend the knee, prostrate oneself, kowtow, salaam.

bowl[1]

■ **bowl over** 1 = **knock down**, bring, down, floor, fell. 2 = **astound**, amaze, astonish, stagger, dumbfound, stun, surprise; [inf] flabbergast.

bowl[2] NOUN = **basin**, dish, pan, container, vessel.

box[1] NOUN = **container**, receptacle, crate, case, carton, pack, package,

box

110

b

chest, trunk, bin, coffer, casket.

box² VERB = **fight**, spar, punch, thump, cuff, batter, pummel; [inf] belt, sock, clout, whack, slug, slam.

boxer NOUN = **fighter**, pugilist, sparring partner, prizefighter.

boy NOUN = **youth**, lad, youngster, stripling, schoolboy; [inf] kid, whippersnapper.

boycott VERB **1** = **shun**, ostracize, stay away from, avoid, spurn, reject, eschew, send to Coventry, blacklist, blackball. **2** = **ban**, bar, prohibit, embargo, proscribe, blacklist, debar.

brace VERB **1** = **strengthen**, support, reinforce, shore up, prop up, buttress. **2** = **steady**, secure, stabilize, make fast. **3** = **prepare**, ready, fortify, tense.

brag VERB = **boast**, show off, blow one's own trumpet, crow, sing one's own praises.

brain NOUN **1** = **cerebrum**, cerebral matter, encephalon; [inf] grey matter. **2** = **intelligence**, intellect, mind, sense, cleverness, wit, understanding, acumen; [inf] nous, savvy.

brainy ADJ = **clever**, intelligent, bright, brilliant, gifted; [inf] smart.
Opposites: stupid.

branch NOUN **1** = **bough**, limb, stem, twig, shoot, sprig, arm.
2 = **department**, division, subdivision, section, subsection, part, wing, office.
▶ VERB = **fork**, divide, diverge, separate, bifurcate, split, subdivide.
■ **branch out** = **extend**, spread out, diversify, expand, proliferate, multiply.

brand NOUN **1** = **make**, variety, line, trade name, trademark. **2** = **kind**, type, sort, variety, style, stamp, cast.
▶ VERB **1** = **stamp**, mark, burn, scorch, sear, tag,

identify. 2 = **stigmatize**, characterize, mark, taint, vilify, disgrace, discredit, denounce.

brandish VERB = **flourish**, wave, wield, raise, swing, display, shake, wag, flaunt, show off.

brash ADJ = **bold**, self-confident, cocky, audacious, assertive, brazen, aggressive, forward, insolent, impudent, bumptious.
Opposites: meek.

bravado NOUN = **bluster**, swaggering, arrogance, boldness, audacity, bombast, braggadocio.

brave ADJ = **courageous**, valiant, fearless, intrepid, plucky, unafraid, heroic, bold, daring, resolute, indomitable, audacious, unshrinking, determined, undaunted, lion-hearted, spirited, dauntless, gallant, valorous, stalwart, doughty, stout-hearted, venturesome, game; [inf] gutsy, spunky.
Opposites: cowardly, fearful.

bravery NOUN = **courage**, courageousness, fearlessness, pluck, pluckiness, intrepidity, boldness, heroism, audacity, daring, nerve, fortitude, resolution, grit, spirit, dauntlessness, mettle, valour, tenacity, doughtiness, hardihood; [inf] guts, spunk; [Brit. inf] bottle.
Opposites: cowardice.

brawl NOUN = **fight**, scuffle, fracas, rumpus, altercation, clash, free-for-all, tussle, brouhaha, quarrel, wrangle, commotion, uproar, ruckus; [inf] punch-up, scrap; [Law, dated] affray.
▶ VERB = *see* **fight** VERB (**1**).

brawny ADJ = **muscular**, powerful, burly, strong, powerfully built, robust, sturdy, strapping, sinewy.
Opposites: scrawny, puny.

brazen ADJ = **bold**, shameless, unashamed, unabashed, audacious, defiant, brash, forward, pushy, presumptuous, brassy, impudent, insolent, cheeky, immodest, pert; [inf] saucy.

Opposites: reserved, modest.

breach NOUN **1** = **break**, rupture, split, opening, crack, gap, hole, fissure, rent, fracture, rift, cleft, aperture, gulf, chasm. **2** = **breaking**, violation, infringement, contravention, transgression, infraction. **3** = **breaking off**, severance, estrangement, parting, parting of the ways, rift, split, falling-out, schism, alienation, disaffection, quarrel, discord.

▶ VERB **1** = **break through**, split, rupture, open up, burst through, make a gap in. **2** = **break**, contravene, violate, infringe, transgress against, defy, disobey, flout.

break VERB **1** = **smash**, crack, shatter, split, burst, fracture, fragment, splinter, crash, snap, rend, tear, divide, sever, separate, part, demolish, disintegrate. **2** = **violate**, contravene, infringe, breach, disobey, defy,

flout, transgress against. **3** = **stop**, take a break, pause, rest, discontinue, give up; [inf] knock off, take five. **4** = **beat**, surpass, outdo, better, exceed, outstrip, top, cap.

Opposites: repair, mend, obey.

▶ NOUN **1** = **crack**, hole, gap, opening, chink, split, fissure, tear, rent, gash, rupture, rift, chasm, cleft. **2** = **interval**, pause, stop, halt, intermission, rest, respite, breathing space, interlude; [inf] breather, let-up, time out. **3** = **breach**, split, rupture, rift, discontinuation, schism, disaffection, alienation.

▪ **break away** = **leave**, break with, separate from, part company with, detach oneself from, secede from.

▪ **break down 1** = **stop working**, give out, go wrong, malfunction; [inf] conk out; [Brit. inf] pack up **2** = See **analyse**. **3** = See **collapse** VERB **(3)**.

■ **break in** = *see* **interrupt (1)**.

■ **break off** = **end**, bring to an end, finish, cease, discontinue, call a halt to, suspend.

■ **break out** = *see* **escape** VERB **(1)**.

■ **break up 1** = *See* **disperse**. **2** = *See* **separate** VERB **(4)**.

breakdown NOUN **1** = **stoppage**, failure, malfunctioning, seizing up; [inf] conking out. **2** = **collapse**, failure, disintegration, foundering, falling through. **3** = **analysis**, classification, itemization, categorization, explanation, examination, dissection.

breakthrough NOUN = **advance**, step/leap forward, leap, quantum leap, discovery, find, invention, innovation, development, improvement, revolution.

breast NOUN = **bust**, bosom, chest, front, thorax; [inf] boob, knocker.

breath NOUN **1** = **inhalation**, pant, gasp, gulp of air, inspiration, exhalation, expiration. **2** = **puff**, waft, gust, breeze.

breathe VERB **1** = **inhale**, = **exhale**, respire, puff, pant, gasp, wheeze, gulp. **2** = **whisper**, murmur, purr, sigh, say.

breathless ADJ = **out of breath**, panting, wheezing, wheezy, puffing, gasping, winded, choking.

breathtaking ADJ = **spectacular**, magnificent, impressive, awesome, awe-inspiring, astounding, exciting, astonishing, amazing, thrilling, stunning; [inf] out of this world.

breed VERB **1** = **reproduce**, procreate, multiply, give birth, bring forth young, propagate; [poetic/literary] beget. **2** = **produce**, bring about, give rise to, create, generate, stir up, engender, make for, foster, arouse, induce, originate, occasion.

breeze

b

▶ NOUN **1** = **family**, variety, type, kind, class, strain, stock, line. **2** = **stock**, species, race, lineage, extraction, pedigree.

breeze NOUN = **breath of wind**, gentle wind, draught, puff of air, gust, flurry, current of air; [poetic/literary] zephyr.

breezy ADJ = **windy**, blowy, blustery, gusty, squally, fresh.

brevity NOUN = **shortness**, briefness, conciseness, concision, terseness, compactness, pithiness, succinctness, economy, curtness, condensation, pointedness.

brew VERB **1** = **make**, prepare, infuse, ferment, mash. **2** = **be imminent**, loom, gather, form, be threatening, be impending, impend.
▶ NOUN = **drink**, beverage, liquor, ale, beer, tea, infusion, mixture, potion.

bribe VERB = **corrupt**, entice, suborn, get at, buy off, pay off; [inf] grease someone's palm, sweeten, fix,

square.
▶ NOUN = **inducement**, enticement, incentive; [inf] backhander, sweetener, graft, kickback.

bridge NOUN **1** = **arch**, span, overpass, flyover, viaduct. **2** = **bond**, link, tie, connection, cord, binding.
▶ VERB = **span**, cross, go over, pass over, traverse, extend across, reach across, arch over.

brief ADJ **1** = **concise**, short, succinct, to the point, terse, economic, abbreviated, pithy, pointed, curt, crisp, condensed, compressed, sparing, thumbnail, epigrammatic. **2** = **short-lived**, short, fleeting, momentary, temporary, impermanent, passing, fading, transitory, ephemeral, transient.
Opposites: long.
▶ VERB = **instruct**, inform, direct, guide, advise, enlighten, prepare, prime; [inf] fill in, put in the picture, give someone the low-down.

▶ NOUN **1** = **information**, advice, instructions, directions, guidance, briefing, preparation, priming, intelligence; [inf] low-down, rundown. **2** = **argument**, case, proof, defence, evidence, contention, demonstration.

briefly ADV **1** = **concisely**, succinctly, to the point, tersely, sparingly, economically. **2** = **fleetingly**, temporarily, momentarily, ephemerally. **3** = **in short**, in brief, to cut a long story short, in a word, in a nutshell, in essence.

briefs PL NOUN = **underpants**, pants, Y-fronts, knickers; [Brit.] camiknickers; [N. Amer.] shorts; [inf] panties.

bright ADJ **1** = **shining**, brilliant, vivid, intense, blazing, dazzling, beaming, sparkling, glittering, gleaming, radiant, glowing, glistening, shimmering, luminous, lustrous, incandescent. **2** = **vivid**, intense, rich, brilliant, bold, glowing. **3** = **clear**, cloudless, unclouded, sunny, pleasant, clement. **4** = **intelligent**, clever, sharp, quick-witted, astute, acute, ingenious, resourceful, accomplished; [inf] brainy, smart. **5** = **promising**, optimistic, favourable, hopeful, auspicious, propitious, encouraging, lucky, golden. **Opposites**: dark, dull, stupid.

brighten VERB **1** = **make bright/brighter**, light up, lighten, illuminate, irradiate; [poetic/literary] illumine. **2** = **cheer up**, gladden, liven up, enliven, perk up, animate; [inf] buck up, pep up.

brilliant ADJ **1** = **bright**, shining, intense, radiant, beaming, gleaming, sparkling, dazzling, lustrous. **2** = **clever**, intelligent, astute, masterly, inventive, resourceful, discerning; [inf] smart. **3** = **excellent**, superb, very good,

outstanding, exceptional;
[Brit. inf] brill, smashing.
Opposites: dull, bad.

brim NOUN = **rim**, lip, edge,
brink, margin,
circumference, perimeter,
verge.
▶ VERB = **be full**, be filled up,
be full to capacity,
overflow, run over, well
over.

bring VERB 1 = **fetch**, carry,
bear, take, convey,
transport, deliver, lead,
guide, conduct, usher,
escort. 2 = **cause**, create,
produce, result in,
engender, give rise to,
precipitate, occasion,
wreak, effect, contribute
to.
■ **bring about** = *see sense*
(2) *above*.
■ **bring in** = *see* **earn** (1).
■ **bring off** = *see* **achieve**.
■ **bring up** 1 = *see* **raise** (3).
2 = *see* **broach** (2).

brink NOUN 1 = **edge**, verge,
margin, limit, rim,
extremity, boundary,
fringe. 2 = **verge**, edge,
threshold, point.

brisk ADJ 1 = **quick**, rapid,
fast, swift, speedy,
energetic, lively,
vigorous, sprightly,
spirited. 2 = **abrupt**,
brusque, no-nonsense,
sharp, curt, crisp;
[inf] snappy.
Opposites: slow, leisurely.

bristle NOUN = **hair**,
stubble, whisker, prickle,
spine, quill, thorn, barb.
▶ VERB = **grow angry/
indignant**, be irritated,
bridle, flare up, draw
oneself up, rear up.

brittle ADJ 1 = **breakable**,
hard, crisp, fragile, frail,
delicate; [formal] frangible.
2 = **edgy**, nervous, on
edge, tense, stiff;
[inf] uptight.
Opposites: flexible,
relaxed.

broach VERB 1 = **pierce**,
puncture, tap, draw off.
2 = **introduce**, raise, bring
up, mention, suggest,
open, put forward,
propound.

broad ADJ 1 = **wide**, large,
extensive, vast, spacious,
expansive, sweeping,
boundless, ample,
capacious, open.
2 = **wide-ranging**, wide,
general, comprehensive,
inclusive, encyclopedic,

all-embracing, universal, unlimited. **3 = general**, non-specific, unspecific, imprecise, vague, loose, sweeping.
Opposites: narrow.

broadcast VERB
1 = transmit, relay, send out, put on the air, beam, televise, telecast.
2 = announce, make public, report, publicize, publish, advertise, proclaim, air, spread, circulate, disseminate, promulgate.
▸ NOUN = **programme**, show, transmission, telecast.

broaden VERB **1 = widen**, make broader, extend, spread, enlarge.
2 = expand, widen, enlarge, extend, increase, augment, add to, develop, amplify, swell.

broad-minded ADJ
= **open-minded**, liberal, tolerant, unprejudiced, flexible, unbiased, undogmatic, catholic, fair, progressive, freethinking, enlightened, permissive.
Opposites: narrow-minded.

brochure NOUN = **booklet**, catalogue, prospectus, leaflet, pamphlet, handbill, handout, advertisement.

broke ADJ = **penniless**, insolvent, bankrupt, poverty-stricken, impoverished, impecunious, destitute, indigent, ruined; [inf] flat broke, strapped for cash, cleaned out, on one's uppers; [Brit. inf] skint, stony broke.

broken-hearted ADJ
= **grief-stricken**, desolate, despairing, devastated, inconsolable, miserable, overwhelmed, wretched, forlorn, woeful, crestfallen.

brood NOUN = **offspring**, young, family, clutch, nest, litter, children, youngsters.
▸ VERB **1 = worry**, agonize, fret, dwell on, meditate, mull over. **2 = sit on**, hatch, incubate.

brook¹ NOUN = **stream**, streamlet, channel, rivulet, runnel; [N. English] beck; [Scottish & N. English] burn; [N. Amer. &

Austral./NZ] creek.

brook² VERB = **tolerate**, stand, bear, allow.

browbeat VERB = **bully**, force, coerce, intimidate, compel, badger, hector, harangue, terrorize, tyrannize.

brown ADJ 1 = **hazel**, chestnut, nut-brown, brunette, chocolate, coffee, walnut, ochre, sepia, mahogany, russet, umber, burnt sienna, dun, khaki, beige, tan. 2 = **tanned**, sunburnt, browned, bronze, bronzed, swarthy.
▶VERB = **grill**, toast, sear, seal.

browse VERB 1 = **look through**, skim, scan, glance at, thumb through, leaf through, peruse. 2 = **graze**, feed, eat, crop, nibble.

bruise NOUN = **contusion**, swelling, bump, mark, blemish, welt.
▶VERB = **contuse**, injure, blacken, mark, discolour, make black and blue.

brunt NOUN = **impact**, full force, burden, shock, thrust, violence, pressure, strain, stress, repercussions, consequences.

brush NOUN 1 = **broom**, sweeper, besom, whisk. 2 = **encounter**, clash, confrontation, conflict, skirmish, tussle, fight, engagement.
▶VERB 1 = **sweep**, clean, groom, buff. 2 = **touch**, graze, kiss, glance, contact.
■ **brush aside** = *see* **dismiss** (1).
■ **brush off** = *see* **rebuff** VERB.

brusque ADJ = **abrupt**, curt, blunt, short, terse, caustic, gruff, rude, discourteous, impolite.
Opposites: polite.

brutal ADJ = **savage**, cruel, vicious, sadistic, violent, bloodthirsty, ruthless, callous, murderous, heartless, merciless, pitiless, remorseless, inhuman, barbarous, barbaric, ferocious, wild, brutish, bestial.
Opposites: gentle.

brute NOUN 1 = **animal**, beast, creature. 2 = **savage**, monster, animal, sadist, barbarian, fiend, devil, lout, oaf, boor; [inf] swine.

▶ ADJ = **crude**, rough, mindless, physical, unfeeling.

bubble NOUN = **globule**, bead, drop, air pocket.

▶ VERB = **fizz**, foam, froth, gurgle, effervesce, sparkle, boil, simmer, seethe, percolate.

bubbly ADJ **1** = **fizzy**, foamy, frothy, effervescent, sparkling, sudsy. **2** = **vivacious**, lively, animated, sparkling, excited, effervescent, bouncy, ebullient, elated.

bucket NOUN = **pail**, pitcher, can, scuttle.

buckle NOUN **1** = **clasp**, fastener, clip, catch, fastening, hasp. **2** = **kink**, warp, distortion, wrinkle, bulge.

▶ VERB **1** = **fasten**, hook, secure, do up, strap, tie, clasp, clip. **2** = **bend**, twist, contort, warp, crumple, distort.

bud NOUN = **shoot**, sprout.

▶ VERB = **sprout**, germinate, shoot, burgeon.

budge VERB **1** = **move**, shift, stir, yield, go, proceed. **2** = **persuade**, convince, influence, sway, bend.

budget NOUN = **financial plan**, estimate, statement, account, allowance, means, resources.

▶ VERB **1** = **plan**, allow, set aside, allocate, save. **2** = **plan**, schedule, allocate, ration, apportion.

buff[1] VERB = **polish**, shine, rub, smooth, burnish.

buff[2] NOUN = **fan**, enthusiast, aficionado, devotee, admirer, expert; [inf] freak, nut.

buffer NOUN = **bulwark**, fender, bumper, cushion, guard, safeguard, shield, screen, intermediary.

buffet[1] NOUN = **cafe**, cafeteria, snack bar, refreshment counter/ stall.

buffet[2] VERB = **batter**, strike, knock against, hit, bang, beat against.

buffoon NOUN = **fool**, idiot, dolt, nincompoop; [inf] dope, chump,

b

numbskull, halfwit; [Brit. inf] nitwit.

bug NOUN 1 = **insect**, flea, mite; [inf] creepy-crawly; [Brit. inf] minibeast. 2 = **germ**, virus, bacterium, microbe, micro-organism. 3 = **illness**, sickness, disease, infection, disorder, upset, complaint; [Brit. inf] lurgy. 4 = **fault**, flaw, defect, error, imperfection, failing, obstruction; [inf] gremlin.
▶ VERB 1 = **tap**, wiretap, listen in on, intercept, spy on. 2 = see **annoy**.

build VERB = **construct**, make, erect, put up/ together, assemble, set up, manufacture, fabricate, raise, form.
▶ NOUN = **physique**, body, frame, shape.
■ **build up** = see **intensify**.

building NOUN = **structure**, construction, edifice, pile, erection.

build-up NOUN = **growth**, increase, expansion, enlargement, accumulation, escalation, development.

bulbous ADJ = **distended**, bulging, swollen, rotund, convex, bloated, spherical, rounded.

bulge VERB = **swell**, swell out, project, protrude, stick out, balloon, jut out, enlarge, billow, distend, bloat.
▶ NOUN = **swelling**, bump, protuberance, protrusion, lump, knob, projection, prominence, distension.

bulk NOUN 1 = **size**, volume, quantity, weight, extent, mass, substance, magnitude, dimensions, amplitude. 2 = **majority**, preponderance, greater part, mass, body, generality.

bulky ADJ = **unwieldy**, awkward, large, big, substantial, massive, immense, voluminous, weighty, ponderous; [inf] hulking.

bulldoze VERB 1 = **demolish**, flatten, level, raze. 2 = **force**, push, shove, drive, propel.

bulletin NOUN = **report**, announcement, statement, newsflash, account, message, communiqué, communication, dispatch, notification.

bullish ADJ = **optimistic**, hopeful, confident, positive, assured, cheerful, sanguine.

bully NOUN = **intimidator**, persecutor, oppressor, browbeater, tyrant, tormentor, bully boy, thug; [inf] tough.
▶ VERB = **intimidate**, coerce, browbeat, oppress, domineer, persecute, torment, pressurize, pressure, terrorize, tyrannize, cow; [inf] push around.

bulwark NOUN 1 = **rampart**, embankment, fortification, bastion, redoubt, outwork, breastwork. 2 = **support**, defence, guard, protection, safeguard.

bumbling ADJ = **clumsy**, awkward, blundering, incompetent, bungling, inept, inefficient, stumbling, lumbering, foolish.

bump VERB 1 = **hit**, bang, strike, knock, jar, crash into, collide with, smash into. = *See also* **hit** (1).
2 = **bounce**, jolt, shake, jerk, rattle, jounce.
▶ NOUN 1 = **bang**, crash, thud, thump, knock, smash, collision.
2 = **lump**, swelling, contusion, injury, protrusion, bulge, projection, protuberance, hump, knob, distension.
▪ **bump into** = *see* **meet** (1).

bumpkin NOUN = **yokel**, clodhopper, peasant, rustic, country cousin; [N. Amer. inf] hillbilly, hick, hayseed, rube.

bumptious ADJ = **self-important**, conceited, arrogant, cocky, full of oneself, overconfident, brash, overbearing, puffed up, self-opinionated, egotistical, immodest, boastful, presumptuous, pompous, officious, swaggering, forward, pushy; [inf] big-headed.
Opposites: modest.

bumpy ADJ 1 = **rough**, uneven, rutted, potholed, pitted, lumpy, knobby.

bunch

2 = jolting, jarring, bouncy, jerky, rough.
Opposites: smooth.

bunch NOUN **1 = collection**, cluster, batch, set, quantity, bundle, heap, sheaf, clump.
2 = bouquet, spray, posy, sheaf, corsage, nosegay.
3 = group, crowd, party, band, gathering, swarm, gang, flock, mob, knot, cluster, multitude.
▶ VERB **= gather**, cluster, huddle, group, flock, mass, cram, pack, herd, bundle.
Opposites: disperse.

bundle NOUN **= batch**, pile, collection, heap, stack, bunch, parcel, bale, sheaf, mass, quantity, accumulation.
▶ VERB **1 = tie**, tie up, wrap, bind, fasten together, pack, parcel, roll, truss.
2 = push, shove, hurry, hustle, rush, thrust, throw.

bungle VERB **= make a mess of**, mismanage, spoil, ruin, blunder, muff, mar; [inf] screw up, foul up, mess up, louse up, botch, make a hash of, muck up; [Brit. inf] cock up.

bungling ADJ **= clumsy**, incompetent, inept, unskilful, blundering, maladroit; [inf] ham-fisted, cack-handed.

buoy NOUN **= float**, marker, beacon.

buoyant ADJ **1 = floating**, afloat, floatable, light.
2 = *See* **cheerful (1).**

burden NOUN **1 = load**, weight, cargo, freight.
2 = responsibility, duty, obligation, onus, charge, care, worry, anxiety, problem, trouble, difficulty, strain, stress, affliction, weight, trial, tribulation, encumbrance, millstone, cross, albatross.
▶ VERB **1 = load**, overload, weigh down, encumber, hamper. **2 = trouble**, worry, oppress, bother, distress, afflict, torment, strain, tax, overwhelm, saddle, encumber; [inf] land.

bureau NOUN **1 = agency**, office, department, service. **2 = desk**, writing desk, writing table.

burrow

bureaucracy NOUN
= **officialdom**, officials,
administration, civil
servants, civil service,
government, directorate,
regulations, paperwork,
red tape.

burglar NOUN
= **housebreaker**, thief,
robber, raider, looter, cat
burglar, intruder; [N. Amer.
inf] second-story man.

burglary NOUN
= **housebreaking**,
breaking and entering,
breaking in, break-in,
forced/forcible entry,
theft, robbery.

burial NOUN = **interment**,
burying, entombment,
funeral, obsequies;
[formal] exequies.
Opposites: exhumation.

burly ADJ = **well built**,
muscular, brawny, stout,
thickset, stocky, sturdy,
big, powerful, strong,
strapping, hefty, athletic,
tough, husky; [inf] beefy,
hulking.
Opposites: puny.

burn VERB **1** = **be on fire**, be
alight, be ablaze, go up,
blaze, be aflame,
smoulder, flare, flash,
glow, smoke, flicker.
2 = **set on fire**, set fire to,
set alight, ignite, light,
kindle, put a match to,
incinerate, reduce to
ashes, cremate, consume,
sear, char, scorch.

burning ADJ **1** = **on fire**,
blazing, ablaze, aflame,
alight, flaring, glowing,
smouldering, ignited,
flickering, scorching,
incandescent; [poetic/
literary] afire. **2** = **stinging**,
smarting, biting,
prickling, irritating,
searing, caustic,
corrosive, painful.
3 = **intense**, eager,
passionate, fervent,
ardent, fervid.
4 = **important**, crucial,
significant, urgent,
pressing, critical,
compelling, vital,
essential, acute, pivotal.

burnish VERB = **polish**,
shine, brighten, rub,
buff, buff up, smooth.

burrow NOUN = **tunnel**,
hole, hollow, excavation,
lair, den, earth, warren,
set.
▸ VERB = **dig**, tunnel,
excavate, mine, hollow

b

out, gouge out, scoop
out.

burst VERB 1 = **split**, break
open, rupture, crack,
shatter, explode, give
way, fracture,
disintegrate, fragment,
fly open. 2 = **rush**, thrust,
shove, push, dash, run,
erupt, surge.

bury VERB 1 = **inter**, lay to
rest, entomb, consign to
the grave; [inf] plant.
2 = **conceal**, hide, cover
with, submerge, tuck,
sink, cup.
Opposites: exhume.

bush NOUN 1 = **shrub**,
thicket, undergrowth,
shrubbery. 2 = **scrub**,
brush, wilds, backwoods;
[Austral./NZ] outback.

bushy ADJ = **thick**, shaggy,
dense, tangled, hairy,
bristly, fuzzy, luxuriant,
unruly, untidy,
spreading.

business NOUN
1 = **occupation**,
profession, line, career,
job, trade, vocation,
work, employment,
pursuit, métier. 2 = **trade**,
commerce, industry,
buying and selling,

trading, merchandising,
trafficking, bargaining,
dealing, transactions.
3 = **company**, firm,
enterprise, corporation,
concern, organization,
venture, shop,
establishment,
partnership. 4 = **concern**,
affair, responsibility,
duty, function, task,
assignment, obligation,
problem. 5 = **affair**,
matter, thing, case, set of
circumstances, issue.

businesslike ADJ
1 = **professional**, efficient,
organized, methodical,
systematic, well ordered,
practical, thorough,
painstaking, meticulous,
correct. 2 = **routine**,
conventional,
unimaginative, prosaic,
down-to-earth,
workaday.
Opposites: unprofessional,
disorganized.

bust[1] NOUN = **breasts**,
bosom, chest, torso;
[inf] boobs, knockers.

bust[2] VERB 1 = **break**,
destroy, wreck, rupture,
fracture, crack. 2 = **arrest**,
capture, catch, seize;

[inf] pinch, nab, collar; [Brit. inf] nick.

bustle NOUN = **activity**, flurry, stir, restlessness, movement, hustle, hurly-burly, busyness, commotion, tumult, excitement, agitation, fuss; [inf] to-do.
▶ VERB = **hurry**, rush, dash, scurry, dart, hasten, scramble, fuss, scamper, flutter; [inf] tear.

busy ADJ 1 = **active**, industrious, tireless, energetic, hectic, strenuous, full, bustling, exacting; [inf] on the go. 2 = **occupied**, working, engaged, at work, on duty, otherwise engaged; [inf] tied up. 3 = **ornate**, over-elaborate, over-decorated, fussy, cluttered.
Opposites: idle, simple.

busybody NOUN = **meddler**, interferer, troublemaker, mischief-maker, gossip, scandalmonger, muckraker; [inf] snooper, nosy parker.

butt¹ VERB = **knock**, strike, shove, ram, bump, push, thrust, prod, poke, jab, thump, buffet.
▪ **butt in** = **interrupt**, intrude, interfere in; [inf] stick one's nose/oar in.

butt² NOUN = **target**, victim, object, subject, scapegoat, dupe.

butt³ NOUN 1 = **handle**, shaft, hilt, haft. 2 = **stub**, end, remnant, tail end; [Brit. inf] fag end.

buttocks NOUN = **cheeks**, rump, behind, hindquarters, seat; [Brit.] bottom; [inf] BTM, backside, derrière; [Brit. inf] bum, arse; [N. Amer. inf] butt, fanny; [humorous] posterior, fundament.

buttonhole VERB = **accost**, waylay, importune, detain, grab, catch, take aside.

buttress NOUN = **support**, prop, reinforcement, strut, stanchion, pier.
▶ VERB = **strengthen**, support, reinforce, prop up, shore up, brace, underpin, uphold, defend, back up.

buxom ADJ = **big-breasted**, big-bosomed, full-figured, voluptuous, well rounded, Rubenesque, plump, robust, shapely, ample; [inf] busty, well endowed.

buy VERB = **purchase**, pay for, get, acquire, obtain, come by, procure, invest in.
Opposites: sell.
▶ NOUN = **purchase**, acquisition, bargain, deal.
Opposites: sale.

buzz VERB = **hum**, murmur, drone, whirr, whisper; [poetic/literary] susurrate.

bygone ADJ = **past**, departed, dead, gone, former, previous, one-time, forgotten, lost, old, antiquated, ancient, obsolete, outmoded.

bypass VERB 1 = **go round**, make a detour round, pass round.
2 = **circumvent**, avoid, evade, get round, pass over, ignore, skirt, sidestep, miss out, go over the head of, short-circuit.

bystander NOUN = **onlooker**, spectator, eyewitness, witness, watcher, viewer, passer-by.

Cc

cabin NOUN **1** = **hut**, shack, shed, chalet, lodge, shelter, bothy. **2** = **berth**, compartment, stateroom, sleeping quarters, saloon, deckhouse.

cable NOUN = **rope**, cord, wire, line, lead, hawser, mooring line, chain, guy.

cache NOUN = **hoard**, store, supply, collection, fund; [inf] stash.

cacophonous ADJ = **discordant**, atonal, dissonant, noisy, raucous, harsh, unmusical.
Opposites: harmonious.

cacophony NOUN = **discordance**, dissonance, atonality, noise, racket, din, row, caterwauling, jangle, tumult, stridency, raucousness.

cadaverous ADJ = **corpse-like**, death-like, gaunt, haggard, drawn, emaciated, skeletal, hollow-eyed, ashen, pale, wan, ghostly.

cadence NOUN = **rhythm**, beat, pulse, tempo, measure, metre, swing, lilt, intonation, inflection, accent, modulation.

cafe NOUN = **cafeteria**, snack bar, buffet, coffee bar/shop/house, tea room/shop, diner, bistro, restaurant, brasserie.

cage NOUN = **pen**, enclosure, pound, coop, lock-up, hutch, aviary.
▶ VERB = *see* **confine** (**1**).

cagey ADJ = **guarded**, secretive, cautious, non-committal, wary, careful, chary, wily.

cajole VERB = **coax**, wheedle, beguile, seduce, persuade, flatter, humour, lure, entice, tempt, inveigle; [inf] sweet-talk, soft-soap, butter up.

cake NOUN 1 = **bun**, gateau, pastry. 2 = **block**, bar, slab, piece, lump, cube, mass, loaf, chunk.
▶ VERB 1 = **harden**, solidify, thicken, dry, bake, congeal, coagulate, consolidate. 2 = **cover**, coat, plaster, encrust, clog.

calamitous ADJ = **disastrous**, catastrophic, devastating, cataclysmic, ruinous, dire, dreadful, terrible, tragic, fatal, wretched, woeful, ghastly, unfortunate.

calamity NOUN = **disaster**, catastrophe, tragedy, misfortune, cataclysm, accident, devastation, misadventure, mischance, mishap, ruin, tribulation, woe.

calculate VERB 1 = **work out**, estimate, determine, compute, count up, figure out, reckon up, evaluate, total. 2 = **estimate**, gauge, judge, measure, weigh up, reckon, rate. 3 = **design**, plan, aim, intend.

calculated ADJ = *see* **deliberate** ADJ (**1**).

calculating ADJ = *see* **crafty**.

calibre NOUN 1 = **quality**, worth, stature, distinction, ability, merit, talent, capability, excellence, competence, capacity, endowments, gifts, strengths, scope. 2 = **bore**, gauge, diameter, size.

call VERB 1 = **cry**, cry out, shout, bellow, exclaim, yell, scream, roar, shriek. 2 = **telephone**, phone, call up; [Brit.] ring; [inf] buzz, give someone a buzz/tinkle; [Brit. inf] give someone a ring. 3 = **visit**, pay a visit/call, call on, stop by; [inf] drop in/by, pop in. 4 = **convene**, summon, assemble, announce, order; [formal] convoke. 5 = **name**, christen, baptize, entitle, dub, designate, describe as, label, term. 6 = **send for**, summon, ask for, contact, order, fetch, bid. 7 = **awaken**, wake, arouse, rouse.

▶ NOUN 1 = **cry**, shout, exclamation, yell, scream, shriek, roar, bellow. 2 = **plea**, request, appeal, order, command, summons. 3 = **need**, occasion, reason, cause, justification, grounds, excuse. 4 = **demand**, requirement, request, need, want, requisition.

■ **call for** = **need**, require, be grounds for, justify, necessitate, demand, entail.

■ **call off** = *see* **cancel**.

calling NOUN = **vocation**, occupation, job, line, line of work, career, profession, métier, business, work, employment, trade, craft, pursuit, province, field.

callous ADJ = **insensitive**, unfeeling, hard, hardened, heartless, hard-hearted, hard-bitten, tough, cold, cool, stony-hearted, cruel, uncaring, unsympathetic, indifferent, unresponsive, dispassionate, unconcerned, unsusceptible, merciless, pitiless, soulless; [inf] hard-nosed, hard-boiled.
Opposites: compassionate.

callow ADJ = **immature**, inexperienced, naive, unsophisticated, innocent, uninitiated, raw, green, young, adolescent; [inf] wet behind the ears.
Opposites: mature, experienced.

calm ADJ 1 = **composed**, relaxed, collected, cool, controlled, restrained, self-controlled, self-possessed, quiet, tranquil, unruffled, serene, unexcited, unflappable, undisturbed, imperturbable, unemotional, unmoved, impassive, undemonstrative, poised, level-headed, patient, equable, stoical, pacific; [inf] laid-back, together. 2 = **still**, windless, mild, tranquil, balmy, quiet,

peaceful, restful,
undisturbed, halcyon.
Opposites: excitable,
stormy.

▶ VERB **1** = **soothe**, quieten,
pacify, hush, tranquillize,
mollify, appease, allay,
alleviate, assuage.
2 = **quieten**, settle, settle
down, die down, still.
Opposites: agitate.

▶ NOUN **1** = **composure**,
coolness, self-control,
tranquillity, serenity,
quietness, peace,
peacefulness, harmony,
restfulness, repose.
2 = **stillness**, tranquillity,
serenity, quietness,
quietude.

calumny NOUN = **slander**,
libel, defamation,
misrepresentation, false
accusation, insult, abuse,
denigration, vilification,
vituperation, aspersions,
backbiting, detraction,
disparagement,
deprecation, revilement,
obloquy, smear
campaign; [inf] mud-
slinging.

camouflage NOUN
= **disguise**, mask, screen,
cover, protective

colouring, cloak, cover-
up, front, false front,
guise, facade, blind,
concealment,
masquerade, subterfuge.

▶ VERB = **disguise**, hide,
conceal, mask, screen,
cloak, veil, cover, cover
up, obscure.

camp¹ NOUN
= **encampment**,
settlement, campsite,
camping ground, tents,
bivouac, cantonment.

camp² ADJ = **effeminate**,
effete, mincing, affected,
artificial, mannered,
posturing, studied.
Opposites: macho.

campaign NOUN **1** = **battle**,
war, offensive,
expedition, attack,
crusade. **2** = **drive**, push,
operation, plan,
promotion, strategy,
movement, manoeuvre.

▶ VERB = **fight**, battle, work,
crusade, push, strive,
struggle.

cancel VERB **1** = **call off**,
scrap, drop, axe,
abandon, stop,
discontinue. **2** = **annul**,
declare void, invalidate,
quash, nullify, set aside,

retract, negate,
countermand, rescind,
revoke, repudiate,
abrogate, abolish.
Opposites: confirm.

■ **cancel out**
= **counterbalance**, offset,
counteract, neutralize,
redeem.

cancer NOUN = **malignant
growth**, cancerous
growth, tumour,
malignancy;
[technical] carcinoma,
sarcoma.

candid ADJ = **frank**, open,
honest, truthful, direct,
plain-spoken, blunt,
straightforward, straight
from the shoulder,
outspoken, sincere,
forthright, no-nonsense,
unequivocal,
undisguised, bluff,
brusque.
Opposites: guarded.

candidate NOUN
= **applicant**, contender,
nominee, contestant,
competitor, runner,
entrant, aspirant,
possibility.

candour NOUN
= **frankness**, honesty,
truthfulness, openness,

directness, bluntness,
outspokenness, sincerity,
forthrightness.

canny ADJ = **shrewd**,
sharp, astute, discerning,
penetrating, clever,
perspicacious, judicious,
wise, sagacious,
circumspect.
Opposites: foolish.

canopy NOUN = **awning**,
shade, sunshade, cover,
tarpaulin.

canvass VERB 1 = **seek
votes**, solicit votes,
campaign, electioneer,
drum up support,
persuade, convince.
2 = **investigate**, survey,
find out, enquire into,
look into, examine,
scrutinize, explore, study,
analyse, evaluate.
▶ NOUN = **survey**, poll,
opinion poll, census,
investigation, market
research.

canyon NOUN = **ravine**,
valley, gorge, gully,
defile, chasm, gulf, abyss.

capability NOUN = **ability**,
capacity, potential,
aptitude, faculty, facility,
power, skill, skilfulness,
competence, efficiency,

effectiveness, proficiency, adeptness.

capable ADJ = **able**, competent, effective, efficient, proficient, accomplished, talented, gifted, adept, skilful, experienced, practised, expert, masterly, qualified, adequate, clever, intelligent; [inf] smart.
Opposites: incapable, incompetent.

■ **capable of** = **up to**, equal to, inclined to, disposed to, liable to, prone to, likely to.

capacity NOUN 1 = **space**, room, size, scope, extent, volume, largeness, dimensions, proportions, magnitude, ampleness, amplitude. 2 = **ability**, capability, aptitude, facility, competence, competency, potential, proficiency, skill, talent, accomplishment, cleverness, intelligence. 3 = **position**, role, job, post, office, function, responsibility, appointment, province.

cape[1] NOUN = **cloak**, shawl, wrap, coat, robe, cope.

cape[2] NOUN = **headland**, point, promontory, peninsula, neck, tongue.

caper VERB = **frolic**, romp, skip, gambol, cavort, prance, dance, jig, leap, hop, jump, bound, spring, bounce.

capital NOUN 1 = **first city**, seat of government, metropolis. 2 = **money**, funds, finance, cash, wealth, principal, savings, resources, means, assets, reserves, property, wherewithal.
▶ ADJ = **upper-case**, block.

capitulate VERB = **surrender**, yield, give in/up, back down, submit, concede, throw in the towel/sponge, succumb, cave in, relent, accede, acquiesce.
Opposites: resist.

caprice NOUN = **whim**, impulse, fancy, vagary, notion, fad, quirk.

capricious ADJ = **fickle**, unpredictable, impulsive, changeable, inconstant, mercurial, whimsical, volatile, erratic, variable,

wayward, fitful, quirky, fanciful, uncertain, irregular, unreliable.
Opposites: stable, consistent.

capsize VERB = **overturn**, turn over, upset, upend, tip over, knock over, keel over, turn turtle, invert.

capsule NOUN = **pill**, tablet, caplet, lozenge; [inf] tab.

captain NOUN
1 = **commander**, master, officer in charge; [inf] skipper. **2** = **chief**, head, leader, principal; [inf] boss.

caption NOUN = **heading**, title, wording, head, legend, inscription, description.

captious ADJ = **critical**, criticizing, carping, fault-finding, quibbling, cavilling; [inf] nit-picking.
Opposites: forgiving.

captivate VERB = **charm**, delight, enchant, bewitch, fascinate, dazzle, beguile, entrance, enrapture, attract, hypnotize, mesmerize, enthral, allure, win, infatuate, seduce, ravish, ensnare, steal someone's heart.
Opposites: repel, bore.

captive ADJ = **imprisoned**, locked up, caged, incarcerated, jailed, confined, detained, taken prisoner, interned, penned up, captured, ensnared, restrained, in captivity, in bondage; [inf] under lock and key.
Opposites: free.
▶ NOUN = **prisoner**, detainee, prisoner-of-war, convict, internee, slave; [inf] jailbird, con.

captivity NOUN = **imprisonment**, custody, detention, confinement, internment, incarceration, restraint, constraint, committal, bondage, slavery, servitude, enslavement, subjugation, subjection; [historical] thraldom.
Opposites: freedom.

capture VERB = **catch**, arrest, apprehend, take prisoner, take into custody, seize, trap, take, lay hold of, take captive; [inf] nab, pinch, collar, lift, bag; [Brit. inf] nick.
Opposites: free, liberate.

▶ NOUN = **arrest**, apprehension, detention, imprisonment, seizure, trapping.

car NOUN = **motor car**, motor, automobile; [inf] wheels; [N. Amer. inf] auto.

carcass NOUN 1 = **body**, corpse, remains; [Medicine] cadaver; [inf] stiff. 2 = **frame**, framework, skeleton, remains, structure, shell, hulk.

cardinal ADJ = **fundamental**, basic, main, chief, primary, prime, principal, paramount, key, essential.
Opposites: unimportant.

care NOUN 1 = **worry**, anxiety, sadness, trouble, stress, unease, distress, disquiet, sorrow, anguish, grief, woe, hardship, tribulation, affliction, responsibility, pressure, strain, burden.
2 = **carefulness**, attention, thought, regard, thoroughness, conscientiousness, pains, vigilance, accuracy,

precision, meticulousness, fastidiousness, punctiliousness, mindfulness, solicitude, forethought, heed.
3 = **charge**, supervision, custody, protection, safe keeping, guardianship, control, management, ministration, wardship.
Opposites: happiness, inattention, carelessness.
▶ VERB = **mind**, be concerned, be interested, worry oneself, bother, trouble, have regard.
■ **care for** = see **love** VERB (1), **look after**.

career NOUN = **profession**, occupation, job, vocation, calling, livelihood, employment, work, métier.

carefree ADJ = **cheerful**, light-hearted, happy, nonchalant, unworried, untroubled, cheery, happy-go-lucky, jolly, merry, buoyant, easy-going, relaxed, unconcerned, breezy, jaunty, insouciant, blithe; [inf] upbeat, laid-back.

Opposites: worried, miserable.

careful ADJ **1 = cautious**, alert, attentive, watchful, aware, vigilant, wary, on one's guard, prudent, heedful, circumspect, mindful, observant, chary. **2 = conscientious**, painstaking, meticulous, diligent, attentive, accurate, precise, scrupulous, fastidious, punctilious, methodical, organized, systematic, thorough, well organized.
Opposites: careless.

careless ADJ **1 = inattentive**, thoughtless, negligent, unthinking, irresponsible, lax, slipshod, sloppy, forgetful, absent-minded, remiss. **2 = cursory**, perfunctory, hasty, inaccurate, disorganized, slapdash, slipshod, sloppy, messy. **3 = thoughtless**, unthinking, insensitive, indiscreet, unguarded, ill-considered, reckless, rash, imprudent.

Opposites: careful.
caress VERB = **fondle**, stroke, smooth, touch, pet, cuddle, pat, nuzzle, kiss, embrace, hug.
caretaker NOUN = **janitor**, superintendent, porter, warden, watchman, keeper, steward, curator, concierge.
careworn ADJ = *see* **weary** ADJ **(1)**.
cargo NOUN = **freight**, payload, load, consignment, contents, goods, merchandise, baggage, shipment, boatload, lorryload, truckload, lading.
caricature NOUN = **parody**, mimicry, lampoon, distortion, burlesque, travesty, cartoon, satire, farce; [inf] take-off, send-up. ▶ VERB = **parody**, mimic, lampoon, mock, ridicule, distort, satirize, burlesque; [inf] take off, send up.
carnage NOUN = **slaughter**, massacre, mass murder, butchery, bloodbath, bloodshed, holocaust, pogrom.

carnal ADJ = **sexual**, sensual, erotic, fleshly, lustful, lewd, lecherous, lascivious, libidinous, coarse, gross, prurient, salacious, lubricious.

carnival NOUN = **festival**, celebration, fair, fiesta, fête, gala, jamboree, festivity, revelry.

carouse VERB = **make merry**, party, go on a spree, binge, roister, overindulge; [inf] live it up, paint the town red, go on a bender.

carp VERB = **complain**, find fault, criticize, quibble, grumble, object, reproach, censure, cavil, nag; [inf] nit-pick, gripe, go on.

carpenter NOUN = **woodworker**, cabinetmaker, joiner; [Brit. inf] chippy.

carriage NOUN 1 = **coach**, vehicle. 2 = **bearing**, posture, stance, gait, manner, presence, air, demeanour, mien, behaviour, conduct; [Brit.] deportment; [formal] comportment. 3 = **transport**, transportation, freight, conveyance, delivery, carrying.

carry VERB 1 = **convey**, transport, move, transfer, take, bring, fetch, bear, haul, shift, transmit, relay, manhandle; [inf] lug, cart. 2 = **support**, bear, sustain, maintain, hold up, shoulder. 3 = **affect**, influence, have an effect on, stimulate, motivate, spur on, drive, impel, urge. 4 = **involve**, lead to, result in, require, entail, demand.

■ **carry on** = *see* **continue**.

■ **carry out** = *see* **do** (1).

cart NOUN = **barrow**, wheelbarrow, handcart, pushcart.

▶ VERB = *see* **carry** (1).

carton NOUN = **box**, container, package, case, packet, pack.

cartoon NOUN 1 = **caricature**, parody, lampoon, burlesque, satire; [inf] send-up, take-off. 2 = **animated film**, animation, comic strip, photostory.

cartridge NOUN 1 = **case**, container, cylinder,

capsule, cassette, magazine. **2 = round**, shell.

carve VERB **1 = sculpt**, sculpture, chisel, cut, hew, whittle, form, shape, fashion, mould. **2 = engrave**, etch, incise, notch, cut in. **3 = slice**, cut up.
■ **carve up** = *see* **divide (3)**.

cascade NOUN **= waterfall**, falls, shower, fountain, torrent, flood, deluge, outpouring, avalanche, cataract.
▶ VERB **= gush**, pour, surge, spill, overflow, tumble, descend.

case¹ NOUN **1 = situation**, occasion, context, circumstances, instance, position, conditions, event, occurrence, predicament, contingency, plight. **2 = instance**, example, occurrence, occasion, illustration, specimen. **3 = trial**, proceedings, lawsuit, action, suit. **4 = patient**, victim, sufferer, invalid.

case² NOUN **= container**, box, receptacle, canister, crate, carton, pack, suitcase, trunk, luggage, baggage.

cash NOUN **= money**, funds, finance, capital, resources, currency, change, notes, coins, legal tender; [inf] dough, bread, moolah; [Brit. inf] readies, the ready.
▶ VERB **= exchange**, change, turn into money/cash, realize; [Brit.] encash.

cashier NOUN **= teller**, clerk, banker, treasurer, purser, bursar, controller.

cask NOUN **= barrel**, keg, vat, butt, tub, vessel, tun, hogshead, firkin, pipe.

cast VERB **1 = throw**, toss, fling, pitch, hurl, sling, lob, launch, let fly; [inf] chuck, heave. **2 = emit**, give off, send out, shed, radiate, diffuse, spread. **3 = mould**, form, fashion, sculpt, model.
▶ NOUN **1 = figure**, shape, mould, form, sculpture. **2 = sort**, kind, type, style, stamp.

caste NOUN = **class**, order, rank, level, grade, position, station, place, status, standing, grading.

castle NOUN = **fortress**, fort, citadel, stronghold, fortification, keep, palace, chateau, tower.

casual ADJ **1** = **indifferent**, careless, lax, unconcerned, uninterested, unenthusiastic, easy-going, nonchalant, offhand, throwaway, relaxed, apathetic, lackadaisical, blasé, insouciant, unprofessional; [inf] laid-back. **2** = **slight**, superficial, shallow. **3** = **temporary**, part-time, freelance, irregular. **4** = **accidental**, chance, unintentional, unplanned, unexpected, unforeseen, unanticipated, fortuitous, serendipitous, incidental. **5** = **informal**, relaxed, leisure, unceremonious; [inf] sporty.
Opposites: diligent, permanent, deliberate, formal.

casualty NOUN = **fatality**, victim, sufferer, dead/wounded/injured person.

cat NOUN = **feline**, tomcat, tom, kitten; [inf] pussy, pussy cat, puss, kitty; [Brit. inf] moggie, mog.

catalogue NOUN = **list**, record, register, inventory, index, directory, roll, table, guide, classification, calendar, schedule.
▸ VERB = **list**, file, classify, categorize, register, record, make an inventory of, alphabetize.

catapult VERB = **launch**, hurl, propel, shoot, fling, fire. = *See also* **throw** (1).

cataract NOUN = **waterfall**, falls, cascade, rapids, torrent, downpour.

catastrophe NOUN = **disaster**, calamity, cataclysm, tragedy, misfortune, blow, mishap, misadventure, reverse, debacle, fiasco, trouble, trial, adversity, affliction.

catch VERB **1** = **grasp**, seize, grab, clutch, grip, hold, pluck, clench, intercept, snare, trap, receive,

acquire. **2** = **capture**, apprehend, arrest, seize, take prisoner, lay hold of, trap, snare; [inf] collar, nab, pinch; [Brit. inf] nick. **3** = **hear**, understand, follow, grasp, comprehend, make out, take in, discern, perceive, fathom. **4** = **contract**, get, develop, become infected by, suffer from, succumb to; [Brit.] go down with.
▶ NOUN **1** = **bolt**, lock, fastening, fastener, clasp, hasp, hook, clip, latch, snib. **2** = **snag**, disadvantage, drawback, difficulty, hitch, fly in the ointment, stumbling block, trick, snare. **3** = **yield**, take, haul, bag, net, prize.
■ **catch on 1** = **become popular**, come into fashion, succeed, become all the rage; [inf] become trendy. **2** = *See* **understand** (1).

catching ADJ = **contagious**, infectious, communicable, transmissible, transmittable.

catchy ADJ = **memorable**, popular, haunting, appealing, captivating, melodious, singable.

categorical ADJ = **unqualified**, unconditional, unequivocal, unambiguous, unreserved, definite, absolute, explicit, emphatic, positive, express, firm, direct, conclusive, decided, forceful, downright, utter, out-and-out.
Opposites: equivocal, tentative.

category NOUN = **class**, group, classification, grouping, type, sort, kind, variety, grade, order, rank, division, heading, section, department.

cater
■ **cater for 1** = **feed**, provide food for, provision, serve, cook for; [dated] victual. **2** = **take into account/consideration**, allow for, bear in mind, make provision for, have regard for.

catholic ADJ = **wide**, broad, wide-ranging, all-embracing, general, comprehensive, varied, all-inclusive, eclectic, universal.
Opposites: narrow.

cattle NOUN = **cows**, bovines, livestock, stock, bulls, heifers, calves, bullocks, steers.

cause NOUN **1** = **origin**, source, root, beginning, genesis, occasion, mainspring, author, originator, creator, produce, agent, prime mover, maker. **2** = **reason**, basis, grounds, justification, call, motive, motivation. **3** = **principle**, ideal, belief, conviction, object, end, aim, objective, purpose, charity.
▶ VERB **1** = **bring about**, produce, create, make happen, give rise to, lead to, result in, provoke, originate, generate, engender, arouse, effect, occasion, precipitate.
2 = **force**, make, compel, induce.

caustic ADJ **1** = **corrosive**, acid, corroding, burning, destructive, mordant, acrid. **2** = **cutting**, biting, sarcastic, stinging, scathing, virulent, waspish, trenchant, pungent, astringent, acidulous, acrimonious, mordant.
Opposites: gentle, mild.

caution NOUN **1** = **care**, carefulness, attention, alertness, wariness, prudence, watchfulness, vigilance, heed, heedfulness, guardedness, circumspection, discretion, forethought, mindfulness. **2** = **warning**, reprimand, admonition, injunction; [inf] dressing-down; [Brit. inf] ticking-off.
▶ VERB **1** = **warn**, advise, urge, counsel, inform, alert, forewarn, admonish. **2** = **reprimand**, admonish, warn, give a warning to, censure; [inf] tell off; [Brit. inf] tick off.

cautious ADJ = **careful**, wary, prudent, guarded, alert, circumspect,

watchful, vigilant, mindful, shrewd, chary, tactful, non-committal, tentative; [inf] cagey.
Opposites: incautious, reckless.

cavalier ADJ = **offhand**, arrogant, haughty, disdainful, supercilious, insolent, condescending, lofty, patronizing.

cave NOUN = **cavern**, hollow, grotto, pothole, cavity, dugout, underground chamber.
■ **cave in** = *see* **collapse**.

cavity NOUN = **hole**, hollow, crater, pit, orifice, gap, dent, aperture.

cease VERB = **stop**, finish, end, bring to a halt, halt, break off, discontinue, conclude, suspend, terminate, desist, leave off, refrain from; [inf] quit, knock off, lay off.
Opposites: start, begin.

ceaseless ADJ
= **unending**, endless, constant, continual, continuous, non-stop, perpetual, never-ending, incessant, persistent, relentless, unremitting, interminable, everlasting, untiring, chronic.
Opposites: intermittent.

celebrate VERB **1** = **enjoy oneself**, rejoice, make merry, revel, party; [inf] go out on the town, paint the town red, whoop it up.
2 = **commemorate**, remember, honour, observe, make, keep, toast, drink to.
3 = **perform**, officiate at, observe.

celebrated ADJ = *see* **famous**.

celebration NOUN
1 = **party**, festival, carnival, gala, fête, festivity, revelry, merrymaking, jollification, spree; [inf] bash, shindig; [Brit. inf] beanfeast, rave-up.
2 = **commemoration**, remembrance, observance, honouring, keeping.

celebrity NOUN **1** = *See* **fame**. **2** = **famous person**, star, dignitary, luminary, notable, personage; [inf] bigwig, big shot, big noise.

celestial ADJ
1 = **astronomical**, cosmic, heavenly, stellar, interstellar, extraterrestrial. **2** = **divine**, heavenly, supernatural, transcendental, godlike, ethereal, sublime, spiritual, immortal, angelic, seraphic, cherubic.

celibacy NOUN = **chastity**, purity, abstinence, self-denial, asceticism, virginity, bachelorhood, spinsterhood, monasticism, monkhood, nunhood, continence, abnegation.

celibate ADJ = **chaste**, pure, abstinent, virgin, immaculate, continent.

cell NOUN **1** = **enclosure**, dungeon, lock-up, cubicle, room, apartment, chamber, stall. **2** = **cavity**, compartment, hole, unit.

cement NOUN = **adhesive**, glue, paste, bonding, binder.

cemetery NOUN = **graveyard**, burial ground, churchyard,

necropolis.

censor VERB = **expurgate**, bowdlerize, cut, delete, edit, remove, make cuts/changes to, amend, prohibit, forbid, ban.

censorious ADJ = **critical**, hypercritical, disapproving, condemnatory, judgemental, moralistic, fault-finding, captious, carping, cavilling.

censure VERB = **criticize**, blame, disapprove of, denounce, reprove, rebuke, reproach, reprimand, upbraid, berate, scold, chide, reprehend; [inf] tell off; [Brit. inf] tick off, carpet; [formal] castigate.
▶ NOUN = **criticism**, blame, condemnation, denunciation, disapproval, reproval, reproof, reproach, rebuke, reprimand, scolding, berating, upbraiding, obloquy, reprehension, vituperation; [inf] talking-to, dressing-down; [formal] castigation.

central ADJ 1 = **middle**, mid, median, mean, mesial. 2 = **main**, chief, principal, foremost, basic, fundamental, key, essential, primary, pivotal, core, focal, cardinal.
Opposites: side, outer, subordinate.

centralize VERB = **concentrate**, centre, consolidate, condense, amalgamate, unify, incorporate, streamline, focus, rationalize.

centre NOUN = **middle**, middle point, heart, core, nucleus, midpoint, hub, kernel, focus, focal point, pivot, inside, interior.
Opposites: periphery.
▶ VERB = **concentrate**, focus, converge, close in, pivot.

ceremonial ADJ = **formal**, official, ritual, ritualistic, celebratory, liturgical, stately, dignified, solemn.

ceremonious ADJ = **dignified**, majestic, imposing, impressive, solemn, stately, formal, courtly, scrupulous, precise, punctilious, deferential, stiff, rigid.

Opposites: casual.

ceremony NOUN 1 = **rite**, service, ritual, sacrament, formality, observance, celebration, commemoration, function, event, parade. 2 = **formality**, pomp, decorum, formalities, niceties, etiquette, propriety, ritual, attention to detail, protocol, punctiliousness, pageantry, grandeur, ceremonial.

certain ADJ 1 = **sure**, confident, convinced, satisfied, persuaded, assured, unwavering, secure, unshaken. 2 = **assured**, inevitable, definite, destined, inescapable, bound to happen, inexorable, unarguable, ineluctable. 3 = **definite**, sure, sound, reliable, dependable, trustworthy, unquestionable, beyond question, evident, plain, clear, indubitable, undeniable, obvious, undisputed, incontrovertible, incontestable, conclusive, infallible, foolproof; [inf] sure-fire.

4 = particular, specific, precise, special, individual.

Opposites: doubtful, possible, unlikely.

certainly ADV = **definitely**, surely, assuredly, undoubtedly, undeniably, obviously, plainly, clearly.

certainty NOUN
1 = sureness, authority, positiveness, confidence, assurance, assuredness, conviction, reliability, conclusiveness, authoritativeness, validity. **2 = fact**, inevitability, foregone conclusion, indubitability; [inf] sure thing; [Brit. inf] dead cert.

Opposites: uncertainty.

certificate NOUN
= **certification**, authorization, document, licence, warrant, credentials, pass, permit, guarantee, voucher, diploma, qualification, testimonial.

certify VERB
1 = authenticate, document, verify, validate, confirm, bear witness to, attest to, testify to, substantiate, corroborate, endorse, vouch for, ratify, warrant. **2 = accredit**, license, recognize, authorize, qualify, give a certificate/diploma to.

cessation NOUN = **end**, finish, termination, conclusion, halt, pause, break, respite, let-up.

chain NOUN **1 = shackle**, fetter, manacle, bonds, coupling, link. **2 = series**, succession, progression, sequence, string, set, cycle, line, row, concatenation.
▶ VERB = **fasten**, secure, tie, bind, tether, shackle, fetter, manacle, handcuff, hitch.

chair VERB = **preside over**, lead, direct, manage, control, oversee, supervise.

chalky ADJ = **white**, pale, wan, pallid, ashen, pasty, waxen, blanched, bleached, colourless.

challenge VERB **1 = dare**, summon, invite, throw

down the gauntlet to, defy. **2** = **question**, dispute, call into question, protest against, object to, take exception to, disagree with, argue against, contest, oppose, query, demur against, impugn. **3** = **stimulate**, test, tax, inspire, excite, arouse, spur on.

challenging ADJ = **stimulating**, exciting, inspiring, testing, thought-provoking.
Opposites: easy.

chamber NOUN **1** = **room**, cubicle, bedroom, bedchamber, boudoir. **2** = **cavity**, compartment, hollow, cell.

champion NOUN **1** = **winner**, prizewinner, medallist, record-breaker, victor, title-holder, conqueror, hero. **2** = **supporter**, defender, upholder, advocate, backer, patron, protector, vindicator. **3** = **knight**, hero, warrior, contender, fighter, man-at-arms, paladin. ▶ADJ = **winning**, victorious, unrivalled, leading, great, supreme, record-breaking.
▶VERB = **defend**, support, uphold, stand up for, back, advocate, promote, espouse.

chance NOUN **1** = **accident**, coincidence, luck, fate, destiny, fluke, providence, fortune, serendipity, fortuity. **2** = **possibility**, likelihood, prospect, probability, likeliness, odds, conceivability. **3** = **opportunity**, time, occasion, turn, opening; [inf] shot. ▶ADJ = **accidental**, unforeseen, unexpected, coincidental, lucky, unplanned, unintended, unintentional, unpremeditated, casual, inadvertent, unanticipated, unforeseeable, random, haphazard, unlooked for, fortuitous, serendipitous, adventitious, fluky.
Opposites: intentional, deliberate.
▶VERB **1** = *See* **happen**. **2** = *See* **risk** VERB (**2, 3**).

■ chance on/upon
= **meet**, encounter, come across, stumble on; [inf] bump into, run into.

chancy ADJ = **risky**, dangerous, hazardous, unsafe, uncertain, precarious, perilous, insecure, speculative, unpredictable; [inf] dicey; [Brit. inf] dodgy.
Opposites: safe.

change VERB 1 = **alter**, adjust, transform, modify, convert, vary, amend, rearrange, reorganize, remodel, reorder, reform, reconstruct, restyle, recast, tailor, transmute, accustom, metamorphose, transmogrify, permutate, permute. 2 = **be changed**, alter, be transformed, evolve, develop, move on, mutate, shift, do an about-face, do a U-turn; [Brit. inf] chop and change. 3 = **exchange**, swap, switch, substitute, replace, trade, interchange, barter, transpose.

▶ NOUN 1 = **alteration**, modification, adaptation, difference, transformation, conversion, variation, development, remodelling, reorganization, rearrangement, reconstruction, shift, transition, metamorphosis, mutation, transmutation, transmogrification, innovation, vicissitude, permutation.
2 = **exchange**, switch, swap, trade, substitution, interchange, bartering.
3 = **coins**, silver, small change, cash, petty cash.

changeable ADJ = **variable**, changing, varying, shifting, vacillating, fluctuating, volatile, capricious, wavering, unstable, unsteady, irregular, erratic, unreliable, inconsistent, unpredictable, fickle, inconstant, mercurial, fluid, fitful, kaleidoscopic, protean, mutable, chequered,

vicissitudinous.
Opposites: constant.

channel NOUN 1 = **passage**, sea passage, strait, narrow, neck, waterway, watercourse, fiord. 2 = **gutter**, furrow, groove, conduit, duct, culvert, ditch, gully. 3 = **path**, route, direction, way, approach, course. 4 = **medium**, means, agency, vehicle, route.
▶ VERB = **convey**, conduct, transmit, transport, guide, direct.

chant NOUN = **song**, hymn, chorus, carol, psalm.
▶ VERB = **intone**, recite, sing, cantillate.

chaos NOUN = **disorder**, anarchy, mayhem, bedlam, pandemonium, turmoil, tumult, uproar, disruption, upheaval, confusion, disarray, lawlessness, riot, disorganization.
Opposites: order.

chaotic ADJ = **anarchic**, in chaos, disordered, disorganized, confused, disorderly, unruly, uncontrolled, tumultuous, jumbled, upset, askew, disrupted, in disarray, awry, lawless, riotous, ungovernable, rebellious, orderless; [inf] topsy-turvy, haywire, higgledy-piggledy; [Brit. inf] shambolic.
Opposites: disorderly.

character NOUN 1 = **personality**, nature, disposition, temperament, temper, make-up, constitution, cast, attributes, bent, complexion. 2 = **strength**, honour, integrity, moral fibre, uprightness, rectitude, fortitude, backbone. 3 = **eccentric**, original, individual, oddity; [inf] oddball, odd fellow, queer fish; [inf, dated] card. 4 = **person**, individual, human being; [inf] fellow, guy, type, sort, customer; [Brit. inf] bloke, chap. 5 = **reputation**, name, standing, position, status. 6 = **type**, sign, symbol, mark, figure, hieroglyph, cipher, ideogram.

characteristic NOUN = **quality**, attribute,

feature, trait, property, peculiarity, quirk, mannerism, idiosyncrasy, hallmark, trademark.
▸ ADJ = **typical**, distinctive, distinguishing, particular, special, individual, peculiar, specific, representative, symbolic, idiosyncratic, symptomatic.

characterize VERB
= **portray**, depict, describe, present, identify, draw, brand, typify, delineate, denote, indicate, specify, designate.

charade NOUN = **pretence**, travesty, mockery, fake, sham, deception, pose, farce, absurdity, parody, pantomime, play-acting, masquerade.

charge VERB 1 = **ask in payment**, ask, ask for, expect, make someone pay, impose, levy, require. 2 = **accuse of**, arraign, indict, prosecute, impute, blame, incriminate. 3 = **attack**, storm, assault, rush, open fire on, assail, fall on; [inf] lay into, wade into. 4 = **entrust**, burden, impose on, give, load, encumber, saddle. 5 = **fill**, load, imbue, instil, suffuse, permeate, pervade.
Opposites: absolve.
▸ NOUN 1 = **cost**, rate, price, amount, fee, payment, expense, outlay, expenditure, levy, toll, terms, dues.
2 = **accusation**, allegation, indictment, arraignment, impeachment, citation, imputation, blame, incrimination. 3 = **attack**, assault, offensive, storming, raid, strike, onrush, onslaught, sally, incursion, sortie. 4 = **care**, custody, responsibility, protection, supervision, safe keeping, keeping, trust, guardianship, surveillance.

charitable ADJ
1 = **generous**, kind, giving, philanthropic, magnanimous, liberal, munificent, bountiful, open-handed, benevolent. 2 = **liberal**, generous, tolerant,

understanding, broad-minded, sympathetic.
Opposites: uncharitable.

charity NOUN
1 = **donations**, contributions, handouts, financial assistance, funding, endowments, almsgiving, philanthropy, benefaction.
2 = **compassion**, humanity, goodwill, kindliness, sympathy, love, tolerance, thoughtfulness, generosity, altruism, humanitarianism, benevolence.

charm NOUN
1 = **attractiveness**, attraction, appeal, allure, fascination, desirability, charisma, lure, delightfulness, captivation, allurement.
2 = **spell**, magic words, incantation, sorcery, witchcraft, wizardry.
3 = **amulet**, trinket, talisman, mascot.
▸ VERB = **delight**, please, attract, captivate, fascinate, win over, bewitch, beguile,

enchant, seduce, hypnotize, mesmerize, enthral, intrigue, disarm, enamour, allure, draw.
Opposites: repel.

chart NOUN = **graph**, table, diagram, map, plan, blueprint, guide, scheme, tabulation.
▸ VERB = **map**, map out, plot, graph, delineate, sketch, draft.

chase VERB = **pursue**, run/go after, follow, hunt, hound, track, trail, tail.

chasm NOUN = **abyss**, ravine, pit, canyon, opening, void, crater, crevasse, gap, fissure, rift.

chaste ADJ **1** = **celibate**, virginal, abstinent, pure, innocent, virtuous, undefiled, moral, immaculate, unmarried.
2 = **virtuous**, good, pure, innocent, decent, moral, modest, wholesome, upright, righteous, becoming, restrained, unsullied.
Opposites: promiscuous.

chastity NOUN
= **chasteness**, celibacy, abstinence, virginity,

self-restraint, self-denial,
virtue, purity, innocence,
continence, sinlessness.

chat VERB = **talk**, gossip,
chatter, have a
conversation with,
converse, prattle, jabber.
▸ NOUN = **talk**, gossip,
conversation, heart-to-
heart; [inf] confab,
chinwag; [Brit. inf] natter.

chatty ADJ = **talkative**,
garrulous, loquacious,
voluble, effusive,
gushing, gossipy.
Opposites: taciturn.

chauvinism NOUN
= **jingoism**, prejudice,
bigotry, bias, machismo.

cheap ADJ 1 = **inexpensive**,
low-cost, low-priced,
economical, reasonable,
bargain, economy,
reduced, marked down,
discounted, sale;
[inf] bargain-basement,
knock-down. 2 = **poor-
quality**, inferior, shoddy,
common, tawdry, tatty,
paltry, worthless,
second-rate, gimcrack;
[inf] tacky, trashy.
3 = **despicable**,
contemptible, tasteless,
unpleasant, unworthy,

mean, low, base, sordid,
vulgar.
Opposites: expensive.

cheapen VERB = **degrade**,
debase, belittle, demean,
devalue, denigrate,
discredit, prostitute,
lower the tone of.

cheat VERB 1 = **deceive**,
trick, swindle, take in,
defraud, dupe,
hoodwink, double-cross,
take advantage of,
exploit, gull; [inf] rip off,
take for a ride, con,
diddle, bamboozle,
finagle, bilk, fleece.
2 = **avoid**, elude, evade,
dodge, escape, shun,
eschew.
▸ NOUN 1 = **cheater**, swindler,
fraud, confidence
trickster, deceiver,
trickster, double-crosser,
impostor, crook, hoaxer,
rogue, charlatan,
mountebank, shark;
[inf] con man, phoney;
[Brit. inf] twister.
2 = **swindle**, fraud,
deception, deceit, trick,
trickery, ruse,
misrepresentation,
chicanery, imposture,
artifice; [inf] con, rip-off,

fiddle, racket; [Brit. inf] swizz.

check VERB 1 = **examine**, inspect, look over/at, scrutinize, test, monitor, investigate, probe, enquire into, study; [inf] give the once-over to. 2 = **stop**, halt, arrest, bring to a standstill, slow down, brake, obstruct, inhibit, bar, impede, block, retard, curb, delay, thwart.
▶ NOUN 1 = **examination**, inspection, scrutiny, test, monitoring, investigation, enquiry, probe, study; [inf] once-over, going-over. 2 = **stop**, stoppage, halt, obstruction, break, slowing down, slowdown, delay, interruption, suspension, hiatus, retardation.

cheek NOUN = **impudence**, impertinence, insolence, effrontery, boldness, audacity, temerity, brazenness; [inf] brass, neck, gall, lip; [Brit. inf] sauce.

cheeky ADJ = **impudent**, impertinent, insolent, disrespectful, insulting, impolite, presumptuous, mocking, irreverent, forward, pert; [inf] saucy; [N. Amer. inf] sassy.
Opposites: respectful.

cheep VERB = **chirp**, chirrup, tweet, twitter, warble, trill.

cheer VERB 1 = **acclaim**, applaud, hail, hurrah, encourage, clap, shout/yell at. 2 = **make cheerful**, please, hearten, gladden, brighten, perk up, comfort, console, buoy up, solace, uplift; [inf] buck up.
▶ NOUN 1 = **acclaim**, acclamation, applause, hurray, hurrah, ovation, plaudit, shout, shouting, hailing, clapping, encouragement, approval.
2 = **cheerfulness**, happiness, gladness, merriment, glee, mirth, gaiety, joy, pleasure, jubilation, rejoicing, festivity, revelry.
▪ **cheer up** = **brighten**, liven up, perk up, rally, take heart.

cheerful ADJ **1** = **happy**, bright, glad, merry, sunny, joyful, delighted, good-humoured, jolly, animated, buoyant, light-hearted, carefree, gleeful, breezy, cheery, jaunty, perky, smiling, laughing, optimistic, hopeful, positive, in good spirits, sparkling, happy-go-lucky, sprightly, rapturous; [inf] chirpy; [poetic/literary] blithe. **2** = **bright**, sunny, cheering, pleasant, agreeable, friendly, happy.
Opposites: sad, cheerless, dull.

cheerless ADJ = **gloomy**, miserable, dreary, dull, dismal, depressing, bleak, drab, grim, austere, dark, dingy, desolate, sombre, uninviting, forbidding, melancholy, comfortless, forlorn, joyless, disconsolate, funereal, woeful.
Opposites: cheerful, bright.

cheery ADJ = **cheerful**, happy, bright, merry, glad, in good spirits.

= *See also* **cheerful** (**1**).
Opposites: sad.

chemist NOUN = **pharmacist**, pharmacy; [N. Amer.] drugstore; [archaic] apothecary.

chequered ADJ = **mixed**, varied, diverse, diversified, eventful.

cherish VERB **1** = **treasure**, prize, hold dear, love, adore, dote on, idolize, cosset, nurture, look after, protect, value. **2** = **have**, entertain, harbour, cling to, nurture, foster.
Opposites: neglect.

chest NOUN **1** = **breast**, thorax, sternum, ribcage. **2** = **box**, crate, case, trunk, container, coffer, casket.

chew VERB = **bite**, crunch, gnaw, masticate, champ, grind.

chic ADJ = **stylish**, fashionable, smart, elegant, modish, voguish.

chief NOUN **1** = **chieftain**, head, headman, ruler, leader, overlord, suzerain. **2** = **head**, ruler, principal, leader, director, manager, supervisor, superintendent,

chairman, chairperson, chief executive, proprietor, master, mistress, overseer, foreman, controller, captain, commander; [inf] boss, kingpin, top dog, big cheese, bigwig, number one, supremo; [Brit. inf] gaffer, governor.
▸ ADJ **1** = **supreme**, foremost, principal, highest, leading, pre-eminent, senior, superior, premier, head, directing, grand, top. **2** = **main**, principal, most important, cardinal, key, primary, prime, central, fundamental, predominant, foremost, vital, paramount, uppermost.
Opposites: minor, subordinate.

chiefly ADV = **mainly**, principally, primarily, in the main, predominantly, especially, particularly, mostly, essentially, on the whole, for the most part, above all.

child NOUN **1** = **boy**, = **girl**, youngster, young person, infant, baby, toddler, tot, tiny tot, youth, adolescent, juvenile, minor; [Scottish] bairn; [inf] kid, nipper, shaver, brat, guttersnipe; [Brit. inf] sprog. **2** = **son**, = **daughter**, offspring, progeny, descendant, scion; [Law] issue.

childbirth NOUN = **labour**, delivery, confinement, parturition, accouchement.

childhood NOUN = **youth**, infancy, babyhood, boyhood, girlhood, adolescence, minority; [inf] teens, pre-teens.

childish ADJ = **immature**, infantile, juvenile, puerile, irresponsible, foolish, jejune. = *See also* **silly** (1).
Opposites: mature.

childlike ADJ = **innocent**, simple, unsophisticated, trusting, gullible, naive, ingenuous, guileless, artless, unaffected, credulous.

chill VERB = **cool**, freeze, refrigerate, make cold/cool.
Opposites: heat.

▶ NOUN **1** = **coolness**, chilliness, coldness, iciness, rawness, frigidity, nip, bite. **2** = **coldness**, coolness, aloofness, unfriendliness, hostility, distance, unresponsiveness.
Opposites: warmth.

chilly ADJ **1** = **cold**, cool, icy, freezing, chill, fresh, sharp, biting, raw, brisk, penetrating, wintry, frigid. **2** = **unfriendly**, cool, cold, aloof, distant, unresponsive, reserved, unsympathetic, unwelcoming, hostile, remote, frigid.
Opposites: warm, friendly.

chime VERB = **ring**, peal, toll, strike, sound, clang, tinkle, resound.
▶ NOUN = **peal**, striking, tolling.

china NOUN **1** = **dishes**, tableware, dinner/tea service. **2** = **porcelain**.

chink NOUN = **crack**, gap, cleft, rift, slit, fissure, crevice, split, opening, aperture, cranny, cavity.

chip NOUN **1** = **shard**, flake, fragment, splinter, paring, sliver, bit, fleck, shred, scrap, snippet. **2** = **nick**, crack, notch, snick, scratch, splinter, gash, fault, flaw, dent.
▶ VERB **1** = **nick**, crack, notch, scratch, splinter, gash, damage, snick. **2** = **chisel**, whittle, hew.

chivalrous ADJ
1 = **courteous**, polite, gallant, gentlemanly, gracious, well mannered, thoughtful, protective.
2 = **courtly**, knightly, courageous, brave, valiant, heroic, daring, intrepid, honourable, just, fair, constant, true, magnanimous.
Opposites: rude, boorish.

choice NOUN **1** = **selection**, option, choosing, preference, picking, election, adoption.
2 = **alternative**, option, possibility, solution, answer, way out.
3 = **variety**, range, selection, assortment, mixture, store, supply, display, array, miscellany.
▶ ADJ = **best**, excellent, superior, first-rate, first-class, prize, prime, select,

special, exclusive, rare,
hand-picked.
Opposites: inferior.

choke VERB **1 = strangle**,
asphyxiate, throttle,
suffocate, smother, stifle.
2 = gag, gasp, retch,
struggle for air,
asphyxiate, suffocate.
3 = clog, congest, jam,
block, obstruct, fill up,
constrict, plug, stop up.
■ **choke back** = *see*
suppress (2).

choose VERB **= select**,
pick, pick on/out, decide
on, opt for, settle on,
agree on, fix on, plump
for, prefer, designate,
elect, single out, adopt,
espouse, hand-pick,
name, nominate, vote
for, show a preference
for.

choosy ADJ **= fussy**,
particular,
discriminating, exacting,
finicky, pernickety,
fastidious, hard to please,
selective, discerning;
[inf] picky.

chop VERB **1 = cut down**,
fell, hack down, hew,
bring down, saw down,
lop, split. **2 = cut up**, dice,

cube, fragment, crumble.
3 = *See* **cut (2)**.

choppy ADJ **= rough**,
turbulent, stormy,
squally, blustery,
tempestuous.
Opposites: calm.

chorus NOUN **1 = choir**,
ensemble, choral group,
choristers, singers,
vocalists. **2 = refrain**,
response.

christen VERB **= baptize**,
anoint, name, dub, call,
designate, style, term.

chronic ADJ **1 = persistent**,
long-lasting, long-
standing, lingering,
continual, constant,
incessant, deep-rooted,
deep-seated, ingrained.
2 = habitual, inveterate,
confirmed, hardened.
3 = bad, dreadful,
appalling, awful,
atrocious.
Opposites: acute.

chronicle NOUN **= record**,
account, history, story,
description, calendar,
annals, narrative,
journal, archive, log.
▶ VERB **= record**, report,
document, set down,
relate, tell about, register.

chronological ADJ
= **consecutive**, in
sequence, sequential,
ordered, historical, serial,
progressive.

chubby ADJ = **plump**,
tubby, flabby, dumpy,
paunchy, fleshy, stout,
portly, rotund. = *See also*
fat (1).
Opposites: skinny.

chunk NOUN = **lump**, piece,
block, hunk, slab, square,
portion, mass, wedge;
[inf] dollop.

church NOUN = **place of
worship**, house of God,
cathedral, chapel, abbey,
minster, temple,
tabernacle, mosque,
synagogue.

churlish ADJ = **rude**,
impolite, boorish, oafish,
ill-mannered,
discourteous, surly, curt,
sullen, brusque.
Opposites: polite.

churn VERB 1 = **beat**, whip
up, agitate, stir up, shape
up, disturb. 2 = **seethe**,
foam, boil, froth, swirl,
toss, convulse.

cinema NOUN = **films**,
movies, pictures, motion
pictures; [inf] silver screen,
big screen.

circle NOUN 1 = **ring**, disc,
round, loop,
circumference, ball,
globe, sphere, orb.
2 = **group**, circle of
friends, set, company,
crowd, ring, coterie,
clique, assembly,
fellowship, class.
▶ VERB 1 = **move round**,
revolve, rotate, orbit,
circumnavigate, wheel,
gyrate, whirl, pivot,
swivel. 2 = **surround**, ring,
encircle, enclose,
envelop, hedge in, hem
in, gird, belt,
circumscribe.

circuit NOUN = **lap**, round,
cycle, loop,
circumference, turn,
ambit.

circuitous ADJ = **winding**,
indirect, meandering,
roundabout, twisting,
tortuous, rambling,
zigzag, labyrinthine,
maze-like, serpentine.
Opposites: direct.

circular ADJ = **round**,
spherical, spheroid, ring-
shaped, globular,
annular.

▶ NOUN = **pamphlet**, leaflet, notice, advertisement.

circulate VERB 1 = **spread**, spread round, make known, broadcast, publish, distribute, give out, disseminate, propagate, issue, pronounce, advertise; [inf] put about. 2 = **move/ go round**, flow, revolve, rotate, whirl, gyrate.

circumference NOUN = **perimeter**, border, boundary, periphery, bounds, limits, confines, edge, rim, verge, margin, fringe, outline, skirt, circuit, compass, extremity.

circumspect ADJ = **cautious**, wary, careful, guarded, vigilant, watchful, prudent, suspicious, apprehensive, observant, leery, chary, judicious, politic.
Opposites: unguarded.

circumstances PL NOUN 1 = **situation**, set of affairs, conditions, facts, position, context, occurrence, event, background, particulars, surroundings. 2 = **state**, situation, conditions, financial position, plight, predicament, means, resources, station.

circumstantial ADJ = **indirect**, incidental, presumed, conjectural, inferential.

citadel NOUN = **fortress**, fort, fortification, stronghold, bastion, castle, tower, keep, fastness.

citation NOUN = **quotation**, quote, reference, extract, excerpt, allusion, passage, source.

cite VERB = **quote**, mention, refer to, allude to, name, adduce, specify, excerpt, extract.

citizen NOUN = **subject**, national, native, passport-holder, resident, inhabitant, denizen, dweller, householder, taxpayer, voter, freeman, freewoman, burgher, burgess.

city NOUN = **town**, conurbation, metropolis, urban area, municipality; [inf] concrete jungle, urban sprawl.

civil ADJ **1** = **polite**, courteous, well mannered, well bred, gentlemanly, ladylike, refined, urbane, polished, cultured, cultivated, cordial, civilized, genial, pleasant. **2** = **civic**, public, municipal, community, local.
Opposites: rude.

civility NOUN = **courtesy**, politeness, courteousness, good manners, graciousness, cordiality, pleasantness, geniality, affability, amiability, urbanity, gallantry.
Opposites: rudeness.

civilization NOUN
1 = **development**, advancement, progress, enlightenment, culture, cultivation, refinement, sophistication.
2 = **society**, culture, community, nation, country, people, way of life.

civilize VERB = **enlighten**, educate, cultivate, instruct, improve, refine, polish, domesticate, socialize, humanize, edify.

civilized ADJ
= **enlightened**, advanced, developed, cultured, cultivated, educated, sophisticated, refined, sociable, urbane, well behaved.
Opposites: uncivilized, barbarous.

claim VERB **1** = **demand**, request, ask for, lay claim to, require, insist on, command, exact, requisition. **2** = **profess**, maintain, state, declare, assert, allege, protest, insist, contend, hold, avow, affirm, postulate; [formal] aver.

clairvoyant NOUN
= **psychic**, fortune teller, crystal-gazer; medium, spiritualist; telepath.

clamber VERB = **scramble**, climb, scrabble, scale, ascend, mount, shin, shinny, claw one's way.

clammy ADJ = **moist**, damp, humid, sweaty, sticky, close, muggy, dank.

clamour NOUN = **noise**, uproar, outcry, racket, row, din, shouts, shouting, yelling, babel,

classic

commotion, hubbub, hullabaloo, brouhaha, vociferation.
▸ VERB = **shout**, yell, call/cry out, exclaim.

clamp NOUN = **vice**, press, brace, clasp, fastener, hasp.
▸ VERB = **grip**, hold, press, squeeze, clench, fix, secure, make fast.

clandestine ADJ = **secret**, undercover, surreptitious, furtive, concealed, hidden, underhand, cloak-and-dagger.

clarify VERB 1 = **make clear**, explain, clear up, make plain, illuminate, resolve, throw light on, make simple, simplify. 2 = **purify**, refine.
Opposites: confuse.

clash VERB 1 = **bang**, strike, crash, clang, clatter, rattle, jangle. 2 = **fight**, contend, quarrel, wrangle, do battle, feud, grapple, cross swords. 3 = See **coincide** (1).

clasp NOUN 1 = **catch**, fastener, fastening, clip, hook, buckle, pin, hasp. 2 = **embrace**, hug, cuddle, hold, grip, grasp.

▸ VERB = **embrace**, hug, squeeze, clutch, grip, grasp, hold.

class NOUN 1 = **category**, group, sort, type, kind, set, division, order, rank, classification, grade, section, denomination, species, genus, genre, domain. 2 = **social order/division**, rank, stratum, level, status, standing, station, group, grouping, caste, lineage, pedigree, descent. 3 = **quality**, excellence, distinction, ability, stylishness, elegance, chic.
▸ VERB = *see* **classify**.

classic ADJ 1 = **excellent**, memorable, notable, lasting, brilliant, finest, first-rate, first-class, outstanding, exemplary, consummate, masterly, legendary, immortal. 2 = **typical**, archetypal, definitive, standard, model, stock, prototypical, paradigmatic, copybook. 3 = **traditional**, simple, timeless, ageless, enduring, abiding, long-lasting, time-honoured,

long-established.
▶ NOUN = **masterpiece**,
master work, great work,
standard work.

classical ADJ **1** = **ancient**,
Greek, Grecian, Hellenic,
Attic, Roman, Latin.
2 = **serious**, symphonic,
traditional, highbrow.
3 = **elegant**, balanced,
well proportioned,
symmetrical, austere,
pure, simple, plain,
harmonious, restrained.

classification NOUN
= **categorization**,
ordering, organization,
grouping, arrangement,
grading, systemization,
codification, tabulation,
taxonomy.

classify VERB = **categorize**,
class, arrange, order, sort,
organize, group,
catalogue, systematize,
type, rank, index, file,
bracket.

clause NOUN = **section**,
subsection, paragraph,
article, item, point,
passage, part, heading,
provision, proviso,
stipulation, note.

claw NOUN = **nail**, talon,
pincer, nipper, chela.

▶ VERB = **scratch**, tear,
scrape, lacerate, rip,
maul.

clean ADJ **1** = **unstained**,
spotless, unsoiled,
unblemished, unsullied,
immaculate, speckless,
hygienic, sanitary,
disinfected, sterile,
sterilized, washed,
cleansed, laundered,
scrubbed. **2** = **pure**, clear,
unpolluted, natural,
unadulterated,
uncontaminated,
untainted. **3** = **good**,
upright, virtuous, pure,
decent, respectable,
moral, upstanding,
exemplary, chaste,
undefiled. **4** = **unused**,
unmarked, blank,
untouched, new, vacant,
void. **5** = **fair**, honest,
sporting, sportsmanlike,
honourable.
Opposites: dirty.
▶ VERB = **wash**, cleanse,
wipe, sponge, scour,
swab, dry-clean, launder,
tidy, vacuum, hoover,
dust, mop, sweep.
Opposites: dirty, soil.

cleanse VERB = **wash**,
clean, bathe, rinse,

disinfect.

clear ADJ **1** = **bright**, cloudless, fine, fair, light, sunny, sunshiny. **2** = **transparent**, translucent, limpid, pellucid, crystalline, diaphanous. **3** = **obvious**, plain, evident, apparent, sure, definite, unmistakable, beyond question, indisputable, patent, manifest, incontrovertible, irrefutable, palpable. **4** = **comprehensible**, plain, intelligible, understandable, lucid, coherent, distinct. **5** = **open**, empty, unobstructed, unimpeded, free, unhindered, unlimited. **6** = **untroubled**, undisturbed, innocent, guilt-free, guiltless, clean, peaceful, tranquil, serene, sinless, stainless. **Opposites:** cloudy, opaque, vague, incoherent. ▶ ADV **1** = **away from**, at a distance from, apart from, out of contact with. **2** = **completely**, entirely, fully, wholly, thoroughly. ▶ VERB **1** = **unblock**, unclog, unstop, clean out, free. **2** = **empty**, vacate, evacuate. **3** = **acquit**, absolve, discharge, let go, exonerate, vindicate, excuse, pardon. **4** = **jump**, vault, leap, hop, pass over. **5** = **authorize**, sanction, give consent to, approve, permit, allow, pass; [inf] give the go-ahead to. ▪ **clear up** = *see* **explain** (**1**).

clearance NOUN **1** = **clearing**, removal, emptying, evacuation, eviction, depopulation, withdrawal. **2** = **gap**, space, headroom, allowance, margin, leeway, room to spare. **3** = **authorization**, permission, consent, sanction, leave, endorsement; [inf] go-ahead, green light.

clear-cut ADJ = **definite**, specific, precise, explicit, unequivocal.

clearly ADV = **obviously**, plainly, undoubtedly,

undeniably, surely, certainly, incontestably, patently, incontrovertibly.

cleave VERB = **split**, crack, lay open, divide, hew, hack, chop/slice up, sever, sunder, rend.

cleft NOUN = **split**, crack, fissure, gap, crevice, rift, break, fracture.

clemency NOUN = **mercy**, leniency, compassion, kindness, humanity, pity, sympathy, fairness, magnanimity, moderation, indulgence.
Opposites: ruthlessness.

clench VERB = **grip**, grasp, clutch, hold, seize, clamp, squeeze.

clergyman NOUN = **minister**, priest, pastor, preacher, vicar, rabbi, imam, cleric, churchman, churchwoman, man of the cloth, bishop, archbishop, cardinal, prelate, ecclesiastic, divine.

clerical ADJ 1 = **office**, secretarial.
2 = **ecclesiastical**, spiritual, priestly, episcopal, churchly, pastoral, canonical, rabbinical, sacerdotal, apostolic, prelatic.

clever ADJ 1 = **intelligent**, bright, sharp, quick-witted, quick, gifted, talented, brilliant, able, capable, knowledgeable, educated, sagacious; [inf] brainy, smart.
2 = **shrewd**, cunning, ingenious, astute, skilful, skilled, resourceful, wily, inventive, subtle, canny, artful, adroit, guileful; [inf] foxy; [N. Amer. inf] cute. 3 = **dexterous**, skilful, deft, nimble, handy.
Opposites: stupid, awkward.

cliché NOUN = **hackneyed/ well-worn phrase**, platitude, commonplace, banality, truism, saw, maxim; [inf] old chestnut.

click VERB 1 = **clink**, clack, snap, tick. 2 = **become clear**, make sense, fall into place, come home to one. 3 = **take to each other**, get on, feel a rapport, be compatible, be on the same

wavelength; [inf] hit it off.
4 = be successful, prove popular, succeed, be a success, go down well.

client NOUN = **customer**, patron, regular, buyer, purchaser, shopper, consumer, user, patient.

cliff NOUN = **precipice**, rock face, crag, bluff, escarpment, scar, scarp, promontory, tor.

climate NOUN = **atmosphere**, mood, environment, temper, spirit, feeling, ambience, aura, ethos.

climax NOUN = **culmination**, high point, crowning point, height, peak, pinnacle, summit, top, highlight, acme, zenith, apex, apogee, ne plus ultra. **Opposites:** anticlimax, nadir.

climb VERB **1 = go up**, ascend, mount, scale, clamber up, shin up. **2 = rise**, increase, shoot up, soar. **3 = slope upward**, incline, bank. **Opposites:** descend, fall.
■ **climb down 1 = descend**, go down, shin down. **2 = back down**, retreat, retract, eat one's words, eat humble pie.

clinch VERB = **complete**, settle, secure, seal, set the seal on, confirm, conclude, assure, cap, close, wind up.

cling VERB = **stick**, adhere, hold, grip, clasp, clutch.
■ **cling to = embrace**, clutch, hold on to, grasp, grip, cleave to.

clinic NOUN = **medical centre**, health centre, infirmary, surgery, sickbay.

clip¹ VERB = **pin**, staple, fasten, fix, attach, hold.
▶ NOUN = **fastener**, clasp, pin.

clip² VERB = **cut**, crop, trim, snip, shear, prune.
▶ NOUN = **excerpt**, cutting, snippet, fragment, portion, bit, passage, section, trailer.

clique NOUN = **coterie**, in-crowd, set, group, gang, faction, band, ring, fraternity.

cloak NOUN **1 = cape**, robe, wrap, poncho, mantle. **2 = cover**, screen, mask,

veil, shroud, cloud,
shield, camouflage,
disguise.
▸ VERB = **hide**, conceal,
cover, screen, mask, veil,
shroud, shield,
camouflage, obscure,
disguise.

clog VERB = **obstruct**,
block, jam, congest, stop
up, plug, dam, bung up,
impede, hinder, hamper.

close[1] ADJ 1 = **near**,
adjacent, neighbouring,
in close proximity,
adjoining, abutting, hard
by. 2 = **similar**, like, alike,
near, comparable,
corresponding, akin,
parallel. 3 = **accurate**,
precise, near, true,
faithful, literal,
conscientious.
4 = **intimate**, devoted,
loving, inseparable,
bosom, close-knit,
confidential. 5 = **dense**,
condensed, crowded,
compact, packed, solid,
tight, cramped,
congested, squeezed.
6 = **hard-fought**, well
matched, evenly
matched, sharply
contested; [inf] neck-and-

neck, nose-to-nose, fifty-
fifty. 7 = **careful**, keen,
rigorous, thorough,
vigilant, alert,
concentrated, minute,
detailed, intent,
assiduous, painstaking,
searching. 8 = **humid**,
muggy, airless, stuffy,
suffocating, oppressive,
stifling, musty,
unventilated; [Brit.
inf] fuggy. 9 = **mean**,
miserly, parsimonious,
niggardly, penny-
pinching, near;
[inf] tight-fisted, tight,
stingy.
Opposites: distant,
remote.

close[2] VERB 1 = **shut**, slam,
fasten, secure, lock, bolt,
bar, latch. 2 = **seal off**,
stop up, obstruct, block,
clog, choke. 3 = **end**,
bring to an end,
conclude, finish,
terminate, wind up,
adjourn, discontinue.
4 = **narrow**, lessen, grow
smaller, dwindle, reduce.
Opposites: open.

closet NOUN = **cupboard**,
wardrobe, cabinet,
locker, storage room.

▶ VERB = **shut away**, sequester, cloister, seclude, confine, isolate.

▶ ADJ = **secret**, undisclosed, hidden, concealed, furtive.

clot NOUN = **lump**, clump, mass, obstruction, thrombus; [inf] glob.

▶ VERB = **coagulate**, set, congeal, solidify, thicken, jell, cake, curdle.

cloth NOUN = **fabric**, material, textile, stuff.

clothe VERB = **dress**, attire, garb, robe, outfit, fit out, turn out, deck out, rig out, drape, accoutre; [inf] doll up, kit out; [archaic] apparel.
Opposites: undress.

clothes PL NOUN = **garments**, clothing, dress, attire, costume, garb, wardrobe, outfit, finery, ensemble, vestments; [inf] get-up, gear, togs, weeds; [Brit. inf] clobber; [formal] apparel; [dated] raiment.

cloud NOUN **1** = **haze**, pall, shroud, cloak, screen, cover. **2** = **shadow**, threat, gloom, darkness.

cloudy ADJ **1** = **overcast**, dark, grey, hazy, sombre, leaden, heavy, gloomy, dim, sunless, starless. **2** = **opaque**, murky, muddy, milky, turbid. **3** = **blurred**, vague, indistinct, hazy, obscure, confused, muddled, nebulous.
Opposites: cloudless, clear.

clown NOUN **1** = **jester**, fool, buffoon, harlequin, pierrot. **2** = **joker**, comedian, comic, humorist, funny man, wag, wit, prankster.

club¹ NOUN = **society**, group, association, organization, circle, set, league, union, federation, fellowship, fraternity, brotherhood, sisterhood, sorority.

■ **club together** = **combine**, join forces, pool resources, divide costs; [inf] have a whip-round.

club² NOUN = **cudgel**, baton, truncheon, bludgeon, staff; [Brit. inf] cosh.

▶ VERB = *see* **hit** (1).

clue NOUN = **sign**, lead, hint, indication, indicator, suggestion, pointer, evidence, information, guide, tip, tip-off, suspicion, trace, inkling.

clump NOUN = **cluster**, bunch, bundle, collection, mass, assembly, assemblage. = *See also* **group** NOUN (**2**).

clumsy ADJ **1** = **awkward**, uncoordinated, ungainly, blundering, inept, bungling, bumbling, maladroit, fumbling, lumbering, heavy-handed, unhandy, unskilful, inexpert, graceless, ungraceful; [inf] cack-handed, ham-fisted, butterfingered, like a bull in a china shop. **2** = **unwieldy**, awkward, cumbersome, bulky, heavy, solid, inconvenient, inelegant, ponderous; [inf] hulking. **3** = **crude**, boorish, crass, inappropriate, ill-judged, tactless, graceless, insensitive, uncouth, inept, gauche, unpolished.

Opposites: graceful, adroit.

cluster NOUN = **bunch**, clump, group, collection, gathering, crowd, assembly, assemblage, knot.
▶ VERB = **gather**, collect, assemble, congregate, group, come together, flock together.

clutch VERB = **grip**, grasp, clasp, cling to, hang on to, clench.
▪ **clutch at** = **grab**, seize, catch at, snatch at, claw at, reach for.

clutches PL NOUN = **hands**, power, control, hold, grip, grasp, claws, possession, keeping, custody.

clutter NOUN = **mess**, jumble, litter, disorder, junk, untidiness, chaos, confusion, heap, odds and ends, hotchpotch, tangle.
▶ VERB = **litter**, make untidy, make a mess of, be strewn about, be scattered about; [inf] mess up.

coach¹ NOUN = **bus**, carriage; [dated] omnibus;

[historical] charabanc.

coach² NOUN = **instructor**, trainer, teacher, tutor, mentor.

▸ VERB = **instruct**, train, teach, tutor, guide, prepare, direct, drill, cram, prime, put someone through their paces.

coagulate VERB = **congeal**, clot, thicken, set, gel, solidify, stiffen, curdle.

coalesce VERB = **combine**, unite, join together, blend, fuse, amalgamate, integrate, affiliate, commingle.

coalition NOUN = **union**, alliance, league, affiliation, association, federation, bloc, confederacy, amalgamation, merger, conjunction, fusion.

coarse ADJ **1** = **rough**, uneven, harsh, lumpy, bristly, prickly, gritty, hairy, shaggy, scratchy. **2** = **rude**, ill-mannered, uncivil, boorish, loutish, uncouth, crass, churlish. **3** = **vulgar**, indecent, obscene, crude, smutty, offensive, indelicate, bawdy, immodest, unrefined, earthy, ribald, lewd, improper, foul, prurient, pornographic; [inf] blue, raunchy. **Opposites:** fine, refined.

coast NOUN = **shore**, seashore, coastline, shoreline, beach, foreshore, seaboard, water's edge; [poetic/ literary] strand.

▸ VERB = **glide**, cruise, freewheel, drift, taxi, sail, skim, slide.

coat NOUN **1** = **jacket**, overcoat. **2** = **fur**, hair, wool, fleece, hide, pelt. **3** = **layer**, covering, coating, overlay, film, patina, veneer, wash, glaze, finish, membrane.

▸ VERB = *see* **cover** VERB (**1**).

coax VERB = **cajole**, persuade, wheedle, beguile, inveigle, talk into, induce, entice, win over, prevail upon; [inf] sweet-talk, soft-soap.

cocky ADJ = **arrogant**, conceited, egotistical, vain, swollen-headed, cocksure, swaggering, brash.

Opposites: modest.

code NOUN **1** = **cipher**, secret writing, cryptograph. **2** = **system**, laws, rules, regulations, rule book.

coerce VERB = **force**, compel, pressure, pressurize, drive, bully, intimidate, frighten, terrorize, browbeat, impel, constrain, oblige; [inf] lean on, twist someone's arm, strong-arm, put the screws on.

coffer NOUN = **box**, chest, case, casket, strongbox, safe, trunk, cabinet.

cogent ADJ = **convincing**, persuasive, compelling, forceful, effective, conclusive, indisputable, sound, unanswerable, powerful, strong, weighty, potent, influential, telling, authoritative, well argued.
Opposites: unconvincing.

coherent ADJ = **logical**, rational, reasoned, consistent, lucid, articulate, systematic, orderly, structured, well structured, well ordered, cohesive, organized, comprehensible, intelligible, unified, integrated.
Opposites: incoherent, muddled.

cohort NOUN = **troop**, brigade, squad, squadron, group, company, body, band, legion, column.

coil VERB = **loop**, wind, spiral, curl, twist, snake, turn, wreathe, entwine, twine, convolute.

coin NOUN **1** = **piece**, bit. **2** = **change**, small/loose change, silver, copper, coppers, coinage, specie.
▶ VERB **1** = **mint**, stamp, mould, die, forge. **2** = **invent**, create, make up, devise, conceive, originate, introduce, think/dream up, formulate, concoct, produce, fabricate.

coincide VERB **1** = **occur simultaneously**, fall together, be concurrent, concur, coexist, synchronize, happen together, clash. **2** = **agree**, accord, match, correspond, concur, square, tally, harmonize.

coincidence NOUN
= **chance**, accident, luck, fluke, fortuity, serendipity.

coincidental ADJ
= **accidental**, chance, unintentional, unplanned, lucky, casual, fortuitous, serendipitous.

cold ADJ 1 = **chilly**, cool, freezing, bitter, icy, chill, wintry, frosty, raw, perishing, biting, glacial, numbing, piercing, frigid, inclement, windy, Siberian, crisp, sunless, polar; [inf] nippy; [Brit. inf] parky. 2 = **shivery**, shivering, cool, chilly, chilled, freezing, frozen, frozen stiff, frostbitten. 3 = **distant**, reserved, aloof, remote, unfriendly, unresponsive, unfeeling, unemotional, indifferent, dispassionate, stand-offish, frigid, glacial, passionless, unmoved, unexcitable, phlegmatic, lukewarm, apathetic, spiritless, unsympathetic, uncaring, heartless, callous, cold-hearted, stony-hearted, inhospitable.

Opposites: hot, warm.

cold-blooded ADJ
= **ruthless**, callous, savage, inhuman, barbaric, heartless, pitiless, merciless, hard-hearted.
Opposites: kind, humane.

collaborate VERB
1 = **cooperate**, work together, join forces, join, unite, combine; [inf] team up, pull together. 2 = **collude**, connive, turn traitor, conspire, fraternize; [inf] rat.

collaborator NOUN 1 = **co-worker**, colleague, associate, fellow worker, partner, helper, confederate, accomplice, team mate, co-author; [humorous] partner in crime. 2 = **traitor**, turncoat, quisling, colluder, fraternizer, conspirator; [inf] Judas, blackleg.

collapse VERB 1 = **fall in/down**, cave in, give way, crumple, disintegrate, subside, buckle, tumble down, fall to pieces, come apart, break up,

fold up, sink, give in.
2 = **faint**, pass out, black out, fall down, lose consciousness, fall unconscious, swoon; [inf] keel over. 3 = **break down**, fail, fold, fall through, founder, come to nothing, disintegrate, fall flat, miscarry, crash; [inf] flop.

▶ NOUN 1 = **cave-in**, fall-in, subsidence, disintegration, break-up.
2 = **fainting**, loss of consciousness, swoon.
3 = **breakdown**, failure, disintegration, foundering.

collate VERB = **arrange**, put in order, order, sort, categorize.

colleague NOUN = **co-worker**, fellow worker, associate, workmate, partner, collaborator, confederate.

collect VERB 1 = **put together**, gather, accumulate, pile up, assemble, stockpile, amass, store, hoard, put by, save, reserve, heap up, aggregate. 2 = **come together**, gather, assemble, congregate, converge, mass, flock together, convene, rally.
3 = **raise**, gather, solicit, obtain, acquire, secure.
4 = **fetch**, call for, go and get, pick up, bring.
Opposites: disperse.

collected ADJ
= **composed**, cool, poised, unperturbed, serene, unruffled, unshaken. = *See also* **calm** ADJ (**1**).

collection NOUN
1 = **accumulation**, pile, stockpile, store, stock, supply, heap, hoard, mass, conglomeration, array, aggregation.
2 = **donations**, contributions, gifts, offerings, alms.

collective ADJ = **joint**, united, combined, shared, common, cooperative, concerted, collaborative, corporate, aggregate.
Opposites: individual.

college NOUN = **university**, polytechnic, institute, college of further education, school, conservatory.

collide VERB = **crash**, come into collision, bang into, smash into, knock into, run into, slam into, cannon into.

collision NOUN = **crash**, impact, accident, smash, pile-up, bump, scrape, knock, clash, wreck.

colloquial ADJ = **conversational**, informal, casual, familiar, chatty, everyday, idiomatic, demotic, vernacular.
Opposites: formal.

collusion NOUN = **complicity**, connivance, collaboration, secret understanding, plotting, intrigue; [inf] cahoots.

colonize VERB = **occupy**, settle, populate, people, subjugate, pioneer, open up, found.

colony NOUN 1 = **dependency**, possession, settlement, territory, province, dominion, protectorate, satellite state. 2 = **community**, group, ghetto, quarter.

colossal ADJ = **enormous**, huge, immense, gigantic, vast, massive, mammoth, gargantuan, monumental, prodigious, monstrous, titanic, mountainous, towering, elephantine, Brobdingnagian.
Opposites: small.

colour NOUN 1 = **hue**, tint, shade, tone, tinge, coloration, colouring, pigmentation, pigment. 2 = **pinkness**, rosiness, redness, ruddiness, blush, flush, glow, bloom. ▶ VERB 1 = **tint**, dye, paint, colour-wash, tinge, stain, shade, pigment. 2 = **influence**, affect, prejudice, distort, bias, slant, taint, sway, pervert, warp.

colourful ADJ 1 = **bright**, vivid, intense, brilliant, vibrant, multi-coloured, deep-coloured, iridescent, psychedelic, gaudy, variegated. 2 = **vivid**, graphic, lively, interesting, animated, rich, striking, picturesque, stimulating, telling. 3 = **interesting**, eccentric, unusual, flamboyant, dynamic,

flashy.
Opposites: colourless, dull.

colourless ADJ
1 = uncoloured, achromatic, white, bleached, faded. **2 = dull**, boring, uninteresting, tame, lifeless, dreary, insipid, lacklustre, characterless, vapid, vacuous.
Opposites: colourful.

column NOUN **1 = pillar**, post, support, upright, shaft, pilaster, obelisk, caryatid. **2 = line**, row, file, queue, procession, train, rank, string, progression, cavalcade. **3 = article**, piece, item, feature, editorial, leader, leading article.

comb VERB **1 = groom**, arrange, tidy, smarten up, spruce up, untangle, curry, dress. **2 = search**, hunt through, scour, ransack, rummage, rake, sift, go over with a fine-tooth comb.

combat NOUN **= battle**, fighting, conflict, hostilities, fight, clash, skirmish, duel, contest, engagement, encounter.
▶ VERB **= fight**, battle against, oppose, resist, contest, make a stand against, stand up to, grapple with, struggle against, tackle, withstand, defy, strive against. **= See also fight** VERB.

combative ADJ **= aggressive**, belligerent, pugnacious, bellicose, quarrelsome, argumentative, antagonistic, contentious, truculent.
Opposites: conciliatory.

combination NOUN **1 = blend**, mixture, compound, amalgamation, amalgam, mix, alloy, composite, aggregate, fusion, marriage, synthesis, concoction. **2 = union**, association, alliance, federation, merger, grouping, confederation, confederacy, cooperation, coalition, partnership, league, consortium, syndication.

combine VERB **1 = join**, join forces, unite, form

an alliance, get together, cooperate, ally, pool resources, associate, unify, integrate; [inf] team up, gang together, club together. **2 = mix**, blend, add together, fuse, compound, mingle, merge, amalgamate, bind, alloy, bond, incorporate, synthesize, interweave.
Opposites: separate, part.

combustible ADJ
= flammable, inflammable, incendiary, explosive.
Opposites: incombustible.

come VERB **1 = move towards**, approach, advance, draw near, near, reach, bear down on, close in on. **2 = arrive**, appear, turn up, put in an appearance, materialize; [inf] show up, fetch up, blow in. **3 = be available**, be made, be produced, be on offer.
Opposites: go, leave.
■ **come about** = *see* **happen**.
■ **come across** = *see* **meet** (1), **find** (1).

■ **come clean** = *see* **confess**.
■ **come off** = *see* **succeed** (2).
■ **come out with** = *see* **say** (2).

comedian NOUN **1 = comic**, stand-up comedian, humorist. **2 = wit**, wag, joker, clown, jester; [inf] laugh; [inf, dated] card.

comedy NOUN **= humour**, joking, funniness, wit, wittiness, fun, farce, hilarity, levity, slapstick, clowning, buffoonery, facetiousness, drollery.

comfort NOUN **1 = ease**, well-being, affluence, contentment, tranquillity, luxury, opulence, serenity, repose, cosiness, plenty, sufficiency. **2 = solace**, help, support, sympathy, consolation, succour, cheer, condolence, relief, easement, alleviation, gladdening.
Opposites: discomfort, grief, pain.
▶ VERB **= help**, support, bring comfort to, console, sympathize with, solace, reassure,

succour, cheer, soothe, hearten, gladden, assuage.
Opposites: distress.

comfortable ADJ **1** = **well fitting**, snug, loose-fitting, roomy. **2** = **cosy**, homely, snug, relaxing, tranquil. **3** = **pleasant**, well off, affluent, prosperous, well-to-do, luxurious, opulent, free from hardship, untroubled, happy, contented.
Opposites: uncomfortable.

comic ADJ = **funny**, humorous, amusing, entertaining, comical, witty, hilarious, farcical, jocular, hysterical, diverting, joking, droll, zany, side-splitting, ridiculous, facetious, whimsical, uproarious, waggish; [inf] rich, priceless.
Opposites: serious.
▶ NOUN = *see* **comedian**.

command VERB **1** = **order**, give orders to, direct, instruct, charge, require, prescribe, ordain, demand, compel, bid, summon, enjoin;

[formal] adjure. **2** = **be in charge of**, have charge of, control, have control of, lead, head, rule, direct, supervise, manage, govern, preside over, superintend.
▶ NOUN **1** = **order**, instruction, decree, directive, edict, direction, dictate, injunction, requirement, prescription, bidding, mandate, fiat, commandment, precept. **2** = **charge**, control, authority, power, direction, mastery, government, management, supervision, administration, dominion, sway, domination, ascendancy. **3** = **knowledge**, grasp, mastery.

commander NOUN = **leader**, head, chief, director, officer-in-charge; [inf] boss, top dog, kingpin, big cheese.
= *See also* **chief**.

commemorate VERB = **celebrate**, remember, honour, salute, mark, memorialize, pay tribute to, pay homage to, immortalize, solemnize.

commence VERB = **begin**, start, initiate, originate, embark on, go ahead, inaugurate, launch; [inf] set the ball rolling, get the show on the road.
Opposites: finish, end, conclude.

commend VERB = **praise**, applaud, speak highly of, acclaim, extol, compliment, approve of, eulogize; [formal] laud.
Opposites: criticize.

commendable ADJ = **admirable**, praiseworthy, laudable, creditable, worthy, estimable, meritorious, reputable, deserving.
Opposites: reprehensible.

comment VERB **1** = **say**, observe, state, remark, speak, express an opinion on, interpose, interject, opine.
2 = **explain**, annotate, write notes, interpret, elucidate, clarify, shed light on.

▶ NOUN **1** = **remark**, opinion, observation, view, statement, reaction, criticism, animadversion.
2 = **note**, annotation, explanation, interpretation, footnote, gloss, exposition, interpolation, marginalia.

commentary NOUN
1 = **narration**, description, account, review, analysis.
2 = **annotation**, notes, interpretation, analysis, critique, elucidation, exegesis.

commerce NOUN
= **business**, trade, trading, dealing, dealings, financial transactions, buying and selling, merchandising, trafficking.

commercial ADJ
1 = **business**, trade, profit-making, marketing, mercantile, merchandising, sales.
2 = **profit-orientated**, materialistic, mercenary, mercantile.
▶ NOUN = **advertisement**, advertising break; [inf] ad, plug; [Brit. inf] advert.

commission NOUN
1 = **task**, employment, piece of work, work, duty, charge, mission, responsibility.
2 = **percentage**, brokerage, share, fee, compensation; [inf] cut, rake-off. **3** = **performance**, perpetration, execution, committal.
▶ VERB **1** = **engage**, employ, appoint, contract, book, authorize. **2** = **order**, place an order for, contract for, pay for, authorize.

commit VERB **1** = **perform**, carry out, perpetrate, execute, enact, effect, do.
2 = **entrust**, trust, deliver, hand over, give, consign, assign, transfer.
■ **commit oneself** = **promise**, pledge, engage, bind oneself, obligate oneself, covenant.

commitment NOUN
1 = **dedication**, involvement in, devotion, zeal, loyalty, allegiance, adherence.
2 = **promise**, pledge, undertaking, vow, assurance, guarantee, covenant. **3** = **obligation**, duty, responsibility, undertaking, appointment, arrangement, liability, task, engagement, tie.

committed ADJ
= **dedicated**, enthusiastic, devoted, keen, passionate, resolute, earnest, single-minded, whole-hearted, unwavering, ardent, zealous; [inf] card-carrying.
Opposites: apathetic.

common ADJ **1** = **ordinary**, average, normal, conventional, typical, unexceptional, plain, commonplace, run-of-the-mill, simple, habitual, undistinguished, unsurprising, pedestrian, humdrum, everyday, workaday, customary, stock; [Brit. inf] common or garden.
2 = **widespread**, general, universal, popular, accepted, prevalent, prevailing, shared, public, communal, collective. **3** = **vulgar**,

coarse, rude, uncouth, unrefined, boorish, churlish, inferior, disreputable, lower-class, plebeian, lowly, proletarian; [Brit. inf] yobbish.
Opposites: exceptional, rare, refined.
▶ NOUN = **park**, heath, parkland.

commonplace ADJ
= **ordinary**, unexceptional, undistinguished, routine, pedestrian, mediocre, dull, uninteresting, humdrum, trite, hackneyed.
Opposites: remarkable.

commotion NOUN
= **disturbance**, racket, uproar, disorder, chaos, tumult, clamour, pandemonium, rumpus, hubbub, riot, fracas, hullabaloo, row, furore, brouhaha, confusion, upheaval, disruption, bother, turmoil, agitation, contretemps, excitement, fuss, disquiet, ferment, bustle, hustle and bustle; [inf] to-do, bedlam, stir, palaver.

communal ADJ
= **common**, collective, shared, joint, general, public, community, cooperative.
Opposites: individual, private.

communicable ADJ
= **infectious**, contagious, catching, transmittable, transmissible, transferable.

communicate VERB
1 = **make known**, pass on, convey, spread, impart, get across, publish, transmit, broadcast, announce, report, relay, disseminate, proclaim, promulgate, divulge, disclose, express, mention, reveal, intimate, transfer. 2 = **get one's ideas/message across**, talk, get in touch, converse, confer, correspond, commune, have dealings, interface. 3 = **transmit**, pass on, spread, give, infect with, transfer. 4 = **connect**, be connected to, lead to, adjoin, abut on.

communication NOUN
1 = **contact**, interaction,

getting in touch, link, dissemination, communion.
2 = **message**, dispatch, letter, report, statement, news, information, data, intelligence, word.

communicative ADJ
= **talkative**, chatty, open, frank, candid, expansive, forthcoming, voluble, loquacious, informative, conversational.
Opposites: uncommunicative, reserved.

communion NOUN
= **empathy**, rapport, sympathy, affinity, closeness, togetherness, unity, accord, fellowship, harmony, fusion; [formal] concord.

commute VERB **1** = **travel to and from**, travel back and forth, shuttle.
2 = **lessen**, reduce, shorten, curtail, mitigate, modify.

compact[1] ADJ **1** = **dense**, compressed, condensed, packed close, tight-packed, solid, firm, close, consolidated. **2** = **concise**, succinct, terse, brief,

condensed, pithy, to the point, epigrammatic, abridged, abbreviated, compendious. **3** = **small**, neat, portable, handy.
Opposites: loose, rambling, large.

compact[2] NOUN
= **agreement**, contract, pact, covenant, treaty, alliance, bargain, deal, settlement, entente.

companion NOUN
1 = **escort**, friend, partner, consort, chaperone, confederate, colleague, associate, ally, crony, comrade.
2 = **counterpart**, fellow, match, twin, complement, mate.

companionship NOUN
= **friendship**, company, fellowship, togetherness, society, camaraderie, intimacy, rapport, comradeship.

company NOUN
1 = **business**, firm, organization, corporation, conglomerate, consortium, concern, enterprise, house, establishment,

antagonist, opposition.

compile VERB = **collect**, gather, accumulate, amass, assemble, put together, marshal, organize, arrange, collate, anthologize.

complain VERB
1 = **criticize**, make/lodge a complaint, find fault, carp, make a fuss; [inf] kick up a fuss.
2 = **grumble**, whine, lament, bewail; [inf] moan, gripe, grouch, grouse, bellyache, bitch.

complaint NOUN
1 = **grievance**, criticism, protest, accusation, charge, remonstrance, objection, grumble; [inf] gripe, grouse, moan, beef, whine, whinge.
2 = **illness**, disease, sickness, ailment, disorder, affliction, malady, infection, malaise. = *See also* **illness**.

complement NOUN
1 = **companion**, addition, supplement, accessory, finishing/final touch.
2 = **amount**, total, allowance, aggregate, load, capacity, quota.
▶ VERB = **complete**, round/ set off, go well with, add the finishing/final touch to, supplement.

complementary ADJ
= **matching**, finishing, perfecting, interdependent, reciprocal.

complete ADJ 1 = **entire**, whole, full, total, intact, comprehensive, undivided, uncut, unshortened, unabridged, unexpurgated.
2 = **finished**, completed, accomplished, achieved, done, concluded, ended, finalized. 3 = **absolute**, utter, total, out-and-out, downright, thorough, thoroughgoing, unmitigated, unqualified, sheer, rank, dyed-in-the-wool.
Opposites: incomplete, partial, unfinished.
▶ VERB 1 = **finish**, conclude, end, accomplish, achieve, do, perform, execute, fulfil, effect, discharge, realize, settle, clinch; [inf] wrap up,

polish off. **2** = **round off**, finish off, make perfect, crown, cap, add the final/finishing touch.

completely ADV = **totally**, utterly, absolutely, thoroughly, quite, wholly, altogether.

complex ADJ
1 = **complicated**, difficult, intricate, convoluted, involved, knotty, puzzling, perplexing, cryptic, problematic, enigmatic, tortuous, labyrinthine; [inf] tricky.
2 = **composite**, compound, elaborate, multiple, manifold, heterogeneous, multiplex.
Opposites: simple, elementary.

complicate VERB = **make difficult**, confuse, make involved/intricate, muddle, jumble, entangle, compound; [inf] snarl up, screw up.
Opposites: simplify.

complicated ADJ = *see* **complex** (**1**).

complication NOUN
1 = **problem**, difficulty, obstacle, snag, drawback,

setback. **2** = **confusion**, difficulty, complexity, muddle, intricacy.

compliment NOUN
= **praise**, tribute, admiration, flattery, commendation, congratulations, accolade, honour, plaudits, bouquet, testimonial, eulogy, panegyric;
[formal] encomium.
▶ VERB = **congratulate**, praise, speak highly of, commend, flatter, acclaim, honour, pay tribute to, salute, admire, sing someone's praises, extol, felicitate, eulogize;
[formal] laud.
Opposites: insult, criticize.

complimentary ADJ
= **congratulatory**, admiring, approving, appreciative, flattering, commendatory, eulogistic, panegyrical;
[formal] encomiastic, laudatory.
Opposites: insulting, abusive.

comply VERB = **obey**, conform to, observe, abide by, keep to, adhere

to, assent to, consent to, agree with, accord with, acquiesce in, follow, respect, yield, submit, defer to.
Opposites: disobey, ignore.

component NOUN = **part**, piece, element, bit, section, constituent, ingredient, unit, item, module.

compose VERB 1 = **write**, make up, create, think up, produce, devise, invent, concoct, compile, fashion, formulate.
2 = **comprise**, form, make up, constitute. 3 = **calm**, quiet, collect, control, soothe, pacify, assuage, still.

composed ADJ = see **calm** ADJ (**1**).

composition NOUN
1 = **structure**, make-up, organization, layout, configuration, constitution, character, formulation. 2 = **story**, article, essay, poem, novel, work of art, piece, work, opus.
3 = **arrangement**, proportions, balance,

harmony, symmetry.

compound NOUN = **blend**, mixture, amalgam, combination, fusion, alloy, conglomerate, synthesis, medley, hybrid;
[technical] admixture.
▶ ADJ = **composite**, blended, complex, fused, conglomerate.
▶ VERB 1 = See **combine**.
2 = **worsen**, make worse, add to, exacerbate, aggravate, magnify, intensify, heighten.

comprehend VERB
= **understand**, grasp, take in, follow, appreciate, see, realize, assimilate, fathom, perceive, discern, apprehend; [Brit. inf] twig.

comprehensible ADJ
= **understandable**, clear, straightforward, intelligible, self-explanatory, lucid, explicit, discernible, graspable, fathomable.
Opposites: incomprehensible.

comprehensive ADJ
= **complete**, all-inclusive, full, all-embracing, total,

encyclopedic, wholesale, universal, exhaustive, detailed, thorough, extensive, widespread, broad, wide-ranging, far-reaching, blanket, umbrella, catholic.
Opposites: selective.

compress VERB
1 = compact, squeeze, press down/together, crush, squash, flatten, cram, condense, constrict, tamp; [inf] jam together. **2 = shorten**, abbreviate, abridge, reduce, contract, summarize, truncate.
Opposites: expand.

comprise VERB **1 = consist of**, include, contain, be composed of, take in, embrace, encompass. **2 = make up**, form, constitute, compose.

compromise VERB
1 = come to an understanding, make concessions, strike a balance, meet halfway, come to terms, make a deal, give and take, find the middle ground, find a happy medium, reach a formula, negotiate a settlement. **2 = damage**, injure, undermine, discredit, dishonour, bring into disrepute, shame, embarrass, endanger, jeopardize, imperil, weaken.
▶ NOUN = **understanding**, deal, balance, concession, happy medium, trade-off, middle course, give and take, adjustment.

compulsion NOUN
1 = obligation, force, constraint, duress, coercion, pressure, oppression. **2 = urge**, need, desire, drive, necessity, addiction, preoccupation, obsession.

compulsive ADJ
1 = uncontrollable, obsessive, irresistible, compelling, overwhelming, driving, urgent, besetting. **2 = obsessional**, obsessive, addicted, habitual, incorrigible, incurable, dependent, out of control; [inf] hooked.

compulsory ADJ
= obligatory, mandatory, required, binding, forced,

necessary, essential,
unavoidable, inescapable,
requisite, prescribed, set,
statutory, de rigueur,
stipulated.
Opposites: optional.

compunction NOUN
= **remorse**, regret, guilt,
scruples, qualms,
contrition, pangs of
conscience, penitence,
repentance, contriteness.

compute VERB = **calculate**,
count, add up, work out,
reckon, determine, total,
figure out, estimate, tally,
measure, evaluate, rate,
enumerate, sum.

comrade NOUN = **friend**,
companion, colleague,
partner, associate,
confederate, co-worker,
fellow worker, teammate,
ally; [inf] pal; [Brit.
inf] mate.

con VERB = **deceive**,
swindle, trick, cheat,
mislead, hoodwink,
delude; [inf] bamboozle.

conceal VERB 1 = **hide**,
cover, keep hidden, keep
out of sight, obscure,
screen, mask, disguise,
camouflage, shelter, bury,
tuck away. 2 = **keep**
secret, hide, keep dark,
cover up, hush up,
dissemble; [inf] keep the
lid on.
Opposites: reveal, expose.

concealed ADJ = *see*
hidden.

concede VERB 1 = **admit**,
acknowledge, accept,
allow, grant, accede,
confess, recognize, own.
2 = **give up**, yield,
surrender, hand over,
relinquish, cede.
Opposites: deny, retain.

conceit NOUN = **pride**,
arrogance, vanity,
egotism, self-importance,
self-satisfaction, self-
admiration, boasting,
swagger, narcissism;
[poetic/literary] vainglory.
Opposites: humility.

conceited ADJ = **proud**,
arrogant, vain, self-
important, swollen-
headed, haughty,
immodest, egotistical,
egocentric, self-satisfied,
smug, cocky, boastful,
swaggering, narcissistic,
supercilious,
overweening,
complacent, bumptious;
[inf] big-headed, stuck up,

toffee-nosed, snooty;
[poetic/literary] vainglorious.
Opposites: modest,
humble.

conceivable ADJ
= **credible**, believable,
thinkable, imaginable,
possible, understandable,
comprehensible.
Opposites: inconceivable.

conceive VERB 1 = **become
pregnant**, be
impregnated. 2 = **think
up**, formulate, create,
work out, form, devise,
originate, produce,
frame, draw up, develop,
imagine, dream up,
contrive, envisage;
[inf] cook up.

concentrate VERB 1 = **give
one's attention to**, be
absorbed in, focus on, be
engrossed in, put one's
mind to, consider
closely. 2 = **collect**,
gather, crowd, mass,
accumulate, congregate,
amass, cluster, converge,
rally. 3 = **condense**,
reduce, compress, boil
down, distil.
Opposites: disperse,
dilute.

concentrated ADJ
= **intensive**, intense,
rigorous, vigorous, all-
out.
Opposites: half-hearted.

concern NOUN 1 = **worry**,
anxiety, disquiet,
distress, apprehension,
disturbance,
perturbation. 2 = **interest**,
importance, relevance,
bearing, applicability.
3 = **affair**, matter of
interest, department,
involvement, business,
responsibility, duty, job,
task, occupation.
4 = **business**, company,
firm, enterprise,
organization,
corporation,
establishment.
Opposites: indifference.
▶ VERB 1 = **affect**, be the
business of, be relevant
to, involve, apply to, be
of interest to, touch.
2 = **worry**, disturb,
trouble, bother, make
anxious, perturb, distress.

concerned ADJ
1 = **involved**, implicated,
relevant, party to,
connected, interested.
2 = **worried**, disturbed,

anxious, upset, bothered, apprehensive, uneasy, distressed, perturbed, exercised.

concerning PREP = **about**, relating to, regarding, as regards, involving, with reference to, with respect to, in the matter of, re, apropos.

concerted ADJ = **joint**, combined, united, collective, coordinated, collaborative, cooperative, synchronized.

conciliate VERB = **placate**, calm down, appease, pacify, mollify, assuage, soothe.
Opposites: provoke.

concise ADJ = **succinct**, brief, short, compact, condensed, terse, compressed, to the point, pithy, laconic, epigrammatic, synoptic, compendious.
Opposites: lengthy, wordy.

conclude VERB **1** = **end**, finish, come/bring to an end, halt, stop, cease, terminate, discontinue; [inf] wind up. **2** = **come to**

a **conclusion**, deduce, infer, gather, judge, assume, presume, suppose, conjecture, surmise.
Opposites: start.

conclusion NOUN **1** = **end**, finish, halt, stop, close, completion, termination, cessation, culmination, discontinuance.
2 = **deduction**, inference, decision, opinion, judgement, verdict, conviction, assumption, presumption, interpretation, resolution, solution.
Opposites: beginning.

conclusive ADJ = **decisive**, definitive, certain, incontestable, unquestionable, unequivocal, final, clinching, ultimate, categorical, irrefutable, convincing, cogent.
Opposites: inconclusive.

concoct VERB = **invent**, devise, think up, dream up, put together, plan, fabricate, formulate, form, hatch, plot, forge, design, fashion, brew; [inf] cook up.

concrete ADJ = **actual**, real, definite, genuine, factual, substantial, solid, physical, visible, material, tangible, palpable, specific, objective, firm, existing. **Opposites:** abstract, unreal.

concur VERB = **agree**, assent, acquiesce, accord, be of the same mind. **Opposites:** disagree.

concurrent ADJ = **simultaneous**, parallel, coexisting, overlapping, coexistent, coincident, contemporaneous, synchronous, side by side.

condemn VERB **1** = **denounce**, criticize, censure, damn, deplore, berate, reprove, upbraid, reproach, blame, reprehend, deprecate, disapprove of, disparage, revile, execrate, decry, reprobate; [inf] slam; [Brit. inf] slate; [formal] castigate. **2** = **sentence**, pass sentence on, convict. **3** = **damn**, doom, compel, coerce, impel. **Opposites:** praise, acquit.

condense VERB **1** = **shorten**, abridge, abbreviate, cut, reduce, compress, curtail, summarize, contract, compact, synopsize, encapsulate. **2** = **thicken**, concentrate, reduce, distil, solidify, coagulate. **Opposites:** lengthen.

condescend VERB = **deign**, lower oneself, stoop, descend, unbend, humble/demean oneself.

condescending ADJ = **patronizing**, supercilious, disdainful, superior, snobbish, lofty, lordly; [inf] snooty, snotty, toffee-nosed.

condition NOUN **1** = **state**, state of affairs, situation, circumstance, position, predicament, plight, quandary. **2** = **shape**, fitness, health, state of health, order, trim; [inf] nick, fettle, kilter. **3** = **restriction**, proviso, provision, stipulation, prerequisite, rule, limitation, terms, limit. **4** = **disease**, illness, disorder, complaint, problem, ailment, malady.

▸ VERB = **train**, accustom, habituate, adapt, influence, mould, determine, govern, educate, inure.

conditional ADJ = **provisional**, dependent, contingent, qualified, limited, restricted, provisory; [inf] with strings attached.
Opposites: unconditional.

condone VERB = **allow**, tolerate, excuse, pardon, make allowances for, forgive, overlook, disregard, turn a blind eye to, let pass; [inf] wink at.
Opposites: condemn.

conducive ADJ = **contributory**, helpful, favourable, useful, instrumental, advantageous, supportive, beneficial.

conduct NOUN
1 = **behaviour**, actions, habits, practices, bearing, manners; [N. Amer.] deportment; [formal] comportment.
2 = **running**, handling, operation, direction, management, organization, administration, control, regulation, guidance, supervision, leadership.

▸ VERB 1 = **behave**, act, acquit, deport; [formal] comport.
2 = **direct**, run, manage, administer, be in charge of, lead, organize, handle, control, supervise, regulate, preside over. 3 = **show**, guide, lead, escort, accompany, take.

confer VERB 1 = **bestow**, present, award, grant, give, hand out, invest, accord. 2 = **talk**, have discussions, exchange views, consult, debate, deliberate, compare notes, converse, seek advice; [inf] put their/your/our heads together.

conference NOUN = **meeting**, seminar, discussion, deliberation, convention, council, congress, forum, symposium, colloquium, convocation.

confess VERB = **admit**, acknowledge, own up to,

make known, disclose, reveal, divulge, accept responsibility, make a clean breast of, unburden oneself, come clean; [inf] spill the beans, get something off one's chest, blurt out, fess up.

confidant NOUN = **friend**, crony, intimate, familiar, alter ego; [inf] pal, chum; [Brit. inf] mate.

confide VERB = **confess**, reveal, disclose, tell, divulge, admit, unburden oneself, unbosom oneself, open one's heart.

confidence NOUN
1 = **belief**, reliance, faith, certainty, trust, credence, dependence. 2 = **self-assurance**, self-confidence, self-reliance, self-possession, nerve, poise, courage, boldness, conviction, panache, composure, mettle, fortitude, verve.
Opposites: distrust, uncertainty, doubt.

confident ADJ 1 = **certain**, sure, convinced, positive, sanguine. 2 = **self-assured**, self-possessed, self-confident, unafraid, fearless, secure, bold, assertive, cocksure.
Opposites: uncertain.

confidential ADJ
1 = **secret**, top secret, private, classified, restricted, off the record, suppressed, personal, intimate. 2 = **close**, trusted, intimate, faithful, reliable, trustworthy.

confine VERB 1 = **enclose**, cage, lock up, imprison, detain, jail, shut up, intern, hold captive, incarcerate, restrain, impound, keep, pen, coop up, box up, immure, wall up.
2 = **restrict**, limit, keep within the limits of, circumscribe, curb.
Opposites: free.

confirm VERB 1 = **verify**, prove, bear out, corroborate, validate, endorse, authenticate, establish, substantiate, give credence to, evidence. 2 = **ratify**, endorse, approve, sanction, authorize, underwrite, warrant, accredit. 3 = **guarantee**,

overcrowded, crowded, blocked, obstructed, overflowing, teeming. Opposites: clear.

congratulate VERB = **compliment**, offer good wishes to, wish joy to, praise, felicitate. Opposites: criticize.

congregate VERB = **gather**, assemble, come together, collect, mass, group, convene, flock together, converge, meet, crowd, cluster, throng, swarm, rendezvous, muster, rally, foregather. Opposites: disperse.

conjecture NOUN = **guess**, suspicion, theory, hypothesis, presumption, presupposition, notion, fancy, surmise, inference; [inf] guesstimate.

connect VERB 1 = **attach**, link, fix, couple, affix, clamp, secure, tie, rivet, fuse, solder, weld. 2 = **associate**, link, relate to, equate, identify, bracket, draw a parallel with. Opposites: separate.

connection NOUN 1 = **attachment**, fastening, coupling, clamp, joint, clasp. 2 = **link**, relationship, association, relation, correspondence, parallel, analogy.

connive VERB = **conspire**, collude, be in collusion with, collaborate, plot, scheme, abet, be a party to, intrigue.

connotation NOUN = **nuance**, undertone, intimation, hint, suggestion, implication, allusion, insinuation, reference.

conquer VERB 1 = **defeat**, beat, vanquish, overpower, overthrow, subdue, rout, trounce, subjugate, triumph over, overwhelm, crush, overrun, prevail over, quell, worst; [inf] thrash, lick. 2 = **seize**, occupy, invade, annex, overrun, win, appropriate. 3 = **overcome**, master, get the better of, surmount, quell, vanquish.

conquest NOUN 1 = **victory**, beating, defeat, overthrow, overpowering, subjugation, trouncing,

rout, triumph, mastery, crushing. **2** = **occupation**, seizure, possession, annexation, invasion, overrunning, appropriation.
3 = **admirer**, worshipper, fan, adherent, follower, supporter.

conscience NOUN = **moral sense**, morals, principles, ethics, scruples, standards, qualms, reservations, misgivings.

conscientious ADJ = **diligent**, careful, meticulous, thorough, attentive, precise, accurate, exact, punctilious, dedicated, hard-working, painstaking, scrupulous, rigorous, detailed.
Opposites: casual.

conscious ADJ **1** = **awake**, aware, alert, sentient, responsive. **2** = **deliberate**, premeditated, intentional, intended, on purpose, calculated, voluntary, studied, knowing, volitional.
Opposites: unconscious.

consecrate VERB = **sanctify**, bless, make holy/sacred, devote, hallow.

consecutive ADJ = **successive**, succeeding, following, in sequence, sequential, serial, in turn, progressive, continuous, uninterrupted, unbroken, chronological.

consensus NOUN = **agreement**, common consent, consent, unanimity, harmony, unity, concurrence; [formal] concord.
Opposites: disagreement.

consent NOUN = **agreement**, assent, acceptance, approval, permission, acquiescence, sanction, compliance, concurrence; [inf] go-ahead, green light.
▶ VERB = **agree to**, accept, approve, go along with, acquiesce in, accede to, concede to, yield to, give in to, submit to, comply with, abide by, concur with.
Opposites: dissent, refuse.

consequence NOUN **1** = **result**, effect, outcome, aftermath, repercussion, upshot,

reverberation, by-product, event, issue, end. **2 = importance**, significance, note, value, concern, substance, weight, import, moment, portent.
Opposites: cause.

consequent ADJ
= resulting, subsequent, following, ensuing, resultant, consequential, successive, sequential.

conservation NOUN
= preservation, protection, safe keeping, safeguarding, saving, guarding, care, charge, custody, husbandry, upkeep, maintenance.
Opposites: destruction.

conservative ADJ
1 = right-wing, reactionary, Tory; [N. Amer.] Republican. **2 = conventional**, traditional, reactionary, orthodox, cautious, prudent, careful, moderate, middle-of-the-road, unadventurous, temperate, stable, unchanging, old-fashioned, hidebound, sober. **3 = moderate**,

reasonable, cautious.
Opposites: radical.

conserve VERB
= preserve, save, keep, protect, take care of, use sparingly, husband, hoard, store up, nurse.
Opposites: squander, waste.

consider VERB **1 = think about**, weigh up, give thought to, examine, study, ponder, contemplate, deliberate over, mull over, meditate on, ruminate over, chew over, turn over in one's mind. **2 = think**, believe, regard as, deem, hold to be, judge, rate.

considerable ADJ
1 = substantial, sizeable, appreciable, tolerable, goodly, fair, reasonable, ample, plentiful, abundant, marked, noticeable, comfortable, decent, great, lavish. **2 = distinguished**, noteworthy, noted, important, significant, influential, illustrious, renowned.
Opposites: negligible.

considerate ADJ
= **thoughtful**, kind, helpful, concerned, attentive, solicitous, kindly, unselfish, compassionate, sympathetic, charitable, patient, generous, obliging, accommodating, neighbourly, altruistic. **Opposites:** thoughtless.

consign VERB = **hand over**, give over, deliver, send, pass on, transfer, assign, entrust, commend, remit, bequeath.

consignment NOUN = **load**, batch, delivery, shipment, cargo, container load.

consist VERB = **be composed of**, be made up of, comprise, contain, include, incorporate, add up to, involve, embody.

consistent ADJ
1 = **constant**, unchanging, unvarying, undeviating, steady, dependable, steadfast, stable, reliable, faithful, uniform, true to type. 2 = **compatible**, conforming to, consonant, agreeing, congruous, accordant. **Opposites:** inconsistent.

consolation NOUN = **comfort**, sympathy, solace, compassion, pity, commiseration, relief, help, support, cheer, encouragement, soothing, assuagement, alleviation.

consolidate VERB = **make stronger**, strengthen, make secure, secure, make stable, stabilize, reinforce, fortify, cement. **Opposites:** weaken.

consort
▪ **consort with** = **associate with**, keep company with, mix with, spend time with, fraternize with, have dealings with; [inf] hang around with.

conspicuous ADJ = **clear**, visible, obvious, evident, apparent, prominent, notable, noticeable, marked, plain, unmistakable, observable, recognizable, discernible, perceptible, distinguishable, manifest, patent, vivid, striking, glaring, blatant, flagrant,

obtrusive, showy, bold, ostentatious, eminent.
Opposites: inconspicuous, unobtrusive.

conspiracy NOUN = **plot**, scheme, plan, stratagem, machinations, cabal, intrigue, collusion, connivance, machination, treason.

conspirator NOUN = **plotter**, conspirer, schemer, intriguer, colluder, collaborator, confederate, traitor; [inf] wheeler-dealer.

conspire VERB = **plot**, scheme, form conspiracy, hatch a plot, intrigue, collude, collaborate, connive, combine, be in league; [inf] be in cahoots.

constant ADJ **1** = **even**, regular, uniform, stable, steady, unchanging, fixed, consistent, invariable, unvarying, sustained, immutable.
2 = **continual**, unending, non-stop, sustained, incessant, endless, unceasing, perpetual, persistent, interminable, unflagging, unremitting, relentless, unrelenting.

3 = **loyal**, faithful, devoted, dependable, staunch, true, trustworthy, trusty, resolute, steadfast, unwavering, unswerving.
Opposites: variable, fickle.

consternation NOUN = **dismay**, anxiety, bewilderment, distress, alarm, surprise, astonishment, amazement, confusion, mystification, panic, fear, fright, dread, horror, trepidation, shock, terror, awe.

construct VERB = **build**, make, assemble, erect, put up, set up, manufacture, produce, put together, fabricate, fashion, forge, establish, raise, elevate, engineer, form.
Opposites: demolish.

construction NOUN
1 = **building**, assembly, erection, manufacture, fabrication, elevation.
2 = **structure**, building, edifice, framework.
3 = **interpretation**, meaning, reading, explanation, inference.

constructive ADJ
= **useful**, helpful,
productive, practical,
positive, valuable,
worthwhile, beneficial,
creative.
Opposites: destructive,
negative.

consult VERB 1 = **confer**,
discuss, talk, talk over,
speak to, exchange views,
deliberate; [inf] put heads
together, talk turkey.
2 = **ask**, seek advice from,
call in, turn to, take
counsel from.

consume VERB 1 = **eat**,
drink, swallow, ingest,
devour, guzzle;
[inf] gobble, tuck into;
[Brit. inf] scoff. 2 = **use**,
utilize, expend, deplete,
absorb, exhaust, waste,
squander, drain,
dissipate.

contact VERB
= **communicate with**,
get/be in touch with, be
in communication with,
approach, write to,
phone, call, ring up,
speak to, reach, get hold
of, notify, sound out.
▶ NOUN = **touch**, proximity,
exposure, joining,

junction, contiguity,
tangency.

contagious ADJ
= **catching**,
communicable,
transmittable,
transmissible, infectious,
spreadable, pandemic.

contain VERB 1 = **hold**,
carry, have capacity for,
accommodate, seat.
2 = **include**, comprise,
take in, embrace,
incorporate, involve.
3 = **restrain**, hold in/back,
control, keep in check,
keep under control,
suppress, repress, curb,
stifle.

container NOUN
= **receptacle**, vessel,
holder, repository.

contaminate VERB
= **adulterate**, pollute,
debase, defile, corrupt,
taint, dirty, infect, foul,
spoil, tarnish, sully, soil,
stain, befoul.

contemplate VERB
1 = **think about**, meditate
over/on, consider,
ponder over/on, reflect
over/on, muse on, dwell
on, deliberate over,
ruminate over, cogitate

on. **2** = **envisage**, think about, consider, intend, plan, propose, foresee, expect to. **3** = **look at**, view, regard, examine, inspect, observe, scrutinize, survey, eye.

contemplative ADJ = **thoughtful**, pensive, reflective, meditative, ruminative, musing, intent, rapt, lost in thought.

contemporary ADJ **1** = **current**, modern, present-day, up to date, latest, fashionable, recent, newest; [inf] trendy, with it. **2** = **contemporaneous**, concurrent, coexistent, coeval, synchronous.
Opposites: old-fashioned.

contempt NOUN = **scorn**, disdain, disgust, loathing, abhorrence, detestation, disrespect, derision, mockery, condescension. = *See also* **hatred**.
Opposites: admiration.

contemptible ADJ = **despicable**, detestable, beneath contempt, disgraceful, loathsome, odious, ignominious, lamentable, pitiful, discreditable, low, mean, shameful, abject, unworthy, worthless, base, vile, shabby, cheap, sordid, wretched, degenerate.
Opposites: admirable.

contemptuous ADJ = **scornful**, disdainful, insulting, disrespectful, derisive, derisory, insolent, mocking, sneering, jeering, belittling, dismissive, condescending, patronizing, haughty, lofty, supercilious, arrogant, superior, snide, imperious; [inf] snooty, high and mighty, snotty; [formal] contumelious.
Opposites: respectful, admiring.

contend VERB **1** = **compete**, oppose, challenge, contest, vie, clash, strive, struggle, grapple, tussle, wrestle. **2** = **cope with**, face, grapple with, take on. **3** = **state**, declare, assert, maintain, hold, claim, profess, allege, affirm; [formal] aver.

content¹ NOUN = *see*
contentment.

▶ ADJ = *see* **contented**.

▶ VERB = *see* **satisfy (2)**.

content² NOUN
= **constituent**, part,
ingredient, element.

contented ADJ
= **satisfied**, content,
pleased, happy, cheerful,
glad, gratified, fulfilled,
at ease, at peace,
comfortable, relaxed,
serene, tranquil,
unworried, untroubled,
uncomplaining,
complacent.
Opposites: discontented,
dissatisfied.

contentment NOUN
= **satisfaction**, content,
contentedness,
happiness, pleasure,
cheerfulness, gladness,
gratification, fulfilment,
relaxation, ease, comfort,
peace, serenity,
equanimity, tranquillity,
complacency.
Opposites: dissatisfaction.

contest NOUN **1** = *See*
competition (1).
2 = **struggle**, conflict,
battle, fight, combat,
tussle, skirmish.

▶ VERB **1** = **compete for**,
contend for, fight for/
over, vie for, battle for,
struggle for, tussle over;
[inf] make a bid for.
2 = **challenge**, question,
call into question,
oppose, doubt, dispute,
object to, query, resist.

contestant NOUN
= **competitor**, entrant,
candidate, contender,
participant, rival,
opponent, adversary,
player.

context NOUN
= **circumstances**,
situation, conditions,
state of affairs,
background,
environment, setting,
frame of reference,
framework, surroundings,
milieu.

contingency NOUN
= **event**, eventuality,
incident, happening,
occurrence, juncture,
accident, chance,
possibility, emergency,
uncertainty, fortuity.

continual ADJ
1 = **constant**, perpetual,
endless, interminable.
= *See also* **continuous**.

2 = **frequent**, regular, constant, habitual, persistent, recurrent, repeated.
Opposites: occasional, temporary.

continue VERB **1** = **carry on**, go on, keep on, persist, persevere, stay, endure, remain, survive, last, sustain, linger; [inf] stick at. **2** = **prolong**, extend, sustain, maintain, protract, perpetuate. **3** = **resume**, carry on with, recommence, restart, start again, return to, take up.
Opposites: stop.

continuous ADJ = **constant**, uninterrupted, non-stop, perpetual, sustained, ceaseless, incessant, relentless, unceasing, unremitting, endless, never-ending, interminable, lasting, everlasting, unbroken.
Opposites: sporadic, intermittent.

contour NOUN = **outline**, silhouette, profile, figure, shape, form, line, curve.

contract NOUN = **agreement**, pact, arrangement, settlement, covenant, compact, understanding, treaty, bargain, deal, convention, concordat, entente.
▸ VERB **1** = **get/become/make smaller**, shrink, reduce, shrivel, narrow, tighten, draw in, constrict, tense, diminish, decrease, shorten, compress, curtail, concentrate, abbreviate, abridge. **2** = **agree**, arrange, come to terms, reach an agreement, negotiate, bargain, strike a bargain, engage, settle, covenant. **3** = **catch**, develop, get, become infected with; [Brit.] go down with.
Opposites: expand.

contradict VERB = **say the opposite of**, oppose, challenge, counter, be at variance with, clash with, dissent from, rebut, refute, controvert, impugn, confute.
Opposites: agree.

contradictory ADJ = **opposing**, opposite,

opposed, conflicting, clashing, contrasting, incompatible, inconsistent, irreconcilable, dissenting, contrary, dissident, antithetical.

contraption NOUN
= **device**, machine, mechanism, gadget, contrivance, apparatus, appliance; [inf] whatsit, thingamajig, thingamabob, thingummy, whatchamacallit, gizmo, doodah.

contrary ADJ
1 = **opposing**, opposite, contradictory, conflicting, contrasting, clashing, incompatible, irreconcilable, inconsistent, incongruous, antithetical. 2 = **awkward**, wilful, perverse, obstinate, stubborn, headstrong, wayward, intractable, unaccommodating, recalcitrant, intransigent, refractory, cantankerous; [inf] pig-headed, cussed; [Brit. inf] stroppy.

Opposites: compatible, accommodating.

contrast NOUN
= **difference**, dissimilarity, disparity, distinction, differentiation, divergence, opposition, dissimilitude.
▶ VERB 1 = **compare**, set side by side, juxtapose, distinguish, differentiate, discriminate. 2 = **form a contrast**, differ, contradict, clash, conflict, be at variance, be contrary, diverge.

contribute VERB 1 = **give**, donate, provide, subscribe, put up, present, supply, grant, endow, bestow, confer, furnish; [inf] chip in. 2 = **lead to**, be conducive to, be instrumental in, help, add to, promote, advance; [inf] have a hand in.

contribution NOUN
1 = **donation**, gift, subscription, offering, present, grant, allowance, subsidy, endowment; [inf] handout.
2 = **participation**, input;

[inf] one's pennyworth.

contrite ADJ = **penitent**, repentant, remorseful, regretful, sorry, conscience-stricken, guilt-stricken, chastened, in sackcloth and ashes. **Opposites:** unrepentant.

control NOUN 1 = **authority**, power, charge, management, command, direction, rule, government, supervision, oversight, regulation, jurisdiction, dominance, mastery, leadership, reign, supremacy, sway, superintendence, guidance. 2 = **limitation**, restriction, regulation, check, restraint, curb, brake. 3 = **instrument**, switch, dial, knob, lever. ▶ VERB 1 = **be in charge of**, be in control of, manage, head, direct, command, rule, govern, oversee, dominate, preside over, conduct, reign over; [inf] be the boss of, be in the driver's seat, be in the saddle. 2 = **regulate**, restrain, keep in check, restrict, curb, hold back, contain, limit, subdue,

bridle.

controversial ADJ = **disputed**, contentious, at issue, open to question/discussion, disputable, debatable, under discussion, problematical, doubtful, questionable, contended, controvertible.

controversy NOUN = **dispute**, argument, debate, disagreement, dissension, contention, altercation, wrangle, wrangling, quarrelling, squabbling, bickering, war of words, polemic.

convalesce VERB = **get better**, recover, recuperate, improve, return to health, be on the mend, regain strength.

convene VERB 1 = **call**, call together, summon, round up, rally; [formal] convoke. 2 = **assemble**, gather, meet, collect, congregate, muster.

convenient ADJ 1 = **suitable**, suited, appropriate, fitting, fit, favourable,

advantageous,
opportune, timely, well
timed, expedient, useful,
serviceable.
2 = accessible, nearby,
close at hand, handy, at
hand, within reach, just
round the corner.
Opposites: inconvenient.

convention NOUN **1 =** *See*
assembly. **2 = protocol**,
formality, code, custom,
tradition, practice, usage,
etiquette, propriety.

conventional ADJ
1 = accepted, expected,
customary, usual,
normal, standard,
regular, correct, proper,
orthodox, traditional,
prevailing, prevalent,
conformist, decorous,
conservative, formal,
ritual. **2 = commonplace**,
common, run-of-the-
mill, everyday, prosaic,
routine, stereotyped,
pedestrian, hackneyed,
unoriginal, clichéd, trite,
platitudinous, bourgeois;
[Brit. inf] common or
garden.
Opposites:
unconventional.

converge VERB **= meet**,
intersect, join, merge,
unite, come together,
become one, coincide,
concur.
Opposites: diverge,
separate.

conversant ADJ
= acquainted with,
familiar with,
knowledgeable about,
well versed in, informed
about, apprised of, au fait
with, experienced in,
proficient in, practised
in, skilled in; [inf] well up
on.

conversation NOUN **= talk**,
discussion, chat,
dialogue,
communication, gossip,
exchange of views,
conference, tête-à-tête,
discourse, colloquy,
intercourse, heart to
heart, palaver;
[inf] powwow, confab,
chinwag; [Brit. inf] natter.

convert VERB **1 = change**,
transform, alter, modify,
reshape, refashion,
remodel, remake, rebuild,
reorganize,
metamorphose,
transfigure, transmogrify,

transmute. **2** = **convince**, persuade, reform, re-educate, baptize, save, proselytize.

convey VERB **1** = **transport**, carry, bring, fetch, take, move, deliver, bear, shift, transfer, ship, conduct, channel, transmit; [inf] cart, lug. **2** = **transmit**, communicate, pass on, send, make known, tell, announce, relate, impart, hand on, dispatch, reveal, disclose.

convict NOUN = **prisoner**, criminal, offender, felon, law-breaker, malefactor; [inf] jailbird, con, old lag.
▶ VERB = **declare/find guilty**, sentence, condemn.
Opposites: acquit.

conviction NOUN
1 = **confidence**, assurance, belief, certainty, persuasion, firmness, earnestness, certitude.
2 = **belief**, view, principle, opinion, thought, idea, creed, tenet, persuasion.
Opposites: uncertainty.

convince VERB
= **persuade**, prove to, satisfy, assure, talk round, bring round, win

over, sway.

convincing ADJ
= **persuasive**, powerful, plausible, credible, conclusive, cogent, incontrovertible.
Opposites: unconvincing.

convivial ADJ = **friendly**, genial, cordial, sociable, affable, amiable, congenial, agreeable, jolly, cheerful.

convoy NOUN = **group**, company, line, fleet, cortège, caravan, assemblage.
▶ VERB = **escort**, accompany, attend, protect, guard, defend, guide, shepherd, flank.

cook VERB = **prepare**, make, put together, concoct, improvise.

cool ADJ **1** = **chilled**, chilly, fresh, refreshing, unheated, breezy, draughty; [inf] nippy.
= See also **cold** (1).
2 = **calm**, relaxed, composed, collected, self-possessed, level-headed, self-controlled, unexcited, unmoved, unperturbed, unruffled, unemotional, placid,

serene. **3** = **aloof**, distant, reserved, stand-offish, unfriendly, offhand, indifferent, uninterested, undemonstrative, unwelcoming, uncommunicative, chilly, frigid, impassive, dispassionate.
4 = **sophisticated**, urbane, cosmopolitan, elegant.
Opposites: warm.
▸ VERB **1** = **chill**, refrigerate, freeze. **2** = **lessen**, diminish, reduce, dampen, abate, moderate, temper, soothe, assuage, allay, mollify.
Opposites: heat, inflame.

cooperate VERB = **work together**, join forces, unite, help each other, act jointly, combine, collaborate, pool resources, conspire, connive, coordinate; [inf] pull together, pitch in, play ball.

cooperative ADJ **1** = **joint**, united, shared, unified, combined, concerted, collective, collaborative, coordinated. **2** = **helpful**, of assistance, obliging, accommodating, supportive, responsive, willing.
Opposites: uncooperative.

coordinate VERB = **arrange**, organize, order, integrate, correlate, systematize, synchronize, harmonize.

cope VERB = **manage**, succeed, survive, carry on, get through, get on, get by, subsist, come through; [inf] make out.
■ **cope with** = **handle**, deal with, take care of, contend with, grapple with, struggle with.

copious ADJ = **abundant**, plentiful, ample, profuse, full, extensive, generous, lavish, superabundant, rich, liberal, bountiful, exuberant, luxuriant, overflowing, abounding; [poetic/literary] plenteous, bounteous.
Opposites: scarce.

copy NOUN
1 = **reproduction**, imitation, replica, likeness, representation, twin, counterfeit, forgery, fake, sham. **2** = **duplicate**, photocopy, facsimile,

carbon copy, transcript; [trademark] Xerox, photostat.

▶ VERB **1** = **imitate**, mimic, emulate, mirror, echo, follow, simulate, ape, parrot. **2** = **duplicate**, photocopy, xerox, photostat. **3** = **reproduce**, replicate, forge, counterfeit.

cord NOUN = **string**, rope, twine, cable, line, ligature.

cordon NOUN = **barrier**, line, chain, ring, picket line.

■ **cordon off** = **close off**, fence off, shut off, separate off, isolate, enclose, encircle, surround, picket.

core NOUN = **centre**, heart, nucleus, nub, kernel, crux, essence, heart of the matter, substance, gist, pith; [inf] nitty-gritty.

corner NOUN **1** = **bend**, angle, curve, turn, crook. **2** = **junction**, turn, intersection, crossroads, fork, convergence. **3** = **nook**, cranny, recess, crevice, hideaway, niche, cavity, hole; [inf] hidey-hole.

▶ VERB = **trap**, capture, run to earth, bring to bay.

corpse NOUN = **body**, remains, cadaver, carcass; [inf] stiff.

correct ADJ **1** = **right**, accurate, true, actual, exact, precise, unerring, faithful, strict, faultless, flawless, confirmed, verified; [inf] on the mark; [Brit. inf] spot on, bang on. **2** = **proper**, suitable, appropriate, accepted, fit, fitting, seemly, apt, approved, conventional, usual, customary. **Opposites:** wrong, incorrect, improper.

▶ VERB **1** = **rectify**, amend, set right, remedy, repair, emend, redress, cure, improve, better. **2** = **adjust**, regulate, fix, set, standardize, normalize. **3** = *See* **reprimand** VERB.

correspond VERB **1** = **agree**, be in agreement, accord, concur, coincide, conform, match, fit together, square, tally, dovetail, correlate.

2 = exchange letters, write to, communicate, keep in touch/contact.

correspondence NOUN = **letters**, mail, post, notes, messages.

corroborate VERB = **confirm**, verify, bear out, authenticate, validate, certify, endorse, ratify, substantiate, uphold, attest to; [inf] back up.

corrode VERB **1 = eat away**, wear away, erode, abrade, destroy, consume, rust, oxidize. **2 = wear away**, rust, deteriorate, disintegrate, crumble, fragment.

corrugated ADJ = **furrowed**, ridged, wrinkled, creased, grooved, crinkled, ribbed, channelled, puckered, fluted.

corrupt ADJ **1 = dishonest**, fraudulent, unscrupulous, dishonourable, untrustworthy, venal; [inf] crooked, bent, shady. **2 = immoral**, depraved, wicked, evil, sinful, degenerate, perverted, dissolute, debauched, decadent, abandoned, lascivious, lecherous. **Opposites:** honest, pure.
▶ VERB **1 = bribe**, buy, buy off, pay off, suborn, induce, lure, entice; [inf] grease someone's palm. **2 = deprave**, pervert, warp, debauch, lead astray.

cosmic ADJ **1 = universal**, worldwide. **2 = vast**, huge, enormous, immense, immeasurable, infinite, limitless.

cosmopolitan ADJ **1 = international**, global, universal. **2 = sophisticated**, liberal, urbane, worldly, worldly-wise, well travelled. **Opposites:** parochial.

cost NOUN = **price**, charge, amount, rate, value, quotation, payment, expense, outlay; [inf] damage.
▶ VERB = **be priced at**, be worth, come to, fetch, amount to, realize; [inf] set someone back.

costly ADJ **1 = expensive**, dear, exorbitant,

extortionate, extravagant; [inf] steep.
2 = **disastrous**, harmful, ruinous, catastrophic, pyrrhic.
Opposites: cheap, inexpensive.

cosy ADJ = **comfortable**, snug, restful, warm, relaxed, homely, sheltered, secure, safe; [inf] comfy, snug as a bug.
Opposites: uncomfortable.

counsel NOUN **1** = *See* **advice**. **2** = *See* **lawyer**.
▶ VERB = **advise**, guide, direct, recommend, warn, admonish, caution.

count VERB **1** = **add up**, keep a count of, calculate, work out, total, estimate, reckon up, enumerate, check, tally, compute, tell; [inf] tot up.
2 = **regard**, consider, think, look upon, hold, judge, deem. **3** = **matter**, be of account, signify, enter into consideration, mean anything, amount to anything, rate.
■ **count on** = *see* **rely on**.

countenance NOUN = **face**, features, expression, look, mien, appearance, visage, air.
▶ VERB = *see* **permit** VERB, **stand** VERB (**4**).

counter¹ NOUN **1** = **top**, surface, worktop, table, checkout, stand.
2 = **token**, disc, piece, marker, wafer, man.

counter² VERB = **oppose**, resist, combat, dispute, argue against, rebut, contradict, retaliate, ward off, parry; [inf] hit back at, come back at.

counteract VERB = **offset**, balance, counterbalance, neutralize, act counter to, be an antidote to, oppose, work against, thwart, negate, annul, impede, hinder, invalidate, countervail.

counterbalance VERB = **balance**, compensate for, make up for, offset, neutralize, equalize, set off, undo, counterpoise.

counterfeit ADJ = **fake**, faked, forged, copied, imitation, pseudo, fraudulent, sham, bogus, spurious, feigned, ersatz; [inf] phoney.
Opposites: genuine.

▶ NOUN = **fake**, copy, forgery, imitation, reproduction, fraud, sham.

▶ VERB = **fake**, copy, imitate, reproduce, simulate, feign, falsify, pretend.

counterpart NOUN
= **equivalent**, equal, opposite number, parallel, complement, match, twin, mate, fellow, analogue, correlative, copy, duplicate.

countless ADJ
= **innumerable**, incalculable, infinite, immeasurable, endless, limitless, without limit/ end, untold, inexhaustible, boundless, myriad, legion, no end of.

country NOUN 1 = **state**, nation, realm, kingdom, land, territory, power, commonwealth, domain, people, principality.
2 = **land**, terrain, landscape, territory, scenery, region, area, district, neighbourhood.

coupon NOUN = **voucher**, token, ticket, slip, stub, certificate.

courage NOUN = **bravery**, fearlessness, valour, heroism, intrepidity, pluck, nerve, grit, boldness, daring, audacity, mettle, spirit, fortitude, firmness, resolution, tenacity, determination, lion-heartedness, gallantry, stout-heartedness, dauntlessness, indomitability, hardihood, fibre;
[inf] guts, spunk; [Brit. inf] bottle.
Opposites: cowardice, fear.

courageous ADJ = **brave**, fearless, heroic, bold, daring, plucky, audacious, unshrinking, dauntless, lion-hearted, intrepid, valiant, valorous, gallant, tenacious, indomitable, resolute, determined, game, spirited, stout-hearted, undaunted, stalwart.
Opposites: cowardly.

course NOUN 1 = **route**, way, track, direction, path, trail, line, road, passage, lane, tack, trajectory, circuit, ambit, orbit. **2 = way**, method, line of action, procedure, process, system, policy, programme, regimen. **3 = duration**, passing, passage, period, lapse, term, span. **4 = classes**, lectures, curriculum, schedule, syllabus, programme.

court NOUN **1 = law court**, court of law, tribunal, forum, bench, chancery, assizes. **2 = attendants**, household, retinue, entourage, train, suite. **3 = homage**, suit, wooing, courtship, respects, blandishments.
▶ VERB **1 = woo**, pursue, run after, go out (with); [inf] date, go steady (with). **2 = invite**, risk, provoke, lead to, cause, bring on, elicit.

courteous ADJ **= polite**, well mannered, civil, gentlemanly, gracious, mannerly, well bred, civilized, urbane.
Opposites: discourteous, rude.

courtier NOUN **= attendant**, follower, steward, page, squire, cup-bearer, train-bearer, liegeman.

cove NOUN **= bay**, inlet, sound, creek, bight, anchorage; [Scottish] firth.

cover VERB **1 = place over**, spread over, protect, shield, shelter, conceal, coat, extend over, cloak, overlay, blanket, carpet, drape, overlie, overspread, shroud, surface, veil, enclose, mask, screen, obscure, enshroud, house, secrete, bury, hide, submerge, layer, film, mantle, pave, clothe, wrap, swaddle, attire, garb, robe, encase, sheathe. **2 = deal with**, involve, take in, contain, encompass, embrace, incorporate, treat, examine, survey. **3 = report**, write up, describe, tell of, give an account of, give details of, investigate.
▶ NOUN **1 = covering**, surface, top, lid, cap, screen, layer, coat, coating, carpet, canopy, crust, mantle, blanket, overlay, mask, cloak, veil, film, sheath, shield, veneer,

wrapping, housing, cocoon, casing, cladding, skin, tarpaulin, encrustation, rind.
2 = **disguise**, front, camouflage, pretence, facade, false front, smokescreen, window-dressing, pretext, cloak, veil, mask. **3** = **insurance**, protection, compensation, indemnity, indemnification.

covert ADJ = **secret**, concealed, hidden, surreptitious, furtive, stealthy, private, underground.
Opposites: overt.

covet VERB = **desire**, want, wish for, long/yearn for, crave, hanker after, lust after, thirst for, hunger for, set one's heart on, aspire to, aim for, envy, begrudge.

cowardly ADJ = **fearful**, timid, timorous, faint-hearted, spineless, lily-livered, chicken-hearted, craven, base, shrinking, pusillanimous, afraid of one's shadow, submissive, unheroic, unchivalrous, ungallant; [inf] chicken, yellow, yellow-bellied, gutless, wimpish.
Opposites: brave, courageous.

cower VERB = **cringe**, shrink, flinch, draw back, recoil, crouch, wince, slink, blench, quail, quake, tremble, quiver, grovel, skulk.

coy ADJ = **coquettish**, arch, kittenish, evasive, shy, modest, unforthcoming, demure, bashful, reticent, diffident, retiring, self-effacing, hesitant, shrinking, withdrawn, timid, prudish, lacking confidence, unsure.
Opposites: brazen.

crack NOUN **1** = **fracture**, break, chip, split, fissure, crevice, breach, rupture, rift, chink, gap, cavity, slit, cleft, cranny.
2 = **attempt**, try, shot, opportunity; [inf] go, stab.
3 = *See* **joke** NOUN (**1**).
▶ VERB **1** = **fracture**, break, fragment, chip, split, splinter, snap. **2** = **break down**, give way, collapse, yield, succumb; [inf] go to

pieces, come apart at the seams.

cradle NOUN **1** = **crib**, cot, carrycot, bassinet.

2 = **birthplace**, source, fount, wellspring, beginnings, nursery.

▶ VERB = **hold**, rock, nestle, shelter, support.

craft NOUN **1** = **skill**, skilfulness, expertise, ability, mastery, artistry, art, technique, aptitude, dexterity, talent, flair, knack, genius. **2** = **trade**, occupation, vocation, calling, pursuit, business, line, work, employment. **3** = **vessel**, ship, boat, aircraft, plane, spacecraft.

crafty ADJ = **cunning**, artful, calculating, designing, scheming, wily, sly, devious, tricky, foxy, shrewd, astute, canny, sharp, Machiavellian, shifty, guileful, deceitful, duplicitous, insidious, treacherous, fraudulent, underhand; [inf] crooked. **Opposites:** honest.

crag NOUN = **cliff**, bluff, escarpment, scarp, ridge, peak, pinnacle, tor.

cram VERB **1** = **stuff**, push into, force into, pack in, ram down, press into, squeeze into, compress, compact, condense.

2 = *See* **study** (**1**).

cramped ADJ = **confined**, crowded, packed, narrow, small, restricted, limited, uncomfortable, closed in, hemmed in, tight, overfull, squeezed, jammed in, congested. **Opposites:** spacious.

crash VERB **1** = **collide with**, bump into, smash into, plough into, pitch into, jolt, jar. **2** = **fall**, topple, tumble, overbalance, pitch, plunge, hurtle, lurch.

▶ NOUN **1** = **collision**, accident, smash, pile-up, bump; [Brit. inf] prang. **2** = **clash**, clang, clank, bang, smash, clangour, racket, din, boom, explosion. **3** = **collapse**, failure, fall, plummet, ruin, downfall, depression, debacle.

crate NOUN = **box**, case, chest, carton, basket, hamper, receptacle.

crater NOUN = **hole**, hollow, pit, cavity, depression, dip, chasm, abyss.

crawl VERB 1 = **creep**, move on hands and knees, go on all fours, slither, squirm, wriggle, writhe, worm one's way, sneak. 2 = **fawn**, flatter, grovel, cringe, toady; [inf] suck up.

craze NOUN = **trend**, fashion, fad, vogue, enthusiasm, passion, obsession, mania, fixation, whim, fascination, preoccupation, rage, infatuation.

crazy ADJ 1 = **mad**, insane, unbalanced, demented, lunatic, crazed, of unsound mind, deranged, unhinged, touched, berserk; [inf] batty, loony, nuts, nutty, cuckoo, bonkers, mental, round the bend/twist; [Brit. inf] potty. 2 = **absurd**, idiotic, stupid, ridiculous, silly, foolish, peculiar, odd, strange, queer, eccentric, bizarre, weird, fantastic, inane, fatuous, unwise, preposterous; [inf] half-baked; [Brit. inf] potty. 3 = **enthusiastic**, mad, keen, passionate, smitten, fanatical, devoted, fervent, excited. Opposites: sensible, uninterested.

cream NOUN = **lotion**, paste, ointment, salve, unguent, liniment, emulsion.

crease NOUN = **wrinkle**, furrow, line, fold, crinkle, ridge, corrugation, pucker, ruck, pleat, tuck.
▶VERB = **crumple**, wrinkle, rumple, crinkle, ruck up, pucker, ridge, furrow, corrugate, pleat, tuck.

create VERB 1 = **produce**, originate, generate, design, establish, set up, invent, make, build, construct, develop, initiate, engender, frame, fabricate, erect, found, institute, constitute, inaugurate, shape, form, mould, forge, concoct, hatch. 2 = **bring into being**, give birth/life to, father, sire, spawn, procreate; [poetic/

literary] beget. **3 = result in**, make, produce, bring about, give rise to, lead to.
Opposites: destroy.

creative ADJ **= inventive**, imaginative, original, artistic, inspired, visionary, talented, gifted, resourceful, ingenious, clever, productive, fertile, fecund.

creator NOUN **1 = inventor**, originator, author, maker, designer, initiator, deviser, producer, manufacturer, architect, builder, prime mover, parent, generator; [poetic/literary] begetter.
2 = God, the Almighty.

creature NOUN **1 = animal**, beast, being, living thing, organism; [N. Amer. inf] critter. **2 = person**, human being, individual, character, soul, mortal; [inf] fellow. **3 = lackey**, minion, puppet, toady, sycophant, hireling, retainer, dependant, hanger-on, vassal.

credentials PL NOUN **= documents**, references, documentation, qualifications, certificate, diploma, testimonial, warrant, licence, permit, card, voucher, passport, letter of introduction.

credible ADJ
1 = believable, plausible, convincing, likely, conceivable, imaginable, persuasive, tenable.
2 = acceptable, reliable, trustworthy, dependable.
Opposites: incredible, untrustworthy.

credit NOUN **1 = praise**, acclaim, approval, commendation, acknowledgement, tribute, kudos, glory, recognition, esteem, regard, respect, merit, veneration; [formal] laudation.
2 = financial standing/ status, solvency.
▶ VERB **1 = believe**, accept, trust, have faith in, rely on, depend on, put confidence in; [inf] fall for, swallow, buy.
2 = ascribe to, attribute to, assign to, give credit to, accredit to, impute to, chalk up to, put down to.

creditable ADJ
= **praiseworthy**,
admirable,
commendable, laudable,
meritorious, exemplary,
worthy, respectable,
reputable, estimable,
honourable,
deserving.
Opposites: discreditable.

credulous ADJ = **gullible**,
easily taken in, over-
trusting, naive,
unsuspicious, uncritical;
[inf] green, wet behind
the ears.
Opposites: suspicious.

creed NOUN = **belief**,
principle, teaching,
doctrine, dogma, tenet,
catechism, article of
faith.

creek NOUN = **inlet**, bay,
cove, estuary, bight;
[Scottish] firth.

creep VERB = **crawl**, move
on hands and knees, go
on all fours, slither,
squirm, wriggle, writhe,
move stealthily, sneak,
tiptoe, slink, skulk, worm
one's way.
▶ NOUN = **sycophant**, toady,
fawner, sneak;
[inf] bootlicker.

creepy ADJ = **horrifying**,
horrific, horrible,
frightening, scary,
terrifying, hair-raising,
awful, disturbing, eerie,
sinister, weird,
nightmarish, macabre,
ominous, menacing,
threatening, disgusting,
repellent, repulsive,
revolting.

crest NOUN 1 = **comb**, tuft,
cockscomb, plume.
2 = **summit**, top, peak,
crown, brow, apex, ridge,
heights. 3 = **badge**,
emblem, regalia, insignia,
device, coat of arms, seal,
shield, sign, symbol.

crestfallen ADJ
= **downcast**, dejected,
depressed, glum,
downhearted,
disheartened,
discouraged, dispirited,
despondent,
disconsolate; [inf] down in
the dumps, in the
doldrums.
Opposites: cheerful.

crevice NOUN = **fissure**,
cleft, crack, cranny, split,
rift, slit, gash, rent,
fracture, opening, gap,
hole, interstice.

crisp

crick NOUN = **pain**, stiffness, rick, ache, cramp, twinge, spasm.

crime NOUN 1 = **offence**, violation, felony, misdemeanour, misdeed, wrong, transgression, fault, injury; [archaic] trespass.
2 = **lawbreaking**, illegality, misconduct, wrongdoing, delinquency, villainy, wickedness, evil; [Law] malfeasance.

criminal ADJ 1 = **unlawful**, illegal, illicit, lawless, felonious, delinquent, indictable, culpable, wrong, villainous, corrupt, evil, wicked, iniquitous, nefarious; [inf] crooked, bent.
2 = **deplorable**, scandalous, shameful, reprehensible, senseless, foolish, ridiculous, sinful, immoral.
Opposites: lawful, commendable.
▸ NOUN = **offender**, lawbreaker, wrongdoer, malefactor, felon, delinquent, miscreant, culprit, villain, gangster, racketeer, hoodlum, bandit, transgressor, sinner; [inf] crook, con, baddy; [archaic] trespasser.

cringe VERB = **cower**, shrink, draw back, quail, flinch, recoil, start, shy, dodge, duck, crouch, wince, tremble, quiver, shake.

cripple VERB 1 = **disable**, incapacitate, lame, debilitate, impair, damage, maim, weaken, enfeeble, paralyse.
2 = **damage**, injure, ruin, destroy, weaken, hamstring, enfeeble, paralyse, bring to a standstill.

crisis NOUN = **emergency**, disaster, catastrophe, calamity, predicament, plight, mess, trouble, difficulty, extremity, dilemma, quandary, exigency; [inf] fix, pickle, scrape.

crisp ADJ 1 = **brittle**, breakable, crunchy, crispy, friable. 2 = **brisk**, decisive, vigorous, brusque, curt, abrupt.
Opposites: limp, soft, rambling.

criterion NOUN = **measure**, standard, benchmark, norm, yardstick, scale, touchstone, barometer, exemplar, canon.

critic NOUN 1 = **reviewer**, commentator, pundit, arbiter, judge, evaluator. 2 = **attacker**, fault-finder, detractor, reviler, vilifier, carper, backbiter; [inf] knocker, nit-picker.

critical ADJ 1 = **censorious**, disapproving, disparaging, derogatory, fault-finding, carping, depreciatory, niggling, cavilling, judgemental, uncomplimentary, scathing, unfavourable, captious; [inf] nit-picking. 2 = **evaluative**, analytic, interpretative, expository, explanatory, explicative, elucidative, annotative. 3 = **crucial**, decisive, pivotal, key, important, vital, urgent, pressing. 4 = **dangerous**, grave, serious, risky, perilous, hazardous, precarious. **Opposites:** complimentary, unimportant.

criticism NOUN 1 = **condemnation**, censure, disapproval, disparagement, fault-finding, reproof, carping, cavilling, captiousness, animadversion; [inf] nit-picking, brickbats, flak, knocking, slamming. 2 = **evaluation**, comment, commentary, assessment, appreciation, appraisal, analysis, interpretation, judgement, elucidation, explication, annotation.

criticize VERB = **find fault with**, censure, denounce, condemn, disapprove of, disparage, cast aspersions on, snipe at, impugn, scold, decry, carp at, cavil at, excoriate, animadvert on; [inf] nit-pick, pick holes in, knock, slam, pan, lash, get at, pitch into, rap, flay, hand out brickbats; [Brit. inf] slate. **Opposites:** praise.

crockery NOUN = **dishes**, tableware, pottery, porcelain, china, earthenware.

crook NOUN **1** = *See* **criminal**. **2** = **bend**, curve, curvature, angle, bow, hook.

crooked ADJ **1** = *See* **criminal** ADJ (**1**). **2** = **bent**, curved, twisted, warped, contorted, angled, bowed, irregular, hooked, flexed, winding, twisting, zigzag, misshapen, out of shape, lopsided, off-centre, meandering, sinuous, tortuous, serpentine.
Opposites: straight.

crop NOUN = **harvest**, growth, yield, produce, vintage, fruits, gathering, reaping.
▸ VERB = **cut**, trim, clip, shear, lop, snip, prune, mow, graze, nibble, browse.

cross NOUN **1** = **affliction**, trouble, worry, burden, trial, disaster, tribulation, misfortune, misery, adversity, woe, pain, suffering, catastrophe, calamity. **2** = **hybrid**, mixture, cross-breed, amalgam, blend, combination, mongrel.
▸ VERB **1** = **go across**, span, stretch/extend across, pass over, bridge, ford, traverse. **2** = **intersect**, meet, join, converge, criss-cross, interweave, intertwine. **3** = **oppose**, resist, thwart, frustrate, obstruct, foil, impede, hinder, hamper, check, contradict.
▸ ADJ = **annoyed**, irritated, vexed, bad-tempered, short-tempered, irascible, touchy, fractious, peevish, crotchety, grouchy, querulous, cantankerous, testy, waspish; [inf] snappy.
Opposites: pleased, good-humoured.
■ **cross out** = *see* **delete**.

crossing NOUN
1 = **junction**, crossroads, intersection.
2 = **pedestrian/pelican crossing**, underpass, subway, level crossing, bridge, ford, causeway, flyover.

crouch VERB = **squat**, bend, duck, stoop, hunch over, hunker, cower, cringe.

crowd NOUN **1** = **horde**, throng, mob, mass, multitude, host, rabble, army, herd, flock, drove, swarm, troupe, pack, press, crush, flood, assembly, gathering, collection, congregation, convention. **2** = **audience**, house, turnout, gate, attendance, spectators, viewers, listeners.
▶ VERB **1** = **gather**, cluster, flock, swarm, throng, huddle, concentrate, foregather. **2** = **press**, push, shove, thrust, jostle, elbow, squeeze, pile, pack, cram, jam, bundle, stuff.

crowded ADJ = **full**, busy, packed, congested, overflowing, teeming, swarming, crammed, thronged, populous; [inf] jam-packed, full to bursting.
Opposites: empty.

crown NOUN **1** = **royalty**, monarchy, monarch, king, queen, emperor, empress. **2** = **top**, crest, summit, apex, tip, head, pinnacle.

▶ VERB **1** = **invest**, enthrone, inaugurate, install, induct, anoint. **2** = **cap**, be the culmination/climax of, round off, complete, perfect, conclude, top off.

crucial ADJ = **important**, vital, critical, decisive, pivotal, central, urgent, pressing, high-priority, essential.
Opposites: unimportant.

crude ADJ **1** = **raw**, unrefined, natural, coarse, unprocessed, unpolished. **2** = **rough**, primitive, rudimentary, rough and ready, unpolished, makeshift, rough-hewn, unskilful, amateurish, clumsy, inartistic, awkward, inept. **3** = see **vulgar** (1).
Opposites: refined.

cruel ADJ = **brutal**, savage, barbaric, inhuman, barbarous, vicious, ferocious, fierce, evil, callous, pitiless, fiendish, sadistic, venomous, cold-blooded, ruthless, merciless, unrelenting, implacable, remorseless, unfeeling, heartless,

malevolent, inhumane, severe, harsh, stern, stony-hearted, hard-hearted, flinty, bestial, tyrannical.
Opposites: kind, merciful.

cruelty NOUN = **brutality**, savagery, savageness, inhumanity, barbarism, barbarousness, viciousness, ferocity, fierceness, callousness, heartlessness, evil, fiendishness, sadism, ruthlessness, pitilessness, relentlessness, severity, harshness, inclemency.
Opposites: kindness, compassion.

cruise NOUN = **trip**, voyage, sail.
▶ VERB = **sail**, voyage, journey, drift, coast.

crumb NOUN = **bit**, fragment, morsel, particle, grain, speck, scrap, snippet, atom, sliver.

crumble VERB 1 = **crush**, break up, pulverize, pound, grind, powder, fragment.
2 = **disintegrate**, fall apart, break down/up, collapse, deteriorate, decompose, rot, rot away, perish.

crumple VERB = **crush**, crease, rumple, wrinkle, crinkle, fold, pucker, dent, mangle.

crunch VERB = **bite**, chew, gnaw, masticate, champ, chomp, munch, crush, grind, pulverize.

crusade NOUN = **campaign**, drive, movement, push, struggle, cause, war.
▶ VERB = **fight**, campaign, work, take up arms, take up a cause.

crush VERB 1 = **squash**, squeeze, press, mash, compress, mangle, pound, pulverize, smash, crunch, grind, pulp, shiver. 2 = **put down**, defeat, suppress, subdue, overpower, overwhelm, quash, stamp out, conquer, extinguish.
3 = **humiliate**, mortify, shame, abash, chagrin.
▶ NOUN = **crowd**, jam, congestion.

crust NOUN = **casing**, outer layer, rind, shell, husk, covering, skin, encrustation, scab, concretion.

crusty ADJ = **crisp**, crispy, brittle, hard, well done, friable.

cry VERB 1 = **weep**, sob, wail, snivel, blubber, whimper, whine, bawl, howl. 2 = **call out**, yell, exclaim, screech, bellow, howl.
▶ NOUN 1 = **sob**, wail, blubbering, keening. 2 = **call**, exclamation, scream, screech, yell, shout, bellow, howl.

crypt NOUN = **tomb**, vault, burial chamber, sepulchre, catacomb, undercroft.

cryptic ADJ = **mysterious**, obscure, enigmatic, arcane, esoteric, puzzling, perplexing, secret, concealed, coded, unintelligible, hidden, unclear, veiled.
Opposites: clear.

cuddle VERB = **hug**, embrace, clasp, fondle, pet, snuggle, nestle, curl up, enfold, nurse, dandle; [inf] canoodle, neck, smooch.

cudgel NOUN = **club**, bludgeon, stick, truncheon, blackjack, baton, bat, bastinado; [Brit. inf] cosh.
▶ VERB = **bludgeon**, club, beat, strike, pound, pummel, thrash, thump; [inf] clobber, thwack; [Brit. inf] cosh.

cue NOUN = **signal**, sign, hint, indication, suggestion, reminder, intimation.

culminate VERB = **peak**, come to/reach a climax, come to an end, come to a head, end, finish, close, conclude, terminate; [inf] wind up.

culpable ADJ = **guilty**, in the wrong, at fault, blameworthy, to blame, answerable, wrong, reprehensible, reproachable, sinful.
Opposites: blameless, innocent.

culprit NOUN = **guilty party**, person responsible, sinner, evil-doer, miscreant, lawbreaker, criminal, delinquent, reprobate, transgressor, malefactor.

cult NOUN 1 = **sect**, church, religion, body,

denomination, faith, belief, persuasion.
2 = **craze**, fashion, fad, vogue, trend, obsession.

cultivate VERB **1** = **till**, farm, work, plough, dig, prepare, fertilize.
2 = **educate**, improve, better, develop, train, civilize, enlighten, refine, elevate, enrich. **3** = **woo**, court, pursue, ingratiate oneself with, curry favour with; [inf] butter up, suck up to. **4** = **foster**, develop, pursue, devote oneself to, encourage, support, further, aid.

cultivated ADJ = *see* **cultured**.

cultural ADJ = **artistic**, aesthetic, educational, improving, educative, enlightening, intellectual, civilizing, elevating, broadening, developmental.

culture NOUN
1 = **cultivation**, enlightenment, education, accomplishment, edification, erudition, refinement, polish, sophistication, urbanity,

discernment, discrimination, good taste, breeding, politeness, savoir faire.
2 = **civilization**, way of life, lifestyle, customs, habits, ways, mores.

cultured ADJ = **artistic**, cultivated, educated, learned, enlightened, intellectual, knowledgeable, highbrow, scholarly, well informed, well read, erudite, accomplished, well versed, refined, genteel, polished, sophisticated, urbane.

cunning ADJ **1** = **crafty**, devious, wily, sly, artful, shrewd, astute, knowing, sharp, Machiavellian, deceitful, shifty, guileful; [inf] tricky, foxy.
2 = **clever**, ingenious, resourceful, inventive, imaginative, skilful, deft, subtle, adroit.
Opposites: ingenuous.
▶ NOUN **1** = **craftiness**, artfulness, wiliness, slyness, shrewdness, guile, astuteness, sharpness. **2** = **cleverness**, ingenuity,

resourcefulness, inventiveness, skill, deftness, adroitness, finesse, capability.

cup NOUN **1** = **mug**, teacup, beaker, tumbler, tankard, wine glass, chalice, goblet. **2** = **trophy**, prize, award.

curator NOUN = **keeper**, caretaker, custodian, guardian, conservator, steward.

curb VERB = **restrain**, check, keep in check, control, contain, hold back, repress, suppress, moderate, dampen, put a brake on, impede, retard, subdue, bridle, muzzle.
Opposites: encourage.

curdle VERB = **congeal**, turn, coagulate, clot, solidify, thicken, condense.

cure NOUN = **remedy**, antidote, treatment, therapy, alleviation, medicine, restorative, panacea, corrective.
▶ VERB **1** = **heal**, make better, rehabilitate, remedy, put right, repair, fix, restore, palliate, rectify, relieve.
2 = **preserve**, smoke, salt,

dry, kipper, pickle.
Opposites: aggravate.

curiosity NOUN
= **inquisitiveness**, interest, questioning, prying, meddling; [inf] snooping, nosiness.

curious ADJ **1** = **inquisitive**, inquiring, interested, searching, querying, questioning, interrogative, puzzled, intrusive, prying, interfering; [inf] snooping.
2 = *See* **strange** (**1**).
Opposites: incurious.

curl VERB **1** = **spiral**, coil, bend, twist, wind, loop, twirl, wreathe, meander, snake, corkscrew.
2 = **crimp**, perm, crinkle, frizz, wave.
▶ NOUN **1** = **spiral**, twist, coil, whorl, helix. **2** = **ringlet**, coil, kink, wave, curlicue, corkscrew.

curly ADJ = **curled**, crimped, kinked, crinkly, wavy, frizzy, permed, fuzzy.
Opposites: straight.

current ADJ = **present**, present-day, contemporary, up to date, up to the minute,

existing, modern, fashionable, popular, prevailing, prevalent, accepted, common, general, widespread, rife; [inf] trendy, now, in.
Opposites: obsolete.
▶ NOUN = **flow**, stream, tide, river, channel, drift, jet, draught, undercurrent, undertow.

curse NOUN **1** = **damnation**, execration, imprecation, evil eye, malediction, anathema; [inf] jinx.
2 = **swear word**, obscenity, oath, profanity, expletive, blasphemy, bad language.
▶ VERB **1** = **put a curse on**, damn, execrate, put the evil eye on, anathematize. **2** = **swear**, use bad/foul language, utter oaths, blaspheme, be foul-mouthed.

cursory ADJ = **hasty**, rapid, hurried, quick, perfunctory, slapdash, casual, superficial, desultory, fleeting, passing, ephemeral, transient.
Opposites: thorough.

curt ADJ = **terse**, abrupt, brusque, blunt, short, sharp, crisp, tart, gruff, uncommunicative, laconic, offhand, rude, summary, impolite, unceremonious, ungracious, uncivil, brief, concise, succinct, pithy, compact; [inf] snappy, snappish.
Opposites: expansive.

curtail VERB = **reduce**, shorten, cut, cut back/down, decrease, lessen, diminish, slim down, tighten up, pare down, trim, dock, lop, truncate, abridge, abbreviate, contract, compress, shrink.
Opposites: lengthen, expand.

curtain NOUN = **drape**, hanging, blind, screen.

curtsy VERB = **bow**, genuflect, bend the knee, bob, salaam.

curve NOUN = **bend**, arch, arc, bow, turn, loop, hook, crescent, spiral, twist, swirl, whorl, corkscrew, curvature, undulation, camber, meander.

▶ VERB = **bend**, arc, arch, bow, turn, swerve, twist, wind, hook, loop, spiral, coil, meander, snake, swirl, bulge, camber, inflect, incurve.

curved ADJ = **bent**, arched, rounded, bowed, twisted, crooked, humped, concave, serpentine, whorled, undulating, tortuous, sinuous.
Opposites: straight.

cushion NOUN = **pillow**, bolster, pad, headrest, hassock, mat, squab, pillion, scatter cushion, beanbag.
▶ VERB 1 = **pillow**, bolster, cradle, support, prop up.
2 = **soften**, lessen, diminish, mitigate, allay, deaden, muffle, stifle.

custody NOUN 1 = **care**, charge, guardianship, keeping, safe keeping, protection, supervision, superintendence, control, tutelage. 2 = **detention**, imprisonment, incarceration, confinement, restraint, constraint, duress.

custom NOUN 1 = **habit**, practice, routine, way, policy, rule, convention, procedure, ritual, ceremony, form, usage, observance, fashion, mode, style. 2 = **trade**, business, patronage, support, customers, buyers.

customary ADJ = **usual**, accustomed, regular, typical, common, habitual, traditional, routine, fixed, set, established, familiar, everyday, prevailing, confirmed, normal, ordinary, expected, favourite, popular, stock, well worn; [poetic/ literary] wonted.
Opposites: unusual, exceptional.

customer NOUN = **buyer**, purchaser, shopper, consumer, patron, client.

cut VERB 1 = **gash**, slash, lacerate, slit, nick, pierce, notch, penetrate, wound, lance, incise, score.
2 = **carve**, slice, chop, sever, divide, cleave.
3 = **shape**, fashion, form, mould, chisel, carve, sculpt, chip away, whittle. 4 = **trim**, clip,

crop, snip, shear, dock, shave, pare, mow.
5 = reduce, decrease, lessen, lower, diminish, contract, prune, curb, curtail, slash, rationalize, economize on.
6 = shorten, abridge, condense, abbreviate, contract, compact, precis, summarize.
▶ NOUN **1 = gash**, laceration, slash, incision, slit.
2 = cutback, decrease, reduction, curtailment, contraction. **3 = share**, portion, proportion.
cutting ADJ **= wounding**, hurtful, caustic, acid, barbed, acrimonious, sarcastic, spiteful, sardonic, vicious, malicious, sharp, trenchant, mordant.

cycle NOUN **1 = series**, sequence, succession, round, run, rotation.
2 = bicycle, bike, tandem, tricycle, monocycle.

cynical ADJ **= sceptical**, pessimistic, doubting, unbelieving, disbelieving, distrustful, suspicious, misanthropic, critical, sardonic, scoffing.
Opposites: optimistic.

Dd

dab VERB = **pat**, blot, press, touch, smudge, besmear, bedaub.
▶ NOUN **1** = **pat**, blot, press, touch, smudge. **2** = **bit**, speck, touch, trace, dash, drop, tinge, suggestion, hint, modicum.

dabble VERB **1** = **paddle**, dip, splash, slosh. **2** = **flirt with**, toy with, dally with, dip into.

dabbler NOUN = **dilettante**, amateur, trifler.

daily ADJ **1** = **everyday**, quotidian, diurnal.
2 = **common**, regular, commonplace, usual, habitual, customary.
▶ ADV = **every day**, once a day, day after day, day by day, per diem.

dainty ADJ **1** = **petite**, delicate, neat, exquisite, graceful, elegant, trim, pretty, fine, refined.

2 = **particular**, discriminating, fastidious, fussy, choosy, finicky, refined, scrupulous, meticulous, squeamish, nice.
3 = **tasty**, delicious, appetizing, palatable, choice, savoury, flavoursome, luscious, juicy, succulent.
Opposites: unwieldy, undiscriminating, unpalatable.
▶ NOUN = **titbit**, delicacy, confection, sweetmeat, bonne bouche.

dally VERB = **dawdle**, loiter, delay, linger, take one's time, loaf, saunter, procrastinate, waste time; [inf] dilly-dally, hang about; [archaic] tarry.
Opposites: hurry.

dam NOUN = **barrier**, wall, obstruction, barricade, embankment, barrage,

danger

bank, weir.

▶ VERB = **block**, obstruct, hold back, check, stop, staunch, stem.

damage NOUN 1 = **harm**, injury, destruction, hurt, impairment, defacement, abuse, defilement, vandalism, ruin, devastation, havoc, detriment, mischief, outrage, accident, loss, suffering. 2 = **cost**, charge, expense, bill, total.

▶ VERB = **harm**, injure, do damage to, spoil, vandalize, destroy, wreck, ruin, mar, deface, devastate, defile, play havoc with, do mischief to, mutilate, impair, disable, sabotage, warp.

damaging ADJ = *see* **harmful**.

damn VERB 1 = **curse**, execrate, anathematize, imprecate. 2 = **criticize**, censure, condemn, attack, flay; [inf] pan, slam, knock, blast, take apart; [Brit. inf] slate.
Opposites: bless, praise.

damning ADJ
= **incriminating**,

condemnatory, condemning, implicating, accusatorial.

damp ADJ 1 = **moist**, soggy, wettish, dank. 2 = **rainy**, wettish, drizzly, humid, clammy, muggy, misty, foggy, vaporous.
Opposites: dry.

▶ VERB 1 = **moisten**, dampen, sprinkle, humidify.
2 = **discourage**, dampen, check, curb, restrain, stifle, inhibit; [inf] put a damper on, pour cold water on. 3 = **reduce**, lessen, diminish, decrease, moderate.

dance VERB = **caper**, trip, jig, skip, prance, cavort, hop, frolic, gambol, jump, leap, romp, bounce, whirl, spin.

dandy NOUN = **fop**, man about town, boulevardier; [inf] sharp dresser; [dated] beau, popinjay, blade; [archaic] coxcomb.

danger NOUN 1 = **risk**, peril, hazard, jeopardy, endangerment, precariousness, insecurity, instability.
2 = **chance**, possibility,

threat, risk.
Opposites: safety.

dangerous ADJ **1** = **risky**, perilous, unsafe, hazardous, precarious, insecure, exposed, defenceless, uncertain, unsound, critical, alarming; [inf] hairy, chancy. **2** = **menacing**, threatening, ruthless, nasty, violent, desperate, treacherous, unmanageable, wild, volatile.
Opposites: safe, harmless.

dangle VERB **1** = **hang**, swing, sway, trail, droop, flap, wave. **2** = **tempt with**, entice with, lure with, hold out.

dank ADJ = **damp**, wet, moist, humid, clammy, chilly.
Opposites: dry.

dappled ADJ = **spotted**, marked, mottled, flecked, stippled, freckled, dotted, streaked, patchy, marbled, blotchy, blotched, piebald, motley, brindled, pinto, variegated, particoloured.

dare VERB **1** = **risk**, hazard, venture, have the courage, take the risk, be brave enough, make bold. **2** = **challenge**, provoke, goad, taunt.

daring ADJ = **bold**, adventurous, brave, courageous, audacious, intrepid, fearless, undaunted, unshrinking, rash, reckless, foolhardy.

dark ADJ **1** = **black**, pitch-black, pitch-dark, jet-black, inky, unlit, shadowy, shady, murky, dim, indistinct, dingy, foggy, misty, cloudy, overcast, sunless, gloomy, funereal.
2 = **dark-skinned**, sallow, swarthy, black, olive-skinned, ebony, tanned, bronzed. **3** = **moody**, brooding, angry, sullen, dour, glum, morose, sulky, frowning, glowering, forbidding, ominous. **4** = **evil**, wicked, villainous, sinful, iniquitous, vile, base, foul, horrible, atrocious, nefarious, fiendish, satanic, damnable.
5 = *See* **mysterious**.
Opposites: light, pale, cheerful.

darken VERB **1** = **grow dark/darker**, blacken, cloud over, dim, grow dim. **2** = **make dark/darker**, blacken, black, dim, shade, overshadow, eclipse.
Opposites: lighten, brighten.

darling NOUN **1** = **dear**, dearest, sweetheart, love, beloved, honey. **2** = **charmer**, pet, sweetheart; [inf] sweetie, poppet.

dart NOUN = **arrow**, bolt, missile.
▶ VERB = **rush**, dash, bolt, sprint, run, tear, hurtle, fly, bound, flash, shoot, leap, spring, scuttle, flit; [inf] scoot, zip, whizz.

dash VERB **1** = **rush**, run, hurry, race, sprint, tear, speed, fly, dart, bolt, hasten. **2** = **shatter**, destroy, ruin, spoil, frustrate, thwart, blight, baulk, check.
▶ NOUN **1** = **rush**, bolt, run, race, flight, dart, sprint, sortie, spurt. **2** = **bit**, pinch, drop, sprinkling, touch, trace, tinge.

dashing ADJ = **debonair**, stylish, lively, spirited, dynamic, energetic, animated, gallant, bold, daring, swashbuckling, dazzling.

data PL NOUN = **information**, facts, figures, details, statistics, material, input.

date NOUN **1** = **day**, point in time. **2** = **meeting**, appointment, engagement, rendezvous, assignation; [poetic/ literary] tryst. **3** = **partner**, escort, girlfriend, boyfriend; [dated] beau.

dated ADJ = **out of date**, outdated, old-fashioned, outmoded, antiquated; [inf] old hat.
Opposites: up to date, modern.

daunt VERB = **intimidate**, frighten, overawe, scare, alarm, dismay, unnerve, abash, cow, dishearten, dispirit.

dawdle VERB = **loiter**, delay, move slowly, linger, take one's time, waste time, idle, dally, straggle, trail behind, potter about, move at a snail's pace.

Opposites: hurry, hasten.

dawn NOUN 1 = **daybreak**, break of day, sunrise, first light, cockcrow.
2 = **beginning**, start, birth, rise, commencement, onset, advent, arrival, appearance, emergence, origin, inception, genesis, unfolding, development.
Opposites: dusk.

day NOUN 1 = **daytime**, daylight, daylight hours, broad daylight.
2 = **period**, time, epoch, age, era, generation.

daze VERB = **stun**, stupefy, confuse, bewilder, befuddle, addle, numb, benumb, paralyse.

dazzle VERB 1 = **blind**, bedazzle, daze.
2 = **overpower**, overwhelm, overawe, awe, stagger, fascinate, dumbfound, amaze, astonish.

dead ADJ 1 = **deceased**, lifeless, gone, passed on/away, departed, no more, late, inanimate, defunct; [inf] done for.
2 = **obsolete**, extinct, outmoded, outdated, lapsed, inactive. 3 = **dull**, boring, uninteresting, tedious, uneventful, flat, wearisome, humdrum, stale, moribund, vapid.
Opposites: alive, lively.
▸ ADV = **completely**, totally, absolutely, entirely, utterly, thoroughly, categorically.

deaden VERB
1 = **desensitize**, numb, anaesthetize, paralyse, dull. 2 = **reduce**, suppress, moderate, blunt, dull, muffle, diminish, mitigate, alleviate, smother, stifle.

deadlock NOUN
= **stalemate**, impasse, stand-off, standstill, halt, stop.

deadly ADJ = **fatal**, lethal, dangerous, destructive, toxic, poisonous, venomous, virulent, noxious. = See also **harmful** (1).
Opposites: harmless.

deafening ADJ = **loud**, ear-splitting, thunderous, resounding, ringing, reverberating.

deal NOUN 1 = **agreement**, transaction,

arrangement, contract, bargain, understanding, settlement, compact, pact. **2** = **amount**, quantity, volume.
▶ VERB **1** = **trade**, do business, buy and sell, traffic. **2** = **distribute**, share out, allocate, divide out, hand out, dole out, apportion, mete out. **3** = **administer**, deliver, give, direct, aim.
■ **deal with** = **attend to**, see to, take care of, cope with, handle, manage, tackle.

dealer NOUN = **trader**, broker, retailer, wholesaler, supplier, purveyor, distributor, vendor, tradesman, merchant, trafficker, pedlar.

dear ADJ **1** = **beloved**, loved, adored, cherished, intimate, close, esteemed, respected. **2** = **expensive**, costly, overpriced, exorbitant, high-priced; [inf] pricey, steep.
Opposites: cheap.

dearth NOUN = **lack**, scarcity, scarceness, shortage, deficiency, insufficiency, paucity.
Opposites: abundance.

death NOUN **1** = **dying**, demise, end, final exit, passing on/away. **2** = **killing**, murder, massacre, slaughter; [poetic/literary] slaying.
Opposites: life.

debacle NOUN = **fiasco**, disaster, catastrophe, failure, collapse, ruin, defeat, rout, havoc.

debase VERB = **degrade**, devalue, demean, disgrace, dishonour, shame, discredit, cheapen, humble, humiliate, diminish, ruin, soil, sully, vulgarize.
Opposites: enhance.

debatable ADJ = **arguable**, questionable, open to question, disputable, controversial, contentious, doubtful, open to doubt, dubious, uncertain, unsure, undecided, borderline, moot.
Opposites: certain.

debate NOUN = **argument**, dispute, discussion, difference of opinion,

d

altercation, disputation, wrangle, controversy, war of words, polemic.
▶ VERB = **argue**, dispute, argue the pros and cons of, discuss, bandy words, wrangle, contend, moot; [inf] kick around.

debauched ADJ = **degenerate**, dissipated, dissolute, immoral, abandoned, promiscuous, wanton.
Opposites: wholesome.

debris NOUN = **rubble**, wreckage, detritus, rubbish, litter, waste, flotsam, remains, ruin, fragments.

debt NOUN **1** = **bill**, account, money owing, score, tally, dues, arrears.
2 = **obligation**, liability, indebtedness.

decamp VERB = **run off/ away**, make off, flee, take off, abscond, escape; [inf] cut and run, skedaddle, vamoose, skip, hightail it; [Brit. inf] do a moonlight flit.

decay VERB **1** = **rot**, decompose, go bad, putrefy, spoil, perish, corrode. **2** = **degenerate**,

decline, deteriorate, fail, wane, ebb, dwindle, crumble, disintegrate, wither, die, atrophy.

deceit NOUN = **deception**, cheating, dishonesty, duplicity, double-dealing, fraud, fraudulence, trickery, subterfuge, untruthfulness, duping, chicanery, underhandedness, cunning, wiliness, dissimulation, pretence, artifice, treachery.
Opposites: honesty.

deceitful ADJ = **deceptive**, misleading, fraudulent, double-dealing, sneaky, treacherous, untruthful, dishonest, underhand, false, untrustworthy, lying, unfaithful, two-faced, duplicitous, mendacious, insincere, disingenuous, sham, bogus, spurious, perfidious; [inf] crooked, tricky.
Opposites: honest.

deceive VERB = **mislead**, take in, fool, delude, misguide, lead on, trick, hoodwink, dupe, hoax, swindle, outwit, ensnare, entrap, double-cross, gull; [inf] con, take for a ride, pull someone's leg, pull the wool over someone's eyes, pull a fast one on, bamboozle, diddle.

decelerate VERB = **slow down**, go slower, reduce speed, brake, put the brakes on, ease up.
Opposites: accelerate.

decent ADJ 1 = **proper**, acceptable, respectable, correct, appropriate, seemly, fitting, fit, suitable, modest, becoming, tasteful, decorous, pure. 2 = **honest**, trustworthy, dependable, respectable, worthy, upright, kind, thoughtful, obliging, helpful, generous, courteous, civil. 3 = **sufficient**, acceptable, reasonable, adequate, ample.
Opposites: indecent.

deception NOUN 1 = **trick**, ruse, dodge, subterfuge, fraud, cheat, swindle, sham, pretence, bluff, stratagem, confidence trick, imposture; [inf] con.

2 = *See* **deceit**.

deceptive ADJ 1 = **misleading**, false, illusory, ambiguous, unreliable, wrong, distorted, deceiving, delusive, spurious, treacherous. 2 = *See* **deceitful**.
Opposites: genuine.

decide VERB 1 = **come to a decision**, reach/make a decision, make up one's mind, resolve, choose, come to a conclusion, conclude, commit oneself, opt for, select. 2 = **judge**, adjudicate, arbitrate, make a judgement on, make a ruling, give a verdict.

decided ADJ = **clear**, distinct, definite, obvious, certain, marked, pronounced, emphatic, categorical, unequivocal.

decision NOUN = **conclusion**, resolution, judgement, verdict, pronouncement, determination, outcome, findings.

decisive ADJ 1 = **determined**, resolute, firm, sure, purposeful, unhesitating, unswerving, unwavering, unfaltering, incisive, emphatic. **2 = deciding**, determining, conclusive, final, critical, crucial, significant, influential. **Opposites:** irresolute, inconclusive.

declaration NOUN **1 = statement**, announcement, proclamation, pronouncement, broadcast, promulgation, edict, notification, manifesto. **2 = assertion**, protestation, insistence, profession, claim, allegation, avowal, contention, affirmation, swearing; [formal] averment.

declare VERB **= state**, announce, proclaim, make known, assert, pronounce, broadcast, report, trumpet, profess, claim, allege, affirm, maintain, swear, emphasize, insist, avow, attest.

decline VERB **1 = refuse**, turn down, reject, say no, rebuff, forgo, send one's regrets; [inf] give the thumbs down to. **2 = lessen**, decrease, dwindle, wane, fade, ebb, fall/taper off, tail off, flag, abate. **3 = deteriorate**, diminish, weaken, fail, degenerate, wither, fade away, sink. **Opposites:** accept, flourish, increase.

▸ NOUN **= decrease**, reduction, lessening, downturn, downswing, slump, plunge, diminution, ebb, waning, falling-off, deterioration, degeneration; [inf] nosedive.

decode VERB **= decipher**, unravel, make out, unscramble, solve, explain, interpret, read; [inf] crack, figure out. **Opposites:** encode.

decompose VERB **= rot**, decay, putrefy, go bad, go off, break down, disintegrate, fester.

decor NOUN **= decoration**, furnishings, furbishing, colour scheme, ornamentation.

decorate VERB **1 = adorn**, ornament, festoon,

beautify, prettify, embellish, garnish, trim, enhance, garland.
2 = paint, wallpaper, paper, renovate, refurbish, furbish; [inf] do up. **3 = honour**, give a medal to, pin a medal on, confer an award on.

decoration NOUN
1 = adornment, ornamentation, embellishment, beautification, prettification, enhancement.
2 = ornament, trinket, bauble, frill, flourish, frippery, knick-knack, tinsel, trimming.
3 = medal, award, order, badge, star, ribbon, laurel, colours, insignia.

decorative ADJ
= ornamental, ornate, fancy, elaborate.

decorous ADJ **= proper**, seemly, decent, becoming, fitting, tasteful, in good taste, correct, appropriate, suitable, presentable, apt, apposite, polite, well mannered, well behaved, refined, genteel, well bred, respectable, dignified.
Opposites: indecorous, unseemly.

decorum NOUN
= propriety, decency, correctness, appropriateness, seemliness, respectability, good taste, politeness, courtesy, refinement, breeding, etiquette, protocol, conformity, good form; [inf] the thing to do.

decoy NOUN **= lure**, bait, temptation, diversion, distraction, snare, trap, inducement, attraction, enticement.
▶ VERB **= lure**, attract, tempt, seduce, inveigle, draw, lead, ensnare, entrap, snare, trap, trick.

decrease VERB **1 = lessen**, reduce, grow less, diminish, drop, fall off, decline, contract, dwindle, shrink, lower, cut down/back, curtail.
2 = die down, abate, subside, let up, slacken, ebb, wane, taper off, peter out, tail off.
Opposites: increase.

▶ NOUN = **reduction**, drop, lessening, decline, falling-off, downturn, cutback, diminution, curtailment, contraction, shrinkage.
Opposites: increase.

decree NOUN 1 = **edict**, order, law, statute, act, ordinance, regulation, injunction, rule, enactment, command, mandate, proclamation, precept, dictum.
2 = **ruling**, verdict, judgement, decision, finding.
▶ VERB = **ordain**, rule, order, command, dictate, lay down, prescribe, pronounce, declare, proclaim, direct, determine, decide, promulgate, enact, adjudge, enjoin.

decrepit ADJ = **dilapidated**, battered, ramshackle, derelict, broken-down, run-down, worn out, rickety, antiquated; [inf] the worse for wear, on its last legs.
Opposites: sound.

dedicate VERB 1 = **devote**, commit, give, give over, pledge, surrender.
2 = **inscribe**, address, assign, name.

dedicated ADJ = **committed**, devoted, wholehearted, enthusiastic, keen, zealous, single-minded, sworn.

deduce VERB = **conclude**, come to the conclusion that, infer, gather, work out, reason, understand, come to understand, surmise, divine, assume, presume, glean; [inf] put two and two together; [Brit. inf] suss out.

deduct VERB = **subtract**, take away, take off, withdraw, remove, discount, abstract.
Opposites: add.

deduction NOUN 1 = **conclusion**, inference, reasoning, assumption, presumption, findings, result. 2 = **subtraction**, reduction, decrease, taking off, removal, withdrawal, discount.

deed NOUN 1 = **act**, action, feat, exploit, performance, undertaking, effort,

defect

accomplishment, enterprise, achievement, endeavour, stunt.
2 = **document**, title, contract, instrument, indenture.

deep ADJ **1** = **fathomless**, bottomless, yawning, cavernous, profound, unplumbed, abyssal.
2 = **profound**, extreme, intense, great, deep-seated, deep-rooted, grave. **3** = **intense**, heartfelt, fervent, ardent, impassioned. **4** = **low**, low-pitched, bass, rich, powerful, resonant, sonorous, rumbling, booming, resounding.
Opposites: shallow, light, high.

deface VERB = **spoil**, disfigure, blemish, mar, deform, ruin, sully, tarnish, damage, mutilate, vandalize, injure, uglify.

defame VERB = **slander**, libel, blacken someone's name, cast aspersions on, smear, malign, insult, speak evil of, vilify, traduce, besmirch, drag through the mud, defile, stigmatize, disparage, denigrate.

defeat VERB **1** = **beat**, conquer, get the better of, win a victory over, vanquish, rout, trounce, overcome, overpower, overwhelm, crush, quash, subjugate, subdue, quell; [inf] thrash, wipe the floor with, lick, smash, clobber, zap.
2 = **baffle**, puzzle, perplex, confound, frustrate.
3 = **reject**, throw out, outvote.
Opposites: lose.
▶ NOUN = **conquest**, beating, vanquishing, thrashing, rout, overpowering, overthrow, reverse, setback, subjugation, humiliation, failure, repulse; [inf] drubbing, licking.

defect¹ NOUN = **fault**, flaw, imperfection, deficiency, shortcoming, weak spot/point, weakness, mistake, error, failing, inadequacy, omission, absence, snag, kink, deformity, blemish, crack, break, tear, scratch; [inf] bug.

defect² VERB = **desert**, change sides, go over, apostatize.

defective ADJ = **faulty**, flawed, imperfect, malfunctioning, broken, in disrepair, inadequate, deficient, incomplete, weak, unsatisfactory, cracked, torn, scratched, insufficient, wanting. **Opposites**: intact.

defence NOUN
1 = **protection**, guard, shield, security, safeguard, cover, shelter, fortification, screen, resistance, deterrent.
2 = **justification**, argument, apology, apologia, vindication, plea, explanation, excuse, extenuation, exoneration.

defenceless ADJ = **vulnerable**, helpless, exposed, weak, powerless, unguarded, unprotected, unarmed, open to attack, wide open.

defend VERB **1** = **protect**, guard, watch over, safeguard, keep from harm, preserve, secure, shelter, screen, shield, cover, fight for.
2 = **justify**, argue for, speak on behalf of, make a case for, give reasons for, plead for, champion, stand up for, explain, exonerate. **Opposites**: attack.

defendant NOUN
= **accused**, prisoner at the bar, respondent, appellant, litigant.

defensive ADJ
1 = **protective**, watchful, shielding, opposing.
2 = **oversensitive**, prickly, apologetic, thin-skinned. **Opposites**: offensive.

defer VERB = **postpone**, put off, delay, adjourn, hold over, suspend, stay, hold in abeyance, prorogue; [inf] put on ice, shelve.

deference NOUN
= **respect**, reverence, homage, veneration, dutifulness, consideration, regard, attentiveness, attention, thoughtfulness.

defiant ADJ = **challenging**, aggressive, provocative, rebellious, disobedient, uncooperative, insolent, resistant, insubordinate, mutinous, obstinate, headstrong, antagonistic, refractory, contemptuous, scornful, bold, brazen, daring, audacious, truculent, unruly, self-willed.

deficiency NOUN 1 = **lack**, shortage, scarcity, scantiness, want, dearth, insufficiency, inadequacy, deficit, absence, paucity. 2 = *See* **defect¹**.

defile VERB = **corrupt**, contaminate, taint, tarnish, pollute, foul, dirty, soil, sully, pervert, infect, besmirch, desecrate, dishonour.

define VERB 1 = **explain**, give the meaning of, spell out, elucidate, describe, interpret, expound, clarify. 2 = **mark out/off**, fix, establish, determine, settle, bound, demarcate, delineate, delimit, circumscribe, describe.

definite ADJ 1 = **specific**, precise, particular, exact, well defined, clear, clear-cut, explicit, fixed, established, confirmed, determined, express. 2 = **certain**, sure, decided, positive, settled, guaranteed, assured, conclusive, final. 3 = **fixed**, marked, delimited, demarcated, circumscribed. **Opposites:** indefinite, uncertain, indeterminate.

definitely ADV = **certainly**, surely, for sure, without doubt/question, beyond any doubt, undoubtedly, indubitably, positively, absolutely, undeniably, unmistakably, plainly, clearly, obviously, decidedly.

definition NOUN 1 = **meaning**, description, elucidation, exposition, interpretation, clarification. 2 = **sharpness**, clearness, clarity, distinctness, focus, precision.

definitive ADJ = **conclusive**, authoritative, final, decisive, unconditional, unqualified, absolute, categorical, settled,

official, ultimate,
decided, agreed,
standard, complete,
correct.

deflect VERB = **turn aside**,
turn, divert, parry, fend
off, ward off, intercept,
glance off, veer, swerve,
deviate, switch, avert,
sidetrack.

deformed ADJ
= **misshapen**, malformed,
distorted, contorted,
twisted, crooked,
crippled, maimed,
disfigured, damaged,
mutilated, marred,
warped, gnarled,
mangled, perverted,
corrupted, depraved.

defraud VERB = **cheat**,
swindle, rob, trick, fool;
[inf] rip off, fleece, con,
gyp.

deft ADJ = **dexterous**,
nimble, adroit, agile,
skilful, skilled, adept,
proficient, able, clever,
expert, quick.
Opposites: clumsy,
maladroit.

defy VERB **1** = **disobey**,
disregard, rebel, ignore,
flout, deride, slight,
scorn; [inf] thumb one's
nose at, scoff at, snap
one's fingers at. **2** = **resist**,
stand up to, confront,
face, repel, repulse,
thwart, frustrate, foil,
withstand, brave;
[inf] meet head-on.
Opposites: obey.

degenerate ADJ = *see*
debauched.
▸VERB = **deteriorate**,
decline, worsen, decay,
rot, regress, fail, fall off,
sink, slide, slip; [inf] go to
the dogs, go to pot, hit
the skids.
Opposites: improve.

degrade VERB **1** = **debase**,
discredit, cheapen,
belittle, demean, lower,
devalue, reduce, shame,
disgrace, dishonour,
humble, humiliate,
abase, mortify;
[formal] vitiate. **2** = **demote**,
downgrade, strip of rank,
cashier, unseat, dethrone.
Opposites: dignify.

degree NOUN **1** = **level**,
stage, grade, step, rung,
point, mark, measure,
gradation, limit.
2 = **extent**, measure,
magnitude, level,
amount, intensity,

quality, proportion, ratio.

deign VERB = **condescend**, lower oneself, stoop, think/see fit, deem worthy, consent.

deity NOUN = **god**, goddess, supreme being, divinity, godhead, divine being, demiurge.

dejected ADJ = **depressed**, dispirited, discouraged, disheartened, downhearted, crestfallen, downcast, disappointed, unhappy, sad, miserable, despondent, forlorn, woebegone, disconsolate, morose; [inf] down in the dumps, blue, long-faced. **Opposites:** cheerful.

delay VERB 1 = **postpone**, put off, hold over, adjourn, defer, stay, hold in abeyance; [inf] shelve, put on ice, put on the back burner. 2 = **hold up/ back**, detain, hinder, obstruct, hamper, impede, check, restrain, arrest; [inf] bog down. 3 = **linger**, loiter, dawdle, dally, lag/fall behind, procrastinate; [inf] dilly-dally; [archaic] tarry.

Opposites: advance, hurry.
▸ NOUN 1 = **postponement**, adjournment, deferment, suspension, stay. 2 = **hold-up**, wait, setback, check, stoppage, halt, interruption, detention, hindrance, obstruction, impediment.

delegate VERB 1 = **appoint**, designate, nominate, name, depute, commission, mandate, choose, select, elect, ordain. 2 = **pass on**, hand over, transfer, give, entrust, assign, commit.
▸ NOUN = **representative**, agent, envoy, legate, emissary.

delegation NOUN = **deputation**, legation, mission, commission, embassy.

delete VERB = **erase**, cross out, rub out, cut out, cancel, edit out, remove, take out, expunge, obliterate, blue-pencil, efface.

deliberate ADJ 1 = **intentional**, planned, intended, calculated, considered, designed,

studied, conscious,
purposeful, wilful,
premeditated, pre-
arranged, preconceived,
aforethought. **2 = careful**,
unhurried, cautious,
thoughtful, steady,
regular, measured,
unwavering,
unhesitating, unfaltering,
determined, resolute,
ponderous, laborious.
Opposites: unintentional,
hasty.

▶ VERB = *see* **think (3)**.

deliberately ADV
= **intentionally**, on
purpose, purposefully, by
design, knowingly,
wittingly, consciously,
premeditatedly,
calculatingly; [inf] in cold
blood.

delicate ADJ **1 = fine**,
fragile, dainty, exquisite,
slender, slight, elegant,
graceful, flimsy, wispy,
gossamer. **2 = frail**, sickly,
weak, unwell, in poor
health, infirm, ailing,
debilitated. **3 = careful**,
sensitive, tactful, discreet,
considerate, diplomatic,
politic. **4 = subtle**,
subdued, muted, pastel,

pale, understated.
5 = difficult, awkward,
tricky, sensitive, critical,
precarious; [inf] ticklish,
touchy. **6 = deft**, skilled,
skilful, expert.
Opposites: coarse, robust.

delicious ADJ
1 = appetizing, tasty,
delectable, mouth-
watering, savoury,
palatable, luscious,
flavoursome, toothsome,
ambrosial; [inf] yummy,
scrumptious.
2 = delightful,
enchanting, enjoyable,
pleasant, agreeable,
charming, pleasurable,
entertaining, amusing,
diverting.
Opposites: revolting,
disgusting.

delight NOUN = **joy**,
pleasure, happiness,
gladness, bliss, ecstasy,
rapture, elation,
jubilation, satisfaction,
excitement,
entertainment,
amusement, transports.
Opposites: dismay.

▶ VERB = **please**, gladden,
thrill, cheer, gratify,
enchant, excite,

transport, captivate, charm, entertain, amuse, divert.
Opposites: dismay, displease.

delighted ADJ = *see* **happy** (**1, 2**).

delightful ADJ = **pleasing**, agreeable, enjoyable, pleasant, pleasurable, amusing, entertaining, diverting, gratifying, delectable, enchanting, captivating, entrancing, ravishing, attractive, beautiful, engaging, winning, joyful, exciting, thrilling.

delinquent NOUN = **offender**, wrongdoer, lawbreaker, criminal, hooligan, culprit, ruffian, hoodlum, miscreant, transgressor, malefactor; [Brit.] tearaway.

delirious ADJ **1** = **raving**, incoherent, babbling, light-headed, irrational, deranged, demented, unhinged, insane; [inf] off one's head. **2** = **ecstatic**, euphoric, carried away, wild with excitement, frantic, transported.

deliver VERB **1** = **distribute**, carry, bring, take, transport, convey, send, dispatch, remit. **2** = **give**, give voice to, pronounce, enunciate, announce, proclaim, declare, read, recite, broadcast, promulgate. **3** = **set free**, save, liberate, free, release, rescue, set loose, emancipate, redeem.
4 = **direct**, aim, give, deal, administer, inflict, throw, pitch.

delivery NOUN
1 = **distribution**, transport, carriage, conveyance, dispatch.
2 = **consignment**, batch, load. **3** = **enunciation**, articulation, intonation, elocution, utterance, presentation.
4 = **childbirth**, labour, confinement, parturition.

deluge NOUN = **flood**, downpour, inundation, spate, rush.
▸ VERB = **flood**, inundate, swamp, engulf, drown, submerge, soak, drench, douse, overwhelm.

delusion NOUN
= **misconception**,

illusion, fallacy,
misapprehension,
mistake,
misunderstanding,
hallucination, fantasy,
fancy.

delve VERB = **search**,
rummage, dig into, hunt
through, investigate,
probe, examine.

demand VERB 1 = **ask for**,
request, insist on, press
for, urge, clamour for,
claim, lay claim to.
2 = **expect**, impose, insist
on, order, requisition.
3 = **require**, need,
necessitate, involve,
want, call for, cry out
for. 4 = **ask**, inquire,
question, interrogate.
▶ NOUN 1 = **request**, entreaty,
claim, requisition.
2 = **requirement**, need,
necessity, claim,
imposition, exigency.
3 = **inquiry**, question,
interrogation, challenge.

demanding ADJ = *see*
difficult (1).

demean VERB = **degrade**,
lower, debase, devalue,
humble, abase,
humiliate, disgrace,
shame, belittle.

demeanour NOUN = **air**,
appearance, bearing,
conduct, behaviour,
mien, deportment,
carriage;
[formal] comportment.

demolish VERB = **knock
down**, pull/tear down,
flatten, bring down, raze,
level, bulldoze, wreck,
topple, dismantle, break
up, pulverize.
Opposites: build.

demonic ADJ = **hellish**,
diabolical, satanic,
infernal, evil, wicked,
fiendish.
Opposites: angelic.

demonstrable ADJ
= **provable**, verifiable,
indisputable,
incontrovertible,
irrefutable, conclusive,
undeniable,
unquestionable,
confirmable, attestable,
evincible.

demonstrate VERB
1 = **show**, indicate,
display, exhibit,
manifest, evince,
evidence. 2 = **prove**,
indicate, show,
determine, confirm,
validate, verify, establish.

3 = protest, march, parade, rally, picket.

demonstration NOUN
1 = explanation, exposition, illustration, description.
2 = indication, confirmation, substantiation, verification, validation, affirmation. **3 = protest**, march, parade, rally, vigil, lobby, picket; [inf] demo, sit-in.

demonstrative ADJ
= emotional, unrestrained, expressive, open, effusive, expansive, gushing, affectionate, loving, warm.
Opposites: undemonstrative, reserved.

demoralize VERB
= discourage, dishearten, dispirit, depress, crush, shake, undermine.
Opposites: hearten.

demure ADJ = **modest**, unassuming, bashful, retiring, shy, meek, diffident, reticent, timid, shrinking, timorous, sober.
Opposites: brazen.

denial NOUN
1 = contradiction, repudiation, disaffirmation, negation, dissent, abjuration.
2 = refusal, rejection, dismissal, veto, repulse; [inf] thumbs down.
Opposites: confession.

denigrate VERB
= disparage, belittle, diminish, deprecate, detract from, decry, defame, slander, libel, cast aspersions on, malign, vilify, besmirch, abuse, revile; [inf] bad-mouth, put down.
Opposites: praise.

denomination NOUN
1 = creed, faith, church, sect, persuasion, communion, order, school. **2 = category**, type, classification, group, grouping.

denote VERB = **be a sign of**, indicate, mean, stand for, signify, represent, symbolize, express, betoken.

denounce VERB
1 = condemn, attack, criticize, censure, decry, fulminate against,

inveigh against, revile;
[formal] castigate.
2 = accuse, inform
against, incriminate,
implicate, charge,
inculpate, indict,
impeach.

dense ADJ **1 = tightly
packed**, close-packed,
crowded, jammed
together, crammed,
compressed, compacted,
closely set.
2 = concentrated, heavy,
condensed, thick,
viscous, impenetrable,
opaque. **3 = stupid**, slow-
witted, slow, dull-witted,
obtuse, blockheaded;
[inf] thick, dim.
Opposites: sparse, light,
clever.

deny VERB **1 = repudiate**,
dispute, reject,
contradict, disagree with,
disclaim, dissent from,
negate, disaffirm, abjure,
controvert. **2 = refuse**,
reject, turn down,
decline, dismiss, repulse,
veto; [inf] give the thumbs
down to, give the red
light to.
Opposites: admit, allow,
grant.

depart VERB **1 = leave**, go,
take one's leave/
departure, withdraw,
absent oneself, set off,
start out, get under way,
quit, make an exit,
decamp, retire, retreat;
[inf] make tracks, shove
off, split, vamoose,
hightail it. **2 =** See
deviate.

departed ADJ **= dead**,
deceased, late, gone,
passed away/on.

department NOUN
1 = section, division,
unit, branch, office,
bureau, agency,
compartment. **2 = area of
responsibility**, area,
concern, sphere, line,
province, domain, field,
realm, jurisdiction.

departure NOUN **= leaving**,
going, starting out,
embarkation, escape,
exit, withdrawal, retreat,
retirement.
Opposites: arrival.

depend VERB **1 = be
dependent on**, turn/
hinge on, be subject to,
rest on, be contingent
on, revolve around, be
influenced by. **2 = rely on**,

count/bank on, trust in, put one's faith in, swear by, be sure of, be supported by.

dependable ADJ
= **reliable**, trustworthy, trusty, faithful, steady, responsible, sure, stable, unfailing, sound.
Opposites: unreliable.

dependent ADJ
1 = **depending on**, conditional on, contingent on, subject to, determined by, connected with, relative to. 2 = **relying on**, reliant on, supported by, sustained by. 3 = **reliant**, helpless, weak, defenceless, vulnerable.
Opposites: independent.

depict VERB = **portray**, represent, draw, paint, sketch, illustrate, delineate, outline, reproduce, render, describe, set out, relate, detail, narrate, recount, chronicle.

deplete VERB = **exhaust**, use up, consume, expend, spend, drain, empty, milk.

Opposites: augment, increase.

deplorable ADJ
= **disgraceful**, shameful, reprehensible, scandalous, shocking, dishonourable, discreditable, despicable, contemptible, blameworthy, abominable, lamentable, dire, pitiable, calamitous, base, sordid, vile, execrable, opprobrious.
Opposites: admirable.

deplore VERB 1 = *See* **condemn** (1). 2 = **be scandalized by**, be shocked by, be offended by, disapprove of, abhor.
Opposites: applaud.

deploy VERB 1 = **arrange**, position, dispose, distribute, station.
2 = **use**, utilize, set out/ up, bring into play, have recourse to.

deport VERB = **expel**, banish, evict, transport, oust, expatriate, extradite.

depose VERB = **unseat**, oust, remove, dismiss, dethrone, discharge, cashier; [inf] sack, fire, give someone the boot; [Brit. inf] give someone the push.

deposit NOUN **1** = **down payment**, instalment, retainer, security, pledge, stake. **2** = **sediment**, accumulation, layer, precipitation, deposition, sublimate, dregs, silt, alluvium.
▶ VERB **1** = **bank**, lodge, consign, entrust, store, hoard, stow, put away, lay in; [inf] squirrel away. **2** = **put**, place, lay, drop, let fall; [inf] dump, park.

depot NOUN **1** = **station**, garage, terminus, terminal. **2** = **store**, storehouse, warehouse, repository, depository, magazine, arsenal, cache.

deprave VERB = **corrupt**, debauch, lead astray, pervert, debase, degrade, defile, pollute, contaminate.

depraved ADJ = *see* **corrupt** ADJ (**2**).

depreciate VERB **1** = **decrease in value**, lose value, decline in price. **2** = *See* **disparage**.

depress VERB **1** = **sadden**, make gloomy/ despondent, dispirit, dishearten, discourage, weigh down, grieve, oppress, dampen someone's spirits, burden. **2** = **slow down/ up**, weaken, lower, reduce, impair, enfeeble, drain, sap, debilitate, devitalize.
Opposites: cheer.

depressed ADJ = *see* **sad** (**1**).

depression NOUN **1** = **sadness**, unhappiness, despair, gloom, dejection, downheartedness, despondency, melancholy, desolation, moodiness, moroseness, pessimism; [inf] the dumps, the blues. **2** = **hollow**, indentation, cavity, dip, valley, pit, hole, bowl, excavation, concavity. **3** = **recession**, slump, slowdown, stagnation, decline.
Opposites: happiness, boom.

deprive VERB = **dispossess**, take away

from, strip, deny, expropriate, divest, wrest, rob.

deprived ADJ = *see* **poor** (**1**).

deputize VERB = **take the place of**, stand in for, act for, do someone's job, substitute for, take over from, replace, cover for, understudy.

deputy NOUN = **substitute**, representative, stand-in, delegate, envoy, proxy, agent, ambassador, commissioner, legate.

derelict ADJ
1 = **abandoned**, deserted, neglected, rejected, discarded, forsaken, relinquished, cast off.
2 = **dilapidated**, ramshackle, tumbledown, run-down, broken-down, in disrepair, crumbling, rickety.
▶ NOUN = **vagrant**, beggar, down and out, tramp, outcast; [N. Amer.] hobo; [Brit. inf] dosser.

deride VERB = **mock**, ridicule, jeer at, scoff at, sneer at, make fun of, poke fun at, laugh at, scorn, lampoon, satirize, taunt, insult, rag, tease, chaff, disparage, slight, vilify; [inf] pooh-pooh.

derogatory ADJ
= **disparaging**, deprecatory, depreciatory, detracting, disapproving, unflattering, insulting, defamatory.
Opposites: complimentary.

descend VERB **1** = **go/come down**, climb down, fall, drop, sink, subside, plunge, plummet, tumble, slump. **2** = **get down**, get off, alight, disembark, dismount, detrain, deplane.
Opposites: ascend.

descent NOUN **1** = **slope**, incline, dip, drop, gradient, declivity, slant. **2** = **ancestry**, parentage, origins, lineage, extraction, heredity, genealogy, succession, stock, line, pedigree, blood, strain.
Opposites: ascent.

describe VERB **1** = **give details of**, detail, tell, narrate, put into words, express, recount, relate, report, set out, chronicle, illustrate, characterize, portray, depict. **2** = **draw**, mark out, delineate, outline, trace, sketch.

description NOUN
= **account**, statement, report, chronicle, narration, recounting, commentary, explanation, illustration, designation, characterization, portrayal, depiction, elucidation, relation.

descriptive ADJ
= **detailed**, graphic, vivid, striking, expressive, illustrative, depictive, pictorial.

desecrate VERB = **defile**, profane, blaspheme, pollute, treat sacrilegiously, contaminate, befoul, infect, debase, degrade, dishonour.
Opposites: honour.

desert[1] VERB **1** = **abandon**, forsake, give up, leave, turn one's back on, betray, jilt, strand, leave stranded, maroon, neglect, shun, relinquish;

[inf] walk out on, leave in the lurch, leave high and dry. **2** = **abscond**, defect, run away, flee, decamp, bolt, depart, quit; [inf] go AWOL, turn tail, take French leave.

desert[2] ADJ = **arid**, dry, parched, scorched, torrid.
▸ NOUN = **wasteland**, wilderness, barrenness, wilds.

deserted ADJ
= **abandoned**, empty, neglected, vacant, uninhabited, unoccupied, untenanted, desolate, lonely, solitary, godforsaken.
Opposites: crowded.

deserter NOUN
1 = **absconder**, runaway, defector, fugitive, truant, escapee. **2** = **renegade**, turncoat, traitor, betrayer, apostate; [inf] rat.

deserve VERB = **merit**, warrant, be worthy of, rate, justify, earn, be entitled to, have a right to, have a claim on.

deserving ADJ = *see* **worthy**.

design NOUN **1 = plan**, blueprint, drawing, sketch, outline, map, plot, diagram, draft, scheme, model. **2 = pattern**, style, arrangement, composition, configuration, shape. **3 = intention**, aim, purpose, plan, objective, goal, end, target, point, hope, desire, wish, aspiration. ▶ VERB **1 = plan**, draw, sketch, outline, map out, block out, delineate, draft, depict. **2 = create**, invent, think up, originate, conceive, fashion. **3 = intend**, aim, contrive, plan, tailor, mean, destine.

designer NOUN **= creator**, inventor, deviser, originator, architect, author.

desire VERB **1 = wish for**, want, long for, yearn for, thirst for, hunger after, crave, ache for, set one's heart on, hanker after, fancy, have a fancy for, covet, aspire to; [inf] have a yen for. **2 = lust after**, burn for; [inf] have the hots for. ▶ NOUN **1 = wish**, want, fancy, inclination, preference, longing, yearning, craving, eagerness, enthusiasm, hankering, predilection, aspiration. **2 = lust**, lustfulness, passion, lechery, sexual appetite, libido, sensuality, sexuality, lasciviousness, salaciousness, libidinousness; [inf] the hots.

desolate ADJ **1 = abandoned**, deserted, barren, uninhabited, unoccupied, lonely, isolated, bare, desert, bleak, depopulated, forsaken, unfrequented, remote, cheerless, dismal, godforsaken. **2 = sad**, unhappy, miserable, broken-hearted, wretched, downcast, dejected, downhearted, melancholy, gloomy, depressed, forlorn, disconsolate, despondent, distressed, grieving, bereft.

Opposites: populous, joyful.

despair NOUN
= **hopelessness**, depression, dejection, despondency, pessimism, melancholy, gloom, misery, wretchedness, distress, anguish.
▸ VERB = **lose hope**, give up hope, give up, lose heart, be discouraged, resign oneself.

desperate ADJ
1 = **reckless**, rash, foolhardy, risky, hazardous, daring, wild, imprudent, incautious, injudicious, ill-conceived, precipitate. 2 = **urgent**, pressing, acute, critical, crucial, drastic, serious, grave, dire, extreme, great. 3 = **bad**, appalling, grave, intolerable, deplorable, lamentable.

despise VERB = **disdain**, scorn, hate, detest, loathe, be contemptuous of, abhor, abominate, look down on, deride, spurn, shun, scoff at, jeer at, mock, revile, execrate, undervalue.
Opposites: admire.

despondent ADJ
= **downcast**, miserable, sad, sorrowful, disheartened, discouraged, disconsolate, low-spirited, dispirited, downhearted, in despair, despairing, melancholy, gloomy, glum, morose, woebegone.
Opposites: cheerful, happy.

despotic ADJ = **autocratic**, dictatorial, tyrannical, authoritarian, absolute, oppressive, totalitarian, domineering, imperious, arrogant, high-handed, arbitrary.

destination NOUN
= **journey's end**, stop, terminus, port of call, goal.

destined ADJ 1 = **bound for**, en route for, heading for/towards, directed towards, scheduled for. 2 = **fated**, ordained, preordained, predestined, predetermined, doomed, certain, sure, bound.

destiny NOUN 1 = **fate**, lot, portion, due, future, doom. 2 = **chance**, fortune, predestination, luck, fate, karma, kismet.

destitute ADJ = **penniless**, impoverished, poverty-stricken, poor, impecunious, penurious, indigent, insolvent, deprived, down-and-out, beggarly; [inf] on one's uppers; [Brit. inf] skint. **Opposites:** rich, wealthy.

destroy VERB **1** = **demolish**, wreck, smash, annihilate, knock down, pull down, tear down, level, raze, shatter, dismantle, blow up, wipe out, bomb, torpedo, ruin, spoil, devastate, lay waste to, ravage, wreak havoc on, extinguish, vaporize, extirpate. **2** = **kill**, slaughter, put to sleep, exterminate, wipe out, massacre, liquidate, decimate. **Opposites:** build, construct.

destruction NOUN **1** = **demolition**, annihilation, devastation, levelling, razing, blowing up, wiping out, tearing down, ruination,

desolation, ruin, havoc, termination, extinction. **2** = **killing**, slaughter, massacre; [poetic/ literary] slaying.

destructive ADJ **1** = **ruinous**, devastating, disastrous, catastrophic, calamitous, cataclysmic, fatal, deadly, dangerous, lethal, damaging, noxious, pernicious, injurious, harmful, detrimental, deleterious. **2** = **negative**, adverse, unfavourable, contrary, antagonistic, hostile, unfriendly, derogatory, disparaging, disapproving, undermining. **Opposites:** constructive.

desultory ADJ = **half-hearted**, rambling, aimless, irregular, fitful, haphazard, erratic, inconsistent. **Opposites:** keen.

detach VERB = **disconnect**, unfasten, remove, undo, take off, release, unhitch, separate, uncouple, loosen, free, sever, tear off, disengage, part. **Opposites:** attach.

detached ADJ
= **dispassionate**,
impersonal, indifferent,
aloof, unconcerned,
reserved, remote, cool.
Opposites: passionate,
involved.

detail NOUN **1** = **item**, point,
particular, factor, nicety,
fact, element, aspect,
circumstance, intricacy,
feature, respect, attribute,
component, part, unit.
2 = **unit**, detachment, task
force, patrol.

detailed ADJ = **full**,
comprehensive,
exhaustive, thorough,
all-inclusive, itemized,
precise, exact, specific,
meticulous,
particularized.
Opposites: general.

detain VERB **1** = **delay**, hold
up/back, keep, slow
down/up, hinder,
impede, check, retard,
inhibit, stay. **2** = **put/keep
in custody**, imprison,
confine, lock up, jail,
incarcerate, intern,
restrain, hold, arrest,
impound; [inf] collar; [Brit.
inf] nick.

detect VERB **1** = **find out**,
discover, turn up,
uncover, bring to light,
expose, unearth, reveal,
unmask, unveil; [inf] track
down, ferret out.
2 = **notice**, note, perceive,
discern, make out,
observe, spot, become
aware of, recognize,
distinguish, identify,
catch, sense, see, smell.

detective NOUN
= **investigator**, police
officer; [inf] private eye,
sleuth, tec, dick; [N. Amer.
inf] gumshoe.

detention NOUN
= **custody**, confinement,
imprisonment,
incarceration,
internment, detainment,
arrest, quarantine.

deter VERB = **prevent**, put
off, stop, discourage, talk
out of, dissuade, check,
restrain, caution,
frighten, intimidate,
daunt, scare off, warn
against, prohibit, hinder,
impede, obstruct.
Opposites: encourage.

deteriorate VERB **1** = **get
worse**, worsen, decline,
degenerate, go downhill,

sink, slip, lapse, fall, drop; [inf] go to the dogs, go to pot.
2 = **disintegrate**, crumble, fall apart, fall to pieces, break up, decay, decompose.
Opposites: improve.

determination NOUN
= **firmness**, persistence, resoluteness, tenacity, perseverance, steadfastness, single-mindedness, resolve, drive, fortitude, dedication, backbone, stamina, mettle, conviction, doggedness, stubbornness, intransigence, obduracy, push, thrust, pertinacity; [inf] grit, guts.

determine VERB
1 = **decide**, agree on, fix, settle, establish, judge, arbitrate, decree, ordain.
2 = **find out**, discover, learn, establish, calculate, work out, check, ascertain, verify.
3 = **affect**, influence, act/ work on, regulate, decide, condition, direct, control, rule, dictate, govern, form, shape.

determined ADJ = **firm**, resolute, purposeful, single-minded, steadfast, tenacious, strong-willed, dedicated, persistent, persevering, dogged, unflinching, tough, assertive, mettlesome, plucky, unwavering, stubborn, obdurate, intransigent, indomitable, inflexible.
Opposites: irresolute, hesitant.

deterrent NOUN
= **disincentive**, inhibition, restraint, discouragement, curb, check, impediment, hindrance, obstacle, block, obstruction, barrier, warning, threat.
Opposites: incentive.

detest VERB = **loathe**, hate, abhor, despise, abominate, execrate.
= *See also* **hate** VERB (**1**).
Opposites: love.

detestable ADJ
= **loathsome**, abhorrent, hateful, odious, despicable, contemptible, disgusting, repugnant, distasteful, abominable.

detract VERB = **take away from**, diminish, reduce, lessen, lower, devalue.

detrimental ADJ = **harmful**, damaging, injurious, hurtful, destructive, pernicious, deleterious, inimical, prejudicial, unfavourable. **Opposites:** benign.

devastate VERB
1 = **destroy**, ruin, lay waste to, demolish, wreck, flatten, obliterate, level, raze, annihilate, ravage, despoil, sack.
2 = See **dismay** VERB (**1**).

develop VERB 1 = **grow**, evolve, mature, improve, expand, spread, enlarge, advance, progress, flourish, prosper, make headway. 2 = **elaborate**, unfold, work out, enlarge on, expand, broaden, add to, augment, amplify, dilate on, magnify, supplement, reinforce. 3 = **acquire**, begin to have, contract, pick up, get. 4 = **begin**, start, come about, follow, happen, result, ensue, break out.

development NOUN
1 = **growth**, evolution, advance, improvement, expansion, spread, progress, maturing, furtherance, extension, headway. 2 = **event**, turn of events, occurrence, happening, incident, circumstance, situation, issue, outcome, upshot.
3 = **estate**, complex, building, structure, conglomeration.

deviate VERB = **diverge**, branch off, turn aside, depart from, make a detour, digress, deflect, differ, vary, change, veer, swerve, wander, bend, drift, stray, tack, slew.

device NOUN 1 = **appliance**, gadget, implement, tool, utensil, piece of equipment, apparatus, instrument, machine, contraption, contrivance, invention; [inf] gizmo.
2 = **scheme**, ploy, plan, plot, stratagem, trick, deception, artifice, ruse, dodge, stunt, gambit, subterfuge, manoeuvre, expedient, fraud, imposture. 3 = **emblem**,

symbol, insignia, crest, coat of arms, seal, badge, token, motif, design, figure, motto, slogan, legend.

devilish ADJ = **demonic**, diabolical, fiendish, satanic, infernal, hellish, demoniacal.

devious ADJ 1 = **cunning**, underhand, sly, crafty, wily, artful, scheming, designing, calculating, deceitful, dishonest, double-dealing, guileful, treacherous, furtive, secretive; [inf] slippery, crooked. 2 = **indirect**, roundabout, circuitous, rambling, winding, tortuous, wandering, erratic, digressive.
Opposites: honest, direct.

devise VERB = **create**, invent, originate, concoct, work out, contrive, plan, form, formulate, plot, scheme, compose, frame, construct, think up, imagine, fabricate, hatch, put together, prepare.

devoted ADJ = **committed**, faithful, loyal, true, dedicated, staunch, devout, steadfast, constant, unswerving, zealous.

devotee NOUN = **fan**, enthusiast, admirer, follower, adherent, disciple, supporter, champion, advocate, fanatic, zealot; [inf] buff, freak.

devotion NOUN = **faithfulness**, loyalty, steadfastness, commitment, staunchness, allegiance, dedication, devoutness, fervour, zeal.
Opposites: disloyalty, indifference.

devour VERB = **eat greedily**, consume, swallow, gorge oneself on, guzzle down, feast on; [inf] tuck into, pig out on.

devout ADJ = **pious**, religious, godly, churchgoing, reverent, holy, righteous, orthodox, saintly.
Opposites: impious.

dexterity NOUN = **deftness**, adroitness, nimbleness, agility, skilfulness, adeptness, expertise, talent, craft, mastery, finesse.

diabolical ADJ
1 = **devilish**, demonic, fiendish, satanic, infernal, hellish, demoniacal. **2** = **very bad**, horrible, dreadful, appalling, shocking, outrageous, atrocious.

diagnose VERB = **identify**, detect, find, determine, recognize, distinguish, isolate, pinpoint.

diagonal ADJ
= **crossways**, crosswise, slanting, slanted, sloping, oblique, angled, cornerways, cornerwise.

diagram NOUN = **plan**, picture, representation, blueprint, sketch, illustration, outline, draft, table, chart, figure.

dialect NOUN = **regional language**, vernacular, patois, regionalism, localism, provincialism; [inf] lingo.

dialogue NOUN
= **conversation**, talk, chat, communication, debate, argument, exchange of views, discussion, conference,

discourse, parley, colloquy, interlocution, palaver; [inf] powwow, chinwag, rap session.

diary NOUN = **journal**, chronicle, account, record, log, history, annals, calendar.

dictate VERB **1** = **read aloud**, read out, speak, say, utter, recite.
2 = **order**, command, decree, ordain, direct, enjoin, give orders, order about, impose one's will, domineer, lay down the law; [inf] boss about, throw one's weight about.

dictator NOUN = **absolute ruler**, despot, autocrat, tyrant, oppressor.

dictatorial ADJ
= **tyrannical**, oppressive, despotic, overbearing, domineering, repressive, imperious, high-handed, authoritarian, totalitarian, peremptory, dogmatic, arbitrary, fascistic; [inf] bossy.

diction NOUN
= **enunciation**, articulation, elocution, pronunciation,

intonation, inflection, delivery.

dictum NOUN = **utterance**, pronouncement, direction, injunction, statement, dictate, command, order, decree, edict.

die VERB **1** = **expire**, perish, pass on/away, lose one's life, meet one's end, lay down one's life, breathe one's last, be no more, go to one's last resting place; [inf] give up the ghost, kick the bucket, bite the dust, be pushing up daisies, croak, turn up one's toes, cash in one's chips, pop off; [Brit. inf] snuff it, pop one's clogs. **2** = **come to an end**, end, pass, disappear, vanish, fade, decline, ebb, dwindle, melt away, wane, wither, subside. **3** = **fail**, break down, halt, stop, lose power. **Opposites:** live.

diehard ADJ = **intransigent**, inflexible, uncompromising, indomitable, unyielding, rigid, immovable, adamant, dyed-in-the-wool, conservative, reactionary.

differ VERB **1** = **be different**, vary, contrast, diverge, be dissimilar, be distinguishable. **2** = **disagree**, be in dispute, dissent, be at variance, oppose, take issue, contradict, dispute, conflict, clash, quarrel, argue, wrangle, squabble, quibble, altercate. **Opposites:** agree.

difference NOUN **1** = **dissimilarity**, contrast, distinction, variance, variation, divergence, deviation, contradiction, disparity, imbalance, incongruity, dissimilitude, differentiation, antithesis, nonconformity, contrariety. **2** = **difference of opinion**, dispute, disagreement, argument, debate, misunderstanding, quarrel, altercation, wrangle, clash, contretemps, feud, vendetta; [inf] row, tiff, set-to. **3** = **balance**,

remainder, rest, residue, excess.
Opposites: similarity.

different ADJ
1 = dissimilar, contrasting, diverse, disparate, divergent, incompatible, opposed, inconsistent, at variance, at odds, clashing, conflicting, discrepant, unlike. **2 = changed**, altered, modified, transformed, metamorphosed.
3 = various, several, many, numerous, sundry, assorted, diverse.
4 = unusual, uncommon, out of the ordinary, distinctive, rare, unique, novel, special, remarkable, singular, noteworthy, unconventional, atypical, strange, odd, bizarre.
Opposites: similar, ordinary.

difficult ADJ **1 = hard**, demanding, laborious, onerous, burdensome, tough, strenuous, arduous, exhausting, exacting, tiring, wearisome, back-breaking, painful, oppressive; [inf] no picnic.
2 = complex, complicated, hard, problematic, intricate, involved, puzzling, baffling, perplexing, knotty, thorny, delicate, obscure, abstruse, enigmatic, abstract, recondite, profound, deep.
3 = troublesome, demanding, tiresome, unmanageable, intractable, perverse, recalcitrant, obstreperous, refractory, fractious, uncooperative, unamenable.
4 = inconvenient, ill-timed, unfavourable.
Opposites: easy, simple.

difficulty NOUN
1 = problem, complication, snag, hitch, obstacle, hindrance, hurdle, pitfall, impediment, obstruction, barrier.
2 = protest, objection, complaint, gripe, demur, cavil. **3 = predicament**, quandary, dilemma, plight, distress, embarrassment, trouble,

straits; [inf] fix, jam, spot, scrape. **4 = hardship**, trial, tribulation, ordeal, exigency.

diffident ADJ **= shy**, modest, bashful, sheepish, unconfident, timid, unassertive, fearful, timorous, shrinking, apprehensive, reserved, withdrawn, hesitant, tentative, reluctant, doubtful, unsure, insecure, unobtrusive, self-effacing, unassuming, humble, meek, distrustful, suspicious.
Opposites: bold, assertive.

diffuse ADJ **1 = spread out**, scattered, dispersed, diffused. **2 = wordy**, verbose, long-winded, prolix, discursive, rambling, wandering, meandering, digressive, circumlocutory; [inf] waffly.
Opposites: concentrated, concise.

dig VERB **1 = cultivate**, turn over, work, spade, till, harrow, fork over.
2 = excavate, dig out, burrow, mine, quarry, hollow out, scoop out, tunnel, gouge. **3 = poke**, nudge, prod, jab, thrust, punch.
■ **dig up = exhume**, unearth, disinter.

digest VERB **1 = absorb**, assimilate, break down, dissolve, process, macerate. **2 = understand**, take in, absorb, comprehend, grasp, master, consider, think about, mull over, weigh up.
▶ NOUN **= summary**, abstract, precis, outline, review, compendium, abridgement, epitome.

dignified ADJ **= formal**, grave, solemn, stately, noble, decorous, reserved, ceremonious, courtly, majestic, august, lofty, exalted, regal, lordly, imposing, grand, impressive.
Opposites: undignified.

dignitary NOUN **= luminary**, worthy, notable, VIP, big name, leading light, celebrity, star, lion, pillar of society; [inf] somebody, bigwig, big shot, big noise, celeb, top brass, lord/lady muck; [N. Amer. inf] big wheel.

dignity NOUN = **stateliness**, nobleness, nobility, formality, solemnity, gravity, gravitas, decorum, propriety, respectability, reserve, courtliness, ceremoniousness, majesty, augustness, loftiness, exaltedness, regality, grandeur, lordliness, impressiveness.

digress VERB = **stray from the point**, get off the subject, go off at a tangent, ramble, wander, deviate, turn aside, depart, drift, meander, maunder; [inf] lose the thread.

dilapidated ADJ = **run-down**, ramshackle, broken-down, in ruins, ruined, tumbledown, falling to pieces, falling apart, in disrepair, shabby, battered, rickety, shaky, crumbling, decayed, decrepit, worn out, neglected, uncared for.

dilate VERB = **enlarge**, widen, expand.
Opposites: contract.

dilemma NOUN = **difficulty**, problem, quandary, predicament, puzzle, plight, trouble, perplexity, confusion, embarrassment; [inf] catch-22, tight spot.

■ **in a dilemma** on the horns of a dilemma, between the devil and the deep blue sea, between a rock and a hard place, in a cleft stick.

diligent ADJ = **assiduous**, industrious, conscientious, hard-working, painstaking, meticulous, thorough, careful, attentive, heedful, earnest, studious, persevering, persistent, tenacious, zealous, active, busy, untiring, tireless, indefatigable, dogged, plodding, laborious.
Opposites: lazy.

dilute VERB = **water down**, weaken, thin out, cut, adulterate, mix.
Opposites: concentrate.

dim ADJ **1** = **dull**, muted, faint, weak, feeble, pale, dingy, lustreless. **2** = **dark**, gloomy, badly lit, poorly lit, dingy, dismal. **3** = **vague**, ill-defined, indistinct, unclear, shadowy, blurred, blurry, fuzzy, imperceptible, obscured, nebulous, bleary, obfuscated. **4** = *See* **stupid** (1).
Opposites: bright, clear.
▸ VERB **1** = **dip**, turn down, lower. **2** = **grow darker**, darken, cloud over.
Opposites: brighten.

dimension NOUN **1** = **size**, extent, length, width, area, volume, capacity, proportions. **2** = **aspect**, facet, side, feature, element.

diminish VERB **1** = **lessen**, grow less, decrease, reduce, shrink, contract, abate, grow weaker, lower, curtail, cut, narrow, constrict, truncate. **2** = **subside**, wane, recede, dwindle, slacken, fade, decline, peter out. **3** = **disparage**, denigrate, belittle, deprecate, devalue, detract from, cheapen, defame, vilify.
Opposites: increase, boost.

diminutive ADJ = **small**, tiny, little, petite, minute, miniature, microscopic, undersized, dwarfish.
Opposites: enormous.

din NOUN = **noise**, uproar, row, racket, commotion, hullabaloo, tumult, hubbub, clamour, outcry, shouting, yelling, pandemonium, bedlam, rumpus, brouhaha, babel.

dingy ADJ = **dark**, dull, dim, gloomy, drab, dismal, dreary, cheerless, dusky, sombre, murky, smoggy, dirty, sooty, grimy, discoloured, faded, shabby, worn, seedy, run-down, tacky.
Opposites: bright.

dip VERB **1** = **go down**, descend, sink, subside, fall, drop, decline, sag, droop. **2** = **immerse**, plunge, submerge, duck, dunk, lower, sink, soak, drench, steep, bathe.
Opposites: rise.
▸ NOUN **1** = **swim**, bathe, plunge, dive, paddle.

2 = **hollow**, hole, basin, concavity, depression, declivity, slope, incline, slant.

diplomacy NOUN
= **tactfulness**, tact, discretion, subtlety, sensitivity, delicacy, politeness, finesse, prudence, judiciousness, cleverness, artfulness, cunning, care, skill.

diplomatic ADJ = **tactful**, subtle, discreet, careful, delicate, sensitive, thoughtful, considerate, prudent, judicious, polite, politic, clever, skilful, artful.
Opposites: tactless.

dire ADJ = **terrible**, dreadful, awful, appalling, frightful, horrible, atrocious, grim, cruel, disastrous, ruinous, wretched, miserable, woeful, calamitous, catastrophic.

direct ADJ 1 = **straight**, uncircuitous, unswerving, undeviating.
2 = **non-stop**, straight through, through, uninterrupted, unbroken.
3 = **frank**, blunt, straightforward, straight to the point, straight, clear, plain, explicit, candid, open, honest, sincere, unambiguous, unequivocal, outspoken, plain-spoken, forthright, matter-of-fact.
Opposites: indirect.
▶ VERB 1 = **show the way**, give directions, guide, steer, lead, conduct, usher, navigate, pilot.
2 = **be in charge of**, lead, run, command, control, supervise, oversee, superintend, regulate, govern, conduct, handle, preside over, mastermind, orchestrate; [inf] call the shots. 3 = **aim at**, address to, intend/ mean for, destine for, point at, train on, fix on.
4 = **command**, order, instruct, charge, bid, enjoin; [formal] adjure.

directive NOUN
= **command**, direction, order, instruction, charge, bidding, injunction, ruling, regulation, dictate, decree, edict, notice, ordinance, prescription,

mandate, fiat.

director NOUN = **manager**, administrator, executive, head, chief, chairperson, leader, governor, president, superintendent, supervisor, overseer; [inf] boss; [Brit. inf] gaffer.

dirge NOUN = **lament**, elegy, requiem, keen, funeral song, threnody.

dirt NOUN 1 = **grime**, dust, soot, muck, mud, filth, sludge, slime, ooze, waste, dross, pollution, smudge, stain, tarnish; [inf] crud; [Brit. inf] gunge. 2 = **earth**, soil, clay, silt, loam. 3 = See **obscenity** (1).

dirty ADJ 1 = **unclean**, filthy, stained, grimy, soiled, grubby, messy, dusty, mucky, sooty, muddy, bedraggled, slimy, polluted, sullied, foul, smudged, tarnished, defiled, spotted; [inf] cruddy, yucky; [Brit. inf] grotty, gungy. 2 = **obscene**, indecent, vulgar, ribald, salacious, smutty, coarse, bawdy, suggestive, prurient, lewd, lascivious, licentious. 3 = **unfair**, unsporting, dishonourable, dishonest, unscrupulous, illegal, deceitful, double-dealing, treacherous; [inf] crooked. 4 = **malevolent**, bitter, angry, annoyed, resentful, indignant, offended, smouldering. **Opposites:** clean. ▶ VERB = **soil**, stain, muddy, begrime, blacken, mess up, spatter, smudge, smear, spot, splash, sully, pollute, foul, defile; [poetic/literary] besmirch. **Opposites:** clean.

disability NOUN = **handicap**, infirmity, impairment, affliction, disorder, complaint, ailment, illness, malady, disablement.

disable VERB = **incapacitate**, impair, damage, injure, cripple, lame, handicap, debilitate, indispose, weaken, enfeeble, render infirm, immobilize, paralyse, hamstring, maim, prostrate, mutilate.

disadvantage NOUN
1 = **drawback**, snag, weak point, downside, fly in the ointment, weakness, flaw, defect, fault, handicap, liability, trouble, hindrance, obstacle; [inf] minus.
2 = **detriment**, prejudice, harm, damage, loss, injury, hurt.
Opposites: advantage.

disaffected ADJ
= **alienated**, estranged, unfriendly, disunited, dissatisfied, disgruntled, discontented, disloyal, rebellious, mutinous, seditious, hostile, antagonistic; [inf] up in arms.
Opposites: contented.

disagree VERB 1 = **differ**, fail to agree, be in dispute, dissent, be at variance/odds, quarrel, argue, bicker, wrangle, squabble, dispute, debate, take issue; [inf] have words, fall out.
2 = **be different**, be dissimilar, vary, conflict, clash, contrast, diverge.
Opposites: agree.

disagreeable ADJ
= **unpleasant**, objectionable, disgusting, horrible, nasty, dreadful, hateful, detestable, offensive, repulsive, obnoxious, odious, repellent, revolting, sickening.
Opposites: pleasant.

disallow VERB = **reject**, say no to, refuse, dismiss, forbid, prohibit, veto, embargo, proscribe, rebuff, repel, repudiate, repulse, ban, bar, cancel, disclaim, disown, abjure, disavow.

disappear VERB 1 = **vanish**, pass from sight, be lost to view, fade, recede, dematerialize, evaporate.
2 = *See* **leave**[1] VERB (**1**).
3 = **die out**, come to an end, end, pass away, vanish, expire, perish, fade away, leave no trace, pass into oblivion.
Opposites: appear.

disappoint VERB = **let down**, fail, dishearten, depress, dispirit, upset, sadden, dash someone's hopes, dismay, chagrin, disgruntle, disenchant,

disillusion, dissatisfy, vex.
Opposites: delight.

disappointed ADJ
= **saddened**, let down, disheartened, downhearted, downcast, depressed, despondent, dispirited, disenchanted, disillusioned.
Opposites: pleased.

disapproval NOUN
= **disapprobation**, displeasure, criticism, blame, censure, condemnation, dislike, disfavour, discontent, dissatisfaction, reproach, reproof, remonstration, deprecation, animadversion.
Opposites: approval.

disapprove VERB = **find unacceptable**, dislike, deplore, have a poor opinion of, be displeased with, frown on, criticize, look askance at, censure, condemn, denounce, object to, take exception to, reprove, remonstrate, disparage, deprecate;
[inf] take a dim view of, look down one's nose at.
Opposites: approve.

disarray NOUN = **disorder**, confusion, untidiness, chaos, mess, muddle, clutter, jumble, mix-up, tangle, shambles, dishevelment;
[Scottish] guddle.
Opposites: tidiness.

disaster NOUN
= **catastrophe**, calamity, cataclysm, tragedy, act of God, accident, mishap, misadventure, mischance, stroke of bad luck, heavy blow, shock, adversity, trouble, misfortune, ruin, ruination.
Opposites: success.

disastrous ADJ
= **catastrophic**, cataclysmic, calamitous, devastating, tragic, dire, terrible, shocking, appalling, dreadful, harmful, black, ruinous, unfortunate, unlucky, ill-fated, ill-starred, injurious, detrimental, hapless.
Opposites: successful.

disbelieve VERB = **reject**, discount, give no credence to, be incredulous, question,

suspect, challenge, scoff at, mistrust, distrust.
Opposites: believe.

discard VERB = **throw out/ away**, dispose of, get rid of, jettison, toss out, dispense with, scrap, cast aside, reject, repudiate, abandon, relinquish, forsake, shed; [inf] have done with, dump, ditch.
Opposites: keep.

discern VERB = **see**, notice, observe, perceive, make out, distinguish, detect, recognize, determine.

discernible ADJ = **visible**, noticeable, observable, perceptible, perceivable, detectable, recognizable, apparent, obvious, clear, manifest, conspicuous, patent.

discerning ADJ = **discriminating**, astute, shrewd, ingenious, clever, perceptive, penetrating, perspicacious, percipient, judicious, sensitive, knowing.

discharge VERB **1** = **emit**, exude, release, give off, eject, send out, leak, dispense, void, gush, excrete, ooze, belch, secrete, spew, spit out. **2** = **dismiss**, expel, get rid of, oust, cashier; [inf] fire, sack, axe, send packing, give someone the boot, boot out. **3** = **fire**, shoot, let off, set off, detonate. **4** = **set free**, free, release, liberate, acquit, clear, absolve, exonerate, pardon, emancipate, exculpate. **5** = **carry out**, perform, do, accomplish, achieve, fulfil, execute.

disciple NOUN = **apostle**, follower, supporter, adherent, devotee, advocate, student, pupil, believer, proponent, partisan, votary.

disciplinarian NOUN = **martinet**, authoritarian, hard taskmaster, tyrant, despot, stickler for order, autocrat, dictator, hardliner; [inf] slave-driver.

discipline NOUN **1** = **control**, self-control, self-restraint, strictness, restraint, orderliness, regulation, direction, restriction, limitation,

check, curb.
2 = **punishment**, correction, chastisement, penalty, reprimand, rebuke, reproof. **3** = **field of study**, subject, area, course, speciality, specialty.
▶ VERB **1** = **control**, restrain, regulate, restrict, govern, limit, check, curb.
2 = **punish**, chastise, correct, penalize, reprimand, rebuke, reprove; [formal] castigate.

disclaim VERB = **deny**, renounce, repudiate, reject, refuse, decline, disown, abandon, abjure; [inf] wash one's hands of.

disclose VERB = **reveal**, divulge, tell, impart, communicate, broadcast, unveil, leak, let slip, blurt out.

discolour VERB = **stain**, soil, mark, streak, spot, tarnish, tinge, fade, bleach.

discomfort NOUN **1** = **pain**, ache, soreness, irritation, pang, throb, smart.
2 = **hardship**, unpleasantness, trouble, distress.

disconcert VERB
= **unsettle**, shake, disturb, take aback, perturb, ruffle, upset, agitate, worry, discomfit, discompose, confound, throw off balance, distract, confuse, nonplus; [inf] throw, put someone off their stroke, faze, rattle.

disconnect VERB = **undo**, detach, disengage, uncouple, unfasten, unhook, unhitch, unplug, cut off, break off, sever, part, turn off, switch off.
Opposites: connect.

disconnected ADJ
= **disjointed**, confused, garbled, jumbled, mixed up, incoherent, unintelligible, rambling, disordered, wandering.

discontented ADJ
= **dissatisfied**, displeased, disgruntled, unhappy, miserable, disaffected; [inf] fed up, browned off, hacked off; [Brit. inf] cheesed off.

discord NOUN
1 = **disagreement**, dispute, argument,

conflict, friction, strife, opposition, hostility, disharmony, incompatibility, disunity. = *See also* **quarrel** NOUN.
2 = **disharmony**, dissonance, cacophony.
Opposites: harmony.

discordant ADJ

1 = **conflicting**, differing, contrary, opposed, opposing, opposite, contradictory, contentious, hostile, divergent, incompatible, incongruous.
2 = **dissonant**, atonal, tuneless, cacophonous, inharmonious, jangling, grating, jarring, harsh, strident, shrill.
Opposites: harmonious.

discount NOUN

= **reduction**, price cut, rebate, concession;
[inf] mark-down.
▶VERB = **disregard**, ignore, dismiss, overlook, pass over, pay no attention to, take no notice of, gloss over, brush off.

discourage VERB

1 = **dishearten**, dispirit, depress, demoralize, deject, disappoint, disenchant, dismay, cast down, frighten, put off, scare, daunt, intimidate, cow, unnerve, unman;
[inf] pour cold water on.
2 = **dissuade**, put off, deter, talk out of, advise against, urge against, caution against, restrain, inhibit, divert from.
3 = **oppose**, disapprove of, repress, deprecate;
[inf] put a damper on.
Opposites: encourage.

discouragement NOUN

1 = **opposition**, disapproval, repression, deprecation.
2 = **deterrent**, disincentive, impediment, hindrance, obstacle, barrier, curb, damper, check, restraint, constraint.
Opposites: encouragement.

discourse NOUN

1 = **address**, speech, lecture, oration, sermon, homily, essay, treatise, dissertation, paper, study, disquisition. **2** = *See* **conversation**.
▶VERB = *see* **speak** (**1**), **talk** VERB (**1**).

discover VERB 1 = **find**, come across/upon, locate, stumble upon, chance upon, light upon, bring to light, unearth, uncover, turn up; [inf] dig up. 2 = **find out**, come to know, learn, realize, detect, ascertain, determine, recognize, see, spot, notice, perceive; [inf] get wise to; [Brit. inf] twig. 3 = **invent**, devise, originate, pioneer, conceive of, contrive.

discoverer NOUN 1 = **inventor**, originator, pioneer, deviser, designer, initiator. 2 = **founder**, explorer, pioneer.

discovery NOUN 1 = **detection**, recognition, disclosure, finding, determination, revelation. 2 = **innovation**, invention, breakthrough, finding, find.

discredit VERB 1 = **attack**, denigrate, disparage, defame, slur, slander, libel, detract from, cast aspersions on, vilify, bring into disrepute, deprecate, decry, dishonour, devalue, degrade, belittle, disgrace, censure. 2 = **disprove**, invalidate, refute, dispute, challenge, reject, deny.

discreet ADJ = **careful**, circumspect, cautious, wary, guarded, sensitive, prudent, judicious, chary, tactful, reserved, diplomatic, muted, understated, delicate, considerate, politic, wise, sensible, sagacious. **Opposites:** indiscreet, tactless.

discrepancy NOUN = **inconsistency**, disparity, deviation, variance, variation, divergence, incongruity, difference, disagreement, dissimilarity, conflict, discordance, gap, lacuna. **Opposites:** similarity.

discretionary ADJ = **optional**, voluntary, open, open to choice, elective, non-mandatory, unrestricted, volitional. **Opposites:** compulsory.

discriminate VERB 1 = **distinguish**,

differentiate, tell the difference, tell apart, separate, discern. **2 = be biased against**, show prejudice against/towards, treat differently, favour.

discriminating ADJ = *see* **perceptive**.

discrimination NOUN
1 = discernment, good taste, taste, perception, penetration, perspicacity, shrewdness, astuteness, acumen, judgement, refinement, sensitivity, insight, subtlety, cultivation, artistry.
2 = prejudice, bias, intolerance, bigotry, narrow-mindedness, favouritism, chauvinism, racism, sexism, unfairness.

discuss VERB = **talk over**, talk/chat about, debate, argue about/over, exchange views about, converse about, deliberate, consider, go into, examine, review, analyse, weigh up, consult about, ventilate; [inf] kick about, thrash out.

discussion NOUN
= **conversation**, talk, dialogue, chat, argument, dispute, conference, debate, discourse, exchange of views, seminar, consultation, symposium, deliberation, review, analysis; [inf] confab. = *See also* **talk** NOUN (**1**).

disdainful ADJ = **scornful**, contemptuous, derisive, sneering, disparaging, arrogant, proud, supercilious, haughty, superior, lordly, pompous, snobbish, aloof, indifferent.
Opposites: respectful.

disease NOUN = *see* **illness**.

diseased ADJ = **unhealthy**, unwell, sick, sickly, infected, abnormal, blighted, unsound, cankerous. = *See also* **ill** ADJ (**1**).

disembark VERB = **land**, arrive, get off, step off, alight, go ashore, deplane, detrain.
Opposites: embark.

disfigure VERB = **mutilate**, deface, deform, blemish,

scar, spoil, mar, damage, injure, maim, vandalize, ruin, make ugly, uglify.

disgrace NOUN **1 = shame**, humiliation, dishonour, scandal, ignominy, degradation, discredit, infamy, debasement.
2 = scandal, black mark, stain, blemish, stigma, blot, smear.
Opposites: honour.

disgraceful ADJ
= scandalous, outrageous, shocking, shameful, dishonourable, disreputable, contemptible, despicable, ignominious, reprehensible, improper, unseemly.
Opposites: admirable.

disgruntled ADJ
= dissatisfied, displeased, unhappy, discontented, annoyed, exasperated, irritated, vexed, grumpy, testy, petulant; [inf] fed up; [Brit. inf] cheesed off.

disguise NOUN
= camouflage, costume, pretence, mask, cover, cloak; [inf] get-up, smokescreen.

▸ VERB **1 = dress up**, camouflage, cover up, conceal, hide, mask, veil, cloak, shroud. **2 = cover up**, falsify, misrepresent, fake, feign, dissemble, dissimulate, varnish.

disgust NOUN **= revulsion**, repugnance, repulsion, aversion, abhorrence, loathing, detestation, distaste, nausea.
▸ VERB **= sicken**, nauseate, revolt, repel, put off, offend, outrage, shock, appal, scandalize, displease, dissatisfy, annoy, anger; [inf] turn someone's stomach.

dish NOUN **1 = plate**, platter, bowl, basin, container, receptacle, salver.
2 = food, recipe, fare, concoction, item on the menu.
▪ **dish up = serve**, serve up, spoon, ladle, scoop.

dishearten VERB
= discourage, dispirit, depress, crush, sadden, disappoint, deter, weigh down; [inf] put a damper on.
Opposites: encourage.

dishevelled ADJ = **untidy**, rumpled, messy, scruffy, bedraggled, disordered, disarranged, tousled, unkempt, slovenly, uncombed, slatternly, blowsy, frowzy. **Opposites:** tidy, neat.

dishonest ADJ = **untruthful**, deceitful, lying, underhand, cheating, fraudulent, false, misleading, dishonourable, unscrupulous, unprincipled, corrupt, deceptive, crafty, cunning, designing, mendacious, double-dealing, two-faced, treacherous, perfidious, unfair, unjust, unethical, disreputable, rascally, knavish, roguish; [inf] crooked, shady, bent, slippery. **Opposites:** honest.

dishonour NOUN = **disgrace**, shame, humiliation, discredit, blot, blemish, stigma, scandal, infamy, ignominy, disrepute, disfavour, abasement, odium, opprobrium, obloquy.

▶ VERB = **disgrace**, bring shame to, shame, discredit, degrade, humiliate, sully, stain, stigmatize, insult, abuse, affront, slight, offend.

dishonourable ADJ
1 = **unprincipled**, unscrupulous, untrustworthy, corrupt, treacherous, perfidious, traitorous, disreputable, discreditable; [inf] shady; [archaic] blackguardly.
2 = **disgraceful**, shameful, ignoble, shameless, ignominious, contemptible, blameworthy, despicable, reprehensible, base. **Opposites:** honourable.

disillusion VERB = **disabuse**, disenchant, shatter someone's illusions, open someone's eyes, set straight, enlighten, disappoint; [inf] make sadder and wiser.

disinclined ADJ = **reluctant**, unenthusiastic, unwilling, hesitant, loath, averse, resistant, antipathetic, opposed, recalcitrant, not in the mood.

disinfect VERB = **sterilize**, sanitize, clean, cleanse, purify, fumigate, decontaminate.

disingenuous ADJ = **insincere**, deceitful, feigned, underhand, duplicitous, two-faced, false, untruthful, artful, cunning, wily, scheming, calculating.

disintegrate VERB = **fall apart**, fall to pieces, break up, break apart, shatter, crumble, come apart, crack up, smash, splinter, decompose, decay, rot, dissolve, degenerate, erode, moulder.

disinterested ADJ = **unbiased**, unprejudiced, impartial, detached, objective, dispassionate, impersonal, open-minded, neutral, fair, just, even-handed.
Opposites: biased, partial.

disjointed ADJ = **incoherent**, rambling, unconnected, disconnected, wandering, disorganized, confused, muddled, jumbled, disordered, aimless, directionless, uncoordinated, fitful, spasmodic, dislocated, discontinuous.
Opposites: coherent.

dislike VERB = **have no liking for**, have an aversion to, regard with distaste, feel hostility towards, be unable to stomach, have no taste for, object to, hate, detest, loathe, abominate, abhor, despise, scorn, execrate, shun, have a grudge against.
Opposites: like.
▸ NOUN = **aversion**, distaste, disapproval, animosity, hostility, antipathy, hate, antagonism, detestation, loathing, disgust, repugnance, enmity, abhorrence, animus.

dislocate VERB = **displace**, put out, disjoint, disengage, disconnect, put out of joint; [Medicine] luxate.

disloyal ADJ = **unfaithful**, faithless, false, untrue, inconstant, untrustworthy, treacherous, traitorous, perfidious, disaffected, seditious, subversive, unpatriotic, renegade, apostate, dissident, double-dealing, two-faced, deceitful.
Opposites: loyal.

disloyalty NOUN = **unfaithfulness**, faithlessness, infidelity, breaking of faith, breach of trust, falseness, falsity, inconstancy, untrustworthiness, treachery, treason, perfidiousness, disaffection, sedition, subversion, apostasy, dissidence, double-dealing.
Opposites: loyalty.

dismal ADJ = **gloomy**, sad, bleak, miserable, wretched, drab, dreary, dingy, cheerless, desolate, depressing, grim, funereal, uninviting.
Opposites: cheerful, bright.

dismantle VERB = **take apart**, take to pieces, disassemble, pull apart, strip down, tear down, demolish.
Opposites: assemble.

dismay NOUN = **disappointment**, distress, consternation, discouragement, anxiety, apprehension, gloom, horror, agitation.
Opposites: pleasure, relief.
▶ VERB **1** = **discourage**, dishearten, dispirit, put off, depress, disappoint, daunt, abash, cast down, devastate. **2** = **shock**, horrify, take aback, startle, alarm, frighten, scare, surprise, disturb, perturb, upset, unsettle, unnerve.
Opposites: encourage.

dismiss VERB **1** = **banish**, put away, lay/set aside, reject, drop, put out of one's mind, brush aside, think no more of, spurn, repudiate; [inf] pooh-pooh. **2** = **expel**, discharge, give notice to, lay off, make redundant, remove, oust, cashier; [inf] sack, fire, boot out, give the boot/push to, give someone their marching orders, send packing. **3 = disperse**, send away, disband, let go, release, free, discharge.

disobedient ADJ
= **insubordinate**, rebellious, defiant, unruly, wayward, undisciplined, mutinous, recalcitrant, intractable, wilful, refractory, fractious, obdurate, stubborn, obstreperous, disorderly, delinquent, uncontrollable, disruptive, wild, non-compliant, perverse, naughty, mischievous, contrary; [formal] contumacious. **Opposites:** obedient.

disobey VERB = **defy**, not comply with, disregard, ignore, oppose, contravene, flout, infringe, resist, overstep, rebel against, transgress, violate; [inf] fly in the face of.

disobliging ADJ
= **unhelpful**, uncooperative, unaccommodating, unfriendly, unsympathetic, discourteous, uncivil. **Opposites:** helpful.

disorder NOUN **1 = mess**, untidiness, chaos, muddle, clutter, jumble, confusion, disorderliness, disarray, disorganization, shambles. **2 = disturbance**, disruption, riot, tumult, fracas, rumpus, unrest. **3 = disease**, complaint, affliction, illness, sickness, malady. **Opposites:** tidiness, peace.

disorderly ADJ **1** = *See* **untidy**. **2** = *See* **undisciplined** (**1**).

disorganized ADJ
= **confused**, disorderly, untidy, chaotic, jumbled, muddled, in disarray, unsystematic, haphazard, random, unorganized, scatterbrained, unmethodical, careless, sloppy, slipshod, slapdash, messy, hit-or-miss, aimless, unplanned, unstructured; [Brit. inf] shambolic.

Opposites: organized, systematic.

disown VERB = **renounce**, repudiate, reject, abandon, forsake, disclaim, disavow, deny, disallow, abnegate, disinherit; [inf] turn one's back on.

disparage VERB = **belittle**, slight, deprecate, denigrate, depreciate, dismiss, ridicule, malign, scorn, insult, impugn, vilify, traduce; [inf] put down, bad-mouth; [Brit. inf] rubbish.
Opposites: praise.

disparity NOUN = **discrepancy**, difference, dissimilarity, contrast, gap, inequality, unevenness, inconsistency, imbalance, incongruity.

dispassionate ADJ = **calm**, level-headed, cool, unflappable, unruffled, collected, nonchalant, sober, equable, serene, unperturbed, detached, objective, disinterested, indifferent.
Opposites: emotional.

dispatch VERB 1 = **send**, post, mail, forward, transmit, consign, remit, convey. 2 = *See* **kill** (1).
▶ NOUN = **letter**, message, bulletin, communication, report, account, missive, document.

dispense VERB
1 = **distribute**, hand out, share out, measure out, divide out, dole out, allocate, assign, apportion, allot, supply, disburse, bestow, mete out, confer. 2 = **make up**, prepare, mix, supply.
■ **dispense with** = **omit**, do without, waive, forgo, give up, relinquish, renounce.

disperse VERB 1 = **go separate ways**, break up, disband, separate, scatter, dissolve, leave, vanish, melt away. 2 = **drive away**, break up, scatter, dissipate, dispel, banish.
Opposites: gather.

displace VERB 1 = **remove**, dismiss, discharge, depose, dislodge, eject, expel, force out; [inf] sack, fire. 2 = **replace**, take the place of, take over from, succeed, oust, supersede, supplant.

display VERB 1 = **put on show/view**, show, exhibit, present, unveil, set forth, demonstrate, advertise, publicize. 2 = **manifest**, show, evince, betray, show evidence of, reveal, disclose. **Opposites:** conceal, hide. ▶ NOUN 1 = **exhibition**, show, exhibit, presentation, demonstration, array. 2 = **spectacle**, show, parade, pageant.

displease VERB = **annoy**, irritate, anger, put out, dissatisfy, irk, vex, offend, pique, gall, nettle, incense, exasperate, disgust, perturb; [inf] aggravate.

dispose VERB 1 = **arrange**, order, position, place, range, line up, array, marshal, organize, group, rank, regulate. 2 = **incline**, make willing, predispose, make, prompt, lead, induce, motivate. ▪ **dispose of** = *see* **discard**.

disposed ADJ = **inclined**, willing, predisposed, minded, of a mind to, in the mood to, prepared, ready, prone, liable, given, apt.

disprove VERB = **prove false**, invalidate, refute, negate, confute, rebut, give the lie to, deny, contradict, discredit, controvert, expose, demolish. **Opposites:** prove.

dispute NOUN = **argument**, quarrel, altercation, clash, wrangle, squabble, feud, disturbance, fracas, brawl; [inf] row. ▶ VERB 1 = **debate**, discuss, argue, disagree, clash, quarrel, bicker, wrangle, squabble. 2 = **question**, call into question, challenge, contest, doubt, deny, object to, oppose, controvert, impugn, gainsay. **Opposites:** agree.

disqualify VERB = **rule out**, bar, exclude, reject, turn down, prohibit, debar, preclude.

disquiet NOUN = **uneasiness**, anxiety,

nervousness, agitation, upset, worry, concern, distress, alarm, fear, fretfulness, dread, foreboding.
Opposites: calm.

disregard VERB = **ignore**, pay no attention to, take no notice of, neglect, discount, set aside, brush aside, overlook, turn a blind eye to, pass over, forget, gloss over, make light of, play down, laugh off, skip, snub, cold-shoulder; [inf] pooh-pooh.
Opposites: attention.

disrepair NOUN = **dilapidation**, decay, collapse, shabbiness, ruin, deterioration, decrepitude.

disreputable ADJ = **infamous**, notorious, dishonourable, dishonest, unprincipled, villainous, corrupt, unworthy, questionable, unsavoury, contemptible, unscrupulous, despicable, disgraceful, reprehensible, discreditable, shocking, outrageous, scandalous.

Opposites: reputable.

disrespectful ADJ = **impolite**, discourteous, ill-mannered, rude, uncivil, irreverent, insolent, inconsiderate, impertinent, impudent, cheeky, scornful, contemptuous, insulting, churlish, derisive, uncomplimentary.
Opposites: respectful.

disrupt VERB = **upset**, interrupt, break up, throw into disorder, cause turmoil in, disturb, interfere with, obstruct, impede, hamper, unsettle; [Brit.] throw a spanner in the works.

dissatisfaction NOUN = **discontent**, displeasure, disappointment, disapproval, frustration, unhappiness, dismay, disquiet, annoyance, irritation, anger, exasperation, resentment, malaise, restlessness, disapprobation.
Opposites: satisfaction.

dissatisfied ADJ = **discontented**, displeased, disgruntled,

unsatisfied, disapproving, disappointed, frustrated, unhappy, angry, vexed, irritated, annoyed, resentful, restless, unfulfilled.
Opposites: satisfied.

disseminate VERB
= **spread**, circulate, broadcast, publish, publicize, proclaim, promulgate, propagate, dissipate, scatter, distribute, disperse, diffuse, bruit abroad.

dissident NOUN
= **dissenter**, rebel, objector, protestor, nonconformist, recusant, apostate.
Opposites: conformist.

dissimilar ADJ = **different**, distinct, unlike, varying, disparate, unrelated, divergent, deviating, diverse, various, contrasting, mismatched.
Opposites: similar.

dissipate VERB
1 = **disperse**, scatter, drive away, dispel, dissolve. 2 = **squander**, waste, fritter away, misspend, deplete, use up, consume, run

through.

dissipated ADJ = *see* **debauched**.

dissociate VERB
= **separate**, set apart, segregate, isolate, detach, disconnect, sever, divorce.
Opposites: associate.

dissolve VERB 1 = **liquefy**, become liquid, melt, deliquesce. 2 = **end**, bring to an end, break up, terminate, discontinue, wind up, disband, suspend. 3 = **be overcome with**, break into, collapse into.

dissuade VERB = **persuade against**, advise against, warn against, put off, stop, talk out of, argue out of, discourage from, deter from, divert, turn aside from.
Opposites: persuade.

distance NOUN 1 = **space**, extent, interval, gap, separation, span, stretch, measurement, length, width, breadth, depth, range, mileage.
2 = **aloofness**, reserve, coolness, remoteness, reticence, coldness,

stiffness, frigidity,
restraint, formality,
unresponsiveness,
unfriendliness;
[inf] stand-offishness.

■ **distance oneself**
= **separate oneself**,
dissociate oneself, keep
one's distance, set
oneself apart, remove
oneself, stay away, keep
away, detach oneself, be
unfriendly.

distant ADJ 1 = **far**,
faraway, far-off, remote,
out of the way, outlying,
far-flung, inaccessible.
2 = **away**, off, apart,
separated, dispersed,
scattered. 3 = **reserved**,
aloof, uncommunicative,
remote, withdrawn,
unapproachable,
restrained, reticent, cool,
cold, stiff, formal,
unfriendly, unresponsive,
haughty, condescending.
Opposites: close, friendly.

distasteful ADJ
= **disagreeable**,
unpleasant, displeasing,
undesirable, off-putting,
objectionable, offensive,
obnoxious, repugnant,
disgusting, unsavoury,

revolting, nauseating,
sickening, loathsome,
abhorrent, detestable.
Opposites: pleasant.

distinct ADJ 1 = **clear**,
clear-cut, well defined,
marked, sharp, decided,
visible, perceptible,
definite, unmistakable,
obvious, recognizable,
plain, plain as day,
evident, apparent,
manifest, patent,
unambiguous, palpable,
unequivocal.
2 = **separate**, individual,
different, unconnected,
contrasting, discrete,
disparate, dissimilar,
detached, unassociated.
Opposites: indistinct,
vague.

distinction NOUN
1 = **contrast**, difference,
dissimilarity, division,
dividing line, separation,
differentiation,
contradistinction,
peculiarity. 2 = **note**,
consequence,
importance, account,
significance, greatness,
prestige, eminence,
prominence, renown,
fame, celebrity, mark,

honour, merit, worth, excellence, name, rank, quality, superiority.
Opposites: similarity, mediocrity.

distinctive ADJ = **distinguishing**, characteristic, typical, individual, particular, special, peculiar, different, uncommon, unusual, remarkable, singular, extraordinary, noteworthy, original, idiosyncratic.
Opposites: ordinary.

distinguish VERB **1** = **tell apart**, differentiate, discriminate, tell the difference between, decide between, determine. **2** = **set apart**, single out, separate, characterize, individualize. **3** = **make out**, see, perceive, discern, observe, notice, recognize, pick out, espy.

distinguished ADJ = **famous**, renowned, well known, prominent, famed, noted, notable, illustrious, celebrated, respected, acclaimed, esteemed, legendary.

Opposites: obscure.

distort VERB **1** = **twist**, bend, warp, contort, buckle, deform, misshape, mangle, wrench. **2** = **misrepresent**, pervert, twist, falsify, slant, bias, colour, tamper with, alter, change, garble.

distract VERB **1** = **divert**, deflect, sidetrack, interrupt, interfere, draw away, turn aside. **2** = **amuse**, entertain, divert, beguile, engage, occupy. **3** = **confuse**, bewilder, disturb, fluster, agitate, disconcert, discompose, harass, annoy, trouble; [inf] hassle.

distracted ADJ = *see* **distraught**.

distraction NOUN **1** = **diversion**, interruption, disturbance, interference, obstruction. **2** = **confusion**, bewilderment, agitation, befuddlement, harassment. **3** = **amusement**, diversion, entertainment, recreation, pastime, divertissement.

distraught ADJ
= **distressed**, disturbed, excited, overcome, overwrought, frantic, distracted, beside oneself, wild, hysterical, grief-stricken, mad, maddened, insane, crazed, deranged; [inf] out of one's mind, worked up.
Opposites: calm.

distress NOUN 1 = **anguish**, suffering, pain, agony, affliction, torment, misery, wretchedness, torture, sorrow, grief, sadness, discomfort, heartache, desolation, trouble, worry, anxiety, uneasiness, perturbation, angst. 2 = **hardship**, adversity, trouble, misfortune, poverty, need, destitution, privation, impoverishment, indigence, penury, beggary, dire straits.
Opposites: happiness, prosperity.
▸VERB = **upset**, pain, trouble, worry, bother, disturb, perturb, torment,

grieve, sadden, make miserable, vex, shock, scare, alarm.
Opposites: calm.

distribute VERB 1 = **give out**, hand out, share out, divide out, dole out, measure out, parcel out, mete out, allocate, allot, issue, dispense, apportion, administer, deal out, dish out, assign, dispose. 2 = **circulate**, pass around, hand out, deliver, convey, transmit. 3 = **disseminate**, disperse, scatter, strew, spread, sow, diffuse.

district NOUN = **area**, region, place, locality, neighbourhood, sector, vicinity, quarter, territory, domain, precinct, province, zone, ward, department, parish, community.

distrust VERB = **mistrust**, be suspicious of, have doubts about, doubt, be wary/chary of, have misgivings about, question, wonder about, suspect, disbelieve; [inf] be leery of.
Opposites: trust.

disturb VERB **1** = **interrupt**, distract, bother, trouble, intrude on, butt in on, interfere with, harass, plague, pester, hinder; [inf] hassle. **2** = **muddle**, disorder, disarrange, confuse, throw into confusion; [inf] jumble up, mess about with. **3** = **concern**, trouble, worry, perturb, upset, fluster, agitate, discomfit, alarm, frighten, dismay, distress, unsettle, ruffle.

disturbed ADJ **1** = **upset**, troubled, worried, concerned, agitated, alarmed, dismayed, unsettled, ruffled. **2** = **unbalanced**, disordered, maladjusted, neurotic, psychotic; [inf] screwed up.

disused ADJ = **unused**, neglected, abandoned, discontinued, obsolete, superannuated, withdrawn, discarded, idle, closed.

ditch NOUN = **trench**, channel, dyke, canal, drain, gutter, gully, moat, furrow, rut.

▶ VERB = **throw out**, abandon, discard, drop, jettison, scrap, get rid of, dispose of; [inf] dump.

dive VERB = **plunge**, plummet, jump, leap, bound, spring, nosedive, fall, descend, submerge, drop, swoop, dip, pitch, bellyflop.

diverge VERB = **separate**, fork, branch off, radiate, spread out, bifurcate, divide, split, part, go off at a tangent, divaricate, ramify.
Opposites: converge.

diverse ADJ = **assorted**, various, miscellaneous, mixed, varied, diversified, variegated, heterogeneous, different, differing, distinct, unlike, dissimilar, distinctive, contrasting, conflicting.

diversify VERB = **branch out**, expand, bring variety to, develop, extend, enlarge, spread out, vary, mix, change, transform.

diversion NOUN **1** = **detour**, deviation, alternative route. **2** = **amusement**, entertainment,

distraction, fun,
relaxation, recreation,
pleasure, enjoyment,
delight, divertissement.

divert VERB **1** = **deflect**,
turn aside, change the
course of, redirect, draw
away, switch, sidetrack.
2 = **amuse**, entertain,
distract, delight, beguile,
give pleasure to, enchant,
interest, occupy, absorb,
engross.

diverting ADJ = **amusing**,
entertaining, distracting,
fun, enjoyable,
pleasurable, interesting,
absorbing, engrossing.
Opposites: boring.

divide VERB **1** = **split**, cut
up, separate, sever, halve,
bisect, sunder, rend, part,
segregate, partition,
detach, disconnect,
disjoin. **2** = **branch**, fork,
diverge, split in two.
3 = **share out**, allocate,
allot, apportion,
distribute, dispense,
hand out, dole out,
measure out, parcel out,
carve up. **4** = **break up**,
separate, alienate, split
up, disunite, set/pit
against one another, set

at odds, come between,
sow dissension.
Opposites: unite.

divine¹ ADJ **1** = **heavenly**,
celestial, holy, angelic,
spiritual, saintly,
seraphic, sacred,
consecrated, godlike,
godly, supernatural.
2 = **lovely**, beautiful,
wonderful, glorious,
marvellous, admirable;
[inf] super, stunning.
Opposites: mortal.

divine² VERB = **foretell**,
predict, foresee, forecast,
presage, augur, portend,
prognosticate.

divinity NOUN **1** = **divine
nature**, divineness, deity,
godliness, holiness,
sanctity. **2** = **theology**,
religious studies, religion,
scripture.

division NOUN **1** = **dividing
line**, boundary, limit,
border, partition,
demarcation, frontier,
margin. **2** = **section**, part,
portion, slice, fragment,
chunk, component,
share, compartment,
category, class, group,
family, grade. **3** = **branch**,
department, section,

arm, sector, unit.
4 = **disagreement**, conflict, dissension, discord, difference of opinion, feud, breach, rupture, split, variance, disunion, estrangement, alienation, schism.

divorce NOUN = **break-up**, split, dissolution, annulment, separation, breach, rupture.
▶ VERB = **break up**, split up, separate, part, annul/end the marriage.

dizzy ADJ = **light-headed**, giddy, faint, shaky, off balance, reeling, staggering; [inf] weak at the knees, wobbly, woozy.

do VERB **1** = **perform**, carry out, undertake, execute, accomplish, discharge, achieve, implement, complete, finish, bring about, effect, produce, engineer. **2** = **act**, behave, conduct oneself; [formal] comport oneself. **3** = **be enough**, be adequate, suffice, be sufficient, be satisfactory, serve the purpose, fit the bill, pass muster, measure up. **4** = **grant**, bestow, render, pay, give, afford. **5** = **get on/along**, progress, fare, make out, manage, continue.

docile ADJ = **amenable**, compliant, tractable, manageable, accommodating, obedient, pliant, biddable, submissive, dutiful, malleable.
Opposites: disobedient.

dock¹ NOUN = **pier**, quay, wharf, jetty, berth, harbour, port, slipway, marina, waterfront.

dock² VERB **1** = **cut**, shorten, crop, lop, truncate. **2** = **deduct**, subtract, remove, take off.

doctor NOUN = **physician**, medical practitioner, GP, general practitioner, consultant, registrar; [inf] medic, doc; [Brit. inf] quack.

doctrine NOUN = **creed**, belief, teaching, credo, dogma, conviction, tenet, principle, maxim, axiom, precept, article of faith, canon, theory, thesis, orthodoxy, postulate.

document NOUN = **paper**, form, certificate, record, report, deed, voucher, charter, instrument, licence, parchment, visa, warrant.

▶ VERB = **record**, detail, report, register, chart, cite, instance.

documentary ADJ
1 = **documented**, recorded, written, registered. **2** = **factual**, non-fiction, true-to-life, real-life, realistic.

dodge VERB **1** = **dart**, duck, dive, swerve, veer, jump, move aside. **2** = **evade**, avoid, elude, fend off, parry, fudge, escape, steer clear of, shun, shirk, deceive, trick.

▶ NOUN = **ruse**, ploy, stratagem, trick, subterfuge, wile, deception, manoeuvre, contrivance, expedient; [Brit. inf] wheeze.

dog NOUN = **hound**, bitch, cur, mongrel, tyke, pup, puppy, whelp; [inf] doggy, pooch, mutt, bow-wow.

▶ VERB = **follow**, pursue, track, shadow, trail, hound, plague, trouble, haunt.

dogged ADJ = **determined**, obstinate, stubborn, tenacious, relentless, single-minded, unflagging, unwavering, persistent, obdurate, firm, steadfast, staunch.

dogmatic ADJ
= **opinionated**, peremptory, assertive, insistent, pushy, emphatic, categorical, authoritarian, domineering, imperious, arrogant, overbearing, dictatorial, intolerant, biased, prejudiced.

dole NOUN = **benefit**, welfare, social security, income support.

▪ **dole out** = *see* **distribute** (**1**).

doleful ADJ = **mournful**, sad, sorrowful, dejected, depressed, miserable, disconsolate, wretched; [inf] blue, down in the dumps.

domestic ADJ **1** = **home**, family, household, private. **2** = **domesticated**, tame, pet, trained; [Brit.] house-trained;

[N. Amer.] housebroken.

domesticate VERB
1 = **tame**, train, break in;
[Brit.] house-train;
[N. Amer.] housebreak.
2 = **naturalize**,
acclimatize, habituate,
accustom, familiarize,
assimilate.

dominant ADJ
1 = **commanding**, ruling,
controlling, presiding,
governing, supreme,
ascendant, domineering,
most influential, most
assertive, authoritative.
2 = **chief**, most important,
predominant, main,
leading, principal,
paramount, pre-eminent,
primary, outstanding,
prevailing.
Opposites: submissive.

dominate VERB 1 = **rule**,
govern, control, exercise
control over, have the
whip hand, command,
direct, preside over, have
mastery over, domineer,
tyrannize, intimidate;
[inf] call the shots, have
under one's thumb, be in
the driver's seat, wear the
trousers. 2 = **overlook**,
tower above, stand over,

project over, hang over,
loom over, bestride.

domineering ADJ
= **overbearing**,
authoritarian, autocratic,
imperious, high-handed,
peremptory, arrogant,
dictatorial, haughty,
masterful, forceful,
pushy, tyrannical,
despotic, oppressive,
iron-fisted; [inf] bossy.
Opposites: meek, servile.

donate VERB = **give**,
contribute, present, make
a gift of, hand over,
grant, subscribe; [inf] chip
in, kick in.

donation NOUN
= **contribution**, gift,
subscription, present,
grant, offering, gratuity,
charity, benefaction,
largesse.

donor NOUN = **contributor**,
giver, benefactor,
benefactress, supporter,
backer, philanthropist;
[inf] angel.

doom NOUN 1 = **ruin**,
ruination, downfall,
destruction, disaster,
catastrophe,
annihilation, extinction,
death, termination,

quietus. **2 = fate**, destiny, fortune, lot, portion.

▶ VERB **= destine**, condemn, ordain, preordain, consign, predestine.

doomed ADJ **= damned**, cursed, hopeless, accursed, ill-fated, ill-starred, ruined, bedevilled.

door NOUN **1 = doorway**, opening, portal, entrance, exit, way out, barrier. **2 = entry**, entrance, opening, access, gateway, way, path, road, ingress.

dormant ADJ **1 = sleeping**, asleep, hibernating, resting, slumbering, inactive, inert, comatose, quiescent. **2 = hidden**, latent, potential, untapped, unused.
Opposites: awake, active.

dose NOUN **1 = amount**, quantity, measure, portion, draught.
2 = bout, attack, spell.

dot NOUN **= spot**, speck, fleck, point, mark, dab, particle, atom, iota, jot, mote, mite.

dote

■ **dote on = adore**, idolize, love, treasure, prize, make much of, lavish affection on, indulge, spoil, pamper.

double ADJ **1 = duplicate**, twinned, twin, paired, in pairs, dual, coupled, twofold. **2 = ambiguous**, dual, ambivalent, equivocal, double-edged.

▶ NOUN **= twin**, clone, lookalike, doppelgänger, duplicate, replica, copy, facsimile, counterpart, match, mate, fellow; [inf] spitting image, dead ringer.

double-cross VERB **= betray**, cheat, defraud, trick, mislead, deceive, swindle, hoodwink; [inf] two-time, take for a ride.

doubt VERB **1 = be suspicious of**, suspect, distrust, mistrust, have misgivings about, feel uneasy about, call into question, question, query. **2 = have doubts**, be dubious, be undecided, lack conviction, have

scruples.
Opposites: trust.
▶ NOUN **1 = distrust**, mistrust,
suspicion, scepticism,
lack of confidence,
uneasiness, reservations,
misgivings, qualms.
2 = uncertainty,
indecision, hesitancy,
hesitation, vacillation,
wavering, irresolution,
lack of conviction.

doubtful ADJ **1 = in doubt**,
uncertain, unsure,
improbable, unlikely.
2 = distrustful,
mistrustful, doubting,
suspicious, sceptical,
having reservations,
apprehensive, uneasy,
questioning, unsure,
incredulous.
3 = uncertain, dubious,
open to question,
questionable, debatable,
inconclusive, unresolved,
unconfirmed. **4 = unclear**,
dubious, ambiguous,
equivocal, obscure,
vague, nebulous.
5 = suspect, dubious,
suspicious, questionable,
under suspicion,
unreliable, disreputable.
Opposites: certain.

dour ADJ **= morose**,
unsmiling, gloomy,
sullen, sour, gruff,
churlish,
uncommunicative,
unfriendly, forbidding,
grim, stern, austere,
severe, harsh, dismal,
dreary.
Opposites: cheerful.

dowdy ADJ **= frumpish**,
drab, dull,
unfashionable, inelegant,
unstylish, slovenly,
shabby, dingy, untidy,
frowzy.
Opposites: smart.

downcast ADJ = *see*
dejected.

downright ADV
= completely, totally,
absolutely, utterly,
thoroughly, profoundly,
categorically, positively.

downward ADJ
= declining, descending,
falling, downhill, going
down, earthbound.
Opposites: upward.

drab ADJ **1 = dull**,
colourless, grey, mousy,
dingy, dreary, cheerless,
gloomy, sombre,
depressing.
2 = uninteresting, boring,

tedious, dry, dreary, lifeless, lacklustre, uninspired.
Opposites: bright, interesting.

draft NOUN **1** = **outline**, plan, rough version, skeleton, abstract, notes. **2** = **money order**, cheque, bill of exchange, postal order.

drag VERB **1** = **pull**, haul, draw, tug, yank, trail, tow, lug. **2** = **go on too long**, go on and on, become tedious, pass slowly, be boring, crawl, creep.

■ **drag out** = **protract**, prolong, draw out, spin out, stretch out, lengthen, extend.

drain VERB **1** = **draw off**, extract, remove, pump out, bleed, milk, tap, filter. **2** = **flow out**, seep out, leak, trickle, ooze, well out, discharge, exude, effuse. **3** = **use up**, exhaust, deplete, consume, sap, bleed, tax, strain.

▶ NOUN = **trench**, channel, duct, sewer, gutter, ditch, culvert, pipe, outlet, conduit.

dramatic ADJ **1** = **theatrical**, stage, thespian, dramaturgical. **2** = **exciting**, sensational, startling, spectacular, thrilling, tense, suspenseful, electrifying, stirring, affecting. **3** = **striking**, impressive, vivid, breathtaking, moving, affecting, graphic.

dramatist NOUN = **playwright**, scriptwriter, screenwriter, dramaturge.

dramatize VERB **1** = **adapt**, put into dramatic form. **2** = **exaggerate**, make a drama of, overstate, overdo; [inf] ham it up, lay it on thick.

drape VERB = **cover**, envelope, swathe, blanket, cloak, veil, shroud, decorate, adorn, deck, festoon, array, overlay.

▶ NOUN = **curtain**, drapery, screen, hanging, tapestry, valance.

drastic ADJ = **severe**, extreme, strong, vigorous, draconian, desperate, radical, dire, harsh, forceful, rigorous, sharp.

draw VERB **1 = pull**, haul, drag, tug, yank, tow, trail, lug. **2 = attract**, lure, entice, invite, engage, interest, win, capture, captivate, tempt, seduce, fascinate, allure.
3 = sketch, portray, depict, delineate, make a drawing of, represent, paint, design, trace, map out, chart, mark out.
4 = pull out, take out, bring out, extract, withdraw, unsheathe.
▸NOUN **1 = lure**, attraction, pull, enticement, allure, magnetism. **2 = lottery**, raffle, sweepstake. **3 = tie**, dead heat, stalemate.
▪**draw on = make use of**, have recourse to, exploit, employ, rely on.
▪**draw out = extend**, protract, prolong, lengthen, drag out, spin out.

drawback NOUN **= disadvantage**, catch, problem, snag, difficulty, trouble, flaw, hitch, fly in the ointment, stumbling block, handicap, obstacle, impediment, hindrance, barrier, hurdle, deterrent, nuisance, defect.
Opposites: benefit.

drawing NOUN **= picture**, sketch, illustration, portrayal, representation, depiction, composition, study, outline, diagram.

dread NOUN **= fear**, fearfulness, terror, alarm, nervousness, uneasiness, anxiety, apprehension, trepidation, horror, concern, foreboding, dismay, perturbation; [inf] blue funk, the heebie-jeebies.
▸VERB **= fear**, be afraid of, be terrified by, worry about, have forebodings about, shrink from, flinch from; [inf] have cold feet about.

dreadful ADJ **1 = terrible**, horrible, frightful, awful, dire, frightening, terrifying, distressing, alarming, shocking, appalling, harrowing, ghastly, fearful, hideous, gruesome, horrendous, calamitous, grievous.
2 = nasty, unpleasant,

disagreeable, repugnant, distasteful, odious.
Opposites: pleasant, agreeable.

dream NOUN **1 = vision**, nightmare, hallucination, fantasy, daydream, reverie, illusion, delusion. **2 = ambition**, aspiration, goal, design, plan, aim, hope, desire, wish, daydream, fantasy.
▶ VERB **1 = daydream**, be in a reverie, be in a trance, be lost in thought, muse, be preoccupied. **2 = think**, consider, conceive, suppose, visualize.
■ **dream up = think up**, invent, concoct, devise, create, hatch; [inf] cook up.

dreamy ADJ **= dreamlike**, vague, dim, hazy, shadowy, misty, faint, indistinct, unclear.

dreary ADJ **= dull**, drab, uninteresting, colourless, lifeless, dry, flat, tedious, boring, humdrum, monotonous, wearisome, routine, unvaried.
Opposites: interesting.

drench VERB **= soak**, drown, saturate, flood, inundate, steep, permeate, douse, souse, wet, slosh.

dress NOUN **1 = frock**, gown, garment, robe.
2 = clothes, garments, attire, costume, outfit, ensemble, garb; [inf] get-up, togs, duds.
▶ VERB **1 = clothe**, attire, garb, fit out, turn out, robe, accoutre; [archaic] apparel.
2 = bandage, bind up, cover.
Opposites: undress.

dribble VERB **1 = drool**, slaver, slobber; [Scottish] slabber. **2 = drip**, trickle, leak, run, ooze, seep, exude.

drift VERB **1 = be carried along**, float, coast, be borne, be wafted.
2 = wander, roam, rove, meander, stray. **3 = pile up**, accumulate, gather, form heaps, bank up, amass.
▶ NOUN **1 = gist**, essence, substance, meaning, significance, import, purport, tenor. **2 = pile**, heap, bank, mound, mass, accumulation.

drill VERB 1 = **train**, instruct, coach, teach, exercise, rehearse, ground, inculcate, discipline; [inf] put someone through their paces. 2 = **bore a hole in**, pierce, penetrate, puncture, perforate.
▶ NOUN 1 = **training**, instruction, coaching, teaching, indoctrination. 2 = **procedure**, routine, practice.

drink VERB 1 = **swallow**, sip, gulp down, drain, guzzle, imbibe, quaff, partake of; [inf] swig, swill, toss off. 2 = **take alcohol**, indulge, imbibe, tipple; [inf] booze, take a drop, hit the bottle, knock back a few.
▶ NOUN 1 = **swallow**, gulp, sip, draught; [inf] swill, swig. 2 = **alcohol**, liquor, spirits; [inf] booze, the hard stuff, hooch.

drip VERB = **dribble**, trickle, drizzle, leak, ooze, splash, sprinkle; [inf] plop.
▶ NOUN = **drop**, dribble, splash, trickle, leak, bead.

drive VERB 1 = **operate**, steer, handle, guide, direct, manage. 2 = **move**, herd, get going, urge, press, impel, push, round up. 3 = **force**, make, compel, coerce, oblige, impel, pressure, goad, spur, prod. 4 = **hammer**, thrust, ram, strike, bang, sink, plunge.
▶ NOUN 1 = **trip**, run, outing, journey, jaunt, tour, excursion; [inf] spin, joyride. 2 = **energy**, determination, enthusiasm, industry, vigour, push, motivation, persistence, keenness, enterprise, initiative, aggressiveness, zeal, verve; [inf] get-up-and-go, pizzazz, zip. 3 = **campaign**, effort, push, crusade.

drop VERB 1 = **fall**, descend, plunge, dive, plummet, tumble, dip, sink, subside, swoop. 2 = **decrease**, fall, lessen, diminish, dwindle, sink, plunge, plummet. 3 = **leave**, finish with, desert, abandon, jilt, reject, discard, renounce, disown; [inf] ditch, chuck, run out on. 4 = **fall down**, collapse, faint, swoon, drop/fall dead.

Opposites: rise, increase.

▶ NOUN **1** = **droplet**, globule, bead, bubble, blob, spheroid, oval. **2** = **bit**, dash, trace, pinch, dab, speck, modicum, dribble, splash, trickle, sprinkle. **3** = **decrease**, fall, decline, reduction, cut, lowering, depreciation, slump. **4** = **incline**, slope, descent, declivity, plunge, abyss, chasm, precipice, cliff.

drown VERB **1** = **flood**, submerge, inundate, deluge, swamp, engulf, drench. **2** = **be louder than**, muffle, overpower, overwhelm, stifle.

drowsy ADJ = **sleepy**, tired, lethargic, weary, dozy, dozing, sluggish, somnolent, heavy-eyed; [inf] dopey.
Opposites: alert.

drug NOUN **1** = **medicine**, medication, medicament, remedy, cure, panacea; [inf] magic bullet; [dated] physic. **2** = **narcotic**, opiate; [inf] dope, junk.
▶ VERB = **anaesthetize**, tranquillize, sedate, knock out, render

unconscious, stupefy, poison, narcotize, befuddle; [inf] dope.

drum VERB = **tap**, beat, rap, knock, tattoo, strike, thrum.

drunk ADJ = **intoxicated**, inebriated, blind drunk, the worse for drink, under the influence, befuddled, merry, tipsy, incapable, tight; [inf] tiddly, squiffy, plastered, smashed, paralytic, sloshed, blotto, sozzled, drunk as a lord, pie-eyed, three sheets to the wind, well oiled, stewed, pickled, tanked up, steaming, out of it, one over the eight, canned, tired and emotional; [Brit. inf] legless, bevvied.
Opposites: sober.
▶ NOUN = **drunkard**, heavy drinker, alcoholic, dipsomaniac, inebriate; [inf] soak, boozer, alky, lush, wino.

dry ADJ **1** = **arid**, parched, dehydrated, scorched, waterless, moistureless, desiccated, withered, shrivelled, wizened,

rainless, torrid, barren, unproductive, sterile. **2** = **dull**, uninteresting, boring, tedious, dreary, monotonous, tiresome, wearisome, flat, unimaginative, prosaic, humdrum. **3** = **cool**, cold, indifferent, aloof, unemotional, remote, impersonal.
Opposites: wet.

▸ VERB **1** = **dry up**, mop, blot, towel, drain. **2** = **make dry**, dry up, parch, scorch, dehydrate, sear, desiccate, wither, wilt, shrivel, mummify.

dub VERB = **call**, name, christen, designate, term, entitle, style, label, tag, nickname, denominate, nominate.

dubious ADJ **1** = **doubtful**, uncertain, unsure, hesitant, undecided, wavering, vacillating, irresolute, suspicious, sceptical; [inf] iffy.
2 = **suspicious**, questionable, suspect, untrustworthy, unreliable, undependable; [inf] shady, fishy, iffy.

Opposites: certain, trustworthy.

duck VERB **1** = **bend**, bob down, crouch, stoop, squat, hunch down, hunker down.
2 = **immerse**, submerge, dip, plunge, douse, souse, dunk.

duct NOUN = **pipe**, tube, conduit, channel, passage, canal, culvert.

due ADJ **1** = **owing**, owed, payable, outstanding, receivable. **2** = **deserved**, merited, earned, justified, appropriate, fitting, suitable, right. **3** = **proper**, correct, rightful, fitting, appropriate, apt, adequate, ample, satisfactory, requisite, apposite.

dull ADJ **1** = **drab**, dreary, sombre, dark, subdued, muted, toned down, lacklustre, lustreless, faded, washed out.
2 = **overcast**, cloudy, gloomy, dismal, dreary, dark, leaden, murky, sunless, lowering.
3 = **uninteresting**, boring, tedious, tiresome, wearisome, dry,

monotonous, flat, bland,
unimaginative,
humdrum, prosaic,
vapid. **4 = muted**,
muffled, indistinct,
feeble, deadened.
Opposites: bright,
interesting.

dumbfound VERB
= astound, amaze,
astonish, startle, surprise,
stun, stagger, take aback,
bewilder, overwhelm,
confound, baffle,
confuse, disconcert;
[inf] throw, knock
sideways; [Brit. inf] knock
for six.

dummy NOUN **1 = model**,
mannequin, figure, doll.
2 = copy, reproduction,
imitation, representation,
sample, substitute,
counterfeit, sham. **3 =** *See*
idiot.

dump VERB **1 = dispose of**,
get rid of, discard, throw
away/out, scrap, jettison.
2 = leave, abandon,
desert, walk out on,
forsake; [inf] leave in the
lurch.
▶ NOUN **1 = tip**, rubbish
dump, scrapyard,
junkyard. **2 = pigsty**,

hovel, slum, shack;
[inf] hole.

dunce NOUN **= fool**, dolt,
idiot, ass, ignoramus,
imbecile, simpleton;
[inf] chump, booby,
nincompoop, ninny,
dunderhead, blockhead,
fathead, halfwit, cretin,
moron, dummy,
numbskull, dimwit; [Brit.
inf] twerp, clot, twit,
nitwit.

duplicate NOUN **1 = replica**,
copy, reproduction,
likeness, twin, double,
clone, match;
[inf] lookalike, spitting
image, dead ringer.
2 = copy, carbon copy,
photocopy;
[trademark] photostat,
Xerox.
▶ ADJ **= matching**, twin,
identical, corresponding,
second, paired.
▶ VERB **1 = copy**, photocopy,
reproduce, replicate,
clone, photostat, xerox.
2 = repeat, do again,
replicate, perform again.

duplicity NOUN
= deceitfulness, double-
dealing, dishonesty,
two-facedness, trickery,

guile, chicanery, artifice.

durable ADJ 1 = **long-lasting**, hard-wearing, strong, sturdy, tough, resistant, imperishable. 2 = **lasting**, long-lasting, enduring, persistent, abiding, continuing, stable, constant, firm, permanent, unchanging, dependable, reliable. **Opposites:** flimsy, ephemeral.

dusk NOUN = **twilight**, sunset, sundown, nightfall, evening, dark.

dust NOUN 1 = **dirt**, grime, powder, soot. 2 = **earth**, soil, clay, ground, dirt.

dusty ADJ 1 = **dust-covered**, dirty, grimy, grubby, unclean, sooty, undusted. 2 = **powdery**, chalky, crumbly, sandy, fine, friable.

dutiful ADJ = **conscientious**, obedient, submissive, compliant, deferential, respectful, filial, reverent, reverential, devoted, considerate, thoughtful, pliant, docile.

Opposites: disrespectful, remiss.

duty NOUN 1 = **responsibility**, obligation, service, loyalty, allegiance, obedience, faithfulness, respect, deference, fidelity, homage. 2 = **task**, job, assignment, requirement, responsibility, obligation, mission, commission, function, office, charge, role, burden, onus. 3 = **tax**, levy, tariff, excise, toll, fee, impost.

dwarf VERB = **tower over**, overshadow, dominate, stand head and shoulders above, diminish, minimize.

dwell VERB = **live**, reside, stay, lodge; [inf] hang out; [formal] abide.

dwindle VERB = **become/grow less**, diminish, decrease, lessen, shrink, contract, fade, wane. **Opposites:** increase, grow.

dye NOUN = **colour**, shade, tint, hue.
▸ VERB = **colour**, tint, stain, pigment, shade.

dynamic ADJ = **energetic**, active, lively, spirited, aggressive, pushy, enthusiastic, driving, eager, motivated, zealous, alive, vigorous, strong, forceful, powerful, high-powered, potent, vital, effective; [inf] go-ahead, go-getting, zippy, peppy.

Ee

eager ADJ **1** = **keen**, enthusiastic, avid, fervent, impatient, zealous, passionate, wholehearted, earnest, diligent, ambitious, enterprising; [inf] bright-eyed and bushy-tailed, raring to go. **2** = **longing**, yearning, anxious, intent, agog, wishing, desirous, hopeful, thirsty, hungry, greedy; [inf] dying, itching, hot.
Opposites: indifferent, apathetic.

early ADV **1** = **ahead of time**, too soon, beforehand, before the appointed time, prematurely. **2** = **in good time**, ahead of schedule, before the appointed time.
Opposites: late.
▶ ADJ **1** = **advanced**, forward, premature, untimely, precocious. **2** = **primitive**, primeval, prehistoric, primordial.
Opposites: overdue.

earn VERB **1** = **get**, make, receive, obtain, draw, clear, collect, bring in, take home, gross, net; [inf] pull in, pocket. **2** = **gain**, win, attain, merit, achieve, rate, secure, obtain, deserve, be entitled to, be worthy of, warrant.

earnest ADJ **1** = **serious**, solemn, grave, intense, thoughtful, studious, staid, diligent, steady, hard-working, committed, dedicated, assiduous, keen, zealous. **2** = **sincere**, fervent, intense, ardent, passionate, heartfelt, wholehearted, enthusiastic, urgent, zealous, fervid, warm.

Opposites: flippant.

earnings PL NOUN
= **income**, salary, wage, pay, remuneration, fee, stipend, emolument, honorarium.

earth NOUN = **soil**, clay, loam, turf, clod, dirt, sod, ground.

earthly ADJ 1 = **worldly**, temporal, secular, mortal, human, material, materialistic, non-spiritual, mundane, carnal, fleshly, physical, corporeal, gross, sensual, base, sordid, vile, profane. 2 = **possible**, feasible, conceivable, imaginable, likely.
Opposites: spiritual.

earthy ADJ
1 = **unsophisticated**, down-to-earth, unrefined, homely, simple, plain, unpretentious, natural, uninhibited, rough, robust. 2 = **crude**, bawdy, coarse, ribald, indecent, obscene, indecorous; [inf] blue.

ease NOUN
1 = **effortlessness**, no difficulty, simplicity, deftness, proficiency, facility, adroitness, dexterity, mastery.
2 = **comfort**, contentment, enjoyment, content, affluence, wealth, prosperity, luxury, opulence.
3 = **peace**, peacefulness, calmness, tranquillity, composure, serenity, restfulness, quiet, security.
Opposites: difficulty.
▶ VERB 1 = **lessen**, mitigate, reduce, lighten, diminish, moderate, ameliorate, relieve, assuage, allay, soothe, palliate, appease.
2 = **guide**, manoeuvre, edge, inch, steer, glide, slip. 3 = **comfort**, console, soothe, solace, calm, quieten, pacify.
Opposites: aggravate.

easy ADJ 1 = **simple**, uncomplicated, straightforward, undemanding, effortless, painless, trouble-free, facile; [inf] idiot-proof.
2 = **natural**, casual, informal, unceremonious, easy-

going, amiable,
unconcerned, affable,
carefree, nonchalant,
composed, urbane,
insouciant, suave;
[inf] laid-back.
3 = **untroubled**,
unworried, relaxed, at
ease, calm, tranquil,
composed, serene,
comfortable, contented,
secure. **4** = **moderate**,
steady, regular,
undemanding, leisurely,
unhurried.
Opposites: difficult,
formal, uneasy.

easy-going ADJ = **even-tempered**, relaxed,
carefree, happy-go-lucky,
placid, serene,
nonchalant, insouciant,
tolerant, undemanding,
amiable, patient,
understanding,
imperturbable; [inf] laid-back, together.
Opposites: intolerant.

eat VERB = **consume**,
devour, swallow, chew,
munch, gulp down, bolt,
wolf, ingest; [inf] tuck
into, put away; [Brit.
inf] scoff.

■ **eat away** = **erode**, wear
away, corrode, gnaw
away, dissolve, waste
away, rot, decay, destroy.

eavesdrop VERB = **listen in**, spy, monitor, tap,
wire-tap, overhear;
[inf] bug, snoop.

ebb VERB **1** = **go out**, flow
back, retreat, fall back,
draw back, recede, abate,
subside. **2** = *See* **decline**
VERB **(2, 3)**.

ebullience NOUN
= **exuberance**, buoyancy,
high spirits, exhilaration,
elation, euphoria, high-spiritedness, jubilation,
animation, sparkle,
vivacity, zest,
irrepressibility.

eccentric ADJ = **odd**,
strange, queer, peculiar,
unconventional,
idiosyncratic, quirky,
bizarre, weird,
outlandish, irregular,
uncommon, abnormal,
freakish, aberrant,
anomalous, capricious,
whimsical; [inf] offbeat,
way-out, dotty, nutty,
screwy.
Opposites: ordinary,
conventional.

▶ NOUN = **character**, oddity, crank; [inf] queer fish, weirdo, oddball, nut; [Brit. inf] nutter; [N. Amer. inf] screwball.

echo VERB **1** = **reverberate**, resound, ring, repeat, reflect. **2** = **copy**, imitate, repeat, reproduce, reiterate, mirror, parrot, reflect, parallel, parody, ape.

eclipse VERB **1** = **block**, cover, blot out, obscure, conceal, cast a shadow over, darken, shade, veil, shroud. **2** = **outshine**, overshadow, dwarf, put in the shade, surpass, exceed, outstrip, transcend.

economical ADJ **1** = **thrifty**, sparing, careful, prudent, frugal, scrimping, mean, niggardly, penny-pinching, parsimonious; [inf] stingy; [Brit. inf] tight. **2** = **cheap**, inexpensive, reasonable, low-price, low-cost, budget. Opposites: extravagant.

economize VERB = **budget**, cut back, scrimp, save, be economical, be sparing, retrench; [inf] cut corners, tighten one's belt, draw in one's horns.

economy NOUN **1** = **wealth**, resources, financial state. **2** = **thriftiness**, carefulness, prudence, frugality, thrift, care, restraint, meanness, stinginess, miserliness, niggardliness, parsimony, penny-pinching, husbandry, conservation.

ecstasy NOUN = **bliss**, delight, rapture, joy, joyousness, happiness, elation, euphoria, jubilation, exultation, transports of delight, rhapsodies; [inf] seventh heaven, cloud nine. Opposites: misery.

ecstatic ADJ = **blissful**, enraptured, rapturous, joyful, joyous, overjoyed, jubilant, gleeful, exultant, elated, in transports of delight, delirious, in a frenzy of delight, rhapsodic, orgasmic, transported; [inf] on cloud nine, in seventh heaven, over the moon.

Opposites: miserable.

eddy NOUN = **whirl**, whirlpool, vortex, maelstrom, swirl, countercurrent, counterflow.
▸ VERB = **swirl**, whirl, spin, turn.

edge NOUN 1 = **border**, boundary, side, rim, margin, fringe, outer limit, extremity, verge, brink, lip, contour, perimeter, periphery, parameter, ambit. 2 = **sting**, bite, sharpness, severity, pointedness, acerbity, acidity, acrimony, virulence, trenchancy, pungency. 3 = **advantage**, lead, superiority, upper hand, whip hand, dominance, ascendancy; [inf] head start.
▸ VERB 1 = **trim**, hem, border, fringe, rim, bind, verge. 2 = **inch**, creep, sidle, steal, ease, elbow, worm, work, sidestep.

edgy ADJ = **nervous**, nervy, tense, anxious, apprehensive, on tenterhooks, uneasy, irritable, touchy, irascible, tetchy; [inf] twitchy, uptight.
Opposites: calm.

edit VERB = **revise**, correct, emend, polish, check, modify, rewrite, rephrase, prepare, adapt, amend, alter.

edition NOUN 1 = **issue**, number, version, printing. 2 = **printing**, impression, publication, issue.

educate VERB = **teach**, instruct, tutor, coach, school, train, drill, inform, enlighten, inculcate, prime, indoctrinate, edify, cultivate, develop, improve, prepare, rear, nurture, foster.

educated ADJ = **literate**, well read, informed, knowledgeable, learned, enlightened, erudite, cultivated, refined, cultured, schooled.
Opposites: illiterate, ignorant.

education NOUN 1 = **teaching**, schooling, instruction, tuition, training, tutelage, enlightenment,

edification, cultivation, development, improvement, preparation, indoctrination, drilling.
2 = **literacy**, knowledge, scholarship, letters, cultivation, refinement, culture.

eerie ADJ = **uncanny**, unearthly, ghostly, mysterious, strange, weird, unnatural, frightening, chilling, fearful, spine-chilling, blood-curdling, spectral; [inf] spooky, scary, creepy.

effect NOUN **1** = **result**, outcome, consequence, upshot, repercussion, impact, aftermath, conclusion, issue, fruit.
2 = **effectiveness**, success, influence, efficacy, weight, power. **3** = **sense**, meaning, drift, essence, tenor, significance, import, purport.
▶ VERB = **bring about**, carry out, execute, initiate, cause, make, create, produce, perform, achieve, accomplish, complete, fulfil, implement, actuate.

effective ADJ
1 = **successful**, competent, productive, capable, able, efficient, useful, efficacious, adequate, active.
2 = **valid**, in force, in operation, operative, active, effectual.
3 = **forceful**, powerful, telling, cogent, compelling, persuasive, convincing, moving.
Opposites: ineffective.

effeminate ADJ
= **womanish**, unmanly, girlish, effete, weak, camp; [inf] wimpish, sissy, pansy-like.
Opposites: manly, virile.

efficient ADJ = **well organized**, organized, capable, competent, effective, productive, proficient, adept, skilful, businesslike, workmanlike.
Opposites: inefficient.

effigy NOUN = **image**, likeness, statue, bust, model, dummy, representation, carving.

effort NOUN **1** = **exertion**, force, power, energy, work, application,

muscle, labour, striving, endeavour, toil, struggle, strain, stress; [inf] elbow grease. **2 = attempt**, try, endeavour; [inf] go, shot, crack, stab.
3 = achievement, accomplishment, attainment, creation, result, production, feat, deed, opus.

effrontery NOUN
= impertinence, insolence, impudence, cheek, audacity, temerity, presumption, gall, rashness, bumptiousness; [inf] nerve, neck, brass neck.

effusive ADJ **= gushing**, unrestrained, extravagant, fulsome, lavish, enthusiastic, expansive, profuse, demonstrative, exuberant, verbose, wordy, long-winded; [inf] over the top, OTT.

egotistic, **egotistical** ADJ **= egocentric**, self-absorbed, egoistic, narcissistic, conceited, vain, proud, arrogant, self-important, boastful, superior, bragging, self-

admiring.

eject VERB **1 = emit**, discharge, expel, cast out, exude, excrete, spew out, disgorge, spout, vomit, ejaculate. **2 = evict**, expel, turn out, put out, remove, oust, banish, deport, exile; [inf] kick out, chuck out, turf out, boot out.

elaborate ADJ
1 = complicated, detailed, complex, involved, intricate, studied, painstaking, careful.
2 = complex, detailed, ornate, fancy, showy, fussy, ostentatious, extravagant, baroque, rococo.
Opposites: simple.
▪**elaborate on = expand on**, enlarge on, flesh out, amplify, add detail to, expatiate on.

elastic ADJ **= stretchy**, stretchable, flexible, springy, pliant, pliable, supple, yielding, rubbery, plastic, resilient.
Opposites: rigid.

elderly ADJ **= old**, aging, aged, ancient, superannuated, long in

e

the tooth, past one's prime; [Biology] senescent; [inf] getting on, over the hill.
Opposites: young, youthful.

elect VERB = **vote for**, cast one's vote for, choose by ballot, choose, pick, select, appoint, opt for, plump for, decide on, designate.

election NOUN = **ballot**, poll, vote, referendum, plebiscite, general election.

electric ADJ
1 = **electrically operated**, battery-operated; [Brit.] mains-powered.
2 = **exciting**, charged, tense, thrilling, stirring, galvanizing, stimulating, jolting.

electrify VERB = **thrill**, excite, startle, arouse, rouse, stimulate, move, stir, animate, fire, charge, invigorate, galvanize.

elegant ADJ = **stylish**, graceful, tasteful, artistic, fashionable, cultured, beautiful, lovely, charming, exquisite, polished, cultivated, refined, suave, debonair, modish, dignified, luxurious, sumptuous, opulent.
Opposites: inelegant.

element NOUN **1** = **part**, piece, ingredient, factor, feature, component, constituent, segment, unit, member, subdivision, trace, detail, module. **2** = **environment**, habitat, medium, milieu, sphere, field, domain, realm, circle, resort, haunt.

elementary ADJ **1** = **basic**, introductory, preparatory, fundamental, rudimentary, primary.
2 = **easy**, simple, straightforward, uncomplicated, facile, simplistic.
Opposites: advanced, difficult.

elevate VERB **1** = **raise**, lift, hoist, hike. **2** = **promote**, upgrade, advance, prefer, exalt, aggrandize.
Opposites: lower, demote.

elevated ADJ **1** = **raised**, upraised, lifted up, aloft, high up. **2** = **high**, great, grand, lofty, dignified, noble, exalted, magnificent, inflated. **3** = **lofty**, exalted, inflated, pompous, bombastic, orotund, fustian.

elf NOUN = **fairy**, pixie, sprite, goblin, hobgoblin, imp, puck, troll.

elicit VERB = **bring out**, draw out, obtain, extract, extort, exact, wrest, evoke, derive, educe, call forth.

eligible ADJ = **suitable**, fitting, fit, appropriate, proper, acceptable, qualified, worthy, authorized, competent, allowed.
Opposites: ineligible.

elite NOUN **1** = **the best**, the pick, the cream, the elect. **2** = **aristocracy**, nobility, gentry, high society, beau monde; [inf] beautiful people, jet set.

eloquent ADJ = **articulate**, expressive, well spoken, fluent, silver-tongued, smooth-tongued, well expressed, vivid, graphic, pithy, persuasive, glib, forceful, effective,

plausible.
Opposites: inarticulate, tongue-tied.

elude VERB = **avoid**, dodge, evade, lose, escape, duck, flee, circumvent; [inf] shake off, give the slip to, throw off the scent, slip away from.

elusive ADJ **1** = **difficult to find/catch**, slippery, evasive; [inf] shifty, cagey. **2** = **evasive**, ambiguous, misleading, equivocal, deceptive, baffling, puzzling, fraudulent.

emaciated ADJ = **thin**, skinny, wasted, skeletal, gaunt, anorexic, starved, scrawny, cadaverous, shrunken, haggard, withered, shrivelled, drawn, pinched, wizened, attenuated, atrophied.
Opposites: fat.

emancipate VERB = **free**, set free, liberate, release, let loose, deliver, unchain, discharge, unfetter, unshackle, unyoke; [historical] manumit.

emasculate VERB = **weaken**, enfeeble,

debilitate, erode, undermine, cripple, pull the teeth of; [inf] water down.

embargo NOUN = **ban**, bar, prohibition, stoppage, proscription, restriction, restraint, blockage, check, barrier, obstruction, impediment, hindrance.

embarrass VERB = **make uncomfortable/awkward**, make self-conscious, upset, disconcert, discomfit, discompose, confuse, fluster, agitate, distress, chagrin, shame, humiliate, abash, mortify, discountenance, nonplus; [inf] show up, put one on the spot.

embed VERB = **insert**, drive in, hammer in, ram in, sink, implant, plant, set/fix in, root.

embellish VERB = **decorate**, adorn, ornament, dress up, beautify, festoon, enhance, garnish, trim, gild, varnish, embroider, deck, bedeck, emblazon, bespangle; [inf] tart up.

embezzle VERB = **steal**, rob, thieve, pilfer, misappropriate, pocket, appropriate, purloin, abstract; [inf] filch, put one's hand in the till, rip off; [formal] peculate.

emblazon VERB = **decorate**, adorn, ornament, embellish, illuminate, colour, paint.

emblem NOUN = **crest**, insignia, badge, symbol, sign, device, representation, token, image, figure, mark.

embody VERB
1 = **personify**, represent, symbolize, stand for, typify, exemplify, incarnate, manifest, incorporate, realize, reify.
2 = **incorporate**, combine, bring together, comprise, include, collect, contain, integrate, constitute, consolidate, encompass, assimilate, systematize.

embrace VERB 1 = **take/hold in one's arms**, hold, hug, cuddle, clasp, squeeze, clutch, seize, grab, enfold, enclasp, encircle; [inf] canoodle with, neck with.

2 = **welcome**, accept, take up, adopt, espouse.

emerge VERB **1** = **come out**, come into view, appear, become visible, surface, crop up, spring up, materialize, arise, proceed, issue, come forth, emanate.
2 = **become known**, come out, come to light, become apparent, transpire, come to the fore.

emergency NOUN = **crisis**, difficulty, predicament, danger, accident, quandary, plight, dilemma, crunch, extremity, exigency; [inf] pickle.

eminence NOUN = **importance**, greatness, prestige, reputation, fame, distinction, renown, pre-eminence, prominence, illustriousness, rank, standing, note, station, celebrity.

eminent ADJ = **important**, great, distinguished, well known, celebrated, famous, renowned, noted, prominent, esteemed, noteworthy, pre-eminent, outstanding, superior, high-ranking, exalted, revered, elevated, august, paramount.
Opposites: unimportant.

emit VERB = **discharge**, give out/off, throw out, issue, disgorge, vent, vomit, send forth, eject, spew out, emanate, radiate, ejaculate, exude, ooze, leak, excrete.

emotional ADJ
1 = **passionate**, demonstrative, feeling, hot-blooded, warm, responsive, tender, loving, sentimental, ardent, fervent, sensitive, excitable, temperamental, melodramatic.
2 = **moving**, touching, affecting, poignant, emotive, tear-jerking, pathetic, heart-rending, soul-stirring, impassioned.
Opposites: unfeeling.

emotive ADJ = **sensitive**, delicate, controversial, touchy, awkward.

emphasis NOUN **1** = **stress**, attention, importance, priority, weight, significance, prominence, urgency, force, insistence, accentuation, pre-eminence, import, mark. **2** = **accent**, stress, accentuation, weight.

emphasize VERB = **lay/put stress on**, stress, accent, dwell on, focus on, underline, accentuate, call attention to, highlight, give prominence to, point up, spotlight, insist on, play up, feature, intensify, strengthen, heighten, deepen, underscore. **Opposites:** understate, minimize.

emphatic ADJ **1** = **forceful**, forcible, categorical, unequivocal, definite, decided, certain, determined, absolute, direct, earnest, energetic, vigorous. **2** = **marked**, pronounced, decided, positive, definite, distinctive, unmistakable, important, significant, striking, strong, powerful, resounding, telling, momentous. **Opposites:** hesitant.

employ VERB **1** = **hire**, engage, take on, sign up, put on the payroll, enrol, apprentice, commission, enlist, retain, indenture. **2** = **use**, make use of, utilize, apply, exercise, bring to bear.

employed ADJ **1** = **working**, in work, in employment, in a job. **2** = **occupied**, busy, engaged, preoccupied. **Opposites:** unemployed, unoccupied.

employee NOUN = **worker**, member of staff, hand, hired hand, hireling, labourer, assistant.

employer NOUN = **manager**, owner, proprietor, patron, contractor, director; [Brit. inf] gaffer, governor.

empower VERB **1** = **authorize**, license, certify, accredit, qualify, sanction, warrant, commission, delegate. **2** = **allow**, enable, give strength to, equip.

empty ADJ **1** = **unfilled**, vacant, unoccupied,

hollow, void, uninhabited, bare, desolate, unadorned, barren, blank, clear.
2 = **meaningless**, futile, ineffective, ineffectual, useless, worthless, insubstantial, fruitless, idle. **3** = **purposeless**, aimless, hollow, barren, senseless, unsatisfactory, banal, inane, frivolous, trivial, worthless, valueless, profitless.
4 = **blank**, expressionless, vacant, deadpan, vacuous, absent.
Opposites: full.
▶ VERB = **vacate**, clear, evacuate, unload, unburden, void, deplete, sap.

enable VERB = **allow**, permit, make possible, give the means to, equip, empower, facilitate, prepare, entitle, authorize, sanction, fit, license, warrant, validate, accredit, delegate, legalize.
Opposites: prevent.

enchant VERB = **bewitch**, hold spellbound, fascinate, charm, captivate, entrance, beguile, enthral, hypnotize, mesmerize, enrapture, delight, enamour.

enchanting ADJ
= **bewitching**, charming, delightful, attractive, appealing, captivating, irresistible, fascinating, engaging, endearing, entrancing, alluring, winsome, ravishing.

enclose VERB
1 = **surround**, circle, hem in, ring, shut in, hedge in, wall in, confine, encompass, encircle, circumscribe, encase, gird. **2** = **include**, send with, put in, insert, enfold.

enclosure NOUN
= **compound**, yard, pen, pound, ring, fold, paddock, stockade, corral, run, sty, cloister, close, kraal.

encompass VERB
= **include**, cover, embrace, contain, comprise, take in, incorporate, envelop, embody.

encounter VERB **1** = **meet**, run into/across, come upon, stumble across, chance upon, happen upon; [inf] bump into. **2** = **be faced with**, contend with, confront, tussle with.
▶ NOUN = **fight**, battle, clash, conflict, confrontation, engagement, skirmish, scuffle, tussle, brawl; [inf] run-in, set-to, brush.

encourage VERB **1** = **cheer**, rally, stimulate, motivate, inspire, stir, incite, hearten, animate, invigorate, embolden; [inf] buck up. **2** = **urge**, persuade, prompt, influence, exhort, spur, goad, egg on. **3** = **promote**, advance, foster, help, assist, support, aid, advocate, back, boost, abet, forward, strengthen.
Opposites: discourage.

encroach VERB = **trespass**, intrude, invade, infringe, infiltrate, overrun, impinge, usurp, appropriate; [inf] tread on someone's toes, muscle in on, invade someone's space.

encumber VERB = **inconvenience**, constrain, handicap, hinder, impede, obstruct, retard, check, restrain.

encyclopedic ADJ = **comprehensive**, complete, wide-ranging, all-inclusive, exhaustive, all-embracing, thorough, universal, all-encompassing, compendious, vast.

end NOUN **1** = **ending**, finish, close, conclusion, cessation, termination, completion, resolution, climax, finale, culmination, denouement, epilogue, expiry; [inf] wind-up, pay-off. **2** = **edge**, border, boundary, limit, extremity, margin, point, tip, extent. **3** = **remainder**, remnant, fragment, vestige, leftover. **4** = **aim**, goal, purpose, intention, objective, design, motive, aspiration, intent, object.
Opposites: beginning, start.

▸ VERB **1** = **come to an end**, finish, stop, close, cease, conclude, terminate, discontinue, break off, fade away, peter out; [inf] wind up. **2** = **bring to an end**, finish, stop, cease, conclude, close, terminate, break off, complete, dissolve, resolve.
Opposites: begin, start.

endanger VERB = **threaten**, put at risk, put in danger, jeopardize, imperil, risk, expose, hazard, compromise.
Opposites: protect.

endearing ADJ
= **charming**, adorable, lovable, attractive, engaging, disarming, appealing, winning, sweet, captivating, enchanting, winsome.

endearment NOUN
1 = **sweet talk**, sweet nothings, soft words, blandishments.
2 = **affection**, love, fondness, liking, attachment.

endeavour VERB = **try**, attempt, strive, venture, aspire, undertake, struggle, labour, essay; [inf] work at, have a go/ stab at.

endless ADJ **1** = **unending**, unlimited, infinite, limitless, boundless, continual, perpetual, constant, everlasting, unceasing, unfading, interminable, incessant, measureless, untold, incalculable.
2 = **continuous**, unbroken, uninterrupted, never-ending, whole, entire. **3** = **non-stop**, interminable, overlong, unremitting, monotonous, boring.
Opposites: finite, limited.

endorse VERB **1** = **sign**, countersign, validate, autograph, superscribe, underwrite. **2** = **approve**, support, back, favour, recommend, advocate, champion, subscribe to, uphold, authorize, sanction, ratify, affirm, warrant, confirm, vouch for, corroborate.

endow VERB = **provide**, give, present, confer, bestow, gift, enrich, supply, furnish, award,

invest; [poetic/
literary] endue.

endurance NOUN
1 = **stamina**, staying
power, perseverance,
tenacity, fortitude,
durability, continuance,
longevity. **2** = **toleration**,
sufferance, forbearance,
acceptance, patience,
resignation.

endure VERB **1** = **last**,
continue, persist, remain,
live on, hold on, survive,
abide; [archaic] bide, tarry.
2 = **stand**, bear, put up
with, tolerate, suffer,
abide, submit to,
countenance, stomach,
swallow; [Brit. inf] stick;
[formal] brook.
Opposites: fade.

enemy NOUN = **adversary**,
opponent, foe, rival,
antagonist, competitor.
Opposites: friend.

energetic ADJ **1** = **active**,
lively, vigorous,
strenuous, dynamic,
brisk, spirited, animated,
vibrant, sprightly, vital,
tireless, indefatigable;
[inf] zippy, peppy, bright-
eyed and bushy-tailed.
2 = **forceful**, forcible,

determined, aggressive,
emphatic, driving,
powerful, effective,
potent.
Opposites: lethargic.

energy NOUN = **vigour**,
strength, stamina, power,
forcefulness, drive, push,
exertion, enthusiasm,
life, animation,
liveliness, vivacity,
vitality, spirit,
spiritedness, fire, zest,
exuberance, buoyancy,
verve, dash, sparkle,
effervescence, brio,
ardour, zeal, passion,
might, potency,
effectiveness, efficiency,
efficacy, cogency;
[inf] vim, zip, zing.

enfold VERB = **enclose**,
fold, envelop, encircle,
swathe, shroud, swaddle.

enforce VERB **1** = **apply**,
carry out, administer,
implement, bring to
bear, impose, prosecute,
execute, discharge, fulfil.
2 = **force**, compel, insist
on, require, coerce,
necessitate, urge, exact.

engage VERB **1** = **employ**,
hire, take on, appoint,
enlist, enrol,

commission. **2 = occupy**, absorb, hold, engross, grip, secure, preoccupy, fill. **3 = take part**, enter into, become involved in, undertake, embark on, set about, join in, participate in, tackle, launch into. **4 = fit together**, join together, mesh, intermesh, interconnect.
Opposites: dismiss.

engender VERB = **cause**, produce, create, bring about, give rise to, lead to, arouse, rouse, provoke, excite, incite, induce, generate, instigate, effect, hatch, occasion, foment; [formal] effectuate.

engine NOUN = **motor**, mechanism, machine, power source, generator.

engineer VERB = **bring about**, cause, plan, plot, contrive, devise, orchestrate, mastermind, originate, manage, control, superintend, direct, conduct, handle, concoct.

engrave VERB = **inscribe**, etch, carve, cut, chisel, imprint, impress, mark.

enhance VERB = **add to**, increase, heighten, stress, emphasize, strengthen, improve, augment, boost, intensify, reinforce, magnify, amplify, enrich, complement.

enjoy VERB **1 = take pleasure in**, delight in, appreciate, like, love, rejoice in, relish, revel in, savour, lap up, luxuriate in; [inf] fancy. **2 = have**, possess, benefit from, own, have the advantage of, be blessed with.
Opposites: dislike.

■ **enjoy oneself = have fun**, have a good time, make merry, celebrate, party, have the time of one's life; [inf] have a ball, let one's hair down.

enjoyable ADJ = **entertaining**, amusing, delightful, diverting, satisfying, gratifying, pleasant, lovely, agreeable, pleasurable, fine, good, great, nice.
Opposites: boring, disagreeable.

enlarge VERB = **make bigger/larger**, expand,

extend, add to, augment, amplify, supplement, magnify, multiply, widen, broaden, lengthen, elongate, deepen, thicken, distend, dilate, swell, inflate.

enlighten VERB = **inform**, make aware, advise, instruct, teach, educate, tutor, illuminate, apprise, counsel, edify, civilize, cultivate.

enlist VERB **1** = **enrol**, sign up, conscript, recruit, hire, employ, take on, engage, muster, obtain, secure. **2** = **join**, join up, enrol in, sign up for, enter into, volunteer for.

enliven VERB = **brighten up**, cheer up, perk up, hearten, gladden, excite, stimulate, exhilarate, invigorate, revitalize, buoy up, give a boost to, wake up, rouse, refresh; [inf] jazz up, ginger up, light a fire under.

enormous ADJ = **huge**, immense, massive, vast, gigantic, colossal, mammoth, astronomic, gargantuan, mountainous, prodigious, tremendous, stupendous, titanic, excessive, Herculean, Brobdingnagian; [inf] jumbo.
Opposites: tiny.

enough ADJ = **sufficient**, adequate, ample, abundant.
Opposites: insufficient, inadequate.

enquire VERB = *see* **inquire**.

enrage VERB = **madden**, infuriate, incense, exasperate, provoke, annoy, irritate, inflame, incite, irk, agitate; [inf] make someone's hackles rise, make someone's blood boil, get someone's back up; [Brit. inf] wind up.
Opposites: placate.

enrapture VERB = **delight**, thrill, captivate, charm, fascinate, enchant, beguile, bewitch, entrance, enthral, transport, ravish; [inf] blow someone's mind, turn on.

ensue VERB = **follow**, come next/after, result, occur, happen, turn up, arise, transpire, proceed, succeed, issue, derive, stem, supervene; [poetic/literary] come to pass, befall.

ensure VERB = **make certain**, make sure, guarantee, confirm, certify, secure, effect, warrant.

entail VERB = **involve**, require, call for, necessitate, demand, impose, cause, bring about, produce, result in, lead to, give rise to, occasion.

enter VERB 1 = **come/go into**, pass/move into, invade, infiltrate, penetrate, pierce, puncture. 2 = **begin**, start, commence, embark on, engage in, undertake, venture on. 3 = **take part in**, participate in, go in for, gain entrance/admittance to. 4 = **submit**, put forward, present, proffer, register, tender. 5 = **record**, register, put down, note, mark down, document, list, file, log.

enterprise NOUN
1 = **venture**, undertaking, project, operation, endeavour, task, effort, plan, scheme, campaign. 2 = **resourcefulness**, initiative, drive, push, enthusiasm, zest, energy, vitality, boldness, audacity, courage, imagination, spirit, spiritedness, vigour; [inf] get-up-and-go, vim, oomph. 3 = **business**, firm, industry, concern, operation, corporation, establishment, house.

enterprising ADJ = **resourceful**, entrepreneurial, energetic, determined, ambitious, purposeful, pushy, adventurous, audacious, bold, daring, active, vigorous, imaginative, spirited, enthusiastic, eager, keen, zealous, vital, courageous, intrepid; [inf] go-ahead, up-and-coming, peppy.

entertain VERB 1 = **amuse**, divert, delight, please, charm, cheer, interest, beguile, engage, occupy.

2 = **play host/hostess**, receive guests, provide hospitality, have people round, have company, keep open house, hold/throw a party.

3 = **consider**, give consideration to, take into consideration, give some thought to, think about/over, contemplate, weigh up, ponder, muse over, bear in mind.

entertainment NOUN
1 = **amusement**, fun, enjoyment, recreation, diversion, distraction, pastime, hobby, sport.
2 = **show**, performance, concert, play, presentation, spectacle, pageant.

enthralling ADJ
= **captivating**, enchanting, spellbinding, fascinating, bewitching, gripping, riveting, charming, delightful, intriguing, mesmerizing, hypnotic.

enthusiasm NOUN
= **eagerness**, keenness, fervour, ardour, passion, zeal, warmth, vehemence, zest, fire, excitement, exuberance, ebullience, avidity, wholeheartedness, commitment, devotion, fanaticism, earnestness.
Opposites: apathy.

enthusiast NOUN
= **supporter**, follower, fan, devotee, lover, admirer, fanatic, zealot, aficionado; [inf] buff, freak.

enthusiastic ADJ = **eager**, keen, fervent, ardent, passionate, warm, zealous, vehement, excited, spirited, exuberant, ebullient, avid, wholehearted, hearty, committed, devoted, fanatical, earnest; [inf] mad about.
Opposites: apathetic, indifferent.

entice VERB = **tempt**, lure, seduce, inveigle, lead on/astray, beguile, coax, wheedle, cajole, decoy, bait.

entire ADJ **1** = **whole**, complete, total, full, continuous, unbroken.
2 = **intact**, undamaged, unbroken, sound, unmarked, perfect,

unimpaired,
unblemished, unspoiled.
Opposites: partial.

entirely ADV = **completely**,
absolutely, totally, fully,
wholly, altogether,
utterly, in every respect,
without exception,
thoroughly, perfectly.

entitle VERB 1 = **give the
right to**, make eligible,
qualify, authorize, allow,
sanction, permit, enable,
empower, warrant,
enfranchise, accredit.
2 = **call**, name, term,
style, dub, designate.

entity NOUN = **being**, body,
person, creature,
individual, organism,
object, thing, article,
substance, quantity,
existence.

entourage NOUN = **retinue**,
escort, cortège, train,
suite, bodyguard,
attendants, companions,
followers, associates;
[inf] groupies.

entrails PL NOUN
= **intestines**, internal
organs, bowels, vital
organs, viscera; [inf] guts,
insides, innards.

entrance NOUN 1 = **way in**,
entry, means of entry/
access, access, door,
doorway, gate, gateway,
drive, driveway, foyer,
lobby, porch, threshold,
portal. 2 = **coming in**,
entry, appearance,
arrival, introduction,
ingress. 3 = **admission**,
entry, permission to
enter, right of entry,
access, ingress.
Opposites: exit, departure.

entrant NOUN
1 = **newcomer**, beginner,
new arrival, probationer,
trainee, novice, tyro,
initiate, neophyte;
[inf] cub, rookie; [N. Amer.
inf] greenhorn.
2 = **contestant**,
competitor, participant,
player, candidate,
applicant, rival,
opponent.

entreat VERB = **beg**,
implore, plead with,
appeal to, petition,
solicit, pray, crave,
exhort, enjoin,
importune, supplicate;
[poetic/literary] beseech.

entrenched ADJ = **deep-
seated**, deep-rooted,

rooted, well established, fixed, set, firm, ingrained, unshakeable, immovable, indelible, dyed in the wool.

envelop VERB = **enfold**, cover, wrap, swathe, swaddle, cloak, blanket, surround, engulf, encircle, encompass, conceal, hide, obscure.

envelope NOUN = **wrapper**, wrapping, cover, covering, case, casing, jacket, shell, sheath, skin, capsule, holder, container.

enviable ADJ = **exciting envy**, desirable, covetable, worth having, tempting, excellent, fortunate, lucky, favourable.

envious ADJ = **jealous**, covetous, desirous, green-eyed, green, grudging, begrudging, resentful, bitter, jaundiced; [inf] green with envy.

environment NOUN = **surroundings**, habitat, territory, domain, medium, element, milieu, situation, location, scene, locale, background, conditions, circumstances, setting, context, atmosphere, ambience, mood.

envisage VERB = **predict**, foresee, imagine, visualize, picture, anticipate, envision, contemplate, conceive of, think of, dream of.

envy NOUN = **enviousness**, jealousy, covetousness, desire, cupidity, longing, resentment, bitterness, resentfulness, discontent, spite, dissatisfaction.
▶ VERB = **be envious of**, be jealous of, covet, be covetous of, begrudge, grudge, resent.

ephemeral ADJ = **fleeting**, short-lived, transitory, transient, momentary, brief, short, temporary, passing, impermanent, evanescent, fugitive.
Opposites: permanent.

epidemic NOUN = **outbreak**, pandemic, plague, scourge, upsurge, wave, upswing, upturn, increase, growth, rise, mushrooming.

▸ ADJ = **rife**, rampant, widespread, extensive, wide-ranging, prevalent, sweeping, predominant.

episode NOUN 1 = **part**, instalment, chapter, section, passage, scene. 2 = **incident**, occurrence, event, happening, experience, adventure, matter, occasion, affair, business, circumstance, interlude.

epitome NOUN = **personification**, embodiment, essence, quintessence, archetype, representation, model, typification, example, exemplar, prototype.

epoch NOUN = **era**, age, period, time, date.

equal ADJ 1 = **identical**, alike, like, comparable, commensurate, equivalent, the same as, on a par with. 2 = **even**, evenly matched, balanced, level, evenly proportioned; [Brit.] level pegging; [inf] fifty-fifty, neck and neck. 3 = **capable of**, up to, fit for, good enough for, adequate for, sufficient for, suited, ready for.

▸ NOUN = **equivalent**, match, parallel, peer, twin, alter ego, counterpart.

▸ VERB 1 = **be equal/level with**, be equivalent to, match, measure up to, equate with, vie with, rival, emulate. 2 = **match**, reach, achieve, parallel, come up to, measure up to.

equality NOUN 1 = **sameness**, identity, parity, likeness, similarity, uniformity, evenness, levelness, balance, correspondence, comparability. 2 = **fairness**, justice, justness, impartiality, egalitarianism, even-handedness. **Opposites:** inequality.

equanimity NOUN = **composure**, presence of mind, self-control, self-possession, level-headedness, equilibrium, poise, aplomb, sangfroid, calmness, calm, coolness, serenity, placidity, tranquillity, phlegm, imperturbability, unflappability.

Opposites: anxiety.

equilibrium NOUN
1 = **balance**, stability, steadiness, evenness, symmetry, equipoise, counterpoise. 2 = *See* **equanimity**.

equip VERB = **fit out**, rig out, provide, supply, furnish, prepare, stock, arm, attire, array, dress, outfit, accoutre, endow; [inf] kit out.

equitable ADJ = **fair**, fair-minded, just, even-handed, right, rightful, proper, reasonable, honest, impartial, unbiased, unprejudiced, open-minded, non-discriminatory, disinterested, dispassionate.
Opposites: inequitable, unfair.

equivalent ADJ = **equal**, identical, similar, the same, alike, like, comparable, corresponding, commensurate, matching, interchangeable, on a par, tantamount, synonymous, homologous.
Opposites: different, dissimilar.

equivocal ADJ = **ambiguous**, ambivalent, vague, unclear, obscure, roundabout, non-committal, hazy, oblique, evasive, misleading, duplicitous, indeterminate, uncertain.
Opposites: unequivocal.

era NOUN = **age**, epoch, period, time, eon, generation, stage, cycle, season.

eradicate VERB = **remove**, get rid of, wipe out, eliminate, do away with, extirpate, abolish, annihilate, stamp out, obliterate, extinguish, excise, expunge, destroy, kill.

erase VERB = **delete**, rub out, wipe out, remove, cross out, strike out, blot out, efface, expunge, obliterate, cancel.

erect ADJ 1 = **upright**, straight, vertical. 2 = **rigid**, stiff, hard, firm.
▶ VERB = **build**, construct, put up, assemble, put

together, raise, elevate, mount.

erode VERB = **wear away**, wear, eat away at, corrode, abrade, gnaw away at, grind down, consume, devour, spoil, disintegrate, destroy, excoriate.

erotic ADJ = **arousing**, stimulating, aphrodisiac, exciting, titillating, seductive, sensual, sexy, carnal, salacious, suggestive, pornographic; [inf] steamy.

err VERB = **be wrong**, be incorrect, make a mistake, be mistaken, blunder, misjudge, miscalculate, misunderstand, misconstrue, get it wrong, be wide of the mark; [inf] be barking up the wrong tree, slip up; [Brit. inf] boob.

errand NOUN = **task**, job, commission, chore, assignment, undertaking, message, charge, mission.

erratic ADJ
1 = **inconsistent**, variable, irregular, unstable, unpredictable, unreliable, capricious, whimsical, fitful, wayward, abnormal, eccentric, aberrant, deviant.
2 = **wandering**, meandering, wavering, directionless, haphazard.
Opposites: consistent.

error NOUN **1** = **mistake**, inaccuracy, miscalculation, blunder, fault, flaw, oversight, misprint, erratum, misinterpretation, misreading, fallacy, misconception, delusion; [Brit.] literal; [inf] slip-up, boo-boo, howler, typo; [Brit. inf] boob; [Brit. inf, dated] bloomer.
2 = **wrongness**, misconduct, misbehaviour, lawlessness, criminality, delinquency, sinfulness, evil.

erupt VERB **1** = **eject**, gush, pour forth, spew, vent, boil over, vomit.
2 = **break out**, flare up, blow up, explode.

escalate VERB = **grow**, increase, be stepped up, mushroom, intensify, heighten, accelerate, be extended, be magnified, be amplified.

escapade NOUN = **stunt**, prank, adventure, caper, romp, frolic, fling, spree, antics; [inf] lark, scrape, shenanigans.

escape VERB 1 = **get away**, break out, run away, break free, flee, bolt, abscond, decamp, fly, steal away, slip away; [inf] skedaddle, vamoose, fly the coop; [Brit. inf] do a bunk, do a runner. 2 = **avoid**, evade, dodge, elude, circumvent, sidestep, steer clear of, shirk; [inf] duck, bilk; [Brit. inf] skive (off). 3 = **leak**, seep, pour out, gush, spurt, issue, flow, discharge, emanate, drain. ▶ NOUN 1 = **breakout**, getaway, flight. 2 = **avoidance**, evasion, dodging, eluding, elusion, circumvention. 3 = **leak**, leakage, seepage, gush, spurt, issue, flow, discharge, outflow, emanation, efflux.

escort NOUN 1 = **entourage**, retinue, attendants, train, cortège, bodyguard, protector, convoy, defender, contingent. 2 = **partner**, companion, gigolo, hostess, geisha; [inf] date; [dated] beau. ▶ VERB 1 = **accompany**, guide, conduct, lead, usher, shepherd, guard, protect, safeguard, defend. 2 = **partner**, accompany, take out, go out with, attend on.

esoteric ADJ = **abstruse**, obscure, cryptic, arcane, recondite, abstract, mysterious, hidden, secret, mystic, magical, occult, cabbalistic.

essence NOUN 1 = **fundamental nature**, substance, crux, quintessence, heart, lifeblood, kernel, marrow, pith, reality, actuality; [Philosophy] quiddity. 2 = **extract**, concentrate, distillate, tincture, elixir, abstraction.

essential ADJ 1 = **necessary**, important, indispensable, vital, crucial, needed, requisite. 2 = **basic**, fundamental,

chief, intrinsic, inherent, innate, elemental, characteristic, principal, cardinal.
Opposites: unimportant.

establish VERB 1 = **set up**, found, institute, form, start, begin, bring about, create, inaugurate, organize, build, construct, install, plant. 2 = **prove**, show to be true, show, demonstrate, confirm, attest to, certify, verify, evidence, substantiate, corroborate, validate, authenticate, ratify.
Opposites: disprove.

established ADJ = **accepted**, official, proven, settled, conventional, traditional, fixed, entrenched, inveterate, dyed in the wool.

establishment NOUN 1 = **formation**, foundation, founding, setting up, creation, inception, inauguration, building, construction, organization, installation. 2 = **residence**, house,

household, home, estate; [formal] dwelling, abode, domicile. 3 = **firm**, business, company, shop, store, concern, office, factory, organization, enterprise, corporation, conglomerate.

estate NOUN 1 = **property**, landholding, lands, manor, domain. 2 = **area**, piece of land, region, tract, development. 3 = **assets**, resources, effects, possessions, belongings, wealth, fortune, property.

esteem VERB = **respect**, admire, value, honour, look up to, think highly of, revere, venerate, appreciate, favour, approve of, like, love, cherish, prize, treasure.

estimate VERB = **work out**, calculate, assess, gauge, reckon, weigh up, evaluate, judge, appraise, guess, compute.
▶ NOUN 1 = **estimation**, valuation, costing, assessment, appraisal, evaluation. 2 = **opinion**, estimation, judgement, consideration, thinking,

mind, point of view, viewpoint, feeling, conviction, deduction, conclusion, guess, conjecture, surmise.

estimation NOUN = *see* **estimate** NOUN (**2**).

estrangement NOUN = **alienation**, parting, separation, divorce, break-up, split, breach, severance, division, hostility, antagonism, antipathy, disaffection.

estuary NOUN = **river mouth**; [Scottish] firth.

eternal ADJ = **endless**, everlasting, never-ending, without end, immortal, infinite, enduring, deathless, undying, permanent, indestructible, imperishable, immutable, ceaseless, incessant, constant, continuous, unchanging, unremitting, interminable, relentless, perpetual.

eternity NOUN = **immortality**, afterlife, everlasting life, the hereafter, the next world, heaven, paradise,

nirvana.

ethical ADJ = **moral**, honourable, upright, righteous, good, virtuous, decent, principled, honest, just, fair, right, correct, proper, fitting, seemly, high-minded, decorous.
Opposites: unethical, immoral.

euphoric ADJ = **elated**, joyful, ecstatic, jubilant, enraptured, rapturous, blissful, exhilarated, gleeful, excited, high-spirited, exalted, buoyant, intoxicated, merry; [inf] on cloud nine, in seventh heaven, over the moon, on a high.

evacuate VERB **1** = **leave**, abandon, vacate, move out of, pull out of, quit, withdraw from, retreat from, flee, depart from, go away from, retire from, decamp from, desert, forsake. **2** = **expel**, excrete, eject, discharge, eliminate, void, purge, drain.

evade VERB **1** = **avoid**, dodge, escape from, elude, circumvent,

sidestep, shake off, keep out of the way of, keep one's distance from, steer clear of, shun, shirk; [inf] duck, give the slip to, chicken out of.
2 = **dodge**, avoid, parry, fend off, quibble about, fudge, not give a straight answer to; [inf] duck, cop out of.

evaluate VERB = **assess**, put a price on, appraise, weigh up, size up, gauge, judge, rate, estimate, rank, calculate, reckon, measure, determine.

evaporate VERB
1 = **become vapour**, vaporize, volatilize.
2 = **dry**, dry up/out, dehydrate, desiccate, sear, parch. **3** = **vanish**, fade, disappear, melt away, dissolve, dissipate.

evasive ADJ = **equivocal**, equivocating, prevaricating, quibbling, indirect, roundabout, circuitous, oblique, cunning, artful, casuistic; [inf] cagey, waffling.

even ADJ **1** = **flat**, level, smooth, plane, uniform, flush, true. **2** = **constant**, steady, uniform, consistent, stable, unvarying, unchanging, unwavering, regular, unfluctuating. **3** = **equal**, identical, the same, alike, like, similar, comparable, commensurate, parallel, on a par.
Opposites: bumpy, uneven.
▶ ADV **1** = **yet**, still, more so, all the more, all the greater. **2** = **at all**, so much as, hardly, barely, scarcely.
▶ VERB **1** = **smooth**, level, flatten, make flush.
2 = **equalize**, make equal, make the same, balance up, standardize, regularize.

evening NOUN = **night**, close of day, twilight, dusk, nightfall, sunset, sundown.

event NOUN **1** = **occasion**, affair, business, matter, occurrence, happening, episode, circumstance, fact, eventuality, experience, phenomenon.
2 = **competition**, contest, fixture, engagement,

game, tournament, round, bout, race.
3 = end, conclusion, outcome, result, upshot, consequence, effect, aftermath.

eventful ADJ = **busy**, action-packed, lively, full, active, important, noteworthy, memorable, notable, remarkable, outstanding, fateful, momentous, significant, crucial, historic, critical, decisive, consequential. **Opposites:** uneventful, dull, insignificant.

eventual ADJ = **final**, closing, concluding, end, last, ultimate, resulting, resultant, later, ensuing, consequent, subsequent.

eventually ADV = **in the end**, ultimately, finally, at the end of the day, in the long run, when all is said and done, one day, some day, sooner or later, sometime.

everlasting ADJ = **never-ending**, endless, without end, eternal, perpetual, undying, immortal, deathless, indestructible, abiding, enduring,

infinite, boundless, timeless.

evermore ADV = **forever**, always, for all time, endlessly, without end, ceaselessly, unceasingly, constantly.

evict VERB = **turn out**, throw out, eject, expel, remove, oust, dispossess, dislodge; [inf] throw out on the streets, throw someone out on their ear, chuck out, kick/turf out, give the heave-ho to, give the bum's rush to.

evidence NOUN **1 = proof**, verification, confirmation, substantiation, corroboration, authentication, support, grounds. **2 = testimony**, sworn statement, deposition, declaration, allegation, affidavit, attestation.

evident ADJ = **obvious**, clear, apparent, plain, unmistakable, noticeable, conspicuous, perceptible, visible, discernible, transparent, manifest, patent, tangible, palpable, indisputable, undoubted, incontrovertible, incontestable.

evil ADJ **1** = **wicked**, wrong, bad, immoral, sinful, corrupt, vile, base, depraved, iniquitous, heinous, villainous, nefarious, sinister, reprobate, vicious, atrocious, malevolent, demonic, malicious, devilish, diabolic. **2** = **bad**, harmful, injurious, destructive, deleterious, pernicious, mischievous, malignant, venomous, noxious.
3 = **unfavourable**, adverse, unfortunate, unhappy, disastrous, catastrophic, ruinous, calamitous, unpropitious, inauspicious, dire, woeful.
Opposites: good.
▶ NOUN **1** = **wickedness**, wrong, bad, wrongdoing, sin, sinfulness, immorality, vice, iniquity, vileness, baseness, corruption, depravity, villainy, malevolence,

devilishness. **2** = **harm**, hurt, pain, misery, sorrow, suffering, disaster, misfortune, catastrophe, ruin, calamity, affliction, woe.
Opposites: goodness.

evoke VERB = **bring about**, cause, produce, bring forth, induce, arouse, excite, awaken, give rise to, stir up, stimulate, kindle, elicit, educe, summon up, call forth, conjure up, invoke, raise.

evolution NOUN
= **development**, progress, growth, progression, unrolling, expansion, natural selection, Darwinism.

evolve VERB = **develop**, grow, progress, emerge, mature, expand, unfold, unroll, open out, work out.

exacerbate VERB
= **aggravate**, make worse, worsen, intensify; [inf] add fuel to the fire, put salt on the wound.

exact ADJ **1** = **accurate**, precise, correct, faithful, close, true, unerring, literal, strict; [inf] on the nail; [Brit. inf] spot on, bang on; [formal] veracious.

2 = **careful**, precise, meticulous, painstaking, methodical, conscientious, punctilious, rigorous, scrupulous, exacting.

Opposites: inaccurate, careless.

▶ VERB = **require**, demand, extract, extort, insist on, request, compel, call for, command, impose, wring, wrest, squeeze.

exacting ADJ = see **difficult (1)**.

exaggerate VERB = **overstate**, overemphasize, overstress, overestimate, overvalue, magnify, embellish, amplify, embroider, colour, add colour, over-elaborate, aggrandize, overdraw, hyperbolize; [inf] make a mountain out of a molehill, lay it on thick, lay it on with a trowel.

Opposites: understate, minimize.

exalted ADJ 1 = **high**, high-ranking, lofty, grand, eminent, elevated, prestigious, august.

2 = **elated**, exultant, jubilant, triumphant, joyful, rapturous, ecstatic, blissful, rhapsodic, transported.

examination NOUN 1 = **study**, inspection, scrutiny, investigation, review, analysis, research, observation, exploration, consideration, appraisal.

2 = **check-up**, inspection, observation, assessment.

3 = **questioning**, cross-examination, cross-questioning.

examine VERB 1 = **look at/into**, study, investigate, inquire into, survey, analyse, review, research, explore, sift, probe, check out, consider, appraise, weigh, weigh up, scan, inspect, vet. 2 = **inspect**, look at, check over, assess, observe, give a check-up to, scrutinize.

3 = **put questions to**, question, interrogate, quiz, test, cross-examine, cross-question; [inf] give the third-degree to, grill, pump.

example NOUN 1 = **sample**, specimen, instance, representative, case, case in point, illustration. 2 = **model**, pattern, ideal, standard, paradigm, criterion.

exasperate VERB = **anger**, infuriate, annoy, irritate, madden, incense, enrage, provoke, irk, vex, gall, pique, try someone's patience; [inf] get on someone's nerves, make someone's blood boil, bug, needle, get to, rile.

excavate VERB = **dig**, dig out, quarry, mine, burrow, hollow out, scoop out, gouge, cut out, unearth.

exceed VERB = **be greater than**, surpass, beat, outdo, outstrip, outshine, transcend, go beyond, better, pass, top, cap, overshadow, eclipse.

exceedingly ADV = **extremely**, very, extraordinarily, unusually, tremendously, enormously, vastly, greatly, highly, supremely, hugely, inordinately, superlatively.

excellence NOUN = **eminence**, merit, pre-eminence, distinction, greatness, fineness, quality, superiority, transcendence, supremacy, value, worth, skill.

excellent ADJ = **very good**, first-rate, first-class, of a high standard, of high quality, great, fine, distinguished, superior, superb, outstanding, marvellous, eminent, pre-eminent, noted, notable, supreme, admirable, superlative, sterling, worthy, prime, select, model, exemplary, consummate, remarkable; [inf] A1, top-notch, ace, tip-top, super; [Brit. inf] smashing, brilliant, brill.
Opposites: poor, inferior.

except PREP = **with the exception of**, excepting, excluding, besides, leaving out, barring, bar, other than, omitting, saving, save.

exception NOUN 1 = **exclusion**, omission.

2 = special case, anomaly, irregularity, peculiarity, oddity, deviation, departure, quirk, freak.

■ **take exception = object**, be offended, take offence, resent, take umbrage, demur, disagree, cavil.

exceptional ADJ
1 = unusual, uncommon, abnormal, out of the ordinary, atypical, rare, odd, anomalous, singular, peculiar, inconsistent, aberrant, deviant, divergent.
2 = unusually good, excellent, extraordinary, remarkable, outstanding, special, phenomenal, prodigious.
Opposites: normal, usual, average.

excerpt NOUN = **extract**, quote, citation, quotation, passage, selection, highlight, part, section, fragment, piece, portion.

excess NOUN **1 = surplus**, over-abundance, glut, surfeit, superfluity, plethora, superabundance, overkill.
2 = remainder, residue, leftovers, overflow, overload.
3 = immoderation, lack of restraint, overindulgence, intemperance, debauchery, dissipation, dissolution.
Opposites: shortage, moderation.
▶ ADJ = **extra**, additional, too much, surplus, spare, superfluous, redundant.

excessive ADJ = **too much**, immoderate, extravagant, lavish, superabundant, unreasonable, undue, uncalled for, extreme, inordinate, unjustifiable, unwarranted, unnecessary, needless, disproportionate, exorbitant, outrageous, intemperate, unconscionable.

exchange VERB = **trade**, swap, barter, interchange, reciprocate, bandy.
▶ NOUN = **trade**, trade-off, barter, swapping, traffic, dealings, interchange, giving and taking,

reciprocity.

excise VERB 1 = **cut out/off**, remove, eradicate, extirpate; [technical] resect. 2 = **delete**, remove, cut out, cross/strike out, erase, expunge, eliminate, blue-pencil, expurgate, bowdlerize.

excitable ADJ = **temperamental**, emotional, highly strung, nervous, edgy, mercurial, volatile, tempestuous, hot-tempered, quick-tempered, hot-headed, passionate, fiery, irascible, testy, moody, choleric. **Opposites:** calm.

excite VERB 1 = **stimulate**, animate, rouse, arouse, move, thrill, inflame, provoke, stir up, electrify, intoxicate, titillate, discompose; [inf] turn on, get going, work up; [Brit. inf] wind up. 2 = **bring about**, cause, rouse, arouse, awaken, incite, provoke, stimulate, kindle, evoke, stir up, elicit, engender, foment, instigate.

excited ADJ = **aroused**, animated, stimulated, thrilled, agitated, impassioned, hysterical, frenzied, delirious, enthusiastic, lively, exuberant, exhilarated, overwrought, feverish, wild; [inf] wound up, high, turned on. **Opposites:** calm, indifferent.

excitement NOUN 1 = **animation**, enthusiasm, passion, agitation, emotion, exhilaration, anticipation, elation, feverishness, ferment, tumult, discomposure, perturbation. 2 = **thrill**, adventure, stimulation, pleasure; [inf] kick. 3 = **arousal**, stimulation, awakening, evocation, kindling.

exciting ADJ = **thrilling**, exhilarating, stimulating, gripping, dramatic, stirring, intoxicating, rousing, electrifying, invigorating, spine-tingling, riveting, moving, inspiring, provocative, titillating,

sensational.
Opposites: boring, uninteresting.

exclaim VERB = **call**, cry, call/cry out, shout, yell, roar, bellow, shriek, proclaim, utter, vociferate;
[dated] ejaculate.

exclamation NOUN = **call**, cry, shout, yell, roar, bellow, shriek, utterance, interjection, expletive;
[dated] ejaculation.

exclude VERB **1** = **bar**, debar, keep out, shut out, prohibit, forbid, prevent, disallow, refuse, ban, veto, blackball, proscribe, interdict, stand in the way of.
2 = **eliminate**, rule out, preclude, reject, set aside, omit, pass over, leave out, ignore, repudiate, except. **3** = **be exclusive of**, not include, not be inclusive of, omit, leave out.
Opposites: include.

exclusive ADJ **1** = **select**, selective, restrictive, restricted, private, closed, limited, discriminating, cliquish, snobbish,
fashionable, chic, elegant, upmarket;
[inf] ritzy; [Brit. inf] posh, swish. **2** = **not including**, excluding, with the exception of, except for, not counting, leaving out, omitting.
Opposites: inclusive.

excommunicate VERB = **exclude**, expel, cast out, banish, eject, remove, bar, debar, proscribe, anathematize, interdict, repudiate.

excrement NOUN = **waste matter**, excreta, faeces, stools, droppings, ordure, dung, manure.

excrete VERB = **defecate**, urinate, pass, void, discharge, eject, evacuate, expel, eliminate, emit.

excruciating ADJ = **agonizing**, unbearable, insufferable, harrowing, searing, acute, piercing, racking, torturous, severe, intense.

excusable ADJ = **forgivable**, pardonable, defensible, justifiable, understandable, condonable, venial.

excuse NOUN
1 = **explanation**, reason, grounds, justification, defence, apology, vindication, mitigation, mitigating circumstances.
2 = **pretext**, pretence, cover-up, front, subterfuge, fabrication, evasion. 3 = **apology**, travesty, mockery, pitiful example.
▶ VERB 1 = **forgive**, pardon, absolve, acquit, exonerate, make allowances for, bear with, tolerate, indulge, exculpate. 2 = **let off**, exempt, spare, release, absolve, relieve, free, liberate.
Opposites: condemn.

execute VERB 1 = **put to death**, kill, carry out a sentence of death.
2 = **carry out**, accomplish, perform, implement, effect, bring off, achieve, complete, fulfil, enact, enforce, put into effect, do, engineer, prosecute, discharge, realize, attain, render.

exemplary ADJ = **model**, ideal, perfect, excellent, admirable, commendable, faultless, praiseworthy, laudable, honourable, meritorious.

exemplify VERB = **typify**, personify, epitomize, represent, embody, illustrate, show, demonstrate, symbolize.

exempt VERB = **free from**, release from, make an exception for, exclude from, excuse from, absolve from, spare, liberate from, relieve of, discharge from, dismiss from; [inf] let off.

exercise NOUN 1 = **activity**, exertion, effort, action, work, movement, training, gymnastics, sports, aerobics, callisthenics, keep-fit, workout, warm-up, limbering up, drill.
2 = **employment**, use, application, utilization, implementation, practice, operation, exertion, discharge.
▶ VERB 1 = **work out**, train, do exercises, exert oneself, drill. 2 = **employ**, use, make use of, utilize, apply, implement, exert.

3 = worry, disturb, trouble, perplex, distress, preoccupy, annoy, make uneasy, perturb, vex.

exert VERB **1 = employ**, exercise, use, make use of, utilize, apply, wield, bring to bear, set in motion, expend, spend. **2 = apply oneself**, make an effort, spare no effort, try hard, do one's best, give one's all, strive, endeavour, struggle, labour, toil, strain, work, push, drive; [inf] put one's back into it.

exhaust VERB **1 = tire**, wear out, fatigue, drain, weary, sap, debilitate, prostrate, enfeeble, disable; [inf] knock out; [Brit. inf] knacker, fag out; [N. Amer. inf] poop. **2 = use up**, deplete, consume, finish, expend, run through, waste, squander, dissipate, fritter away; [inf] blow. **Opposites:** invigorate, replenish.

exhausting ADJ **= tiring**, fatiguing, wearing, gruelling, punishing, strenuous, arduous, back-breaking, taxing, laborious, enervating, sapping, debilitating.

exhaustion NOUN **= tiredness**, fatigue, weariness, weakness, collapse, debility, prostration, faintness, lassitude, enervation.

exhaustive ADJ **= all-inclusive**, comprehensive, intensive, all-out, in-depth, total, all-embracing, thorough, encyclopedic, complete, full, thoroughgoing, extensive, profound, far-reaching, sweeping. **Opposites:** perfunctory.

exhibit VERB **1 = put on display**, show, display, demonstrate, set out/forth, present, model, expose, air, unveil, flaunt, parade. **2 = show**, express, indicate, reveal, display, demonstrate, betray, give away, disclose, manifest, evince, evidence.

exhibition NOUN **= display**, show, fair, demonstration, presentation, exposition, spectacle.

exhilarate VERB = **make happy**, elate, delight, gladden, brighten, enliven, excite, thrill, animate, invigorate, lift, perk up, stimulate, raise someone's spirits, revitalize, exalt, inspirit; [inf] pep up.

exhilaration NOUN = **elation**, joy, happiness, delight, gladness, high spirits, excitement, gaiety, glee, animation, vivacity, exaltation, mirth, hilarity.

exhort VERB = **urge**, persuade, press, encourage, prompt, sway, advise, counsel, incite, goad, stimulate, push, entreat, bid, enjoin, admonish, warn.

exile VERB = **banish**, deport, expatriate, expel, drive out, eject, oust, uproot.
▸ NOUN 1 = **banishment**, deportation, expatriation, uprooting, separation. 2 = **expatriate**, deportee, refugee, displaced person, outcast, pariah.

exist VERB 1 = **live**, be, have existence, have being, have life, breathe, draw breath, subsist, be extant, be viable. 2 = **survive**, live, stay alive, subsist, eke out a living.
Opposites: die.

existing ADJ = **in existence**, existent, extant, living, surviving, remaining, enduring, prevailing, abiding, present, current.

exit NOUN 1 = **way out**, door, doorway, gate, gateway, opening, egress, portal. 2 = **departure**, withdrawal, leaving, going, retirement, leave-taking, retreat, flight, exodus, farewell, adieu.
Opposites: entrance, arrival.

exonerate VERB = **absolve**, clear, acquit, discharge, vindicate, exculpate, dismiss, let off, excuse, pardon, justify.
Opposites: incriminate.

exorbitant ADJ = **excessive**, unreasonable, extortionate, extreme, immoderate, outrageous, inordinate, preposterous, monstrous, unwarranted, undue, unconscionable. **Opposites:** moderate.

exotic ADJ **1** = **foreign**, tropical, imported, alien, novel, introduced, external, extraneous. **2** = **striking**, outrageous, colourful, extraordinary, sensational, extravagant, unusual, remarkable, astonishing, strange, outlandish, bizarre, peculiar, impressive, glamorous, fascinating, mysterious, curious, different, unfamiliar.

expand VERB **1** = **grow/ become/make larger**, enlarge, increase in size, swell, inflate, magnify, amplify, add to, distend, lengthen, heighten, broaden, thicken, prolong, stretch, extend, multiply, dilate. **2** = **open out**, spread out, unfold, unfurl, unravel, unroll. **Opposites:** contract.

expanse NOUN = **area**, stretch, region, tract, extent, breadth, space, sweep, field, plain, surface, extension.

expansive ADJ = **sociable**, outgoing, friendly, affable, talkative, communicative, uninhibited, open, frank, genial, extrovert, garrulous, loquacious.

expect VERB **1** = **suppose**, assume, believe, imagine, think, presume, surmise, calculate, conjecture; [inf] reckon. **2** = **anticipate**, envisage, predict, forecast, await, look for, look forward to, watch for, hope for, contemplate, bargain for, have in prospect. **3** = **demand**, insist on, require, count on, rely on, call for, look for, wish, want, hope for.

expectant ADJ **1** = **hopeful**, eager, anticipating, anticipatory, ready, watchful, in suspense, anxious, on tenterhooks; [inf] keyed up. **2** = **pregnant**, expecting, in the family way; [technical] gravid.

expectation NOUN **1** = **assumption**, belief,

supposition, presumption, assurance, conjecture, surmise, reckoning, calculation, confidence.
2 = **prospects**, hopes, outlook, good fortune.

expedient ADJ
= **convenient**, useful, pragmatic, advantageous, beneficial, profitable, gainful, practical, desirable, appropriate, suitable, advisable, apt, fit, effective, helpful, politic, judicious, timely, opportune, propitious.
▶ NOUN = **means**, measure, stratagem, plan, scheme, plot, manoeuvre, trick, ploy, ruse, device, artifice, contrivance, invention.

expel VERB 1 = **evict**, banish, oust, drive out, exile, throw out, cast out, expatriate, deport, proscribe, outlaw; [inf] chuck out, kick out, boot out, turf out, heave out, send packing, give the bum's rush to.
2 = **discharge**, eject, eliminate, excrete, evacuate, void, belch, spew out.

expend VERB = **spend**, pay out, lay out, disburse, lavish, squander, waste, fritter away, use up, consume, exhaust, deplete, sap, empty, finish off.

expendable ADJ
= **disposable**, dispensable, replaceable, non-essential, inessential, unimportant.
Opposites: indispensable.

expense NOUN = **cost**, price, outlay, payment, expenditure, outgoings, charge, amount, fee, rate, figure, disbursement.

expensive ADJ
= **overpriced**, exorbitant, steep, costly, dear, high-priced, extortionate, extravagant, lavish. = *See also* **exorbitant**.
Opposites: cheap.

experience NOUN
1 = **familiarity**, knowledge, involvement, practice, practical knowledge, participation, contact, acquaintance, exposure, observation, understanding. 2 = **event**, incident, occurrence,

happening, affair, episode, adventure, encounter, circumstance, test, trial, case, ordeal.
▸ VERB = **have experience of**, undergo, encounter, meet, feel, become familiar with, come into contact with, go through, live through, suffer, sustain.

experienced ADJ = **practised**, proficient, accomplished, skilful, seasoned, trained, expert, competent, adept, capable, knowledgeable, qualified, well versed, professional, mature, veteran, master.
Opposites: novice.

experiment NOUN = **test**, investigation, trial, trial run, try-out, examination, observation, enquiry, demonstration, venture.
▸ VERB = **conduct experiments**, carry out tests/trials, conduct research, test, examine, investigate, explore, observe.

experimental ADJ = **trial**, exploratory, pilot, tentative, speculative, preliminary, under review.

expert NOUN = **authority**, specialist, professional, master, adept, pundit, maestro, virtuoso, connoisseur; [inf] old hand, ace, wizard, buff, pro; [Brit. inf] dab hand.
▸ ADJ = **accomplished**, brilliant, competent, adept, master, able, proficient, skilful, experienced, practised, qualified, knowledgeable, capable, specialist, adroit, deft, dexterous, clever; [inf] crack, top-notch, wizard.
Opposites: incompetent.

expire VERB 1 = **run out**, lapse, finish, end, come to an end, terminate, conclude, discontinue, stop, cease. 2 = *See* **die** (1).

explain VERB 1 = **describe**, give an explanation of, make clear/plain, teach, illustrate, demonstrate, define, spell out, interpret, clear up, throw light on, clarify, elucidate, explicate, decipher, expound, decode, delineate, expose, resolve, solve, gloss, unravel, unfold; [inf] get across. **2 = account for**, justify, give a reason for, give a justification for, excuse, defend, vindicate, legitimize, rationalize, mitigate.

explanation NOUN **1 = description**, interpretation, elucidation, explication, demonstration, definition, clarification, deciphering, decoding, expounding, illustration, exposure, resolution, solution. **2 = account**, justification, reason, excuse, defence, apology, vindication, mitigation, apologia.

explanatory ADJ **= expository**, descriptive, interpretative, illustrative, demonstrative, elucidative, elucidatory, explicative, justificatory, exegetic.

expletive NOUN **= swear word**, oath, curse, obscenity, epithet, exclamation, four-letter word, dirty word.

explicit ADJ **1 = clear**, understandable, detailed, crystal-clear, direct, plain, obvious, precise, exact, straightforward, definite, categorical, specific, unequivocal, unambiguous. **2 = unrestrained**, unreserved, uninhibited, open, candid, frank, direct, full-frontal, no holds barred.
Opposites: vague, implicit.

explode VERB **1 = blow up**, detonate, go off, erupt, burst, fly apart, fly into pieces; [inf] go bang. **2 = disprove**, invalidate, refute, discredit, debunk, repudiate, belie, give the lie to, ridicule; [inf] blow up, blow sky-high, knock the bottom from.

exploit VERB **1 = make use of**, use, put to use, utilize, turn/put to good use, profit from/by, turn to account, capitalize on, make capital out of; [inf] milk, cash in on. **2 = take advantage of**, abuse, impose on,

e

misuse; [inf] take for a ride, walk all over, put one over on.

▶ NOUN = **feat**, deed, adventure, stunt, achievement, accomplishment, attainment.

explore VERB 1 = **travel**, tour, range over, traverse, survey, inspect, scout, reconnoitre, prospect. 2 = **investigate**, look into, enquire into, consider, examine, scrutinize, research, study, review, take stock of.

explosion NOUN 1 = **blast**, bang, detonation, eruption, discharge, boom, rumble, report, thunder, crash, clap, crack. 2 = **outburst**, flare-up, fit, outbreak, eruption, paroxysm.

explosive ADJ 1 = **volatile**, unstable, inflammable, eruptive. 2 = **tense**, charged, serious, critical, dangerous, hazardous, overwrought, ugly, volcanic.

exponent NOUN 1 = **advocate**, supporter, upholder, backer, defender, champion, spokesperson, promoter, proponent, propagandist. 2 = **practitioner**, performer, interpreter, player, presenter, executant.

expose VERB 1 = **uncover**, bare, lay bare, strip, reveal, denude. 2 = **reveal**, show, display, exhibit, make obvious, disclose, manifest, unveil. 3 = **disclose**, bring to light, reveal, uncover, divulge, let out, denounce, unearth, unmask, detect, betray; [inf] spill the beans on, blow the whistle on. **Opposites:** cover, conceal.

express VERB = **communicate**, convey, put across/over, utter, voice, air, articulate, state, give vent to, phrase, word, put into words, indicate, show, demonstrate, reveal.

expression NOUN 1 = **statement**, utterance, pronouncement, assertion, proclamation, articulation, voicing. 2 = **word**, phrase, term, choice of words, turn of phrase, wording, language, phrasing, speech, diction, idiom, style, delivery, intonation; [formal] locution. **3 = look**, countenance, appearance, air, mien, aspect. **4 = feeling**, emotion, passion, intensity, power, force, imagination, artistry, poignancy, depth, spirit, vividness, ardour.

expressionless ADJ
1 = blank, deadpan, inscrutable, emotionless, impassive, poker-faced, straight-faced, vacuous. **2 = dull**, dry, boring, wooden, undemonstrative, apathetic, devoid of feeling.
Opposites: expressive.

expressive ADJ
1 = eloquent, demonstrative, emotional, suggestive, telling, vivid. **2 = passionate**, intense, emotional, moving, poignant, striking, eloquent, vivid, evocative, artistic, sympathetic.
Opposites: expressionless, unemotional.

expressly ADV
1 = absolutely, explicitly, clearly, plainly, distinctly, specifically, unequivocally, precisely. **2 = specially**, especially, particularly, solely, specifically, singularly.

extend VERB **1 = expand**, increase, enlarge, lengthen, widen, broaden, stretch, draw out, elongate. **2 = increase**, widen, add to, expand, augment, enhance, develop, supplement, amplify. **3 = prolong**, increase, lengthen, protract, drag out, stretch out, spin out. **4 = offer**, give, proffer, present, hold out, confer, advance, impart. **5 = continue**, stretch, carry on, run on, last, unroll, range.
Opposites: contract, curtail.

extensive ADJ **1 = large**, sizeable, substantial, spacious, considerable,

vast, immense. **2 = broad**, wide, wide-ranging, comprehensive, thorough, complete, all-embracing, inclusive.
Opposites: small, limited.

extent NOUN **1 = length**, area, expanse, stretch, range, scope. **2 = breadth**, range, scope, degree, comprehensiveness, completeness, thoroughness.

exterior NOUN **= outside**, surface, front, covering, facade, shell, skin.
▶ ADJ **= outer**, outside, outermost, outward, external, surface, superficial.
Opposites: interior.

exterminate VERB **= kill**, destroy, annihilate, eradicate, extirpate, abolish, eliminate; [inf] wipe out, bump off.

extinguish VERB **1 = put out**, blow out, quench, smother, douse, snuff out, dampen down, stifle, choke off.
2 = destroy, kill, end, remove, annihilate, wipe out, eliminate, abolish, eradicate, erase, expunge,

suppress, extirpate.
Opposites: light, kindle.

extol VERB **= praise**, sing someone's praises, applaud, acclaim, pay tribute to, commend, exalt, congratulate, compliment, celebrate, glorify, eulogize; [formal] laud.
Opposites: condemn.

extra ADJ **1 = additional**, further, supplementary, supplemental, added, subsidiary, auxiliary, ancillary, other, accessory. **2 = spare**, surplus, left over, excess, redundant, superfluous, reserve, unused.

extract VERB **1 = pull out**, draw out, take out, pluck out, wrench out, prise out, tear out, uproot, withdraw. **2 = extort**, exact, force, coerce, elicit, wring, wrest, squeeze.
▶ NOUN **1 = concentrate**, essence, distillate, juice, solution, decoction.
2 = excerpt, passage, cutting, clipping, abstract, citation, selection, quotation,

fragment.

extraordinary ADJ
1 = **exceptional**, unusual,
rare, uncommon, unique,
singular, outstanding,
striking, remarkable,
phenomenal, marvellous,
wonderful, signal,
peculiar, unprecedented.
2 = **amazing**, surprising,
unusual, remarkable,
strange, astounding, odd.
3 = **odd**, strange, curious,
bizarre, unconventional,
weird.
Opposites: ordinary,
commonplace.

extravagant ADJ
1 = **spendthrift**, profligate,
wasteful, lavish, reckless,
imprudent, excessive,
improvident, prodigal,
thriftless.
2 = **exaggerated**,
excessive, unrestrained,
outrageous, immoderate,
preposterous, absurd,
irrational, reckless, wild;
[inf] over-the-top, OTT.
3 = **exorbitant**, excessive,
unreasonable,
extortionate, inordinate,
immoderate, expensive,
steep, dear, costly,
overpriced.

Opposites: thrifty,
restrained.

extreme ADJ 1 = **great**,
greatest, acute, intense,
severe, highest, utmost,
maximum, supreme,
high, ultimate,
exceptional,
extraordinary. 2 = **severe**,
harsh, Draconian,
stringent, drastic, strict,
stern, unrelenting,
relentless, unbending,
uncompromising,
unyielding, radical,
overzealous. 3 = **fanatical**,
immoderate,
intemperate, militant,
radical, intransigent,
extremist, exaggerated,
excessive, unreasonable,
overzealous, outrageous.
Opposites: moderate.
▶ NOUN = **maximum**, highest
point, pinnacle, climax,
acme, zenith, apex, ne
plus ultra.

extremely ADV = **very**,
exceedingly,
exceptionally, intensely,
greatly, acutely, utterly,
excessively, inordinately,
markedly,
extraordinarily,
uncommonly, severely,

terribly; [inf] awfully.

extrovert ADJ = **outgoing**, extroverted, sociable, friendly, social, lively, cheerful, effervescent, exuberant.

Opposites: introverted.

exuberant ADJ **1** = **elated**, exhilarated, cheerful, sparkling, full of life, animated, lively, high-spirited, spirited, buoyant, effervescent, vivacious, excited, ebullient, exultant, enthusiastic, irrepressible, energetic, vigorous, zestful; [inf] upbeat, bouncy. **2** = **profuse**, luxuriant, lush, thriving, abundant, superabundant, prolific, teeming, lavish, copious, rich, plentiful, abounding, overflowing, rank.

Opposites: depressed, meagre.

exultant ADJ = **joyful**, overjoyed, jubilant, triumphant, delighted, ecstatic, cock-a-hoop, gleeful, enraptured, transported.

eyeful NOUN **1** = **look**, good look, view, stare, gaze; [inf] load, gander; [Brit. inf] butcher's, shufti. **2** = **vision**, dream, beauty, dazzler; [inf] stunner, knockout, sight for sore eyes, bobby-dazzler.

eyesore NOUN = **blemish**, blot, scar, blight, disfigurement, defacement, defect, monstrosity, carbuncle, atrocity, disgrace, ugliness.

eyewitness NOUN = **witness**, observer, onlooker, bystander, passer-by, spectator, watcher, viewer, beholder.

Ff

fabric NOUN **1** = **cloth**, material, textile, stuff. **2** = **structure**, make-up, framework, frame, constitution, essence.

fabricate VERB **1** = **assemble**, construct, build, make, manufacture, erect, put together, form, produce, fashion, frame, shape. **2** = **make up**, invent, concoct, think up, hatch, devise, trump up, coin.

fabulous ADJ **1** = *See* **marvellous**. **2** = **mythical**, legendary, fantastical, imaginary, fictional, fictitious, unreal, made up, fanciful, apocryphal.

face NOUN **1** = **countenance**, visage, physiognomy, features, lineaments; [inf] mug, clock, dial; [Brit. inf] phizog, phiz. **2** = **expression**, look, demeanour, air, aspect.
▶ VERB **1** = **look on to**, overlook, look towards, give on to, be opposite to. **2** = **encounter**, meet, confront, withstand, cope with, deal with, brazen out, defy, brave, oppose; [inf] get to grips with, meet head-on. **3** = **dress**, finish, polish, smooth, level, coat, surface, clad, veneer. Opposites: evade.

facet NOUN = **aspect**, feature, characteristic, factor, element, angle, side, point, part.

facetious ADJ = **flippant**, jocular, frivolous, light-hearted, tongue-in-cheek, waggish, jocose. Opposites: serious.

facile ADJ **1** = **insincere**, superficial, glib, shallow, slick, urbane, suave, bland. **2** = **easy**, simple, uncomplicated, unchallenging.

facility NOUN **1 = ease**, effortlessness, skill, adroitness, smoothness, fluency, slickness.
2 = amenity, resource, service, benefit, convenience, equipment, aid, opportunity.

fact NOUN **1 = truth**, actuality, reality, certainty, certitude.
2 = detail, particular, information, point, item, factor, element, feature, circumstance, specific.
Opposites: falsehood.

faction NOUN **= group**, section, side, party, band, set, ring, division, contingent, lobby, camp, bloc, clique, coalition, confederacy, coterie, caucus, cabal, junta, ginger group, splinter group, pressure group; [inf] gang, crew.

factor NOUN **= element**, part, component, ingredient, constituent, point, detail, item, facet, aspect, feature, characteristic, consideration, influence, circumstance, thing, determinant.

factual ADJ **= real**, realistic, true, fact-based, true-to-life, truthful, authentic, genuine, accurate, sure, exact, precise, honest, faithful, literal, matter-of-fact, verbatim, word-for-word, objective, unbiased, unprejudiced, unvarnished, unadorned, unadulterated, unexaggerated.
Opposites: untrue, fictitious.

fad NOUN **= craze**, mania, enthusiasm, vogue, fashion, trend, mode, fancy, whim.

fade VERB **1 = grow pale**, lose colour, become paler, become bleached, become washed out, dull, dim, lose lustre. **2 = grow less**, dwindle, diminish, decline, die away, disappear, vanish, die, peter out, dissolve, melt away, grow faint, wane, fail, evanesce.
Opposites: increase.

fail VERB **1 = not succeed**, be unsuccessful, fall

through, be frustrated, break down, be defeated, be in vain, collapse, founder, misfire, meet with disaster, come to grief, come to nothing, run aground, go astray; [inf] come a cropper, bite the dust, fizzle out, miss the mark, not come up to scratch. **2 = go bankrupt**, collapse, crash, go under, become insolvent, go into receivership, cease trading, be closed, close down; [inf] fold, flop, go bust, go broke. **3 = let down**, desert, neglect, abandon, forsake, disappoint. **4 = omit**, neglect, forget, be unable.
Opposites: succeed.

failing NOUN = **fault**, shortcoming, weakness, imperfection, defect, flaw, blemish, frailty, foible, drawback.
Opposites: strength.

failure NOUN **1 = fiasco**, vain attempt, defeat, debacle, blunder; [inf] botch, flop, washout. **2 = loser**, incompetent,

non-achiever, disappointment, ne'er-do-well; [inf] no-hoper, dud, flop, washout. **3 = omission**, neglect, negligence, dereliction, remissness, delinquency. **Opposites:** success.

faint ADJ **1 = indistinct**, unclear, obscure, dim, pale, faded, bleached. **2 = soft**, muted, indistinct, low, weak, feeble, subdued, stifled, whispered. **3 = slight**, small, remote, vague, minimal. **4 = dizzy**, giddy, light-headed, muzzy, weak, weak-headed, vertiginous; [inf] woozy. **Opposites:** clear, loud.
▶ VERB = **lose consciousness**, black out, pass out, collapse, swoon; [inf] keel over, conk out, flake out.

fair¹ ADJ **1 = just**, impartial, unbiased, unprejudiced, objective, even-handed, disinterested, dispassionate, equitable, detached, above board, lawful, legal, legitimate, proper, square; [inf] on the level. **2 = reasonable**, tolerable, passable, satisfactory, respectable, decent, goodish, moderate, average, middling, adequate, sufficient, ample, so-so. **3 = blond/blonde**, light, yellow, golden, flaxen, light brown, strawberry blonde. **4 = beautiful**, pretty, lovely, attractive, good-looking; [Scottish & N. English] bonny; [poetic/literary] beauteous; [archaic] comely. **5 = fine**, dry, bright, clear, sunny, cloudless, unclouded. **Opposites:** unfair, ugly.

fair² NOUN **1 = exhibition**, display, show, exhibit, exposition, expo. **2 = festival**, carnival, fête, gala.

fairly ADV **1 = justly**, equitably, impartially, even-handedly, without prejudice, objectively. **2 = reasonably**, quite, pretty, passably, tolerably, moderately, satisfactorily, rather, somewhat, adequately.

faith NOUN **1 = trust**, belief, confidence, conviction, credence, reliance, credit, optimism, hopefulness. **2 = religion**, church, denomination, belief, creed, persuasion, teaching, doctrine, sect. **Opposites:** mistrust.

faithful ADJ **1 = loyal**, devoted, constant, dependable, true, reliable, trustworthy, staunch, unswerving, unwavering, steadfast, dutiful, dedicated, committed. **2 = accurate**, true, exact, precise, close, strict, unerring; [Brit. inf] spot on, bang on. **Opposites:** unfaithful, inaccurate.

fake ADJ **1 = sham**, imitation, false, counterfeit, forged, fraudulent, bogus, spurious, pseudo, mock, simulated, artificial, synthetic, reproduction, ersatz; [inf] phoney. **2 = assumed**, affected, feigned, put on, pseudo, insincere; [inf] phoney. **Opposites:** genuine, authentic.
▶ NOUN **1 = sham**, imitation, forgery, counterfeit, copy, reproduction,

hoax. **2** = **fraud**, charlatan, impostor, hoaxer, cheat, humbug, mountebank, quack; [inf] phoney.

fall VERB **1** = **drop**, descend, come/go down, sink, plummet, cascade, gravitate. **2** = **fall down/ over**, collapse, fall in a heap, trip, trip over, stumble, slip, tumble, slide, topple over, keel over, go head over heels, take a spill. **3** = **decrease**, dwindle, go down, grow less, diminish, plummet, depreciate, slump, deteriorate.
▸ NOUN **1** = **tumble**, trip, spill, stumble, slide, collapse. **2** = **downfall**, demise, collapse, ruin, failure, decline, deterioration, destruction, overthrow. **3** = **decrease**, lessening, cut, dip, reduction, depreciation, slump.
▪ **fall apart** = see **disintegrate**.
▪ **fall back** = see **retreat** VERB (**1**).
▪ **fall back on** = **resort to**, have recourse to, call into play, call upon, make use of, use, employ, rely on.

fallacy NOUN = **misconception**, false notion, error, mistake, misapprehension, miscalculation, delusion, misjudgement.

false ADJ **1** = **untrue**, untruthful, fictitious, inaccurate, misleading, invented, concocted, fabricated, incorrect, wrong, faulty, erroneous, unfounded, invalid, forged, fraudulent, spurious. **2** = **treacherous**, disloyal, unfaithful, faithless, traitorous, two-faced, double-dealing, untrustworthy, deceitful, untrue, deceiving, deceptive, duplicitous, dishonourable, perfidious, dishonest, hypocritical, unreliable, unsound, lying, mendacious.
Opposites: true, loyal, faithful.

falsehood NOUN = **lie**, untruth, false statement, fib, falsification, fabrication, invention, piece of fiction, fairy

story, exaggeration;
[inf] whopper.
Opposites: truth.

falsify VERB **= alter**, doctor, tamper with, forge, counterfeit, distort, pervert, adulterate.

falter VERB **1 = hesitate**, waver, delay, drag one's feet, vacillate, shilly-shally, blow hot and cold, be undecided, sit on the fence, oscillate, fluctuate; [Brit.] hum and haw. **2 = stammer**, stutter, speak haltingly.

fame NOUN **= renown**, celebrity, eminence, notability, note, distinction, prominence, mark, esteem, importance, greatness, account, pre-eminence, glory, honour, illustriousness, stardom, reputation, repute, notoriety, infamy.
Opposites: obscurity.

familiar ADJ **1 = well known**, known, recognized, accustomed, common, customary, everyday, ordinary, commonplace, frequent, habitual, usual, repeated, stock, routine, mundane, run-of-the-mill, conventional, household; [Brit. inf] common or garden. **2 = overfamiliar**, presumptuous, disrespectful, forward, bold, impudent, impertinent, intrusive, pushy.
Opposites: unfamiliar.

■ **familiar with**
= acquainted with, knowledgeable about, informed about, expert in, conversant with, well up on, au fait with, at home with, no stranger to, au courant with.

family NOUN **1 = household**, ménage, clan, tribe. **2 = children**, offspring, progeny, brood, descendants; [inf] kids; [Law] issue, scions. **3 = ancestry**, extraction, parentage, pedigree, birth, background, descent, lineage, genealogy, line, bloodline, stock, dynasty, house, forebears, forefathers.

famine NOUN
1 = starvation, hunger,

lack of food. **2** = **scarcity**, shortage, insufficiency, lack, want, dearth, paucity, deficiency.

famished ADJ = **starving**, starved, ravenous, hungry, undernourished.

famous ADJ = **well known**, renowned, celebrated, famed, noted, prominent, notable, eminent, great, pre-eminent, distinguished, esteemed, respected, venerable, illustrious, acclaimed, honourable, exalted, glorious, remarkable, signal, popular, legendary, much publicized.
Opposites: unknown, obscure.

fan NOUN = **admirer**, follower, devotee, enthusiast, aficionado, disciple, adherent, supporter, backer, champion; [inf] buff, freak, nut, groupie.

fanatic NOUN **1** = **extremist**, zealot, militant, activist, partisan, bigot, sectarian. **2** = **devotee**, addict, enthusiast, fan, lover.

fanatical ADJ
1 = **extremist**, extreme, zealous, radical, militant, sectarian, bigoted, dogmatic, prejudiced, intolerant, narrow-minded, partisan, rabid.
2 = **enthusiastic**, eager, keen, fervent, passionate, obsessive, immoderate, frenzied, frenetic; [inf] wild, gung-ho.

fanciful ADJ **1** = **unreal**, imaginary, illusory, made up, fantastic, romantic, mythical, legendary, fairy-tale. **2** = **imaginative**, inventive, whimsical, capricious, visionary, impractical.

fancy NOUN **1** = **desire**, urge, wish, want, yearning, longing, inclination, bent, hankering, impulse, fondness, liking, love, partiality, preference, taste, predilection, relish, penchant; [inf] yen, itch.
2 = **imagination**, creativity, conception, images, visualizations.
▶ VERB **1** = **have an idea**, think, guess, believe, suppose, reckon, suspect,

conjecture, surmise.
2 = find attractive, be
attracted to, be
infatuated by, take to,
desire, lust after; [inf] go
for, be wild/mad about,
have taken a shine to.
▶ ADJ = **ornate**, elaborate,
ornamented, decorative,
embellished, intricate,
lavish, ostentatious,
showy, luxurious,
sumptuous; [inf] jazzy,
snazzy, ritzy.

fantastic ADJ **1 = fanciful**,
imaginary, unreal,
illusory, romantic,
make-believe,
extravagant, irrational,
wild, mad, absurd,
incredible, strange,
eccentric, whimsical.
2 = strange, weird, queer,
peculiar, outlandish,
eccentric, bizarre,
grotesque, freakish,
fanciful, quaint, exotic,
elaborate, ornate,
intricate, rococo,
baroque. **3** = *See*
marvellous.
Opposites: ordinary.

fantasy NOUN
1 = imagination, fancy,
creativity, invention,
originality, vision, myth,
romance. **2 = speculation**,
fancy, daydreaming,
reverie, flight of fancy,
fanciful notion, dream,
daydream, pipe dream.

far ADV = **a long way**, a
great distance, a good
way, afar.
▶ ADJ = **faraway**, far-flung,
distant, remote, out of
the way, far removed,
outlying, inaccessible.
Opposites: near.

farcical ADJ = **ridiculous**,
ludicrous, absurd,
laughable, preposterous,
nonsensical, silly,
foolish, asinine.

farewell NOUN = **goodbye**,
adieu, leave-taking,
parting, send-off,
departure, departing.
▶ EXCLAMATION = **goodbye**, so
long, adieu, au revoir, see
you, see you later; [Brit.
inf] cheerio, cheers.

far-fetched ADJ
= **improbable**, unlikely,
implausible, remote,
incredible, unbelievable,
doubtful, dubious,
unconvincing, strained,
laboured, fanciful,
unrealistic; [inf] hard to

take/swallow.
Opposites: likely.

fascinate VERB
= **captivate**, enchant,
beguile, bewitch,
infatuate, enthral,
enrapture, entrance, hold
spellbound, rivet,
transfix, mesmerize,
hypnotize, lure, allure,
tempt, entice, draw,
tantalize, charm, attract,
intrigue, delight, absorb,
engross.
Opposites: bore, repel.

fashion NOUN 1 = **style**,
vogue, trend, latest
thing, taste, mode, craze,
rage, fad, convention,
custom, practice.
2 = **clothes**, design,
couture; [inf] rag trade.
3 = **way**, manner, style,
method, system, mode,
approach.
▶ VERB = **make**, build,
construct, manufacture,
create, devise, shape,
form, mould, forge, hew,
carve.

fashionable ADJ = **stylish**,
in fashion, up to date, up
to the minute,
contemporary, modern,
voguish, in vogue,
modish, popular, all the
rage, trendsetting, latest,
smart, chic, elegant;
[inf] trendy, natty, with it,
ritzy.
Opposites: unfashionable.

fast ADJ 1 = **quick**, rapid,
swift, speedy, brisk,
hurried, breakneck,
hasty, accelerated, flying,
express, fleet; [inf] nippy.
2 = **loyal**, devoted,
faithful, steadfast, firm,
staunch, constant,
lasting, unchanging,
unwavering, enduring.
3 = **licentious**,
promiscuous, dissolute,
loose, wanton. 4 = **wild**,
dissipated, debauched,
dissolute, promiscuous,
intemperate, immoderate,
unrestrained, reckless,
profligate, extravagant.
Opposites: slow.
▶ ADV 1 = **quickly**, rapidly,
swiftly, speedily, briskly,
hastily, hurriedly, in a
hurry, post-haste,
expeditiously; [inf] hell for
leather, like a shot, like a
bat out of hell, lickety-
split. 2 = **firmly**, tightly,
securely, immovably,
fixedly.

fasten VERB **1** = **bolt**, lock, secure, chain, seal. **2** = **attach**, fix, affix, clip, pin, tack, stick. **3** = **tie**, bind, tether, hitch, anchor, lash. **4** = **direct**, aim, point, focus, fix, concentrate, rivet, zero in.

fastidious ADJ = **fussy**, finicky, over-particular, critical, hard to please, overcritical, hypercritical; [inf] choosy, picky, pernickety.
Opposites: easy-going.

fat ADJ **1** = **plump**, stout, overweight, obese, heavy, large, solid, corpulent, tubby, chubby, portly, rotund, pudgy, flabby, pot-bellied, gross, paunchy, bloated, dumpy, bulky, fleshy, stocky, well fed, massive, elephantine; [inf] beefy, roly-poly. **2** = **substantial**, large, major, sizeable, significant, considerable.
Opposites: thin, lean.

fatal ADJ **1** = **mortal**, deadly, lethal, terminal, final, incurable.
2 = **ruinous**, disastrous, destructive, catastrophic, calamitous, cataclysmic.
3 = **critical**, fateful, decisive, crucial, pivotal, determining, momentous, important.

fatalism NOUN = **stoicism**, resignation, acceptance.

fatality NOUN = **death**, casualty, mortality, loss.

fate NOUN **1** = **destiny**, providence, predestination, predetermination, kismet, chance, one's lot in life, the stars.
2 = **future**, outcome, issue, upshot, end.

father NOUN = **male parent**, paterfamilias, patriarch; [inf] dad, daddy, pop, poppa, pa, old boy, old man; [Brit. inf, dated] pater.

fathom VERB
= **understand**, comprehend, grasp, perceive, divine, penetrate, search out, get to the bottom of, ferret out.

fatigue NOUN = **tiredness**, weariness, exhaustion, lethargy, prostration, lassitude, debility, listlessness, enervation.

Opposites: vigour.

▸ VERB = **tire**, tire out, weary, exhaust, wear out, drain, prostrate, enervate; [inf] take it out of, do in, whack; [Brit. inf] fag out; [N. Amer. inf] poop.

fatuous ADJ = **silly**, foolish, stupid, senseless, nonsensical, idiotic, puerile, brainless, mindless, asinine, vacuous, moronic, witless.
Opposites: sensible.

fault NOUN 1 = **defect**, flaw, imperfection, blemish, failing, weakness, weak point, deficiency, snag, error, mistake, inaccuracy, blunder, oversight. 2 = **misdeed**, wrongdoing, offence, misdemeanour, sin, vice, misconduct, lapse, indiscretion, transgression, peccadillo; [archaic] trespass.

▸ VERB = **find fault with**, criticize, complain about, censure, quibble about, find lacking, impugn; [inf] pick holes in.

■ **at fault** = to blame, in the wrong, culpable, responsible, accountable, answerable, blameworthy.

faultless ADJ 1 = **perfect**, flawless, without fault, unblemished, impeccable, accurate, correct, exemplary, model. 2 = **innocent**, blameless, guiltless, above reproach, irreproachable, pure, sinless, unsullied.
Opposites: imperfect.

faulty ADJ
1 = **malfunctioning**, defective, broken, out of order, damaged, unsound; [inf] on the blink, kaput.
2 = **defective**, flawed, unsound, wrong, inaccurate, incorrect, erroneous, fallacious, impaired, weak, invalid.
Opposites: working, correct.

favour NOUN 1 = **service**, good turn, kindness, courtesy, good deed.
2 = **approval**, approbation, good will, esteem, kindness, benevolence, friendliness. 3 = **backing**,

support, patronage, aid, assistance, championship.
Opposites: disservice, disfavour.
▶ VERB **1** = **approve of**, advocate, recommend, support, back, endorse, sanction. **2** = **be to the advantage of**, be advantageous to, benefit, help, assist, aid, advance, abet, succour.
Opposites: oppose.

favourable ADJ
1 = **approving**, good, enthusiastic, well disposed, commendatory. **2** = **advantageous**, in one's favour, beneficial, on one's side, helpful, good, hopeful, promising, fair, auspicious, propitious, opportune, timely, encouraging, conducive, convenient, suitable, fitting, appropriate. **3** = **good**, pleasing, agreeable, successful, positive.
Opposites: unfavourable.

favourite ADJ = **best-loved**, most-liked, favoured, preferred,

chosen, ideal, treasured, pet, well liked.
▶ NOUN = **first choice**, pick, beloved, darling, idol, god, goddess, jewel; [inf] teacher's pet; [Brit. inf] blue-eyed boy.

fear NOUN **1** = **fearfulness**, fright, terror, alarm, panic, trepidation, apprehensiveness, dread, nervousness, timidity, disquiet, trembling, anxiety, worry, unease, agitation, concern, foreboding, misgiving, doubt, angst, quaking, quivering, consternation, dismay, shivers, tremors; [inf] funk, blue funk, butterflies. **2** = **likelihood**, probability, chance, prospect, possibility.
▶ VERB = **be afraid of**, be scared of, dread, live in fear of, go in terror of, take fright at, shudder at, shrink from, quail at, tremble at, have cold feet.

fearful ADJ **1** = **afraid**, frightened, scared, terrified, apprehensive, alarmed, uneasy, nervous, tense, panicky,

timid, faint-hearted, timorous, diffident, intimidated, hesitant, trembling, quaking, quivering, cowering, cowardly, pusillanimous; [inf] jumpy, jittery.
2 = **terrible**, dreadful, appalling, frightful, ghastly, horrific, horrible, horrendous, shocking, awful, hideous, atrocious, monstrous, dire, grim, unspeakable, gruesome, distressing, harrowing, fearsome, alarming.
Opposites: fearless.

fearless ADJ = **unafraid**, brave, courageous, intrepid, valiant, gallant, plucky, lion-hearted, stout-hearted, heroic, bold, daring, confident, game, audacious, indomitable, doughty, undaunted, unflinching, unshrinking, unabashed; [inf] gutsy, spunky.
Opposites: fearful, cowardly.

fearsome ADJ = *see* **fearful (2)**.

feasible ADJ = **practicable**, possible, achievable, doable, likely, attainable, workable, accomplishable, realizable, viable, reasonable, realistic, within reason.
Opposites: impractical, impossible.

feast NOUN **1** = **banquet**, dinner, repast, junket, revels; [inf] blowout, spread, bash, thrash; [Brit. inf] beanfeast, beano.
2 = **feast day**, festival, saint's day, holy day, holiday, fête, gala, festivity.
▶ VERB = **eat one's fill of**, gorge on, indulge in; [inf] stuff one's face with, stuff oneself with.

feat NOUN = **deed**, act, action, exploit, achievement, accomplishment, performance, attainment, manoeuvre, move, stunt.

feather NOUN = **plume**, quill, pinion, plumule, pinna, plumage, down, hackles.

feature NOUN **1** = **aspect**, characteristic, facet, side, point, attribute, quality, property, trait, mark, hallmark, trademark, peculiarity, idiosyncrasy. **2 = article**, piece, item, report, story, column. ▶ VERB **1 = present**, give prominence to, promote, star, spotlight, highlight, emphasize, accentuate, play up. **2 = play a part**, have a place, have prominence.

federation NOUN **= confederation**, confederacy, league, alliance, coalition, union, syndicate, association, amalgamation, combination, entente, fraternity.

feeble ADJ **1 = weak**, weakly, weakened, frail, infirm, sickly, puny, delicate, slight, failing, ailing, helpless, powerless, debilitated, decrepit, doddering, tottering, enfeebled, enervated, effete, etiolated. **2 = inadequate**, ineffectual, ineffective, weak, indecisive, wishy-washy. **3 = unconvincing**, unsuccessful, ineffective, ineffectual, poor, weak, futile, tame, paltry, slight.

Opposites: strong.

feed VERB **1 = nourish**, sustain, cater for, provide for, wine and dine. **2 = eat**, take nourishment, graze, browse. **3 = give**, supply, provide, furnish.

feel VERB **1 = touch**, stroke, caress, fondle, handle, finger, manipulate, paw, maul. **2 = be aware of**, notice, be conscious of, perceive, observe, be sensible of. **3 = experience**, undergo, have, know, go through, bear, endure, suffer. **4 = think**, believe, consider, be of the opinion, hold, judge, deem. ▪ **feel for = sympathize with**, be sorry for, pity, empathize with, feel compassion for, be moved by, weep for, grieve for, commiserate with.

feeling NOUN **1 = sensation**, sense, perception, awareness, consciousness. **2 = idea**, suspicion, funny feeling, impression, notion, inkling, hunch, apprehension,

presentiment, premonition, foreboding.
3 = **sympathy**, pity, compassion, understanding, concern, sensitivity, tenderness, commiseration, empathy, fellow-feeling.

felicitous ADJ **1** = **apt**, well chosen, well expressed, well put, fitting, suitable, appropriate, pertinent, apposite, germane.
2 = **happy**, joyful, fortunate, lucky, successful, prosperous.
Opposites: inappropriate, unfortunate.

fell VERB **1** = **cut down**, chop down, saw down.
2 = **knock down**, bring down, knock out; [inf] deck, floor, lay out.

fellow NOUN = **man**, male, boy, person, individual; [inf] guy, character, customer, codger; [Brit. inf] bloke, chap.

feminine ADJ = **womanly**, girlish, ladylike, soft, delicate, gentle, tender, graceful, refined, modest.
Opposites: masculine.

fence NOUN = **barrier**, railing, rail, paling, wall, hedge, barricade, rampart, stockade, palisade.
▶ VERB **1** = **enclose**, surround, encircle, circumscribe, encompass.
2 = **shut in**, confine, pen, separate off, secure, imprison.

fend
■ **fend for oneself**
= **provide for oneself**, take care of oneself, get by, look after oneself, support, oneself, survive.
■ **fend off** = **ward off**, stave off, parry, turn aside, keep off, divert, deflect, avert, defend oneself against, guard against, forestall.

ferment NOUN
1 = **fermentation agent**, yeast, mould, bacteria, leaven, leavening.
2 = **frenzy**, furore, fever, tumult, commotion, uproar, agitation, turbulence, stir, confusion, fuss, brouhaha, hubbub, stew, hurly-burly, racket, imbroglio.
▶ VERB **1** = **undergo fermentation**, foam,

froth, bubble, effervesce, seethe, boil, rise, work. **2 = excite**, inflame, agitate, incite.

ferocious ADJ **1 = fierce**, savage, brutal, brutish, ruthless, cruel, pitiless, merciless, vicious, barbarous, violent, barbaric, inhuman, inexorable, bloodthirsty, murderous, wild, untamed, predatory, rapacious. **2 = intense**, very great, fierce, extreme, acute.
Opposites: gentle.

ferry VERB **= carry**, transport, convey, run, ship, shuttle, chauffeur.

fertile ADJ **1 = fruitful**, productive, rich, fecund. **2 = inventive**, creative, original, ingenious, resourceful, productive, visionary, constructive.
Opposites: sterile.

fertilize VERB **1 = add fertilizer to**, feed, enrich, mulch, dress, compost, top-dress. **2 = impregnate**, inseminate, make pregnant, fecundate.

fertilizer NOUN **= plant food**, manure, dung, compost, dressing, top-dressing, bonemeal, guano, marl.

fervent ADJ **= passionate**, ardent, impassioned, intense, vehement, heartfelt, emotional, fervid, emotive, warm, devout, sincere, eager, zealous, earnest, enthusiastic, excited, animated, spirited; [poetic/literary] perfervid.
Opposites: apathetic, unemotional.

fervour NOUN **= passion**, ardour, intensity, vehemence, emotion, warmth, devoutness, sincerity, eagerness, zeal, enthusiasm, earnestness, excitement, animation, spirit, vigour.
Opposites: apathy, indifference.

fester VERB **1 = suppurate**, run, discharge, ulcerate, rot, decay, go bad, go off, decompose, disintegrate, gather, come to a head. **2 = rankle**, chafe, cause bitterness/resentment, gnaw.

festival NOUN **1 = saint's day**, holy day, feast day,

holiday, anniversary, day of observance.
2 = **carnival**, gala day, fête, celebrations, festivities.

festive ADJ = **joyful**, joyous, happy, jolly, merry, jovial, light-hearted, cheerful, cheery, jubilant, convivial, gleeful, mirthful, uproarious, rollicking, backslapping, celebratory, carnival, sportive, festal.

festoon VERB = **garland**, wreathe, hang, drape, decorate, adorn, ornament, array, deck, bedeck, swathe, beribbon.
▶ NOUN = **garland**, wreath, chaplet, lei, swathe, swag.

fetch VERB 1 = **get**, go and get, bring, carry, deliver, convey, transport, escort, conduct, lead, usher in.
2 = **sell for**, realize, go for, bring in, yield, earn, cost, afford.

fetching ADJ = **attractive**, charming, enchanting, sweet, winsome, captivating, fascinating, alluring.

feud NOUN = **vendetta**, conflict, quarrel, argument, hostility, enmity, strife, discord, bad blood, animosity, grudge, antagonism, estrangement, schism, unfriendliness.

fever NOUN = **feverishness**, high temperature, delirium; [formal] pyrexia.

feverish ADJ 1 = **fevered**, febrile, hot, burning.
2 = **frenzied**, excited, frenetic, agitated, nervous, overwrought, frantic, distracted, worked up, flustered, impatient, passionate.

few ADJ 1 = **not many**, hardly any, scarcely any, one or two, a handful of, a sprinkling of, a couple of, few and far between, infrequent, sporadic, irregular. 2 = **scarce**, rare, negligible, scant, thin on the ground.
Opposites: many.

fiasco NOUN = **failure**, disaster, debacle, catastrophe, mess, ruination, abortion; [inf] flop, washout.

fibre NOUN = **thread**, strand, tendril, filament, fibril.

fickle ADJ = **capricious**, unpredictable, mercurial, changeable, variable, volatile, inconstant, unstable, vacillating, unsteady, unfaithful, faithless, undependable, inconsistent, irresolute, flighty, giddy, erratic, fitful, irregular, mutable.
Opposites: constant, stable.

fiction NOUN 1 = **story telling**, narration, romance, fable, fantasy, legend. 2 = **fabrication**, lie, piece of fiction, untruth, falsehood, invention, concoction, fib, improvisation, prevarication; [inf] cock and bull story, whopper.
Opposites: fact.

fictional ADJ = **fictitious**, invented, made up, imaginary, unreal, non-existent, make-believe, fabricated, mythical, fanciful.
Opposites: real, actual.

fictitious ADJ 1 = **invented**, made up, imaginary, imagined, untrue, false, apocryphal. 2 = **false**, bogus, sham, counterfeit, fake, fabricated, spurious, concocted.
Opposites: true, genuine.

fidelity NOUN = **faithfulness**, loyalty, devotedness, devotion, allegiance, commitment, constancy, trustworthiness, dependability, reliability, staunchness, obedience.
Opposites: disloyalty.

fidget VERB 1 = **move restlessly**, wriggle, squirm, twitch, jiggle; [inf] have ants in one's pants. 2 = **fiddle with**, play with, fuss with.

fidgety ADJ = **restless**, restive, on edge, uneasy, nervous, nervy, twitchy; [inf] jittery, jumpy, like a cat on hot bricks.

field NOUN 1 = **pasture**, meadow, grassland, paddock, sward; [literary] lea, mead, greensward; [archaic] glebe. 2 = **area**, area of activity, sphere, province, department, subject, discipline, line, speciality, domain,

territory, regime.
3 = **range**, scope, limits, confines, purview.

fiend NOUN 1 = **devil**, demon, evil spirit.
2 = **brute**, monster, savage, beast, barbarian, sadist, ogre; [archaic] blackguard.

fiendish ADJ = **wicked**, cruel, savage, brutal, brutish, barbaric, barbarous, inhuman, vicious, bloodthirsty, ferocious, ruthless, heartless, pitiless, merciless, black-hearted, unfeeling, malevolent, villainous, odious, malignant, devilish, diabolical, demonic, satanic.

fierce ADJ 1 = **ferocious**, savage, wild, vicious, bloodthirsty, dangerous, brutal, cruel, murderous, menacing, threatening, slaughterous, terrible, grim, tigerish, wolfish, feral. 2 = **passionate**, intense, ardent, impassioned, fervent, fiery, uncontrolled, fervid. 3 = **keen**, strong, intense, relentless, cut-

throat.
Opposites: gentle, mild.

fight VERB 1 = **attack/ assault each other**, hit each other, come to blows, exchange blows, grapple, scuffle, brawl, box, skirmish, tussle, collide, spar, joust, clash, wrestle, battle, do battle, give battle, war, wage war, go to war, make war, take up arms, combat, engage, meet; [inf] scrap. 2 = **quarrel**, argue, feud, bicker, squabble, fall out, wrangle, dispute, be at odds, disagree, battle, altercate. 3 = **oppose**, contest, take a stand against, object to, resist, defy, withstand, struggle against, take issue with.
▶ NOUN 1 = **brawl**, scuffle, tussle, skirmish, struggle, fracas, battle, engagement, clash, conflict, combat, contest, encounter, exchange, brush; [inf] set-to, scrap, punch-up, dust-up; [Law, dated] affray. 2 = **quarrel**, disagreement, difference of opinion, dispute,

argument, altercation, feud.

- **fight back 1 = defend oneself**, put up a fight, retaliate, counter-attack. **2 = suppress**, repress, check, curb, restrain, contain, bottle up.
- **fight off = ward off**, beat off, stave off, repel, repulse, hold at bay, resist.

figurative ADJ
= **metaphorical**, symbolic, allegorical, non-literal, representative, emblematic, imagistic. **Opposites:** literal.

figure NOUN **1 = number**, numeral, digit, integer, sum, value, symbol, cipher. **2 = cost**, price, amount, value, total, sum, aggregate. **3 = shape**, form, outline, silhouette. **4 = body**, physique, build, frame, torso, proportions. **5 = diagram**, illustration, picture, drawing, sketch, chart, plan, map.
▶ VERB **1 = appear**, feature, play a part, be featured, be conspicuous. **2 = be likely**, be probable, be understandable, make sense.

- **figure out 1 =** *See* **calculate**. **2 =** *See* **understand** (1).

file¹ NOUN **1 = folder**, portfolio, box, document case, filing cabinet. **2 = dossier**, information, documents, records, data, particulars, case notes.
▶ VERB **= record**, enter, store, categorize, classify, put in place, put in order, put on record, pigeonhole.

file² NOUN **= line**, column, row, string, chain, queue.
▶ VERB **= walk/march in a line**, march, parade, troop, stream.

fill VERB **1 = occupy all of**, crowd, overcrowd, congest, cram, pervade. **2 = pack**, load, stack, supply, furnish, provide, replenish, restock, refill. **3 = stop up**, block up, plug, seal, bung up, close, clog. **4 = carry out**, execute, perform, complete, fulfil.

film NOUN **1 = movie**, picture, motion picture, video; [inf] flick. **2 = layer**,

coat, coating, covering, cover, dusting, sheet, blanket, skin, tissue, membrane, pellicle.
3 = **haze**, mist, cloud, blur, veil, murkiness.

filter NOUN = **strainer**, sieve, riddle, sifter, colander, gauze, netting.
▸VERB = **strain**, sieve, sift, riddle, filtrate, clarify, purify, clear, refine.

filth NOUN = **dirt**, muck, grime, mud, sludge, mire, slime, excrement, dung, manure, ordure, sewage, rubbish, refuse, garbage, trash, contamination, pollution; [inf] crud; [Brit. inf] gunge.

filthy ADJ = **dirty**, unclean, mucky, muddy, slimy, murky, squalid, foul, nasty, polluted, contaminated, unwashed, grubby, dirt-encrusted, black, blackened, begrimed, rotten, decaying, smelly, fetid, putrid, faecal.
Opposites: clean, spotless.

final ADJ **1** = **last**, closing, concluding, finishing, terminal, end, ultimate, eventual, endmost.

2 = **absolute**, conclusive, irrevocable, unalterable, incontrovertible, indisputable, decisive, definite, definitive, settled.
Opposites: first.

finale NOUN = **end**, finish, close, conclusion, climax, culmination, denouement, last act, final scene, final curtain, epilogue; [inf] wind-up.

finalize VERB = **complete**, conclude, settle, decide, agree on, work out, tie up, wrap up, put the finishing touches to, clinch, sew up.

finance NOUN **1** = **money matters**, financial affairs, economics, commerce, business, investment, banking, accounting.
2 = **money**, funds, cash, resources, assets, capital, wealth, wherewithal, revenue, stock.
▸VERB = **pay for**, fund, back, support, subsidize, underwrite, capitalize, guarantee, provide capital for.

financial ADJ = **monetary**, fiscal, pecuniary,

economic, budgetary.

find VERB 1 = **discover**, come across, chance upon, stumble on, light on, bring to light, turn up, happen upon, come up with, hit upon, uncover, unearth, locate, lay one's hands on, encounter. 2 = **obtain**, get, achieve, attain, acquire, gain, earn, procure. 3 = **realize**, discover, learn, conclude, detect, observe, notice, note, perceive.

finding NOUN = **decision**, conclusion, verdict, judgement, pronouncement, decree, order, recommendation.

fine ADJ 1 = **excellent**, first-class, first-rate, great, exceptional, outstanding, admirable, superior, magnificent, splendid, quality, beautiful, exquisite, choice, select, prime, supreme, rare; [inf] A1, top-notch; [Brit. inf, dated] top-hole. 2 = **fair**, dry, bright, clear, cloudless, sunny, balmy, clement. 3 = **sheer**, light, lightweight, thin, flimsy, diaphanous, filmy, chiffony, gossamer, gauze-like, gauzy, transparent, translucent, airy, ethereal. 4 = **elegant**, stylish, expensive, smart, chic, fashionable, modish, high-fashion, lavish. 5 = **all right**, satisfactory, acceptable, agreeable, convenient, suitable; [inf] OK.

finish VERB 1 = **complete**, conclude, accomplish, carry out, execute, discharge, deal with, do, get done, fulfil, achieve, attain, end, close, bring to a conclusion, finalize, terminate, round off, put the finishing touches to; [inf] wind up, wrap up, sew up, polish off, knock off. 2 = **stop**, cease, give up, suspend, have done with, discontinue. 3 = **use**, use up, consume, exhaust, empty, deplete, drain, expend, dispatch, dispose of.
Opposites: start, begin.
▶ NOUN 1 = **end**, completion, conclusion, close, closing, cessation, final act, finale,

accomplishment, fulfilment, achievement, consummation, execution. **2 = surface**, veneer, coating, texture, glaze, lustre, gloss, polish, shine, patina.

finite ADJ **= limited**, restricted, bounded, delimited, demarcated, subject to limitations, determinate, measurable, countable.
Opposites: infinite.

fire NOUN **1 = blaze**, conflagration, inferno, flames, combustion.
2 = gunfire, sniping, bombardment, flak, shelling, barrage, fusillade, salvo.
3 = passion, intensity, ardour, zeal, energy, spirit, vivacity, sparkle, vigour, fervour, enthusiasm.
▶ VERB **1 = set fire to**, set on fire, set alight, set ablaze, light, ignite, kindle, put a match to. **2 = shoot**, let off, discharge, trigger.
3 = stimulate, animate, arouse, rouse, stir up, excite, enliven, inflame, inspire, motivate, incite,

galvanize, electrify, impassion. **4 = dismiss**, discharge, get rid of, oust, depose, cashier; [inf] give someone their marching orders, show someone the door, sack, give someone the sack, axe, give someone the bullet.

firebrand NOUN **= troublemaker**, agitator, rabble-rouser, demagogue, tub-thumper.

fireproof ADJ **= non-flammable**, non-inflammable, fire-resistant, flame-resistant, flame-retardant, incombustible, unburnable.
Opposites: inflammable.

firm¹ ADJ **1 = hard**, hardened, stiff, rigid, inflexible, unyielding, inelastic, resistant, solid, solidified, compacted, compressed, condensed, dense, close-grained, congealed, frozen, set, jelled, stony. **2 = settled**, fixed, decided, definite, established, unalterable, unchangeable. **3 = strong**,

vigorous, sturdy,
powerful. **4 = constant**,
unchanging, enduring,
abiding, durable, deep-
rooted, long-standing,
long-lasting, steady,
stable, staunch.
5 = determined, resolute,
decided, resolved,
unfaltering, unwavering,
unflinching, unswerving,
unyielding, unbending,
inflexible, obstinate,
stubborn, obdurate,
strict, intransigent,
unmalleable.
Opposites: soft.

firm² NOUN = **business**,
company, concern,
establishment,
organization,
corporation,
conglomerate,
partnership; [inf] outfit.

first ADJ **1 = initial**, earliest,
original, introductory,
opening, primitive,
premier, primordial,
primeval. **2 = basic**,
fundamental,
rudimentary, key,
cardinal, primary,
beginning.
Opposites: last.

▶ ADV **1 = at first**, to begin
with, at the beginning, at
the outset, initially.
2 = firstly, before
anything else, first and
foremost, in the first
place.

fish VERB = **go fishing**,
angle, cast, trawl.

fishy ADJ = **suspicious**,
dubious, questionable,
doubtful, suspect, odd,
queer, peculiar, strange,
not quite right;
[inf] funny, shady, not
kosher.

fit¹ ADJ **1 = well**, healthy, in
good health, in shape, in
good shape, in good
trim, in good condition,
strong, robust, hale and
hearty, sturdy, hardy,
vigorous. **2 = capable**,
able, competent, good
enough, adequate, ready,
prepared, satisfactory,
qualified, trained,
equipped, worthy,
eligible; [inf] up to
scratch. **3 = fitting**, proper,
seemly, decent, right,
decorous, correct, apt,
appropriate, suitable,
apposite, relevant,
pertinent.

Opposites: unfit, inappropriate.

▶ VERB **1** = **agree with**, be in agreement with, accord with, concur with, correspond with, match, tally with, suit, go with, conform to, dovetail with, be consonant with, be congruent with. **2** = **join**, connect, put together, put in place, fix, arrange, insert, adjust, shape.

fit² NOUN **1** = **convulsion**, spasm, paroxysm, seizure, attack. **2** = **bout**, burst, outburst, outbreak.

fix VERB **1** = **fasten**, secure, attach, connect, join, couple, stick, glue, cement, pin, nail, screw, bolt, clamp, bind, tie, pinion, anchor, plant, embed, establish, position, station. **2** = **decide on**, settle, set, agree on, arrange, arrive at, determine, establish, name, specify. **3** = **repair**, mend, put right, patch up, put to rights, restore, adjust, rectify, sort out, see to.

▶ NOUN = **predicament**, difficulty, quandary, plight, dilemma, trouble, muddle, mess, corner, tricky situation, tight spot; [inf] pickle, jam, hole, scrape; [Brit. inf] spot of bother.

fixation NOUN = **obsession**, preoccupation, compulsion, complex, mania, monomania; [inf] hang-up, thing.

fizz VERB = **bubble**, effervesce, froth, sparkle, foam, fizzle, sputter.

fizzy ADJ = **bubbly**, bubbling, sparkling, effervescent, gassy, carbonated.

flag¹ NOUN = **standard**, ensign, banner, pennant, streamer, bunting, colours, pennon, gonfalon.

flag² VERB **1** = **tire**, become tired/weary, weaken, grow weak, lose one's strength. **2** = **fade**, decline, fail, wane, diminish, ebb, decrease, taper off.

flagrant ADJ = **obvious**, glaring, blatant,

outrageous, shameless, disgraceful, shocking, scandalous, terrible, dreadful.

flair NOUN **1** = **ability**, capability, aptitude, facility, skill, talent, gift, knack, bent, genius. **2** = **style**, panache, dash, elan, good taste, discrimination, discernment.

flap VERB = **flutter**, beat, thresh, thrash, wave, wag, agitate, waggle, swing, shake, oscillate.

flash VERB **1** = **glare**, beam, gleam, shine out, glint, sparkle, flicker, shimmer, twinkle, glimmer, glisten, scintillate, coruscate. **2** = **show off**, flaunt, flourish, display, exhibit.

flat ADJ **1** = **level**, horizontal, levelled, even, smooth, unbroken, plane. **2** = **stretched out**, prone, spreadeagled, prostrate, supine, recumbent. **3** = **deflated**, punctured, burst, collapsed, ruptured. **4** = **monotonous**, boring, dull, tedious, uninteresting, lifeless, dead, lacklustre, bland, insipid, vapid, prosaic. **5** = **outright**, direct, out-and-out, definite, positive, downright, firm, conclusive, utter, complete, categorical, unconditional.

flatten VERB **1** = **level**, level out/off, even out, smooth, compress, trample, press down, crush, squash, compact. **2** = **demolish**, tear down, knock down, raze, raze to the ground. **3** = **knock someone off their feet**, knock to the ground, floor, prostrate, fell.

flatter VERB = **compliment**, praise, sing someone's praises, praise to excess, praise to the skies, pay court to, pay blandishments to, fawn upon, cajole, humour, flannel, wheedle; [inf] sweet-talk, soft-soap, butter up, lay it on thick, play up to. **Opposites:** insult.

flattering ADJ **1** = **complimentary**, adulatory, fulsome, laudatory, honeyed,

sugary, ingratiating, cajoling. **2 = enhancing**, becoming.
Opposites: unflattering.

flattery NOUN **= praise**, adulation, fulsomeness, unctuousness, fawning, puffery, cajolery, wheedling, compliments, blandishments, honeyed words; [inf] sweet talk, soft soap, flannel.

flaunt VERB **= show off**, parade, display, exhibit, draw attention to, make a show of, wave, dangle, brandish.

flavour NOUN **1 = taste**, savour, tang, relish.
2 = flavouring, seasoning, tastiness, tang, relish, piquancy, spiciness, zest.
3 = atmosphere, spirit, essence, nature, character, soul, quality, feel, feeling, ambience, tone, style.

flaw NOUN **1 = shortcoming**, defect, imperfection, fault, failing, blemish, weakness, weak spot, foible. **2 = defect**, fault, crack, chip, fracture, break, crevice, fissure, rent, split, tear.

Opposites: strength.

flawless ADJ **1 = perfect**, impeccable, faultless.
2 = unblemished, perfect, blemish-free, unmarred, unimpaired. **3 = perfect**, whole, intact, sound, undamaged, unbroken.
Opposites: imperfect, flawed.

flee VERB **= run away**, run off, make off, fly, take flight, beat a hasty retreat, bolt, abscond, retreat, depart hastily, make a quick exit, run for it, make a run for it, take off, take to one's heels, decamp, escape, make one's getaway, vanish; [inf] do a disappearing act, cut and run, beat it, skedaddle, split, scram, light out; [Brit. inf] scarper, do a bunk, do a runner.

fleeting ADJ **= brief**, short-lived, transient, momentary, rapid, swift, transitory, ephemeral, temporary, impermanent, here today and gone tomorrow, evanescent, fugitive, vanishing, flying,

passing, flitting.
Opposites: lasting.

flesh NOUN = **muscle**, tissue, meat, brawn, body.

flexible ADJ **1** = **bendable**, pliable, pliant, elastic, plastic, springy, mouldable, rubbery. **2** = **supple**, agile, limber, lithe, lissom, double-jointed. **3** = **adaptable**, adjustable, changeable, open to change, variable, open, open-ended, provisional, mutable. **4** = **cooperative**, accommodating, tractable, compliant, manageable, amenable, malleable, biddable, docile, submissive, yielding.
Opposites: inflexible, rigid.

flick VERB **1** = **strike**, hit, whip, rap, tap, touch. **2** = **click**, switch, snap, flip.
■ **flick through** = **skim**, glance over/through, browse through, thumb through.

flight NOUN **1** = **aviation**, flying, air transport, aeronautics. **2** = **flock**, group, skein, bevy, covey, migration.

flimsy ADJ
1 = **insubstantial**, fragile, frail, slight, makeshift, rickety, shaky, jerry-built, ramshackle, gimcrack.
2 = **thin**, light, fine, delicate, lightweight, sheer, filmy, diaphanous, transparent, gossamer, gauzy. **3** = **feeble**, weak, poor, inadequate, thin, unconvincing, transparent, implausible, unsatisfactory, trivial, shallow, paltry.
Opposites: strong.

flinch VERB = **draw back**, shrink back, pull back, start back, recoil, withdraw, shy away, cringe, cower, quail, crouch, wince, blench.
■ **flinch from** = **shirk**, evade, avoid, shy away from, dodge, duck, baulk at.

fling VERB = **throw**, hurl, toss, pitch, cast, launch, catapult, propel, send flying, let fly, shy, lob; [inf] chuck, heave.

flippant ADJ = **frivolous**, glib, offhand, impertinent, insouciant, impudent, irreverent, superficial, carefree, thoughtless, shallow, cheeky, pert; [inf] flip. **Opposites:** serious.

flirt VERB = **chat up**, make eyes at, toy with, lead on, trifle with, dally with, tease.
▶ NOUN = **coquette**, tease, vamp, heartbreaker, trifler, philanderer.

flirtatious ADJ = **provocative**, teasing, coquettish, playful, amorous, philandering, come-hither.

float VERB 1 = **stay afloat**, be buoyant, sail, bob, glide, drift, slip. 2 = **move aimlessly**, drift, wander, meander; [N. Amer. inf] bum around. **Opposites:** sink.

flock NOUN 1 = **herd**, drove. 2 = **flight**, bevy, gaggle, skein. 3 = **crowd**, gathering, assembly, group, company, collection, congregation, throng, mass, host, multitude, troop, convoy.

flog VERB = **whip**, lash, horsewhip, flay, flagellate, birch, scourge, belt, cane, strap, thrash, beat, whack, wallop, chastise, trounce; [inf] tan someone's hide.

flood NOUN 1 = **deluge**, torrent, inundation, spate, overflow, flash flood. 2 = **abundance**, superabundance, profusion, glut, surfeit, plethora, superfluity; [inf] tons, heaps, loads. **Opposites:** trickle.
▶ VERB 1 = **inundate**, deluge, pour over, immerse, submerge, swamp, drown, engulf, saturate. 2 = **oversupply**, saturate, overfill, glut, overwhelm. **Opposites:** trickle.

floor NOUN = **storey**, level, tier, deck.

flop VERB 1 = **collapse**, slump, drop, fall, tumble, droop, sag, dangle. 2 = **fail**, be unsuccessful, be a disaster, miss the mark, founder, fall flat; [inf] bomb, go down like a lead balloon. **Opposites:** succeed.

florid ADJ **1** = **red**, ruddy, flushed, high-coloured, rubicund, rubescent, erubescent. **2** = **flowery**, over-elaborate, verbose, purple, grandiloquent.
Opposites: pale, plain.

flounder VERB **1** = **thrash**, struggle, blunder, stumble, fumble, grope. **2** = **struggle**, falter, be in difficulties, be confused, be in the dark, be out of one's depth.

flourish VERB **1** = **brandish**, wave, wield, swing, hold aloft, display, exhibit, flaunt, show off, parade, vaunt. **2** = **thrive**, grow, do well, develop, burgeon, bloom, blossom, bear fruit, flower, succeed, prosper.

flout VERB = **defy**, disdain, scorn, show contempt for, scoff at, mock, laugh at, deride, ridicule, sneer at.
Opposites: obey, observe.

flow VERB **1** = **move**, course, run, go along, proceed, glide, stream, ripple, swirl, surge, sweep, roll, whirl, rush, drift, slide, trickle, gurgle. **2** = **gush**, stream, well, spurt, spout, squirt, spew, jet, spill, leak, seep, ooze, drip.
▶ NOUN **1** = **current**, course, drift, stream, tide, spate. **2** = **gush**, stream, outflow, outpouring, welling.

flower NOUN **1** = **bloom**, blossom, floweret, floret, annual, perennial. **2** = **best**, finest, pick, cream, elite.

fluctuate VERB **1** = **rise and fall**, go up and down, see-saw, yo-yo, be unstable, vary, change, alter, swing, oscillate, ebb and flow, undulate. **2** = **waver**, vacillate, hesitate, change one's mind, blow hot and cold, shilly-shally, alternate, veer, teeter, totter; [Brit.] hum and haw.

fluent ADJ **1** = **articulate**, eloquent, silver-tongued, smooth-spoken, voluble. **2** = **smooth**, flowing, fluid, natural, effortless, graceful, elegant, mellifluous, euphonious.
Opposites: inarticulate.

fluff NOUN = **down**, fuzz, lint, nap, pile, dust.

fluid ADJ **1** = **liquid**, liquefied, gaseous, gassy, melted, molten, running, flowing, uncongealed.
2 = **smooth**, fluent, flowing, graceful, elegant, effortless, easy, natural.
3 = **flexible**, open to change, adaptable, not fixed, adjustable, variable, mutable.
4 = **unstable**, likely to change, unsteady, fluctuating, shifting.
Opposites: solid.
▸ NOUN = **liquid**, gas, solution.

flush VERB **1** = **blush**, turn red, redden, colour, colour up, crimson, burn up, flame up, glow, suffuse with colour.
2 = **wash out**, rinse out, cleanse, hose down, swab. **3** = **expel**, eject.

fluster VERB = **agitate**, ruffle, unsettle, upset, bother, put on edge, panic, disconcert, discompose, confuse, throw off balance, confound, nonplus; [inf] hassle, rattle, faze, throw into a tizz.

flutter VERB **1** = **beat**, flap, quiver, agitate, vibrate, ruffle. **2** = **bat**, flicker, flit. **3** = **flap**, wave, flop, ripple, quiver, shiver, tremble.

fly VERB **1** = **soar**, take wing, take to the air, wing, wing its way, hover, swoop. **2** = **display**, show, exhibit, wave, hoist, raise, hang out. **3** = **dash**, race, rush, tear, bolt, zoom, dart, speed, hurry, career, hasten; [inf] hare off, be off like a shot.
4 = **flee**, run away, bolt, take flight, make off, abscond, beat a retreat, run for it, decamp, make one's escape; [inf] cut and run, skedaddle; [Brit. inf] scarper, do a bunk.

foam VERB = **froth**, froth up, bubble, fizz, cream, lather, spume, effervesce.
▸ NOUN = **froth**, bubbles, fizz, head, spume, lather, effervescence, suds.

focus NOUN **1** = **centre**, central point, focal point, centre of attention, core, hub, pivot, magnet, cynosure.
2 = **focal point**, point of

conversion.

▶ VERB = **aim**, fix, concentrate, bring to bear, zero in on, zoom in on, centre, pinpoint, rivet.

foe NOUN = **enemy**, opponent, adversary, rival, antagonist, combatant, contestant. **Opposites:** friend.

fog NOUN = **mist**, smog, haze, murk, murkiness, gloom; [inf] pea-souper.

foggy ADJ 1 = **misty**, smoggy, dark, grey, dim, overcast, murky, hazy, gloomy. 2 = **vague**, indistinct, cloudy, hazy, unclear, obscure, befuddled, confused, muddled, dazed. **Opposites:** clear.

foible NOUN = **weakness**, weak point, failing, shortcoming, flaw, blemish, defect, frailty, quirk, idiosyncrasy; [inf] hang-up.

foil VERB = **thwart**, frustrate, stop, baffle, defeat, check, checkmate, circumvent, counter, baulk, disappoint, impede, obstruct,

hamper, hinder.

fold NOUN 1 = **layer**, pleat, overlap, turn, gather, crease, knife-edge. 2 = **wrinkle**, pucker, furrow, crinkle, crows feet.

▶ VERB 1 = **double up**, turn under, turn up, bend, tuck, crease, gather, pleat, crimp, crumple. 2 = **wrap**, enfold, clasp, embrace, envelop, hug, squeeze. 3 = **fail**, collapse, go out of business, go bankrupt, crash, go to the wall; [inf] go bust, go under, flop.

folk NOUN = **people**, populace, population, citizenry, general public, public, clan, tribe.

follow VERB 1 = **go/come behind**, walk behind, go with, escort, accompany, keep pace with, attend, chase, pursue, run after, trail, shadow, hunt, stalk, track, dog, hound; [inf] tread on someone's heels, tail, tag after. 2 = **obey**, observe, comply with, heed, conform to, pay attention to, stick to, adhere to, note, have regard to, mind, be guided by, accept, yield to. **3 = result from**, arise from, be consequent on, develop from, ensue from, emanate from, issue from, proceed from, spring from, flow from. **4 = understand**, comprehend, take in, see, grasp, fathom, get, catch on to, appreciate. **5 = be a follower of**, be a supporter of, be interested in, be devoted to, support, keep abreast of, keep up to date with.

■**follow through** = **continue**, complete, bring to completion, see something through.

■**follow up** = **investigate**, research, find out about, look into, check out, pursue.

following ADJ = **next**, ensuing, succeeding, subsequent, successive.

▶NOUN = **supporters**, backers, fans, admirers, devotees, public, audience, adherents, patrons.

foment VERB = **incite**, instigate, stir up, provoke, excite, arouse, encourage, initiate, agitate. = *See also* **stimulate**.

fond ADJ **1 = adoring**, devoted, loving, affectionate, caring, warm, tender, amorous, doting, indulgent. **2 = foolish**, naive, deluded, delusory, absurd, vain, empty. **Opposites:** hostile.

fondle VERB = **caress**, stroke, pat, pet, cuddle, hug, nuzzle.

food NOUN = **nourishment**, sustenance, nutriment, subsistence, diet, fare, menu, bread, board, provender, cooking, cuisine, foodstuffs, refreshments, edibles, meals, provisions, rations, stores, commons, comestibles, solids; [inf] nosh, grub, eats, chow; [Brit. inf] scoff; [dated] victuals.

fool NOUN **1 = idiot**, dolt, dunce, ass, ignoramus, imbecile, simpleton; [inf] chump, booby, nincompoop, ninny, dunderhead, blockhead,

fathead, halfwit, cretin, moron, dummy, numbskull, dimwit; [Brit. inf] twerp, clot, twit, nitwit. **2** = **dupe**, butt, laughing stock, gull, easy mark, cat's paw; [inf] stooge, sucker, pushover, sap, fall guy; [Brit. inf] mug.
▶ VERB **1** = **trick**, deceive, hoax, make a fool of, dupe, take in, mislead, hoodwink, bluff, delude, beguile, gull; [inf] con, bamboozle, kid, have on. **2** = **pretend**, make believe, feign, put on an act, sham, fake.

foolish ADJ = **silly**, stupid, idiotic, senseless, brainless, dense, moronic, half-witted, doltish, imprudent, incautious, injudicious, irresponsible, mad, crazy, unwise, ill-advised, ill-considered; [inf] dotty, batty, nutty, dippy, screwy; [Brit. inf] daft, potty, barmy.
Opposites: sensible.

foolproof ADJ = **infallible**, certain, sure, guaranteed, safe, dependable, trustworthy, never-failing.

forbid VERB = **prohibit**, ban, bar, debar, outlaw, veto, proscribe, disallow, preclude, interdict, exclude, rule out, stop.
Opposites: allow.

forbidden ADJ = **prohibited**, out of bounds, banned, outlawed, vetoed, proscribed, taboo, debarred, interdicted.

forbidding ADJ **1** = **stern**, harsh, grim, hard, tough, hostile, unfriendly, disagreeable, nasty, mean, repellent, off-putting. **2** = **frightening**, ominous, threatening, menacing, sinister, daunting, foreboding.
Opposites: friendly.

force NOUN **1** = **power**, strength, vigour, energy, potency, muscle, might, effort, impact, exertion, pressure, stamina, vitality, stimulus, dynamism. **2** = **coercion**, duress, compulsion, pressure, constraint, enforcement, violence; [inf] arm-twisting.

3 = **persuasiveness**, validity, weight, effectiveness, influence, power, strength, vehemence, efficacy; [inf] punch, bite.
4 = **detachment**, unit, squad, squadron, battalion, division, regiment, army, patrol.
▶ VERB **1** = **compel**, coerce, make, bring pressure on, use force on, pressure, pressurize, impel, drive, oblige, necessitate, constrain, urge, press-gang; [inf] use strong-arm tactics on, put the squeeze on. **2** = **drive**, push, propel, thrust, shove, press. **3** = **wrest**, extract, extort, wring, drag.

forceful ADJ **1** = **powerful**, vigorous, strong, potent, dynamic, energetic, assertive. **2** = **persuasive**, telling, convincing, compelling, effective, cogent, impressive, valid.
Opposites: weak, unconvincing.

forecast VERB = **predict**, foretell, foresee, prophesy, forewarn, prognosticate, augur, divine, guess, conjecture, speculate, calculate.
▶ NOUN = **prediction**, prophecy, prognostication, augury, prognosis, guess, conjecture, projection.

foregoing ADJ = **preceding**, prior, previous, former, above, aforesaid, antecedent, anterior.

foreign ADJ **1** = **overseas**, distant, remote, alien, exotic. **2** = **strange**, unfamiliar, unknown, exotic, outlandish, odd, unheard of, novel, new. **3** = **irrelevant**, unrelated, not pertinent, unconnected, inappropriate, extraneous, outside, extrinsic, inapposite.
Opposites: domestic, native, familiar.

foreigner NOUN = **alien**, non-native, immigrant, incomer, newcomer, stranger, outsider.
Opposites: native.

foremost ADJ = **leading**, principal, premier, top, first, primary, front, paramount, chief, main, most important, supreme, highest.

forerunner NOUN
= **predecessor**, precursor, antecedent, ancestor, forefather, harbinger, herald, usher, advance guard.

foresee VERB = **anticipate**, expect, envisage, envision, see, predict, forecast, foretell, prophesy.

foreshadow VERB
= **forebode**, bode, presage, augur, portend, indicate, show, signify, point to, prefigure, promise.

foresight NOUN = **far-sightedness**, perspicacity, anticipation, forethought, presence of mind, preparedness, readiness, prescience, provision, discernment, care, caution.

forest NOUN = **woodland**, wood, woods, trees, plantation.

forestall VERB = **pre-empt**, anticipate, intercept, thwart, frustrate, stave

off, ward off, fend off, prevent, avert, hinder, impede, obstruct; [inf] steal a march on, get ahead of.

foretell VERB 1 = **predict**, forecast, prophesy, foresee, forewarn, prognosticate, augur, divine. 2 = **presage**, augur, forebode, portend, foreshadow, prefigure, point to, indicate, betoken.

forethought NOUN
= **foresight**, far-sightedness, anticipation, provision, circumspection, prudence, judiciousness, care, precaution.

forever ADV = **always**, evermore, ever, for all time, until the end of time, eternally, perpetually; [inf] till the cows come home, till hell freezes over, for keeps, for good and all.

forfeit NOUN = **fine**, penalty, confiscation, damages, loss, relinquishment.
▶ VERB = **give up**, hand over, relinquish, be stripped

of.

forge VERB 1 = **beat into shape**, hammer out, shape, form, fashion, mould, cast, found, make, manufacture, frame, construct, create. 2 = **fake**, fabricate, falsify, counterfeit, copy, imitate.

forgery NOUN = **fake**, counterfeit, sham, fraud, imitation, reproduction; [inf] phoney.

forget VERB 1 = **fail to remember**, lose track of, overlook, let slip. 2 = **disregard**, put out of one's mind, ignore, let bygones be bygones. 3 = **leave behind**, omit to take, overlook. Opposites: remember.

forgetful ADJ 1 = **absent-minded**, vague, apt to forget, abstracted, amnesiac. 2 = **neglectful**, negligent, careless, heedless, unmindful, inattentive, lax, remiss, oblivious.

forgive VERB = **pardon**, excuse, absolve, exonerate, acquit, let off, let bygones be bygones, bury the hatchet, bear no malice, harbour no grudge; [inf] let someone off the hook.

forgiveness NOUN = **pardon**, amnesty, reprieve, absolution, exoneration, acquittal, remission, clemency, tolerance, compassion, exculpation, indulgence, leniency.

forgiving ADJ = **merciful**, lenient, magnanimous, understanding, compassionate, humane, clement, soft-hearted, forbearing, tolerant, mild. Opposites: unforgiving.

forgo VERB = **do/go without**, waive, renounce, sacrifice, relinquish, abjure, surrender, cede, abandon, yield, abstain from, refrain from, eschew; [formal] forswear.

fork VERB = **branch**, branch off, diverge, bifurcate, divide, split, separate, go separate ways, divaricate.

forlorn ADJ = **unhappy**, sad, miserable, wretched, pathetic, woebegone, disconsolate, lonely, cheerless, desolate, pitiable, pitiful, uncared for.

form NOUN **1** = **shape**, formation, configuration, structure, construction, conformation, arrangement, appearance, exterior. **2** = **appearance**, shape, character, guise, description, manifestation, semblance. **3** = **type**, kind, sort, variety, species, genre, stamp, kidney, genus. **4** = **structure**, organization, order, planning, symmetry, proportion, orderliness, framework, format. **5** = **condition**, fitness, health, shape, trim, fettle. **6** = **application**, document, paper, sheet of paper.
▶ VERB **1** = **make**, fashion, shape, model, mould, forge, construct, build, assemble, put together, set up, erect, produce, concoct. **2** = **devise**, formulate, think up, plan, draw up, frame, hatch, forge, develop, organize, dream up. **3** = **bring about**, set up, establish, found, organize, institute, inaugurate. **4** = **take shape**, appear, materialize, show, become visible, come into being. **5** = **acquire**, get into, contract, develop, get, pick up, grow into.

formal ADJ **1** = **correct**, proper, conventional, reserved, aloof, remote, precise, exact, punctilious, stiff, unbending, inflexible, stand-offish, prim, stuffy, strait-laced. **2** = **official**, set, fixed, conventional, standard, regular, customary, approved, prescribed, pro forma, legal, lawful, ceremonial, ritual. **3** = **orderly**, arranged, symmetrical, regular, methodical. **Opposites:** informal.

formation NOUN **1** = **arrangement**, pattern, order, grouping, configuration, structure, format, layout,

disposition, design.
2 = establishment, setting up, institution, founding, creation, inauguration.
3 = composition, make-up, constitution, organization.

former ADJ **1 = previous**, ex-, prior, preceding, earlier, late, sometime, erstwhile, one-time, foregoing, antecedent, anterior, ci-devant; [formal] quondam.
2 = earlier, past, long past, bygone, long departed, long gone, old, ancient, of yore.

formidable ADJ
1 = intimidating, daunting, alarming, frightening, terrifying, horrifying, dreadful, awesome, fearsome, menacing, threatening, dangerous; [inf] scary.
2 = strong, powerful, impressive, mighty, great, redoubtable, terrific, indomitable, invincible. **3 = difficult**, arduous, onerous, tough, mammoth, colossal, challenging, overwhelming, staggering.
Opposites: weak, easy.

formula NOUN **1 = form of words**, set expression, wording, rubric, formulary. **2 = recipe**, prescription, method, blueprint, procedure, convention, modus operandi, ritual, principles, rules, precepts, rubric.

formulate VERB **1 = draw up**, work out, plan, map out, prepare, compose, devise, think up, conceive, create, invent, coin, design. **2 = define**, state clearly, set down, frame, give form to, specify, itemize, detail, indicate, systematize.

forsake VERB **1 = desert**, abandon, leave, quit, jilt, throw over, cast off, discard, repudiate, reject, disown; [inf] leave in the lurch, leave flat. **2 = give up**, renounce, relinquish, forgo, turn one's back on, repudiate, have done with, discard, set aside.

forthcoming ADJ
1 = future, coming, expected, prospective,

imminent, impending.
2 = communicative,
informative, talkative,
expansive, voluble,
chatty, loquacious, open.

forthright ADJ **= direct**,
frank, open, candid,
blunt, outspoken, plain-
speaking, plain-spoken,
straightforward, honest.
Opposites: evasive.

fortify VERB **1 = build
defences round**, protect,
secure, garrison, cover,
guard, buttress, shore up.
2 = strengthen,
invigorate, energize,
revive, embolden, give
courage to, encourage,
cheer, hearten, buoy up,
reassure, make confident,
brace, sustain.

fortitude NOUN **= strength**,
firmness, courage, nerve,
grit, backbone, bravery,
pluck, mettle,
fearlessness, valour,
intrepidity, stout-
heartedness, forbearance,
tenacity, perseverance,
resolution, resoluteness,
determination.
Opposites: cowardice.

fortunate ADJ **= lucky**,
blessed, favoured, in

luck, having a charmed
life, happy, felicitous,
prosperous, well off,
successful, flourishing;
[inf] sitting pretty, born
with a silver spoon in
one's mouth; [Brit.
inf] jammy.

fortune NOUN **1 = wealth**,
affluence, treasure,
opulence, prosperity,
riches, property, assets,
means, possessions.
2 = huge amount, mint,
king's ransom;
[inf] packet, bundle,
bomb, pile. **3 = chance**,
accident, luck,
coincidence, happy
chance, fortuity,
serendipity, contingency,
providence.
Opposites: pittance.

fortune-teller NOUN
= seer, soothsayer,
prophet, prophetess,
augur, diviner, sibyl,
oracle, clairvoyant,
astrologer.

forward ADJ **1 = onward**,
advancing, progressing,
progressive, frontal.
2 = advanced, well
advanced, early,
premature, precocious.

3 = **front**, at the front/
fore, fore, frontal,
foremost, head, leading,
advance. **4** = **bold**, brash,
brazen, audacious,
presumptuous, cocky,
familiar, assertive,
confident, overweening,
aggressive, pushy,
thrusting, pert,
impudent, impertinent,
cheeky, insolent;
[inf] brass-necked, fresh.
Opposites: backward, shy.
▸ ADV **1** = **towards the front**,
onward, onwards, on,
ahead, forth. **2** = **out**, into
view, into the open, into
public view.
▸ VERB **1** = **send on**, pass on,
dispatch, transmit, post,
mail, ship, freight,
deliver. **2** = **advance**,
further, hasten, speed up,
hurry along, accelerate,
expedite, step up, aid,
assist, help, encourage,
foster, promote, favour,
support, back, give
backing to.

foster VERB **1** = **encourage**,
promote, further,
stimulate, boost,
advance, forward,
cultivate, foment, help,

aid, assist, support,
uphold, back, give
backing to, facilitate.
2 = **bring up**, rear, raise,
care for, look after, take
care of, mother, parent.
3 = **cherish**, harbour,
hold, entertain, nurse,
nourish, nurture, sustain.

foul ADJ **1** = **disgusting**,
revolting, repulsive,
nauseating, sickening,
loathsome, odious,
abominable, offensive,
nasty. **2** = **evil-smelling**,
stinking, high, rank,
fetid; [poetic/
literary] mephitic,
noisome. **3** = **impure**,
contaminated, polluted,
adulterated, infected,
tainted, defiled, filthy,
dirty, unclean.
4 = **blasphemous**,
profane, obscene, vulgar,
offensive, coarse, filthy,
dirty, indecent,
indelicate, smutty,
salacious, suggestive, off
colour, low, ribald, lewd,
scatological; [inf] blue.
5 = **abhorrent**, detestable,
hateful, loathsome,
despicable, contemptible,
offensive, odious,

disgusting, revolting, dishonourable, disgraceful, base, low, mean, sordid, vile, wicked, heinous, execrable, iniquitous, nefarious, infamous.

6 = unfair, dishonourable, dishonest, underhand, unsportsmanlike, unsporting, dirty, unprincipled, unscrupulous, immoral, fraudulent; [inf] crooked.

▶ VERB **= dirty**, soil, stain, blacken, muddy, begrime, smear, spatter, besmear, defile, pollute, contaminate, taint, sully; [poetic/literary] besmirch.

found VERB **= establish**, set up, institute, originate, initiate, bring into being, create, start, inaugurate, constitute, endow, organize, develop.

foundation NOUN **1 = base**, bottom, substructure, bedrock, substratum, understructure, underpinning. **2 = basis**, groundwork, principles, fundamentals, rudiments. **3 = establishment**, founding, institution, inauguration, initiation, constitution, endowment.

founder NOUN **= establisher**, builder, constructor, maker, initiator, institutor, beginner, inventor, discoverer, framer, designer, architect, creator, author, originator, organizer, developer, generator, prime mover, father, patriarch.

fountain NOUN **1 = spray**, jet, spout, well, fount, stream, fountainhead. **2 = source**, fount, fountainhead, origin, wellspring, commencement, beginning, cause, birth, genesis, root, mainspring, derivation, inception, inspiration.

fractious ADJ **= bad-tempered**, cross, irritable, ill-humoured, ill-natured, petulant, testy, querulous, touchy, irascible, sulky, sullen, morose; [inf] snappish.

fracture NOUN = **break**, breakage, rupture, split, crack, fissure, cleft, rift, rent, chink, crevice, gap, opening, aperture.

▶ VERB = **break**, crack, split, rupture, splinter.

fragile ADJ **1** = **flimsy**, breakable, frail, delicate, insubstantial, brittle, dainty, fine. **2** = **ill**, unwell, sickly, ailing, delicate, weak, infirm. **Opposites:** strong.

fragment NOUN = **piece**, part, particle, shred, chip, shard, sliver, splinter, scrap, bit, snip, snippet, wisp, tatter, remnant, remainder, fraction.

▶ VERB = *see* **break** VERB (**1**).

fragmentary ADJ = **incomplete**, partial, piecemeal, disconnected, broken, disjointed, discontinuous, uneven, incoherent, scrappy, bitty, sketchy, unsystematic. **Opposites:** complete, whole.

fragrance NOUN = **scent**, smell, perfume, aroma, bouquet, balm, balminess; [poetic/ literary] redolence.

fragrant ADJ = **sweet-smelling**, aromatic, scented, perfumed, balmy, odorous, odoriferous; [poetic/ literary] redolent. **Opposites:** smelly.

frail ADJ **1** = **fragile**, breakable, delicate, easily broken; [formal] frangible. **2** = **weak**, infirm, ill, unwell, sickly, ailing, delicate, slight, slender, puny, unsound. **Opposites:** strong, robust.

frame NOUN **1** = **structure**, framework, foundation, body, chassis, skeleton, scaffolding, shell, casing, support. **2** = **body**, physique, build, figure, shape, size, carcass. **3** = **mount**, mounting, setting, border.

▶ VERB **1** = **formulate**, put together, draw up, plan, think up, draft, map out, shape, compose, form, devise, create, establish, conceive. **2** = **incriminate**, fabricate charges/ evidence against; [Brit. inf] fit up.

framework NOUN **1** = *See* **frame** NOUN (**1**). **2** = **order**, organization, frame, scheme, fabric.

frank ADJ **1** = **candid**, direct, straightforward, plain, plain-spoken, straight, outspoken, blunt, open, sincere, honest, truthful, artless, guileless, explicit, downright. **2** = **open**, obvious, transparent, patent, undisguised, manifest, unmistakable, evident, noticeable, visible.
Opposites: evasive.

frantic ADJ = **distraught**, overwrought, panic-stricken, panicky, beside oneself, at one's wits' end, frenzied, wild, hysterical, frenetic, berserk, worked up, fraught, distracted, agitated, distressed, out of control, uncontrolled, unhinged, mad, crazed, out of one's mind, maniacal.
Opposites: calm.

fraud NOUN
1 = **fraudulence**, sharp practice, cheating, swindling, crookedness, embezzlement, trickery, deceit, double-dealing, duplicity, treachery, chicanery, imposture, skulduggery; [inf] monkey business. **2** = **ruse**, trick, deception, swindle, hoax, subterfuge, wile, stratagem, artifice.
3 = **impostor**, fake, sham, cheat, cheater, swindler, trickster, charlatan, quack, mountebank; [inf] phoney, con man.

fraudulent ADJ
= **dishonest**, cheating, swindling, criminal, deceitful, double-dealing, duplicitous, unscrupulous, dishonourable; [inf] crooked, shady, sharp.
Opposites: honest.

fraught ADJ **1** = **filled with**, full of, attended by, teeming with, accompanied by.
2 = **anxious**, distraught, overwrought, agitated, worked up, distracted, distressed.

fray VERB **1** = **unravel**, wear, wear thin, wear out/

away, become threadbare, become tattered/ragged. **2 = strain**, tax, overtax, irritate, put on edge, make edgy/tense.

freak NOUN **1 = aberration**, abnormality, oddity, irregularity, monster, monstrosity, mutant, malformation. **2 = oddity**, peculiar person; [inf] queer fish, odd bod, oddball, weirdo, nutcase, nut. **3 = fan**, enthusiast, fanatic, addict, aficionado, devotee; [inf] buff, fiend, nut.
▸ ADJ **= abnormal**, unusual, aberrant, atypical, exceptional, unaccountable, unpredictable, unforeseeable, bizarre, queer, odd, unparalleled, fluky.

free ADJ **1 = free of charge**, complimentary, for nothing, without charge, gratis, at no cost, for free, on the house.
2 = available, unoccupied, at leisure, with time on one's hands, with time to spare. **3 = unoccupied**, empty, vacant, available, spare, untaken, uninhabited.
4 = independent, self-governing, autonomous, sovereign, emancipated, democratic, enfranchised. **5 = at liberty**, at large, loose, on the loose, unconfined, unchained, unrestrained, unshackled, unfettered.
6 = unobstructed, unimpeded, clear, unblocked, unhampered.
7 = familiar, overfamiliar, bold, assertive, presumptuous, cocky, forward, cheeky, aggressive, impudent.
▸ VERB **1 = set free**, release, let go, set at liberty, liberate, turn loose, untie, unchain, unfetter, unshackle, uncage, unleash, deliver.
2 = rescue, release, extricate, get loose, disentangle, disengage, disencumber. **3 = exempt**, make exempt, excuse, except, relieve.
▪ **free of/from = without**, devoid of, lacking in, exempt from, not liable to, safe from, immune

to, unaffected by, clear of, unencumbered by, relieved of, released from, rid of.

freedom NOUN **1 = liberty**, emancipation, release, deliverance, independence, autonomy, sovereignty, self-government, enfranchisement; [historical] manumission. **2 = scope**, latitude, flexibility, wide margin, elbow room, licence, facility, free rein. **3 = naturalness**, openness, lack of reserve, informality, lack of ceremony, spontaneity. **Opposites:** captivity.

freeze VERB **1 = ice over/ up**, glaciate, solidify, harden. **2 = chill**, cool, make cold, deep-freeze. **3 = stand still**, stop dead, stop in one's tracks, go rigid, become motionless. **4 = fix**, hold, peg, suspend.

freezing ADJ **= bitterly cold**, chilling, frosty, glacial, arctic, wintry, raw, biting, piercing, penetrating, cutting, numbing, Siberian.

freight NOUN **= cargo**, load, consignment, lading, merchandise, goods.

frenzy NOUN **= madness**, mania, insanity, wild excitement, wildness, hysteria, agitation, distraction, fit, seizure, paroxysm, outburst, spasm.

frequent ADJ **1 = many**, numerous, several, repeated, recurrent, persistent, continuing, quite a lot/few. **2 = regular**, habitual, common, customary, usual, familiar, everyday, continual, constant, incessant. **Opposites:** infrequent.
▶ VERB **= visit**, attend, haunt, patronize; [inf] hang out at.

fresh ADJ **1 = natural**, unprocessed, raw, newly harvested, crisp, unwilted, undried, uncured. **2 = new**, brand new, recent, latest, up to date, modern, new-fangled, innovative, different, original, novel, unusual, unconventional, unorthodox.

3 = energetic, vigorous, invigorated, lively, vibrant, spry, sprightly, bright, alert, bouncing, refreshed, rested, restored, revived, fresh as a daisy; [inf] full of beans, bright-eyed and bushy-tailed. **4 = additional**, more, further, extra, supplementary.

5 = healthy, clear, bright, wholesome, blooming, glowing, fair, rosy, pink, ruddy. **6 = clear**, bright, cool, crisp, sparkling, pure, clean, refreshing.

7 = familiar, overfamiliar, forward, presumptuous, cocky, bold, audacious, brazen, cheeky, impudent, impertinent, insolent, disrespectful; [inf] brass-necked.

Opposites: stale, old, tired.

fret VERB **1 = worry**, be upset, be distressed, be anxious, agonize, pine, brood, mope, fuss, complain, grumble, whine. **2 =** See **annoy** (**2**).

friction NOUN **1 = abrasion**, attrition, rubbing, chafing, scraping, rasping. **2 = dissension**, dissent, disagreement, discord, strife, conflict, contention, dispute, argument, quarrelling, bickering, squabbling, hostility, rivalry, animosity, antagonism, resentment, bad feeling.

Opposites: harmony.

friend NOUN **= companion**, crony, bosom friend, comrade, playmate, soul mate, intimate, confidante, alter ego, ally, acquaintance, associate, familiar, shadow; [inf] pal, chum; [Brit. inf] mate; [N. Amer. inf] buddy.

Opposites: enemy.

friendless ADJ **= alone**, companionless, by oneself, lone, lonely, lonesome, with no one to turn to, solitary, with no ties, unattached, single, forlorn, unpopular, unloved, forsaken, deserted, ostracized, abandoned.

friendliness NOUN **= amiability**, affability, geniality, warmth, affection, companionability, cordiality, conviviality, sociability, neighbourliness, approachability, communicativeness, good-naturedness, amenability, benevolence. **Opposites:** hostility.

friendly ADJ **1 = amiable**, affable, warm, genial, agreeable, companionable, cordial, convivial, sociable, hospitable, comradely, neighbourly, outgoing, approachable, accessible, communicative, open, unreserved, easy-going, good-natured, kindly, benign, amenable, well disposed, sympathetic, benevolent; [inf] chummy; [Brit. inf] matey.
2 = amicable, close, cordial, congenial, intimate, familiar, peaceable, conciliatory. **Opposites:** unfriendly.

friendship NOUN **1 = close relationship**, companionship, intimacy, rapport,

affinity, attachment, alliance, harmony, fellowship, mutual understanding, amity, comradeship.
2 = friendliness, affability, amiability, warmth, geniality, cordiality, neighbourliness, good-naturedness, kindliness.

fright NOUN **1 = fear**, terror, alarm, horror, dread, fearfulness, apprehension, trepidation, consternation, dismay, disquiet, nervousness, panic; [inf] blue funk, jitters, heebie-jeebies, willies. **2 = scare**, shock, shivers.

frighten VERB **= scare**, terrify, startle, alarm, terrorize, give a shock to, shock, panic, appal, throw into a panic, unnerve, unman, intimidate, cow, daunt, dismay, make someone's blood run cold, freeze someone's blood; [inf] scare the living daylights out of, scare stiff, scare someone out of their wits, scare witless, make someone's hair stand on end, make someone's hair curl, throw into a blue funk, make someone jump out of their skin, spook; [Brit. inf] put the wind up.

frightful ADJ 1 = **dreadful**, terrible, horrible, horrid, hideous, ghastly, gruesome, grisly, macabre, grim, dire, abhorrent, revolting, repulsive, loathsome, odious, fearful, fearsome, terrifying, alarming, shocking, harrowing, appalling, daunting, unnerving. 2 = **disagreeable**, unpleasant, dreadful, horrible, terrible, awful, ghastly, insufferable, unbearable, annoying, irritating. 3 = **very bad**, terrible, dreadful, awful, ghastly, nasty.

frigid ADJ 1 = **cold**, icy, distant, austere, aloof, remote, unapproachable, forbidding, stiff, formal, unbending, cool, unfeeling, unemotional, unfriendly, hostile, unenthusiastic.

2 = **passionless**, cold, unresponsive, passive. 3 = **very cold**, bitterly cold, freezing, frozen, icy, frosty, chilly, wintry, arctic, glacial, Siberian, polar, gelid.

fringe NOUN 1 = **border**, frill, ruffle, gathering, trimming, tassels, edging. 2 = **outer edge**, edge, border, perimeter, periphery, margin, rim, limits, outskirts, verge.

frisky ADJ = **lively**, bouncy, active, playful, spirited, romping, rollicking, sportive, in high spirits, high-spirited, exuberant, joyful, sprightly, perky, jaunty; [inf] full of beans; [poetic/literary] frolicsome.

frivolity NOUN 1 = **light-heartedness**, gaiety, levity, fun, silliness, foolishness. 2 = **empty-headedness**, frivolousness, giddiness, flightiness, dizziness, flippancy, silliness, zaniness.

frivolous ADJ 1 = **silly**, flighty, foolish, dizzy, facetious, flippant, senseless, giddy, light-

hearted, merry, superficial, shallow, empty-headed, feather-brained. **2 = flippant**, ill-considered, inane, facetious, superficial, shallow; [inf] flip.
Opposites: serious.

frolic VERB **= gambol**, cavort, skip, frisk, caper, cut capers, dance, leap, romp, trip, prance, hop, jump, bounce, rollick, sport, curvet.
▶ NOUN **= romp**, lark, antics, caper, escapade, prank, revels, spree, high jinks.

front NOUN **1 = face**, facade, frontage, fore, forepart, foremost part, forefront, foreground, anterior. **2 = head**, top, lead, beginning. **3 = front line**, vanguard, van, firing line. **4 = cover**, blind, facade, disguise, pretext, mask.
Opposites: back.
▶ ADJ **= leading**, lead, first, foremost.
▪ **front on = face towards**, look out on, overlook, lie opposite to.

frontier NOUN **= border**, boundary, limit, edge, rim, bounds, confines, marches.

frosty ADJ **1 = freezing**, frozen, cold, glacial, frigid, arctic, icy, wintry, bitter. **2 = unfriendly**, cold, unwelcoming, unenthusiastic, icy, glacial.

froth NOUN **= foam**, fizz, lather, head, scum, effervescence, bubbles, suds, spume.

frown VERB **1 = scowl**, glare, glower, knit one's brows, lower, lour; [inf] look daggers at, give a dirty look to. **2 = disapprove of**, view with dislike/disfavour, dislike, not take kindly to, not think much of, take a dim view of, look askance at.

frugal ADJ **= thrifty**, economical, sparing, careful, prudent, abstemious, scrimping, niggardly, cheese-paring, penny-pinching, miserly, parsimonious; [inf] stingy.
Opposites: extravagant, spendthrift.

fruitful ADJ **1 = fertile**, fecund, potent,

abundant, flourishing, lush, copious, bountiful; [poetic/literary] bounteous. **2 = useful**, worthwhile, productive, well spent, profitable, advantageous, beneficial, rewarding, gainful, successful, effective. **Opposites**: barren, futile, fruitless.

fruition NOUN **= fulfilment**, realization, materialization, achievement, attainment, success, completion, consummation, actualization, perfection, maturation, maturity, ripening.

fruitless ADJ **= futile**, useless, vain, in vain, to no avail, worthless, pointless, abortive, to no effect, idle, ineffectual, ineffective, inefficacious, unproductive, unrewarding, profitless, unsuccessful, unavailing. **Opposites**: fruitful, productive.

frustrate VERB **1 = discourage**, dishearten, dispirit, depress, dissatisfy, make discontented, anger, annoy, vex, irritate, embitter, irk. **2 = defeat**, thwart, obstruct, impede, hamper, hinder, check, block, counter, foil, baulk, forestall, disappoint, baffle, stymie, stop, cripple, spoil, circumvent.

fudge VERB **= evade**, dodge, avoid, shift ground about.

fuel VERB **= supply with fuel**, fire, stoke up, charge, power.

fugitive NOUN **= escapee**, runaway, deserter, refugee, renegade. ▸ ADJ **= transient**, transitory, fleeting, ephemeral, passing, impermanent, momentary, short-lived, short, brief, evanescent, fugacious.

fulfil VERB **1 = accomplish**, achieve, carry out, execute, perform, discharge, complete, implement, finish, conclude, effect; [formal] effectuate. **2 = satisfy**, realize, attain, consummate. **3 = conform to**, satisfy, fill, answer, meet, comply with, obey.

full ADJ **1** = **filled up**, filled, filled to the brim, brimming, overflowing, filled to capacity. **2** = **crowded**, packed, crammed, solid with people, chock-a-block, chock-full; [inf] jam-packed. **3** = **satisfied**, sated, gorged, replete, glutted, cloyed. **4** = **complete**, entire, whole, comprehensive, thorough, exhaustive, detailed, all-inclusive, all-encompassing, extensive, unabridged. **5** = **baggy**, voluminous, loose-fitting, capacious. **6** = **rich**, deep, resonant, loud, strong; [inf] fruity. **Opposites:** empty, incomplete.

fully ADV = **completely**, entirely, wholly, totally, thoroughly, in all respects, utterly, amply, satisfactorily.

fumble VERB **1** = **fail to catch**, miss, drop, mishandle, misfield. **2** = **grope**, feel about, search blindly, scrabble about/around.

fume VERB = **be enraged**, seethe, boil, be livid, rage, rant and rave, be furious, be incensed, flare up; [inf] be up in arms, get hot under the collar, fly off the handle, foam at the mouth, get all steamed up, flip one's lid, blow one's top.

fumes PL NOUN = **vapour**, gas, exhaust, smoke, pollution, smog, fog.

fun NOUN **1** = **amusement**, entertainment, recreation, relaxation, enjoyment, pleasure, diversion, play, playfulness, tomfoolery, buffoonery, distraction, good time, jollification, merrymaking, junketing; [inf] living it up, skylarking. **2** = **merriment**, gaiety, mirth, laughter, hilarity, glee, cheerfulness, gladness, jollity, joy, high spirits, zest. **Opposites:** misery.
■ **make fun of** = **ridicule**, deride, mock, scoff at, sneer at, taunt, jeer at, lampoon, parody; [inf] send up, rib, take off.

function NOUN 1 = **role**, capacity, responsibility, duty, task, job, post, situation, office, occupation, employment, business, charge, province, concern, activity, operation, mission.
2 = **social event**, gathering, affair, reception, party; [inf] do; [Brit. inf] beanfeast.
▶ VERB = **work**, go, run, be in working order, operate.

functional ADJ
1 = **practical**, useful, serviceable, utilitarian, working, workaday, hard-wearing.
2 = **working**, in working order, going, running, operative, in commission.

fund NOUN = **reserve**, collection, pool, kitty, endowment, foundation, grant, investment, capital, savings.
▶ VERB = **finance**, pay for, back, subsidize, stake, endow, support.

fundamental ADJ = **basic**, rudimentary, elemental, underlying, primary, cardinal, initial, original, prime, first, principal, chief, key, central, structural, organic, inherent, intrinsic, vital, essential, important, indispensable, necessary. **Opposites:** unimportant.

fundamentally ADV
= **basically**, at heart, at bottom, deep down, essentially, intrinsically.

funds PL NOUN = **money**, ready money, cash, hard cash, capital, the wherewithal, means, assets, resources, savings; [inf] dough, bread; [Brit. inf] dosh.

funny ADJ 1 = **amusing**, comical, comic, humorous, hilarious, entertaining, diverting, laughable, hysterical, side-splitting, witty, jocular, riotous, droll, absurd, rich, facetious, ludicrous, ridiculous, farcical, risible, silly, slapstick, waggish.
2 = **peculiar**, odd, strange, curious, queer, bizarre, mysterious, suspicious, dubious; [inf] weird.

Opposites: serious.

furious ADJ **1 = enraged**, very angry, raging, infuriated, livid, fuming, boiling, incensed, inflamed, frenzied, indignant, mad, maddened, wrathful, beside oneself, in high dudgeon; [inf] hot under the collar, up in arms, foaming at the mouth. **2 = violent**, fierce, wild, intense, vehement, unrestrained, tumultuous, tempestuous, stormy, turbulent, boisterous. Opposites: calm.

furnish VERB **1 = provide with furniture**, fit out, outfit, appoint. **2 = supply**, provide, give, present, offer, equip, grant, bestow, endow, provision.

furniture NOUN **= furnishings**, house fittings, effects, movables, appointments, chattels.

furore NOUN **= commotion**, uproar, disturbance, hullabaloo, turmoil, tumult, brouhaha, tempest, stir, excitement, outburst, outcry; [inf] to-do.

furrow NOUN **1 = groove**, trench, channel, rut, trough, ditch, seam, hollow. **2 = crease**, line, wrinkle, crinkle, corrugation, crow's foot.

further ADJ **= additional**, more, extra, supplementary, other, new, fresh.
▶ ADV **= furthermore**, moreover, what's more, also, besides, additionally, as well, to boot, on top of that, over and above that, by the same token.
▶ VERB **= advance**, forward, facilitate, aid, assist, help, lend a hand to, promote, back, contribute to, encourage, foster, champion.

furthest ADJ **= farthest**, furthermost, most distant, most remote, outermost, outmost, extreme, uttermost, ultimate.

furtive ADJ **= secretive**, secret, stealthy, surreptitious, clandestine,

sneaky, sneaking, hidden, disguised, shifty, skulking, covert, cloaked, conspiratorial, sly, underhand, under the table, wily.
Opposites: open, above board.

fury NOUN 1 = **anger**, rage, wrath, madness, passion, frenzy; [poetic/literary] ire.
2 = **fierceness**, violence, ferocity, intensity, force, power, severity, turbulence, tempestuousness.

fuse VERB = **combine**, amalgamate, join, put together, unite, blend, intermix, intermingle, merge, coalesce, integrate, meld, compound, agglutinate, weld, solder.
Opposites: separate.

fuss NOUN = **fluster**, agitation, excitement, bother, commotion, stir, confusion, uproar, tumult, upset, worry; [inf] palaver, storm in a teacup, flap, tizzy, stew.
▸ VERB = **be worried/ agitated**, worry, rush about, dash about; [inf] get worked up, be in a tizzy, flap, be in a stew, make a big thing out of it.

fussy ADJ 1 = **particular**, over-particular, finicky, pernickety, fastidious, hard to please, difficult, exacting, demanding, selective, discriminating, faddish; [inf] choosy, picky, nit-picking; [Brit. inf] faddy. 2 = **cluttered**, busy, over-decorated, ornate, overdone, over-elaborate, rococo, over-embellished.

futile ADJ = **useless**, vain, in vain, to no avail, ineffectual, unsuccessful, unproductive, unprofitable, abortive, unavailing, inefficacious, barren, impotent, hollow.
Opposites: fruitful.

future NOUN 1 = **time to come**, time ahead, hereafter, coming times.
2 = **prospects**, expectations, anticipation, outlook, likely success/ advancement.

▶ ADJ = **forthcoming**, coming, impending, approaching, prospective, expected, planned, destined, awaited.

fuzzy ADJ 1 = **downy**, down-covered, frizzy, woolly, furry, fleecy, fluffy, linty, napped.

2 = **out of focus**, unfocused, blurred, blurry, indistinct, unclear, misty, distorted, ill-defined, bleary.

Gg

gadget NOUN = **appliance**, apparatus, device, contrivance, mechanism, instrument, tool, implement, invention, contraption; [inf] widget, gizmo.

gaffe NOUN = **mistake**, blunder, slip, indiscretion, faux pas, solecism, gaucherie; [inf] clanger, howler, boo-boo; [Brit. inf] boob; [Brit. inf, dated] bloomer.

gag NOUN = **joke**, witticism, jest, quip, funny remark, hoax, prank; [inf] crack, wisecrack.

gaiety NOUN
1 = **cheerfulness**, light-heartedness, merriment, glee, happiness, high spirits, gladness, delight, joy, joyfulness, joyousness, pleasure, exuberance, elation, jollity, hilarity, mirth, joviality, liveliness, animation, vivacity, effervescence, buoyancy, sprightliness, exultation; [poetic/literary] blitheness.
2 = **colourfulness**, brightness, sparkle, brilliance, glitter, showiness, gaudiness, garishness.
Opposites: gloom.

gain VERB 1 = **obtain**, get, acquire, secure, procure, attain, build up, achieve, arrive at, come to have, win, capture, pick up, net, reap, gather.
2 = **increase in**, add on, get more of. 3 = **catch up with**, get nearer to, close in on, narrow the gap between, overtake, come up to, approach.
4 = **reach**, arrive at, get to, come to, attain.
Opposites: lose.

▶ NOUN **1** = **increase**, addition, rise, augmentation, increment, accumulation, accretion. **2** = **profit**, earnings, income, advantage, benefit, reward, yield, return, winnings, proceeds, dividend, interest, emolument; [inf] pickings.

gainful ADJ = **profitable**, rewarding, remunerative, lucrative, productive, beneficial, fruitful, advantageous, worthwhile, useful.

gait NOUN = **walk**, step, stride, pace, tread, manner of walking, bearing, carriage.

gale NOUN = **storm**, tempest, hurricane, squall, tornado, cyclone, typhoon.

gallant ADJ **1** = **chivalrous**, gentlemanly, courtly, courteous, polite, attentive, gracious, considerate, thoughtful, obliging, deferential. **2** = **brave**, courageous, valiant, bold, daring, plucky, fearless, intrepid, dashing, heroic, lion-hearted, mettlesome. **Opposites:** rude, cowardly.

galvanize VERB = **electrify**, shock, stir, startle, jolt, arouse, awaken, spur, prod, stimulate, invigorate, fire, animate, vitalize, energize, thrill, inspire.

gamble VERB **1** = **bet**, wager, lay a bet, place a wager, stake, game, try one's luck; [inf] punt; [Brit. inf] have a flutter. **2** = **take a chance/risk**, speculate, venture; [inf] stick one's neck out, go out on a limb, take a flier.

game NOUN **1** = **pastime**, diversion, recreation, entertainment, amusement, sport, play, distraction, frolic, romp, fun, merriment. **2** = **match**, contest, tournament, meeting, event, round, bout. **3** = **business**, line, trade, occupation, profession, industry, activity, calling. **4** = **wild animals**, quarry, prey, big game.

gang NOUN = **group**, band, company, crowd, gathering, pack, horde, mob, herd.

gangly ADJ = **lanky**, rangy, skinny, angular, spindly, awkward.

gangster NOUN = **racketeer**, crook, criminal, hoodlum, Mafioso, gang member, mobster, robber, brigand, bandit, desperado, thug; [inf] tough; [N. Amer. inf] hood.

gap NOUN **1** = **opening**, hole, aperture, cavity, space, breach, break, fracture, rift, fissure, rent, cleft, chink, crack, crevice, divide, cranny, orifice, interstice. **2** = **pause**, break, intermission, interval, interlude, lull, respite, breathing space, rest, suspension, hiatus, recess. **3** = **omission**, blank, lacuna, void, vacuity. **4** = **difference**, disparity, inconsistency, incompatibility, disagreement, divergence, breach, discrepancy, distance, division.

gape VERB **1** = **stare**, gaze, goggle, ogle; [inf] gawk, rubberneck. **2** = **open wide**, open up, yawn, part, split, crack.

garb NOUN = **clothes**, garments, clothing, dress, attire, costume, outfit, wear, uniform, vestments, livery, trappings; [inf] gear, get-up, togs, rig-out, duds; [formal] apparel; [archaic] habit.
▶ VERB = **clothe**, dress, attire, array, robe, cover, outfit, fit; [inf] kit out, rig out; [archaic] apparel.

garbage NOUN = **waste**, rubbish, refuse, litter, debris, junk, filth, detritus, scraps, leftovers, remains, slops.

garble VERB = **distort**, twist, warp, slant, doctor, falsify, pervert, corrupt, misstate, misquote, misreport, misrepresent, misinterpret, misunderstand.

garish ADJ = **flashy**, flash, showy, loud, gaudy, lurid, bold, glaring, brassy, tinselly, vivid,

tawdry, tasteless, in poor taste, vulgar.
Opposites: sober, tasteful.

garner VERB = **gather**, collect, accumulate, heap, pile up, amass, stack up, assemble, hoard, stockpile, deposit, husband, reserve, save, preserve.

garrison NOUN 1 = **force**, detachment, unit, brigade, platoon, squadron. 2 = **barracks**, base, fort, fortress, fortification, stronghold, camp, encampment, citadel.
▶ VERB = **station**, post, assign, position, billet, send in.

garrulous ADJ = **talkative**, chatty, verbose, loquacious, long-winded, effusive; [inf] mouthy, gabby.
Opposites: taciturn.

gash VERB = **cut**, slash, tear, lacerate, wound, gouge, incise, slit, rend, split, rent, nick, cleave.

gasp VERB = **pant**, puff, puff and blow, blow, catch one's breath, gulp, choke, fight for breath, wheeze; [inf] huff and puff.

gate NOUN = **barrier**, door, gateway, doorway, access, entrance, exit, opening, turnstile, passage, egress, portal, wicket, postern.

gather VERB 1 = **come together**, collect, assemble, congregate, meet, group, cluster, mass, crowd, flock together, convene, foregather, muster, converge, accumulate.
2 = **call together**, summon, assemble, collect, convene, round up, muster, marshal.
3 = **collect**, accumulate, assemble, amass, store, garner, stockpile, heap up, pile up, stack up, hoard; [inf] stash away.
4 = **understand**, be given to understand, believe, hear, learn, infer, deduce, conclude, come to the conclusion, surmise, assume. 5 = **harvest**, pick, collect, reap, glean, garner, cull, pluck.
6 = **increase**, grow, rise, build, expand, enlarge,

swell, extend, intensify, deepen, heighten, thicken.
Opposites: disperse.

gathering NOUN
= **assembly**, congregation, company, collection, group, crowd, band, throng, mass, horde, meeting, convention, conclave, rally, congress, convocation.

gauche ADJ = **awkward**, clumsy, ungainly, bumbling, maladroit, lumbering, inept, inelegant, unpolished, graceless, unsophisticated, uncultured, uncultivated.
Opposites: sophisticated, adroit.

gaudy ADJ = *see* **garish**.

gauge NOUN **1** = **size**, measure, extent, degree, capacity, magnitude, height, width, thickness, span, bore. **2** = **measure**, basis, standard, guide, guideline, touchstone, yardstick, benchmark, criterion, rule, norm, example, model, pattern, exemplar, sample, test,

indicator.

gaunt ADJ **1** = **haggard**, drawn, cadaverous, skeletal, emaciated, skinny, skin and bone, spare, bony, angular, lanky, lean, raw-boned, spindly, pinched, hollow-cheeked, scrawny, scraggy, wasted, shrivelled, withered.
2 = **bleak**, barren, desolate, bare, dreary, dismal, forlorn, grim, stern, harsh, forbidding.
Opposites: fat, lush.

gay ADJ = **homosexual**, lesbian, homoerotic; [inf] queer; [Brit. inf] bent, poofy.
Opposites: heterosexual.

gaze VERB = **stare**, gape, take a good look, look fixedly, goggle, stand agog, watch in wonder, ogle, eye, contemplate; [inf] gawk, rubberneck, give the once-over.

gear NOUN **1** = **equipment**, tools, kit, apparatus, implements, tackle, appliances, utensils, supplies, accessories, paraphernalia, accoutrements, contrivances, trappings; [inf] stuff. **2 = belongings**, possessions, things, luggage, baggage, kit, effects, goods, paraphernalia, impedimenta, chattels.

genealogy NOUN **= family tree**, ancestry, pedigree, line, lineage, descent, parentage, birth, derivation, extraction, family, strain, stock, bloodline, heritage, roots.

general ADJ **1 = usual**, customary, common, ordinary, normal, standard, regular, everyday, typical, conventional, habitual, run-of-the-mill. **2 = common**, accepted, widespread, shared, broad, wide, prevalent, prevailing, universal, popular, public, generic, extensive. **3 = universal**, blanket, comprehensive, all-inclusive, across-the-board, broad-ranging, broad, sweeping, indiscriminate, catholic, encyclopedic. **4 = mixed**, assorted, miscellaneous, diversified, variegated,

composite, heterogeneous. **5 = broad**, loose, rough, approximate, non-specific, vague, ill-defined, indefinite, inexact, imprecise. **Opposites:** unusual, specific, detailed.

generally ADV **1 = usually**, in general, as a rule, normally, ordinarily, almost always, customarily, habitually, typically, regularly, for the most part, mainly, by and large, on average, on the whole, in most cases. **2 = commonly**, widely, extensively, universally, comprehensively.

generate VERB **= cause**, give rise to, produce, make, bring into being, create, engender, originate, initiate, occasion, arouse, whip up, propagate.

generosity NOUN **= liberality**, kindness, magnanimity, benevolence, munificence, open-handedness, bounty, hospitality, charitableness, lavishness.

generous ADJ **1** = **liberal**, kind, magnanimous, benevolent, munificent, beneficent, bountiful, hospitable, open-handed, charitable, ungrudging, lavish, unstinting, free-handed, princely; [poetic/literary] bounteous. **2** = **noble**, magnanimous, high-minded, honourable, good, unselfish, altruistic, unprejudiced, disinterested. **3** = **abundant**, liberal, plentiful, lavish, ample, rich, copious, superabundant, overflowing.
Opposites: mean, selfish, meagre.

genial ADJ = **amiable**, affable, friendly, sociable, congenial, amicable, convivial, good-humoured, good-natured, agreeable, warm, pleasant, cordial, amenable, well disposed, cheerful, cheery, kind, kindly, benign, happy, sunny, jovial, easy-going,

sympathetic.
Opposites: unfriendly.

genius NOUN **1** = **brilliant person**, mental giant, prodigy, virtuoso, master, mastermind, maestro, intellectual, intellect, expert, adept; [inf] brain, Einstein. **2** = **brilliance**, intelligence, cleverness, capability, flair, talent, aptitude, ability, capacity, endowment.

genteel ADJ
1 = **respectable**, refined, patrician, ladylike, gentlemanly, well bred, aristocratic, noble, blue-blooded, well born. **2** = **polite**, well mannered, courteous, mannerly, civil, gracious, decorous, courtly, polished, cultivated, stylish, elegant.
Opposites: uncouth.

gentle ADJ **1** = **tender**, kind, kindly, humane, benign, merciful, lenient, compassionate, tender-hearted, placid, sweet-tempered, mild, serene, soft, quiet, tranquil, still, peaceful, pacific, meek, dove-like. **2** = **mild**,

moderate, light,
temperate, soft, balmy.
3 = **soft**, tender, light,
smooth, soothing.
4 = **placid**, docile, tame,
biddable, tractable,
manageable, meek, easily
handled, broken, trained,
schooled. **5** = **gradual**,
slight, easy,
imperceptible.
Opposites: cruel, fierce,
rough.

genuine ADJ **1** = **real**,
authentic, true, pure,
actual, bona fide,
veritable, sound, pukka,
sterling, legitimate,
lawful, legal, valid,
original, unadulterated,
unalloyed; [inf] kosher,
honest-to-goodness.
2 = **sincere**, truthful,
honest, frank, candid,
open, natural,
unaffected, artless,
ingenuous; [inf] upfront.
Opposites: fake, insincere.

germ NOUN **1** = **microbe**,
micro-organism, bacillus,
bacterium, virus; [inf] bug.
2 = **beginning**, start,
genesis, seed, embryo,
root, bud, origin, source,
fount, fountain,
rudiment.

gesture NOUN = **signal**,
motion, sign, wave,
indication, gesticulation.
▶ VERB = **gesticulate**, signal,
make a sign, motion,
wave, indicate.

get VERB **1** = **acquire**,
obtain, come by, come
into possession of,
secure, procure, buy,
purchase. **2** = **receive**, be
sent, be given. **3** = **go for**,
fetch, bring, collect,
carry, transport, convey.
4 = **earn**, be paid, make,
bring in, clear, gross, net,
take home, pocket;
[inf] pull in. **5** = **capture**,
seize, arrest, apprehend,
take, trap, lay hold of,
grab, bag, take captive,
grasp; [inf] collar, nab; [Brit.
inf] nick. **6** = **understand**,
comprehend, grasp, see,
fathom, work out,
follow; [inf] make head or
tail of, catch on, get the
hang of. **7** = **persuade**,
induce, coax, talk into,
wheedle into, prevail
upon, influence, sway,
convince, win over.
8 = **become**, grow, come
to be, turn.

Opposites: lose.

■ **get ahead** = **succeed**, do well, make good, be successful, prosper, flourish, rise in the world.

■ **get at 1** = **find fault with**, pick on, criticize, carp, nag, taunt. **2** = **suggest**, mean, imply, hint, intend, lead up to.

■ **get by** = **survive**, cope, manage, subsist, exist, get along, fare, make both ends meet; [inf] keep one's head above water, make out.

■ **get out of** = **avoid**, dodge, evade, shirk, escape.

getaway NOUN = **escape**, flight, breakout, break, absconding.

ghastly ADJ **1** = **terrible**, horrible, frightful, dreadful, awful, horrid, horrendous, hideous, shocking, grim, gruesome, terrifying, frightening. **2** = **loathsome**, odious, nasty, contemptible, dreadful, appalling, foul. **3** = **very bad**, serious, grave, critical,

unforgivable, awful, terrible.

ghost NOUN **1** = **apparition**, spectre, spirit, phantom, wraith, shade; [inf] spook; [poetic/literary] phantasm. **2** = **suggestion**, hint, trace, glimmer, shadow, impression, semblance.

ghostly ADJ = **spectral**, phantom, ghost-like, wraithlike, unearthly, supernatural, other-worldly, illusory, insubstantial, shadowy, eerie, creepy, scary, weird, uncanny; [inf] spooky; [poetic/literary] phantasmal.

giant NOUN = **colossus**, behemoth, man mountain, titan, Goliath. ▶ ADJ = **gigantic**, enormous, huge, colossal, immense, vast, mammoth, gargantuan, titanic, elephantine, prodigious, stupendous, Brobdingnagian; [inf] jumbo.

gibe NOUN = see **jibe**.

giddy ADJ = **dizzy**, faint, light-headed, unsteady, reeling, vertiginous; [inf] woozy.

gift NOUN **1** = **present**, offering, donation, contribution, grant, bonus, bounty, largesse, boon, gratuity, benefaction, bequest, legacy, inheritance, endowment. **2** = **talent**, aptitude, flair, facility, knack, bent, ability, faculty, capacity, capability, skill, attribute, expertise, genius, mind for.

gifted ADJ = **talented**, brilliant, clever, bright, intelligent, ingenious, sharp, able, accomplished, capable, masterly, skilled, adroit, proficient, expert; [inf] smart.
Opposites: inept.

gigantic ADJ = *see* **giant** ADJ.

giggle VERB = **titter**, snigger, snicker, chuckle, chortle, laugh, cackle; [inf] tee-hee.

gingerly ADV = **cautiously**, warily, carefully, attentively, heedfully, vigilantly, watchfully, guardedly, prudently, circumspectly, judiciously, suspiciously, hesitantly, reluctantly, timidly, timorously.
Opposites: recklessly.

girl NOUN **1** = **young woman**, female, young lady, miss; [Scottish & N. English] lass, lassie; [inf] chick, filly; [Brit. inf] bird; [N. Amer. inf] babe, broad; [Austral./NZ inf] sheila. **2** = **girlfriend**, lover, sweetheart, mistress, inamorata.

girth NOUN = **circumference**, perimeter, size, bulk, measure.

gist NOUN = **essence**, substance, drift, sense, crux, significance, idea, import, core, quintessence, nucleus, kernel, nub, pith, marrow, burden.

give VERB **1** = **present**, hand, hand over, bestow, donate, contribute, confer, turn over, award, grant, accord, leave, will, bequeath, make over, entrust, consign, vouchsafe. **2** = **provide**, supply, furnish, proffer, offer. **3** = **produce**, yield,

afford, result in.
4 = cause, be a source of,
make, create. **5 = let out**,
utter, emit, issue, voice.

- **give away = reveal**,
disclose, divulge, let slip,
leak, let out, expose,
uncover.
- **give in = give up**,
surrender, admit defeat,
concede, yield,
capitulate, submit,
comply, succumb,
retreat; [inf] quit.
- **give off = emit**, send
out, throw out,
discharge, exude, release,
vent, produce.
- **give up = stop**, cease,
leave off, desist from,
swear off, renounce,
abandon, discontinue;
[inf] quit, cut out, chuck;
[formal] forswear.

glad ADJ **1 = happy**,
pleased, delighted,
thrilled, gratified,
overjoyed, elated,
satisfied, contented;
[inf] over the moon,
tickled pink; [Brit.
inf] chuffed. **2 = willing**,
eager, ready, prepared,
happy, pleased.
3 = welcome, joyful,
cheering, happy,
cheerful, pleasing,
gratifying.
Opposites: unhappy,
reluctant.

gladden VERB **= make
happy**, delight, cheer,
cheer up, hearten,
brighten up, raise
someone's spirits, please,
elate, buoy up, give a lift
to; [inf] buck up.
Opposites: sadden.

glamorous ADJ
1 = alluring, dazzling,
smart, elegant, beautiful,
lovely, attractive,
charming, fascinating,
exciting, beguiling,
bewitching, enchanting,
entrancing, irresistible,
tantalizing. **2 = exciting**,
fascinating, stimulating,
thrilling, glossy,
glittering; [inf] ritzy,
glitzy.
Opposites: dowdy, boring.

glamour NOUN **1 = beauty**,
loveliness, attractiveness,
allure, attraction,
elegance, charm,
fascination.
2 = excitement, allure,
charm, fascination,
enchantment,

captivation, magic, spell.

glance VERB = **look quickly/hurriedly**, take a quick look, glimpse, catch a glimpse, peek, peep, sneak a look.

glare VERB **1** = **scowl**, glower, frown, look threateningly, look daggers, give someone dirty looks, lour.
2 = **dazzle**, beam, flare, blaze, flame.

glaring ADJ **1** = **dazzling**, blazing, flaring.
2 = **obvious**, conspicuous, manifest, overt, patent, visible, flagrant, blatant, outrageous, egregious, gross.

glass NOUN = **tumbler**, flute, schooner, balloon, goblet, beaker.

glasses PL NOUN = **spectacles**, eyeglasses, bifocals, sunglasses, monocle, lorgnette, pince-nez, field glasses, binoculars, opera glasses.

glassy ADJ **1** = **shiny**, glossy, smooth, mirror-like, clear, transparent, translucent, limpid, pellucid. **2** = **glazed**, blank, expressionless, empty, vacant, deadpan, vacuous, fixed, unmoving, lifeless, motionless.

glaze VERB = **varnish**, coat, polish, enamel, lacquer, gloss, burnish.
▶ NOUN = **gloss**, lustre, finish, lacquer, enamel.

gleam VERB = **shine**, radiate, flash, glow, glint, flare, glisten, glitter, beam, shimmer, glimmer, sparkle, twinkle, scintillate.
▶ NOUN **1** = **beam**, flash, glow, shaft, ray, flare, glint. **2** = **lustre**, glow, shine, gloss, sheen, brightness, flash, brilliance, coruscation.

glee NOUN = **mirth**, merriment, gaiety, delight, joy, joyfulness, joyousness, gladness, happiness, pleasure, jollity, hilarity, jocularity, joviality, exhilaration, high spirits, cheerfulness, exaltation, elation, exuberance, liveliness, verve, triumph; [poetic/literary] blitheness.

gloom

glib ADJ = **smooth-talking**, fast-talking, slick, smooth, fluent, smooth-tongued, silver-tongued, plausible, talkative, voluble, loquacious, unctuous, having the gift of the gab; [inf] sweet-talking.
Opposites: tongue-tied, inarticulate.

glimpse VERB = **catch sight of**, catch a glimpse of, spot, spy, discern, make out, distinguish, notice, observe, sight, espy, descry.
▸ NOUN = **glance**, brief look, peek, peep, look, sight, view.

glint VERB = **shine**, sparkle, flash, twinkle, glitter, glimmer, blink, gleam, wink, shimmer, glisten, dazzle, scintillate.

glisten VERB = **shine**, shimmer, sparkle, twinkle, flicker, glint, blink, wink, gleam, flash, scintillate, coruscate.

glitter VERB = **sparkle**, twinkle, flicker, blink, wink, shimmer, glimmer, glint, flash, gleam.
▸ NOUN 1 = **sparkle**, twinkle, flicker, blink, winking.
2 = **showiness**, flashiness, glamour, ostentation, pageantry, splendour, fanfare; [inf] razzle-dazzle, glitz, pizzazz.

gloat VERB = **relish**, revel in, glory in, rejoice in, exult in, triumph over, crow about; [inf] rub it in.

global ADJ 1 = **worldwide**, universal, international, planetary. 2 = **general**, comprehensive, all-encompassing, exhaustive, encyclopedic, thorough, total, with no exceptions, across-the-board.

globule NOUN = **bead**, drop, ball, droplet, pearl, particle.

gloom NOUN 1 = **dimness**, darkness, dark, blackness, murkiness, shadowiness, shadiness, dullness, obscurity, dusk, twilight. 2 = **sadness**, melancholy, unhappiness, sorrow, woe, grief, despondency, misery, dejection, glumness, desolation, depression, despair, pessimism, hopelessness.

Opposites: light, cheer.

gloomy ADJ **1 = dark**, overcast, cloudy, dull, sunless, dim, shadowy, black, unlit, murky, sombre, dismal, dreary, shady, dingy. **2 = sad**, melancholy, unhappy, miserable, sorrowful, despondent, woebegone, disconsolate, dejected, downcast, downhearted, glum, dispirited, desolate, depressed, blue, pessimistic, morose; [inf] down in the mouth.
Opposites: bright, cheerful.

glorious ADJ
1 = illustrious, celebrated, noble, famous, famed, renowned, distinguished, honoured, eminent, magnificent, excellent, majestic, splendid, resplendent, supreme, triumphant, sublime, victorious. **2 = beautiful**, bright, sunny, brilliant, perfect. **3 = marvellous**, splendid, wonderful, delightful, enjoyable, pleasurable, fine, excellent, great; [inf] fab, terrific.

glory NOUN **1 = exaltation**, worship, adoration, honour, reverence, extolment, veneration, thanksgiving.
2 = distinction, fame, kudos, renown, honour, prestige, acclaim, illustriousness, credit, accolade, recognition; [formal] laudation.
3 = splendour, resplendence, magnificence, grandeur, majesty, pomp, pageantry, beauty.
Opposites: disgrace.
■ **glory in = exult in**, rejoice in, take pleasure in, be proud of, delight in, revel in, boast about, crow about, gloat about.

gloss NOUN **1 = shine**, sheen, lustre, gleam, brightness, brilliance, sparkle, polish, shimmer, burnish. **2 = front**, facade, disguise, mask, semblance, camouflage, show, veneer, surface.
■ **gloss over = evade**, avoid, smooth over, conceal, hide, cover up, disguise, mask, veil, whitewash.

glossy ADJ = **shining**, shiny, gleaming, bright, smooth, lustrous, glistening, brilliant, polished, burnished, glazed, silky, silken, sleek, waxed.
Opposites: dull, lustreless.

glow VERB 1 = **gleam**, shine, glimmer, smoulder, shed a glow, light up.
2 = **blush**, flush, redden, grow pink, go scarlet, colour, crimson, radiate, thrill, tingle.
▶ NOUN 1 = **gleam**, glimmer, luminosity, incandescence, phosphorescence, lambency. 2 = **brightness**, vividness, colourfulness, brilliance, radiance, splendour, richness.
3 = **blush**, rosiness, flush, pinkness, redness, crimson, reddening, scarlet, bloom.

glower VERB = **scowl**, stare angrily, glare, frown, give someone black/dirty looks, look daggers, lour.
Opposites: smile.

glowing ADJ 1 = **luminous**, bright, vivid, brilliant, radiant, rich, smouldering, incandescent, phosphorescent, aglow, lambent. 2 = **favourable**, enthusiastic, complimentary, laudatory, adulatory, ecstatic, rhapsodic, eulogistic, panegyrical; [inf] rave.

glue NOUN = **adhesive**, gum, fixative, paste, cement, epoxy resin, mucilage.
▶ VERB = **stick**, paste, gum, fix, affix, cement, bond, seal.

glum ADJ = **gloomy**, melancholy, sad, despondent, miserable, dejected, downcast, downhearted, dispirited, depressed, in low spirits; [inf] down in the mouth.
Opposites: cheerful.

glut NOUN = **surplus**, excess, surfeit, over-abundance, superabundance, oversupply, overprovision, saturation, superfluity.
Opposites: dearth.

glutinous ADJ = **sticky**, viscous, tacky, mucous,

gummy, adhesive, viscid, glue-like, mucilaginous.

gluttonous ADJ = **greedy**, voracious, insatiable, ravenous, gormandizing; [inf] piggish, hoggish.

gnaw VERB = **chew**, munch, bite, nibble, masticate, worry.

go VERB 1 = **move**, proceed, progress, walk, pass, travel, journey, repair. 2 = **leave**, go away, depart, withdraw, retire, set off, set out, decamp; [inf] beat it, scram. 3 = **work**, be in working order, function, operate, be operative, run, perform. 4 = **become**, grow, get, come to be, turn. 5 = **belong**, have a place, fit in, be located, be situated, be found, lie, stand. 6 = **stop**, cease, disappear, vanish, be no more, fade away, melt away. 7 = **turn out**, work out, fare, progress, develop, result, end, end up, eventuate. 8 = **match**, go together, be compatible, blend, suit each other, complement each other, harmonize,

accord, be in accord.
▶ NOUN = **try**, attempt, turn, opportunity, effort, bid, endeavour, essay; [inf] shot, stab, crack, whirl, whack.
■ **go down** 1 = **sink**, submerge, founder, go under. 2 = **decrease**, fall, drop, be reduced, decline, plummet.
■ **go far** = **do well**, be successful, succeed, make progress, get on, get ahead, make a name for oneself, advance; [inf] set the world on fire.
■ **go in for** = **engage in**, take part in, participate in, practise, pursue, take up, adopt, espouse, embrace.
■ **go off** 1 = **explode**, detonate, blow up, erupt, burst; [inf] go bang. 2 = **go bad**, go stale, go sour, be rotten.

goad NOUN = **stimulus**, incentive, incitement, inducement, stimulation, impetus, motivation, pressure, spur, jolt, prod, poke.
▶ VERB = **prompt**, stimulate, induce, motivate, spur,

urge, chivvy.

go-ahead NOUN
= **permission**,
authorization, assent,
consent, sanction, leave,
confirmation,
imprimatur; [inf] green
light, OK, okay, thumbs
up.
▸ADJ = **enterprising**,
ambitious, pioneering,
progressive; [inf] up-and-
coming, go-getting.

goal NOUN = **aim**, objective,
end, purpose, ambition,
target, design, intention,
intent, aspiration, ideal.

go-between NOUN
= **intermediary**, mediator,
middleman, liaison,
contact, messenger,
agent, broker, medium,
dealer, factor, pander.

godforsaken ADJ
= **desolate**, dismal,
dreary, bleak, wretched,
miserable, gloomy,
deserted, abandoned,
forlorn, neglected,
remote, backward, in the
back of beyond.

godless ADJ = **atheistic**,
agnostic, sceptical,
faithless, pagan, heathen,
ungodly, impious,

irreligious, unrighteous,
sinful, wicked, evil,
depraved.

godsend NOUN = **piece of
good fortune**, stroke of
luck, blessing, boon,
windfall, bonanza, gift,
benediction.
Opposites: curse.

goggle VERB = **stare**, gape,
gaze, ogle; [inf] gawk,
rubberneck.

good ADJ 1 = **virtuous**,
moral, ethical, righteous,
right-minded, right-
thinking, honourable,
upright, honest, high-
minded, noble, worthy,
admirable, estimable,
exemplary.
2 = **satisfactory**,
acceptable, good enough,
passable, tolerable,
adequate, fine, excellent;
[inf] great, hunky-dory,
OK. 3 = **well behaved**,
well mannered, obedient,
manageable, tractable,
malleable. 4 = **correct**,
right, proper, fitting,
suitable, appropriate,
decorous, seemly.
5 = **competent**, capable,
able, accomplished,
skilful, efficient, adept,

proficient, expert, excellent, first-rate, first-class; [inf] top-notch, tip-top, A1. **6** = **fine**, healthy, sound, robust, strong, vigorous. **7** = **kind**, kindly, kind-hearted, good-hearted, friendly, obliging, well disposed, charitable, gracious, sympathetic, benevolent, altruistic, benign. **8** = **wholesome**, healthy, nutritious, nutritional, beneficial. **9** = **delicious**, tasty, appetizing; [inf] scrumptious, yummy. **10** = **valid**, legitimate, genuine, authentic, sound, bona fide. **11** = **considerable**, substantial, goodly, sizeable, large, sufficient, ample; [inf] tidy. **12** = **fine**, fair, mild, clear, bright, cloudless, sunny, calm, balmy, tranquil, clement, halcyon. **Opposites:** bad.

▶ NOUN **1** = **benefit**, advantage, gain, profit, interest, well-being, welfare. **2** = **virtue**, goodness, righteousness, morality, ethics, rectitude, honour, uprightness, honesty, integrity, probity, worth, merit.

goodbye EXCLAMATION = **farewell**, adieu, au revoir; [inf] bye, bye-bye, see you later, see you, so long, ciao; [Brit. inf] cheerio, cheers, ta-ta.

good-humoured ADJ = **amiable**, affable, easy-going, genial, cheerful, cheery, happy, pleasant, good-tempered. **Opposites:** grumpy.

good-looking ADJ = **attractive**, handsome, pretty, lovely, beautiful, personable, well favoured; [archaic] comely, fair.

goodly ADJ = **considerable**, substantial, sizeable, significant, large, great, ample, sufficient; [inf] tidy. **Opposites:** paltry.

good-natured ADJ = **kind**, kindly, kind-hearted, warm-hearted, generous, benevolent, charitable, friendly, helpful, accommodating, amiable, tolerant.

goods PL NOUN = **property**, belongings, possessions, effects, things, paraphernalia, chattels, movables, appurtenances, trappings, accoutrements; [inf] stuff, gear.

gorge NOUN = **chasm**, canyon, ravine, abyss, defile, pass, cleft, crevice, rift, fissure.

gorgeous ADJ
1 = **beautiful**, attractive, lovely, good-looking, sexy; [inf] stunning.
2 = **splendid**, magnificent, superb, grand, impressive, sumptuous, imposing, dazzling, brilliant, glittering, breathtaking.

gory ADJ = **bloody**, bloodstained, horrific, violent, bloodthirsty, brutal, murderous, savage.

gossip NOUN **1** = **rumours**, scandal, tittle-tattle, tattle, hearsay, whispering campaign; [inf] mud-slinging, dirt.
2 = **gossipmonger**, rumour-monger, scandalmonger, busybody, babbler, chatterer, prattler.
▶ VERB = **spread rumours**, chat, chit-chat, blather, blether, talk, tattle, babble, gabble, prattle, prate; [inf] chinwag, jaw, yack.

gouge VERB = **dig**, incise, chisel, gash, scoop, hollow.

govern VERB **1** = **rule**, reign over, be in power over, exercise control over, hold sway over, preside over, administer, lead, be in charge of, control, command, direct, order, guide, manage, conduct, oversee, supervise, superintend, pilot, steer.
2 = **control**, restrain, keep in check, check, curb, hold back, keep back, rein in, bridle, subdue, constrain, arrest, contain.
3 = **determine**, decide, sway, rule, influence, have an influence on, be a factor in.

government NOUN
= **administration**, regime, parliament, ministry, executive, rule, leadership, command,

g

direction, control, guidance, management, conduct, supervision, superintendence.

gown NOUN = **dress**, frock, garment, costume, garb, habit.

grab VERB 1 = **grasp**, clutch, grip, clasp, lay hold of, catch hold of, take hold of, fasten upon; [inf] collar. 2 = **seize**, snatch, pluck, snap up, appropriate, capture; [inf] bag, nab.

grace NOUN 1 = **elegance**, refinement, charm, attractiveness, beauty, loveliness, polish, suaveness, culture, cultivation, good taste, taste, tastefulness, smoothness, suppleness, fluidity. 2 = **manners**, courtesy, decency, consideration, tact, breeding, decorum, propriety. 3 = **favour**, good will, generosity, kindness, kindliness, indulgence, benefaction, mercy, mercifulness, compassion, clemency. 4 = **blessing**, prayer, thanksgiving, thanks, benediction.
▶ VERB = **adorn**, decorate, ornament, embellish, enhance, beautify, prettify, set off, deck.

graceful ADJ = **elegant**, refined, smooth, agile, flowing, nimble, cultured, cultivated, polished, suave, charming, appealing, attractive, beautiful, lovely; [archaic] comely. **Opposites:** inelegant.

gracious ADJ 1 = **courteous**, cordial, kindly, kind-hearted, warm-hearted, benevolent, friendly, amiable, considerate, affable, pleasant, polite, civil, well mannered, chivalrous, charitable, indulgent, obliging, accommodating, beneficent, benign. 2 = **elegant**, tasteful, comfortable, luxurious. 3 = **merciful**, compassionate, gentle, mild, humane, clement.

grade NOUN 1 = **level**, degree, stage, echelon, rank, standing, station, position, order, class.

2 = **category**, class, classification, type, brand. **3** = **gradient**, slope, incline, hill, rise, bank, declivity.

▸ VERB = **classify**, class, categorize, sort, group, order, brand, size, rank, evaluate, rate, value, range, graduate.

gradient NOUN = **slope**, incline, hill, rise, bank, acclivity, declivity, grade.

gradual ADJ = **progressive**, regular, steady, even, moderate, slow, measured, unhurried, step-by-step, successive, continuous, systematic.
Opposites: sudden, abrupt.

gradually ADV = **slowly**, steadily, moderately, evenly, bit by bit, little by little, by degrees, step by step, inch by inch, piece by piece, drop by drop.

graduate VERB **1** = **take a degree**, receive one's degree, become a graduate. **2** = **mark off**, measure off, divide into degrees, grade, calibrate.

3 = **move up**, progress, advance, gain promotion, be promoted.

graft NOUN **1** = **shoot**, bud, scion, new growth, slip, sprout, splice.
2 = **transplant**, implant, implantation.

grain NOUN **1** = **particle**, granule, bit, piece, scrap, crumb, fragment, morsel, speck, trace, scintilla, mite, iota. **2** = **texture**, weave, fibre, pattern, nap.

grand ADJ **1** = **impressive**, imposing, magnificent, splendid, superb, striking, palatial, stately, large, monumental, majestic. **2** = **splendid**, sumptuous, luxurious, lavish, magnificent, opulent, princely.
3 = **great**, noble, aristocratic, distinguished, august, illustrious, eminent, elevated, esteemed, celebrated, pre-eminent, leading, prominent, notable, renowned, famous.
Opposites: unimpressive, lowly.

grandiose ADJ
1 = **overambitious**, ambitious, extravagant, high-flown, high-sounding, pompous, flamboyant, pretentious; [inf] OTT. **2** = **grand**, impressive, magnificent, imposing, striking, splendid, superb, stately, majestic.
Opposites: modest.

grant VERB **1** = **agree to**, consent to, assent to, accede to, permit, give one's permission for, allow, concede, accord, vouchsafe.
2 = **acknowledge**, concede, accept, cede, yield, go along with.
▶ NOUN = **award**, endowment, contribution, donation, allowance, subsidy, allocation, allotment, gift, present, subvention, sponsorship, honorarium; [Brit.] bursary.

granule NOUN = **grain**, particle, fragment, crumb, bit, scrap, molecule, atom, mite, iota, jot.

graphic ADJ = **vivid**, striking, expressive, descriptive, illustrative, lively, forcible, detailed, well defined, well drawn, telling, effective, cogent, clear, lucid, explicit.
Opposites: dull.

grapple VERB **1** = **fight with**, wrestle with, struggle with, tussle with, clash with, engage with, close with, battle with, combat with, brawl with.
2 = **tackle**, face, cope with, deal with, handle, manage, confront, address oneself to, attack, get down to, come to grips with.

grasp VERB **1** = **grip**, clutch, hold, clasp, clench, grab, snatch, get/take hold of, seize. **2** = **understand**, comprehend, follow, see, take in, realize, apprehend, perceive; [inf] get, get the picture, get the drift, catch on.

grasping ADJ = **greedy**, acquisitive, avaricious, rapacious, covetous, mean, parsimonious, niggardly, penny-pinching, selfish,

possessive; [inf] grabby, tight-fisted, stingy.
Opposites: generous.

grate VERB **1 = shred**, pulverize, mince, grind, granulate, triturate.
2 = rasp, scrape, jar, scratch, grind, creak, rub, grit. **3 = irritate**, annoy, jar on, irk, vex, gall, rankle with, anger, rile, exasperate, chafe; [Brit.] rub up the wrong way; [inf] set someone's teeth on edge, get on someone's nerves, aggravate.

grateful ADJ **= thankful**, appreciative, obliged, indebted, obligated, beholden, filled with gratitude.
Opposites: ungrateful.

gratify VERB **= please**, make happy, delight, give pleasure to, gladden, satisfy, thrill; [inf] warm the cockles of the heart.

gratitude NOUN **= gratefulness**, thankfulness, thanks, appreciation, thanksgiving, indebtedness, acknowledgement, recognition, sense of obligation.
Opposites: ingratitude.

gratuitous ADJ
1 = unprovoked, unjustified, groundless, without cause, without reason, unfounded, baseless, uncalled for, unwarranted, unmerited, needless, unnecessary, superfluous. **2 = free**, complimentary, voluntary, unpaid, unrewarded, unasked for, without charge, at no cost.

gratuity NOUN **= tip**, bonus, gift, present, donation, reward, recompense, largesse.

grave ADJ **1 = solemn**, serious, earnest, sober, sombre, severe, unsmiling, long-faced, stony-faced, grim-faced, grim, gloomy, preoccupied, thoughtful, pensive, subdued, muted, quiet, dignified, sedate, dour, staid. **2 = serious**, important, significant, weighty, momentous, urgent, pressing, vital, crucial, life-and-death, acute, pivotal, perilous, hazardous, dangerous, threatening, menacing. **Opposites:** carefree, trivial.

graveyard NOUN = **cemetery**, burial ground, churchyard, memorial park, necropolis, charnel house; [inf] boneyard; [N. Amer. inf] potter's field.

gravitate VERB 1 = **move towards**, head towards, be drawn to, be pulled towards, be attracted to, drift towards, lean towards, incline towards. 2 = **sink**, fall, drop, descend, precipitate, be precipitated, settle.

gravity NOUN 1 = **solemnity**, seriousness, earnestness, sobriety, sombreness, severity, grimness, thoughtfulness, pensiveness, sedateness, dignity, dourness, staidness. 2 = **seriousness**, importance, significance, momentousness, weightiness, acuteness, criticalness, consequence, perilousness, peril,

hazard, danger.

graze VERB 1 = **brush**, touch, rub, glance off, shave, skim, kiss. 2 = **scrape**, abrade, skin, scratch, chafe, bark, bruise, contuse.

greasy ADJ 1 = **fatty**, fat, oily, buttery, oleaginous, sebaceous, adipose. 2 = **slippery**, slippy, slimy. 3 = **slimy**, oily, unctuous, smooth, smooth-tongued, glib, suave, slick, fawning, ingratiating, grovelling, sycophantic, toadying, flattering, gushing; [inf] smarmy.

great ADJ 1 = **large**, big, extensive, vast, immense, boundless, unlimited, huge, spacious, enormous, gigantic, colossal, mammoth, monstrous, prodigious, tremendous, stupendous. 2 = **major**, main, most important, leading, chief, principal, capital, paramount, primary. 3 = **impressive**, grand, magnificent, imposing, splendid, majestic, glorious, sumptuous.

4 = **prominent**, eminent, pre-eminent, distinguished, illustrious, august, celebrated, renowned, noted, notable, noteworthy, famous, famed, leading, top, high, high-ranking, noble. 5 = **gifted**, talented, outstanding, remarkable, exceptional, first-rate, incomparable, expert, skilful, skilled, able, masterly, adept, proficient, adroit; [inf] crack, ace.
6 = **excellent**, enjoyable, marvellous, wonderful, first-class, first-rate, fine, very good, admirable; [inf] fab, super.

greatly ADV = **very much**, considerably, to a great extent, extremely, exceedingly, vastly, enormously, immensely, tremendously, hugely, markedly, mightily, remarkably, abundantly.

greed NOUN 1 = **gluttony**, voraciousness, voracity, ravenousness, insatiability; [inf] hoggishness, piggishness, swinishness.

2 = **avarice**, acquisitiveness, rapacity, covetousness, cupidity, miserliness, parsimony; [inf] tight-fistedness.
3 = **desire**, eagerness, avidity, hunger, craving, longing, enthusiasm, impatience.

greedy ADJ 1 = **gluttonous**, voracious, ravenous, ravening, famished, gourmandizing, insatiable, omnivorous; [inf] piggish, hoggish, gutsy; [archaic] esurient.
2 = **avaricious**, acquisitive, grasping, rapacious, grabbing, covetous, miserly, hoarding, niggardly, close-fisted, parsimonious; [inf] grabby, money-grubbing, tight-fisted. 3 = **eager**, hungry, avid, desirous, anxious, impatient, enthusiastic, longing, craving.
Opposites: generous.

greenhouse NOUN = **hothouse**, glasshouse, conservatory.

greet VERB = **say hello to**, address, salute, hail, nod to, wave to, raise one's hat to, acknowledge, accost, receive, meet, welcome.

greeting NOUN = **hello**, salute, salutation, address, nod, wave, acknowledgement, welcome.

greetings PL NOUN = **good wishes**, best wishes, regards, kind regards, congratulations, compliments, respects.

grey ADJ **1** = **cloudy**, overcast, dull, dark, sunless, gloomy, dim, dreary, dismal, cheerless, depressing, misty, foggy, murky. **2** = **dull**, uninteresting, boring, characterless, anonymous, colourless. **3** = **unclear**, doubtful, uncertain, indistinct, mixed.

grief NOUN = **sorrow**, mourning, mournfulness, bereavement, lamentation, misery, sadness, anguish, pain, distress, agony, suffering, affliction, heartache, heartbreak, broken-heartedness, heaviness of heart, trouble, woe,

tribulation, desolation, trial, despondency, dejection, despair, remorse, regret.
Opposites: joy, delight.

grievance NOUN
1 = **complaint**, protest, charge, moan, axe to grind, bone to pick; [inf] grouse, gripe, beef.
2 = **injustice**, unfairness, injury, damage, hardship, offence, affront, insult.

grieve VERB **1** = **mourn**, lament, be sorrowful, sorrow, be sad, weep and wail, cry, sob, suffer, ache, be in anguish, be distressed, bemoan, bewail; [inf] eat one's heart out. **2** = **hurt**, wound, pain, sadden, break someone's heart, upset, distress, cause suffering to, crush.
Opposites: rejoice.

grim ADJ **1** = **stern**, forbidding, fierce, formidable, threatening, ferocious, menacing, harsh, sombre, cross, crabbed, churlish, morose, surly, ill-tempered, sour, implacable, cruel, ruthless, merciless.

2 = resolute, determined, firm, decided, obstinate, adamant, unyielding, unwavering, unfaltering, unshakeable, obdurate, inflexible, unrelenting, relentless, inexorable, dead set. **3 = dreadful**, horrible, horrendous, terrible, horrid, dire, ghastly, awful, appalling, frightful, shocking, unspeakable, harrowing, grisly, hideous, gruesome, macabre. **Opposites:** amiable.

grimy ADJ **= dirty**, grubby, stained, soiled, dusty, sooty, muddy, filthy, besmeared; [poetic/literary] besmirched. **Opposites:** clean.

grind VERB **1 = crush**, pound, pulverize, mill, powder, granulate, crumble, mash, smash, triturate, kibble, levigate. **2 = sharpen**, file, whet, smooth, polish, sand. **3 = gnash**, grit, grate, scrape, rasp.
■ **grind down = oppress**, persecute, ill-treat,

torture, torment, harass, harry.

grip VERB **1 = grasp**, clutch, hold, clasp, clench, take/lay hold of, grab, seize, catch, latch on to. **2 = absorb**, engross, rivet, spellbind, hold spellbound, entrance, fascinate, enthral, hold, catch, mesmerize, hypnotize, compel.
▶ NOUN **1 = grasp**, clutch, clasp, clench, handshake, clinch. **2 = understanding**, comprehension, awareness, perception.

grisly ADJ **= gruesome**, frightful, horrifying, horrid, grim, horrendous, awful, dreadful, terrible, fearful, disgusting, hideous, repulsive, revolting, repugnant, repellent, macabre, spine-chilling, sickening, appalling, loathsome, abhorrent, odious, abominable. **Opposites:** pleasant.

grit NOUN **1 = gravel**, sand, dust, dirt. **2 = pluck**, courage, bravery, mettle, backbone, spirit, gameness, fortitude, toughness, determination, resolution, tenacity; [inf] guts, spunk; [Brit. inf] bottle.

groan VERB **1 = moan**, cry, call out, sigh, murmur, whine, whimper.
2 = complain, grumble, object, lament; [inf] moan, grouse, gripe, beef, bellyache, bitch.
3 = creak, grate, squeak, screech.

groove NOUN **1 = channel**, furrow, trench, trough, canal, gouge, rut, gutter, cutting, cut, score, rabbet, rebate. **2 = rut**, routine, habit, treadmill, daily grind.

grope VERB **1 = feel**, fumble, move blindly, pick. **2 = fumble for**, fish for, scrabble for, cast about for, search for, hunt for, look for.

gross ADJ **1 = obese**, massive, huge, immense, colossal, big, large, overweight, fat, corpulent, bloated, bulky, lumpish, cumbersome, unwieldy; [inf] hulking. **2 = coarse**, crude, vulgar, obscene, rude, lewd, ribald, bawdy, dirty, filthy, smutty, earthy, risqué, indecent, indelicate, improper, unseemly, impure, offensive, sexual, sensual, pornographic; [inf] blue. **3 = boorish**, loutish, oafish, coarse, vulgar, crass, ignorant, unrefined, unsophisticated, uncultured, uncultivated, undiscriminating, tasteless, insensitive, unfeeling, imperceptive, callous; [Brit. inf] yobbish. **4 = flagrant**, blatant, glaring, outrageous, shocking, serious, egregious, manifest, obvious, plain, apparent. **5 = total**, whole, entire, aggregate, before deductions, before tax.
Opposites: slender, refined, net.
▶ VERB **= earn**, make, bring in, take home, rake in.

grotesque ADJ **1 = bizarre**, weird, outlandish, freakish, strange, odd, peculiar, unnatural, surreal, macabre, queer, fantastic, whimsical, fanciful, ridiculous, ludicrous, absurd, incongruous, preposterous, extravagant. **2** = **distorted**, misshapen, twisted, deformed, malformed, misproportioned. **Opposites:** normal.

ground NOUN **1** = **earth**, floor, terra firma; [inf] deck. **2** = **soil**, earth, dirt, land, terrain, clay, turf, loam, clod, sod, dust. **3** = **pitch**, stadium, field, arena, park. = *See also* **grounds**.
▶ VERB **1** = **base**, establish, settle, set, found. **2** = **teach**, instruct, train, tutor, coach, educate, drill, school, prepare, familiarize with, acquaint with, inform.

groundless ADJ = **without basis**, baseless, without foundation, unfounded, unsupported, imaginary, illusory, false, unsubstantiated, unwarranted, unjustified, unjustifiable, uncalled for, unprovoked, without cause/reason, unreasonable, irrational, illogical, empty, idle, chimerical.

grounds PL NOUN **1** = **surroundings**, land, property, estate, acres, lawns, gardens, park, parkland, area, domain, holding, territory. **2** = **reason**, cause, basis, base, foundation, justification, call, rationale, argument, premise, occasion, factor, excuse, pretext, motive, inducement. **3** = **dregs**, deposit, lees, sediment, precipitate, settlings, grouts.

group NOUN **1** = **set**, lot, category, classification, class, batch, family, species, genus, bracket. **2** = **company**, band, party, body, gathering, congregation, assembly, collection, bunch, cluster, crowd, flock, pack, troop, gang, batch. **3** = **faction**, set, coterie, clique, circle. **4** = **society**, association, league, guild, circle, club, work party.

g

▶ VERB **1** = **classify**, class, categorize, sort, grade, rank, bracket.
2 = **assemble**, collect, gather together, arrange, organize, marshal, range, line up, dispose.
3 = **collect**, gather, assemble, cluster. **4** = **get together**, band together, associate, consort.

grouse VERB = **complain**, grumble, groan, protest; [inf] moan, gripe, bellyache, beef, bitch, grouch, whinge.

grovel VERB **1** = **abase oneself**, toady, fawn, flatter, curry favour, humble oneself, kowtow, bow and scrape, lick someone's boots; [inf] crawl, butter someone up. **2** = **prostrate oneself**, fall on one's knees, crawl, creep, kneel, slither.

grow VERB **1** = **get bigger**, get larger, get taller, stretch, lengthen, heighten, enlarge, extend, expand, spread, thicken, widen, fill out, swell, increase, multiply.
2 = **develop**, sprout, shoot up, spring up, germinate, bud, burgeon, flourish, thrive, pullulate.
3 = **flourish**, thrive, prosper, succeed, progress, make progress, make headway, advance, improve, expand.
4 = **arise**, originate, stem, issue, spring. **5** = **become**, come to be, get to be, get, turn, wax.
6 = **produce**, cultivate, farm, propagate, raise.
Opposites: shrink.

grown-up NOUN = **adult**, grown man, man, grown woman, woman, mature man/woman.

growth NOUN **1** = **increase**, expansion, enlargement, development, augmentation, proliferation, multiplication, extension, evolution, magnification, amplification, growing, deepening, heightening, widening, thickening, broadening, swelling, aggrandizement.
2 = **development**, maturation, germination, burgeoning, sprouting,

shooting up, blooming, vegetation, pullulation.
3 = expansion, rise, progress, success, advance, advancement, improvement, headway.
4 = tumour, lump, cancer, swelling, excrescence, intumescence, tumefaction.

grubby ADJ = **dirty**, filthy, unwashed, grimy, messy, soiled, scruffy, shabby, untidy, unkempt, slovenly, sordid, squalid; [inf] mucky, cruddy; [Brit. inf] gungy.
Opposites: clean.

grudge NOUN
= **resentment**, spite, malice, bitterness, ill will, pique, umbrage, grievance, hard feelings, rancour, malevolence, venom, hatred, dislike, aversion, animosity, animus.
▶ VERB **1 = begrudge**, give unwillingly, give reluctantly. **2 = resent**, mind, take ill, begrudge, envy, be jealous of.

gruelling ADJ
= **exhausting**, tiring, fatiguing, wearying, taxing, demanding, trying, arduous, laborious, back-breaking, strenuous, punishing, crushing, draining, hard, difficult, harsh, severe, grinding, stiff, brutal, relentless, unsparing, inexorable.

gruesome ADJ = **grisly**, ghastly, frightful, horrible, horrifying, horrid, horrendous, awful, dreadful, grim, terrible, fearful, hideous, disgusting, repulsive, revolting, repugnant, repellent, macabre, spine-chilling, sickening, appalling, shocking, abominable, loathsome, abhorrent, odious.

grumble VERB = **complain**, groan, protest, object, find fault, carp, whine; [inf] moan, grouse, gripe, bellyache, beef, bitch, grouch, whinge.

grumpy ADJ = **bad-tempered**, surly, churlish, crotchety, tetchy, crabby, crusty, ill-natured, bearish; [inf] grouchy.

Opposites: good-humoured.

guarantee NOUN
1 = **warranty**, warrant, covenant, bond, contract, guaranty.
2 = **pledge**, promise, assurance, word, word of honour, oath, bond.
▸ VERB 1 = **underwrite**, sponsor, back, support, provide collateral for, vouch for, provide surety for. 2 = **promise**, pledge, give a pledge, give an assurance, give one's word, swear.

guard VERB 1 = **defend**, shield, safeguard, stand guard over, protect, watch over, cover, patrol, police, preserve, save, conserve, secure, screen, shelter. 2 = **beware**, keep watch, be alert, take care, be on the lookout; [inf] keep an eye out, keep one's eyes peeled/skinned.
▸ NOUN 1 = **defender**, guardian, bodyguard, custodian, sentry, sentinel, watchman, nightwatchman, lookout, scout, watch, picket, garrison, escort, convoy, patrol; [inf] minder. 2 = **warder**, jailer, keeper; [inf] screw.

guarded ADJ = **careful**, cautious, circumspect, wary, chary, reluctant, non-committal, reticent, restrained, reserved, discreet, prudent; [inf] cagey.

guess NOUN = **conjecture**, surmise, estimate, hypothesis, guesswork, theory, reckoning, judgement, supposition, feeling, assumption, inference, prediction, speculation, notion; [inf] guesstimate.
▸ VERB 1 = **conjecture**, surmise, estimate, reckon, hypothesize, postulate, predict, speculate. 2 = **suppose**, believe, think, imagine, judge, consider, feel, suspect, dare say, fancy, divine, deem, surmise, reckon.

guest NOUN 1 = **visitor**, caller, company. 2 = **resident**, boarder, lodger, patron, tenant.

guidance NOUN
1 = **direction**, leadership, management, auspices, control, handling, conduct, government, charge, rule, teaching, instruction. **2** = **advice**, counselling, counsel, direction, recommendation, suggestion, tip, hint, pointer, intelligence, information, instruction.

guide VERB **1** = **lead**, lead the way, conduct, show, usher, shepherd, direct, show the way, pilot, steer, escort, accompany, convoy, attend.
2 = **control**, direct, manage, steer, command, be in charge of, govern, rule, preside over, superintend, supervise, handle, regulate, manipulate, manoeuvre.
3 = **advise**, give advice to, counsel, give counselling to, make suggestions/ recommendations to, give someone pointers/ tips, inform, instruct.
▶ NOUN **1** = **escort**, chaperone, leader, courier, pilot, usher,

attendant, director.
2 = **adviser**, counsellor, mentor, tutor, teacher, guru, confidant.
3 = **guidebook**, handbook, manual, ABC, instructions, key, catalogue.

guile NOUN = **cunning**, duplicity, craftiness, artfulness, craft, wiliness, artifice, foxiness, slyness, deception, deceit, underhandedness, double-dealing, trickery, trickiness, sharp practice, treachery, chicanery, skulduggery, fraud, gamesmanship, knavery. **Opposites:** candour.

guilty ADJ **1** = **to blame**, blameworthy, culpable, blameable, at fault, responsible, censurable, convicted, criminal, reproachable, condemnable, erring, errant, wrong, delinquent, offending, sinful, wicked, evil, unlawful, illegal, illicit, reprehensible, felonious, iniquitous.
2 = **remorseful**, ashamed, conscience-stricken,

shamefaced, regretful, contrite, repentant, penitent, rueful, sheepish, hangdog, compunctious.
Opposites: innocent, unrepentant.

guise NOUN **1** = **costume**, clothes, likeness, outfit, dress, appearance, style. **2** = **pretence**, disguise, screen, cover, blind, appearance, form.

gulf NOUN **1** = **bay**, cove, inlet, bight. **2** = **chasm**, abyss, hollow, pit, hole, opening, rift, cleft, fissure, split, crevice, gully, canyon, gorge, ravine.

gullible ADJ = **credulous**, trustful, over-trustful, easily deceived, easily taken in, unsuspecting, unsuspicious, ingenuous, naive, innocent, simple, inexperienced, green, foolish, silly; [inf] wet behind the ears.
Opposites: cynical, suspicious.

gulp VERB **1** = **swallow**, quaff, toss off, drain one's glass; [inf] swig, swill. **2** = **bolt**, wolf,

gobble, guzzle, devour; [inf] tuck into. **3** = **fight back**, suppress, stifle, smother, choke back, strangle.
▶ NOUN = **swallow**, mouthful, draught; [inf] swig.

gunman NOUN = **armed robber**, sniper, gangster, terrorist, assassin, murderer, killer, bandit; [inf] gunslinger, hit man, hired gun, trigger man, gunfighter; [N. Amer. inf] hood.

gurgle VERB = **bubble**, murmur, babble, burble, lap, splash, tinkle, plash, purl.

gush VERB **1** = **stream**, rush, spout, spurt, surge, jet, well, pour, burst, cascade, flood, flow, run, issue, emanate. **2** = **be effusive**, enthuse, wax lyrical, bubble over, get carried away, fuss, babble, prattle, jabber, gabble, blather, chatter, make too much, overstate the case.
▶ NOUN = **stream**, outpouring, spurt, jet, spout, rush, burst, surge,

cascade, flood, torrent, spate, freshet.

gusto NOUN = **zest**, enthusiasm, relish, zeal, fervour, verve, enjoyment, delight, exhilaration, pleasure, appreciation, liking, fondness, appetite, savour, taste.
Opposites: apathy, indifference.

gut NOUN = **stomach**, belly, abdomen, bowels, colon, intestines, entrails, vital organs, viscera; [inf] insides, innards.
▶ VERB **1** = **eviscerate**, disembowel, dress, clean, draw. **2** = **strip**, ransack, empty, plunder, loot, rob, rifle, ravage, sack, clear out, destroy, devastate, lay waste.

guts PL NOUN = **courage**, bravery, valour, nerve, fortitude, pluck, mettle, spirit, boldness, audacity, daring, hardiness, toughness, forcefulness, will power, tenacity; [inf] grit, gumption, spunk; [Brit. inf] bottle.

gutter NOUN = **drain**, sewer, sluice, culvert, conduit, pipe, duct, channel, trench, trough, ditch, furrow.

guttural ADJ = **husky**, throaty, gruff, gravelly, harsh, croaking, rasping, deep, low, rough, thick.

gyrate VERB = **rotate**, revolve, wheel round, turn round, circle, whirl, pirouette, twirl, swirl, spin, swivel.

Hh

habit NOUN **1** = **custom**, practice, wont, procedure, way, routine, matter of course, style, pattern, convention, policy, mode, rule.
2 = **tendency**, propensity, predisposition, proclivity, penchant, leaning, bent, inclination, custom, practice, quirk.
3 = **addiction**, dependence, weakness, obsession, fixation.
4 = **costume**, dress, garb, attire, clothes, clothing, garments, livery, uniform; [formal] apparel.

habitable ADJ = **inhabitable**, liveable in, usable, fit to live in, fit to occupy, tenantable.
Opposites: uninhabitable.

habitual ADJ **1** = **usual**, customary, accustomed, regular, normal, set, fixed, established, routine, common, ordinary, familiar, traditional; [poetic/literary] wonted.
2 = **persistent**, constant, continual, repeated, recurrent, perpetual, non-stop, continuous, frequent. **3** = **confirmed**, addicted, chronic, inveterate, hardened, ingrained.
Opposites: unaccustomed, infrequent, occasional.

hackneyed ADJ = **banal**, trite, overused, overworked, tired, worn out, time-worn, stale, clichéd, platitudinous, unoriginal, commonplace, common, unimaginative, pedestrian, prosaic, run-of-the-mill, stock, conventional; [inf] corny, old hat, played out.
Opposites: fresh, original.

haggard ADJ = **gaunt**, drawn, pinched, hollow-cheeked, scraggy, scrawny, withered, exhausted, ghost-like, death-like, wan, pallid, ghastly, cadaverous, peaked, drained, careworn, emaciated, wasted, thin.
Opposites: plump.

hail VERB **1** = **greet**, salute, acknowledge, lift one's hat to. **2** = **signal**, make a sign, flag, flag down, wave down, call, shout to. **3** = *See* **acclaim**.

hair NOUN **1** = **locks**, tresses, shock of hair, mop of hair, head of hair.
2 = **coat**, fur, pelt, hide, wool, fleece, mane.

hair-raising ADJ = **spine-chilling**, blood-curdling, terrifying, horrifying, petrifying, frightening, alarming, shocking, exciting, thrilling; [inf] scary, creepy.

hairy ADJ = **hirsute**, woolly, shaggy, bushy, fuzzy, bristly, fleecy, downy, bearded, unshaven, bewhiskered, stubbly.

half-hearted ADJ = **lukewarm**, unenthusiastic, apathetic, indifferent, uninterested, unconcerned, cool, listless, unemotional, lacklustre, dispassionate, cursory, perfunctory, superficial, passive, neutral.
Opposites: enthusiastic.

hallmark NOUN = **mark**, trademark, stamp, sign, badge, device, symbol, indicator, indication.

hallucinate VERB = **imagine things**, see things, have hallucinations, dream, fantasize, be delirious; [inf] be on a trip.

hallucination NOUN = **illusion**, delusion, figment of the imagination, vision, fantasy, apparition, dream, mirage, chimera, delirium, phantasmagoria.

halt VERB **1** = **come to a halt**, stop, come to a stop/standstill, pull up, draw up, wait. **2** = **finish**, stop, cease, break off, call it a day, desist,

discontinue; [inf] knock off; [Brit. inf] down tools. **3** = **block**, arrest, terminate, stop, curb, put an end/stop to, bring to an end, crush, frustrate, obstruct, baulk, impede, hold back.
Opposites: begin.

▶ NOUN = **stop**, stoppage, cessation, close, end, standstill, pause, interval, interlude, intermission, break, hiatus, rest, respite.

hammer VERB = **beat**, batter, pound, pummel, hit, strike, cudgel, slap, bludgeon, club; [inf] wallop, clobber.

hamper VERB = **hinder**, obstruct, impede, hold back, inhibit, retard, slow down, hold up, restrain, block, check, frustrate, thwart, foil, curb, interfere with, cramp, restrict, bridle, handicap, stymie, hamstring, shackle, fetter, encumber, trammel, cumber; [Brit.] throw a spanner in the works.
Opposites: expedite.

hand NOUN **1** = **fist**, palm; [inf] mitt, paw, duke. **2** = **pointer**, indicator, needle. **3** = **worker**, workman, employee, operative, hired hand, labourer, artisan.
▶ VERB = **give**, pass, pass over, hand over, deliver, present.
▪ **hand on/down** = **pass on/down**, bequeath, will, give, transfer.
▪ **hand out** = **distribute**, give out, pass out, deal out, dole out, mete out, dispense, apportion, disseminate, disburse, dish out.

handicap NOUN **1** = **disability**, impairment, abnormality, disadvantage, defect. **2** = **impediment**, disadvantage, hindrance, obstruction, obstacle, encumbrance, check, block, curb, barrier, stumbling block, constraint, restriction, limitation, drawback, shortcoming.
Opposites: advantage.
▶ VERB = **disadvantage**, put

at a disadvantage, impede, hinder, impair, hamper, obstruct, check, block, encumber, curb, trammel, bridle, hold back, constrain, restrict, limit.

handiwork NOUN
1 = **handicraft**, craft, craftsmanship. **2** = **action**, achievement, work, doing, creation, design, product, production, result.

handle VERB **1** = **touch**, feel, hold, finger, grasp, grip, pick up, lift, pat, caress, stroke, fondle, poke, maul; [inf] paw.
2 = **cope with**, deal with, treat, manage, control.
3 = **be in charge of**, control, manage, administer, direct, guide, conduct, supervise, take care of. **4** = **drive**, steer, operate, manoeuvre.
5 = **deal in**, trade in, traffic in, market, sell, stock, carry.
▶ NOUN = **shaft**, grip, handgrip, hilt, haft, knob, stock, helve.

handsome ADJ **1** = **good-looking**, attractive, personable; [inf] dishy.
2 = **attractive**, good-looking, lovely, elegant, fine, personable, well formed, well proportioned, stately, dignified. **3** = **generous**, magnanimous, liberal, lavish, considerable, sizeable, large, ample, abundant, plentiful; [poetic/literary] bounteous.
Opposites: ugly.

handy ADJ **1** = **to hand**, at hand, within reach, available, accessible, near, nearby, close, at one's fingertips, convenient; [inf] on tap.
2 = **useful**, helpful, practicable, practical, serviceable, functional, expedient, easy-to-use, neat, convenient. **3** = **deft**, dexterous, nimble-fingered, adroit, proficient, adept, skilful, skilled, expert, clever/good with one's hands.
Opposites: inaccessible, useless, inept.

hang VERB **1** = **be suspended**, dangle,

swing, sway, be pendent.
2 = **send to the gallows**,
send to the gibbet,
execute; [inf] string up.
3 = **stick up**, attach, fix,
fasten on, paste, glue,
cement. **4** = **adorn**,
decorate, deck,
ornament, drape, cover,
furnish.

- **hang about/around**
= **wait**, linger, loiter,
dally, waste time;
[archaic] tarry.
- **hang back** = **hold back**,
stay back, stay in the
background, be reluctant,
hesitate, recoil, demur,
shrink back.
- **hang on** = **wait**, hold
on, stop, stay, remain,
persevere.

hang-up NOUN = **fixation**,
preoccupation, obsession,
phobia, problem;
[inf] thing, bee in one's
bonnet.

hanker
- **hanker after/for** = **long
for**, have a longing for,
yearn for, crave, desire,
hunger for, thirst for, be
bent on, covet, want,
wish for, set one's heart
on, pine for, lust after;
[inf] be itching for, be
dying for, have a yen for.

haphazard ADJ
= **unplanned**, random,
indiscriminate,
undirected, unforeseen,
chaotic, chance,
unsystematic,
unorganized,
unmethodical, orderless,
aimless, irregular,
slapdash, thrown
together, careless, casual,
hit-or-miss.
Opposites: methodical,
systematic.

hapless ADJ = **unlucky**,
unfortunate, out of luck,
ill-starred, forlorn,
wretched, unhappy,
woebegone; [inf] down on
one's luck.
Opposites: lucky.

happen VERB = **take place**,
occur, come about,
present itself, arise,
materialize, appear, come
into being, chance,
arrive, transpire, crop up,
develop, eventuate,
supervene; [poetic/
literary] come to pass.

happening NOUN
= **occurrence**, event,
incident, occasion, affair,

circumstance, action, case, phenomenon, eventuality, episode, experience, adventure, scene, proceedings, chance.

happiness NOUN = **cheerfulness**, cheeriness, merriness, gaiety, good spirits, high spirits, light-heartedness, joy, joyfulness, glee, joviality, carefreeness, enjoyment, gladness, delight, exuberance, elation, ecstasy, bliss, blissfulness, euphoria, transports; [poetic/literary] blitheness.
Opposites: unhappiness, sadness.

happy ADJ **1** = **cheerful**, cheery, merry, in good/high spirits, joyful, joyous, light-hearted, jovial, gleeful, buoyant, carefree, untroubled, smiling, glad, delighted, elated, ecstatic, blissful, euphoric, overjoyed, exuberant, in seventh heaven, floating/walking on air; [inf] over the moon, on cloud nine, on top of the world;

[dated] gay; [poetic/literary] blithe. **2** = **glad**, pleased, delighted, contented, satisfied, gratified, thrilled.
3 = **lucky**, fortunate, advantageous, favourable, beneficial, opportune, helpful, timely, convenient, welcome, propitious, auspicious, felicitous, fortuitous.
4 = **appropriate**, fitting, apt, fit, good, right, proper, seemly.
Opposites: unhappy, sad, displeased, unfortunate.

harangue NOUN = **lecture**, tirade, diatribe, speech, talk, sermon, exhortation, declamation, oration, address, homily, peroration; [inf] spiel.

harass VERB **1** = **bother**, pester, annoy, exasperate, worry, fret, disturb, agitate, provoke, badger, hound, torment, plague, persecute, harry, tease, bait, nag, molest, bedevil; [inf] hassle, give someone a hard time, drive someone up the wall. **2 = harry**, attack repeatedly, raid, beleaguer, press hard, oppress.

harassed ADJ **= stressed**, under pressure, distraught, under stress, strained, worried, careworn, troubled, vexed, agitated, fretting; [inf] hassled.
Opposites: carefree.

harbour NOUN **1 = port**, anchorage, dock, haven, marina. **2 = refuge**, shelter, haven, sanctuary, retreat, asylum, sanctum, covert.
▶ VERB **1 = shelter**, give shelter to, house, lodge, put up, take in, billet, provide refuge for, shield, protect, conceal, hide, secrete. **2 = nurse**, maintain, nurture, hold on to, cherish, cling to, retain, entertain.

hard ADJ **1 = firm**, solid, compact, compacted, compressed, condensed, dense, rigid, stiff, unyielding, resistant, inflexible, unpliable, tough, strong, stony, unmalleable, close-packed, rock-like.
2 = strenuous, arduous, heavy, tiring, fatiguing, exhausting, back-breaking, laborious, rigorous, exacting, formidable, tough, difficult, uphill, toilsome, Herculean. **3 = difficult**, complicated, complex, involved, intricate, puzzling, perplexing, baffling, knotty, thorny, bewildering, insoluble, enigmatic, unfathomable, incomprehensible.
4 = harsh, severe, stern, hard-hearted, cold, unfeeling, unsympathetic, grim, ruthless, oppressive, tyrannical, pitiless, merciless, unrelenting, unsparing, callous, cruel, vicious, implacable, obdurate, unyielding, unjust, unfair.
5 = unpleasant, grim, harsh, difficult, disagreeable, uncomfortable, intolerable, unendurable, unbearable, insupportable, distressing, painful,

disastrous, calamitous.
6 = forceful, violent, heavy, strong, powerful, fierce, harsh, sharp.
Opposites: soft, easy.

harden VERB **1 = solidify**, become hard, set, stiffen, cake, congeal, clot, coagulate, bake, anneal. **2 = toughen**, make insensitive/unfeeling, deaden, numb, benumb.

hard-hitting ADJ **= tough**, uncompromising, unsparing, strongly worded, vigorous, straight-talking, blunt, frank, critical; [inf] pulling no punches.

hardly ADV **= scarcely**, barely, only just, just, almost not, with difficulty, with effort.
Opposites: fully.

hardship NOUN
= adversity, deprivation, privation, want, need, destitution, poverty, austerity, desolation, misfortune, distress, suffering, affliction, pain, misery, wretchedness, tribulation, trials, burdens, calamity, catastrophe, disaster,

ruin, ruination, torment, torture; [poetic/literary] travail.
Opposites: ease, comfort.

hardy ADJ **= healthy**, fit, strong, robust, sturdy, tough, rugged, vigorous, in good condition, resilient, lusty, stalwart, hale and hearty, fit as a fiddle, sound in body and limb, in fine fettle, in good kilter.
Opposites: delicate.

harm NOUN **1 = hurt**, injury, pain, suffering, trauma, destruction, loss, ruin, havoc, adversity, disservice, abuse, damage, mischief, detriment, defacement, defilement, impairment. **2 = evil**, badness, wrongdoing, wrong, wickedness, vice, iniquity, sin, sinfulness, immorality, nefariousness.
▶ VERB **= hurt**, injure, wound, inflict pain/suffering on, abuse, maltreat, ill-treat, ill-use, molest, do violence to, destroy, damage, do mischief to, deface,

h

defile, impair, spoil, mar, blemish.

harmful ADJ **1** = **hurtful**, injurious, wounding, abusive, detrimental, damaging, deleterious, disadvantageous, destructive, dangerous, pernicious, noxious, baneful, toxic. **2** = **bad**, evil, wicked, malign, corrupting, subversive.
Opposites: harmless.

harmless ADJ **1** = **safe**, innocuous, non-toxic, mild, non-irritant.
2 = **inoffensive**, innocuous, unoffending, innocent, blameless, gentle.
Opposites: harmful.

harmonious ADJ
1 = **melodious**, tuneful, musical, harmonizing, sweet-sounding, mellifluous, dulcet, euphonious, symphonious, consonant. **2** = **peaceful**, peaceable, friendly, amicable, cordial, amiable, agreeable, congenial, united, cooperative, in harmony, in tune, attuned, in

accord, compatible, sympathetic.
Opposites: discordant, hostile.

harmonize VERB **1** = **be in accord**, coincide, agree, correspond, tally, be in unison, be congruent, be of one mind.
2 = **reconcile**, settle differences, restore harmony to, make peaceful, patch up, negotiate peace between, heal the breach, pour oil on troubled waters.

harmony NOUN
1 = **agreement**, accord, accordance, concordance, concurrence, unanimity, cooperation, unity, unison, oneness, amicability, good will, amity, affinity, rapport, sympathy, like-mindedness, friendship, fellowship, comradeship, peace, peacefulness.
2 = **compatibility**, congruity, consonance, coordination, blending, balance, symmetry, suitability;
[formal] concord. **3** = **tune**, melody, tunefulness,

melodiousness, mellifluousness, euphony.
Opposites: disagreement, incongruity, dissonance.

harrowing ADJ
= **distressing**, agonizing, excruciating, traumatic, heart-rending, heartbreaking, painful, racking, afflicting, chilling, disturbing, vexing, alarming, perturbing, unnerving, horrifying, terrifying.

harsh ADJ **1** = **abrupt**, brusque, blunt, curt, gruff, short, surly, concise, clipped, impolite, discourteous, uncivil, ungracious.
2 = **cruel**, brutal, savage, barbarous, hard-hearted, despotic, tyrannical, ruthless, unfeeling, merciless, pitiless, relentless, unrelenting, inhuman. **3** = **severe**, stringent, stern, grim, austere, uncompromising, inflexible, punitive, draconian. **4** = **grating**, jarring, grinding, rasping, strident, jangling,
raucous, ear-piercing, discordant, dissonant, unharmonious. **5** = **rough**, coarse, guttural, hoarse, croaking, raucous, strident, gravelly.
6 = **bleak**, grim, desolate, stark, severe, austere, barren, rough, wild, bitter, inhospitable, comfortless, spartan.
7 = **garish**, gaudy, glaring, bold, loud, flashy, showy, crass, crude, vulgar.
Opposites: lenient, gentle.

harvest NOUN = **reaping**, crop, yield, produce, vintage, ingathering.
▶ VERB = **gather**, gather in, reap, glean, pick, pluck, collect, amass, accumulate, garner.

hassle VERB = **annoy**, badger, harass, hound, pester, bother, trouble, worry, torment, plague; [inf] give someone a hard time.
▶ NOUN = **trouble**, bother, inconvenience, annoyance, nuisance, harassment, difficulty, problem, struggle, fight, quarrel, altercation,

disagreement, dispute, wrangle, tussle.

haste NOUN = **speed**, swiftness, rapidity, rapidness, quickness, fastness, briskness, urgency, alacrity, promptness, dispatch, expeditiousness, promptitude, expedition, celerity, fleetness.

hasty ADJ **1** = **swift**, rapid, quick, fast, speedy, hurried, hurrying, running, prompt, expeditious, brisk, urgent, fleet. **2** = **quick**, short, brief, rushed, short-lived, fleeting, transitory, cursory, perfunctory, superficial, slight. **3** = **hurried**, rushed, impetuous, reckless, rash, foolhardy, precipitate, impulsive, headlong, thoughtless, heedless, careless, ill-conceived.
Opposites: slow, cautious.

hatch VERB **1** = **incubate**, brood, sit on, cover.
2 = **devise**, concoct, contrive, plan, scheme, design, invent, formulate, originate, conceive, dream up, think up; [inf] cook up.

hate VERB **1** = **loathe**, detest, abhor, dislike, despise, abominate, execrate, have an aversion to, feel hostile towards, be unable to stand/bear, view with dislike, be sick of, be tired of, shudder at, be repelled by, recoil from.
2 = **be reluctant**, be loath, be unwilling, feel disinclined, be sorry, dislike, not have the heart, shy away from, flinch from.
Opposites: love, relish.
▸ NOUN = *see* **hatred**.

hateful ADJ = **detestable**, loathsome, abhorrent, abominable, despicable, execrable, odious, revolting, repugnant, repellent, disgusting, obnoxious, offensive, insufferable, horrible, unpleasant, nasty, disagreeable, foul, vile, heinous.
Opposites: admirable.

hatred NOUN = **hate**, loathing, detestation, abhorrence, dislike, aversion, hostility, ill will, enmity, animosity, antagonism, antipathy, animus, revulsion, repugnance, odium, rancour, grudge, execration, abomination. **Opposites:** love.

haughty ADJ **= arrogant**, proud, conceited, self-important, egotistical, vain, swollen-headed, overweening, overbearing, pompous, smug, presumptuous, condescending, supercilious, lofty, patronizing, snobbish, imperious, boastful, scornful, lordly, high-handed; [inf] snooty, on one's high horse, high and mighty, stuck up, hoity-toity, uppity, uppish. **Opposites:** modest, humble.

haul VERB **= drag**, pull, tug, draw, heave, trail, lug, tow, take in tow, cart, carry, convoy, ship.

haunt VERB **1 = frequent**, visit regularly, patronize; [inf] hang out in. **2 = obsess**, prey on someone's mind, prey on, torment, plague, disturb, trouble, worry, oppress, burden, beset, harry, weigh on, come back to, stay with.

have VERB **1 = own**, possess, keep, keep for one's use, use, hold, retain. **2 = get**, be given, receive, accept, obtain, acquire, procure, secure, gain. **3 = contain**, include, comprise, embrace, take in, incorporate, embody, comprehend.
4 = experience, undergo, go through, encounter, meet, find, be subjected to, submit to, suffer from, endure, tolerate, put up with. **5 = feel**, entertain, have/keep/bear in mind, harbour, foster, nurse, cherish. **6 = give birth to**, bear, deliver, be delivered of, bring into the world, bring forth.
▪ **have had it = be finished**, be out, be defeated, have lost, have no chance, have no hope.
▪ **have to = must**, have got to, be bound to, be

h

obliged to, be forced to, be compelled to.

haven NOUN = **refuge**, shelter, sanctuary, asylum, retreat, sanctum, sanctum sanctorum, covert.

havoc NOUN
1 = **devastation**, destruction, damage, ruination, ruin, rack and ruin, despoliation, waste, gutting, wreckage, desolation, disaster, catastrophe, cataclysm.
2 = **chaos**, disorder, confusion, disruption, disorganization, mayhem; [inf] shambles.

hazard NOUN **1** = **danger**, peril, risk, jeopardy, threat, menace.
2 = **chance**, accident, luck, contingency, fortuity, fortuitousness.
▶ VERB **1** = **risk**, put at risk, endanger, expose to danger, imperil, put in jeopardy, jeopardize.
2 = **venture**, put forward, proffer, offer, submit, advance, volunteer.

hazardous ADJ
= **dangerous**, risky, perilous, fraught with

danger/risk, chancy, uncertain, unpredictable, precarious, parlous, unsafe, insecure; [inf] dicey, hairy, tricky.
Opposites: safe.

haze NOUN = **mist**, mistiness, fog, cloud, cloudiness, smog, vapour.

hazy ADJ **1** = **misty**, foggy, cloudy, smoggy, overcast.
2 = **vague**, indefinite, blurred, fuzzy, faint, confused, muddled, unclear, obscure, dim, indistinct, ill-defined.
Opposites: clear.

head NOUN **1** = **skull**, cranium; [inf] nut; [Brit. inf] bonce; [inf, dated] conk, noodle, noddle. **2** = **mind**, intelligence, intellect, brain, brains, mentality, wit, sense, wisdom, reasoning, rationality, understanding. **3** = **leader**, chief, commander, director, manager, superintendent, controller, administrator, supervisor, principal, captain. **4** = **front**, fore, forefront, van, vanguard.

▸ VERB **1** = **lead**, be at the head of, be in charge of, be in command/control of, command, control, run, supervise, rule, govern, guide. **2** = **make for**, go to, go in the direction of, aim for, set out for, start out for, go towards, steer towards, make a beeline for.

■ **head off** = **divert**, intercept, deflect, turn aside, block off, cut off, forestall.

headlong ADV **1** = **head first**, head on, on one's head. **2** = **hastily**, hurriedly, impatiently, without thinking, rashly, recklessly, wildly, prematurely, carelessly, precipitately, heedlessly. **Opposites:** cautiously.

headquarters NOUN = **centre of operations**, base, command post, main office/branch, head office.

heal VERB **1** = **cure**, make well, make better, remedy, treat, mend, restore, regenerate. **2** = **recuperate**, get better/well, mend, be cured, be on the mend, improve, be restored. **3** = **reconcile**, patch up, settle, set right, put right, harmonize, conciliate.

health NOUN **1** = **healthiness**, fitness, well-being, good condition, good shape, soundness, robustness, strength, vigour, fine fettle, salubrity. **2** = **state of health**, constitution, physical state, shape, condition, form, tone.

healthy ADJ **1** = **in good health**, fit, in good condition, robust, strong, vigorous, hardy, flourishing, blooming, hale and hearty, hale; [inf] in the pink. **2** = **health-giving**, beneficial, invigorating, bracing, stimulating, refreshing, nutritious, nourishing, wholesome, good for one. **Opposites:** unhealthy.

heap NOUN **1** = **pile**, stack, mound, mass, stockpile, accumulation, collection, agglomeration, conglomeration, hoard, store, stock, supply.

2 = a lot, lots, a great deal, abundance, plenty, a mint; [inf] oodles, loads, tons, pots, stacks; [Brit. inf] lashings.

▶ VERB **= pile up**, stack, amass, stockpile, mound, accumulate, collect, assemble, hoard, store, stock up, set aside, lay by.

hear VERB **1 = take in**, catch, perceive, overhear; [inf] get, latch on to. **2 = be informed**, be told of, be made aware, receive information, find out, discover, learn, gather, pick up, hear tell, get wind of. **3 = try**, judge, pass judgement on, adjudicate, examine, investigate, inquire into, consider.

hearing NOUN **= inquiry**, trial, inquest, investigation, review.

heart NOUN **1 = passion**, love, affection, emotions, feelings. **2 = tenderness**, compassion, sympathy, empathy, humanity, responsiveness, fellow feeling, goodwill, kindness, kindliness. **3 = spirit**, enthusiasm, keenness, eagerness, liveliness. **4 = essence**, crux, substance, core, quintessence.

heartache NOUN **= sorrow**, grief, sadness, anguish, pain, hurt, agony, suffering, misery, wretchedness, despair, desolation, woe, despondency; [poetic/literary] dolour.
Opposites: happiness.

heartbreaking ADJ **= sad**, pitiful, tragic, poignant, painful, agonizing, distressing, affecting, grievous, bitter, cruel, harsh, tear-jerking, harrowing, excruciating.

hearten VERB **= cheer**, raise someone's spirits, revitalize, energize, invigorate, animate, exhilarate, uplift, elate, comfort, encourage, buoy up; [inf] buck up, give someone a shot in the arm.

heartfelt ADJ **= deeply felt**, deep, profound, wholehearted, sincere, earnest, honest, devout, genuine, unfeigned, ardent, fervent, passionate, warm, enthusiastic, eager.

heartless ADJ = **unfeeling**, unsympathetic, unkind, uncaring, unmoved, untouched, cold, cold-hearted, cold-blooded, hard-hearted, cruel, harsh, stern, hard, brutal, merciless, pitiless, ruthless.
Opposites: compassionate.

heat NOUN 1 = **hotness**, warmth, warmness, torridness, torridity, sultriness, calefaction.
2 = **passion**, warmth, intensity, vehemence, ardour, fervour, fervency, zeal, eagerness, enthusiasm, animation, earnestness, excitement, agitation.
Opposites: cold, apathy.
▶ VERB 1 = **warm**, warm up, make hot/warm, reheat, cook. 2 = **grow hot/warm**, become hotter/warmer.

heated ADJ = **vehement**, passionate, fierce, angry, furious, stormy, tempestuous, frenzied, raging, intense, impassioned, violent,

animated, inflamed, enraged.

heathen NOUN
= **unbeliever**, infidel, pagan, disbeliever, atheist, heretic, idolater/idolatress.
▶ ADJ = **pagan**, godless, infidel, heathenish, irreligious, idolatrous, atheistic, heretical.

heave VERB 1 = **lift**, haul, tug, raise, hoist.
2 = **throw**, cast, toss, fling, hurl, let fly, pitch; [inf] sling, chuck.
3 = **vomit**, gag, retch; [Brit.] be sick; [N. Amer.] get sick; [inf] throw up, puke.

heaven NOUN 1 = **paradise**, the next life, the hereafter, the life to come, the next world, the afterlife, nirvana.
2 = **ecstasy**, bliss, rapture, joy, happiness, contentment, seventh heaven. 3 = **sky**, skies; [poetic/literary] firmament, empyrean, ether.
Opposites: hell.

heavenly ADJ 1 = **celestial**, divine, angelic, seraphic, cherubic, beatific, blessed, holy, god-like,

immortal, paradisiacal.
2 = delightful, pleasurable, enjoyable, marvellous, wonderful, gratifying, blissful, rapturous, sublime, glorious, divine.
3 = beautiful, exquisite, perfect, superb, ravishing, enchanting, alluring.
Opposites: hellish.

heavy ADJ **1 = weighty**, bulky, hefty, big, large, substantial, massive, enormous, unwieldy, cumbersome, burdensome. **2 = onerous**, burdensome, oppressive, difficult, unbearable, intolerable. **3 = hard**, forceful, strong, severe, harsh, intense, sharp. **4 = overweight**, fat, stout, obese, tubby, corpulent, paunchy, lumbering, bulky; [inf] hulking. **5 = severe**, intense, serious, grave.
Opposites: light.

heavy-handed ADJ = *see* **clumsy (1, 3)**.

hectic ADJ = **busy**, active, frantic, frenetic, frenzied, bustling, flurried, fast and furious, turbulent,

tumultuous, confused, exciting, excited, wild.
Opposites: leisurely.

hedge NOUN **1 = hedgerow**, row of bushes, quickset, barrier, screen, protection, windbreak. **2 = safeguard**, guard, protection, shield, cover, insurance.
▸VERB **1 = surround**, enclose, encircle, circle, border, edge, skirt. **2 = equivocate**, prevaricate, be vague/ambivalent, be non-committal, dodge the question/issue, beat about the bush, sidestep the question/issue, temporize, quibble; [Brit.] hum and haw; [N. Amer. inf] waffle.

heed NOUN = **attention**, attentiveness, notice, note, regard, mindfulness, mind, respect, consideration, thought, care, caution, watchfulness, wariness, chariness.
▸VERB = **pay heed/attention to**, attend to, take notice/note of, notice, note, bear in mind, be

mindful of, mind, mark, take into account, follow, obey, adhere to, observe, take to heart, be alert to, be cautious of, watch out for.

heedful ADJ = **attentive**, careful, mindful, cautious, prudent, circumspect, wary, observant, watchful, vigilant, alert, on guard. Opposites: heedless.

heedless ADJ = **inattentive**, unheeding, careless, incautious, unmindful, regardless, unthinking, thoughtless, unwary, oblivious, unobservant, negligent, neglectful, rash, reckless, foolhardy, precipitate. Opposites: heedful.

heft VERB = **lift**, lift up, raise, hoist, hike up, heave, boost.

hefty ADJ 1 = **heavy**, bulky, big, large, stout, massive, huge, muscular, brawny, strapping, sturdy, solidly built, strong; [inf] beefy, hulking. 2 = **substantial**, sizeable, huge, colossal, expensive. Opposites: light.

height NOUN 1 = **highness**, altitude, loftiness, elevation, tallness, stature. 2 = **top**, mountain top, hilltop, summit, peak, crest, crown, pinnacle, apex, vertex, apogee. 3 = **peak**, zenith, apex, culmination, crowning point, climax, consummation, perfection.

heighten VERB 1 = **raise**, make higher, lift, elevate. 2 = **make greater**, intensify, raise, increase, add to, build up, augment, boost, strengthen, amplify, magnify, aggravate, enhance. Opposites: lower.

heinous ADJ = **abominable**, atrocious, abhorrent, odious, detestable, loathsome, hateful, wicked, monstrous, horrible, ghastly, shocking, flagrant, contemptible, reprehensible, despicable.

hellish ADJ 1 = **demonic**, diabolical, devilish, fiendish, satanic, infernal. 2 = **unpleasant**, nasty, disagreeable, horrible, horrid, awful.

help VERB **1** = **assist**, aid, give someone a (helping) hand, lend a hand, guide, be of service to, be useful to, succour, befriend. **2** = **support**, back, contribute to, promote, boost. **3** = **soothe**, relieve, ameliorate, alleviate, mitigate, assuage, cure, heal, improve, ease. ▶ NOUN **1** = **assistance**, aid, service, helping hand, guidance, benefit, advantage, support, backing, succour. **2** = **relief**, alleviation, amelioration, mitigation, remedy, cure, improvement, ease, corrective, balm. **3** = **servant**, maid, worker, hired help; [Brit. inf] daily. ▪ **help oneself to** = **take**, appropriate, commandeer, steal, make free with; [inf] walk off with; [Brit. inf] pinch, nick.

helper NOUN = **assistant**, aide, deputy, adjutant, second-in-command, auxiliary, right-hand man/woman, henchman, colleague, associate, co-worker, partner, ally, collaborator.

helpful ADJ **1** = **useful**, of use, of service, beneficial, valuable, advantageous, constructive, practical, productive, instrumental. **2** = **supportive**, kind, friendly, obliging, accommodating, cooperative, sympathetic, considerate, caring, neighbourly, charitable, benevolent.
Opposites: useless, unhelpful.

helping NOUN = **portion**, serving, ration, piece, plateful, amount, share.

helpless ADJ **1** = **weak**, feeble, disabled, incapable, infirm, debilitated, powerless, dependent, unfit, invalid, bedridden, paralysed; [inf] laid up. **2** = **defenceless**, unprotected, vulnerable, exposed, abandoned, destitute, forlorn, desolate.
Opposites: independent.

hem NOUN = **border**, edge, edging, trim, trimming, fringe, frill, flounce, valance.
▸ VERB **1** = **bind**, edge, trim, fringe. **2** = **border**, edge, skirt, surround, encircle, circle, enclose, encompass. **3** = **shut in**, hedge in, close in, pen in, confine, constrain, restrict, limit, trap, keep within bounds.

herd NOUN = **flock**, pack, mob, crowd, throng, swarm, press, multitude.
▸ VERB = **drive**, round up, assemble, collect, muster, shepherd, guide, lead, force, urge, goad.

hereditary ADJ
1 = **genetic**, congenital, innate, inborn, inherent, family, inbred, transmissible, transferable. **2** = **inherited**, handed down, bequeathed, willed, transferred, transmitted, family, ancestral.

heresy NOUN = **apostasy**, dissent, nonconformity, unorthodoxy, free thinking, dissidence, scepticism, agnosticism, atheism, heterodoxy, revisionism, idolatry, paganism.

heretic NOUN = **dissenter**, apostate, unbeliever, sceptic, agnostic, atheist, nonconformist, free thinker, renegade, revisionist, schismatic, pagan, idolater, recusant.

heretical ADJ = **dissident**, sceptical, nonconformist, atheistical, agnostic, freethinking, unorthodox, heterodox, renegade, revisionist, schismatic, idolatrous, pagan, recusant.
Opposites: orthodox.

heritage NOUN = **history**, tradition, background, ancestry, lineage, descent, family, extraction, heredity, birth.

hermit NOUN = **recluse**, solitary, anchorite, anchoress, eremite, stylite.

heroic ADJ **1** = **brave**, courageous, valiant, intrepid, fearless, gallant, valorous, stout-hearted, lion-hearted, bold, daring, undaunted, dauntless, manly, virile, doughty, chivalrous.

2 = legendary, mythological, classic, classical, fabulous.

3 = epic, epical, Homeric, grandiloquent, high-flown, high-sounding, extravagant, grandiose, bombastic, rhetorical, pretentious, turgid, magniloquent, orotund, elevated.

Opposites: cowardly.

heroism NOUN **= bravery**, courage, courageousness, valour, intrepidity, fearlessness, gallantry, stout-heartedness, lion-heartedness, boldness, daring, dauntlessness, doughtiness, manliness, virility, mettle, spirit, fortitude, chivalry.

hesitant ADJ **1 = uncertain**, unsure, doubtful, dubious, sceptical, irresolute, indecisive, vacillating, wavering, oscillating, shilly-shallying, stalling, delaying, disinclined, unwilling, half-hearted, lacking confidence, diffident, timid, shy.

2 = reluctant, unwilling, disinclined, diffident, having qualms about.

Opposites: determined, decisive.

hesitate VERB **1 = delay**, pause, hang back, wait, be uncertain, be unsure, be doubtful, be indecisive, vacillate, waver, dither, shilly-shally, dally, stall, temporize, dilly-dally.

2 = be reluctant, be unwilling, be disinclined, shrink from, hang back from, think twice about, baulk at, demur from, scruple to, have misgivings about, be diffident about.

3 = stammer, stumble, falter, fumble for words; [Brit.] hum and haw.

hew VERB **1 = chop**, hack, axe, cut, saw, fell, lop, sever, trim, prune.

2 = carve, sculpt, sculpture, shape, fashion, form, model, whittle, chip, hammer, chisel, rough-hew.

hidden ADJ **1 = out of sight**, secret, unseen, not visible, not on view,

covered, concealed, masked, shrouded, unrevealed. **2 = secret**, obscure, indistinct, indefinite, unclear, vague, cryptic, mysterious, covert, concealed, under wraps, abstruse, arcane, recondite, clandestine, ulterior, unfathomable, inexplicable, occult, mystical.
Opposites: obvious.

hide VERB **1 = conceal oneself**, go into hiding, take cover, find a hiding place, lie low, keep out of sight, secrete oneself, go to ground, go underground, cover one's tracks; [inf] hole up. **2 = stow away**, secrete, store away, lock up; [inf] stash. **3 = obscure**, block, obstruct, darken, eclipse, cloud. **4 = keep secret**, keep dark, withhold, conceal, suppress, mask, veil, shroud, camouflage, disguise, hush up; [inf] keep mum about, keep under one's hat.
Opposites: reveal.

hideous ADJ **1 = ugly**, unsightly, grotesque, monstrous, repulsive, repellent, revolting, gruesome, disgusting, grim, ghastly, macabre. **2 = awful**, horrible, horrific, horrendous, horrifying, frightful, shocking, dreadful, outrageous, monstrous, appalling, terrible, terrifying, heinous, abominable, foul, vile, odious, loathsome, contemptible, execrable.
Opposites: beautiful.

hiding NOUN **= beating**, thrashing, whipping, caning, spanking, flogging, drubbing, battering; [inf] licking, walloping, tanning, whaling, lathering.

hierarchy NOUN **= social order**, ranking, grading, class system, pecking order.

high ADJ **1 = tall**, lofty, elevated, soaring, towering, steep. **2 = high-ranking**, leading, top, powerful, important, prominent, eminent, principal, chief,

influential, distinguished, notable, illustrious, exalted. **3** = **intense**, strong, powerful, extreme, forceful, vigorous, potent, violent. **4** = **drugged**, intoxicated, inebriated, delirious, hallucinating; [inf] stoned, on a trip, turned on.
Opposites: low.

highbrow NOUN = **intellectual**, scholar, genius, mastermind; [inf] egghead, brain; [Brit. inf] brainbox.
▶ADJ = **intellectual**, scholarly, bookish, cultured, cultivated, educated, sophisticated; [inf] brainy.
Opposites: lowbrow.

high-handed ADJ = **autocratic**, tyrannical, despotic, domineering, oppressive, overbearing, imperious, haughty, lordly; [inf] bossy.

hike VERB **1** = **walk**, march, tramp, trek, trudge, plod, ramble, wander, backpack. **2** = **hitch up**, pull up, jack up, lift up. **3** = **raise**, increase, add to, put up, jack up.

▶NOUN = **walk**, march, tramp, trek, ramble, trudge, wander.

hilarious ADJ = **very funny**, extremely amusing, comical, uproarious, humorous, entertaining, side-splitting; [inf] priceless.

hill NOUN **1** = **elevation**, heights, hillock, hilltop, knoll, hummock, mound, mount, fell, ridge. **2** = **slope**, incline, rise, gradient, ramp, acclivity, declivity.

hinder VERB = **impede**, hamper, hold back, interfere with, delay, hold up, slow down, retard, obstruct, inhibit, handicap, hamstring, block, interrupt, check, trammel, forestall, curb, baulk, thwart, frustrate, baffle, foil, stymie, stop, bring to a halt, arrest, defer, abort, prevent, debar.
Opposites: facilitate.

hindrance NOUN = **impediment**, obstacle, obstruction, interference, handicap, block, restraint, interruption,

check, bar, barrier, drawback, snag, difficulty, stumbling block, encumbrance, curb, stoppage, trammel, deterrent, prevention, debarment.
Opposites: aid, help.

hinge
▪ **hinge on** = **depend on**, turn on, hang on, be contingent on, pivot on, revolve around, rest on, centre on.

hint NOUN 1 = **clue**, inkling, suggestion, innuendo, tip-off, insinuation, implication, indication, mention, allusion, intimation, whisper, a word to the wise. 2 = **tip**, pointer, advice, help, suggestion. 3 = **touch**, trace, suggestion, dash, soupçon, sprinkling, tinge, whiff, breath, taste, scent.
▶ VERB = **suggest**, insinuate, imply, indicate, mention, allude to, intimate, let it be known, signal, refer to, make a reference to.

hire VERB 1 = **rent**, lease, charter, engage. 2 = **appoint**, sign on, take on, engage, employ, secure someone's services, enlist, contract with.

historic ADJ = **famed**, notable, famous, celebrated, renowned, momentous, significant, important, consequential, memorable, remarkable, outstanding, extraordinary, epoch-making, red-letter.

historical ADJ = **documented**, recorded, factual, chronicled, archival, authentic, actual, attested, verified, confirmed.

history NOUN 1 = **annal**, records, chronicles, account, study, tale, saga, narrative, recital, reports, memoirs, biography. 2 = **life story**, background, antecedents, experiences, adventures, fortunes. 3 = **the past**, former times, bygone days, yesterday, the old days, the good old days, time gone by, antiquity.

hit VERB 1 = **strike**, smack, slap, punch, box, cuff,

buffet, thump, batter, pound, pummel, thrash, hammer, bang, knock, club, swat; [inf] whack, wallop, bash, belt, clout, clip, clobber, sock, biff, swipe. **2** = **run into**, collide with, bang into, smash into, crash into, knock into, bump, meet head-on.

hoard VERB = **store**, store up, stock up, stockpile, put by, put away, lay by, lay in, set aside, pile up, stack up, stow away, husband, save, buy up, accumulate, amass, heap up, collect, gather, squirrel away, garner.
▶ NOUN = **store**, stockpile, supply, reserve, fund, cache, reservoir, accumulation, heap, pile, mass, aggregation, conglomeration; [inf] stash.

hoarse ADJ = **croaky**, croaking, gruff, rough, throaty, harsh, husky, gravelly, rasping, guttural, raucous, cracked.
Opposites: smooth.

hoax NOUN = **practical joke**, joke, prank, jest, trick, ruse, deception, fraud, imposture, cheat, swindle; [inf] con, fast one, spoof, scam.
▶ VERB = **trick**, fool, deceive, hoodwink, delude, bluff, dupe, take in, cheat, swindle, defraud, gull; [inf] con, pull a fast one on, pull the wool over someone's eyes, take for a ride, spoof.

hobble VERB = **walk with difficulty**, limp, falter, shuffle, totter, stagger, reel; [Scottish] hirple.

hobby NOUN = **interest**, pursuit, pastime, diversion, recreation, relaxation, sideline, divertissement, entertainment, amusement.

hold VERB **1** = **clasp**, clutch, grasp, grip, clench, seize, cling to. **2** = **bear**, carry, take, support, hold up, buttress, keep up, sustain, prop up, brace, suspend. **3** = **detain**, hold in custody, confine, impound, constrain, lock up, imprison, put behind

bars, incarcerate.
4 = keep, maintain, occupy, engage, involve, absorb, engross, monopolize, catch, arrest, fascinate, rivet.
5 = contain, take, accommodate, have a capacity for. **6 = call**, convene, assemble, conduct, run, preside over, officiate at.
▸ NOUN **1 = grip**, grasp, clutch, clasp. **2 = control**, grip, power, dominance, influence, mastery, dominion, authority, ascendancy.
■ **hold out = stand fast**, stand firm, resist, withstand, maintain one's position, stay put.
■ **hold up = delay**, hinder, impede, obstruct, retard, slow down, set back, stop, bring to a halt, prevent.

holder NOUN **1 = owner**, possessor, bearer, proprietor, keeper, custodian, purchaser, incumbent; [Brit.] occupier.
2 = container, case, casing, receptacle, stand,

cover, covering, housing, sheath.

hole NOUN **1 = opening**, aperture, gap, orifice, space, breach, break, fissure, crack, rift, puncture, perforation, cut, incision, split, gash, rent, slit, vent, notch.
2 = pit, crater, excavation, mine, shaft, dugout, cave, cavern, pothole, depression, hollow, chamber, pocket, cavity, dip.

holiness NOUN **= sanctity**, sanctitude, saintliness, sacredness, divineness, divinity, godliness, blessedness, spirituality, religiousness, piety, righteousness, goodness, virtue, purity, sanctimoniousness.

hollow ADJ **1 = empty**, vacant, not filled, not solid, hollowed out.
2 = sunken, deep-set, indented, depressed, concave, caved in, cavernous, incurvate.
3 = muffled, muted, low, dull, deep, rumbling, flat, dead, sepulchral.
4 = worthless, valueless,

empty, profitless,
fruitless, unprofitable,
pointless, meaningless,
insignificant, specious,
pyrrhic. **5 = insincere**,
false, dissembling,
deceitful, sham, untrue,
spurious.
Opposites: solid.

▶ NOUN = **indentation**,
depression, concavity,
dent, dip, dint, dimple,
hole, crater, cavern, pit,
cavity, well, trough.

holocaust NOUN
1 = devastation,
destruction, inferno,
conflagration,
demolition. **2 = genocide**,
mass murder,
annihilation, massacre,
carnage, slaughter,
extermination, butchery,
ethnic cleansing.

holy ADJ **1 = devout**, God-
fearing, pious, spiritual,
religious, righteous,
good, virtuous, moral,
saintly, saintlike, sinless,
pietistic. **2 = sacred**,
blessed, blest, sanctified,
consecrated, hallowed,
sacrosanct, dedicated,
venerated, divine,
religious.

Opposites: impious.

home NOUN **1 = house**,
residence, habitation;
[formal] dwelling, abode,
domicile. **2 = homeland**,
birth place, native land,
fatherland, motherland,
country of origin.
3 = habitat, environment,
natural element,
territory, ground, haunts,
domain; [formal] abode.

▪ **home in on = aim at**,
focus on, focus attention
on, concentrate on,
pinpoint, zero in on,
zoom in on.

homeless ADJ **= of no
fixed abode**, destitute,
derelict, without a roof
over one's head, down-
and-out, vagrant,
itinerant, nomadic,
dispossessed, rootless.

homely ADJ
1 = comfortable, cosy,
snug, welcoming,
informal, relaxed,
modest, unassuming,
unpretentious, simple,
natural, plain. **2 = plain**,
unattractive, ugly, plain-
featured, ill-favoured;
[inf] not much to look at,
short on looks.

Opposites: grand, beautiful.

homicide NOUN = **murder**, manslaughter, killing, slaughter, assassination, patricide, matricide, infanticide; [poetic/literary] slaying.

homily NOUN = **sermon**, lecture, speech, address, discourse, lesson, talk, oration.

homosexual ADJ = **gay**, lesbian, homoerotic; [inf] queer; [Brit. inf] bent, poofy.
Opposites: heterosexual.

honest ADJ **1** = **principled**, upright, honourable, ethical, moral, righteous, right-minded, virtuous, good, worthy, decent, law-abiding, high-minded, upstanding, just, fair, truthful, incorruptible, true, trustworthy, trusty, reliable, conscientious, scrupulous, reputable, dependable, loyal, faithful; [formal] veracious.
2 = **truthful**, frank, candid, direct, forthright, straightforward, open, genuine, plain-speaking,

matter-of-fact, outspoken, blunt, undisguised, unfeigned, unequivocal.
Opposites: dishonest.

honestly ADV **1** = **lawfully**, legally, legitimately, fairly, by fair means, honourably, decently, ethically, morally, without corruption; [inf] on the level, on the straight and narrow.
2 = **speaking truthfully**, truthfully, to be honest, speaking frankly, in all sincerity, candidly, frankly, openly, plainly, in plain language, to someone's face, without dissembling; [inf] straight out, straight up, Scout's honour.

honorary ADJ = **nominal**, titular, in name only, unofficial, ex officio, complimentary, unpaid.

honour NOUN **1** = **honesty**, uprightness, integrity, ethics, morals, high principles, righteousness, virtue, rectitude, goodness, decency, probity, worthiness, worth, fairness, justness,

justice, truthfulness,
trustworthiness,
reliability, dependability,
faithfulness, fidelity.
2 = glory, prestige,
renown, fame,
illustriousness, notability,
esteem, distinction,
credit, kudos. **3 = acclaim**,
acclamation, applause,
accolades, tributes,
homage, praise,
compliments, eulogy,
paeans, adoration,
reverence, adulation.
Opposites: dishonour.
▶ VERB **1 = esteem**, respect,
hold in esteem, have a
high regard for, admire,
defer to, revere, venerate,
worship, adore, idolize.
2 = acclaim, applaud, pay
homage to, pay tribute
to, lionize, cheer, praise,
eulogize. **3 = fulfil**,
discharge, carry out,
observe, keep, be true to,
live up to.

honourable ADJ = **honest**,
upright, ethical, moral,
principled, upstanding,
righteous, right-minded,
virtuous, good, decent,
worthy, fair, just, true,
truthful, trustworthy,

trusty, reliable,
dependable, faithful.
hook VERB **1 = fasten**,
secure, fix, close the
clasp. **2 = snare**, trap,
ensnare, entrap, enmesh.
hooligan NOUN = **thug**,
vandal, lout, rowdy,
delinquent, ruffian,
mugger, hoodlum;
[Brit.] tearaway; [inf] tough,
yahoo; [Brit. inf] yob,
yobbo.
hoop NOUN = **ring**, band,
circle, loop, wheel,
girdle.
hop VERB = **jump**, leap,
bound, spring, vault,
bounce, skip, caper,
dance, frisk.
hope NOUN = **expectation**,
hopefulness, expectancy,
anticipation, desire,
longing, wish, wishing,
craving, yearning,
aspiration, ambition,
dream, belief, assurance,
confidence, assumption,
conviction, faith, trust,
optimism.
Opposites: despair,
pessimism.
▶ VERB = **be hopeful of**,
expect, anticipate, look
forward to, await,

contemplate, desire, long, wish, crave, yearn, aspire, be ambitious, dream, believe, assume, have confidence, be convinced, rely on, count on, trust in.

hopeful ADJ 1 = **full of hope**, expectant, optimistic, confident, positive, assured, buoyant, sanguine. 2 = **encouraging**, promising, heartening, reassuring, gladdening, optimistic, favourable, auspicious, propitious, cheerful, bright, pleasant, rosy. **Opposites:** hopeless.

hopefully ADV 1 = **with hope**, full of hope, expectantly, optimistically, confidently, with assurance, buoyantly, sanguinely. 2 = **it is to be hoped that**, with luck, all being well, if all goes well, probably, conceivably, feasibly.

hopeless ADJ 1 = **without hope**, despairing, in despair, desperate, pessimistic, dejected, downhearted, despondent, demoralized, disconsolate, downcast, wretched, forlorn, suicidal, woebegone. 2 = **impossible**, impracticable, futile, useless, vain, pointless, worthless, unattainable, unachievable, no-win. 3 = **poor**, incompetent, inadequate, inferior, ineffective, ineffectual; [inf] no good, useless. **Opposites:** hopeful, accomplished.

horde NOUN = **crowd**, throng, mob, mass, group, multitude, host, army, pack, gang, troop, drove, crew, band, flock, swarm, gathering, assembly.

horrible ADJ 1 = **awful**, dreadful, terrible, horrid, horrifying, terrifying, frightful, fearful, horrendous, shocking, gruesome, hideous, grim, ghastly, harrowing, disgusting, revolting, repulsive, loathsome, abhorrent, detestable, hateful, abominable.

2 = disagreeable, nasty, unpleasant, obnoxious, odious, awful, dreadful, ghastly, frightful, hideous, revolting, appalling.
Opposites: pleasant.

horrify VERB **= shock**, appal, outrage, scandalize, disgust, revolt, repel, nauseate, sicken, offend, dismay; [inf] turn off.

horror NOUN **1 = terror**, fear, fearfulness, alarm, fright, dread, awe, panic, trepidation, apprehensiveness, uneasiness, nervousness, dismay, consternation.
2 = abhorrence, abomination, loathing, hate, detestation, repulsion, revulsion, disgust, distaste, aversion, hostility, antipathy, animosity.

horse NOUN **= steed**, mount, hack, cob, nag; [Brit. inf] gee-gee.

horseman, horsewoman NOUN **= rider**, equestrian, jockey, horse soldier, cavalryman, dragoon, cavalier, cowboy, cowgirl.

horseplay NOUN **= clowning**, fooling, tomfoolery, buffoonery, pranks, antics, capers, high jinks, rough and tumble, skylarking; [inf] shenanigans, monkey business.

hospitable ADJ **= welcoming**, generous, open-handed, sociable, friendly, bountiful, neighbourly, kind, warm, helpful.
Opposites: inhospitable.

hospital NOUN **= clinic**, infirmary, health centre, medical centre, sanatorium, nursing home, hospice, sick bay.

host NOUN **1 = proprietor**, proprietress, landlord, landlady, innkeeper, hotel-keeper, hotelier.
2 = presenter, compère, master of ceremonies, MC, anchorman, anchorwoman.

hostage NOUN **= captive**, prisoner, pawn, pledge, security.

hostile ADJ **1 = opposed**, antagonistic, averse, ill-disposed, against, inimical; [inf] anti.
2 = aggressive, angry, belligerent, bellicose, warlike, warring, militant, antagonistic, unfriendly, unkind, unsympathetic, malevolent, malicious, spiteful, wrathful.
3 = adverse, unfavourable, inauspicious, unpropitious, disadvantageous.
Opposites: favourable, friendly.

hostility NOUN
1 = antagonism, opposition, ill will, aversion, animosity, enmity. **2 = aggression**, belligerence, anger, bellicosity, militancy, antagonism, unfriendliness, unkindness, malevolence, spite, malice, wrath.
Opposites: friendship.

hot ADJ **1 = heated**, very warm, boiling, boiling hot, piping hot, scalding, red-hot, sizzling, steaming, scorching, roasting, searing, blazing hot, sweltering, blistering, baking, oven-like, torrid, sultry.
2 = spicy, peppery, piquant, fiery, pungent, sharp, biting, acrid.
3 = violent, furious, heated, fierce, ferocious, stormy, tempestuous, savage.
Opposites: cold, mild.

hot-headed ADJ **= hot-tempered**, quick-tempered, short-tempered, fiery, excitable, volatile, hasty, rash, impetuous, impulsive, reckless, foolhardy, wild, unruly.

house NOUN **1 = residence**, home, habitation; [inf] pad; [Brit. inf] gaff; [formal] dwelling, abode, domicile. **2 = family**, clan, line, dynasty, lineage, ancestry.
▶ VERB **1 = accommodate**, lodge, put up, take in, have room for, sleep, shelter, harbour.
2 = cover, sheathe,

h

protect, shelter, guard, contain, keep.

household NOUN = **family**, home, house, ménage, establishment.
▶ ADJ = **domestic**, family, ordinary, everyday, common, usual, run-of-the-mill.

hover VERB **1** = **float**, fly, be suspended, hang, drift, be wafted, flutter.
2 = **linger**, loiter, hang about, wait, stay.
3 = **vacillate**, fluctuate, oscillate, alternate, see-saw; [Scottish] swither.

however ADV
= **nevertheless**, be that as it may, nonetheless, notwithstanding, anyway, anyhow, regardless, despite that, still, yet, just the same, though.

howl VERB = **bay**, yowl, ululate, yelp, wail, bawl, scream, bellow, caterwaul, cry.

hub NOUN **1** = **pivot**, axis, nave. **2** = **centre**, middle, core, heart, focus, focal point.

huddle VERB **1** = **crowd**, throng, press, pack, cluster, cram, herd, squeeze, gather, congregate. **2** = **curl up**, snuggle, cuddle, nestle, hunch up.
▶ NOUN = **gathering**, crowd, cluster, pack, press.

hue NOUN **1** = **colour**, tone, shade, tint, tinge, dye.
2 = **complexion**, cast, aspect, light.

hug VERB **1** = **embrace**, cuddle, take in one's arms, hold close, enfold in one's arms, clasp/press to one's bosom, squeeze, snuggle against.
2 = **keep close to**, stay near, follow closely.

huge ADJ = **enormous**, immense, great, massive, colossal, vast, prodigious, gigantic, giant, gargantuan, mammoth, monumental, monstrous, elephantine, bulky, extensive, mountainous, titanic, Brobdingnagian, Herculean; [inf] jumbo.
Opposites: tiny.

hulk NOUN **1** = **wreck**, shipwreck, derelict, ruin, shell, skeleton, hull, frame. **2** = **oaf**, lout, lump, lubber.

hull NOUN = **framework**, body, frame, skeleton, structure, casing, covering.

hum VERB **1** = **murmur**, drone, vibrate, thrum, buzz, whirr, purr. **2** = **sing**, croon, whisper, mumble.

human ADJ **1** = **mortal**, physical, bodily, fleshly, carnal, corporal. **2** = **kind**, kindly, considerate, understanding, sympathetic, compassionate, approachable, humane, accessible. **3** = **flesh and blood**, fallible, weak, frail, vulnerable, erring.

humane ADJ = **kind**, kindly, kind-hearted, good, good-natured, compassionate, understanding, considerate, sympathetic, forgiving, merciful, lenient, forbearing, gentle, tender, mild, benign, clement, benevolent, charitable, generous, magnanimous, approachable, accessible. **Opposites:** cruel, inhumane.

humble ADJ **1** = **modest**, unassuming, self-effacing, meek, unassertive, unpretentious, unostentatious, servile, docile, submissive, obsequious, subservient, deferential, over-respectful, slavish, sycophantic. **2** = **common**, ordinary, simple, poor, low-born, of low birth, low-ranking, low, lowly, inferior, plebeian, proletarian, base, mean, unrefined, vulgar, unimportant, insignificant, inconsequential, undistinguished, ignoble. **Opposites:** arrogant, important.
▶ VERB **1** = **humiliate**, mortify, subdue, chasten, shame, put to shame, abash, degrade. **2** = **defeat**, crush, trounce, rout, break, conquer, vanquish, overwhelm, bring someone to their knees.

humdrum ADJ = **commonplace**, routine, run-of-the-mill, unvaried,

unvarying, ordinary, everyday, mundane, monotonous, repetitious, dull, uninteresting, boring, tedious, banal, tiresome, wearisome.
Opposites: remarkable.

humiliate VERB = **mortify**, shame, humble, put to shame, make ashamed, disgrace, embarrass, discomfit, chasten, subdue, deflate, abash, debase, abase, degrade, crush, demean; [inf] take someone down a peg or two, make someone eat humble pie, put down, show up; [N. Amer.] make someone eat crow.

humiliation NOUN = **mortification**, loss of pride, humbling, disgrace, loss of face, dishonour, indignity, discredit, embarrassment, discomfiture, affront, abasement, debasement, degradation, submission; [inf] put-down.

humility NOUN = **humbleness**, lack of pride, modesty, meekness, self-effacement,

unpretentiousness, unobtrusiveness, diffidence, servility, submissiveness, obsequiousness, subservience, deference, sycophancy.
Opposites: arrogance, pride.

humorous ADJ = **funny**, comic, comical, entertaining, witty, jocular, amusing, hilarious, side-splitting, rib-tickling, farcical, facetious, ridiculous, ludicrous, absurd, droll.
Opposites: serious.

humour NOUN
1 = **funniness**, comic side, funny side, comical aspect, comedy, farce, jocularity, hilarity, ludicrousness, absurdness, absurdity, drollness. **2** = **comedy**, jokes, joking, jests, jesting, wit, wittiness, witticisms, waggishness, pleasantries, buffoonery; [inf] gags, wisecracks.
3 = **mood**, temper, temperament, frame of mind, state of mind,

disposition, spirits.

hump NOUN = **protrusion**, protuberance, projection, bulge, swelling, lump, bump, knob, hunch, mass, nodule, node, intumescence, tumefaction.
▶ VERB **1** = **hunch**, arch, curve, curl up, crook.
2 = **carry**, lift, lug, heave, shoulder, hoist.

hunch NOUN **1** = **feeling**, presentiment, premonition, intuition, sixth sense, suspicion, inkling, impression, idea.
2 = *See* **hump** NOUN.

hunger NOUN
1 = **hungriness**, lack of food, starvation, ravenousness, emptiness, famine, voracity, greediness. **2** = **longing**, craving, yearning, desire, want, need, thirst, appetite, hankering, lust; [inf] itch.

hungry ADJ **1** = **famished**, famishing, ravenous, starving, starved, half-starved, empty, greedy, voracious; [dated] sharp-set. **2** = **longing**, yearning, craving, in need/want of,

eager, keen, desirous of, covetous of.
Opposites: full.

hunt VERB **1** = **chase**, give chase, pursue, stalk, track, trail, follow, shadow, hound, tail.
2 = **search for**, look for, seek, try to find, scour for, forage for, fish for, rummage for, scrabble for.

hurdle NOUN **1** = **fence**, barrier, railing, rail, wall, hedge, hedgerow, bar, barricade. **2** = **obstacle**, barrier, hindrance, impediment, obstruction, stumbling block, snag, complication, difficulty, handicap.

hurl VERB = **throw**, fling, pitch, cast, toss, heave, fire, launch, let fly, shy, propel, project, dart, catapult; [inf] sling, chuck.

hurried ADJ **1** = **quick**, rapid, fast, swift, speedy, hasty, breakneck.
2 = **hasty**, quick, swift, rushed, cursory, superficial, perfunctory, offhand, passing, fleeting, transitory.

h

Opposites: slow.

hurry VERB 1 = **move quickly**, hurry up, be quick, make haste, hasten, speed, lose no time, press on, push on, run, dash, rush; [inf] go hell for leather, get a move on, put one's foot down, step on it, get cracking, shake a leg, go like a bat out of hell, hightail it, hotfoot it. 2 = **speed up**, quicken, hasten, accelerate, expedite, urge on, drive on, push on, goad, prod, hustle.
Opposites: dawdle.

hurt VERB 1 = **be sore**, be painful, cause pain, ache, smart, sting, nip, throb, tingle, burn. 2 = **injure**, wound, bruise, cut, scratch, lacerate, maim, damage, mutilate, disable, incapacitate, impair, debilitate. 3 = **upset**, sadden, grieve, wound, distress, pain, cut to the quick, sting, offend, give offence to, discompose. 4 = **harm**, damage, spoil, blight, mar, blemish, impair.

hurtful ADJ 1 = **upsetting**, wounding, injurious, distressing, unkind, nasty, mean, spiteful, malicious, cutting, cruel, mischievous, offensive. 2 = **harmful**, damaging, injurious, detrimental, deleterious, destructive, prejudicial, ruinous, inimical.

husband NOUN = **spouse**, partner, consort, groom, bridegroom; [inf] hubby, old man; [Brit. inf] other half.

hush VERB = **silence**, quieten, quieten down, shush, shut up.
▸ NOUN = **quiet**, quietness, silence, stillness, still, peace, calm, tranquillity.

hustle VERB 1 = **push**, shove, thrust, crowd, jostle, elbow, nudge, shoulder. 2 = See **hurry**. 3 = **coerce**, force, impel, pressure, badger, urge, goad, prod, spur, propel.

hut NOUN = **shed**, lean-to, shack, cabin, shanty, hovel; [Scottish] bothy.

hygiene NOUN
= **cleanliness**, sanitation, public health, sanitary measures.

hygienic ADJ = **sanitary**, clean, germ-free, disinfected, sterilized, sterile, aseptic, unpolluted, uncontaminated, healthy, pure.
Opposites: dirty, unsanitary.

hypnotic ADJ = **mesmeric**, mesmerizing, sleep-inducing, soporific, somniferous, numbing, sedative, stupefacient.

hypnotize VERB **1** = **put under**, put out, send into a trance, mesmerize, put to sleep. **2** = **fascinate**, bewitch, entrance, beguile, spellbind, magnetize.

hypocrisy NOUN
= **insincerity**, falseness, sanctimoniousness, falsity, deceptiveness, deceit, deceitfulness, deception, dishonesty, duplicity, imposture, cant, two-facedness, double-dealing, pretence, Pharisaism, pietism.

Opposites: sincerity.

hypocritical ADJ = **false**, insincere, sanctimonious, fraudulent, deceitful, deceptive, dishonest, untruthful, lying, dissembling, duplicitous, two-faced, double-dealing, untrustworthy, perfidious, specious, spurious; [inf] phoney.

hypothesis NOUN
= **theory**, thesis, theorem, proposition, axiom, premise, postulate, supposition, assumption, presumption, conjecture, speculation.

hypothetical ADJ
= **assumed**, presumed, theoretical, putative, speculative, conjectured, imagined, notional, academic.

hysteria NOUN = **hysterics**, frenzy, loss of control, agitation, madness, delirium; [inf] the screaming habdabs.

hysterical ADJ
1 = **frenzied**, in a frenzy, frantic, out of control, berserk, beside oneself, distracted, distraught, overwrought, agitated, in

a panic, mad, crazed, delirious, raving. **2 = very funny/amusing**, hilarious, uproarious, side-splitting, comical, farcical, screamingly funny.
Opposites: calm.

Ii

ice NOUN = **frozen water**, frost, icicle, iceberg, glacier, rime.

icy ADJ 1 = **freezing**, chill, chilly, frigid, frosty, biting, raw, bitter, arctic, glacial, Siberian, polar, gelid. 2 = **frozen**, ice-bound, frosty, rimy, glassy, slippery, slippy. 3 = **cold**, cool, frigid, frosty, stiff, aloof, distant, unfriendly, unresponsive, uncommunicative, reserved, reticent, restrained.

idea NOUN 1 = **concept**, thought, conception, conceptualization, image, abstraction, perception, notion. 2 = **thought**, theory, view, viewpoint, opinion, feeling, outlook, belief, judgement, conclusion. 3 = **impression**, feeling, notion, suspicion, inkling. 4 = **estimation**, approximation, guess, surmise; [inf] guesstimate. 5 = **plan**, design, aim, scheme, intention, objective, object, purpose, end, goal, target.

ideal ADJ 1 = **perfect**, consummate, supreme, absolute, complete, flawless, exemplary, classic, archetypal, model, quintessential. 2 = **unattainable**, utopian, unreal, impracticable, imaginary, ivory-towered, romantic, visionary, fanciful. ▶ NOUN 1 = **archetype**, prototype, model, pattern, exemplar, paradigm, example, criterion, yardstick. 2 = **principle**, standard, moral value, morals, ethics.

idealistic ADJ
= **impractical**, utopian, perfectionist, visionary, romantic, quixotic, unrealistic; [inf] starry-eyed.
Opposites: practical, realistic.

ideally ADV = **in a perfect world**, all things being equal, theoretically, hypothetically, in theory.

identical ADJ 1 = **the same**, the very same, one and the same, selfsame.
2 = **alike**, like, similar, much the same, indistinguishable, corresponding, matching, twin.
Opposites: different.

identify VERB
1 = **recognize**, single out, pick out, spot, point out, pinpoint, discern, distinguish, name; [inf] put the finger on.
2 = **establish**, find out, ascertain, diagnose, select, choose.
3 = **associate**, connect, think of in connection with. 4 = **relate to**, empathize with,

sympathize with, have a rapport with, respond to, feel for.

identity NOUN 1 = **name**, specification.
2 = **personality**, self, selfhood, ego, individuality, distinctiveness, singularity, uniqueness.
3 = **identification**, recognition, naming.
4 = **sameness**, interchangeability, likeness, similarity, closeness, accordance.

ideology NOUN = **doctrine**, creed, credo, teaching, dogma, theory, thesis, tenets, beliefs, opinions, principles, convictions, attitudes.

idiocy NOUN = **stupidity**, foolishness, absurdity, inanity, fatuity, fatuousness, asininity, lunacy, craziness, insanity, dumbness; [Brit. inf] daftness.
Opposites: sense.

idiom NOUN 1 = **phrase**, expression, locution, turn of phrase, set phrase, fixed expression.
2 = **language**, style of

speech, speech, talk, usage, parlance, vernacular, jargon, patois; [inf] lingo.

idiomatic ADJ = **colloquial**, informal, vernacular, natural.

idiosyncrasy NOUN = **peculiarity**, oddity, eccentricity, trait, singularity, mannerism, quirk, habit, characteristic, speciality, quality, feature.

idiot NOUN = **fool**, dolt, dunce, ass, ignoramus, imbecile, simpleton; [inf] chump, booby, nincompoop, ninny, dunderhead, blockhead, fathead, halfwit, cretin, moron, dummy, numbskull, dimwit; [Brit. inf] twerp, clot, twit, nitwit.

idiotic ADJ = **stupid**, foolish, senseless, absurd, fatuous, inane, asinine, unintelligent, half-witted, hare-brained, lunatic, crazy, insane, mad, moronic, dumb, irrational, nonsensical, ridiculous; [Brit. inf] daft. **Opposites:** sensible.

idle ADJ **1** = **lazy**, indolent, slothful, sluggish, apathetic, torpid, slow, shiftless, loafing, dronish. **2** = **inoperative**, not in operation, inactive, out of action, unused, mothballed. **3** = **empty**, unfilled, unoccupied, vacant. **4** = **groundless**, baseless, worthless, futile, casual. **5** = **trivial**, unimportant, insignificant, trifling, superficial, shallow, foolish, inane, fatuous. **Opposites:** industrious, busy.
▶ VERB **1** = **while**, loaf, lounge, loiter, dawdle, fritter, dally, potter. **2** = **do nothing**, laze, loaf, be inactive, mark time, shirk, slack, vegetate, take it easy, rest on one's oars.

idol NOUN **1** = **god**, icon, effigy, image, graven image, fetish, likeness. **2** = **hero**, heroine, favourite, darling, pet, beloved, star, superstar, apple of one's eye; [Brit. inf] blue-eyed boy/girl.

idolize VERB **1** = **worship**, bow down before, glorify, exalt, revere, deify. **2** = **hero-worship**, worship, adulate, adore, love, look up to, admire, dote on, lionize, revere, venerate.

ignite VERB **1** = **set fire to**, light, set on fire, set alight, fire, kindle, inflame, touch off, put a match to. **2** = **catch fire**, catch, burst into flames, burn up, burn, flame up, kindle.
Opposites: extinguish.

ignominious ADJ
1 = **shameful**, dishonourable, disgraceful, humiliating, mortifying, discreditable, disreputable, undignified, infamous, ignoble, inglorious, scandalous, abject, sorry, base.
2 = **contemptible**, despicable, offensive, revolting, wicked, vile, base, low.
Opposites: glorious.

ignorance NOUN
= **unfamiliarity**, unconsciousness, lack of knowledge, inexperience, greenness, innocence; [poetic/literary] nescience.
Opposites: knowledge.

ignorant ADJ **1** = **unaware of**, unfamiliar with, unconscious of, unacquainted with, uninformed about, unconversant with, unenlightened about, inexperienced in, blind to, unschooled in, naive about, innocent about; [inf] in the dark about.
2 = **uneducated**, unschooled, illiterate, unlettered, uninformed, unknowledgeable, unintelligent, stupid, benighted.
Opposites: knowledgeable.

ignore VERB **1** = **disregard**, pay no attention to, take no notice of, brush aside, pass over, shrug off, shut one's eyes to, be oblivious to, turn a blind eye to, turn a deaf ear to.
2 = **slight**, spurn, cold-shoulder, look right through, look past, turn one's back on, send to Coventry, cut, cut dead.
Opposites: acknowledge.

ill ADJ 1 = **sick**, unwell, not well, poorly, ailing, sickly, infirm, feeling bad, afflicted, indisposed, out of sorts, diseased, bedridden, invalided, weak, feeble; [Brit.] off colour; [inf] under the weather, laid up, queasy, funny, seedy; [Brit. inf, dated] queer. 2 = **hostile**, unfriendly, antagonistic, acrimonious, belligerent, bellicose, unkind, spiteful, rancorous, malicious, resentful, malevolent, bitter. 3 = **bad**, infamous, notorious, wicked, nefarious, vile, evil, foul, sinful, corrupt, depraved, degenerate. **Opposites:** healthy.
▶ ADV = **badly**, unfavourably, with disfavour, with disapproval, with hostility, unkindly, maliciously, spitefully.

ill-advised ADJ = **unwise**, ill-considered, imprudent, incautious, injudicious, ill-judged, impolitic, misguided, foolish, foolhardy, rash, hasty, overhasty, short-sighted, thoughtless, careless, reckless.

illegal ADJ = **unlawful**, illegitimate, illicit, lawless, criminal, felonious, actionable, unlicensed, unauthorized, unsanctioned, unwarranted, unofficial, outlawed, banned, forbidden, barred, prohibited, proscribed, contraband, black-market, under the counter, bootleg. **Opposites:** legal.

illegible ADJ = **indecipherable**, unreadable, unintelligible, scrawled, scribbled, unclear, obscure, squiggly. **Opposites:** legible.

illegitimate ADJ 1 = **illegal**, illicit, unlawful, lawless, criminal, unauthorized, unsanctioned, irregular, invalid. 2 = **born out of wedlock**; [dated] love, born on the wrong side of the blanket; [archaic] bastard, natural.

3 = **unsound**, illogical, invalid, incorrect, spurious.
Opposites: legitimate.

ill-fated ADJ = **unlucky**, luckless, unfortunate, hapless, unhappy, doomed, blighted, ill-starred, ill-omened.

ill-judged ADJ = *see* **ill-advised**.

illness NOUN = **sickness**, ailment, disease, complaint, malady, disorder, affliction, disability, attack, indisposition, infection, contagion, ill health, poor health.

illogical ADJ = **unsound**, fallacious, unproved, invalid, specious, unreasonable, unreasoned, fallible, untenable, unscientific, casuistic, sophistic, inconsistent, incorrect, wrong, absurd, preposterous, meaningless, senseless.
Opposites: logical.

ill-treat VERB = **treat badly**, abuse, harm, injure, damage, handle roughly, mishandle, ill-use, maltreat, misuse; [inf] knock about.

illuminating ADJ = **instructive**, informative, enlightening, explanatory, revealing, helpful.

illusion NOUN **1** = **delusion**, misapprehension, misconception, deception, false/mistaken impression, fallacy, error, misjudgement, fancy.
2 = **hallucination**, figment of the imagination, spectre, phantom, mirage, fantasy, will-o'-the-wisp; [poetic/literary] phantasm.

illusory ADJ = **false**, mistaken, deceptive, delusory, delusional, delusive, fallacious, erroneous, misleading, untrue, specious, unreal, imagined, imaginary, fancied, non-existent, fanciful, notional, chimerical, dreamlike.
Opposites: genuine.

illustrate VERB **1** = **add pictures to**, adorn, decorate, ornament, embellish.

2 = **demonstrate**, exemplify, show, point up, instance, make plain/clear, clarify, bring home, emphasize, interpret.

illustration NOUN
1 = **picture**, drawing, sketch, figure, plate, artwork. **2** = **example**, demonstration, typical case, case in point, instance, specimen, sample, exemplar, analogy.

image NOUN **1** = **likeness**, representation, painting, picture, portrait, effigy, figure, statue, sculpture, bust. **2** = **double**, twin, replica, clone, copy, reproduction, counterpart, doppelgänger; [inf] spit, spitting image, ringer, dead ringer. **3** = **figure of speech**, conceit, trope, expression.

imaginary ADJ = **unreal**, non-existent, illusory, fanciful, unsubstantial, chimerical, notional, assumed, supposed, supposititious, fictitious, fictional, mythical, mythological, made up, invented, hallucinatory, ghostly, spectral, dreamlike, visionary, shadowy; [poetic/literary] phantasmic.
Opposites: real, actual.

imagination NOUN
1 = **creativity**, vision, inspiration, inventiveness, originality, innovation, ingenuity, insight, fancifulness. **2** = **illusion**, figment of the imagination, fancy, vision, dream, unreality.

imaginative ADJ
= **creative**, inventive, original, innovative, visionary, inspired, fanciful, resourceful, ingenious, enterprising, clever, whimsical.
Opposites: unimaginative.

imagine VERB **1** = **picture**, visualize, see in the mind's eye, envision, envisage, conjure up, dream about, dream up, think up, conceive, fantasize about, conceptualize, plan, scheme, project.
2 = **assume**, presume,

expect, suppose, think, believe, be of the opinion that, take it, gather, fancy, judge, deem, infer, deduce, conjecture, surmise, guess, reckon, suspect, realize.

imbue VERB = **fill**, impregnate, inject, inculcate, instil, ingrain, inspire, permeate, charge.

imitate VERB 1 = **copy**, emulate, simulate, mirror, follow someone's example, take after, follow, follow suit, take a page from someone's book, follow in someone's footsteps, echo. 2 = **mimic**, ape, impersonate, do an impression of, parody, mock, caricature, burlesque, travesty; [inf] send up, take off, spoof, do.

imitation NOUN 1 = **copy**, reproduction, forgery, fake, counterfeit, resemblance, emulation, duplication, likeness, replica, simulation. 2 = **mimicking**, mimicry, aping, impersonation,

impression, parody, mockery, caricature, burlesque, travesty; [inf] send-up, take-off, spoof.

▸ ADJ = **artificial**, simulated, synthetic, man-made, mock, sham, fake, reproduction, pseudo, ersatz; [inf] phoney.

immature ADJ 1 = **unripe**, undeveloped, unformed, imperfect, unfinished, incomplete, half-grown, crude, raw, green, unfledged, untimely. 2 = **childish**, juvenile, adolescent, infantile, babyish, puerile, callow, jejune, inexperienced, green; [inf] wet behind the ears.
Opposites: mature.

immediate ADJ
1 = **instant**, instantaneous, prompt, swift, speedy, sudden, abrupt. 2 = **near**, nearest, next, next-door, close, closest, adjacent, adjoining, abutting, contiguous, proximate. 3 = **current**, present, existing, actual, existent, extant, urgent, pressing.

Opposites: delayed, distant.

immediately ADV = **right away**, right now, straight away, at once, instantly, now, this minute, directly, promptly, without delay; [inf] before you can say Jack Robinson, pronto.

immense ADJ = **huge**, vast, massive, enormous, gigantic, colossal, giant, great, extensive, infinite, immeasurable, illimitable, monumental, tremendous, prodigious, elephantine, monstrous, titanic, Brobdingnagian; [inf] mega; [Brit. inf] ginormous.
Opposites: tiny, minute.

immerse VERB
1 = **submerge**, plunge, dip, dunk, duck, sink, souse, soak, drench, imbue, saturate.
2 = **absorb**, engross, occupy, engage, preoccupy, involve, engulf, lose oneself in.

immigrant NOUN = **settler**, alien, incomer, non-native, new arrival, migrant, naturalized citizen, expatriate.

imminent ADJ = **impending**, approaching, close, fast-approaching, at hand, near, coming, forthcoming, on the way, about to happen, upon us, in the offing, on the horizon, in the air, brewing, threatening, menacing, looming.
Opposites: distant.

immobile ADJ = **unmoving**, motionless, immovable, still, static, at rest, stationary, at a standstill, stock-still, dormant, rooted, fixed to the spot, rigid, frozen, stiff, riveted, like a statue; [technical] immotile, immotive.

immobilize VERB = **stop**, halt, bring to a standstill, paralyse, put out of action, inactivate, disable, cripple, freeze, transfix.

immodest ADJ = **bold**, brazen, forward, impudent, unblushing, shameless, wanton, improper, indecent, cheeky.

immoral ADJ = **bad**, wicked, evil, unprincipled, dishonest, unethical, sinful, impure, corrupt, iniquitous, depraved, vile, base, degenerate, debauched, abandoned, dissolute, villainous, nefarious, reprobate, indecent, lewd, licentious, pornographic, unchaste, bawdy, of easy virtue. **Opposites:** ethical, chaste.

immortal ADJ **1** = **undying**, eternal, deathless, everlasting, never-ending, endless, imperishable, timeless, indestructible, unfading, perennial, evergreen, perpetual, lasting, enduring, constant, abiding, immutable, indissoluble; [poetic/literary] sempiternal, perdurable. **2** = **famous**, celebrated, renowned. **Opposites:** mortal.

immortalize VERB = **commemorate**, memorialize, eternalize, eternize, perpetuate, exalt, glorify; [formal] laud.

immovable ADJ **1** = **fixed**, set fast/firm, fast, firm, secure, stable, rooted, riveted, moored, anchored, stuck, jammed, stiff, unbudgeable. **2** = **motionless**, unmoving, stationary, still, stock-still, at a standstill, dead still, statue-like. **3** = **firm**, adamant, steadfast, unwavering, unswerving, resolute, determined, tenacious, stubborn, dogged, obdurate, inflexible, unyielding, unbending, uncompromising, unshakeable, inexorable.

immune ADJ = **not subject to**, not liable to, protected from, safe from, unsusceptible to, secure against, exempt from, clear of, free from, absolved from, released from, excused from, relieved of, spared from, exempted from, unaffected by, resistant to, proof against. **Opposites:** liable, susceptible.

immunize VERB
= **inoculate**, vaccinate,
protect, shield, safeguard.

impact NOUN 1 = **collision**,
crash, contact, smash,
striking, clash, bump,
knock, bang, jolt, thump,
whack, thwack, slam,
smack, slap. 2 = **influence**,
effect, impression,
results, consequences,
repercussions.

impair VERB = **weaken**,
lessen, decrease, reduce,
blunt, diminish,
enfeeble, debilitate,
enervate, damage, mar,
spoil, injure, harm,
hinder, disable, cripple,
impede, undermine;
[formal] vitiate.
Opposites: improve,
enhance.

impart VERB = **pass on**,
convey, communicate,
transmit, relate, tell,
make known, report,
disclose, reveal, divulge,
proclaim, broadcast.

impartial ADJ = **unbiased**,
unprejudiced,
disinterested, objective,
detached, neutral,
equitable, even-handed,
fair, fair-minded, open-

minded, non-partisan,
without fear or favour,
with no axe to grind.
Opposites: biased,
partisan.

impartiality NOUN
= **detachment**, disinterest,
objectivity, neutrality,
even-handedness,
fairness, justness, open-
mindedness.

impassable ADJ 1 = **close**,
blocked, obstructed,
unnavigable,
untraversable,
impenetrable.
2 = **insurmountable**,
insuperable,
unconquerable.

impatient ADJ 1 = **eager**,
keen, anxious, avid,
desirous, yearning,
longing. 2 = **restless**,
restive, excitable,
agitated, nervous, edgy,
impetuous. 3 = **abrupt**,
brusque, terse, short,
irritated, angry, testy,
short-tempered, quick-
tempered, curt,
querulous, peevish,
intolerant; [inf] snappy.
Opposites: patient.

impede VERB = **hinder**,
obstruct, hamper,

handicap, block, check, curb, bar, hold back, hold up, delay, interfere with, disrupt, retard, slow, slow down, brake, restrain, thwart, frustrate, baulk, stop; [Brit.] throw a spanner in the works.
Opposites: facilitate.

impediment NOUN
= **hindrance**, obstruction, obstacle, handicap, block, stumbling block, check, encumbrance, bar, barrier, curb, brake, restraint, drawback, difficulty, snag, setback.

impel VERB = **urge**, press, exhort, force, oblige, constrain, necessitate, require, demand, make, apply pressure, pressure, pressurize, spur, goad, incite, prompt, chivvy, persuade, inspire.

impending ADJ = *see* **imminent**.

impenetrable ADJ
1 = **impervious**, impermeable, solid, dense, thick, hard, closed, sealed, resistant, waterproof, tight, unpierceable.
2 = **impassable**, inaccessible, thick, dense, overgrown.
3 = **incomprehensible**, baffling, puzzling, abstruse, obscure, inexplicable, unfathomable, recondite, inscrutable, enigmatic.

imperceptible ADJ
= **unnoticeable**, unobtrusive, unapparent, slight, small, gradual, subtle, faint, fine, inconsequential, tiny, minute, minuscule, microscopic, infinitesimal, undetectable, indistinguishable, indiscernible, invisible, indistinct, unclear, obscure, vague, indefinite, shadowy, inaudible, muffled, impalpable.
Opposites: obvious.

imperceptibly ADV
= **unnoticeably**, unobtrusively, unseen, gradually, slowly, subtly, undetectably, little by little, bit by bit.

imperfect ADJ **1** = **faulty**, flawed, defective, blemished, damaged,

broken, impaired.
2 = **deficient**, inadequate, insufficient, rudimentary, limited, patchy, sketchy.
Opposites: flawless.

imperfection NOUN
1 = **fault**, flaw, defect, blemish, deformity, crack, break, scratch, cut, tear, stain, spot.
2 = **failing**, foible, deficiency, weakness, weak point, shortcoming, fallibility, frailty, infirmity, peccadillo.

imperious ADJ
= **overbearing**, overweening, domineering, peremptory, high-handed, assertive, commanding, authoritative, lordly, masterful, dictatorial, tyrannical.
Opposites: humble.

impersonal ADJ
1 = **objective**, detached, disinterested, dispassionate, neutral, unbiased, unprejudiced, fair, equitable, even-handed. **2** = **cold**, cool, aloof, frigid, stiff, rigid, wooden, starchy, stilted, stuffy, businesslike, bureaucratic, matter-of-fact.
Opposites: biased.

impersonate VERB
= **imitate**, mimic, personate, ape, mock, parody, caricature, masquerade as, burlesque, pose as, pass oneself off as; [inf] take off, do.

impertinent ADJ
= **insolent**, impudent, cheeky, rude, impolite, unmannerly, ill-mannered, uncivil, coarse, uncouth, crude, discourteous, disrespectful, bold, brazen, audacious, presumptuous, forward, pert, brash, shameless; [inf] saucy, brass-necked, fresh, flip.
Opposites: polite.

imperturbable ADJ
= **self-possessed**, composed, collected, calm, cool, tranquil, serene, unexcitable, unflappable, even-tempered, easy-going, at ease, unruffled, untroubled, undismayed,

unmoved, nonchalant.
Opposites: nervous,
excitable.

impetuous ADJ
1 = **impulsive**, hasty,
impatient, excitable,
headstrong, rash,
reckless, foolhardy, wild,
uncontrolled, eager,
enthusiastic,
spontaneous, passionate,
ardent, zealous. 2 = **hasty**,
precipitate, impulsive,
spontaneous,
impromptu, spur-of-the-
moment, unthinking,
unplanned, ill-conceived,
ill-considered,
unreasoned, heedless,
reckless, rash.
Opposites: cautious.

impetus NOUN
1 = **momentum**, energy,
force, power, propulsion,
motion. 2 = **stimulus**,
motivation, incentive,
inducement, inspiration,
encouragement,
influence, push, urging,
pressing, spur, goading,
goad, instigation,
actuation.

impinge
■ **impinge on**
1 = **encroach on**, infringe,

intrude on, invade,
trespass on, violate,
usurp, make inroads on,
obtrude on. 2 = **affect**,
have an effect on, have a
bearing on, impress,
touch, exert influence
on, bear upon.

implausible ADJ
= **unlikely**, improbable,
hard to believe,
incredible, unbelievable,
unimaginable,
inconceivable, debatable,
questionable, doubtful.
Opposites: plausible.

implement NOUN = **tool**,
utensil, appliance,
instrument, gadget,
device, apparatus,
contrivance; [inf] gizmo.
▶ VERB = **carry out**, fulfil,
execute, perform,
discharge, accomplish,
achieve, realize, put into
effect, bring about, effect,
enforce.

implicate VERB
= **incriminate**, involve,
compromise, accuse,
charge, blame, entangle,
impeach, inculpate.
Opposites: absolve.

implication NOUN
1 = **incrimination**,

involvement, connection, entanglement, embroilment, association.
2 = **suggestion**, inference, insinuation, innuendo, hint, allusion, reference, assumption, presumption.

implicit ADJ **1** = **implied**, indirect, inferred, unspoken, undeclared, unexpressed, unstated, tacit, understood, suggested. **2** = **absolute**, complete, total, wholehearted, utter, unqualified, unconditional, unreserved, unquestioning, firm, steadfast.
Opposites: explicit.

implore VERB = **beg**, appeal to, entreat, plead with, ask, pray, request, solicit, supplicate, importune, press, crave, plead for, appeal for; [poetic/literary] beseech.

imply VERB = **insinuate**, hint, suggest, intimate, give to understand, signal, indicate.

impolite ADJ = *see* **rude** (**1**).

important ADJ
1 = **significant**, crucial, of great consequence/ import, far-reaching, critical, pivotal, momentous, substantial, weighty, valuable, serious, grave, urgent, of great moment, consequential, salient, chief, main, principal, major, of concern, of interest, relevant, of value, necessary, essential. **2** = **eminent**, prominent, pre-eminent, leading, foremost, outstanding, distinguished, esteemed, notable, noteworthy, of note, influential, of influence, powerful, high-ranking, high-level, top-level, prestigious.
Opposites: unimportant.

importunate ADJ
= **persistent**, insistent, dogged, unremitting, relentless, pertinacious, pressing, urgent, demanding, exacting, clamorous, entreating, solicitous, imprecatory.

importune VERB = **beg**, implore, plead with, appeal to, call upon, supplicate, petition, press; [poetic/literary] beseech.

impose VERB 1 = **enforce**, apply, exact, levy, charge, lay on, set, establish, fix, ordain, introduce, promulgate, decree. 2 = **force**, inflict, foist, thrust, obtrude.

imposing ADJ = **impressive**, striking, grand, splendid, majestic, august, lofty, stately.

impossible ADJ 1 = **not possible**, out of the question, inconceivable, unthinkable, unimaginable, impracticable, unattainable, unachievable, unobtainable, beyond one, hopeless. 2 = **unbelievable**, incredible, absurd, ludicrous, ridiculous, preposterous, outlandish. 3 = **unmanageable**, intractable, recalcitrant, wayward, intolerable, unbearable.

Opposites: possible, plausible.

impostor NOUN = **deceiver**, pretender, fake, fraud, sham, charlatan, mountebank, hoodwinker, bluffer, trickster, cheat, cheater, swindler, confidence man/woman, rogue; [inf] con man/woman, con artist.

impracticable ADJ = **impossible**, out of the question, unfeasible, unworkable, unattainable, unrealizable, unsuitable. Opposites: feasible, possible.

impractical ADJ 1 = **useless**, ineffective, ineffectual, unrealistic, impossible, unviable. 2 = **unrealistic**, idealistic, romantic, quixotic, starry-eyed. Opposites: practical.

imprecise ADJ 1 = **inexact**, approximate, estimated, rough, inaccurate, incorrect. 2 = **vague**, loose, hazy, blurred, indefinite, woolly, confused, ambiguous,

equivocal.
Opposites: precise.

impregnate VERB
= **suffuse**, permeate,
imbue, penetrate, fill,
infuse, pervade, soak,
steep, saturate, drench,
inundate.

impress VERB 1 = **make an
impression/impact on**,
move, sway, influence,
affect, stir, rouse, excite,
inspire, galvanize.
2 = **stamp**, imprint, print,
mark, engrave, emboss.

impression NOUN
1 = **effect**, influence,
impact, sway, hold,
power, control. 2 = **mark**,
indentation, dent,
hollow, outline, stamp,
imprint. 3 = **feeling**,
sense, sensation,
awareness, perception,
notion, idea, thought,
belief, opinion,
conviction, suspicion,
inkling, intuition,
hunch, funny feeling.
4 = **impersonation**,
imitation, mimicry,
parody, caricature, take-
off, send-up, burlesque,
travesty.

impressionable ADJ
= **suggestible**,
susceptible, persuadable,
receptive, responsive,
sensitive, open, gullible,
ingenuous, pliable,
malleable, mouldable.

impressive ADJ
= **imposing**, striking,
magnificent, splendid,
moving, touching,
affecting, stirring,
rousing, exciting,
powerful, inspiring.
Opposites: ordinary,
unexciting.

imprison VERB = **put in
prison**, send to prison,
jail, lock up, take into
custody, put under lock
and key, put away,
incarcerate, confine, shut
in/up, intern, detain,
constrain, immure;
[inf] send down.

imprisonment NOUN
= **custody**, incarceration,
internment,
confinement, detention,
restraint; [Brit.
inf] porridge.

improbable ADJ
= **unlikely**, doubtful,
questionable, dubious,
implausible, far-fetched,

unconvincing, unbelievable, incredible, ridiculous, ludicrous, preposterous.
Opposites: probable.

impromptu ADJ
= **unrehearsed**, ad lib, unprepared, extempore, extemporized, extemporaneous, spontaneous, improvised, unscripted, unpremeditated, unstudied; [inf] off-the-cuff, off the top of one's head, on the spur of the moment.
Opposites: rehearsed.

improper ADJ
1 = **unseemly**, unbecoming, indecorous, unfitting, indiscreet, injudicious. 2 = **indecent**, off colour, indelicate, risqué, suggestive, smutty, obscene, lewd, pornographic; [inf] blue. 3 = **incorrect**, inaccurate, wrong, erroneous, false, fallacious.
Opposites: proper.

improve VERB 1 = **make better**, better, ameliorate, mend, amend, reform, rehabilitate, set/put right, correct, rectify, help, advance, upgrade, revamp, modernize; [inf] give something a facelift. 2 = **get/grow better**, advance, come along, make headway, develop, progress, make progress, pick up, perk up, take a turn for the better, take on a new lease of life, rally, look up. 3 = **get better**, recuperate, be on the mend, turn the corner, recover, gain strength, convalesce.
Opposites: worsen.

improvident ADJ
= **unthrifty**, thriftless, spendthrift, wasteful, prodigal, extravagant, uneconomical, shiftless.
Opposites: thrifty.

improvise VERB
1 = **extemporize**, ad lib; [inf] speak off the cuff, play it by ear, make it up as you go along.
2 = **throw/put together**, contrive, devise, concoct, rig, jury-rig.

impudent ADJ
= **impertinent**, insolent, cheeky, bold, audacious,

brazen, cocky, pert, presumptuous, forward, bumptious, impolite, rude, disrespectful, ill-mannered, unmannerly, ill-bred, shameless, immodest; [inf] saucy, brass-necked.

impulse NOUN **1** = **drive**, urge, instinct, appetite, proclivity. **2** = **stimulus**, inspiration, stimulation, incitement, incentive, inducement, motivation.

impulsive ADJ **1** = **hasty**, sudden, quick, precipitate, impetuous, impromptu, spontaneous, snap, ill-considered, unplanned, unpremeditated, thoughtless, rash, reckless. **2** = **impetuous**, rash, reckless, spontaneous, instinctive, passionate, intuitive, emotional, foolhardy, madcap, devil-may-care.
Opposites: deliberate, cautious.

impure ADJ **1** = **adulterated**, debased, contaminated, polluted, tainted, infected, dirty, foul, unclean, filthy, sullied, defiled, unwholesome, poisoned, feculent. **2** = **lewd**, lustful, obscene, indecent, lecherous, ribald, smutty, pornographic, improper, crude, vulgar, coarse, gross.
Opposites: pure.

inaccessible ADJ = **unreachable**, out of reach, cut off, beyond reach, unapproachable, impenetrable, unattainable, out of the way, isolated, lonely, remote, godforsaken, off the beaten track.
Opposites: accessible.

inaccurate ADJ **1** = **incorrect**, wrong, erroneous, faulty, inexact, imprecise, out. **2** = **wrong**, false, not true, erroneous, fallacious, not right, imperfect, flawed, defective, unsound, unreliable, wide of the mark; [inf] full of holes.
Opposites: accurate.

inactive ADJ **1** = **immobile**, motionless, inert, stationary, idle, sluggish, slow, indolent, lazy, lifeless, slothful, lethargic, stagnant, vegetating, dilatory, torpid. **2 = inoperative**, idle, out of service, unused, out of use, unoccupied, mothballed, unemployed. **3 = dormant**, quiescent, latent, passive.

inadequate ADJ
1 = insufficient, not enough, too little, too few, lacking, found wanting, deficient, short, in short supply, meagre, scanty, scant, niggardly, scarce, sparse, skimpy, sketchy, incomplete. **2 = incapable**, incompetent, unfit, ineffective, ineffectual, inefficient, unskilful, inexpert, inept; [inf] not up to scratch.
Opposites: adequate.

inadvertent ADJ
= accidental, unintentional, chance, unpremeditated, unplanned, unconscious, uncalculated, unwitting, involuntary.
Opposites: deliberate.

inadvisable ADJ
= unwise, ill-advised, ill-judged, misguided, injudicious, imprudent, foolish, impolitic, inexpedient.
Opposites: shrewd.

inanimate ADJ **1 = lifeless**, without life, dead, inert, insentient, insensate, extinct, defunct. **2 = apathetic**, spiritless, lazy, inactive, listless, lethargic, sluggish, torpid.
Opposites: living.

inappropriate ADJ
= unsuitable, unfitting, out of place, unseemly, unbecoming, improper, indecorous, inapposite, incongruous, out of keeping, inexpedient, inadvisable, injudicious, infelicitous, untimely.
Opposites: appropriate.

inarticulate ADJ
1 = unintelligible, incomprehensible, incoherent, unclear, indistinct, blurred, muffled, mumbled, muttered. **2 = poorly spoken**, faltering, hesitating, halting, stumbling, stuttering, stammering.

3 = **unspoken**, unuttered, unexpressed, unvoiced, wordless, silent, mute, dumb, speechless, voiceless, soundless, taciturn, tongue-tied.
Opposites: articulate.

inattentive ADJ
1 = **neglectful**, negligent, remiss, forgetful, careless, thoughtless, heedless, indifferent, unconcerned, inconsiderate.
2 = **distracted**, preoccupied, absent-minded, daydreaming, wool-gathering, lost in thought; [inf] in a world of one's own, miles away, with one's head in the clouds, in a brown study.
Opposites: attentive.

inauspicious ADJ
= **unpropitious**, unpromising, unlucky, unfortunate, unhappy, infelicitous, unfavourable, ill-omened, ominous, ill-fated, ill-starred, untoward, untimely.
Opposites: auspicious.

incapable ADJ
1 = **incompetent**, ineffective, ineffectual, inadequate, inefficacious, unfit, unfitted, unqualified, inept, inapt, useless, feeble; [inf] not up to scratch. **2** = **unable to**, not capable of, lacking the ability to.
Opposites: capable.

inception NOUN
= **beginning**, commencement, start, starting point, outset, opening, debut, inauguration, initiation, institution, birth, dawn, origin, rise; [inf] kick-off.
Opposites: end.

incessant ADJ
= **unceasing**, ceaseless, non-stop, endless, unending, never-ending, everlasting, eternal, constant, continual, perpetual, continuous, uninterrupted, unbroken, on-going, unremitting, persistent, recurrent.
Opposites: intermittent.

incident NOUN **1** = **event**, happening, occurrence, episode, experience, proceeding, adventure, occasion, circumstance, fact, matter.

2 = **disturbance**, commotion, scene, row, fracas, contretemps, skirmish, clash, conflict, confrontation, brush.

incidental ADJ
1 = **accidental**, by chance, chance, random, fortuitous. 2 = **related**, connected, associated, accompanying, attendant, concomitant, contingent.
3 = **secondary**, subsidiary, subordinate.

incise VERB = **cut**, cut into, make an incision in, slit, slit open, gash, slash, notch, nick, furrow.

incite VERB 1 = **instigate**, provoke, foment, whip up, stir up, prompt.
2 = **encourage**, urge, egg on, goad, spur on, prod, stimulate, drive on, excite, arouse, agitate, inflame, stir up, provoke.
Opposites: discourage.

inclination NOUN
1 = **tendency**, leaning, propensity, proclivity, predisposition, weakness, penchant, predilection, partiality, preference, affinity, attraction, fancy, liking, fondness, affection, love. 2 = **bend**, bow, nod, lowing, stooping.

incline VERB 1 = **tend**, lean, swing, veer, have a preference for, be attracted to, have an affinity for. 2 = **bend**, slope, slant, bank, cant, bevel, tilt, lean, tip, list, deviate.
▶ NOUN = **slope**, gradient, hill, drop, declivity, descent, ascent, ramp, rise.
▪ **be inclined to** = **have a tendency to**, be liable to, be likely to, be predisposed to.

include VERB 1 = **contain**, hold, take in, admit, incorporate, embrace, encompass, comprise, embody, comprehend, subsume. 2 = **add**, insert, allow for, put in, enter, introduce, count in, take account of, build in, number, incorporate.
Opposites: exclude.

incoherent ADJ
= **unconnected**, disconnected, disjointed, disordered, confused,

mixed up, muddled, jumbled, scrambled, rambling, wandering, discursive, illogical, unintelligible, inarticulate, mumbled, muttered, stuttered, stammered.
Opposites: coherent.

income NOUN = **salary**, pay, earnings, wages, remuneration, takings, profits, revenue, gains, proceeds, means.

incomparable ADJ = **beyond compare**, inimitable, unequalled, matchless, nonpareil, unrivalled, peerless, unparalleled, unsurpassed, superlative, supreme, transcendent.

incompatible ADJ
1 = **unsuited**, mismatched, ill-assorted, incongruous, antagonistic, conflicting, antipathetic, discordant; [Brit.] like chalk and cheese. 2 = **clashing**, discordant, jarring, inharmonious.
3 = **contrary to**, differing from, at odds with, inconsistent with, in opposition to, diametrically opposed to.
Opposites: compatible.

incompetent ADJ
1 = **incapable**, inept, inefficient, ineffectual, unqualified, unable, unfitted, unsuitable, useless, inadequate, deficient. 2 = **inexpert**, unskilful, inept, bungling, awkward, maladroit, clumsy, floundering, gauche; [inf] botched.
Opposites: competent.

incomplete ADJ
1 = **unfinished**, partial, unaccomplished, undone, undeveloped, unexecuted, unperformed.
2 = **imperfect**, broken, defective, lacking, wanting, deficient.
3 = **shortened**, deficient, curtailed, abridged, expurgated, bowdlerized.
Opposites: complete.

incomprehensible ADJ
1 = **unintelligible**, too difficult/hard, complicated, complex, involved, intricate; [inf] over one's head.

2 = illegible, indecipherable, unintelligible, unreadable.
Opposites: intelligible, clear.

inconceivable ADJ
= unimaginable, unthinkable, incomprehensible, incredible, unbelievable, implausible, impossible, out of the question, preposterous, ridiculous, ludicrous.
Opposites: plausible.

inconclusive ADJ
= indefinite, indeterminate, indecisive, undetermined, open to question, open to doubt, vague, unsettled, unresolved, questionable, ambiguous, equivocal, unestablished; [inf] up in the air.
Opposites: conclusive.

incongruous ADJ = **out of place**, inappropriate, incompatible, discordant, jarring, out of keeping, inconsistent, contrary, unsuited, at odds, in opposition, opposed, conflicting, irreconcilable, strange, odd, absurd, unsuitable.
Opposites: appropriate, suitable.

inconsequential ADJ
= insignificant, negligible, unimportant, trivial, trifling, petty; [inf] piddling.
Opposites: important.

inconsiderate ADJ
= thoughtless, unthinking, uncaring, heedless, unmindful, regardless, undiscerning, insensitive, tactless, uncharitable, unkind, ungracious, selfish, self-centred, egotistical.
Opposites: considerate.

inconsistent ADJ
1 = incompatible, out of keeping, out of place, contrary, at odds, at variance, in opposition, conflicting, in conflict, irreconcilable, discordant, discrepant.
2 = unstable, unsteady, changeable, erratic, irregular, unpredictable, capricious, fickle, whimsical, mercurial, volatile.

Opposites: consistent.

inconspicuous ADJ
= **unobtrusive**,
unnoticeable, indistinct,
ordinary, plain, run-of-
the-mill, unremarkable,
undistinguished,
unostentatious,
unimposing, hidden,
insignificant, quiet,
retiring, unassuming, in
the background;
[inf] low-key.
Opposites: conspicuous.

inconvenience NOUN
1 = **trouble**, bother,
disruption, disturbance,
vexation, worry,
annoyance, disadvantage,
difficulty,
embarrassment.
2 = **awkwardness**,
unwieldiness,
cumbersomeness,
unhandiness.
▸ VERB = **disturb**, bother,
trouble, worry, disrupt,
put out, impose upon,
burden, distract, annoy,
discommode.

inconvenient ADJ
1 = **awkward**, unsuitable,
inappropriate,
inopportune,
disadvantageous,

inexpedient, disturbing,
troublesome,
bothersome, tiresome,
vexatious, annoying,
embarrassing, ill-timed,
untimely, unseasonable.
2 = **unwieldy**,
cumbersome, awkward,
unmanageable, unhandy,
difficult.
Opposites: convenient.

incorporate VERB
1 = **include**, embrace,
absorb, embody,
assimilate, subsume.
2 = **merge**, coalesce, fuse,
blend, mix, amalgamate,
combine, unite,
integrate, unify,
compact.
Opposites: exclude.

incorrect ADJ 1 = **wrong**,
inaccurate, erroneous,
wide of the mark.
2 = **mistaken**, inaccurate,
faulty, inexact, untrue,
false, fallacious, non-
factual, flawed; [inf] full of
holes. 3 = **improper**,
unsuitable, indecorous,
inappropriate, lacking in
propriety, unseemly,
ungentlemanly,
unladylike.
Opposites: correct.

incorrigible ADJ
= **inveterate**,
irredeemable, hardened,
dyed-in-the-wool,
incurable, irreformable,
hopeless, beyond hope,
beyond redemption,
impenitent, uncontrite,
unrepentant, obdurate,
habitual, shameless.

incorruptible ADJ
1 = **virtuous**, honest,
upright, honourable,
moral, ethical,
trustworthy, straight,
unbribable, high-
principled.
2 = **imperishable**,
indestructible,
indissoluble, everlasting,
non-biodegradable.
Opposites: corrupt.

increase VERB 1 = **grow**,
become greater/larger/
bigger, expand, extend,
multiply, intensify,
heighten, mount,
escalate, mushroom,
snowball, swell, wax.
2 = **add to**, enhance, build
up, enlarge, augment,
expand, extend, spread,
heighten, raise, intensify,
strengthen, magnify,
proliferate, inflate, step

up.
Opposites: decrease.
▶ NOUN = **growth**, rise,
enlargement, expansion,
extension, increment,
addition, development,
intensification,
escalation, heightening,
boost, augmentation,
snowballing,
mushrooming,
strengthening,
magnification, inflation.
Opposites: decrease.

incredible ADJ
1 = **unbelievable**, hard to
believe, beyond belief,
far-fetched,
inconceivable,
unimaginable,
unthinkable, impossible,
implausible, highly
unlikely, improbable,
absurd, preposterous,
questionable, dubious,
doubtful, fictitious,
mythical.
2 = **extraordinary**,
wonderful, great,
supreme, tremendous,
marvellous, amazing,
astounding, prodigious,
awe-inspiring, awesome,
superhuman;
[inf] fantastic, fab, magic.

Opposites: credible.

incredulous ADJ
= **disbelieving**, unbelieving, sceptical, cynical, distrusting, distrustful, mistrusting, mistrustful, doubtful, doubting, dubious, unconvinced, suspicious, uncertain.
Opposites: credulous.

incriminate VERB
= **implicate**, involve, inculpate, inform against, charge, blame, pin the blame on, accuse, indict, impeach, arraign, stigmatize, blacken someone's name; [inf] point the finger at, finger, rat on; [Brit. inf] grass on.

incumbent ADJ
1 = **binding**, obligatory, mandatory, necessary, compulsory. 2 = **current**, existing, present, in office, in power.

incur VERB = **bring upon oneself**, expose oneself to, lay oneself open to, provoke, be liable to, contract, meet with, experience.

incurable ADJ
1 = **untreatable**, inoperable, beyond cure, fatal, terminal, irremediable. 2 = See **incorrigible**.

indecent ADJ
1 = **improper**, suggestive, indelicate, impure, risqué, off colour, ribald, bawdy, foul, vulgar, gross, crude, obscene, dirty, smutty, coarse, lewd, lascivious, salacious, licentious, pornographic, scatological; [inf] blue, raunchy. 2 = **unseemly**, improper, inappropriate, unsuitable, unfitting, unacceptable, offensive, outrageous.
Opposites: proper, seemly.

indecisive ADJ
= **irresolute**, hesitant, in two minds, wavering, vacillating, ambivalent, undecided, uncertain, unresolved, sitting on the fence, blowing hot and cold.

indefatigable ADJ
= **tireless**, untiring, unflagging, persistent, tenacious, dogged,

assiduous, industrious, indomitable, relentless, unremitting.

indefensible ADJ
1 = inexcusable, unjustifiable, unpardonable, unforgivable, inexpiable.
2 = untenable, insupportable, flawed, faulty, implausible, specious, unarguable.

indefinite ADJ **1 = vague**, unclear, imprecise, inexact, ambiguous, ambivalent, equivocal, confused, evasive.
2 = indeterminate, unspecified. **3 = blurred**, ill-defined, indistinct, fuzzy, hazy, dim, vague, obscure.
Opposites: definite.

indemnify VERB **= insure**, underwrite, guarantee, protect, secure, make secure, give security to, endorse.

independence NOUN
1 = self-government, autonomy, self-determination, sovereignty, freedom, home rule, autarchy.
2 = freedom, liberty, self-sufficiency, self-reliance.

independent ADJ **1 = self-governing**, autonomous, free, sovereign, self-determining, non-aligned, neutral, autarchic.
2 = freethinking, bold, liberated, individualistic, unconventional, unrestrained, untrammelled, unfettered, unconstrained.
3 = separate, unconnected, unrelated, unattached, distinct, individual.
Opposites: subservient, biased, related.

indescribable ADJ
= inexpressible, undefinable, beyond words/description, incommunicable, ineffable, unutterable, incredible, extraordinary, remarkable, prodigious.

indestructible ADJ
= unbreakable, imperishable, durable, enduring, infrangible, inextinguishable, perennial, deathless, undying, immortal,

endless, everlasting.
Opposites: fragile.

indeterminate ADJ
= **unfixed**, indefinite,
undetermined,
unspecified, unstipulated,
unknown, uncertain,
unpredictable,
uncounted, uncalculated.

index NOUN = **key**, guide,
directory, catalogue,
table of contents.

indicate VERB 1 = **show**,
demonstrate, exhibit,
display, manifest, evince,
express, make known,
tell, state, reveal,
disclose, register, record,
signal, denote, betoken,
suggest, imply. 2 = **point
to/at**, designate, specify.

indication NOUN 1 = **sign**,
symptom, mark,
manifestation, signal,
omen, augury, portent,
warning, hint. 2 = **show**,
demonstration,
exhibition, display,
manifestation, revelation,
disclosure.

indicator NOUN 1 = **pointer**,
needle, marker, meter,
display. 2 = **index**, guide,
mark, sign, signal,
symbol, signpost.

indifferent ADJ
1 = **unconcerned**,
apathetic, heedless,
uncaring, uninterested,
unimpressed, aloof,
detached, distant, cold,
cool, impassive,
dispassionate,
unresponsive,
unemotional,
emotionless, unmoved,
unexcited, unfeeling,
unsympathetic, callous.
2 = **mediocre**, middling,
moderate, fair, not bad,
passable, adequate,
barely adequate, average,
ordinary, commonplace,
undistinguished,
uninspired; [inf] so-so, OK.
Opposites: enthusiastic.

indigenous ADJ = **native**,
original, aboriginal,
autochthonous.

indignant ADJ = **angry**,
angered, irate, furious,
incensed, infuriated,
annoyed, irritated,
wrathful, enraged,
exasperated, heated,
riled, in a temper, in
high dudgeon, provoked,
piqued, disgruntled,
fuming, livid, mad,
seeing red; [inf] miffed, in

a huff, up in arms, huffy;
[Brit. inf] narked.

indirect ADJ **1 = circuitous**,
roundabout, wandering,
meandering, winding,
curving, tortuous, zigzag,
divergent, deviant.
2 = discursive, oblique,
digressive, long-drawn-
out, rambling,
circumlocutory,
periphrastic, allusive.
3 = backhanded, devious,
insidious, underhand,
sneaky, surreptitious.
Opposites: direct.

indiscreet ADJ
= imprudent, unwise,
incautious, injudicious,
ill-advised, ill-judged, ill-
thought-out, ill-
considered, foolish,
impolitic, careless,
unwary, hasty, rash,
reckless, impulsive,
precipitate, foolhardy,
tactless, insensitive,
undiplomatic.

indiscriminate ADJ
1 = unselective,
undiscriminating,
uncritical, careless,
aimless, hit-or-miss,
haphazard, random,
unsystematic,

unmethodical, sweeping,
general, broad-based,
wholesale. **2 = jumbled**,
mixed, haphazard,
motley, miscellaneous,
diverse, varied, confused,
mongrel, chaotic, thrown
together; [inf] higgledy-
piggledy.
Opposites: systematic.

indispensable ADJ
= essential, vital, crucial,
imperative, key,
necessary, requisite,
needed, important,
urgent, pressing, high-
priority, fundamental.
Opposites: superfluous.

indisputable ADJ
= incontestable,
incontrovertible,
undeniable, irrefutable,
unquestionable,
indubitable, beyond
dispute/question, beyond
the shadow of a doubt,
unassailable, certain,
sure, positive, definite,
absolute, final,
conclusive.
Opposites: debatable.

indistinct ADJ **1 = blurred**,
fuzzy, out of focus,
bleary, hazy, misty,
shadowy, dim, obscure,

indefinite, indistinguishable, barely perceptible. **2 = muffled**, muted, low, muttered, mumbled, slurred.
Opposites: distinct.

indistinguishable ADJ = **identical**, alike, very similar, interchangeable, the same; [inf] like two peas in a pod.
Opposites: different.

individual ADJ **1 = single**, separate, lone, sole, solitary, distinct, distinctive, particular, specific, peculiar, isolated.
2 = characteristic, distinctive, peculiar, personal, personalized, own, private, special, singular, original, unique, idiosyncratic.

indolent ADJ = **lazy**, idle, slothful, lethargic, slow-moving, slack, lackadaisical, apathetic, listless, inert, torpid.
Opposites: active.

induce VERB **1 = persuade**, talk into, get, prevail upon, move, prompt, inspire, instigate, influence, press, urge, incite, encourage, impel, motivate, inveigle, coax, wheedle. **2 = bring about**, bring on, cause, produce, effect, create, give rise to, generate, originate, engender, occasion, set in motion, develop, lead to.

inducement NOUN = **incentive**, encouragement, attraction, bait, carrot, lure, reward, incitement, stimulus, spur, goad, impetus, motive, provocation; [inf] come-on.

indulge VERB = **pamper**, spoil, coddle, mollycoddle, cosset, pander to, humour, go along with, baby, pet.

indulgent ADJ = **permissive**, easy-going, compliant, fond, doting, forbearing, compassionate, humane, kind, understanding, sympathetic, liberal, forgiving, lenient, merciful, clement.
Opposites: intolerant.

industrious ADJ = **hard-working**, diligent,

assiduous, conscientious, sedulous, laborious, steady, busy, active, bustling, energetic, on the go, vigorous, determined, dynamic, indefatigable, tireless, persistent, pertinacious, zealous, productive. **Opposites:** idle, lazy.

industry NOUN
1 = manufacturing, production, fabrication, construction, business, trade, field, line, craft.
2 = industriousness, diligence, assiduity, application, activity, energy, vigour, effort, determination, dynamism, tirelessness, persistence, zeal, pertinacity, productiveness, sedulousness, sedulity, conscientiousness.

ineffective ADJ
1 = unavailing, useless, to no avail, ineffectual, worthless, unsuccessful, futile, fruitless, unproductive, profitless, abortive, inadequate, inefficient, inefficacious, impotent, idle, feeble,

weak, incompetent, inept, lame, barren, sterile. **2 = incompetent**, inept, unproductive, inadequate, ineffectual, feeble, weak, impotent. **Opposites:** effective.

inelegant ADJ
1 = awkward, clumsy, ungainly, ungraceful, graceless. **2 = unrefined**, uncultured, uncultivated, unpolished, unsophisticated, unfinished, gauche, crude, uncouth, ill-bred, coarse, vulgar. **Opposites:** graceful, refined.

ineligible ADJ
= unsuitable, unqualified, unfit, unfitted, inappropriate, unequipped, unacceptable, undesirable, disqualified. **Opposites:** eligible.

inept ADJ **1 = incompetent**, incapable, unskilled, inexpert, clumsy, awkward, maladroit, heavy-handed; [inf] cack-handed.
2 = inappropriate, badly timed, inapt, unsuitable,

infelicitous.
Opposites: competent,
appropriate.

inequality NOUN
= **disparity**, imbalance,
lack of balance,
disproportion, variation,
variability, difference,
discrepancy, contrast,
dissimilarity, unevenness,
incongruity.
Opposites: equality.

inequitable ADJ = **unfair**,
unjust, prejudiced,
biased, discriminatory,
partisan, partial,
preferential, one-sided,
intolerant, bigoted.
Opposites: fair.

inert ADJ **1** = **unmoving**,
inactive, motionless,
immobile, still, stock-
still, stationary, static,
lifeless, inanimate,
unconscious, passive, out
cold, comatose, dormant,
dead. **2** = **idle**, inactive,
indolent, slack, lazy,
slothful, dull, sluggish,
lethargic, stagnant,
languid, lackadaisical,
listless, torpid.
Opposites: active.

inertia NOUN = **inertness**,
inactivity, inaction,
motionlessness,
immobility, stagnation,
passivity, stasis, idleness,
indolence, laziness, sloth,
slothfulness, dullness,
sluggishness, lethargy,
languor, listlessness,
torpor.
Opposites: activity.

inescapable ADJ
= **unavoidable**, inevitable,
unpreventable,
inexorable, assured,
certain, bound to
happen, ineludible,
ineluctable.
Opposites: avoidable.

inestimable ADJ
= **immeasurable**,
measureless, incalculable,
priceless, precious,
invaluable, unparalleled,
supreme, superlative.

inevitable ADJ
= **unavoidable**,
unpreventable,
inexorable, inescapable,
fixed, settled, irrevocable,
fated, destined,
predestined, ordained,
decreed, out of one's
hands, assured, certain,
bound/sure to happen,
for sure, necessary,
ineluctable.

Opposites: avoidable.

inexhaustible ADJ
= **unlimited**, limitless,
illimitable, infinite,
boundless, endless,
never-ending,
unrestricted, bottomless,
measureless, copious,
abundant.
Opposites: limited.

inexpensive ADJ = *see*
cheap (1).

inexperienced ADJ
= **untrained**, untutored,
unqualified, undrilled,
unpractised, amateur,
unskilled, uninitiated,
uninformed, ignorant,
unacquainted, unversed,
naive, unsophisticated,
unfledged, untried,
unseasoned, new, callow,
immature, fresh, green,
raw; [inf] wet behind the
ears.

inexplicable ADJ
= **unexplainable**,
unaccountable,
incomprehensible,
beyond comprehension,
unintelligible,
unfathomable, baffling,
puzzling, mysterious,
strange, weird, abstruse,
enigmatic, inscrutable.

Opposites:
understandable.

infallible ADJ 1 = **unfailing**,
foolproof, dependable,
trustworthy, reliable,
sure, certain; [inf] sure-fire.
2 = **unerring**, unfailing,
error-free, faultless,
flawless, impeccable,
unimpeachable, perfect.
Opposites: fallible.

infamous ADJ = **notorious**,
disreputable, ill-famed, of
ill-repute, iniquitous,
ignominious,
dishonourable,
discreditable, villainous,
wicked, evil, vile,
nefarious.

infant NOUN = **baby**, little
child, little one, tot,
toddler; [Scottish] bairn.

infantile ADJ = **childish**,
babyish, puerile,
immature, juvenile,
adolescent.
Opposites: mature.

infatuated ADJ
= **besotted**, enamoured,
captivated, bewitched,
beguiled, spellbound,
fascinated, enraptured,
carried away, obsessed,
swept off one's feet,
smitten.

infinite

infatuation NOUN
= **passing fancy**, crush, fancy, passion, obsession, fixation, craze, mania.

infect VERB
1 = **contaminate**, pollute, taint, blight, spoil, mar.
2 = **influence**, affect, imbue, infuse, stimulate, inspire, corrupt, pervert.

infectious ADJ
1 = **contagious**, infective, communicable, transmittable, transmissible, catching, spreading. **2** = **germ-laden**, pestilential, contaminating, toxic, noxious, virulent, poisonous. **3** = **catching**, spreading, contagious, communicable, irresistible, compelling.

infer VERB = **deduce**, conclude, work out, derive, reason, gather, understand, presume, conjecture, surmise, theorize, hypothesize; [inf] figure; [Brit. inf] suss.

inferior ADJ **1** = **lower**, lesser, subordinate, junior, secondary, subsidiary, ancillary, minor, subservient,
lowly, humble, servile, menial. **2** = **faulty**, imperfect, defective, substandard, low-quality, low-grade, shoddy, cheap, reject, gimcrack; [Brit. inf] grotty.
3 = **second-rate**, indifferent, mediocre, incompetent, poor, bad, awful.
Opposites: superior.

infernal ADJ = **hellish**, diabolical, devilish, demonic, demoniac, fiendish, satanic.

infest VERB = **spread through**, overrun, take over, pervade, permeate, penetrate, infiltrate, invade, swarm over, beset, plague.

infidelity NOUN
= **unfaithfulness**, adultery, cheating, cuckoldry, affair, liaison, intrigue, amour.

infinite ADJ **1** = **boundless**, unbounded, unlimited, limitless, without end, extensive, vast.
2 = **countless**, without number, numberless, innumerable, immeasurable,

incalculable, untold,
uncountable,
inestimable,
indeterminable, vast,
enormous, stupendous,
prodigious. **3 = unlimited**,
boundless, endless,
unending, never-ending,
inexhaustible,
interminable, absolute,
total.
Opposites: limited.

infinity NOUN
= limitlessness,
boundlessness,
unlimitedness,
endlessness, infinitude.

infirm ADJ **= feeble**,
enfeebled, weak, frail,
debilitated, decrepit,
disabled, in poor health,
failing, ailing, doddery,
lame, crippled.
Opposites: fit.

inflame VERB **= incite**,
excite, arouse, rouse, stir
up, work up, whip up,
agitate, fire, ignite,
kindle, foment,
impassion, provoke,
stimulate, actuate.
Opposites: cool.

inflammable ADJ
= flammable,
combustible, burnable,

ignitable, incendiary.
Opposites: incombustible.

inflate VERB **1 = blow up**,
pump up, puff up/out,
dilate, distend, swell,
aerate. **2 = exaggerate**,
increase, extend, amplify,
augment, expand,
intensify.
Opposites: deflate.

inflexible ADJ **1 = rigid**,
stiff, non-flexible,
unbendable, unyielding,
taut, hard, firm, inelastic,
unmalleable.
2 = unchangeable,
unalterable, immutable,
unvarying, firm, fixed,
hard and fast,
uncompromising,
stringent, rigorous,
inexorable. **3 = adamant**,
firm, immovable,
unaccommodating,
dyed-in-the-wool,
stubborn, obdurate,
obstinate, intractable,
unbending, intolerant,
relentless, merciless,
pitiless,
uncompromising,
inexorable, steely, iron-
willed.
Opposites: flexible.

inflict VERB = **administer**, deal out, mete out, serve out, deliver, apply, lay on, impose, levy, exact, wreak.

influence NOUN = **effect**, impact, control, sway, ascendancy, power, mastery, agency, guidance, domination, rule, supremacy, leadership, direction, pressure.
▶ VERB **1** = **affect**, have an effect on, impact on, sway, bias, incline, motivate, determine, guide, control, change, alter, transform. **2** = **persuade**, induce, impel, incite, manipulate, prompt.

influential ADJ **1** = **powerful**, important, leading, authoritative, controlling, dominant, predominant, prestigious. **2** = **instrumental**, guiding, significant, important, persuasive, telling, meaningful.
Opposites: unimportant.

influx NOUN = **rush**, inflow, inundation, flood, invasion, intrusion, incursion, ingress, convergence.

inform VERB **1** = **tell**, let know, advise, apprise, notify, announce to, impart to, relate to, communicate to, acquaint, brief, instruct, enlighten, make conversant, send word to; [inf] put in the picture, fill in, clue in, put wise, spill the beans to, tip off, tip the wink to, give the inside story to. **2** = **denounce**, betray, incriminate, inculpate; [inf] blab on, rat on, squeal on, tell on, blow the whistle on, put the finger on, finger, sell down the river, snitch on, peach on; [Brit. inf] grass on.

informal ADJ **1** = **casual**, non-formal, unceremonious, unofficial, simple, unpretentious, everyday, relaxed, easy. **2** = **colloquial**, vernacular, non-literary, simple, natural, unofficial, unpretentious; [inf] slangy.

Opposites: formal.

information NOUN 1 = **data**, facts. 2 = **knowledge**, intelligence, news, notice, word, advice, counsel, instruction, enlightenment, tidings, message, report, communiqué, communication; [inf] info, gen, low-down, dope, inside story, bumf, dirt.

informative ADJ = **instructive**, illuminating, enlightening, edifying, educational, revealing, telling, communicative, newsy, chatty, gossipy.
Opposites: uninformative.

informed ADJ = **knowledgeable**, well briefed, posted, abreast of the facts, well versed, primed, up to date, au fait, au courant.

informer NOUN = **informant**, betrayer, traitor, Judas, whistle-blower; [inf] rat, squealer, stool pigeon, canary, snitch, peacher; [Brit. inf] grass, nark, snout.

infrequent ADJ = **rare**, occasional, irregular, sporadic, uncommon, unusual, exceptional, few and far between, intermittent; [inf] once in a blue moon.
Opposites: frequent.

infringe VERB = **break**, disobey, violate, contravene, transgress, breach, disregard, take no notice of, defy, flout.

ingenious ADJ = **clever**, intelligent, shrewd, astute, sharp, bright, talented, brilliant, masterly, resourceful, inventive, creative, original, subtle, crafty, wily, cunning, skilful, adroit, deft, capable; [inf] smart.
Opposites: stupid, unimaginative.

ingenuous ADJ = **open**, sincere, honest, frank, candid, direct, forthcoming, artless, guileless, simple, naive, innocent, genuine, unaffected, trustful, trusting, truthful, unsuspicious.
Opposites: insincere, artful.

ingratiating ADJ
= **sycophantic**, toadying,
fawning, unctuous,
obsequious, servile,
crawling, flattering,
wheedling;
[inf] bootlicking.

inhabit VERB = **live in**,
dwell in, reside in,
occupy, lodge in, tenant,
make one's home in,
settle in, people,
populate.

inhabitant NOUN
= **resident**, dweller,
occupant, habitant,
settler, native, tenant;
[Brit.] occupier.

inherent ADJ **1** = **intrinsic**,
innate, built-in,
inseparable, essential,
basic, fundamental,
ingrained. **2** = **inborn**,
inbred, innate,
hereditary, inherited, in
the family, congenital,
familial.

inherit VERB = **be left**, be
willed, be bequeathed,
come into, fall heir to,
succeed to, accede to,
assume, take over.

inheritance NOUN
= **legacy**, bequest,
endowment, birthright,
heritage, patrimony.

inhibit VERB = **impede**,
hold back, prevent, stop,
hamper, hinder, obstruct,
interfere with, curb,
check, restrict, restrain,
constrain, bridle, rein in,
baulk, frustrate, arrest.
Opposites: assist,
encourage.

inhibited ADJ = **shy**,
reticent, self-conscious,
reserved, constrained,
repressed, embarrassed,
tongue-tied, subdued,
withdrawn; [inf] uptight.
Opposites: uninhibited.

inhibition NOUN
1 = **obstruction**,
prevention, stopping,
hindrance, hampering,
impediment, curb, check,
restriction, restraint,
frustration, arrest.
2 = **shyness**, reticence,
reserve, self-
consciousness,
repression, constraint,
embarrassment.

inhospitable ADJ
1 = **unwelcoming**,
unfriendly, unsociable,
unsocial, antisocial,
uncivil, discourteous,
ungracious, ungenerous,

cool, cold, chilly, aloof, unkind, unsympathetic, ill-disposed, hostile, inimical, xenophobic.
2 = bleak, bare, uninviting, barren, desolate, lonely, empty, forbidding, hostile.
Opposites: hospitable.

initial ADJ **= first**, beginning, starting, commencing, opening, early, prime, primary, elementary, introductory, inaugural, foundational, inceptive.
Opposites: final.

initiate VERB **1 = begin**, start, commence, open, institute, inaugurate, get under way, set in motion, lay the foundations of, launch, actuate, instigate, trigger off, originate, pioneer, sow the seeds of; [inf] start the ball rolling. **2 = teach**, instruct, coach, tutor, school, train, prime, familiarize, indoctrinate.
Opposites: finish.

initiative NOUN **= enterprise**, resourcefulness, inventiveness, resource, originality, creativity, drive, push, dynamism, ambition, ambitiousness, verve, dash, leadership; [inf] get-up-and-go, pep, zip.

injunction NOUN **= command**, instruction, order, ruling, direction, directive, dictate, dictum, mandate, enjoinment, admonition, precept, ultimatum.

injure VERB **= hurt**, harm, damage, wound, maim, cripple, lame, disable, mutilate, deform, mangle, impair, weaken, enfeeble, blight, blemish.

injurious ADJ **= harmful**, hurtful, damaging, deleterious, detrimental, disadvantageous, unfavourable, destructive, pernicious, ruinous, disastrous, calamitous, malignant.
Opposites: innocuous.

injury NOUN **1 = harm**, hurt, wounding, damage, impairment, affliction. **2 = wound**, sore, cut, bruise, gash, laceration, abrasion, lesion, contusion, trauma.

injustice NOUN
= **unfairness**, unjustness, inequity, bias, prejudice, favouritism, partiality, one-sidedness, discrimination, partisanship.
Opposites: justice.

inkling NOUN = **hint**, clue, intimation, suggestion, indication, whisper, suspicion, insinuation, notion, glimmering; [inf] the foggiest idea, the foggiest.

innate ADJ = **inborn**, inbred, congenital, hereditary, inherited, inherent, intrinsic, ingrained, natural, native, indigenous.

inner ADJ = **interior**, inside, central, middle, further in.
Opposites: outer.

innocence NOUN
1 = **guiltlessness**, blamelessness, irreproachability, clean hands. 2 = **simpleness**, ingenuousness, naivety, guilelessness, openness, credulity, inexperience, gullibility.
Opposites: guilt.

innocent ADJ 1 = **not guilty**, guiltless, blameless, clear, in the clear, above suspicion, above reproach, unimpeachable, irreproachable.
2 = **harmless**, innocuous, safe, unobjectionable, inoffensive, playful.
3 = **simple**, naive, ingenuous, unsophisticated, artless, guileless, childlike, frank, open, trustful, trusting, credulous, inexperienced, unworldly, green, gullible; [inf] wet behind the ears.
Opposites: guilty.

innocuous ADJ 1 = **safe**, harmless, non-poisonous.
2 = **inoffensive**, harmless, unobjectionable, unexceptionable, mild, peaceful, bland, commonplace, insipid.

innuendo NOUN
= **insinuation**, implication, suggestion, hint, overtone, allusion, inkling, imputation, aspersion.

innumerable ADJ = **very many**, numerous,

countless, untold,
incalculable, numberless,
unnumbered, infinite,
myriad; [inf] umpteen,
masses, oodles.
Opposites: few.

inquire VERB = **ask**, make
inquiries about,
investigate, question,
query, research, look
into, examine, explore,
probe, scan, scrutinize,
study.

inquiry NOUN
1 = **investigation**,
examination,
exploration, probe,
review, search, scrutiny,
scrutinization,
inspection, study,
interrogation.
2 = **question**, query.

inquisitive ADJ
= **inquiring**, questioning,
probing, scrutinizing,
curious, burning with
curiosity, interested,
intrusive, meddlesome,
prying; [inf] nosy, nosy-
parker, snooping.
Opposites: uninterested.

insane ADJ = **mad**, crazy,
deranged, demented,
unhinged, out of one's
mind, non compos

mentis; [inf] not all there,
bonkers, cracked, batty,
bats, cuckoo, loony,
loopy, nuts, nutty, screw,
bananas, off one's rocker,
round the bend; [Brit.
inf] barmy, crackers, off
one's trolley.
Opposites: sane.

inscrutable ADJ
= **enigmatic**,
impenetrable,
unreadable, cryptic,
deadpan, sphinx-like,
poker-faced.
Opposites: transparent.

insecure ADJ
1 = **vulnerable**, open to
attack, defenceless,
unprotected, unguarded,
exposed, in danger,
dangerous, perilous,
hazardous.
2 = **unconfident**, lacking
confidence, timid,
diffident, uncertain,
unsure, doubtful,
hesitant, anxious, fearful,
apprehensive, worried.
Opposites: secure.

insensitive ADJ
1 = **impervious to**,
immune to, oblivious to,
unmoved by, indifferent
to, proof against,

insusceptible to, unaffected by, unreactive to. **2** = **heartless**, uncaring, unfeeling, callous, tactless, thick-skinned, unconcerned, unsympathetic.
Opposites: sensitive.

insert VERB = **drive in**, push in, put in, press in, stick in, thrust in, work in, slide in, slip in, tuck in, pop in.
Opposites: extract.
▸ NOUN = **insertion**, inset, supplement, circular, advertisement, ad.

inside NOUN **1** = **interior**, inner part, contents.
2 = **stomach**, abdomen, gut, intestines, viscera, entrails, bowels, vital organs.
▸ ADJ = **interior**, inner, internal, innermost, inward, on the inside, intramural.

insidious ADJ
= **surreptitious**, sneaky, cunning, crafty, stealthy, subtle, artful, Machiavellian, sly, wily, slick, deceitful, deceptive, underhand, double-dealing, duplicitous,

dishonest, insincere, treacherous, perfidious; [inf] tricky.
Opposites: straightforward.

insignificant ADJ
= **unimportant**, trivial, trifling, negligible, inconsequential, of no consequence, not worth mentioning, nugatory, meagre, paltry, scanty, petty, insubstantial, flimsy, irrelevant, immaterial.
Opposites: significant, important.

insincere ADJ
= **untruthful**, dishonest, deceptive, not candid, not frank, disingenuous, dissembling, dissimulating, pretended, devious, hypocritical, deceitful, duplicitous, underhand, double-dealing, false, faithless, disloyal, treacherous, two-faced, lying, mendacious, evasive, shifty, slippery.
Opposites: sincere.

insinuate VERB = **imply**, hint, whisper, suggest, indicate, give the impression, intimate, mention.

insist VERB **1 = be firm**, stand one's ground, stand firm, make a stand, be resolute, be determined, be emphatic, not take no for an answer; [formal] brook no refusal. **2 = maintain**, assert, state, declare, contend, pronounce, proclaim, avow, vow, swear, stress, reiterate; [formal] aver.

insistent ADJ **= firm**, emphatic, determined, resolute, tenacious, persistent, unyielding, obstinate, dogged, unrelenting, unremitting, relentless, inexorable, importunate.

insolence NOUN **= impertinence**, impudence, cheek, cheekiness, rudeness, disrespect, incivility, insubordination, contempt, abuse, offensiveness, audacity, boldness, brazenness, brashness, pertness, forwardness, effrontery, insults; [inf] gall, chutzpah; [Brit. inf] sauce, backchat.

insolent ADJ **= impertinent**, impudent, cheeky, rude, ill-mannered, disrespectful, insubordinate, contemptuous, insulting, abusive, offensive, audacious, bold, brash, brazen, pert, forward; [inf] saucy, fresh. **Opposites:** respectful.

insoluble ADJ **1 = unsolvable**, baffling, unfathomable, indecipherable, perplexing, complicated, intricate, involved, impenetrable, inscrutable, enigmatic, obscure, mystifying, inexplicable, incomprehensible, mysterious. **2 = indissoluble**.

insolvent ADJ **= bankrupt**, ruined, penniless, impoverished, penurious, impecunious; [inf] gone bust, in the red, broke, strapped for cash.

inspect VERB **= examine**, check, go over, look over, survey, scrutinize, vet, audit, study, pore over, view, scan, observe, investigate, assess, appraise; [inf] give the once-over to.

inspection NOUN
= **examination**, check, check-up, survey, scrutiny, view, scan, observation, investigation, probe, assessment, appraisal; [inf] once-over, look-see.

inspector NOUN
= **examiner**, checker, scrutinizer, scrutineer, auditor, surveyor, observer, investigator, overseer, supervisor, assessor, appraiser, critic.

inspiration NOUN
1 = **stimulus**, stimulation, motivation, fillip, encouragement, influence, muse, goad, spur, incitement, arousal.
2 = **creativity**, originality, inventiveness, genius, insight, vision, afflatus.
3 = **bright idea**, revelation, illumination, enlightenment.

inspire VERB 1 = **stimulate**, motivate, encourage, influence, rouse, stir,

goad, energize, galvanize, animate. 2 = **arouse**, excite, touch off, spark off, ignite, kindle, give rise to, produce, bring about, prompt, instigate.

instability NOUN
1 = **unsteadiness**, unsoundness, shakiness, frailty, flimsiness, insubstantiality.
2 = **impermanence**, temporariness, transience, inconstancy.
3 = **capriciousness**, volatility, changeableness, flightiness, vacillation, wavering, fitfulness, oscillation.
Opposites: stability.

install VERB 1 = **put in**, insert, put in place, position, place, fix, locate, situate, station, lodge. 2 = **invest**, ordain, establish, initiate, ensconce, induct, institute.
Opposites: remove.

instalment NOUN = **part**, portion, section, segment, chapter, episode, division.

instance NOUN = **case**, case in point, example, illustration, occasion, occurrence.
▸ VERB = **cite**, mention, name, specify, quote, adduce.

instant ADJ
1 = **instantaneous**, immediate, prompt, rapid, sudden, abrupt.
2 = **pre-prepared**, ready-prepared, ready-mixed, pre-cooked.
▸ NOUN = **moment**, minute, second, split second, trice, twinkling, twinkling of an eye, flash; [inf] jiffy, tick, shake.

instigate VERB **1** = **bring about**, start, initiate, generate, actuate, incite, provoke, inspire, foment, kindle, stir up, whip up.
2 = **incite**, encourage, egg on, urge, prompt, goad, prod, induce, impel, constrain, press, persuade, prevail upon, sway, entice.
Opposites: discourage.

instigator NOUN = **inciter**, prime mover, motivator, agitator, fomenter, troublemaker, mischief-maker, ringleader, leader.

instil VERB = **imbue**, infuse, inculcate, introduce, inject, implant, insinuate, ingrain, indoctrinate, teach, drill, arouse.

instinct NOUN **1** = **natural feeling**, tendency, inclination, intuition, sixth sense, inner prompting. **2** = **talent**, gift, ability, capacity, faculty, aptitude, knack, bent, trait, characteristic.

instinctive ADJ
1 = **automatic**, reflex, mechanical, spontaneous, involuntary, impulsive, intuitive, unthinking, unpremeditated.
2 = **inborn**, inbred, innate, inherent, natural, intuitive, untaught, unlearned.
Opposites: learned.

institute VERB **1** = **begin**, start, commence, set in motion, put into operation, initiate.
2 = **found**, establish, launch, bring into being, set up, constitute,

organize, develop, create, originate, pioneer.
▶ NOUN = **institution**, establishment, organization, foundation, society, association, league, guild, consortium.

institutional ADJ
1 = **organized**, established, bureaucratic, accepted, orthodox, conventional, customary, formal, systematic, methodical, orderly.
2 = **uniform**, same, unvarying, unvaried, unchanging, monotonous, bland, dull, insipid. 3 = **cold**, cheerless, clinical, dreary, drab, unwelcoming, uninviting, impersonal, formal, forbidding.

instruct VERB 1 = **tell**, order, direct, command, bid, charge, enjoin, demand, require.
2 = **teach**, educate, tutor, coach, train, school, drill, ground, prepare, prime, guide, inform, enlighten, discipline, edify.

instruction NOUN
1 = **teaching**, education, tutoring, tutelage, coaching, training, schooling, drilling, grounding, preparation, priming, guidance, information, enlightenment, edification, lessons, classes, lectures.
2 = **directive**, direction, briefing, order, command, charge, injunction, requirement, ruling, mandate.

instructive ADJ
= **informative**, educational, educative, enlightening, illuminating, revealing, useful, helpful, edifying, uplifting, informational, cultural, academic, didactic, doctrinal.

instructor NOUN = **teacher**, schoolmaster, schoolmistress, educator, lecturer, professor, tutor, coach, trainer, adviser, counsellor, guide, mentor, demonstrator.

instrument NOUN
= **implement**, tool, appliance, apparatus, mechanism, utensil, gadget, contrivance,

device, aid.

instrumental ADJ
= **helpful**, of use, of help, of assistance, useful, of service, contributory, active, involved, influential, significant, important, valuable, beneficial.

insubordinate ADJ
= **defiant**, rebellious, mutinous, disobedient, refractory, recalcitrant, undisciplined, ungovernable, uncontrollable, unmanageable, unruly, disorderly, seditious, riotous, insurgent, contumacious.
Opposites: obedient.

insufferable ADJ
= **intolerable**, unbearable, unendurable, insupportable, impossible, dreadful, excruciating, grim, outrageous.
Opposites: bearable.

insufficient ADJ
= **inadequate**, deficient, in short supply, scarce, meagre, scant, scanty, too small/few/little, not enough, lacking,

wanting, at a premium.
Opposites: sufficient.

insular ADJ 1 = **isolated**, detached, separate, solitary, insulated, self-sufficient. 2 = **narrow**, narrow-minded, illiberal, prejudiced, biased, bigoted, provincial, blinkered, parochial, limited, restricted.
Opposites: broad-minded.

insulate VERB 1 = **cover**, wrap, encase, enwrap, envelop, pad, cushion, seal, heatproof, soundproof. 2 = **separate**, segregate, isolate, detach, cut off, keep apart, exclude, sequester, protect, shield.

insult NOUN = **slight**, affront, gibe, snub, barb, slur, dig, abuse, disparagement, depreciation, impugnment, revilement, insolence, rudeness, aspersions.
▶ VERB = **offend**, affront, slight, hurt someone's feelings, hurt, abuse, injure, wound, mortify, humiliate, disparage, discredit, depreciate,

impugn, slur, revile.
Opposites: compliment.

insuperable ADJ
= **insurmountable**,
impassable,
overwhelming,
invincible,
unconquerable,
unassailable.

insure VERB = **assure**,
indemnify, cover,
underwrite, guarantee,
warrant.

intact ADJ = **whole**,
complete, entire, perfect,
in one piece, sound,
unbroken, undamaged,
unblemished, faultless,
flawless.
Opposites: damaged.

intangible ADJ
1 = **impalpable**,
untouchable,
incorporeal, phantom,
spectral, ghostly.
2 = **indefinable**,
indescribable, vague,
subtle, unclear, obscure,
mysterious.
Opposites: tangible.

integral ADJ 1 = **essential**,
necessary, indispensable,
requisite, basic,
fundamental, inherent,
intrinsic, innate.

2 = **entire**, complete,
whole, total, full, intact,
unified, integrated,
undivided.
Opposites: peripheral,
fragmented.

integrate VERB = **join**,
unite, combine,
amalgamate, consolidate,
blend, incorporate,
coalesce, fuse, merge,
intermix, mingle,
commingle, assimilate,
homogenize, mesh,
harmonize, concatenate.
Opposites: separate.

integrity NOUN
1 = **honesty**, uprightness,
rectitude, righteousness,
virtue, probity, morality,
honour, goodness,
decency, truthfulness,
fairness, sincerity,
candour. 2 = **unity**,
wholeness, entirety,
completeness, totality,
cohesion.
Opposites: dishonesty.

intellect NOUN
= **intelligence**,
understanding, reason,
comprehension, mind,
brain, thought, sense,
judgement.

intellectual ADJ
1 = **mental**, cerebral, academic, rational, logical. **2** = **intelligent**, academic, well educated, well read, erudite, learned, bookish, donnish, highbrow, scholarly, studious.
▶ NOUN = **intellect**, genius, thinker, mastermind, academic, don, man/woman of letters, bluestocking, highbrow, pedant; [inf] egghead, bookworm.

intelligence NOUN
1 = **intellect**, mind, brain, brainpower, mental capacity, aptitude, reason, understanding, comprehension, acumen, wit, cleverness, brightness, sharpness, brilliance, quickness of mind, discernment, alertness, perception, perspicacity, penetration, sense, brains, sagacity; [inf] grey matter, nous.
2 = **information**, news, notice, notification, knowledge, account, advice, rumour, facts, data, reports, tidings;
[inf] gen, low-down, dope.
3 = **spying**, observation, information collection, investigation, surveillance.

intelligent ADJ = **clever**, bright, sharp, brilliant, quick, quick-witted, perceptive, penetrating, discerning, sagacious, thinking, well informed, educated, knowledgeable, enlightened; [inf] brainy, smart.

intelligentsia PL NOUN
= **intellectuals**, academics, literati, cognoscenti, illuminati, highbrows, pedants, the enlightened.

intelligible ADJ
= **understandable**, comprehensible, clear, lucid, plain, explicit, unambiguous, legible, decipherable, straightforward, meaningful.
Opposites: unintelligible, incomprehensible.

intemperate ADJ
= **immoderate**, self-indulgent, excessive, inordinate, extreme, extravagant,

unreasonable, outrageous.
Opposites: moderate.

intend VERB = **mean**, plan, have in mind/view, propose, aim, resolve, be resolved, be determined, expect, purpose, contemplate, think of.

intense ADJ **1** = **acute**, fierce, severe, extreme, harsh, strong, powerful, potent, vigorous, great, profound, deep, concentrated, consuming. **2** = **earnest**, ardent, eager, keen, enthusiastic, zealous, excited, impassioned, passionate, fervent, burning, fervid, consuming, vehement, fanatical. **3** = **nervous**, nervy, tense, overwrought, fraught, highly strung, emotional.
Opposites: mild.

intensify VERB = **strengthen**, increase, deepen, heighten, enhance, add to, fuel, build up, reinforce, magnify, fan, extend, boost, augment, escalate, step up, aggravate,

exacerbate, worsen, inflame, raise.
Opposites: reduce, decrease.

intensive ADJ = **concentrated**, in-depth, thorough, exhaustive, all-out, thoroughgoing, total, all-absorbing, high-powered, unremitting, comprehensive.
Opposites: cursory.

intent ADJ **1** = **concentrated**, concentrating, fixed, steady, steadfast, absorbed, attentive, engrossed, focused, occupied, preoccupied, rapt, enrapt, wrapped up, observant, watchful, alert, earnest, committed, intense. **2** = **set on**, bent on, committed to, firm about, determined to, resolved to; [inf] hell-bent on.

intention NOUN **1** = **aim**, purpose, objective, goal, intent, end, end in view, target, aspiration, wish, ambition, plan, design, resolve, resolution, determination.

2 = **premeditation**, design, plan, calculation, preconception.

intentional ADJ
= **intended**, deliberate, meant, done on purpose, wilful, purposeful, planned, calculated, designed, premeditated, preconceived, predetermined, pre-arranged, considered, weighed up, studied.
Opposites: accidental, inadvertent.

inter VERB = **bury**, entomb, consign to the grave, lay to rest; [inf] put six feet under.

intercept VERB = **cut off**, stop, deflect, head off, catch, check, arrest, block, obstruct, impede, interrupt, thwart.

intercourse NOUN
1 = **dealings**, trade, traffic, commerce, association, communication, connection, contact, correspondence, congress, communion.
2 = **sex**, sexual intercourse, sexual relations, copulation, coitus, coition, carnal knowledge, lovemaking, sexual congress, congress, intimacy.

interest NOUN
1 = **attentiveness**, attention, absorption, engrossment, heed, regard, notice, scrutiny, curiosity, inquisitiveness.
2 = **curiosity**, attraction, appeal, fascination, charm, allure.
3 = **concern**, importance, consequence, import, moment, significance, note, relevance, seriousness, weight, gravity, priority, urgency.
4 = **pastime**, hobby, activity, diversion, amusement, pursuit, relaxation; [inf] thing, scene. 5 = **share**, stake, portion, claim, investment, involvement, participation, stock, equity.
Opposites: boredom.
▶ VERB = **attract**, absorb, hold/engage someone's interest, engross, fascinate, rivet, grip, captivate, amuse, intrigue, arouse curiosity

in, concern.
Opposites: bore.

interested ADJ
1 = **attentive**, intent, absorbed, engrossed, curious, fascinated, riveted, gripped, captivated, intrigued. **2** = **concerned**, involved, implicated. **3** = **partial**, involved, partisan, biased, prejudiced.
Opposites: uninterested, disinterested.

interesting ADJ
= **absorbing**, engrossing, fascinating, riveting, gripping, compelling, compulsive, spellbinding, captivating, appealing, engaging, amusing, entertaining, stimulating, thought-provoking, diverting, exciting, intriguing.
Opposites: boring, uninteresting.

interfere VERB **1** = **hinder**, inhibit, impede, obstruct, get in the way of, check, block, hamper, handicap, cramp, frustrate, trammel, thwart, baulk.
2 = **meddle with**, butt into, pry into, intrude

into, intervene in, get involved in, tamper with, intercede in; [inf] poke one's nose into, horn in, stick one's oar in.

interim ADJ = **temporary**, provisional, pro tem, stopgap, caretaker, acting, makeshift, improvised.

interior ADJ = **inner**, internal, inside, inward.
Opposites: exterior, outer.
▶ NOUN **1** = **inside**, inner part, centre, middle, nucleus, core, heart.
2 = **hinterland**, centre, heartland.
Opposites: exterior.

interject VERB
= **introduce**, interpose, interpolate, add, insinuate, intersperse.

interlude NOUN = **interval**, intermission, break, pause, recess, rest, respite, halt, stop, stoppage, breathing space, delay, wait, hiatus.

intermediary NOUN
= **mediator**, go-between, broker, agent, middleman, arbitrator, negotiator.

intermediate ADJ
= **halfway**, in-between, middle, in the middle, mid, midway, intervening, interposed, transitional, medial, median, intermediary.

interminable ADJ
= **endless**, never-ending, everlasting, incessant, ceaseless, unlimited, infinite, boundless, countless, untold, innumerable, incalculable, immeasurable, indeterminable.

intermittent ADJ = **fitful**, spasmodic, irregular, sporadic, occasional, periodic, cyclic, recurrent, recurring, broken, discontinuous, on and off, erratic.
Opposites: continuous.

internal ADJ **1** = **inner**, inside, inward, interior. **2** = **domestic**, home, civil, interior, in-house.
Opposites: external, foreign.

international ADJ
= **worldwide**, cosmopolitan, global, universal,

intercontinental.

interpolate VERB = **insert**, interject, interpose, introduce, add, inject, insinuate, put in, work in, intercalate.

interpret VERB
1 = **translate**, transliterate, transcribe, paraphrase.
2 = **explain**, elucidate, expound, explicate, clarify, make clear, illuminate, shed light on, gloss, simplify, spell out.
3 = **decode**, decipher, solve, crack, unravel, untangle. **4** = **understand**, take, take to mean, read.

interrogate VERB
= **question**, put/pose questions to, examine, cross-examine, give the third degree to, inquire of, quiz, probe; [inf] put the screws on, pump, grill.

interrogation NOUN
= **questioning**, cross-examination, inquisition, investigation, grilling, probing, inquiry; [inf] the third degree.

interrogative ADJ
= **inquisitive**, questioning, quizzical,

inquiring, curious, investigative, inquisitorial, probing.

interrupt VERB 1 = **cut in on**, break in on, barge in on, intrude on, butt in on, disturb, heckle, interfere with; [inf] chime in on, horn in on, muscle in on; [Brit. inf] chip in on.
2 = **suspend**, discontinue, break, break off, hold up, delay, lay aside, leave off, postpone, stop, put a stop to, halt, bring to a halt/standstill, cease, end, cancel, sever.

interruption NOUN
1 = **interference**, disturbance, intrusion, butting in, obtrusion; [inf] horning in.
2 = **suspension**, discontinuance, breaking off, delay, postponement, stopping, halt, cessation.
3 = **intermission**, interval, interlude, break, pause, recess, gap, hiatus.

intersect VERB 1 = **cut across/through**, cut in two, divide, bisect.
2 = **cross**, criss-cross, meet, connect.

intersection NOUN
= **junction**, interchange, crossroads, roundabout, spaghetti junction.

interval NOUN 1 = **interlude**, interim, intervening time, time, period, meantime, meanwhile, wait, space.
2 = **intermission**, break, half-time, pause, lull, respite, breather, breathing space, gap, hiatus, delay.

intervene VERB 1 = **come/ occur between**, occur, happen, arise, take place, ensue, supervene, succeed; [poetic/ literary] come to pass.
2 = **intercede**, mediate, arbitrate, negotiate, step in, involve oneself, come into, interpose, interfere, intrude.

interview NOUN
1 = **appraisal**, evaluation, discussion, meeting, talk, dialogue. 2 = **audience**, question and answer session, exchange, dialogue, colloquy, interlocution.
▸VERB = **talk to**, have a discussion/dialogue with,

hold a meeting with, confer with, question, put questions to, sound out, examine, interrogate, cross-examine, evaluate.

interweave VERB
1 = **weave**, intertwine, twine, twist, interlace, braid, plait.
2 = **intermingle**, mingle, interlink, intermix, mix, blend, interlock, knit, connect, associate.

intimate¹ ADJ **1** = **close**, near, dear, nearest and dearest, cherished, bosom, familiar, confidential, warm, friendly, comradely, amicable. **2** = **informal**, warm, cosy, friendly, comfortable, snug.
3 = **personal**, private, confidential, secret, privy.
Opposites: distant.

intimate² VERB
1 = **announce**, make known, state, tell, inform, communicate, impart. **2** = **imply**, suggest, let it be known, hint, insinuate, give an inkling that, indicate, signal;

[inf] tip someone the wink.

intimidate VERB
= **frighten**, terrify, scare, alarm, terrorize, overawe, awe, cow, subdue, daunt, domineer, browbeat, bully, tyrannize, coerce, compel, bulldoze, pressure, pressurize, threaten; [inf] push around, lean on, twist someone's arm.

intolerable ADJ
= **unbearable**, unendurable, beyond endurance, insufferable, insupportable, not to be borne, more than one can stand, impossible, painful, excruciating, agonizing.

intolerant ADJ = **bigoted**, illiberal, narrow-minded, narrow, parochial, provincial, insular, small-minded, prejudiced, biased, partisan, one-sided, warped, twisted, fanatical, chauvinistic, jingoistic, racist, xenophobic, sexist, ageist, homophobic.
Opposites: tolerant.

intonation NOUN = **pitch**, tone, timbre, cadence, lilt, inflection, accentuation, emphasis, stress.

intoxicate VERB
1 = **inebriate**, make drunk, befuddle, fuddle, stupefy.
2 = **exhilarate**, elate, thrill, invigorate, animate, enliven, excite, arouse, inflame, enrapture.

intoxicated ADJ = *see* **drunk**.

intractable ADJ
= **unmanageable**, ungovernable, uncontrollable, stubborn, obstinate, obdurate, perverse, disobedient, indomitable, refractory, recalcitrant, insubordinate, rebellious, wild, unruly, rowdy.
Opposites: manageable.

intricate ADJ **1** = **tangled**, entangled, ravelled, twisted, knotty, convoluted, involute, maze-like, labyrinthine, winding, serpentine, circuitous, sinuous, fancy, elaborate, ornate, Byzantine, rococo.
2 = **complex**, complicated, difficult, involved, perplexing, puzzling, thorny, mystifying, enigmatic, obscure.
Opposites: simple.

intrigue VERB **1** = **interest**, absorb, arouse someone's curiosity, attract, draw, pull, rivet someone's attention, rivet, fascinate, charm, captivate, divert, pique, titillate. **2** = **plot**, conspire, scheme, connive, manoeuvre, machinate, devise.
Opposites: bore.
▶ NOUN = **plot**, conspiracy, collusion, cabal, scheme, ruse, stratagem, wile, dodge, artifice, manoeuvre, machination, trickery, sharp practice, double-dealing.

intrinsic ADJ = **inherent**, inborn, inbred, congenital, natural, native, indigenous, constitutional, built-in, ingrained, implanted, basic, fundamental, elemental, essential, true, genuine, real, authentic.

introduce VERB
1 = **present**, make known,

acquaint, make acquainted, announce, give an introduction to. **2** = **preface**, precede, lead into, commence, start off, begin. **3** = **bring in**, bring into being, originate, launch, inaugurate, institute, initiate, establish, found, set in motion, organize, develop, start, begin, commence, usher in, pioneer. **4** = **insert**, inject, interject, interpose, interpolate, intercalate, add, bring, infuse, instil.

introduction NOUN
= **foreword**, preface, front matter, preamble, prologue, prelude, exordium, lead-in; [inf] intro, prelims.
Opposites: afterword.

introductory ADJ
1 = **prefatory**, preliminary, precursory, lead-in, initiatory, opening, initial, starting.
2 = **preparatory**, elementary, basic, basal, rudimentary, fundamental, initiatory.
Opposites: closing.

introspective ADJ
= **inward-looking**, inner-directed, introverted, self-analysing, self-examining, subjective, contemplative, reflective, meditative, musing, pensive, brooding, preoccupied.

intrude VERB **1** = **interrupt**, push/thrust oneself in, gatecrash, barge in, encroach, butt in, interfere, obtrude.
2 = **encroach on**, invade, impinge on, infringe on, trespass on, obtrude on, violate.

intruder NOUN **1** = **burglar**, housebreaker, thief, raider, invader, prowler, trespasser. **2** = **unwelcome guest/visitor**, gatecrasher, interloper, infiltrator.

intuition NOUN **1** = **instinct**, sixth sense, divination, presentiment, clairvoyance, second sight, extrasensory perception, ESP.
2 = **feeling**, feeling in one's bones, hunch, inkling, presentiment, foreboding.

inundate VERB 1 = **flood**, deluge, overrun, swamp, submerge, engulf, drown, cover, saturate, soak. 2 = **overwhelm**, overpower, overburden, swamp, bog down, glut.

inure VERB = **harden**, toughen, season, temper, habituate, familiarize, accustom, naturalize, acclimatize.

invade VERB 1 = **attack**, assail, assault, overrun, occupy, storm, take over, descend upon, make inroads on, raid, plunder. 2 = **intrude on**, obtrude on, encroach on, infringe on, trespass on, burst in on, violate.
Opposites: withdraw.

invalid ADJ 1 = **inoperative**, legally void, null, null and void, void, not binding, nullified, revoked, rescinded, abolished. 2 = **unjustified**, unsubstantiated, unwarranted, untenable, illogical, irrational, unscientific, false, faulty, fallacious, spurious, unacceptable, inadequate, unconvincing, ineffectual, unsound, weak, useless, worthless.

invaluable ADJ = **priceless**, beyond price, inestimable, precious, costly, worth its weight in gold, worth a king's ransom.
Opposites: worthless.

invariable ADJ = **unchanging**, changeless, unchangeable, constant, unvarying, unvaried, invariant, unalterable, immutable, fixed, stable, set, steady, unwavering, static, uniform, regular, consistent.
Opposites: varied.

invariably ADV = **always**, every/each time, on every occasion, at all times, without fail/ exception, regularly, consistently, repeatedly, habitually, unfailingly, infallibly, inevitably.

invasion NOUN 1 = **overrunning**, occupation, incursion, offensive, attack, assailing, assault, raid, foray, onslaught, plundering. **2 = intrusion**, obtrusion, encroachment, infringement, breach, infraction, trespass, violation.

inveigle VERB **= persuade**, talk into, cajole, wheedle, coax, beguile, tempt, decoy, lure, entice, seduce, deceive; [inf] sweet-talk.

invent VERB **1 = originate**, create, innovate, discover, design, devise, contrive, formulate, think up, conceive, come up with, hit upon, compose, frame, coin. **2 = make up**, fabricate, concoct, hatch, trump up, forge; [inf] cook up.

invention NOUN **1 = origination**, creation, innovation, discovery, design, contrivance, construction, coinage; [inf] brainchild. **2 = inventiveness**, originality, creativity, creativeness, imagination, artistry, inspiration, ingenuity, resourcefulness, genius.

inventive ADJ **= original**, creative, innovational, imaginative, artistic, inspired, ingenious, resourceful, innovative, gifted, talented, skilful, clever. **Opposites:** unimaginative.

inventor NOUN **= originator**, creator, innovator, discoverer, author, architect, designer, deviser, developer, initiator, coiner, father, prime mover, maker, framer, producer.

inventory NOUN **= list**, listing, checklist, catalogue, record, register, tally, account, description, statement.

inverse ADJ **= opposite**, converse, contrary, reverse, counter.

invert VERB **= turn upside down**, upturn, overturn, upset, turn turtle, capsize.

invest VERB **1 = put/sink money into**, lay out money on, provide capital for, fund, subsidize. **2 = spend**, expend, lay out, put in,

use up, devote,
contribute, donate, give.
3 = **vest**, endow, confer,
bestow, grant, entrust,
give, place.

investigate VERB
= **inquire into**, make
inquiries about, go/look
into, research, probe,
explore, search,
scrutinize, study,
examine, inspect,
consider, sift, analyse;
[inf] check out; [Brit.
inf] suss out.

investigation NOUN
= **inquiry**, fact-finding,
search, scrutinization,
scrutiny, research, probe,
exploration, study,
survey, review,
examination, inspection,
consideration, sifting,
analysis, inquest,
hearing, questioning,
inquisition.

inveterate ADJ
= **confirmed**, habitual,
inured, hardened,
chronic, die-hard, deep-
dyed, dyed-in-the-wool,
long-standing, addicted,
hard-core, incorrigible.

invidious ADJ
1 = **discriminatory**, unfair,

prejudicial, slighting,
offensive, objectionable,
deleterious, detrimental.
2 = **unpleasant**, awkward,
unpopular, repugnant,
hateful.
Opposites: fair, pleasant.

invigorate VERB
= **revitalize**, energize,
fortify, strengthen, put
new strength/life/heart
in, brace, refresh,
rejuvenate, enliven, liven
up, animate, exhilarate,
perk up, stimulate,
motivate, rouse, excite,
wake up, galvanize,
electrify; [inf] pep up.
Opposites: tire.

invincible ADJ
1 = **unconquerable**,
undefeatable, unbeatable,
unassailable,
invulnerable,
indestructible,
impregnable,
indomitable, unyielding,
unflinching, dauntless.
2 = **insuperable**,
unsurmountable,
overwhelming,
overpowering.
Opposites: vulnerable.

inviolable ADJ
= **inalienable**,

untouchable, unalterable, sacrosanct, sacred, holy, hallowed.

invisible ADJ = **unseeable**, out of sight, undetectable, imperceptible, indiscernible, indistinguishable, unseen, unnoticed, unobserved, hidden, concealed, inconspicuous, unnoticeable.

invite VERB **1** = **ask**, bid, summon, request someone's company/ presence. **2** = **ask for**, request, call for, solicit, look for, seek, appeal for, petition, summon. **3** = **cause**, bring on, bring upon oneself, induce, provoke.

inviting ADJ = **attractive**, appealing, pleasant, agreeable, delightful, engaging, tempting, enticing, alluring, irresistible, ravishing, seductive.
Opposites: repellent.

invocation NOUN = **call**, prayer, request, petition, appeal, supplication, entreaty, solicitation, imploring, importuning; [poetic/literary] beseeching.

invoke VERB = **call for**, call up, pray for, request, supplicate, entreat, solicit, beg, implore, importune, call on, petition, appeal to; [poetic/literary] beseech.

involuntary ADJ
1 = **reflexive**, reflex, automatic, mechanical, unconditioned, spontaneous, instinctive, instinctual, unconscious, unthinking, unintentional, uncontrolled.
2 = **unwilling**, against one's will/wishes, reluctant, grudging, forced, coerced, coercive, compelled, compulsory, obligatory.
Opposites: deliberate, voluntary.

involve VERB **1** = **entail**, imply, mean, denote, betoken, connote, require, necessitate, presuppose. **2** = **include**, count in, cover, embrace, take in, number, incorporate, encompass, comprise, contain, comprehend. **3 = interest**, be of interest to, absorb, engage, engage/hold someone's attention, rivet, grip, occupy, preoccupy, engross. **Opposites:** preclude, exclude.

involved ADJ
= complicated, difficult, intricate, complex, elaborate, confused, confusing, mixed up, jumbled, tangled, entangled, convoluted, knotty, tortuous, labyrinthine, Byzantine.

iota NOUN **= bit**, mite, speck, atom, jot, whit, particle, fraction, morsel, grain; [inf] smidgen.

ironic ADJ **1 = satirical**, mocking, derisive, scornful, sardonic, wry, double-edged, sarcastic.
2 = paradoxical, incongruous.

irrational ADJ **= illogical**, unreasonable, groundless, unsound, implausible, absurd, ridiculous, silly, foolish, senseless, nonsensical, muddled, confused,

ludicrous, preposterous, crazy, demented, insane. **Opposites:** rational.

irrefutable ADJ
= incontrovertible, incontestable, indisputable, undeniable, unquestionable, beyond question, indubitable, beyond doubt, conclusive, decisive, definite.

irregular ADJ
1 = asymmetric, unsymmetrical, uneven, broken, jagged, ragged, serrated, crooked, curving, craggy.
2 = uneven, unsteady, shaky, fitful, variable, erratic, spasmodic, wavering, fluctuating, aperiodic.
3 = inconsistent, erratic, sporadic, variable, inconstant, desultory, haphazard, intermittent, occasional. **4 = out of order**, against the rules, unofficial, unorthodox, unconventional, abnormal.

irrelevant ADJ
= immaterial, unrelated, unconnected, inapposite,

inapt, inapplicable, non-germane, inappropriate, extraneous, beside the point, not to the point, out of place; [inf] nothing to do with it, neither here nor there.

irreparable ADJ = **beyond repair**, past mending, irreversible, irrevocable, irretrievable, irrecoverable, irremediable, incurable, ruinous.

irreplaceable ADJ = **priceless**, invaluable, precious, unique, worth its weight in gold, rare.

irrepressible ADJ
1 = **inextinguishable**, unquenchable, uncontainable, uncontrollable, unstoppable, unreserved, unchecked, unbridled.
2 = **buoyant**, effervescent, ebullient, vivacious, animated, spirited, lively.

irresistible ADJ
1 = **overwhelming**, overpowering, compelling, irrepressible, forceful, potent, imperative, urgent.
2 = **fascinating**, alluring,

enticing, seductive, captivating, enchanting, ravishing, tempting, tantalizing.

irresolute ADJ
= **uncertain**, unsure, doubtful, dubious, undecided, indecisive, unresolved, undetermined, unsettled, vacillating, wavering, hesitant, hesitating, tentative, in two minds, oscillating.
Opposites: resolute.

irresponsible ADJ
1 = **undependable**, unreliable, untrustworthy, careless, reckless, rash, flighty, giddy, scatterbrained, erratic, hare-brained, feather-brained, immature.
2 = **thoughtless**, ill-considered, unwise, injudicious, careless, reckless, immature.
Opposites: sensible.

irreverent ADJ
1 = **disrespectful**, impertinent, insolent, impudent, rude, cheeky, discourteous, impolite, uncivil. 2 = **impious**,

irreligious, heretical, sacrilegious, ungodly, blasphemous, profane. **Opposites:** respectful.

irrevocable ADJ = **unalterable**, unchangeable, irreversible, fixed, settled, fated, immutable, predetermined, predestined.

irrigation NOUN = **watering**, wetting, spraying, sprinkling, moistening, soaking, flooding, inundating.

irritable ADJ = **bad-tempered**, ill-tempered, ill-humoured, irascible, cross, edgy, testy, touchy, crabbed, peevish, petulant, cantankerous, grumpy, grouchy, crusty, dyspeptic, choleric, splenetic; [inf] snappish, snappy. **Opposites:** good-humoured, cheerful.

irritate VERB 1 = **annoy**, vex, provoke, irk, nettle, get on someone's nerves, exasperate, infuriate, anger, enrage, incense, make someone's hackles rise, ruffle, disturb, put out, bother, pester, try someone's patience; [Brit.] rub up the wrong way; [inf] aggravate, peeve, get someone's goat, get someone's back up, get up someone's nose, drive up the wall, drive bananas. **2** = **chafe**, fret, rub, pain, hurt, inflame, aggravate.

irritation NOUN 1 = **irritability**, annoyance, impatience, vexation, exasperation, indignation, crossness, ill temper, anger, fury, rage, wrath, displeasure; [inf] aggravation; [poetic/literary] ire. **2** = **source of annoyance**, annoyance, irritant, pest, nuisance, thorn in the flesh; [inf] pain in the neck, pain.

isolate VERB = **set apart**, segregate, cut off, separate, detach, abstract, quarantine, keep in solitude, sequester, insulate.

isolated ADJ 1 = **alone**, solitary, lonely, separated, exiled, forsaken, forlorn.

2 = remote, out of the way, off the beaten track, outlying, secluded, hidden, unfrequented, lonely, desolate, godforsaken. **3 = single**, solitary, unique, random, unrelated, unusual, uncommon, exceptional, abnormal, atypical, untypical, anomalous, freak.

issue NOUN **1 = matter**, matter in question, point at issue, question, subject, topic, affair, problem, bone of contention, controversy, argument. **2 = result**, outcome, decision, upshot, end, conclusion, consequence, termination, effect, denouement. **3 = edition**, number, printing, print run, impression, copy, instalment, version. **4 = issuing**, issuance, publication, circulation, distribution, supplying, supply, dissemination, sending out, delivery. ▸ VERB **1 = put out**, give out, deal out, send out, distribute, circulate, release, disseminate, announce, proclaim, broadcast. **2 = come out/forth**, emerge, emanate, appear, pour out/forth, exude, gush, seep, ooze.

itch VERB **1 = tingle**, prickle, tickle, be irritated, be itchy. **2 = long**, have a longing, yearn, hanker, pine, ache, burn, hunger, thirst, lust, desire greatly, crave. ▸ NOUN **1 = tingling**, irritation, itchiness, prickling, tickling; [Medicine] formication, paraesthesia. **2 = great desire**, longing, yearning, craving, hankering, ache, burning, hunger, thirst, lust; [inf] yen.

item NOUN **1 = article**, thing, piece of merchandise, goods. **2 = point**, detail, matter, consideration, particular, feature, circumstance, aspect, element, ingredient.

Jj

jab NOUN = **poke**, prod, dig, nudge, elbow, thrust, stab, bump, tap, punch; [inf] sock, biff.

jacket NOUN = **casing**, case, encasement, sheath, sheathing, envelope, cover, covering, wrapping, wrapper, wrap.

jaded ADJ = **tired**, weary, fatigued, worn out, exhausted, spent; [inf] played out, bushed, done, done in; [Brit. inf] fagged out; [N. Amer. inf] pooped.
Opposites: fresh.

jagged ADJ = **serrated**, toothed, notched, indented, nicked, pointed, snaggy, spiked, barbed, uneven, rough, ridged, ragged, craggy, broken, cleft.
Opposites: smooth.

jam VERB 1 = **wedge**, sandwich, insert, force, ram, thrust, push, stick, press, cram, stuff.
2 = **cram**, pack, crowd, squeeze, crush.
3 = **become stuck**, stick, stall, halt, stop.
▶ NOUN 1 = **traffic jam**, hold-up, obstruction, congestion, bottleneck, stoppage, gridlock.
2 = **predicament**, plight, straits, trouble, quandary; [inf] fix, pickle, hole, spot, tight spot, scrape; [Brit. inf] spot of bother.

jar VERB 1 = **grate**, rasp, scratch, squeak, screech.
2 = **grate on**, irritate, disturb, upset, discompose, irk, annoy, nettle, vex. 3 = **clash**, conflict, be in opposition, be at variance, be at odds.

jargon NOUN = **cant**, slang, argot, idiom, usage, vernacular, dialect, patois; [inf] lingo.

jaundiced ADJ = **cynical**, pessimistic, sceptical, distrustful, suspicious, misanthropic, bitter, resentful, jealous, envious.

jaunt NOUN = **trip**, outing, excursion, expedition, tour, holiday, break, airing, stroll, ramble.

jaunty ADJ = **sprightly**, bouncy, buoyant, lively, breezy, perky, frisky, merry, blithe, carefree, joyful. = See also **happy** (1).

jazzy ADJ = **flashy**, fancy, stylish, smart, gaudy; [inf] flash, snazzy.

jealous ADJ 1 = **envious**, begrudging, grudging, resentful, green with envy, green-eyed, covetous, desirous, emulous. 2 = **suspicious**, possessive, distrustful, mistrustful, doubting, insecure. 3 = **protective**, vigilant, watchful, heedful, mindful, careful, solicitous, on guard, wary.
Opposites: trusting.

jeer VERB = **mock**, ridicule, deride, taunt, gibe, scorn, cry down, hector, barrack, boo, hiss, tease, scoff at, laugh at, sneer at; [inf] knock.
Opposites: cheer.

jeopardy NOUN = **risk**, danger, endangerment, peril, hazard, precariousness, insecurity, vulnerability, threat, menace.
Opposites: safety.

jerk VERB 1 = **pull**, yank, tug, wrench, tweak, pluck. 2 = **jolt**, lurch, bump, jump, bounce, jounce.
▸ NOUN 1 = **pull**, yank, tug, wrench, tweak. 2 = **jolt**, lurch, bump, start, jar. 3 = See **idiot**.

jerky ADJ 1 = **spasmodic**, fitful, convulsive, twitchy, shaking, shaky, tremulous, uncontrolled. 2 = **jolting**, lurching, bumpy, bouncy, jouncing, rough; [inf] jumpy.
Opposites: smooth.

jobless

jester NOUN **1** = **comic**, comedian, humorist, wag, wit. **2** = **fool**, clown, buffoon, merry andrew, harlequin, pantaloon.

jet NOUN **1** = **stream**, gush, spurt, spout, spray, rush, fountain, spring. **2** = **nozzle**, spout, nose, sprinkler, sprinkler head, spray, rose, atomizer. ▶ VERB = **shoot**, gush, spurt, spout, well, rush, spray, squirt, spew, stream, surge, flow, issue.

jetty NOUN = **pier**, wharf, quay, harbour, dock, breakwater, mole, groyne.

jewel NOUN = **gem**, gemstone, precious stone, stone, brilliant; [inf] sparkler, rock.

jib VERB = **balk at**, recoil from, shrink from, stop short of, refuse.

jibe NOUN = **taunt**, sneer, jeer, mocking, sneering, scoffing, scorn, derision, ridicule, teasing, sarcasm; [inf] dig.

jilt VERB = **reject**, cast aside, discard, throw over, leave, forsake; [inf] ditch, dump, give the brush-off

to, give the heave-ho, give the elbow.

jingle VERB **1** = **clink**, chink, jangle, rattle, clank. **2** = **tinkle**, ding, go ding-dong, go ting-a-ling, ring, chime. ▶ NOUN = **ditty**, chorus, refrain, short song, limerick, piece of doggerel, carol, melody, tune, catchy tune.

job NOUN **1** = **work**, piece of work, task, undertaking, chore, assignment, venture, enterprise, activity, business, affair. **2** = **occupation**, profession, trade, employment, vocation, calling, career, field of work, means of livelihood, métier, pursuit, position, post, situation, appointment. **3** = **duty**, task, chore, errand, responsibility, concern, role, charge, office, commission, capacity, contribution.

jobless ADJ = **unemployed**, without employment, out of work, without work, workless, idle, inactive,

unoccupied.
Opposites: employed.

jocular ADJ = **humorous**, funny, witty, comic, comical, facetious, joking, jesting, playful, roguish, waggish, whimsical, droll, jocose, teasing, sportive, amusing, entertaining, diverting, hilarious, farcical, laughable.
Opposites: serious.

jog VERB **1** = **go jogging**, run slowly, dogtrot, trot, canter, lope. **2** = **nudge**, prod, poke, push, elbow, tap. **3** = **stimulate**, activate, stir, arouse, prompt.

join VERB **1** = **fasten**, attach, tie, bind, couple, connect, unite, link, splice, yoke, knit, glue, cement, fuse, weld, solder. **2** = **join forces with**, team up with, band together with, cooperate with, collaborate with, affiliate with. **3** = **enlist**, sign up, enrol, become a member of, enlist in, sign up for, enrol in. **4** = **adjoin**, conjoin, abut on, border, border on,

touch, meet, verge on, reach to, extend to.
Opposites: detach, leave.

joint NOUN = **join**, junction, juncture, intersection, nexus, knot, seam, coupling.
▶ ADJ = **common**, shared, joined, mutual, combined, collective, cooperative, allied, united, concerted, consolidated.
Opposites: separate.

jointly ADV = **together**, in combination, in conjunction, as one, mutually, in partnership, cooperatively, in cooperation, in league, in collusion; [inf] in cahoots.

joke NOUN **1** = **jest**, witticism, quip, yarn, pun, sally; [inf] wisecrack, crack, gag, funny. **2** = **practical joke**, prank, trick, hoax, jape; [inf] leg-pull, lark. **3** = **laughing stock**, butt, figure of fun, target, fair game, Aunt Sally.
▶ VERB **1** = **tell jokes**, crack jokes, jest, banter, quip, wisecrack. **2** = **fool**, fool around, tease, pull

someone's leg; [inf] kid, have someone on.

jolly ADJ = **merry**, joyful, joyous, jovial, happy, glad, mirthful, gleeful, cheerful, cheery, carefree, buoyant, lively, bright, light-hearted, jocund, sprightly, elated, exuberant, exhilarated, jubilant, high-spirited, sportive, playful; [dated] gay; [poetic/ literary] blithe.
Opposites: miserable.

jolt VERB 1 = **bump against**, knock against, bump into, bang into, collide with, jostle, push, shove, elbow, nudge, jar.
2 = **bump**, bounce, jounce, start, jerk, lurch, jar. 3 = **upset**, disturb, perturb, shake, shake up, shock, stun, disconcert, discompose, disquiet, startle, surprise, astonish, amaze, stagger.

jostle VERB 1 = **bump against**, knock against, bump into, bang into, collide with, jolt, push, shove, elbow. 2 = **push**, thrust, shove, press, squeeze, elbow, force.

jot NOUN = **iota**, whit, bit, scrap, fraction, atom, grain, particle, morsel, mite, speck, trace, trifle, tinge; [inf] smidgen, tad.

journal NOUN 1 = **diary**, daybook, notebook, commonplace book, log, logbook, chronicle, record, register.
2 = **periodical**, magazine, trade magazine, review, publication.
3 = **newspaper**, paper, daily newspaper, daily, weekly newspaper, weekly, gazette.

journalist NOUN
= **reporter**, newspaperman/woman, newsman/woman, news hound, pressman/ woman, feature writer, columnist, correspondent, contributor, commentator, reviewer, editor, subeditor; [inf] stringer, sub.

journey NOUN = **trip**, expedition, excursion, travels, tour, trek, voyage, cruise, safari, peregrination, roaming, roving, globetrotting,

odyssey, pilgrimage, outing, jaunt.
▶ VERB = *see* **travel** (1).

jovial ADJ = **jolly**, jocular, jocose, jocund, happy, cheerful, cheery, glad, in good spirits, merry, mirthful, buoyant, animated, convivial, sociable, cordial; [dated] gay; [poetic/literary] blithe.
Opposites: miserable.

joy NOUN 1 = **delight**, pleasure, gladness, enjoyment, gratification, happiness, rapture, glee, bliss, ecstasy, elation, rejoicing, exultation, jubilation, euphoria, ravishment, transport, felicity. 2 = **source of joy**, treasure, prize, gem, jewel, pride and joy, delight. 3 = **success**, satisfaction, good fortune, luck, achievement.
Opposites: misery.

joyful ADJ 1 = **overjoyed**, elated, beside oneself, thrilled, delighted, pleased, gratified, happy, glad, gleeful, jubilant, ecstatic, exultant,

euphoric, enraptured; [inf] over the moon, in seventh heaven, on cloud nine, tickled pink; [poetic/literary] blithe.
2 = **glad**, happy, good, pleasing, cheering, gratifying, heart-warming. 3 = **joyous**, happy, cheerful, merry, festive, celebratory; [dated] gay.
Opposites: unhappy.

judge VERB 1 = **adjudicate**, adjudge, umpire, referee, arbitrate, mediate.
2 = **assess**, appraise, evaluate, weigh up, size up, gauge, examine, review, criticize, diagnose. 3 = **estimate**, assess, reckon, guess, surmise; [inf] guesstimate.
4 = **consider**, believe, think, form the opinion, deduce, gather, conclude.
▶ NOUN 1 = **magistrate**, sheriff, His/Her/Your Honour; [Brit.] m'lud; [Brit. inf] beak. 2 = **appraiser**, assessor, evaluator, critic, expert. 3 = **adjudicator**, umpire, referee, arbiter, arbitrator, mediator.

judgement NOUN
1 = **discernment**, acumen, shrewdness, common sense, good sense, sense, perception, perspicacity, percipience, penetration, discrimination, wisdom, judiciousness, prudence, sagacity, understanding, intelligence, powers of reasoning. **2** = **verdict**, decision, adjudication, ruling, finding, opinion, conclusion, decree, sentence. **3** = **opinion**, view, belief, conviction, estimation, evaluation, assessment, appraisal.

judicial ADJ **1** = **judiciary**, juridical, judicatory, legal. **2** = **judgelike**, impartial, unbiased, critical, analytical, discriminating, discerning, perceptive.

judicious ADJ = **wise**, prudent, politic, sagacious, shrewd, astute, sensible, common-sense, sound, well advised, well considered, well judged, considered, thoughtful, expedient, practical, discerning, discriminating, informed, intelligent, clever, enlightened, logical, rational, discreet, careful, cautious, circumspect, diplomatic; [inf] smart.
Opposites: injudicious, foolish.

jug NOUN = **pitcher**, carafe, decanter, jar, urn, crock, vessel, receptacle, container.

juggle VERB = **change around**, alter, tamper with, falsify, fake, manipulate, manoeuvre, rig, massage; [inf] fix, doctor, cook.

juice NOUN = **extract**, sap, secretion, liquid, liquor, fluid, serum.

juicy ADJ **1** = **succulent**, moist, lush, sappy, watery, wet, flowing.
2 = **racy**, risqué, spicy, sensational, thrilling, fascinating, colourful, exciting, vivid.
Opposites: dry, dull.

jumble VERB
= **disorganize**, muddle, confuse, disarrange, disorder, dishevel, tangle, shuffle, mix, mix up, mingle, put in disarray, make a shambles of,

throw into chaos.

▶ NOUN = **clutter**, muddle, confusion, litter, mess, hodgepodge, hotchpotch, mishmash, confused heap, miscellany, motley collection, mixture, medley, gallimaufry, farrago.

jump VERB 1 = **spring**, leap, bound, hop, bounce, skip, caper, gambol, frolic, frisk, cavort. 2 = **leap over**, vault, pole-vault, hurdle, clear, go over, sail over. 3 = **start**, flinch, jerk, recoil, twitch, quiver, shake, wince; [inf] jump out of one's skin. 4 = **set upon**, mug, pounce on, fall on, swoop down on, attack, assault.

▶ NOUN 1 = **spring**, leap, vault, bound, hop, bounce, skip. 2 = **hurdle**, fence, rail, hedge, obstacle, barrier, gate. 3 = **gap**, break, hiatus, interruption, space, lacuna, breach, interval. 4 = **start**, flinch, jerk, twitch, quiver, shake, wince.

jumpy ADJ = **nervous**, nervy, edgy, on edge, agitated, fidgety, anxious, uneasy, restive, tense, alarmed, apprehensive, panicky; [inf] jittery. Opposites: calm.

junction NOUN 1 = **join**, joint, juncture, link, bond, connection, seam, joining, coupling, linking, welding, union. 2 = **crossroads**, crossing, intersection, interchange.

juncture NOUN = **point**, point in time, time, stage, period, critical point, crucial moment, moment of truth, turning point, crisis, crux, extremity.

junior ADJ = **younger**, subordinate, lesser, lower, minor, secondary, inferior. Opposites: senior, older.

junk NOUN = **rubbish**, refuse, litter, scrap, waste, garbage, trash, debris, leavings, leftovers, remnants, cast-offs, rejects, odds and ends, bric-a-brac, oddments.

▶ VERB = **throw out**, throw away, discard, get rid of,

dispose of, scrap; [inf] dump.

just ADJ **1 = fair**, fair-minded, equitable, even-handed, impartial, unbiased, objective, neutral, disinterested, unprejudiced, open-minded. **2 = valid**, sound, well founded, well grounded, justified, justifiable, warrantable, defensible, reasonable.
Opposites: unjust, undeserved.

justice NOUN **1 = justness**, fairness, fair play, fair-mindedness, equitableness, equity, even-handedness, impartiality, lack of bias, objectivity, neutrality, disinterestedness, lack of prejudice, open-mindedness. **2 = validity**, justification, soundness, reasonableness.
3 = amends, recompense, redress, compensation, reparation, requital, retribution, penalty, punishment.
Opposites: injustice.

justifiable ADJ **= valid**, sound, well founded, lawful, legitimate, legal, tenable, right, defensible, supportable, sustainable, warrantable, reasonable, within reason, sensible, acceptable, plausible, vindicable.

justify VERB **1 = give grounds for**, give reasons for, show just cause for, explain, give an explanation for, rationalize, defend, stand up for, uphold.
2 = warrant, substantiate, bear out, show to be reasonable, prove to be right, confirm.

jut VERB **= stick out**, project, protrude, poke out, bulge out, overhang, beetle.

juvenile ADJ **1 = young**, junior, minor.
2 = childish, puerile, infantile, immature, inexperienced, callow, green, unsophisticated, naive; [inf] wet behind the ears.

Kk

keen ADJ **1** = **eager**, enthusiastic, willing, avid, earnest, intent, diligent, assiduous, conscientious, zealous, fervent, fervid, impatient, yearning; [inf] raring to, itching to. **2** = **fond of**, devoted to, eager for, hungry for, thirsty for. **3** = **acute**, sharp, discerning, perceptive, sensitive, discriminating. **4** = **astute**, sharp, quick-witted, sharp-witted, shrewd, perceptive, penetrating, perspicacious, clever, bright, intelligent, brilliant, wise, canny, sagacious; [inf] brainy, smart; [formal] sapient.
Opposites: apathetic, stupid.

keep VERB **1** = **carry on**, continue, maintain, persist, persevere. **2** = **hold**
on to, keep hold of, retain; [inf] hang on to.
3 = **save up**, accumulate, store, hoard, amass, pile up, collect, garner.
4 = **look after**, keep in good order, tend, mind, maintain, keep up, manage, superintend.
5 = **provide for**, support, maintain, sustain, subsidize, feed, nurture.
6 = **keep to**, abide by, comply with, fulfil, carry out, keep faith with, stand by, honour, obey, observe; [formal] effectuate.
7 = **observe**, hold, celebrate, commemorate, respect, ritualize, solemnize, ceremonialize.
8 = **keep back**, hold back, hold up, delay, detain, retard, hinder, obstruct, impede, hamper, constrain, check, block.

■ **keep at 1 = persist**, persevere, be persistent, be pertinacious, carry on, keep going, continue, work away, see it through; [inf] stick at it, stay the distance, hang on in there. **2 = keep on at**, keep after, go on at, chivvy, badger, harp on at, nag, harass.

■ **keep back = withhold**, keep secret, keep hidden, hide, conceal, suppress.

keeper NOUN **1 = jailer**, warder, warden, guard, custodian, sentry; [inf] screw. **2 = curator**, conservator, attendant, caretaker, steward, superintendent, overseer, administrator.

keepsake NOUN **= memento**, souvenir, remembrance, reminder, token of remembrance, relic, favour.

kernel NOUN **1 = seed**, nut, grain, germ. **2 = nub**, nucleus, core, centre, heart, marrow, pith, substance, essence, essential part, gist, quintessence; [inf] nitty-gritty, nuts and bolts.

key NOUN **1 = answer**, solution, explanation, guide, clue, cue, pointer, interpretation, explication, clarification, exposition. **2 = tone**, pitch, timbre, tonality.

kick VERB **1 = boot**, punt. **2 = recoil**, spring back. **3 = give up**, stop, abandon, leave off, desist from; [inf] quit.

kill VERB **1 = take someone's life**, murder, do away with, do to death, slaughter, butcher, massacre, assassinate, liquidate, wipe out, destroy, erase, eradicate, exterminate, dispatch, put to death, execute; [inf] bump off, do in, knock off, top; [poetic/literary] slay. **2 = destroy**, put an end to, ruin, extinguish, scotch, quell. **3 = exhaust**, overtire, tire out, fatigue, wear out, debilitate, enervate, prostrate, tax, overtax, strain; [Brit. inf] fag out. **4 = hurt**, cause pain, cause discomfort, be uncomfortable, be painful.

k

killer NOUN = **murderer**, slaughterer, butcher, assassin, liquidator, destroyer, exterminator, executioner, gunman; [inf] hit man; [poetic/literary] slayer.

killing NOUN **1** = **murder**, manslaughter, homicide, slaughter, butchery, massacre, bloodshed, carnage, liquidation, destruction, extermination, execution. **2** = **financial success**, bonanza, fortune, windfall, gain, profit, booty, coup; [inf] bomb, clean-up.

killjoy NOUN = **spoilsport**, dampener, damper; [inf] wet blanket, party-pooper.

kin NOUN = **relatives**, relations, family, connections, folks, people, kindred, kith and kin, kinsfolk, kinsmen, kinswomen.

kind¹ NOUN **1** = **sort**, type, variety, brand, class, category, genus, species. **2** = **nature**, character, manner, aspect, disposition, humour, style, stamp, mould.

kind² ADJ = **kind-hearted**, kindly, generous, charitable, giving, benevolent, magnanimous, big-hearted, warm-hearted, altruistic, philanthropic, humanitarian, humane, tender-hearted, soft-hearted, gentle, mild, lenient, merciful, clement, pitying, forbearing, patient, tolerant, sympathetic, compassionate, understanding, considerate, helpful, thoughtful, good, nice, pleasant, benign, friendly, genial, congenial, amiable, amicable, cordial, courteous, gracious, good-natured, warm, affectionate, loving, indulgent, obliging, accommodating, neighbourly; [Brit. inf] decent; [poetic/literary] bounteous. **Opposites:** unkind, nasty.

kindle VERB **1** = **light**, set alight, set on fire, set fire to, ignite, start, torch.

2 = **stimulate**, rouse, arouse, excite, stir, awaken, inspire, inflame, incite, induce, provoke, actuate, activate, touch off.
Opposites: extinguish.

kindred ADJ **1** = **related**, connected, of the same blood, of the same family, consanguineous, cognate. **2** = **like**, similar, resembling, corresponding, matching, congenial, allied.

kink NOUN **1** = **twist**, bend, coil, corkscrew, curl, twirl, knot, tangle, entanglement. **2** = **flaw**, defect, imperfection, hitch, snag, difficulty, complication.

kinky ADJ **1** = **quirky**, peculiar, odd, strange, queer, bizarre, eccentric, idiosyncratic, weird, outlandish, unconventional, unorthodox, whimsical, capricious, fanciful. **2** = **perverted**, warped, deviant, unnatural, abnormal, depraved, degenerate, lascivious, licentious, lewd, sadistic, masochistic.

kit NOUN **1** = **equipment**, apparatus, set of tools, tools, implements, instruments, utensils, tackle, supplies, paraphernalia, accoutrements, effects, trappings, appurtenances; [inf] gear, stuff. **2** = **outfit**, clothing, dress, uniform, colours; [inf] rig-out, gear, strip.

■ **kit out** = **equip**, supply, provide, fit out, fix up, furnish, outfit, deck out, rig out, arm, accoutre.

knack NOUN = **talent**, aptitude, gift, flair, bent, forte, ability, capability, capacity, expertise, expertness, skill, genius, facility, propensity, dexterity, ingenuity, proficiency, competence, handiness.

knead VERB = **work**, manipulate, press, squeeze, massage, rub, form, shape.

kneel VERB = **get down on one's knees**, fall to one's knees, genuflect, bow, bow down, stoop, make obeisance, kowtow.

knife NOUN = **blade**, cutting tool.

▶VERB = **stab**, pierce, run through, impale, bayonet, transfix, cut, slash, lacerate, wound. = *See also* **wound** VERB.

knit VERB 1 = **loop**, weave, interweave, crochet.
2 = **link**, bind, unite, draw together, ally.

knob NOUN 1 = **doorknob**, handle, door handle, switch, on/off switch.
2 = **bump**, bulge, swelling, lump, knot, node, nodule, pustule, growth, tumour, protuberance, tumescence.

knock VERB 1 = **tap**, rap, bang, pound, hammer.
2 = **strike**, hit, slap, smack, box, punch, cuff, buffet, thump, thwack, batter, pummel.
3 = **knock into**, bang into, bump into, collide with, run into, crash into, crash against, smash into, dash against, jolt.
4 = **criticize**, find fault with, take apart, take to pieces, pick holes in, run down, carp at, cavil at, deprecate, belittle,

disparage, censure, condemn.

knot NOUN = **loop**, twist, bend, intertwinement, interlacement, ligature.
▶VERB = **tie**, loop, bind, secure, tether, lash, leash.

know VERB 1 = **be aware of**, notice, perceive, realize, be conscious of, be cognizant of, sense, recognize; [inf] latch on to. 2 = **have knowledge of**, understand, comprehend, apprehend, be conversant with, be familiar with, be acquainted with. 3 = **be familiar with**, be acquainted with, experience, undergo, go through. 4 = **have met**, be acquainted with, have dealings with, associate with, be friends with, socialize with, fraternize with, be intimate with, be close to, be on good terms with.

knowing ADJ 1 = **astute**, shrewd, perceptive, meaningful, well informed, significant, eloquent, expressive.
2 = **aware**, astute, shrewd,

perceptive, sophisticated, worldly, worldly-wise.
3 = **conscious**, intentional, intended, deliberate, wilful, purposeful, calculated, on purpose, by design.

knowledge NOUN
1 = **learning**, erudition, scholarship, letters, education, enlightenment, wisdom.
2 = **understanding**, grasp, comprehension, apprehension, cognition, adeptness, skill, expertise, proficiency; [inf] know-how.
3 = **acquaintanceship**, familiarity, conversance.

knowledgeable ADJ
1 = **well informed**, informed, educated, learned, erudite, scholarly, well read, cultured, cultivated, enlightened. **2** = **having a knowledge of**, acquainted with, familiar with, experienced in, expert in, conversant with, having an understanding of.
Opposites: ill-informed.

known ADJ = **recognized**, acknowledged, admitted, declared, proclaimed, avowed, confessed, published, revealed.

k

LI

label NOUN
1 = **identification tag**, tag, ticket, tab, sticker, marker, docket.
2 = **epithet**, name, nickname, title, sobriquet, designation, description, characterization; [formal] denomination.
▶ VERB 1 = **attach labels to**, tag, tab, ticket, stamp, mark, put stickers on, docket. 2 = **describe**, designate, identify, classify, class, categorize, brand, call, name, term, dub.

laborious ADJ 1 = **hard**, heavy, difficult, arduous, strenuous, fatiguing, tiring, wearying, wearisome, tedious.
2 = **painstaking**, careful, meticulous, diligent, assiduous, industrious, hard-working, scrupulous, persevering, pertinacious, zealous.
3 = **laboured**, strained, forced.
Opposites: easy, natural.

labour NOUN 1 = **work**, employment, job, toil, exertion, effort, industry, industriousness, hard work, hard labour, drudgery, slog, donkey work, sweat of one's brow; [poetic/literary] travail. 2 = **task**, job, chore, undertaking, commission, assignment, charge, venture.
3 = **employees**, workers, workmen, workforce, working people, hands, labourers. 4 = **childbirth**, birth, parturition, delivery, contractions, labour pains; [poetic/literary] travail; [dated] confinement.

▶ VERB = **work hard**, work away, toil, slave away, drudge, grub away, plod on/away, grind/sweat away, struggle, exert oneself, work like a slave, work one's fingers to the bone, work like a Trojan; [poetic/literary] travail.

laboured ADJ 1 = **difficult**, strained, forced, heavy, awkward. 2 = **contrived**, affected, studied, stiff, strained, stilted, forced, unnatural, artificial, overdone, overworked, heavy, ponderous, ornate, elaborate, over-elaborate, intricate, convoluted, complex, laborious.

labyrinth NOUN = **maze**, warren, network, convolution, entanglement.

labyrinthine ADJ
1 = **maze-like**, meandering, winding, wandering, twisting, circuitous, tangled.
2 = **intricate**, complicated, complex, involved, tortuous, convoluted, tangled, entangled, confusing, puzzling, perplexing, mystifying, bewildering.

lacerate VERB = **cut**, tear, gash, slash, cut open, rip, rend, mangle, mutilate, hurt, wound, injure, maim.

lack NOUN = **absence**, want, need, deprivation, deficiency, privation, dearth, insufficiency, shortage, scarcity, scarceness, paucity.
Opposites: plenty.
▶ VERB = **be lacking**, be without, have need of, need, stand in need of, require, want, be short of, be deficient in, miss.

laconic ADJ = **brief**, concise, terse, succinct, short, elliptical, crisp, pithy, to the point, incisive, abrupt, blunt, curt.
Opposites: verbose.

laden ADJ = **loaded**, burdened, heavily laden, weighed down, weighted, encumbered, hampered, oppressed, taxed.

lady NOUN 1 = **woman**, female. 2 = **noblewoman**, gentlewoman, aristocrat.

ladylike ADJ = **genteel**, refined, well bred, cultivated, polished, decorous, proper, correct, respectable, well mannered, courteous, polite, civil, gracious. **Opposites:** coarse.

lag VERB = **fall behind**, fall back, trail, not keep pace, bring up the rear, loiter, linger, dally, straggle, dawdle, hang back, delay, move slowly, drag one's feet.

laid-back ADJ = **relaxed**, at ease, easy, leisurely, unhurried, casual, easy-going, free and easy, informal, nonchalant, unexcitable, imperturbable, unflappable. **Opposites:** tense.

lair NOUN 1 = **tunnel**, dugout, hollow, cave, haunt. 2 = **retreat**, hideaway, refuge, sanctuary, sanctum, sanctum sanctorum.

lake NOUN = **pond**, tarn, pool, reservoir, lagoon; [Scottish] loch; [N. Amer.] bayou.

lame ADJ 1 = **limping**, hobbling, halting, crippled, game, disabled, incapacitated, defective; [Brit. inf] gammy. 2 = **weak**, feeble, thin, flimsy, unconvincing, unsatisfactory, inadequate, insufficient, deficient, defective, ineffectual.

lament VERB 1 = **mourn**, grieve, sorrow, wail, moan, groan, weep, cry, sob, complain, keen, ululate, howl, beat one's breast. 2 = **complain about**, bemoan, bewail, deplore.

lamentable ADJ 1 = **deplorable**, regrettable, tragic, terrible, wretched, woeful, sorrowful, distressing, grievous. 2 = **miserable**, pitiful, poor, meagre, low, unsatisfactory, inadequate; [inf] measly.

lamp NOUN = **lantern**, table lamp, standard lamp, night light, light bulb, headlight, headlamp, sidelight, fog light, fog lamp.

land NOUN **1** = **dry land**, ground, solid ground, earth, terra firma. **2** = **ground**, fields, open space, expanse, stretch, tract. **3** = **property**, ground, acres, estate, realty, real estate. **4** = **country**, nation, fatherland, motherland, state, realm, province, territory, district, region, area, domain.
▶ VERB **1** = **touch down**, alight, make a landing, come in to land. **2** = **make a landing**, bring down, put down, take down. **3** = **berth**, dock, reach the shore, come ashore, disembark, debark. **4** = **deal**, deliver, deposit, give, catch; [inf] fetch.

landlady, **landlord** NOUN **1** = **innkeeper**, hotel keeper, hotelier, host, mine host; [Brit.] publican, pub-owner. **2** = **owner**, proprietor, lessor, householder, freeholder.

landscape NOUN = **countryside**, scene, scenery, outlook, view, aspect, prospect, vista, panorama, perspective.

landslide NOUN **1** = **avalanche**, landslip, rockfall. **2** = **decisive victory**, runaway victory, overwhelming majority.

language NOUN **1** = **speech**, speaking, talking, words, vocabulary, utterances, verbal expression, verbalization, vocalization, communication, conversation, discourse, interchange. **2** = **tongue**, speech, parlance, mother tongue, native tongue; [inf] lingo.

languid ADJ = **languishing**, listless, languorous, lackadaisical, spiritless, vigourless, lacking energy, lethargic, torpid, idle, inactive, inert, indolent, lazy, sluggish, slow-moving, unenthusiastic, apathetic, indifferent.
Opposites: energetic, vigorous.

languish VERB **1** = **droop**, flag, wilt, wither, fade, fail, weaken, decline, go into a decline, go downhill, waste away.

2 = waste away, rot, decay, wither away, be abandoned, be neglected, be forgotten, be disregarded.
Opposites: thrive.

languor NOUN
= listlessness, lethargy, torpor, idleness, inactivity, inertia, indolence, laziness, sluggishness, sleepiness, drowsiness, somnolence, dreaminess, relaxation.
Opposites: vigour.

lank ADJ **= lifeless**, lustreless, limp, straggling, straight, long.

lanky ADJ **= tall**, spindly, gangling, gangly, lean, thin, angular, scraggy, bony, gaunt, raw-boned, gawky, rangy; [inf] weedy.
Opposites: sturdy.

lap NOUN **1 = circuit**, circle, loop, orbit, round, compass, ambit.
2 = round, tour, section, stage.

lapse NOUN **1 = slip**, error, mistake, blunder, failing, fault, failure, omission, oversight, negligence, dereliction; [inf] slip-up.
2 = interval, gap, pause, intermission, interlude, lull, hiatus, break, passage. **3 = decline**, downturn, fall, falling, falling away, slipping, drop, deterioration, worsening, degeneration, backsliding.

▶ VERB **1 = decline**, fall, fall off, drop, go downhill, deteriorate, worsen, degenerate, go to pot.
2 = become void, become invalid, expire, run out, terminate, become obsolete. **3 = slide**, slip, drift, sink, subside, submerge.

larder NOUN **= pantry**, storage room, storeroom, store, still room, cooler, scullery.

large ADJ **1 = big**, great, of considerable size, sizeable, substantial, goodly, tall, high, huge, immense, enormous, colossal, massive, mammoth, vast, prodigious, gigantic, giant, monumental, stupendous, gargantuan, man-size, king-size, giant-size, outsize, considerable; [inf] jumbo,

whopping. **2** = **burly**, big, heavy, bulky, thickset, powerfully built, heavy-set, chunky, strapping, hefty, ample, fat, obese, corpulent; [inf] hulking. **3** = **abundant**, copious, plentiful, ample, liberal, generous. **4** = **wide**, wide-ranging, large-scale, broad, extensive, far-reaching, sweeping, comprehensive, exhaustive.
Opposites: small.

■ **at large** = **at liberty**, free, unconfined, unrestrained, roaming, on the loose, on the run, fugitive.

largely ADV = **to a large extent**, to a great degree, chiefly, for the most part, mostly, mainly, in the main, principally, in great measure.

lascivious ADJ = **lewd**, lecherous, lustful, licentious, promiscuous, libidinous, prurient, salacious, lubricious, concupiscent, debauched, depraved, degenerate, dissolute, dissipated.

lash VERB = **whip**, horsewhip, scourge, birch, switch, flog, flail, flagellate, thrash, beat, strike, batter, hammer; [inf] wallop, whack.

last[1] ADJ **1** = **final**, closing, concluding, ending, finishing, terminating, ultimate, terminal.
2 = **hindmost**, rearmost, at the end, at the back, final, aftermost. **3** = **least likely**, most unlikely, least suitable, least wanted, least favourite.
4 = **latest**, most recent.

last[2] VERB **1** = **continue**, go on, carry on, remain, persist, keep on.
2 = **survive**, exist, live, subsist, hold on, hold out. **3** = **last long**, wear well, stand up to wear, keep, endure.

late ADJ **1** = **behind schedule**, behind, not on time, tardy, overdue, delayed, dilatory, slow.
2 = **deceased**, dead, departed, defunct, non-extant. **3** = **former**, previous, preceding, past, prior.
Opposites: punctual.

latent ADJ = **dormant**, quiescent, inactive, passive, hidden, unrevealed, concealed, unapparent, indiscernible, imperceptible, invisible, covert, undeveloped, unrealized, potential, possible.
Opposites: evident.

lateral ADJ = **sidewise**, sideways, sidelong, sideward, edgewise, edgeways, indirect, oblique, slanting.

latitude NOUN **1** = **parallel**. **2** = **scope**, freedom of action, freedom, liberty, free play, carte blanche, leeway, elbow room, licence, indulgence.
Opposites: longitude, restriction.

latter ADJ **1** = **last-mentioned**, second-mentioned, second of the two, second. **2** = **later**, hindmost, closing, end, concluding, final.
Opposites: former.

laudable ADJ = **praiseworthy**, commendable, admirable, worthy of admiration, meritorious, deserving, creditable, worthy, estimable, of note, noteworthy, exemplary, excellent.
Opposites: shameful.

laugh VERB = **chuckle**, chortle, guffaw, giggle, titter, snigger, tee-hee, burst out laughing, roar/hoot with laughter, shake/be convulsed with laughter, split one's sides, be rolling in the aisles, be doubled up; [inf] be in stitches, die laughing, be creased up, fall about, crack up, break up.

▪ **laugh at** = **mock**, ridicule, deride, scoff at, jeer at, sneer at, make fun of, poke fun at, make a fool of, lampoon, satirize, taunt, tease; [inf] send up, take the mickey out of.

laughter NOUN = **laughing**, chuckling, chortling, guffawing, giggling, tittering, sniggering, amusement, entertainment, humour, mirth, merriment, gaiety, hilarity, glee, light-heartedness; [poetic/ literary] blitheness.

launch VERB 1 = **fire**, discharge, propel, project, send forth, throw, cast, hurl, let fly, blast off. 2 = **set in motion**, get going, begin, start, commence, embark upon, initiate, instigate, institute, inaugurate, establish, set up, organize, introduce, usher in.

lavatory NOUN = **toilet**, public convenience, cloakroom, powder room, privy, urinal, latrine; [Brit.] WC, ladies, gents; [N. Amer.] bathroom, washroom, rest room; [Nautical] head; [inf] little girls' room, little boys' room; [Brit. inf] loo, bog, khazi, lav; [N. Amer. inf] can, john; [dated] water closet.

lavish ADJ 1 = **copious**, abundant, superabundant, plentiful, profuse, prolific, unlimited. 2 = **extravagant**, excessive, immoderate, wasteful, squandering, profligate, prodigal, thriftless, improvident, intemperate, unrestrained. 3 = **generous**, liberal, bountiful, open-handed, unstinting, free, munificent, extravagant. 4 = **luxuriant**, lush, gorgeous, sumptuous, costly, opulent, pretentious, showy. **Opposites:** meagre.

▶ VERB = **heap**, shower, pour, deluge, give freely, give generously, bestow freely, waste, squander, dissipate.

law NOUN 1 = **statute**, regulation, rule, enactment, act, decree, edict, command, order, ordinance, commandment, directive, pronouncement, covenant. 2 = **principle**, precept, standard, criterion, formula, tenet, doctrine, canon. 3 = **generalization**, general truth, axiom, maxim, truism. 4 = **litigation**, legal action, legal proceedings, lawsuit.

law-abiding ADJ = **lawful**, righteous, honest, honourable, upright, upstanding, good, virtuous, orderly, peaceable, peaceful, dutiful, duteous, obedient, compliant, complying.
Opposites: lawless.

lawful ADJ 1 = **legal**, legitimate, licit, just, valid, permissible, allowable, rightful, proper, constitutional, legalized, sanctioned, authorized, warranted, approved, recognized.
2 = see **law-abiding**.
Opposites: illegal.

lawless ADJ 1 = **without law and order**, anarchic, disorderly, ungoverned, unruly, insurrectionary, insurgent, revolutionary, rebellious, insubordinate, riotous, mutinous, seditious, terrorist.
2 = **unlawful**, illegal, law-breaking, illicit, illegitimate, criminal, felonious, miscreant, transgressing, violating.

Opposites: orderly, legal.

lawyer NOUN = **solicitor**, legal practitioner, legal adviser, barrister, advocate, counsel, Queen's Counsel, QC; [inf] brief; [N. Amer.] attorney.

lax ADJ = **slack**, slipshod, negligent, neglectful, remiss, careless, heedless, unmindful, inattentive, casual, easy-going, lenient, permissive, indulgent, overindulgent, complaisant, over-tolerant.

laxative NOUN = **purgative**, aperient, cathartic, senna, ipecacuanha, castor oil.

lay VERB 1 = **set**, deposit, plant, settle, position.
2 = **position**, set out, arrange, dispose.
3 = **attribute**, assign, ascribe, allocate, allot, impute. 4 = **impose**, inflict, encumber, saddle, tax, charge, burden, apply.
■ **lay aside** = **put aside**, put to one side, keep, save, store.

■ **lay down 1 = surrender**, relinquish, give up, yield, cede, turn over. **2 = set down**, stipulate, prescribe, order, command, ordain, postulate, demand, proclaim, assert, maintain.

■ **lay in = stock up with/ on**, stockpile, store, accumulate, amass, heap up, hoard, collect.

layabout NOUN **= good-for-nothing**, ne'er-do-well, do-nothing, idler, loafer, lounger, shirker, wastrel, sluggard, laggard; [inf] waster; [Brit. inf] skiver.

layman NOUN **= amateur**, non-professional, dilettante.

laze VERB **= idle**, do nothing, loaf, lounge, lounge about, loll around, waste time, fritter away time.

laziness NOUN **= idleness**, indolence, slothfulness, sloth, inactivity, inertia, lethargy, languor, remissness, laxity.

lazy ADJ **= idle**, indolent, slothful, work-shy, inactive, inert, sluggish, lethargic, languorous, listless, torpid, slow-moving, remiss, negligent, lax.
Opposites: industrious.

lead VERB **1 = guide**, show someone the way, conduct, lead the way, usher, escort, steer, pilot. **2 = cause**, induce, prompt, move, incline, dispose, predispose, persuade, sway, influence, prevail upon, bring round. **3 = be at the head of**, be at the front of, head. **4 = command**, direct, govern, rule, manage, be in charge of, regulate, preside over, head, supervise, superintend, oversee; [inf] head up. **5 = be in the lead**, be in front, be out in front, be ahead, be first, come first, precede. **6 = have**, live, pass, spend, experience, undergo.

▶ NOUN **1 = leading position/ place**, first place, advance position, van, vanguard. **2 = margin**, gap, interval. **3 = example**, model, pattern, standard of excellence. **4 = leading role**, star/starring role, star part, title role, principal part. **5 = leash**, tether, rein, cord, rope, chain.

- **lead off = begin**, start, start off, commence, open; [inf] kick off.
- **lead to = cause**, result in, bring on, call forth, provoke, contribute to.
- **lead up to = prepare the way for**, pave the way for, open the way for, do the groundwork for, work round/up to, make overtures about, make advances about, hint at, approach the subject of, introduce the subject of.

leader NOUN **1 = ruler**, head, chief, commander, director, governor, principal, captain, manager, superintendent, supervisor, overseer, foreman, kingpin; [inf] boss, number one, skipper. **2 = pacesetter**, pacemaker, trendsetter, front runner, innovator, pioneer, trailblazer, pathfinder, groundbreaker, originator.
Opposites: follower, supporter.

leading ADJ **= chief**, main, most important, principal, foremost, supreme, paramount, dominant, superior, first-rate, greatest, best, outstanding, preeminent; [inf] number-one.
Opposites: subordinate, minor.

leaflet NOUN **= pamphlet**, booklet, brochure, advertisement, handbill, flyer, bill, circular; [Brit. inf] advert.

league NOUN **= alliance**, confederation, confederacy, federation, union, association, coalition, combine, consortium, affiliation, guild, corporation, conglomerate, cooperative, partnership, fellowship, syndicate, band, group.

leak NOUN **1 = drip**, leaking, leakage, escape, seeping, seepage, oozing, percolation, discharge.

2 = opening, crack, crevice, chink, fissure, puncture, cut, gash, slit, rent, break, rift.
3 = disclosure, divulgence, revelation, uncovering.
▶ VERB **1 = escape**, drip out, seep out/through, ooze out, exude, discharge, issue, gush out.
2 = disclose, divulge, reveal, make known, make public, impart, pass on, relate, give away, let slip; [inf] let the cat out of the bag, spill the beans about, take the lid off.

lean VERB **1 = be supported**, be propped up, recline, repose.
2 = incline, bend, slant, tilt, be at an angle, slope, bank, list, heel. **3 = incline towards**, tend towards, have a tendency towards, have a propensity for, have a proclivity for, have a preference for, be attracted to, have a liking for, gravitate towards, have an affinity with.
4 = depend on, be dependent on, rely on, count on, pin one's faith on, have faith in, trust, have every confidence in.

leaning NOUN **= tendency**, inclination, bent, proclivity, propensity, penchant, predisposition, predilection, proneness, partiality, preference, bias, attraction, liking, fondness, taste.

leap VERB **1 = jump**, bound, bounce, hop, skip, romp, caper, spring, frolic, frisk, cavort, gambol, dance.
2 = jump over, jump, vault over, vault, spring over, bound over, hurdle, clear, cross over, sail over. **3 = increase rapidly**, soar, rocket, skyrocket, shoot up, escalate, mount.

learn VERB **1 = acquire a knowledge of**, gain an understanding of, acquire skill in, become competent in, grasp, master, take in, absorb, assimilate, pick up.
2 = learn by heart, get by heart, memorize, commit to memory, become word-perfect in, get off pat. **3 = discover**, find out, detect, become

aware of, gather, hear, be informed, have it brought to one's attention, understand, ascertain, discern, perceive, get word of, get wind of.

learned ADJ = **erudite**, scholarly, well educated, knowledgeable, well read, widely read, well versed, well informed, lettered, cultured, intellectual, academic, literary, bookish.
Opposites: ignorant.

learner NOUN = **beginner**, trainee, apprentice, pupil, student, novice, tyro, neophyte, initiate; [inf] rookie; [N. Amer. inf] greenhorn.
Opposites: veteran.

lease VERB 1 = **rent**, hire, charter. 2 = **let**, let out, rent, rent out, hire, hire out, sublet.

leash NOUN 1 = **lead**, rein, tether, rope, cord, chain. 2 = **rein**, curb, control, check, restraint, hold.

leathery ADJ 1 = **wrinkled**, wizened, weather-beaten, rough, rugged, coriaceous. 2 = **tough**, hard, hardened.

leave[1] VERB 1 = **depart**, go away, go, withdraw, retire, take oneself off, exit, take one's leave, make off, pull out, quit, be gone, decamp, disappear, say one's farewells/goodbyes; [inf] push off, shove off, cut, split, vamoose; [Brit. inf] do a bunk. 2 = **set off**, set sail. 3 = **abandon**, desert, forsake, give up, discard, turn one's back on, leave in the lurch; [inf] quit. 4 = **leave behind**, forget, mislay. 5 = **assign**, allot, consign, hand over, give over, refer, commit, entrust. 6 = **bequeath**, will, endow, hand down, transfer, convey.
7 = **cause**, leave behind, produce, generate, result in.

■ **leave out** = **miss out**, omit, fail to include, overlook.

leave[2] NOUN
1 = **permission**, consent, authorization, sanction, warrant, dispensation, concession, indulgence.
2 = **holiday**, vacation,

break, time off, furlough, sabbatical, leave of absence; [inf] hols, vac.
3 = **leaving**, leave-taking, departure, parting, withdrawal, exit, farewell, goodbye, adieu.

lecherous ADJ = **lustful**, promiscuous, carnal, sensual, licentious, lascivious, lewd, salacious, libertine, libidinous, lubricious, concupiscent, debauched, dissolute, wanton, intemperate, dissipated, degenerate, depraved; [inf] horny, raunchy.
Opposites: chaste.

lecture NOUN **1** = **talk**, speech, address, discourse, disquisition, lesson, sermon, homily.
2 = **scolding**, reprimand, rebuke, reproof, reproach, remonstration, upbraiding, berating, tirade, diatribe; [inf] dressing-down, telling-off, talking-to.
▶ VERB **1** = **teach**, tutor in, instruct in, give instruction in, give lessons in. **2** = **scold**,

reprimand, rebuke, reprove, reproach, remonstrate with, upbraid, berate; [formal] castigate.

lecturer NOUN = **teacher**, college teacher, tutor, reader, instructor, academic, academician.

ledge NOUN = **shelf**, sill, mantel, mantelpiece, mantelshelf, projection, protrusion, overhang, ridge, step.

leer VERB = **ogle**, look lasciviously at, look suggestively at, eye, wink at, watch, stare, goggle, sneer, smirk grin; [inf] give someone the glad eye, give someone the once-over.

left ADJ **1** = **left-hand**, sinistral; [Nautical] port; [Heraldry] sinister. **2** = **left-wing**, leftist, socialist, radical, progressive, liberal, communist, communistic.
Opposites: right.

leg NOUN **1** = **lower limb**, limb, member, shank; [inf] stump, peg, pin.
2 = **support**, upright, prop, brace,

underpinning. **3** = **part**, portion, segment, section, bit, stretch, stage, lap.

legal ADJ **1** = **lawful**, legitimate, licit, legalized, valid, right, proper, sound, permissible, permitted, allowable, allowed, above board, admissible, acceptable, authorized, sanctioned, warranted, licensed; [inf] legit. **2** = **judicial**, juridical, forensic.
Opposites: illegal.

legalize VERB = **make legal**, decriminalize, legitimize, legitimatize, legitimate, validate, ratify, permit, allow, admit, accept, authorize, sanction, warrant, license.

legend NOUN = **myth**, saga, epic, folk tale, folk story, traditional story, tale, story, narrative, fable, romance.

legendary ADJ
1 = **mythical**, heroic, traditional, fabled, fictitious, fictional, storybook, romantic, fanciful, fantastical,

fabulous. **2** = **celebrated**, acclaimed, illustrious, famous, famed, renowned, well known, popular, immortal.

legitimate ADJ **1** = **legal**, lawful, licit, within the law, going by the rules; [inf] legit. **2** = **lawful**, rightful, genuine, authentic, real, true, proper, correct, authorized, sanctioned, warranted, acknowledged, recognized, approved. **3** = **valid**, sound, admissible, acceptable, well founded, justifiable, reasonable, plausible, credible, believable, reliable, logical, rational.
Opposites: illegitimate.

legitimize VERB = **legalize**, pronounce lawful, declare legal, legitimate, decriminalize, validate, permit, warrant, authorize, sanction, license, give the stamp of approval to.

leisure NOUN = **free time**, spare time, idle hours, inactivity, time off, relaxation, recreation, freedom, holiday, vacation, breathing space, breathing spell, respite; [inf] time to kill.

leisurely ADJ = **unhurried**, relaxed, easy, easy-going, gentle, comfortable, restful, slow, lazy, lingering; [inf] laid-back. Opposites: hurried.

lend VERB 1 = **loan**, give someone the loan of, let someone have the use of, advance. 2 = **impart**, add, give, bestow, confer, provide, supply, furnish. Opposites: borrow.

length NOUN 1 = **distance**, extent, linear measure, span, reach. 2 = **period**, stretch, duration, term, span. 3 = **piece**, portion, section, measure, segment, swatch.

lengthen VERB 1 = **make longer**, elongate, let down. 2 = **grow longer**, get longer, draw out, stretch. 3 = **prolong**, make longer, increase, extend, expand, protract, stretch out, draw out. Opposites: shorten.

lengthy ADJ = **long**, long-lasting, prolonged, extended, protracted, long-drawn-out. Opposites: short.

lenient ADJ = **merciful**, clement, sparing, moderate, compassionate, humane, forbearing, tolerant, liberal, magnanimous, indulgent, kind, gentle, easy-going, mild. Opposites: severe.

less ADJ = **smaller**, slighter, not so much, not so great.
▸ PRON = **a smaller amount**, not so much.
▸ ADV = **to a lesser degree**, to a smaller extent, not so much.
▸ PREP = **minus**, subtracting, excepting, without.

lessen VERB 1 = **grow less**, abate, decrease, diminish, subside, moderate, slacken, die down, let up, ease off, tail off, ebb, wane. 2 = **relieve**, soothe, allay, assuage, alleviate, palliate, ease, dull, deaden, blunt, take the edge off. Opposites: increase.

lesson NOUN 1 = **class**, period of instruction,

exercise, schoolwork, homework, assignment, task. **2 = example**, warning, deterrent, message, moral, precept.

let VERB **1 = allow**, permit, give permission to, give leave to, authorize, sanction, grant, license, assent to, consent to, agree to; [inf] give the thumbs up to, give the go-ahead to, give the green light to. **2 = let out**, rent, rent out, lease, hire, sublet.

■ **let down = fail**, disappoint, disillusion, forsake, abandon, desert, leave, betray, leave in the lurch.

■ **let off 1 = explode**, detonate. **2 = acquit**, release, discharge, reprieve, absolve, exonerate, pardon, forgive, exempt, spare.

■ **let up = lessen**, abate, decrease, diminish, subside, moderate, slacken, die down, ease off, tail off, ebb, wane.

let-down NOUN **= disappointment**, disillusionment, fiasco, anticlimax; [inf] washout.

lethal ADJ **= fatal**, deadly, mortal, death-dealing, murderous, poisonous, toxic, dangerous, virulent, noxious, destructive, disastrous, calamitous, ruinous.
Opposites: harmless.

lethargic ADJ **= sluggish**, inactive, slow, slothful, torpid, listless, languid, apathetic, passive, weary, enervated, fatigued, sleepy, indolent, dull, comatose.
Opposites: energetic.

lethargy NOUN **= sluggishness**, inertia, inactivity, slowness, sloth, idleness, torpor, torpidity, lifelessness, dullness, listlessness, languor, languidness, apathy, passivity, weariness, lassitude, fatigue, sleepiness, drowsiness, somnolence, narcosis.
Opposites: energy.

letter NOUN **1 = character**, sign, symbol.
2 = message, note, line, missive, epistle, dispatch.

level ADJ **1** = **flat**, smooth, even, uniform, plane, flush, horizontal.
2 = **even**, uniform, regular, consistent, constant, stable, steady, unchanging, unvarying, unfluctuating. **3** = **equal**, on a level, close together, neck and neck, level-pegging, side by side, on a par, with nothing to choose between them.
Opposites: uneven, unsteady, unequal.
▸ NOUN **1** = **height**, highness, altitude, elevation.
2 = **level of achievement**, position, rank, standing, status, station, degree, grade, stage, standard.
3 = **layer**, stratum, bed.
▸ VERB **1** = **level out**, make level, even off, even out, make flat, flatten, smooth, smooth out, plane. **2** = **raze**, raze to the ground, pull down, knock down, tear down, demolish, flatten, bulldoze, lay waste, destroy.

liable ADJ **1** = **responsible**, accountable, answerable, chargeable, blameworthy, at fault, censurable.
2 = **exposed**, open, subject, susceptible, vulnerable, in danger of, at risk of. **3** = **apt**, likely, inclined, tending, disposed, predisposed, prone.

liar NOUN = **fibber**, perjurer, falsifier, false witness, fabricator, deceiver, spinner of yarns.

libel NOUN = **defamation**, denigration, vilification, disparagement, aspersions, calumny, slander, false report, traducement, obloquy, abuse, slur, smear; [formal] derogation, calumniation.
▸ VERB = **defame**, vilify, blacken someone's name, denigrate, disparage, cast aspersions on, slander, traduce, abuse, revile, malign, slur, smear, fling mud at; [formal] derogate, calumniate.

libellous ADJ
= **defamatory**, denigratory, vilifying, disparaging, derogatory, slanderous, false, misrepresentative,

traducing, abusive, reviling, malicious, scurrilous, muckraking.

liberal ADJ **1 = abundant**, copious, ample, plentiful, lavish, profuse, munificent, bountiful, rich, handsome, generous. **2 = generous**, magnanimous, open-handed, unsparing, unstinting, lavish, munificent, bountiful, big-hearted, kind, philanthropic, charitable, altruistic, unselfish; [poetic/literary] bounteous. **3 = unprejudiced**, unbiased, unbigoted, impartial, disinterested, broad-minded, enlightened, catholic, indulgent, permissive. **4 = loose**, flexible, free, general, inexact, imprecise. **5 = advanced**, forward-looking, progressive, reformist, radical, latitudinarian. **Opposites:** conservative.

liberate VERB **= set free**, free, release, let out, let go, discharge, set loose, unshackle, unfetter, unchain, deliver, rescue, emancipate, unyoke; [historical] manumit.

liberty NOUN **1 = freedom**, independence, autonomy, sovereignty, self-government, self-rule. **2 = liberation**, freeing, release, discharge, deliverance, emancipation; [historical] manumission.

■ **at liberty = free**, loose, on the loose, at large, unconfined.

licence NOUN **1 = permit**, certificate, credentials, document, documentation, pass. **2 = permission**, leave, liberty, freedom, consent, authority, authorization, sanction, approval, warranty.

license VERB **1 = grant a licence to**, authorize, warrant, accredit, charter, franchise. **2 = give permission to**, permit, allow, grant leave to, entitle, give the freedom to, sanction, give one's approval to, empower. **Opposites:** ban.

lid NOUN **= cover**, top, cap, cork, stopper, plug.

lie¹ NOUN = **untruth**, falsehood, fib, white lie, fabrication, made-up story, trumped-up story, invention, piece of fiction, falsification, falsity, fairy story, cock and bull story, dissimulation, departure from the truth; [inf] terminological inexactitude, tall tale, whopper.
▸ VERB = **tell a lie**, perjure oneself, fib, fabricate, invent/make up a story, falsify, dissemble, dissimulate, prevaricate, depart from the truth, be economical with the truth, bear false witness.

lie² VERB 1 = **recline**, be recumbent, be prostrate, be supine, be prone, be stretched out, sprawl, rest, repose, relax, lounge, loll. 2 = **be**, be situated, be located, be placed, be positioned, be found.
▪ **lie in** = **consist**, be inherent, inhere, be present, exist, reside.
▪ **lie low** = **hide**, go into hiding, hide out, conceal oneself, keep out of sight, keep a low profile, take cover, go to earth, go to ground, go underground; [inf] hole up.

life NOUN 1 = **existence**, being, animation, aliveness, viability. 2 = **living things**, living beings, living creatures, human/animal/plant life, fauna, flora. 3 = **person**, human being, individual, mortal, soul. 4 = **lifetime**, days, duration of life, course of life, lifespan, time on earth, existence, career; [inf] one's born days.

lifeless ADJ 1 = **dead**, deceased, gone, cold, defunct. 2 = **barren**, sterile, bare, desolate, stark, arid, unproductive, uncultivated, empty, uninhabited, unoccupied. 3 = **spiritless**, lacking vitality, lacklustre, apathetic, uninspired, colourless, dull, flat, stiff, wooden, tedious, uninspiring.
Opposites: alive, lively.

lifelike ADJ = **true-to-life**, realistic, photographic, faithful, authentic, exact, vivid, graphic, natural. **Opposites:** unrealistic.

lift VERB 1 = **pick up**, uplift, hoist, heave up, raise, raise up, heft. 2 = **remove**, raise, withdraw, revoke, cancel, annul, void, countermand, relax, end, stop, terminate. 5 = **steal**, thieve, rob, pilfer, purloin, pocket, take, appropriate; [inf] filch, swipe; [Brit. inf] pinch, nick.

light¹ NOUN 1 = **illumination**, luminescence, luminosity, shining, gleaming, brightness, brilliance, blaze, glare, incandescence, effulgence, refulgence, lambency, radiance, lustre. 2 = **daylight**, daylight hours, daytime, day, hours of sunlight. 3 = **aspect**, angle, slant, approach, viewpoint, point of view.
▶ VERB 1 = **set burning**, set fire to, set a match to, ignite, kindle. 2 = **illuminate**, brighten, lighten, irradiate, flood with light, floodlight; [poetic/literary] illumine.
▶ ADJ 1 = **full of light**, bright, well lit, well illuminated, sunny. 2 = **light-coloured**, light-toned, pale, pastel, whitish, faded, bleached.

light² ADJ 1 = **lightweight**, underweight, portable. 2 thin, flimsy, insubstantial, delicate, floaty, gossamer. 3 = **gentle**, slight, delicate, soft, weak, faint, indistinct. 4 = **moderate**, easy, simple, undemanding, untaxing, effortless, facile; [inf] cushy. 5 = **light-hearted**, entertaining, diverting, recreational, amusing, humorous, funny, frivolous, superficial, trivial, trifling. **Opposites:** heavy.

lighten¹ VERB = **make lighter**, lessen, reduce, ease, alleviate, mitigate, allay, relieve, assuage, ameliorate. **Opposites:** increase.

lighten² VERB 1 = **become lighter**, grow brighter,

brighten. 2 = **make lighter**, make brighter, brighten, light up, illuminate, shed light on, cast light on, irradiate. Opposites: darken.

lightly ADV 1 = **slightly**, thinly, softly, gently. 2 = **sparingly**, sparsely, slightly. 3 = **airily**, carelessly, heedlessly, uncaringly, indifferently, thoughtlessly, flippantly, frivolously, slightingly.

like¹ VERB 1 = **be fond of**, have a liking for, be attracted to, be keen on, love, adore, have a soft spot for. 2 = **enjoy**, be keen on, find/take pleasure in, be partial to, love, adore, find agreeable, delight in, relish, revel in; [inf] get a kick from. 3 = **wish**, want, desire, prefer, had sooner, had rather. Opposites: dislike.

like² ADJ = **similar**, comparable, corresponding, resembling, analogous, parallel, equivalent, of a kind, identical, matching, akin.

Opposites: dissimilar.

▸ PREP 1 = **in the same way as**, in the manner of, in a similar way to, after the fashion of, along the lines of. 2 = **typical of**, characteristic of, in character with.

▸ NOUN = **equal**, match, counterpart, fellow, twin, mate, parallel, peer, compeer.

likeable ADJ = **pleasant**, nice, friendly, agreeable, amiable, genial, charming, engaging, pleasing, appealing, winning, attractive, winsome, lovable, adorable. Opposites: unpleasant.

likelihood NOUN = **likeliness**, probability, good chance, chance, prospect, good prospect, possibility.

likely ADJ 1 = **probable**, possible, to be expected, on the cards, odds-on. 2 = **apt**, inclined, tending, liable, prone. 3 = **suitable**, appropriate, fit, fitting, acceptable, proper, right, qualified, relevant, reasonable. 4 = **promising**,

talented, gifted; [inf] up-
and-coming.
Opposites: unlikely.

liken VERB = **compare**,
equate, analogize, draw
an analogy between,
draw a parallel between,
parallel, correlate, link,
associate.

likeness NOUN
1 = **resemblance**,
similarity, sameness,
similitude,
correspondence, analogy.
2 = **guise**, semblance,
appearance, outward
form, form, shape,
character. **3** = **picture**,
drawing, sketch,
painting, portrait,
photograph, study,
representation, image,
bust, statue, statuette,
sculpture.

liking NOUN = **fondness**,
love, affection, desire,
preference, partiality,
penchant, bias,
weakness, weak spot, soft
spot, appreciation, taste,
predilection, fancy,
inclination, bent,
leaning, affinity,
proclivity, propensity,
proneness, tendency.

Opposites: dislike,
aversion.

limb NOUN **1** = **arm**, leg,
wing, member,
extremity, appendage.
2 = **branch**, bough.

limelight NOUN = **focus of
attention**, public
attention, public notice,
public eye, public
recognition, publicity,
fame, renown, celebrity,
stardom, notability,
eminence, prominence,
spotlight.

limit NOUN **1** = **boundary**,
border, bound, frontier,
edge, perimeter, confines,
periphery. **2** = **maximum**,
ceiling, limitation,
restriction, curb, check,
restraint.
▶ VERB **1** = **place a limit on**,
restrict, curb, check, keep
within bounds, hold in
check, restrain, confine,
control, ration, reduce.
2 = **restrict**, curb, restrain,
constrain, hinder,
impede, hamper, check,
trammel.

limitation NOUN
1 = **restriction**, curb,
restraint, constraint,
qualification, control,

check, hindrance, impediment, obstacle, obstruction, bar, barrier, block, deterrent. **2** = **inability**, incapability, incapacity, defect, frailty, weakness.

limited ADJ = **restricted**, scanty, sparse, cramped, narrow, basic, minimal, little, inadequate, insufficient. **Opposites:** ample, boundless.

limitless ADJ **1** = **infinite**, endless, never-ending, interminable, immense, vast, extensive, measureless. **2** = **unlimited**, boundless, unbounded, illimitable, infinite, endless, unceasing, interminable, inexhaustible, constant, perpetual.

limp ADJ **1** = **floppy**, drooping, droopy, soft, flaccid, flabby, loose, slack. **2** = **tired**, fatigued, weary, exhausted, worn out, lethargic, enervated, feeble, frail, puny, debilitated. **3** = **weak**, characterless, ineffectual, insipid, wishy-washy, vapid; [inf] wet. **Opposites:** stiff.

line NOUN **1** = **rule**, bar, score, underline, underscore, stroke, slash. **2** = **band**, stripe, strip, belt, seam. **3** = **furrow**, wrinkle, crease, crow's foot, groove, scar. **4** = **outline**, contour, configuration, shape, figure, delineation, silhouette, profile. **5** = **boundary**, boundary line, limit, border, borderline, frontier, edge, margin, perimeter, periphery. **6** = **row**, queue, procession, column, file, string, chain, array; [Brit. inf] crocodile. **7** = **lineage**, descent, ancestry, parentage, family, extraction, heritage, stock, strain, race, breed. **8** = **rope**, string, cord, cable, wire, thread, twine, strand, filament.
▶ VERB = **border**, edge, fringe, bound, skirt, hem, rim, verge.
■ **line up** = **form a line**, get into rows/columns, file, form a queue, queue up, group together, fall in.

linger VERB **1** = **stay**, remain, wait around, hang around, delay, dawdle, loiter, dally, take one's time; [inf] dilly-dally; [archaic] tarry. **2** = **persist**, continue, remain, stay, hang around, be protracted, endure.

link NOUN **1** = **chain ring**, loop, connection, connective, coupling, joint, knot. **2** = **component**, constituent, element, part, piece, member, division. **3** = **connection**, relationship, relatedness, association, tie-up. **4** = **bond**, tie, attachment, connection, relationship, association, affiliation, mutual interest. ▸ VERB **1** = **connect**, fasten together, attach, bind, unite, couple, yoke. **2** = **join**, connect, associate, relate, bracket. **Opposites**: detach, separate.

lip NOUN = **edge**, rim, brim, margin, border, verge, brink.

liquid NOUN = **fluid**, liquor, solution, juice, sap.

liquidate VERB **1** = **convert to cash**, cash, cash in, sell off, sell up, realize. **2** = **kill**, murder, put to death, do away with, assassinate, put an end to, eliminate, dispatch, finish off, destroy, obliterate; [inf] do in, bump off, rub out, wipe out.

liquidize VERB = **blend**, crush, purée, pulverize, process.

list¹ NOUN = **catalogue**, inventory, record, register, roll, file, index, directory, listing, enumeration, table, tabulation, schedule, syllabus, calendar, programme, series. ▸ VERB = **note down**, write down, record, register, set down, enter, itemize, enumerate, catalogue, file, tabulate, schedule, chronicle, classify, alphabetize.

list² VERB = **lean**, lean over, tilt, tip, heel, heel over, careen, cant, incline, slant, slope.

listen VERB = **pay attention to**, be attentive to, hear, attend, hark, give ear to, lend an ear to, hang on someone's words, keep one's ears open, prick up one's ears; [inf] be all ears, pin back one's ears.

listless ADJ = **languid**, lethargic, languishing, enervated, lackadaisical, spiritless, lifeless, inactive, inert, indolent, apathetic, passive, dull, heavy, sluggish, slothful, limp, languorous, torpid, supine, indifferent, uninterested, impassive. **Opposites:** energetic.

literal ADJ = **word-for-word**, verbatim, line-for-line, exact, precise, faithful, close, strict, undeviating, true, accurate.

literary ADJ **1** = **well read**, widely read, educated, well educated, scholarly, learned, intellectual, cultured, erudite, bookish, studious, lettered. **2** = **formal**, poetic.

literate ADJ **1** = **able to read and write**, educated, schooled. **2** = **educated**, well educated, well read, scholarly, learned, intellectual, erudite, cultured, cultivated, knowledgeable, well informed. **3** = **well written**, stylish, polished, articulate, lucid, eloquent.

literature NOUN **1** = **written works**, writings, printed works, published works, letters. **2** = **printed matter**, brochure, leaflet, pamphlet, circular, information, data, facts; [inf] bumf.

lithe ADJ = **agile**, flexible, supple, limber, loose-limbed, pliant, pliable, lissom.

litigation NOUN = **lawsuit**, legal case, case, legal dispute, legal contest, legal action, legal proceedings, suit, suit at law.

litter NOUN **1** = **rubbish**, debris, refuse, junk, odds and ends, fragments, detritus, flotsam; [N. Amer.] trash, garbage. **2** = **brood**, young, offspring, progeny,

little

family. **3** = **stretcher**, portable bed/couch, palanquin.

▶ VERB = **make untidy**, mess up, make a mess of, clutter up, throw into disorder, disarrange; [inf] make a shambles of.

little ADJ **1** = **small**, short, slight, petite, tiny, wee, miniature, mini, diminutive, minute, infinitesimal, microscopic, minuscule, young, dwarf, midget, pygmy, bantam; [inf] teeny, teeny-weeny, pint-sized.
2 = **unimportant**, insignificant, minor, trivial, trifling, petty, paltry, inconsequential, negligible, nugatory.
3 = **hardly any**, small, scant, meagre, skimpy, sparse, insufficient, exiguous; [inf] piddling.
Opposites: big, important.

▶ ADV = **hardly**, barely, scarcely, not much, only slightly, only just.

liturgy NOUN = **ritual**, worship, service, ceremony, rite, observance, celebration,

office, sacrament.

live ADJ **1** = **alive**, living, having life, breathing, animate, vital, existing, existent; [inf] in the land of the living. **2** = **not prerecorded**, unedited, with an audience.
3 = **charged**, connected, active, switched on.
4 = **current**, topical, active, prevalent, important, of interest, lively, vital, pressing, burning, pertinent, controversial, debatable, unsettled.
Opposites: dead.

livelihood NOUN = **living**, subsistence, means of support, income, keep, maintenance, sustenance, upkeep, work, employment, occupation, trade, profession, career.

lively ADJ **1** = **full of life**, active, animated, energetic, alive, vigorous, alert, spirited, high-spirited, vivacious, enthusiastic, keen, cheerful, buoyant, sparkling, bouncy, perky, sprightly, spry, frisky,

loan

agile, nimble; [inf] chirpy, chipper, peppy. **2 = brisk**, quick, rapid, swift, speedy, vigorous.
3 = animated, spirited, stimulating, heated, enthusiastic, forceful.
4 = busy, crowded, bustling, hectic, swarming, teeming, astir, buzzing, thronging.
Opposites: apathetic.

liven
■ **liven up = enliven**, put some life into, brighten up, cheer up, perk up, put some spark into, add some zest to, give a boost to, animate, vitalize, vivify; [inf] pep up; [Brit. inf] hot up.

living ADJ **= alive**, live, having life, breathing, animate, vital, existing, existent; [inf] in the land of the living.
▶ NOUN **= livelihood**, subsistence, means of support, income, keep, maintenance, sustenance, upkeep, job, work, employment, occupation.

load NOUN **1 = cargo**, freight, charge, burden, lading, contents, consignment, shipment, lorryload, shipload, containerload, busload.
2 = burden, onus, weight, responsibility, duty, charge, obligation, tax, strain, trouble, worry, encumbrance, affliction, oppression, handicap, trial, tribulation, cross, millstone, albatross, incubus.
▶ VERB **1 = fill**, fill up, lade, freight, charge, pack, pile, heap, stack, stuff, cram. **2 = burden**, weigh down, weight, saddle, charge, tax, strain, encumber, hamper, handicap, overburden, overwhelm, oppress, trouble, worry. **3 = prime**, charge, fill. **4 = weight**, add weight to, bias, rig.

loaf VERB **= laze**, lounge, do nothing, idle, lie around, hang about, waste time, fritter away time, take things easy, twiddle one's thumbs, sit on one's hands.

loan NOUN **= advance**, credit, mortgage.

▶ VERB = **lend**, advance, give credit, give on loan, let out.

loath ADJ = **reluctant**, unwilling, disinclined, not in the mood, against, averse, opposed, resisting.
Opposites: eager.

loathe VERB = **hate**, detest, abhor, despise, abominate, have an aversion to, not be able to bear, dislike, shrink from, recoil from, feel repugnance towards, be unable to stomach, execrate.
Opposites: like, love.

loathing NOUN = **hatred**, hate, detestation, abhorrence, aversion, abomination, repugnance, disgust, revulsion, odium, antipathy, dislike, ill will, enmity, execration.

loathsome ADJ = **hateful**, detestable, abhorrent, odious, repugnant, disgusting, repulsive, revolting, nauseating, abominable, vile, nasty, obnoxious, horrible, offensive, disagreeable, despicable, contemptible, reprehensible, execrable; [inf] yucky.

local NOUN 1 = **local person**, native, inhabitant, resident, parishioner. 2 = **bar**, inn, tavern; [Brit.] = **pub**, public house; [inf] watering hole; [Brit. inf] boozer.

locale NOUN = **place**, site, spot, position, location, venue, area, neighbourhood, locality, setting, scene.

locality NOUN 1 = **vicinity**, surrounding area, area, neighbourhood, district, region, environs, locale. 2 = **location**, position, place, whereabouts, bearings; [technical] locus.

localize VERB = **confine**, restrict, contain, limit, circumscribe, delimit.

locate VERB 1 = **find**, find out, discover, identify, pinpoint, detect, uncover, track down, run to earth, unearth, hit upon, come across, reveal, pin down. 2 = **situate**, site, position, place, put, build, establish, station, set, fix, settle.

location NOUN = **position**, place, situation, whereabouts, bearings, site, spot, point, scene, setting, venue, locale; [technical] locus.

lock VERB **1** = **bolt**, fasten, bar, secure, make secure, padlock. **2** = **jam**, become immovable, become rigid.
Opposites: unlock.
▶ NOUN = **bolt**, catch, fastener, clasp, bar, hasp.
■ **lock up** = see **imprison**.

locker NOUN = **cupboard**, compartment, cabinet, cubicle, storeroom, storage room.

lodge VERB **1** = **board**, have lodgings, put up, reside, dwell, sojourn, stop; [inf] have digs.
2 = **register**, submit, put forward, place, file, lay, put on record, record.
3 = **become fixed**, become embedded, become implanted, stick, become caught, come to rest.

lofty ADJ **1** = **towering**, soaring, tall, high, elevated, sky-high, sky-scraping. **2** = **arrogant**, haughty, proud, self-important, conceited, overweening, disdainful, supercilious, condescending, patronizing, lordly, snobbish, scornful, contemptuous, insulting, cavalier; [inf] high and mighty, stuck up, snooty, toffee-nosed, uppity.
3 = **noble**, exalted, grand, sublime, imposing, esoteric.
Opposites: low, modest, base.

log NOUN **1** = **block**, piece, chunk, billet, stump, trunk, branch, bole.
2 = **logbook**, record, register, journal, diary, daybook, chart, account, tally.

logic NOUN **1** = **line of reasoning**, reasoning, argument, argumentation.
2 = **reason**, sound judgement, judgement, wisdom, sense, good sense, common sense, rationale, relevance, coherence.

logical ADJ **1** = **reasoned**, well reasoned, rational,

sound, cogent, coherent, clear, consistent, relevant. **2 = most likely**, likeliest, plausible, obvious. **3 = reasoning**, thinking, straight-thinking, rational, consistent.
Opposites: illogical.

loiter VERB **= hang around/about**, linger, wait, skulk, loaf, lounge, idle, waste time, dawdle, take one's time, go at a snail's pace, dally, stroll, saunter, delay, loll.

lone ADJ **= single**, solitary, sole, unaccompanied.

lonely ADJ **1 = friendless**, companionless, lonesome, forlorn, forsaken, abandoned, rejected, isolated, outcast, sad, unhappy, despondent. **2 = desolate**, barren, isolated, out of the way, remote, secluded, off the beaten track, deserted, uninhabited, unfrequented, unpopulated, godforsaken.
Opposites: popular, crowded.

long¹ ADJ **1 = lengthy**, extended, extensive, stretched out, spread out. **2 = prolonged**, lengthy, protracted, extended, long-drawn-out, spun out, dragged out, interminable.
Opposites: short.

long²
▪ **long for = wish for**, desire, want, yearn for, crave, hunger for, thirst for, covet, lust after, hope for, dream of, pine for, eat one's heart out over, have a fancy for, hanker for/after; [inf] itch for, have a yen for.

longing NOUN **= wish**, desire, wanting, yearning, craving, hunger, thirst, covetousness, lust, hope, dream, aspiration, pining, fancy, urge, hankering; [inf] itch, yen.

look VERB **1 = see**, take a look, glance, fix one's gaze, focus, observe, view, regard, eye, take in, watch, examine, study, inspect, scan, scrutinize, survey, check, contemplate, consider, pay attention to, run the eyes over, peep, peek, glimpse, gaze, stare, gape, ogle; [inf] take a gander, have a squint, gawp, rubberneck; [Brit. inf] take a butcher's, take a dekko, take a shufti; [N. Amer. inf] eyeball. **2** = **seem**, seem to be, appear, appear to be, give every appearance/indication of being, look to be, strike someone as being. **3** = **face**, overlook, front, front on, give on to.

▸ NOUN **1** = **sight**, glance, observation, view, examination, study, inspection, scan, survey, peep, peek, glimpse, gaze, stare, gape, ogle; [inf] eyeful, gander, look-see, once-over, squint; [Brit. inf] butcher's, dekko, shufti. **2** = **expression**, face, countenance, features, mien.

▪ **look after** = **take care of**, care for, attend to, tend, mind, keep an eye on, watch, sit with, nurse, take charge of, supervise, protect, guard.

▪ **look down on** = **regard with contempt**, scorn, disdain, hold in disdain, sneer at, spurn, disparage, despise; [inf] look down one's nose at, turn up one's nose at.

▪ **look for** = **search for**, hunt for, seek, look around for, cast about for, forage for.

loom VERB **1** = **appear**, emerge, become visible, take shape, materialize, reveal itself. **2** = **be imminent**, impend, be close, be ominously close, threaten, menace.

loop NOUN = **coil**, hoop, noose, circle, ring, oval, spiral, curl, twirl, whorl, twist, convolution.

▸ VERB = **form a hoop with**, make a circle with, bend into spirals/whorls.

loophole NOUN = **let-out clause**, means of avoidance, means of escape, escape clause, escape route, ambiguity, omission.

loose ADJ **1** = **at large**, at liberty, free, on the loose, unconfined, untied, unchained, untethered, unsecured, unshackled, unfastened,

unrestricted, unbound, freed, let go, liberated, released, set loose.
2 = **wobbly**, not secure, insecure, rickety, unsteady, movable.
3 = **untied**, unpinned, hanging free, flowing, floppy. **4** = **loose-fitting**, easy-fitting, generously cut, slack, baggy, saggy, sloppy. **5** = **inexact**, imprecise, vague, indefinite, ill-defined, broad, general, non-specific.

■ **let loose** = **set free**, unloose, turn loose, set loose, untie, unchain, untether, unfasten, detach, unleash, let go, release, free, liberate.

loosen VERB **1** = **slacken**, slack, unstick, work loose, work free.
2 = **loose**, relax, slacken, weaken, lessen, moderate.
Opposites: tighten.

■ **loosen up** = **relax**, ease up/off; [inf] let up, hang loose, lighten up.

loot NOUN = **booty**, spoils, plunder, haul, stolen goods, pillage, prize;

[inf] swag, the goods, hot goods, boodle.
▶ VERB = **plunder**, pillage, rob, burgle, steal from, ransack, sack, maraud, ravage, despoil.

lop VERB = **cut off**, chop, chop off, hack off, prune, sever, clip, dock, crop, remove, detach.

lose VERB **1** = **mislay**, misplace, fail to keep/ retain, fail to keep sight of, drop, forget. **2** = **be deprived of**, suffer the loss of. **3** = **escape from**, evade, elude, dodge, give the slip to, shake off, throw off, throw off the scent, duck, get rid of.
4 = **suffer defeat**, be defeated, be the loser, be worsted, get/have the worst of it, be beaten, be conquered, be vanquished, be trounced, come off second-best, fail, come to grief, meet one's Waterloo; [inf] come a cropper.

loser NOUN = **runner-up**, also-ran, the defeated, the vanquished, failure, born loser; [inf] flop, dud, non-starter, no-hoper,

washout.
Opposites: winner, success.

loss NOUN **1** = **mislaying**, misplacement, dropping, forgetting. **2** = **losing**, deprivation, privation, forfeiture, bereavement, disappearance, waste, squandering, dissipation. **3** = **casualty**, fatality, dead, death toll, number killed. **4** = **deficit**, debit, debt, lack of profit, deficiency, losing, depletion.

lost ADJ **1** = **missing**, strayed, gone missing/astray, mislaid, misplaced, vanished, disappeared, forgotten. **2** = **stray**, astray, off course, off-track, disorientated, having lost one's bearings, adrift, going round in circles, at sea. **3** = **missed**, passed, forfeited, neglected, wasted, squandered, dissipated, gone by the board; [inf] down the drain.

lotion NOUN = **cream**, salve, ointment, moisturizer, balm, emollient, lubricant, unguent, liniment, embrocation, pomade, hand lotion, body lotion.

lottery NOUN = **draw**, raffle, sweepstake, game of chance, gamble, drawing of lots, bingo, tombola.

loud ADJ **1** = **blaring**, booming, noisy, deafening, resounding, reverberant, sonorous, stentorian, roaring, thunderous, tumultuous, clamorous, head-splitting, ear-splitting, ear-piercing, piercing, strident, harsh, raucous. **2** = **brash**, brazen, bold, loud-mouthed, vociferous, raucous, aggressive, pushy, coarse, crude, rough, crass, vulgar, brassy. **3** = **garish**, gaudy, flashy, bold, flamboyant, lurid, glaring, showy, obtrusive, vulgar, tawdry, tasteless, meretricious; [inf] flash, kitsch, camp, tacky; [Brit. inf] naff.
Opposites: quiet.

lounge VERB = **laze**, lie, lie around, recline, relax, take it easy, sprawl,

slump, loll, repose, loaf, idle, loiter, hang about, linger, skulk, waste time; [inf] hang out.
▶ NOUN = **sitting room**, drawing room, living room, parlour.

lousy ADJ **1 = very bad**, poor, incompetent, inadequate, unsatisfactory, inferior, careless, second-rate, terrible, miserable; [inf] rotten, no-good, poxy; [Brit. inf] duff.
2 = dirty, low, mean, base, despicable, contemptible, hateful, detestable, loathsome, vile, wicked, vicious.

lout NOUN = **boor**, oaf, dolt, churl, bumpkin, yahoo, barbarian; [inf] slob, clodhopper; [Brit. inf] yob, yobbo; [N. Amer. inf] lummox.

lovable ADJ = **adorable**, dear, sweet, cute, charming, lovely, likeable, attractive, delightful, captivating, enchanting, engaging, bewitching, pleasing, appealing, winsome, winning, endearing, warm-hearted, cuddly.
Opposites: hateful, loathsome.

love VERB **1 = be in love with**, be fond of, feel affection for, be attracted to, be attached to, care fore, hold dear, adore, think the world of, dote on, worship, idolize, treasure, prize, cherish, be devoted to, desire, want, be infatuated with, lust after, long for, yearn for, adulate; [inf] have a crush on, lech after, have the hots for, be soft on; [Brit. inf] fancy. **2 = like**, have a liking for, have a weakness for, be partial to, have a soft spot for, be addicted to, enjoy, find enjoyment in, relish, savour, appreciate, take pleasure in, delight in; [inf] get a kick out of, have a thing about.
Opposites: hate.
▶ NOUN **1 = affection**, fondness, care, concern, attachment, regard, warmth, intimacy, devotion, adoration, passion, ardour, desire, lust, yearning,

infatuation, adulation.
2 = liking for, weakness for, partiality for, enjoyment of, appreciation of, delight in, relish, passion for.
3 = beloved, loved one, true love, love of one's life, dear, dearest, dear one, darling, sweetheart, sweet, sweet one, angel, lover, inamorato/inamorata.

love affair NOUN **= affair**, romance, relationship, liaison, amour, intrigue, affair of the heart, affaire de cœur.

lovely ADJ **1 = beautiful**, pretty, attractive, good-looking, glamorous, handsome, sweet, fair, charming, adorable, enchanting, engaging, bewitching, winsome, seductive, ravishing; [archaic] comely.
2 = delightful, pleasant, nice, agreeable, pleasing, marvellous, wonderful; [inf] fabulous, terrific.
Opposites: ugly, horrible.

lover NOUN **1 = boyfriend**, girlfriend, mistress, lady-love, other man, other woman, beau, loved one, beloved, sweetheart, inamorato/inamorata; [inf] bit on the side, bit of fluff, toy boy, fancy man, fancy woman; [archaic] paramour.
2 = admirer, devotee, fan, enthusiast, aficionado; [inf] buff, freak.

loving ADJ **= affectionate**, fond, devoted, caring, adoring, doting, solicitous, demonstrative, tender, warm, warm-hearted, friendly, kind, sympathetic, charitable, cordial, amiable, amorous, ardent, passionate.

low ADJ **1 = short**, small, little, squat, stubby, stunted, truncated, dwarfish, knee-high.
2 = sparse, meagre, scarce, scanty, scant, few, little, deficient, inadequate, paltry, measly, trifling, reduced, depleted, diminished.
3 = depressed, dejected, despondent, disheartened, downhearted, downcast, gloomy, glum, unhappy,

sad, miserable, blue, morose, moody, heavy-hearted, forlorn; [inf] fed up, down in the mouth, down in the dumps; [Brit. inf] brassed off, cheesed off. **4 = low-grade**, inferior, substandard, below par, second-rate, deficient, defective, wanting, lacking, inadequate, mediocre, unacceptable, worthless. **5 = unfavourable**, poor, bad, adverse, hostile, negative.

lower[1] ADJ **1 = lesser**, lower-level, lower-grade, subordinate, junior, inferior, minor, secondary. **2 = cheaper**, reduced, decreased, lessened, cut, slashed, curtailed, pruned.
Opposites: higher.

lower[2] VERB **1 = let down**, take down, haul down, drop, let fall, let sink.
2 = soften, quieten, hush, tone down, muffle, turn down, mute. **3 = degrade**, debase, demean, downgrade, discredit, devalue, dishonour, disgrace, belittle,

humble, humiliate, disparage. **4 = reduce**, bring down, decrease, lessen, cut, slash, curtail, prune. **5 = abate**, die down, subside, let up, moderate, slacken, dwindle, lessen, ebb, fade away, wane, taper off, lull.
Opposites: raise.

lowly ADJ **1 = humble**, low-born, low-ranking, plebeian, peasant, poor, common, ordinary, inferior, subordinate.
2 = ordinary, simple, plain, commonplace, run-of-the-mill, modest, unambitious, unpretentious, unaspiring.
Opposites: aristocratic, exalted.

loyal ADJ **= faithful**, true, true-hearted, tried and true, trusted, trustworthy, trusty, true-blue, steadfast, staunch, dependable, reliable, devoted, dutiful, patriotic, constant, unchanging, unwavering, unswerving, firm, stable.

Opposites: disloyal, treacherous.

loyalty NOUN
= **faithfulness**, fidelity, allegiance, trueness, true-heartedness, trustiness, trustworthiness, steadfastness, staunchness, dependability, reliability, devotion, duty, patriotism, constancy, stability; [historical] fealty.
Opposites: disloyalty, treachery.

lucid ADJ **1** = **clear**, clear-cut, crystal-clear, comprehensible, intelligible, understandable, plain, simple, direct, straightforward, graphic, explicit. **2** = **sane**, rational, in one's right mind, in possession of one's faculties, of sound mind, compos mentis, sensible, clear-headed.
Opposites: confusing.

luck NOUN **1** = **fate**, fortune, destiny, chance, fortuity, accident, hazard, serendipity. **2** = **good luck**, good fortune, success, prosperity, advantage, advantageousness, felicity; [inf] lucky break.

lucky ADJ **1** = **fortunate**, blessed with good luck, favoured, born under a lucky star, charmed, successful, prosperous, happy, advantaged.
2 = **fortuitous**, fortunate, providential, advantageous, timely, opportune, expedient, auspicious, propitious.
Opposites: unlucky.

lucrative ADJ = **profitable**, profit-making, moneymaking, paying, high-income, well paid, high-paying, gainful, remunerative, productive, fat, fruitful, rewarding, worthwhile.
Opposites: unprofitable.

ludicrous ADJ = **absurd**, ridiculous, laughable, risible, derisible, comic, comical, farcical, silly, crazy, zany, nonsensical, odd, outlandish, eccentric, incongruous, preposterous.
Opposites: sensible.

lull VERB = **soothe**, quiet, hush, silence, calm, still, quell, assuage, allay, ease, alleviate, pacify.
▶ NOUN = **respite**, interval, break, hiatus, let-up, calm, calmness, stillness, quiet, quietness, tranquillity, silence, hush.

lumber VERB = **clump**, stump, plod, trudge, stamp, shuffle, shamble, stumble, waddle, lump along.

lumbering ADJ = **awkward**, clumsy, heavy-footed, blundering, bumbling, inept, maladroit, ungainly, like a bull in a china shop, ungraceful, lumpish, ponderous; [inf] clodhopping.
Opposites: graceful, agile.

luminous ADJ = **illuminated**, shining, bright, brilliant, radiant, dazzling, glowing, effulgent, luminescent, phosphorescent, vivid, resplendent.

lump NOUN 1 = **chunk**, wedge, hunk, piece, mass, cake, nugget, ball, dab, pat, clod, gobbet, wad, clump, cluster, mound; [Brit. inf] gob.
2 = **bump**, swelling, bruise, bulge, protuberance, growth, carbuncle, tumour, tumescence, node.

lunacy NOUN = **insanity**, madness, mental illness/ derangement, dementia, dementedness, loss of reason, unsoundness of mind, mania, frenzy, psychosis; [inf] craziness.
Opposites: sanity.

lunatic NOUN = **maniac**, madman, madwoman, imbecile, idiot, psychopath; [inf] loony, nut, nutcase, head case, headbanger, psycho; [Brit. inf] nutter; [N. Amer. inf] screwball.

lunge VERB 1 = **spring**, jump, leap, bound, dash, charge, pounce, dive.
2 = **stab**, jab, poke, thrust at, pitch into, lash out at, take a swing at, aim a blow at; [inf] take a swipe at.

lurch VERB = **stagger**, sway, reel, weave, stumble, totter.

lure VERB = **entice**, cajole, attract, induce, inveigle, decoy, draw, lead, allure, tempt, seduce, beguile, ensnare.

lurid ADJ **1** = **brilliant**, glaring, flaming, dazzling, glowing, intense, vivid, showy, gaudy. **2** = **sensational**, melodramatic, exaggerated, extravagant, graphic, explicit, unrestrained, shocking, startling.
Opposites: muted, restrained.

lurk VERB = **skulk**, lie in wait, lie low, hide, conceal oneself, take cover, crouch, sneak, slink, prowl, steal, tiptoe.

luscious ADJ = **juicy**, sweet, succulent, mouth-watering, tasty, appetizing, delectable, palatable, toothsome, nectar-like; [inf] scrumptious, yummy.

lush ADJ **1** = **luxuriant**, abundant, profuse, exuberant, dense, thick, riotous, overgrown, prolific, rank, flourishing, verdant, green.

2 = **luxurious**, sumptuous, grand, palatial, opulent, lavish, elaborate, extravagant; [inf] plush, ritzy.

lustful ADJ = **lecherous**, lascivious, lewd, libidinous, licentious, salacious, prurient, concupiscent, wanton, unchaste, hot-blooded, passionate, sensual, sexy; [inf] horny; [Brit. inf] randy.
Opposites: chaste.

lusty ADJ **1** = **healthy**, strong, vigorous, robust, hale and hearty, hearty, energetic, lively, blooming, rugged, sturdy, tough, stalwart, brawny, hefty, husky, burly, solidly built, powerful, virile, red-blooded. **2** = **loud**, vigorous, hearty, powerful, forceful.

luxuriant ADJ **1** = **lush**, abundant, profuse, exuberant, dense, thick, riotous, overgrown, prolific, teeming, verdant. **2** = **ornate**, elaborate, fancy, adorned, decorated, embellished,

embroidered,
extravagant, flamboyant,
ostentatious, showy,
baroque, rococo.

luxurious ADJ = **opulent**,
affluent, sumptuous,
expensive, rich, costly,
de luxe, lush, grand,
splendid, magnificent,
lavish, well appointed,
comfortable, extravagant,
ornate, fancy; [inf] plush,
ritzy, swanky; [Brit.
inf] posh.
Opposites: spartan.

luxury NOUN
1 = **luxuriousness**,
opulence, affluence,
sumptuousness,
grandeur, splendour,
magnificence, lavishness,
lap of luxury, bed of
roses. **2** = **extra**, non-
essential, frill,
extravagance,
indulgence, treat,
refinement.

Opposites: simplicity,
necessity.

lying NOUN
= **untruthfulness**,
fabrication, fibbing,
perjury, falseness, falsity,
dishonesty, mendacity,
storytelling,
dissimulation,
dissembling,
prevarication, deceit,
guile; [inf] crookedness.
▶ ADJ = **untruthful**,
fabricating, false,
dishonest, mendacious,
dissimulating,
dissembling,
prevaricating, deceitful,
guileful, double-dealing,
two-faced; [inf] crooked.
Opposites: truthful.

lyrical ADJ = **rhapsodic**,
effusive, rapturous,
ecstatic, euphoric, carried
away, emotional,
impassioned.
Opposites: unenthusiastic.

Mm

macabre ADJ = **gruesome**, grisly, grim, gory, morbid, ghastly, hideous, horrific, horrible, horrifying, horrendous, frightening, frightful, fearsome, shocking, dreadful.

machine NOUN = **appliance**, apparatus, instrument, tool, device, contraption, gadget, mechanism, engine, motor, vehicle, car, bicycle, motor cycle, aeroplane.

machismo NOUN = **masculinity**, manliness, virility, toughness, male chauvinism, sexism.

mad ADJ **1** = **insane**, deranged, crazy, demented, of unsound mind, crazed, lunatic, non compos mentis, unbalanced, unhinged, unstable, distracted, manic, frenzied, raving, distraught, frantic, hysterical, delirious, psychotic; [inf] not quite right, mad as a hatter, mad as a March hare, foaming at the mouth, off one's head, out of one's mind, off one's nut, nuts, nutty, off one's rocker, round the bend, raving mad, batty, bonkers, crackpot, cuckoo, loopy, loony, bananas, loco, dippy, screwy, with a screw loose, off the wall, not all there, not right upstairs; [Brit. inf] barmy, crackers, round the twist, not the full shilling, off one's trolley. **2** = *See* **angry**. **3** = **foolish**, insane, stupid, lunatic, foolhardy, idiotic, crackbrained, irrational, unreasonable, illogical,

senseless, nonsensical, absurd, impractical, silly, inane, asinine, ludicrous, wild, unwise, imprudent, preposterous. **4** = *see* **enthusiastic**.
Opposites: sane, sensible.

madden VERB = **anger**, infuriate, enrage, incense, exasperate, irritate, inflame, annoy, provoke, upset, agitate, vex, irk, pique, gall, make someone's hackles rise, make someone's blood boil; [inf] make someone see red, get someone's back up.

madman NOUN = **maniac**, lunatic, psychopath; [inf] loony, nut, nutcase, head case, headbanger, psycho; [Brit. inf] nutter; [N. Amer. inf] screwball.

madness NOUN = **insanity**, craziness, dementia, mental illness, derangement, dementedness, instability of mind, unsoundness of mind, lunacy, distraction, mania, frenzy, psychosis.
Opposites: sanity, calm.

magazine NOUN = **periodical**, journal, publication, supplement, colour supplement; [inf] glossy.

magic NOUN **1** = **sorcery**, witchcraft, wizardry, enchantment, spell-working, necromancy, the supernatural, occultism, the occult, black magic, black art, voodoo, hoodoo, thaumaturgy. **2** = **sleight of hand**, legerdemain, conjuring, illusion, prestidigitation, deception, trickery, juggling.
▶ ADJ **1** = **magical**, enchanting, entrancing, spellbinding, fascinating, captivating, charming, glamorous, magnetic, irresistible, hypnotic.
2 = **marvellous**, wonderful, excellent; [inf] terrific, fab; [Brit. inf] brilliant, brill.

magician NOUN = **sorcerer**, sorceress, witch, wizard, warlock, enchanter, enchantress, spell-worker, spell-caster, necromancer, thaumaturge.

magnanimity NOUN
= **generosity**,
charitableness, charity,
benevolence,
beneficence, open-
handedness, big-
heartedness, kindness,
munificence,
bountifulness, largesse,
altruism, philanthropy,
unselfishness,
selflessness, self-sacrifice,
mercy, leniency.
Opposites: meanness,
selfishness.

magnanimous ADJ
= **generous**, charitable,
benevolent, beneficent,
open-handed, big-
hearted, great-hearted,
kind, kindly, munificent,
bountiful, liberal,
altruistic, philanthropic,
noble, unselfish, selfless,
self-sacrificing,
ungrudging, unstinting,
forgiving, merciful,
lenient, indulgent.
Opposites: mean.

magnificent ADJ
1 = **splendid**, resplendent,
grand, grandiose,
impressive, imposing,
striking, glorious, superb,
majestic, august, noble,
stately, exalted, awe-
inspiring, royal, regal,
kingly, princely,
sumptuous, opulent,
luxurious, lavish, rich,
brilliant, radiant, elegant,
gorgeous; [inf] ritzy; [Brit.
inf] posh. 2 = **excellent**,
masterly, skilful,
virtuoso, splendid,
impressive, fine,
marvellous, wonderful.
Opposites: ordinary, poor.

magnify VERB 1 = **augment**,
enlarge, expand, amplify,
intensify, heighten,
deepen, broaden, widen,
dilate, boost, enhance.
2 = **exaggerate**, overstate,
overdo, overemphasize,
overplay, dramatize,
colour, embroider,
embellish, enhance,
inflate, make a mountain
out of a molehill.
Opposites: minimize.

magnitude NOUN = **size**,
extent, measure,
proportions, dimensions,
volume, weight,
quantity, mass, bulk,
amplitude, capacity.

mail NOUN = **post**, letters,
packages, parcels,

correspondence.

main ADJ = **head**, chief, principal, leading, foremost, most important, central, prime, premier, primary, supreme, predominant, pre-eminent, paramount, cardinal, crucial, vital, critical, pivotal, urgent. **Opposites:** minor.

mainly ADV = **for the most part**, mostly, in the main, on the whole, largely, by and large, to a large extent, to a great degree, predominantly, chiefly, principally, substantially, overall, in general, generally, usually, commonly, as a rule.

maintain VERB
1 = **continue**, keep going, keep up, keep alive, keep in existence, carry on, preserve, conserve, prolong, perpetuate, sustain. 2 = **keep in good condition**, keep in repair, keep up, conserve, preserve, keep intact, care for, take good care of, look after. 3 = **support**, provide for, keep, finance, feed, nurture, nourish, sustain.
4 = **insist on**, hold to, declare, assert, state, announce, affirm, avow, profess, claim, allege, contend; [formal] aver.

maintenance NOUN
1 = **upkeep**, repairs, preservation, conservation, care.
2 = **alimony**, support, allowance, keep, upkeep, subsistence.

majestic ADJ = **regal**, royal, kingly, queenly, princely, imperial, noble, lordly, august, exalted, awesome, elevated, lofty, stately, dignified, distinguished, magnificent, grand, splendid, resplendent, glorious, impressive, imposing, marvellous, superb, proud.

major ADJ 1 = **greatest**, best, most important, leading, foremost, chief, main, outstanding, first-rate, notable, eminent, pre-eminent, supreme.
2 = **important**, significant, crucial, vital, great, weighty, paramount,

utmost, prime.
3 = **serious**, radical, complicated.
Opposites: minor.

majority NOUN **1** = **larger part/number**, greater part/number, most, more than half, bulk, mass, main body, preponderance, lion's share. **2** = **legal age**, coming-of-age, seniority, adulthood, manhood, womanhood, maturity, age of consent.
Opposites: minority.

make VERB **1** = **build**, construct, assemble, put together, put up, erect, manufacture, produce, fabricate, create, form, fashion, model, mould, shape, forge. **2** = **force to**, compel to, coerce into, press into, drive into, pressure into, pressurize into, oblige to, require to, prevail upon to, dragoon into, impel to, constrain to, urge to; [inf] railroad into, put the heat on, put the screws on, use strong-arm tactics on. **3** = **cause**, create, give rise to, produce, bring about, generate, engender, occasion, effect. **4** = **create**, appoint, designate, name, nominate, select, elect, vote in, install, invest, ordain, assign. **5** = **gain**, acquire, obtain, get, realize, secure, win, earn, net, gross, clear, bring in, take home, pocket. **6** = **prepare**, get ready, put together, concoct, cook; [inf] whip up. **7** = **come to**, add up to, total, amount to. **8** = **give**, deliver, utter, give voice to, enunciate, recite, pronounce. **9** = **be**, act as, serve as, constitute, perform the function of, play the part of, represent, embody.
▸ NOUN = **brand**, label, sort, type, variety, style, mark, marque.

make-believe NOUN = **pretence**, fantasy, daydreaming, dreaming, fabrication, play-acting, charade, masquerade.
▸ ADJ = **pretended**, feigned, made up, fantasy, dream, imagined, imaginary,

unreal, fictitious, mock, sham, pretend.

maker NOUN
= **manufacturer**, builder, constructor, producer, creator, fabricator, author, architect, framer.

makeshift ADJ = **stopgap**, make-do, provisional, temporary, rough and ready, substitute, improvised, standby, jerry-built, thrown together.

malice NOUN
= **malevolence**, maliciousness, malignity, malignancy, evil intentions, ill will, ill feeling, animosity, animus, hostility, enmity, bad blood, hatred, hate, spite, spitefulness, vindictiveness, rancour, bitterness, grudge, venom, spleen, defamation;
[inf] bitchiness, cattiness.
Opposites: benevolence.

malicious ADJ
= **malevolent**, malign, malignant, evil, evil-intentioned, ill-natured, hostile, spiteful, baleful, vindictive, rancorous, bitter, venomous, pernicious, hurtful, destructive, defamatory;
[inf] bitchy, catty.
Opposites: friendly.

malign VERB = **slander**, libel, defame, smear, blacken someone's name/character, vilify, speak ill of, spread lies about, cast aspersions on, misrepresent, traduce, denigrate;
[formal] calumniate.
Opposites: praise.

malnutrition NOUN
= **undernourishment**, lack of food, starvation, famine, anorexia.

maltreat VERB = **treat badly**, ill-treat, ill-use, mistreat, misuse, abuse, handle/treat roughly, bully, injure, harm, hurt, molest.

maltreatment NOUN = **ill-treatment**, ill use, mistreatment, abuse, rough handling, mishandling, manhandling, bullying, injury, harm.

manage VERB **1** = **be in charge of**, run, be head

of, head, direct, control,
preside over, lead,
govern, rule, command,
superintend, supervise,
oversee, administer,
organize, conduct,
handle, guide, be at the
helm of; [inf] head up.
2 = succeed in, contrive,
engineer, bring about/off,
achieve, accomplish,
effect. **3 = cope**, deal with
the situation, get along/
on, carry on, survive,
make do.

manageable ADJ **1 = easy**,
doable, practicable,
possible, feasible, viable.
2 = controllable,
governable, tractable,
pliant, compliant, docile,
accommodating,
amenable, yielding,
submissive.
Opposites: unmanageable.

management NOUN
1 = managers, employers,
owners, proprietors,
directors, board of
directors, board,
directorate, executives,
administration;
[inf] bosses, top brass.
2 = running, charge, care,
direction, leadership,

control, governing,
ruling, command,
superintendence,
supervision,
administration.

mandatory ADJ
= obligatory, compulsory,
binding, required,
requisite, essential,
imperative, necessary.
Opposites: voluntary.

mangle VERB **= mutilate**,
hack, cut about, lacerate,
maul, tear at, rend,
butcher, disfigure,
deform.

mangy ADJ **1 = scabby**,
scaly, diseased.
2 = shabby, moth-eaten,
worn, shoddy, dirty,
mean, squalid, filthy,
seedy; [Brit. inf] grotty.

manhandle VERB
1 = handle roughly, push,
pull, shove, maul,
mistreat, ill-treat, abuse,
injure, damage, beat,
batter; [inf] knock about,
rough up. **2 = heave**,
haul, push, shove, pull,
tug, manoeuvre;
[inf] hump.

mania NOUN **1 = frenzy**,
violence, wildness,
hysteria, raving,

derangement, dementia.
2 = **obsession**,
compulsion, fixation,
fetish, fascination,
preoccupation, passion,
enthusiasm, urge.

maniac NOUN = *see*
madman.

manifest ADJ = **obvious**,
clear, plain, apparent,
patent, noticeable,
perceptible, visible,
transparent, conspicuous,
unmistakable, distinct,
blatant, glaring.
Opposites: secret.
▶ VERB = *see* **show** VERB (**1, 3**).

manifestation NOUN
1 = **display**, show,
exhibition,
demonstration,
presentation, exposition,
illustration,
exemplification,
indication, declaration,
expression, profession.
2 = **evidence**, proof,
testimony,
substantiation, sign,
indication, mark,
symbol, token, symptom.

manifold ADJ
= **multifarious**, multiple,
numerous, many, several,
multitudinous, various.

manipulate VERB
1 = **handle**, wield, ply,
work. **2** = **influence**,
control, use to one's
advantage, exploit,
manoeuvre, direct, guide,
pull the strings.
3 = **juggle**, massage,
falsify, doctor, tamper
with, fiddle with, tinker
with.

manipulator NOUN
= **handler**, wielder,
operator.

mankind NOUN = **man**,
homo sapiens, the
human race, the human
species, humankind,
human beings, humans,
people.

manly ADJ = **masculine**,
all-male, macho, virile,
strong, robust, vigorous,
muscular, powerful, well
built, strapping, sturdy,
rugged, tough.
Opposites: effeminate.

manner NOUN **1** = **way**,
means, method, system,
approach, technique,
procedure, process,
methodology, routine,
practice, fashion, mode,
style, habit, custom.
2 = **air**, appearance,

demeanour, aspect, mien, bearing, deportment, cast, behaviour, conduct. **3 = kind**, sort, type, variety, form, nature, breed, brand, stamp, class, category.

mannerism NOUN = **habit**, characteristic, trait, idiosyncrasy, quirk, foible, peculiarity.

manoeuvre NOUN **1 = movement**, move, measure. **2 = trick**, stratagem, tactic, machination, manipulation, artifice, subterfuge, device, dodge, ploy, ruse, scheme, plan, plot, intrigue; [inf] wangle. ▸ VERB **1 = move**, work, negotiate, steer, guide, direct, manipulate. **2 = scheme**, intrigue, plot, use trickery/artifice, machinate; [inf] pull strings.

manufacture VERB = **make**, produce, mass-produce, build, construct, assemble, put together, create, fabricate, turn out, process, form, fashion, model, mould, shape, forge.

manufacturer NOUN = **maker**, producer, builder, constructor, creator, fabricator, factory owner, industrialist, captain of industry.

many ADJ = **a lot of**, lots of, numerous, innumerable, a large/great number of, countless, scores of, myriad, great quantities of, multitudinous, multiple, copious, abundant. **Opposites:** few.

mar VERB = **spoil**, detract from, impair, damage, ruin, wreck, disfigure, blemish, scar, deface, harm, hurt, injure, deform, mutilate, maim, mangle. **Opposites:** enhance.

marauder NOUN = **raider**, plunderer, pillager, looter, ravager, robber, pirate, freebooter.

march NOUN = **walk**, step, pace, stride, tramp, hike, demonstration, parade, procession; [inf] demo.

m

margin NOUN 1 = **edge**, side, verge, border, perimeter, boundary, limits, periphery, brim. 2 = **leeway**, latitude, scope, room, room for manoeuvre, space, allowance, extra, surplus.

marginal ADJ = **slight**, small, tiny, minute, low, minor, insignificant, minimal, negligible.

maritime ADJ = **naval**, marine, nautical, seafaring, seagoing.

mark NOUN 1 = **stain**, blemish, blot, smear, trace, spot, speck, dot, blotch, smudge, bruise, scratch, scar, dent, pit, pock, chip, notch, nick, line, score, cut, incision, gash; [inf] splotch. 2 = **marker**, guide, pointer, landmark, direction post, signpost, milestone, waymark. 3 = **sign**, symbol, indication, symptom, feature, token, badge, emblem, evidence, proof, clue, hint.
▶ VERB 1 = **stain**, smear, smudge, scratch, scar, dent, chip, notch, score, cut, gash. 2 = **put one's name on**, initial, label, tag, stamp, brand, earmark. 3 = **correct**, assess, evaluate, appraise, grade. 4 = **celebrate**, commemorate, honour, observe, recognize, acknowledge, solemnize.

marked ADJ = **pronounced**, decided, striking, clear, glaring, blatant, unmistakable, remarkable, prominent, signal, conspicuous, noticeable.
Opposites: inconspicuous.

maroon VERB = **abandon**, forsake, leave behind, desert, strand, leave stranded, leave isolated.

marriage NOUN 1 = **married state**, matrimony, holy matrimony, wedlock, conjugal bond, union, match. 2 = **marriage ceremony**, wedding, wedding ceremony, nuptials. 3 = **alliance**, union, merger, unification, amalgamation, combination, affiliation, association, connection, coupling; [inf] hook-up.

marry VERB = **be married**, wed, be wed, become man and wife, become espoused; [inf] tie the knot, walk down the aisle, take the plunge, get spliced, get hitched, get yoked.

marsh NOUN = **marshland**, bog, peat bog, swamp, swampland, morass, mire, quagmire, quag, slough, fen, fenland; [N. Amer.] bayou.

marshal VERB = **gather together**, assemble, collect, muster, draw up, line up, align, set/put in order, arrange, deploy, dispose.

martial ADJ = **militant**, warlike, combative, belligerent, bellicose, aggressive, pugnacious.

marvel NOUN = **wonder**, amazing thing, prodigy, sensation, spectacle, phenomenon, miracle.

■ **marvel at** = **be amazed by**, be filled with amazement at, be awed by, be full of wonder at, wonder at.

marvellous ADJ
1 = **amazing**, astounding, astonishing, awesome, breathtaking, sensational, remarkable, spectacular, stupendous, phenomenal, prodigious, miraculous, extraordinary; [poetic/literary] wondrous.
2 = **excellent**, splendid, wonderful, magnificent, superb, glorious, great; [inf] super, fantastic, terrific, fabulous, awesome, ace, mean, bad, wicked; [Brit. inf] smashing.

masculine ADJ = **male**, manly, manlike, virile, all-male, robust, vigorous, muscular, strapping, rugged, macho.
Opposites: feminine.

mash VERB = **crush**, pulp, purée, smash, squash, pound, beat.
▶ NOUN = **pulp**, mush, paste, purée, slush, pap.

mask NOUN = **disguise**, guise, concealment, cover, cover-up, cloak, camouflage, veil, screen, front, false front, facade, blind, semblance, false colours, pretence.

▶ VERB = **disguise**, hide, conceal, cover up, obscure, cloak, camouflage, veil, screen.

mass NOUN

1 = **concentration**, conglomeration, aggregation, assemblage, collection. 2 = **majority**, greater part, major part, most, bulk, main body, preponderance.

▶ ADJ = **wholesale**, universal, widespread, general, large-scale, extensive, pandemic, popular.

▶ VERB = **amass**, accumulate, assemble, gather, collect, draw together, join together.

massacre VERB = *see* **kill** (1).

massage VERB = **rub**, knead, pummel, manipulate.

master NOUN = **lord**, overlord, ruler, overseer, superintendent, director, manager, controller, governor, commander, captain, chief, head, headman, principal, owner, employer; [inf] boss, top dog, big cheese.

▶ VERB 1 = **conquer**, vanquish, defeat, overcome, overpower, subdue, subjugate, govern, quell, quash, suppress, control, curb, check, bridle, tame. 2 = **learn**, become proficient in, grasp; [inf] get the hang of, get clued up about.

masterful ADJ = **authoritative**, powerful, controlling, domineering, dictatorial, overbearing, overweening, imperious, peremptory, high-handed, arrogant, haughty.
Opposites: weak.

masterly ADJ = **expert**, adept, clever, skilful, deft, adroit, skilled, dexterous, accomplished, polished; [inf] ace.
Opposites: inept.

mastermind VERB = **direct**, manage, plan, organize, arrange, engineer, conceive, devise, forge, originate, initiate, think up, come up with; [inf] be the brains behind.

masterpiece NOUN
= **magnum opus**, masterwork, chef-d'œuvre, work of art, creation, pièce de resistance.

match VERB
1 = **complement**, blend with, harmonize with, go with, tone with, coordinate with, team with, tally with, correspond to, accord with. 2 = **be equal to**, be a match for, measure up to, rival, vie with, compete with, compare with. 3 = **pair up**, mate, couple, unite, join, combine, link, ally; [inf] hitch up, yoke.

matching ADJ
= **corresponding**, equivalent, parallel, analogous, complementary, the same, paired, twin, coupled, double, duplicate, identical, like. **Opposites:** different.

mate NOUN 1 = **friend**, companion, comrade, crony; [inf] pal, chum; [N. Amer. inf] buddy.

2 = **assistant**, helper, apprentice, subordinate.
▶ VERB = **breed**, copulate, couple.

material NOUN 1 = **matter**, substance, stuff, medium, constituent elements. 2 = **fabric**, cloth, stuff, textile. 3 = **data**, information, facts, facts and figures, evidence, details.
▶ ADJ = **corporeal**, physical, bodily, fleshly, tangible, substantial, concrete.

materialize VERB 1 = **come into being**, happen, occur, come about, take place; [poetic/literary] come to pass. 2 = **appear**, turn up, become visible, come into view, come into sight, show oneself/itself, come to light, emerge.

matrimonial ADJ
= **marital**, conjugal, connubial, nuptial, spousal.

matter NOUN 1 = **material**, substance, stuff. 2 = **affair**, business, proceeding, situation, circumstance, event, happening, occurrence, incident, occasion, experience.

m

3 = **subject**, topic, issue, question, point, case.

▶ VERB = **be of importance**, be of consequence, make a difference, signify, be relevant, carry weight, count.

mature ADJ **1** = **adult**, grown up, grown, fully grown, full-grown, of age. **2** = **ripe**, ripened, mellow, ready, seasoned.
Opposites: immature.

▶ VERB = **grow up**, develop fully, become adult, reach adulthood, come of age.

maverick NOUN = **nonconformist**, rebel, dissenter, dissident, individualist, bohemian, eccentric.
Opposites: conformist.

maxim NOUN = **aphorism**, proverb, adage, saw, saying, axiom, precept, epigram, gnome.

maximum NOUN = **most**, utmost, uttermost, upper limit, ceiling, top, summit, peak, apogee, acme.

▶ ADJ = **highest**, greatest, biggest, largest, topmost, most, utmost, supreme.

Opposites: minimum.

mayhem NOUN = **havoc**, disorder, confusion, chaos, bedlam.

meadow NOUN = **field**, grassland, pasture, paddock, lea.

meagre ADJ = **paltry**, sparse, scant, scanty, spare, inadequate, insufficient, insubstantial, skimpy, miserly, niggardly, pathetic; [inf] stingy.
Opposites: abundant.

mean[1] VERB **1** = **indicate**, signify, express, convey, denote, designate, stand for, represent, symbolize, portend, connote, imply, purport, suggest, allude to, intimate, hint at, insinuate, drive at. **2** = **intend**, have in mind, have in view, contemplate, set out, aim, aspire, desire, want, wish. **3** = **involve**, entail, lead to, result in, give rise to, bring about, cause.

mean[2] ADJ **1** = **miserly**, niggardly, parsimonious, close-fisted, penny-pinching, grasping,

greedy, avaricious, ungenerous, illiberal, close, near; [inf] stingy, tight, tight-fisted, mingy. **2 = nasty**, disagreeable, unpleasant, unfriendly, offensive, obnoxious, cross, ill-natured, bad-tempered, irritable, churlish, surly, cantankerous, crotchety, crabbed. **3 = low**, lowly, low-born, humble, modest, common, ordinary, base, proletarian, plebeian, obscure.
Opposites: generous, kind, noble.

meander VERB **= wind**, zigzag, snake, curve, turn, bend.

meaning NOUN
1 = definition, explanation, interpretation, elucidation, explication. **2 = significance**, point, value, worth, consequence, account.

meaningful ADJ
1 = significant, important, serious, sincere, in earnest. **2 = pointed**, significant, suggestive, eloquent, expressive, pregnant.
Opposites: meaningless.

meaningless ADJ
1 = senseless, unintelligible, incomprehensible, incoherent. **2 = pointless**, senseless, purposeless, motiveless, irrational. **3 = empty**, futile, pointless, aimless, valueless, worthless, trivial, insignificant.
Opposites: meaningful.

means PL NOUN **= way**, method, expedient, process, mode, manner, agency, medium, instrument, channel, avenue, course.

meanwhile ADV **1 = in the meantime**, for the time being, for now, for the moment, in the interim, in the interval. **2 = at the same time**, simultaneously, concurrently, coincidentally.

measure NOUN **1 = size**, dimension, proportions, magnitude, amplitude, mass, bulk, volume, capacity, quantity,

weight. **2** = **rule**, ruler, tape measure, gauge, meter, scale, level, yardstick. **3** = **share**, portion, division, allotment, part, piece, quota, lot, ration, percentage; [inf] rake-off. **4** = **action**, act, course, course of action, deed, proceeding, procedure, step, means, expedient.
▶ VERB = **calculate**, compute, estimate, quantify, weigh, size, evaluate, rate, assess, appraise, gauge, measure out, determine, judge, survey.

measured ADJ = **carefully chosen**, selected with care, well thought out, studied, calculated, planned, considered, deliberate, reasoned.

mechanical ADJ
1 = **automated**, automatic, machine-driven, motor-driven, power-driven.
2 = **automatic**, unthinking, unconscious, unfeeling, unemotional, cold, involuntary, instinctive, routine, habitual.
Opposites: manual.

mechanism NOUN
1 = **machine**, apparatus, appliance, tool, device, instrument, contraption, contrivance. **2** = **process**, procedure, system, operation, method, means, medium, agency, channel.

meddle VERB = **interfere**, butt in, intrude, intervene, interlope, pry, nose; [inf] stick one's nose in, horn in, snoop.

mediate VERB = **arbitrate**, negotiate, conciliate, intervene, intercede, interpose, moderate, umpire, referee, act as peacemaker, reconcile, restore harmony, make peace, bring to terms, step in.

mediator NOUN
= **arbitrator**, arbiter, negotiator, go-between, middleman, intermediary, honest broker, peacemaker, intervenor, interceder, moderator, umpire, referee, judge, conciliator, reconciler.

medicinal ADJ = **medical**, therapeutic, curative,

healing, remedial, restorative, health-giving, analeptic.

medicine NOUN
1 = **medication**, medicament, drug, remedy, cure; [archaic] physic.
2 = **medical science**, practice of medicine, healing art.

mediocre ADJ
1 = **indifferent**, average, middle-of-the-road, middling, ordinary, commonplace, pedestrian, run-of-the-mill, tolerable, passable, adequate, uninspired, undistinguished, unexceptional; [inf] so-so, fair-to-middling, nothing to write home about, no great shakes. 2 = **inferior**, second-rate, second-class, low-grade, poor, shabby, minor.
Opposites: exceptional.

meditate VERB
= **contemplate**, think about/over, muse on/about, ponder on/over, consider, concentrate on, reflect on, deliberate about/on, ruminate about/on/over, brood over, mull over, be in a brown study over.

meditation NOUN
= **contemplation**, thought, musing, pondering, consideration, reflection, deliberation, rumination.

medium NOUN 1 = **median**, mid-point, middle, centre point, average, norm, standard, middle course, compromise, happy medium, golden mean. 2 = **means**, agency, channel, avenue, vehicle, organ, instrument.
▸ ADJ = **middle**, mean, medial, median, midway, midpoint, intermediate.

meek ADJ = **docile**, modest, humble, unassuming, unpretentious, submissive, yielding, unresisting, patient, long-suffering, forbearing, resigned, gentle, peaceful, compliant, acquiescent, deferential, weak, timid, frightened, spineless, spiritless; [inf] weak-kneed.
Opposites: assertive.

meet VERB **1 = encounter**, come face to face with, make contact with, run into, run across, come across, come upon, chance upon, happen upon, light upon; [inf] bump into. **2 = come together**, abut, adjoin, join, link up, unite, connect, touch, converge, intersect. **3 = gather**, assemble, come together, foregather, congregate, convene, muster, rally; [formal] convoke.
Opposites: avoid.

meeting NOUN **1 = encounter**, contact, assignation, rendezvous; [poetic/literary] tryst. **2 = gathering**, assembly, conference, congregation, convention, convocation, conclave; [inf] get-together. **3 = abutment**, junction, conjunction, union, convergence, confluence, concourse, intersection. **4 = meet**, race meeting, athletics meeting, sports meeting.

melancholy ADJ **= despondent**, dejected, depressed, down, downhearted, downcast, disconsolate, glum, gloomy, sunk in gloom, miserable, dismal, dispirited, low, in low spirits, in the doldrums, blue, mournful, lugubrious, woeful, woebegone, doleful, sorrowful, unhappy, heavy-hearted, low-spirited, sombre, pessimistic; [inf] down in the dumps, down in the mouth.
Opposites: cheerful.

mellifluous ADJ **= sweet**, sweet-sounding/toned, dulcet, honeyed, mellow, soft, soothing, smooth, silvery, euphonious, musical.

mellow ADJ **1 = mature**, well matured, soft, juicy, tender, luscious, sweet. **2 = gentle**, easy-going, pleasant, kindly, kind-hearted, amicable, amiable, good-natured, affable, gracious. **3 = genial**, jovial, jolly, cheerful, happy, merry.

melodious ADJ = **melodic**, musical, tuneful, harmonious, lyrical, dulcet, sweet, sweet-sounding, sweet-toned, silvery, silvery-toned, euphonious.
Opposites: discordant.

melodramatic ADJ = **theatrical**, stagy, overdramatic, histrionic, over-sensational, extravagant, exaggerated, overdone, overemotional; [inf] actressy, camp, hammy.

melody NOUN = **tune**, air, strain, music, refrain, theme, song.

melt VERB = **dissolve**, deliquesce, thaw, unfreeze, defrost, soften, fuse.

member NOUN
1 = **adherent**, associate, fellow. 2 = **organ**, limb, appendage, extremity.

memorable ADJ
= **unforgettable**, not to be forgotten, momentous, significant, historic, notable, noteworthy, important, consequential, remarkable, outstanding, extraordinary, striking, impressive, distinctive, distinguished.
Opposites: forgettable.

memorial NOUN
= **monument**, statue, plaque, shrine, tombstone.

memorize VERB = **commit to memory**, remember, learn by heart, get by heart, learn off, learn, learn by rote.

memory NOUN
1 = **recollection**, remembrance, powers of recall, recall, powers of retention, retention.
2 = **commemoration**, remembrance, honour, tribute.

menace NOUN = **threat**, danger, hazard, jeopardy.
▸ VERB = **threaten**, intimidate, frighten, scare, alarm, terrify, bully, browbeat, cow, terrorize.

mend VERB 1 = **repair**, fix, put back together, patch up, restore, rehabilitate, renew, renovate, make whole, make well, cure, heal. 2 = **get better**, recover, recuperate, improve, be well, be cured. **3** = **put right**, set straight, rectify, put in order, correct, amend, emend, improve.

menial ADJ = **lowly**, humble, low-grade, low-status, unskilled, routine, humdrum, boring, dull. **Opposites:** elevated.

▶ NOUN = **servant**, domestic, drudge, underling, lackey, flunkey; [Brit. inf] dogsbody, skivvy.

mentality NOUN **1** = **cast of mind**, frame of mind, turn of mind, way of thinking, mind, psychology, mental attitude, outlook, character, disposition, make-up. **2** = **intellect**, intellectual capabilities, intelligence, IQ, brainpower, brains, mind, comprehension, understanding; [inf] grey matter.

mention VERB **1** = **refer to**, allude to, touch on, speak briefly of, hint at. **2** = **say**, state, name, cite, quote, call attention to, adduce. **3** = **tell**, speak about/of, utter,

communicate, let someone know, disclose, divulge, breathe a word of, reveal, intimate, whisper; [inf] let on about.

▶ NOUN = **reference**, allusion, observation, remark, statement, announcement, indication.

mentor NOUN = **adviser**, counsellor, guide, guru, spiritual leader, confidant, teacher, tutor, coach, instructor.

mercenary ADJ = **money-oriented**, grasping, greedy, acquisitive, avaricious, covetous, bribable, venal; [inf] money-grubbing.

merchandise NOUN = **goods**, wares, stock, commodities, produce, vendibles.

merchant NOUN = **trader**, dealer, trafficker, wholesaler, broker, seller, salesman/woman/person, vendor, retailer, shopkeeper, distributor.

merciful ADJ = **lenient**, clement, compassionate, pitying, forgiving, forbearing, sparing,

humane, mild, soft-hearted, tender-hearted, kind, sympathetic, liberal, tolerant, generous, beneficent, benignant.
Opposites: merciless, cruel.

merciless ADJ
= **unmerciful**, ruthless, relentless, inexorable, harsh, pitiless, unforgiving, unsparing, unpitying, implacable, barbarous, inhumane, inhuman, hard-hearted, heartless, callous, cruel, unsympathetic, unfeeling, illiberal, intolerant, rigid, severe, stern.
Opposites: merciful, compassionate.

mercy NOUN = **leniency**, clemency, compassion, pity, charity, forgiveness, forbearance, quarter, humanity, humaneness, mildness, soft-heartedness, tender-heartedness, kindness, sympathy, liberality, tolerance, generosity, beneficence, benignancy.

Opposites: severity, cruelty.

mere ADJ = **nothing more than**, no better than, no more important than, just a, only a, pure and simple.

merge VERB 1 = **join together**, join forces, amalgamate, unite, combine, incorporate, coalesce, team up.
2 = **blend**, fuse, mingle, mix, intermix, homogenize.
Opposites: separate.

merit NOUN 1 = **excellence**, goodness, quality, worth, worthiness, value.
2 = **good point**, strong point, advantage, asset, plus.
▶ VERB = **deserve**, be deserving of, earn, be worthy of, be worth, be entitled to, have a right to, have a claim to, warrant, rate, incur.

merriment NOUN
= **cheerfulness**, gaiety, high-spiritedness, high spirits, buoyancy, carefreeness, levity, sportiveness, joy, joyfulness, joyousness,

jolliness, jollity,
rejoicing, conviviality,
festivity, merrymaking,
revelry, mirth, glee,
gleefulness, laughter,
hilarity, amusement, fun.
Opposites: misery.

merry ADJ = **cheerful**,
cheery, in good spirits,
high-spirited, light-
hearted, buoyant,
carefree, sportive, joyful,
joyous, rejoicing, jolly,
jocund, convivial, festive,
mirthful, gleeful, happy,
glad, laughing;
[dated] gay; [poetic/
literary] frolicsome.
Opposites: miserable.

mesh NOUN 1 = **netting**, net,
tracery, web, lattice,
latticework, lacework,
trellis, reticulation,
plexus. 2 = **tangle**,
entanglement, web,
snare, trap.
▶ VERB 1 = **be engaged**,
connect, interlock.
2 = **harmonize**, fit
together, go together,
coordinate, match, be on
the same wavelength,
dovetail.

mesmerize VERB
1 = **hypnotize**, put into a

trance, put under.
2 = **hold spellbound**,
spellbind, entrance,
enthral, bewitch,
captivate, enchant,
fascinate, grip,
magnetize, hypnotize.

mess NOUN 1 = **disorder**,
untidiness, disarray,
dirtiness, filthiness,
clutter, shambles, litter,
jumble, muddle, chaos,
confusion,
disorganization, turmoil.
2 = **plight**, predicament,
tight spot, tight corner,
difficulty, trouble,
quandary, dilemma,
muddle, mix-up,
confusion, imbroglio;
[inf] jam, fix, pickle, stew,
hole. 3 = **muddle**, bungle;
[inf] botch, screw-up; [Brit.
inf] cock-up.
▪ **mess up** 1 = **dirty**,
befoul, litter, pollute,
clutter up, disarrange,
throw into disorder,
dishevel; [poetic/
literary] besmirch.
2 = **bungle**, muff, make a
mess of, mar, spoil, ruin;
[inf] botch, make a hash
of, muck up, foul up,
screw up; [Brit. inf] cock

up, make a muck of.

message NOUN
1 = **communication**, piece of information, news, word, tidings, note, memorandum, letter, missive, bulletin, communiqué, dispatch, memo. 2 = **meaning**, import, idea, point, purport, intimation, theme, moral.

messenger NOUN
= **message-bearer**, courier, errand boy/girl, runner, envoy, emissary, agent, go-between, herald, harbinger.

messy ADJ = **untidy**, disordered, dirty, filthy, grubby, slovenly, cluttered, littered, muddled, in a muddle, chaotic, confused, disorganized, sloppy, in disarray, disarranged, dishevelled, unkempt; [Brit. inf] shambolic.
Opposites: orderly.

metamorphosis NOUN
= **transformation**, transfiguration, change, alteration, conversion, changeover, mutation, transmutation, sea change; [inf] transmogrification.

method NOUN
1 = **procedure**, technique, system, practice, modus operandi, process, approach, way, course of action, scheme, plan, rule, arrangement, form, style, manner, mode. 2 = **order**, orderliness, sense of order, organization, arrangement, structure, form, planning, plan, design, purpose, pattern, regularity.

methodical ADJ = **orderly**, well ordered, organized, systematic, structured, logical, well regulated, planned, efficient, businesslike.
Opposites: disorganized.

meticulous ADJ
= **conscientious**, careful, scrupulous, punctilious, painstaking, demanding, exacting, thorough, perfectionist, fastidious, particular.
Opposites: careless, slapdash.

microscopic ADJ
= **infinitesimal**,

minuscule, tiny, minute.
Opposites: massive.

middle ADJ = **mid**, mean,
medium, medial,
median, midway,
halfway, central,
equidistant,
intermediate,
intermediary.
▸ NOUN = **mean**, median,
mid-point, halfway
point, centre, dead
centre.

middling ADJ = **average**,
medium, ordinary, fair,
moderate, adequate,
passable, tolerable,
mediocre, indifferent,
run-of-the-mill,
unexceptional,
unremarkable; [inf] fair-
to-middling, so-so.

might NOUN = **force**, power,
strength, mightiness,
powerfulness,
forcefulness, potency,
toughness, robustness,
sturdiness, muscularity.

mighty ADJ 1 = **forceful**,
powerful, strong, potent,
tough, robust, sturdy,
muscular, strapping,
vigorous, energetic.
2 = **huge**, massive, vast,
enormous, colossal,
giant, gigantic,
monumental,
mountainous, towering.
Opposites: puny, tiny.

migrant ADJ = **migratory**,
wandering, drifting,
nomadic, itinerant,
peripatetic, vagrant.

mild ADJ 1 = **tender**, gentle,
soft, soft-hearted,
tender-hearted, sensitive,
sympathetic, warm,
compassionate, humane,
forgiving, conciliatory,
forbearing, placid, meek,
docile, calm, tranquil,
serene, peaceful,
peaceable, good-natured,
amiable, affable, genial,
easy, easy-going, mellow.
2 = **gentle**, soft, moderate,
warm, balmy. 3 = **bland**,
insipid, tasteless.
Opposites: cruel, harsh,
spicy.

milieu NOUN
= **environment**,
surroundings,
background, setting,
scene, location, sphere,
element.

militant ADJ = **aggressive**,
combative, pugnacious,
fighting, warring,
combating, contending,

embattled, in arms, belligerent, bellicose. **Opposites:** peaceful.

▶ NOUN = **activist**, extremist, partisan.

military ADJ = **army**, service, soldierly, soldier-like, armed, martial.

▶ NOUN = **army**, armed forces, services, militia, soldiery, navy, air force, marines.

militate

■ **militate against** = **operate against**, go against, count against, tell against, weigh against, be detrimental to, be disadvantageous to, be to the disfavour of, be counter to the interests of, conflict with the interests of.

milk VERB **1** = **draw**, draw off, express, siphon, tap, drain, extract. **2** = **exploit**, take advantage of, impose on, bleed, suck dry.

milky ADJ = **white**, milk-white, whitish, creamy, pearly, nacreous, ivory, alabaster, off-white, clouded, cloudy.

mill NOUN = **factory**, plant, foundry, works, workshop, shop, industrial centre.

▶ VERB = **grind**, pulverize, pound, crush, powder, crunch, granulate; [technical] comminute, triturate.

■ **mill about/around** = **move around**, wander around, amble, meander, crowd, swarm, throng.

mimic VERB **1** = **impersonate**, give an impersonation of, imitate, copy, ape, caricature, parody; [inf] take off. **2** = **resemble**, look like, have/take on the appearance of, echo, mirror, simulate.

▶ NOUN = **mimicker**, impersonator, impressionist, imitator, parodist, copyist, parrot, ape.

mince VERB = **chop/cut into tiny pieces**, grind, crumble, hash.

mind NOUN **1** = **brain**, head, seat of intellect, psyche, ego, subconscious. **2** = **brainpower**, powers of thought, intellect, intellectual capabilities, mentality, intelligence, powers of reasoning, brain, brains, wits, understanding, comprehension, sense, ratiocination; [inf] grey matter. **3 = opinion**, way of thinking, thoughts, outlook, view, viewpoint, point of view, belief, judgement, attitude, feeling, sentiment. **4 = genius**, intellect, intellectual, thinker; [inf] brain, egghead.

▶ VERB **1 = be offended by**, take offence at, object to, care about, be bothered by, be upset by, be affronted by, resent, dislike, disapprove of, look askance at. **2 = take heed of**, heed, pay heed to, pay attention to, attend to, concentrate on, listen to, note, mark, observe, respect, obey, follow, comply with, adhere to. **3 = look after**, take care of, attend to, tend, have charge of, keep an eye on, watch.

▪ **never mind = do not bother about**, pay no attention to, do not worry about, disregard, forget, do not take into consideration, do not give a second thought to.

mindful ADJ **= paying attention to**, heedful of, watchful of, careful of, wary of, chary of, cognizant of, aware of, conscious of, alert to, alive to, sensible of. **Opposites:** heedless.

mindless ADJ **= stupid**, foolish, senseless, witless, empty-headed, unintelligent, dull, slow-witted, obtuse; [inf] birdbrained, dumb, dopey, moronic. **Opposites:** intelligent.

mine NOUN **1 = colliery**, pit, quarry, lode, vein, deposit, coal mine. **2 = source**, reservoir, repository, store, storehouse, wealth.

▶ VERB **= excavate**, quarry for, dig for, dig up, extract, unearth.

mingle VERB **1 = mix**, blend, combine, compound, homogenize, merge, unite, join, amalgamate, fuse. **2 = circulate**, socialize,

hobnob, fraternize, meet people.
Opposites: separate.

miniature ADJ = **small-scale**, scaled down, mini, midget, baby, toy, pocket, dwarf; [inf] pint-sized.
Opposites: giant.

minimal ADJ = **minimum**, least, smallest, slightest, nominal, token.
Opposites: maximum.

minimize VERB **1** = **keep at/to a minimum**, reduce, decrease, curtail, cut back on, prune, slash.
2 = **belittle**, make light of, decry, discount, play down, deprecate, depreciate, underestimate, underrate.
Opposites: maximize, exaggerate.

minimum NOUN = **lowest level**, bottom level, bottom, depth, nadir, least, lowest, slightest.
▸ ADJ = **minimal**, lowest, smallest, littlest, least, least possible, slightest.
Opposites: maximum.

minion NOUN = **lackey**, flunkey, henchman, creature, toady, underling, hireling, servant, dependant, hanger-on, parasite.

minor ADJ = **lesser**, insignificant, unimportant, inconsequential, inferior, trivial, negligible, trifling, lightweight, subordinate.
Opposites: major.

mint NOUN = **fortune**, small fortune, vast sum, king's ransom; [inf] pile, stack, heap, packet, bundle.
▸ ADJ = **brand new**, as new, unused, perfect, unblemished, undamaged, fresh.
▸ VERB = **stamp**, punch, die, cast, strike, coin, make, manufacture, produce.

minute ADJ = **tiny**, minuscule, microscopic, miniature, diminutive, Lilliputian, little, small.
Opposites: gigantic, huge.

minutely ADV = **in detail**, exhaustively, meticulously, punctiliously, painstakingly, closely.

miracle NOUN = **wonder**, marvel, prodigy, phenomenon.

m

miraculous ADJ
= **supernatural**, fantastic, magical, inexplicable, unaccountable, preternatural, superhuman, thaumaturgic, phenomenal, prodigious, wonderful, remarkable; [poetic/literary] wondrous.

mire NOUN = **marsh**, bog, swamp, morass, quagmire, quag, slough, fen, fenland; [N. Amer.] bayou.
▸ VERB = **sink**, sink down, bog down, stick in the mud.

mirror VERB = **reflect**, imitate, emulate, simulate, copy, follow, mimic, echo, ape, parrot, impersonate.

mirth NOUN = **gaiety**, merriment, high spirits, cheerfulness, cheeriness, hilarity, glee, laughter, jocularity.

misapprehension NOUN = **misunderstanding**, misinterpretation, misconstruction, misreading, misjudgement, misconception, the wrong idea, a false impression, delusion.

misappropriate VERB = **embezzle**, steal, thieve, swindle, pocket, help oneself to; [Brit. inf] nick, pinch; [formal] peculate.

misbehave VERB = **behave badly**, be bad, be naughty, be disobedient, get up to mischief, misconduct oneself, be guilty of misconduct, be bad-mannered, show bad/poor manners, be rude, fool around; [inf] carry on, act up.

misbehaviour NOUN = **misconduct**, bad behaviour, disorderly conduct, badness, naughtiness, mischief, mischievousness, delinquency, misdeed, misdemeanour, bad/poor manners, rudeness; [inf] carrying on, acting up, shenanigans.

miscalculate VERB = **calculate wrongly**, make a mistake, go wrong, err, blunder, be wide of the mark; [inf] slip up, make a boo-boo; [Brit. inf] boob.

miscarriage NOUN
1 = **failure**, foundering, ruination, non-fulfilment, misfiring, breakdown, mismanagement, perversion, thwarting, frustration.
2 = **spontaneous abortion**, termination.

miscarry VERB **1** = **have a miscarriage**, abort, lose the baby. **2** = **go wrong**, go awry, go amiss, be unsuccessful, fail, misfire, founder, come to nothing, come to grief, meet with disaster, fall through, be ruined, fall flat.
Opposites: succeed.

miscellaneous ADJ
= **varied**, assorted, mixed, diverse, sundry, variegated, diversified, motley, multifarious, jumbled, confused, indiscriminate, heterogeneous.

miscellany NOUN
= **assortment**, mixture, mixed bag, variety, collection, medley, pot-pourri, conglomeration, jumble, confusion, mix,

mishmash, hotchpotch, hodgepodge, pastiche, patchwork, farrago, gallimaufry.

mischief NOUN
1 = **mischievousness**, naughtiness, badness, bad behaviour, misbehaviour, misconduct, pranks, wrongdoing, delinquency; [inf] monkey business, shenanigans.
2 = **harm**, hurt, injury, damage, disruption, trouble.

mischievous ADJ
1 = **naughty**, bad, badly behaved, misbehaving, disobedient, troublesome, vexatious, playful, rascally, roguish, delinquent; [poetic/literary] frolicsome.
2 = **playful**, teasing, impish, roguish, waggish, arch.
Opposites: well behaved.

misconception NOUN
= *see* **misapprehension**.

miserable ADJ
1 = **unhappy**, sorrowful, dejected, depressed, downcast, downhearted, down, despondent,

disconsolate, desolate,
wretched, glum, gloomy,
dismal, blue,
melancholy, low-spirited,
mournful, woeful,
woebegone, sad, doleful,
forlorn, crestfallen;
[inf] down in the mouth,
down in the dumps.
2 = **wretched**, mean, poor,
shabby, squalid, filthy,
foul, sordid, seedy,
dilapidated. **3** = **meagre**,
paltry, scanty, low, poor,
niggardly, pathetic.
4 = **unpleasant**,
disagreeable, displeasing,
uncomfortable, wet,
rainy, stormy.
Opposites: happy.

miserly ADJ = **mean**,
niggardly, parsimonious,
close-fisted, penny-
pinching, cheese-paring,
penurious, grasping,
greedy, avaricious,
ungenerous, illiberal,
close, near; [inf] stingy,
mingy, tight, tight-fisted,
money-grabbing; [N. Amer.
inf] cheap.
Opposites: generous.

misery NOUN **1** = **distress**,
wretchedness, hardship,
suffering, affliction,

anguish, torment,
torture, agony, pain,
discomfort, deprivation,
poverty, grief, sorrow,
heartbreak, despair,
depression, dejection,
desolation, gloom,
melancholy, woe,
sadness, unhappiness.
2 = **misfortune**, trouble,
adversity, affliction,
ordeal, pain, sorrow,
burden, load, blow, trial,
tribulation, woe,
torment, catastrophe,
calamity, disaster.
Opposites: happiness.

misfortune NOUN **1** = **bad
luck**, ill luck, ill fortune,
poor/hard luck, accident,
misadventure,
mischance. **2** = **mishap**,
trouble, setback, reverse,
adversity, misadventure,
blow, failure, accident,
disaster, tragedy,
affliction, sorrow, misery,
woe, trial, tribulation,
catastrophe, calamity.

misgiving NOUN = **qualm**,
doubt, reservation,
suspicion, apprehension,
unease, uncertainty.

misguided ADJ
= **mistaken**, deluded,

erroneous, fallacious, wrong, unwarranted, uncalled for, misplaced, ill-advised, unwise, injudicious, imprudent, foolish.

mishap NOUN = **accident**, trouble, setback, reverse, adversity, misadventure, misfortune, stroke of bad luck, blow, disaster, trial, tribulation, catastrophe, calamity.

mislay VERB = **lose**, misplace, lose track of, miss, be unable to find. **Opposites:** find.

mislead VERB = **misinform**, misdirect, delude, take in, deceive, fool, hoodwink, lead astray, throw off the scent, send on a wild-goose chase; [inf] lead up the garden path, take for a ride, pull the wool over someone's eyes.

misleading ADJ = *see* **deceptive**.

miss VERB 1 = **fail to attend**, be too late for, absent oneself from, skip, be absent from, play truant from, take French leave from. 2 = **fail to seize/**grasp, let slip, let go, pass up, overlook, disregard. 3 = **regret the absence/loss of**, feel the loss of, feel nostalgic for, long to see, long for, pine for, yearn for, ache for.

misshapen ADJ = **deformed**, malformed, ill-proportioned, misproportioned, twisted, distorted, contorted, warped, curved, crooked, wry, bent, hunchbacked.

missing ADJ = **lost**, mislaid, misplaced, nowhere to be found, absent, not present, gone, gone astray, unaccounted for. **Opposites:** present.

mission NOUN 1 = **assignment**, commission, task, job, errand, sortie, operation, work, chore, undertaking, duty, charge, trust. 2 = **vocation**, calling, pursuit, goal, aim, quest. 3 = **delegation**, deputation, commission, legation.

mistake NOUN = **error**, fault, inaccuracy, slip, blunder, miscalculation, misunderstanding, oversight, gaffe, faux pas, solecism, misapprehension, misreading; [inf] slip-up, boo-boo, howler; [Brit. inf] boob; [Brit. inf, dated] bloomer.

▶ VERB = **get wrong**, misunderstand, misapprehend, misinterpret, misconstrue, misread.

■ **be mistaken** = **be wrong**, be in error, be at fault, be under a misapprehension, be misinformed, be misguided, be wide of the mark, be barking up the wrong tree, get the wrong end of the stick.

■ **mistake for** = **take for**, mix up with, confuse with, misinterpret as.

mistakenly ADV = **by mistake**, wrongly, in error, erroneously, incorrectly, falsely, fallaciously, misguidedly. Opposites: correctly.

mistreat VERB = **maltreat**, treat badly, ill-treat, ill-use, misuse, abuse, mishandle, harm, hurt, molest; [inf] beat up, rough up.

mistress NOUN = **lover**, girlfriend, partner, lady-love, kept woman, inamorata; [archaic] paramour, concubine.

mistrust VERB = **feel mistrustful of**, distrust, feel distrustful of, have doubts about, be suspicious of, suspect, have reservations about, have misgivings about, be wary of, have no confidence in, question, doubt, lack faith in. Opposites: trust.

misty ADJ = **hazy**, foggy, cloudy, blurred, fuzzy, dim, indistinct, vague, obscure, nebulous. Opposites: clear.

misunderstand VERB = **misapprehend**, misinterpret, misconstrue, misread, get the wrong idea, receive a false impression; [inf] get the wrong end of the stick, be barking up the wrong tree.

misunderstanding NOUN
1 = **misapprehension**, mistake, error, mix-up, misinterpretation, misconstruction, misreading, misconception, misbelief, the wrong idea, a false impression; [inf] the wrong end of the stick.
2 = **disagreement**, difference of opinion, falling-out, clash of views, dispute, quarrel, argument, squabble, conflict; [inf] spat, scrap, tiff.

misuse VERB 1 = **put to wrong use**, misapply, misemploy, abuse, squander, waste, dissipate. 2 = **maltreat**, mistreat, treat badly, ill-treat, ill-use, abuse, mishandle, manhandle, harm, hurt, bully, molest, beat up, rough up.
▶ NOUN 1 = **wrong use**, misapplication, misemployment, abuse, squandering, waste, dissipation. 2 = **misusage**,

malapropism, barbarism, catachresis.
3 = **maltreatment**, mistreatment, ill-treatment, ill use, abuse, rough handling, mishandling, manhandling, bullying, injury, harm, molesting.

mitigate VERB = **alleviate**, reduce, diminish, lessen, weaken, attenuate, allay, assuage, palliate, appease, soothe, relieve, ease, soften, temper, mollify, lighten, still, quieten, quiet, tone down, moderate, modify, extenuate, calm, lull, pacify, placate, tranquillize.
Opposites: aggravate.

mix VERB 1 = **blend**, combine, mingle, compound, homogenize, alloy, merge, unite, join, amalgamate, fuse, coalesce, interweave.
2 = **socialize**, mingle, associate with others, meet people.
Opposites: separate.
▶ NOUN = **mixture**, blend, combination, compound, alloy, merger, union,

amalgamation, fusion.
- ■ **mix up** 1 = **confuse**, muddle up, mistake, scramble. 2 = **involve**, implicate, entangle, embroil, draw into, incriminate.

mixed ADJ 1 = **assorted**, varied, miscellaneous, diverse, diversified, motley, heterogeneous. 2 = **hybrid**, cross-bred, interbred, mongrel. 3 = **ambivalent**, equivocal, unsure, uncertain.
Opposites: homogeneous.

mixture NOUN
1 = **compound**, blend, mix, brew, combination, concoction, alloy.
2 = **assortment**, variety, melange, collection, medley, pot-pourri, conglomeration, jumble, mix, mishmash, hotchpotch, pastiche, farrago, mixed bag.
3 = **cross**, cross-breed, mongrel, hybrid.

moan NOUN = **groan**, lament, lamentation, wail, whimper, whine.
▶ VERB 1 = **groan**, wail, whimper, whine.
2 = **complain**, whine,

carp; [inf] grouse, gripe, grouch, whinge, beef.

mob NOUN = **crowd**, horde, multitude, rabble, mass, body, throng, host, gang, gathering, assemblage.
▶ VERB = **crowd around**, swarm around, surround, besiege, jostle.

mobile ADJ 1 = **able to move**, moving, walking, motile, ambulatory. 2 = **transportable**, portable, travelling, peripatetic, locomotive. 3 = **expressive**, animated, ever-changing, changeable.
Opposites: immobile.

mobilize VERB 1 = **muster**, rally, marshal, assemble, call to arms, organize, make ready, prepare, ready. 2 = **get ready**, prepare, ready oneself.

mock VERB = **ridicule**, jeer at, sneer at, deride, scorn, make fun of, poke fun at, laugh at, tease, taunt, twit, chaff, gibe at, insult; [inf] rag, kid, rib, take the mickey out of.
▶ ADJ = **imitation**, artificial, simulated, synthetic, ersatz, so-called, fake,

sham, false, spurious, bogus, counterfeit, forged, pseudo, pretended.

mockery NOUN **1** = **ridicule**, jeering, derision, contempt, scorn, disdain, gibe, insult; [inf] ribbing. **2** = **parody**, travesty, caricature, lampoon, burlesque.

mocking ADJ = **sneering**, derisive, derisory, contemptuous, scornful, disdainful, sardonic, insulting, satirical.

model NOUN **1** = **replica**, representation, mock-up, copy, dummy, imitation, facsimile, image. **2** = **prototype**, archetype, type, mould, original, pattern, design, paradigm, sample, example, exemplar. **3** = **style**, design, mode, form, mark, version, type, variety, kind, sort. **4** = **ideal**, paragon, perfect example, perfect specimen, exemplar, epitome, nonpareil, acme.

moderate ADJ **1** = **middle-of-the-road**, non-radical.

2 = **reasonable**, within reason, within due limits, fair, just. **3** = **not given to excesses**, restrained, controlled, temperate, sober, steady. **4** = **average**, middling, ordinary, fair, fairish, modest, tolerable, passable, adequate. Opposites: immoderate.

▶ VERB **1** = **abate**, let up, die down, calm down, lessen, decrease, diminish, slacken. **2** = **lessen**, decrease, diminish, mitigate, alleviate, allay, assuage, ease, palliate.

moderately ADV = **quite**, rather, somewhat, fairly, reasonably, to a certain degree, to some extent, within reason, within limits.

modern ADJ **1** = **contemporary**, present-day, present, current, twentieth-century, existing, existent. **2** = **up to date**, up to the minute, fashionable, in fashion, in, in style, in vogue, voguish, modish, the latest, new, newfangled,

fresh, advanced, progressive; [inf] trendy, with it.
Opposites: old-fashioned.

modernize VERB = **make modern**, update, bring up to date, renovate, remodel, remake, redo, refresh, revamp, rejuvenate; [inf] do over.

modest ADJ 1 = **self-effacing**, humble, unpretentious, unassuming, free from vanity. 2 = **shy**, bashful, self-conscious, diffident, reserved, retiring, reticent, quiet, coy, embarrassed, blushing, timid, fearful, meek. 3 = **moderate**, fair, tolerable, passable, adequate, satisfactory, acceptable, unexceptional, small, limited.
Opposites: conceited, grand.

modesty NOUN 1 = **lack of vanity**, humility, self-effacement, lack of pretension, unpretentiousness. 2 = **shyness**, bashfulness, self-consciousness,

reserve, reticence, timidity, meekness.

modify VERB = **alter**, change, adjust, adapt, revise, recast, reform, reshape, refashion, rework, remould, redo, revamp, reorganize, refine, transform.

moist ADJ = **wet**, damp, clammy, humid, dank, rainy, drizzly, dewy, soggy, succulent, juicy, soft, spongy.

moisture NOUN = **water**, liquid, wetness, wet, dampness, damp, humidity, dankness, rain, dew, drizzle, perspiration, sweat.

molest VERB = **pester**, annoy, plague, torment, harass, badger, harry, persecute, bother, worry, trouble, provoke; [inf] bug, needle, hassle.

mollify VERB = **calm down**, pacify, placate, appease, soothe, quiet.
Opposites: enrage.

moment NOUN 1 = **short time**, minute, second, instant; [inf] tick, jiffy. 2 = **point in time**, time, instant, minute, juncture, stage.

momentary ADJ = **brief**, short, short-lived, fleeting, passing, transient, transitory, ephemeral, evanescent, temporary, impermanent.
Opposites: lengthy.

momentous ADJ = **crucial**, critical, vital, decisive, pivotal, serious, grave, important, significant, consequential, fateful, historic; [inf] earth-shattering.
Opposites: insignificant.

momentum NOUN = **impetus**, impulse, propulsion, thrust, push, driving power, drive, power, energy, force.

money NOUN = **cash**, hard cash, ready money, finance, capital, funds, banknotes, currency, coin, coinage, silver, copper, legal tender, specie; [inf] wherewithal, dough, bread, loot, the necessary, the needful, shekels, tin, gelt, moolah, filthy lucre; [Brit. inf] dosh, brass, lolly, spondulicks, the ready, readies; [N. Amer. inf] mazuma.

monitor NOUN = **detector**, scanner, recorder, security camera, observer, watchdog, overseer, supervisor, invigilator.
▸ VERB = **observe**, scan, record, survey, follow, keep an eye on, keep track of, check, oversee, supervise, invigilate.

monopolize VERB
1 = **corner**, control, take over, have sole rights in.
2 = **dominate**, take over, not let anyone else take part in.
Opposites: share.

monotonous ADJ = **unvarying**, lacking/without variety, unchanging, repetitious, all the same, uniform, routine, humdrum, run-of-the-mill, commonplace, mechanical, uninteresting, unexciting, prosaic, wearisome, dull, boring, tedious, tiresome.
Opposites: varied, interesting.

m

monster NOUN 1 = **fiend**, beast, brute, barbarian, savage, villain, ogre, devil, demon.
2 = **monstrosity**, malformation, abortion, freak, freak of nature, mutant.

monstrous ADJ
1 = **malformed**, unnatural, abnormal, grotesque, gruesome, repellent, freakish, mutant.
2 = **outrageous**, shocking, disgraceful, scandalous, atrocious, heinous, evil, abominable, terrible, horrible, dreadful, hideous, foul, vile, nasty, ghastly, odious, loathsome, intolerable, contemptible, despicable, vicious, cruel, savage.
Opposites: lovely.

monument NOUN
1 = **memorial**, statue, shrine, reliquary, sepulchre, mausoleum, cairn, obelisk, dolmen, cromlech, megalith.
2 = **commemoration**, memorial, remembrance, reminder, testament, witness, token.

monumental ADJ
1 = **great**, huge, enormous, immense, vast, exceptional, extraordinary, tremendous, stupendous, prodigious, staggering.
2 = **massive**, impressive, striking, remarkable, magnificent, awe-inspiring, marvellous, majestic, stupendous, prodigious.

mood NOUN = **humour**, temper, disposition, frame of mind, state of mind, spirit, tenor, vein.

moody ADJ
= **temperamental**, changeable, unpredictable, volatile, mercurial, unstable, unsteady, erratic, fitful, impulsive, capricious.

moon VERB = **languish**, idle, mope, daydream, be in a reverie, be in a brown study.

moot ADJ = **debatable**, open to question, open, doubtful, disputable, arguable, contestable, controversial, unresolved, undecided.

moral NOUN = **lesson**, teaching, message, meaning, significance, point.

morale NOUN = **confidence**, heart, spirit, hope, hopefulness, optimism, determination, zeal.

morality NOUN = **morals**, moral code, moral standards, ethics, principles of right and wrong, standards/ principles of behaviour.

morbid ADJ = **gruesome**, grisly, macabre, hideous, dreadful, horrible, unwholesome.
Opposites: wholesome.

more ADV = **to a greater extent**, further, longer, some more.
▶ PRON = **additional amount/number**, greater quantity/part, addition, supplement, extra, increase, increment.
Opposites: less.

moreover ADV = **besides**, furthermore, further, what is more, in addition, also, as well, into the bargain, to boot.

moron NOUN = **fool**, idiot, dolt, dunce, ass, ignoramus, imbecile, simpleton; [inf] chump, booby, nincompoop, ninny, dunderhead, blockhead, fathead, halfwit, cretin, dummy, numbskull, dimwit; [Brit. inf] twerp, clot, twit, nitwit; [N. Amer. inf] schmuck.

morsel NOUN = **bite**, nibble, bit, crumb, grain, particle, fragment, piece, scrap, segment, soupçon, taste.

mortal ADJ 1 = **temporal**, transient, ephemeral, passing, impermanent, perishable, human, earthly, worldly, corporeal, fleshly.
2 = **deadly**, sworn, irreconcilable, bitter, implacable, unrelenting, remorseless.
Opposites: immortal.

mortify VERB = **humiliate**, humble, bring low, disgrace, shame, abash, chasten, degrade, abase, deflate, crush, discomfit, embarrass.

mostly ADV = **for the most part**, on the whole, in the main, largely, mainly, chiefly, predominantly.

mother NOUN = **female parent**, materfamilias, matriarch; [inf] ma, mam, mammy, old lady, old woman; [Brit. inf] mum, mummy; [N. Amer. inf] mom, mommy; [Brit. inf, dated] mater.

motherly ADJ = **maternal**, protective, comforting, caring, loving, affectionate, fond, warm, tender.

motion NOUN = **mobility**, locomotion, movement, moving, travel, travelling, progress, passing, passage, flow, action, activity.

motionless ADJ = **unmoving**, stock-still, at a standstill, stationary, immobile, immovable, static, at rest, frozen, inert, lifeless.
Opposites: mobile.

motivate VERB = **move**, cause, lead, persuade, prompt, actuate, drive, impel, spur, induce, provoke, incite, inspire.

motive NOUN = **motivation**, reason, rationale, grounds, cause, basis, occasion, incentive, inducement, incitement, influence, stimulus, spur, goad; [inf] what makes one tick.

motley ADJ = **assorted**, varied, miscellaneous, mixed, diverse, diversified, variegated.

mottled ADJ = **blotched**, blotchy, speckled, spotted, streaked, marbled, flecked, freckled, dappled, stippled; [inf] splotchy.

motto NOUN = **maxim**, aphorism, adage, saying, saw, axiom, truism, precept, epigram, proverb.

mould VERB = **shape**, form, fashion, model, create, design, carve, sculpt, chisel, forge.

mouldy ADJ = **mildewed**, blighted, musty, fusty, decaying, rotting, rotten, bad, spoiled.

mound NOUN = **hillock**, knoll, rise, hummock, tump, embankment, bank, dune.

mount VERB 1 = **ascend**, go up, climb up, clamber up, make one's way up, scale. 2 = **increase**, grow, escalate, intensify. 3 = **stage**, put on, install, prepare, organize, arrange, set in motion, get up.
Opposites: descend.

mountain NOUN = **peak**, mount, height, elevation, eminence, pinnacle, fell, alp; [Scottish] ben.

mountainous ADJ = **hilly**, high, highland, steep, lofty, towering, soaring, alpine, rocky.

mourn VERB = **grieve**, sorrow, keen, lament, bewail, bemoan.

mournful ADJ = **sad**, sorrowful, doleful, gloomy, sombre, melancholy, lugubrious, funereal, dejected, depressed, downcast, miserable, woeful, unhappy.
Opposites: cheerful.

mouth NOUN 1 = **lips**, jaws, maw, muzzle; [inf] trap, chops, kisser; [Brit. inf] gob. 2 = **opening**, entrance, entry, inlet, door, doorway, gateway, hatch, aperture, orifice.

mouthful NOUN = **bite**, swallow, nibble, sip, sup, taste, drop, bit, piece, morsel, sample.

mouthpiece NOUN = **spokesman**, spokeswoman, spokesperson, negotiator, intermediary, mediator, agent, representative.

move VERB 1 = **go**, walk, march, proceed, progress, advance. 2 = **carry**, transport, transfer, transpose, change over, shift, switch. 3 = **take action**, act, do something, get moving. 4 = **move house**, relocate, move away, leave, go away. 5 = **affect**, touch, impress, upset, disturb, disquiet, agitate, make an impression on, have an impact on. 6 = **provoke**, incite, actuate, rouse, excite, urge, incline, stimulate, motivate, influence, persuade, lead, prompt, cause, impel, induce. 7 = **propose**, put forward, advocate, recommend, urge, suggest.

▶ NOUN **1** = **movement**, motion, moving, action, activity, gesture, gesticulation. **2** = **action**, act, deed, measure, step, tack, manoeuvre, tactic, stratagem, ploy, ruse, trick. **3** = **turn**, go.

■ **get a move on** = **hurry up**, make haste, speed up, move faster, get moving; [inf] get cracking, make it snappy, step on it, shake a leg.

movement NOUN
1 = **moving**, carrying, transportation, transferral, shifting.
2 = **move**, motion, action, activity, gesture, gesticulation.
3 = **mechanism**, machinery, works, workings, action.
4 = **campaign**, crusade, drive, group, party, organization, coalition, front.

moving ADJ **1** = **affecting**, touching, emotive, emotional, poignant, stirring, arousing, upsetting, disturbing.

2 = **movable**, mobile, motile, unfixed.
3 = **driving**, dynamic, impelling, motivating, stimulating, inspirational.

mow VERB = **cut**, trim, crop, clip, scythe, shear.

muck NOUN **1** = **dirt**, grime, filth, mud, slime, sludge, scum, mire; [inf] gunk; [Brit. inf] gunge. **2** = **dung**, manure, ordure, excrement, guano, droppings, faeces.

■ **muck up** = **bungle**, muff, make a mess of, mess up, mar, spoil, ruin, foul up; [inf] botch, screw up.

muddle VERB **1** = **mix up**, get confused, confuse, jumble, scramble, throw into disorder, get into a tangle, make a mess of, mess up. **2** = **bewilder**, disorientate, confuse, befuddle, daze, perplex, puzzle, baffle, nonplus, confound.

muddy VERB **1** = **dirty**, begrime, soil. **2** = **make unclear**, cloud, confuse, mix up, jumble, scramble, get into a tangle.

muffle VERB **1** = **wrap up**, cover up, swathe, swaddle, envelop, cloak. **2** = **deaden**, dull, dampen, stifle, smother, suppress, soften, quieten, mute.

mug VERB = **assault**, attack, beat up, knock down, rob; [inf] rough up, do over.

muggy ADJ = **close**, stuffy, sultry, oppressive, airless, humid, clammy, sticky. Opposites: fresh.

multiple ADJ = **several**, many, numerous, various, collective, manifold. Opposites: single.

multiply VERB **1** = **breed**, reproduce. **2** = **increase**, grow, accumulate, augment, proliferate, spread.

multitude NOUN = **crowd**, assembly, throng, host, horde, mass, mob, legion, army.

munch VERB = **chew**, champ, chomp, masticate, crunch, eat.

mundane ADJ = **common**, ordinary, everyday, workaday, usual, prosaic, pedestrian, routine, customary, regular, normal, typical, commonplace, banal, hackneyed, trite, stale, platitudinous. Opposites: extraordinary.

municipal ADJ = **civic**, civil, city, metropolitan, urban, town, borough.

murder NOUN = **killing**, manslaughter, homicide, slaughter, assassination, butchery, carnage, massacre; [poetic/ literary] slaying. ▶ VERB = see **kill** (**1**).

murderer NOUN = **killer**, slaughterer, cut-throat, assassin, butcher; [poetic/ literary] slayer.

murderous ADJ = **fatal**, lethal, deadly, mortal, homicidal, savage, barbarous, brutal, bloodthirsty.

murky ADJ = **dark**, dim, gloomy, dirty, muddy, dingy, dull, cloudy, turbid, opaque. Opposites: clear.

murmur NOUN **1** = **whisper**, undertone, mutter, mumble. **2** = **babble**,

burble, whisper, purl,
rustle, buzzing, drone.

▶ VERB **1** = **whisper**, speak in
an undertone, speak
sotto voce, mutter,
mumble. **2** = **babble**,
burble, whisper, purl,
rustle, buzz, drone.

muscular ADJ = **brawny**,
strapping, powerfully
built, solidly built, hefty,
sturdy, rugged, burly;
[inf] beefy.
Opposites: weak, puny.

muse VERB = **think**,
meditate, ruminate,
contemplate, reflect,
deliberate, day dream, be
in a reverie.

musical ADJ = **tuneful**,
melodic, melodious,
harmonious, mellifluous,
dulcet, euphonious.

muster VERB = **assemble**,
bring together, call/
gather together, call up,
summon, rally, mobilize,
round up, marshal,
collect; [formal] convoke.

musty ADJ = **mouldy**,
mildewed, fusty,
decaying, stale, stuffy,
airless, damp, dank.

mutation NOUN = **change**,
variation, alteration,

modification,
transformation,
metamorphosis,
evolution, transmutation,
transfiguration.

mute ADJ = **silent**,
speechless, wordless,
unspeaking, taciturn,
uncommunicative;
[inf] mum.

▶ VERB = *see* **muffle (2)**.

muted ADJ = **soft**,
softened, subdued,
subtle, discreet, toned
down, quiet, understated.

mutinous ADJ
= **rebellious**, insurgent,
insurrectionary,
revolutionary, subversive,
seditious, traitorous,
insubordinate,
disobedient, riotous,
unruly, restive,
contumacious, refractory;
[Brit. inf] bolshie.

mutiny NOUN = **rebellion**,
revolt, insurrection,
insurgence, insurgency,
uprising, rising,
revolution, disobedience,
defiance,
insubordination.

mysterious ADJ
= **enigmatic**,
impenetrable,

inscrutable,
incomprehensible,
inexplicable,
unexplainable,
unfathomable,
unaccountable, dark,
obscure, arcane, abstruse,
cryptic, unknown,
recondite, secret,
preternatural,
supernatural, uncanny,
mystical, peculiar,
strange, weird, curious,
bizarre, undisclosed,
mystifying, baffling,
puzzling, perplexing,
bewildering.

mystery NOUN = **enigma**,
puzzle, secret, riddle,
conundrum, question,
question mark, closed
book, unexplored
ground, terra incognita.

mystic, **mystical** ADJ
= **spiritual**, paranormal,
transcendental, other-
worldly, supernatural,
preternatural, occult,
metaphysical.

mystify VERB = **confuse**,
bewilder, confound,
perplex, baffle, nonplus,
puzzle, elude, escape;
[inf] stump, beat,
bamboozle.

myth NOUN 1 = **legend**,
saga, tale, story, fable,
folk tale, allegory,
parable, fairy story/tale.
2 = **fantasy**, delusion,
invention, fabrication,
untruth, lie.

mythical ADJ
1 = **legendary**,
mythological, fabled,
chimerical, fabulous,
fantastical, fairy-tale,
storybook, fictitious,
allegorical. 2 = **imagined**,
imaginary, pretend,
make-believe, unreal,
fictitious, invented,
fabricated, made up,
untrue.
Opposites: real.

m

Nn

nadir NOUN = **the lowest point**, rock bottom, the depths, all-time low, as low as one can get; [inf] the pits.
Opposites: zenith.

nag VERB = **scold**, carp, pick on, keep on at, harp on at, henpeck, bully, upbraid, berate, chivvy, criticize, find fault with, complain to, grumble to.
▶ NOUN = **shrew**, scold, harpy, termagant, carper, caviller, complainer, grumbler.

naive ADJ = **innocent**, artless, childlike, simple, ingenuous, guileless, trusting, unsophisticated, unworldly, jejune, natural, unaffected, unpretentious, frank, open, candid.
Opposites: worldly.

naked ADJ = **stark naked**, nude, in the nude, bare, stripped, unclothed, undressed, uncovered, undraped, disrobed, au naturel; [inf] in the buff, butt naked; [Brit. inf] starkers; [N. Amer. inf] buck naked.
Opposites: clothed.

name NOUN = **designation**, title, label, tag, cognomen, sobriquet, epithet, first name, given name, surname, family name, maiden name, nickname, pet name, stage name, pseudonym, alias; [inf] moniker, handle; [formal] denomination, appellation.
▶ VERB = **christen**, baptize, call, entitle, label, style, term, title, dub, denominate.

nameless ADJ = **unnamed**, untitled, unlabelled, untagged, anonymous, unidentified, undesignated, unspecified.

nap NOUN = **short sleep**, catnap, doze, light sleep, rest, lie-down; [inf] snooze, forty winks, shut-eye; [Brit. inf] kip.

narrate VERB = **tell**, relate, recount, recite, unfold, chronicle, describe, detail, portray, sketch out, rehearse, repeat.

narrator NOUN = **reporter**, describer, chronicler, annalist, storyteller, raconteur.

narrow ADJ 1 = **slender**, thin, slim, slight, spare, attenuated, tapering. 2 = **limited**, restricted, select, exclusive. **Opposites:** wide.

narrow-minded ADJ = **intolerant**, illiberal, reactionary, close-minded, unreasonable, prejudiced, bigoted, biased, discriminatory, jaundiced, parochial, provincial, insular, small-minded, petty-minded, petty, mean-spirited, prudish, strait-laced.
Opposites: broad-minded.

nasty ADJ = **unpleasant**, disagreeable, distasteful, horrible, vile, foul, hateful, loathsome, revolting, disgusting, odious, obnoxious, repellent, repugnant, ugly, offensive, objectionable, squalid, dirty, filthy, impure, polluted, tainted, unpalatable, unsavoury, unappetizing, evil-smelling, foul-smelling, stinking, rank, fetid, malodorous; [poetic/literary] mephitic, noisome.
Opposites: pleasant.

nation NOUN = **country**, land, state, kingdom, empire, realm, republic, commonwealth, people, race, tribe, society.

national ADJ = **nationwide**, countrywide, state, coast-to-coast, widespread, comprehensive, general.
▶ NOUN = **citizen**, subject, native.

native ADJ **1 = inborn**, inherent, innate, intrinsic, instinctive, intuitive, natural, congenital, hereditary. **2 = indigenous**, home-grown, domestic, local.

natural ADJ **1 = organic**, pure, unrefined, unmixed, whole, plain, real, chemical-free, additive-free. **2 = native**, inborn, inherent, innate, intrinsic, instinctive, intuitive, congenital, hereditary, inherited, ingrained. **3 = genuine**, real, authentic, simple, unaffected, unpretentious, spontaneous, artless, ingenuous, candid, open, frank, relaxed, unstudied. **Opposites:** unnatural.

nature NOUN **1 = natural forces**, creation, the environment, the earth, mother earth, landscape, scenery. **2 = kind**, sort, type, variety, description, category, class, classification. **3 = temperament**, temper, personality, disposition, humour, mood, outlook.

naughty ADJ **= mischievous**, badly behaved, misbehaving, disobedient, defiant, unruly, roguish, wayward, delinquent, undisciplined, unmanageable, ungovernable, fractious, refractory, perverse, errant. **Opposites:** well behaved.

nausea NOUN **= sickness**, vomiting, retching, gagging, biliousness, queasiness, faintness.

nauseous ADJ **1 = sick**, queasy, unwell, indisposed; [Brit.] off colour; [inf] green about the gills. **2 = disgusting**, revolting, repulsive, repellent, repugnant, offensive, loathsome, abhorrent, odious.

nautical ADJ **= maritime**, naval, marine, seagoing, seafaring.

navigable ADJ **= negotiable**, passable, traversable, clear, unobstructed.

near ADJ **1 = close**, nearby, alongside, at close range/quarters,

accessible, within reach, close/near at hand, at hand, neighbouring, adjacent, adjoining, bordering, contiguous, proximate.
2 = **approaching**, coming, imminent, forthcoming, in the offing, impending, looming.
Opposites: distant.

nearly ADV = **almost**, virtually, next to, close to, well-nigh, about, just about, practically, roughly, approximately, not quite.

neat ADJ **1** = **tidy**, orderly, well ordered, in good order, spick and span.
2 = **smart**, spruce, trim, tidy, dapper, well groomed, well turned out. **3** = **adroit**, skilful, expert, practised, dexterous, deft, accurate, precise, nimble, agile.
Opposites: untidy.

necessary ADJ = **needed**, needful, essential, required, requisite, vital, indispensable, imperative, mandatory, obligatory, compulsory, de rigueur.

Opposites: unnecessary.

need VERB = **require**, necessitate, demand, call for, have occasion for, want, lack, be without.
▸ NOUN = **requirement**, want, wish, demand, prerequisite, requisite, essential, desideratum.

needless ADJ
= **unnecessary**, uncalled for, gratuitous, undesired, unwanted, pointless, useless, dispensable, expendable, inessential.
Opposites: necessary.

negative ADJ
= **pessimistic**, defeatist, gloomy, gloom-laden, cynical, jaundiced, critical, fault-finding, complaining, unhelpful, uncooperative.
Opposites: positive.

neglect VERB **1** = **fail to look after**, fail to provide for, abandon, forsake, leave alone. **2** = **let slide**, skimp on, shirk, be remiss about, be lax about, not attend to, leave undone, procrastinate about.

▶ NOUN = **negligence**, neglectfulness, remissness, carelessness, heedlessness, slackness, laxity, laxness, dereliction.
Opposites: care, attention.

negligent ADJ
= **neglectful**, remiss, lax, careless, inattentive, heedless, thoughtless, unmindful, uncaring, forgetful, indifferent, offhand, cursory, slack, sloppy, slapdash, slipshod, procrastinating, dilatory.
Opposites: attentive.

negligible ADJ = **trivial**, trifling, insignificant, of no account, paltry, petty, tiny, minute, small, minor, inconsequential, inappreciable, imperceptible.
Opposites: significant.

negotiate VERB = **bargain**, drive a bargain, hold talks, confer, debate, discuss, discuss terms, discuss a settlement, consult together, parley, haggle.

neighbourhood NOUN = **district**, area, region, locality, part, quarter, precinct, community; [inf] neck of the woods, stamping ground.

neighbouring ADJ
= **adjacent**, adjoining, bordering, abutting, contiguous, nearby, near, very near, close/near at hand, not far away, in the vicinity.

nervous ADJ = **on edge**, edgy, tense, strained, anxious, nervy, agitated, worried, fretful, uneasy, disquieted, on tenterhooks, fidgety, ruffled, flustered, apprehensive, perturbed, fearful, frightened, scared, with one's heart in one's mouth, quaking, trembling, shaking, shaky; [inf] jittery, twitchy, jumpy, in a state, uptight, wired.
Opposites: calm.

nestle VERB = **snuggle**, curl up, huddle together, cuddle up, nuzzle.

net NOUN = **netting**, fishnet, mesh, latticework, lattice, openwork, webbing, tracery.

▶ VERB = **catch**, trap, snare, ensnare, entangle, enmesh, bag.

nettle VERB = **irritate**, provoke, ruffle, annoy, incense, exasperate, irk, vex, pique, bother, pester, harass, torment, plague.

neurotic ADJ = **unstable**, maladjusted, obsessive, phobic, fixated, compulsive, oversensitive, hysterical, irrational.
Opposites: stable.

neuter ADJ = **asexual**, sexless, unsexed.
▶ VERB = **castrate**, geld, emasculate, spay, dress; [inf] fix, doctor.

neutral ADJ = **impartial**, unbiased, unprejudiced, open-minded, non-partisan, without favouritism, even-handed, disinterested, non-aligned, dispassionate, objective, detached, uninvolved, uncommitted.

neutralize VERB = **counteract**, cancel, nullify, negate, annul, undo, invalidate, frustrate, be an antidote to.

new ADJ = **modern**, recent, advanced, state-of-the-art, present-day, contemporary, current, latest, up to date, up to the minute, new-fashioned, modish, brand new, newly arrived, modernist, ultra-modern, avant-garde, futuristic, newfangled.
Opposites: old.

newcomer NOUN = **arrival**, incomer, immigrant, settler, stranger, outsider, foreigner, alien, intruder, interloper; [inf] johnny-come-lately.

news PL NOUN
= **information**, facts, data, report, story, news item, news flash, account, statement, announcement, press release, communiqué, message, bulletin, dispatch, disclosure, revelation, word, talk, the latest; [inf] gen, info.

newspaper NOUN = **paper**, gazette, journal, tabloid, broadsheet, weekly, scandal sheet; [inf] rag.

n

next ADJ **1** = **following**, succeeding, successive, subsequent, later, ensuing. **2** = **neighbouring**, adjacent, adjoining, bordering, contiguous. Opposites: previous.

nice ADJ **1** = **good**, pleasant, enjoyable, pleasurable, agreeable, delightful, marvellous. **2** = **fine**, ultra-fine, subtle, minute, precise, exact, accurate, strict, close. Opposites: unpleasant, rough.

nicety NOUN = **finer point**, subtlety, nuance, detail.

niggardly ADJ = **mean**, miserly, parsimonious, penny-pinching, cheese-paring; [inf] tight-fisted, stingy. Opposites: generous.

nimble ADJ = **agile**, lithe, sprightly, spry, graceful, skilful, deft. Opposites: clumsy.

nippy ADJ = **icy**, chilly, bitter, raw, piercing, stinging. Opposites: warm.

no ADV = **absolutely not**, under no circumstances, by no means, never; [inf] not on your life, no way, nope.

noble ADJ **1** = **aristocratic**, patrician, blue-blooded, titled, landed. **2** = **noble-minded**, magnanimous, generous, self-sacrificing, honourable, virtuous, brave. Opposites: common, dishonourable.

nod VERB = **incline**, bob, bow, dip, duck.

noise NOUN = **sound**, din, hubbub, clamour, racket, row, uproar, tumult, commotion, rumpus, pandemonium. Opposites: silence.

noisy ADJ **1** = **rowdy**, clamorous, boisterous, obstreperous, turbulent; [inf] rackety. **2** = **loud**, blaring, blasting, deafening, ear-splitting. Opposites: quiet.

nomad NOUN = **itinerant**, traveller, migrant, wanderer, transient, vagabond, vagrant, tramp.

nominal ADJ **1** = **in name only**, titular, formal, theoretical, self-styled,

purported, supposed.
2 = **token**, symbolic,
minimal, trivial,
insignificant.

nominate VERB = **name**,
propose, put forward,
submit, present,
recommend; [inf] put up.

nonchalant ADJ = **self-possessed**,
imperturbable, calm,
cool, collected, cool as a
cucumber, unconcerned,
indifferent, blasé, casual,
offhand, carefree,
insouciant, easy-going,
careless; [inf] laid-back.
Opposites: anxious.

nonplus VERB = **take aback**, stun, dumbfound,
confound, astound,
astonish, amaze, surprise,
disconcert, stump,
confuse, bewilder,
embarrass, fluster;
[inf] faze, flummox, floor.

nonsense NOUN = **rubbish**,
balderdash, drivel,
gibberish, blather, trash,
claptrap; [inf] twaddle,
waffle, tripe, bilge, bull,
tosh, bosh,
gobbledegook, mumbo-jumbo, poppycock, stuff
and nonsense; [Brit.

inf] flannel; [inf,
dated] bunkum,
tommyrot.
Opposites: sense.

nonsensical ADJ
= **meaningless**,
incomprehensible,
unintelligible, senseless,
foolish, absurd, silly,
inane, stupid, ridiculous,
ludicrous, preposterous,
hare-brained, irrational,
idiotic, insane; [inf] crazy,
crackpot, nutty, wacky.
Opposites: sensible.

non-stop ADJ = **incessant**,
unceasing, ceaseless,
constant, continuous,
continual, unbroken,
unfaltering, steady,
unremitting, relentless,
persistent, endless,
never-ending, unending,
interminable.

nook NOUN = **corner**,
cranny, recess, alcove,
niche, opening, cavity,
crevice, gap.

normal ADJ **1** = **usual**,
standard, average,
common, ordinary,
natural, general,
commonplace,
conventional, typical,
regular, routine, run-of-

the-mill, everyday,
accustomed, habitual,
prevailing, popular,
accepted, acknowledged.
2 = well adjusted, well
balanced, rational,
compos mentis, sane.
Opposites: abnormal.

normally ADV = **usually**,
ordinarily, as a rule, as a
general rule, generally, in
general, mostly,
commonly, habitually.

nose NOUN = **proboscis**,
bill, beak, snout, muzzle;
[inf] snoot, hooter; [Brit.
inf] conk; [N. Amer.
inf] schnozz.

nosy ADJ = **inquisitive**,
curious, interfering,
meddlesome, intrusive;
[inf] snooping, snoopy.

notable ADJ
1 = noteworthy,
remarkable, outstanding,
important, significant,
momentous, memorable,
unforgettable,
pronounced, marked,
striking, impressive,
uncommon, unusual,
particular, special,
extraordinary. **2 = noted**,
of note, distinguished,
eminent, pre-eminent,

well known, prominent,
illustrious, great, famous,
famed, renowned,
celebrated, acclaimed.
Opposites: insignificant.

note NOUN **1 = record**,
account, entry, item,
notation, comment,
jotting, inscription.
2 = letter, message,
memorandum, memo,
epistle, missive,
communication.
3 = footnote, annotation,
commentary, gloss,
marginalia, explanation,
explication, exposition,
exegesis. **4 = distinction**,
eminence, pre-eminence,
illustriousness, greatness,
prestige, fame, renown.
5 = tone, intonation,
inflection, sound,
indication, hint,
element.
▶ VERB **1 = write down**, jot
down, mark down, enter,
mark, record, register.
2 = take note of, take
notice of, see, observe,
perceive, behold, detect,
take in.

noted ADJ = **notable**,
distinguished, eminent,
pre-eminent, well

known, prominent,
illustrious, great, famous,
famed, renowned,
celebrated, acclaimed.
Opposites: unknown.

notice NOUN 1 = **attention**,
attentiveness, heed, note,
observation, cognizance,
regard, consideration,
watchfulness, vigilance.
2 = **bulletin**, poster,
handbill, bill, circular,
leaflet, pamphlet,
advertisement.
▶ VERB = **see**, note, take
note of, observe,
perceive, discern, detect,
behold, spot, distinguish,
make out, take heed of,
heed, pay attention to,
take notice of, mark,
regard.
Opposites: overlook.

noticeable ADJ
= **observable**, visible,
discernible, perceptible,
detectable,
distinguishable, distinct,
evident, obvious,
apparent, manifest,
patent, plain, clear,
conspicuous,
unmistakable,
pronounced, striking,
blatant.

Opposites: imperceptible.

notify VERB = **inform**, tell,
advise, acquaint, apprise,
warn, alert, caution.

notion NOUN = **idea**, belief,
opinion, thought,
impression, view,
conviction, concept,
assumption,
presumption, hypothesis,
theory, postulation,
apprehension,
understanding.

notorious ADJ = **infamous**,
ill-famed, disreputable,
dishonourable, of ill
repute, well known,
prominent, scandalous,
opprobrious, legendary.

nourishing ADJ
= **nutritious**, nutritive,
wholesome, healthy,
health-giving, healthful,
beneficial, good for one.
Opposites: unhealthy.

nourishment NOUN
= **food**, nutriment,
nutrition, sustenance,
subsistence, provisions;
[inf] grub, chow; [Brit.
inf] scoff; [dated] victuals.

novel ADJ = **new**, fresh,
different, original,
unusual, rare, unique,
imaginative,

unconventional, innovative, ground-breaking, trailblazing, modern, advanced.

novice NOUN = **beginner**, newcomer, apprentice, trainee, learner, probationer, student, pupil, recruit, tyro, initiate, neophyte; [inf] rookie; [N. Amer. inf] greenhorn.

now ADV = **at present**, at the present time, at this time, at the moment, for the time being, currently.

noxious ADJ = **unwholesome**, unhealthy, poisonous, toxic, harmful, injurious, malignant, detrimental, deleterious.
Opposites: innocuous.

nuance NOUN = **shade**, shading, gradation, subtlety, nicety, refinement, degree.

nucleus NOUN = **core**, kernel, centre, heart, nub.

nude ADJ = *see* **naked**.

nudge VERB = **poke**, jab, prod, dig, jog, elbow, touch, push, shove.

nuisance NOUN = **pest**, bother, plague, irritant, annoyance, trouble, burden, problem, difficulty, worry; [inf] drag.
Opposites: blessing.

numb ADJ = **without feeling**, deadened, benumbed, insensible, insensate, dull, anaesthetized, dazed, stunned, stupefied, paralysed, immobilized, frozen.
Opposites: sensitive.
▶VERB = **deaden**, dull, anaesthetize, benumb, daze, stun, stupefy, paralyse, immobilize, freeze.

number NOUN 1 = **figure**, digit, numeral, cipher, character, symbol, unit, integer. 2 = **total**, aggregate, score, tally, count, sum.
▶VERB = **count**, add up, enumerate, total, calculate, compute, reckon, tell, estimate, assess.

numerous ADJ = **many**, a lot, lots, innumerable, myriad, multitudinous,

several, quite a few,
various, diverse.
Opposites: few.

nurse VERB 1 = **take care
of**, care for, look after,
tend, attend to, minister
to. 2 = **suckle**, breast-feed,
feed, wet-nurse.

nurture VERB = **feed**,
nourish, provide for, care
for, take care of, tend,
attend to, bring up, rear.
nutritious ADJ = *see*
nourishing.
nuzzle VERB = **nose**,
nudge, prod, push.

Oo

oaf NOUN = **lout**, blunderer, bungler, boor, churl, bumpkin, yokel, brute, galoot; [inf] clodhopper; [N. Amer. inf] lummox.

oath NOUN 1 = **vow**, promise, pledge, avowal, affirmation, attestation, bond, word of honour, word. 2 = **curse**, swear word, expletive, blasphemy, profanity, imprecation, malediction, obscenity, epithet, four-letter word, dirty word.

obedient ADJ = **compliant**, acquiescent, biddable, dutiful, deferential, respectful, tractable, amenable, malleable, governable, well trained, submissive, docile, meek, subservient, obsequious, servile.
Opposites: disobedient.

obese ADJ = *see* **fat** (1).

obey VERB 1 = **abide by**, comply with, adhere to, observe, conform to, respect, acquiesce in, consent to, agree to, follow. 2 = **perform**, carry out, execute, put into effect, fulfil, act upon.
Opposites: disobey.

object NOUN 1 = **thing**, article, body, entity, item, device, gadget; [inf] thingamajig, thingamabob, thingummy, whatchamacallit, whatsit. 2 = **objective**, aim, goal, target, end, ambition, purpose, design, intent, intention, idea, point.
▶ VERB = **protest**, demur, beg to differ, remonstrate, expostulate, take exception, argue against, oppose, be in opposition to, complain about.

objection NOUN = **protest**, protestation, complaint, demurral, opposition, remonstration, remonstrance, expostulation, dissatisfaction, disapproval, grievance, scruple, qualm; [inf] niggle.
Opposites: approval.

objectionable ADJ = **offensive**, obnoxious, unpleasant, disagreeable, unacceptable, nasty, disgusting, repulsive, repellent, abhorrent, repugnant, revolting, loathsome, hateful, detestable, reprehensible, deplorable, insufferable, intolerable, despicable, contemptible, odious, vile, obscene, foul, horrible, horrid, noxious.
Opposites: agreeable.

objective ADJ = **unbiased**, unprejudiced, impartial, neutral, uninvolved, non-partisan, disinterested, detached, dispassionate, even-handed, equitable, fair, just, open-minded.
Opposites: subjective.

▶ NOUN = **object**, aim, goal, target, end, ambition, aspiration, intent, intention, purpose, design, plan, scheme, plot.

obligatory ADJ = **compulsory**, mandatory, enforced, necessary, essential, required, requisite, imperative, de rigueur, unavoidable, inescapable.
Opposites: voluntary.

oblige VERB 1 = **compel**, require, necessitate, obligate, impel, force, constrain, press, pressure, pressurize. 2 = **do someone a favour**, do someone a kindness, do someone a service, help, accommodate, meet someone's wants/needs, put oneself out for, indulge, assist.

obliging ADJ = see **helpful** (2).

oblique ADJ 1 = **slanting**, slanted, sloping, italic, sloped, inclined, at an angle, angled, tilted, listing, diagonal. 2 = **indirect**, implied, roundabout, circuitous,

circumlocutory, ambiguous, evasive, backhanded.
Opposites: direct.

obliterate VERB = **erase**, eradicate, efface, blot out, rub out, wipe out, expunge, delete, destroy, annihilate, eliminate, extirpate, decimate, liquidate, demolish.

oblivious ADJ = **heedless of**, unmindful of, unaware of, unconscious of, insensible of, ignorant of, blind to, unobservant of, deaf to, inattentive to, neglectful of, forgetful of, absent-minded, careless of, unconcerned with, abstracted, preoccupied, absorbed, far away.
Opposites: conscious.

obscene ADJ = **indecent**, pornographic, off colour, risqué, lewd, salacious, smutty, lecherous, lascivious, licentious, prurient, lubricious, ribald, scatological, scabrous, bawdy, suggestive, vulgar, dirty, filthy, foul, coarse, gross, vile, nasty, offensive,

immoral, impure, immodest, shameless, unchaste, improper, unwholesome, erotic, carnal, sexy; [inf] raunchy, blue.
Opposites: decent.

obscenity NOUN
1 = **indecency**, lewdness, salaciousness, lasciviousness, licentiousness, prurience, lubricity, ribaldry, scabrousness, bawdiness, suggestiveness, vulgarity, dirtiness. 2 = **curse**, oath, swear word, expletive, imprecation, blasphemy, epithet, profanity, four-letter word, dirty word.

obscure ADJ 1 = **unclear**, indeterminate, opaque, abstruse, recondite, unexplained, concealed, hidden, arcane, enigmatic, deep, cryptic, mysterious, puzzling, perplexing, confusing, involved, unfathomable, incomprehensible, impenetrable, vague, indefinite, hazy, uncertain, doubtful, dubious, ambiguous, equivocal. 2 = **indistinct**,

vague, shadowy, hazy, blurred, fuzzy, cloudy.
3 = little known, unknown, unheard of, undistinguished, insignificant, inconspicuous, minor, unimportant, unrecognized, unsung.
Opposites: clear, famous.

obsequious ADJ = **servile**, subservient, submissive, slavish, menial, abject, fawning, grovelling, cringing, toadying, truckling, sycophantic, ingratiating, unctuous, oily, Uriah Heepish; [inf] bootlicking.

observant ADJ = **alert**, sharp-eyed, sharp, eagle-eyed, attentive, vigilant, wide awake, watchful, heedful, on the lookout, on guard, mindful, intent, aware, conscious; [inf] not missing a thing/ trick, on the ball.
Opposites: inattentive.

observation NOUN
1 = scrutiny, scrutinization, watch, monitoring, surveillance, inspection, attention, consideration, study, review, examination.
2 = remark, comment, statement, utterance, pronouncement, declaration.

observe VERB **1 = see**, catch sight of, notice, note, perceive, discern, detect, espy, behold, watch, view, spot, witness; [inf] get a load of.
2 = keep, obey, adhere to, abide by, heed, follow, comply with, conform to, acquiesce in, consent to, accept, respect, defer to. **3 = carry out**, perform, execute, discharge, fulfil.
4 = celebrate, keep, recognize, commemorate, mark, remember, solemnize.

observer NOUN = **watcher**, looker-on, onlooker, witness, eyewitness, spectator, bystander, beholder, viewer, spotter.

obsess VERB = **preoccupy**, haunt, have a hold on, possess, consume, engross, have a grip on, grip, dominate, rule, control, be on someone's mind, prey on, plague, torment, hound, bedevil.

obsession NOUN
= **preoccupation**, fixation, consuming passion, mania, enthusiasm, infatuation, compulsion, phobia, complex, fetish, craze; [inf] bee in one's bonnet, hang-up.

obsessive ADJ
= **excessive**, overdone, consuming, compulsive, besetting, gripping, haunting.

obsolete ADJ = **outworn**, discarded, discontinued, extinct, bygone, outmoded, antiquated, out of date, superannuated, old-fashioned, behind the times, old, dated, antique, archaic, ancient, antediluvian, time-worn, past its prime.
Opposites: current.

obstacle NOUN = **bar**, barrier, obstruction, impediment, hindrance, hurdle, barricade, blockade, stumbling block, blockage, curb, check, snag, difficulty, catch, drawback.
Opposites: advantage, aid.

obstinate ADJ = **stubborn**, mulish, pig-headed, wilful, self-willed, strong-minded, perverse, refractory, recalcitrant, contumacious, unmanageable, firm, steadfast, unyielding, inflexible, unbending, immovable, intransigent, intractable, uncompromising, persistent, tenacious, dogged, single-minded.
Opposites: amenable, tractable.

obstruct VERB = **block**, barricade, bar, cut off, shut off, choke, clog, hold up, bring to a standstill, stop, halt, hinder, impede, hamper, interfere with, frustrate, thwart, baulk, inhibit, curb, hamstring, encumber.
Opposites: clear, facilitate.

obtain VERB **1** = **get**, get hold of, acquire, come by, procure, secure, gain, earn, achieve, attain, get one's hands on, seize, grab, pick up. **2** = **be in force**, be effective, exist, stand, prevail, hold, be the case, reign, rule, hold sway.

obtrusive ADJ
= **noticeable**, conspicuous, obvious, unmistakable, blatant, flagrant, bold, audacious, intrusive.
Opposites: unobtrusive.

obtuse ADJ = *see* **stupid** (1).

obvious ADJ = **clear**, plain, visible, noticeable, perceptible, discernible, detectable, recognizable, evident, apparent, manifest, palpable, patent, conspicuous, unconcealed, overt, pronounced, transparent, prominent, unmistakable, indisputable, undeniable; [inf] sticking out like a sore thumb, sticking out a mile.
Opposites: imperceptible, inconspicuous.

occasion NOUN 1 = **time**, juncture, point, situation, instance, case, circumstance. 2 = **event**, incident, occurrence, happening, episode, affair, experience.

▶ VERB = **cause**, give rise to, bring about, result in, lead to, prompt, provoke, produce, create, generate, engender.

occasional ADJ
= **infrequent**, intermittent, irregular, sporadic, odd, rare, casual, incidental.
Opposites: regular, habitual.

occasionally ADV = **now and then**, now and again, from time to time, sometimes, at times, every so often, once in a while, on occasion, periodically, at intervals, irregularly, sporadically, infrequently, intermittently, off and on.

occupation NOUN 1 = **job**, profession, business, employment, employ, career, calling, vocation, trade, craft, line, field, province, area.
2 = **occupancy**, tenancy, tenure, residence, inhabitancy, habitation, possession, holding.
3 = **invasion**, seizure, takeover, conquest,

capture, overthrow, subjugation, subjection.

occupy VERB **1 = live in**, inhabit, reside in, dwell in, tenant, have one's residence/abode in, make one's home in. **2 = fill**, fill up, take up, use up, utilize, cover. **3 = invade**, overrun, seize, take over.

occur VERB **1 = happen**, take place, come about, materialize, transpire, arise, crop up, turn up, eventuate; [poetic/literary] come to pass, befall. **2 = be found**, be met with, be present, exist, obtain, appear, present itself, show itself, manifest itself.

occurrence NOUN **1 = happening**, event, incident, circumstance, affair, episode, proceedings, adventure. **2 = existence**, appearance, manifestation, materialization.

odd ADJ **1 = strange**, eccentric, queer, peculiar, idiosyncratic, unconventional, outlandish, weird, bizarre, freakish; [inf] offbeat, wacky, freaky. **2 = occasional**, casual, temporary, part-time, seasonal, periodic, irregular, miscellaneous. **3 = random**, irregular, periodic, haphazard, chance, fortuitous. **4 = unmatched**, unpaired, left over, spare, remaining, surplus, superfluous, lone, single, solitary, sole. **Opposites:** ordinary.

odious ADJ **= abhorrent**, offensive, repugnant, disgusting, repulsive, repellent, revolting, foul, vile, unpleasant, disagreeable, loathsome, detestable, hateful, despicable, contemptible. **Opposites:** delightful.

odour NOUN **= aroma**, smell, scent, perfume, fragrance, bouquet, essence, stench, stink; [Brit. inf] niff, pong; [poetic/literary] redolence.

offence NOUN **1 = crime**, illegal act, wrongdoing, wrong, misdemeanour, misdeed, peccadillo, sin, transgression,

shortcoming, fault, lapse; [Law] malfeasance.
2 = annoyance, anger, indignation, exasperation, wrath, displeasure, disapproval, dislike, animosity, resentment; [poetic/literary] ire.

offend VERB **1 = give offence to**, affront, upset, displease, annoy, anger, incense, exasperate, vex, pique, put out, gall, irritate, provoke, ruffle, disgruntle, rankle with, outrage, insult, slight, humiliate; [inf] put someone's back up.
2 = commit a crime, break the law, do wrong, sin, go astray, fall from grace, err, transgress.

offender NOUN
= wrongdoer, culprit, criminal, lawbreaker, miscreant, delinquent, sinner, transgressor, malefactor.

offensive ADJ **1 = hurtful**, wounding, abusive, affronting, displeasing, annoying, exasperating, vexing, galling, irritating, provocative, objectionable, outrageous, insulting, rude, discourteous, uncivil, impolite.
2 = disagreeable, unpleasant, nasty, foul, vile, objectionable, odious, abominable, detestable, loathsome, repugnant, disgusting, obnoxious, repulsive, repellent.
Opposites: complimentary.

offer VERB **1 = put forward**, propose, advance, submit, propound, suggest, recommend.
2 = volunteer one's services, volunteer, offer one's service, offer assistance/help, make oneself available.

offering NOUN
= contribution, donation, subscription, gift, present, handout.

offhand ADJ **= casual**, unceremonious, cavalier, careless, indifferent, perfunctory, cursory, abrupt, brusque, discourteous, uncivil, impolite, rude.

office NOUN 1 = **place of business**, base, workplace. 2 = **post**, position, role, place, situation, station, function, responsibility, obligation, charge, tenure.

official ADJ = **authorized**, accredited, approved, validated, authenticated, certified, endorsed, sanctioned, licensed, recognized, accepted, legitimate, legal, lawful, bona fide, proper, ex cathedra; [inf] kosher. **Opposites:** unofficial.

officiate VERB = **take charge**, be in charge, preside, oversee, superintend, conduct, run, take the chair.

officious ADJ = **overzealous**, interfering, intrusive, meddlesome, importunate, forward, obtrusive, self-important, opinionated, dictatorial, domineering, pushy; [inf] nosy. **Opposites:** self-effacing.

offset VERB = **counterbalance**, counteract, countervail, balance, balance out, cancel out, neutralize, compensate for, make up for, make good.

offshoot NOUN = **branch**, subsidiary, adjunct, appendage.

offspring NOUN = **children**, family, progeny, young, descendants, heirs, successors, spawn; [inf] kids; [Law] issue.

often ADV = **frequently**, a lot, many a time, repeatedly, again and again, time and again, time after time, over and over, over and over again, day in, day out; [poetic/literary] oft, oft-times. **Opposites:** seldom, never.

oily ADJ 1 = **greasy**, fatty, buttery. 2 = **smooth**, smooth-talking, flattering, fulsome, glib, unctuous, subservient, servile, oleaginous.

ointment NOUN = **cream**, lotion, emollient, salve, balm, liniment, embrocation, unguent, gel.

old ADJ **1 = older**, elderly, aged, advanced in years, long in the tooth, mature, grey-haired, grizzled, hoary, past one's prime, ancient, decrepit, senile, venerable, senior; [Biology] senescent; [inf] getting on, past it, over the hill. **2 = out of date**, outdated, old-fashioned, outmoded, passé, archaic, obsolete, extinct, antiquated, antediluvian, superannuated; [inf] old hat. **3 = bygone**, past, early, earlier, primeval, primordial, prehistoric. **4 = age-old**, long-standing, long-lived, long-estab... -ring, ... -ex-, former, ...rous, one-time, sometime, erstwhile; [formal] quondam.
Opposites: young.

old age NOUN **= oldness**, elderliness, age, declining years, advanced years, winter/autumn of one's life, twilight years, senility, dotage; [Biology] senescence.

old-fashioned ADJ **= out of fashion**, outmoded, unfashionable, out of style, out of date, outdated, dated, out, dead, old-time, behind the times, past, bygone, passé, archaic, obsolescent, obsolete, ancient, antiquated, superannuated, antediluvian, old-fangled; [inf] old hat, not with it.
Opposites: up to date, fashionable.

omen NOUN **= portent**, sign, token, foretoken, harbinger, premonition, forewarning, warning, prediction, forecast, prophecy, augury.

ominous ADJ **= threatening**, menacing, minatory, black, dark, gloomy, heavy, sinister, bad, unpromising, unpropitious, pessimistic, inauspicious, unfavourable, unlucky.
Opposites: auspicious.

omission NOUN **1 = exclusion**, exception, deletion, erasure,

elimination, expunction.
2 = neglect, negligence,
dereliction, forgetfulness,
oversight, disregard,
default, failure.

omit VERB **1 = leave out**,
exclude, except, miss
out, miss, fail to
mention, pass over, drop;
[inf] give something a
miss. **2 = forget to**,
neglect to, fail to, leave
undone, overlook, skip.

omnipotent ADJ **= all-
powerful**, almighty,
supreme, pre-eminent,
invincible.

onerous ADJ **= arduous**,
strenuous, difficult, hard,
burdensome, crushing,
back-breaking, taxing,
demanding, exacting,
wearing, wearisome,
fatiguing.
Opposites: easy.

ongoing ADJ **= in
progress**, current,
progressing, advancing,
successful, developing,
evolving, growing,
extant.

onset NOUN **= start**,
beginning,
commencement,
inception, outbreak;

[inf] kick-off.
Opposites: end.

onslaught NOUN **= assault**,
attack, charge, storming,
sortie, sally, raid, foray,
push, thrust, drive, blitz.

onus NOUN **= burden**,
weight, load,
responsibility, liability,
obligation, duty, charge,
encumbrance.

open ADJ **1 = not shut**, not
closed, unlocked,
unbolted, unlatched,
unbarred, unfastened,
unsecured, ajar, wide
open, agape, gaping,
yawning. **2 = uncovered**,
topless, unsealed.
3 = exposed, unsheltered,
wide, wide open,
spacious, broad,
uncrowded, sprawling, airy,
undeveloped. **4 = candid**, honest, uncovered,
forthright, direct, blunt,
plain-spoken, downright.
5 = obvious, clear,
noticeable, visible,
apparent, evident,
manifest, overt,
conspicuous, patent,
unconcealed, unhidden,
undisguised, blatant,

flagrant. **6 = wide open to**, allowing of, permitting, vulnerable to, exposed to, susceptible to, liable to, at the mercy of, an easy target for. **7 = unbiased**, unprejudiced, non-partisan, impartial, objective, disinterested, dispassionate, detached.

▶ VERB **1 = throw open**, unlock, unbolt, unlatch, unbar, unfasten. **2 = unwrap**, undo, untie, unseal. Opposites: close.

opening NOUN **1 = gap**, aperture, space, hole, orifice, vent, slot, breach, crack, split, fissure, cleft, crevice, chink, interstice, rent, rupture. **2 = vacancy**, position, job, opportunity, chance; [inf] break, lucky break.

operate VERB **1 = function**, work, go, run, perform, act. **2 = manage**, run, work, use, utilize, employ, handle, be in charge of. **3 = perform an operation**, perform surgery; [inf] put under the knife.

operational ADJ **= operative**, workable, in operation, working, in working order, functioning, functional, going, in use, usable, in action, ready for action.

operative ADJ **1 = in operation**, in force, effective, valid. **2 = operational**, workable, working, functioning, functional, usable. Opposites: inoperative.

▶ NOUN **= worker**, workman, machinist, operator, mechanic, factory hand/employee.

opinion NOUN **= point of view**, view, viewpoint, belief, thought, thinking, way of thinking, standpoint, theory, judgement, estimation, feeling, sentiment, impression, notion, assumption, conception, conviction, persuasion, creed, dogma.

opponent NOUN **= opposition**, rival, adversary, opposer, contestant, competitor, enemy, foe, antagonist, contender, dissenter,

disputant.
Opposites: ally.

opportune ADJ
= **advantageous**,
favourable, auspicious,
propitious, good, lucky,
happy, timely, well
timed, fortunate,
providential, felicitous,
convenient, expedient,
suitable, apt, fitting,
relevant, pertinent.
Opposites: unfavourable.

opportunity NOUN
= **chance**, good time,
golden opportunity,
favourable time/
occasion/moment, right
set of circumstances,
appropriate time;
[inf] break.

oppose VERB = **be hostile
to**, take a stand against,
stand up to, take issue
with, take on, contradict,
counter, argue against,
counter-attack, confront,
resist, withstand, defy,
fight, put up a fight
against, combat, fly in
the face of.
Opposites: support.

opposite ADJ **1** = **facing**,
face to face with;
[inf] eyeball to eyeball

with. **2** = **opposing**,
differing, different,
unlike, contrary, reverse,
contradictory,
conflicting, clashing,
discordant, dissident, at
variance, incompatible,
irreconcilable,
antipathetic, poles apart.

opposition NOUN
1 = **hostility**, dislike,
disapproval, resistance,
defiance. **2** = **opponent**,
opposing side, other
side/team, rival,
adversary, competition,
antagonist, enemy, foe.

oppress VERB = **subjugate**,
enslave, suppress, crush,
subdue, quash, quell,
bring someone to their
knees, tyrannize, repress,
abuse, maltreat,
persecute, rule with a rod
of iron, trample on,
trample underfoot, ride
roughshod over.

oppressed ADJ
= **enslaved**, crushed,
subdued, repressed,
persecuted, abused,
maltreated, misused,
browbeaten,
downtrodden,
disadvantaged,

underprivileged.

oppression NOUN
= **subjugation**, subduing,
tyranny, suppression,
persecution, abuse,
maltreatment, cruelty,
brutality, injustice,
ruthlessness, harshness.

oppressive ADJ
1 = **tyrannical**, despotic,
Draconian, iron-fisted,
high-handed, repressive,
domineering, harsh,
crushing, cruel, brutal,
ruthless, merciless,
pitiless, unjust.
2 = **muggy**, close, airless,
stuffy, stifling,
suffocating, sultry, torrid.
Opposites: lenient.

oppressor NOUN = **tyrant**,
despot, autocrat,
persecutor, bully, iron
hand, slave-driver, hard
taskmaster, scourge,
dictator.

optimistic ADJ = **positive**,
sanguine, hopeful,
confident, bullish,
cheerful, buoyant;
[inf] upbeat.
Opposites: pessimistic.

optimum ADJ 1 = **most
favourable**, best, most
advantageous, most

appropriate, ideal,
perfect. 2 = **peak**, top,
best, perfect, ideal,
flawless, superlative,
optimal.

option NOUN = **choice**,
freedom of choice,
alternative, other
possibility, preference.

optional ADJ = **non-
compulsory**, not
required, voluntary,
discretionary, at one's
discretion, elective.
Opposites: compulsory.

opulent ADJ 1 = **luxurious**,
sumptuous, lavishly
appointed; [inf] plush,
plushy, ritzy. 2 = **affluent**,
wealthy, rich, well off,
well-to-do, moneyed,
prosperous; [inf] well
heeled, rolling in it.
Opposites: spartan, poor.

orbit NOUN 1 = **revolution**,
circle, circuit, cycle,
rotation. 2 = **sphere**,
sphere of influence,
range, reach, scope,
ambit, sweep, domain.

ordeal NOUN = **trial**, test,
tribulation, suffering,
affliction, distress, agony,
anguish, torture,
torment, calamity,

o

trouble, nightmare.

order NOUN **1 = orderliness**, neatness, tidiness, trimness, harmony. **2 = method**, organization, system, plan, uniformity, regularity, symmetry, pattern. **3 = condition**, state, shape, situation. **4 = arrangement**, grouping, system, organization, form, structure, disposition, classification, categorization, codification, series, sequence, progression, succession, layout, set-up. **5 = command**, direction, directive, instruction, decree, edict, injunction, law, rule, regulation, ordinance, stipulation, dictate. **6 = request**, call, requirement, requisition, demand, booking, reservation, commission. **7 = brotherhood**, sisterhood, community. ▶ VERB **1 = give the order to**, command, instruct, direct, bid, enjoin. **2 = put in/place an order for**, request, call for, requisition, book, reserve, contract for, apply for, send away for.

orderly ADJ **1 = in order**, neat, tidy, trim, shipshape, shipshape and Bristol fashion, in apple-pie order. **2 = organized**, well organized, methodical, systematic, efficient, businesslike. **3 = well behaved**, disciplined, quiet, peaceful, controlled, restrained.
Opposites: disorderly.

ordinary ADJ **1 = usual**, normal, standard, typical, stock, common, customary, habitual, accustomed, everyday, quotidian, regular, routine, established, settled, fixed, prevailing, humdrum; [poetic/literary] wonted. **2 = run-of-the-mill**, common, conventional, standard, typical, average, commonplace, workaday, humdrum, unremarkable, unexceptional, undistinguished, unmemorable,

pedestrian, prosaic,
unpretentious, modest,
plain, simple.
Opposites: unusual.

organization NOUN
1 = **arrangement**,
regulation, coordination,
systematization,
categorization,
administration, running,
management.
2 = **company**, firm,
concern, operation,
corporation, institution,
group, consortium,
conglomerate, combine,
syndicate, federation,
confederation,
association, body.

organize VERB 1 = **arrange**,
dispose, regulate,
marshal, put in order,
put straight, coordinate,
systematize, methodize,
standardize, collocate,
group, sort, sort out,
classify, categorize,
catalogue, codify,
tabulate. 2 = **be**
responsible for, be in
charge of, take care of,
administrate, run,
manage, lick/knock into
shape, see to.

orientate VERB 1 = **find**
one's bearings, get the
lie of the land, establish
one's location. 2 = **adapt**,
adjust, accommodate,
familiarize, acclimatize,
find one's feet. 3 = **direct**,
guide, lead, point
someone in the direction
of, turn.

orifice NOUN = **opening**,
hole, vent, aperture, gap,
space, breach, break,
rent, slot, slit, cleft,
cranny, fissure, crevice,
rift, crack, chink.

origin NOUN 1 = **source**,
basis, base, derivation,
root, roots, provenance,
etymology, genesis,
spring, wellspring,
fountain, fountainhead,
aetiology. 2 = **descent**,
ancestry, pedigree,
lineage, heritage,
parentage, extraction,
beginnings.

original ADJ 1 = **aboriginal**,
indigenous, early,
earliest, first, primary,
primordial, primal,
primeval, primitive,
autochthonous.
2 = **innovative**,
innovatory, inventive,

new, novel, fresh, creative, imaginative, individual, ingenious, unusual, unconventional, unorthodox, unprecedented, ground-breaking.
Opposites: unoriginal, derivative.

originate VERB 1 = **arise**, stem, spring, result, derive, start, begin, commence. 2 = **give birth to**, set in motion, set up, invent, dream up, conceive, discover, initiate, create, formulate, inaugurate, pioneer, introduce, establish, found, evolve, develop, generate.

ornament NOUN 1 = **knick-knack**, trinket, bauble, gewgaw, accessory, decoration, frill, whatnot, doodah. 2 = **decoration**, adornment, embellishment, trimming, garnish, garnishing.

ornamental ADJ = **decorative**, attractive, showy, embellishing, ornamenting.

ornate ADJ = **elaborate**, over-elaborate, decorated, embellished, adorned, ornamented, fancy, fussy, busy, ostentatious, showy, baroque, rococo; [inf] flash.
Opposites: plain.

orthodox ADJ 1 = **doctrinal**, of the faith, of the true faith, sound, conservative, correct, faithful, true, devoted, strict, devout. 2 = **conventional**, accepted, approved, correct, proper, conformist, established, traditional, usual, regular.
Opposites: unconventional.

ostensible ADJ = **apparent**, seeming, professed, outward, alleged, claimed, purported, pretended, feigned, supposed.
Opposites: genuine.

ostentation NOUN = **showiness**, show, conspicuousness, obtrusiveness, loudness, extravagance, flamboyance, gaudiness, flashiness, pretentiousness, affectation, exhibitionism; [inf] swank.

ostentatious ADJ
= **showy**, conspicuous, obtrusive, loud, extravagant, flamboyant, gaudy, flashy, pretentious, affected, overdone; [inf] flash, swanky.
Opposites: unobtrusive.

ostracize VERB = **cold-shoulder**, give someone the cold shoulder, send to Coventry, exclude, shut out, shun, spurn, avoid, boycott, repudiate, cast out, reject, blackball, blacklist.
Opposites: welcome.

other ADJ 1 = **different**, unlike, variant, dissimilar, distinct, separate, alternative.
2 = **more**, additional, further, extra.

outbreak NOUN = **eruption**, flare-up, upsurge, outburst, start, rash.

outburst NOUN = **burst**, explosion, eruption, outbreak, flare-up, attack, fit, spasm, paroxysm.

outcome NOUN = **result**, upshot, issue, product, conclusion, after-effect, aftermath, wake; [inf] pay-off.

outdated ADJ = **out of date**, out of fashion, old-fashioned, unfashionable, outmoded, dated, passé, behind the times, antiquated, archaic.
Opposites: modern.

outdo VERB = **surpass**, top, exceed, excel, get the better of, outstrip, outshine, eclipse, overshadow, outclass, overcome, beat, defeat.

outer ADJ 1 = **outside**, outermost, outward, exterior, external, surface, superficial.
2 = **outlying**, distant, remote, faraway, peripheral, fringe, perimeter.
Opposites: inner.

outgoing ADJ 1 = **extrovert**, demonstrative, affectionate, warm, friendly, genial, cordial, affable, sociable, communicative, open, expansive, talkative,

gregarious, approachable.
2 = **retiring**, departing,
leaving, withdrawing,
ex-, former.
Opposites: reserved,
incoming.

outlandish ADJ = **strange**,
unfamiliar, unknown,
unheard of, odd,
unusual, extraordinary,
peculiar, queer, curious,
singular, eccentric,
quaint, bizarre,
grotesque, preposterous,
weird; [inf] freaky, wacky,
far out, off-the-wall.
Opposites: ordinary.

outline NOUN **1** = **thumbnail
sketch**, rough idea, quick
rundown, abbreviated
version, summary,
synopsis, main points,
bones, bare bones.
2 = **contour**, silhouette,
profile, lineaments,
delineation,
configuration, perimeter,
circumference.

outlook NOUN **1** = **point of
view**, viewpoint, view,
perspective, attitude,
frame of mind,
standpoint, slant, angle,
interpretation, opinion.
2 = **vista**, view, prospect,
panorama, aspect.

outlying ADJ = **outer**,
outermost, out of the
way, remote, distant,
far-flung, peripheral,
isolated, inaccessible, off
the beaten track.

output NOUN = **production**,
product, productivity,
yield, harvest, crop.

outrage NOUN **1** = **atrocity**,
crime, horror, enormity,
brutality. **2** = **offence**,
affront, insult, injury,
abuse, scandal,
desecration, violation.
3 = **anger**, fury, rage,
indignation, wrath,
annoyance, shock,
resentment, horror.

outrageous ADJ
1 = **intolerable**,
insufferable,
insupportable,
unendurable, unbearable,
impossible, exasperating,
offensive, provocative,
maddening, distressing.
2 = **atrocious**, heinous,
abominable, wicked, vile,
foul, monstrous, horrible,
horrid, dreadful, terrible,
horrendous, hideous,
ghastly, unspeakable,
gruesome.

outside ADJ 1 = **outer**, outermost, outward, exterior, external. 2 = **outdoor**, out of doors. 3 = **unlikely**, improbable, slight, slender, slim, small, faint, negligible, marginal, remote, distant, vague.
Opposites: inside.

outsider NOUN = **alien**, stranger, foreigner, outlander, immigrant, incomer, newcomer, parvenu/parvenue, arriviste, interloper, intruder, gatecrasher, outcast, misfit.

outskirts PL NOUN = **vicinity**, neighbourhood, environs, outlying districts, fringes, margin, periphery, borders, boundary, suburbs.

outspoken ADJ = **candid**, frank, forthright, direct, straightforward, plain-spoken, explicit, blunt.
Opposites: diplomatic.

outstanding ADJ 1 = **excellent**, remarkable, exceptional, superlative, pre-eminent, eminent, well known, notable, noteworthy, distinguished, important, famous, famed, renowned, celebrated, great. 2 = **unpaid**, unsettled, owing, due.
Opposites: unexceptional.

outwardly ADV 1 = **externally**, on the outside. 2 = **on the surface**, superficially, on the face of it, to all appearances, as far as one can see, to all intents and purposes, apparently, evidently.

outwit VERB = **get the better of**, be cleverer than, outsmart, outmanoeuvre, steal a march on, trick, dupe, make a fool of; [inf] put one over on, pull a fast one on.

overall ADJ = **comprehensive**, universal, all-embracing, inclusive, all-inclusive, general, sweeping, complete, blanket, umbrella, global.
▶ ADV = **on the whole**, in general, generally speaking.

overawe VERB
= **intimidate**, daunt, disconcert, abash, dismay, frighten, alarm, scare, terrify, terrorize.

overcome VERB
= **conquer**, defeat, vanquish, beat, prevail over, get the better of, triumph over, best, worst, trounce, rout, master, overpower, overwhelm, overthrow, subdue, subjugate, quell, quash, crush; [inf] thrash, lick, clobber, whip.
▸ ADJ = **overwhelmed**, emotional, moved, affected, speechless, at a loss for words; [inf] bowled over.

overdue ADJ **1** = **late**, behind schedule, delayed, belated, tardy, unpunctual. **2** = **unpaid**, owed, owing, outstanding, unsettled, in arrears.

overflow VERB = **flow over**, run over, spill over, brim over, well over, pour forth, stream forth, discharge, surge, debouch.

overhead ADV = **above**, up above, high up, up in the sky, on high, aloft.

overlook VERB **1** = **fail to notice**, miss, leave, neglect; [inf] slip up on. **2** = **leave undone**, ignore, disregard, omit, neglect, forget. **3** = **look over**, look on to, front on to, have/ afford a view of, command a view of.

overpowering ADJ
= **overwhelming**, burdensome, weighty, unbearable, unendurable, intolerable, shattering; [inf] mind-blowing.

overriding ADJ = **most important**, predominant, principal, primary, paramount, chief, main, major, foremost, central.

oversight NOUN
1 = **carelessness**, inattention, neglect, inadvertence, laxity, dereliction, omission.
2 = **mistake**, error, blunder, gaffe, fault, omission, slip, lapse.

overt ADJ = **obvious**, noticeable, undisguised, unconcealed, apparent, plain, manifest, patent,

open, public, blatant, conspicuous.
Opposites: covert.

overtake VERB = **pass**, get past, go past, go by, overhaul, leave behind, outstrip, go faster than.

overthrow VERB = *see* **overcome**.

overtone NOUN
= **implication**, innuendo, hint, suggestion, insinuation, association, connotation, undercurrent, nuance.

overwhelm VERB
1 = **overcome**, move, make emotional, daze, dumbfound, shake, take aback, leave speechless, stagger. 2 = **inundate**, flood, deluge, engulf, submerge, swamp, bury, overload, overburden, snow under.

overwhelming ADJ
1 = **uncontrollable**, irrepressible, irresistible, overpowering. 2 = **vast**, massive, great, large.

owe VERB = **be in debt**, be indebted, be under an obligation, be obligated, be beholden.

own VERB = **possess**, have in one's possession, have, keep, retain, maintain, hold, enjoy.
■ **own up** = *see* **confess**.

Pp

pace NOUN 1 = **step**, stride.
2 = **gait**, walk, tread.
3 = **speed**, swiftness,
fastness, quickness,
rapidity, velocity.

pacify VERB = **calm down**,
placate, conciliate,
propitiate, appease,
mollify, soothe,
tranquillize, quieten.
Opposites: enrage.

pack NOUN 1 = **packet**,
container, package,
carton. 2 = **backpack**,
rucksack, knapsack,
kitbag, satchel.
▶ VERB 1 = **fill**, store, stow,
load, bundle, stuff, cram.
2 = **fill**, crowd, throng,
mob, cram, jam, press
into, squeeze into.

packed ADJ = **full**, filled to
capacity, crowded,
thronged, mobbed,
crammed, jammed,
brimful, chock-full,
chock-a-block, jam-
packed.

pact NOUN = **agreement**,
treaty, deal, contract,
settlement, bargain,
compact, covenant,
bond, concordat,
entente.

pad NOUN 1 = **padding**,
wadding, stuffing, buffer.
2 = **cushion**, pillow,
bolster. 3 = **notepad**,
writing pad, notebook;
[Brit.] jotter; [inf] memo
pad.
▶ VERB = **pack**, stuff, line,
cushion, protect.

paddle VERB = **row**, pull,
oar, scull, pole, punt.

paddock NOUN = **field**,
meadow, enclosure, yard,
pen, pound, corral.

pagan NOUN = **unbeliever**,
heathen, infidel, idolater,
pantheist, polytheist.
▶ ADJ = **heathen**, infidel,
idolatrous, pantheistic,

polytheistic.

pageantry NOUN
= **spectacle**,
magnificence, pomp,
splendour, grandeur,
glamour, theatricality,
show, showiness;
[inf] pizzazz.

pain NOUN 1 = **soreness**,
hurt, ache, aching,
agony, throb, throbbing,
smarting, twinge, pang,
spasm, cramp,
discomfort, irritation,
tenderness. 2 = **suffering**,
hurt, sorrow, grief,
heartache, sadness,
unhappiness, distress,
misery, wretchedness,
anguish, affliction, woe.

pained ADJ = **hurt**,
aggrieved, reproachful,
offended, insulted, upset,
unhappy, distressed;
[inf] miffed.

painful ADJ 1 = **sore**,
hurting, aching,
throbbing, smarting,
tender, inflamed,
agonizing, excruciating.
2 = **disagreeable**,
unpleasant, nasty,
distressing, disquieting,
disturbing, miserable,
wretched, agonizing,

harrowing.

painless ADJ 1 = **pain-free**,
without pain. 2 = **easy**,
simple, trouble-free,
effortless, plain sailing;
[inf] as easy as pie, as easy
as falling off a log,
child's play, a cinch.
Opposites: painful,
difficult.

painstaking ADJ
= **careful**, thorough,
assiduous, conscientious,
meticulous, punctilious,
sedulous, scrupulous.
Opposites: careless.

painting NOUN = **picture**,
illustration, portrayal,
depiction, delineation,
representation, likeness.

pair NOUN = **couple**, duo,
brace, two, twosome,
matched set, matching
set.

▪ **pair off** = **arrange/group
in pairs**, pair up, put
together, get together,
join up, link up, team
up.

palatable ADJ 1 = **tasty**,
appetizing, pleasant-
tasting, flavoursome,
delicious, mouth-
watering, savoury;
[inf] scrumptious, yummy.

2 = **agreeable**, pleasant, pleasing, pleasurable, nice, attractive, acceptable, satisfactory.
Opposites: unpalatable.

palatial ADJ = **luxurious**, imposing, splendid, grand, magnificent, stately, majestic, opulent, sumptuous, plush.
Opposites: humble.

pale ADJ 1 = **white**, white-faced, colourless, anaemic, wan, drained, pallid, pasty, peaky, ashen, waxen, as white as a sheet/ghost, deathly pale. 2 = **light**, pastel, muted, low-key, restrained, faded, bleached, washed out, etoliated. 3 = **dim**, faint, weak, feeble, thin.
Opposites: dark.
▶ VERB = **grow/become pale**, go/turn white, blanch, lose colour.

pallid ADJ = *see* **pale** ADJ (1).

palpable ADJ = **tangible**, feelable, touchable, solid, concrete.
Opposites: intangible.

paltry ADJ 1 = **small**, meagre, trifling, minor, insignificant, trivial,

derisory; [inf] piddling. 2 = **worthless**, despicable, contemptible, miserable, wretched, sorry, puny.
Opposites: considerable.

pamper VERB = **spoil**, cosset, indulge, overindulge, humour, coddle, mollycoddle.

pamphlet NOUN = **leaflet**, booklet, brochure, circular.

panache NOUN = **style**, verve, flamboyance, zest, dash, flourish, brio, elan; [inf] pizzazz.

pander VERB = **gratify**, indulge, humour, give in to, please, satisfy, cater for.

panic NOUN = **alarm**, fright, fear, terror, horror, agitation, hysteria.
Opposites: calm.
▶ VERB = **be alarmed**, take fright, be terrified/horrified, be agitated, be hysterical, lose one's nerve, overreact.

panoramic ADJ = **wide**, extensive, sweeping, bird's-eye, comprehensive.

pant VERB = **puff**, huff and puff, blow, gasp, wheeze.

paper NOUN 1 = **newspaper**, magazine, journal, gazette, broadsheet, tabloid; [inf] rag.
2 = **essay**, article, work, dissertation, treatise, thesis, monograph, study, report.

parade NOUN = **procession**, progression, cavalcade, spectacle, pageant, array.
▶ VERB 1 = **march**, go in columns, file by.
2 = **display**, show off, exhibit, show, demonstrate, make a show of, flaunt.

paradox NOUN = **contradiction**, inconsistency, incongruity, anomaly, enigma, puzzle, absurdity, oxymoron.

paradoxical ADJ = **self-contradictory**, inconsistent, incongruous, anomalous, enigmatic, puzzling, absurd.

parallel ADJ 1 = **side by side**, equidistant, collateral. 2 = **similar**, like, resembling, analogous, comparable, equivalent, corresponding, matching.
▶ NOUN = **counterpart**, equivalent, analogue, match, duplicate, equal.
▶ VERB = **be similar to**, be like, resemble, be analogous to, correspond to, compare with, be comparable/equivalent to.

paralyse VERB = **immobilize**, numb, deaden, dull, incapacitate, debilitate, disable, cripple.

paralysis NOUN = **immobility**, powerlessness, lack of feeling, numbness, palsy, incapacity, debilitation; [Medicine] paresis.

parameter NOUN = **limit**, limitation, limiting factor, restriction, specification, guidelines, framework.

parched ADJ = **dried up/out**, dry, baked, burned, scorched, seared, desiccated, dehydrated, withered, shrivelled.

pardon NOUN
1 = **forgiveness**, forbearance, indulgence, clemency, lenience;

p

leniency, mercy. **2 = free pardon**, reprieve, release, acquittal, absolution, amnesty, exoneration, exculpation.
▶ VERB **1 = excuse**, condone, let off. **2 = reprieve**, release, acquit, absolve, exonerate, exculpate.

pardonable ADJ = **forgivable**, excusable, allowable, condonable, understandable, minor, slight, venial.
Opposites: inexcusable.

parentage NOUN = **family**, birth, origins, extraction, ancestry, lineage, descent, heritage, pedigree.

parliament NOUN = **legislative assembly**, congress, senate, chamber, house, convocation, diet.

parody NOUN = **lampoon**, spoof, send-up, satire, pastiche, caricature, mimicry, take-off, burlesque.
▶ VERB = **lampoon**, satirize, caricature, mimic, take off, send up, burlesque.

parry VERB = **ward off**, fend off, stave off, turn aside, avert, deflect, block, rebuff, repel, repulse, hold at bay.

part NOUN **1 = portion**, division, section, segment, bit, piece, fragment, scrap, slice, fraction, chunk.
2 = section, area, region, sector, quarter, territory, neighbourhood.
3 = function, role, job, task, work, responsibility, capacity, participation.
4 = role, character.
▶ VERB **1 = divide**, separate, split, break up, sever, disjoin. **2 = leave**, go away, say goodbye, say one's goodbyes, separate; [inf] split, push off, hit the road.

partial ADJ **1 = part**, in part, limited, incomplete, imperfect, fragmentary.
2 = biased, prejudiced, partisan, one-sided, discriminatory, preferential, unjust, unfair.
Opposites: complete, impartial.
■**be partial to** = *see* **like**[1] **(2)**.

participate VERB = **take part in**, join in, engage in, play a part in, contribute to, be involved in, share in, have a hand in.

participation NOUN = **part**, contribution, association, involvement, partaking.

particle NOUN **1** = **bit**, piece, speck, spot, atom, molecule. **2** = **iota**, jot, whit, grain, bit, scrap, shred, morsel, atom, hint, touch, trace, suggestion.

particular ADJ **1** = **specific**, individual, single, distinct, precise. **2** = **special**, especial, singular, peculiar, exceptional, unusual, uncommon, notable, noteworthy, remarkable. **3** = **fastidious**, discriminating, selective, fussy, painstaking, meticulous, punctilious, demanding, critical, finicky; [inf] pernickety, choosy, picky. **Opposites:** general, careless.

particularly ADV **1** = **especially**, specially, singularly, peculiarly, distinctly, markedly, exceptionally, unusually, uncommonly. **2** = **in particular**, specifically, explicitly, expressly, specially, especially.

partisan NOUN **1** = **guerrilla**, resistance fighter, underground fighter. **2** = **supporter**, adherent, devotee, backer, follower, disciple.
▶ ADJ = see **partial** (**2**).

partition VERB = **divide**, divide up, subdivide, separate, separate off, screen off, wall off, fence off.

partly ADV = **in part**, partially, not wholly, not fully, half, somewhat, to some extent/degree, in some measure, fractionally, slightly. **Opposites:** completely.

partnership NOUN **1** = **association**, cooperation, collaboration, alliance, union, fellowship, companionship. **2** = **collaboration**, collusion, connivance, conspiracy.

party NOUN **1** = **gathering**, function, reception, celebration, festivity, at-home, soirée, bacchanal; [inf] do, bash, shindig; [Brit. inf] rave-up. **2** = **political party**, alliance, association, grouping, faction, camp, set, caucus.

pass VERB **1** = **go**, move, proceed, progress, drive, run, travel, roll, flow, course. **2** = **go past**, move past, go/get ahead of, go by, overtake, outstrip. **3** = **hand over**, reach, let someone have, give, transfer. **4** = **elapse**, go by, proceed, progress, advance. **5** = **spend**, occupy, fill, take up, use, employ, while away. **6** = **gain a pass in**, get through, be successful in, succeed in, pass muster in. **7** = **vote for**, accept, approve, adopt, authorize, ratify.
▶ NOUN = **permit**, warrant, authorization, licence, passport, visa, safe conduct, exeat.
■ **pass for** = **be taken for**, be accepted as, be

mistaken for.
■ **pass out** = **faint**, collapse, black out, keel over, swoon.

passable ADJ **1** = **adequate**, all right, tolerable, fair, acceptable, satisfactory, mediocre, middling, ordinary, average, run-of-the-mill, not too bad, unexceptional, indifferent. **2** = **open**, clear, crossable, traversable, navigable, unblocked, unobstructed.

passage NOUN **1** = **passing**, progress, advance, process, flow, course. **2** = **journey**, voyage, transit, trek, crossing, trip, tour. **3** = **passageway**, corridor, hall, hallway, entrance hall, entrance, vestibule, lobby. **4** = **extract**, excerpt, quotation, citation, section, verse.

passer-by NOUN = **bystander**, onlooker, witness, spectator.

passion NOUN **1** = **intensity**, fervour, ardour, zeal, vehemence, fire, emotion, feeling, zest, eagerness, excitement, animation.

2 = fascination, keen interest, obsession, fixation, craze, mania.

passionate ADJ
1 = impassioned, intense, fervent, fervid, ardent, zealous, vehement, fiery, emotional, heartfelt, animated. **2 = ardent**, aroused, desirous, hot, sexy, amorous, sensual, erotic, lustful.
Opposites: apathetic, frigid.

passive ADJ **1 = inactive**, unassertive, uninvolved, unresisting, yielding, submissive, compliant, pliant, acquiescent, quiescent, resigned, obedient, tractable, malleable. **2 = impassive**, emotionless, unmoved, unresponsive, undemonstrative, dispassionate, detached, distant, remote, aloof, indifferent.
Opposites: active.

past ADJ **1 = gone by**, gone, bygone, elapsed, over, ended, former, long ago. **2 = former**, previous,

prior, erstwhile, one-time, sometime.
Opposites: present.

pastel ADJ **= pale**, soft, delicate, muted, subdued, faint, low-key.
Opposites: vivid.

pastime NOUN **= hobby**, leisure activity, sport, game, recreation, diversion, amusement, entertainment, distraction, relaxation.

pastoral ADJ **= rural**, country, rustic, simple, idyllic, innocent, Arcadian, agricultural, bucolic, georgic.

pasture NOUN **= pasturage**, grazing, grassland, grass, field, meadow.

patch NOUN **1 = cover**, covering, pad, shield.
2 = plot, area, piece, tract, parcel.
▸ VERB **= cover**, mend, repair, fix, sew up, stitch.

patent ADJ **= obvious**, clear, plain, evident, apparent, manifest, transparent, conspicuous, blatant, unmistakable.

path NOUN **1 = pathway**, footpath, footway, track, trail, towpath, walk.

p

2 = course, route, circuit, track, orbit, trajectory.

pathetic ADJ **1 = piteous**, pitiful, moving, touching, poignant, affecting, heartbreaking, heart-rending, sad, wretched, mournful, woeful. **2 = lamentable**, deplorable, miserable, wretched, feeble, pitiful, woeful, poor, contemptible, inadequate, unsatisfactory, worthless.

pathological ADJ **= compulsive**, obsessive, irrational, unreasonable, illogical.

patience NOUN **1 = calmness**, composure, even-temperedness, equanimity, serenity, tranquillity, restraint, imperturbability, tolerance, indulgence, forbearance, endurance, resignation, stoicism, fortitude. **2 = perseverance**, persistence, endurance, tenacity, assiduity, diligence, staying power, indefatigability, doggedness, singleness of purpose.
Opposites: impatience.

patient ADJ **= uncomplaining**, serene, calm, composed, even-tempered, tranquil, restrained, imperturbable, tolerant, accommodating, long-suffering, forbearing, indulgent, resigned, stoical, unflappable; [inf] cool.
Opposites: impatient.

patriotic ADJ **= nationalist**, nationalistic, chauvinistic, flag-waving, jingoistic.

patrol VERB **= make the rounds of**, range, police, keep watch on, guard, keep guard on, monitor.
▶ NOUN **1 = patrolling**, round, policing, watch, guard, monitoring. **2 = sentry**, guard, watchman, watch, nightwatchman, policeman/policewoman.

patron NOUN **1 = sponsor**, backer, benefactor/benefactress, promoter, friend; [inf] angel. **2 = customer**, client, shopper, regular, frequenter.

patronize VERB **1 = look down on**, talk down to, condescend to, treat condescendingly, treat scornfully/ contemptuously, be snobbish to. **2 = be a customer of**, be a client of, frequent, shop at, buy from, do business with, deal with, trade with.

patronizing ADJ **= condescending**, supercilious, superior, haughty, lofty, lordly, snobbish; [inf] snooty, toffee-nosed.

pattern NOUN **1 = decoration**, design, motif, ornamentation, device, figure. **2 = plan**, guide, blueprint, model, design, template, instructions.

pause VERB **= stop**, halt, cease, discontinue, take a break, desist, rest, hold back, delay, hesitate, waver; [inf] take a breather.
▸ NOUN **= break**, halt, stoppage, cessation, interruption, lull, respite, stay, discontinuation, gap, interlude, intermission, interval, rest, delay, hesitation.

pay VERB **1 = settle up with**, remunerate, reimburse, recompense. **2 = pay out**, spend, expend, lay out, part with, disburse, hand over, remit, render; [inf] shell out, fork out, cough up. **3 = make money**, be profitable, make a profit, be remunerative, make a return. **4 = repay**, be advantageous to, be of advantage to, be of benefit to, be beneficial to, be profitable to, be worthwhile to.
▸ NOUN **= payment**, salary, wages, earnings, fee, remuneration, recompense, reimbursement, reward, stipend, emoluments.

payment NOUN **1 = settlement**, discharge, clearance, squaring, liquidation. **2 =** See **pay** NOUN. **3 = instalment**, premium, amount, remittance.

peace NOUN **1 = tranquillity**, peacefulness, serenity,

calm, calmness,
composure, placidity,
rest, repose,
contentment.
2 = harmony,
peaceableness,
peacefulness, accord,
amity, amicableness,
goodwill, friendship,
cordiality;
[formal] concord. **3 = treaty**,
truce, agreement,
armistice, cessation of
hostilities, non-
aggression, ceasefire.
Opposites: anxiety, war.

peaceable ADJ = **peace-
loving**, non-violent,
easy-going, placid,
gentle, mild, good-
natured, even-tempered,
amiable, amicable,
pacific, pacifist, dovelike,
dovish.
Opposites: aggressive.

peaceful ADJ = **tranquil**,
restful, quiet, calm, still,
serene, composed, placid,
reposeful, undisturbed,
untroubled, unworried,
anxiety-free.
Opposites: noisy, agitated.

peacemaker NOUN
= **conciliator**, mediator,
arbitrator, pacifier,

appeaser, peace-monger.

peak NOUN **1 = top**, summit,
crest, pinnacle,
mountain, hill, height,
alp. **2 = height**, high
point, climax,
culmination, zenith,
acme, meridian, apogee,
prime, heyday.
Opposites: nadir.

peculiar ADJ **1 = strange**,
odd, queer, funny,
curious, unusual,
abnormal, eccentric,
unconventional, bizarre,
weird, quaint,
outlandish, out of the
way, grotesque, freakish,
offbeat, droll, comical;
[inf] far out, way-out.
2 = characteristic,
distinctive, distinct,
individual,
distinguishing, special,
unique, idiosyncratic.
Opposites: ordinary.

peculiarity NOUN
1 = strangeness, oddness,
queerness, abnormality,
eccentricity,
unconventionality,
bizarreness, weirdness,
outlandishness,
grotesqueness,
freakishness.

2 = characteristic, feature, quality, property, trait, attribute, mark, stamp, hallmark.

pedantic ADJ **= precise**, exact, scrupulous, over-scrupulous, punctilious, meticulous, overnice, perfectionist, formalist, dogmatic, literalist, literalistic, quibbling, hair-splitting, casuistic, casuistical, pettifogging; [inf] nit-picking.

pedestal NOUN **= base**, support, stand, foundation, pillar, column, plinth.

pedestrian NOUN **= walker**, person on foot, hiker, footslogger.
▶ ADJ **1 = pedestrianized**, for pedestrians. **2 = plodding**, unimaginative, uninspired, unexciting, dull, flat, prosaic, turgid, stodgy, mundane, humdrum, banal, run-of-the-mill, commonplace, ordinary, mediocre.
Opposites: inspired.

peek VERB **= peep**, glance, sneak a look, cast a brief look, look hurriedly, look; [inf] take a gander, have a look-see.

peephole NOUN **= aperture**, opening, spyhole, judas, slit, crack, chink, crevice, fissure.

peer¹ VERB **= look closely**, try to see, narrow one's eyes, screw up one's eyes, squint.

peer² NOUN **1 = noble**, nobleman, aristocrat, lord, patrician.
2 = compeer, fellow, equal, match, like, co-equal.

peeve VERB **= irritate**, annoy, anger, vex, provoke, upset, exasperate, irk, pique, nettle, get on someone's nerves; [Brit.] rub up the wrong way; [inf] aggravate, miff; [Brit. inf] nark.

penalize VERB **= punish**, discipline, fine, correct; [formal] castigate.
Opposites: reward.

penalty NOUN **= penance**, fine, forfeit, sentence, mulct.

penance NOUN
= atonement, reparation, amends, mortification.

p

penchant NOUN = **liking**, fondness, preference, taste, partiality, inclination, bent, proclivity, predilection.

pending ADJ = **imminent**, impending, on the way, coming, approaching, forthcoming, near, nearing, close, close at hand, in the offing.

penetrate VERB 1 = **pierce**, bore, perforate, stab, prick, gore, spike.
2 = **permeate**, pervade, fill, imbue, suffuse, seep through, saturate.

penitent ADJ = **repentant**, contrite, regretful, remorseful, sorry, apologetic, rueful, ashamed, abject, sorrowful.
Opposites: unrepentant.

penniless ADJ = **impecunious**, penurious, impoverished, indigent, poor, poverty-stricken, destitute, bankrupt, hard up; [inf] broke; [Brit. inf] skint.
Opposites: wealthy.

pensive ADJ = **thoughtful**, reflective, lost in thought, contemplative, meditative, cogitative, ruminative, absorbed, preoccupied.

people NOUN 1 = **persons**, individuals, human beings, humans, mortals, living souls, men, women, and children.
2 = **race**, tribe, clan, nation, country, population, populace.
3 = **the general public**, the public, the masses, the rank and file, commonalty, the mob, the multitude, the hoi polloi.

perceive VERB 1 = **see**, catch sight of, spot, observe, glimpse, notice, make out, discern, behold, espy, detect, witness, remark.
2 = **discern**, appreciate, recognize, be aware of, be conscious of, know, grasp, understand, comprehend, apprehend, see, sense.

perceptible ADJ = **perceivable**, discernible, noticeable, detectable, distinguishable, appreciable, visible,

observable, distinct, palpable, tangible.
Opposites: imperceptible.

perception NOUN
1 = **discernment**, appreciation, recognition, awareness, consciousness, knowledge, grasp, understanding, comprehension, apprehension, notion, conception, idea, sense. **2** = **perspicacity**, discernment, perceptiveness, understanding, discrimination, insight, intuition, feeling, sensitivity.

perceptive ADJ
= **penetrating**, astute, shrewd, discerning, perspicacious, percipient, understanding, discriminating, intuitive, responsive, sensitive.
Opposites: obtuse.

perch NOUN = **pole**, rod, branch, roost, rest.
▸ VERB = **sit**, rest, roost, settle, alight, land.

peremptory ADJ
= **imperious**, high-handed, overbearing,

dogmatic, autocratic, dictatorial, domineering, arbitrary, tyrannical, despotic, arrogant.

perfect ADJ **1** = **flawless**, faultless, unmarred, ideal, impeccable, consummate, immaculate, exemplary, superb, superlative, supreme, excellent, complete, full, whole, entire. **2** = **exact**, precise, accurate, faithful, strict; [Brit. inf] spot on.
3 = **absolute**, complete, out-and-out, thorough, thoroughgoing, downright, utter, sheer, consummate, unmitigated, unqualified.
▸ VERB = **make perfect**, render faultless/flawless, polish, refine, complete, consummate, put the finishing touches to.

perfection NOUN
1 = **perfecting**, polishing, refinement, completion, consummation. **2** = **flawlessness**, faultlessness, impeccability, immaculateness, exemplariness,

superbness.

perfidious ADJ
= **treacherous**, traitorous, treasonous, false, untrue, disloyal, faithless, unfaithful, deceitful.
Opposites: faithful.

perform VERB 1 = **do**, carry out, execute, discharge, conduct, effect, bring about, bring off, accomplish, achieve, fulfil, complete. 2 = **act**, play, appear. 3 = **function**, work, operate, run, go.

performance NOUN
1 = **execution**, discharge, accomplishment, achievement, fulfilment.
2 = **show**, production, entertainment, act, presentation; [inf] gig.

performer NOUN = **actor/ actress**, player, entertainer, artist, artiste, Thespian, musician, singer, dancer.

perfume NOUN 1 = **smell**, fragrance, aroma, scent, bouquet; [poetic/ literary] redolence.
2 = **fragrance**, scent, eau de Cologne, cologne.

perfunctory ADJ
= **cursory**, superficial, desultory, mechanical, automatic, routine, sketchy, brief, hasty, hurried, rapid, fleeting, quick, fast, offhand, casual, indifferent, careless, inattentive, negligent.
Opposites: careful, thorough.

perhaps ADV = **maybe**, possibly, it is possible that, conceivably, feasibly, for all one knows; [poetic/ literary] peradventure.

peril NOUN = **danger**, jeopardy, risk, hazard, menace, threat.
Opposites: safety.

perilous ADJ = **dangerous**, risky, precarious, hazardous, chancy, threatening, unsafe.
Opposites: safe.

perimeter NOUN
= **boundary**, border, frontier, limits, outer limits, confines, edge, margin, fringe, periphery.

period NOUN = **space**, spell, interval, term, stretch, span, age, era, epoch, aeon.

periodic ADJ = **periodical**, recurrent, recurring, repeated, cyclical, cyclic, regular, intermittent, occasional, infrequent, sporadic.

peripheral ADJ **1** = **outer**, on the edge/outskirts, surrounding, neighbouring. **2** = **minor**, lesser, secondary, subsidiary, ancillary, unimportant, superficial, irrelevant.
Opposites: central.

perish VERB **1** = **die**, lose one's life, be killed, lay down one's life, meet one's death, breathe one's last, draw one's last breath; [inf] bite the dust, kick the bucket. **2** = **go bad**, go off, go sour, rot, decay, decompose.

perk NOUN = **benefit**, advantage, bonus, dividend, extra, plus; [inf] freebie; [formal] perquisite.

perk
▪ **perk up** = **cheer up**, brighten up, take heart; [inf] buck up, pep up.

permanent ADJ = **lasting**, long-lasting, stable, fixed, established, everlasting, perpetual, eternal, enduring, perennial, abiding, constant, persistent, unending, endless, never-ending, immutable, unchangeable, unalterable, invariable.
Opposites: impermanent.

permeate VERB = **spread through**, pass through, pervade, saturate, fill, diffuse through, extend throughout, imbue, penetrate, infiltrate, percolate through.

permissible ADJ = **permitted**, allowable, admissible, acceptable, tolerated, authorized, sanctioned, legal, lawful, legitimate, licit, within bounds; [inf] legit.
Opposites: forbidden.

permission NOUN = **authorization**, sanction, leave, licence, dispensation, empowerment, allowance, consent, assent, acquiescence, agreement, approval, approbation, tolerance, sufferance; [inf] green light, go-ahead, thumbs up.

permissive ADJ = **liberal**, tolerant, broad-minded, open-minded, easy-going, indulgent, lenient, overindulgent, lax, unprescriptive.
Opposites: intolerant, strict.

permit VERB = **give permission**, allow, let, authorize, give leave, sanction, grant, license, consent to, assent to, acquiesce in, agree to, approve of, tolerate, countenance, suffer; [inf] give the green light to, give the go-ahead to, give the thumbs up to; [formal] brook.
Opposites: forbid.
▶ NOUN = **licence**, authorization, warrant, sanction, pass, passport.

perpetual ADJ
1 = **everlasting**, eternal, never-ending, unending, endless, undying, perennial, permanent, lasting, abiding, persisting, enduring, constant, unfailing, unchanging, unvarying,

invariable; [poetic/literary] perdurable.
2 = **incessant**, unceasing, ceaseless, unending, endless, non-stop, continuous, uninterrupted, unbroken, unremitting.
3 = **interminable**, persistent, frequent, continual, recurrent, repeated; [inf] eternal.

perpetuate VERB = **keep alive**, keep going, keep up, preserve, conserve, sustain, maintain, continue.

perplex VERB = **puzzle**, baffle, mystify, stump, bewilder, confound, confuse, nonplus, disconcert, dismay, dumbfound; [inf] bamboozle.

persecute VERB = **oppress**, tyrannize, abuse, mistreat, maltreat, ill-treat, molest, afflict, torment, torture, victimize, martyr.

persevere VERB = **persist**, go on, keep on, keep at, keep going, continue, carry on, struggle, work, hammer away, be tenacious, be persistent, be pertinacious, be resolute, be purposeful, be obstinate, be insistent, be intransigent, be patient, be diligent; [inf] plug away. **Opposites:** give up.

persist VERB = *see* **persevere**.

persistent ADJ
1 = **persevering**, tenacious, pertinacious, determined, resolute, purposeful, obstinate, stubborn, insistent, intransigent, obdurate, intractable, patient, diligent. 2 = **constant**, continual, continuous, continuing, interminable, incessant, unceasing, endless, unremitting, unrelenting, relentless. **Opposites:** irresolute, intermittent.

person NOUN = **individual**, human being, human, creature, living soul, soul, mortal.

personable ADJ = **pleasant**, agreeable, amiable, affable, likeable, charming, nice, attractive, presentable, good-looking. **Opposites:** disagreeable.

personal ADJ
1 = **individual**, private, confidential, secret, one's own business. 2 = **personalized**, individual, idiosyncratic, characteristic, unique, peculiar. 3 = **insulting**, slighting, derogatory, disparaging, pejorative, offensive. **Opposites:** public, general.

personality NOUN
1 = **nature**, disposition, character, temperament, temper, make-up, psyche. 2 = **force of personality**, character, charisma, magnetism, powers of attraction, charm. 3 = **celebrity**, VIP, household name, dignitary, notable, personage, luminary, worthy.

personally ADV = **for my part**, for myself, from my own point of view, as far as I am concerned.

personification NOUN = **embodiment**, incarnation, epitome, quintessence, essence, symbol, representation, image.

personnel NOUN = **staff**, employees, workers, workforce, labour force, manpower, human resources, liveware.

perspective NOUN
1 = **outlook**, view, viewpoint, point of view, standpoint, stance, angle, slant, attitude. **2** = **view**, vista, bird's-eye view, prospect, scene, outlook, panorama, aspect, sweep.

persuade VERB = **prevail upon**, induce, convince, win over, talk into, bring round, influence, sway, prompt, coerce, inveigle, cajole, wheedle; [inf] sweet-talk, soft-soap. Opposites: discourage.

persuasive ADJ = **effective**, effectual, convincing, cogent, plausible, compelling, forceful, eloquent, weighty, influential, telling. Opposites: ineffective.

pertain VERB = **be connected**, relate, be relevant, have relevance, concern, apply to, be pertinent to, have reference to, have a bearing upon.

pertinent ADJ = **relevant**, appropriate, suitable, fitting, fit, apt, apposite, to the point, applicable, material, germane, to the purpose, apropos. Opposites: irrelevant.

perturb VERB = **disturb**, make anxious, worry, alarm, trouble, upset, disquiet, discompose, disconcert, vex, bother, agitate, unsettle, fluster, ruffle, harass. Opposites: reassure.

pervade VERB = **spread through**, permeate, fill, pass through, suffuse, diffuse through, imbue, infuse, penetrate, infiltrate, percolate.

pervasive ADJ = **pervading**, permeating, prevalent, extensive, ubiquitous, omnipresent, rife, widespread, universal, suffusive.

perverse ADJ = **contrary**, wayward, troublesome, difficult, awkward, unreasonable,

disobedient,
unmanageable,
uncontrollable,
rebellious, wilful,
headstrong, capricious,
stubborn, obstinate,
obdurate, pertinacious,
mulish, pig-headed,
wrong-headed,
querulous, fractious,
intractable, refractory,
intransigent,
contumacious; [Brit.
inf] bolshie, stroppy.

perversion NOUN
1 = **distortion**, misuse,
misrepresentation,
falsification,
misinterpretation,
misconstruction.
2 = **deviation**, aberration,
abnormality, irregularity,
unnaturalness,
corruption, debauchery,
depravity, vice;
[inf] kinkiness.

pervert VERB **1** = **misapply**,
misuse, distort, garble,
warp, twist, misinterpret,
misconstrue. **2** = **lead
astray**, corrupt, warp,
deprave, debauch,
debase, degrade.
▶ NOUN = **deviant**, deviate,
degenerate, debauchee;

[inf] perv.

perverted ADJ
= **depraved**, debauched,
debased, corrupt,
deviant, abnormal,
aberrant, warped,
distorted, twisted, sick,
unhealthy, immoral, evil,
vile; [inf] kinky.

pessimist NOUN = **prophet
of doom**, cynic, defeatist,
fatalist, alarmist, doubter,
doubting Thomas;
[inf] doom merchant,
gloom merchant.
Opposites: optimist.

pessimistic ADJ
= **gloomy**, gloom-ridden,
cynical, defeatist,
fatalistic, hopeless,
distrustful, alarmist,
doubting, suspicious,
bleak, resigned,
depressed, dejected,
despairing.
Opposites: optimistic.

pest NOUN = **nuisance**,
bother, irritant, thorn in
the flesh, problem,
trouble, worry,
inconvenience, trial,
tribulation, the bane of
one's life; [inf] pain, pain
in the neck.

pester VERB = **badger**, hound, irritate, annoy, bother, irk, nag, harass, chivvy, torment, plague, bedevil, harry; [inf] bug, hassle.

pet NOUN = **favourite**, darling, idol, apple of one's eye; [Brit. inf] blue-eyed boy/girl; [N. Amer. inf] fair-haired boy/girl.
▶ VERB = **stroke**, caress, fondle, pat.

peter
▪ **peter out** = **fade**, wane, ebb, diminish, taper off, come to nothing, die out, fail, fall through, come to a halt, come to an end.

petition NOUN = **appeal**, request, entreaty, supplication, plea, prayer, application, suit.
▶ VERB = **appeal to**, request, ask, apply to, entreat, beg, plead with, make a plea to; [poetic/ literary] beseech.

petrify VERB 1 = **terrify**, frighten, horrify, fill with fear, panic, alarm, scare someone out of their wits, paralyse, stun, stupefy, transfix. 2 = **turn to stone**, fossilize, calcify, ossify.

petulant ADJ = **querulous**, complaining, peevish, fretful, impatient, cross, irritable, moody, crabbed, crabby, crotchety, touchy, bad-tempered, irascible, sulky; [inf] snappish; [Brit. inf] ratty.

phantom NOUN = **ghost**, apparition, spectre, shade, spirit, revenant, wraith, shadow; [inf] spook; [poetic/ literary] phantasm.

phenomenal ADJ = **extraordinary**, remarkable, exceptional, singular, uncommon, unheard of, unique, unparalleled, unprecedented, amazing, astonishing, astounding, unusual, marvellous, prodigious, sensational, miraculous; [inf] mind-blowing.

phenomenon NOUN 1 = **fact**, experience, occurrence, happening, event, incident, episode. 2 = **marvel**, prodigy, rarity, wonder, sensation, miracle, nonpareil.

philanthropic ADJ
= **benevolent**, beneficent,
benignant, charitable,
almsgiving, generous,
kind, munificent,
bountiful, liberal, open-
handed, giving, helping;
[poetic/literary] bounteous.
Opposites: selfish.

philistine ADJ
= **uncultured**,
uncultivated,
uneducated,
unenlightened, unread,
ignorant, boorish,
barbaric.

philosophical ADJ
1 = **thoughtful**, reflective,
pensive, meditative,
contemplative. 2 = **calm**,
composed, cool,
collected, self-possessed,
serene, tranquil, stoical,
impassive, phlegmatic,
unperturbed,
imperturbable,
dispassionate, unruffled,
patient, resigned,
rational, logical, realistic,
practical.

philosophy NOUN
1 = **thought**, thinking,
reasoning, logic, wisdom.
2 = **beliefs**, convictions,

ideology, ideas, doctrine,
tenets, values, principles,
attitude, view, viewpoint,
outlook.

phlegmatic ADJ = **calm**,
cool, composed,
collected, serene,
tranquil, placid,
impassive, imperturbable,
dispassionate,
philosophical.
Opposites: excitable.

phobia NOUN = **aversion**,
fear, dread, horror, terror,
dislike, hatred, loathing,
detestation, distaste,
antipathy, revulsion,
repulsion; [inf] thing,
hang-up.

phone VERB = **telephone**,
call, give someone a call;
[Brit.] ring, ring up;
[inf] buzz, get on the
blower to.

phoney ADJ = **bogus**,
sham, counterfeit,
imitation, spurious,
mock, ersatz, fake,
forged, feigned,
simulated, make-believe,
false, fraudulent.
Opposites: genuine.

photograph NOUN
= **photo**, snap, snapshot,
picture, likeness, shot,

print, slide, transparency.

photographic ADJ
1 = **pictorial**, in photographs. **2** = **detailed**, graphic, exact, accurate, precise.

phrase NOUN = **expression**, idiom, remark, saying, utterance, witticism, tag.
▶ VERB = **put into words**, put, word, express, formulate, couch, frame.

phraseology NOUN = **phrasing**, wording, words, choice of words, language, vocabulary, terminology.

physical ADJ = **material**, substantial, solid, concrete, tangible, palpable, visible, real, bodily, non-mental, corporeal, corporal.
Opposites: mental, spiritual.

physician NOUN = **doctor**, medical practitioner, general practitioner, GP, specialist, consultant; [inf] doc, medic, medico; [Brit. inf] quack.

physique NOUN = **body**, build, shape, frame, form, figure.

pick VERB **1** = **choose**, select, opt for, plump for, single out, hand-pick, decide upon, settle upon, fix upon, prefer, favour, elect. **2** = **harvest**, gather, collect, take in, pluck, pull, cull.
▶ NOUN **1** = **choice**, selection, option, preference.
2 = **best**, choicest, prime, cream, flower, prize.
■ **pick on** = **bully**, victimize, tyrannize, torment, persecute, harass, hound, taunt.
■ **pick up** = **improve**, get better, recover, rally, perk up, be on the mend, make headway, make progress, take a turn for the better.

picture NOUN **1** = **painting**, drawing, sketch, oil painting, watercolour, print, canvas, delineation, portrait, portrayal, illustration, likeness, representation, similitude, semblance.
2 = See **photograph**.
▶ VERB **1** = **see in one's mind/mind's eye**, imagine, call to mind, visualize, see, evoke.

2 = **paint**, draw, sketch, depict, delineate, portray, illustrate, reproduce, represent.

picturesque ADJ
1 = **beautiful**, pretty, lovely, attractive, scenic, charming, quaint, pleasing, delightful.
2 = **vivid**, graphic, colourful, impressive, striking.
Opposites: ugly.

pie NOUN = **pastry**, tart, tartlet, pasty, quiche.

piece NOUN **1** = **part**, bit, section, segment, length, quantity, unit, slice, chunk, lump, hunk, wedge, remnant, scrap, snippet. **2** = **fragment**, smithereens, shard, shred, tatter. **3** = **share**, slice, portion, allotment, allocation, quota, percentage, fraction.
■ **piece together** = **put together**, assemble, join up, fit together, unite.

piecemeal ADV = **piece by piece**, bit by bit, gradually, in stages, in steps, little by little, by degrees, in fits and starts.

pier NOUN **1** = **jetty**, quay, wharf, dock, landing, landing place, promenade. **2** = **support**, upright, pillar, post, column, pile, piling, buttress.

pierce VERB = **penetrate**, puncture, perforate, prick, stab, spike, enter, pass through, transfix, bore, drill.

piercing ADJ **1** = **shrewd**, sharp, keen, searching, alert, penetrating, perceptive, probing.
2 = **shrill**, penetrating, ear-splitting, high-pitched, loud. **3** = **severe**, sharp, stabbing, shooting, penetrating, intense, fierce, excruciating, agonizing, exquisite.

piety NOUN = **piousness**, religiousness, holiness, godliness, devoutness, devotion, veneration, reverence, religious duty, spirituality, sanctity, religious zeal.
Opposites: impiety.

pile NOUN **1** = **heap**, bundle, stack, mound, mass, accumulation, collection,

p

assemblage, store, stockpile, hoard, load, mountain. **2 = great deal**, a lot, lots, quantity, abundance, mountain; [inf] heap, ocean, stacks, oodles, scuds.
▶ VERB **1 = heap**, stack. **2 = accumulate**, amass, collect, gather, stockpile, hoard, store up, assemble, lay by/in. **3 = form piles**, form heaps, heap up, amass, accumulate.

pile-up NOUN **= crash**, collision, smash, smash-up, accident, road accident.

pill NOUN **= tablet**, capsule, pellet, lozenge, bolus.

pillage VERB **= plunder**, rob, raid, loot, maraud, sack, ransack, ravage, lay waste, despoil.
▶ NOUN **= plunder**, robbery, raiding, looting, marauding, sacking, ransacking, ravaging, rapine, despoiling, laying waste, spoliation, depredation.

pillory VERB **= stigmatize**, cast a slur on, denounce, hold up to shame, hold up to ridicule, ridicule, heap scorn on; [inf] show up.

pilot NOUN **1 = airman/airwoman**, aviator, flier, captain, commander, co-pilot. **2 = navigator**, guide, steersman, helmsman.
▶ VERB **= fly**, drive, operate, navigate, guide, steer, control, handle, manoeuvre.

pimple NOUN **= spot**, pustule, boil, swelling, papule; [inf] zit.

pin VERB **1 = attach**, fasten, affix, fix, stick, tack, nail. **2 = pinion**, hold, press, restrain, constrain, hold fast, immobilize, pin down.

pinch VERB **1 = nip**, tweak, squeeze, compress. **2 =** *See* **steal (1, 2)**. **3 =** *See* **arrest**.

pinched ADJ **= drawn**, haggard, worn, peaky, pale, wan, strained, stressed, drained.
Opposites: healthy.

pinnacle NOUN **= peak**, height, culmination, high point, acme, zenith, climax, crowning point,

summit, apex, vertex, apogee.
Opposites: nadir.

pinpoint VERB = **identify**, discover, distinguish, locate, spot, home in on, put one's finger on.

pioneer NOUN 1 = **settler**, colonist, colonizer, explorer. 2 = **developer**, innovator, ground-breaker, trailblazer, founder, founding father, architect.
▶ VERB = **develop**, introduce, launch, instigate, initiate, institute, originate, create, open up, blaze a trail, break new ground.

pious ADJ 1 = **religious**, holy, godly, spiritual, devout, devoted, dedicated, reverent, God-fearing, righteous, faithful. 2 = **sanctimonious**, hypocritical, self-righteous, unctuous, pietistic, holier-than-thou, goody-goody.
Opposites: impious.

pipe NOUN = **tube**, cylinder, conduit, main, duct, channel, pipeline, drainpipe.

▶ VERB = **convey**, duct, channel, transmit, bring in, siphon.

piquant ADJ 1 = **spicy**, flavoursome, peppery, tangy, pungent, sharp, tart, zesty, biting, stinging. 2 = **stimulating**, intriguing, interesting, fascinating, alluring, racy, salty, provocative.
Opposites: insipid.

pirate NOUN = **freebooter**, marauder, raider; [historical] privateer; [archaic] buccaneer, corsair.

pit NOUN = **abyss**, chasm, crater, hole, cavity, excavation, quarry, coal mine, mine, diggings, working.

pitch VERB 1 = **throw**, cast, fling, hurl, toss, lob, launch; [inf] chuck, heave, bung. 2 = **put up**, set up, erect, raise. 3 = **fall headlong**, fall, tumble, topple, plunge, dive.
▶ NOUN 1 = **field**, ground, park, stadium, arena, playing field. 2 = **level**, point, degree, height, extent, intensity.

■ **pitch in** = **help**, assist, lend a hand, join in, participate, play a part, do one's bit, cooperate, collaborate.

piteous ADJ = **pitiful**, pitiable, pathetic, distressing, affecting, moving, sad, heart-rending, heartbreaking, poignant, emotional, emotive.

pitfall NOUN = **trap**, snare, catch, stumbling block, hazard, peril, danger, difficulty. ·

pitiful ADJ **1** = *See* **piteous**. **2** = **contemptible**, despicable, poor, sorry, miserable, inadequate, worthless, base, shabby, pathetic.

pitiless ADJ = **merciless**, ruthless, relentless, cruel, severe, harsh, heartless, callous, brutal, inhuman, inhumane, cold-hearted, hard-hearted, unfeeling, uncaring, unsympathetic. **Opposites:** merciful.

pity NOUN **1** = **commiseration**, condolence, sympathy, compassion, fellow feeling, understanding, forbearance, distress, sadness, emotion, mercy, clemency, kindness. **2** = **shame**, crying shame, misfortune, sad thing, sin. **Opposites:** indifference.

▶ VERB = **feel sorry for**, commiserate with, feel sympathy for, sympathize with, feel for.

pivot NOUN = **axis**, fulcrum, axle, swivel, spindle, central shaft.

placate VERB = **calm**, pacify, soothe, appease, conciliate, propitiate, mollify.

place NOUN **1** = **location**, spot, scene, setting, position, site, situation, venue, area, region, whereabouts; [technical] locus. **2** = **position**, status, grade, rank, station, standing, footing, role, niche.

▶ VERB **1** = **put**, position, set/ lay down, deposit, rest, settle, station, situate. **2** = **order**, rank, grade, group, arrange, sort, class, classify, categorize, bracket.

placid ADJ **1** = **still**, calm, peaceful, at peace, pacific, tranquil, motionless, smooth, unruffled, undisturbed. **2** = **calm**, cool, composed, self-possessed, serene, tranquil, equable, even-tempered, peaceable, easy-going, unmoved, undisturbed, unperturbed, imperturbable, unexcited, unexcitable, unruffled, unemotional. **Opposites:** excitable, bustling.

plagiarize VERB = **copy**, pirate, poach, borrow, reproduce, appropriate; [inf] rip off, crib.

plague NOUN **1** = **contagion**, disease, pestilence, sickness, epidemic, pandemic. **2** = **multitude**, host, swarm, influx, infestation.
▶ VERB = **afflict**, cause suffering to, torture, torment, bedevil, trouble.

plain ADJ **1** = **clear**, crystal-clear, obvious, evident, apparent, manifest, transparent, patent, unmistakable. **2** = **clear-cut**, simple, straightforward, uncomplicated, comprehensible, intelligible, understandable, lucid, unambiguous. **3** = **simple**, austere, stark, severe, basic, ordinary, unsophisticated, spartan. **4** = **unattractive**, ugly, unprepossessing, unlovely, homely. **Opposites:** obscure, fancy, attractive.
▶ ADV = **downright**, utterly, completely, totally, thoroughly, positively, incontrovertibly, unquestionably, simply.

plaintive ADJ = **mournful**, doleful, melancholy, sad, sorrowful, unhappy, disconsolate.

plan NOUN **1** = **plan of action**, scheme, system, procedure, method, programme, schedule, project, way, means, strategy, tactics, formula. **2** = **scale drawing**, blueprint, layout, sketch, diagram, chart, map, illustration, representation,

p

delineation.
▶ VERB **1** = **arrange**, organize, line up, schedule, programme. **2** = **make plans**, intend, aim, propose, mean, purpose, contemplate, envisage, foresee.

plane ADJ = **flat**, level, horizontal, even, flush, smooth, regular, uniform.

plant NOUN **1** = **flower**, vegetable, herb, shrub, weed. **2** = **machinery**, equipment, apparatus; [inf] gear. **3** = **factory**, works, foundry, mill, workshop, shop, yard.
▶ VERB **1** = **implant**, set out, sow, scatter. **2** = **place**, position, set, situate.

plaster VERB = **cover thickly**, spread, coat, smear, overlay, bedaub.

plastic ADJ **1** = **mouldable**, malleable, workable, ductile, pliant, pliable, supple, flexible, soft. **2** = **false**, artificial, synthetic, spurious, sham, bogus; [inf] phoney.

plate NOUN **1** = **dish**, platter, dinner plate, side plate. **2** = **plaque**, tablet, sign;

[Brit.] brass. **3** = **illustration**, picture, photograph, print, lithograph. **4** = **sheet**, panel, slab.

platform NOUN **1** = **dais**, rostrum, podium, stage, stand. **2** = **programme**, policy, manifesto, plan, objectives, principles, tenets.

platitude NOUN = **truism**, hackneyed expression, commonplace, stock expression, trite phrase, banality, bromide, inanity.

platter NOUN = **serving plate**, salver, plate, dish, tray.

plausible ADJ = **believable**, credible, convincing, persuasive, likely, probable, conceivable, imaginable, tenable, cogent, reasonable.
Opposites: implausible.

play VERB **1** = **amuse oneself**, entertain oneself, enjoy oneself, have fun, play games, frolic, frisk, gambol, romp, cavort. **2** = **play the part of**, act, act the part of, perform, portray,

represent, execute.
3 = perform, carry out, execute, do, accomplish.
4 = take part in, participate in, engage in, be involved in.
5 = compete against, contend against, oppose, take on, challenge, vie with, rival.

▶ NOUN **1 = amusement**, entertainment, recreation, diversion, leisure, enjoyment, fun, merrymaking, revelry.
2 = movement, freedom of movement, free motion, slack, give.

■ **play at = pretend to be**, give the appearance of, assume/affect the role of; [inf] make like.

■ **play down = make light of**, make little of, gloss over, minimize, diminish, set little store by, underrate, underestimate, undervalue, think little of; [inf] soft-pedal.

player NOUN
1 = competitor, contestant, participant, team member, sportsman/sportswoman.

2 = actor/actress, performer, entertainer, artist, artiste, trouper, Thespian. **3 = performer**, musician, instrumentalist, artist, artiste, virtuoso.

playful ADJ **1 = fun-loving**, full of fun, high-spirited, frisky, skittish, coltish, sportive, mischievous, impish, puckish; [poetic/literary] frolicsome. **2 = in fun**, joking, jesting, humorous, facetious, waggish, tongue-in-cheek, arch, roguish.
Opposites: serious.

plea NOUN **1 = appeal**, entreaty, supplication, petition, prayer, request, solicitation, suit, invocation. **2 = excuse**, pretext, claim, vindication.

plead VERB **1 = appeal to**, beg, entreat, implore, petition, supplicate, importune, pray to, solicit, request, ask earnestly; [poetic/literary] beseech. **2 = put forward**, state, assert, argue, claim, allege.

p

pleasant ADJ **1** = **pleasing**, pleasurable, agreeable, enjoyable, entertaining, amusing, delightful, satisfying, gratifying, nice, good, fine.
2 = **agreeable**, friendly, amiable, affable, genial, likeable, nice, good-humoured, charming, engaging, winning, delightful.
Opposites: unpleasant.

please VERB **1** = **give pleasure to**, be agreeable to, make pleased/happy/glad etc., gladden, delight, cheer up, charm, divert, entertain, amuse.
2 = **want**, wish, see fit, will, like, desire, be inclined, prefer.
Opposites: displease.

pleased ADJ = **happy**, glad, cheerful, delighted, thrilled, elated, contented, satisfied, gratified, fulfilled; [inf] over the moon; [Brit. inf] chuffed.

pleasure NOUN = **happiness**, gladness, delight, joy, enjoyment, entertainment, amusement, diversion, satisfaction, gratification, fulfilment, contentment.

pledge NOUN **1** = **promise**, word, word of honour, vow, assurance, undertaking, oath, covenant, warrant.
2 = **security**, surety, guarantee, collateral.
▶ VERB **1** = **promise**, give one's word, vow, give an undertaking, undertake, take an oath, swear, vouch, engage, contract.
2 = **mortgage**, put up as collateral, guarantee, plight, pawn.

plentiful ADJ = **abundant**, copious, ample, profuse, lavish, liberal, generous, large, huge, bumper, infinite.
Opposites: scanty.

plenty NOUN = **plentifulness**, affluence, prosperity, wealth, opulence, luxury, abundance, copiousness, fruitfulness, profusion; [poetic/literary] plenteousness.
▪ **plenty of** = **enough**, sufficient, a good deal of, a great deal of, masses of; [inf] lots of, heaps of,

stacks of, piles of.

plethora NOUN = **over-abundance**, superabundance, excess, superfluity, surplus, surfeit, glut.
Opposites: dearth.

pliable ADJ **1** = **flexible**, bendable, bendy, pliant, elastic, supple, stretchable, ductile, plastic. **2** = **malleable**, compliant, docile, biddable, tractable, manageable, governable, controllable, amenable.
Opposites: rigid, obdurate.

plot NOUN **1** = **piece of ground**, parcel, patch; [Brit.] allotment; [N. Amer.] lot.
2 = **conspiracy**, intrigue, stratagem. **3** = **action**, theme, subject, story line, story, scenario, thread.
▸ VERB **1** = **map out**, draw, draw a diagram of, draw the layout of, make a blueprint/chart of, sketch out, outline. **2** = **take part in a plot**, scheme, conspire, participate in a conspiracy, intrigue, form an intrigue.

plough VERB = **till**, work, cultivate, break up, turn up.

ploy NOUN = **dodge**, ruse, scheme, trick, stratagem, manoeuvre, move.

plummet VERB = **fall**, fall headlong, plunge, hurtle, nosedive, dive, drop.

plump ADJ = **chubby**, well rounded, of ample proportions, rotund, buxom, stout, fat, obese, corpulent, fleshy, portly, tubby, dumpy, roly-poly, well covered; [Brit. inf] podgy.
Opposites: slim, skinny.

plunder VERB = **rob**, pillage, loot, raid, ransack, strip, fleece, lay waste, despoil, maraud, sack, rape.
▸ NOUN = **loot**, booty, spoils, prize, pillage, ill-gotten gains; [inf] swag.

plunge VERB **1** = **thrust**, stick, jab, push, drive.
2 = **dive**, nosedive, jump, plummet, drop, fall, descend.

plush ADJ = **luxurious**, luxury, sumptuous, lavish, gorgeous, opulent, rich, costly;

[inf] ritzy, classy.
Opposites: plain.

pocket NOUN = **pouch**, compartment, receptacle.

▶ ADJ = **small**, little, miniature, compact, concise, abridged, potted.

▶ VERB = **misappropriate**, steal, thieve, purloin; [inf] lift, filch, swipe, snaffle; [Brit. inf] pinch, nick.

poet NOUN = **versifier**, rhymester, sonneteer, balladeer, lyricist, bard, minstrel.

poetic ADJ = **imaginative**, creative, figurative, symbolic, flowery.

poignant ADJ = **moving**, affecting, touching, tender, emotional, sentimental, heartfelt, sad, sorrowful, tearful, evocative.

point NOUN 1 = **tip**, top, extremity, prong, spike, tine. 2 = **promontory**, headland, head, foreland, cape, bluff. 3 = **place**, position, location, situation, site, spot, area, locality. 4 = **time**, juncture, stage, period, moment, instant.

5 = **main point**, central point, essential point, focal point, salient point, keynote, heart of the matter, essence, nub, core, pith, marrow, meat, crux. 6 = **meaning**, significance, signification, import, essence, gist, substance, drift, thrust, burden, theme, tenor, vein. 7 = **aim**, purpose, object, objective, goal, intention, reason for, use, utility. 8 = **characteristic**, trait, attribute, quality, feature, property, predisposition, streak, peculiarity, idiosyncrasy.

▶ VERB = **direct**, aim, level, train.

▪ **point out** = **call attention to**, draw attention to, indicate, show, specify, designate, identify, mention, allude to.

pointed ADJ 1 = **sharp**, sharp-edged, edged; [formal] cuspidate, acicular. 2 = **cutting**, trenchant, biting, incisive, penetrating,

p

forceful, telling, significant.

pointless ADJ = **futile**, useless, in vain, unavailing, to no purpose, valueless, unproductive, senseless, absurd, foolish, nonsensical, stupid, silly. **Opposites:** useful.

poise NOUN = **composure**, equanimity, self-possession, aplomb, self-assurance, calmness, coolness, serenity, dignity, imperturbability, suaveness, urbanity; [inf] cool.
▶ VERB = **balance**, steady, position, support.

poised ADJ **1** = **composed**, serene, self-possessed, self-assured, calm, cool, imperturbable, unruffled, unflappable. **2** = **ready**, prepared, all set, standing by, waiting. **Opposites:** flustered.

poison NOUN **1** = **venom**, toxin. **2** = **blight**, contagion, cancer, canker, malignancy, corruption, pollution.
▶ VERB **1** = **contaminate**, pollute, blight, spoil.

2 = **corrupt**, warp, pervert, deprave, defile, debauch.

poisonous ADJ = **venomous**, deadly, fatal, lethal, noxious. **Opposites:** non-toxic.

poke VERB = **jab**, prod, dig, elbow, nudge, push, thrust, shove, stick.

poky ADJ = **confined**, cramped, narrow, cell-like, small, little, tiny. **Opposites:** spacious.

pole NOUN = **post**, upright, pillar, stanchion, standard, support, prop, rod, shaft, mast.

police NOUN = **police force**, police officers; [Brit.] constabulary; [inf] the cops, the fuzz, the law, the boys in blue; [Brit. inf] the (Old) Bill, the rozzers, the force, the pigs, the filth.
▶ VERB = **guard**, keep guard over, keep watch on, protect, keep in order, control, keep under control, regulate.

police officer NOUN = **policeman**, = **policewoman**; [Brit.] constable, PC, WPC; [N. Amer.] patrolman, trooper; [inf] cop; [Brit. inf] bobby, copper, rozzer.

policy NOUN = **plan**, scheme, programme, schedule, code, system, approach, procedure, guideline, theory.

polish VERB 1 = **wax**, buff, rub up, burnish, shine. 2 = **perfect**, refine, improve, brush up, touch up, finish off.

polished ADJ 1 = **waxed**, buffed, burnished, shining, shiny, glossy, gleaming, lustrous, glassy, slippery. 2 = **refined**, cultivated, civilized, well bred, polite, well mannered, genteel, courtly, urbane, suave, sophisticated. 3 = **expert**, accomplished, masterly, skilful, proficient, adept, impeccable, flawless, faultless, perfect, consummate, outstanding, remarkable. **Opposites:** dull, gauche, inexpert.

polite ADJ 1 = **well mannered**, mannerly, courteous, civil, respectful, deferential, well behaved, well bred, genteel, polished, tactful, diplomatic. 2 = **well bred**, civilized, cultured, refined, polished, genteel, urbane, sophisticated, elegant, courtly. **Opposites:** rude.

politic ADJ = **wise**, prudent, sensible, advisable, judicious, well judged, sagacious, expedient, shrewd, astute, discreet, tactful, diplomatic. **Opposites:** unwise.

political ADJ 1 = **governmental**, ministerial, public, civic, administrative, bureaucratic. 2 = **factional**, partisan, bipartisan, power, status.

poll NOUN 1 = **vote**, ballot, canvass, headcount. 2 = **returns**, count, tally. ▶ VERB 1 = **register**, record, return, get, gain. 2 = **ballot**, canvass, question, interview, survey, sample.

pollute VERB = **contaminate**, adulterate, infect, taint,

populace

poison, befoul, foul.
Opposites: purify.

pomp NOUN = **ceremony**, ritual, display, pageantry, show, spectacle, splendour, grandeur, magnificence, majesty.

pompous ADJ = **self-important**, presumptuous, imperious, overbearing, grandiose, affected, pretentious, arrogant, vain, haughty, proud, conceited, egotistic, supercilious, condescending, patronizing; [inf] uppity, uppish.
Opposites: humble.

ponder VERB = **think about**, give thought to, consider, reflect on, mull over, contemplate, meditate on, deliberate about/on, dwell on, brood on/over, ruminate about/on/over, puzzle over, cogitate about/on, weigh up, review.

pontificate VERB = **hold forth**, expound, declaim, preach, lay down the law, sound off, dogmatize, sermonize;
[inf] preachify.

poor ADJ **1** = **penniless**, hard up, badly off, poverty-stricken, needy, deprived, in need, needful, in want, indigent, impoverished, impecunious, destitute, penurious, beggared, in straitened circumstances, in the red, on one's beam-ends; [inf] broke, flat broke, on one's uppers; [Brit. inf] skint, stony broke. **2** = **inferior**, unsatisfactory, below standard, below par, imperfect, bad, low-grade, inadequate, deficient, insufficient, sparse, scanty, meagre, scarce, skimpy, paltry, miserable.
3 = **unfortunate**, wretched, pitiable, pitiful, unlucky, luckless, unhappy, hapless, ill-fated, ill-starred.
Opposites: rich.

populace NOUN = **the general public**, the public, the people, the population, the common people, the masses.

popular ADJ 1 = **well liked**, liked, favoured, in favour, favourite, well received, approved, admired, accepted. 2 = **public**, general, civic. 3 = **current**, prevalent, prevailing, accepted, recognized, widespread, universal, general, common, customary, usual, standard, stock, conventional.
Opposites: unpopular.

popularity NOUN 1 = **favour**, approval, approbation, admiration, acceptance. 2 = **demand**, fashionableness, vogue.

populate VERB 1 = **inhabit**, dwell in, occupy, people. 2 = **settle**, colonize, people.

population NOUN = **inhabitants**, residents, community, people, citizenry, populace, society.

populous ADJ = **densely populated**, heavily populated, thickly populated, overpopulated, crowded.
Opposites: deserted.

pore NOUN = **opening**, orifice, hole, outlet.

pornographic ADJ = **obscene**, indecent, erotic, dirty, smutty, filthy, salacious, lewd, prurient; [inf] porno, blue.

porous ADJ = **absorbent**, permeable, penetrable, pervious, spongy, sponge-like.
Opposites: impermeable.

port NOUN = **harbour**, harbourage, haven, anchorage, dock, mooring, marina.

portable ADJ = **transportable**, movable, conveyable, easily carried, lightweight, compact, handy, manageable.

portend VERB = **be a sign of**, be a warning of, point to, be an omen of, herald, bode, augur, presage, forebode, foreshadow, foretell.

portion NOUN 1 = **helping**, serving, piece, quantity. 2 = **share**, division, quota, part, bit, allocation, allotment, piece; [inf] cut; [Brit. inf] whack.

portly ADJ = **stout**, plump, fat, corpulent, obese, tubby, stocky.
Opposites: slim.

portrait NOUN = **portrayal**, representation, likeness, image, study, depiction.

portray VERB 1 = **paint**, draw a picture of, draw, sketch, depict, represent, delineate. 2 = **describe**, depict, characterize, put into words.

pose VERB 1 = **sit**, model, take up a position.
2 = **arrange**, position, lay out, set out, dispose, place, put, locate, situate.
3 = **strike an attitude**, posture, put on an act, play-act, attitudinize, put on airs, show off.
4 = **present**, set, create, cause, give rise to.
▸ NOUN 1 = **posture**, stance, position, attitude. 2 = **act**, pretence, facade, front, masquerade, attitudinizing, affectation, airs.

poser¹ NOUN = **vexed question**, enigma, dilemma, puzzle, mystery, conundrum.

poser² NOUN = **poseur**, attitudinizer, posturer, play-actor, impostor, exhibitionist, show-off; [inf] phoney.

posh ADJ 1 = **luxurious**, luxury, sumptuous, opulent, lavish, rich, fancy; [inf] plushy, ritzy, swanky. 2 = **upper-class**, aristocratic, upmarket, fancy; [inf] upper-crust.

position NOUN
1 = **situation**, location, site, place, spot, area, locality, locale, scene, setting. 2 = **posture**, stance, attitude, pose, bearing. 3 = **state**, condition, situation, circumstance, predicament, plight, pass. 4 = **point of view**, viewpoint, opinion, way of thinking, outlook, attitude, stand, standpoint, stance.
5 = **post**, job, situation, appointment, role, office, place, capacity, duty.
6 = **place**, level, grade, grading, rank, status, standing.
▸ VERB = **place**, locate, situate, put, arrange, set,

p

settle, dispose, array.

positive ADJ **1** = **confident**, optimistic, assured, assertive, firm, forceful, determined, resolute, emphatic, dogmatic. **2** = **good**, favourable, effective, promising, encouraging, heartening. **3** = **constructive**, productive, helpful, practical, useful, beneficial.
Opposites: negative.

possess VERB **1** = **own**, be the owner of, have, be the possessor of, count among one's possessions, have to one's name, hold, be blessed with, enjoy, be endowed with, be gifted with. **2** = **influence**, control, dominate, have mastery over, bewitch, enchant, put under a spell, obsess.

possessions PL NOUN = **belongings**, things, property, assets, luggage, baggage, personal effects, goods and chattels, accoutrements, paraphernalia, appendages, impedimenta.

possessive ADJ **1** = **acquisitive**, greedy, grasping, covetous, selfish. **2** = **overprotective**, clinging, controlling, dominating, jealous.

possibility NOUN = **feasibility**, practicability, attainability, likelihood, potentiality, conceivability, probability.

possible ADJ **1** = **feasible**, able to be done, practicable, doable, attainable, achievable, realizable, within reach; [inf] on. **2** = **likely**, potential, conceivable, imaginable, probable, credible, tenable.
Opposites: impossible.

possibly ADV **1** = **perhaps**, maybe, for all one knows, very likely. **2** = **conceivably**, by any means, by any chance, at all.

post NOUN = **stake**, upright, pole, shaft, prop, support, column, stanchion, standard, stock, picket, pillar, palisade, baluster, newel.

▶ VERB **1** = **put up**, stick, stick up, pin, pin up, tack, tack up, attach, affix, hang, display.
2 = **announce**, make known, advertise, publish, publicize, circulate, broadcast.

poster NOUN = **placard**, bill, notice, public notice, sticker, advertisement, announcement, bulletin; [Brit. inf] advert.

postpone VERB = **defer**, put off, put back, delay, hold over, adjourn, shelve, table, pigeonhole; [inf] put on ice, put on the back burner.
Opposites: advance.

postscript NOUN = **PS**, subscript, afterthought, afterword, addendum, appendix, codicil, supplement.

posture NOUN **1** = **position**, pose, attitude, carriage, bearing, stance.
2 = **attitude**, position, point of view, viewpoint, opinion, outlook, stand, standpoint, stance, angle, slant.

▶ VERB = **pose**, strike an attitude, put on an act, act, play-act, attitudinize, show off.

potent ADJ = **powerful**, forceful, strong, vigorous, mighty, influential, authoritative, commanding, compelling, dominant, energetic, dynamic, convincing, cogent, effective, persuasive, eloquent; [poetic/literary] puissant.
Opposites: impotent.

potential ADJ **1** = **budding**, embryonic, developing, promising, prospective, likely, possible, probable.
2 = **likely**, possible, probable.

▶ NOUN = **promise**, possibilities, capability, capacity, ability, aptitude.

potion NOUN = **drink**, beverage, brew, concoction, mixture, draught, elixir, philtre.

potter VERB = **dawdle**, loiter, dally, dilly-dally; [inf] mess about/around.

pouch NOUN = **bag**, purse, wallet, container.

p

pounce VERB = **swoop on**, spring on, lunge at, leap at, jump at/on, ambush, take by surprise, take unawares, attack suddenly.

pound¹ VERB **1** = **crush**, beat, pulverize, powder, smash, mash, grind; [technical] comminute, triturate. **2** = **beat**, pulsate, pulse, throb, thump, pump, palpitate.

pound² NOUN = **compound**, enclosure, pen, yard.

pour VERB **1** = **gush**, rush, stream, flow, course, spout, jet, spurt. **2** = **let flow**, decant, splash, spill.

poverty NOUN
1 = **pennilessness**, neediness, need, want, hardship, deprivation, indigence, impoverishment, impecuniousness, destitution, penury, privation, beggary.
2 = **deficiency**, dearth, shortage, scarcity, paucity, insufficiency, lack, want, meagreness.
Opposites: wealth.

powder VERB **1** = **dust**, sprinkle, scatter, strew.
2 = *See* **pound¹** (**1**).

powdery ADJ = **powder-like**, fine, dusty, chalky, floury, friable, granulated, ground, crushed, pulverized.

power NOUN **1** = **ability**, capability, capacity, faculty, potential, potentiality. **2** = **strength**, force, might, weight.
3 = **control**, authority, mastery, domination, dominance, rule, command, ascendancy, supremacy, dominion, sway.

powerful ADJ **1** = **strong**, sturdy, strapping, stout, robust, vigorous, tough.
2 = **influential**, dominant, authoritative, commanding, forceful, strong, vigorous, potent.
3 = **forceful**, strong, effective, cogent, compelling, convincing, persuasive, eloquent, impressive.
Opposites: weak.

powerless ADJ = **weak**, feeble, impotent, helpless, unfit,

ineffectual, inadequate, paralysed, disabled, incapacitated, debilitated.
Opposites: powerful, strong.

practicable ADJ
= **feasible**, possible, viable, workable, doable, achievable, attainable, accomplishable.
Opposites: theoretical.

practical ADJ 1 = **applied**, empirical, pragmatic, workaday, hands-on.
2 = **functional**, useful, utilitarian, sensible.
3 = **businesslike**, sensible, down-to-earth, pragmatic, realistic, hard-headed; [inf] hard-nosed.
Opposites: impractical.

practically ADV = **almost**, nearly, virtually, all but, in effect; [inf] pretty nearly/well.

practice NOUN 1 = **action**, operation, application, effect, exercise, use.
2 = **training**, preparation, study, exercise, drill, workout, rehearsal.
3 = **procedure**, method, system, usage, tradition, convention.

practise VERB 1 = **perform**, carry out, do, execute, follow, pursue, observe.
2 = **rehearse**, go through, run through, go over, work at, polish, refine.
3 = **work in**, have a career in, pursue a career in, engage in.

praise VERB 1 = **express admiration for**, applaud, acclaim, express approval of, cheer, compliment, congratulate, commend, pay tribute to, extol, sing the praises of, eulogize; [formal] laud. 2 = **worship**, glorify, honour, exalt, adore, pay tribute to, give thanks to; [formal] laud.
Opposites: condemn.
▶ NOUN 1 = **approbation**, applause, acclaim, approval, acclamation, compliments, congratulations, commendation, tributes, accolades, plaudits, eulogy, panegyric, encomium, extolment; [formal] laudation.
2 = **worship**, glory, honour, devotion, exaltation, adoration.

p

praiseworthy ADJ
= **commendable**,
laudable, admirable,
estimable, creditable,
deserving, meritorious,
worthy, excellent,
exemplary, sterling, fine.

prance VERB 1 = **leap**,
spring, jump, skip,
cavort, caper, frisk,
gambol. 2 = **parade**,
cavort, strut, swagger;
[inf] swank.

prank NOUN = **trick**,
practical joke, joke, hoax,
caper, stunt; [inf] lark.

pray VERB 1 = **offer prayers
to**, say prayers to.
2 = **appeal for**, beg for,
petition for, solicit, plead
for.

prayer NOUN = **devotion**,
communion, litany,
collect.

preach VERB = **give/deliver
a sermon**, sermonize,
spread the gospel,
evangelize.
■ **preach at** = **lecture**,
moralize at, admonish,
harangue, sermonize.

preacher NOUN = **minister**,
parson, clergyman,
churchman, cleric,
missionary, revivalist,
evangelist, televangelist.

precarious ADJ = **risky**,
hazardous, insecure,
unstable, shaky, tricky,
perilous, dangerous,
touch-and-go; [inf] dicey,
hairy.
Opposites: safe.

precaution NOUN
1 = **preventive measure**,
preventative measure,
safety measure,
safeguard, provision.
2 = **foresight**,
foresightedness,
forethought, far-
sightedness, anticipation,
prudence,
circumspection, caution,
care, attentiveness,
chariness, wariness.

precede VERB 1 = **go
before**, come before, go/
come ahead of, lead,
usher in. 2 = **lead to**, lead
up to, antedate,
antecede, usher in,
herald, pave the way for.
Opposites: follow.

precedence NOUN = **rank**,
seniority, superiority,
pre-eminence, eminence,
supremacy, primacy,
ascendancy.

precedent NOUN
= **previous case**, prior case, previous instance, prior instance, pattern, model, example, exemplar, paradigm, criterion, yardstick, standard.

precious ADJ 1 = **valuable**, costly, expensive, dear, priceless, rare, choice.
2 = **valued**, cherished, prized, treasured, favourite, dear, beloved, adored, revered, venerated.

precipitate VERB
= **hasten**, accelerate, expedite, speed up, push forward, bring on, trigger.
▶ ADJ = **hurried**, rapid, swift, speedy, headlong, abrupt, sudden, unexpected, breakneck, precipitous.

precipitous ADJ 1 = **steep**, sheer, perpendicular, abrupt, high. 2 = See **precipitate** ADJ.

precise ADJ 1 = **exact**, literal, actual, close, faithful, strict, express, minute, accurate, correct.
2 = **exact**, very, actual, particular, specific, distinct.
Opposites: imprecise.

preclude VERB = **prevent**, prohibit, make impossible, rule out, eliminate, debar, interdict, block, bar, hinder, impede.

precocious ADJ
= **advanced**, ahead, forward, gifted, brilliant, quick, smart.
Opposites: backward.

preconception NOUN
= **preconceived idea**, assumption, presupposition, presumption, prejudgement, prejudice, bias.

predatory ADJ 1 = **hunting**, predacious, rapacious, raptorial. 2 = **exploitative**, greedy, acquisitive, rapacious, vulturine.

predecessor NOUN
= **precursor**, forerunner, antecedent, ancestor, forefather, forebear, progenitor.
Opposites: successor.

predestine VERB = **fate**, predetermine, destine, foreordain, predestinate.

predicament NOUN
= **difficult situation**,
plight, tight corner,
mess, emergency, crisis,
dilemma, quandary,
trouble; [inf] jam, hole,
fix, pickle, scrape, tight
spot.

predict VERB = **forecast**,
foretell, prophesy,
foresee, divine,
prognosticate, forewarn,
forebode, portend,
presage, augur.

predictable ADJ
= **foreseeable**, expected,
anticipated, probable,
likely, certain, sure;
[inf] on the cards.

predilection NOUN
= **liking**, fondness,
preference, love,
partiality, taste,
weakness, penchant,
fancy, inclination,
leaning.
Opposites: dislike.

predominate VERB = **be
dominant**, be in control,
rule, hold ascendancy,
hold sway, have the
upper hand, carry most
weight.

pre-eminent ADJ
= **outstanding**, leading,
foremost, chief,
excellent, distinguished,
prominent, eminent,
important, superior,
unrivalled, unsurpassed.
Opposites:
undistinguished.

preface NOUN
= **introduction**, foreword,
preamble, prologue,
prelude, front matter,
proem, exordium,
prolegomenon;
[inf] prelims, intro.
▶ VERB = **precede**, prefix,
introduce, begin, open,
launch.

prefer VERB = **like better**,
favour, fancy, be more
partial to, incline
towards, choose, select,
pick, opt for, go for,
plump for, single out.

preferable ADJ = **better**,
superior, more desirable,
more suitable.

preference NOUN
1 = **choice**, first choice,
first option, liking, fancy,
desire, wish, inclination,
partiality, predilection,
leaning, bias, bent.
2 = **preferential treatment**,
favour, precedence,
priority, advantage.

preferential ADJ
= **special**, better, advantageous, favoured, privileged, partial, partisan.

pregnant ADJ 1 = **having a baby/child**, expectant, expecting, in the family way, with child, enceinte; [inf] preggers, with a bun in the oven; [Brit. inf] in the club; [technical] gravid.
2 = **meaningful**, significant, eloquent, expressive, suggestive, pointed, telling.

prejudice NOUN = **bias**, discrimination, partisanship, partiality, preference, one-sidedness, chauvinism, bigotry, narrow-mindedness, intolerance, unfairness, unjustness, racism, sexism, ageism, heterosexism.
▸ VERB = **be prejudicial to**, be disadvantageous to, damage, injure, harm, hurt, mar, spoil, impair, undermine.

prejudiced ADJ = **biased**, discriminatory, partisan, partial, one-sided, jaundiced, chauvinistic, bigoted, intolerant, narrow-minded, unfair, unjust, racist, sexist, ageist.
Opposites: impartial.

prejudicial ADJ
= **detrimental**, deleterious, unfavourable, damaging, injurious, harmful, hurtful, inimical.
Opposites: beneficial.

preliminary ADJ
= **introductory**, prefatory, prior, precursory, opening, initial, beginning, preparatory, initiatory.
Opposites: final.

prelude NOUN
1 = **precursor**, forerunner, curtain-raiser, harbinger, herald, preliminary, introduction, start, beginning.
2 = **introduction**, preface, prologue, preamble, proem, exordium, prolegomenon; [inf] intro.

premature ADJ = **too soon**, too early, early, untimely, overhasty, precipitate, impulsive, impetuous, rash.
Opposites: overdue.

premeditated ADJ
= **planned**, pre-planned, pre-arranged, intentional, intended, deliberate, calculated, wilful.
Opposites: spontaneous.

premier NOUN = **head of government**, president, prime minister, PM.
▶ ADJ = **leading**, foremost, chief, principal, head, top, first, highest, main.

premonition NOUN
= **foreboding**, presentiment, intuition, feeling, hunch, suspicion, sneaking suspicion, misgiving, apprehension, fear, feeling in one's bones, funny feeling.

preoccupied ADJ = **lost in thought**, deep in thought, in a brown study, absorbed, engrossed, pensive, absent-minded, distracted, abstracted, distrait, oblivious, faraway, rapt.

preparation NOUN
1 = **arrangement**, provision, preparatory measure, necessary step, groundwork, spadework.

2 = **coaching**, training, grooming, priming.
3 = **mixture**, compound, concoction, composition, tincture.

prepare VERB 1 = **get ready**, make ready, arrange, develop, put together, assemble, draw up, produce, construct, compose, concoct, fashion, work up.
2 = **revise**, study, cram, do homework; [Brit. inf] swot. 3 = **coach**, train, groom, prime.

preposterous ADJ
= **absurd**, ridiculous, foolish, ludicrous, farcical, asinine, senseless, unreasonable, crazy, insane, outrageous, unbelievable, incredible, unthinkable.
Opposites: sensible.

prerequisite ADJ
= **necessary**, needed, required, called for, essential, requisite, vital, indispensable, imperative, obligatory, mandatory.
Opposites: unnecessary.
▶ NOUN = **requirement**, necessity, essential,

requisite, precondition, condition, sine qua non; [inf] must.

prescribe VERB **1** = **advise**, recommend, commend, suggest. **2** = **lay down**, require, stipulate, specify, decree, order, command, ordain, enjoin.

presence NOUN **1** = **existence**, being. **2** = **company**, proximity, neighbourhood, vicinity, closeness, nearness. **3** = **magnetism**, aura, charisma, personality, attraction, poise. Opposites: absence.

present¹ ADJ **1** = **existing**, existent, extant. **2** = **present-day**, existing, current, contemporary. **3** = **in attendance**, near, nearby, available, at hand, ready. Opposites: absent.
▶ NOUN = **today**, now, here and now, the present moment, the time being.

present² VERB **1** = **give**, hand over, confer, bestow, donate, award, grant, accord. **2** = **introduce**, make known, announce. **3** = **put**

on, produce, perform, stage, mount.

present³ NOUN = **gift**, donation, offering, contribution, gratuity, handout, presentation, award, bounty, benefaction; [inf] freebie; [Brit. inf] pressie.

presentable ADJ = **well groomed**, smartly dressed, tidily dressed, tidy, spruce, of smart appearance, fit to be seen.

preserve VERB = **conserve**, protect, care for, safeguard, guard, defend, shield, save, keep, maintain, perpetuate, uphold. Opposites: neglect.

preside VERB = **be in charge of**, control, direct, run, conduct, supervise, govern, rule.

press VERB **1** = **depress**, push down, force down, bear down on. **2** = **crush**, squeeze, compress, mash, reduce. **3** = **smooth out**, flatten, iron. **4** = **urge**, entreat, exhort, implore, put pressure on, pressurize, force, compel,

p

coerce.

▶ NOUN = **newspapers**, the media, journalists, reporters; [Brit.] Fleet Street.

pressing ADJ = *see* **urgent (1)**.

pressure NOUN 1 = **force**, weight, heaviness, compression. 2 = **coercion**, compulsion, force, constraint, duress. 3 = **strain**, stress, tension, burden, load, weight, trouble; [inf] hassle.

▶ VERB = **put pressure on**, pressurize, press, force, compel, coerce, constrain, bulldoze, dragoon.

prestige NOUN = **status**, kudos, standing, stature, importance, reputation, fame, renown, esteem, influence, authority, supremacy, eminence, superiority, predominance.

prestigious ADJ = **important**, prominent, impressive, high-ranking, reputable, respected, esteemed, eminent, distinguished, of high standing, well known,

celebrated, illustrious, renowned, famous.

presume VERB 1 = **assume**, take for granted, take it, take as read, suppose, presuppose, believe, think, imagine, judge, guess, surmise, conjecture, hypothesize, infer, deduce. 2 = **have the temerity**, have the audacity, be so bold as, have the effrontery, go so far as, dare, venture.

presumptuous ADJ = **overconfident**, cocksure, arrogant, egotistical, conceited, bold, audacious, forward, pushy, insolent, impudent, bumptious; [inf] too big for one's boots.

pretence NOUN 1 = **false show**, show, semblance, appearance, false front, guise, facade, masquerade, mask, veneer, cover, charade. 2 = **pretext**, false excuse, guise, sham, ruse, wile, trickery, lie, falsehood. 3 = **pretentiousness**, display, ostentation, affectation, showiness, flaunting, posturing.

pretend VERB 1 = **put on an act**, act, play-act, put it on, dissemble, sham, feign, fake, dissimulate, make believe, put on a false front, posture, go through the motions. 2 = **claim**, make believe, purport, affect, profess, make out, fabricate.

pretender NOUN = **claimant**, claimer, aspirant.

pretentious ADJ = **affected**, ostentatious, showy, pompous, artificial, mannered, high-flown, high-sounding, flowery, grandiose, elaborate, extravagant, flamboyant, grandiloquent, bombastic, orotund; [inf] highfalutin. Opposites: plain, simple.

pretty ADJ = **lovely**, attractive, good-looking, nice-looking, personable, prepossessing, appealing, charming, delightful, nice, engaging, pleasing, winning, winsome, as pretty as a picture; [Scottish & N.

English] bonny; [N. Amer. inf] cute; [archaic] fair, comely. Opposites: ugly.
▶ ADV = **quite**, rather, fairly, somewhat, moderately, reasonably; [inf] kind of.

prevail VERB = **win**, triumph, be victorious, carry the day, conquer, overcome, gain mastery.

prevalent ADJ 1 = **prevailing**, current, frequent, usual, common, general, widespread, pervasive, universal, set, established, accepted, popular, fashionable, in fashion, in style, in vogue. 2 = **widespread**, extensive, frequent, usual, endemic, universal, ubiquitous, rampant, rife. Opposites: uncommon.

prevaricate VERB = **be evasive**, shilly-shally, dodge the issue, hedge, beat about the bush, equivocate, quibble; [Brit.] hum and haw.

prevent VERB = **put a stop to**, halt, arrest, avert, nip in the bud, fend off, turn

aside, stave off, ward off, block, check, hinder, impede, hamper, obstruct, baulk, foil, thwart, frustrate, forestall, inhibit, hold back, restrain, prohibit, bar, deter.
Opposites: encourage.

preventative,
preventive ADJ
= **precautionary**, protective, deterrent, prophylactic.

previous ADJ **1** = **former**, ex-, past, sometime, one-time, erstwhile; [formal] quondam.
2 = **preceding**, foregoing, earlier, prior, above, precursory, antecedent, anterior.
Opposites: following.

previously ADV
= **formerly**, earlier on, before, until now, hitherto, heretofore, once, at one time, in the past, in years gone by.

price NOUN **1** = **cost**, asking price, charge, fee, payment, rate, amount, figure, value, valuation, bill. **2** = **result**, cost, penalty, sacrifice, forfeit,

forfeiture, punishment.
▶ VERB = **fix/set the price of**, cost, value, rate, evaluate, assess, estimate, appraise, assay.

priceless ADJ
1 = **invaluable**, precious, rare, incomparable, expensive, costly, rich, dear, irreplaceable, treasured, prized. **2** = *See* **hilarious**.
Opposites: worthless.

prick VERB = **pierce**, puncture, perforate, stab, nick, gash, slit, bore, spike.

prickle NOUN **1** = **thorn**, needle, barb, spike, spine, spur. **2** = **tingle**, tingling, sting, stinging, smarting, itching.
▶ VERB = **tingle**, sting, smart, itch.

pride NOUN **1** = **self-esteem**, self-respect, ego, amour propre, self-worth, self-image, feelings, sensibilities. **2** = **conceit**, vanity, arrogance, haughtiness, self-importance, self-love, egotism, presumption, hauteur, superciliousness, disdain; [inf] big-

headedness.
3 = **satisfaction**, gratification, pleasure, joy, delight.

Opposites: humility.

▶ VERB = **be proud of**, take pride in, take satisfaction in, congratulate oneself on, revel in, glory in, exult in, boast about, brag about, crow about.

priest NOUN = **clergyman**, cleric, man/woman of the cloth, man/woman of God, father, padre.

prim ADJ = **proper**, demure, formal, precise, stuffy, starchy, strait-laced, prudish, prissy, old-maidish, priggish, puritanical.

primarily ADV = **basically**, essentially, in essence, fundamentally, in the first place, first and foremost, chiefly, mainly, in the main, principally, mostly, for the most part, on the whole, predominantly, predominately.

primary ADJ **1** = **prime**, chief, main, principal, leading, predominant, most important,

paramount, basic, fundamental, elemental, rudimentary, essential.
2 = **earliest**, original, initial, beginning, first, opening.

Opposites: secondary.

prime ADJ **1** = *See* **primary** (1). **2** = **top-quality**, highest, top, best, first-class, high-grade, grade A, superior, choice, select.

Opposites: inferior.

▶ NOUN = **best part**, peak, pinnacle, best days, height, zenith, acme, culmination, apex, heyday, full flowering.

primitive ADJ **1** = **ancient**, earliest, primeval, primordial, primal, pristine. **2** = **crude**, simple, rudimentary, undeveloped, unrefined, rough, unsophisticated, rude. **3** = **uncivilized**, barbarian, barbaric, savage, wild.

Opposites: advanced.

principal ADJ **1** = **foremost**, chief, leading, pre-eminent, most important, most influential, dominant,

controlling, ruling, in charge. **2 = major**, main, chief, leading, key, primary, prime, paramount.
Opposites: subsidiary.
▶ NOUN **1 = head teacher**, headmaster, headmistress, head, rector, master, dean.
2 = leading player/ performer, leading man/ lady, lead, star.

principle NOUN **1 = theory**, basis, fundamental, essence, assumption, rule, law, canon, tenet, code, maxim, axiom, dictum, postulate.
2 = morals, ethics, integrity, uprightness, righteousness, probity, rectitude, honour, conscience, scruples.

print VERB **1 = set in print**, send to press, publish, issue, run off, put to bed.
2 = imprint, stamp, mark.
▶ NOUN **1 = type**, letters, lettering, typeface, newsprint. **2 = copy**, reproduction, replica.

prior ADJ **= earlier**, previous, anterior.
Opposites: subsequent.

■ **prior to = before**, until, up to, earlier than, preceding.

priority NOUN **1 = first/ prime concern**, most important thing.
2 = precedence, preference, urgency.

prison NOUN **= jail**, lock-up, penal institution, place of detention, place of confinement, dungeon; [N. Amer.] penitentiary, correctional facility; [inf] clink, cooler, slammer, stir, jug; [Brit. inf] nick; [N. Amer. inf] can, pen; [Brit. inf, dated] chokey.

prisoner NOUN **= convict**, captive, detainee, internee, hostage; [inf] con, lag, lifer, jailbird.

pristine ADJ **= unmarked**, unblemished, unspoilt, spotless, immaculate, clean, in mint/perfect condition.
Opposites: dirty, spoilt.

private ADJ
1 = confidential, secret, unofficial, off-the-record, in camera, closet, privileged; [inf] hush-

hush. **2** = **personal**, intimate, secret.
3 = **secluded**, secret, remote, out of the way, quiet. **4** = **reserved**, retiring, self-contained, uncommunicative, diffident, secretive.
Opposites: public, open, extrovert.

privileged ADJ
1 = **advantaged**, socially advantaged, favoured, elite, indulgent, spoilt.
2 = **confidential**, private, off-the-record, secret, top secret; [inf] hush-hush.
Opposites: disadvantaged, public.

prize NOUN = **trophy**, medal, award, accolade, reward, premium, honour, laurels, palm, bays.
▶ ADJ = **prizewinning**, award-winning, winning, champion.
▶ VERB = **value**, treasure, cherish, hold dear, esteem, hold in high regard.

probable ADJ = **likely**, most likely, odds-on, expected, anticipated, predictable, foreseeable,

on the cards, credible, quite possible, possible.
Opposites: improbable.

probably ADV = **in all probability**, in all likelihood, as likely as not, it is to be expected that, perhaps.

probe NOUN
= **investigation**, scrutiny, inquest, exploration, examination, study.
▶ VERB **1** = **feel**, feel around, prod, poke, explore.
2 = **investigate**, scrutinize, inquire into, examine, study, research, analyse.

problem NOUN
1 = **difficulty**, complication, trouble, mess, predicament, plight, dilemma, quandary; [inf] pickle, can of worms. **2** = **puzzle**, poser, enigma, riddle, conundrum; [inf] teaser, brain-teaser.

problematic ADJ
1 = **problematical**, difficult, troublesome, complicated, puzzling, knotty, thorny, ticklish, tricky; [Brit. inf] dodgy.
2 = **doubtful**, uncertain, unsettled, questionable,

p

open to question, debatable, arguable.
Opposites: straightforward.

procedure NOUN
1 = **course of action**, plan of action, policy, system, method, methodology, modus operandi, technique, means, practice, operation, strategy. **2** = **step**, process, measure, move, operation, transaction.

proceed VERB **1** = **make one's way**, go, advance, carry on, move on, press on, progress. **2** = **arise**, originate, spring, stem, come, derive, result, follow, ensue, emanate, issue, flow.

proceedings PL NOUN
1 = **activities**, events, action, process, affairs, doings, happenings.
2 = **case**, lawsuit, litigation, trial.
3 = **minutes**, report, account, record, transactions.

proceeds PL NOUN
= **takings**, profits, returns, receipts, income, earnings.

process NOUN **1** = **method**, system, technique, means, practice, way, procedure.
2 = **development**, evolution, changes, stages, steps.

procession NOUN
1 = **parade**, march, column, file, train, cortège, cavalcade, motorcade. **2** = **stream**, steady stream, succession, series, sequence, run.

proclaim VERB
1 = **announce**, declare, make known, give out, notify, circulate, advertise, publish, broadcast, promulgate.
2 = **pronounce**, announce, declare to be.

procrastinate VERB
= **delay**, postpone action, defer action, be dilatory, use delaying tactics, stall, temporize, play for time, play a waiting game, dally, dilly-daily, drag one's feet/heels.

prod VERB **1** = **poke**, jab, dig, nudge, elbow, butt, push, shove, thrust.
2 = *See* **urge** VERB **(1)**.

prodigious ADJ
= **impressive**, striking, startling, extraordinary, remarkable, exceptional, amazing, staggering, stupendous, phenomenal, miraculous. **Opposites:** small, unexceptional.

prodigy NOUN = **child genius**, wonder child, wunderkind, gifted child, wonder, marvel, phenomenon, sensation.

produce VERB **1** = **make**, manufacture, create, construct, build, fabricate, put together, assemble, turn out, compose, originate, prepare, develop, fashion. **2** = **present**, offer, set forth, proffer, advance, show, exhibit, demonstrate, disclose, reveal. **3** = **yield**, bear, give, bring forth, supply, provide, furnish. **4** = **give birth to**, bring forth, bear, breed, give life to, bring into the world, procreate. **5** = **mount**, stage, put on, present.
▶ NOUN = **yield**, crops, harvest, output.

product NOUN
1 = **commodity**, artefact, goods, wares, merchandise. **2** = **result**, outcome, effect, consequence, upshot, fruit, spin-off, legacy.

productive ADJ **1** = **fertile**, fruitful, fecund, rich, high-yielding. **2** = **prolific**, energetic, vigorous, efficient, effective, valuable.
Opposites: sterile, unproductive.

profess VERB = **declare**, announce, proclaim, assert, state, utter, affirm, avow; [formal] aver.

profession NOUN
1 = **career**, job, calling, business, vocation, occupation, line of work, métier, position, situation. **2** = **declaration**, announcement, proclamation, assertion, statement, affirmation, avowal; [formal] averment.

professional ADJ
1 = **skilled**, skilful, proficient, expert, adept, competent, efficient, experienced. **2** = **skilful**, expert, adept, masterly,

excellent, fine, polished, finished. **3 = non-amateur**, paid.
Opposites: amateurish, amateur.

proffer VERB **= offer**, tender, present, extend, give, submit, volunteer, suggest.
Opposites: withdraw.

profile NOUN **1 = outline**, silhouette, contour, lines, shape, form, figure.
2 = short biography, sketch, thumbnail sketch, portrait, vignette.

profit NOUN **1 = takings**, proceeds, gain, yield, return, receipts, income, earnings, winnings.
2 = gain, benefit, advantage, good, value, use, avail.
Opposites: loss.
▶ VERB **= benefit**, be of benefit to, be of advantage to, be of use/value to, serve, help, be helpful to, assist, aid, stand in good stead.

profitable ADJ **1 = money-making**, commercial, gainful, remunerative, paying, lucrative.
2 = beneficial,

advantageous, rewarding, helpful, productive, useful, worthwhile, valuable.
Opposites: unprofitable.

profound ADJ **1 = serious**, weighty, deep, learned, discerning, penetrating, thoughtful, philosophical, erudite, wise, sagacious.
2 = sincere, intense, keen, great, extreme, deep, heartfelt. **3 = far-reaching**, radical, extensive, exhaustive, thoroughgoing.
Opposites: shallow, superficial.

profuse ADJ **1 = copious**, prolific, abundant, liberal, effusive, lavish, extravagant, inordinate.
2 = luxuriant, plentiful, lush, rich, exuberant, riotous, rank, rampant.
Opposites: meagre.

programme NOUN **1 = agenda**, calendar, schedule, syllabus, list of events, order of the day.
2 = production, presentation, show, performance, broadcast.
3 = syllabus, prospectus,

schedule, list, curriculum, literature.

progress NOUN **1 = forward movement**, headway, advance, going, passage, advancement, progression. **2 = progression**, improvement, betterment, upgrading, development, growth.
▶ VERB **1 = go forward**, move forward/on, make one's way, advance, go on, continue, proceed, push forward, forge ahead. **2 = make progress**, get better, improve, recover, recuperate.
Opposites: regress.

progressive ADJ **1 = increasing**, growing, intensifying, accelerating, escalating. **2 = modern**, advanced, radical, reforming, innovative, revolutionary, forward-looking, enlightened, avant-garde; [inf] go-ahead.
Opposites: conservative.

prohibit VERB **1 = forbid**, ban, bar, disallow, proscribe, veto, interdict, outlaw. **2 = prevent**, stop, rule out, preclude, make impossible, hinder, impede, hamper, obstruct, restrict, constrain.
Opposites: allow.

prohibitive ADJ **= exorbitant**, steep, extortionate, excessive, preposterous, high-priced, high-cost, sky-high.

project NOUN **= scheme**, plan, programme, enterprise, undertaking, venture, activity, operation, campaign.
▶ VERB **1 = plan**, propose, map out, devise, design, outline. **2 = launch**, discharge, propel, hurl, throw, cast, fling, shoot. **3 = jut out**, protrude, extend, stick out, stand out, hang over, obtrude.

proliferate VERB **= increase**, multiply, extend, expand, burgeon, accelerate, escalate, rocket, snowball, mushroom.
Opposites: decrease.

prolong VERB **= lengthen**, make longer, elongate, extend, stretch out, draw

out, drag out, protract,
spin out.

prominent ADJ
1 = **protruding**,
protuberant, jutting,
projecting, standing out,
bulging. **2** = **conspicuous**,
noticeable, obvious,
unmistakable, obtrusive,
eye-catching, striking.
3 = **eminent**, important,
pre-eminent,
distinguished, notable,
noted, illustrious,
celebrated, well known,
famous, renowned,
leading.
Opposites: inconspicuous.

promiscuous ADJ
= **dissolute**, dissipated,
fast, licentious, loose,
profligate, abandoned,
immoral, debauched,
wanton, of easy virtue,
unchaste.
Opposites: chaste.

promise VERB **1** = **give
one's word**, give an
undertaking, give one's
assurance, swear, vow,
pledge, contract.
2 = **augur**, indicate,
denote, signify, be a sign
of, show signs of,
suggest, betoken, presage.

▶ NOUN **1** = **word**,
undertaking, assurance,
guarantee, commitment,
vow, oath, pledge, bond,
contract, covenant.
2 = **potential**, flair, talent,
ability, aptitude,
capability, capacity.

promising ADJ
= **encouraging**, hopeful,
favourable, auspicious,
propitious, optimistic,
bright.
Opposites: unfavourable,
hopeless.

promontory NOUN
= **headland**, point, cape,
foreland, bluff, cliff,
precipice, overhang,
height, projection,
prominence.

promote VERB **1** = **elevate**,
advance, move up,
upgrade, prefer,
aggrandize. **2** = **advance**,
further, assist, aid, help,
contribute to, foster,
boost. **3** = **advertise**,
publicize, push, puff,
beat the drum for;
[inf] plug, give a plug to,
hype.
Opposites: demote,
obstruct.

promotion NOUN
1 = **upgrading**, elevation, advancement, preferment, aggrandizement.
2 = **advancement**, furtherance, furthering, assistance, aid, help, contribution to, fostering, boosting.
3 = **advertising**, publicity, hard sell, puff; [inf] plug, hype, hyping.

prompt ADJ **1** = **immediate**, instant, instantaneous, swift, rapid, speedy, quick, fast, expeditious, early, punctual, in good time, timely. **2** = **swift**, rapid, speedy, quick, fast, ready, willing, eager.
Opposites: slow.
▶ VERB **1** = **cause**, make, encourage, move, induce, urge, incite, impel, spur on, motivate, stimulate, inspire, provoke.
2 = **remind**, jog someone's memory, refresh someone's memory, cue, help out.

pronounce VERB
1 = **enunciate**, articulate, say, utter, sound, voice, vocalize. **2** = **announce**, declare, proclaim, assert, affirm, rule, decree.

pronounced ADJ
1 = **marked**, noticeable, obvious, evident, conspicuous, striking, distinct, unmistakable.
2 = **decided**, definite, clear, strong, positive, distinct.
Opposites: slight.

pronunciation NOUN
= **enunciation**, articulation, accent, saying, uttering, utterance, sounding, voicing, vocalization.

proof NOUN = **evidence**, demonstration, substantiation, corroboration, confirmation, attestation, testimony, certification, verification, authentication, validation.
▶ ADJ = **impervious**, impenetrable, resistant, repellent.

prop NOUN = **support**, upright, brace, buttress, stay, bolster, stanchion, truss, column, post, rod, pole, shaft.

▶ VERB = **lean**, rest, set, lay, stand, balance, steady.

■ **prop up** = **hold up**, shore up, bolster up, buttress, support, brace, underpin, reinforce, strengthen.

propaganda NOUN = **publicity material**, publicity, promotion, advertising, advertisement, information, agitprop.

propagate VERB 1 = **grow**, breed, multiply, reproduce. 2 = **spread**, communicate, circulate, disseminate, transmit, distribute, broadcast, publish, publicize, proclaim, promulgate.

propel VERB = **move**, set in motion, push forward, drive, thrust forward, force, impel.

propensity NOUN = *see* **tendency**.

proper ADJ 1 = **suitable**, fitting, appropriate, apt. 2 = **correct**, right, precise, accepted, established, orthodox, conventional, formal. 3 = **seemly**, decorous, respectable, decent, refined, genteel,

formal, conventional, orthodox, strict, punctilious.
Opposites: improper.

property NOUN 1 = **possessions**, belongings, things, goods, effects, chattels, assets, resources. 2 = **real estate**, buildings, land. 3 = **quality**, attribute, characteristic, feature, power, peculiarity, idiosyncrasy, quirk.

prophecy NOUN = **prediction**, forecast, prognostication, divination, augury.

prophesy VERB = **predict**, foretell, forecast, foresee, forewarn of, presage, prognosticate, divine, augur.

prophet NOUN = **seer**, soothsayer, diviner, clairvoyant, prophesier, oracle, augur, sibyl, Cassandra.

proportion NOUN 1 = **ratio**, distribution, relative amount/number, relationship. 2 = **portion**, part, segment, share, quota, division, percentage, fraction,

measure; [inf] cut.
3 = balance, symmetry, harmony, correspondence, congruity, agreement.

proportional ADJ
= proportionate, corresponding, commensurate, equivalent, comparable.
Opposites: disproportionate.

proposal NOUN = **scheme**, plan, project, programme, motion, bid, proposition, presentation, suggestion, recommendation, tender, terms.

propose VERB **1 = put forward**, advance, offer, proffer, present, submit, tender, propound, suggest, recommend, advocate. **2 = intend**, mean, plan, have in mind, aim, purpose.
3 = nominate, name, put forward, put up, suggest, recommend.

proprieties PL NOUN
= etiquette, social niceties, protocol, civilities, formalities, rules of conduct,

accepted behaviour, good manners, good form, the done thing, punctilio.

proprietor NOUN = **owner**, possessor, title-holder, deed-holder, landowner, landlord/landlady.

prosaic ADJ
= unimaginative, ordinary, uninspired, commonplace, dull, tedious, boring, dry, humdrum, mundane, pedestrian, lifeless, spiritless, stale, bland, vapid, banal, hackneyed, trite, insipid, monotonous, flat.
Opposites: imaginative.

prosecute VERB
1 = charge, prefer charges against, bring an action against, try, bring to trial, put on trial, sue, bring a suit against, interdict, arraign.
2 = carry on, conduct, direct, engage in, work at, proceed with, continue with.

prospect NOUN
1 = likelihood, likeliness, hope, expectation, anticipation, chance, chances, odds,

p

probability, possibility.
2 = **view**, vista, outlook,
perspective, panorama,
scene, spectacle.
▶ VERB = **explore**, search,
inspect, survey, examine,
check out.

prospective ADJ = **future**,
to-be, soon-to-be,
intended, expected,
would-be, potential,
possible, likely, hoped
for, looked for, awaited,
anticipated.

prospects PL NOUN
= **potential**, promise,
possibilities,
expectations, scope.

prosper VERB = **do well**,
get on well, thrive,
flourish, be successful,
succeed, get ahead,
progress, advance, get on
in the world, make
headway, make good,
become rich, be in
clover.
Opposites: fail.

prosperity NOUN
= **affluence**, wealth,
riches, prosperousness,
success, good fortune,
ease, plenty, the good
life, luxury.
Opposites: hardship.

prosperous ADJ = **well
off**, well-to-do, affluent,
wealthy, rich, successful,
moneyed, opulent, in
clover; [inf] well heeled,
in the money, on Easy
Street.
Opposites: poor.

prostitute NOUN = **call girl**,
whore; [inf] tart, pro,
working girl, member of
the oldest profession;
[Brit. inf] tom; [N. Amer.
inf] hooker, hustler;
[dated] loose woman,
woman of ill repute,
streetwalker, woman of
the streets, fallen woman;
[archaic] courtesan,
strumpet, harlot, trollop,
wench.

prostrate ADJ = **prone**,
lying down, flat,
stretched out, horizontal,
procumbent.
▶ VERB = **knock flat**, flatten,
knock down, floor, level.

protect VERB 1 = **keep safe**,
save, safeguard, shield,
preserve, defend, shelter,
secure. 2 = **guard**,
mount/stand guard on,
defend, secure, watch
over, look after, take care
of.

proud

Opposites: endanger.

protection NOUN 1 = **safe keeping**, safety, care, charge, keeping, preservation, defence, security. 2 = **safeguard**, shield, barrier, buffer, screen, cover.

protective ADJ 1 = **protecting**, safeguarding, shielding, covering. 2 = **careful**, watchful, vigilant, paternal/maternal, fatherly/motherly, overprotective, possessive, clinging.

protector NOUN = **defender**, champion, bodyguard, guardian, guardian angel.

protest VERB 1 = **object**, raise objections, take issue, make/take a stand, put up a fight, take exception, complain, demur, remonstrate, make a fuss, demonstrate; [inf] kick up a fuss, beef, bitch. 2 = **declare**, announce, profess, proclaim, assert, affirm, argue, attest, maintain, insist on, avow; [formal] aver.

▶ NOUN = **objection**, opposition, exception, complaint, disapproval, disagreement, dissent, demurral, remonstration, fuss, outcry, demonstration, protestation.

protocol NOUN = **etiquette**, rules of conduct, code of behaviour, conventions, formalities, customs, propriety, proprieties, decorum, manners, courtesies, civilities, good form, politesse.

protract VERB = **prolong**, extend, stretch out, draw out, lengthen, make longer, drag out, spin out, keep going, continue.
Opposites: curtail, shorten.

proud ADJ 1 = **pleased**, glad, happy, satisfied, gratified, content, appreciative. 2 = **arrogant**, conceited, vain, self-important, egotistical, boastful, haughty, disdainful, scornful, supercilious, snobbish, imperious, overbearing,

p

prove

overweening, high-
handed; [inf] high and
mighty, stuck up, snooty,
toffee-nosed.
3 = **gratifying**, satisfying,
happy, memorable,
notable, red-letter,
glorious, marvellous.
Opposites: ashamed,
humble.

prove VERB = **establish**,
determine, demonstrate,
show beyond doubt,
substantiate, corroborate,
verify, validate,
authenticate, confirm.
Opposites: disprove.

proverb NOUN = **saying**,
adage, maxim, saw,
axiom, aphorism,
dictum, apophthegm.

proverbial ADJ
= **legendary**, notorious,
infamous, famous,
famed, renowned, well
known, acknowledged,
accepted, traditional,
time-honoured.

provide VERB **1** = **supply**,
furnish, equip,
accommodate, provision,
outfit. **2** = **give**, bring,
afford, present, offer,
accord, yield, impart,
lend.

■ **provide for** = **support**,
maintain, keep, sustain,
take care of, care for,
look after.

provided CONJUNCTION
= **providing that**, on
condition that, if, as long
as, given, with the
provision/proviso that,
contingent upon, on the
assumption that.

provident ADJ = **far-
sighted**, prudent,
judicious, shrewd,
cautious, careful, thrifty,
canny, economical,
frugal.

provincial ADJ **1** = **local**,
small-town, rural,
country.
2 = **unsophisticated**,
parochial, limited,
small-minded, insular,
inward-looking, illiberal,
narrow, narrow-minded,
inflexible, bigoted,
prejudiced, intolerant.
Opposites: metropolitan,
sophisticated.

provisional ADJ
= **provisory**, temporary,
interim, stopgap, to be
confirmed, transitional,
conditional, tentative,
contingent, pro tem.

Opposites: permanent.

provisions PL NOUN
= **supplies**, stores, groceries, food and drink, foodstuffs, staples, rations, provender, eatables, edibles, comestibles; [poetic/literary] viands; [dated] victuals.

proviso NOUN = **condition**, stipulation, provision, clause, rider, qualification, restriction, reservation, limitation.

provocative ADJ
1 = **provoking**, annoying, irritating, exasperating, infuriating, maddening, vexing, galling, affronting, insulting, inflaming, goading; [inf] aggravating.
2 = **seductive**, sexy, tempting, suggestive, arousing, exciting, alluring, erotic, titillating.

provoke VERB 1 = **annoy**, anger, incense, enrage, irritate, exasperate, infuriate, madden, pique, nettle, vex, harass, irk, gall, affront, insult; [inf] make someone's

blood boil, aggravate.
2 = **incite**, rouse, stir, move, stimulate, motivate, excite, inflame, prompt, induce, spur, goad, prod, egg on.
Opposites: allay, pacify.

prowess NOUN = **skill**, skilfulness, expertise, facility, ability, capability, talent, genius, adroitness, adeptness, aptitude, competence, proficiency; [inf] know-how.

prowl VERB = **roam**, range, move stealthily, slink, skulk, steal, sneak, stalk.

proxy NOUN
= **representative**, deputy, substitute, agent, delegate, surrogate.

prudent ADJ 1 = **wise**, well judged, judicious, sagacious, sage, shrewd, sensible, circumspect, far-sighted, politic.
2 = **cautious**, careful, discreet, wary, vigilant, heedful, thrifty, economical, canny, sparing, frugal, provident.
Opposites: imprudent.

prudish ADJ = **priggish**, prim, strait-laced, prissy, puritan, puritanical, stuffy, starchy, Victorian, Grundyish, old-maid, old-maidish, schoolmarmish; [inf] goody-goody.
Opposites: permissive.

prune VERB = **cut**, lop, chop, clip, snip, remove.

pry VERB = **be inquisitive**, interfere, meddle, intrude, be nosy, be a busybody; [inf] stick/poke one's nose in, stick one's oar in, snoop; [Austral./NZ inf] stickybeak.

pseudonym NOUN = **assumed name**, alias, false name, nom de plume, pen-name, stage name, professional name, sobriquet, nickname, nom de guerre.

psychological ADJ = **mental**, of the mind, cerebral, psychic, psychical.

pub NOUN = **bar**, tavern, inn; [Brit.] public house; [Brit. inf] local, boozer.

puberty NOUN = **pubescence**, adolescence, young adulthood, teenage years, teens.

public ADJ 1 = **popular**, general, common, universal, widespread. 2 = **known**, widely known, acknowledged, overt, in circulation, published, publicized, plain, obvious. 3 = **prominent**, well known, important, eminent, respected, influential, prestigious, famous.
Opposites: private.
▶ NOUN = **people**, population, country, nation, community, citizens, populace, the masses, the multitude, the mob, the hoi polloi.

publication NOUN 1 = **publishing**, production, issuing, issuance. 2 = **book**, newspaper, magazine, periodical, journal, daily, weekly, monthly, quarterly, booklet, brochure, leaflet, pamphlet, handbill.

publicize VERB 1 = **make public**, make known, announce, publish, broadcast, distribute, disseminate, promulgate. **2** = **give publicity to**, promote, advertise, puff, puff up, push, beat the drum for; [inf] hype, plug. Opposites: conceal.

publish VERB **1** = **produce**, issue, print, bring out. **2** = See **publicize** (1).

pucker VERB = **screw up**, wrinkle, crease, furrow, knit, crinkle, corrugate.

puerile ADJ = **childish**, immature, infantile, juvenile, adolescent, foolish, silly, inane, asinine. Opposites: mature.

puff NOUN = **gust**, blast, whiff, breath, flurry, draught.
▶ VERB **1** = **pant**, blow, gasp, gulp. **2** = **swell**, distend, inflate, dilate, bloat. **3** = See **publicize** (2).

pugnacious ADJ = **belligerent**, bellicose, combative, aggressive, antagonistic, argumentative, disputatious, hostile, threatening, irascible, ill-tempered, bad-tempered. Opposites: peaceable.

pull VERB **1** = **haul**, drag, draw, trail, tow, tug. **2** = **strain**, sprain, wrench, stretch, tear, dislocate, damage. Opposites: push.
▪ **pull back** = **withdraw**, retreat, draw back, fall back.
▪ **pull down** = **knock down**, demolish, raze, level, destroy, bulldoze.
▪ **pull oneself together** = **regain one's composure/calm**, get a grip on oneself; [inf] snap out of it.
▪ **pull out** = **withdraw**, retreat from, leave, abandon, give up, quit.

pulp NOUN = **purée**, mush, mash, pap, triturate.
▶ VERB = **crush**, squash, mash, purée, pulverize, triturate.

pulsate VERB = **beat**, throb, vibrate, pulse, palpitate, pound, thud, thump, drum.

pulse NOUN = **beat**, rhythm, throb, throbbing, vibration, pulsation, pounding, thud, thumping, thump, drumming.

▶ VERB = *see* **pulsate**.

pump VERB **1** = **drive**, force, push, send. **2** = **question**, quiz, interrogate, cross-examine; [inf] grill.

punch VERB = **strike**, hit, knock, thump, thwack, box, jab, cuff, slug, smash, slam, batter, pound, pummel; [inf] sock, biff, bash, bop, wallop, whack, clout.

punctilious ADJ = **careful**, scrupulous, meticulous, conscientious, exact, precise, particular, strict, nice, finicky, fussy.
Opposites: careless.

punctual ADJ = **on time**, on the dot, prompt, in good time, when expected, timely, well timed.
Opposites: late.

puncture NOUN = **hole**, perforation, flat, prick, rupture, cut, nick, slit, leak.

▶ VERB = **make a hole in**, hole, perforate, pierce, bore, prick, penetrate, rupture, cut, nick, slit.

pungent ADJ **1** = **sharp**, acrid, acid, sour, biting, stinging, burning, bitter, tart, tangy, spicy, highly flavoured, aromatic, piquant, peppery, hot, fiery. **2** = **caustic**, acid, biting, cutting, sharp, incisive, scathing, pointed, acrimonious, trenchant, mordant.
Opposites: bland, mild.

punish VERB **1** = **discipline**, teach someone a lesson, penalize, chastise, smack, slap, beat, cane, whip, flog, lash, scourge; [formal] castigate.
2 = **maltreat**, mistreat, abuse, manhandle, damage, harm.

punishing ADJ = **arduous**, demanding, taxing, strenuous, hard, exhausting, fatiguing, wearing, tiring, gruelling, uphill, back-breaking.

punitive ADJ **1** = **penal**, disciplinary, corrective, correctional. **2** = **harsh**, severe, stiff, cruel, savage.

puny ADJ = **weak**, weakly, frail, feeble, undersized, underdeveloped, stunted, small, slight, little.
Opposites: strong.

pupil NOUN = **schoolboy/ girl**, schoolchild, scholar,

purpose

student.

puppet NOUN
1 = **marionette**, string puppet, glove puppet, finger puppet. 2 = **tool**, instrument, cat's-paw, pawn, creature, dupe, mouthpiece; [Brit. inf] poodle.

purchase VERB = *see* **buy**.
▶ NOUN 1 = **acquisition**, order, investment; [inf] buy. 2 = **grip**, hold, foothold, footing, toehold, support, grasp, leverage.

pure ADJ 1 = **unalloyed**, unmixed, unadulterated, uncontaminated, flawless, perfect, genuine, real, true. 2 = **clean**, clear, fresh, unpolluted, untainted, unadulterated, uncontaminated, uninfected, wholesome, natural. 3 = **virginal**, chaste, maidenly, virtuous, undefiled, unsullied. 4 = **stainless**, spotless, unsullied, unblemished, impeccable, immaculate, blameless, sinless. 5 = **sheer**, utter, absolute, downright, out-and-out,

complete, total, perfect, unmitigated, unqualified. **Opposites:** adulterated, polluted, immoral.

purely ADV = **entirely**, completely, totally, wholly, solely, only, simply, just, merely.

purge VERB 1 = **cleanse**, clear, purify, make pure. 2 = **remove**, clear out, expel, eject, dismiss, oust, depose, eradicate, root out, weed out.

purify VERB = **make pure**, clean, cleanse, decontaminate, filter, refine, disinfect, sterilize, sanitize, fumigate. **Opposites:** contaminate.

puritanical ADJ = **prudish**, prim, priggish, prissy, puritan, ascetic, austere, strait-laced, narrow-minded, rigid, stiff. **Opposites:** broad-minded.

purpose NOUN 1 = **reason**, point, basis, motivation, cause, justification. 2 = **aim**, intention, object, objective, goal, end, target, ambition, aspiration, desire, wish, hope. 3 = **determination**, resolution, resolve,

firmness, steadfastness, single-mindedness, persistence, perseverance, tenacity, doggedness.
▶ VERB = *see* **intend (1)**.

purposeful ADJ
= **determined**, resolute, resolved, firm, steadfast, single-minded, persistent, tenacious, dogged, unfaltering, unwavering.
Opposites: aimless.

purposely ADV = **on purpose**, intentionally, deliberately, by design, wilfully, wittingly, knowingly, consciously.

pursue VERB 1 = **go after**, run after, follow, chase, hunt, stalk, track, trail, shadow; [inf] tail.
2 = **proceed with**, go on with, follow, keep/carry on with, continue with, continue, persist in.
3 = **work at**, engage in, follow, practise, prosecute, apply oneself to.

push VERB 1 = **shove**, thrust, propel, drive, ram, butt, jostle. 2 = **urge**, press, egg on, spur on, prod, goad, incite, impel, dragoon, force, coerce, constrain, browbeat, strong-arm. 3 = **promote**, advertise, publicize, puff, puff up, boost, beat the drum for; [inf] plug, hype.
■ **push around** = **bully**, ride roughshod over, browbeat, tyrannize, intimidate, domineer.

pushy ADJ = **assertive**, self-assertive, aggressive, forceful, forward, bold, brash, bumptious, presumptuous, cocksure, loud, obnoxious.
Opposites: submissive.

put VERB 1 = **place**, lay, set down, deposit, position, rest, stand, locate, situate, settle, install.
2 = **lay**, present, bring forward, forward, submit, tender, offer, proffer, put forward, set forth, advance.
■ **put about** = **spread**, bandy about, circulate, disseminate, make public, make known, give out, publicize, broadcast, propagate, announce, bruit.
■ **put away** = **imprison**, confine, lock up, shut away/up.

p

■ **put down** 1 = **put to sleep**, put out of its misery, destroy, do away with, kill;
[N. Amer.] euthanize.
2 = **snub**, disparage, deprecate, belittle, denigrate, deflate, slight, humiliate, crush, mortify.

■ **put out**
1 = **inconvenience**, trouble, bother, impose upon, discommode, incommode.
2 = **extinguish**, quench, douse, stamp out.

puzzle VERB = **perplex**, baffle, stump, beat, mystify, confuse, bewilder, nonplus, stagger, dumbfound, daze, confound;
[inf] flummox.

puzzling ADJ = **difficult**, hard, unclear, perplexing, knotty, baffling, enigmatic, abstruse, mystifying, bewildering, unfathomable, inexplicable, incomprehensible, beyond one, above one's head.
Opposites: clear.

p

Qq

quail VERB = **flinch**, shrink, recoil, shy away, pull back, draw back, cower, cringe, shudder, shiver, tremble, shake, quake, blench, blanch.

quake VERB = **shake**, tremble, quiver, shiver, shudder, rock, vibrate, pulsate, throb.

qualification NOUN **1** = **certification**, training, competence, competency, accomplishment, eligibility, acceptability, suitableness, preparedness, fitness, proficiency, skilfulness, adeptness, capability, aptitude, skill, ability, attribute, endowment. **2** = **modification**, limitation, restriction, reservation, stipulation, allowance, adaptation, adjustment, condition, proviso, provision, caveat.

qualified ADJ **1** = **trained**, certificated, equipped, prepared, competent, accomplished, proficient, skilled, skilful, adept, practised, experienced, expert, capable, able. **2** = **modified**, limited, conditional, restricted, bounded, contingent, confined, circumscribed, reserved, guarded, equivocal.

qualify VERB **1** = **certify**, license, empower, authorize, allow, permit, sanction, warrant, fit, equip. **2** = **count**, be considered, be designated, be eligible, meet the requirements of. **3** = **modify**, limit, make conditional, restrict.

quality NOUN 1 = **degree of excellence**, standard, grade, level, sort, type, kind, variety. 2 = **feature**, trait, attribute, characteristic, aspect, property, peculiarity.

qualm NOUN = **doubt**, misgiving, scruple, hesitation, hesitancy, reluctance, anxiety, apprehension, disquiet, uneasiness, concern.

quantity NOUN = **number**, amount, total, aggregate, sum, quota, weight, capacity, mass, volume, bulk, extent, length, area.

quarrel NOUN = **argument**, fight, disagreement, difference of opinion, dispute, disputation, squabble, altercation, wrangle, misunderstanding, feud, vendetta; [inf] row, spat, scrap, tiff.
▶ VERB = **argue**, have a fight, fight, dispute, squabble, bicker, spar, wrangle, have a misunder-standing, fall out; [inf] row, have a row.
Opposites: agree.

quarrelsome ADJ = **argumentative**, belligerent, disputatious, contentious, pugnacious, combative, ready for a fight, bellicose, litigious, hot-tempered, irascible, choleric, irritable.
Opposites: peaceable.

quarry NOUN = **prey**, victim, prize.

quarter NOUN 1 = **district**, area, region, part, side, neighbourhood, locality, zone. 2 = **mercy**, leniency, clemency, compassion, pity.
▶ VERB = **put up**, house, board, billet, accommodate, lodge, install.

quarters PL NOUN = **accommodation**, billet, residence, habitation, lodgings, rooms, barracks; [inf] digs, pad; [formal] dwelling, abode, domicile.

quash VERB 1 = **annul**, declare null and void, nullify, invalidate, void, cancel, overrule, override, overthrow, reject, set aside, reverse, revoke, rescind, repeal.

q

2 = **crush**, put down, squash, quell, subdue, suppress, repress, quench, extinguish, stamp out, put a stop to, end, terminate, defeat, destroy.
Opposites: validate.

quaver VERB = **quiver**, vibrate, tremble, shake, waver.

queasy ADJ = **sick**, nauseated, ill, indisposed, dizzy, sick to one's stomach.

queer ADJ **1** = **odd**, strange, unusual, extraordinary, funny, curious, peculiar, weird, outlandish, singular, eccentric, unconventional, unorthodox, atypical, abnormal, irregular, anomalous, deviant, offbeat; [inf] off-the-wall.
2 = **suspicious**, suspect, irregular, questionable, dubious, doubtful; [inf] fishy, shady.

quell VERB **1** = **allay**, lull, quiet, silence, calm, soothe, appease, assuage, abate, deaden, dull, pacify. **2** = *See* **quash** (2).

quench VERB **1** = **satisfy**, slake, sate, satiate.
2 = **extinguish**, put out, snuff out, blow out, douse.

quest NOUN **1** = **search**, seeking, pursuit, chase, hunt. **2** = **adventure**, expedition, journey, voyage, exploration, crusade.

question NOUN **1** = **query**, enquiry, interrogation.
2 = **issue**, problem, matter, point, subject, topic, theme, bone of contention.
Opposites: answer.
▶ VERB **1** = **ask questions of**, interrogate, cross-examine, quiz, interview, sound out, examine; [inf] grill, pump. **2** = **call into question**, query, raise doubts about, throw doubt on, have suspicions about, challenge.

questionable ADJ = **open to question/doubt**, doubtful, dubious, uncertain, debatable, in dispute, arguable, controversial, controvertible.

q

Opposites: indisputable.

queue NOUN = **line**, row, column, file, chain, string, train, succession, sequence, series, concatenation.

quibble NOUN = **criticism**, complaint, protest, objection, niggle, cavil, nicety.

▶ VERB = **cavil**, carp, pettifog, split hairs, chop logic; [inf] nit-pick.

quick ADJ 1 = **fast**, rapid, speedy, swift, fleet, express. 2 = **prompt**, without delay, immediate, instantaneous, expeditious. 3 = **brief**, brisk, fleeting, momentary, hasty, hurried, cursory, perfunctory. 4 = **quick-witted**, sharp-witted, alert, intelligent.
Opposites: slow, long.

quicken VERB 1 = **become/ grow faster**, speed up, accelerate, hurry, hasten. 2 = *see* **arouse**.

quiet ADJ 1 = **silent**, hushed, noiseless, soundless, peaceful. 2 = **soft**, low, inaudible.

3 = **peaceful**, sleepy, undisturbed, unfrequented, secluded, isolated, out of the way, off the beaten track.
Opposites: noisy.

quieten VERB 1 = **silence**, hush, shush, quiet, still; [inf] shut up. 2 = **allay**, soothe, calm, appease, lull, pacify, mollify, palliate.

quit VERB 1 = **give up**, stop, cease, leave off, abandon, abstain from, desist from. 2 = **leave**, depart from, vacate, walk out on.

quite ADV 1 = **completely**, fully, entirely, totally, wholly, absolutely, in all respects. 2 = **fairly**, relatively, moderately, reasonably, to some extent/degree, rather, somewhat.

quiver VERB = **tremble**, shiver, vibrate, quaver, quake, shudder, pulsate, convulse, palpitate.

quota NOUN = **share**, allowance, allocation, portion, ration, part, slice, measure, proportion; [inf] cut; [Brit. inf] whack.

q

quotation NOUN

1 = citation, reference, quote, allusion, excerpt, extract, selection, passage, line.
2 = estimate, estimated price, quote, cost, charge, figure.

quote VERB **1 = repeat**, iterate, recite, reproduce.
2 = cite, give, name, instance, mention, refer to, make reference to, allude to. **3 = estimate for**, price, set a price for.

rabble NOUN = **mob**, horde, swarm, crowd, throng.

race¹ NOUN **1** = **contest**, competition, chase, pursuit, relay.
2 = **channel**, waterway, watercourse, sluice, spillway.
▸ VERB **1** = **run against**, compete against, be pitted against. **2** = **run**, sprint, dash, dart, bolt, speed, hare, fly, tear, zoom, accelerate, career.

race² NOUN = **ethnic group**, people, bloodline, stock, line, lineage, breed, strain.

racial ADJ = **race-related**, ethnic, ethnological.

racism NOUN = **racialism**, racial discrimination, racial prejudice/bigotry, chauvinism, xenophobia.

racist NOUN = **racialist**, bigot.
▸ ADJ = **racialist**, discriminatory, prejudiced, bigoted, intolerant, illiberal.

rack NOUN = **frame**, framework, stand, form, trestle, structure, holder, shelf.

racket NOUN = **noise**, din, row, commotion, disturbance, uproar, hubbub, hullabaloo, clamour, pandemonium, tumult.

radiant ADJ **1** = **shining**, bright, illuminated, brilliant, luminous, luminescent, lustrous.
2 = **joyful**, happy, elated, ecstatic, delighted, pleased. = *See also* **happy** (**1**).
Opposites: dark, gloomy.

radiate VERB = **send out/forth**, give off/out, emit, emanate, scatter, disperse, diffuse, spread, shed.

radical ADJ
1 = **fundamental**, basic, rudimentary, elementary, elemental, constitutional.
2 = **thorough**, complete, total, entire, absolute, utter, comprehensive, exhaustive, sweeping, far-reaching, profound, drastic. **3** = **extremist**, extreme, immoderate, revolutionary, rebel, rebellious, militant.
Opposites: superficial, moderate.

raffle NOUN = **lottery**, draw, sweepstake, sweep, tombola.

rage NOUN = **fury**, anger, wrath, high dudgeon, frenzy, madness; [poetic/literary] ire.
▶ VERB = **be furious**, be infuriated, be angry, seethe, be beside oneself, lose one's temper, boil over, rant, rave, storm, fume, fulminate; [inf] blow one's top, flip one's lid, freak out.

ragged ADJ **1** = **tattered**, threadbare, frayed, the worse for wear, torn, rent, in holes, worn to shreds, falling to pieces.
2 = **jagged**, uneven, irregular, notched, serrated, saw-toothed, craggy.
Opposites: smart.

raid NOUN = **surprise attack**, assault, onslaught, invasion, incursion, thrust, sortie, sally.
▶ VERB **1** = **attack**, assault, invade, assail, storm, rush, set upon, descend upon, swoop upon.
2 = **plunder**, pillage, loot, rifle, forage, ransack, steal from.

rain NOUN = **rainfall**, precipitation, raindrops, drizzle, shower, rainstorm, cloudburst, torrent, downpour, deluge.
▶ VERB = **pour**, pour/come down, precipitate; [inf] rain cats and dogs, come down in buckets.

rainy ADJ = **wet**, showery, drizzly, damp.

raise VERB **1** = **lift**, lift up, raise aloft, elevate, uplift, hoist, heave up.
2 = **increase**, put up,

escalate, inflate, heighten, augment, amplify, intensify; [inf] step up, hike, jack up. **3 = bring up**, rear, nurture, educate. **Opposites:** lower.

rally VERB **1 = come/get together**, assemble, group, band together, convene, unite. **2 = call/ bring together**, assemble, summon, round up, muster, marshall, mobilize. **3 = recover**, recuperate, revive, get better/well, improve, perk up. ▶ NOUN = **meeting**, gathering, assembly, convention, convocation.

ram VERB **1 = force**, cram, stuff, compress, jam, squeeze, thrust, tamp. **2 = strike**, hit, run into, crash into, collide with, bump, slam.

ramble VERB **1 = walk**, hike, wander, stroll, amble, roam, range, rove, traipse. **2 = digress**, wander, gabble; [inf] rattle on; [Brit. inf] rabbit on, witter on.

rambling ADJ **1 = digressive**, wandering, roundabout, circuitous, periphrastic, disconnected, disjointed, maundering, long-winded, verbose, wordy, prolix. **2 = sprawling**, spreading, unsystematic, straggling. **Opposites:** concise.

ramification NOUN = **consequence**, aftermath, outcome, result, upshot, issue, sequel, complication, implication.

ramp NOUN = **slope**, incline, gradient, acclivity, rise.

rampage VERB = **run riot**, run amok, charge, tear, storm, go berserk. ▶ NOUN = **uproar**, furore, mayhem, turmoil.

rampant ADJ = **out of control/hand**, unrestrained, unchecked, unbridled, widespread, pandemic, epidemic. **Opposites:** controlled.

random ADJ = **haphazard**, chance, accidental, fortuitous, serendipitous, adventitious, arbitrary,

hit-or-miss,
indiscriminate, sporadic,
stray, spot, casual,
unsystematic,
unmethodical,
disorganized, unplanned.
Opposites: systematic.

range NOUN **1** = **scope**,
compass, limits, bounds,
confines, radius, span,
scale, gamut, reach,
sweep, extent, area, field,
orbit, province, domain,
latitude. **2** = **assortment**,
variety, kind, sort, type,
class, rank, order, genus,
species.
▶ VERB **1** = **extend**, stretch,
reach, cover, go, run,
pass, fluctuate between,
vary between. **2** = **roam**,
rove, ramble, traverse,
travel over, wander,
meander, amble, stroll,
stray, drift.

rank¹ NOUN **1** = **grade**, level,
echelon, stratum, class,
status, position, station.
2 = **nobility**, aristocracy,
eminence, distinction.
▶ VERB **1** = **classify**, class,
categorize, grade. **2** = **have
a rank**, be graded, be
placed, be positioned.

rank² ADJ **1** = see **lush** (**1**).
2 = see **foul** ADJ (**2**).

rankle VERB = **fester**,
annoy, anger, irk, vex,
irritate, rile, chafe, gall,
embitter; [inf] get
someone's goat.

ransack VERB **1** = See
plunder VERB. **2** = See
search VERB (**1**).

rapid ADJ = **quick**, fast,
swift, speedy, fleet,
hurried, hasty,
expeditious, express,
brisk, lively, prompt,
precipitate.
Opposites: slow.

rapport NOUN = **affinity**,
bond, empathy,
sympathy,
understanding.

rapture NOUN = **joy**,
ecstasy, elation,
exaltation, exhilaration,
bliss, euphoria, rhapsody,
enchantment, delight.

rare ADJ **1** = **unusual**,
uncommon, out of the
ordinary, exceptional,
atypical, singular,
remarkable, unique.
2 = **infrequent**, few and
far between, scarce,
sparse, sporadic,
scattered.

Opposites: common.

rascal NOUN **1** = **imp**, scamp, scallywag, mischief-maker, little devil. **2** = **scoundrel**, rogue, ne'er-do-well, good-for-nothing, wastrel, reprobate; [dated] cad; [inf] creep, rat; [inf, dated] rotter; [archaic] blackguard.

rash ADJ = **reckless**, impetuous, hasty, impulsive, bold, madcap, audacious, brash, daredevil, foolhardy, foolish, harum-scarum, devil-may-care, headstrong, hot-headed, incautious, careless, heedless, thoughtless, unthinking, imprudent, injudicious.
Opposites: prudent.

rate NOUN **1** = **percentage**, ratio, proportion, scale, degree, standard.
2 = **pace**, stride, gait, motion, speed, tempo, velocity, measure.
▸ VERB **1** = **judge**, assess, appraise, evaluate, value, measure, weigh up, grade, rank, adjudge.
2 = **regard as**, consider, deem, reckon, account.

rather ADV **1** = **sooner**, preferably, more readily.
2 = **quite**, fairly, a bit, a little, slightly, somewhat; [inf] sort of, kind of, pretty.

ratify VERB = **confirm**, endorse, sign, sanction, warrant, approve, authorize, validate.
Opposites: revoke.

ratio NOUN = **proportion**, comparative size/extent, correlation, correspondence, percentage, fraction, quotient.

ration NOUN = **allowance**, quota, allotment, portion, share, measure, part, lot, amount, helping, proportion, percentage.
▸ VERB = **limit**, restrict, control, conserve, budget.

rational ADJ = **sensible**, reasonable, logical, sound, intelligent, wise, judicious, sagacious, prudent, circumspect, politic, astute, shrewd, perceptive, well advised, well grounded.

Opposites: irrational.

rationalize VERB
1 = **explain away**, account for, make excuses, make plausible, try to vindicate/justify.
2 = **streamline**, trim, make cuts in, cut back on, retrench on.

rattle VERB 1 = **bang**, knock, rap, clatter, clang, clank, jangle, clink.
2 = **disconcert**, disturb, fluster, upset, shake, perturb, faze, discompose, discomfit.

raucous ADJ = **strident**, piercing, ear-splitting, shrill, screeching, harsh, sharp, grating, rasping, discordant, dissonant, jarring.
Opposites: soft, quiet.

ravage VERB = **devastate**, lay waste, ruin, wreak havoc on, destroy, level, raze, demolish.

rave VERB 1 = **rant and rave**, rage, storm, fulminate, explode in anger; [inf] fly off the handle, flip one's lid.
2 = **rhapsodize over**, enthuse about, praise to the skies, gush over.

ravenous ADJ = **starving**, starved, famished, ravening, wolfish, voracious, insatiable, insatiate.

ravishing ADJ = **beautiful**, lovely, stunning, gorgeous, dazzling, radiant, enchanting, bewitching, charming.
Opposites: hideous.

raw ADJ 1 = **uncooked**, fresh. 2 = **unrefined**, crude, green, coarse, unprocessed, unprepared, untreated.
3 = **inexperienced**, untrained, unskilled, untutored, new, callow, immature, green; [inf] wet behind the ears. 4 = **cold**, chilly, freezing, bitter, biting, nippy, piercing, penetrating.
Opposites: cooked, processed.

ray NOUN = **beam**, shaft, streak, stream, gleam, glint, flash, glimmer.

raze VERB = **tear/pull down**, knock down, level, bulldoze, flatten, demolish, ruin, wreck.

reach VERB 1 = **stretch**, extend, hold out, thrust

out, stick out. **2 = get as far as**, get to, arrive at, come to. **3 = contact**, get in touch with, get hold of, get through to, communicate with.

▶ NOUN = **scope**, range, compass, latitude, ambit, orbit, sphere, area.

react VERB **1 = have a reaction/response to**, respond. **2 = behave**, act, conduct oneself, proceed, operate, function, cope.

reactionary ADJ = **ultra-conservative**, conservative, obscurantist, diehard, rightist, right-wing; [Brit.] Colonel Blimp. **Opposites:** progressive.

read VERB **1 = peruse**, study, scan, pore over, scrutinize; [inf] wade through, dip into. **2 = interpret**, construe, decipher, deduce, understand, comprehend. **3 = register**, record, display, show, indicate.

readable ADJ **1 = legible**, easy to read, decipherable, clear, intelligible, understandable, comprehensible. **2 = enjoyable**, entertaining, interesting, gripping, enthralling, stimulating. **Opposites:** unreadable.

readily ADV **1 = willingly**, gladly, happily, cheerfully, eagerly. **2 = easily**, without difficulty, effortlessly. **Opposites:** reluctantly.

ready ADJ **1 = finished**, completed, prepared, organized. **2 = prepared**, equipped, organized, all set, in a fit state; [inf] fit. **3 = within reach**, available, on hand, present, near, near at hand, accessible, handy, convenient, on call, at one's fingertips; [inf] on tap. **4 = about to**, on the verge/brink of, in danger of, liable to, likely to. **5 = eager**, prepared, enthusiastic, anxious, keen; [inf] psyched up, geared up.

real ADJ **1 = actual**, existent, factual, non-fictitious. **2 = authentic**, genuine, bona fide.

r

3 = sincere, heartfelt, earnest, fervent, unfeigned, unaffected, honest, truthful. **Opposites:** imaginary, false.

realistic ADJ **1 = practical**, pragmatic, rational, down-to-earth, matter-of-fact, sensible, no-nonsense, commonsensical, level-headed, hard-headed, businesslike, hard-boiled, sober, unromantic, unsentimental, with both feet on the ground. **2 = lifelike**, true-to-life, true, faithful, close, representational, graphic, naturalistic, authentic, genuine. **Opposites:** unrealistic.

reality NOUN **1 = real world**, actuality, physical existence, corporeality, substantiality, materiality. **2 = fact**, actuality, truth. **Opposites:** fantasy.

realize VERB **1 = understand clearly**, grasp, take in, know, comprehend, apprehend, appreciate, recognize, perceive, discern, conceive; [inf] latch on; [Brit. inf] twig. **2 = fulfil**, achieve, accomplish, bring about, bring off, bring to fruition, consummate, effect, perform, execute, actualize, reify; [formal] effectuate. **3 = make**, clear, acquire, gain, bring in, obtain, earn.

realm NOUN **= kingdom**, country, land, state, province, empire, domain, monarchy, principality.

reap VERB **1 = cut**, crop, harvest, gather in, bring in, take in. **2 = realize**, receive, obtain, get, acquire, secure, procure.

rear[1] VERB **1 = bring up**, raise, care for, nurture, parent, educate, train, instruct. **2 = raise**, lift up, hold up, elevate, upraise.

rear[2] NOUN **= back**, back part, hind part, back end, tail, tail end. **Opposites:** front.

reason NOUN **1 = grounds**, cause, basis, motive, motivation, impetus.

2 = **explanation**, justification, argument, case, defence, vindication, apologia, rationalization, excuse, apology. **3** = **reasoning**, intellect, intelligence, intellectuality, mind, judgement, logic, rationality, thought, understanding, apprehension, comprehension, ratiocination. **4** = **sanity**, mind, soundness of mind, senses.

▶ VERB **1** = **think**, think straight, use one's mind, use one's brain/head, analyse, cogitate, cerebrate, intellectualize, ratiocinate; [inf] put on one's thinking cap. **2** = **use logic on**, argue with, debate with, dispute with, try to persuade, plead with.

reasonable ADJ **1** = **logical**, practical, rational, sensible, intelligent, wise, sound, judicious, advisable, well thought out, tenable, plausible. **2** = **open to reason**, fair, just, equitable, impartial, dispassionate, unbiased, disinterested. **3** = **moderate**, low, modest, cheap, within one's means. **4** = **tolerable**, passable, acceptable, average; [inf] OK.
Opposites: unreasonable.

reasoned ADJ = **logical**, rational, well thought out, clear, systematic, methodical, organized, well expressed, well presented.

reassure VERB = **put one's mind at rest**, put at ease, restore/give confidence to, encourage, hearten, buoy up, cheer up.

rebel NOUN = **revolutionary**, revolutionist, insurrectionist, insurgent, mutineer.
▶ VERB = **mutiny**, riot, revolt, rise up, rise up in arms, take to the streets.
Opposites: conform.

rebellion NOUN **1** = **revolt**, revolution, insurrection, uprising, rising, mutiny. **2** = **defiance**, disobedience, resistance,

r

dissent, nonconformity, heresy, apostasy, schism, recusancy.

rebellious ADJ **1** = **defiant**, disobedient, unruly, ungovernable, unmanageable, turbulent, disorderly, intractable, recalcitrant, incorrigible; [formal] contumacious. **2** = **revolutionary**, insurrectionary, insurgent, mutinous. **Opposites:** obedient.

rebound VERB **1** = **bounce back**, recoil, ricochet, boomerang. **2** = **misfire**, backfire, come back on, redound on.

rebuff NOUN = **rejection**, repudiation, discouragement, snub, slight; [inf] brush-off, slap in the face.
▶ VERB = **reject**, refuse, turn down, turn away, spurn, brush off, repudiate, snub, slight.

rebuke VERB = **reprimand**, tell off, scold, chide, admonish, reproach, reprove, remonstrate with, lecture, reprehend, berate, upbraid, take to task; [inf] bawl out; [Brit. inf] tick off, tear off a strip, carpet; [formal] castigate. **Opposites:** praise.

recalcitrant ADJ = **intractable**, refractory, unmanageable, ungovernable, disobedient, insubordinate, defiant, contrary, wayward. **Opposites:** compliant.

recall VERB **1** = **summon back**, call back, bring back. **2** = *See* **remember (1)**.

receive VERB **1** = **be in receipt of**, accept delivery of, accept, take into one's possession. **2** = **undergo**, experience, meet with, encounter, be subjected to, bear, suffer. **3** = **welcome**, greet, entertain, be at home to. **Opposites:** give, send.

recent ADJ **1** = **new**, fresh, novel, latest, late, modern, contemporary, latter-day, current, up to date. **2** = **occurring/appearing recently**, not long past.

recently ADV = **lately**, of late, latterly, in recent times, not along ago.

receptacle NOUN = **container**, holder, repository.

receptive ADJ = **open**, open to suggestions, flexible, willing, perceptive, sensitive, alert, bright, quick, keen.
Opposites: unresponsive.

recess NOUN 1 = **alcove**, niche, nook, corner, cavity, bay, oriel.
2 = **break**, respite, rest, interval, intermission, holiday, time off, vacation.

recession NOUN = **downturn**, depression, slump.
Opposites: boom.

recipe NOUN = **directions**, instructions, guide, method, system, procedure.

reciprocal ADJ = **mutual**, shared, common, exchanged, give and take, complementary, corresponding, correlative.

reciprocate VERB = **return**, requite, repay, give back.

recital NOUN
1 = **performance**, concert, show. 2 = **account**, report, telling, relation, description, detailing, rendering, record, chronicle.

recite VERB = **say**, repeat, read aloud, deliver, declaim, speak, render.

reckless ADJ = **rash**, careless, thoughtless, incautious, heedless, unheeding, regardless, daredevil, devil-may-care, madcap, harum-scarum, wild, precipitate, hasty, headlong, irresponsible, hare-brained, foolhardy, imprudent, unwise, indiscreet, mindless, negligent.
Opposites: cautious.

reckon VERB 1 = **be of the opinion**, think, believe, suppose, assume.
2 = **count**, calculate, add up, compute, total, tally, put a figure on, give a figure to.

reclaim VERB = **have returned**, get back, take back, regain, retrieve, recover.

recline VERB = **lie down**, be recumbent, rest, repose, loll, lounge, sprawl, stretch out.

recluse NOUN = **hermit**, anchorite, eremite, solitary, lone wolf, loner.

recognize VERB **1** = **know**, know again, identify, place, spot, recall, recollect, remember, call to mind. **2** = **realize**, see, be aware of, be conscious of, perceive, discern, appreciate, understand, apprehend, acknowledge, accept, admit, concede, allow, grant, confess, own. **3** = **acknowledge**, accept, admit, concede, allow, grant, endorse, sanction, approve, validate, ratify, uphold.

recoil VERB = **draw back**, jump back, pull back, shrink, shy away, flinch, start, wince, cower, quail.

recollect VERB = **remember**, recall, call to mind, think of, summon up, place; [inf] put one's finger on.
Opposites: forget.

recommend VERB = **advocate**, commend, put in a good word for, speak favourably of, endorse, approve, vouch for, suggest, offer, put forward, propose, advance.

recommendation NOUN = **commendation**, endorsement, suggestion, tip, hint, proposal, good word, favourable mention, praise; [inf] plug.

reconcile VERB = **reunite**, bring together, restore harmony between, make peace between, bring to terms, pacify, appease, placate, propitiate, mollify.
Opposites: estrange, quarrel.

reconnaissance NOUN = **survey**, exploration, scouting, probe, inspection, observation; [inf] recce.

reconnoitre VERB = **survey**, see how the land lies, spy out, take stock of, explore, scout, investigate, scrutinize, scan, inspect, observe; [inf] recce, check out.

reconsider VERB
= **rethink**, review, re-examine, re-evaluate, reassess, think again, think twice, have second thoughts, change one's mind.

reconstruct VERB
= **rebuild**, remake, reassemble, refashion, recreate, remodel, revamp, renovate, recondition.

record NOUN 1 = **document**, register, log, logbook, file, official report/ account, chronicle, documentation, minutes, notes, annals, archives.
2 = **disc**, album, single, recording, release; [inf] platter.
▶ VERB 1 = **put on record**, set down, write down, put in writing, take down, put down, enter, make a note of, document.
2 = **register**, read, indicate, show, display.

recount VERB = **describe**, detail, enumerate, list, specify, itemize, cite, particularize, catalogue.

recover VERB 1 = **get back**, win back, regain, recoup, retrieve, reclaim, repossess, redeem, recuperate, recapture.
2 = **get better**, get well, recuperate, convalesce, heal, get back on one's feet, feel oneself again, improve, mend, pick up, perk up, rally, revive, pull through, bounce back.
Opposites: deteriorate.

recovery NOUN
1 = **recouping**, regaining, retrieval, reclamation, repossession, recapture.
2 = **recuperation**, convalescence, healing, rallying, revival.

recreation NOUN
1 = **relaxation**, leisure, refreshment, amusement, entertainment, distraction, diversion.
2 = **activity**, pastime, hobby, diversion, distraction.

recrimination NOUN
= **counter-accusation**, countercharge, counter-attack, retaliation, reprisal.

recruit VERB = **enlist**, enrol, sign up, draft, conscript, levy, engage,

obtain, acquire, procure, take on, round up, muster.
▶ NOUN 1 = **draftee**, conscript. 2 = **newcomer**, initiate, beginner, learner, trainee, apprentice.

rectify VERB = **put/set right**, right, correct, amend, emend, remedy, repair, fix, make good.

rectitude NOUN = **righteousness**, virtue, honour, integrity, principle, probity, uprightness, good character, decency, honesty.

recuperate VERB = *see* **recover**.

recur VERB = **reoccur**, happen/occur again, come back, return, reappear, be repeated, happen repeatedly.

recurrent ADJ = **recurring**, repeated, repetitive, reiterative, periodic, cyclical, regular, habitual, continual, frequent, intermittent, chronic.

recycle VERB = **reuse**, reprocess, salvage, save.

redden VERB = **go red**, blush, flush, colour, colour up, crimson.

redeem VERB
1 = **exchange**, cash in, convert, turn in, trade in.
2 = **save**, deliver from sin, turn from sin, convert, purge/absolve of sin.

redolent ADJ
1 = **evocative**, suggestive, reminiscent. 2 = **sweet-smelling**, fragrant, scented, perfumed, aromatic.

reduce VERB 1 = **make smaller**, lessen, lower, decrease, diminish, cut, curtail, contract, shorten, abbreviate, moderate, dilute, alleviate, abate.
2 = **bring to**, bring to the point of, force to, drive to. 3 = **demote**, downgrade, lower, lower in rank/status, humble.
4 = **lower/cut in price**, lower, make cheaper, cheapen, cut, mark down, slash, discount, put on sale.
Opposites: increase.

reduction NOUN
1 = **lessening**, lowering, decrease, diminution, cut, contraction, abbreviation,

moderation, dilution, alleviation, abatement. **2 = discount**, deduction, cut, concession, allowance. **3 = demotion**, downgrading, lowering, humbling.

redundant ADJ **= surplus to requirements**, not required, unnecessary, inessential, unwanted, surplus, supernumerary.

reel VERB **1 = stagger**, lurch, sway, stumble, totter, wobble, falter, waver, pitch, roll. **2 = feel giddy/dizzy**, feel confused, be shaken, be in shock, be upset.

refer VERB **1 = consult**, turn to, look at, look up, have recourse to. **2 = pass**, hand on, send on, transfer, remit, direct. **3 = mention**, make mention of, make reference to, allude to, touch on, speak of, cite, hint at; [formal] advert to. **4 = apply to**, be relevant to, have relevance to, concern, relate to, belong to.

referee NOUN **= umpire**, judge, adjudicator, arbitrator, arbiter, mediator; [inf] ref.

reference NOUN **1 = mention**, allusion, citation, hint. **2 = regard**, respect, relation, bearing, relevance, pertinence. **3 = source**, citation, authority, bibliography. **4 = testimonial**, recommendation, good word, credentials.

refine VERB **= purify**, rarefy, clarify, clear, cleanse, strain, sift, filter, distil, process.

refined ADJ **1 = purified**, pure, rarefied, clarified, clear, filtered, distilled, processed. **2 = cultivated**, cultured, polished, civilized, civil, gracious, stylish, elegant, sophisticated, urbane, courtly, well mannered, well bred, gentlemanly, ladylike, genteel.
Opposites: crude.

refinement NOUN **1 = purification**, processing, distillation, filtration. **2 = cultivation**, culture, taste, discrimination, polish, finish, civility, grace,

r

graciousness, style, elegance, finesse, sophistication, urbanity, courtliness, good breeding, politeness, good manners, gentility. **3 = subtlety**, nicety, nuance, fine point.

reflect VERB **1 = throw back**, cast back, send back, give back, scatter, diffuse. **2 = mirror**, echo. **3 = think**, consider, mull over, contemplate, deliberate, ponder, meditate, muse, ruminate, cogitate, brood.

reflection NOUN **1 = image**, mirror image, echo. **2 = thinking**, thought, consideration, contemplation, deliberation, meditation, rumination, cogitation. **3 = opinion**, thought, view, idea, impression, comment, findings.

reform VERB **1 = improve**, make better, ameliorate, amend, mend, rectify, correct, rehabilitate, change, make over, revamp, renovate. **2 = mend one's ways**,

change for the better, turn over a new leaf, improve; [inf] go straight.

refrain VERB **= desist**, abstain, hold back, forbear, forgo, do without, avoid, eschew, cease, stop, give up, leave off, renounce; [inf] quit.

refresh VERB **1 = freshen**, invigorate, revitalize, revive, brace, fortify, enliven, perk up, stimulate, energize, exhilarate, rejuvenate, regenerate, breathe new life into, inspirit. **2 = stimulate**, prompt, prod, jog, activate, rouse, arouse.
Opposites: weary.

refreshing ADJ **= freshening**, invigorating, revitalizing, reviving, bracing, stimulating, exhilarating, energizing.

refuge NOUN **1 = shelter**, safety, security, protection, asylum, sanctuary. **2 = place of safety**, shelter, haven, retreat, bolt-hole, sanctuary, harbour.

refund VERB = **give back**, return, repay, pay back, reimburse, make good, restore, replace.
▶ NOUN = **repayment**, reimbursement.

refuse¹ VERB 1 = **turn down**, decline, say no to, reject, spurn, rebuff, repudiate; [inf] pass up, knock back. 2 = **decline**, be unwilling, baulk at, demur at, avoid, resist, protest at.
Opposites: accept.

refuse² NOUN = **rubbish**, waste, debris, litter, dross, dregs, leavings, sweepings; [N. Amer.] garbage, trash; [inf] junk.

refute VERB = **prove wrong**, disprove, negate, invalidate, discredit.

regain VERB = **get back**, win back, recover, recoup, retrieve, reclaim, repossess, redeem, recuperate, take back, retake, recapture.

regal ADJ = **royal**, majestic, noble, proud, kingly, queenly, princely, fit for a king/queen/prince/princess.

regard VERB 1 = **watch**, look at, gaze at, keep an eye on, stare at, observe, view, study, scrutinize, eye, mark, behold. 2 = **look upon**, view, consider, contemplate, think of, weigh up, mull over, reflect on, deliberate on.
▶ NOUN 1 = **look**, gaze, stare, observation, scrutiny. 2 = **heed**, attention, notice, consideration, thought, mind. 3 = **respect**, esteem, admiration, approval, approbation, favour.

regarding PREP = **with/in regard to**, as regards, as to, with reference to, on the subject/matter of, apropos, concerning, about, respecting.

regardless
▪ **regardless of** = **without regard to**, disregarding, unmindful of, heedless of, without consideration of, indifferent to, negligent of.

regards PL NOUN = **best/good wishes**, greetings, salutations, respects, compliments.

regenerate VERB = **renew**, breathe new life into, restore, invigorate, refresh, revitalize, revive, revivify, rejuvenate.

regiment VERB = **organize**, order, control, discipline, keep a tight rein on, bring into line, rule with a rod of iron.

region NOUN = **area**, province, territory, division, section, sector, zone, tract, part, quarter, locality.

register NOUN = **list**, listing, roll, roster, index, directory, catalogue.
▶ VERB **1** = **record**, put on record, enter, set down, chronicle, write down, take down, note, minute, list, catalogue. **2** = **read**, record, indicate, show, display. **3** = **show**, express, display, exhibit, evince, betray, reveal, manifest, demonstrate, reflect. **4** = **make an impression**, get through, sink in, penetrate, have an effect.

regret VERB **1** = **feel sorry/ contrite about**, feel remorse about, wish undone, repent, rue.
2 = **lament**, bemoan, be upset/disappointed about, mourn, grieve over, weep over, fret about, pine over, deplore.
Opposites: welcome.
▶ NOUN **1** = **sorrow**, remorse, contrition, repentance, pangs of conscience, compunction, ruefulness, self-reproach, penitence.
2 = **disappointment**, lamentation, grief, mourning, pining.
Opposites: satisfaction.

regretful ADJ = **sorry**, apologetic, remorseful, contrite, repentant, conscience-stricken, rueful, penitent.
Opposites: unrepentant.

regrettable ADJ = **deplorable**, reprehensible, disgraceful, blameworthy, unfortunate, unwelcome, ill-advised.

regular ADJ **1** = **usual**, normal, customary, habitual, routine, typical, everyday, daily, unvarying, common,

r

average, commonplace.
2 = **rhythmic**, steady,
even, uniform, constant,
consistent, orderly.
3 = **real**, thorough,
absolute, utter, complete.
Opposites: occasional,
erratic.

regulate VERB **1** = **control**,
direct, guide, govern,
rule, manage, order,
organize, conduct, run,
supervise, oversee,
superintend, monitor.
2 = **adjust**, balance, set,
synchronize, modulate.

regulation NOUN
1 = control, direction,
guidance, government,
rule, management,
administration,
organization,
supervision. **2** = **rule**,
ruling, order, directive,
act, law, decree, statute,
edict, ordinance.

rehearsal NOUN
= **practice**, preparation,
trial performance, run-
through, going-over.

rehearse VERB = **practise**,
try out, run through, go
over.

reign VERB **1** = **be king/
queen**, sit on the throne,

occupy the throne, wear
the crown, wield the
sceptre. **2** = **be in power**,
govern, rule, be in
charge/control,
administer, hold sway.
▶ NOUN **1** = **monarchy**,
sovereignty. **2** = **power**,
government, rule,
command, control,
administration, charge.

rein
■ **rein in** = **check**, curb,
restrain, constrain, hold
back, restrict, control,
bridle.

reinforce VERB
1 = **strengthen**, fortify,
bolster up, shore up,
buttress, prop up, brace,
support, back up,
uphold, stress, underline,
emphasize. **2** = **augment**,
increase, add to,
supplement.

reiterate VERB = **repeat**,
say again, go over again,
belabour, dwell on, harp
on, hammer away at.

reject VERB **1** = **refuse**, turn
down, decline, say no to,
spurn, rebuff, repudiate,
veto, deny; [inf] pass up,
knock back, give the
thumbs down to. **2** = **cast**

out, cast aside, discard, jettison, renounce, abandon, forsake, scrap, exclude, eliminate.
Opposites: accept.
▶ NOUN **1 = substandard article**, discard, second. **2 = failure**, outcast, derelict; [inf] drop-out.

rejoice VERB **= be joyful**, be happy, be pleased, be glad, be delighted, be elated, be overjoyed, be jubilant, be euphoric, exult.
Opposites: mourn.

rejoinder NOUN **= answer**, response, reply, riposte, retort; [inf] comeback.

relapse VERB **= lapse**, regress, retrogress, revert, backslide, fall away, go backwards, slip back, degenerate.
Opposites: improve.
▶ NOUN **= lapse**, regression, retrogression, reversion, backsliding, recidivism.

relate VERB **1 = recount**, tell, narrate, describe, report, impart, communicate, recite, rehearse, present, detail, delineate, chronicle, set forth. **2 = connect**, associate, link, correlate, ally, couple, join.
3 = apply to, be relevant to, have relevance to, concern, refer to, have reference to, pertain to, bear on.

related ADJ **1 = connected**, interconnected, associated, linked, correlated, allied, affiliated, accompanying, concomitant, akin. **2 = of the same family**, connected, akin, kindred, agnate, cognate, consanguineous.
Opposites: unrelated.

relation NOUN
1 = connection, association, link, tie-in, correlation, alliance, bond, relationship, interdependence.
2 = relative, family member, kinsman, kinswoman, connection, kin.

relationship NOUN **1 =** See **relation (1)**. **2 = friendship**, love affair, affair, liaison.

relative ADJ
1 = comparative, comparable, respective, correlative, parallel,

corresponding.
2 = **proportionate**, in proportion/ratio, based.
▸ NOUN = *see* **relation** (2).

relax VERB **1** = **loosen**, slacken, weaken, lessen, let up, reduce, diminish.
2 = **become less tense/ stiff/rigid**, loosen, slacken. **3** = **moderate**, make less strict/formal, soften, ease. **4** = **loosen up**, ease up/off;
[inf] unwind, take it easy, let it all hang out, hang loose.
Opposites: tense, tighten.

relaxation NOUN
1 = **loosening**, slackening, weakening, letting up.
2 = **lessening**, reduction, easing off, abatement.
3 = **leisure**, recreation, enjoyment, amusement, entertainment, pleasure, rest, refreshment.

relay VERB = **pass on**, hand on, communicate, send, transmit, broadcast, spread, circulate.

release VERB **1** = **set free**, free, let go, set/turn loose, let out, liberate, untie, undo, unloose, unbind, unchain,

unfetter, unshackle, extricate, deliver, emancipate;
[historical] manumit.
2 = **make public**, make known, issue, break, announce, reveal, divulge, unveil, present, disclose, publish, broadcast, put out, circulate, disseminate, distribute, spread.
Opposites: imprison, suppress.

relent VERB = **soften**, become merciful/lenient, show mercy/pity, give quarter, capitulate, yield, give way, give in, unbend, come round, forbear, change one's mind.

relentless ADJ
1 = **unceasing**, unrelenting, unremitting, persistent, unswerving, persevering, unflagging, unfaltering, unstoppable, incessant. **2** = **harsh**, ruthless, merciless, pitiless, remorseless, unforgiving, implacable, inexorable, cruel, grim, hard, cold-hearted, fierce, strict, obdurate,

r

unyielding, inflexible, unbending.
Opposites: lenient.

relevant ADJ = **applicable**, pertinent, apposite, material, appurtenant, to the point/purpose, germane, admissible, appropriate, apt, fitting.
Opposites: irrelevant.

reliable ADJ
1 = **trustworthy**, dependable, trusty, true, faithful, devoted, steady, steadfast, constant, unfailing, certain, sure.
2 = **well founded**, well grounded, sound, trustworthy, dependable, credible, authentic, genuine.
Opposites: unreliable.

relic NOUN 1 = **ancient/ historical object**, artefact, antique, heirloom. 2 = **vestige**, trace, survivor, remnant.

relief NOUN 1 = **alleviation**, mitigation, assuagement, palliation, ease, appeasement, abatement.
2 = **aid**, help, assistance, succour. 3 = **respite**, remission, interruption, break, variation,

diversion; [inf] let-up.
Opposites: intensification.

relieve VERB 1 = **alleviate**, mitigate, assuage, allay, soothe, soften, palliate, appease, ease, dull, abate, reduce, lessen, diminish.
2 = **bring aid to**, aid, help, assist, rescue, save, succour. 3 = **bring respite to**, interrupt, break up, vary, lighten.
Opposites: aggravate.

religious ADJ 1 = **church**, holy, divine, theological, doctrinal, spiritual, sectarian.
2 = **churchgoing**, God-fearing, godly, pious, devout. 3 = **scrupulous**, conscientious, meticulous, zealous, strict, rigid, rigorous.
Opposites: irreligious.

relinquish VERB = **give up**, renounce, resign, abdicate, surrender, sign away.
Opposites: retain.

relish NOUN = **enjoyment**, delight, pleasure, satisfaction, gratification, appreciation, liking, zest, gusto.

▶ VERB = **enjoy**, delight in, like, love, adore, appreciate, revel in, luxuriate in.
Opposites: dislike.

reluctant ADJ = **unwilling**, disinclined, hesitant, unenthusiastic, grudging, loath, averse, slow, chary.
Opposites: eager.

rely

■ **rely on** = **depend on**, count on, bank on, trust, lean on, be confident/ sure of, swear by.

remain VERB 1 = **be left**, be left over, stay behind, survive, last, abide, endure, prevail. 2 = **wait**, stay, linger; [inf] stay put; [archaic] tarry. 3 = **stay**, continue to be, persist in being.

remainder NOUN = **remnant**, residue, leavings, dregs, residuum, balance, surplus, excess, superfluity.

remains PL NOUN 1 = **remnants**, leftovers, leavings, scraps, residue, debris, detritus. 2 = **relics**, reliquiae, fragments, shards. 3 = **corpse**, dead body, body, carcass; [Medicine] cadaver; [inf] stiff.

remark VERB 1 = **mention**, say, state, declare, pronounce, assert, observe. 2 = **note**, notice, observe, mark, perceive, discern.
▶ NOUN = **comment**, statement, utterance, declaration, pronouncement, observation, reference, opinion.

remarkable ADJ = **out of the ordinary**, extraordinary, unusual, uncommon, conspicuous, singular, notable, noteworthy, memorable, signal, rare, exceptional, outstanding, striking, impressive, considerable, pre-eminent, significant, important, momentous, phenomenal, wonderful.
Opposites: ordinary, commonplace.

remedy NOUN 1 = **cure**, treatment, medicine, medication, medicament, therapy, antidote, restorative, nostrum, panacea. **2 = corrective**, solution, redress, panacea.

▶ VERB **1 = cure**, heal, treat, counteract, control.
2 = rectify, solve, set to rights, put right, redress, fix, sort out.

remember VERB **1 = recall**, call to mind, recollect, think of, keep/bear in mind, not forget.
2 = reminisce about, look/think back on, hark back to, summon up.
Opposites: forget.

remind VERB **= cause to remember**, jog/refresh someone's memory, prompt.

reminiscent ADJ **= evocative**, suggestive, redolent.

remiss ADJ **= negligent**, neglectful, lax, slack, slipshod, sloppy, careless, forgetful, inattentive, heedless, thoughtless, unthinking, culpable, delinquent.
Opposites: careful, diligent.

remission NOUN
1 = cancellation, revocation, repeal, rescinding. **2 = easing**, moderation, abatement, lessening, decrease, dwindling, wane, waning, ebb, ebbing, subsidence.

remit VERB **1 = cancel**, revoke, repeal, rescind, stop, halt. **2 = ease**, moderate, abate, lessen, decrease, dwindle, wane, ebb, subside. **3 = send**, dispatch, forward, transmit, post, mail.

remnant NOUN
1 = remainder, residue, balance, remains, vestiges. **2 = piece**, fragment, scrap.

remonstrate
▪ **remonstrate with**
= take issue with, argue with, dispute with, protest to, complain to, expostulate with.

remorse NOUN **= regret**, sorrow, contrition, penitence, repentance, guilty conscience, guilt, shame, self-reproach, ruefulness, pangs of conscience, compunction.

remorseful ADJ = **sorry**, regretful, contrite, apologetic, penitent, repentant, guilt-ridden, conscience-stricken, ashamed, chastened, rueful.
Opposites: unrepentant.

remorseless ADJ = *see* **relentless**.

remote ADJ **1** = **distant**, far, far-off, faraway, out of the way, outlying, inaccessible, off the beaten track, isolated, secluded, lonely, godforsaken. **2** = **unlikely**, improbable, implausible, negligible, insignificant, doubtful, dubious, slight, slender, slim, small, poor. **3** = **aloof**, distant, detached, withdrawn, reserved, uncommunicative, unapproachable, stand-offish, cool, haughty, uninvolved, indifferent, unconcerned.
Opposites: near, likely, friendly.

removal NOUN
1 = **dismissal**, eviction, ejection, expulsion, ousting, dislodgement, deposition. **2** = **taking away**, withdrawal, deprivation, abolition. **3** = **deletion**, elimination, erasure, effacing, obliteration.

remove VERB **1** = **take away**, carry away, move, shift, convey, transfer, transport. **2** = **dismiss**, get rid of, eject, expel, cast out, oust, throw out, dislodge, relegate, unseat, depose, displace; [inf] sack, fire. **3** = **take off**, pull off, strip off; [Brit. inf] peel off. **4** = **delete**, eliminate, erase, rub out, cross out, strike out, blue-pencil, efface, obliterate. **5** = **take out**, pull out, uproot, eradicate, extirpate, destroy, exterminate, annihilate. **6** = **cut off**, amputate, lop off, chop off, excise.

remunerative ADJ = **profitable**, moneymaking, paying, lucrative, gainful, financially rewarding, rich.

render VERB **1** = **make**, cause to be/become,

leave. **2** = **give**, contribute, make available, provide, supply, furnish. **3** = **present**, send in, submit, tender. **4** = **act**, perform, play, execute, interpret.

rendezvous NOUN = **appointment**, date, engagement, meeting, assignation.

renegade NOUN = **defector**, deserter, turncoat, traitor, apostate, revolutionary, rebel, mutineer.

renege VERB = **go back on one's word**, break one's promise, default, back out, welsh, pull out; [inf] cop out.
Opposites: honour.

renounce VERB
1 = **relinquish**, give up, resign, abdicate, surrender, sign away, waive, forego. **2** = **disown**, repudiate, cast off, discard, reject, disinherit, wash one's hands of, spurn, shun. **3** = **abstain from**, give up, desist from, swear off, eschew.
Opposites: embrace.

renovate VERB = **modernize**, recondition, refurbish, rehabilitate, overhaul, restore, revamp, remodel, repair, redecorate, refit; [inf] do up, fix up.

renown NOUN = **fame**, repute, acclaim, celebrity, distinction, illustriousness, eminence, pre-eminence, prominence, mark, note, consequence, prestige.

renowned ADJ = **famous**, famed, well known, of repute, acclaimed, celebrated, distinguished, illustrious, eminent, pre-eminent, prominent, noted, notable, of note, of consequence, prestigious.
Opposites: obscure.

rent¹ NOUN = **rental**, payment, hire fee.
▸ VERB **1** = **lease**, hire, charter. **2** = **let**, lease, hire, hire/let out, farm out.

rent² NOUN = **tear**, rip, split, gash, slash, hole, perforation, break, crack, fracture, crevice, fissure, cleft.

repair VERB 1 = **mend**, fix, put right, restore, adjust, regulate, overhaul. 2 = **put right**, make good, rectify, correct, redress, compensate for.

repay VERB 1 = **pay back**, refund, reimburse, recompense, remunerate, square accounts with, settle up with. 2 = **get back at**, hit back, retaliate against, get even with, settle the score with; [inf] get one's own back on.

repeal VERB = **revoke**, rescind, abrogate, annul, nullify, make void, void, invalidate, quash, set aside, cancel, countermand, retract, overrule, override, reverse.

repeat VERB 1 = **say again**, restate, retell, reiterate, recapitulate, recap, echo, parrot, quote. 2 = **do again**, redo, duplicate, replicate.

repeated ADJ = **recurrent**, frequent, continual, incessant, constant, endless.

repel VERB 1 = **repulse**, drive back, push back, thrust back, force back, beat back, ward off, fend off, keep at bay, keep at arm's length. 2 = **revolt**, disgust, sicken, nauseate, make someone sick, turn someone's stomach, be repugnant to, make someone's flesh creep; [inf] give someone the creeps.
Opposites: welcome, attract.

repellent ADJ = **repulsive**, revolting, disgusting, sickening, nauseating, distasteful, repugnant, abhorrent, offensive, obnoxious, loathsome, off-putting, hateful, vile, nasty, odious, abominable, horrible, horrid, foul, heinous, obscene.
Opposites: attractive.

repent VERB = **be sorry**, be contrite, be conscience-stricken, reproach oneself, be ashamed, regret, rue, be penitent.

repentant ADJ = **penitent**, sorrowful, apologetic, regretful, contrite,

r

remorseful, conscience-stricken, rueful, ashamed, guilt-ridden.
Opposites: unashamed.

repercussion NOUN
= **effect**, result, consequence, reverberation, backlash.

repetitive ADJ
= **recurrent**, unchanging, unvaried, monotonous, humdrum, tedious, boring, mechanical, automatic; [Brit. inf] samey.

replace VERB 1 = **put back**, return, restore. 2 = **take the place of**, succeed, supersede, follow after, come after, supplant, substitute for, stand in for, act for, fill in for, cover for.

replacement NOUN
= **successor**, substitute, stand-in, fill-in, locum, understudy, proxy, surrogate.

replenish VERB = **refill**, top up, fill up, recharge, reload.

replica NOUN = **copy**, carbon copy, duplicate, facsimile, model, reproduction, imitation.

reply VERB = **answer**, respond, write back, rejoin, retort, return, riposte, come back, counter.
▶ NOUN = **answer**, response, acknowledgement, rejoinder, retort, return, riposte; [inf] comeback.

report NOUN 1 = **account**, statement, record, exposition. 2 = **article**, piece, story, write-up, communiqué, dispatch, bulletin. 3 = **explosion**, bang, boom, crack, crash.
▶ VERB 1 = **announce**, pass on, communicate, relay, relate, tell, recount, give an account of, set forth, document, narrate, describe, delineate, detail, divulge, disclose, circulate. 2 = **tell on**, inform on, accuse, make a charge/complaint against; [inf] squeal on, rat on; [Brit. inf] grass on.
3 = **present oneself**, be present, appear, arrive, come, turn up, clock in; [Brit.] clock on; [inf] show up.

reporter NOUN = **journalist**, newsman, newswoman,

pressman, correspondent, writer, broadcaster, announcer, presenter; [inf] newshound, hack.

reprehensible ADJ
= **blameworthy**, culpable, erring, errant, wrong, bad, shameful, disgraceful, discreditable, dishonourable, objectionable, unpardonable, indefensible, unjustifiable, inexcusable.
Opposites: praiseworthy.

represent VERB **1** = **stand for**, symbolize, personify, epitomize, typify, embody, incorporate, exemplify. **2** = **depict**, portray, delineate, illustrate, picture, denote, paint, draw, sketch, exhibit, show, display, evoke. **3** = **act for**, appear for, speak for, be the representative of.

representation NOUN
= **depiction**, portrayal, portrait, delineation, illustration, picture, painting, drawing, sketch, image, model.

representative ADJ
1 = **typical**, archetypal, exemplary, characteristic, indicative, illustrative.
2 = **elected**, elective, chosen, delegated.
Opposites: unrepresentative.
▸ NOUN **1** = **spokesman**, spokeswoman, spokesperson, agent, deputy, proxy.
2 = **Member of Parliament**, MP, Member, deputy, councillor.

repress VERB
1 = **subjugate**, conquer, vanquish, overpower, overcome, crush, master, dominate, domineer, bully, intimidate, oppress. **2** = **hold/keep back**, hold in, bite back, restrain, suppress, keep in check, check, inhibit, bottle up, silence, muffle, stifle, smother.

repressed ADJ
1 = **subjugated**, oppressed, tyrannized.
2 = **restrained**, suppressed, muffled, smothered. **3** = **inhibited**, withdrawn, restrained.

r

repression NOUN
1 = **oppression**, dictatorship, authoritarianism, tyranny, despotism, domination, coercion, suppression, subjugation.
2 = **holding back**, biting back, restraint, suppression, smothering.

repressive ADJ
= **tyrannical**, despotic, dictatorial, authoritarian, oppressive, coercive, suppressive, harsh, severe, strict, cruel.

reprieve VERB
= **postpone/cancel punishment of**, grant a stay of execution to, let off, spare, pardon, let off the hook, show clemency to.

reprimand VERB = **rebuke**, scold, chide, reproach, reprove, lecture, admonish, berate, upbraid, correct, take to task, haul over the coals; [inf] tell off, give someone a dressing-down, bawl out; [Brit. inf] tick off; [formal] castigate.
Opposites: praise

▶ NOUN = **rebuke**, scolding, chiding, reproach, reproof, admonition, berating, upbraiding, tongue-lashing; [inf] talking-to, telling-off, dressing-down, bawling-out; [Brit. inf] ticking-off, wigging; [formal] castigation.
Opposites: commendation.

reprisal NOUN = **retaliation**, revenge, vengeance, retribution, redress, requital, recrimination, an eye for an eye; [inf] tit for tat.

reproach VERB & NOUN = see **reprimand**.

reproachful ADJ
= **disapproving**, disappointed, critical, censorious, admonitory, condemnatory, disparaging, reproving; [formal] castigatory.
Opposites: approving.

reproduce VERB 1 = **copy**, duplicate, replicate, photocopy, recreate, redo, remake, imitate, follow, emulate, echo, mirror, parallel, match, mimic, ape. 2 = **breed**, procreate, bear young, produce offspring, give birth, multiply, propagate, proliferate, spawn.

reproduction NOUN
1 = **copy**, duplicate, replica, facsimile, imitation, print.
2 = **breeding**, procreation, propagation, proliferation.

repudiate VERB = **disown**, reject, cast off, cut off, abandon, forsake, desert, discard, renounce, disavow, abjure, turn one's back on, have nothing to do with, wash one's hands of.
Opposites: embrace.

repugnant ADJ
= **abhorrent**, revolting, repulsive, repellent, disgusting, sickening, nauseating, disagreeable, distasteful, offensive, objectionable, obnoxious, loathsome, off-putting, hateful, despicable, reprehensible, contemptible, abominable, horrible, horrid, foul, nasty, vile, ugly, odious, heinous.

Opposites: agreeable.

repulsive ADJ = *see* **repugnant**.

reputable ADJ
= **respectable**, respected, well thought of, esteemed, estimable, of good repute, worthy, creditable, reliable, dependable, conscientious, trustworthy, above board, legitimate, upright, virtuous, good, excellent.
Opposites: disreputable.

reputation NOUN = **repute**, standing, name, character, position, status, station.

request NOUN = **entreaty**, appeal, petition, plea, application, demand, solicitation, call, suit.
▸ VERB = **ask for**, solicit, seek, apply for, put in for, call for, beg for, plead for, pray for, petition, implore, sue for, supplicate for, requisition, demand, desire; [poetic/ literary] beseech.

require VERB **1** = **need**, have need of, lack, be

short of, want, wish, desire, crave, miss.
2 = call for, demand, necessitate, involve, take.

required ADJ
= **compulsory**, obligatory, mandatory, prescribed, recommended, requisite, set, essential, necessary, vital.
Opposites: optional.

requirement NOUN
= **need**, want, lack, must, necessity, demand, prerequisite, requisite, precondition, specification, qualification, sine qua non, stipulation.

requisite ADJ = *see* **required**.

requisition NOUN
1 = application, order, claim, request, call, demand.
2 = commandeering, appropriation, possession, occupation, seizure, confiscation.
▶ VERB **1 = apply for**, order, put in a claim for, request, call for, demand.
2 = commandeer, appropriate, take over, take possession of,

occupy, seize, confiscate.

rescue VERB = **save**, come to someone's aid, free, set free, release, liberate, emancipate, get out, extricate, redeem, salvage, relieve.
▶ NOUN = **deliverance**, freeing, release, liberation, emancipation, extrication, redemption, salvage, relief.

research NOUN
= **experiment**, assessment, study, tests, investigation, experimentation, fact-finding, testing, exploration.
▶ VERB = **do tests on**, investigate, inquire into, look into, probe, explore, analyse, study, examine.

resemblance NOUN
= **likeness**, similarity, semblance, sameness, uniformity, correspondence, comparability, affinity, closeness, nearness, agreement, congruity, concurrence, conformity.

resemble VERB = **be like**, look like, bear a resemblance to, be similar to, remind one of, take after, echo, mirror, parallel, favour.

resent VERB = **take offence/umbrage at**, take exception to, take amiss, be annoyed/angry at, begrudge, feel bitter about, dislike.
Opposites: welcome.

resentful ADJ = **aggrieved**, offended, indignant, irritated, displeased, annoyed, angry, irate, incensed, piqued, in high dudgeon, grudging, bitter, embittered, wounded; [inf] in a huff.

resentment NOUN = **offence**, indignation, irritation, displeasure, annoyance, anger, pique, grudgingness, bitterness, animosity, hostility, hard feelings; [poetic/literary] ire.

reservation NOUN
1 = **booking**, engagement, appointment.
2 = **condition**, stipulation, qualification, proviso, provision, qualm, scruple, hesitancy, doubt.

reserve VERB 1 = **put/set/lay aside**, put away, keep back, keep, withhold, conserve, save, retain, store, hoard, stockpile; [inf] hang on to. 2 = **book**, engage, arrange for, charter, hire.
▶ NOUN 1 = **store**, stock, supply, reservoir, pool, cache, fund, stockpile, accumulation, backlog, hoard. 2 = **aloofness**, detachment, distance, remoteness, formality, coolness, coldness, frigidity, reticence, unapproachability, uncommunicativeness, shyness, diffidence, taciturnity. 3 = **preserve**, reservation, sanctuary, park.

reserved ADJ = **aloof**, detached, remote, formal, unemotional, undemonstrative, cool, cold, frigid, reticent, unapproachable, uncommunicative, unsociable, unfriendly, unresponsive, unforthcoming, shy, retiring, diffident, secret, secretive, taciturn, silent.
Opposites: outgoing.

reside
■ **reside in** = **live in**, dwell

in, stay in, inhabit,
occupy.

residence NOUN = **house**,
home, habitation,
quarters, lodgings;
[formal] dwelling,
domicile.

resident NOUN
= **inhabitant**, occupant,
householder, denizen;
[Brit.] occupier.

residue NOUN = **remainder**,
remnant, residuum, rest,
surplus, extra, excess,
remains, leftovers, dregs,
lees.

resign VERB 1 = **give
notice**, hand in one's
notice, leave; [inf] quit.
2 = **renounce**, relinquish,
give up, abdicate,
surrender, cede.

resilient ADJ 1 = **elastic**,
springy, rubbery,
whippy, flexible, pliant,
supple, pliable, plastic.
2 = **tough**, strong, hardy,
quick to recover, difficult
to keep down,
irrepressible.

resist VERB 1 = **withstand**,
be proof against, repel.
2 = **stop**, halt, prevent,
check stem, curb,
obstruct, hinder,

impede, block, thwart,
frustrate, inhibit,
restrain.

resistant ADJ = **proof
against**, impervious to,
unaffected by, immune
to.

resolute ADJ
= **determined**, resolved,
decided, firm, fixed, set,
intent, steadfast,
constant, earnest,
staunch, bold,
courageous, serious,
purposeful, deliberate,
inflexible, unyielding,
unwavering, unfaltering,
unhesitating,
unswerving, unflinching,
obstinate, obdurate,
strong-willed, dogged,
persevering, persistent,
tenacious, relentless,
unshakeable, dedicated.
Opposites: irresolute.

resolution NOUN
1 = **resolve**,
determination, firmness,
intentness, steadfastness,
constancy, staunchness,
boldness, courage,
seriousness,
purposefulness,
obstinacy, obduracy, will
power, doggedness,

perseverance, persistence, tenacity, staying power, dedication. **2 = motion**, declaration, decree, verdict, judgement. **3 = solving**, solution, answer, sorting out, working out, unravelling, disentanglement, cracking.

resolve VERB **1 = decide**, make up one's mind, determine, settle on, undertake. **2 = solve**, answer, sort out, work out, clear up, fathom, unravel, disentangle, crack.
▶ NOUN = *see* **resolution** (1).

resort VERB **= fall back on**, turn to, have recourse to, look to, make use of, use, avail oneself of, bring into play/service, exercise.
▶ NOUN **1 = holiday/tourist centre**, centre, spot, retreat. **2 = recourse**, source of help, expedient, alternative, choice, possibility, hope.

resound VERB **= reverberate**, resonate, echo, ring.

resource NOUN **1 = asset**, reserve, reservoir, store, stock, supply, pool, fund, stockpile. **2 = resourcefulness**, initiative, ingenuity, inventiveness, quick-wittedness, cleverness, native wit, talent, ability, capability.

respect NOUN **1 = esteem**, high regard, regard, high opinion, admiration, approval, appreciation, veneration, reverence, deference, honour, praise, homage. **2 = aspect**, facet, feature, way, sense, characteristic, particular, point, detail. **Opposites:** contempt.
▶ VERB **= esteem**, have a high opinion of, think highly of, admire, approve of, appreciate, venerate, revere, honour, praise. **Opposites:** despise.

respectable ADJ **1 = reputable**, of good repute, upright, honest, honourable, trustworthy, above board, worthy, decent, good, virtuous, admirable, well bred,

proper, decorous.
2 = reasonable, fairly good, fair, considerable, ample, sizable, substantial; [inf] not to be sneezed at.
Opposites: disreputable, paltry.

respective ADJ
= individual, separate, personal, own, particular, specific.

respects PL NOUN
= regards, best wishes, greetings, compliments, remembrances.

respite NOUN **= rest**, break, interval, intermission, recess, lull, pause, hiatus, halt, relief, relaxation; [inf] breather, let-up.

respond VERB **1 = answer**, reply to, say in response to, acknowledge. **2 = say in response**, answer, reply, rejoin, retort, return, riposte, come back, counter.

response NOUN **= answer**, reply, acknowledgement, rejoinder, retort, return, riposte; [inf] comeback.
Opposites: question.

responsibility NOUN
1 = duty, charge, onus, task, role, liability, accountability, answerability. **2 = blame**, fault, guilt, culpability.

responsible ADJ **1 = in charge/control of**, at the helm of, accountable for, liable for.
2 = accountable, answerable, to blame, blameworthy, at fault, guilty, culpable.
3 = sensible, level-headed, rational, reasonable, sound, stable, reliable, dependable, trustworthy, competent, conscientious, hard-working, industrious.
Opposites: irresponsible.

responsive ADJ **= quick to react**, reactive, receptive, forthcoming, sensitive, perceptive, sympathetic, susceptible, impressionable, open, alive, awake, aware, sharp.

rest NOUN **1 = repose**, relaxation, leisure, ease, inactivity, respite, time off, breathing space, sleep, slumber. **2 = break**, interval, interlude, intermission, lull, pause, time off. **3** = **stand**, base, holder, support, prop, shelf.

▶ VERB **1** = **take a rest**, relax, sit down, lie down, go to bed, sleep, take a nap, nap, catnap, doze, slumber; [inf] take it easy. **2** = **be supported by**, be propped up by, lie on, be laid on, recline on, stand on, sit on. **3** = **depend**, rely, hang, hinge, be based, be founded.

restful ADJ = **quiet**, calm, tranquil, relaxed, peaceful, placid, still, languid, undisturbed, unhurried, sleepy. **Opposites:** hectic.

restless ADJ **1** = **sleepless**, wakeful, tossing and turning, fitful. **2** = **uneasy**, ill at ease, on edge, agitated. **3** = **unsettled**, roaming, roving, wandering, itinerant, travelling, nomadic, peripatetic.

restore VERB **1** = **renovate**, repair, fix, mend, set to rights, recondition, rehabilitate, refurbish, rebuild, reconstruct, remodel, revamp,

redecorate, touch up; [inf] do up, fix up. **2** = **return**, give back, hand back, send back. **3** = **re-establish**, reinstitute, reinstate, reinstall, reimpose.

restrain VERB = **control**, keep under control, check, hold in check, curb, keep within bounds, subdue, suppress, repress, contain, smother, stifle, bottle up, rein in; [inf] keep the lid on.

restraint NOUN **1** = **constraint**, check, curb, block, hindrance, impediment, deterrent, inhibition. **2** = **self-restraint**, self-control, self-discipline, moderation, temperateness, prudence, judiciousness.

restrict VERB **1** = **hinder**, impede, hamper, retard, handicap, cramp. **2** = **limit**, set/impose limits on, keep under control, regulate, control, moderate.

restriction NOUN = **constraint**, limitation,

control, check, curb, regulation, condition, provision, proviso, stipulation, qualification, demarcation.

result NOUN **1 = outcome**, consequence, issue, upshot, sequel, effect, repercussion, end, conclusion, termination, aftermath, product, by-product, fruits.
2 = answer, solution.
Opposites: cause.
▶ VERB **= follow**, ensue, issue, develop, stem, evolve, emerge, emanate, occur, happen, come about, eventuate.
■ **result in = end in**, culminate in, finish in, terminate in.

resume VERB **= carry on**, continue, recommence, begin again, reopen, reinstitute.

resurrect VERB **= raise from the dead**, restore to life, bring back to life, revive, breathe new life into, give new life to.

retain VERB **1 = keep**, keep possession/hold of, hold on to, hang on to, preserve, maintain.

2 = hire, employ, engage, commission.

retaliate VERB **= take/exact/wreak revenge**, avenge oneself, exact retribution, give as good as one gets, get one's own back, get back at, make reprisals, get even with, even the scores, settle a score.

retard VERB **= slow down**, slow up, hold back, set back, hold up, delay, hinder, hamper, obstruct, impede, decelerate, put a brake on, check, arrest, interfere with, interrupt, thwart, frustrate.
Opposites: expedite.

reticent ADJ **=** see **reserved**.

retire VERB **1 = give up work**, stop working, be pensioned off; [inf] be put out to grass. **2 = withdraw**, go out, depart, exit, leave, absent oneself.
3 = go to bed, go to sleep, turn in, call it a day; [inf] hit the sack.

retiring ADJ **= shy**, diffident, bashful, self-effacing, shrinking, unassuming, reserved,

reticent, timid, timorous, nervous, modest, demure.
Opposites: brash.

retract VERB **1** = **draw in**, pull in, pull back. **2** = **take back**, withdraw, revoke, repeal, rescind, annul, cancel, abrogate, disavow, abjure, renounce, recant, disclaim, backtrack on, renege on.

retreat VERB **1** = **withdraw**, pull back, fall back, back off, give way/ground, decamp, depart, leave, flee, take flight, turn tail, beat a retreat, beat a hasty retreat. **2** = **go back**, recede, ebb.
▶ NOUN **1** = **withdrawal**, pulling back, departure, flight, evacuation. **2** = **refuge**, haven, shelter, sanctuary, sanctum sanctorum, hideaway, resort, asylum.

retribution NOUN = **reprisal**, retaliation, revenge, vengeance, punishment, justice, nemesis, reckoning, requital, an eye for an eye, tit for tat.

retrieve VERB = **get back**, recover, regain, win back, recoup, redeem, reclaim, repossess, recapture, salvage, rescue.

retrograde ADJ = **retrogressive**, backwards, deteriorating, declining, on the wane.

retrospect
▪ **in retrospect** = **on reflection**, on looking/ thinking back, with hindsight.

return VERB **1** = **go back**, come back, reappear, reoccur, come again, come round again. **2** = **give back**, send back, take back, carry back, put back, replace, restore, reinstate, reinstall. **3** = **reciprocate**, repay, requite, send/give in response to.
Opposites: depart.
▶ NOUN **1** = **homecoming**, reappearance, reoccurrence. **2** = **replacement**, restoration, reinstatement, reinstallation. **3** = **profit**, yield, gain, income, revenue, interest.

r

Opposites: departure.

reveal VERB **1** = **show**, display, exhibit, expose to view. **2** = **bring to light**, uncover, expose to view, lay bare, unearth, unveil, unmask. **3** = **disclose**, divulge, tell, let out, let on, let slip, give away, give out, leak, betray, make known/public, broadcast, publicize, publish, proclaim.
Opposites: conceal, hide.

revel VERB = **celebrate**, make merry, have a party, party, carouse, roister.

■ **revel in** = **delight in**, take pleasure in, bask in, rejoice in, relish, savour, gloat over, luxuriate in, wallow in.

revelation NOUN = **disclosure**, divulgence, telling, leak, betrayal, broadcasting, publicizing, communication, publishing, proclamation.

revelry NOUN = **celebrations**, festivities, jollification, merrymaking, carousal.

revenge NOUN = **vengeance**, retaliation, retribution, reprisal, redress.
▶ VERB = **take revenge for**, avenge, retaliate, exact retribution for, take reprisals for, requite.

revenue NOUN = **income**, return, yield, interest, profits, returns, receipts, proceeds, takings, rewards.
Opposites: expenditure.

reverberate VERB = **resound**, echo, ring, vibrate.

revere VERB = **look up to**, think highly of, admire, respect, esteem, defer to, honour, venerate, exalt, put on a pedestal, idolize.
Opposites: despise.

reverence NOUN = **esteem**, admiration, respect, deference, honour, veneration, worship, homage, adoration, devotion, awe, exaltation.
Opposites: scorn.

reverent ADJ = **reverential**, admiring, respectful, deferential, adoring, loving, devoted, awed, submissive, humble, meek.

reversal NOUN
1 = **turnaround**, turnabout, about-face, volte-face, U-turn, change of heart; [Brit.] about-turn.
2 = **change**, exchange, trading, trade-off, swapping. 3 = **overturn**, overthrow, revocation, repeal, rescinding, annulment, invalidation.

reverse VERB 1 = **turn round**, put back to front, turn upside down, upend, invert. 2 = **move/ direct backwards**, back. 3 = **change**, exchange, trade, swap. 4 = **set aside**, overturn, overthrow, revoke, repeal, rescind, annul, nullify, declare null and void, void, invalidate, quash.
▶ ADJ = **reversed**, backwards, inverted, transposed, turned round.
▶ NOUN 1 = **opposite**, contrary, converse, antithesis. 2 = **other side**, back, rear, underside, flip

side. 3 = **reversal**, upset, setback, failure, misfortune, mishap, blow, disappointment.

review NOUN 1 = **study**, analysis, survey, examination, scrutiny, assessment, appraisal.
2 = **criticism**, critique, notice, assessment, evaluation, rating.
▶ VERB 1 = **analyse**, examine, study, survey, scrutinize, assess, appraise.
2 = **criticize**, evaluate, assess, appraise, judge, weigh up, discuss.

revise VERB 1 = **amend**, emend, correct, alter, change, edit, rewrite, redraft, rework, update, revamp. 2 = **go over**, reread, run through, study; [inf] bone up on; [Brit. inf] swot up on.

revival NOUN
= **resuscitation**, resurrection, rebirth, renaissance, comeback, restoration, reintroduction.

revive VERB 1 = **bring round**, resuscitate, give artificial respiration to, save, restore to health;

[inf] give the kiss of life to. **2 = refresh**, restore, cheer up, comfort, enliven, revitalize.

revoke VERB **= repeal**, rescind, abrogate, countermand, annul, nullify, declare null and void, void, invalidate, quash.
Opposites: enact.

revolt VERB **1 = rise up**, take to the streets, take up arms, rebel, mutiny. **2 = repel**, disgust, sicken, nauseate, turn someone's stomach, be repugnant to, make someone's flesh creep, put off, offend, shock.

revolting ADJ **= see repellent**.

revolution NOUN
1 = rebellion, revolt, insurrection, uprising, rising, insurgence, coup, putsch. **2 = drastic change**, metamorphosis, sea change, upheaval, upset, transformation. **3 = rotation**, single turn, whirl, round, spin, wheel.

revolutionary ADJ
1 = rebellious, insurrectionary, mutinous, seditious, subversive, extremist. **2 = progressive**, radical, innovative, new, novel, avant-garde, experimental, different, drastic.
▶ NOUN **= rebel**, insurgent, insurrectionist.

revolve VERB **= go round**, turn round, rotate, spin, circle, orbit, gyrate, whirl.

revulsion NOUN
= repulsion, disgust, nausea, distaste, aversion, repugnance, abhorrence, loathing.
Opposites: delight.

reward NOUN
= recompense, payment, remuneration, bonus, bounty, present, gift, tip, gratuity, prize.
Opposites: punishment.
▶ VERB **= recompense**, pay, remunerate, give a present to, tip.

rewarding ADJ
= satisfying, fulfilling, enriching, edifying, beneficial, profitable, advantageous, productive, valuable.

rhetoric NOUN = **bombast**, grandiloquence, magniloquence, hyperbole, pomposity, verbosity, prolixity, turgidity.

rhetorical ADJ = **pompous**, high-flown, flamboyant, showy, flowery, florid, oratorical, declamatory, bombastic, grandiloquent, magniloquent, hyperbolical, verbose, long-winded, prolix, turgid, periphrastic.

rhythm NOUN = **beat**, cadence, tempo, pulse, metre, pattern.

ribald ADJ = **bawdy**, risqué, smutty, vulgar, coarse, earthy, off colour, rude, naughty, racy, suggestive, indecent, indelicate. = See also **obscene**.

rich ADJ 1 = **wealthy**, affluent, well off, well-to-do, prosperous, moneyed, propertied; [inf] well heeled, filthy rich, loaded, made of money, rolling in it/ money, flush, worth a packet/bundle, on Easy Street. 2 = **opulent**, expensive, costly, precious, valuable, priceless, beyond price, lavish, luxurious, lush, sumptuous, palatial, splendid, superb, resplendent, elegant, fine, exquisite, magnificent, grand, gorgeous. 3 = **well provided**, well supplied, well stocked, abounding, overflowing, replete, rife. 4 = **fertile**, productive, fecund, fruitful, lush. 5 = **creamy**, fatty, heavy. Opposites: poor, plain, barren.

riches PL NOUN = **wealth**, affluence, prosperity, money, capital, property, treasure, assets, resources.

richly ADV 1 = **expensively**, lavishly, luxuriously, sumptuously, palatially, splendidly, superbly, magnificently. 2 = **fully**, in full measure, well, thoroughly, completely, amply, utterly. Opposites: meanly.

rid VERB = **do away with**, remove, get rid of, dispense with, eliminate, dump, dispose of,

r

unload, expel, eject,
weed out, clear, cleanse,
purge, purify.

riddle NOUN = **puzzle**,
poser, conundrum,
brain-teaser, problem,
enigma, mystery.

ride VERB 1 = **sit on**, mount,
be mounted on, bestride,
manage, control.
2 = **travel**, go, move,
progress.
▶ NOUN = **trip**, outing,
journey, jaunt; [inf] spin.

ridicule NOUN = **derision**,
mockery, laughter, scorn,
jeering, gibing, teasing,
taunting, chaff, banter,
badinage, raillery, satire,
sarcasm, irony;
[inf] kidding, ribbing,
ragging.
Opposites: respect.
▶ VERB = **deride**, mock,
laugh at, scoff at, scorn,
jeer at, gibe at, make fun
of, poke fun at, make a
fool of, tease, taunt,
chaff; [inf] kid, rib, rag,
take the mickey out of,
send up.

ridiculous ADJ 1 = **absurd**,
comical, funny,
laughable, hilarious,
humorous, droll, farcical,
facetious, ludicrous,
risible, derisory.
2 = **pointless**, senseless,
foolish, inane, fatuous,
nonsensical, mindless.
3 = **unbelievable**,
incredible, outrageous,
preposterous, shocking,
monstrous.
Opposites: sensible.

rife ADJ = **widespread**,
common, prevalent,
predominant, general,
extensive, ubiquitous,
universal, global,
rampant.

rifle
▪ **rifle through** = **ransack**,
rummage through, go
through, rake through,
search.

rift NOUN 1 = **split**, break,
breach, fissure, cleft,
crevice, gap, crack,
cranny, slit.
2 = **disagreement**, fight,
falling-out, breach,
division, estrangement,
schism, split, alienation,
quarrel, altercation,
conflict, feud; [inf] row.

rig[1]
▪ **rig out** = **clothe**, dress,
attire, accoutre, array,
deck, bedeck, drape.

▪ **rig up** = **put together**, erect, assemble, throw together, cobble together.

rig² VERB = **falsify**, fake, tamper with, doctor, engineer, manipulate.

right ADJ **1** = **just**, fair, equitable, impartial, good, upright, righteous, virtuous, proper, moral, ethical, honourable, honest, principled, lawful, legal. **2** = **correct**, accurate, unerring, exact, precise, valid; [inf] on the mark; [inf] spot on, bang on. **3** = **suitable**, appropriate, fit, proper, desirable, ideal, opportune, favourable, convenient, propitious. **4** = **right-hand**, dextral; [Nautical] starboard; [Heraldry] dexter. **5** = **conservative**, right-wing, Tory, reactionary. **Opposites:** wrong, left.
▶ NOUN **1** = **lawfulness**, legality, goodness, righteousness, virtue, virtuousness, integrity, rectitude, propriety, justice, justness, fairness, equity, equitableness.

2 = **prerogative**, privilege, authority, power, licence, permission, entitlement.
▶ VERB = **put to rights**, sort out, straighten out, rectify, fix, put in order, repair.

righteous ADJ = **good**, virtuous, upright, moral, ethical, law-abiding, honest, honourable, pure, noble, God-fearing. **Opposites:** sinful.

rigid ADJ **1** = **stiff**, hard, taut, inflexible, unbendable, unbending, unyielding, inelastic, non-pliant. **2** = **strict**, severe, stern, stringent, rigorous, austere, spartan, harsh, inflexible, intransigent, uncompromising. **Opposites:** flexible.

rigorous ADJ **1** = **meticulous**, painstaking, thorough, laborious, scrupulous, conscientious, nice, exact, precise, accurate. **2** = **harsh**, severe, bad, bleak, extreme, inclement. **Opposites:** slapdash, mild.

rim NOUN = **brim**, edge, lip, circumference, border, verge, margin, brink.

rind NOUN = **outer layer**, peel, skin, husk, crust.

ring[1] NOUN 1 = **band**, circle, loop, circuit, halo, disc, round. **2** = **arena**, enclosure, area. **3** = **gang**, syndicate, cartel, association, league.
▶ VERB = **circle**, encircle, circumscribe, encompass, loop, gird, enclose, surround, hem in, fence in, seal off.

ring[2] NOUN 1 = **ringing**, tolling, peal, pealing, knell, chime, clang, tinkle. **2** = **call**, telephone call, phone call; [inf] phone, buzz.
▶ VERB 1 = **toll**, peal, sound, chime, ding, ding-dong, clang, tinkle. **2** = **call**, telephone, phone; [inf] buzz.

rinse VERB = **wash**, wash out, clean, sluice, flush, drench.

riot NOUN = **street fight**, commotion, disturbance, uproar, tumult, melee, scuffle, fracas, fray, brawl, free-for-all, uprising, insurrection.
▶ VERB = **run riot**, rampage, go on the rampage, run wild/amok, go berserk, fight, brawl, take to the streets.

riotous ADJ 1 = **disorderly**, uncontrollable, ungovernable, unmanageable, rowdy, wild, violent, brawling, lawless, anarchic, rebellious, mutinous. **2** = **loud**, noisy, boisterous, uproarious, rollicking, orgiastic. **3** = **hilarious**, funny, uproarious, side-splitting.
Opposites: peaceable.

ripe ADJ 1 = **mature**, developed, full grown, ready to eat, ready, mellow, seasoned, tempered. **2** = **ready**, fit, suitable, right.
Opposites: immature.

ripen VERB = **mature**, come to maturity, develop, mellow.

riposte NOUN = **retort**, rejoinder, reply, response, sally; [inf] comeback.

rise VERB 1 = **arise**, come/ go up, move up, ascend,

climb up. **2 = rise up**, tower, soar, loom, rear up. **3 = go up**, get higher, increase, soar, rocket, escalate. **4 = stand up**, get to one's feet, get up, jump up. **5 = get up**, get out of bed, wake up, surface.
Opposites: fall.
▸ NOUN **1 = incline**, elevation, slope, acclivity, rising ground, hillock, hill. **2 = increase**, escalation, upsurge, upswing.

risk NOUN **1 = chance**, possibility. **2 = danger**, peril, jeopardy.
Opposites: impossibility, safety.
▸ VERB **1 = put at risk**, endanger, imperil, jeopardize. **2 = take the risk of**, chance, venture. **3 = bet**, gamble, hazard, chance, venture.

risky ADJ **= dangerous**, hazardous, perilous, unsafe, precarious, touch-and-go, tricky, uncertain; [inf] chancy, dicey; [Brit. inf] dodgy.

rite NOUN **= ritual**, ceremony, ceremonial, observance, service, sacrament, celebration, performance, act, practice, tradition, convention, formality, procedure, usage.

rival NOUN **= opponent**, opposition, adversary, antagonist, contestant, competitor, challenger, contender.
Opposites: ally.
▸ VERB **= compete with**, vie with, match, equal, emulate, measure up to, compare with, parallel.
▸ ADJ **= opposing**, competing, in competition, contending, in conflict, conflicting.

rivalry NOUN **= opposition**, competition, competitiveness, vying, contention, conflict.

road NOUN **= street**, thoroughfare, highway.

roam VERB **= wander**, rove, ramble, meander, drift, range, travel, walk, tramp, traverse, trek, peregrinate.

roar VERB **= bellow**, yell, bawl, shout, howl, thunder, shriek, scream, cry, bay.

r

rob VERB = **steal from**, burgle, burglarize, hold up, break into, mug, defraud, swindle, cheat, mulct; [inf] rip off, diddle, bilk, do out of.

robber NOUN = **burglar**, thief, mugger, pilferer, housebreaker, looter, raider, bandit, brigand, pirate, highwayman.

robbery NOUN = **theft**, burglary, stealing, housebreaking, larceny, pilfering, embezzlement, misappropriation, swindling, fraud, mugging, hold-up, break-in, raid; [inf] filching.

robe NOUN 1 = **vestment**, habit, costume, gown. 2 = **dressing gown**, housecoat, wrapper, peignoir.

robust ADJ = **sturdy**, tough, rugged, strong, healthy, vigorous, hale and hearty, muscular, powerful, strapping, burly. Opposites: weak.

rock¹ VERB 1 = **move to and fro**, swing, sway, roll, lurch, pitch. 2 = **stun**, shock, stagger, astound, astonish, dumbfound, shake, take aback.

rock² NOUN = **boulder**, stone.

rocky¹ ADJ = **rock-strewn**, stony, pebbly, rough.

rocky² ADJ = **unsteady**, unstable, shaky, tottering, teetering, wobbly. Opposites: steady, stable.

rod NOUN = **bar**, stick, pole, baton, staff.

rogue NOUN = **villain**, scoundrel, rascal, reprobate, swindler, fraudster, cheat, deceiver, confidence trickster, charlatan, mountebank, sharper, wretch, ne'er-do-well, wastrel, good-for-nothing, crook; [inf, dated] rotter, bounder; [dated] cad; [archaic] blackguard.

role NOUN 1 = **part**, character, representation, portrayal. 2 = **capacity**, function, position, place, situation, job, post, task.

roll VERB 1 = **go round**, turn, turn round, rotate, revolve, spin, whirl, wheel. 2 = **furl**, coil, fold.

3 = **pass**, go, flow, travel.
4 = **flatten**, level, smooth, even, press down, crush.
▶ NOUN **1** = **turn**, rotation, revolution, spin, whirl.
2 = **spool**, reel, bobbin, cylinder. **3** = **register**, list, file, index, roster, directory, catalogue.

romance NOUN **1** = **fantasy**, fancy, whimsy, fabrication, glamour, mystery, legend, fairy tale, idyll. **2** = **love affair**, affair, liaison, attachment, intrigue, courtship, amour.

romantic ADJ **1** = **loving**, amorous, passionate, fond, tender, sentimental, sloppy; [inf] mushy; [Brit. inf] soppy. **2** = **unrealistic**, idealistic, visionary, utopian, starry-eyed, optimistic, hopeful.
3 = **fascinating**, mysterious, glamorous, exotic, exciting.
Opposites: unsentimental.
▶ NOUN = **dreamer**, visionary, idealist, utopian.
Opposites: realist.

room NOUN **1** = **space**, area, territory, expanse, extent, volume, elbow room.
2 = **scope**, capacity, margin, leeway, latitude, occasion, opportunity.

roomy ADJ = **spacious**, commodious, capacious, voluminous, ample, generous, sizeable, large, broad, wide, extensive.
Opposites: cramped.

root NOUN **1** = **rootstock**, tuber, tap root; [Botany] rhizome, radicle.
2 = **source**, origin, starting point, basis, foundation, beginnings, seat, cause, reason, rationale, occasion; [formal] radix.
▶ VERB = **take root**, grow roots, become established, set.

rope NOUN = **cord**, cable, line, strand, hawser.

roster NOUN = **list**, listing, rota, roll, register, schedule, agenda, calendar, directory, index, table.

rot VERB **1** = **decompose**, decay, crumble, disintegrate, corrode, perish. **2** = **go bad**, spoil,

r

rotary

go sour, putrefy, fester;
[inf] go off.
▶ NOUN **1** = **decomposition**,
decay, disintegration,
corrosion, putrefaction,
mould, blight.
2 = **rubbish**, nonsense,
claptrap, drivel; [inf] bosh,
twaddle, poppycock,
guff, tosh; [Brit.
inf] codswallop; [inf,
dated] bunkum, bunk.

rotary ADJ = **rotating**,
rotational, revolving,
turning, gyrating,
gyratory, spinning,
whirling.

rotate VERB **1** = **go round**,
move round, turn,
revolve, spin, whirl,
swivel, reel, wheel,
gyrate. **2** = **alternate**, take
turns, take in turn.

rotten ADJ **1** = **bad**, off,
mouldy, mouldering,
spoiled, tainted, sour,
rancid, rank, decaying,
decomposed, putrid,
putrescent, festering,
fetid, stinking. **2** = **nasty**,
foul, mean, bad, dirty,
filthy, contemptible,
despicable.
Opposites: fresh, kind.

rough ADJ **1** = **uneven**,
irregular, bumpy, broken,
stony, rugged, craggy,
lumpy, nodulous.
2 = **boisterous**, rowdy,
disorderly, wild, violent,
savage. **3** = **turbulent**,
tumultuous, choppy.
4 = **stormy**, squally, wild,
tempestuous, wintry.
5 = **coarse**, crude,
uncouth, vulgar,
unrefined, loutish,
boorish, churlish,
brutish, ill-mannered,
unmannerly, impolite,
discourteous, uncivil.
6 = **harsh**, severe, hard,
tough, difficult,
unpleasant, disagreeable,
nasty, cruel. **7** = **rough
and ready**, hasty, quick,
cursory, crude,
incomplete, rudimentary,
basic. **8** = **approximate**,
inexact, imprecise, vague,
hazy. **9** = **ill**, sick, unwell,
unhealthy, below par;
[Brit.] off colour.
Opposites: smooth, exact.

round ADJ **1** = **circular**,
ring-shaped, cycloid,
discoid, disk-like,
cylindrical, spherical,
spheroid, ball-shaped,

globe-like, convex, curved. **2** = **well rounded**, ample, rotund, chubby, buxom, roly-poly, tubby, portly, stout, corpulent, fat, obese; [Brit. inf] podgy.
▶ NOUN **1** = **succession**, sequence, series, cycle. **2** = **circuit**, course, beat, routine, schedule. **3** = **stage**, level, division, lap, heat.
▶ VERB = **go round**, travel round, sail round, circumnavigate.

roundabout ADJ = **indirect**, circuitous, meandering, winding, tortuous, discursive, oblique, circumlocutory, periphrastic.
Opposites: direct.

rouse VERB **1** = **wake**, wake up, rise, call, get up. **2** = **stir up**, excite, incite, egg on, induce, impel, inflame, agitate, whip up, galvanize, stimulate.
Opposites: calm, pacify.

rout VERB = **defeat**, trounce, worst, conquer, subjugate, overthrow, crush, beat; [inf] lick, thrash, give someone a pasting.

Opposites: victory.
route NOUN = **course**, way, itinerary, road, path.
routine NOUN **1** = **pattern**, procedure, practice, custom, habit, programme, schedule, formula, method, system, order. **2** = **act**, performance, piece; [inf] spiel.
▶ ADJ = **usual**, normal, everyday, workaday, common, ordinary, typical, customary, habitual, scheduled, conventional, standard.
Opposites: unusual.

row¹ NOUN = **line**, column, queue, procession, chain, string; [Brit. inf] crocodile.
row² NOUN **1** = **argument**, dispute, disagreement, falling-out, controversy, quarrel, squabble, fight, conflict, altercation, wrangle; [inf] set-to, tiff. **2** = **noise**, din, clamour, commotion, rumpus, uproar, tumult, hubbub, pandemonium.

rowdy ADJ = **unruly**, disorderly, noisy, boisterous, loud, obstreperous, wild,

rough, unrestrained, lawless.
Opposites: quiet.

royal ADJ = **kingly**, queenly, kinglike, queenlike, princely, regal, monarchical, sovereign.

rub VERB 1 = **massage**, knead, stroke, caress, fondle. 2 = **scrub**, scour, wipe, clean.
■ **rub out** = **erase**, wipe off, efface, obliterate, expunge, remove.

rubbish NOUN 1 = **waste**, refuse, litter, lumber, junk, debris, detritus, dross, rubble, sweepings, leavings, dregs, offscourings; [N. Amer.] garbage, trash. 2 = See **nonsense**.

rude ADJ 1 = **ill-mannered**, bad-mannered, mannerless, impolite, discourteous, impertinent, insolent, impudent, cheeky, uncivil, disrespectful, churlish, curt, brusque, blunt, offhand, short, offensive. 2 = **vulgar**, coarse, indelicate, smutty, dirty, naughty, risqué, ribald, bawdy, licentious; [inf] blue. 3 = **primitive**, crude, rudimentary, rough, rough-hewn, simple.
Opposites: polite.

rudimentary ADJ 1 = **elementary**, basic, fundamental, introductory, early, primitive, crude, rough, simple. 2 = **undeveloped**, immature, incomplete, vestigial.

rudiments PL NOUN = **basics**, fundamentals, beginnings, elements, essentials, foundation; [inf] nuts and bolts.

rueful ADJ = **regretful**, apologetic, sorry, remorseful, contrite, repentant, penitent, woebegone, woeful, plaintive.

ruffle VERB 1 = **rumple**, dishevel, tousle, disarrange, discompose, disorder, derange, tangle, mess up; [inf] muss up. 2 = **fluster**, agitate, harass, upset, disturb, discompose, perturb, unsettle, disconcert, worry, alarm, trouble,

confuse, rattle, shake up.
Opposites: smooth,
soothe.

rugged ADJ 1 = **rough**,
uneven, irregular,
bumpy, rocky, stony,
broken up, jagged,
craggy. 2 = **wrinkled**,
furrowed, lined, gnarled,
weather-beaten, leathery.
3 = **tough**, hardy, robust,
sturdy, strong, vigorous,
stalwart, hale and hearty,
muscular, brawny.
Opposites: smooth,
flimsy.

ruin NOUN 1 = **destruction**,
devastation, wreckage,
demolition,
disintegration, decay,
disrepair. 2 = **ruination**,
loss, failure, bankruptcy,
insolvency, penury,
impoverishment,
indigence, destitution,
calamity, disaster.
▶ VERB 1 = **destroy**,
devastate, lay waste, raze,
demolish, damage, spoil,
wreak havoc on.
2 = **bankrupt**, make
insolvent, impoverish,
pauperize.
Opposites: save.

ruined ADJ = **in ruins**,
ruinous, dilapidated,
decaying, in disrepair,
derelict, ramshackle,
decrepit.

ruinous ADJ
1 = **disastrous**,
devastating, calamitous,
catastrophic, cataclysmic,
dire, injurious,
damaging, crippling.
2 = *see* **ruined**.

rule NOUN 1 = **ruling**, law,
regulation, statute,
ordinance, tenet, order,
decree, commandment,
directive. 2 = **principle**,
precept, standard, axiom,
maxim. 3 = **government**,
administration,
jurisdiction, reign,
authority, control,
direction, mastery,
leadership, command.
▶ VERB 1 = **preside over**,
govern, control,
dominate, direct,
administer, manage,
regulate. 2 = **order**,
decree, direct,
pronounce, make a
judgement, judge,
adjudge, adjudicate, lay
down, decide, determine,
resolve, settle, establish.

r

■ **rule out** = *see* **exclude**
(2).

ruling NOUN = **judgement**, adjudication, finding, verdict, resolution, decree, pronouncement.

rumour NOUN = **report**, story, whisper, word, news, tidings, gossip, hearsay, talk.
▶ VERB = **say**, report.

run VERB **1** = **race**, rush, hasten, hurry, dash, sprint, bolt, dart, gallop, career along, tear along, charge along, speed along, jog along; [inf] scoot, hare, step on it, hotfoot it. **2** = **move**, go, get along, travel. **3** = **glide**, course, roll, slide. **4** = **operate**, be in operation, be valid, be current, continue. **5** = **go**, continue, proceed, extend, stretch. **6** = **flow**, issue, stream, pour, gush, cascade, spurt, jet, trickle, leak. **7** = **own**, operate, conduct, carry on, direct, manage, administer, be in charge of, control, head, lead, look after, organize, coordinate, supervise, superintend, oversee.
▶ NOUN **1** = **jog**, sprint, dash, gallop, canter, headlong rush, scamper. **2** = **drive**, ride, trip, outing, excursion, jaunt, short journey; [inf] spin.
3 = **spell**, stretch, streak, chain, string, round, cycle, sequence, series, succession.

■ **run after** = *see* **pursue**
(1).

■ **run into** = *see* **meet** (1).

runner NOUN **1** = **racer**, sprinter, hurdler, harrier, jogger, athlete.
2 = **branch**, shoot, offshoot, tendril.

rupture NOUN = **break**, fracture, crack, split, burst, rent, tear, rift, fissure.
▶ VERB **1** = **break**, fracture, crack, split, breach, burst, rend, tear, puncture.
2 = **sever**, cut off, break off, disrupt, breach.

rural ADJ = **country**, rustic, bucolic, pastoral, agricultural, agrarian, Arcadian.
Opposites: urban.

rush VERB = **hurry**, hasten, run, race, dash, sprint,

bolt, dart, gallop, career, tear, charge, speed, scurry, scamper; [inf] step on it, get a move on, hotfoot it.
Opposites: dawdle.
▶ NOUN **1** = **onslaught**, attack, assault, charge. **2** = **surge**, flow, gush, stream, flood. **3** = **hurry**, haste, speed, swiftness, rapidity, dispatch.

rushed ADJ = **hurried**, hasty, speedy, quick, fast, swift, rapid, expeditious, prompt.

rustle VERB **1** = **swish**, whisper, whoosh. **2** = **steal**, purloin, plunder, abduct, kidnap; [inf] filch.

rusty ADJ **1** = **rusted**, corroded, oxidized.

2 = **weak**, below par, unpractised, out of practice, neglected, not what it was.

rut NOUN **1** = **furrow**, groove, track, crack, hollow, hole, pothole. **2** = **humdrum existence**, routine job, boring routine, treadmill, dead end.

ruthless ADJ = **merciless**, pitiless, relentless, unrelenting, remorseless, unforgiving, unsparing, inexorable, implacable, heartless, unfeeling, hard, harsh, severe, grim, cruel, vicious, brutal, barbarous, callous, savage, fierce, ferocious.
Opposites: compassionate.

r

Ss

sabotage NOUN = **damage**, destruction, vandalism, disruption, ruining, wrecking.
▶ VERB = **damage**, destroy, wreck, ruin, impair, incapacitate, cripple, vandalize, disrupt; [Brit.] throw a spanner in the works; [inf] foul up.

sack NOUN 1 = **bag**, pack. 2 = **dismissal**, discharge, redundancy; [inf] the boot, the chop, the axe; [Brit. inf] the push.
▶ VERB 1 = **discharge**, dismiss, declare redundant; [inf] kick out, give someone their marching orders, boot out, give someone the sack/boot/chop/axe, give someone the old heave-ho; [Brit. inf] give someone the push, give someone their cards. 2 = *See* **plunder** VERB.

sacred ADJ 1 = **holy**, blessed, blest, hallowed, consecrated, sanctified. 2 = **religious**, spiritual, devotional, church, churchly, ecclesiastical.
Opposites: profane.

sacrifice NOUN 1 = **giving up**, renunciation, abandonment, surrender, relinquishment, yielding, ceding, forfeiture. 2 = **offering**, gifts, oblation.
▶ VERB 1 = **give up**, forgo, renounce, abandon, surrender, relinquish, yield, cede, forfeit. 2 = **offer up**, offer, immolate.

sacrilege NOUN = **desecration**, profanity, blasphemy, impiety, irreverence, irreligion, godlessness, disrespect.
Opposites: piety.

sad ADJ **1** = **unhappy**, miserable, sorrowful, gloomy, melancholy, blue, mournful, woebegone, wretched, dejected, downcast, despondent, in low spirits, low-spirited, low, downhearted, depressed, doleful, glum, cheerless, dispirited, disconsolate, heartbroken, broken-hearted, sick at heart, grief-stricken, grieving; [inf] down, down in the dumps, down in the mouth, in the pits.
2 = **unfortunate**, unhappy, sorrowful, miserable, sorry, depressing, upsetting, distressing, dispiriting, heartbreaking, heart-rending, pitiful, pitiable, grievous, tragic, disastrous, calamitous.
3 = **sorry**, wretched, deplorable, lamentable, regrettable, unfortunate, pitiful, pitiable, pathetic, shameful, disgraceful.
Opposites: happy.

sadden VERB = **cast down**, deject, depress, dishearten, dispirit, dampen someone's spirits, cast a gloom upon, desolate, upset, distress, grieve, break someone's heart, make someone's heart bleed.
Opposites: cheer.

sadness NOUN = **unhappiness**, misery, sorrow, gloom, melancholy, wretchedness, dejection, despondency, low spirits, depression, dolefulness, glumness, cheerlessness, disconsolateness, broken-heartedness, heartache, grief.
Opposites: happiness.

safe ADJ **1** = **safe and sound**, secure, protected, sheltered, guarded, defended, free from harm/danger, out of harm's way.
2 = **unharmed**, all right, alive and well, well, unhurt, uninjured, unscathed, undamaged, out of danger; [inf] OK, out of the woods.
3 = **cautious**, circumspect, prudent, unadventurous, conservative, timid, unenterprising.

s

4 = **harmless**, innocuous, non-toxic, non-poisonous, wholesome.
Opposites: dangerous.

▶ NOUN = **strongbox**, safety-deposit box, safe-deposit box, cash box, repository, depository, locker, vault, crypt.

safeguard NOUN = **protection**, defence, preventive, precaution, security, surety.

▶ VERB = **protect**, look after, defend, guard, preserve, secure.
Opposites: endanger.

safety NOUN **1** = **safeness**, security, secureness, soundness, impregnability. **2** = **reliability**, dependability, responsibility, trustworthiness. **3** = **shelter**, sanctuary, refuge.

sag VERB = **sink**, subside, slump, curve down.

saga NOUN = **epic**, chronicle, legend, history, romance.

sail VERB **1** = **cruise**, ride the waves, go by water, go on a sea voyage, voyage. **2** = **set sail**, embark, put to sea, leave port/dock, raise sail, put off, shove off. **3** = **steer**, captain, pilot, navigate.

sailor NOUN = **seaman**, seafarer, mariner, salt, sea dog, boatman, yachtsman/woman; [Brit. inf] matelot; [inf, dated] tar, Jack Tar.

saintly ADJ = **saintlike**, sainted, holy, godly, pious, God-fearing, religious, devout, blessed, virtuous, righteous, good, innocent, sinless, blameless, pure, angelic.
Opposites: ungodly.

sake NOUN = **well-being**, welfare, behalf, benefit, advantage, interest, gain, profit, consideration, regard, concern, account, respect.

salary NOUN = **pay**, wages, earnings, remuneration, fee, emolument, stipend, honorarium.

sale NOUN = **selling**, marketing, trade, traffic, vending, bargaining.

■ **on sale** = **for sale**, in stock, on the market, purchasable, available, obtainable.

salubrious ADJ = **healthy**, health-giving, beneficial, good for one's health, wholesome, salutary, refreshing, invigorating, bracing.
Opposites: unhealthy.

salute NOUN **1** = **greeting**, salutation, address, welcome. **2** = **tribute**, testimonial, honour, homage, recognition, acknowledgement.
▶ VERB **1** = **greet**, address, hail, acknowledge, pay one's respects to. **2** = **pay tribute to**, pay homage to, honour, recognize, acknowledge; [inf] take one's hat off to.

salvage NOUN **1** = **rescue**, saving, recovery, reclamation, salvation. **2** = **waste material**, scrap, remains.
▶ VERB = **rescue**, save, recover, retrieve, reclaim, get back.

salvation NOUN = **redemption**, deliverance, saving, rescue.
Opposites: damnation, destruction.

same ADJ **1** = **identical**, the very same, selfsame, one and the same, the very. **2** = **exactly similar**, identical, alike, duplicate, twin, indistinguishable, interchangeable, corresponding, equivalent. **3** = **unchanging**, unchanged, unvarying, unvaried, invariable, constant, consistent, uniform.
Opposites: different.

sample NOUN **1** = **specimen**, example, instance, illustration, exemplification, representative type, model, pattern. **2** = **cross-section**, sampling, test.
▶ VERB = **try**, try out, test, examine, inspect, taste.

sanctify VERB = **consecrate**, make holy/sacred, bless, hallow, set apart, dedicate.

sanctimonious ADJ = **self-righteous**, holier-than-thou, pietistic, unctuous, smug, mealy-mouthed, hypocritical,

Pharisaic, Tartuffian;
[inf] goody-goody.

sanction NOUN
1 = authorization,
warrant, accreditation,
licence, endorsement,
permission, consent,
approval, backing,
support, seal/stamp of
approval, approbation,
acceptance; [inf] thumbs
up, go-ahead, the green
light, OK. **2 = penalty**,
punishment,
penalization, penance,
sentence.
▶ VERB **= authorize**, warrant,
accredit, license, endorse,
permit, allow, consent
to, back, support,
approve, accept; [inf] give
the thumbs up to, give
the green light to, OK.
Opposites: reject.

sanctity NOUN
1 = sacredness, holiness,
inviolability. **2 = holiness**,
godliness, saintliness,
spirituality, religiosity,
piety, devoutness,
devotion, righteousness,
goodness, virtue, purity.

sanctuary NOUN
1 = refuge, haven, shelter,
retreat, hideout, hiding

place. **2 = holy place**,
church, temple, shrine,
altar, sanctum.
3 = preserve, reserve,
wildlife reserve,
reservation. **4 = safety**,
safe keeping, protection,
shelter, security,
immunity.

sane ADJ **1 = of sound
mind**, in one's right
mind, compos mentis,
rational, lucid, in
possession of one's
faculties; [inf] all there.
2 = sensible, reasonable,
balanced, judicious,
responsible, prudent,
wise, advisable.
Opposites: insane.

sanguine ADJ
= optimistic, confident,
assured, hopeful,
buoyant, cheerful,
spirited.
Opposites: gloomy.

sanitary ADJ **= hygienic**,
clean, germ-free,
antiseptic, aseptic, sterile,
unpolluted, salubrious,
healthy.

sanity NOUN **1 = saneness**,
soundness of mind,
mental health, reason,
rationality, lucidity.

2 = **sense**, sensibleness, common sense, good sense, reasonableness, rationality, soundness, judiciousness, prudence, wisdom, advisability.

sap NOUN **1** = **fluid**, moisture, juice, secretion. **2** = **vigour**, energy, vitality, vivacity, enthusiasm, spirit; [inf] pep, zip, oomph. ▸ VERB = **drain**, enervate, exhaust, weaken, enfeeble, debilitate, devitalize. = *See also* **exhaust** (1).

sarcasm NOUN = **derision**, scorn, mockery, ridicule, irony, satire, trenchancy, acerbity, asperity, mordancy, bitterness, spitefulness.

sarcastic ADJ = **derisive**, derisory, scornful, mocking, sneering, jeering, scoffing, taunting, ironic, sardonic, satirical, caustic, trenchant, acerbic, acrimonious, mordant, bitter, spiteful; [Brit. inf] sarky.

sardonic ADJ = **dry**, wry, derisory, cynical, ironic, sarcastic, caustic, trenchant, acerbic, mordant, bitter.

satanic ADJ = **diabolical**, fiendish, devilish, demonic, demoniac, demoniacal, hellish, infernal, accursed, wicked, evil, sinful, iniquitous, malevolent, vile, foul.

satire NOUN **1** = **take-off**, spoof, send-up, burlesque, parody, travesty, caricature, lampoon, pasquinade. **2** = **mockery**, ridicule, irony, sarcasm.

satirical ADJ = **mocking**, ridiculing, taunting, ironic, sarcastic, sardonic, caustic, biting, cutting.

satirize VERB = **mock**, ridicule, hold up to ridicule, take off, send up, deride, make fun of, poke fun at, parody, lampoon, burlesque, travesty, criticize, censure.

satisfaction NOUN = **fulfilment**, gratification, pleasure, enjoyment, delight, happiness, pride, comfort, content,

S

contentment, smugness.
Opposites: dissatisfaction.

satisfactory ADJ
= **adequate**, all right,
acceptable, fine, good
enough, sufficient,
competent, up to
standard, up to the mark,
up to par, up to scratch,
passable, average; [inf] OK,
okay.
Opposites: unsatisfactory.

satisfy VERB 1 = **satiate**,
sate, slake, quench.
2 = **fulfil**, gratify, appease,
assuage, meet, indulge,
content. 3 = **convince**,
persuade, assure,
reassure, remove/dispel
doubts, put someone's
mind at rest.
Opposites: frustrate.

saturate VERB = **wet
through**, wet, soak,
drench, souse, steep,
douse, permeate, imbue,
pervade, suffuse.

sauce NOUN 1 = **relish**,
dressing, condiment,
flavouring. 2 = See
insolence.

saucy ADJ = **impudent**,
cheeky, impertinent,
insolent, rude,
disrespectful, audacious,

presumptuous, bold,
brash; [inf] fresh.
Opposites: demure, polite.

saunter VERB = **stroll**,
amble, wander, meander,
walk, promenade;
[inf] mosey.

savage ADJ 1 = **vicious**,
ferocious, fierce, brutal,
cruel, bloody, murderous,
bloodthirsty, inhuman,
harsh, grim, terrible,
merciless, ruthless,
pitiless, sadistic,
barbarous. 2 = **untamed**,
wild, undomesticated,
feral. 3 = **uncivilized**,
uncultivated, barbarous,
barbaric, wild, primitive.
Opposites: mild, tame.
▶ NOUN = **barbarian**, wild
man/woman, primitive,
heathen.
▶ VERB = **maul**, lacerate,
mangle, tear to pieces,
attack.

save VERB 1 = **rescue**, free,
set free, liberate, deliver,
snatch, bail out, salvage,
redeem. 2 = **protect**,
safeguard, guard, keep,
keep safe, shield, screen,
preserve, conserve.
3 = **prevent**, obviate,
forestall, spare, make

unnecessary, rule out.
4 = put aside, set aside, put by, put away, lay by, keep, reserve, conserve, salt away, stockpile, store, hoard.

savings PL NOUN = **capital**, assets, resources, reserves, funds, nest egg.

saviour NOUN = **rescuer**, liberator, deliverer, emancipator, champion, knight in shining armour, Good Samaritan, friend in need.

savour NOUN = **taste**, flavour, tang, relish, smack, smell, aroma, fragrance.
▶ VERB = **taste**, enjoy, appreciate, delight in, take pleasure in, relish, revel in.

savoury ADJ
1 = appetizing, mouth-watering, fragrant, flavoursome, palatable, tasty, delicious, delectable, luscious, toothsome; [inf] scrumptious.
2 = salty, piquant, tangy.
Opposites: unpalatable, sweet.

say VERB **1 = mention**, voice, pronounce, put into words, give utterance to, give voice to, vocalize. **2 = state**, remark, announce, affirm, assert, maintain, declare, allege, profess, avow, opine; [inf] come out with; [formal] aver.
3 = estimate, judge, guess, hazard a guess, predict, speculate, conjecture, surmise, imagine, assume, suppose, presume. **4 = propose**, advance, bring forward, offer, introduce, adduce, plead.

saying NOUN = **proverb**, maxim, aphorism, axiom, adage, saw, epigram, dictum, gnome, apothegm, platitude, cliché.

scaffold NOUN
1 = scaffolding, frame, framework, gantry.
2 = gallows, gibbet.

scale[1] NOUN **1 = plate**, flake; [technical] lamella, lamina, squama. **2 = coating**, coat, crust, encrustation, limescale; [Brit.] fur.

S

scale² NOUN
1 = **progression**, succession, sequence, series, ranking, register, ladder, hierarchy; [inf] pecking order.
2 = **extent**, scope, range, degree, reach.
▶ VERB = **climb**, ascend, go up, clamber, mount, clamber up.
▪ **scale down** = **reduce**, cut down, cut back on, decrease, lessen, lower.

scaly ADJ = **flaky**, scurfy, rough, scabrous.

scamp NOUN = **rascal**, rogue, imp, devil, monkey, scallywag, mischief-maker, troublemaker, prankster, tyke.

scan VERB 1 = **study**, examine, scrutinize, survey, inspect, take stock of, search, scour, sweep. **2** = **skim**, look over, glance over, run one's eye over, read through, leaf through, thumb through.

scandal NOUN 1 = **disgrace**, shame, dishonour, disrepute, discredit, odium, opprobrium, censure, obloquy.
2 = **slander**, libel, calumny, defamation, aspersion, gossip, malicious rumours, dirt, muckraking, smear campaign.

scandalous ADJ
1 = **disgraceful**, shameful, dishonourable, outrageous, shocking, monstrous, disreputable, improper, unseemly, discreditable, infamous, opprobrious.
2 = **slanderous**, libellous, defamatory, scurrilous, malicious, gossiping.

scant ADJ = **little**, minimal, limited, insufficient, inadequate, deficient.
Opposites: abundant.

scanty ADJ = **meagre**, scant, sparse, small, paltry, slender, negligible, skimpy, thin, poor, insufficient, inadequate, deficient, limited, restricted, exiguous.
Opposites: ample, copious.

scapegoat NOUN
= **whipping boy**, Aunt Sally; [inf] fall guy;

[N. Amer. inf] patsy.

scar NOUN **1 = mark**, blemish, blotch, discoloration, cicatrix, disfigurement, defacement. **2 = damage**, trauma, shock, injury, suffering, upset.

▶ VERB **1 = mark**, blemish, blotch, discolour, disfigure, deface. **2 = damage**, traumatize, shock, injure, upset.

scarce ADJ **1 = in short supply**, short, meagre, scant, scanty, sparse, paltry, not enough, too little, insufficient, deficient, inadequate, lacking, at a premium, exiguous. **2 = rare**, infrequent, few and far between, seldom seen/found, sparse, uncommon, unusual. **Opposites**: plentiful, abundant.

scarcely ADV **= hardly**, barely, only just.

scarcity NOUN **1 = dearth**, shortage, undersupply, paucity, meagreness, sparseness, insufficiency, deficiency, inadequacy, lack, exiguity. **2 = rarity**, rareness, infrequency, sparseness, uncommonness.

scare VERB **= frighten**, alarm, startle, make fearful, make nervous, terrify, terrorize, petrify, horrify, appal, shock, intimidate, daunt, awe, cow, panic, put the fear of God into, scare stiff, make someone's blood run cold, make someone's flesh creep, make someone's hair stand on end; [inf] scare the pants off; [Brit. inf] put the wind up.

▶ NOUN **= fright**, alarm, start, fearfulness, nervousness, terror, horror, shock, panic.

scathing ADJ **= virulent**, savage, fierce, ferocious, brutal, stinging, biting, mordant, trenchant, caustic, vitriolic, withering, scornful, harsh, severe, stern. **Opposites**: mild.

scatter VERB **1 = disseminate**, diffuse, spread, sow, sprinkle, strew, broadcast, fling, toss, throw. **2 = break up**,

S

disperse, disband,
separate, dissolve.
Opposites: gather,
assemble.

scavenge VERB = **search**,
look for, hunt, forage for,
rummage for.

scenario NOUN = **plot**,
outline, synopsis,
summary, precis,
rundown, storyline,
structure, scheme, plan,
sequence of events.

scene NOUN 1 = **place**,
location, site, position,
spot, setting, locale,
whereabouts, arena,
stage. 2 = **event**, incident,
happening, situation,
episode, affair, moment,
proceeding. 3 = **fuss**,
exhibition, outburst,
commotion, to-do, row,
upset, tantrum, furore,
brouhaha.

scenery NOUN 1 = **view**,
outlook, landscape, vista,
panorama, prospect.
2 = **set**, stage set, setting,
background, backdrop.

scenic ADJ = **picturesque**,
pretty, beautiful,
pleasing.

scent NOUN 1 = **aroma**,
perfume, fragrance,

smell, bouquet, odour;
[poetic/literary] redolence.
2 = **track**, trail, spoor.

sceptic NOUN
= **questioner**, doubter,
agnostic, unbeliever,
doubting Thomas,
disbeliever, dissenter,
scoffer, cynic.

sceptical ADJ = **doubting**,
doubtful, dubious,
questioning, distrustful,
mistrustful, suspicious,
hesitant, disbelieving,
misbelieving,
incredulous,
unconvinced, scoffing,
cynical.
Opposites: certain,
convinced.

scepticism NOUN = **doubt**,
doubtfulness, dubiety,
agnosticism, distrust,
mistrust, suspicion,
hesitancy, disbelief,
misbelief, incredulity,
cynicism.

schedule NOUN = **plan**,
scheme, timetable,
programme, diary,
calendar, itinerary,
agenda.
▶ VERB = **arrange**, timetable,
organize, plan,
programme, book.

scheme NOUN 1 = **plan**, programme, project, course of action, system, procedure, strategy, design, tactics, contrivance.
2 = **arrangement**, system, organization, disposition, schema. 3 = **plot**, ruse, ploy, stratagem, manoeuvre, machinations, intrigue, conspiracy; [inf] game, racket.
▶ VERB = **plot**, conspire, intrigue, manoeuvre, plan, lay plans.

scheming ADJ = **calculating**, designing, conniving, wily, crafty, cunning, sly, artful, slippery, underhand, duplicitous, devious, Machiavellian; [inf] tricky.
Opposites: ingenuous, honest.

schism NOUN = **division**, breach, split, rift, break, rupture, separation, severance, detachment, discord, disagreement.

scholar NOUN = **man/ woman of letters**, learned person, academic, highbrow, intellectual, pundit, savant; [inf] bookworm, egghead.

scholarly ADJ = **learned**, erudite, academic, well read, intellectual, highbrow, scholastic, literary, studious, bookish, lettered.
Opposites: ignorant.

scholarship NOUN
1 = **learning**, knowledge, education, erudition, letters. 2 = **grant**, fellowship, endowment; [Brit.] bursary.

school NOUN
1 = **educational institution**, academy.
2 = **school of thought**, outlook, persuasion, opinion, point of view, belief, faith, creed.
▶ VERB = **educate**, teach, instruct, train, coach, drill, discipline, direct, guide, prepare, prime, verse.

scientific ADJ
= **systematic**, methodical, orderly, regulated, controlled, exact, precise, mathematical.

scintillating ADJ
= **sparkling**, dazzling,

vivacious, effervescent, lively, animated, ebullient, bright, brilliant, witty, exciting, stimulating, invigorating. **Opposites:** dull, boring.

scoff VERB = **jeer at**, mock at, sneer at, gibe at, taunt, laugh at, ridicule, poke fun at, make a fool of, make sport of, rag, revile, deride, belittle, scorn, knock; [inf] pooh-pooh.

scold VERB = *see* **reprimand** VERB.

scoop NOUN 1 = **ladle**, spoon, dipper.
2 = **exclusive story**, revelation, exposé.
■ **scoop out** = **hollow out**, gouge out, dig, excavate.
■ **scoop up** = **gather up**, pick up, lift.

scope NOUN 1 = **extent**, range, sphere, area, field, realm, compass, orbit, reach, span, sweep, confine, limit.
2 = **opportunity**, freedom, latitude, capacity.

scorch VERB = **burn**, singe, char, sear, discolour, blacken.

score NOUN 1 = **number of points/goals**, total, result, outcome.
2 = **notch**, mark, scratch, scrape, groove, cut, nick, chip, gouge.
▶ VERB 1 = **win**, gain, achieve, chalk up, notch up.
2 = **make a notch in**, mark, scratch, scrape, groove, cut, nick, chip, gouge.

scorn NOUN = **contempt**, contemptuousness, disdain, haughtiness, disparagement, derision, mockery, contumely. **Opposites:** praise.
▶ VERB 1 = **be contemptuous**, hold in contempt, look down on, disdain, disparage, slight, deride, mock, scoff at, sneer at.
2 = **rebuff**, spurn, shun, refuse, reject, turn down.

scornful ADJ = **contemptuous**, disdainful, haughty, supercilious, disparaging, slighting, scathing, derisive, mocking, scoffing, sneering, contumelious. **Opposites:** respectful.

scoundrel NOUN = **villain**, rogue, rascal, miscreant, reprobate, scapegrace, good-for-nothing, ne'er-do-well, wastrel; [dated] cad; [inf, dated] rotter, bounder.

scour[1] VERB = **scrub**, rub, clean, cleanse, abrade, wash, wipe, polish, buff, burnish.

scour[2] VERB = **search**, comb, go over, look all over, ransack, hunt through, rake through, rummage through, leave no stone unturned.

scourge NOUN = **bane**, curse, affliction, plague, trial, torment, torture, suffering, burden, cross to bear, thorn in one's flesh/side, nuisance, pest, punishment, penalty.

scout NOUN = **lookout**, outrider, spy.
▶ VERB = **reconnoitre**, make a reconnaissance of, spy out, survey, inspect, investigate, examine, scan.

scowl VERB = **frown**, glower, glare, lower, look daggers.
Opposites: smile.

▶ NOUN = **frown**, glower, glare, black look, dirty look.

scraggy ADJ = *see* **scrawny**.

scramble VERB
1 = **clamber**, climb, crawl.
2 = **hurry**, hasten, rush, race, scurry. 3 = **mix up**, jumble, tangle, throw into confusion, disorganize.
▶ NOUN 1 = **clamber**, climb, trek. 2 = **hurry**, rush, race, scurry.

scrap NOUN 1 = **fragment**, piece, bit, snippet, remnant, leftover, tatter, morsel, particle, sliver.
2 = **waste**, junk, rubbish.
▶ VERB = **throw away**, get rid of, discard, toss out, abandon, jettison, dispense with, shed; [inf] ditch, junk.
Opposites: keep, preserve.

scrape VERB 1 = **scour**, rub, scrub, abrade, remove, erase, grate, rasp, grind, file, sandpaper. 2 = **graze**, scratch, skin, cut, lacerate, bark.
▶ NOUN = **graze**, scratch, abrasion, cut, laceration,

wound.

scratch VERB = **scrape**, abrade, graze, score, cut, lacerate.

▶ NOUN = **scrape**, abrasion, graze, cut, laceration, wound, mark, line.

scream VERB = **shriek**, howl, shout, cry out, call out, yell, screech, wail, squawk, bawl; [inf] holler.

▶ NOUN = **shriek**, howl, shout, yell, cry, screech, wail, squawk.

screen NOUN **1** = **shield**, protection, shelter, guard, safeguard, buffer. **2** = **cover**, cloak, veil, mask, camouflage, disguise, facade, front, blind. **3** = **sieve**, riddle, strainer, colander, filter.

▶ VERB **1** = **partition off**, divide off, conceal, hide. **2** = **shelter**, shield, protect, guard, safeguard. **3** = **vet**, check, test, examine, investigate, scan.

scribble VERB = **dash off**, jot down, scrawl.

scrimp VERB = **skimp**, economize, be frugal, be thrifty, husband one's resources, tighten one's

belt, draw in one's horns.

script NOUN **1** = **handwriting**, writing, hand, pen, calligraphy. **2** = **text**, book, libretto, score, lines, words, manuscript.

scrounge VERB = **beg**, borrow; [inf] sponge, cadge, bum; [N. Amer. inf] mooch.

scrounger NOUN = **beggar**, borrower, parasite; [inf] sponger, cadger, freeloader.

scrub VERB = **rub**, scour, clean, cleanse, wash, wipe.

scruffy ADJ = **untidy**, unkempt, dishevelled, ungroomed, ill-groomed, shabby, down at heel, ragged, tattered, slovenly, messy, slatternly, sluttish.

Opposites: smart.

scruple VERB = **have qualms about**, hesitate to, think twice about, balk at, demur about, be reluctant to, recoil from, shrink from, waver about, vacillate about.

scruples PL NOUN = **qualms**, compunction,

hesitation, second thoughts, doubt, misgivings, uneasiness, reluctance, restraint, wavering, vacillation.

scrupulous ADJ
1 = **meticulous**, careful, painstaking, thorough, rigorous, strict, conscientious, punctilious, exact, precise, fastidious.
2 = **honest**, honourable, upright, righteous, right-minded, moral, ethical.
Opposites: careless, unscrupulous.

scrutinize VERB
= **examine**, study, inspect, survey, scan, look over, investigate, go over, peruse, probe, inquire into, sift, analyse, dissect.

scrutiny NOUN
= **examination**, study, inspection, perusal, investigation, exploration, probe, inquiry, analysis, dissection.

sculpture NOUN = **statue**, statuette, bust, figure, figurine.

▶ VERB = **sculpt**, chisel, model, fashion, shape, cast, carve, cut, hew.

scum NOUN **1** = **film**, crust, algae, filth, dirt.
2 = **lowest of the low**, dregs of society, riff-raff, rabble.

scupper VERB **1** = **sink**, submerge. **2** = **ruin**, defeat, demolish, wreck, smash.

scurrilous ADJ = **abusive**, insulting, offensive, disparaging, defamatory, slanderous, gross, foul, scandalous.

scurry VERB = **hurry**, hasten, make haste, rush, race, dash, run, sprint, scuttle, scamper, scramble.

seal NOUN **1** = **emblem**, symbol, insignia, badge, crest, token, mark, monogram. **2** = **sealant**, sealer, adhesive.
▶ VERB **1** = **fasten**, secure, shut, close up. **2** = **make airtight**, make watertight, close, shut, cork, stopper.
3 = **secure**, clinch, settle, decide, complete.
■ **seal off** = **close off**, shut off, cordon off, fence off.

S

seam NOUN 1 = **joint**, join, junction. 2 = **layer**, stratum, vein, lode.

sear VERB = **burn**, singe, scorch, char, dry up, wither, discolour, brown.

search VERB 1 = **go through**, look through, hunt through, rummage through, forage through, rifle through, scour, ransack, comb, go through with a fine-tooth comb, sift through, turn upside down, turn inside out, leave no stone unturned in.
2 = **look for**, seek, hunt for, look high and low for, cast around for, ferret about for, scout out. 3 = **examine**, inspect, check; [inf] frisk.
▶ NOUN 1 = **hunt**, rummage, forage, ransacking.
2 = **exploration**, quest, probe.

season NOUN = **period**, time, time of year, spell, term.
▶ VERB 1 = **flavour**, add flavouring to, spice, add spices to; [inf] pep up, add zing to. 2 = **mature**, age, mellow, prime, prepare.

seasonable ADJ
= **opportune**, timely, well timed, appropriate, suitable, apt.

seasoned ADJ
= **experienced**, practised, well versed, established, long-serving, veteran, hardened, battle-scarred.
Opposites: inexperienced.

seat NOUN 1 = **chair**, bench, settle, stool, stall.
2 = **headquarters**, location, site, base, centre, hub, heart.
3 = **buttocks**, rump, hindquarters;
[Brit.] bottom; [inf] behind, backside; [Brit. inf] bum; [N. Amer. inf] butt, tail, fanny; [humorous] posterior.
▶ VERB 1 = **place**, position, put, situate, deposit.
2 = **hold**, take, have room for, accommodate.

secluded ADJ = **sheltered**, concealed, hidden, private, solitary, lonely, sequestered, retired, out of the way, remote, isolated, off the beaten track, tucked away, cut-off.
Opposites: accessible.

seclusion NOUN = **privacy**, solitude, retreat, retirement, withdrawal, sequestration, isolation, concealment, hiding, secrecy.

second¹ ADJ
1 = **secondary**, lower, subordinate, lesser, lower-grade, inferior.
2 = **additional**, extra, further.
▶ NOUN = **assistant**, attendant, helper, supporter, backer, right-hand man/woman.
▶ VERB = **support**, give one's support to, back, approve, give one's approval to, endorse, promote.

second² NOUN = **moment**, instant, trice, twinkling, twinkling of an eye; [inf] sec, jiffy, tick, two shakes of a lamb's tail, two shakes.

secondary ADJ **1** = **lesser**, subordinate, minor, ancillary, subsidiary, non-essential, unimportant. **2** = **non-primary**, derived, derivative, indirect, resulting, resultant.

3 = **reserve**, back-up, relief, auxiliary, extra, alternative, subsidiary.
Opposites: primary.

second-hand ADJ = **used**, pre-owned, worn, nearly new, handed down, hand-me-down; [Brit. inf, dated] reach-me-down.
Opposites: new.
▶ ADV = **at second hand**, indirectly.
Opposites: directly.

second-rate ADJ = **second-class**, low-class, inferior, lesser, substandard, poor-quality, low-quality, low-grade, shoddy, rubbishy, tawdry.
Opposites: first-rate, excellent.

secret ADJ **1** = **confidential**, private, unrevealed, undisclosed, under wraps, unpublished, untold, unknown; [inf] hush-hush.
2 = **hidden**, concealed, camouflaged, disguised, clandestine, furtive, conspiratorial, undercover, surreptitious, stealthy, cloak-and-dagger, covert.

S

Opposites: open, obvious.

secrete¹ VERB
= **discharge**, emit, excrete, exude, ooze, leak, give off, send out.
Opposites: absorb.

secrete² VERB = **hide**, conceal, cover up, stow away, sequester, cache; [inf] stash away.
Opposites: reveal.

secretive ADJ = **secret**, reticent, uncommunicative, unforthcoming, reserved, taciturn, silent, quiet, tight-lipped, close-mouthed, close, playing one's cards close to one's chest; [inf] cagey.
Opposites: open.

secretly ADV = **in secret**, confidentially, privately, behind closed doors, in camera, sub rosa.

sectarian ADJ = **bigoted**, prejudiced, doctrinaire, partisan, narrow-minded, insular, hidebound, extreme, fanatic, fanatical.
Opposites: tolerant.

section NOUN = **part**, segment, division, department, component, piece, portion, bit, slice, fraction, fragment.

sector NOUN 1 = **part**, division, area, branch, department, category, field. 2 = **zone**, quarter, district, area, region.

secular ADJ = **lay**, non-religious, non-spiritual, non-church, laical, temporal, worldly, earthly.
Opposites: religious.

secure ADJ 1 = **safe**, free from danger, out of harm's way, invulnerable, unharmed, undamaged, protected, sheltered, shielded. 2 = **fastened**, closed, shut, locked, sealed. 3 = **stable**, fixed, steady, strong, sturdy, solid. 4 = **unworried**, at ease, comfortable, confident, assured.
Opposites: insecure.
▶ VERB 1 = **make safe**, make sound, fortify, strengthen, protect. 2 = **fasten**, close, shut, lock, bolt, chain, seal. 3 = **acquire**, obtain, gain, get, get hold of, procure, get possession of, come

by; [inf] get one's hands on, land.

sedate¹ VERB = **give a sedative to**, put under sedation, tranquillize.

sedate² ADJ 1 = **calm**, tranquil, placid, dignified, formal, decorous, proper, demure, sober, earnest, staid, stiff. 2 = **slow**, slow-moving, leisurely, measured, deliberate, dignified.
Opposites: exciting, fast.

sedative NOUN = **tranquillizer**, calmative, depressant, sleeping pill, narcotic, opiate; [inf] downer.
▸ ADJ = **calming**, tranquillizing, soothing, relaxing, assuaging, lenitive, soporific, narcotic.

sedentary ADJ = **sitting**, seated, desk-bound, desk, inactive.
Opposites: active.

sediment NOUN = **dregs**, lees, grounds, deposit, residue, precipitate, settlings.

seduce VERB 1 = **persuade to have sex**; [inf] have one's (wicked) way with, take advantage of; [dated] debauch. 2 = **attract**, lure, tempt, entice, beguile, ensnare.

seductive ADJ = **attractive**, alluring, appealing, inviting, tempting, enticing, beguiling, provocative, exciting, arousing, sexy.

see VERB 1 = **make out**, catch sight of, glimpse, spot, notice, observe, view, perceive, discern, espy, descry, distinguish, identify, recognize. 2 = **watch**, look at, view. 3 = **understand**, grasp, get, comprehend, follow, take in, know, realize, get the drift of, make out, fathom. 4 = **find out**, discover, learn, ascertain, determine, ask, enquire, make enquiries, investigate. 5 = **foresee**, predict, forecast, anticipate, envisage, picture, visualize.
▪ **see about** = **see to**, deal with, attend to, cope with, look after, take care of.

■ **see through** = not be taken in by, be wise to, get the measure of, penetrate; [inf] have someone's number.

seed NOUN 1 = **ovule**, pip, kernel, stone, germ. 2 = **source**, origin, root, cause, reason.

seek VERB 1 = **search for**, look for, be on the lookout for, be after, hunt for, be in quest of, be in pursuit of. 2 = **ask for**, request, solicit, entreat, beg for.

seem VERB = **appear**, appear to be, have the appearance of being, give the impression of being, look, look like, look to be, have the look of.

seep VERB = **ooze**, leak, exude, drip, drain, percolate.

see-saw VERB = **fluctuate**, go from one extreme to the other, swing, oscillate.

seethe VERB 1 = **boil**, bubble, fizz, foam, froth, ferment, churn. 2 = **be furious**, be livid, be incensed, storm, fume.

segment NOUN = **section**, part, division, component, piece, portion, slice, wedge.

segregate VERB = **separate**, set apart, isolate, cut off, sequester, ostracize, discriminate against.
Opposites: amalgamate.

segregation NOUN = **separation**, setting apart, isolation, dissociation, sequestration, discrimination, apartheid, partition.

seize VERB 1 = **grab**, grab hold of, take hold of, grasp, take a grip of, grip, clutch at. 2 = **confiscate**, impound, commandeer, appropriate, sequester, sequestrate. 3 = **snatch**, abduct, take captive, kidnap, hijack.

seizure NOUN 1 = **confiscation**, commandeering, appropriation, sequestration. 2 = **snatching**, abduction, kidnapping, hijacking.

seldom ADV = **rarely**, hardly ever, scarcely ever,

infrequently, only occasionally; [inf] once in a blue moon.
Opposites: frequently.

select VERB = **choose**, pick, hand-pick, single out, opt for, decide on, settle on, prefer, favour.
▶ ADJ **1** = **choice**, hand-picked, prime, first-rate, first-class, finest, best, high-quality, top-quality. **2** = **exclusive**, elite, limited, privileged, cliquey, cliquish; [Brit. inf] posh.
Opposites: inferior.

selection NOUN **1** = **choice**, pick, option. **2** = **variety**, assortment, anthology, miscellany, collection, range.

selective ADJ = **particular**, discriminating, discriminatory, discerning, fussy, careful, cautious; [inf] choosy, picky.

self-centred ADJ = **egocentric**, egotistical, self-absorbed, self-seeking, wrapped up in oneself, selfish, narcissistic.

self-confidence NOUN = **self-assurance**, confidence, self-reliance, self-dependence, self-possession, poise, aplomb, composure, sangfroid.

self-conscious ADJ = **awkward**, shy, diffident, bashful, blushing, timorous, nervous, timid, retiring, shrinking, ill at ease, embarrassed, uncomfortable.
Opposites: confident.

self-control NOUN = **self-restraint**, restraint, self-discipline, will power, strength of will.

self-important ADJ = **pompous**, vain, conceited, arrogant, swollen-headed, egotistical, presumptuous, overbearing, overweening, haughty, swaggering, strutting.
Opposites: humble.

self-indulgence NOUN = **self-gratification**, lack of self-restraint, intemperance, immoderation, excess,

S

pleasure-seeking, sensualism, dissipation.

selfish ADJ = **self-seeking**, self-centred, egocentric, egotistic, egoistic, self-interested, self-regarding, self-absorbed; [inf] looking out for number one.
Opposites: unselfish, selfless.

selfless ADJ = **unselfish**, altruistic, generous, self-sacrificing, self-denying, magnanimous, liberal, ungrudging.
Opposites: selfish.

self-respect NOUN = **self-esteem**, self-regard, pride in oneself, pride in one's abilities, belief in one's worth, faith in oneself, amour propre.

self-righteous ADJ = **sanctimonious**, pious, holier-than-thou, pietistic, too good to be true, Pharisaic, unctuous, mealy-mouthed; [inf] goody-goody.
Opposites: humble.

self-sacrifice NOUN = **self-denial**, selflessness, unselfishness, altruism.

self-seeking ADJ = **self-interested**, opportunistic, ambitious, mercenary, out for what one can get, fortune-hunting, gold-digging; [inf] on the make, looking out for number one.
Opposites: altruistic.

sell VERB 1 = **put up for sale**, put on sale, dispose of, vend, auction off, trade, barter, trade in, deal in, traffic in, stock, market, handle, peddle, hawk. 2 = **bought**, be purchased, go, move, be in demand. 3 = **retail**, go for, be, be found for. 4 = **get acceptance for**, win approval for, get support for, get across, promote.
Opposites: buy.

seller NOUN = **vendor**, retailer, salesman/woman/person, shopkeeper, trader, merchant, dealer, agent, representative, rep.

semblance NOUN = **appearance**, show, air, guise, pretence, facade, front, veneer, mask, cloak, disguise, camouflage, pretext.

send VERB 1 = **dispatch**, forward, mail, post, remit. 2 = **throw**, fling, hurl, cast, let fly, propel, project. 3 = **drive**, make, cause someone to be/ become.
Opposites: receive.

■ **send for** = **call for**, summon, request, order.

senile ADJ = **doddering**, decrepit, failing, in one's dotage, in one's second childhood; [inf] past it.

senior ADJ 1 = **high-ranking**, higher-ranking, superior. 2 = **older**, elder.
Opposites: junior.

sensation NOUN
1 = **feeling**, sense, awareness, consciousness, perception, impression.
2 = **stir**, excitement, agitation, commotion, furore, scandal.

sensational ADJ
1 = **spectacular**, stirring, exciting, startling, staggering, dramatic, amazing, shocking, scandalous, lurid.
2 = **marvellous**, superb, excellent, exceptional, remarkable; [inf] fabulous, fab, out of this world.

sense NOUN 1 = **feeling**, sensation, faculty, sensibility.
2 = **appreciation**, awareness, understanding, comprehension.
3 = **common sense**, practicality, wisdom, sagacity, sharpness, discernment, perception, wit, intelligence, cleverness, understanding, reason, logic, brains, nous.
4 = **meaning**, definition, import, signification, significance, implication, nuance, drift, gist, purport, denotation.
▶ VERB = **feel**, get the impression of, be aware of, be conscious of, observe, notice, perceive, discern, grasp, pick up, suspect, divine, intuit.

senseless ADJ
1 = **nonsensical**, stupid, foolish, silly, inane, idiotic, mindless, unintelligent, unwise, irrational, illogical, meaningless, pointless, absurd, ludicrous, fatuous, asinine,

moronic, imbecilic.
2 = unconscious, insensible, out cold, out, stunned, numb, numbed, insensate.
Opposites: wise.

sensible ADJ = **practical**, realistic, down-to-earth, wise, prudent, judicious, sagacious, shrewd, discerning, perceptive, intelligent, clever, reasonable, rational, logical.
Opposites: foolish.

sensitive ADJ **1 = delicate**, fine, soft, fragile.
2 = responsive, receptive, perceptive, discerning, discriminatory, sympathetic, understanding, empathetic.
3 = problematic, difficult, delicate, ticklish.
Opposites: resilient, impervious, uncontroversial.

■ **sensitive to** = **responsive to**, easily affected by, susceptible to, reactive to, sentient of.

sensual ADJ **1 = physical**, carnal, bodily, fleshly, animal, voluptuous, epicurean, sybaritic.
2 = voluptuous, sexual, sexy, erotic.
Opposites: spiritual.

sensuous ADJ = **pleasing**, pleasurable, gratifying, aesthetic.

sentence NOUN
1 = judgement, verdict, ruling, decision, decree.
2 = prison sentence, jail sentence, prison term; [inf] time; [Brit. inf] porridge.
▶ VERB = **impose a sentence on**, pass judgement on, penalize, punish, condemn, doom.

sentiment NOUN
1 = emotion, emotionalism, finer feelings, tender feelings, tenderness, softness.
2 = feelings, attitude, belief, opinion, view, point of view.

sentimental ADJ
1 = romantic, emotional, mawkish, maudlin; [inf] mushy, slushy, schmaltzy, corny; [Brit. inf] soppy. **2 = nostalgic**, emotional, affectionate, loving, tender, warm.

sentiments PL NOUN
= **feeling**, attitude, belief, thoughts, way of thinking, opinion, view, point of view, idea, judgement.

sentry NOUN = **guard**, lookout, watch, watchman, sentinel.

separate ADJ
1 = **individual**, distinct, different, particular, autonomous, independent.
2 = **unconnected**, distinct, different, disconnected, unrelated, detached, divorced, divided, discrete.
▸ VERB 1 = **disconnect**, detach, sever, uncouple, divide, sunder. 2 = **divide**, come between, stand between, keep apart, partition. 3 = **part**, part company, go their/your/our separate ways, go different ways, diverge, split, divide. 4 = **break up**, split up, part, become estranged, divorce.
Opposites: join, unite.

separately ADV 1 = **apart**, individually, independently,

autonomously.
2 = **individually**, one by one, one at a time, singly, severally, independently.

septic ADJ = **infected**, festering, poisoned, putrefying, putrefactive, putrid.

sequel NOUN = **follow-up**, development, result, consequence, outcome, issue, upshot.

sequence NOUN = **chain**, course, cycle, series, progression, succession, set, arrangement, order, pattern.

serene ADJ = **calm**, composed, tranquil, peaceful, placid, still, quiet, unperturbed, imperturbable, undisturbed, unruffled, unworried, unexcited, unexcitable, unflappable.
Opposites: excitable.

series NOUN = **succession**, progression, sequence, chain, course, string, train, run, cycle, set, row, arrangement, order.

serious ADJ 1 = **solemn**, earnest, unsmiling, thoughtful, preoccupied,

pensive, grave, sombre, sober, long-faced, dour, stern, grim, poker-faced. **2** = **important**, significant, consequential, of consequence, momentous, weighty, far-reaching, urgent, pressing, crucial, vital, life-and-death. **3** = **acute**, grave, bad, critical, grievous, dangerous, perilous. **4** = **earnest**, in earnest, sincere, honest, genuine, firm, resolute, resolved, determined, fervent.
Opposites: cheerful, minor, trivial.

sermon NOUN = **homily**, address, oration, lecture, preaching, teaching.

servant NOUN = **domestic**, help, domestic help, maid, handyman, menial, drudge, scullion, retainer, attendant, lackey; [Brit. inf] char; [Brit. dated] charwoman.

serve VERB **1** = **have/hold a place on**, be on, perform duties, carry out duties. **2** = **act as**, do duty as, function as, do the work of, be suitable for.

3 = **dish up**, give out, distribute, set out, present, provide. **4** = **attend to**, look after, take care of, assist.

service NOUN **1** = **good turn**, assistance, help, advantage, benefit. **2** = **work**, employment, labour, duty, business. **3** = **ceremony**, ritual, rite, sacrament. **4** = **servicing**, overhaul, check, maintenance, repair.
▶ VERB = **check**, go over, overhaul, maintain, repair.

serviceable ADJ **1** = **functional**, utilitarian, practical, useful, durable, hard-wearing, tough, strong. **2** = **usable**, of use, functioning, operative, repairable.
Opposites: impractical, unusable.

servile ADJ **1** = **menial**, low, lowly, humble, mean, base. **2** = **subservient**, obsequious, sycophantic, fawning, toadying, grovelling, submissive; [inf] bootlicking.
Opposites: assertive.

serving NOUN = **helping**, portion, plateful.

session NOUN 1 = **period**, time, spell, stretch. 2 = **meeting**, sitting, assembly, conference, discussion.

set¹ VERB 1 = **put**, place, lay, lay down, deposit, position, rest, locate, lodge, situate, station; [inf] stick, park, plonk. 2 = **fix**, embed, insert, lodge, mount, arrange, install. 3 = **adjust**, regulate, synchronize, coordinate, harmonize, calibrate, rectify, set right. 4 = **style**, fix, arrange, curl, wave. 5 = **solidify**, stiffen, thicken, jell, harden, cake, congeal, coagulate. 6 = **decide on**, fix, fix on, agree on, appoint, name, specify, stipulate, determine, designate, select, choose, arrange, schedule.

set² NOUN 1 = **collection**, group, assemblage, series, batch, array, assortment, selection. 2 = **stage set**, setting, scenery, backdrop.

set³ ADJ 1 = **fixed**, prescribed, scheduled, specified, determined, arranged, appointed, established, decided, agreed. 2 = **ready**, prepared, equipped, primed; [inf] fit. Opposites: variable, unprepared.

setback NOUN = **reversal**, reverse, upset, check, hitch, hold-up, hindrance, impediment, obstruction, disappointment, misfortune, blow. Opposites: breakthrough.

setting NOUN 1 = **environment**, surroundings, milieu, background, location, place, site. 2 = **stage setting**, set, scene, stage, scenery, backdrop. 3 = **mount**, frame.

settle VERB 1 = **make one's home**, set up home, take up residence, put down roots, establish oneself, go to live, move to, emigrate to. 2 = **establish/found a colony**, colonize, occupy, people, inhabit,

populate. 3 = **calm down**, quieten down, be quiet, be still, relax. 4 = **light**, land, come down, descend, repose, rest. 5 = **resolve**, clear up, patch up, reconcile, conclude, bring to an end. 6 = **put in order**, order, arrange, set to rights, straighten out, organize, regulate, adjust, clear up.
Opposites: agitate, rise.

■**settle for**
= **compromise on**, accept, agree to, accede to, acquiesce in.

■**settle on** = **decide on**, agree on, determine, confirm, arrange, fix, choose, appoint, select.

settlement NOUN
1 = **community**, colony, village, hamlet, encampment, outpost. 2 = **resolution**, reconciliation, conclusion, agreement, contract, pact, compact.

settler NOUN = **colonist**, colonizer, pioneer, immigrant.

sever VERB 1 = **cut off**, chop off, lop off, hack off, break off, tear off. 2 = **divide**, split, cleave, dissect, halve. 3 = **break off**, discontinue, suspend, dissolve, end, terminate, stop, cease, conclude.
Opposites: join, maintain.

several ADJ = **some**, a number of, a few.

severe ADJ 1 = **harsh**, hard, stringent, rigorous, unsparing, relentless, merciless, ruthless, painful, sharp, caustic, biting, cutting, scathing, serious, extreme. 2 = **extreme**, very bad, serious, grave, acute, critical, dire, dangerous, perilous. 3 = **fierce**, strong, violent, intense, powerful, forceful. 4 = **stern**, grim, cold, chilly, austere, forbidding, dour, disapproving, unsmiling, sombre, grave, sober, serious. 5 = **austere**, stark, spartan, ascetic, plain, simple, modest, bare, unadorned, unembellished, restrained, functional, classic.

Opposites: mild, friendly, ornate.

sew VERB = **stitch**, seam, embroider, mend, darn.

sex NOUN 1 = **sexuality**, sexual attraction, sexual chemistry, sexual desire, desire, sex drive, sexual appetite, libido. 2 = **facts of life**, sexual reproduction, reproduction; [inf] the birds and the bees. 3 = **sexual intercourse**, making love, intimacy, coitus, coition, coupling, copulation, carnal knowledge, mating, fornication. 4 = **gender**.

sexuality NOUN 1 = **sex**, gender, sexual characteristics. 2 = **sexual desire**, sexual appetite, sexiness, carnality, physicalness, eroticism, lust, sensuality, voluptuousness. 3 = **sexual orientation**, sexual preferences.

sexy ADJ 1 = **erotic**, titillating, suggestive, arousing, exciting, stimulating. 2 = **arousing**, provocative, seductive, sensuous, slinky.

3 = **attractive**, alluring, seductive, shapely.

shabby ADJ
1 = **dilapidated**, broken-down, run-down, tumbledown, ramshackle, in disrepair, scruffy, dingy, seedy, squalid, tatty; [inf] tacky. 2 = **worn**, worn out, threadbare, ragged, frayed, tattered, faded, scruffy, tatty, the worse for wear. 3 = **contemptible**, despicable, rotten, dishonourable, disreputable, mean, base, low, dirty, odious, shameful, ignoble, unworthy, cheap, shoddy.
Opposites: smart.

shackle VERB = **chain**, fetter, put in irons, manacle, tie up, bind, tether, hobble, handcuff.

shade NOUN 1 = **shadiness**, shadow, shadowiness, shadows, shelter, cover. 2 = **colour**, hue, tone, tint, tinge. 3 = **nuance**, degree, gradation, difference, variety.
Opposites: light.

▶ VERB **1** = **shut out the light from**, block off light to, cast a shadow over, screen, darken, dim. **2** = **cover**, obscure, mute, hide, conceal, veil, curtain.

shadow NOUN **1** = *See* **shade** NOUN **(1).** **2** = **silhouette**, outline, shape. **3** = **a trace**, a hint, a suggestion, a suspicion, a ghost.

shadowy ADJ **1** = **shady**, shaded, dim, dark, gloomy, murky, crepuscular, tenebrous. **2** = **indistinct**, indeterminate, indefinite, unclear, vague, nebulous, ill-defined. **Opposites:** bright, distinct.

shady ADJ **1** = *See* **shadowy (1).** **2** = **disreputable**, suspicious, suspect, questionable, dishonest, dishonourable, untrustworthy, devious, shifty, slippery, underhand, unscrupulous; [inf] crooked, tricky, fishy. **Opposites:** honest.

shaft NOUN **1** = **pole**, stick, rod, staff, shank, stem, handle, upright. **2** = **ray**, beam, gleam, streak, pencil. **3** = **passage**, duct, tunnel, well, flue.

shaggy ADJ = **hairy**, hirsute, long-haired, rough, coarse, matted, tangled, unkempt, untidy. **Opposites:** sleek.

shake VERB **1** = **rock**, bump, jolt, bounce, roll, sway, judder, swing, jar, oscillate, wobble, rattle, vibrate, jerk, joggle, jounce. **2** = **shiver**, tremble, quiver, quake, shudder. **3** = **jiggle**, joggle, jolt, jerk, rattle, agitate, jounce. **4** = **agitate**, upset, distress, shock, alarm, disturb, perturb, fluster, unsettle, discompose, disquiet, disconcert, unnerve, ruffle; [inf] rattle.

shaky ADJ **1** = **trembling**, tremulous, quivering, quivery, unsteady, wobbly, weak, tottering, teetering, doddering, staggering. **2** = **infirm**, unsound, unwell, ill, below par, indisposed;

[inf] under the weather.
3 = **questionable**,
dubious, tenuous, flimsy,
weak, unsound,
unreliable.
Opposites: steady, sound.

shallow ADJ **1** = **frivolous**,
foolish, unintelligent,
unthinking, trivial,
insincere, superficial.
2 = **superficial**,
unsubstantial, trifling,
trivial, petty, empty,
meaningless.
Opposites: serious, deep.

sham VERB = **fake**, pretend,
feign, counterfeit, put
on, simulate, affect,
imitate.
▶ NOUN **1** = **counterfeit**, fake,
forgery, copy, imitation,
hoax, pretence,
simulation. **2** = **impostor**,
fake, fraud, pretender,
masquerader, dissembler,
charlatan; [inf] phoney.
▶ ADJ = **pretend**, feigned,
artificial, synthetic,
ersatz, fake, pseudo,
contrived, simulated,
affected, put on,
insincere, false, bogus,
spurious; [inf] phoney.
Opposites: genuine.

shamble VERB = **shuffle**,
hobble, limp, falter,
totter, dodder.

shambles PL NOUN
= **chaos**, muddle, mess,
confusion, disorder,
disarray, disorganization,
anarchy; [inf] disaster area.

shame NOUN
1 = **humiliation**,
ignominy, mortification,
loss of face, remorse,
guilt, compunction,
embarrassment,
discomfort,
discomposure.
2 = **disgrace**, dishonour,
scandal, discredit,
degradation, ignominy,
disrepute, infamy,
odium, opprobrium.
3 = **pity**, misfortune, bad
luck, ill luck, source of
regret.
Opposites: pride, honour.

s

shamefaced ADJ
1 = **ashamed**,
embarrassed, guilty,
conscience-stricken,
remorseful, contrite,
penitent, regretful,
humiliated, mortified,
shamed. **2** = **shy**, bashful,
timid, timorous,
shrinking, coy, sheepish.

Opposites: unrepentant.

shameful ADJ
1 = **disgraceful**, base, mean, low, vile, outrageous, shocking, dishonourable, unbecoming, unworthy, discreditable, deplorable, despicable, contemptible, reprehensible, scandalous, atrocious, heinous. **2** = **shaming**, humiliating, mortifying, embarrassing; [inf] blush-making.
Opposites: admirable.

shameless ADJ
1 = **unashamed**, without shame, unabashed, uncontrite, impenitent.
2 = **brazen**, impudent, bold, brash, forward, audacious, immodest, unseemly, improper, unbecoming, indecorous, wanton, abandoned, indecent.
Opposites: modest.

shape NOUN **1** = **form**, figure, configuration, formation, conformation, contour, outline, silhouette, profile, outward form, external appearance. **2** = **guise**, form, appearance, likeness, look, semblance, image, aspect. **3** = **condition**, state, health, trim, fettle.
▶ VERB = **form**, fashion, make, mould, model, cast, frame, block, carve, sculpt.

shapeless ADJ
1 = **amorphous**, formless, unformed, unshaped, unfashioned, undeveloped, embryonic. **2** = **formless**, badly cut, sack-like, ill-proportioned, inelegant.

shapely ADJ = **well formed**, well proportioned, elegant, curvaceous, curvy.

share NOUN = **allowance**, ration, allocation, division, quota, allotment, portion, part, lot, measure, helping, serving; [inf] cut, rake-off, piece of the cake, piece of the action; [Brit. inf] whack.
▶ VERB **1** = **divide**, split, have in common, go halves in; [inf] go fifty-fifty in, go Dutch. **2** = **distribute**, divide, apportion, parcel

out, deal out, dole out, give out.

sharp ADJ **1 = edged**, razor-edged, keen, cutting, serrated, knife-like, pointed, needle-like, barbed, spiky. **2 = steep**, sheer, abrupt, precipitous, vertical. **3 = sudden**, abrupt, rapid, unexpected. **4 = intense**, acute, keen, piercing, cutting, extreme, severe, stabbing, shooting, stinging. **5 = pungent**, biting, bitter, acid, sour, tart, vinegary. **6 = harsh**, curt, brusque, bitter, hard, cutting, scathing, caustic, biting, barbed, acrimonious, trenchant, venomous, malicious, vitriolic, hurtful, unkind, cruel. **7 = intelligent**, bright, clever, quick. **8 = keen**, acute, quick, ready, knowing, shrewd, discerning, perceptive, penetrating; [inf] smart. **Opposites:** blunt.

sharpen VERB **= put an edge on**, edge, whet, hone, strop, grind.

shatter VERB **1 = smash**, break, break into pieces, splinter, fracture, pulverize, crush, crack; [inf] bust. **2 = destroy**, demolish, wreck, ruin, dash, blight, wipe out, devastate; [inf] torpedo.

shave VERB **1 = cut off**, trim, snip off, crop. **2 = pare**, plane, shear. **3 = brush**, graze, touch, scrape, rub.

sheath NOUN **1 = case**, casing, cover, covering, envelope, wrapper. **2 = condom**, contraceptive; [Brit. inf] rubber johnny; [N. Amer. inf] rubber.

shed¹ NOUN **= hut**, outhouse, lean-to, shack.

shed² VERB **1 = let fall**, let drop, cast off, slough off. **2 = take off**, remove, strip off, doff. **3 = send forth**, radiate, disperse, scatter.

sheen NOUN **= shine**, lustre, gleam, sparkle, gloss, burnish, polish, patina.

sheer ADJ **1 = utter**, complete, thoroughgoing, total, absolute, veritable, downright, out-and-out, unqualified, unconditional, unmitigated, unalloyed, unadulterated. **2 = steep**, abrupt, sharp, precipitous, vertical. **3 = diaphanous**, transparent, see-through, translucent, fine, thin. **Opposites:** gradual, thick.

sheet NOUN **1 = bedsheet**, bedlinen. **2 = piece**, pane, panel, plate, slab. **3 = piece of paper**, leaf, page, folio. **4 = expanse**, stretch, span, reach, sweep, covering, blanket, carpet.

shell NOUN **1 = carapace**, case, casing, husk, pod, integument. **2 = bullet**, grenade, shot, shrapnel. **3 = framework**, frame, structure, chassis, hull, skeleton. ▸ VERB = **bomb**, bombard, blitz, strafe, fire on.

shelter NOUN **1 = protection**, shield, cover, screen, safety, security, defence. **2 = refuge**, sanctuary, retreat, haven, harbour. **Opposites:** exposure. ▸ VERB **1 = protect**, shield, screen, safeguard, provide refuge/sanctuary from, guard, harbour, conceal, hide. **2 = take shelter**, take refuge, seek protection, seek refuge/sanctuary. **Opposites:** expose.

sheltered ADJ **1 = shady**, shaded, protected, screened, shielded, secluded. **2 = quiet**, withdrawn, retired, isolated, protected, cloistered, reclusive.

shepherd VERB = **escort**, conduct, usher, convoy, guide, marshal, steer.

shift VERB = **move**, carry, transfer, switch, reposition, rearrange. ▸ NOUN **1 = move**, movement, transference, switch, repositioning. **2 = stint**, spell/period of work.

shifty ADJ = **evasive**, slippery, devious, duplicitous, deceitful, underhand, untrustworthy, double-dealing, dishonest, wily, crafty, artful, sly, scheming, contriving. **Opposites:** honest.

shimmer VERB = **glisten**, glint, flicker, twinkle, sparkle, gleam, glow, scintillate, dance.

shine VERB 1 = **gleam**, glow, glint, sparkle, twinkle, flicker, glitter, glisten, shimmer, flash, dazzle, beam, radiate, illuminate, luminesce, incandesce. 2 = **polish**, burnish, buff, wax, gloss. 3 = **excel**, be expert, be brilliant, be very good, be outstanding.
▶ NOUN 1 = **light**, brightness, gleam, glow, glint, sparkle, twinkle, flicker, glitter, glisten, shimmer, flash, dazzle, glare, beam, radiance, illumination, luminescence, luminosity, lambency, effulgence. 2 = **polish**, burnish, gleam, gloss, lustre, sheen, patina.

shiny ADJ = **shining**, polished, burnished, gleaming, glossy, satiny, lustrous.
Opposites: dull.

shirk VERB = **avoid**, evade, dodge, sidestep, shrink from, shun, get out of, play truant from; [inf] funk; [Brit. inf] skive off.

shirker NOUN = **slacker**, truant, absentee, malingerer, layabout, loafer, idler; [Brit. inf] skiver.

shiver VERB = **tremble**, quiver, shake, shudder, quaver, quake, vibrate.
▶ NOUN = **tremble**, quiver, shake, quaver, shudder.

shock NOUN 1 = **impact**, blow, collision, crash, dash, jolt, bump, jar, jerk. 2 = **blow**, upset, bombshell, bolt from the blue, disturbance, state of agitation/perturbation, source of distress, revelation; [inf] eye-opener.
▶ VERB = **appal**, horrify, scandalize, outrage, repel, revolt, disgust, nauseate, sicken, offend, traumatize, make someone's blood run cold, distress, upset, perturb, disturb, disquiet, unsettle, astound, dumbfound, stagger, amaze, astonish, stun.

shoddy ADJ = **poor-quality**, inferior, second-rate,

tawdry, rubbishy, trashy, junky, gimcrack, cheapjack, jerry-built; [inf] tacky, tatty.
Opposites: quality.

shoot VERB 1 = **hit**, shoot down, bring down, pick off, bag, fell, kill; [inf] plug, zap; [poetic/ literary] slay. 2 = **fire**, discharge, launch, let fly, send forth. 3 = **race**, dash, sprint, charge, dart, fly, hurtle, bolt, streak, flash, whisk, run, speed.
4 = **bud**, burgeon, sprout, germinate, appear, spring up.
▶ NOUN = **bud**, offshoot, slip, scion, sucker, sprout, branch, twig, sprig, cutting, graft.

shop NOUN = **store**, retail outlet, retailer, establishment, emporium, trading post.

shore[1] NOUN = **seashore**, seaside, beach, coast, seaboard, waterside, foreshore; [poetic/ literary] strand.

shore[2]
▪ **shore up** = **prop up**, support, hold up, underpin, strengthen, brace, buttress.

short ADJ 1 = **small**, little, slight, petite, tiny, squat, dwarfish, diminutive, dumpy, Lilliputian; [Scottish] wee; [inf] pint-sized, pocket-sized, knee-high to a grasshopper. 2 = **brief**, concise, succinct, to the point, compact, terse, summary, crisp, pithy, epigrammatic, abridged, abbreviated, condensed, summarized, contracted, curtailed, truncated.
3 = **short-lived**, momentary, temporary, brief, impermanent, short-term, cursory, fleeting, passing, transitory, transient, ephemeral, fugacious, evanescent. 4 = **deficient**, lacking, wanting, insufficient, inadequate, scarce, scanty, meagre, sparse, tight, low.
5 = **curt**, sharp, abrupt, blunt, brusque, terse, gruff, surly, testy, tart, rude, discourteous, uncivil, impolite.
Opposites: tall, long, plentiful.

shortage NOUN = **dearth**, scarcity, lack, deficiency, insufficiency, paucity, deficit, inadequacy, shortfall, want, poverty. Opposites: abundance.

shortcoming NOUN = **defect**, fault, flaw, imperfection, failing, drawback, weakness, weak point, foible, frailty, infirmity. Opposites: strength.

shorten VERB = **abbreviate**, condense, abridge, cut, cut down, contract, compress, reduce, lessen, decrease, diminish, curtail, duck, trim, pare down. Opposites: extend.

shortly ADV = **soon**, in a short while, in a little while, presently, before long, directly; [inf] before you can say Jack Robinson.

short-sighted ADJ 1 = **myopic**, near-sighted. 2 = **imprudent**, injudicious, unwise, ill-advised, thoughtless, unthinking, heedless, rash, incautious.

shot NOUN 1 = **crack**, bang, report, blast, explosion, gunfire. 2 = **pellet**, bullet, slug, projectile, ammunition. 3 = **photograph**, photo, snap, snapshot.

shout VERB = **cry out**, call out, yell, roar, howl, bellow, scream, bawl, call at the top of one's voice, raise one's voice; [inf] holler. Opposites: whisper.

shove VERB = **push**, thrust, drive, force, shoulder, elbow, jostle, jolt.

shovel NOUN = **spade**, scoop. ▸ VERB = **scoop up**, dig, excavate, spade.

show VERB 1 = **be visible**, be seen, be in view, appear, put in an appearance. 2 = **exhibit**, display, present, demonstrate, set forth, uncover, reveal. 3 = **indicate**, express, manifest, reveal, make known, make plain, make obvious, evince, evidence, disclose, betray, divulge. 4 = **demonstrate**, point

out, explain, expound,
teach, instruct in, give
instructions in, tutor in,
indoctrinate in.
5 = **escort**, accompany,
usher, conduct, attend,
guide, lead, direct, steer.
6 = **appear**, put in an
appearance, make an
appearance, turn up,
come, arrive, be present.
Opposites: conceal.
▶ NOUN **1** = **display**, array,
arrangement, exhibition,
presentation, exposition,
spectacle. **2** = **exhibition**,
demonstration, display,
exposition, presentation.
3 = **performance**,
production; [inf] gig.
4 = **appearance**, outward
appearance, air, guise,
semblance, pretence,
illusion, pose,
affectation, profession.

shower NOUN **1** = **fall**,
drizzle, flurry, sprinkling.
2 = **abundance**, profusion,
plethora, flood, deluge.
▶ VERB **1** = **deluge**, inundate,
overwhelm. **2** = **lavish**,
pour, load, heap.

show-off NOUN
= **exhibitionist**, extrovert,
bragger, braggart,

boaster; [N. Amer.
inf] blowhard.
showy ADJ = **ostentatious**,
flamboyant, elaborate,
fancy, pretentious,
overdone, glittering.
Opposites: restrained.
shred NOUN **1** = **scrap**,
fragment, wisp, sliver,
bit, piece, remnant,
snippet, tatter. **2** = **trace**,
iota, whit, particle, atom,
modicum, scrap, speck.
▶ VERB = **cut up**, tear up, rip
up, grate.
shrewd ADJ = **astute**,
sharp, clever, intelligent,
alert, quick-witted,
discerning, perspicacious,
perceptive,
discriminating, wise,
sagacious, far-seeing,
canny, cunning, artful,
crafty, wily, calculating;
[inf] smart.
Opposites: stupid.
shriek VERB = **scream**,
screech, squeal, yell,
howl, shout, cry out, call
out, whoop, wail;
[inf] holler.
shrill ADJ = **high-pitched**,
high, sharp, piercing,
ear-piercing, penetrating,
ear-splitting, screeching,

shrieking.

shrine NOUN 1 = **holy place**, temple, church.
2 = **memorial**, monument, cenotaph. 3 = **reliquary**, burial chamber, tomb, sepulchre.

shrink VERB = **get/ become/grow smaller**, contract, diminish, lessen, reduce, dwindle, narrow, decline, fall off, drop off, shrivel.
Opposites: expand, increase.

▪ **shrink from** = **draw back**, pull back, back away, shy away, recoil, retreat, withdraw, flinch, cringe, wince.

shrivel VERB = **dry up**, wither, desiccate, dehydrate, wrinkle, pucker up.

shroud NOUN = **cover**, covering, pall, cloak, mantle, blanket, cloud, veil, screen.
▶ VERB = **cover**, enshroud, swathe, envelop, cloak, blanket, cloud, veil, screen, conceal, hide.

shrug
▪ **shrug off** = **disregard**, take no notice of, not trouble about, dismiss, gloss over, play down, make light of, minimize.

shuffle VERB 1 = **shamble**, hobble, limp, drag one's feet. 2 = **mix**, intermix, shift about, rearrange, reorganize, jumble.

shun VERB = **avoid**, evade, eschew, steer clear of, shy away from, recoil from, keep away from, keep one's distance from, cold-shoulder, give a wide berth to.
Opposites: seek.

shut VERB = **close**, draw to, pull to, fasten, bar, lock, secure, seal.
Opposites: open.

▪ **shut in** = *see* **imprison**.

▪ **shut out** = **exclude**, leave out, omit, keep out, bar, debar, ostracize, blackball, banish, exile, outlaw.

▪ **shut up** = **keep quiet**, be quiet, keep silent, hold one's tongue; [inf] keep mum, pipe down, keep one's trap shut.

shy ADJ = **bashful**, diffident, reserved, reticent, retiring, self-effacing, withdrawn,

timid, timorous, fearful, nervous, hesitant, wary, suspicious, chary, unconfident, self-conscious, embarrassed, abashed, modest.
Opposites: brash, confident.

sick ADJ **1** = **unwell**, ill, ailing, indisposed, poorly, below par, out of sorts, laid up, on the sick list; [inf] under the weather. **2** = **nauseated**, queasy, bilious; [inf] green about the gills. **3** = **tired**, weary, bored, jaded, surfeited, satiated, glutted; [inf] fed up, have had something up to here. **4** = **morbid**, macabre, ghoulish, gruesome, sadistic, perverted, cruel.
Opposites: well.

■ **be sick** = **vomit**, throw up; [inf] spew, puke.

sicken VERB **1** = **make sick**, nauseate, turn someone's stomach, make someone's gorge rise, revolt, disgust, repel, shock, appal. **2** = **take/fall ill**, become ill, become infected, contract, be

stricken.
Opposites: recover.

sickening ADJ = *see* **repellent**, **annoying**.

sickly ADJ **1** = **unhealthy**, in poor health, ill, delicate, frail, weak, feeble, puny. **2** = **sentimental**, cloying, mawkish, maudlin, slushy, mushy, syrupy; [inf] schmaltzy; [Brit. inf] soppy.
Opposites: healthy.

sickness NOUN **1** = **illness**, disease, disorder, ailment, complaint, affliction, malady, infirmity, indisposition; [inf] bug. **2** = **nausea**, queasiness, biliousness.

side NOUN **1** = **edge**, border, verge, boundary, margin, rim, fringe, skirt, flank, brink, brim, periphery. **2** = **part**, quarter, section, sector, neighbourhood. **3** = **aspect**, angle, facet, point of view, viewpoint, view, opinion, standpoint, position, slant. **4** = **camp**, faction, caucus, party, wing, splinter group, sect.

■ **side with** = **take someone's side**, be on someone's side, take someone's part, support, give one's support to, back, give one's backing to, join with, favour.

sidelong ADJ = **side**, sideways, oblique, indirect, covert.
Opposites: overt.

sidetrack VERB = **divert**, deflect, distract, lead away from.

sideways ADV **1** = **side first**, edgeways, edgewise. **2** = **obliquely**, indirectly, sidelong.

sieve NOUN = **strainer**, filter, colander, riddle, screen.

sift VERB **1** = **filter**, strain, riddle, screen.
2 = **examine**, scrutinize, study, investigate, analyse, review.

sigh VERB = **breathe out**, exhale.

■ **sigh for** = **yearn for**, long for, weep for, mourn for.

sight NOUN **1** = **eyesight**, vision, power of sight. **2** = **range of vision**, field of vision, view. **3** = **view**, glimpse, look.
▶ VERB = **catch sight of**, see, behold, spot, make out, descry, espy, perceive, observe, discern.

sign NOUN **1** = **indication**, symptom, hint, suggestion, trace, mark, clue, manifestation, token, evidence, proof.
2 = **signpost**, notice, placard, board, marker.
3 = **gesture**, signal, motion, movement, wave, gesticulation.
4 = **symbol**, mark, cipher, code, hieroglyph.
▶ VERB **1** = **write**, inscribe, autograph, initial. **2** = *See* **signal** VERB (**1**).

signal VERB **1** = **sign**, give a sign to, indicate, beckon, gesture, motion, gesticulate, nod. **2** = **be a sign of**, mark signify, designate.
▶ NOUN = **sign**, indicator, cue, indication, token, evidence, hint.

significance NOUN
1 = **meaning**, sense, import, signification, purport, point, gist, essence, implications.
2 = **importance**,

consequence,
momentousness,
magnitude, seriousness.

significant ADJ
1 = **meaningful**, eloquent,
expressive, pregnant,
knowing. **2** = **important**,
of importance, of
consequence,
momentous, of moment,
weighty, material,
impressive, serious, vital,
critical.
Opposites: insignificant.

signify VERB **1** = **be a sign
of**, indicate, mean,
denote, suggest, point to,
portend. **2** = **mean**,
denote, represent,
symbolize, stand for.
3 = **matter**, be of
importance, be of
consequence, be
important, be significant,
be of significance, carry
weight, count.

silence NOUN **1** = **quiet**,
quietness, hush, still,
stillness, peace,
peacefulness, tranquillity,
noiselessness,
soundlessness.
2 = **speechlessness**,
wordlessness, dumbness,
muteness, taciturnity,

reticence,
uncommunicativeness.
Opposites: noise.
▶ VERB **1** = **quiet**, quieten,
hush, still, calm, pacify,
subdue, quell. **2** = **muffle**,
deaden, abate,
extinguish.

silent ADJ **1** = **quiet**,
hushed, still, peaceful,
tranquil, noiseless,
soundless.
2 = **speechless**,
unspeaking, voiceless,
dumb, mute, taciturn,
reticent, mum,
uncommunicative, tight-
lipped, tongue-tied;
[inf] struck dumb.
3 = **unspoken**, wordless,
unvoiced, unsaid,
unexpressed,
unpronounced, tacit,
implicit, understood,
implied.
Opposites: noisy,
loquacious.

silhouette NOUN = **outline**,
contour, profile,
delineation, form, shape.

silky ADJ = **silken**, smooth,
sleek, velvety,
diaphanous.

silly ADJ **1** = **unintelligent**,
stupid, foolish, idiotic,

brainless, witless, unwise, imprudent, thoughtless, reckless, foolhardy, irresponsible, mad, erratic, unstable, scatterbrained, feather-brained, flighty, frivolous, giddy, fatuous, inane, immature, childish, shallow, naive; [inf] crazy, dotty, scatty, loopy, screwy; [Brit. inf] daft. **2 = senseless**, stupid, foolish, mindless, idiotic, unwise, imprudent, inadvisable, injudicious, misguided, unsound, impractical, pointless, meaningless, purposeless, inappropriate, illogical, irrational, unreasonable, thoughtless, reckless, foolhardy, irresponsible, erratic, hare-brained, absurd, ridiculous, ludicrous, laughable, risible, farcical, preposterous, fatuous, asinine; [inf] half-baked, crazy, screwy; [Brit. inf] daft.
Opposites: sensible.

similar ADJ **= like**, alike, resembling, close, much the same, comparable, corresponding, analogous, parallel, equivalent, kindred, approximate.
Opposites: dissimilar, different.

similarity NOUN **= resemblance**, likeness, sameness, similitude, comparability, correspondence, analogy, parallel, parallelism, equivalence, approximation, closeness, affinity, kinship.
Opposites: dissimilarity, difference.

similarly ADV **= likewise**, in the same way, in like matter, correspondingly, by the same token.

simmer VERB **= boil**, cook, bubble, stew, poach, seethe.

simple ADJ **1 = easy**, uncomplicated, straightforward, uninvolved, effortless, manageable, elementary, facile; [inf] like falling off a log, a piece of cake, a cinch, easy-peasy, no sweat. **2 = clear**, plain,

intelligible,
comprehensible,
understandable, lucid,
direct, straightforward,
uncomplicated,
uninvolved. **3 = plain**,
classic, clean-cut,
unelaborate, unadorned,
undecorated. **4 = simple-
minded**, feeble-minded,
retarded, backward,
slow-witted, slow, dull-
witted.
Opposites: difficult,
complex, ornate.

simplify VERB = **make
simple/simpler**, make
easy/easier, make plainer,
clarify, decipher,
disentangle, explain,
paraphrase, translate.
Opposites: complicate.

simplistic ADJ
= **oversimple**,
oversimplified, facile,
shallow, superficial,
naive.

simply ADV **1** = **clearly**,
plainly, intelligibly,
lucidly, directly,
straightforwardly.
2 = **plainly**, unfussily,
without clutter,
austerely, starkly,
spartanly, with restraint,

naturally, casually.

simultaneous ADJ
= **concurrent**,
contemporaneous,
concomitant, coinciding,
coincident, synchronous,
coexistent, parallel.

sin NOUN = **wrong**,
wrongdoing, act of evil/
wickedness, crime,
offence, misdeed,
misdemeanour,
transgression, error,
lapse, fall from grace;
[archaic] trespass.
Opposites: virtue.
▶ VERB = **commit a sin**, do
wrong, offend, commit
an offence, transgress,
misbehave, go astray,
stray from the straight
and narrow, go wrong,
fall from grace.

sincere ADJ **1** = **genuine**,
real, true, honest,
unfeigned, unaffected,
bona fide, wholehearted,
heartfelt, serious, earnest,
fervent. **2** = **honest**, above
board, trustworthy,
frank, candid,
straightforward, plain-
dealing, no-nonsense,
genuine, artless, guileless,
ingenuous; [inf] upfront.

Opposites: insincere.

sincerely ADV 1 = **with all sincerity**, wholeheartedly, with all one's heart, earnestly, fervently. 2 = **genuinely**, really, truly, in truth, without pretence, honestly, in good faith.

sinful ADJ = **wrong**, evil, wicked, bad, iniquitous, criminal, immoral, corrupt, unrighteous, ungodly, irreligious, irreverent, profane, blasphemous, impious, sacrilegious.
Opposites: virtuous.

sing VERB = **carol**, trill, warble, pipe, quaver, croon, chant, yodel.

singe VERB = **scorch**, burn, sear, char, blacken.

single ADJ 1 = **one**, sole, lone, solitary, unique, isolated, by itself, exclusive. 2 = **individual**, particular, separate, distinct. 3 = **unmarried**, unwed, unwedded, wifeless/husbandless, spouseless, partnerless, unattached, free.
▪ **single out** = **separate out**, set apart, put to one side, pick, choose, select, fix on, decide on.

single-handed ADV = **by oneself**, alone, on one's own, solo, independently, unaided, unassisted, without help.

single-minded ADJ = **unswerving**, unwavering, undeviating, set, fixed, devoted, dedicated, committed, determined, dogged, tireless, purposeful, obsessive, monomaniacal.

singular ADJ 1 = **extraordinary**, exceptional, rare, unusual, unique, remarkable, outstanding, notable, noteworthy, striking, conspicuous, distinctive. 2 = **strange**, unusual, odd, peculiar, curious, queer, bizarre, weird, abnormal, atypical.
Opposites: ordinary.

sinister ADJ 1 = **evil-looking**, villainous, malevolent, menacing, threatening, frightening. 2 = **evil**, wicked, bad, criminal, base, vile, vicious, cruel, malicious, malign. **3** = **ominous**, inauspicious, portentous. **Opposites:** innocent.

sink VERB **1** = **go under**, submerge, founder, capsize. **2** = **fall**, drop, descend, go down, go lower, plunge, plummet, slump. **Opposites:** float, rise.

sinner NOUN = **wrongdoer**, evil-doer, criminal, offender, miscreant, transgressor, reprobate; [archaic] trespasser.

sit VERB **1** = **sit down**, take a seat, settle down, be seated; [inf] take the load/weight off one's feet. **2** = **be placed**, be positioned, be situated, rest, perch. **3** = **be convened**, meet, assemble, be in session.

site NOUN = **location**, situation, position, place, locality, setting, scene. ▶ VERB = *see* **situate**.

situate VERB = **place**, position, locate, site, put, install, station, establish, set up.

situation NOUN **1** = **place**, position, location, site, setting, milieu, environment. **2** = **circumstances**, affairs, state of affairs, condition, case, predicament, plight; [inf] kettle of fish, ball game. **3** = **post**, position, place, job, employment.

size NOUN = **dimensions**, measurements, proportions, bigness, largeness, magnitude, vastness, bulk, area, expanse, extent.

sketch NOUN **1** = **drawing**, outline, diagram, plan, representation, delineation. **2** = **outline**, summary, abstract, precis, skeleton, bones, bare bones, draft, plan. **3** = **skit**, act, scene. ▶ VERB = **draw**, rough out, outline, represent, delineate, depict.

sketchy ADJ **1** = **preliminary**, provisional, unfinished, unrefined, unpolished, rough, crude. **2** = **light**, superficial, cursory, perfunctory, meagre, scrappy, skimpy, bitty, insufficient, inadequate,

imperfect, incomplete.
Opposites: detailed.

skilful ADJ = **skilled**, able, good, accomplished, adept, competent, efficient, adroit, deft, dexterous, masterly, expert, first-rate, experienced, trained, practised, professional, talented, gifted, clever; [inf] smart.
Opposites: incompetent.

skill NOUN = **skilfulness**, ability, accomplishment, adeptness, competence, efficiency, adroitness, deftness, dexterity, aptitude, expertise, expertness, art, finesse, experience, professionalism, talent, cleverness; [inf] smartness.
Opposites: incompetence.

skilled ADJ = *see* **skilful**.

skim VERB = **glide over**, move lightly over, brush, graze.

■ **skim through** = **read quickly**, glance at, scan, run one's eye over, flip through, leaf through, thumb through.

skimp VERB = **be sparing**, be economical, economize, be frugal, be mean, be parsimonious, be niggardly, scrimp, cut corners; [inf] be stingy.
Opposites: lavish.

skin NOUN 1 = **integument**, epidermis, cuticle, corium, derma. 2 = **hide**, pelt, fleece, fell, integument, tegument. 3 = **peel**, rind, hull, husk. 4 = **film**, coating, coat, layer, crust.

skinny ADJ = **thin**, thin as a rake, scraggy, scrawny, emaciated, skeletal; [inf] skin and bone. = *See also* **thin** ADJ **(1)**.

skip VERB 1 = **bound**, jump, leap, spring, hop, bounce, dance, caper, prance, trip, cavort, gambol, frisk, bob. 2 = **omit**, leave out, miss out, pass over, bypass, skim over.

skirmish NOUN = **battle**, fight, clash, conflict, encounter, confrontation, engagement, tussle, scrimmage, fracas.

skirt VERB 1 = **go round**, move round, walk round, circle, circumnavigate.

S

2 = evade, avoid, dodge, steer clear of, sidestep, circumvent, bypass.

skittish ADJ **= playful**, lively, frisky, sportive; [poetic/literary] frolicsome.

sky NOUN **= atmosphere**, air, airspace; [poetic/literary] the heavens, the firmament, the blue, the (wide) blue yonder, the welkin.

slab NOUN **= hunk**, piece, chunk, lump, slice, wedge, portion.

slack ADJ **1 = loose**, baggy, bagging, easy, hanging, flapping. **2 = slow**, quiet, inactive, sluggish. **3 = lax**, negligent, remiss, neglectful, careless, inattentive, offhand, slapdash, slipshod, sloppy, disorderly, disorganized, tardy. **Opposites:** tight.
▶ VERB **= idle**, shirk be inactive, be lazy, be indolent, be neglectful.

slacker NOUN **= idler**, shirker, loafer, dawdler, layabout, malingerer, good-for-nothing, clock-watcher.

slam VERB **= bang**, thump, crash, smash, dash, hurt, fling, throw.

slander NOUN **= defamation**, misrepresentation, calumny, libel, aspersions, vilification, verbal abuse, muckraking, smear campaigning, backbiting, obloquy, disparagement, denigration.
▶ VERB **= defame**, blacken someone's name, libel, cast aspersions on, malign, vilify, verbally abuse, smear, slur, backbite, disparage, denigrate, decry, run down; [formal] calumniate.

slanderous ADJ **= defamatory**, libellous, damaging, abusive, muckraking, malicious, backbiting, disparaging, denigrating; [formal] calumnious. **Opposites:** complimentary.

slang NOUN **1 = colloquialism**, informal language, lingo. **2 = jargon**, cant, argot; [inf] gobbledegook, technospeak, mumbo-jumbo.

slant VERB 1 = **slope**, tilt, be askew, lean, dip, shelve, list. 2 = **give a slant to**, give a bias to, bias, angle, distort, twist.
▶ NOUN 1 = **slope**, tilt, dip, leaning, inclination, shelving, listing. 2 = **bias**, leaning, one-sidedness, prejudice, angle, distortion, twist.

slanting ADJ = **slanted**, aslant, at an angle, sloping, italic, oblique, tilting, tilted, askew, leaning, dipping, shelving, listing, diagonal.

slap VERB = **smack**, strike, hit, cuff; [inf] wallop, clout, whack, biff, belt, sock.

slapdash ADJ = see **careless** (1, 2).

slaughter VERB = **kill**, butcher, massacre, murder, put to death, do to death, put to the sword; [poetic/literary] slay. = See also **kill** (1).
▶ NOUN = **massacre**, murder, butchery, killing, bloodshed, carnage.

slave NOUN [historical] serf, vassal;
[archaic] bondsman/woman.
▶ VERB = **toil**, drudge, slog, labour, grind, work one's fingers to the bone, work day and night, work like a Trojan.

slavery NOUN
= **enslavement**, bondage, servitude, subjugation;
[historical] serfdom, vassalage, thraldom.
Opposites: freedom.

slavish ADJ 1 = **servile**, subservient, obsequious, sycophantic, deferential, grovelling, fawning, cringing, menial, abject. 2 = **imitative**, unoriginal, uninspired, unimaginative.

slay VERB = **kill**, murder, slaughter, put to death, do to death, assassinate, do away with; [inf] rub out.

sleek ADJ = **smooth**, glossy, shiny, lustrous, silken, silky, satiny, burnished.

sleep VERB = **be asleep**, slumber, doze, nap, drowse; [inf] snooze,

S

crash, have forty winks, be in the land of Nod. **Opposites:** wake up.

▶ NOUN = **slumber**, doze, nap, rest, siesta, drowse; [inf] snooze, forty winks, a bit of shut-eye.

sleepiness NOUN = **drowsiness**, tiredness, somnolence, somnolency, languor, languidness, lethargy, sluggishness, inactivity, lassitude, torpor, torpidity.

sleepless ADJ = **without sleep**, wakeful, insomniac, restless, disturbed.

sleepy ADJ 1 = **drowsy**, tired, somnolent, languorous, lethargic, sluggish, inactive, heavy, torpid, comatose. 2 = **inactive**, quiet, peaceful, slow-moving, slumberous. **Opposites:** alert.

slender ADJ 1 = **slim**, thin, slight, lean, svelte, willowy, sylphlike. 2 = **small**, slight, slim, faint, remote, feeble, flimsy, tenuous, fragile. **Opposites:** fat.

sleuth NOUN = **detective**, investigator, private investigator; [inf] private eye, dick; [N. Amer. inf] gumshoe.

slice NOUN = **piece**, portion, segment, sliver, wedge, chunk, hunk; [Brit. inf] wodge.

▶ VERB = **cut up/through**, carve, chop, divide, cleave, sever.

slick ADJ 1 = **well organized**, streamlined, efficient, smooth, polished. 2 = **glib**, smooth, fluent, plausible, specious. 3 = **suave**, urbane, sophisticated, polished, glib, smooth, efficient, professional, smart, sharp, shrewd.

slide VERB = **slip**, skid, slither, skate, skim, glissade, glide.

slight ADJ 1 = **small**, little, tiny, minute, inappreciable, imperceptible, subtle, modest. 2 = **slim**, slender, small, spare, delicate, frail. **Opposites:** large.

▶ VERB = **snub**, insult, affront, rebuff, give the

cold shoulder to, cold-shoulder, keep at arm's length, disregard, ignore, neglect, take no notice of, disdain, scorn.
▸ NOUN = **snub**, insult, affront, rebuff, inattention, scorn, disdain; [inf] slap in the face.

slightly ADV = **a little**, a bit, somewhat, rather, to some degree.
Opposites: very.

slim ADJ 1 = **slender**, thin, slight, lean, narrow, svelte, willowy, sylphlike.
2 = **slight**, small, slender, faint, remote, feeble, flimsy, tenuous, fragile.
Opposites: fat, strong.
▸ VERB = **lose weight**, shed weight, diet, go on a diet.

slime NOUN = **sludge**, muck, ooze, mud; [inf] goo, gunk.

slimy ADJ 1 = **sludgy**, mucky, oozy, muddy, slippery, sticky, viscous, mucous. 2 = **oily**, unctuous, obsequious, sycophantic, servile, grovelling.

sling VERB = **toss**, fling, throw, cast, hurl, pitch, shy, lob; [inf] chuck, heave.

slink VERB = **skulk**, lurk, sneak, creep, steal, slip, slide.

slip VERB 1 = **skid**, slither, lose one's footing, lose one's balance. 2 = **fall**, slide, drop. 3 = **steal**, slide, creep, sneak, slink.
4 = **go down**, decline, decrease, lessen, depreciate, sink, slump, plummet.
▸ NOUN 1 = **slip-up**, mistake, error, blunder, miscalculation, oversight; [inf] boo-boo; [Brit. inf] boob; [Brit. inf, dated] bloomer.
2 = **underskirt**, petticoat.
▪ **slip up** = **make a mistake**, blunder, make a blunder, miscalculate, err; [inf] make a boo-boo, screw up; [Brit. inf] boob; [Brit. inf, dated] make a bloomer.

slippery ADJ 1 = **greasy**, oily, slimy, icy, glassy, smooth, soapy; [inf] slippy, skiddy.
2 = **shifty**, devious,

deceitful, duplicitous, crafty, cunning, sneaky, treacherous, perfidious, two-faced, dishonest, false, unreliable, untrustworthy; [inf] tricky, foxy.

slit VERB = **cut**, split open, slash, gash, rip, make an incision in, tear, rend, pierce.

▶ NOUN = **cut**, split, slash, gash, rip, incision, tear, rent, fissure, opening.

slither VERB = **slide**, slip, skid.

sliver NOUN = **chip**, flake, splinter, shred, fragment, scrap.

slobber VERB = **slaver**, drool, dribble, splutter.

slog

■ **slog away** = **work**, labour, toil, slave, drudge, plough.

slogan NOUN = **motto**, logo, catchword, jingle, rallying cry, shibboleth.

slop VERB = **spill**, overflow, splash, slosh, splatter, spatter.

slope VERB = **drop away**, fall away, slant, incline, lean, tilt, dip.

▶ NOUN = **slant**, inclination, angle, skew, tilt, dip, gradient.

sloping ADJ = **slanting**, oblique, leaning, inclined, angled, italic, askew, tilting, dipping. **Opposites:** level.

sloppy ADJ 1 = **watery**, wet, soggy, splashy, slushy, sludgy. 2 = **careless**, slapdash, slipshod, disorganized, unmethodical, untidy, messy, slovenly. **Opposites:** meticulous.

slot NOUN 1 = **slit**, crack, hole, opening, aperture, groove, notch. 2 = **place**, position, niche, space, opening, time, period.

sloth NOUN = **laziness**, indolence, idleness, sluggishness, inertia, inactivity, lethargy, langour, slothfulness, torpor.

slothful ADJ = **lazy**, indolent, idle, work-shy, sluggish, inert, inactive, lethargic, languorous, torpid. **Opposites:** industrious.

slovenly ADJ = **slatternly**, untidy, dirty, unclean,

messy, unkempt, dishevelled, bedraggled, tousled, rumpled. **Opposites:** tidy.

slow ADJ **1** = **slow-moving**, unhurried, leisurely, measured, deliberate, ponderous, creeping, dawdling, loitering, lagging, laggard, sluggish, snail-like, tortoise-like. **2** = **backward**, retarded, slow-witted, dull-witted, dull, unintelligent, stupid, thick, dense; [inf] dumb, dopey. **3** = **time-consuming**, protracted, drawn-out, prolonged, interminable. **Opposites:** quick, bright. ▶ VERB **1** = **reduce speed**, decelerate, put the brakes on. **2** = **hold back**, keep back, delay, detain, restrain.

slowly ADV = **at a slow pace**, without hurrying, unhurriedly, at a leisurely pace, steadily, ploddingly, taking one's time, in one's own good time, with heavy steps, at a snail's pace.

sluggish ADJ = **inactive**, inert, heavy, lifeless, apathetic, listless, lethargic, languid, languorous, torpid, phlegmatic, indolent, lazy, slothful, drowsy, sleepy. **Opposites:** energetic.

slump NOUN = **plunge**, nosedive, collapse, fall, falling-off, drop, downturn, downswing, slide, decline, decrease, lowering, devaluation, depreciation, depression. ▶ VERB **1** = **collapse**, sink, fall, subside. **2** = **plummet**, plunge, nosedive, fall, drop, go down, slide, decline, decrease, devalue. **Opposites:** rise.

slur NOUN = **insult**, slight, aspersion, imputation, affront, defamation, slander, libel, misrepresentation, smear, stain, stigma.

sly ADJ **1** = **cunning**, crafty, wily, artful, conniving, scheming, devious, underhand, shrewd, astute; [inf] tricky, foxy, smart. **2** = **roguish**, impish, mischievous, playful, arch, knowing.

S

smack NOUN & VERB = **slap**, blow, hit, whack, thump, cuff, punch, spank, buffet, rap, bang; [inf] wallop, clout, belt, sock.

small ADJ **1** = **little**, tiny, petite, slight, minute, miniature, pocket-size, mini, minuscule, diminutive, undersized, puny; [inf] pint-sized, teeny, teeny-weeny, teensy-weensy; [Scottish] wee. **2** = **slight**, minor, unimportant, trifling, trivial, insignificant, inconsequential, inappreciable. **3** = **humble**, modest, lowly, simple, unpretentious, poor, inferior. **4** = **narrow**, narrow-minded, mean, petty.
Opposites: big, large.

smart ADJ **1** = **well dressed**, well turned out, fashionably dressed, fashionable, stylish, modish, elegant, chic, neat, spruce, trim; [inf] natty, snappy, out of a bandbox. **2** = **clever**, bright, intelligent, gifted, sharp, quick-witted, nimble-witted, shrewd, ingenious. **3** = **brisk**, quick, fast, swift, lively, energetic, spirited, vigorous, jaunty; [inf] cracking, spanking.
Opposites: scruffy.
▶ VERB = **sting**, nip, burn, bite, pain.

smash VERB **1** = **break**, shatter, crash, shiver, pulverize, splinter, crack. **2** = **crash**, collide, wreck. **3** = **destroy**, ruin, shatter, devastate.

smattering NOUN = **bit**, modicum, dash, rudiments, elements.

smear VERB **1** = **spread**, daub, slap, plaster. **2** = **smudge**, streak, blur. **3** = **sully**, tarnish, blacken, taint, stain, slur, defame, defile, vilify, slander, libel; [formal] calumniate.
▶ NOUN **1** = **daub**, spot, patch; [inf] splotch. **2** = **smudge**, streak. **3** = **taint**, stain, slur, blot.

smell VERB **1** = **scent**, sniff, get a sniff of; [Brit. inf] get a whiff of. **2** = **have a bad smell**, stink, be stinking,

reek, be malodorous;
[inf] stink to high heaven;
[Brit. inf] pong, whiff,
hum.
▶ NOUN **1** = **odour**, scent,
aroma, perfume,
fragrance, bouquet;
[poetic/literary] redolence.
2 = **stink**, stench, reek;
[Brit. inf] pong, whiff,
hum.

smelly ADJ = **smelling**,
evil-smelling, foul-
smelling, stinking, high,
malodorous, fetid; [Brit.
inf] ponging, humming,
whiffy; [poetic/
literary] noisome,
mephitic.

smirk VERB = **leer**, sneer,
simper, grin.

smitten ADJ = **taken with**,
infatuated with,
enamoured of, attracted
by, charmed by,
captivated by, enchanted
by, beguiled by;
[inf] bowled over by.

smog NOUN = **haze**, fog,
pollution.

smoke VERB **1** = **smoulder**,
reek. **2** = **cure**, dry,
preserve.

smoky ADJ = **smoke-filled**,
hazy, foggy, smoggy,
reeky, murky.

smooth ADJ **1** = **even**,
level, flat, plane, flush,
unwrinkled. **2** = **calm**,
still, tranquil, flat, glassy,
mirror-like. **3** = **easy**,
effortless, trouble-free,
simple, plain sailing.
4 = **steady**, regular,
rhythmic, uninterrupted,
flowing, fluid.
5 = **smooth-tongued**,
suave, urbane,
sophisticated, courteous,
gracious, glib, persuasive,
slick, oily, ingratiating,
unctuous; [inf] smarmy.
Opposites: rough.
▶ VERB **1** = **level**, even,
flatten, plane, press
down, steamroll.
2 = **ease**, make easy/
easier, facilitate, clear the
way for, pave the way
for, open the door for,
expedite, assist, aid, help,
help along.

smother VERB
1 = **suffocate**, stifle,
asphyxiate, choke.
2 = **overwhelm**, shower,
inundate, envelop,
surround, cocoon.

smoulder VERB **1** = **smoke**,
reek. **2** = **seethe**, fume,

burn, boil, foam, rage.

smudge NOUN = **mark**, spot, smear, streak, stain, blotch, blot, blur, smut; [inf] splotch.

smug ADJ = **self-satisfied**, complacent, pleased with oneself, superior, proud of oneself, conceited.

snack NOUN = **light meal**, bite, nibbles, titbit, bite to eat, little something.

snag NOUN 1 = **catch**, drawback, hitch, stumbling block, obstacle, disadvantage, inconvenience, problem, complication. 2 = **rip**, tear, run, hole.
▶ VERB = **catch**, rip, tear.

snap VERB 1 = **break**, fracture, splinter, separate, come apart, crack. 2 = **crack**, click, crackle. 3 = **bite**, gnash, nip. 4 = **speak sharply/brusquely**, bark, snarl, growl, lash out at; [inf] jump down someone's throat, fly off the handle at.

snappy ADJ 1 = **irritable**, irascible, cross, touchy, testy, crabbed, crotchety, grumpy, grouchy,

peppery. 2 = **smart**, fashionable, stylish, chic, modish, dapper; [inf] natty, trendy.
Opposites: peaceable, slovenly.

snare VERB = **trap**, ensnare, catch, get hold of, seize, capture.
▶ NOUN = **trap**, gin, springe, net, noose.

snatch VERB 1 = **seize**, grab, take hold of, pluck. 2 = **grab**, steal, make off with, appropriate; [inf] nab, swipe. 3 = **kidnap**, abduct, grab, take as hostage.

sneak VERB 1 = **creep**, skulk, lurk, prowl, steal, slip, slide, slink, sidle. 2 = **tell tales on**, inform on, report; [inf] tell on, squeal on, peach on; [Brit. inf] grass on.

sneaking ADJ = **secret**, private, hidden, concealed, unexpressed, unvoiced, undisclosed, undivulged, unconfessed, unavowed.

sneer VERB 1 = **curl one's lip**, smirk, snicker, snigger. 2 = **scoff at**, scorn, be contemptuous

of, hold in contempt, disdain, mock, jeer at, gibe at, ridicule, deride, taunt, insult, slight.
▸ NOUN 1 = **smirk**, snicker.
2 = **jeer**, jibe, taunt, insult, slight.

sniff VERB 1 = **snuffle**, inhale, breathe in.
2 = **smell**, catch the scent of, scent; [Brit. inf] get a whiff of.

snigger VERB = **snicker**, sneer, smirk, titter, giggle, chortle.

snip VERB = **cut**, cut into, nick, slit, notch, incise, snick.
▸ NOUN 1 = **cut**, nick, slit, notch, incision, snick.
2 = **bargain**; [inf] good buy, cheap buy, giveaway, steal.

snippet NOUN = **bit**, piece, scrap, fragment, particle, shred, snatch.

snivel VERB 1 = **weep**, cry, sob, whimper; [inf] blub, blubber. 2 = **sniffle**, snuffle, run at the nose, have a runny/running nose.

snobbish ADJ = **snobby**, arrogant, proud, condescending, haughty, disdainful, supercilious, patronizing; [inf] snooty, uppity, stuck up, hoity-toity, toffee-nosed.

snoop VERB = **pry**, spy, interfere, meddle; [inf] poke one's nose in.
▸ NOUN = **busybody**, interferer, meddler; [inf] snooper, nosy parker; [Austral./NZ inf] stickybeak.

snooze VERB = **doze**, nap, catnap, drowse, sleep, slumber; [inf] take forty winks; [Brit. inf] have a kip, kip.
▸ NOUN = **doze**, nap, catnap, siesta, sleep, slumber; [inf] forty winks; [Brit. inf] kip.

snub VERB = **ignore**, disregard, take no notice of, shun, rebuff, repulse, spurn, slight, give the cold shoulder to, cold-shoulder, insult, affront; [inf] give the brush-off to, give the go-by, put down.

snug ADJ 1 = **cosy**, comfortable, warm, homelike, homely, sheltered; [inf] comfy.
2 = **close-fitting**, tight, skin-tight.

S

Opposites: bleak, loose.

snuggle VERB = **nestle**, cuddle, curl up, nuzzle.

soak VERB 1 = **drench**, wet through, saturate, make sopping. 2 = **steep**, immerse, souse.

soaking ADJ = **soaked**, soaked to the skin, wet through, drenched, sodden, saturated, sopping wet, dripping wet, wringing wet, streaming wet.
Opposites: parched.

soar VERB 1 = **fly**, take flight, take off, ascend, climb, rise. 2 = **rise**, go up, increase, climb rapidly, spiral.
Opposites: plummet.

sob VERB = **weep**, cry, shed tears, blubber, snivel, howl, bawl; [Scottish] greet; [inf] boohoo.

sober ADJ 1 = **not drunk/ intoxicated**, abstemious, teetotal, abstinent, temperate; [inf] on the wagon, dry. 2 = **serious**, solemn, thoughtful, grave, earnest, calm, composed, sedate, staid, dignified, steady, level-headed, self-controlled, strict, puritanical. 3 = **dispassionate**, objective, rational, logical, well considered, circumspect, lucid, clear. 4 = **dark**, sombre, quiet, restrained, drab, severe, austere.
Opposites: drunk.

sociable ADJ = **friendly**, affable, cordial, social, neighbourly, companionable, gregarious, convivial, communicative, genial, outgoing, approachable, accessible.
Opposites: unsociable, unfriendly.

social ADJ 1 = **community**, civil, civic, public, societal. 2 = **entertainment**, recreation, amusement. 3 = *See* **sociable**.
Opposites: individual.

socialize VERB = **be sociable/social**, mix, mingle, keep company, fraternize, consort, hobnob, get together, get out and about.

society NOUN 1 = **mankind**, humanity, civilization,

the public, the general public, the people, the population, the world at large, the community. **2** = **community**, group, culture, civilization. **3** = **high society**, polite society, aristocracy, gentry, nobility, upper classes, the elite, the smart set, beau monde, haut monde; [inf] the upper crust, the top drawer, toffs, nobs, swells. **4** = **association**, club, group, band, circle, body, fraternity, brotherhood, sisterhood, league, union, alliance, federation.

sodden ADJ = *see* **soaking**.

soft ADJ **1** = **pliable**, pliant, supple, elastic, flexible, ductile, malleable, plastic, mushy, squashy, pulpy, doughy, spongy; [inf] gooey. **2** = **smooth**, velvety, cushiony, fleecy, downy, furry, silky, silken, satin; [inf] like a baby's bottom. **3** = **low**, dim, shaded, subdued, muted, mellow. **4** = **hushed**, whispered, murmured, stifled,

inaudible, low, quiet, mellow, melodious, mellifluous. **5** = **easy-going**, tolerant, forgiving, forbearing, lenient, indulgent, permissive, liberal, lax. **Opposites:** firm, hard.

soften VERB **1** = **ease**, cushion, temper, mitigate, assuage. **2** = **abate**, moderate, lessen, diminish, calm down. **3** = **moderate**, temper, tone down.

soggy ADJ = **soaking**, saturated, sodden, sopping wet, soft, boggy, swampy, miry, waterlogged, over-moist.

soil[1] NOUN = **earth**, ground, clay, dirt, land.

soil[2] VERB = **dirty**, stain, muddy, spot, smear, splash, smudge, sully, taint, blot; [poetic/literary] besmirch.

soldier NOUN = **fighter**, serviceman, servicewoman, warrior, trooper; [inf] cannon fodder.

solemn ADJ **1** = **serious**, grave, important, formal, profound. **2** = **dignified**,

ceremonious, stately, majestic, imposing, impressive, grand. **3 = sombre**, serious, unsmiling, pensive, thoughtful, gloomy, glum, grim. **4 = earnest**, sincere, honest, genuine, committed, heartfelt.
Opposites: frivolous.

solicit VERB **1 = ask for**, request, apply for, seek, beg, plead for, crave. **2 = work as a prostitute**, engage in prostitution, make sexual advances; [inf] hustle.

solicitous ADJ **= concerned**, caring, attentive, considerate, anxious, worried, nervous, uneasy, apprehensive.

solid ADJ **1 = firm**, hard, thick, dense, concrete, compact, compressed, condensed. **2 = sturdy**, substantial, strong, sound, stout, durable, well built, well constructed, stable. **3 = sound**, well founded, well grounded, concrete, valid, reasonable, logical, cogent, weighty,

authoritative, convincing, plausible, reliable. **4 = sensible**, level-headed, down-to-earth, decent, law-abiding, upright, upstanding, worthy. **5 = staid**, worthy, sound, unexciting, unimaginative, uninspired. **6 = financially sound**, solvent, creditworthy, in good standing, in the black, secure. **7 = continuous**, uninterrupted, unbroken, undivided.
Opposites: liquid, flimsy, unreliable.

solidarity NOUN **= unity**, union, unanimity, singleness of purpose, like-mindedness, team spirit, camaraderie, harmony, esprit de corps.

solidify VERB **= harden**, go hard, set, jell, congeal, cake.
Opposites: liquefy.

solitary ADJ **1 = lonely**, lonesome, companionless, friendless, antisocial, unsocial, unsociable, withdrawn, reclusive,

cloistered, introverted, hermitic. **2 = remote**, out of the way, isolated, secluded, hidden, concealed, private, unfrequented, unvisited, desolate. **3 = lone**, single, sole, alone, by oneself/itself.
Opposites: sociable, accessible.

▸ NOUN **= loner**, lone wolf, recluse, hermit, eremite, anchorite, stylite, coenobite.

solitude NOUN **= loneliness**, remoteness, isolation, seclusion, privacy, retirement, desolation.

solution NOUN **1 = answer**, result, key, resolution, solving, resolving, explanation, clarification, elucidation, unravelling, unfolding. **2 = suspension**, emulsion, mixture, mix, blend, compound.

solve VERB **= find the solution to**, answer, find the answer to, resolve, work out, figure out, fathom, find the key to, decipher, clear up, get to the bottom of, unravel, disentangle, unfold; [inf] crack.

solvent ADJ **= financially sound**, debt-free, creditworthy, in the black, viable.
Opposites: insolvent.

sombre ADJ **1 = dark**, dark-coloured, dull, dull-coloured, drab, dingy. **2 = gloomy**, depressed, sad, melancholy, dismal, doleful, mournful, joyless, cheerless, lugubrious, funereal, sepulchral.
Opposites: bright, cheerful.

somehow ADV **= by some means**, in some way, in one way or other, no matter how, come what may, by fair means or foul, by hook or by crook; [inf] come hell or high water.

sometimes ADV **= occasionally**, on occasion, on occasions, now and then, now and again, from time to time, once in a while, every so often, off and on.

somnolent ADJ = **sleepy**, drowsy, half asleep, heavy-eyed, dozy, groggy, comatose; [inf] dopey.

sonorous ADJ = **deep**, rich, full, round, resonant, resounding, booming, ringing, reverberating, vibrating, pulsating.

soon ADV = **shortly**, in a short time, in a little while, before long, in a minute, in a moment, any minute, in the near future, in a twinkling, in the twinkling of an eye; [inf] before you can say Jack Robinson, pronto, in two shakes of a lamb's tail.

soothe VERB = **ease**, assuage, alleviate, allay, moderate, mitigate, temper, palliate, soften, lessen, reduce.
Opposites: aggravate.

sophisticated ADJ
1 = **worldly-wise**, worldly, experienced, seasoned, suave, urbane, cultured, cultivated, polished, refined, elegant, stylish, cosmopolitan, blasé.

2 = **advanced**, highly developed, ultra-modern, complex, complicated, elaborate, intricate.
Opposites: unsophisticated, crude.

soppy ADJ = **mawkish**, maudlin, sentimental, overemotional, sloppy; [inf] slushy, mushy, schmaltzy, corny.

sorcerer NOUN = **magician**, wizard, enchanter, warlock, necromancer, magus, thaumaturgist.

sorcery NOUN = **magic**, witchcraft, witchery, wizardry, necromancy, black art, enchantment, thaumaturgy.

sordid ADJ **1** = **filthy**, dirty, foul, unclean, grimy, sooty, soiled, stained, mucky, squalid, shabby, seedy, seamy, slummy, sleazy. **2** = **vile**, foul, base, low, debased, degenerate, dishonourable, disreputable, despicable, ignominious, ignoble, abhorrent, abominable.
3 = **mean**, greedy, avaricious, covetous, grasping, mercenary, miserly, niggardly;

[inf] stingy.
Opposites: clean.

sore ADJ **1** = **painful**, in pain, aching, hurting, tender, inflamed, raw, smarting, stinging, burning, irritated, bruised, wounded, injured. **2** = **distressed**, upset, resentful, aggrieved, offended, hurt, pained, annoyed, angry, irritated, irked, nettled; [inf] peeved.
▶ NOUN = **wound**, scrape, abrasion, cut, laceration, graze, boil, abscess, swelling.

sorrow NOUN **1** = **sadness**, unhappiness, grief, misery, distress, heartache, heartbreak, anguish, suffering, pain, woe, affliction, wretchedness, dejection, heaviness of heart, desolation, depression, disconsolateness, mourning. **2** = **trouble**, worry, woe, misfortune, affliction, trial, tribulation.
Opposites: joy.
▶ VERB = **be sad**, feel sad, be miserable, suffer, be

wretched, be dejected, be heavy of heart, pine, weep.

sorrowful ADJ = **unhappy**, heartbroken, wretched, woebegone, tearful, miserable, dejected, desolated, depressed, disconsolate, mournful, doleful, melancholy, lugubrious. = *See also* **sad** (**1**).
Opposites: happy.

sorry ADJ **1** = **regretful**, apologetic, repentant, penitent, remorseful, contrite, ashamed, conscience-stricken, guilt-ridden, in sackcloth and ashes, compunctious. **2** = **sympathetic**, pitying, full of pity, compassionate, moved, commiserative, empathetic.
Opposites: glad, unsympathetic, unrepentant.

sort NOUN **1** = **kind**, type, variety, class, category, style, group, set, genre, genus, family, order, breed, make, brand, stamp. **2** = **person**,

S

individual, soul;
[inf] fellow, guy,
character, customer; [Brit.
inf] bloke, chap.
▸ VERB = **classify**, class,
categorize, catalogue,
grade, rank, group,
divide, arrange, order,
put in order, organize,
assort, systematize,
methodize.
■ **sort out** = **clear up**, put
straight, put right, solve,
find a solution to.

sortie NOUN = **sally**, foray,
charge, rush, onrush,
raid, attack.

soul NOUN 1 = **spirit**,
psyche, inner self, true
being, vital force,
animating principle.
2 = **person**, human being,
individual, creature.

sound[1] NOUN 1 = **noise**,
utterance, cry.
2 = **hearing**, distance,
earshot, range.
Opposites: silence.
▸ VERB 1 = **resound**,
reverberate, resonate.
2 = **pronounce**, utter,
voice, enunciate,
articulate, vocalize.
3 = **appear**, seem, give/
create the impression

that, strike someone that,
give every indication
that.

sound[2] ADJ 1 = **healthy**, in
good health, in good
condition, physically fit,
hale and hearty,
undamaged, unimpaired,
in good shape, in fine
fettle. 2 = **sturdy**,
substantial, solid, well
constructed, intact,
whole, undamaged,
unimpaired. 3 = **well
founded**, well grounded,
solid, valid, reasonable,
logical, cogent, weighty,
authoritative,
convincing, plausible,
reliable. 4 = **solvent**,
creditworthy, in good
financial standing, in the
black, solid, secure.
5 = **thorough**, complete,
without reserve,
unqualified, out-and-out,
drastic, severe.
Opposites: unhealthy,
flimsy, insolvent.

sound[3] VERB = **plumb**,
fathom, probe.
■ **sound out**
= **investigate**, conduct a
survey of, research,
explore, look into,

examine, probe, canvass.

sour ADJ **1** = **acid**, acidy, acid-like, acetic, acidulous, tart, bitter, sharp, vinegary, pungent. **2** = **turned**, curdled, fermented, rancid, bad. **3** = **embittered**, nasty, unpleasant, disagreeable, bad-tempered, ill-tempered, ill-natured, sharp-tongued, irritable, crotchety, cross, crabbed, testy, touchy, peevish, churlish, grumpy; [inf] grouchy, snappish. **Opposites:** sweet, fresh, amiable.

source NOUN **1** = **origin**, derivation, commencement, beginning, start, rise, cause, wellspring, fountainhead, provenance, author, originator; [poetic/literary] begetter. **2** = **wellspring**, well head, headspring. **3** = **reference**, authority.

sovereign NOUN = **ruler**, monarch, king, queen, emperor, empress, tsar, crowned head, potentate.

▶ ADJ **1** = **supreme**, absolute, unlimited, chief, paramount, principal, dominant, predominant, ruling. **2** = **independent**, self-ruling, self-governing, autonomous.

sow VERB = **scatter**, spread, broadcast, disperse, strew, bestrew, disseminate, distribute.

space NOUN **1** = **room**, expanse, extent, capacity, area, volume, spaciousness, scope, elbow room, latitude, margin, leeway. **2** = **gap**, interval, opening, interstice, break. **3** = **time**, duration, period, span, stretch, interval. **4** = **outer space**, the universe, the galaxy, the solar system, infinity.
▶ VERB = **place at intervals**, arrange, line up, range, order, interspace, set apart.

spacious ADJ = **roomy**, commodious, capacious, sizable, ample, large, big, extensive, broad, wide, expansive, vast. **Opposites:** small.

S

span NOUN **1 = length**, extent, reach, stretch, spread, distance. **2 = time**, duration, period, space, stretch, interval.
▶ VERB **= extend over**, stretch across, cover, range over, bridge, cross, traverse, pass over, arch over, vault over.

spare ADJ **1 = extra**, additional, reserve, supplementary, auxiliary, surplus, supernumerary. **2 = free**, leisure, unoccupied. **3 = lean**, thin, slim, slender, skinny, skin and bone, wiry, lank.
▶ VERB **1 = afford**, part with, give, provide, dispense with, do without, manage without, get along without. **2 = be merciful to**, show mercy to, be lenient to, deal leniently with, pardon, leave unpunished; [inf] let off, go easy on.

sparing ADJ **= economical**, frugal, thrifty, careful, prudent, parsimonious, niggardly; [inf] stingy, tight-fisted.
Opposites: extravagant.

spark NOUN **= flicker**, flash, flare, glint.
▶ VERB **= set off**, spark off, start off, trigger off, touch off, precipitate, provoke, stir up, incite.

sparkle VERB **1 = twinkle**, flicker, shimmer, flash, glitter, glint, shine, gleam, glow, coruscate. **2 = be vivacious**, be lively, be animated, be ebullient, be effervescent, be witty, be brilliant.
▶ NOUN **1 = twinkle**, flicker, shimmer, flash, glitter, glint, shining, gleam, glow, coruscation. **2 = vivacity**, liveliness, life, animation, energy, vitality, spirit, enthusiasm, dash, panache; [inf] pizzazz, vim, zip, zing.

sparse ADJ **= scanty**, meagre, slight, light, sparing, inadequate; [inf] thin on the ground.
Opposites: abundant.

spartan ADJ **= austere**, harsh, frugal, stringent, rigorous, strict, severe, bleak, grim, ascetic, abstemious, self-denying.
Opposites: luxurious.

spasm NOUN
1 = **contraction**, convulsion, cramp, twitch. 2 = **fit**, paroxysm, convulsion, attack, bout, seizure, outburst, access.

spasmodic ADJ
= **intermittent**, fitful, irregular, sporadic, erratic, periodic, recurring, recurrent.
Opposites: regular.

spate NOUN = **rush**, flood, deluge, torrent, outpouring, outbreak, cluster.

spatter VERB = **splash**, spray, shower, bespatter, daub.

speak VERB 1 = **utter**, voice, express, say, pronounce, articulate, enunciate, state, discourse upon, tell. 2 = **address**, talk to, converse with, communicate with, have a discussion with, chat with, have a chat with, have a word with, accost; [inf] have a chinwag with, chew the fat/rag with, pass the time of day with.
■ **speak for** 1 = **represent**, act for, act on behalf of, intercede for. 2 = **support**, uphold, defend, stand up for, advocate.
■ **speak out** = **speak boldly**, speak frankly, speak openly, speak one's mind, sound off, stand up and be counted.

speaker NOUN = **public speaker**, lecturer, orator, declaimer, haranguer, demagogue; [inf] tub-thumper, spieler.

spearhead NOUN
= **vanguard**, van, forefront, driving force.
▶ VERB = **lead**, head, set in motion, initiate, launch, pioneer.

special ADJ
1 = **exceptional**, remarkable, unusual, rare, out of the ordinary, extraordinary, singular, distinctive, notable, outstanding, unique.
2 = **specific**, particular, individual, distinctive, exact, precise, definite.
3 = **especial**, extra special, particular, exceptional, out of the ordinary.
4 = **significant**, momentous, memorable, festive, gala, red-letter.

S

Opposites: ordinary.

specialist NOUN = **expert**, authority, professional, consultant, master.

speciality NOUN
1 = **specialty**, area of specialization, field of study. **2** = **distinctive feature**, forte, métier, talent, gift, claim to fame.

species NOUN = **sort**, kind, type, variety, class, category, group, genus, breed, genre.

specific ADJ **1** = **well defined**, clear-cut, unambiguous, unequivocal, exact, precise, explicit, express, detailed. **2** = **particular**, specified, fixed, set, determined, distinct, definite.
Opposites: vague, general.

specify VERB = **state**, mention, name, stipulate, define, set out, itemize, designate, detail, list, spell out, enumerate, particularize, catalogue, be specific about.

specimen NOUN = **sample**, representative, example, illustration, instance, type, exhibit.

specious ADJ
= **misleading**, deceptive, fallacious, unsound, casuistic, sophistic.

speck NOUN **1** = **spot**, fleck, dot, speckle, stain, mark, smudge, blemish.
2 = **particle**, bit, piece, atom, iota, grain, trace.

speckled ADJ = **mottled**, flecked, spotted, dotted, dappled, brindled, stippled.

spectacle NOUN **1** = **sight**, vision, scene, picture.
2 = **display**, show, exhibition, pageant, parade, extravaganza.

spectacles NOUN
= **glasses**, eyeglasses; [inf] specs.

spectacular ADJ
= **impressive**, magnificent, splendid, eye-catching, breathtaking, glorious, dazzling, sensational, stunning, dramatic, exceptional, remarkable, unusual, picturesque; [inf] out of this world.
Opposites: unimpressive, dull.

spectator NOUN = **viewer**, observer, onlooker, looker-on, watcher, beholder, witness, eyewitness, bystander; [inf] rubberneck.
Opposites: participant.

spectre NOUN = **apparition**, ghost, phantom, wraith, spirit, shade, vision, revenant, manes; [inf] spook.

speculate VERB
1 = **conjecture**, theorize, hypothesize, guess, take a guess, surmise, muse, reflect, meditate, deliberate, cogitate, consider, think.
2 = **gamble**, take a risk on, venture on; [inf] have a flutter on.

speculative ADJ
1 = **conjectural**, theoretical, hypothetical, suppositional, notional, academic, tentative, unproven, vague, indefinite. **2** = **risky**, hazardous, gambling; [inf] chancy, dicey.

speech NOUN
1 = **communication**, talk, conversation, discussion, dialogue, colloquy.

2 = **diction**, articulation, enunciation, pronunciation. **3** = **talk**, lecture, address, discourse, oration, sermon, harangue, diatribe, tirade; [poetic/literary] philippic.
4 = **language**, tongue, idiom, dialect, parlance; [inf] lingo.

speechless ADJ **1** = **struck dumb**, dumbstruck, dumbfounded, astounded, thunderstruck. **2** = **silent**, unspoken, unexpressed, unsaid, unvoiced, tacit.

speed NOUN = **rapidity**, swiftness, quickness, fastness, haste, hurry, hurriedness, expeditiousness, expedition, alacrity, promptness, fleetness, celerity, velocity.
▶ VERB **1** = **hurry**, hasten, make haste, rush, race, dash, sprint, scurry, tear, scamper, charge; [inf] scoot. **2** = **drive too fast**, break the speed limit, exceed the speed limit; [inf] put one's foot down, step on it.

3 = **expedite**, hasten, accelerate, advance, further, forward, facilitate, promote, boost, aid, assist.
Opposites: slow, hinder.

■ **speed up** = see **accelerate**.

speedy ADJ = **rapid**, swift, quick, fast, high-speed, expeditious, fleet, prompt, immediate, express.
Opposites: slow, leisurely.

spell[1] VERB = **mean**, signify, amount to, add up to, signal, denote, result in, cause, bespeak, portend, augur, presage.

■ **spell out** = **specify**, set out, itemize, detail, enumerate, particularize, stipulate, make clear, make plain, elucidate, clarify.

spell[2] NOUN **1** = **incantation**, conjuration, charm, abracadabra. **2** = **trance**, entrancement, enthralment, bewitchment.

spell[3] NOUN **1** = **period**, interval, stretch, course, extent, span, patch.
2 = **turn**, stint, term, stretch, shift.

spellbound ADJ = **riveted**, entranced, enthralled, enraptured, transported, rapt, bewitched, fascinated, captivated, mesmerized, hypnotized; [inf] hooked.

spend VERB **1** = **pay out**, lay out, expend, disburse, dish out; [inf] fork out, shell out, splash out, splurge. **2** = **occupy**, fill, take up, use up, pass, while away.

spendthrift NOUN = **squanderer**, prodigal, profligate, wastrel; [inf] big spender.
Opposites: miser.

spent ADJ = **used up**, consumed, exhausted, finished, depleted, drained, emptied; [inf] played out, burnt out.

sphere NOUN **1** = **globe**, ball, orb, globule.
2 = **area**, field, range, scope, extent, compass, jurisdiction. **3** = **social class**, station, rank, status, social circumstances, walk of life.

spherical ADJ = **globe-shaped**, globular, globoid, round, orb-like, orbicular.

spice NOUN 1 = **flavouring**, seasoning, herb, condiment, relish.
2 = **excitement**, interest, colour, piquancy, zest, gusto, pep; [inf] zip, zing, zap.

spicy ADJ 1 = **spiced**, seasoned, tangy, sharp, tart, hot, peppery, piquant, pungent.
2 = **lively**, spirited, suggestive, racy, off colour, improper, indecent, offensive; [inf] raunchy.
Opposites: bland, boring.

spill VERB 1 = **pour**, pour out, flow, overflow, brim over, run over, slop over, well over. 2 = **reveal**, disclose, divulge, leak, make known; [inf] let out, blab.
▶ NOUN = **fall**, tumble; [inf] header, nosedive.

spin VERB 1 = **revolve**, rotate, turn, turn round, circle, whirl, gyrate.
2 = **whirl**, reel, swim, be giddy.

■ **spin out** = see prolong.

spine NOUN 1 = **spinal column**, vertebrae, vertebral column, backbone, dorsum.
2 = **needle**, spike, barb, quill.

spiral ADJ = **coiled**, corkscrew, winding, twisting, whorled, helical, cochlear, cochleate, voluted.
▶ NOUN = **coil**, twist, whorl, corkscrew, wreath, curlicue, helix, volute.
▶ VERB = **coil**, wind, twist, swirl, wreathe.

spirit NOUN 1 = **soul**, psyche, inner self, ego.
2 = **breath of life**, vital spark, animating principle, life force.
3 = **apparition**, ghost, phantom, spectre, wraith, shade, revenant, manes; [inf] spook.
4 = **courage**, bravery, braveness, valour, mettle, pluck, grit, pluckiness, will power, motivation, backbone, determination, firmness of purpose, resoluteness; [inf] guts.
5 = **attitude**, way, state of mind, mood, frame of

mind, point of view, reaction, feeling, humour. 6 = **prevailing tendency**, animating principle, dominating characteristic, ethos, essence, quintessence, embodiment, personification. **Opposites:** body, flesh.

spirited ADJ
1 = **courageous**, brave, valiant, valorous, heroic, mettlesome, plucky, gritty, determined, resolute. 2 = **animated**, lively, vivacious, enthusiastic, fervent, fiery, passionate, energetic. **Opposites:** timid, lifeless.

spiritual ADJ 1 = **non-material**, incorporeal, ethereal, intangible, other-worldly, unworldly. 2 = **religious**, sacred, divine, holy, non-secular, churchly, ecclesiastic, devotional, devout. **Opposites:** physical, secular.

spit VERB = **expectorate**, hawk.

▶ NOUN = **spittle**, saliva, sputum.

spite NOUN = **malice**, maliciousness, ill will, malevolence, venom, malignance, hostility, resentment, resentfulness, snideness, rancour, envy, hate, hatred, vengeance, vengefulness, vindictiveness. **Opposites:** benevolence.

■ **in spite of** = **despite**, despite the fact, notwithstanding, regardless of.

spiteful ADJ = **malicious**, ill-natured, malevolent, venomous, poisonous, malignant, malign, hostile, resentful, snide, rancorous, grudging, envious, vengeful, vindictive, splenetic; [inf] bitchy, catty. **Opposites:** benevolent.

splash VERB 1 = **spatter**, sprinkle, spray, shower, splatter, squirt, slosh, slop; [Brit. inf] splodge. 2 = **paddle**, wade, wallow, dabble. 3 = **blazon**, display, exhibit, plaster, publicize, broadcast, headline, flaunt, trumpet.

splendid ADJ
1 = **magnificent**, imposing, superb, grand, sumptuous, resplendent, opulent, luxurious, plush, de luxe, rich, costly, lavish, ornate, gorgeous, glorious, dazzling, brilliant, showy, elegant, handsome.
2 = **distinguished**, impressive, glorious, illustrious, brilliant, notable, noted, remarkable, outstanding, eminent, celebrated, renowned, noble, venerable. 3 = **excellent**, fine, first-class, first-rate, marvellous, wonderful, great; [inf] fantastic, terrific, fabulous, fab.
Opposites: inferior, undistinguished.

splendour NOUN
1 = **magnificence**, grandeur, sumptuousness, opulence, luxury, luxuriousness, richness, lavishness, gloriousness, elegance.

2 = **illustriousness**, brilliance, notability, eminence, renown, venerableness.
3 = **gloriousness**, brilliance, brightness, gleam, glow, lustre, radiance.

splice VERB = **interweave**, braid, plait, intertwine, interlace, join, unite, connect, bind.

splinter NOUN = **sliver**, fragment, shiver, shard, chip, shaving, shred, piece, bit.
▶ VERB = **shatter**, fracture, split, disintegrate, crumble.

split VERB 1 = **break**, chop, hew, lop, cleave, rend, rip, tear, slash, slit, splinter. 2 = **divide**, separate, set apart, disunite. 3 = **share**, divide, halve, apportion, distribute, dole out, parcel out, allot, allocate; [Brit. inf] divvy. 4 = **break up with/from**, separate from, part from, part company with, reach the parting of the ways, dissociate oneself from.

Opposites: mend, unite, pool, converge.

▶ NOUN 1 = **break**, cut, rent, rip, tear, slash, slit, crack, fissure, breach. 2 = **division**, rift, schism, rupture, separation, break-up, alienation, estrangement. Opposites: marriage.

spoil VERB 1 = **damage**, impair, mar, blemish, disfigure, deface, injure, harm, ruin, destroy, wreck. 2 = **upset**, mess up, disorganize, ruin, destroy, wreck. 3 = **pamper**, overindulge, mollycoddle, cosset, coddle, baby, spoon-feed, feather-bed, wait on hand and foot, kill with kindness. 4 = **go bad**, go off, turn, go sour, become rotten, rot, become tainted, decompose, decay. Opposites: improve, further.

spoilsport NOUN = **killjoy**, damper, dog in the manger; [inf] wet blanket, party-pooper, misery.

spoken ADJ = **oral**, verbal, uttered, voiced, expressed, by word of mouth, unwritten. Opposites: non-verbal, written.

sponge VERB = **clean**, wash, wipe, mop, rub, swab.

spongy ADJ = **soft**, cushiony, squashy, springy, resilient, elastic, porous, absorbent.

sponsor NOUN = **patron**, backer, promoter, subsidizer, guarantor, supporter, angel.

▶ VERB = **be a patron of**, back, put up the money for, fund, finance, promote, subsidize, support, lend one's name to.

spontaneous ADJ 1 = **voluntary**, unforced, unconstrained, unprompted. 2 = **unplanned**, unpremeditated, unrehearsed, impromptu, extempore, spur-of-the-moment, extemporaneous; [inf] off-the-cuff. 3 = **natural**, instinctive, involuntary, automatic, impulsive, impetuous.

Opposites: conscious, voluntary.

sporadic ADJ = **irregular**, intermittent, scattered, random, infrequent, occasional, on and off, isolated, spasmodic.
Opposites: frequent, regular.

sport NOUN 1 = **physical activity**, physical exercise, physical recreation, athletics, game, pastime.
2 = **amusement**, entertainment, diversion, play, fun, pleasure, enjoyment.
▶ VERB 1 = **play**, have fun, amuse oneself, entertain oneself, divert oneself, frolic, gambol, frisk, romp, cavort, caper, disport oneself. 2 = **wear**, exhibit, display, have on show, show off.

sporting ADJ
= **sportsmanlike**, fair, just, honourable, generous.

spot NOUN 1 = **mark**, dot, speck, fleck, smudge, stain, blotch, patch; [inf] splotch. 2 = **pimple**, pustule, papule, boil,

whitehead, blackhead, blemish. 3 = **stain**, taint, blemish, defect, flaw, brand, stigma. 4 = **area**, place, site, location, scene, setting, situation.
▶ VERB 1 = **catch sight of**, see, notice, observe, espy, discern, descry, detect, make out, pick out, recognize. 2 = **mark**, stain, dirty, soil, spatter; [poetic/literary] besmirch.

spotless ADJ 1 = **clean**, snowy-white, whiter-than-white, spick and span, immaculate, shining, gleaming.
2 = **pure**, flawless, faultless, blameless, unstained, unsullied, untainted, unblemished, unimpeachable, above reproach.
Opposites: dirty, impure.

spotlight NOUN = **limelight**, public eye, glare of publicity, publicity, public attention, public interest.

spotted ADJ = **dappled**, mottled, dotted, piebald, speckled.

spotty ADJ 1 = **pimply**, acned. 2 = *See* **spotted**.

3 = **patchy**, irregular, non-uniform.

spouse NOUN = **husband/ wife**, partner, mate, companion, consort, helpmate; [inf] better half, old man/woman/lady, missis.

spout VERB **1** = **spurt**, gush, spew, squirt, jet, spray, emit, erupt, disgorge, pour, stream, flow. **2** = **declaim**, orate, hold forth, ramble, rant, harangue, speechify, sermonize; [inf] spiel.

sprawl VERB **1** = **stretch out**, lounge, lie around, repose, recline, slump, flop, loll, slouch. **2** = **spread**, stretch, spill over, ramble, straggle, trail.

spray¹ NOUN **1** = **shower**, jet, mist, drizzle, spindrift, foam, froth. **2** = **atomizer**, vaporizer, aerosol, sprinkler. ▶ VERB **1** = **sprinkle**, shower, disperse, disseminate. **2** = **jet**, spout, gush.

spray² NOUN = **sprig**, posy, bouquet, nosegay, corsage, wreath, garland.

spread VERB **1** = **stretch**, extend, open out, unfurl, unroll. **2** = **enlarge**, extend, stretch out, grow bigger, widen, broaden, grow, develop, branch out. **3** = **cover**, coat, layer, lay on, put on, apply, smear on; [inf] plaster on. **4** = **disseminate**, circulate, transmit, make public, make known, broadcast, publicize, propagate, promulgate, bruit. ▶ NOUN **1** = **extent**, stretch, span, reach, compass, sweep. **2** = **expansion**, advance, increase, mushrooming, proliferation, escalation, diffusion. **3** = **bedspread**, bedcover, cover, coverlet, counterpane, throw. **4** = **feast**, banquet, repast; [inf] blowout.

spree NOUN = **outing**, fling, revel, junket, orgy, debauch, bacchanal, bacchanalia; [inf] binge, bender, jag.

sprightly ADJ = **spry**, lively, energetic, active, agile, nimble, supple, animated, vivacious, spirited, brisk, vital, light-hearted, cheerful, merry, jolly, jaunty, perky, frisky, playful, sportive; [poetic/literary] frolicsome, blithe. **Opposites:** inactive, lethargic.

spring VERB = **jump**, leap, bound, vault, hop.
▶ NOUN **1** = **jump**, leap, bound, vault, hop.
2 = **bounce**, bounciness, liveliness, light-heartedness, merriment.
▪ **spring from** = **originate**, have its origins in, derive from, stem from, arise in, emanate from, proceed from, start from.
▪ **spring up** = **appear**, come into being, come into existence, shoot up, develop quickly, mushroom, burgeon.

springy ADJ = **bouncy**, elastic, resilient, flexible, stretchy, tensile. **Opposites:** rigid.

sprinkle VERB = **spray**, shower, splash, trickle, spatter, scatter, strew, dust, powder.

sprinkling NOUN
1 = **scattering**, dusting.
2 = **few**, handful, trickle.

sprint VERB = **run**, race, rush, dash, put on a turn/burst of speed; [inf] scoot, tear, hare, hotfoot it.

sprout VERB = **bud**, germinate, put forth shoots, shoot up, spring up, grow, develop, appear, mushroom, proliferate.

spruce ADJ = **neat**, well groomed, well turned out, smart, trim, dapper, elegant, chic; [inf] natty. **Opposites:** dishevelled.

spur NOUN = **goad**, prod, stimulus, stimulant, incentive, inducement, encouragement, impetus. **Opposites:** disincentive.
▶ VERB = **prod**, goad, stimulate, give the incentive to, induce, encourage, motivate, prompt, urge, impel. **Opposites:** discourage.

spurious ADJ
= **counterfeit**, fraudulent, fake, bogus, sham, mock, feigned, pretended, pseudo, make-believe, imitation, contrived, fictitious, deceitful, specious; [inf] phoney.

S

Opposites: authentic, genuine.

spurn VERB = **reject**, turn away, repulse, rebuff, repudiate, snub, slight, cold-shoulder, disdain, look down one's nose at, scorn, despise, condemn; [inf] kick in the teeth, give the go-by. **Opposites:** welcome, accept.

spurt VERB = **gush**, squirt, shoot, surge, well, jet, spring, pour, stream, flow, issue, emanate.
▶ NOUN **1** = **gush**, surge, jet, spray, outpouring. **2** = **burst**, outburst, fit, surge, access.

spy NOUN = **enemy agent**, foreign agent, secret agent, undercover agent, intelligence agent, double agent, fifth columnist; [inf] mole, spook.
▶ VERB = **catch sight of**, spot, see, notice, observe, glimpse, make out, discern, descry, espy.
▪ **spy on** = **keep under surveillance**, watch, keep a watch on, keep an eye on, observe, keep under observation, follow, shadow, trail.

squabble NOUN = **dispute**, argument, wrangle, brawl; [inf] row, scrap, set-to, dust-up, run-in, spat; [Brit. inf] barney.
▶ VERB = **have a dispute**, argue, bicker, have a difference of opinion, have words, wrangle, brawl; [inf] row, have a tiff.

squalid ADJ **1** = **dirty**, filthy, dingy, grubby, grimy, mucky, foul, vile, low, wretched, mean, nasty, seedy, sordid, sleazy, slovenly, repulsive, disgusting, ramshackle, broken-down, tumbledown; [inf] grungy; [Brit. inf] grotty. **2** = **sordid**, vile, nasty, repulsive, horrible, disgraceful, shameful, abominable, odious, filthy, indecent, depraved. **Opposites:** clean, decent.

squander VERB = **waste**, misspend, dissipate, fritter away, run through, lavish, splurge, be prodigal with, spend like water, pour down the drain; [inf] blow. **Opposites:** save.

square NOUN = **piazza**, plaza, market square, marketplace, quadrangle.
▶ ADJ **1** = **equal**, even, level-pegging, drawn. **2** = **fair**, just, equitable, honest, straight, upright, above board, ethical; [inf] on the level.

squash VERB **1** = **crush**, squeeze, flatten, compress, press, smash, pulp, mash, pulverize, macerate. **2** = **crowd**, crush, cram, pack tight, jam, squeeze, wedge. **3** = **put down**, quash, quell, crush, suppress, scotch.

squashy ADJ = **pulpy**, mushy, spongy, squishy, oozy, pappy.
Opposites: firm.

squat ADJ = **dumpy**, stubby, chunky, thickset, stocky, short.

squeak NOUN & VERB = **squeal**, peep, pipe, yelp, whimper.

squeamish ADJ **1** = **easily nauseated**, liable to be made to feel sick, easily

put off, nervous, unable to stand the sight of. **2** = **scrupulous**, particular, punctilious, finicky, fussy, fastidious.

squeeze VERB
1 = **compress**, crush, squash, mash, pulp.
2 = **grip**, clutch, pinch, press, compress.
3 = **crowd**, crush, cram, pack tight, jam, squash, wedge. **4** = **pressure**, pressurize, strong-arm, blackmail; [inf] put the squeeze on, lean on, bleed, put the screws on, put the bite on.

squirm VERB = **wriggle**, wiggle, writhe, twist, turn, shift.

squirt VERB = **spurt**, spout, jet, stream, spray, gush, surge, pour, flow, issue, spew out.

stab VERB = **knife**, pierce, puncture, run through, stick, skewer, gash, slash, wound, injure.
▶ NOUN **1** = **puncture**, gash, slash, incision, wound, injury. **2** = **pang**, twinge, ache, throb, spasm.
3 = **try**, attempt, endeavour, essay, effort,

venture; [inf] go, crack.

stability NOUN = **firmness**, solidity, steadiness, secureness, strength, fastness, stoutness, sturdiness, sureness, durability, constancy, permanence, reliability, dependability.
Opposites: instability.

stable ADJ **1** = **firm**, solid, steady, secure, fixed, strong, fast, stout, sturdy, immovable. **2** = **secure**, solid, strong, steady, firm, sure, steadfast, unwavering, unfaltering, unswerving, long-lasting, deep-rooted, well founded, well grounded, abiding, durable, enduring, lasting, constant, permanent.
3 = **well balanced**, balanced, steady, reasonable, sensible, responsible, equable, self-controlled, sane.
Opposites: unstable.

stack NOUN **1** = **heap**, pile, mass, accumulation, collection, hoard, store, stock, stockpile, mound, mountain.
2 = **abundance**, amplitude, a great deal, a lot; [inf] lots, bags, loads, heaps, tons, oodles, scads.
▶ VERB = **heap**, pile, pile up, amass, accumulate, collect, hoard, store, stockpile.

staff NOUN **1** = **stick**, cane, crook, rod, pole, baton, truncheon. **2** = **mace**, sceptre. **3** = **employees**, workers, workforce, personnel.
▶ VERB = **man**, people, provide with staff.

stage NOUN **1** = **point**, period, step, juncture, time, division, level.
2 = **lap**, leg, phase, step.
3 = **platform**, dais, rostrum, podium.
▶ VERB = **put on**, produce, direct, perform, mount, present.

stagger VERB **1** = **reel**, sway, teeter, totter, wobble, lurch, pitch, roll.
2 = **amaze**, astound, dumbfound, astonish, shock, shake, confound, nonplus, take aback, take someone's breath away, stupefy, stun, strike dumb; [inf] flabbergast.

stagnant ADJ **1** = **still**, motionless, standing, foul, stale, dirty, filthy, brackish. **2** = **sluggish**, slow-moving, quiet, inactive, dull, static. **Opposites: fresh, active.**

stagnate VERB = **do nothing**, be sluggish, lie dormant, be inert, vegetate, idle, be idle, laze, loaf, hang about, languish.

staid ADJ = **sedate**, quiet, serious, grave, solemn, sombre, sober, proper, decorous, formal, demure, stiff, starchy; [inf] stuffy. **Opposites: frivolous.**

stain VERB **1** = **soil**, mark, discolour, dirty, spot, blotch, blemish, smudge, smear, begrime; [poetic/literary] besmirch. **2** = **blacken**, tarnish, sully, blemish, damage, mar, injure, defame, denigrate, dishonour, besmirch, defile, taint, blot, slur. **3** = **varnish**, dye, paint, colour. ▶ NOUN **1** = **mark**, spot, blotch, blemish, smudge, smear. **2** = **blemish**, damage, injury, taint, blot, slur, stigma. **3** = **varnish**, dye, paint, colourant.

stake¹ NOUN = **post**, pole, stick, upright, rod, spike, pale. ▶ VERB **1** = **support**, prop up, hold up, brace, tether. **2** = **establish**, declare, state, lay claim to.

stake² NOUN **1** = **wager**, bet, ante. **2** = **financial interest**, interest, share, investment, involvement, concern. ▶ VERB = **wager**, bet, put on, gamble, pledge, chance, venture, risk, hazard.

stale ADJ **1** = **dry**, dried out, hard, hardened, mouldy, decayed. **2** = **stuffy**, close, musty, fusty; [Brit.] fuggy. **3** = **hackneyed**, tired, worn out, threadbare, banal, trite, stock, stereotyped, run-of-the-mill, commonplace, unoriginal, unimaginative, uninspired, flat, insipid, vapid; [inf] old hat. **Opposites: fresh.**

S

stalemate NOUN
= **deadlock**, impasse, standstill, stand-off.

stalk¹ NOUN = **stem**, branch, shoot, twig.

stalk² VERB 1 = **pursue**, chase, follow, shadow, trail, track down, creep up on, hunt; [inf] tail.
2 = **stride**, march, flounce, strut, prance.

stall NOUN = **booth**, stand, table, counter.
▶ VERB 1 = **play for time**, use delaying tactics, delay, drag one's feet, beat about the bush; [Brit.] hum and haw.
2 = **hold off**, stave off, keep at bay, keep at arm's length, evade, avoid.

stalwart ADJ = **brave**, courageous, valiant, valorous, intrepid, fearless, manly, heroic, indomitable, bold, daring, plucky, spirited, adventurous; [inf] gutsy.
= See also **brave**.
Opposites: timid.

stamina NOUN
= **endurance**, staying power, indefatigability, resilience, fortitude, strength, vigour, energy, staunchness, robustness; [inf] grit, guts.

stammer VERB = **stutter**, stumble, mumble, splutter, hesitate, falter, pause.

stamp VERB 1 = **trample**, step on, tread on, trample on, crush.
2 = **imprint**, inscribe, engrave, emboss, mark, sign.
▶ NOUN = **mark**, hallmark, label, brand, tag, characteristics, quality.
■ **stamp out** = **quash**, suppress, put down, quell, crush, extinguish, scotch, put an end to, eradicate, eliminate.

stampede NOUN = **charge**, rush, flight, scattering.
▶ VERB = **charge**, rush, flee, take flight, dash, race, run.

stance NOUN = **stand**, standpoint, position, line, policy, attitude, angle, slant, viewpoint, point of view, opinion.

stand VERB 1 = **be upright**, be erect, rise, rise/get to one's feet, get up. 2 = **be situated**, be located.

3 = **remain/be in force**, remain/be valid, remain/be effective, hold, hold good, obtain, prevail, be the case. **4** = **put up with**, tolerate, bear, take, endure, abide, countenance, stomach, cope with, handle; [inf] wear; [formal] brook; [archaic] suffer.

▸ NOUN **1** = **standstill**, halt, stop, rest. **2** = See **stance**. **3** = **platform**, stage, staging, dais, rostrum.

▪ **stand by/stand up for** = see **support** VERB (**5**).

▪ **stand out** = **be noticeable**, be noticed, be conspicuous, be striking, attract attention, catch the eye; [inf] stick out a mile, stick out like a sore thumb.

standard NOUN **1** = **yardstick**, benchmark, gauge, measure, criterion, guide, guideline, norm, touchstone, model, pattern, example, exemplar, paradigm, ideal, archetype, specification, requirement, rule, principle, law, canon.

2 = **level**, grade, quality, worth, merit. **3** = **flag**, banner, pennant, streamer, ensign, colours. **4** = **support**, prop, pole, cane, upright.

▸ ADJ **1** = **usual**, ordinary, average, normal, habitual, common, regular, stock, set, fixed, conventional.

2 = **definitive**, established, classic, recognized, approved, accepted, authoritative, official.

Opposites: unusual.

standardize VERB = **make uniform**, regulate, systematize, normalize, homogenize, regiment, bring into line.

standing NOUN = **status**, rank, social position, station, footing, place, circumstances.

stand-off NOUN = **deadlock**, impasse, stalemate.

standpoint NOUN = **point of view**, viewpoint, opinion, perspective, angle, slant, frame of reference.

standstill NOUN = **halt**, stop, dead stop,

stoppage, rest, pause, cessation, stand.

staple ADJ = **chief**, primary, main, principal, basic, fundamental, essential, indispensable.

star NOUN **1** = **heavenly body**, celestial body. **2** = **horoscope**, forecast, augury. **3** = **superstar**, name, lead, celebrity, dignitary, notable, somebody, VIP; [inf] bigwig, big shot, big cheese, big wheel.

stare VERB = **gaze**, gape, goggle, look; [inf] gawp.

stark ADJ **1** = **sharp**, sharply defined, obvious, evident, clear, clear-cut. **2** = **desolate**, bare, barren, arid, vacant, empty, forsaken, bleak, dreary, depressing, grim, harsh; [poetic/literary] drear. **Opposites:** indistinct, ornate.

start VERB **1** = **begin**, commence, make a start, get going, go ahead, set things moving, buckle to/down, turn to, put one's shoulder to the wheel, put one's hand to the plough; [inf] get moving, start the ball rolling, get down to it, get down to business, get one's finger out, get the show on the road, take the plunge, kick off, pitch in, get off one's backside. **2** = **start out**, set out, set off, depart, leave, make a start; [inf] hit the road, push off, get the show on the road. **3** = **set in motion**, set moving, turn on, activate. **4** = **begin working**, start functioning, start operating. **5** = **jump**, leap up, jerk, twitch, recoil, shrink, flinch, blench, wince, shy. **Opposites:** finish.

▶ NOUN **1** = **beginning**, commencement, opening, inception, inauguration, dawn, birth; [inf] kick-off. **2** = **jump**, leap, jerk, twitch, flinch, blench, wince, spasm, convulsion. **Opposites:** end.

startle VERB = **make someone jump**, disturb, agitate, perturb, unsettle, scare, frighten, alarm,

station

surprise, astonish, shock; [inf] give someone a turn.

startling ADJ = **disturbing**, unsettling, alarming, surprising, unexpected, unforeseen, astonishing, amazing, staggering, shocking, extraordinary, remarkable.
Opposites: predictable, ordinary.

starvation NOUN
= **extreme hunger**, lack of food, fasting, famine, undernourishment, malnourishment.

starving ADJ = **starved**, famished, ravenous, very hungry, fasting; [inf] able to eat a horse.

state¹ NOUN 1 = **condition**, shape, situation, circumstances, state of affairs, position, predicament, plight.
2 = **anxiety**, nerves, panic, fluster; [inf] flap, tizzy.
3 = **country**, nation, land, realm, kingdom, republic.

state² VERB = **express**, voice, utter, say, tell, declare, set out, lay down, affirm, assert, announce, make known, reveal, disclose, divulge, pronounce, articulate, proclaim; [formal] aver.

stately ADJ = **ceremonial**, dignified, solemn, majestic, royal, regal, magnificent, grand, glorious, splendid, elegant, imposing, impressive, august, lofty, pompous.

statement NOUN
= **declaration**, account, recitation, report, affirmation, assertion, announcement, revelation, disclosure, divulgence, pronouncement, articulation, proclamation, presentation, promulgation; [formal] averment.

static ADJ = **unmoving**, unvarying, undeviating, changeless, constant, stable, steady, stationary, motionless, at a standstill, frozen.
Opposites: mobile, variable.

station NOUN 1 = **stop**, stopping place, terminus, terminal, depot.

2 = **depot**, base, office, headquarters, seat.
3 = **post**, place, position, location, site. **4** = **class**, level, rank, grade, standing, status, caste.

stationary ADJ
1 = **unmoving**, motionless, at a standstill, parked.
2 = **changeless**, unchanging, constant, unvarying, invariable, undeviating.
Opposites: moving.

statue NOUN = **statuette**, sculpture, effigy, figure, figurine, bust, head.

statuesque ADJ
= **dignified**, stately, majestic, splendid, imposing, impressive, regal.

stature NOUN **1** = **height**, tallness, size. **2** = **status**, importance, import, standing, eminence, prominence, note, renown.

status NOUN = **standing**, rank, level, grade, degree, position, importance, reputation, consequence.

staunch ADJ = **loyal**, faithful, dependable, reliable, steady, constant, stable, firm, steadfast, unswerving, unwavering, unhesitating, unfaltering.
Opposites: disloyal.

stay¹ VERB **1** = **remain**, wait, stay put, continue, linger, pause, rest, delay; [archaic] tarry. **2** = **lodge**, take a room, put up, be accommodated, sojourn, visit, reside, take up residence, dwell, live.
3 = **check**, curb, arrest, stop, delay, hold, prevent, hinder, impede, obstruct.
Opposites: leave.
▸ NOUN **1** = **visit**, sojourn, stop, stopover, holiday, vacation.
2 = **postponement**, suspension, adjournment, deferment, delay.

stay² NOUN = **prop**, support, brace, bolster, buttress.

steadfast ADJ **1** = See **staunch**. **2** = **firm**, determined, resolute, unchanging, unwavering, unfaltering, unswerving, unyielding, inflexible, uncompromising, relentless, implacable. **Opposites:** irresolute.

steady ADJ 1 = **firm**, fixed, stable, secure, immovable. 2 = **still**, motionless, unmoving, sure. 3 = **steadfast**, fixed, immovable, unwavering, unfaltering. 4 = **uniform**, even, regular, rhythmic, consistent. 5 = **well balanced**, balanced, sensible, level-headed, rational, settled, down-to-earth, calm, equable, imperturbable, reliable, dependable, serious-minded, serious. **Opposites:** unstable, shaky, fluctuating.
▸ VERB 1 = **make steady**, hold steady, stabilize, secure, balance, support. 2 = **calm**, calm down, settle, compose, tranquillize, control, get a grip on.

steal VERB 1 = **thieve**, take, appropriate, misappropriate, pilfer, purloin, walk off with, embezzle, pocket, abstract, shoplift; [inf] filch, snitch, swipe, lift, rip off; [Brit. inf] pinch, nick; [formal] peculate. 2 = **plagiarize**, copy, pirate, appropriate; [inf] lift, crib. 3 = **slip**, slide, tiptoe, sneak, creep, slink, slither, flit, glide.

stealthy ADJ = **secret**, furtive, surreptitious, sly, sneaky, clandestine, covert, underhand, undercover; [inf] shady. **Opposites:** above board, open.

steam NOUN = **vapour**, fume, smoke, exhalation.

steamy ADJ 1 = **humid**, muggy, sticky, moist, damp, sweltering, boiling. 2 = **erotic**, sexy, passionate, tempestuous, sensuous, lustful, wanton.

steep ADJ 1 = **sheer**, abrupt, precipitous, sudden, sharp, perpendicular, vertical, declivitous. 2 = **sharp**, rapid, sudden, precipitate. 3 = See **expensive**. **Opposites:** gentle, gradual.

steeple NOUN = **spire**, tower, campanile, turret,

minaret.

steer VERB 1 = **drive**, navigate, pilot, be at the wheel of. 2 = **guide**, lead, direct, conduct, usher.

stench NOUN = **stink**, foul smell/odour, reek; [Brit. inf] pong, whiff.

step NOUN 1 = **stride**, pace, footstep, footfall, tread, tramp. 2 = **walk**, gait, bearing, carriage. 3 = **rung**, tread. 4 = **course of action**, move, act, action, deed, measure, manoeuvre, procedure, expedient, effort. 5 = **stage**, level, grade, rank, degree. ▶ VERB = **walk**, tread, stride, pace, move, advance, proceed; [inf] hoof it.

stereotype NOUN = **received idea**, standardized image, hackneyed conception, cliché. ▶ VERB = **typecast**, pigeonhole, conventionalize, standardize, label, tag, categorize.

sterile ADJ 1 = **infertile**, barren, infecund. 2 = **unfruitful**, unproductive, infertile, unyielding, arid, dry, barren. 3 = **sterilized**, germ-free, antiseptic, disinfected, aseptic, uncontaminated, unpolluted, pure, clean. **Opposites:** fertile, productive.

sterilize VERB 1 = **disinfect**, purify, fumigate. 2 = **make infertile**, make barren, castrate, vasectomize, geld, neuter, spay, emasculate.

stern ADJ 1 = **strict**, harsh, hard, severe, rigorous, stringent, rigid, exacting, demanding, cruel, relentless, unsparing, inflexible, unyielding, authoritarian, tyrannical, despotic, Draconian. 2 = **severe**, forbidding, frowning, unsmiling, sombre, sober, austere. **Opposites:** lax, genial.

stew VERB = **simmer**, boil, casserole, fricassee. ▶ NOUN = **casserole**, ragout, fricassee.

stick¹ NOUN = **piece of wood**, branch, twig, switch.

stick² VERB 1 = **push**, insert, jab, poke. 2 = **glue**, paste, gum, tape, sellotape, fasten, attach, fix, pin, tack. 3 = **become bogged down**, become embedded, become lodged, be unable to move.

sticky ADJ 1 = **adhesive**, adherent, gummy, gluey, tacky. 2 = **gluey**, glutinous, viscous; [inf] gooey. 3 = **close**, humid, muggy, clammy, sultry, sweltering, oppressive. 4 = **awkward**, difficult, tricky, ticklish, delicate, thorny.

stiff ADJ 1 = **rigid**, inflexible, unyielding, inelastic, firm, hard, hardened, brittle. 2 = **tight**, tense, taut, aching; [inf] creaky. 3 = **difficult**, hard, arduous, tough, laborious, exacting, demanding, formidable, challenging, tiring, fatiguing, exhausting, Herculean. 4 = **severe**, harsh, hard, stringent, rigorous, drastic, strong, heavy, Draconian. 5 = **strong**, vigorous, determined, resolute, dogged, tenacious, unflagging, stubborn, obdurate. 6 = **formal**, ceremonial, ceremonious, dignified, proper, decorous, pompous. Opposites: soft.

stiffen VERB 1 = **become stiff**, thicken, set, jell, solidify, harden, congeal, coagulate. 2 = **strengthen**, fortify, brace, steel, reinforce. Opposites: liquefy, weaken.

stifle VERB 1 = **smother**, check, restrain, keep back, hold back, hold in, withhold, choke back, muffle, suppress, curb. 2 = **suppress**, quash, quell, put an end to, put down, stop, extinguish, stamp out, crush, subdue, repress. 3 = **suffocate**, smother, asphyxiate, choke.

stigma NOUN = **shame**, disgrace, dishonour, slur, stain, taint. Opposites: honour.

still ADJ 1 = **motionless**, unmoving, without

moving, immobile, unstirring, inert, lifeless, stock-still, stationary, static. **2** = **quiet**, silent, hushed, soundless, sound-free, noiseless, undisturbed.
Opposites: moving, noisy.

▶ NOUN = **quietness**, quiet, silence, hush, soundlessness, noiselessness, calmness, calm, tranquillity, peace, peacefulness, serenity.

▶ ADV **1** = **at this time**, yet, up to this time, even now, until now.
2 = **nevertheless**, however, in spite of that, notwithstanding, for all that.

stilted ADJ = **stiff**, unnatural, wooden, forced, laboured, constrained, unrelaxed, awkward.
Opposites: natural.

stimulant NOUN **1** = **tonic**, restorative, reviver, energizer, excitant, analeptic; [inf] upper, pick-me-up, bracer.
2 = **stimulus**, incentive, impetus, fillip, spur.

Opposites: sedative, deterrent.

stimulate VERB = **act as a stimulus/incentive to**, encourage, prompt, spur on, activate, stir up, excite, whip up, kindle, incite, instigate, foment, fan.
Opposites: discourage.

stimulating ADJ
1 = **restoring**, restorative, reviving, energizing, analeptic; [inf] pick-me-up. **2** = **interesting**, exciting, stirring, thought-provoking, inspiring, exhilarating, intriguing, provoking, provocative.
Opposites: sedative, boring.

stimulus NOUN
= **stimulant**, incentive, fillip, spur, push, drive, encouragement, inducement, incitement, goad, jog, jolt; [inf] shot in the arm.

sting NOUN = **irritation**, smarting, tingling, tingle, pain, hurt.
▶ VERB **1** = **smart**, tingle, burn, be irritated.
2 = **hurt**, wound, distress,

grieve, vex, pain, anguish, torture, torment, harrow.

stingy ADJ = **mean**, miserly, parsimonious, niggardly, cheese-paring, penny-pinching; [inf] tight, tight-fisted; [N. Amer. inf] cheap.
Opposites: generous.

stink VERB = **smell bad**, give off a bad smell, reek; [inf] smell to high heaven.
▸ NOUN = **bad smell**, foul smell, stench, reek, malodour.

stint VERB = **skimp on**, limit, restrict, hold back on, be sparing with, be economical with, be frugal with, be mean with, be parsimonious with, be niggardly with.

stipulate VERB = **specify**, set down, lay down, state clearly, demand, require, insist upon, make a condition of, make a point of.

stipulation NOUN = **specification**, demand, requirement, condition, precondition, provision, proviso, prerequisite.

stir VERB **1** = **mix**, blend, beat, whip. **2** = **disturb**, move, agitate, rustle. **3** = **get up**, get out of bed, rise, rouse oneself, bestir oneself, move about, be up and about, be active; [inf] shake a leg, look lively. **4** = **stimulate**, excite, rouse, awaken, waken, kindle, quicken, inspire. **5** = **rouse**, incite, provoke, inflame, goad, spur, egg on, urge, encourage, motivate, drive, impel.
▸ NOUN = **excitement**, commotion, disturbance, fuss, uproar, to-do, flurry, ferment, brouhaha.

stirring ADJ = **exciting**, dramatic, thrilling, gripping, riveting, spirited, stimulating, moving, lively, animated, heady, passionate, impassioned.
Opposites: dull, unexciting.

stitch VERB = **sew**, sew up, repair, mend, darn.

stock NOUN **1** = **store**, supply, stockpile, reserve, reservoir, accumulation, pile, heap, load, hoard, cache. **2** = **supplies**, goods, merchandise, wares, articles for sale, commodities. **3** = **farm animals**, livestock, cattle, beasts, herds, sheep, flocks. **4** = **descent**, line of descent, lineage, ancestry, extraction, family, parentage, relatives, pedigree, genealogy, strain, breed, background.

▶ ADJ **1** = **standard**, regular, average, readily available. **2** = **usual**, routine, run-of-the-mill, commonplace, conventional, traditional, stereotyped, clichéd, hackneyed, overused, worn out, banal, trite.
Opposites: unusual, original.

▶ VERB **1** = **sell**, trade in, deal in, market, handle, supply, keep. **2** = **equip**, fit, outfit, kit out, furnish, accoutre, supply, provide.

stockpile VERB = **collect**, gather, accumulate, amass, store, lay in, put away, put down, deposit; [inf] squirrel away, salt away, stash.

stocky ADJ = **heavy-set**, thickset, dumpy, stubby, stumpy, squat, chunky, solid, sturdy, mesomorphic.
Opposites: slender.

stodgy ADJ **1** = **heavy**, solid, substantial, filling, starchy, leaden, indigestible. **2** = **dull**, uninteresting, boring, tedious, dry, wearisome, heavy-going, unimaginative, uninspired, monotonous, laboured, wooden, turgid.
Opposites: light, interesting.

stoical ADJ = **impassive**, dispassionate, unimpassioned, unemotional, self-controlled, self-disciplined, forbearing, patient, long-suffering, resigned, philosophical, fatalistic, imperturbable, calm, cool, unexcitable, unflappable, phlegmatic.
Opposites: excitable.

stolid ADJ = **impassive**, unemotional, apathetic, uninterested,

unimaginative, indifferent, dull, stupid, bovine, lumpish, wooden, doltish, thick, dense.
Opposites: lively, imaginative.

stomach NOUN
= **abdomen**, belly, paunch, pot belly; [inf] tummy, gut, pot, breadbasket.
▸ VERB = **stand**, put up with, bear, take, tolerate, abide, endure, swallow, submit to; [archaic] suffer.

stone NOUN 1 = **pebble**, rock, boulder.
2 = **precious stone**, jewel, gem, brilliant; [inf] rock.
3 = **tombstone**, gravestone, headstone, memorial stone, monument. 4 = **kernel**, pit, nut, seed, pip.

stony ADJ 1 = **rocky**, pebbly, gravelly, shingly, gritty, rough, hard.
2 = **cold**, chilly, frosty, icy, frigid, hard, stern, severe, rigid, fixed, expressionless, blank, poker-faced, deadpan.
3 = **unfeeling**, uncaring, unsympathetic, insensitive, callous, heartless, unmoved, unemotional, dispassionate, unresponsive, stern, severe, harsh, hard, cruel, cold-hearted, merciless, pitiless.
Opposites: sympathetic.

stooge NOUN = **underling**, subordinate, assistant, deputy; [inf] sidekick; [Brit. inf] dogsbody.

stoop VERB 1 = **bend down**, lean over, lean down, crouch down, duck, bow.
2 = **condescend**, deign, lower oneself, humble oneself, demean oneself.
3 = **sink to**, descend to, lower oneself to, demean oneself to, resort to.

stop VERB 1 = **bring to a stop**, halt, bring to a halt, end, bring to an end, put an end to, finish, bring to a close, terminate, bring to a standstill, wind up, discontinue, cut short, interrupt, nip in the bud.
2 = **discontinue**, cease from, refrain from, desist from, leave off, break off, forbear from, abandon;

[inf] quit, knock off, pack in. **3** = **come to a stop**, come to a halt, end, come to an end, finish, come to a close, be over, cease, conclude, terminate, come to a standstill, pause. **4** = **prevent**, hinder, obstruct, impede, block, check. **5** = **plug**, seal, block, bung, staunch, stem.
Opposites: begin, start.

▶ NOUN **1** = **halt**, end, finish, close, cessation, conclusion, termination, standstill, stoppage, discontinuation, discontinuance. **2** = **stopping place**, station, halt, stage, terminus, terminal, depot. **3** = **break**, stop-off, stopover, stay, sojourn, overnight, rest.

stopgap NOUN = **temporary substitute**, substitution, fill-in, makeshift, improvisation, expedient, last resort.

store NOUN **1** = **supply**, stock, stockpile, reserve, accumulation, pile, heap, cache, deposit, reservoir. **2** = **storeroom**, storehouse, warehouse, repository, depository. **3** = **shop**, department store, supermarket, retail outlet, emporium.

▶ VERB = **stock up with**, get in supplies of, stockpile, collect, gather, accumulate, amass, lay in, put away, put down, deposit, hoard; [inf] squirrel away, salt away, stash.

storm NOUN = **gale**, hurricane, cyclone, tempest, squall, cloudburst, downpour, torrent.

▶ VERB = **attack**, charge, rush, make a raid/foray/sortie on, take by storm.

stormy ADJ = **blustery**, blustering, windy, gusty, squally, rainy, wild, tempestuous, turbulent.
Opposites: calm.

story NOUN **1** = **tale**, fairy tale, fable, myth, legend, anecdote, novel, novella, romance, narrative, chronicle; [inf] yarn. **2** = **news item**, news report, article, feature, scoop.

stout ADJ **1 = fat**, fattish, plump, portly, tubby, obese, corpulent, rotund, big, heavy, thickset, overweight, bulky, burly, brawny, fleshy.
2 = strong, heavy, solid, substantial, sturdy.
3 = stout-hearted, brave, courageous, valiant, valorous, gallant, fearless, unafraid, intrepid, bold, plucky, heroic, lion-hearted, daring, tough, doughty; [inf] gutsy, spunky.
Opposites: cowardly.

stow VERB **= place**, deposit, put, put away, pack, store, load, bundle, stuff.
Opposites: unload.

straggle VERB **1 = wander**, ramble, stray, roam, meander, rove, range, spread out. **2 = trail behind**, fall behind, lag, string out, linger, loiter.
3 = grow untidily, be messy, be dishevelled, be unkempt.

straight ADJ **1 = direct**, undeviating, unswerving, straight as an arrow.
2 = successive, consecutive, in a row, running, uninterrupted, solid, non-stop. **3 = in order**, orderly, neat, tidy, spruce, in place, organized, arranged, sorted out. **4 = forthright**, honest, faithful, sincere, frank, candid, direct, straightforward, plain-speaking, matter-of-fact, outspoken, straight from the shoulder, unequivocal, unambiguous, unqualified, unmodified.
Opposites: crooked, evasive.

straighten VERB **= make straight**, adjust, arrange, put in order, make tidy, tidy up, neaten, put to rights.
▪ **straighten out = put in order**, put right, sort out, clear up, settle, resolve, regulate, rectify, disentangle, unsnarl.

straightforward ADJ
1 = straight, direct, honest, frank, candid, forthright, plain-speaking, unambiguous, straight from the shoulder.
2 = uncomplicated, easy,

simple, elementary, effortless, undemanding, routine; [inf] easy as falling off a log, easy as pie.
Opposites: complicated.

strain VERB 1 = **draw tight**, tighten, make taut, tauten, stretch, extend, elongate, distend. 2 = **tax**, overtax, exert to the limit, overwork, push to the limit, fatigue, tire. 3 = **make every effort**, strive one's utmost, push/drive oneself to the limit, struggle, labour; [inf] pull out all the stops, go all out, give it one's all. 4 = **sieve**, silt, screen, riddle, separate.
▶ NOUN 1 = **tightness**, tautness, tension, distension. 2 = **stress**, pressure, tension, overwork, exhaustion, anxiety.

strained ADJ 1 = **forced**, artificial, unnatural, false, constrained, laboured, wooden, stiff, self-conscious. 2 = **awkward**, embarrassed, uneasy, uncomfortable, tense, unrelaxed. 3 = **under**

strain, tense, troubled, uneasy, hostile.
Opposites: natural, relaxed.

strainer NOUN = **sieve**, colander, filter, screen, riddle.

strand NOUN 1 = **thread**, fibre, filament, length. 2 = **element**, component, theme.

stranded ADJ 1 = **left helpless**, left penniless, in dire straits, in difficulties, left in the lurch, left high and dry, abandoned, forsaken. 2 = **grounded**, beached, shipwrecked, wrecked, marooned.

strange ADJ 1 = **peculiar**, odd, bizarre, unusual, atypical, abnormal, surprising, curious, weird, funny, unfamiliar. 2 = **unknown**, unfamiliar. 3 = **inexplicable**, anomalous, unexpected, extraordinary.
Opposites: ordinary, familiar.

stranger NOUN = **new person**, new arrival, newcomer, incomer, foreigner.

■ **a stranger to**
= **unfamiliar with**, unacquainted with, unaccustomed to, new to, fresh to, unused to, inexperienced in, unpractised in, unversed in, unconversant with.

strangle VERB **1** = **throttle**, choke, strangulate, garrotte. **2** = **suppress**, inhibit, repress, check, restrain, hold back, curb, stifle, gag.

strap NOUN = **band**, belt, thong, cord, tie.
▶ VERB **1** = **fasten**, secure, tie, bind, lash, truss, pinion. **2** = **bind**, bandage. **3** = **flog**, lash, whip, scourge, beat; [inf] belt.

strategic ADJ
1 = **calculated**, planned, plotted, tactical, diplomatic, politic, cunning, wily. **2** = **crucial**, key, vital, critical, essential, important.

strategy NOUN = **policy**, approach, programme, scheme, plan of action, master plan, schedule, blueprint, game plan.

stray VERB **1** = **wander**, roam, rove, go astray, ramble, meander, drift. **2** = **digress**, wander, deviate, get off the subject, get sidetracked, go off at a tangent, lose the thread.
▶ ADJ **1** = **strayed**, gone astray, lost, homeless, wandering, vagrant, abandoned, unclaimed. **2** = **odd**, random, isolated, scattered, occasional, incidental, accidental, chance, freak.

streak NOUN **1** = **line**, band, strip, dash, bar, score, striation, vein, slash, smear. **2** = **strain**, vein, element, trace, touch, dash. **3** = **smear**, smudge, mark. **4** = **spell**, period, course, stretch, series.
▶ VERB **1** = **band**, stripe, mark, slash, striate, fleck, daub, smear. **2** = **smear**, smudge, mark. **3** = **race**, rush, speed, dash, sprint, hurtle, scurry, fly, flee, flash, whistle, zoom, zip; [inf] tear, whizz, go hell for leather.

stream NOUN **1** = **river**, brook, rivulet, rill, freshet; [N. English] beck; [Scottish & N. English] burn;

[N. Amer. & Austral./
NZ] creek. **2** = **flow**, rush,
gush, surge, jet,
outpouring, current,
cascade.
▸ VERB **1** = **flow**, run, pour,
course, spill, gush, surge,
flood, cascade, well.
2 = **emit**, issue, shed, spill.
3 = **flutter**, flap, swing,
float, flow. **4** = **surge**,
pour, crowd.

streamlined ADJ
1 = **smooth**, sleek,
elegant. **2** = **efficient**,
smooth-running, well
run, modernized,
rationalized, slick.

street NOUN = **road**,
thoroughfare, terrace,
avenue, drive, row,
crescent.

strength NOUN **1** = **power**,
might, force, brawn,
muscle, muscularity,
sturdiness, robustness,
vigour, toughness,
stamina. **2** = **fortitude**,
courage, bravery, pluck,
firmness, stamina,
backbone; [inf] grit, guts.
3 = **advantage**, asset,
strong point, forte.
Opposites: weakness.

strengthen VERB **1** = **make
strong**, make stronger,
give strength to, nourish,
build up. **2** = **grow strong**,
grow stronger, gain
strength, intensify,
heighten. **3** = **reinforce**,
support, back up, bolster,
authenticate, confirm,
substantiate, corroborate.
Opposites: weaken.

strenuous ADJ
1 = **arduous**, laborious,
taxing, demanding,
difficult, hard, tough,
uphill, heavy, weighty,
burdensome, exhausting,
tiring, fatiguing.
2 = **energetic**, active,
vigorous, forceful, strong,
spirited, bold,
determined, resolute,
tenacious, earnest, keen,
zealous.
Opposites: easy, half-
hearted.

stress NOUN **1** = **strain**,
pressure, tension, worry,
anxiety. **2** = **emphasis**,
priority, importance,
weight, significance,
value, worth, merit.
3 = **accent**, accentuation,
emphasis.

S

▸VERB **1** = **lay stress on**, emphasize, place emphasis on, give emphasis to, accentuate, underline, underscore, point up, highlight, spotlight, press home, dwell on, harp on, belabour. **2** = **lay stress on**, place the accent on, accentuate, emphasize. **3** = **subject to stress/strain/tension**, tax, overtax, pressurize, overwork, overstretch, overburden, push to the limit, push too far. **Opposites:** play down.

stretch VERB **1** = **be stretchy**, be elastic, be tensile. **2** = **extend**, elongate, lengthen, expand, draw out, pull out, get larger, get bigger, enlarge, pull out of shape. **3** = **spread**, extend, unfold, cover, range. **4** = **be a challenge to**, challenge, extend, tax, push to the limit. **5** = **strain**, overstrain, exaggerate, overdraw, push too far. **Opposites:** contract.

▸NOUN **1** = **expanse**, area, tract, extent, spread, sweep. **2** = **period**, time, spell, term, space, run, stint.

strict ADJ **1** = **precise**, exact, close, faithful, true, accurate, scrupulous, meticulous, conscientious, punctilious. **2** = **stringent**, rigorous, severe, harsh, hard, stern, authoritarian, rigid, narrow, austere, illiberal, inflexible, unyielding, uncompromising. **3** = **absolute**, utter, complete, total, perfect. **Opposites:** flexible, easy-going.

stride VERB = **step**, pace, walk, stalk.

strident ADJ = **harsh**, raucous, rough, grating, discordant, rasping, jarring, shrill, loud, screeching, unmelodious, unmusical. **Opposites:** soft.

strife NOUN = **conflict**, friction, discord, disagreement, dissension, dispute, argument, quarrelling, wrangling,

s

bickering, controversy, contention, ill feeling, hostility, animosity. **Opposites:** harmony.

strike VERB **1 = bang**, beat, hit, pound, batter. **2 = hit**, slap, smack, beat, batter, thrash, thump, thwack, punch, cuff, box, rap, buffet, smite, cane, lash, whip; [inf] wallop, belt, clout, whack, bash, clobber, bop, biff, sock, plug. **3 = run into**, knock into, bang into, bump into, smash into, collide with, be in collision with, dash against. **4 = attack**, charge, make an assault on, assault, storm, set upon, fall upon. **5 = go on strike**, take industrial action, walk out; [Brit. inf] down tools.
▶ NOUN **1 = hit**, slap, smack, thump, thwack, punch, cuff, box, knock; [inf] wallop, clout, whack, bop, buffet, plug. **2 = industrial action**, walkout.
■ **strike out = delete**, cross out, erase, rub out, obliterate.

striking ADJ **1 = noticeable**, obvious, conspicuous, evident, visible, distinct, prominent, clear-cut, unmistakable, remarkable, extraordinary, incredible, amazing. **2 = impressive**, imposing, grand, splendid, magnificent, superb, marvellous, wonderful, dazzling; [Brit. inf] smashing. **Opposites:** unremarkable.

string NOUN **1 = twine**, cord, yarn, rope, cable, line. **2 = queue**, line, row, procession, file, column, stream, succession, sequence.
▶ VERB **1 = hang**, suspend, sling. **2 = stretch**, sling, run, fasten, tie, secure together.

stringent ADJ **= strict**, firm, rigid, rigorous, severe, harsh, tough, tight, exacting, demanding, inflexible, hard and fast, uncompromising. **Opposites:** easy.

stringy ADJ **1 = lank**, straggly, straggling.

2 = **tough**, fibrous, gristly, leathery.

strip¹ VERB **1** = **strip naked**, undress, take one's clothes off, remove one's clothes, disrobe. **2** = **peel**, pare, skin, excoriate. **3** = **take away**, dispossess of, deprive of, confiscate. **4** = **dismantle**, take to pieces, take to bits, take apart.

strip² NOUN = **piece**, bit, band, belt, ribbon, stripe, bar, swathe, slip, fillet.

stripe NOUN = **strip**, band, belt, bar.

striped ADJ = **stripy**, banded, barred, striated, variegated.

stripling NOUN = **youth**, adolescent, youngster, boy, lad, teenager, child, juvenile, minor, young man; [inf] kid, nipper, young 'un.

strive VERB = **try**, attempt, endeavour, make an effort, make every effort, exert oneself, do one's best, do all one can, do one's utmost, labour, toil, strain, struggle; [inf] go all out, give it one's best shot.

stroke NOUN **1** = **blow**, hit, slap, smack, thump, thwack, punch, cuff, box, knock, rap, buffet, smite. **2** = **movement**, action, motion. **3** = **thrombosis**, embolism, cerebral vascular accident, CVA, seizure, shock, apoplexy. ▸VERB = **caress**, fondle, pat, touch, rub, massage, soothe.

stroll VERB = **saunter**, amble, wander, meander, ramble, dawdle, promenade, go for a walk, take a walk, stretch one's legs, take the air; [inf] mosey along.

strong ADJ **1** = **powerful**, mighty, brawny, muscular, well built, strapping, sturdy, burly, robust, vigorous, tough, hardy, lusty, Herculean, strong as an ox/horse/ lion. **2** = **courageous**, brave, plucky, firm, resolute, strong-minded; [inf] gutsy. **3** = **determined**, forceful, high-powered, assertive, tough, formidable, aggressive, redoubtable. **4** = **solid**, well built, heavy, heavy-

S

duty, hard-wearing,
sturdy, durable, long-
lasting, tough, secure.
5 = keen, eager,
enthusiastic, deep, acute,
dedicated, passionate,
fierce, loyal, fervent,
zealous. **6 = intense**,
forceful, vehement,
passionate, fervent.
7 = compelling, powerful,
cogent, potent, weighty,
convincing, plausible,
effective, efficacious,
sound, valid, well
founded. **8 = deep**,
intense, vivid, graphic.
9 = bright, brilliant,
intense, radiant,
gleaming, dazzling,
glaring.
10 = concentrated,
undiluted, highly
flavoured.
Opposites: weak.

structure NOUN
1 = building, edifice,
construction, erection,
pile, complex.
2 = construction, form,
configuration,
conformation, shape,
constitution,
composition, make-up,
organization, system,

arrangement, design,
frame, framework.
▶ VERB **= construct**, build,
form, put together,
assemble, shape, design,
organize, arrange, order.

struggle VERB **1 = strive**,
try hard, endeavour,
make every effort, exert
oneself, do one's best, do
all one can, do one's
utmost, battle, labour,
toil, strain; [inf] go all out.
2 = fight, grapple, wrestle,
scuffle, brawl; [inf] scrap.
▶ NOUN **1 = striving**, battle,
endeavour, effort,
exertion, labour, toiling,
pains. **2 = fight**, scuffle,
brawl, tussle; [inf] scrap,
set-to, dust-up.

strut VERB **= swagger**,
prance, parade, flounce;
[N. Amer.] sashay.

stubborn ADJ **= obstinate**,
headstrong, wilful,
strong-willed, pig-
headed, mulish, dogged,
persistent, adamant,
inflexible,
uncompromising,
unbending, unyielding,
unmalleable, obdurate,
intractable, refractory,
recalcitrant,

contumacious.
Opposites: malleable.

stuck ADJ 1 = **immovable**, immobile, fast, fixed, rooted. 2 = **baffled**, beaten, stumped, at a loss, perplexed, nonplussed, at one's wits' ends; [inf] up against a brick wall.

student NOUN = **undergraduate**, pupil, schoolboy, schoolgirl, trainee, apprentice, probationer.

studied ADJ = **deliberate**, wilful, conscious, calculated, purposeful, contrived, affected, forced, feigned, artificial.
Opposites: natural.

studious ADJ = **scholarly**, academic, intellectual, bookish, book-loving, serious, earnest.

study VERB 1 = **apply oneself**, revise, burn the midnight oil; [inf] cram, mug up; [Brit. inf] swot. 2 = **learn**, read up on, read, work at; [inf] mug up on. 3 = **investigate**, inquire into, research, look into, examine, analyse, review, survey, conduct a survey of, scrutinize.

stuff NOUN 1 = **material**, fabric, matter, substance. 2 = **things**, objects, articles, items, luggage, baggage, belongings, possessions, goods, paraphernalia. 3 = **facts**, information, data, subject.
▸ VERB 1 = **fill**, pack, pad. 2 = **pack**, load, cram, squeeze, crowd, stow, press, force, compress, jam, wedge.

stuffy ADJ 1 = **airless**, close, muggy, stifling, suffocating, musty, stale; [Brit. inf] fuggy. 2 = **dull**, boring, dreary, staid, sedate, stiff, formal, pompous, starchy, prim, priggish, strait-laced, conventional, conservative, stodgy; [inf] fuddy-duddy, square.
Opposites: airy, exciting.

stumble VERB 1 = **trip**, slip, blunder, lumber, lurch, stagger, reel. 2 = **stammer**, stutter, hesitate, falter; [inf] fluff one's lines.

stump NOUN = **end**, stub, remnant, remains.

▶ VERB = **baffle**, be too much for, put at a loss, nonplus, mystify, foil, perplex, puzzle, confound, bewilder; [inf] flummox.

stun VERB 1 = **daze**, stupefy, knock senseless, knock out, lay out, knock stupid. **2** = **shock**, astound, dumbfound, stupefy, overwhelm, overcome, overpower, devastate, stagger, amaze, astonish, bewilder, confuse; [inf] flabbergast, knock sideways; [Brit. inf] knock for six.

stunning ADJ
= **sensational**, ravishing, dazzling, wonderful, marvellous, magnificent, glorious, exquisite, impressive, splendid, beautiful, lovely, gorgeous.
Opposites: ordinary.

stupendous ADJ
= **amazing**, fantastic, astounding, astonishing, extraordinary, remarkable, wonderful, prodigious, phenomenal, staggering, breathtaking; [inf] mind-boggling,

mind-blowing.
Opposites: ordinary.

stupid ADJ
1 = **unintelligent**, foolish, dense, brainless, mindless, obtuse, dull-witted, dull, slow-witted, slow, dunce-like, doltish, simple-minded, half-witted, gullible, naive, moronic, imbecilic, cretinous; [inf] thick, dim, dumb, dopey; [Brit. inf] dozy. **2** = **foolish**, silly, idiotic, brainless, mindless, crackbrained, nonsensical, senseless, irresponsible, unthinking, ill-advised, ill-considered, inept, unwise, injudicious, indiscreet, shortsighted, inane, absurd, ludicrous, ridiculous, laughable, fatuous, asinine, pointless, meaningless, futile, fruitless, mad, insane, lunatic; [inf] cock-eyed. **3** = **dazed**, stupefied, unconscious.
Opposites: intelligent, sensible.

stupidity NOUN **1** = **lack of intelligence**, foolishness, denseness, brainlessness, mindlessness, dull-wittedness, dullness, slow-wittedness, slowness, doltishness; [inf] thickness, dimness, dumbness, dopiness, doziness. **2 = foolishness**, folly, silliness, idiocy, brainlessness, senselessness, irresponsibility, injudiciousness, ineptitude, inaneness, inanity, absurdity, ludicrousness, ridiculousness, fatuousness, fatuity, asininity, pointlessness, meaninglessness, futility, fruitlessness, madness, insanity, lunacy.

sturdy ADJ **1 = well built**, well made, muscular, athletic, strong, strapping, brawny, powerfully built, powerful, solid, substantial, robust, vigorous, tough, hardy, stalwart, mighty, lusty. **2 = strong**, vigorous, stalwart, firm, determined, resolute, tenacious, staunch, steadfast, unyielding, unwavering, uncompromising. **3** = See **strong (4)**. **Opposites:** weak.

stutter VERB **= stammer**, stumble, hesitate, falter, splutter.

style NOUN **1 = kind**, type, variety, sort, design, pattern, genre. **2 = technique**, method, methodology, approach, manner, way, mode, system. **3 = stylishness**, smartness, elegance, polish, suavity, urbanity, chic, flair, dash, panache, elan; [inf] pizzazz, ritziness. **4 = fashion**, trend, vogue, mode.

stylish ADJ **= fashionable**, smart, elegant, chic, modish, à la mode, voguish, modern, up to date; [inf] trendy, dressy, natty, classy, nifty, ritzy, snazzy, snappy, with it. **Opposites:** unfashionable.

subdue VERB **1 = conquer**, defeat, vanquish, get the better of, overpower, overcome, overwhelm, subjugate, master, gain the upper hand at, triumph over, crush, quash, quell, tame, humble, bring someone to their knees, hold in check. **2 = control**, curb, restrain, check, hold back, inhibit, rein in, repress, suppress, stifle. **Opposites:** arouse.

subdued ADJ **1 = dim**, muted, toned down, softened, soft, lowered, shaded, low-key, subtle, unobtrusive. **2 = low-spirited**, downcast, dejected, depressed, restrained, repressed, inactive, lifeless, dull, passive, unexcited; [inf] down in the mouth. **Opposites:** bright, lively.

subject NOUN **1 = topic**, theme, question, substance, gist, text, thesis. **2 = branch of knowledge**, course of study, course, discipline. **3 = citizen**, national.
▶ VERB **= submit**, put through, expose, lay open, treat.
■ **subject to 1 = conditional upon**, contingent upon, dependent on.

2 = susceptible to, liable to, prone to, in danger of, vulnerable to.

subjective ADJ **= personal**, personalized, individual, biased, prejudiced, bigoted. **Opposites:** objective.

subjugate VERB **= gain mastery over**, gain control of, bring someone to their knees, bring to heel, bring under the yoke, conquer, vanquish, defeat, crush, quell, quash, overpower, overcome, subdue, tame, break, humble, tyrannize, oppress, enslave. **Opposites:** liberate.

submerge VERB **1 = go under water**, dive, sink, plummet. **2 = immerse**, dip, plunge, duck dunk. **3 = flood**, inundate, deluge, engulf, swamp, overflow.

submission NOUN **1 = surrender**, yielding, capitulation, agreement, acceptance, consent, accession, compliance. **2 = presentation**, tender, proposal, suggestion. **3 = argument**, assertion,

contention, statement, claim; [formal] averment.
Opposites: defiance.

submissive ADJ
= **yielding**, compliant, malleable, acquiescent, accommodating, tractable, manageable, unassertive, passive, obedient, biddable, dutiful, docile, meek, patient, resigned, subdued, humble, self-effacing, deferential, obsequious, servile, self-abasing; [inf] bootlicking.
Opposites: intractable.

submit VERB 1 = **give in**, yield, give way, capitulate, agree, accept, consent, accede, acquiesce, comply, conform. 2 = **put forward**, present, proffer, tender, advance, propose, suggest, table, introduce, move.
Opposites: resist, withdraw.

subordinate ADJ = **lower-ranking**, junior, lower, lesser, inferior, minor, secondary, subsidiary, ancillary, auxiliary.
Opposites: senior.

▶ NOUN = **junior**, assistant, second, deputy, aide, subaltern, underling, inferior, second fiddle.
Opposites: superior.

subscribe
■ **subscribe to** 1 = **pay a subscription to**, buy regularly, take regularly. 2 = **make a donation to**, donate to, give to, give money to, make a contribution to, contribute towards; [inf] chip into. 3 = **agree with**, accede to, consent to, accept, believe in, endorse, back, support.

subscription NOUN 1 = **fee**, membership fee, dues, annual payment. 2 = **donation**, contribution, offering.

subsequent ADJ
= **following**, ensuing, succeeding, later, future, next, consequent.
Opposites: previous.

subservient ADJ = **servile**, submissive, deferential, obsequious, sycophantic, grovelling, fawning, ingratiating, toadying, unctuous, truckling; [inf] bootlicking.

S

Opposites: domineering.

subside VERB **1** = **abate**, let up, moderate, quieten down, calm, slacken, die out, peter out, taper off, recede, lessen, diminish, dwindle. **2** = **go down**, get lower, sink, settle, fall back, recede.
Opposites: strengthen, rise.

subsidize VERB = **pay a subsidy to**, contribute to, give money to, back, support, invest in, sponsor, finance, fund, underwrite, foot the bill for; [inf] pick up the tab for.

subsidy NOUN = **grant**, contribution, backing, support, investment, sponsorship, finance, funding, subvention.

subsist
■ **subsist on** = **live on**, exist on, eke out an existence on, survive on.

substance NOUN **1** = **matter**, material, stuff, medium, mass, fabric. **2** = **solidity**, body, corporeality, reality, actuality, materiality, concreteness, tangibility.

3 = **meaningfulness**, significance, weight, power, soundness, validity. **4** = **wealth**, affluence, prosperity, money, capital, means, resources, assets.

substantial ADJ **1** = **real**, material, weighty, sizeable, considerable, meaningful, significant, important, notable, major, marked, valuable, useful, worthwhile. **2** = **solid**, sturdy, stout, strong, well built, durable. **3** = **essential**, basic, fundamental.
Opposites: insubstantial.

substitute NOUN = **replacement**, deputy, relief, proxy, reserve, surrogate, fill-in, stand-in, standby, locum, stopgap.
▶ VERB **1** = **use as a replacement**, replace with, use instead of, exchange, switch, swap. **2** = **take the place of**, replace, deputize for, act as deputy for, relieve, fill in for, act as stand-in for, cover for, take over from.

subterfuge NOUN = **trick**, ruse, wile, ploy, stratagem, artifice, dodge, manoeuvre, pretext, expedient, intrigue, scheme, deception.

subtle ADJ **1** = **delicate**, faint, understated, low-key, muted, toned down. **2** = **fine**, fine-drawn, nice, slight, minute, tenuous, indistinct, indefinite.
Opposites: crude.

subtract VERB = **take away**, take from, deduct, remove, debit; [inf] knock off.
Opposites: add.

suburb NOUN = **outlying district**, residential area, dormitory area, purlieus.

suburban ADJ = **provincial**, unsophisticated, parochial, insular.
Opposites: cosmopolitan.

subversive ADJ = **undermining**, discrediting, destructive, disruptive, trouble-making, inflammatory, seditious, revolutionary, insurrectionary, treasonous, treacherous.

subvert VERB = **overthrow**, overturn, wreak havoc on, sabotage, ruin, destroy, demolish, wreck, upset, disrupt, undermine, weaken.

subway NOUN = **underground railway**, underground, metro, tube.

succeed VERB **1** = **triumph**, achieve success, be successful, do well, flourish, thrive; [inf] make it, make the grade, make a name for oneself. **2** = **be successful**, turn out well, work, work out, come off; [inf] pan out, do the trick. **3** = **come after**, follow, replace, take the place of, supplant, supersede.
Opposites: fail, precede.

success NOUN **1** = **accomplishment**, achievement, attainment, fulfilment, victory, triumph. **2** = **prosperity**, affluence, wealth, fame, eminence. **3** = **best-seller**, winner, triumph; [inf] hit, smash hit, sensation.
Opposites: failure.

S

successful ADJ
1 = **victorious**, triumphant.
2 = **prosperous**, affluent, wealthy, well-to-do, famous, eminent, at the top, top. 3 = **flourishing**, thriving, booming, profitable, profit-making, moneymaking, lucrative.
Opposites: unsuccessful.

succession NOUN
= **sequence**, series, progression, course, cycle, chain, train, run, continuation.

successor NOUN = **heir**, heir apparent, next-in-line, replacement, supplanter.
Opposites: predecessor.

succinct ADJ = **short**, brief, concise, compact, condensed, crisp, terse, tight, to the point, pithy, summary, short and sweet.
Opposites: lengthy.

succulent ADJ = **juicy**, moist, luscious, mouth-watering.
Opposites: dry.

succumb VERB = **give in**, give way, yield, submit, surrender, capitulate, be overcome/overwhelmed, fall victim.
Opposites: resist.

suck VERB = **suck up**, draw up, absorb, soak up, blot up.

sudden ADJ 1 = **immediate**, instantaneous, abrupt, unexpected, unforeseen, unanticipated, unlooked for, without warning.
2 = **rapid**, swift, speedy, fast, quick, meteoric.
Opposites: gradual.

suddenly ADV = **all of a sudden**, all at once, instantaneously, abruptly, unexpectedly, without warning; [inf] out of the blue.
Opposites: gradually.

sue VERB = **take to court**, bring an action against, prefer/bring charges against, charge, prosecute, bring to trial, summons, indict; [inf] have the law on.
▪ **sue for** = **petition for**, appeal for, solicit, request, ask for, beg for, plead for.

suffer VERB 1 = **be in pain**, feel pain, be racked with pain, hurt, ache. 2 = **be**

distressed, be in distress, be upset, be miserable, be wretched, be hurt, hurt.
3 = experience, undergo, sustain, encounter, meet with, endure.

■ **suffer from = be affected by**, be afflicted by, be troubled with.

suffice VERB **= be enough**, be sufficient, do, serve, fulfil/meet someone's needs; [inf] hit the spot.

sufficient ADJ **= enough**, adequate, plenty of, ample, plenty.
Opposites: insufficient.

suffocate VERB **= smother**, stifle, asphyxiate.

suffuse VERB **= spread over**, cover, bathe, permeate, pervade, imbue.

suggest VERB **1 = propose**, put forward, move, submit, recommend, advocate; [inf] throw out.
2 = indicate, lead to believe, give the impression, give the idea, insinuate, hint, imply, intimate.

suggestion NOUN
1 = proposal, proposition, plan, motion,

submission, recommendation.
2 = hint, trace, touch, suspicion. **3 = insinuation**, hint, implication, intimation.

suggestive ADJ
= provocative, titillating, sexual, sexy, indecent, indelicate, improper, off colour, smutty, ribald, risqué, lewd, salacious; [inf] blue.

suit NOUN **1 = set of clothes**, outfit, costume, ensemble. **2 = lawsuit**, court case, action, proceedings, prosecution.
▶ VERB **1 = become**, look attractive on, go well with, look right on.
2 = be suitable for, be convenient for, be acceptable to, meet someone's requirements, satisfy someone's demands.

suitable ADJ
1 = convenient, acceptable, satisfactory.
2 = suited to, befitting, appropriate to, relevant to, pertinent to, apposite to, in keeping with, in character with, tailor-

made for. **3 = right**, appropriate, fitting, apt, well qualified, ideal.
Opposites: unsuitable.

sulk VERB = **mope**, pout, be sullen, be in a bad mood, be put out, be out of sorts, be grumpy; [inf] be in a huff.

sulky ADJ = **moping**, pouting, moody, sullen, piqued, disgruntled, ill-humoured, out of humour, bad-tempered, grumpy, churlish, glowering.
Opposites: cheerful.

sullen ADJ = **morose**, unresponsive, uncommunicative, unsociable, resentful, sulky, sour, glum, gloomy, dismal, cheerless, surly, cross, angry, frowning, glowering, grumpy.
Opposites: cheerful.

sultry ADJ **1 = close**, airless, stuffy, stifling, suffocating, oppressive, muggy, humid, sticky, hot, sweltering.
2 = sensual, sexy, voluptuous, seductive, provocative, alluring,

tempting, passionate, erotic.

sum NOUN **1 = sum total**, grand total, tally, aggregate, answer.
2 = arithmetical problem, problem, calculation, reckoning, tally.
▪ **sum up = give a summary of**, summarize, encapsulate, put in a nutshell.

summarize VERB = **give/make a summary of**, sum up, give a synopsis of, precis, give a precis of, give a résumé of, give an abstract of, abridge, condense, epitomize, outline, sketch, give the main points of, give a rundown of, review.

summary NOUN
= **synopsis**, precis, résumé, abstract, abridgement, digest, epitome, outline, sketch, rundown, review, summing-up.
▸ ADJ = **immediate**, instant, instantaneous, direct, prompt, rapid, sudden, abrupt, peremptory.

summit NOUN **1 = top**, peak, crest, crown, apex,

vertex, apogee. **2 = peak**, height, pinnacle, culmination, climax, crowning point, zenith, acme.
Opposites: base, nadir.

summon VERB **1 = send for**, call for, bid, request someone's presence.
2 = order, call, convene, assemble, muster, rally; [formal] convoke.

sumptuous ADJ **= lavish**, luxurious, de luxe, opulent, magnificent.
Opposites: plain.

sundry ADJ **= several**, various, varied, miscellaneous, assorted, diverse.

sunken ADJ **1 = at a lower level**, below ground level, lowered. **2 = hollow**, hollowed, concave, drawn, haggard.

sunlight NOUN **= sun**, sunshine, light, daylight, light of day.

sunny ADJ **1 = sunlit**, bright, clear, cloudless, unclouded, without a cloud in the sky. **2 =** *see* **cheerful**.
Opposites: dull.

sunrise NOUN **= dawn**, crack of dawn, daybreak, cockcrow; [N. Amer.] sun-up.

sunset NOUN **= nightfall**, close of day, twilight, dusk; [N. Amer.] sundown.

sunshine NOUN **=** *see* **sunlight**.

superb ADJ **= superlative**, excellent, first-rate, first-class, outstanding, remarkable, dazzling, marvellous, magnificent, wonderful, splendid, exquisite; [inf] fantastic, fabulous; [Brit. inf] brilliant.
Opposites: poor.

supercilious ADJ **= arrogant**, haughty, conceited, proud, vain, disdainful, scornful, condescending, superior, patronizing, imperious, overbearing, lofty, lordly, snobbish, snobby; [inf] hoity-toity, uppity, snooty, stuck up.

superficial ADJ **1 = surface**, exterior, external, outer, outside, peripheral, slight.
2 = cursory, perfunctory, hasty, hurried, casual,

S

sketchy, desultory, slapdash. **3 = shallow**, empty-headed, trivial, frivolous, silly, lightweight, insignificant. **Opposites:** thorough, deep.

superfluous ADJ **= spare**, surplus, extra, unneeded, unrequired, excess, in excess, unnecessary, needless, inessential, uncalled for, unwarranted, gratuitous. **Opposites:** necessary, essential.

superhuman ADJ **1 = Herculean**, phenomenal, prodigious, stupendous, heroic, extraordinary. **2 = divine**, god-like, holy, supernatural, preternatural, paranormal, other-worldly. **Opposites:** mundane.

superior ADJ **1 = better**, finer, higher-quality, higher-grade, greater, more expert, more skilful, more advanced, surpassing. **2 = higher**, higher-ranking, higher up. **3 = haughty**, disdainful, condescending, supercilious, patronizing, lofty, lordly, snobbish, snobby; [inf] high and mighty, hoity-toity, uppity, snooty, stuck up, toffee-nosed. **Opposites:** inferior.

superlative ADJ **= best**, greatest, supreme, consummate, first-rate, first-class, of the first water, of the first order, brilliant, excellent, magnificent, outstanding, unsurpassed, unparalleled, unrivalled, peerless, matchless, transcendent. **Opposites:** poor.

supernatural ADJ **= other-worldly**, unearthly, spectral, ghostly, phantom, magical, mystic, unreal, paranormal, supernormal, psychic, miraculous, extraordinary, uncanny.

supersede VERB **1 = take the place of**, replace, take over from, displace, succeed, supplant, usurp.

2 = **discard**, cast aside, throw out, dispose of, abandon, jettison; [inf] chuck out.

supervise VERB
= **superintend**, be in charge of, direct, administer, manage, run, oversee, keep an eye on, watch, observe, inspect, be responsible for, guide.

supervision NOUN
= **administration**, management, direction, control, charge, superintendence, observation, inspection, guidance.

supervisor NOUN
= **overseer**, superintendent, inspector, controller, manager, director, administrator, chief, guide, adviser; [inf] boss.

supplant VERB = **take the place of**, take over from, replace, displace, supersede, oust, usurp, overthrow, remove, unseat.

supple ADJ **1** = **lithe**, loose-limbed, limber. **2** = **pliant**, pliable, flexible, bendable, stretchable, elastic.
Opposites: stiff.

supplement NOUN
1 = **addition**, supplementation, additive, extra, add-on.
2 = **pull-out**, insert, special-feature section, magazine section.
▶ VERB = **add to**, augment, increase, top up, complement.

supplementary ADJ
1 = **supplemental**, additional, extra, add-on, complementary.
2 = **added**, appended, attached, extra.

suppliant NOUN
= **supplicant**, petitioner, pleader, applicant, suitor, beggar, appellant.

supplicant NOUN = *see* **suppliant**.

supplication NOUN = **plea**, entreaty, begging, petition, appeal, solicitation, request, prayer, invocation; [poetic/literary] beseeching.

supplies NOUN
= **provisions**, stores, rations, food, provender; [dated] victuals.

supply VERB 1 = **provide**, give, furnish, contribute, donate, grant, come up with; [inf] fork out, shell out. 2 = **satisfy**, meet, fulfil.

▶ NOUN 1 = **supplying**, providing, provision, furnishing. 2 = **stock**, store, reserve, reservoir, stockpile, heap, pile, mass, hoard, cache. = *See also* **stock** NOUN (2).

support VERB 1 = **bear**, carry, hold up, prop up, bolster up, brace, keep up, shore up, underpin, buttress. 2 = **maintain**, provide for, sustain, take care of, look after. 3 = **give moral support to**, give strength to, comfort, help, sustain, encourage, buoy up, hearten, fortify; [inf] buck up. 4 = **back up**, substantiate, give force to, bear out, corroborate, confirm, verify, validate, authenticate, endorse, ratify. 5 = **back**, champion, give help to, help, assist, aid, be on someone's side, side with, vote for, stand behind, stand up for, take up the cudgels for; [inf] stick up for. 6 = **advocate**, promote, further, champion, be on someone's side, espouse, be in favour of, recommend, defend.

Opposites: neglect, contradict, oppose.

▶ NOUN 1 = **base**, foundations, pillar, post, prop, underprop, underpinning, substructure, brace, buttress, abutment, bolster, stay. 2 = **keep**, maintenance, sustenance, food and accommodation, subsistence; [archaic] aliment. 3 = **moral support**, friendship, strength, encouragement, buoying up, heartening, fortification; [inf] bucking up. 4 = **backing**, contribution, donation, money, subsidy, funding, funds, finance, capital. 5 = **help**, assistance, comfort, tower of strength, prop, backbone, mainstay.

supporter NOUN 1 = **sponsor**, contributor,

donor, backer, patron, friend, well-wisher.
2 = **champion**, advocate, promoter, backer, defender, apologist, helper. **3** = **fan**, follower.

supportive ADJ = **helpful**, encouraging, caring, sympathetic, understanding, loyal, interested, positive, reassuring.
Opposites: unsympathetic.

suppose VERB **1** = **assume**, take for granted, dare say, take as read, presume, expect, imagine, believe, think, fancy, suspect, guess, surmise, reckon, conjecture, theorize, opine. **2** = **take as a hypothesis**, hypothesize, postulate, posit. **3** = **presuppose**, require, imply.

supposed ADJ = **presumed**, assumed, believed, professed, so-called, alleged, putative, reputed.

supposition NOUN = **assumption**, presumption, suspicion, guess, surmise, conjecture, speculation, theory, hypothesis, postulation.

suppress VERB **1** = **vanquish**, put an end to, crush, quell, conquer, squash, stamp out, extinguish, put out, crack down on, clamp down on. **2** = **restrain**, keep a rein on, hold back, control, keep under control, check, keep in check, curb, bottle up, choke back. **3** = **keep secret**, conceal, hide, keep hidden, keep silent about, withhold, cover up, smother, stifle, muzzle.
Opposites: incite, reveal.

supremacy NOUN = **ascendancy**, dominance, superiority, predominance, paramountcy, dominion, sway, authority, mastery, control, power, rule, sovereignty, lordship.

supreme ADJ **1** = **highest-ranking**, highest, leading, chief, foremost, principal. **2** = **extreme**, greatest, utmost,

uttermost, maximum, extraordinary, remarkable. **3 = final**, last, ultimate.
Opposites: subordinate, minimal.

sure ADJ **1 = certain**, definite, positive, convinced, confident, decided, assured, free from doubt, unhesitating, unwavering, unfaltering. **2 = assured**, certain, guaranteed, inevitable, irrevocable. **3 = reliable**, dependable, trustworthy, trusted, trusty, unfailing, infallible, never-failing, tested, true, foolproof, effective, efficacious; [inf] sure-fire.
Opposites: unsure, uncertain.

surface NOUN **1 = outside**, exterior, top. **2 = outward appearance**, superficial appearance, facade.
▶ ADJ **= superficial**, external, exterior, outward.
▶ VERB **1 = come to the surface**, come up, come to the top. **2 = reappear**, appear, come to light, come up, emerge, crop

up. **3 = get up**, get out of bed, rise, wake, awaken.

surge NOUN **= gush**, rush, outpouring, stream, flow, sweep, efflux.
▶ VERB **1 = gush**, rush, stream, flow. **2 = rise**, swell, heave, billow, roll, eddy, swirl.

surly ADJ **= bad-tempered**, ill-natured, crabbed, grumpy, crotchety, grouchy, cantankerous, irascible, testy, crusty, gruff, abrupt, brusque, churlish, uncivil, morose, sullen, sulky.
Opposites: good-natured, friendly.

surmise VERB **= guess**, conjecture, suspect, deduce, assume, presume, gather, feel, be of the opinion, think, believe, imagine.

surmount VERB **= get over**, overcome, conquer, triumph over, prevail over, get the better of, beat.
Opposites: descend.

surname NOUN **= last name**, family name, patronymic.

surpass VERB = **be greater than**, be better than, beat, exceed, excel, transcend, outdo, outshine, outstrip, overshadow, eclipse.

surplus NOUN = **excess**, remainder, residue, surfeit.
Opposites: dearth, shortage.
▸ ADJ = **excess**, in excess, superfluous, leftover, unused, remaining, extra, spare.

surprise VERB **1** = **astonish**, amaze, nonplus, take aback, startle, astound, stun, stagger, leave open-mouthed, take someone's breath away; [inf] flabbergast, bowl over, blow someone's mind. **2** = **take by surprise**, catch unawares, catch off guard, catch red-handed, catch in the act, catch out, burst in on, spring upon, catch someone with their trousers down; [Brit. inf] catch on the hop.
▸ NOUN **1** = **astonishment**, amazement, incredulity, wonder. **2** = **shock**, bolt from the blue, bombshell, revelation.

surprised ADJ = **astonished**, amazed, nonplussed, startled, astounded, stunned, staggered, open-mouthed, speechless, thunderstruck; [inf] flabbergasted.

surprising ADJ = **astonishing**, amazing, startling, astounding, staggering, incredible, extraordinary, remarkable; [inf] mind-blowing.
Opposites: predictable.

surrender VERB **1** = **give in**, give oneself up, yield, submit, capitulate, lay down one's arms, raise/show the white flag, throw in the towel/sponge. **2** = **give up**, relinquish, renounce, forgo, forsake, cede, abdicate, waive. **3** = **hand over**, give up, deliver up, part with, let go of, relinquish.
Opposites: resist.
▸ NOUN **1** = **yielding**, capitulation, submission. **2** = **relinquishment**,

renunciation, forgoing, ceding, cession, abdication.

surreptitious ADJ
= **stealthy**, clandestine, secret, sneaky, sly, cunning, furtive, underhand, undercover, covert.
Opposites: open, blatant.

surround VERB = **encircle**, enclose, go around, encompass, ring, gird, girdle, fence in, hem in, confine.

surrounding ADJ
= **neighbouring**, nearby, adjacent, adjoining, bordering.

surroundings PL NOUN
= **environment**, setting, location, neighbourhood, vicinity, milieu, element, background.

surveillance NOUN
= **observation**, watch, scrutiny, reconnaissance, spying, espionage.

survey VERB 1 = **look at**, look over, take a look at, observe, view, contemplate, regard, examine, inspect, scrutinize, scan, study, consider, review, take

stock of; [inf] size up.
2 = **make a survey of**, value, carry out a valuation of, estimate the value of, appraise, assess, prospect, triangulate.
▶ NOUN 1 = **study**, consideration, review, overview, examination, inspection, scrutinization, scrutiny.
2 = **valuation**, appraisal.
3 = **investigation**, inquiry, research, study, review, probe, questionnaire.

survive VERB 1 = **remain alive**, live, hold out, pull through, cling to life.
2 = **live on**, continue, remain, last, persist, endure, be extant, exist, be. 3 = **outlive**, outlast, live after, remain alive after.

susceptible ADJ
= **impressionable**, credulous, gullible, innocent, defenceless, vulnerable, easily led, responsive, sensitive, thin-skinned.
Opposites: immune, resistant.
▪ **susceptible to** = **open to**, responsive to,

receptive to, vulnerable to, defenceless against.

suspect VERB **1** = **feel**, have a feeling, be inclined to think, fancy, surmise, guess, conjecture, have a suspicion that, speculate, have a hunch, suppose, believe, think, conclude. **2** = **doubt**, have doubts about, harbour suspicions about, have misgivings about, be sceptical about, distrust, mistrust.

suspend VERB **1** = **hang**, put up, swing, dangle, sling. **2** = **adjourn**, interrupt, cut short, bring to an end, cease, discontinue, break off, arrest, put off, postpone, delay, defer, shelve, pigeonhole; [chiefly US] table; [inf] put on ice. **3** = **debar**, shut out, exclude, keep out, remove.

suspense NOUN = **uncertainty**, doubt, doubtfulness, anticipation, expectation, expectancy, excitement, tension, anxiety, nervousness, apprehension, apprehensiveness.

suspicion NOUN **1** = **doubt**, misgiving, qualm, wariness, chariness, scepticism, distrust, mistrust, funny feeling. **2** = **feeling**, surmise, guess, conjecture, speculation, hunch, supposition, belief, notion, idea, conclusion; [inf] gut feeling. **3** = **trace**, touch, suggestion, hint, soupçon, tinge, shade.

suspicious ADJ **1** = **doubtful**, unsure, wary, chary, sceptical, distrustful, mistrustful, disbelieving. **2** = **guilty-looking**, dishonest-looking, strange-looking, queer-looking, funny-looking; [inf] shifty, shady. **3** = **questionable**, doubtful, odd, strange, irregular, queer, funny; [inf] fishy, shady. **Opposites:** trusting, innocent.

sustain VERB **1** = **bear**, support, carry, keep up, prop up, shore up. **2** = **support**, be a source

of strength to, be a tower
of strength to, comfort,
help, assist, encourage,
buoy up, cheer up,
hearten; [inf] buck up.
3 = **keep alive**, keep
going, maintain,
preserve, feed, nourish.

sustained ADJ
= **continuing**, steady,
continuous, constant,
prolonged, perpetual,
unremitting.
Opposites: intermittent.

sustenance NOUN = **food**,
nourishment, provisions,
rations, comestibles,
provender; [inf] grub,
chow; [Brit. inf] scoff;
[dated] victuals;
[archaic] aliment.

swagger VERB = **strut**,
parade, prance.

swallow VERB **1** = **gulp
down**, eat, drink,
consume, devour, ingest;
[inf] swig, swill; [Brit.
inf] scoff. **2** = **put up with**,
tolerate, endure, stand,
bear, abide, stomach,
brook; [archaic] suffer.
3 = **believe**, accept;
[inf] fall for, buy.
4 = **repress**, restrain, hold
back, control, rein in.

swamp NOUN = **marsh**,
bog, quagmire, mire,
morass, fen, quag.
▶ VERB **1** = **flood**, inundate,
deluge, wash out, soak,
drench, saturate.
2 = **overwhelm**, engulf,
snow under, overload,
overburden, weight
down, besiege, beset.

swap VERB = **exchange**,
interchange, trade,
barter, switch.

swarm NOUN **1** = **hive**,
flight. **2** = **crowd**,
multitude, horde, host,
mob, throng, army,
flock, herd, pack, drove.
▶ VERB = **flock**, crowd,
throng, stream, surge.

swarthy ADJ = **dark**, dark-
coloured, dark-skinned,
dark-complexioned,
dusky, tanned.
Opposites: pale, fair.

swashbuckling ADJ
= **dashing**, daring,
adventurous, bold,
gallant, swaggering.
Opposites: timid.

swathe VERB = **wrap**,
envelop, bind, swaddle,
bandage, bundle up,
cover, shroud, drape.

sway VERB 1 = **swing**, shake, bend, lean, incline. 2 = **waver**, hesitate, fluctuate, vacillate, oscillate. 3 = **influence**, affect, persuade, prevail on, bring round, win over, induce. ▶ NOUN 1 = **jurisdiction**, rule, government, sovereignty, dominion, control, command, power, authority, ascendancy, domination, mastery. 2 = **control**, domination, power, authority, influence, guidance, direction.

swear VERB 1 = **promise**, pledge, vow, give one's word, take an oath, swear on the Bible. 2 = **vow**, insist, declare, assert, maintain, contend; [formal] aver. 3 = **curse**, blaspheme, utter profanities, be foul-mouthed, use bad language, swear like a trooper; [inf] cuss, turn the air blue, eff and blind.

sweat VERB = **perspire**, exude perspiration, drip with sweat, break out in a sweat.

sweaty ADJ = **sweating**, perspiring, clammy, sticky, moist, damp.

sweep VERB = **brush**, clean, clean up, clear up. ▪ **sweep away/aside** = **cast aside**, discard, disregard, ignore, take no notice of, dismiss.

sweet ADJ 1 = **sweetened**, sugary, sugared, honeyed, syrupy, saccharine. 2 = **sweet-smelling**, fragrant, aromatic, perfumed, scented, balmy. 3 = **sweet-sounding**, musical, tuneful, dulcet, mellifluous, soft, harmonious, euphonious, silvery, silver-toned. 4 = **good-natured**, amiable, pleasant, agreeable, friendly, kindly, charming, likeable, appealing, engaging, winning, winsome, taking. 5 = **dear**, dearest, darling, beloved, loved, cherished, precious, treasured.

Opposites: sour, savoury, harsh, disagreeable.

▶ NOUN 1 = **dessert**, pudding; [Brit. inf] afters. 2 = **bonbon**, sweetmeat; [N. Amer.] candy; [inf] sweetie.

sweeten VERB 1 = **make sweet**, add sugar to, sugar. 2 = **soften**, soften up, mellow, pacify, appease, mollify.

sweetheart NOUN = **girlfriend**, boyfriend, lover, love, inamorato, inamorata, beau; [poetic/ literary] swain; [archaic] paramour.

swell VERB 1 = **expand**, bulge, distend, become distended, inflate, become inflated, dilate, become bloated, blow up, puff up, balloon, intumesce. 2 = **increase**, grow larger, rise, mount, escalate, accelerate, step up, snowball, mushroom. 3 = **grow loud**, grow louder, intensify, heighten. Opposites: contract.

▶ ADJ = **expensive**, luxurious, de luxe, fashionable, elegant, grand; [inf] plush, ritzy; [Brit. inf] posh.

swelling NOUN = **bump**, lump, bulge, blister, inflammation, protuberance, tumescence.

swerve VERB = **change direction**, go off course, veer, turn aside, skew, deviate, sheer, twist.

swift ADJ = **fast**, rapid, quick, speedy, fleet-footed, fleet, prompt, brisk, immediate, instantaneous; [inf] nippy. Opposites: slow.

swill VERB = **gulp down**, drink, quaff, swallow, down, drain, guzzle; [inf] swig.
■ **swill out** = **sluice**, wash down, wash out, clean out, flush out, rinse out.

swim VERB = **go swimming**, bathe, dive in; [inf] have a dip.
■ **be swimming in** = **be saturated in**, be drenched in, be soaked in, be steeped in, be immersed in.

swindle VERB = **defraud**, cheat, trick, fleece, dupe, deceive, rook, exploit; [inf] do, con, diddle, rip off, take for a ride, pull a fast one on, bilk.

▶ NOUN = **fraud**, trick, deception, exploitation, sharp practice; [inf] con trick, con, diddle, rip-off, fiddle.

swindler NOUN = **fraudster**, cheat, trickster, rogue, mountebank, exploiter; [inf] con man, con artist, shark, bilker.

swing VERB 1 = **hang**, be suspended, dangle, be pendent. 2 = **move back and forth**, sway, oscillate, wag. 3 = **curve**, veer, turn, lean, incline, wind, twist. 4 = **change**, fluctuate, oscillate, waver, see-saw, yo-yo.

▶ NOUN 1 = **swaying**, oscillation, wagging. 2 = **move**, change, variation, turnaround.

swirl VERB = **whirl**, eddy, circulate, revolve, spin, twist, churn, swish.

switch NOUN 1 = **change**, change of direction, shift, reversal, turnaround, U-turn; [Brit.] about-turn. 2 = **exchange**, trade, swap.

▶ VERB 1 = **change**, shift, reverse. 2 = **exchange**, interchange, trade, barter, swap.

swollen ADJ = **expanded**, bulging, distended, inflated, dilated, bloated, blown up, puffed up, puffy, tumescent.

swoop VERB = **pounce**, dive, descend, sweep down on, drop down on.

sycophant NOUN = **toady**, flatterer, truckler, Uriah Heep; [inf] bootlicker, yes-man.

sycophantic ADJ = **servile**, subservient, obsequious, toadying, flattering, ingratiating, unctuous, truckling, Uriah Heepish; [inf] bootlicking.

symbol NOUN 1 = **emblem**, token, sign, badge, representation, figure, image, type. 2 = **sign**, character, mark.

symbolic ADJ 1 = **emblematic**, representative, typical. 2 = **representative**, illustrative, emblematic, figurative, allegorical.

S

symbolize VERB = **be a symbol of**, stand for, be a sign of, represent, personify, exemplify, typify, betoken, denote, epitomize, signify, mean.

symmetrical ADJ = **balanced**, well proportioned, proportional, in proportion, regular, even, harmonious, uniform, consistent, in agreement. **Opposites:** asymmetrical.

sympathetic ADJ 1 = **compassionate**, commiserating, commiserative, pitying, condoling, consoling, comforting, supportive, caring, concerned, solicitous, considerate, kindly, kind, kind-hearted, warm, warm-hearted, understanding, charitable, empathetic. 2 = **pleasant**, agreeable, likeable, congenial, friendly, sociable, companionable, neighbourly, easy to get along with; [inf] simpatico. 3 = **in sympathy with**, well disposed to, favourably disposed to, approving of, pro, on someone's side. **Opposites:** unsympathetic.

sympathize VERB = **show/feel sympathy for**, be sympathetic towards, show compassion for, be compassionate towards, commiserate with, pity, offer condolences to, console, comfort, be supportive of, show understanding to, empathize with.

sympathy NOUN = **compassion**, commiseration, pity, condolence, consolation, comfort, solace, support, caring, concern, solicitude, solicitousness, consideration, kindness, kind-heartedness, warmth, warm-heartedness, charity, charitableness, understanding, empathy. **Opposites:** indifference.

symptom NOUN = **sign**, indication, signal, warning, mark, characteristic, feature,

token, evidence,
demonstration, display.

symptomatic ADJ
= **indicative of**, signalling,
characteristic of,
suggesting, suggestive of.

synthesis NOUN
= **combination**,
combining, union,
unification, blend,
merging, amalgamation,
fusion, coalescence,
integration.

synthetic ADJ
= **manufactured**, man-
made, fake, artificial,
mock, ersatz.
Opposites: real, natural.

system NOUN 1 = **structure**,
organization, order,
arrangement, set-up.
2 = **method**,
methodology, technique,
process, procedure,
approach, practice, line,
means, way, modus
operandi.
3 = **methodicalness**,
systematization,
orderliness, planning,
logic, method, routine.

systematic ADJ
= **structured**, organized,
methodical, orderly, well
ordered, planned,
systematized, logical,
efficient, businesslike.
Opposites: unsystematic,
chaotic.

S

Tt

table NOUN 1 = **counter**, bar, buffet, bench, stand. 2 = **list**, catalogue, tabulation, inventory, itemization, index.
▶ VERB = **submit**, put forward, propose, suggest, move, enter.

tablet NOUN 1 = **slab**, panel, stone. 2 = **pill**, capsule, lozenge. 3 = **bar**, cake.

taboo ADJ = **forbidden**, prohibited, banned, proscribed, vetoed, ruled out, outlawed, not permitted, not acceptable, frowned on, beyond the pale.
Opposites: acceptable.
▶ NOUN = **prohibition**, proscription, veto, interdiction, interdict, ban.

tacit ADJ = **implicit**, understood, implied, taken for granted, unstated, undeclared, unspoken, silent, wordless.
Opposites: explicit.

taciturn ADJ = **unforthcoming**, uncommunicative, reticent, untalkative, tight-lipped, close-mouthed, quiet, silent.
Opposites: loquacious.

tack NOUN 1 = **drawing pin**, nail, pin, staple, rivet. 2 = **course/line of action**, method, approach, process, way, policy.
▶ VERB = **nail**, pin, staple, fix, fasten, affix, put up/down.

tackle NOUN = **equipment**, apparatus, outfit, tools, implements, accoutrements, paraphernalia, things, trappings; [inf] gear, stuff.
▶ VERB 1 = **undertake**, attempt, apply/address oneself to, get to grips

with, set/go about, get to work at, embark on, set one's hand to, take on, engage in. **2** = **grapple with**, seize, take hold of, confront, face up to; [Brit. inf] have a go at.

tacky[1] ADJ = **sticky**, gluey, gummy; [inf] gooey.

tacky[2] ADJ = **tawdry**, tasteless, kitsch, vulgar, crude, garish, gaudy, flashy; [inf] flash. **Opposites:** tasteful.

tact NOUN = **diplomacy**, discretion, sensitivity, understanding, thoughtfulness, consideration, delicacy, subtlety, finesse, skill, perception, judgement, prudence, judiciousness. **Opposites:** tactlessness.

tactful ADJ = **diplomatic**, politic, discreet, sensitive, understanding, thoughtful, considerate, delicate, subtle, perceptive, prudent, judicious. **Opposites:** tactless.

tactic NOUN = **manoeuvre**, expedient, device, stratagem, trick, scheme, plan, ploy, course/line of action, method, approach, tack, means.

tactical ADJ = **strategic**, politic, planned, shrewd, skilful, adroit, clever, cunning, artful; [inf] smart.

tactless ADJ = **undiplomatic**, impolitic, indiscreet, insensitive, inconsiderate, indelicate, unsubtle, rough, crude, clumsy, awkward, inept, bungling, maladroit, gauche, undiscerning, imprudent, injudicious. **Opposites:** tactful.

tag NOUN **1** = **label**, ticket, sticker, docket. **2** = **quotation**, stock phrase, platitude, cliché, epithet.
▶ VERB = **label**, put a ticket/sticker on, mark.

tail NOUN = **brush**, scut, dock.
▶ VERB = **follow**, shadow, stalk, trail, track, dog, keep under surveillance.

tailor NOUN = **outfitter**, dressmaker, couturier, clothier, costumier.
▶ VERB = **fit**, suit, fashion, style, mould, shape, adapt, adjust, modify,

convert, alter, accommodate.

take VERB **1** = **get/lay hold of**, grasp, grip, clutch. **2** = **obtain**, receive, get, gain, acquire, secure, procure, come by, win. **3** = **seize**, catch, capture, arrest, carry off, abduct. **4** = **remove**, appropriate, make off with, steal, pilfer, purloin, pocket; [inf] filch, swipe; [Brit. inf] pinch, nick. **5** = **reserve**, book, engage, rent, hire, lease. **6** = **travel by/on**, use, make use of, utilize. **7** = **use up**, require, call for, need, necessitate. **8** = **carry**, fetch, bring, bear, transport, convey, cart, ferry. **9** = **escort**, accompany, conduct, guide, lead, usher, convoy. **Opposites:** give.

■ **take off** = *see* **imitate** (**2**).

takings PL NOUN = **proceeds**, returns, receipts, earnings, winnings, pickings, profit, gain, income, revenue.

tale NOUN = **story**, narrative, anecdote, legend, fable, myth, parable, allegory, epic, saga; [inf] yarn.

talent NOUN = **gift**, flair, aptitude, facility, knack, bent, ability, capacity, faculty, aptness, endowment, strong point, forte, genius.

talented ADJ = **gifted**, accomplished, able, capable, apt, deft, adept, proficient, brilliant, expert, artistic. **Opposites:** incapable, inept.

talk VERB **1** = **speak**, give voice/utterance, discourse, chat, chatter, gossip, prattle, prate, gibber, jabber, babble, rattle on, gabble; [inf] yak, gab; [Brit. inf] natter, rabbit. **2** = **communicate**, converse, speak to each other, discuss things, confer, consult each other, have negotiations, parley; [inf] chew the fat/ rag, jaw, rap.

▸ NOUN **1** = **talking**, speaking, chatter, chatting, gossiping, prattling; [Brit.

inf] nattering. **2** = **lecture**, speech, address, discourse, oration, sermon, disquisition. **3** = **gossip**, rumour, hearsay, tittle-tattle.

talkative ADJ = **loquacious**, garrulous, voluble, chatty, gossipy, conversational, long-winded, gushing, effusive; [inf] gabby, mouthy, big-mouthed. **Opposites:** taciturn.

tall ADJ **1** = **big**, colossal, gigantic, lanky, rangy, gangling. **2** = **high**, lofty, towering, soaring, sky-high. **Opposites:** short.

tally NOUN = **count**, record, total, reckoning, enumeration, register, roll, census, poll. ▸ VERB = **agree**, accord, concur, coincide, conform, correspond, match, fit, harmonize. **Opposites:** disagree.

tame ADJ **1** = **domesticated**, gentle. **2** = **unexciting**, uninteresting, uninspired, dull, bland, flat, insipid, vapid, prosaic, humdrum, boring, tedious, wearisome. **Opposites:** wild. ▸ VERB **1** = **domesticate**, break, train. **2** = **subdue**, discipline, curb, control, master, overcome, suppress, repress, humble.

tamper VERB = **meddle**, interfere, monkey around, mess about, tinker, fiddle.

tan VERB = **become suntanned**, suntan, take a suntan/tan, brown, go/turn brown, darken.

tangible ADJ **1** = **touchable**, palpable, tactile, visible. **2** = **concrete**, real, actual, solid, substantial, hard, well documented, definite, clear. **Opposites:** abstract.

tangled ADJ **1** = **entangled**, twisted, snarled, ravelled, knotted, knotty, matted, tousled, messy. **2** = **confused**, jumbled, mixed up, messy, chaotic, complicated, involved, convoluted, complex.

Opposites: neat, straight, simple.

tank NOUN = **container**, receptacle, vat, cistern.

tantalize VERB = **tease**, torment, torture, frustrate, disappoint, thwart, lead on, entice, titillate, allure, beguile.

tantamount
∎ **tantamount to**
= **equivalent to**, equal to, as good as, synonymous with.

tape NOUN 1 = **band**, strip, string, ribbon. 2 = **tape recording**, cassette, videotape, video cassette, video, audio tape, audio cassette.
▶ VERB 1 = **bind**, tie, fasten, stick, seal. 2 = **record**, tape-record, video-record, video.

taper VERB = **narrow**, thin, become narrow/thinner, come to a point.
Opposites: thicken.
∎ **taper off** = see **decline**
VERB (2, 3).

target NOUN 1 = **objective**, goal, object, aim, end, intention. 2 = **butt**, victim, scapegoat.

tariff NOUN 1 = **price list/ schedule**, list of charges. 2 = **tax**, duty, toll, excise, levy, impost.

tarnish VERB 1 = **dull**, dim, discolour, rust. 2 = **sully**, besmirch, blacken, stain, blemish, blot, taint, befoul, drag through the mud.
Opposites: polish, enhance.

tart[1] NOUN = **pastry**, flan, tartlet, quiche, pie.

tart[2] ADJ = **sharp**, sour, tangy, piquant, pungent, bitter, acid, acidulous, vinegary.
Opposites: sweet.

task NOUN = **job**, duty, chore, charge, assignment, commission, mission, engagement, occupation, undertaking, exercise, errand, quest.

taste NOUN 1 = **flavour**, savour, relish, tang. 2 = **morsel**, bite, mouthful, spoonful, sample, sip, drop, swallow, touch, soupçon. 3 = **liking**, love, fondness, fancy, desire, preference, penchant, predilection, inclination, partiality,

leaning, bent, hankering, appetite, palate, thirst, hunger.
4 = discrimination, discernment, judgement, refinement, polish, finesse, elegance, grace, stylishness.
▶ VERB **1 = sample**, test, try, nibble, sip. **2 = make out**, perceive, discern, distinguish, differentiate.

tasteful ADJ = **in good taste**, aesthetic, artistic, harmonious, pleasing, elegant, graceful, beautiful, pretty, charming, handsome, discriminating, refined, restrained.
Opposites: tasteless.

tasteless ADJ
1 = flavourless, bland, insipid, watery, watered down, weak, thin, unappetizing, uninteresting, vapid.
2 = vulgar, crude, tawdry, garish, gaudy, loud, flashy, showy, cheap, gross, meretricious.
Opposites: tasteful.

tasty ADJ = **flavoursome**, full-flavoured, appetizing, palatable, toothsome,

delectable, delicious, luscious, mouth-watering, piquant, pungent, spicy; [inf] scrumptious, yummy, finger-licking.
Opposites: bland.

taunt VERB = **gibe at**, jeer at, sneer at, insult, chaff, tease, torment, provoke, ridicule, deride, mock, poke fun at.

taut ADJ = **tight**, stretched, rigid, flexed, tensed.
Opposites: slack.

tawdry ADJ = **showy**, gaudy, flashy, garish, loud, tasteless, cheap, cheapjack, shoddy, meretricious, Brummagem; [inf] flash, tatty, tacky, kitsch.
Opposites: tasteful.

tax NOUN = **levy**, charge, duty, toll, excise, tariff, impost, tribute.
▶ VERB **1 = levy a tax on**, impose a toll on, charge duty on. **2 = make demands on**, weigh heavily on, weigh down, burden, load, encumber, overload, push, stretch, strain, try, wear out, exhaust, sap, drain,

t

enervate, fatigue, tire, weary, weaken.

teach VERB **1** = **give lessons to**, instruct, educate, school, tutor, coach, train, drill, ground, enlighten. **2** = **give lessons/ instruction in**, instil, inculcate, impart.

teacher NOUN = **schoolteacher**, schoolmaster, schoolmistress, master, mistress, instructor, educator, tutor, coach, trainer, lecturer, professor, don, pedagogue, guide, mentor, guru.

team NOUN = **group**, band, bunch, company, gang, crew, troupe, squad, side, line-up.

tear[1] NOUN = **rip**, split, hole, rent, run, rupture. ▶ VERB = **rip**, split, rend, sever, rive, sunder, rupture.

tear[2] NOUN = **teardrop**, drop, droplet, globule, bead.

tearful ADJ = **in tears**, crying, weeping, weepy, sobbing, blubbering, snivelling, whimpering, wailing; [inf] blubbing. **Opposites:** cheerful.

tease VERB = **mock**, ridicule, poke fun at, torment, provoke, badger, bait, goad, pest, bother, worry, vex, irritate, annoy, gibe; [inf] needle.

technical ADJ **1** = **practical**, mechanical, scientific, technological. **2** = **specialist**, specialized, scientific.

technique NOUN **1** = **method**, system, procedure, style, manner, way, course of action, mode, fashion, means. **2** = **execution**, skill, skilfulness, proficiency, expertise, expertness, mastery, artistry, art, craftsmanship, craft, ability.

tedious ADJ = **wearisome**, wearying, tiresome, tiring, fatiguing, soporific, overlong, long-winded, prolix, dull, deadly dull, boring, uninteresting, dry, dreary, drab, unexciting, lifeless, uninspired, flat,

banal, vapid, insipid, monotonous, unvaried, prosaic, humdrum, run-of-the-mill, routine.
Opposites: interesting.

teem VERB = **abound**, be abundant, be plentiful, be copious, swarm, crawl, bristle, seethe, brim.

teetotaller NOUN = **abstainer**, non-drinker, Rechabite.

telephone NOUN = **phone**, handset, receiver; [inf] blower.
▶ VERB = **call**, call up, phone; [Brit.] ring up, ring; [inf] get on the blower to, buzz.

telescope VERB = **concertina**, crush, squash, squeeze, compress, compact.
Opposites: elongate.

television NOUN = **TV**; [inf] small screen; [Brit. inf] telly, the box, goggle-box; [N. Amer. inf] the tube, idiot box.

tell VERB 1 = **make known**, impart, communicate, announce, proclaim, broadcast, divulge, reveal, disclose, declare, state, mention, utter, voice, say, speak.
2 = **inform**, let know, make aware, apprise, notify. 3 = **instruct**, order, give orders, command, direct, bid, charge, enjoin, dictate to, call upon, require.
4 = **distinguish**, differentiate, discriminate.

telling ADJ = **marked**, significant, substantial, considerable, important, striking, impressive, potent, powerful, forceful, effective, influential, decisive.
Opposites: insignificant.

temper NOUN
1 = **temperament**, disposition, nature, humour, mood, character, frame of mind, mind, attitude, stamp.
2 = **bad mood**, ill humour, fury, rage, passion, fit of temper/pique, tantrum; [Brit. inf] paddy.
▶ VERB 1 = **toughen**, anneal, harden, strengthen, fortify. 2 = **moderate**, soften, tone down, modify, mitigate,

t

alleviate, allay, palliate, mollify, assuage, lessen, weaken.

temperament NOUN
= **disposition**, nature, humour, mood, character, personality, make-up, constitution, complexion, temper, spirit, mettle, frame of mind, cast of mind, mind, attitude, outlook stamp, quality.

temperamental ADJ
1 = **constitutional**, inherent, innate, inborn, congenital, deep-rooted, ingrained. **2** = **excitable**, emotional, volatile, mercurial, oversensitive, capricious, erratic, touchy, moody, hot-headed, explosive, impatient, petulant.
Opposites: calm.

temperance NOUN
= **moderation**, self-control, abstemiousness, continence, abstinence, self-denial.
Opposites: alcoholism.

temperate ADJ
= **moderate**, mild, gentle, clement, balmy, pleasant, agreeable.

Opposites: extreme.

tempestuous ADJ
= **stormy**, turbulent, boisterous, violent, wild, uncontrolled, unrestrained, passionate, impassioned, emotional, intense, fierce.
Opposites: calm.

temple NOUN = **place of worship**, holy place, shrine, sanctuary.

tempo NOUN = **beat**, rhythm, cadence, throb, pulse.

temporal ADJ = **secular**, non-spiritual, worldly, material, earthly, carnal.
Opposites: spiritual.

temporary ADJ **1** = **short-term**, impermanent, interim, provisional, pro tem. **2** = **brief**, fleeting, passing, momentary, short-lived, transient, transitory, ephemeral, fugitive, evanescent.
Opposites: permanent.

tempt VERB = **entice**, lure, attract, appeal to, seduce, tantalize, incite, persuade, induce, egg on, urge, goad, prompt, sway, influence, cajole, coax.

Opposites: discourage, deter.

tempting ADJ = **alluring**, enticing, attractive, captivating, appealing, beguiling, fascinating, tantalizing, appetizing, mouth-watering.
Opposites: off-putting.

tenable ADJ = **justifiable**, defensible, defendable, arguable, maintainable, supportable, plausible, credible, reasonable, rational, sound, viable.
Opposites: untenable.

tenacious ADJ
= **persistent**, pertinacious, determined, dogged, resolute, firm, steadfast, purposeful, unshakeable, unswerving, relentless, inexorable, unyielding, inflexible, stubborn, obstinate, intransigent, obdurate, strong-willed.

tend[1] VERB = **have/show a tendency to**, incline towards, be apt/ disposed/liable to, be likely to.

tend[2] VERB = **look after**, take care of, care for, attend to, minister to, see to, cater to, nurse, wait on, watch over, watch.
Opposites: neglect.

tendency NOUN
= **inclination**, disposition, predisposition, proclivity, propensity, proneness, aptness, bent, leaning, penchant, susceptibility, liability.

tender ADJ 1 = **easily damaged**, breakable, fragile, frail, delicate, sensitive.
2 = **compassionate**, soft-hearted, kind, kindly, sympathetic, warm, caring, humane, gentle, solicitous, generous, benevolent, sentimental.
3 = **loving**, affectionate, warm, emotional, amorous. 4 = **sore**, painful, aching, smarting, throbbing, inflamed, irritated, red, raw, bruised.
Opposites: tough, hard-hearted.

tense ADJ 1 = **tight**, taut, rigid, stretched, strained.
2 = **anxious**, nervous, keyed up, worked up, overwrought, distraught,

uneasy, worried, apprehensive, agitated, jumpy, edgy, on edge, restless, fidgety; [inf] uptight, wound up, jittery.
Opposites: relaxed.

tension NOUN
1 = **tightness**, tautness, rigidity. 2 = **anxiety**, stress, stressfulness, suspense, pressure, strain, unease, disquiet, worry, apprehensiveness, agitation, jumpiness, edginess, restlessness.

tentative ADJ
1 = **speculative**, conjectural, exploratory, trial, provisional, test, pilot, untried, unproven.
2 = **hesitant**, hesitating, faltering, wavering, uncertain, unsure, doubtful, cautious, diffident, timid.
Opposites: definite, confident.

tenuous ADJ = **slight**, flimsy, weak, insubstantial, shaky, sketchy, doubtful, dubious, nebulous, hazy, vague, unspecific, indefinite.

Opposites: definite.

term NOUN 1 = **word**, expression, phrase, name, title, appellation, designation; [formal] denomination.
2 = **period**, time, spell, interval, stretch, span, duration.
▶ VERB = **call**, name, entitle, style, dub, label, tag, designate, denominate.

terminal ADJ = **fatal**, deadly, mortal, lethal, killing, incurable.
▶ NOUN 1 = **terminus**, last stop, depot.
2 = **workstation**, visual display unit, VDU.

terminate VERB = **bring to a close/end/conclusion**, close, end, conclude, finish, stop, wind up, discontinue.
Opposites: commence.

terminology NOUN
= **language**, phraseology, vocabulary, nomenclature, jargon, terms, expressions, words; [inf] lingo.

terrible ADJ 1 = **great**, extreme, incorrigible, outrageous, awful, dreadful, frightful, impossible. **2 = bad**, poor, incompetent, useless, talentless; [inf] rotten; [Brit. inf] duff. **3 = dreadful**, terrifying, frightening, frightful, horrifying, horrible, horrific, horrendous, terrific, harrowing, hideous, grim, unspeakable, appalling, awful, gruesome.

terrific ADJ
1 = tremendous, great, very great, very big, huge, sizeable, considerable, intense, extreme, extraordinary, excessive. **2 = very good**, excellent, superb, remarkable, magnificent, wonderful, marvellous, great, sensational; [inf] super, fantastic, fabulous, fab, A1, ace, unreal, awesome.

terrify VERB = **frighten**, scare stiff, scare, petrify, make someone's hair stand on end, alarm, panic, intimidate.

territory NOUN **1 = region**, area, terrain, tract. **2 = area**, province, field, sector, department.

terror NOUN = **fright**, dread, alarm, panic, intimidation, dismay, consternation, shock, horror; [inf] heebie-jeebies.

terrorize VERB = **strike terror in/into**, terrify, scare stiff, petrify, horrify.

terse ADJ **1 = concise**, succinct, compact, brief, short, to the point, crisp, pithy, elliptical, epigrammatic. **2 = abrupt**, curt, brusque, laconic, short, clipped, blunt. **Opposites:** long-winded.

test NOUN = **examination**, check, assessment, evaluation, appraisal, investigation, inspection, analysis, scrutinization, scrutiny, study, probe, exploration.
▶ VERB = **put to the test**, examine, check, assess, evaluate, appraise, investigate, scrutinize, study, probe.

testify VERB = **give evidence**, bear witness, attest, be a witness.

testimonial NOUN = **reference**, character reference,

recommendation, commendation, credential, endorsement.

testimony NOUN = **evidence**, attestation, sworn statement, deposition, affidavit.

text NOUN 1 = **textbook**, book. 2 = **theme**, subject matter, subject, matter, topic, issue. 3 = **passage**, verse, paragraph.

texture NOUN = **feel**, touch, appearance, surface, grain.

thank VERB = **offer/extend thanks to**, express/show gratitude to, show appreciation to.

thankful ADJ = **grateful**, appreciative, pleased, indebted, obliged, under an obligation, beholden.
Opposites: ungrateful.

thankless ADJ = **unappreciated**, unrewarded, unrewarding, unacknowledged, vain, in vain, fruitless, useless.
Opposites: rewarding.

thanks PL NOUN = **gratitude**, gratefulness, appreciation, acknowledgement,

recognition.

thaw VERB = **defrost**, unfreeze, melt, soften, liquefy.
Opposites: freeze.

theatre NOUN 1 = **drama**, dramaturgy, the stage, show business; [inf] show biz. 2 = **auditorium**, hall, playhouse.

theatrical ADJ 1 = **dramatic**, stage, dramaturgical, thespian. 2 = **ostentatious**, melodramatic, histrionic, emotional, exaggerated, overdone, dramatic, showy, affected, mannered, stilted; [inf] hammy.

theft NOUN = **stealing**, robbery, thieving, thievery, burglary, larceny, misappropriation, pilfering, purloining, shoplifting, embezzlement.

theme NOUN 1 = **topic**, subject, subject matter, matter, thesis, text, argument. 2 = **theme song**, melody, tune, air, leitmotif.

theoretical ADJ
= **hypothetical**,
conjectural,
suppositional,
speculative, notional,
postulatory, assumed,
presumed.
Opposites: proven.

theory NOUN = **hypothesis**,
thesis, conjecture,
supposition, speculation,
guess, notion,
postulation, assumption,
presumption, opinion,
view.

therapy NOUN
1 = **treatment**, remedy,
cure. 2 = **psychotherapy**,
psychoanalysis.

thesis NOUN 1 = **theory**,
hypothesis, contention,
argument, proposal,
proposition, premise,
postulation, idea.
2 = **dissertation**, paper,
treatise, disquisition,
essay, composition,
monograph.

thick ADJ 1 = **broad**, wide,
large, big, bulky, solid,
substantial, fat; [inf] beefy.
2 = **dense**, close-packed,
concentrated, crowded,
condensed. 3 = **opaque**,
heavy, dense, soupy,

murky, impenetrable.
Opposites: thin.

thicken VERB = **set**, gel,
solidify, congeal, clot,
coagulate, cake.

thief NOUN = **robber**,
burglar, housebreaker,
larcenist, pilferer,
shoplifter, pickpocket,
embezzler, bandit,
swindler, fraudster,
mugger.

thieve VERB = **steal**, rob,
pilfer, purloin, embezzle,
swindle; [inf] swipe, filch,
rip off; [Brit. inf] nick,
knock off.

thin ADJ 1 = **slim**, slender,
lean, slight, svelte, light,
skinny, spindly, scrawny,
scraggy, bony, skeletal,
wasted, emaciated,
shrunken, anorexic,
undernourished,
underweight. 2 = **fine**,
light, delicate, flimsy,
diaphanous, gossamer,
sheer, transparent, see-
through, gauzy, filmy,
translucent. 3 = **sparse**,
scarce, scanty, meagre,
paltry, scattered.
4 = **flimsy**, insubstantial,
weak, feeble, lame, poor,
shallow, unconvincing,

t

inadequate, insufficient.
Opposites: fat.
▶ VERB **1** = **dilute**, water down, weaken. **2** = **reduce in number**, lessen, decrease, diminish.

thing NOUN **1** = **object**, article;
[inf] whatchamacallit, what's-its-name, whatsit, thingummy, thingamabob, thingamajig. **2** = **action**, act, deed, exploit, feat, undertaking, task, job, chore.

think VERB **1** = **believe**, suppose, expect, imagine, surmise, conjecture, guess, fancy. **2** = **consider**, deem, hold, reckon, regard as, assume, presume, estimate.
3 = **ponder**, meditate, deliberate, contemplate, muse, cogitate, ruminate, concentrate, brood, rack one's brains, be lost in thought, be in a brown study.

thinker NOUN
= **philosopher**, scholar, sage, theorist, intellect;
[inf] brain.

thirst NOUN **1** = **thirstiness**, dryness, dehydration.
2 = **desire**, craving, longing, hankering, yearning, avidity, keenness, eagerness, hunger, lust, appetite, passion, covetousness;
[inf] yen.
■ **thirst for/after**
= **desire**, crave, long for, hanker after, yearn for, hunger after, lust after, covet.

thirsty ADJ **1** = **parched**, dehydrated, dry.
2 = **thirsting**, avid, keen, eager, hungry, greedy, covetous.

thong NOUN = **strip**, belt, strap, cord, lash, rope, tie, tether.

thorny ADJ **1** = **prickly**, spiky, barbed, spiny, spined, spinose, bristly, sharp, pointed. **2** = *see* **difficult** (2).

thorough ADJ **1** = **in-depth**, exhaustive, complete, comprehensive, intensive, extensive, widespread, sweeping, all-embracing, all-inclusive, detailed.
2 = **meticulous**,

scrupulous, assiduous, conscientious, painstaking, punctilious, methodical, careful.
3 = thoroughgoing, out-and-out, utter, downright, sheer, absolute, unmitigated, unqualified, complete, total, perfect.
Opposites: cursory, careless.

thought NOUN **1 = thinking**, reasoning, pondering, meditation, cogitation, rumination, musing, mulling, reflection, introspection, contemplation, consideration, cerebration. **2 = idea**, notion, line of thinking, theory, opinion.

thoughtful ADJ
1 = pensive, reflective, introspective, meditative, contemplative, ruminative, cogitative, absorbed, rapt/lost in thought, in a brown study. **2 = profound**, deep, serious, pithy, meaty, weighty. **3 = considerate**, attentive, caring, solicitous, helpful, kind, kindly, compassionate, tender, charitable.
Opposites: thoughtless.

thoughtless ADJ
1 = tactless, undiplomatic, indiscreet, insensitive, inconsiderate, careless, selfish, impolite, rude.
2 = unthinking, heedless, careless, unmindful, absent-minded, injudicious, ill-advised, ill-considered, imprudent, unwise, foolish, silly, stupid, reckless, rash, precipitate, negligent, remiss.
Opposites: thoughtful.

thrash VERB **= beat**, whip, horsewhip, flog, lash, birch, cane, flagellate, scourge, leather, spank, chastise, belt, wallop.

thread NOUN **1 = yarn**, cotton, filament, fibre.
2 = strand, line, streak, strip, seam.

threadbare ADJ **= worn**, frayed, tattered, ragged, holey, shabby.

threat NOUN
1 = threatening remark, warning, ultimatum.
2 = danger, peril, hazard,

menace, risk.
3 = possibility, chance, probability, likelihood, risk.

threaten VERB **1 = make threats**, menace, intimidate, browbeat, bully, pressurize, lean on. **2 = be imminent**, impend, hang over, loom, foreshadow.

threatening ADJ **1 = menacing**, warning, intimidating, bullying, minatory. **2 = ominous**, inauspicious, foreboding.

threshold NOUN **1 = doorway**, doorstep, entrance. **2 = beginning**, commencement, start, outset, inception, opening, dawn, brink, verge, debut; [inf] kick-off.

thrifty ADJ **= economical**, careful, frugal, sparing, scrimping, parsimonious, penny-pinching, miserly. **Opposites:** spendthrift.

thrill NOUN **1 = excitement**, sensation of joy, wave of pleasure, glow, tingle; [inf] buzz, charge, kick. **2 = throb**, tremble, tremor, quiver, flutter, shudder, vibration.

▶VERB **= excite**, stimulate, arouse, stir, electrify, move, give joy/pleasure to; [inf] give a buzz/charge/kick to.
Opposites: bore.

thrilling ADJ **= exciting**, stirring, electrifying, rousing, moving, gripping, riveting.
Opposites: boring.

thrive VERB **= flourish**, prosper, do/go well, boom, burgeon, succeed, advance, get ahead, make progress.
Opposites: decline.

throb VERB **= beat**, pulse, pulsate, palpitate, pound, thump.

throng NOUN **= crowd**, horde, mob, mass, host, multitude, swarm, flock, pack, herd, drove, press, assemblage, gathering, congregation.

throttle VERB **= choke**, strangle, strangulate, garrotte.

throw VERB **1 = hurl**, toss, cast, sling, pitch, shy, lob, propel, launch, project, send; [inf] heave, chuck. **2 = cast**, project, send.

thrust VERB = **push**, shove, ram, drive, press, prod, propel.

thrusting ADJ = **forceful**, pushing, forward, pushy, energetic, assertive, aggressive, insistent, ambitious.
Opposites: meek.

thug NOUN = **ruffian**, rough, hoodlum, bully boy, hooligan, villain, gangster; [inf] heavy, bovver boy, tough.

thunder NOUN = **boom**, booming, rumble, rumbling, outburst, roar, roaring.
▶ VERB = **boom**, rumble, roar, blast, resound, reverberate.

thunderous ADJ = **booming**, rumbling, roaring, resounding, reverberating, deafening, ear-splitting, loud, noisy, tumultuous.

thwart VERB = **frustrate**, foil, baulk, check, block, stop, prevent, defeat, impede, obstruct, hinder, hamper, stymie.
Opposites: assist.

tic NOUN = **twitch**, spasm, jerk.

ticket NOUN 1 = **pass**, token, stub, coupon, card. 2 = **label**, tag, tally.

tickle VERB 1 = **stroke**, pet, touch. 2 = **amuse**, entertain, divert, cheer, gladden.

tide NOUN = **tidal flow**, tidewater, tide race, flow, ebb, current, stream.

tidy ADJ 1 = **neat**, trim, orderly, in order, in good order, well ordered, spruce, shipshape, well kept, clean, spick and span. 2 = **orderly**, organized, methodical, systematic, businesslike.
Opposites: untidy.
▶ VERB = **clean**, clean up, put to rights, put in order, straighten, make shipshape, spruce up, groom, smarten, neaten, brush down.

tie VERB 1 = **tie up**, fasten, attach, fix, bind, secure, tether, moor, lash, join, connect, link, couple, rope, chain. 2 = **draw**, be equal, be even, be neck and neck.

tier NOUN = **row**, rank, bank, line, layer, level, storey.

t

tight ADJ **1** = **fast**, secure, fixed, clenched, clinched. **2** = **taut**, rigid, stiff, tense, stretched, strained. **3** = **cramped**, restricted, limited, constricted. **4** = **strict**, rigorous, stringent, tough, rigid, uncompromising, exacting.
Opposites: loose, slack.

tighten VERB **1** = **tauten**, make tight/taut, stretch, make rigid, rigidify, stiffen, tense. **2** = **increase**, make stricter, make rigorous/stringent/rigid.
Opposites: slacken.

till VERB = **cultivate**, work, farm, plough, dig, turn over.

tilt VERB = **lean**, list, slope, slant, incline, tip, cant.

time NOUN **1** = **age**, era, epoch, period. **2** = **while**, spell, stretch, span, period, term. **3** = **occasion**, point, juncture. **4** = **moment**, point, instant, stage. **5** = **rhythm**, measure, tempo, beat, metre.
▸VERB **1** = **clock**, measure, calculate, regulate, count.

2 = **schedule**, arrange, fix, set, timetable, programme.

timeless ADJ = **ageless**, enduring, lasting, permanent, abiding, unending, ceaseless, undying, deathless, eternal, everlasting, immortal, changeless.
Opposites: ephemeral.

timely ADJ = **opportune**, well timed, convenient, appropriate, seasonable, felicitous.
Opposites: ill-timed.

timetable NOUN = **schedule**, programme, calendar, list, agenda.
▸VERB = **schedule**, fix, set, programme.

timid ADJ **1** = **fearful**, apprehensive, timorous, afraid, frightened, scared, faint-hearted, cowardly, pusillanimous; [inf] chicken, yellow, lily-livered. **2** = **shy**, diffident, bashful, reticent, timorous, shrinking, retiring, coy, demure.
Opposites: bold.

tingle VERB = **prickle**, prick, tickle, itch, sting, quiver, tremble.

▶ NOUN = **tingling**, prickling, pricking, tickle, itch, quiver, trembling, pins and needles.

tinker = **fiddle**, play, toy, tamper, fool around, mess about.

tint NOUN = **shade**, colour, tone, tinge, cast, tincture.

tiny ADJ = **minute**, diminutive, miniature, mini, minuscule, infinitesimal, microscopic, dwarfish, midget, pocket-sized, Lilliputian, wee, small, little, insignificant, trifling, negligible, inconsequential; [inf] teeny, teeny-weeny, itsy-bitsy, pint-sized.
Opposites: huge.

tip¹ NOUN **1** = **point**, peak, top, summit, apex, crown. **2** = **end**, extremity, point.
▶ VERB = **cap**, top, crown.

tip² NOUN = **rubbish dump**, dump, refuse dump, rubbish heap, midden.
▶ VERB **1** = **tilt**, lean, list, cant, slant, topple, overturn, fall over, turn topsy-turvy, capsize.
2 = **pour**, empty, unload, dump.

tirade NOUN = **diatribe**, harangue, stream of abuse, verbal onslaught, lecture, upbraiding.

tire VERB **1** = **fatigue**, wear out, weary, exhaust, drain, enervate, debilitate, jade; [inf] take it out of, whack; [Brit. inf] fag out, knacker; [N. Amer. inf] poop; [Austral./NZ inf] bush. **2** = **get/grow/ become tired**, get fatigued, flag, droop.

tired ADJ = **fatigued**, worn out, weary, wearied, exhausted, drained, enervated, debilitated, jaded; [inf] done, done in, all in, dead beat, dog-tired, whacked, dead on one's feet, ready to drop; [Brit. inf] fagged out, knackered; [N. Amer. inf] pooped; [Austral./NZ inf] bush.
Opposites: energetic, fresh.

tireless ADJ = **untiring**, unflagging, indefatigable, energetic, industrious, vigorous, determined, resolute, dogged.
Opposites: lazy.

tiresome ADJ
1 = **wearisome**, laborious, wearing, tedious, boring, monotonous, dull, uninteresting, unexciting, humdrum, routine. **2** = **troublesome**, irksome, vexatious, irritating, annoying, exasperating, trying.
Opposites: interesting, pleasant.

tiring ADJ = **wearying**, wearing, fatiguing, exhausting, draining, enervating, arduous, laborious, strenuous, exacting, taxing.

titillate VERB = **excite**, arouse, stimulate, provoke, thrill, interest, fascinate, tantalize, seduce; [inf] turn on.

title NOUN **1** = **name**, designation, appellation, epithet, sobriquet; [inf] moniker, handle; [formal] denomination.
2 = **entitlement**, right, claim, ownership, proprietorship, possession, holding.
▸ VERB = **entitle**, name, call, designate, label, tag, style, term.

titter NOUN = **snicker**, snigger, giggle, laugh, chuckle, chortle.

toast VERB **1** = **brown**, crisp, warm up, heat, heat up.
2 = **drink the health of**, drink to, pledge, salute.

toddle VERB = **totter**, teeter, wobble, falter, dodder.

together ADV = **with each other**, in conjunction, jointly, in cooperation, as one, in unison, side by side, hand in hand, hand in glove, shoulder to shoulder, cheek by jowl.
Opposites: separately.

toilet NOUN = **lavatory**, ladies' room, powder room, convenience, outhouse, urinal, latrine, privy; [Brit.] WC; [N. Amer.] washroom, bathroom; [inf] loo, bog; [N. Amer. inf] john, can.

token NOUN **1** = **symbol**, sign, emblem, badge, representation, indication, mark, manifestation.
2 = **memento**, souvenir, keepsake, remembrance, reminder, memorial.

▸ ADJ = **perfunctory**, superficial, nominal, slight, hollow.

tolerable ADJ
1 = **endurable**, bearable, sufferable, supportable, acceptable. **2** = **fairly good**, fair, all right, passable, adequate, satisfactory, average, mediocre, ordinary, run-of-the-mill, indifferent, unexceptional; [inf] not bad, OK.
Opposites: intolerable.

tolerance NOUN
1 = **toleration**, open-mindedness, lack of prejudice, broad-mindedness, liberalism, forbearance, patience, magnanimity, understanding, charity, lenience. **2** = **endurance**, sufferance, acceptance.

tolerant ADJ = **open-minded**, unprejudiced, unbiased, broad-minded, liberal, catholic, forbearing, long-suffering, magnanimous, sympathetic, understanding, charitable, lenient, indulgent, permissive, free and easy, easy-going.
Opposites: intolerant.

tolerate VERB **1** = **permit**, allow, sanction, accept, countenance; [formal] brook. **2** = **endure**, bear, suffer, take, stand, put up with, abide, accept, stomach, submit to.

toll NOUN **1** = **charge**, fee, payment, levy, tariff. **2** = **cost**, damage, loss, inroads.

tomb NOUN = **grave**, burial place/chamber, sepulchre, vault, crypt, catacomb, mausoleum.

tone NOUN **1** = **sound**, sound quality, colour, pitch, timbre, tonality. **2** = **tone of voice**, expression, intonation, inflection, modulation, accentuation. **3** = **mood**, air, attitude, character, manner, spirit, temper, tenor, vein, drift.

tonic NOUN = **restorative**, stimulant, analeptic; [inf] pick-me-up.

tool NOUN = **implement**, instrument, utensil, device, apparatus, gadget, appliance, machine,

t

contrivance, contraption, aid.

top NOUN 1 = **highest point/part**, summit, peak, pinnacle, crest, crown, tip, apex, vertex, apogee. 2 = **upper part**, upper surface, upper layer. 3 = **cap**, lid, stopper, cork, cover.
Opposites: bottom.
▶ ADJ 1 = **topmost**, uppermost, highest. 2 = **foremost**, leading, principal, pre-eminent, greatest, finest. 3 = **maximum**, maximal, greatest, utmost.
Opposites: lowest, minimum.
▶ VERB 1 = **cap**, cover, finish, garnish. 2 = **head**, lead, be first in. 3 = **surpass**, exceed, go beyond, transcend, better, best, beat, excel, outstrip, outdo, outshine, eclipse.

topic NOUN = **subject**, theme, issue, matter, question, argument, thesis.

topical ADJ = **current**, up to date, up to the minute, contemporary, popular.

Opposites: out of date.

topple VERB 1 = **fall over**, tip over, keel over, overturn, overbalance, capsize. 2 = **overthrow**, oust, unseat, overturn, bring down, bring low.

torment NOUN = **agony**, suffering, torture, pain, excruciation, anguish, hell, misery, distress, affliction, wretchedness.
▶ VERB = **cause agony/suffering/pain to**, afflict, harrow, plague, torture, distress, worry, trouble.

torn ADJ 1 = **ripped**, split, slit, cut, lacerated, rent. 2 = **divided**, wavering, vacillating, irresolute, uncertain, unsure, undecided.

torrent NOUN = **flood**, deluge, inundation, spate, cascade, rush, stream, current, downpour, rainstorm.
Opposites: trickle.

tortuous ADJ = **twisting**, winding, curving, curvy, sinuous, undulating, coiling, serpentine, snaking, snaky, zigzag, convoluted, meandering.
Opposites: straight.

torture NOUN 1 = **abuse**, ill-treatment, punishment, torment. 2 = **agony**, suffering, pain, excruciation, anguish, misery, distress.
▸ VERB 1 = **inflict pain/ suffering on**, abuse, ill-treat, punish, torment; [inf] work over. 2 = **torment**, afflict, harrow, plague, distress, worry, trouble.

toss VERB 1 = **throw**, hurl, cast, sling, pitch, shy, lob, propel, launch, project; [inf] heave, chuck. 2 = **roll**, sway, undulate, pitch, lurch, heave.

total NOUN = **sum**, sum total, aggregate, whole, entirety, totality.
▸ ADJ 1 = **complete**, entire, whole, full, comprehensive, combined, aggregate, composite, integral. 2 = **thorough**, complete, utter, absolute, downright, out-and-out, outright, unmitigated, unqualified.
▸ VERB 1 = **add up to**, come to, amount to. 2 = **add up**, count, reckon, tot up.

totalitarian ADJ = **autocratic**, authoritarian, absolute, despotic, dictatorial, tyrannical, undemocratic, oppressive.
Opposites: democratic.

totter VERB = **teeter**, wobble, stagger, stumble, reel, sway, roll, lurch.

touch VERB 1 = **be in contact**, come into contact, come together, meet, converge, be contiguous, adjoin, abut. 2 = **press lightly**, tap, brush, graze, feel, stroke, pat, fondle, caress. 3 = **affect**, move, make an impression on, influence, upset, disturb, make sad, arouse sympathy; [inf] get to. 4 = **reach**, attain, arrive at, come to.
▸ NOUN 1 = **feel**, feeling, sense of touch, tactile sense, tactility. 2 = **texture**, feel, grain, finish, surface, coating. 3 = **bit**, trace, dash, taste, spot, drop, pinch, speck, smack, suggestion, hint, soupçon, tinge, whiff,

suspicion; [inf] smidgen.

touching ADJ = **moving**, impressive, affecting, warming, heart-warming.

touchy ADJ = **sensitive**, oversensitive, hypersensitive, thin-skinned, tetchy, testy, irascible, irritable, grouchy, grumpy, peevish, querulous, bad-tempered, captious, crabbed, cross, surly.

tough ADJ **1** = **strong**, durable, resistant, resilient, sturdy, firm, solid, hard, rigid, stiff. **2** = **chewy**, leathery, gristly, stringy, fibrous, sinewy. **3** = **hardy**, strong, fit, sturdy, rugged, stalwart, vigorous, strapping, robust, resilient. **4** = **difficult**, hard, arduous, onerous, laborious, strenuous, exacting, taxing, stressful. **5** = **firm**, strict, stern, severe, harsh, hard-hitting, adamant, inflexible.

6 = **unfortunate**, unlucky, hard, regrettable; [inf] too bad.

Opposites: tender, easy, lax.

toughen VERB = **strengthen**, fortify, reinforce, harden.

tour NOUN = **trip**, excursion, journey, expedition, jaunt, outing, peregrination.
▶ VERB = **travel round/ through**, explore, holiday in, go round, visit.

tourist NOUN = **visitor**, sightseer, holidaymaker, tripper.

tournament NOUN = **competition**, contest, series, meeting, event.

tout
▪ **tout for** = **ask for**, solicit, seek, petition for, appeal for, beg for.

tow VERB = **pull**, draw, drag, haul, tug, trail, lug.

towering ADJ **1** = **high**, tall, lofty, elevated, sky-high. **2** = **outstanding**, extraordinary, pre-eminent, superior, great, incomparable, unrivalled, peerless.

toxic ADJ = **poisonous**, venomous, virulent, noxious.

Opposites: harmless.

trace NOUN 1 = **mark**, sign, vestige, indication, evidence, remains, remnant. 2 = **bit**, hint, suggestion, suspicion, trifle, dash, tinge, jot, iota.

▶ VERB = **find**, discover, detect, unearth, uncover, track down, turn up, ferret out, hunt down; [inf] dig up.

track NOUN 1 = **mark**, trace, impression, footprint, trail, spoor, scent. 2 = **course**, line, path, orbit, route, trajectory. 3 = **path**, trail, route, way.

▶ VERB = **follow**, pursue, trail, trace, tail, shadow, stalk, dog.

trade NOUN 1 = **commerce**, buying and selling, dealing, trafficking, business, merchandising. 2 = **line of work**, line, occupation, job, career, profession, craft, vocation, calling, work, employment.

▶ VERB 1 = **buy and sell**, deal, traffic, market, merchandise. 2 = **swap**, exchange, switch, barter.

trader NOUN = **merchant**, dealer, buyer, seller, marketer, merchandiser, broker, tradesman, tradeswoman.

tradition NOUN = **custom**, belief, practice, convention, ritual, observance, habit, institution, usage, praxis.

traditional ADJ = **customary**, accustomed, conventional, established, ritual, ritualistic, habitual, set, fixed, routine, usual, old, time-honoured, historic, folk; [poetic/ literary] wonted.

tragedy NOUN = **disaster**, calamity, catastrophe, misfortune, misadventure, affliction, adversity.

tragic ADJ 1 = **disastrous**, calamitous, catastrophic, fatal, terrible, dreadful, appalling, dire, awful, miserable, wretched, unfortunate. 2 = **sad**, unhappy, pathetic, moving, distressing, pitiful, piteous, melancholy, doleful,

t

mournful, dismal, gloomy.
Opposites: fortunate, happy.

trail NOUN **1** = **track**, scent, spoor, traces, marks, signs, footprints. **2** = **path**, pathway, footpath, track, road, route.

▶ VERB **1** = **drag**, sweep, dangle, hang down, droop. **2** = **follow**, pursue, track, trace, tail, shadow, stalk, dog. **3** = **lose**, be down, be behind.

train NOUN **1** = **procession**, line, file, column, convoy, caravan. **2** = **retinue**, entourage, following, staff, household, followers, attendants.

▶ VERB **1** = **instruct**, teach, coach, tutor, give lessons to, school, educate, drill, prepare, ground, guide. **2** = **exercise**, do exercises, work out, practise, prepare. **3** = **aim**, point, focus, direct, level, line up.

trait NOUN = **characteristic**, attribute, feature, quality, property, idiosyncrasy, peculiarity, quirk.

traitor NOUN = **betrayer**, turncoat, double-crosser, double-dealer, renegade, defector, deserter, apostate, Judas, quisling, fifth columnist.

trample VERB = **tramp on**, tread on, walk over, stamp on, squash, crush, flatten.

trance NOUN = **daze**, stupor, hypnotic state, dream, reverie, brown study.

tranquil ADJ = **peaceful**, restful, reposeful, calm, quiet, still, serene, placid, undisturbed.

tranquillizer NOUN = **sedative**, opiate; [inf] downer.
Opposites: stimulant.

transaction NOUN = **business**, deal, undertaking, affair, bargain, negotiation.

transcend VERB = **go beyond**, exceed, overstep, rise above, surpass, excel, be superior to, outdo, outstrip.

transfer VERB **1** = **convey**, move, shift, remove, take, carry, transport.

2 = **make over**, turn over, sign over, hand on, hand down, pass on, transmit, assign, delegate.

transform VERB = **change**, alter, convert, metamorphose, revolutionize, transfigure, transmogrify, remodel, redo, reconstruct, rebuild, reorganize, rearrange, renew, translate, transmute.

transformation NOUN = **change**, alteration, conversion, metamorphosis, sea change, revolution, transfiguration, transmogrification, remodelling, reconstruction, reorganization, renewal, transmutation.

transgress VERB = **go beyond**, overstep, exceed, infringe, breach, break, contravene, violate, defy, disobey.

transient ADJ = **transitory**, short-lived, short-term, impermanent, temporary, brief, short, ephemeral, evanescent, momentary, fleeting, flying, passing.
Opposites: permanent.

transit NOUN = **movement**, transport, transportation, conveyance, haulage, travel, journeying, passage.

transition NOUN = **change**, transformation, conversion, metamorphosis, shift, switch, jump, leap, progression, gradation, development, evolution, transmutation.

translate VERB = **render**, interpret, paraphrase, reword, convert, decipher, decode, explain, elucidate.

transmission NOUN
1 = **sending**, conveyance, transport, dispatch, remission.
2 = **broadcasting**, relaying, sending out.
3 = **broadcast**, programme.

transmit VERB 1 = **send**, convey, transport, dispatch, forward, remit.
2 = **transfer**, pass on, hand on, communicate, impart, disseminate, spread, carry, diffuse.

t

3 = **broadcast**, relay, send out, put on air.

transparent ADJ **1** = **clear**, see-through, translucent, pellucid, crystal-clear, crystalline, limpid, glassy, transpicuous. **2** = *See* **obvious**.
Opposites: opaque.

transpire VERB = **come about**, take place, happen, occur, turn up, arise, chance; [poetic/literary] befall.

transport VERB = **convey**, take, transfer, move, shift, bring, fetch, carry, bear, haul, cart, run, ship.
▶ NOUN = **transportation**, conveyance, transit, carriage, freight.

transpose VERB = **interchange**, exchange, switch, swap, transfer, reverse, invert, rearrange, reorder.

transverse ADJ = **crosswise**, crossways, cross, athwart.

trap NOUN = **snare**, net, mesh, gin, ambush, pitfall, booby trap.
▶ VERB **1** = **snare**, ensnare, enmesh, entrap, catch, corner. **2** = **trick**, dupe, deceive, lure, inveigle, beguile.

trappings PL NOUN = **accoutrements**, appurtenances, appointments, trimmings, paraphernalia, fittings, equipment, apparatus, gear, adornment, ornamentation, decoration, finery, frippery, panoply.

trash NOUN **1** = **rubbish**, waste, refuse, litter, garbage. **2** = **riff-raff**, scum, rabble, vermin, good-for-nothings.

traumatic ADJ = **painful**, agonizing, shocking, scarring, disturbing, distressing, damaging, injurious, harmful.

travel VERB = **journey**, take a trip, tour, voyage, cross, traverse, cover, wander, ramble, roam, rove.
▶ NOUN = **travelling**, journeying, touring.

traveller NOUN = **passenger**, tourist, tripper, tourer, explorer, voyager, holidaymaker, sightseer, globetrotter.

traverse VERB = **cross**, go across, travel over, journey over, make one's way across, pass over, wander, roam, range.

treacherous ADJ **1** = *See* **traitorous**. **2** = **hazardous**, dangerous, unsafe, flooded, icy, ice-covered, slippery.

tread VERB = **walk**, step, go, pace, march, tramp.

treason NOUN = **betrayal**, treachery, disloyalty, faithlessness, sedition, subversion, mutiny, rebellion, lese-majesty.

treasure NOUN = **riches**, valuables, wealth, fortune, hoard, jewels, gems, coins, gold.
▶ VERB = **value**, prize, set great store by, think highly of, hold dear.

treat NOUN = **surprise**, celebration, entertainment, amusement, diversion.
▶ VERB **1** = **act towards**, behave towards, deal with, handle, cope with, contend with, manage, use. **2** = **regard**, consider, view, look upon, deal with. **3** = **give treatment to**, medicate, doctor, nurse, care for, attend to, minister to, cure, heal.
4 = **apply to**, put on, use on, ply with. **5** = **pay for**, buy for, pay/foot the bill for, stand, finance, entertain, take out.

treatise NOUN = **discourse**, exposition, disquisition, dissertation, thesis, study, essay, paper, monograph, tract, pamphlet.

treatment NOUN
1 = **action**, behaviour, conduct, handling, management, use, dealings. **2** = **medical care**, medication, medicament, therapy, doctoring, nursing, first aid, care, ministration.

treaty NOUN = **agreement**, pact, deal, compact, covenant, bargain, pledge, contract, alliance, concordat, convention, entente.

trek VERB = **tramp**, hike, trudge, march, slog, footslog, plod, walk, ramble, roam, range, rove, travel, journey;

tremble

[Brit. inf] yomp.
▶ NOUN = **expedition**, trip, journey, trudge, tramp, hike, march, slog, walk, odyssey.

tremble VERB = **shake**, quiver, shudder, judder, teeter, totter, wobble, rock, vibrate, oscillate.

tremendous ADJ **1** = **great**, huge, enormous, immense, massive, vast, colossal, prodigious, stupendous, gigantic, gargantuan, mammoth. **2** = **excellent**, very good, great, marvellous, remarkable, extraordinary, exceptional, wonderful, incredible; [inf] super, fabulous, terrific, fantastic.

tremor NOUN = **tremble**, shake, shaking, shiver, quiver, twitch, judder, spasm, paroxysm.

trend NOUN **1** = **tendency**, drift, course, direction, bearing, current, inclination, bias, leaning, bent. **2** = **fashion**, vogue, style, mode, look, craze; [inf] fad.

trendy ADJ = *see* **fashionable**.

trespass VERB = **intrude**, encroach, infringe, invade, obtrude.

trial NOUN **1** = **court case**, case, hearing, inquiry, tribunal, litigation. **2** = **test**, try-out, trial/test run, check, assay, experiment; [inf] dry run. **3** = **nuisance**, pest, bother, worry, vexation, annoyance, irritant, irritation, bane, affliction, curse, burden, cross to bear; [inf] pain in the neck, hassle.

tribe NOUN = **ethnic group**, family, dynasty, clan, sect.

tribute NOUN = **accolade**, commendation, testimonial, paean, eulogy, panegyric, encomium, applause, praise, homage, honour, exaltation, extolment, glorification, congratulations, compliments, bouquets; [formal] laudation.

trick NOUN **1** = **stratagem**, ploy, artifice, ruse, dodge, wile, device,

manoeuvre, deceit, deception, subterfuge, swindle, fraud; [inf] con.
2 = knack, art, gift, talent, technique, ability, skill, expertise; [inf] know-how.
3 = hoax, practical joke, joke, prank, jape, antic, caper, frolic, lark, gambol; [inf] leg-pull, gag, put-on.
▶ VERB **= deceive**, delude, mislead, take in, cheat, hoodwink, fool, outwit, dupe, hoax, gull, defraud, swindle; [inf] con, pull a fast one on, put one over on; [poetic/literary] cozen.

trickery NOUN **= deceit**, deception, cheating, subterfuge, guile, artifice, wiliness, craftiness, chicanery, dishonesty, fraud, swindling, imposture, double-dealing, duplicity; [inf] monkey/funny business, hanky-panky; [Brit. inf] jiggery-pokery.
Opposites: honesty.

trickle VERB **= drip**, dribble, leak, ooze, seep, exude, percolate.
Opposites: pour, gush.

tricky ADJ **1 = difficult**, problematic, awkward, delicate, sensitive, ticklish, thorny, knotty, touchy, risky.
2 = cunning, crafty, wily, artful, devious, scheming, sly, slippery, subtle, deceitful, deceptive; [inf] foxy.
Opposites: straightforward, honest.

trim ADJ **= neat**, tidy, neat and tidy, smart, spruce, well groomed, well dressed, well turned out, dapper, elegant; [inf] natty.
Opposites: untidy.
▶ VERB **= cut**, clip, snip, shear, prune, pare, even up, neaten, tidy up.

trip NOUN **1 = excursion**, tour, expedition, voyage, jaunt, outing, run.
2 = hallucination, drug experience, vision.
▶ VERB **1 = stumble**, lose one's footing/balance, stagger, slip, slide, misstep, fall, tumble.
2 = skip, dance, hop, prance, bound, spring, gambol, caper, frisk, cavort, waltz.

t

triumph NOUN

1 = **conquest**, victory, win, ascendancy, mastery, success; [inf] walkover.

2 = **exultation**, jubilation, jubilance, elation, rejoicing, joy, joyfulness, pride.
Opposites: failure, despair.

▶ VERB = **win**, succeed, come first, be the victor, be victorious, gain a victory, carry the day, take the honours/prize/crown.

triumphant ADJ

1 = **winning**, victorious, successful, undefeated, unbeaten. **2** = **exultant**, jubilant, elated, rejoicing, joyful, joyous, proud, cock-a-hoop, gloating, boastful.
Opposites: unsuccessful, despondent.

trivial ADJ = **unimportant**, insignificant, inconsequential, flimsy, insubstantial, petty, minor, of no account/matter, negligible, paltry, trifling, foolish, worthless; [inf] piddling.
Opposites: significant.

troops PL NOUN = **armed forces**, army, military, services, soldiers, soldiery, fighting men/women.

trouble NOUN **1** = **problems**, worry, bother, anxiety, disquiet, unease, irritation, vexation, inconvenience, annoyance, agitation, harassment, difficulty, distress. **2** = **difficulty**, misfortune, adversity, hardship, bad luck, distress, pain, suffering, affliction, torment, woe, grief, unhappiness, sadness, heartache.
3 = **bother**, inconvenience, disturbance, fuss, effort, exertion, work, labour, attention, care, thoughtfulness; [inf] hassle. **4** = **disorder**, disease, illness, dysfunction.
5 = **disturbance**, disorder, unrest, fighting, strife, conflict, tumult, commotion, turbulence, law-breaking.

▶ VERB **1** = **worry**, bother, disturb, annoy, irritate,

vex, irk, fret, pester,
torment, plague,
inconvenience, upset,
perturb, agitate,
discompose, harass,
distress; [inf] hassle.
2 = **take the trouble/time**,
bother, make the effort,
exert/disturb oneself, go
out of one's way.

troublemaker NOUN
= **mischief-maker**,
agitator, instigator,
rabble-rouser,
demagogue.

troublesome ADJ
= **worrying**, worrisome,
bothersome, tiresome,
disturbing, annoying,
irritating, irksome,
upsetting, perturbing,
harassing, distressing,
difficult, problematic,
demanding, taxing.

truancy NOUN
= **absenteeism**, absence,
French leave, shirking,
malingering; [inf] bunking
off; [Brit. inf] skiving.

truant NOUN = **absentee**,
dodger, malingerer,
shirker, deserter; [Brit.
inf] skiver.
▶ VERB = **stay away from
school**, play truant; [Brit.

inf] skive (off), bunk off;
[N. Amer. inf] play hookey,
goof off.

truce NOUN = **cease-fire**,
armistice, suspension/
cessation of hostilities,
peace, respite,
moratorium.

true ADJ **1** = **truthful**,
accurate, correct, right,
valid, factual, exact,
precise, faithful, genuine,
reliable, honest;
[formal] veracious. **2** = **real**,
genuine, authentic,
actual, bona fide, valid,
legitimate; [inf] honest-
to-goodness. **3** = **loyal**,
faithful, trustworthy,
trusty, reliable,
dependable, staunch,
firm, fast, steady,
constant, unswerving,
unwavering, devoted,
sincere, dedicated,
supportive, dutiful.
Opposites: untrue, false.

trump VERB = **surpass**,
outperform, outdo.
▪ **trump up** = **invent**,
make up, fabricate,
devise, concoct, hatch,
contrive, fake; [inf] cook
up.

trust NOUN 1 = **faith**, confidence, belief, conviction, credence, assurance, certainty, reliance, hope, expectation.
2 = **responsibility**, duty, obligation, commitment.
▶ VERB 1 = **put/place one's trust in**, have faith/ confidence in, be convinced by, pin one's hopes on. 2 = **hope**, assume, presume, expect, believe, suppose.
Opposites: distrust.

trustful ADJ = **trusting**, unsuspicious, unguarded, unwary, unsuspecting, unquestioning, credulous, gullible, ingenuous, naive, innocent.
Opposites: suspicious.

trustworthy ADJ = **reliable**, dependable, stable, staunch, loyal, faithful, trusty, responsible, sensible, level-headed, honest, honourable, upright, ethical, righteous, principled, virtuous.
Opposites: untrustworthy.

truth NOUN 1 = **truthfulness**, accuracy, correctness, rightness, validity, fact, factualness, factuality, genuineness, veracity, verity, honesty.
2 = **reality**, actuality, factuality.
Opposites: falsehood, fiction.

truthful ADJ 1 = **honest**, trustworthy, candid, frank, open, forthright, straight; [formal] veracious.
2 = **true**, accurate, correct, right, valid, factual, exact, faithful, precise, genuine, reliable, honest; [formal] veracious.
Opposites: untruthful, inaccurate.

try VERB 1 = **attempt**, aim, endeavour, make an effort, exert oneself, undertake, strive, assay, seek, struggle, do one's best; [inf] have a go/shot/ crack/stab. 2 = **try out**, test, put to the test, experiment with, assay, investigate, examine, appraise, evaluate, assess, experience, sample; [inf] check out.

trying ADJ = **troublesome**, bothersome, tiresome, irksome, vexatious, annoying, irritating, exasperating.

tuck VERB = **gather**, push, ease, insert, stuff.

tug VERB = **pull**, jerk, yank, wrench, drag, draw.

tumble VERB = **fall over**, fall down, fall headlong, topple, fall head over heels, fall end over end, lose one's footing/ balance, stumble, stagger, trip up.
Opposites: rise.

tumbledown ADJ = **dilapidated**, ramshackle, crumbling, disintegrating, falling to pieces/bits, decrepit, ruined, in ruins, rickety, shaky, tottering, teetering.

tumour NOUN = **lump**, growth, cancer, cancerous growth, malignant growth, malignancy.

tumult NOUN = **din**, uproar, commotion, racket, hubbub, hullabaloo, clamour, shouting, yelling, pandemonium, babel, bedlam, noise.
Opposites: tranquillity.

tumultuous ADJ = **loud**, noisy, clamorous, ear-shattering, deafening, ear-piercing, blaring, uproarious, unrestrained, boisterous, rowdy, unruly, disorderly, fierce, obstreperous, wild, violent.

tune NOUN = **melody**, air, song, theme, strain, motif.

tunnel NOUN = **underground/ subterranean passage**, underpass, subway, burrow.
▶ VERB = **dig**, excavate, burrow, mine, penetrate.

turbulent ADJ
1 = **tempestuous**, stormy, raging, foaming, rough, choppy, agitated.
2 = **disturbed**, agitated, unsettled, unstable, troubled, distraught, in turmoil.
Opposites: peaceful.

turgid ADJ = **bombastic**, high-flown, high-sounding, rhetorical, oratorical, grandiloquent, magniloquent,

t

extravagant, pretentious, pompous, flowery, fulsome, orotund, fustian.
Opposites: simple.

turmoil NOUN = **agitation**, ferment, confusion, disorder, disarray, upheaval, chaos, pandemonium, bedlam, tumult.
Opposites: peace.

turn VERB **1** = **go round**, rotate, revolve, circle, roll, spin, wheel, whirl, twirl, gyrate, swivel, pivot. **2** = **turn round**, change direction/course, go back, return, reverse direction, make a U-turn. **3** = **turn over**, reverse, invert, flip over, turn topsy-turvy. **4** = **change**, alter, transform, metamorphose, mutate. **5** = **become**, come to be, get, go. **6** = **go/turn sour**, sour, curdle, become rancid, go bad, go off.
▶ NOUN **1** = **rotation**, revolution, circle, spin, whirl, twirl, gyration, swivel. **2** = **turning**, bend, curve, corner, twist, winding. **3** = **time**, opportunity, chance, stint, spell, move, try, attempt; [inf] go, shot, crack.

■ **turn down** = *see* **reject** VERB (**1**).

■ **turn up 1** = **increase**, raise, amplify, make louder, intensify. **2** = **arrive**, appear, put in an appearance, present oneself, be present; [inf] show, show up.

turnover NOUN **1** = **(gross) revenue**, income, volume of business, business, financial flow. **2** = **rate of replacement**, change, movement.

tutor VERB = **teach**, instruct, coach, educate, school, train, drill, direct, guide.

twig NOUN = **branch**, stick, offshoot, shoot, spray, stem.

twilight NOUN = **dusk**, late afternoon, early evening, gloaming; [poetic/ literary] crepuscule.

twin NOUN = **double**, lookalike, image, duplicate, clone; [inf] spitting image, spit, dead spit, dead ringer.

▸ VERB = **join**, link, couple, pair, yoke.

twinge NOUN = **stab of pain**, spasm, pain, pang, ache, throb, tweak, tingle, cramp, stitch.

twist VERB 1 = **bend**, warp, misshape, deform, contort, distort, wrench, wrest. 2 = **wrench**, turn, sprain, rick. 3 = **wind**, curve, bend, twine, zigzag, meander, snake, worm. 4 = **distort**, pervert, warp, garble, misrepresent, falsify, misquote, misreport, change, alter.

▸ NOUN 1 = **bend**, warp, kink, deformity, contortion, distortion. 2 = **wrench**, turn, sprain, rick. 3 = **development**, turn, change, alteration, variation, slant.

twitch VERB = **jerk**, jump, quiver, shiver, quaver.

▸ NOUN = **spasm**, jerk, jump, quiver, tremor, shiver, quaver.

type NOUN 1 = **kind**, sort, variety, form, class, classification, category, group, order, set, genre, strain, species, genus, ilk.

2 = **print**, fount, face, character.

typical ADJ

1 = **representative**, classic, standard, stock, orthodox, conventional, true to type, quintessential, archetypal. 2 = **normal**, average, ordinary, regular, general, customary, habitual, routine.

3 = **characteristic**, in character, in keeping, to be expected.

Opposites: atypical.

typify VERB = **exemplify**, characterize, personify, epitomize, symbolize, embody.

tyrannical ADJ = **despotic**, autocratic, dictatorial, authoritarian, high-handed, imperious, oppressive, coercive, domineering, bullying, harsh, strict, severe, cruel, brutal, unjust.

tyrant NOUN = **despot**, autocrat, dictator, absolute ruler, authoritarian, oppressor, martinet, slave-driver, bully.

t

Uu

ubiquitous ADJ
= **everywhere**,
omnipresent, ever-
present, all-over,
pervasive, universal.
Opposites: rare.

ugly ADJ **1** = **unattractive**,
plain, homely, ill-
favoured,
unprepossessing,
hideous, unlovely,
unsightly, grotesque,
horrible, horrid, frightful,
vile, shocking,
distasteful, disgusting,
revolting; [inf] not much
to look at.
2 = **threatening**,
menacing, ominous,
sinister, dangerous,
nasty, unpleasant,
disagreeable.
Opposites: beautiful.

ulterior ADJ = **hidden**,
concealed, unrevealed,
undisclosed, secret,
covert, unapparent.

Opposites: overt.

ultimate ADJ = **last**, final,
eventual, concluding,
conclusive, terminal,
end, furthest.

umpire NOUN
= **adjudicator**, arbitrator,
arbiter, judge, moderator,
referee; [inf] ref.

unable ADJ = **not able**,
incapable, powerless,
impotent, not up/equal
to, inadequate,
ineffectual, incompetent.
Opposites: able.

unacceptable ADJ
= **unsatisfactory**,
inadmissible, unsuitable,
insupportable,
intolerable,
objectionable, offensive,
obnoxious, undesirable,
disagreeable, distasteful,
improper.
Opposites: acceptable.

unaccompanied ADJ
= **alone**, on one's own,
by oneself, solo, lone,
solitary, single.

unaccustomed ADJ
= **unused**, not used, new,
unpractised, unfamiliar,
inexperienced, unversed.

unanimous ADJ = **in
complete agreement/
accord**, of one mind,
like-minded, in
harmony, at one, of a
piece, with one voice,
united, concordant.
Opposites: divided.

unassailable ADJ
= **impregnable**,
invulnerable, invincible,
secure, well defended.
Opposites: defenceless.

unassuming ADJ = see
modest (1).

unattached ADJ
= **unmarried**, unwed,
unwedded,
uncommitted, free,
available, single, on one's
own, by oneself,
unescorted.
Opposites: married.

unauthorized ADJ
= **unofficial**,
unsanctioned,
uncertified, unaccredited,
unlicensed, unwarranted,
unapproved, disallowed,
prohibited, forbidden,
illegal.
Opposites: official.

unavoidable ADJ
= **inescapable**, inevitable,
bound to happen,
inexorable, ineluctable,
certain, fated,
predestined, necessary,
compulsory, required,
obligatory, mandatory.

unaware ADJ
= **unknowing**,
unconscious, ignorant,
heedless, unmindful,
oblivious, uninformed,
unenlightened; [inf] in the
dark.
Opposites: conscious.

unbelievable ADJ
= **beyond belief**,
incredible, unconvincing,
far-fetched, implausible,
improbable,
inconceivable,
unthinkable,
unimaginable,
impossible, astonishing,
astounding, staggering,
preposterous.
Opposites: credible.

unbending ADJ = see
inflexible (3).

u

unbiased ADJ = **impartial**, unprejudiced, non-partisan, neutral, objective, disinterested, dispassionate, detached, even-handed, open-minded, equitable, fair, fair-minded, just.
Opposites: prejudiced.

unbreakable ADJ = *see* **indestructible**.

uncertain ADJ
1 = **unknown**, undetermined, unsettled, in the balance, up in the air. **2** = **unsure**, doubtful, dubious, undecided, unresolved, indecisive, irresolute, hesitant, wavering, vacillating, equivocating, vague, hazy, unclear, ambivalent, in two minds. **3** = **hesitant**, hesitating, tentative, halting, unsure, unconfident.
Opposites: predictable, sure, confident.

uncharted ADJ
= **unmapped**, unsurveyed, unexplored, unplumbed, unfamiliar, unknown, strange.

uncivilized ADJ
1 = **barbarian**, barbarous, barbaric, primitive, savage, wild. **2** = **uncouth**, coarse, rough, boorish, vulgar, philistine, uneducated, uncultured, uncultivated, unsophisticated, unrefined, unpolished.

unclean ADJ = *see* **dirty** ADJ (1).

uncomfortable ADJ
= **uneasy**, ill at ease, nervous, tense, edgy, self-conscious, awkward, embarrassed, discomfited, disturbed, troubled, worried, anxious, apprehensive.
Opposites: relaxed.

uncommon ADJ = *see* **unusual**.

uncompromising ADJ
= **inflexible**, unbending, unyielding, hard-line, tough, immovable, firm, determined, dogged, obstinate, obdurate, tenacious, relentless, implacable, inexorable, intransigent.
Opposites: flexible.

unconcerned ADJ = *see* **indifferent** (1).

unconditional ADJ
= **complete**, total, entire, full, absolute, downright, utter, all-out, thoroughgoing, unequivocal, conclusive, definite, positive, indubitable.

unconscious ADJ
1 = **senseless**, insensible, comatose, knocked out, stunned, dazed; [inf] out like a light, out cold, out.
2 = **unaware**, heedless, ignorant, in ignorance, oblivious, insensible.
3 = **unintentional**, unintended, accidental, unthinking, unwitting, inadvertent, unpremeditated.
Opposites: aware.

unconventional ADJ
= **unorthodox**, irregular, unusual, uncommon, unwonted, rare, out of the ordinary, atypical, singular, individual, individualistic, different, original, idiosyncratic, nonconformist, bohemian, eccentric, odd.
Opposites: orthodox.

uncouth ADJ = **rough**, coarse, uncivilized, uncultured, uncultivated, unrefined, unpolished, unsophisticated, crude, gross, loutish, boorish, oafish, rude, impolite, discourteous, unmannerly, bad-mannered, ill-bred, vulgar.
Opposites: refined.

uncover VERB 1 = **expose**, lay bare, bare, reveal, unwrap. 2 = *See* **discover** (1).

undaunted ADJ
= **unafraid**, unflinching, indomitable, resolute, intrepid, bold, valiant, brave, courageous.
Opposites: fearful.

undemonstrative ADJ
= **unemotional**, impassive, restrained, self-contained, reserved, uncommunicative, unresponsive, stiff.

underestimate VERB
1 = **miscalculate**, misjudge, set too low.
2 = **underrate**, rate too low, undervalue, set little store by, not do justice to.

u

undergo VERB = **go through**, experience, sustain, endure, bear, tolerate, stand, withstand, put up with, weather.

underground ADJ
1 = **subterranean**, below ground, buried, sunken.
2 = **secret**, clandestine, surreptitious, covert, undercover, concealed, hidden.

underhand ADJ
= **deceitful**, devious, sneaky, furtive, surreptitious, covert, dishonest, dishonourable, unscrupulous, fraudulent.
Opposites: honest.

undermine VERB
1 = **weaken**, impair, damage, injure, sap, threaten, subvert, sabotage. 2 = **tunnel under**, dig under, burrow under, excavate.
Opposites: support.

underprivileged ADJ
= **disadvantaged**, deprived, in need, needy, want, destitute, poor, impoverished,

impecunious.
Opposites: wealthy.

understand VERB
1 = **comprehend**, apprehend, grasp, see, take in, perceive, discern, make out, glean, recognize, appreciate, get to know, follow, fathom; [inf] get the hang/drift of, catch on, latch on to, tumble to, figure out; [Brit. inf] twig.
2 = **appreciate**, accept, commiserate with, feel compassionate towards, sympathize with, empathize with.
3 = **gather**, hear, be informed, learn, believe, think, conclude.
Opposites: misunderstand.

understanding NOUN
1 = **comprehension**, apprehension, grasp, perception, discernment, appreciation, interpretation.
2 = **intelligence**, intellect, mind, brainpower, brains, powers of reasoning; [inf] grey matter. 3 = **compassion**, sympathy, empathy,

insight. **4** = **agreement**, gentleman's agreement, arrangement, bargain, pact, compact, contract.

▸ ADJ = **compassionate**, sympathetic, sensitive, considerate, kind, thoughtful, tolerant, patient, forbearing.

understate VERB = **downplay**, play down, make light of, minimize; [inf] soft-pedal.

Opposites: exaggerate.

undertake VERB = **take on**, set about, tackle, shoulder, assume, enter upon, begin, start, commence, embark on, venture upon, attempt, try.

undertone NOUN **1** = **low tone/voice**, murmur, whisper.

2 = **undercurrent**, hint, suggestion, intimation, insinuation, trace, tinge, touch, atmosphere, aura, tenor, flavour.

undervalue VERB = *see* **underestimate (2)**.

underwear NOUN = **underclothes**, undergarments, underclothing, lingerie; [inf] undies, unmentionables; [Brit. inf] smalls.

undesirable ADJ = **unwanted**, unwished for, unpleasant, disagreeable, nasty, unacceptable.

undisciplined ADJ **1** = **unruly**, disorderly, disobedient, obstreperous, recalcitrant, refractory, uncontrolled, unrestrained, wild, wilful, wayward.

2 = **unsystematic**, unmethodical, disorganized, unorganized.

undisguised ADJ = **open**, obvious, evident, patent, manifest, transparent, overt, unconcealed, unmistakable.

undistinguished ADJ = *see* **ordinary (2)**.

undo VERB **1** = **unfasten**, unhook, unbutton, untie, unlace, loosen, disentangle, release, free, open, unlock. **2** = **destroy**, ruin, wreck, smash, shatter, annihilate, obliterate, overturn.

undoubted ADJ
= **undisputed**, not in doubt, uncontested, unquestioned, not in question, certain, unquestionable, indubitable, incontrovertible, irrefutable.

undress VERB = **take off one's clothes**, remove one's clothes, strip, disrobe; [Brit. inf] peel off.

undue ADJ = **unwarranted**, unjustified, unreasonable, inappropriate, unsuitable, improper, ill-advised, excessive, immoderate.
Opposites: appropriate.

undying ADJ = *see* **eternal**.

uneasy ADJ = **ill at ease**, troubled, worried, anxious, apprehensive, alarmed, disturbed, agitated, nervous, nervy, on edge, edgy, restive, restless, unsettled, discomposed, discomfited, perturbed, upset; [inf] jittery.
Opposites: calm.

unemotional ADJ = **undemonstrative**, passionless, cold, frigid, cool, reserved, restrained, unfeeling, unresponsive, unexcitable, unmoved, impassive, apathetic, indifferent, phlegmatic, detached.

unemployed ADJ = **jobless**, out of work, out of a job, workless, redundant, laid off, idle; [Brit. inf] on the dole.

unequal ADJ 1 = **different**, differing, dissimilar, unlike, unalike, disparate, varying, variable. 2 = **uneven**, asymmetrical, unsymmetrical, unbalanced, lopsided, irregular, disproportionate. 3 = **unfair**, unjust, inequitable, uneven, one-sided, ill-matched.
Opposites: identical, fair.

unequivocal ADJ = **unambiguous**, clear, clear-cut, plain, explicit, unqualified, categorical, direct, straightforward, blunt, point-blank, straight from the shoulder, positive, certain, decisive.

Opposites: ambiguous.

unethical ADJ = *see* **immoral**.

uneven ADJ 1 = **rough**, bumpy, lumpy.
2 = **variable**, varying, changeable, irregular, erratic, patchy.
3 = **unequal**, asymmetrical, unsymmetrical, unbalanced, lopsided, irregular, disproportionate.
Opposites: flat, regular, equal.

uneventful ADJ = **unexciting**, uninteresting, monotonous, boring, dull, tedious, routine, ordinary, run-of-the-mill, pedestrian, commonplace, everyday, unexceptional, unremarkable.
Opposites: exciting.

unexpected ADJ = **unforeseen**, unanticipated, unpredicted, not bargained for, sudden, abrupt, surprising, startling, astonishing, out of the blue, chance,

fortuitous.
Opposites: predictable.

unfair ADJ 1 = **unjust**, inequitable, partial, partisan, prejudiced, biased, one-sided.
2 = **undeserved**, unmerited, uncalled for, unreasonable, unjustifiable, unwarrantable, out of proportion, disproportionate, excessive, extreme, immoderate.
Opposites: just, justified.

unfaithful ADJ 1 = **disloyal**, false-hearted, faithless, perfidious, treacherous, traitorous. 2 = **adulterous**, fickle, untrue, inconstant; [inf] two-timing.
Opposites: loyal.

unfamiliar ADJ = **unknown**, new, strange, alien, unaccustomed, uncommon.

unfashionable ADJ = **out of fashion/date**, old-fashioned, outmoded, outdated, dated, behind the times, passé, archaic, obsolete, antiquated.

u

unfasten VERB = *see* **undo (1)**.

unfavourable ADJ
1 = **adverse**, critical, hostile, inimical, unfriendly, negative, discouraging, poor, bad.
2 = **disadvantageous**, adverse, unfortunate, unhappy, detrimental.
Opposites: positive.

unfeeling ADJ = *see* **callous**.

unfit ADJ 1 = **unsuited**, ill-suited, unsuitable, unqualified, ineligible, unequipped, unprepared, untrained, incapable, inadequate, incompetent, not up to, not equal to.
2 = **out of condition**, in poor condition/shape, flabby, unhealthy, debilitated, weak.
Opposites: suitable.

unfold VERB = **open out**, spread out, stretch out, flatten, straighten out, unfurl, unroll, unravel.

unforgivable ADJ
= **inexcusable**, unpardonable, unjustifiable, indefensible, reprehensible, deplorable, despicable, contemptible, disgraceful, shameful.
Opposites: venial.

unfortunate ADJ
= **unlucky**, out of luck, luckless, ill-starred, star-crossed, hapless, wretched, miserable, unhappy, poor.

unfriendly ADJ
= **uncongenial**, unsociable, inhospitable, unneighbourly, unsympathetic, aloof, cold, cool, distant, disagreeable, unpleasant, surly, sour, hostile, inimical, antagonistic, aggressive, quarrelsome.

ungainly ADJ = *see* **awkward**.

ungrateful ADJ
= **unthankful**, unappreciative, impolite, uncivil, rude.

unhappy ADJ 1 = **sad**, miserable, sorrowful, dejected, despondent, disconsolate, broken-hearted, down, downcast, dispirited, crestfallen, depressed, melancholy, blue, gloomy, glum, mournful, woebegone.

2 = **unfortunate**, regrettable, inappropriate, unsuitable, inapt, tactless, ill-advised, injudicious.

unhealthy ADJ **1** = **in poor health**, unwell, ill, ailing, sick, sickly, poorly, indisposed, unsound, weak, feeble, frail, delicate, debilitated, infirm. **2** = **unwholesome**, unnourishing, detrimental, injurious, damaging, deleterious, noxious.

unheard of ADJ **1** = **unprecedented**, exceptional, extraordinary, undreamed of, unbelievable, inconceivable, unimaginable, unthinkable. **2** = **unknown**, unfamiliar, new.
Opposites: common, well known.

unhurried ADJ = **leisurely**, leisured, easy, slow, slow-moving, deliberate, sedate.
Opposites: hasty.

unidentified ADJ = **nameless**, unnamed, unknown, anonymous, incognito, obscure, unmarked, undesignated, unclassified.

uniform ADJ **1** = **constant**, consistent, invariable, unvarying, unvaried, unchanging, undeviating, stable, regular, even, equal. **2** = **same**, alike, like, selfsame, identical, similar, equal.
Opposites: variable.
▶ NOUN = **livery**, regalia, dress, regimentals.

unify VERB = **unite**, bring together, merge, fuse, amalgamate, coalesce, combine, blend, mix, bind, link up, consolidate.
Opposites: separate.

unimaginable ADJ = **unthinkable**, inconceivable, incredible, unbelievable, unheard of, unthought of, implausible, improbable, unlikely, impossible, undreamed of, fantastic; [inf] mind-boggling, mind-blowing.

u

unimportant ADJ = **of little/no importance**, insignificant, of no consequence, inconsequential, of no account, immaterial, irrelevant, not worth mentioning, minor, slight, trivial, petty, paltry, insubstantial, inferior, worthless, nugatory; [inf] no great shakes; [N. Amer. inf] dinky.

uninhabited ADJ = **vacant**, empty, unoccupied, unpopulated, unpeopled, unsettled, abandoned, deserted, forsaken, barren, desert, desolate.

uninhibited ADJ = **unselfconscious**, spontaneous, free and easy, relaxed, informal, open, candid, outspoken, unrestrained, unrepressed, unconstrained, uncontrolled, uncurbed, unchecked, unbridled. Opposites: repressed.

unintelligible ADJ = *see* **incomprehensible**.

unintentional ADJ = **unintended**, accidental, inadvertent, unplanned, unpremeditated, uncalculated, chance, fortuitous, unconscious, involuntary, unwitting, unthinking. Opposites: deliberate.

uninterested ADJ = **indifferent**, unconcerned, uninvolved, apathetic, unresponsive, impassive, dispassionate, aloof, detached, distant.

uninteresting ADJ = **unexciting**, dull, boring, tiresome, wearisome, tedious, dreary, flat, monotonous, humdrum, commonplace, pedestrian, prosaic, hackneyed, stale. Opposites: interesting.

uninterrupted ADJ = **unbroken**, undisturbed, continuous, continual, constant, steady, sustained, non-stop, unending, endless, incessant, interminable, unremitting.

union NOUN 1 = **joining**, junction, merger, fusion, amalgamation, blend,

bulky, ponderous; [inf] hulking.
Opposites: manageable.

unwilling ADJ = **reluctant**, disinclined, unenthusiastic, grudging, involuntary, averse, loth, opposed, not in the mood.
Opposites: willing.

unwind VERB **1** = *See* **unravel** (1). **2** = *See* **relax** (4).

unwitting ADJ = **unknowing**, unconscious, unintentional, unintended, inadvertent.
Opposites: deliberate.

unworthy ADJ **1** = **not worthy**, not good enough for, undeserving, ineligible for, unqualified for. **2** = **disreputable**, dishonourable, base, contemptible, reprehensible.
Opposites: deserving.

upgrade VERB = **improve**, better, ameliorate, enhance, rehabilitate, refurbish.

upheaval NOUN = **disruption**, disturbance, disorder, confusion,

turmoil, chaos.

uphill ADJ = **arduous**, difficult, laborious, strenuous, hard, tough, burdensome, onerous, taxing, punishing.

uphold VERB = **support**, back up, back, stand by, champion, defend, maintain, sustain.

upkeep NOUN = **maintenance**, running, preservation, conservation, repairs.

upper ADJ **1** = **higher**, further up, loftier. **2** = **superior**, higher-ranking, elevated, greater.
Opposites: lower.

upright ADJ **1** = **erect**, on end, vertical, perpendicular, standing up, rampant. **2** = **honest**, honourable, upstanding, decent, respectable, worthy, reputable, good, virtuous, righteous, law-abiding, ethical, moral.
Opposites: horizontal, dishonourable.

uproar NOUN = **tumult**, turmoil, turbulence, disorder, confusion, commotion, mayhem,

pandemonium, bedlam, din, noise, clamour, hubbub, racket.
Opposites: calm.

upset VERB **1** = **overturn**, knock over, push over, upend, tip over, topple, capsize. **2** = **disturb**, discompose, unsettle, disconcert, dismay, disquiet, trouble, worry, bother, agitate, fluster, ruffle, frighten, alarm, anger, annoy, distress, hurt, grieve. **3** = **throw into disorder/confusion**, disorganize, disarrange, mess up, mix up.

upshot NOUN = **result**, outcome, conclusion, issue, end, end result, denouement, effect, repercussion, reaction; [inf] pay-off.
Opposites: cause.

upstart NOUN = **parvenu/ parvenue**, social climber, nouveau riche, arriviste.

upward ADJ = **rising**, climbing, mounting, ascending, on the rise.
Opposites: downward.

urbane ADJ = **suave**, debonair, sophisticated, smooth, worldly,

cultivated, cultured, civilized, polished.
Opposites: uncouth.

urge VERB **1** = **push**, drive, propel, impel, force, hasten, hurry, spur, incite, stir up, stimulate, prod, goad, egg on, encourage, prompt, entreat, exhort, implore, appeal, beg, plead; [poetic/literary] beseech. **2** = **advise**, counsel, advocate, recommend, suggest, support, endorse, back, champion.
Opposites: discourage.
▶ NOUN = **desire**, need, compulsion, longing, yearning, wish, fancy, impulse.

urgent ADJ **1** = **imperative**, vital, crucial, critical, essential, exigent, top-priority, high-priority, important, necessary, pressing, serious, grave. **2** = **importunate**, insistent, clamorous, earnest, pleading, begging.

usable ADJ = **for use**, to be used, utilizable, available, ready/fit for use, in working order, functional.

use VERB 1 = **make use of**, utilize, employ, work, operate, wield, ply, avail oneself of, put to use, put into service.
2 = **consume**, get through, exhaust, deplete, expend, spend, waste, fritter away.
▶ NOUN 1 = **usefulness**, good, advantage, benefit, service, help, gain, profit, avail. 2 = **need**, necessity, call, demand, purpose.
■ **used to** = **accustomed to**, familiar with, at home with, in the habit of, given to, prone to.

used ADJ = **second-hand**, nearly new, pre-owned, cast-off, hand-me-down.
Opposites: new.

useful ADJ 1 = **of use**, functional, utilitarian, of service, practical, convenient.
2 = **beneficial**, advantageous, of help, helpful, worthwhile, profitable, rewarding, productive, valuable.
Opposites: useless.

useless ADJ 1 = **vain**, in vain, to no avail/ purpose, unavailing, unsuccessful, futile, purposeless, fruitless, unprofitable, unproductive, abortive.
2 = **worthless**, ineffective, ineffectual, incompetent, incapable, inadequate; [inf] no good.
Opposites: useful.

usual ADJ 1 = **habitual**, customary, accustomed, normal, regular, routine, everyday, established, set, familiar; [poetic/ literary] wonted.
2 = **common**, typical, ordinary, average, run-of-the-mill, expected, standard, stock, regular.
Opposites: unusual.

usually ADV = **generally**, as a rule, normally, by and large, in the main, mainly, mostly, for the most part, on the whole.

usurp VERB = **take over**, seize, expropriate, appropriate, commandeer, assume.

utilitarian ADJ = **practical**, functional, useful, to the purpose.

utter VERB = **voice**, say, pronounce, express, put into words, enunciate,

articulate, verbalize,
vocalize.

utterance NOUN **1 = voice**,
expression, articulation,
enunciation,
verbalization,
vocalization. **2 = remark**,
word, comment,
statement, opinion.

utterly ADV **= absolutely**,
completely, totally,
entirely, thoroughly,
positively, extremely,
categorically, perfectly,
consummately, to the
core.

u

Vv

vacancy NOUN
1 = **opening**, position, post, job, opportunity, slot. 2 = **blankness**, lack of expression, lack of emotion/interest, vacuousness.

vacant ADJ 1 = **empty**, void, without contents. 2 = **unoccupied**, unfilled, free, empty, available, unengaged, uninhabited, untenanted, not in use, unused, abandoned, deserted; [inf] up for grabs. 3 = **blank**, expressionless, inexpressive, deadpan, poker-faced, emotionless, uninterested, vacuous, inane.
Opposites: occupied.

vacate VERB = **leave**, quit, depart from, evacuate, abandon, desert.

vacillate VERB = **shilly-shally**, waver, dither, hesitate, equivocate, beat about the bush; [Brit.] hum and haw.

vacuous ADJ = **vacant**, blank, expressionless, deadpan, inane, unintelligent, brainless, stupid.
Opposites: intelligent.

vagrant NOUN = **tramp**, beggar, person of no fixed address, itinerant, nomad, wanderer, vagabond; [N. Amer.] hobo; [N. Amer. inf] bum.

vague ADJ 1 = **indistinct**, indeterminate, ill-defined, unclear, nebulous, amorphous, shadowy, hazy, fuzzy, blurry, bleary, out of focus. 2 = **imprecise**, inexact, inexplicit, non-specific, loose, generalized, ambiguous, equivocal, hazy, woolly. 3 = **absent-minded**,

abstracted, dreamy, vacuous; [inf] with one's head in the clouds.
Opposites: definite.

vaguely ADV **1 = in a general way**, in a way, somehow, slightly, obscurely. **2 = absent-mindedly**, abstractedly, vacantly, vacuously.

vain ADJ **1 = conceited**, self-loving, narcissistic, self-admiring, egotistical, proud, haughty, arrogant, boastful, swaggering, imperious, overweening, cocky, affected.
2 = unsuccessful, futile, useless, unavailing, to no avail, ineffective, inefficacious, fruitless, unproductive, abortive, unprofitable, profitless.
Opposites: modest, successful.

valiant ADJ **= brave**, courageous, valorous, heroic, intrepid, fearless, undaunted, bold, daring, audacious, staunch, stalwart, indomitable, resolute, determined.
Opposites: cowardly.

valid ADJ **= sound**, well founded, well grounded, substantial, reasonable, logical, justifiable, defensible, vindicable, authentic, bona fide, effective, cogent, powerful, convincing, credible, forceful, weighty.
Opposites: invalid.

validate VERB **= ratify**, legalize, legitimize, authorize, sanction, warrant, license, approve, endorse, set one's seal to.
Opposites: invalidate.

valley NOUN **= dale**, dell, hollow, vale, depression; [Brit.] dene, combe; [Scottish] glen, strath.

valuable ADJ **1 = costly**, high-priced, expensive, priceless, precious.
2 = useful, helpful, beneficial, advantageous, worthwhile, worthy, important.
Opposites: worthless.

value NOUN **1 = cost**, face value, price, market price, worth. **2 = worth**, merit, usefulness, advantage, benefit, gain, profit, good, avail, importance, significance.

▶ VERB **1** = **set a price on**, price, evaluate, assess, appraise. **2** = **rate highly**, appreciate, esteem, hold in high regard, think highly of, set store by, respect, admire, prize, cherish, treasure.

vanguard NOUN = **advance guard**, forefront, front, front line, front rank, leading position, van.
Opposites: rear.

vanish VERB = **disappear**, be lost to sight/view, be/become invisible, evaporate, dissipate, disperse, fade, fade away, evanesce, melt away, recede from view, withdraw, depart, leave.
Opposites: appear.

vanity NOUN = **conceit**, conceitedness, narcissism, egotism, pride, haughtiness, arrogance, boastfulness, braggadocio, pretension, affectation, ostentation, show, airs.
Opposites: modesty.

variable ADJ = **varying**, variational, changeable, changing, mutable,

protean, shifting, fluctuating, wavering, vacillating, inconstant, unsteady, unstable, fitful, capricious, fickle; [inf] blowing hot and cold.
Opposites: constant.

variation NOUN **1** = **change**, alteration, modification, diversification. **2** = **variability**, changeability, fluctuation, vacillation, vicissitude. **3** = **difference**, dissimilarity.

varied ADJ = **diverse**, assorted, miscellaneous, mixed, motley, heterogeneous.

variety NOUN **1** = **variation**, diversification, diversity, multifariousness, many-sidedness, change, difference. **2** = **assortment**, miscellany, range, mixture, medley, motley, collection, multiplicity. **3** = **strain**, breed, kind, type, sort, class, category, classification, brand, make.
Opposites: uniformity.

various ADJ **1** = **varying**, diverse, different, differing, dissimilar, disparate, assorted, mixed, miscellaneous, variegated, heterogeneous. **2** = **numerous**, many, several, varied, sundry; [poetic/literary] divers.

varnish VERB = **lacquer**, japan, shellac, enamel, glaze, veneer.

vary VERB **1** = **differ**, be different, be dissimilar, be at variance, disagree, conflict, clash, be at odds. **2** = **change**, be transformed, alter, metamorphose, suffer a sea change, vacillate, fluctuate.

vast ADJ = **immense**, huge, enormous, massive, bulky, tremendous, colossal, prodigious, gigantic, monumental, elephantine, Brobdingnagian, extensive, broad, wide, expansive, boundless, limitless, infinite; [inf] hulking. Opposites: tiny.

vault[1] NOUN = **cellar**, basement, underground chamber, tomb.

vault[2] VERB = **jump**, leap, jump over, leap over, spring over, bound over.

veer VERB = **change course/direction**, turn, swerve, swing, sidestep, sheer, tack, be deflected.

vehemence NOUN = **force**, passion, forcefulness, emphasis, vigour, intensity, violence, earnestness, keenness, enthusiasm, zeal.

vehement ADJ = **passionate**, ardent, impassioned, fervent, fervid, strong, forceful, forcible, powerful, emphatic, vigorous, intense, earnest, keen, enthusiastic, zealous, spirited. Opposites: mild.

vehicle NOUN **1** = **means of transport**, transportation, conveyance, car, bus, lorry. **2** = **channel**, medium, means, agency, instrument, mechanism, organ, apparatus.

veil VERB = **hide**, conceal, cover up, camouflage,

disguise, mask, screen.

vein NOUN 1 = **blood vessel**, artery, capillary. 2 = **lode**, seam, stratum. 3 = **streak**, stripe, line, thread, marking.

veneer NOUN 1 = **facing**, covering, coat, finish. 2 = **facade**, false front, show, outward display, appearance, semblance, guise, mask, pretence, camouflage.

venerable ADJ = **venerated**, respected, revered, reverenced, worshipped, honoured, esteemed, hallowed.

veneration NOUN = **respect**, reverence, worship, adoration, honour, esteem.

vengeance NOUN = **revenge**, retribution, requital, retaliation, reprisal, an eye for an eye, quid pro quo; [inf] tit for tat.

venomous ADJ 1 = **poisonous**, toxic, lethal, deadly, fatal, noxious. 2 = See **spiteful**.

vent NOUN = **opening**, outlet, aperture, hole, gap, duct, flue.

▶ VERB = **give vent/ expression to**, express, air, utter, voice, verbalize, let out, come out with.

ventilate VERB = **air**, aerate, oxygenate, freshen, cool, purify.

venture NOUN = **enterprise**, undertaking, project, speculation, fling, plunge, gamble.

▶ VERB = **dare**, take the liberty, make so bold as, presume to.

verbal ADJ = **oral**, spoken, said, uttered, articulated.

verbatim ADJ = **word for word**, literal, exact, faithful, precise.

verbose ADJ = **wordy**, loquacious, garrulous, long-winded, prolix, diffuse, pleonastic, circumlocutory, periphrastic, tautological. **Opposites:** succinct.

verdict NOUN = **decision**, judgement, adjudication, finding, conclusion, ruling, opinion.

verge NOUN = **edge**, border, margin, rim, limit, boundary, end, extremity.

verge on = **approach**, incline to/towards, tend towards, border on, come near.

verification NOUN = **confirmation**, evidence, proof, substantiation, corroboration, attestation, validation, authentication, endorsement, accreditation, ratification.

verify VERB = **confirm**, substantiate, prove, give credence to, corroborate, attest to, testify to, validate, authenticate, endorse, accredit, ratify. **Opposites:** refute.

vernacular NOUN = **everyday/spoken language**, colloquial/ native speech, conversational language, common parlance, non-standard language, jargon, cant, patois; [inf] lingo, patter.

versatile ADJ 1 = **resourceful**, flexible, all-round, multifaceted, adaptable, ingenious, clever. 2 = **multi-purpose**, all-purpose, adjustable, adaptable, handy.

verse NOUN 1 = **stanza**, canto, couplet. 2 = **poem**, lyric, sonnet, ode, limerick, piece of doggerel, ditty, song, ballad.

version NOUN 1 = **account**, report, story, rendering, interpretation, construction, understanding, reading, impression, side. 2 = **adaptation**, interpretation, translation. 3 = **variant**, variation, form, copy, reproduction.

vertical ADJ = **upright**, erect, on end, perpendicular. **Opposites:** horizontal.

vertigo NOUN = **dizziness**, giddiness, light-headedness, loss of balance/equilibrium; [inf] wooziness.

verve NOUN = **enthusiasm**, vigour, force, energy, vitality, vivacity, liveliness, animation, sparkle, spirit, life, dash, brio, fervour, gusto, passion, zeal, feeling, fire; [inf] zing, zip, vim, get-up-and-go, pizzazz.

very ADV = **extremely**, exceedingly, to a great extent, exceptionally, uncommonly, unusually, decidedly, particularly, eminently, remarkably, really, truly, terribly; [inf] awfully; [Brit. inf] jolly. **Opposites:** slightly.

vessel NOUN 1 = **ship**, boat, yacht, craft; [poetic/literary] barque.
2 = **container**, receptacle.

vet VERB = **check**, check out, investigate, examine, appraise, look over, review, scrutinize; [inf] give the once-over, size up.

veteran NOUN = **old hand**, old-timer, old stager, past master, master; [inf] pro, old warhorse.
Opposites: novice.
▶ ADJ = **long-serving**, seasoned, old, adept, expert.

veto VERB = **reject**, turn down, prohibit, forbid, interdict, proscribe, disallow, outlaw, embargo, ban, bar, preclude, rule out; [inf] give the thumbs down to, put the kibosh on.
Opposites: approve.
▶ NOUN = **rejection**, prohibition, interdict, proscription, embargo, ban.

vex VERB = **anger**, annoy, irritate, incense, irk, enrage, infuriate, exasperate, pique, provoke, nettle, disturb, upset, perturb, discompose, put out, try someone's patience, try; [inf] peeve, miff, bug, hassle, aggravate, drive up the wall.

viable ADJ = **workable**, sound, feasible, practicable, applicable, usable.
Opposites: impractical.

vibrant ADJ 1 = **lively**, energetic, spirited, vigorous, animated, sparkling, vivacious, dynamic, electrifying.
2 = **vivid**, bright, strong, striking.
Opposites: lifeless, pale.

vibrate VERB = **shake**, oscillate, tremble, quiver, throb, pulsate, resonate, resound, reverberate,

v

ring, echo.

vibration NOUN = **shaking**, oscillation, throb, pulsation, resonance, reverberation, quivering, quiver.

vicarious ADJ = **indirect**, second-hand, surrogate, by proxy, at one remove.

vice NOUN 1 = **sin**, sinfulness, wrong, wrongdoing, wickedness, badness, immorality, iniquity, evil, evil-doing, venality, corruption, depravity, degeneracy. 2 = **transgression**, offence, misdeed, error, failing, flaw, defect, imperfection, weakness, foible, shortcoming. Opposites: virtue.

vicinity NOUN = **surrounding district**, neighbourhood, locality, area, district, environs, precincts, purlieus; [inf] neck of the woods.

vicious ADJ 1 = **fierce**, ferocious, savage, dangerous, ill-natured, bad-tempered, hostile. 2 = **malicious**, malevolent, malignant, spiteful, vindictive,

venomous, backbiting, rancorous, caustic, mean, cruel; [inf] bitchy, catty. 3 = **violent**, savage, brutal, fierce, ferocious, inhuman, barbarous, fiendish, sadistic. Opposites: gentle.

vicissitude NOUN = **change**, alteration, transformation, inconstancy, instability, uncertainty, unpredictability, chanciness, fickleness, ups and downs.

victim NOUN 1 = **injured party**, casualty, sufferer. 2 = **offering**, sacrifice, scapegoat.

victimize VERB = **persecute**, pick on, discriminate against, punish unfairly; [inf] have it in for, have a down on.

victor NOUN = **winner**, champion, prizewinner, conquering hero; [inf] champ, top dog, number one. Opposites: loser.

victorious ADJ = **conquering**, vanquishing,

triumphant, winning, champion, successful, prizewinning, top, first.

vie VERB = **compete**, contend, contest, struggle, strive.

view NOUN **1** = **sight**, field/range of vision, vision, eyeshot. **2** = **outlook**, prospect, scene, spectacle, vista, panorama, landscape, seascape. **3** = **point of view**, viewpoint, opinion, belief, judgement, way of thinking, thinking, thought, notion, idea, conviction, persuasion, attitude, feeling, sentiment, impression. ▶ VERB = **look at**, watch, observe, contemplate, regard, behold, scan, survey, examine, scrutinize, see over.

viewpoint NOUN = **point of view**, frame of reference, perspective, angle, slant, standpoint, position, stance, vantage point.

vigilant ADJ = **watchful**, on the lookout, observant, sharp-eyed, eagle-eyed, attentive, alert, on the alert, awake, wide awake, on one's guard, careful, cautious, wary, circumspect, heedful.
Opposites: inattentive.

vigorous ADJ **1** = **robust**, healthy, in good health, hale and hearty, strong, sturdy, fit, in good condition/shape/kilter, tough. **2** = **energetic**, lively, active, spry, sprightly, vivacious, animated, dynamic, full of life, sparkling.
Opposites: weak, feeble.

vigour NOUN = **energy**, activity, liveliness, spryness, sprightliness, vitality, vivacity, verve, animation, dynamism, sparkle, zest, dash, gusto, pep; [inf] zip, zing, oomph, vim.
Opposites: lethargy.

vile ADJ = **foul**, nasty, unpleasant, disagreeable, horrid, horrible, offensive, obnoxious, odious, repulsive, repellent, revolting, repugnant, disgusting, distasteful, loathsome, hateful, nauseating, sickening, base, low, mean, wretched, dreadful, ugly, abominable, monstrous. **Opposites:** pleasant.

vilify VERB = **defame**, run down, impugn, revile, berate, denigrate, disparage, drag through the mud, speak ill of, cast aspersions at, criticize, decry, denounce, fulminate against, malign, slander, libel, traduce; [inf] bad-mouth, do a hatchet job on; [formal] calumniate. **Opposites:** commend.

villain NOUN = **rogue**, scoundrel, wretch, cad, reprobate, evil-doer, wrongdoer, hoodlum, hooligan, miscreant; [inf] baddy, crook, rat, louse; [archaic] blackguard.

vindicate VERB = **acquit**, clear, absolve, free from blame, exonerate, exculpate.

vindictive ADJ = **vengeful**, revengeful, avenging, unforgiving, grudge-bearing, resentful, implacable, unrelenting, spiteful, rancorous,

venomous, malicious, malevolent, malignant. **Opposites:** forgiving.

vintage ADJ = **classic**, ageless, enduring, high-quality, quality, prime, choice, select, superior, best.

violate VERB 1 = **break**, breach, infringe, contravene, infract, transgress, disobey, disregard, ignore. 2 = **desecrate**, profane, defile, blaspheme. 3 = **disturb**, disrupt, intrude on, interfere with, encroach on, invade. **Opposites:** respect.

violence NOUN = **force**, brute force, roughness, ferocity, brutality, savagery; [inf] strong-arm tactics.

violent ADJ 1 = **brutal**, vicious, destructive, savage, fierce, wild, intemperate, bloodthirsty, homicidal, murderous, maniacal. 2 = **uncontrollable**, powerful, uncontrolled, unrestrained, unbridled, ungovernable, wild,

undisguised,
conspicuous, distinct,
distinguishable.
Opposites: invisible.

vision NOUN **1 = eyesight**,
sight, power of seeing.
2 = revelation, dream,
hallucination, chimera,
optical illusion, mirage,
illusion, delusion,
figment of the
imagination.
3 = foresight, far-
sightedness, prescience,
breadth of view,
discernment.

visionary ADJ
1 = idealistic, impractical,
unrealistic, utopian,
romantic, quixotic,
dreamy, dreaming;
[inf] starry-eyed. **2 = far-
sighted**, discerning, wise.
3 = impractical,
unrealistic, unworkable,
unfeasible, theoretical,
hypothetical, idealistic,
utopian.
▶ NOUN = mystic, seer,
prophet, dreamer,
daydreamer, idealist,
romantic, romanticist,
sist, theorist,
an.

visit VERB = **pay a visit to**,
go/come to see, pay a
call on, call on, call/look
in on, stop by; [inf] pop/
drop in on.
▶ NOUN = **call**, social call,
stay, sojourn, stopover.

visitation NOUN
= **affliction**, scourge,
plague, pestilence, blight,
disaster, tragedy,
calamity, catastrophe,
cataclysm.

visual ADJ **1 = seeing**,
optical, ocular. **2 = to be
seen**, seeable,
perceivable, discernible.

visualize VERB = **conjure
up**, envisage, picture,
envision, imagine,
conceive.

vital ADJ **1 = essential**,
necessary, needed,
indispensable, key,
important, significant,
imperative, urgent,
critical, crucial, life-and-
death. **2 = lively**,
animated, spirited,
vivacious, vibrant,
zestful, dynamic,
energetic, vigorous,
forceful.
Opposites: unimportant,
apathetic.

void

vitality NOUN = **life**, liveliness, animation, spirit, spiritedness, vivacity, vibrancy, zest, zestfulness, dynamism, energy, vigour; [inf] zing, zip, pep, get-up-and-go.

vitriolic ADJ = **caustic**, mordant, acrimonious, bitter, acerbic, astringent, acid, acidulous, acrid, trenchant, virulent, spiteful, venomous, malicious, scathing, withering, sarcastic, sardonic; [inf] bitchy.

vivacious ADJ = **lively**, full of life, animated, effervescent, bubbly, ebullient, sparkling, scintillating, light-hearted, spirited, high-spirited, merry, jolly, vibrant, vivid, dynamic, vital; [dated] gay.
Opposites: dull.

vivid ADJ **1** = **strong**, intense, colourful, rich, glowing, bright, brilliant, clear. **2** = **graphic**, clear, lively, stirring, striking, powerful, highly coloured, dramatic, memorable, realistic, lifelike, true to life.

Opposites: dull.

vocal ADJ **1** = **voiced**, vocalized, spoken, said, uttered, expressed, articulated, oral.
2 = **vociferous**, outspoken, forthright, plain-spoken, clamorous, strident, loud, noisy.

vocation NOUN = **profession**, calling, occupation, walk of life, career, life's work, métier, trade, craft, job, work, employment, business, line, speciality.

vogue NOUN = **fashion**, mode, style, trend, taste, fad, craze, rage, latest thing.

voice NOUN **1** = **power of speech/articulation**.
2 = **expression**, utterance, verbalization, vocalization, airing.
▶ VERB = **put into words**, express, give utterance to, utter, articulate, enunciate, mention, talk of, communicate, declare, assert, divulge, air.

void ADJ **1** = **empty**, emptied, vacant, bare, clear, free, unfilled,

unoccupied, uninhabited, untenanted, tenantless.
2 = null and void, nullified, invalid, cancelled, inoperative, ineffective, non-viable, useless, worthless, nugatory.
Opposites: full, valid.

volatile ADJ **1 = mercurial**, changeable, variable, capricious, whimsical, fickle, flighty, giddy, inconstant, erratic, unstable. **2 = explosive**, eruptive, charged, inflammatory, tense, strained.
Opposites: stable.

voluble ADJ **= talkative**, loquacious, garrulous, chatty, gossipy, chattering, articulate, eloquent, forthcoming, fluent, glib.
Opposites: taciturn.

volume NOUN **1 = book**, publication, tome.
2 = space, bulk, capacity.
3 = loudness, sound, amplification.

voluminous ADJ **= capacious**, roomy, commodious, ample, full, big, vast, billowing.
Opposites: small.

voluntary ADJ **= of one's own free will**, volitional, of one's own accord, optional, discretionary, at one's discretion, elective, non-compulsory, non-mandatory.
Opposites: compulsory.

volunteer VERB **= offer one's services**, present oneself, step forward.

voluptuous ADJ
1 = hedonistic, sybaritic, epicurean, self-indulgent, sensual, carnal, licentious, lascivious.
2 = curvy, shapely, full-figured, ample, buxom, seductive, curvaceous.
Opposites: ascetic, scrawny.

vomit VERB **1 = throw up**; [Brit.] be sick; [inf] spew, puke. **2 = bring up**, regurgitate, spew up, spit up.

voracious ADJ
1 = gluttonous, greedy, ravenous, ravening, starving, hungry, insatiable.
2 = compulsive,

enthusiastic, eager.

vote NOUN = **ballot**, poll, election, referendum, plebiscite.

▶ VERB = **cast one's vote**, go to the polls, mark one's ballot paper.

vouch

■ **vouch for** = **attest to**, bear witness to, give assurance of, answer for, be responsible for, guarantee, go/stand bail for.

voucher NOUN = **chit**, slip, ticket, token, document.

vow VERB = **swear**, state under oath, pledge, promise, undertake, give one's word of honour.

voyage NOUN = **journey**, trip, expedition, crossing, cruise, passage.

▶ VERB = **travel**, journey, take a trip, sail, cruise.

vulgar ADJ **1** = **rude**, indecent, indecorous, indelicate, crude, unseemly, offensive, distasteful, obnoxious, suggestive, off colour, ribald, bawdy, obscene, lewd, salacious, licentious, concupiscent, smutty, dirty, filthy, pornographic, scatological; [inf] raunchy, blue. **2** = **tasteless**, gross, crass, unrefined, tawdry, ostentatious, showy, flashy, gaudy.
Opposites: tasteful.

vulnerable ADJ = **exposed**, unprotected, unguarded, open to attack, assailable, defenceless, easily hurt/ wounded/damaged, powerless, helpless, weak, sensitive, thin-skinned.
Opposites: invulnerable.

V

Ww

wad NOUN **1** = **lump**, mass, chunk, hunk, bail, plug, block. **2** = **bundle**, roll.

waddle VERB = **sway**, wobble, totter, toddle, shuffle.

wade VERB = **ford**, cross, traverse, paddle.
- **wade in** = **set to**, set to work, pitch in, buckle down, go to it, put one's shoulder to the wheel; [inf] get cracking, get stuck in.

waffle NOUN = **meaningless talk/ writing**, padding, equivocation, prattle, jabbering, verbiage, logorrhoea; [Brit. inf] wittering.
▶ VERB = **ramble**, prattle, jabber, babble; [Brit. inf] rabbit, witter.

waft VERB **1** = **float**, glide, drift, be carried/borne/ conveyed. **2** = **carry**, bear, convey, transport, transmit.

wag¹ VERB **1** = **swing**, sway, vibrate, quiver, shake, rock, twitch. **2** = **waggle**, wiggle, wobble, wave.

wag² NOUN = **wit**, humorist, jester, joker, jokester, comic, comedian, comedienne, wisecracker, punner, punster.

wage NOUN = **pay**, salary, earnings, payment, fee, remuneration, stipend, emolument.
▶ VERB = **carry on**, conduct, execute, engage in, pursue, undertake, devote oneself to, practise.

wager NOUN = **bet**, gamble, stake, pledge, hazard; [Brit. inf] flutter.
▶ VERB = **lay a wager**, bet, place/make/lay a bet, lay

odds, put money on, speculate.

wail NOUN = **cry of grief/ pain**, lament, lamentation, weeping, sob, moan, groan, whine, complaint, howl, yowl, ululation.
▶ VERB = **cry**, lament, weep, sob, moan, groan, whine, howl, yowl, ululate.

wait VERB 1 = **stay**, remain, rest, linger, abide; [archaic] tarry. 2 = **be patient**, hold back, stand by, bide one's time, hang fire, mark time; [inf] cool one's heels, sit tight, hold one's horses, sweat it out.
▶ NOUN = **interval**, stay, delay, hold-up.
▪ **wait on** = **act as a waiter/waitress to**, serve, attend to.

waiter, **waitress** NOUN = **steward, stewardess**, server, attendant.

waive VERB = **relinquish**, renounce, give up, abandon, surrender, yield, cede, set aside, forgo, disregard, ignore.

wake VERB 1 = **awake**, awaken, waken, wake up, waken up, rouse, stir, come to, get up, arise. 2 = **rouse**, stir up, activate, stimulate, spur, prod, galvanize, provoke. **Opposites:** sleep.
▶ NOUN = **vigil**, death watch, watch.

wakeful ADJ 1 = **unsleeping**, restless, tossing and turning, insomniac. 2 = **alert**, on the alert, vigilant, on the lookout, on one's guard, on the qui vive, watchful, observant, attentive, heedful, wary. **Opposites:** asleep, inattentive.

walk VERB 1 = **go by foot**, travel on foot, foot it; [inf] hoof it. 2 = **stroll**, saunter, amble, plod, trudge, hike, tramp, trek, march, stride, step out. 3 = **accompany**, escort, convey.
▶ NOUN 1 = **stroll**, saunter, amble, promenade, ramble, hike, tramp, march, constitutional, airing. 2 = **manner of walking**, gait, pace, step, stride. 3 = **road**, avenue, drive, promenade, path,

W

pathway, footpath, track, lane, alley.

walkover NOUN = **easy victory**; [inf] piece of cake, child's play, doddle, pushover.

wall NOUN **1** = **partition**, room divider.
2 = **fortification**, rampart, barricade, parapet, bulwark, stockade, breastwork.

wallet NOUN = **purse**, pouch; [N. Amer.] billfold, pocketbook; [Brit. dated] notecase.

wallow VERB **1** = **roll**, tumble about, lie around, splash around.
2 = **luxuriate in**, bask in, take pleasure/satisfaction in, indulge oneself in, delight in, revel in, glory in, enjoy.

wan ADJ = **pale**, pallid, ashen, white, white as a sheet/ghost, anaemic, colourless, bloodless, waxen, pasty, peaky, tired-looking, washed out, sickly.
Opposites: ruddy.

wand NOUN = **baton**, stick, staff, twig, sprig, withe, withy.

wander VERB **1** = **ramble**, roam, meander, rove, range, prowl, saunter, stroll, amble, peregrinate, drift; [inf] traipse; [Brit. inf] mooch. **2** = **stray**, depart, diverge, veer, swerve, deviate. **3** = **be incoherent**, ramble, babble, talk nonsense, rave, be delirious.
▸ NOUN = **ramble**, saunter, stroll, amble.

wanderer NOUN = **rambler**, roamer, rover, drifter, traveller, itinerant, wayfarer, nomad, bird of passage, rolling stone, gypsy, vagabond, vagrant, tramp, derelict, beggar.

wane VERB = **decrease**, decline, diminish, dwindle, shrink, contract, taper off, subside, sink, ebb, dim, fade away, vanish, die out, draw to a close, evanesce, peter out, wind down, be on the way out, abate, fail, become weak, deteriorate, degenerate.
Opposites: strengthen.

W

want VERB 1 = **wish**, wish for, desire, demand, call for, long for, hope for, yearn for, pine for, fancy, crave, hanker after, hunger for, thirst for, lust after, covet, need; [inf] have a yen for. 2 = **need**, be/stand in need of, require. 3 = **lack**, be lacking, be without, be devoid of, be bereft of, be short of, be deficient in, have insufficient of.
▶ NOUN 1 = **lack**, absence, dearth, deficiency, inadequacy, insufficiency, shortness, paucity, shortage, scarcity, scarceness, scantiness. 2 = **wish**, desire, demand, longing, yearning, fancy, craving, hankering, hunger, thirst, lust, covetousness. 3 = **need**, neediness, privation, poverty, destitution, penury, indigence.

wanting ADJ = **lacking**, deficient, inadequate, imperfect, not up to standard/par, not good enough, disappointing, not acceptable, not up to expectations, flawed, faulty, defective, unsound, substandard, inferior, second-rate. **Opposites:** sufficient.

wanton ADJ
1 = **promiscuous**, fast, immoral, loose, immodest, shameless, unchaste, unvirtuous, of easy virtue, impure, abandoned, lustful, lecherous, lascivious, libidinous, licentious, libertine, dissolute, dissipated, debauched, degenerate. 2 = **wilful**, malicious, malevolent, spiteful, wicked, evil, cruel, unmotivated, motiveless, arbitrary, groundless, unjustifiable, unjustified, needless, unnecessary, uncalled for, unprovoked, gratuitous, senseless, pointless, purposeless.

war NOUN = **warfare**, conflict, hostilities, strife, combat, fighting, struggle, armed conflict, battle, fight, confrontation, skirmish. **Opposites:** peace.

w

ward NOUN 1 = **room**, compartment, cubicle. 2 = **administrative district**, district, division, quarter, zone. 3 = **charge**, dependant, protégé/protégée, pupil.

■ **ward off** = **fend off**, stave off, parry, avert, deflect, turn aside, drive back, repel, repulse, beat back, rout, put to flight, scatter, disperse.

warder NOUN = **prison officer**, guard, warden, jailer; [inf] screw.

warehouse NOUN = **store**, storehouse, depot, depository, stockroom.

wares PL NOUN = **goods**, products, commodities, lines, merchandise, produce, stuff, stock.

warily ADV = **carefully**, with care, cautiously, gingerly, circumspectly, guardedly, on one's guard, on the alert, watchfully, vigilantly, suspiciously, distrustfully, mistrustfully, charily. **Opposites:** trustingly.

warlike ADJ = **aggressive**, belligerent, bellicose, pugnacious, combative, militaristic, militant, martial. **Opposites:** peaceful, peaceable.

warm ADJ 1 = **heated**, tepid, lukewarm. 2 = **sunny**, balmy. 3 = **kindly**, friendly, affable, amiable, genial, cordial, sympathetic, affectionate, loving, tender, caring, charitable, sincere, genuine. 4 = **hearty**, cordial, genial, friendly, hospitable, enthusiastic, eager, sincere, heartfelt, ardent, vehement, passionate, intense, fervent, effusive. **Opposites:** cool, cold.

▶ VERB = **warm up**, make warm, heat, heat up, reheat.

warn VERB 1 = **inform**, notify, give notice, give prior notice, tell, let know, acquaint, give fair warning, forewarn; [inf] tip off, put wise. 2 = **advise**, exhort, urge, counsel, caution, forewarn, put on the alert, make aware. 3 = **give a warning to**, admonish, remonstrate with.

warning NOUN
1 = **information**, notification, notice, word, forewarning; [inf] tip-off. 2 = **caution**, advice, exhortation, counselling.
3 = **admonition**, remonstrance. 4 = **omen**, premonition, foretoken, token, augury, signal, sign, threat.

warrant NOUN
1 = **authorization**, consent, sanction, permission, validation, licence, imprimatur, seal of approval. 2 = **official document**, written order, papers.
▶ VERB = **justify**, vindicate, excuse, be a defence of, explain away, account for, be a reason for, offer grounds for, support.

wary ADJ = **careful**, cautious, circumspect, leery, chary, on one's guard, alert, wide awake, on one's toes, on the alert/lookout, on the qui vive, attentive, heedful, watchful, vigilant,

observant.
Opposites: unwary.

wash VERB 1 = **wash oneself**, have a wash, bath, shower, have a bath/shower. 2 = **clean**, cleanse, sponge, scrub, launder, shampoo.
3 = **splash against**, dash against, break against, beat against. 4 = **be accepted**, be plausible, be convincing, hold up, hold water, stand up, bear scrutiny.
▶ NOUN = **clean**, cleaning, cleansing, bath, shower.

waste VERB = **squander**, dissipate, fritter away, misspend, misuse, spend recklessly, throw away, go through, run through; [inf] blow.
Opposites: conserve.
▶ NOUN 1 = **squandering**, dissipation, frittering away, misspending, misuse, prodigality, unthriftiness. 2 = **rubbish**, refuse, debris, dross, dregs, leavings, garbage, trash.
▶ ADJ 1 = **leftover**, unused, superfluous, supernumerary,

w

unwanted, worthless, useless. **2 = desert**, barren, uncultivated, unproductive, arid, bare, desolate, solitary, lonely, empty, void, uninhabited, unpopulated, wild, bleak, cheerless.

■ **waste away = grow weak**, wither, atrophy, become emaciated.

wasteful ADJ = **prodigal**, profligate, thriftless, spendthrift, extravagant, lavish.
Opposites: thrifty.

watch VERB **1 = look at**, observe, view, eye, gaze at, stare at, gape at, peer at, contemplate, behold, inspect, scrutinize, survey, scan, examine. **2 = keep watch on**, keep an eye on, keep in sight, follow, spy on; [inf] keep tabs on. **3 = mind**, take care of, look after, supervise, superintend, tend, guard, protect, keep an eye on.
▶ NOUN **1 = wristwatch**, pocket watch, timepiece, chronometer. **2 = guard**, vigil.

watchful ADJ = **observant**, alert, vigilant, attentive, heedful, sharp-eyed, eagle-eyed, wary, circumspect. = *See also* **wary**, **alert** ADJ **(1)**.

watchman NOUN = **security guard/man**, guard, custodian, caretaker.

water NOUN **1 = Adam's ale**, tap water, mineral water, bottled water. **2 = sea**, river, lake, loch, pool, reservoir.
▶ VERB **1 = sprinkle**, moisten, dampen, wet, water down, douse, hose, spray, drench, saturate, flood. **2 = exude water**, moisten, leak.

■ **water down 1 = add water to**, dilute, thin, weaken, adulterate. **2 = play down**, downplay, tone down, soft-pedal, understate, underemphasize.

waterfall NOUN = **falls**, cascade, cataract.

watertight ADJ **1 = waterproof**, sound. **2 = sound**, flawless, incontrovertible, indisputable, foolproof,

unassailable, impregnable.
Opposites: leaky, flawed.

watery ADJ **1** = **aqueous**, liquid, liquefied, fluid, hydrous. **2** = **wet**, damp, moist, sodden, soggy, squelchy, saturated, waterlogged, marshy, boggy, swampy, miry. **3** = **thin**, runny, weak, dilute, diluted, watered down, adulterated, tasteless, flavourless; [inf] wishy-washy.
Opposites: dry, thick.

wave VERB **1** = **undulate**, ripple, stir, flutter, flap, sway, swing, shake, quiver, oscillate. **2** = **move up and down**, move to and fro, wag, waggle, flutter. **3** = **gesture**, gesticulate, signal, sign, beckon, indicate.
▶ NOUN **1** = **breaker**, roller, comber, ripple, billow, white horse, white cap, swell, surf. **2** = **stream**, flow, rush, surge, flood. **3** = **undulation**, curl, kink. **4** = **surge**, upsurge, groundswell, welling up, rush, outbreak, rash.

■ **wave aside** = **set aside**, dismiss, reject, disregard, ignore.

waver VERB **1** = **become unsteady**, falter, wobble, hesitate. **2** = **be irresolute/indecisive**, hesitate, dither, equivocate, vacillate, shilly-shally, blow hot and cold, pussyfoot around, beat about the bush; [Brit.] hum and haw. **3** = **weave**, reel, totter, teeter, stagger, wobble.

wavy ADJ = **undulating**, curvy, curling, squiggly, rippled, curving, winding.
Opposites: straight.

wax VERB = **get bigger**, increase in size, enlarge, grow, develop, extend, widen, broaden, spread, mushroom.
Opposites: wane.

way NOUN **1** = **direction**, route, course, road, roadway, street, thoroughfare, track, path, pathway, lane, avenue, drive. **2** = **method**, means, course of action, process, procedure, technique, system, plan, scheme, manner, modus operandi. **3** = **manner**, style, fashion, mode. **4** = **distance**, length, stretch, journey.

wayfarer NOUN = **traveller**, walker, hiker, rambler, wanderer, roamer, rover, nomad, gypsy, vagabond, vagrant.

waylay VERB = **lie in wait for**, ambush, hold up, attack, accost, intercept, pounce on, swoop down on.

wayward ADJ = **wilful**, self-willed, headstrong, stubborn, obstinate, obdurate, perverse, contrary, uncooperative, refractory, recalcitrant, contumacious, unruly, ungovernable, unmanageable, incorrigible, intractable, difficult, fractious, disobedient, insubordinate. **Opposites:** docile.

weak ADJ **1** = **frail**, fragile, delicate, feeble, infirm, shaky, debilitated, incapacitated, ailing, indisposed, decrepit, puny, faint, enervated, tired, fatigued, exhausted, spent, worn out. **2** = **cowardly**, pusillanimous, timorous, timid, spineless, ineffectual, useless, inept, effete, powerless, impotent, namby-pamby, soft; [inf] yellow, weak-kneed. **3** = **defective**, faulty, poor, inadequate, deficient, imperfect, substandard, lacking, wanting. **4** = **unsound**, feeble, flimsy, lame, hollow, pathetic, unconvincing, untenable, implausible, unsatisfactory. **5** = **faint**, low, muffled, stifled, muted, scarcely audible. **6** = **under-strength**, dilute, diluted, watery, thinned down, thin, adulterated, tasteless, flavourless, insipid; [inf] wishy-washy. **Opposites:** strong.

weaken VERB **1** = **enfeeble**, debilitate, incapacitate, sap someone's strength, enervate, tire, exhaust, wear out. **2** = **lessen**, reduce, decrease, diminish, moderate, temper, sap, emasculate. **3** = **abate**, lessen, decrease, dwindle, diminish, ease up, let up. **Opposites:** strengthen.

weakling NOUN = **coward**, mouse, milksop, namby-pamby; [inf] wimp, sissy, drip, wet, doormat, chicken, yellow-belly.

weakness NOUN **1** = **frailty**, fragility, delicateness, delicacy, feebleness, infirmity, debility, incapacity, indisposition, decrepitude, puniness, enervation, fatigue. **2** = **cowardliness**, timidity, spinelessness, ineffectuality, ineptness, powerlessness, impotence. **3** = **defectiveness**, faultiness, inadequacy, deficiency. **4** = **unsoundness**, feebleness, flimsiness, lameness, untenability, implausibility. **5** = **faintness**, low intensity, mutedness. **6** = **thinness**, wateriness, tastelessness; [inf] wishy-washiness. **7** = **weak**

point, failing, foible, fault, flaw, defect, shortcoming, imperfection, blemish, Achilles' heel, chink in one's armour. **Opposites:** strength.

wealth NOUN **1** = **money**, cash, capital, affluence, means, fortune, finance, property, riches, assets, possessions, resources, goods, funds. **2** = **mass**, abundance, profusion, copiousness, plenitude, amplitude, bounty, cornucopia. **Opposites:** poverty, scarcity.

wealthy ADJ = **rich**, well off, well-to-do, moneyed, affluent, prosperous, of means, of substance; [inf] well heeled, rolling in it/money, in the money, made of money, filthy/stinking rich, loaded, flush, on easy street, quids in. **Opposites:** poor.

wear VERB **1** = **be dressed in**, dress in, be clothed in, clothe oneself in, have on, put on, don, sport. **2** = **have**, assume,

w

present, show, display, exhibit. **3 = erode**, corrode, abrade, wash away, rub away, rub down, grind away, wear down. **4 = become worn**, wear thin, fray, become threadbare, go into holes.

■ **wear off = lose effectiveness/effect**, lose intensity/strength, fade, peter out, dwindle, decrease, diminish, disappear, subside, ebb, wane.

■ **wear out = fatigue**, tire, weary, exhaust, drain, strain, stress, weaken, enfeeble, prostrate, enervate; [Brit. inf] knacker; [N. Amer. inf] poop.

weariness NOUN **= fatigue**, tiredness, exhaustion, enervation, lassitude, languor, listlessness, lethargy.

wearisome ADJ **= fatiguing**, tiring, exhausting, draining, wearing, trying, irksome, boring, tedious, dull, uninteresting, monotonous, humdrum, routine.
Opposites: refreshing.

weary ADJ **1 = fatigued**, tired, exhausted, drained, worn, worn out, spent, careworn, wearied; [inf] dead tired/beat, dead on one's feet, dog-tired, all in, done in, whacked, bushed; [Brit. inf] fagged out, knackered; [N. Amer. inf] pooped. **2 = bored**, discontented, jaded, uninterested, listless, lethargic; [inf] browned off, fed up, sick and tired; [Brit. inf] cheesed off.
Opposites: fresh, keen.

▶ VERB **1 = fatigue**, tire, exhaust, drain, wear out; [inf] wear to a frazzle; [Brit. inf] knacker. **2 = bore**, irk, make discontented/jaded; [inf] make fed up. **3 = grow weary**, tire, get bored, have enough, grow discontented/jaded.
Opposites: refresh, interest.

weather VERB **1 = dry**, season, expose, expose to the elements. **2 = come/ get through**, survive, withstand, live/pull through, bear up against, stand, endure, ride out, rise above, surmount, overcome, resist; [inf] stick out.

weave¹ VERB **1 = interlace**, intertwine, interwork, twist together, entwine, braid, plait. **2 = make up**, fabricate, put together, construct, invent, create, contrive.

weave² VERB **= zigzag**, wind, criss-cross.

web NOUN **= lacework**, lattice, latticework, mesh, net, netting.

wed VERB **= get married**, marry, become man and wife; [inf] get hitched/ spliced, tie the knot. **Opposites:** divorce, separate.

wedding NOUN **= wedding/ marriage ceremony**, marriage, nuptials.

wedge VERB **= thrust**, stuff, pack, ram, force, cram, squeeze, jam.

weep VERB **= cry**, shed tears, sob, blubber, snivel, whimper, whine, moan, lament, grieve, mourn, keen, wail; [inf] boohoo, blub.

weigh VERB **1 = measure/ gauge the weight of**, put on the scales. **2 = have a weight of**; [inf] tip the scales at. **3 = balance**, compare with, evaluate.

■ **weigh up = consider**, contemplate, think over, mull over, ponder, deliberate upon, meditate on, muse on, brood over, reflect on.

weight NOUN
1 = heaviness, load, quantity, poundage, tonnage, avoirdupois.
2 = burden, load, onus, millstone, albatross, oppression, trouble, worry, strain.
3 = importance, significance, consequence, value, substance, force, influence; [inf] clout.

weird ADJ **1 = strange**, queer, uncanny, eerie, mysterious, mystifying, supernatural, preternatural, unnatural, unearthly, ghostly; [inf] spooky, creepy.
2 = odd, eccentric, bizarre, outlandish, freakish, grotesque; [inf] offbeat, far out, way-out, out on a limb.

w

Opposites: normal, conventional.

welcome NOUN = **greeting**, salutation, reception, warm reception.

▶ VERB 1 = **bid welcome**, greet, receive, embrace, receive with open arms, roll out the red carpet for, meet, usher in. 2 = **be pleased by**, take pleasure in, feel satisfaction at.

▶ ADJ 1 = **wanted**, appreciated, popular, desirable. 2 = **gladly received**, pleasant, pleasing, agreeable, cheering, to one's liking, to one's taste.
Opposites: unwelcome.

welfare NOUN 1 = **well-being**, health, good health, soundness, happiness, comfort, security, prosperity, success, fortune, good fortune. 2 = **state aid/benefit**, public assistance, social security, income support.

well[1] ADJ 1 = **healthy**, in good health, fit, strong, robust, hale and hearty, able-bodied, up to par. 2 = **satisfactory**, all right,

fine, good, thriving, flourishing; [inf] OK, fine and dandy.

well[2] NOUN 1 = **spring**, fountain, waterhole, pool, borehole. 2 = **source**, wellspring, fount, reservoir, repository, mine.

well advised ADJ = **sensible**, wise, prudent, judicious, circumspect, far-sighted, sagacious.

well balanced ADJ 1 = **well adjusted**, sensible, reasonable, rational, level-headed, sound, practical, discerning, logical, sane, in one's right mind. 2 = **balanced**, well proportioned, well ordered.

well built ADJ = **strongly built**, strong, muscular, brawny, sturdy, robust, strapping, husky, burly, big; [inf] hulking, hefty, beefy.
Opposites: puny.

well known ADJ 1 = **known**, widely known, familiar, common, usual, everyday. 2 = **famous**,

famed, renowned, celebrated, noted, notable, illustrious, eminent.
Opposites: unknown.

well-nigh ADV = **virtually**, next to, practically, all but, just about, almost, nearly, more or less.

well off ADJ = **wealthy**, rich, well-to-do, moneyed, affluent, prosperous, of means, of substance; [inf] well heeled, rolling in it/money, in the money, made of money, filthy/stinking rich, loaded, flush, on easy street, quids in.
Opposites: poor.

well spoken ADJ = **articulate**, nicely spoken, educated, polite, refined; [Brit. inf] posh.

wet ADJ 1 = **damp**, moist, moistened, wet through, soaked, drenched, saturated, sopping/dripping/wringing wet, sopping, dripping, soggy, waterlogged. 2 = **rainy**, raining, pouring, showery, drizzling, damp, humid, dank,

misty. 3 = **feeble**, weak, inept, ineffective, ineffectual, effete, timid, timorous, cowardly, spineless, soft; [inf] namby-pamby, weedy.
▶ NOUN = **wetness**, damp, dampness, moisture, moistness, condensation, humidity, water, liquid.
▶ VERB = **dampen**, damp, moisten, sprinkle, spray, splash, water, irrigate, douse.
Opposites: dry.

wharf NOUN = **pier**, quay, jetty, dock, landing stage.

wheel VERB = **turn**, go round, circle, rotate, revolve, spin, swivel round, pivot, whirl/twirl round, make a U-turn.

wheeze VERB = **gasp**, puff, pant, cough, whistle, hiss, rasp.

whereabouts NOUN = **location**, site, position, situation, place, vicinity.

whet VERB = **sharpen**, put an edge on, edge, hone, strop, file, grind, rasp.
Opposites: blunt.

w

whim NOUN = **notion**, fancy, idea, impulse, urge, caprice, vagary, craze, passion, inclination, bent.

whimper VERB = **whine**, cry, sniffle, snivel, moan, wail, groan.

whimsical ADJ = **capricious**, fanciful, fantastical, playful, mischievous, waggish, quaint, unusual, curious, droll, eccentric, peculiar, queer, bizarre, weird, freakish.

whine VERB 1 = **whimper**, cry, wail, groan; [inf] grizzle. 2 = See complain (2).

whip VERB 1 = **lash**, flog, scourge, flagellate, birch, switch, strap, cane, thrash, beat, strike, leather; [inf] belt, tan, give someone a hiding. 2 = **beat**, whisk, mix.
▶ NOUN = **lash**, scourge, horsewhip, bullwhip, cat-o'-nine-tails, knout, crop, riding crop.

whirl VERB = **turn round**, circle, spin, rotate, revolve, wheel, twirl, swirl, gyrate, reel, pirouette, pivot.

whirlpool NOUN = **vortex**, maelstrom, eddy, whirl.

whirlwind NOUN = **tornado**, hurricane, typhoon.
▶ ADJ = **swift**, rapid, quick, speedy, hasty, headlong.

whisk VERB = **whip**, beat, mix, stir.
▶ NOUN = **mixer**, beater.

whisper VERB = **murmur**, mutter, speak softly, speak in muted/hushed tones.
Opposites: roar.
▶ NOUN 1 = **murmur**, mutter, low voice, hushed tone, undertone. 2 = **rumour**, report, insinuation, suggestion, hint, gossip, word.

whit NOUN = **particle**, bit, jot, iota, mite, little, trifle.

white ADJ 1 = **pale**, wan, pallid, ashen, anaemic, colourless, bloodless, waxen, pasty, peaky, whey-faced, grey. 2 = **grey**, silver, hoary, snowy-white, grizzled.

whiten VERB = **make white**, make pale, bleach, blanch, fade, wash out,

w

etiolate.

whole ADJ **1** = **entire**, complete, full, total, solid, integral, unabridged, unreduced, undivided, uncut.
2 = **intact**, sound, flawless, in one piece, unimpaired, undamaged, unharmed, unhurt, uninjured, unmutilated.
Opposites: incomplete.

wholehearted ADJ = **unreserved**, unqualified, unstinting, complete, committed, hearty, emphatic, real, sincere, genuine.
Opposites: half-hearted.

wholesale ADJ = **indiscriminate**, mass, all-inclusive, total, comprehensive, extensive, wide-ranging, sweeping, broad.
Opposites: partial.

wholesome ADJ
1 = **nutritious**, nourishing, health-giving, healthful, good, strengthening.
2 = **moral**, ethical, uplifting, edifying, helpful, beneficial.

wholly ADV = **completely**, fully, entirely, totally, utterly, thoroughly, altogether, comprehensively, in every respect, perfectly, enthusiastically, with total commitment, unreservedly, heart and soul.

wicked ADJ = **evil**, sinful, bad, wrong, unrighteous, villainous, dastardly, black-hearted, iniquitous, heinous, monstrous, atrocious, abominable, base, gross, vile, foul, mean, vicious, hideous, dishonourable, unprincipled, nefarious, criminal, perverted, immoral, amoral, unethical, corrupt, dissolute, dissipated, degenerate, reprobate, debauched, depraved, unholy, impious, irreligious, ungodly, godless, devilish, demonic, diabolic; [archaic] blackguardly.
Opposites: good, righteous.

wide ADJ **1** = **broad**, extensive, spacious.
2 = **broad**, large, outspread, spread out,

W

ample. **3** = **wide-ranging**, extensive, large, large-scale, vast, far-ranging, immense, broad, expansive, sweeping, encyclopedic, comprehensive, general, all-embracing, catholic, compendious. **Opposites:** narrow.

wide-eyed ADJ
1 = **surprised**, amazed, astonished, astounded. **2** = **naive**, impressionable, ingenuous, credulous, trusting, unsuspicious, innocent, simple, unsophisticated, inexperienced, green; [inf] wet behind the ears.

widen VERB **1** = **make wider**, broaden, expand, extend, enlarge, increase, augment, add to, supplement. **2** = **open wide**, dilate.

widespread ADJ
= **universal**, common, general, far-reaching, prevalent, rife, extensive, sweeping, pervasive, epidemic. **Opposites:** limited.

width NOUN **1** = **wideness**, breadth, broadness, span, diameter. **2** = **range**, breadth, scope, span, extensiveness, vastness, immensity, expansiveness, comprehensiveness. **Opposites:** length, narrowness.

wield VERB **1** = **brandish**, flourish, wave, swing, use, employ, handle, ply, manipulate. **2** = **exercise**, exert, be possessed of, have, have at one's disposal, hold, maintain, command, control.

wild ADJ **1** = **untamed**, undomesticated, unbroken, feral, savage, fierce, ferocious. **2** = **uncultivated**, natural, native, indigenous. **3** = **uncivilized**, primitive, ignorant, savage, barbaric, barbarous, brutish, ferocious, fierce. **4** = **stormy**, tempestuous, turbulent, blustery, howling, violent, raging, furious, rough. **5** = **undisciplined**, unrestrained, unconstrained, uncontrolled, out of control, unbridled,

w

unchecked, chaotic, disorderly. **6** = **rowdy**, unruly, disorderly, turbulent, violent, lawless, riotous, out of control, unmanageable, ungovernable, unrestrained, excited, passionate, frantic.
7 = **crazy**, beside oneself, berserk, frantic, frenzied, in a frenzy, hysterical, crazed, mad, distracted, distraught, irrational, deranged, demented, raving, maniacal, rabid.
8 = **extravagant**, fantastical, impracticable, foolish, ill-advised, ill-considered, imprudent, unwise, madcap, impulsive, reckless, rash, outrageous, preposterous. **Opposites:** tame, cultivated, calm, disciplined.

wilderness NOUN = **desert**, wasteland, waste, the wilds, jungle, no-man's-land.

wiles PL NOUN = **tricks**, ruses, ploys, schemes, dodges, manoeuvres, subterfuges, artifices, guile, artfulness, cunning, craftiness.

wilful ADJ **1** = **deliberate**, intentional, intended, conscious, purposeful, premeditated, planned, calculated.
2 = **headstrong**, strong-willed, obstinate, stubborn, mulish, pig-headed, obdurate, intransigent, adamant, dogged, determined, persistent, unyielding, uncompromising, intractable, refractory, recalcitrant, disobedient, contrary, perverse, wayward, self-willed. **Opposites:** accidental.

will NOUN **1** = **volition**, choice, option, decision, discretion, prerogative.
2 = **desire**, wish, preference, inclination, fancy, mind. **3** = **will power**, determination, resolution, resolve, firmness of purpose, purposefulness, doggedness, single-mindedness, commitment, moral fibre, pluck, mettle, grit, nerve. **4** = **last will and testament**, testament,

last wishes.

willing ADJ = **prepared**, ready, game, disposed, content, happy, so-minded, consenting, agreeable, amenable, in the mood, compliant.
Opposites: unwilling.

willingly ADV
= **voluntarily**, of one's own free will, of one's own accord, by choice, by volition, spontaneously, unforced.

wilt VERB **1** = **droop**, wither, shrivel, lose freshness, sag. **2** = **diminish**, dwindle, lessen, grow less, flag, fade, melt away, ebb, wane, weaken, fail.
Opposites: flourish.

wily ADJ = **crafty**, cunning, artful, sharp, astute, shrewd, scheming, intriguing, shifty, sly, guileful, deceitful, deceptive, fraudulent, cheating, underhand; [inf] crooked, foxy; [Brit. inf] fly.
Opposites: naive.

win VERB **1** = **achieve**, attain, earn, gain, receive, obtain, acquire, procure, get, secure, collect, pick up, come away with, net, bag.
2 = **be victorious**, be the victor, gain the victory, overcome, achieve mastery, carry the day, carry all before one, finish first, come out ahead, come out on top, win out, succeed, triumph, prevail.
Opposites: lose.

wind[1] NOUN **1** = **air current**, breeze, gust, blast, gale, storm, hurricane; [poetic/literary] zephyr. **2** = **breath**, respiration; [inf] puff.
3 = **flatulence**, gas; [formal] flatus.

wind[2] VERB = **twist**, twist and turn, curve, bend, loop, zigzag, snake, spiral, meander, ramble.
■ **wind down** = **unwind**, relax, become less tense, ease up, calm down, cool off.
■ **wind up** = **bring to an end/conclusion**, end, conclude, terminate, finish; [inf] wrap up.

windfall NOUN = **piece/stroke of good luck**, unexpected gain, godsend, manna from heaven, bonanza, jackpot.

windy ADJ **1** = **breezy**, blowy, blustery, blustering, gusty, gusting, boisterous, squally, stormy, wild, tempestuous, turbulent.
2 = **long-winded**, loquacious, wordy, verbose, rambling, meandering, prolix, diffuse, turgid.
3 = **nervous**, scared, frightened, alarmed, fearful, timid, timorous, cowardly.
Opposites: still.

wink VERB **1** = **blink**, flutter, bat; [technical] nictate.
2 = **flash**, twinkle, sparkle, glitter, gleam.

winner NOUN = **champion**, victor, vanquisher, conqueror, prizewinner.
Opposites: loser.

winning ADJ **1** = **victorious**, successful, triumphant, vanquishing, conquering.
2 = **captivating**, enchanting, bewitching, beguiling, disarming, taking, engaging, endearing, winsome, charming, attractive, fetching, alluring, sweet, lovely, delightful, darling, pleasing.

wintry ADJ = **cold**, chilly, icy, frosty, freezing, frozen, snowy, arctic, glacial, biting, piercing, nippy.
Opposites: warm.

wipe VERB = **rub**, brush, dust, mop, sponge, swab, clean, dry.

wiry ADJ **1** = **lean**, spare, sinewy, tough, strong.
2 = **bristly**, prickly, thorny, stiff, rigid.

wisdom NOUN
1 = **sageness**, sagacity, cleverness, intelligence, erudition, learning, education, knowledge, enlightenment, reason, discernment, perception, insight. **2** = **sense**, common sense, prudence, judiciousness, judgement, shrewdness, astuteness, circumspection, strategy, foresight, reasonableness, rationality, logic, soundness, saneness; [inf] smartness.
Opposites: folly.

w

wise ADJ **1** = **sage**, sagacious, clever, intelligent, erudite, learned, educated, well read, knowledgeable, informed, enlightened, philosophic, deep-thinking, discerning, perceptive, experienced; [formal] sapient.
2 = **sensible**, prudent, well advised, judicious, politic, shrewd, astute, reasonable, rational, logical, sound, sane; [inf] smart.
Opposites: unwise.

wish VERB = **want**, desire, long for, hope for, yearn for, pine for, have a fancy for, fancy, crave, hunger for, thirst for, lust after, covet, sigh for, set one's heart on, hanker after, have a yen for.
▶ NOUN = **desire**, liking, fondness, longing, hope, yearning, want, fancy, aspiration, inclination, urge, whim, craving, hunger, thirst, lust, hankering, yen.

wistful ADJ = **yearning**, longing, forlorn, disconsolate, melancholy, sad, mournful, dreamy, in a reverie, pensive, reflective, musing, contemplative, meditative.

wit NOUN **1** = **wittiness**, humour, jocularity, funniness, facetiousness, drollery, waggishness, repartee, badinage, banter, raillery.
2 = **humorist**, wag, funny person, comic, jokester, banterer; [inf] card.

witch NOUN = **sorceress**, enchantress, magician, necromancer, hex.

witchcraft NOUN = **witchery**, sorcery, black art/magic, magic, necromancy, wizardry, occultism, the occult, sortilege, thaumaturgy, wonder-working.

withdraw VERB **1** = **take back**, pull back, take away, extract, remove.
2 = **retract**, take back, recall, unsay. **3** = **revoke**, annul, nullify, declare void, rescind, repeal, abrogate. **4** = **pull back**, fall back, retire, retreat, disengage, back down,

depart, go, leave; [inf] make oneself scarce. **Opposites:** insert, enter.

withdrawn ADJ = **retiring**, reserved, uncommunicative, unforthcoming, unsociable, taciturn, silent, quiet, introverted, detached, aloof, self-contained, distant, private, shrinking, timid, timorous, shy, bashful, diffident. **Opposites:** outgoing.

wither VERB **1** = **dry up/out**, shrivel, go limp, wilt, die. **2** = **decline**, fade, ebb, wane, disintegrate, die, perish. **Opposites:** thrive.

withhold VERB **1** = **hold back**, keep back, restrain, hold/keep in check, check, curb, repress, suppress. **2** = **refuse to give/grant/allow**, refuse, decline, keep back.

withstand VERB = **hold out against**, stand up to, stand firm against, resist, fight, combat, oppose, endure, stand, tolerate, bear, put up with, take, cope with, weather, brave.

witness NOUN = **eyewitness**, observer, spectator, onlooker, looker-on, viewer, watcher, beholder, bystander. ▶ VERB = **see**, observe, view, watch, look on at, behold, perceive, be present at, attend.

witticism NOUN = **witty remark**, clever saying, flash of wit, bon mot, quip, sally, pleasantry, riposte, joke, jest, epigram; [inf] wisecrack, crack, one-liner.

witty ADJ = **clever**, original, ingenious, sparkling, scintillating, humorous, amusing, jocular, funny, facetious, droll, waggish, comic.

wizard NOUN = **sorcerer**, warlock, enchanter, witch, necromancer, magician, magus.

wizened ADJ = **withered**, shrivelled, dried up, shrunken, wasted, wrinkled, lined, gnarled, worn.

wobble VERB **1** = **rock**, sway, see-saw, teeter,

W

shake, vibrate. **2 = teeter**, totter, stagger, waddle, waggle.

woe NOUN **1 = misery**, wretchedness, misfortune, disaster, grief, anguish, affliction, suffering, pain, agony, torment, sorrow, sadness, unhappiness, distress, heartache, heartbreak, despondency, desolation, dejection, depression, gloom, melancholy. **2 = trouble**, misfortune, adversity, trial, tribulation, ordeal, burden, affliction, suffering, disaster, calamity, catastrophe. **Opposites:** joy.

woebegone ADJ **= miserable**, sad, unhappy, sorrowful, disconsolate, mournful, downcast, dejected, doleful, desolate, depressed, despairing, tearful. **Opposites:** cheerful.

woeful ADJ **1 = sad**, saddening, unhappy, sorrowful, miserable, dismal, wretched, doleful, gloomy, tragic, pathetic, grievous, pitiful, plaintive, heart-rending, heartbreaking, distressing, anguished, agonizing, dreadful, terrible. **2 = poor**, bad, inadequate, substandard, lamentable, deplorable, disgraceful, wretched, disappointing, feeble; [inf] rotten, lousy, shocking; [Brit. inf] duff. **Opposites:** cheerful, excellent.

woman NOUN **1 = female**, lady, girl, member of the fair/gentle sex; [inf] chick; [Brit. inf] bird; [N. Amer. inf] dame, broad. **2 = girlfriend**, lady-love, sweetheart, partner, lover, wife, spouse.

wonder NOUN **1 = wonderment**, awe, surprise, astonishment, amazement, bewilderment, stupefaction, fascination, admiration. **2 = marvel**, phenomenon, miracle, prodigy, curiosity, rarity, nonpareil, sight, spectacle. ▸ VERB **1 = think**, speculate, conjecture, ponder,

meditate, reflect, deliberate, muse, ask oneself, puzzle, be curious about, be inquisitive about.
2 = **marvel**, stand amazed, stand in awe, be dumbfounded, gape, stare, goggle, look agog; [inf] be flabbergasted, gawk, boggle.

wonderful ADJ
= **marvellous**, awe-inspiring, awesome, remarkable, extraordinary, phenomenal, prodigious, miraculous, amazing, astonishing, astounding, surprising, incredible, unprecedented, unparalleled, unheard of; [poetic/literary] wondrous.
= *See also* **excellent**.
Opposites: dreadful.

wonted ADJ = **customary**, accustomed, habitual, usual, normal, routine, regular, common, frequent, familiar, conventional.

woo VERB **1** = **pay court to**, seek someone's hand, pursue, chase after; [dated] court, set one's cap at. **2** = **importune**, press, urge, entreat, beg, implore, supplicate, solicit, coax, wheedle.

wood NOUN **1** = **forest**, woodland, copse, thicket, coppice, grove.
2 = **timber**, firewood, kindling; [N. Amer.] lumber.

wooded ADJ = **woody**, forested, tree-covered, tree-clad, timbered, sylvan.

wooden ADJ **1** = **made of wood**, wood, woody, timber. **2** = **stiff**, stolid, stodgy, expressionless, graceless, inelegant, ungainly, gauche, awkward, clumsy, maladroit.
3 = **expressionless**, inexpressive, blank, deadpan, empty, vacant, vacuous, glassy, impassive, lifeless, spiritless, unanimated, emotionless, unemotional, unresponsive.

woolly ADJ **1** = **woollen**, made of wool, wool.
2 = **fleecy**, fluffy, shaggy, hairy, furry. **3** = **vague**,

hazy, indefinite,
muddled, confused,
disorganized.

word NOUN **1** = **term**,
expression, name.
2 = **word of honour**,
promise, pledge,
assurance, guarantee,
undertaking, vow, oath.
3 = **news**, intimation,
notice, communication,
information, intelligence,
message, report, account.
▶ VERB = **express**, phrase,
couch, put, say, utter,
state.

wordy ADJ = **long-winded**,
verbose, loquacious,
garrulous, voluble,
prolix, protracted,
discursive, diffuse,
rambling, digressive,
maundering,
tautological, pleonastic.

work NOUN **1** = **effort**,
exertion, labour, toil,
slog, sweat, drudgery,
trouble, industry;
[inf] grind, elbow grease;
[poetic/literary] travail.
2 = **task**, job, chore,
undertaking, duty,
charge, assignment,
commission, mission.
3 = **employment**,

occupation, business,
job, profession, career,
trade, vocation, calling,
craft, line, field, métier,
pursuit.
Opposites: leisure.
▶ VERB **1** = **be employed**,
have a job, hold down a
job, earn one's living, do
business, follow/ply one's
trade. **2** = **exert oneself**,
put in effort, make
efforts, labour, toil, slog,
sweat, drudge, slave;
[inf] grind, plug away,
knock oneself out.
3 = **operate**, control,
drive, manage, direct,
use, handle, manipulate,
manoeuvre, ply, wield.
4 = **go**, operate, function,
perform, run.
5 = **succeed**, be
successful, have success,
go well, be effective, be
effectual.
Opposites: rest, fail.

workable ADJ
= **practicable**, practical,
viable, doable, feasible,
possible.
Opposites: impracticable.

worker NOUN = **employee**,
hand, workman, working
man/woman/person,

blue-collar worker, white-collar worker, labourer, artisan, craftsman, craftswoman, wage-earner, proletarian.

working ADJ 1 = **in work**, employed, in a job, waged. 2 = **functioning**, operating, going, running, in working order.
Opposites: unemployed, broken.

workmanship NOUN = **craftsmanship**, craft, artistry, art, handicraft, handiwork, expertise, skill, technique, work.

workshop NOUN 1 = **factory**, plant, mill, garage. 2 = **workroom**, studio, atelier, shop. 3 = **seminar**, study/discussion group, class.

world NOUN 1 = **earth**, globe, sphere, planet. 2 = **society**, sector, section, group, division.

worldly ADJ 1 = **earthly**, secular, temporal, material, materialistic, human, carnal, fleshly, corporeal, physical. 2 = **worldly-wise**, experienced, knowing, sophisticated, cosmopolitan, urbane.
Opposites: spiritual, naive.

worldwide ADJ = **universal**, global, international, pandemic, general, ubiquitous, extensive, widespread, far-reaching, wide-ranging.
Opposites: local.

worn ADJ 1 = **worn out**, threadbare, tattered, in tatters, ragged, frayed, shabby, shiny. 2 = **haggard**, drawn, strained, careworn; [inf] done in, dog-tired, dead on one's feet, fit to drop, played out, bushed; [Brit. inf] knackered; [N. Amer. inf] pooped.

worried ADJ = **anxious**, disturbed, perturbed, troubled, bothered, distressed, concerned, upset, distraught, uneasy, ill at ease, disquieted, fretful, agitated, nervous, edgy, on edge, tense, overwrought, worked up, distracted, apprehensive, fearful, afraid, frightened; [inf] uptight;

w

[N. Amer. inf] antsy.
Opposites: carefree.

worry VERB **1 = be worried**, be anxious, fret, brood. **2 = make anxious**, disturb, trouble, bother, distress, upset, concern, disquiet, discompose, fret, agitate, unsettle. ▶NOUN **1 = anxiety**, disturbance, perturbation, trouble, bother, distress, concern, care, uneasiness, unease, disquiet, disquietude, fretfulness, agitation, edginess, tenseness, apprehension, fearfulness. **2 = nuisance**, pest, plague, trial, trouble, problem, irritation, irritant, vexation, thorn in one's flesh.

worsen VERB **1 = make worse**, aggravate, exacerbate, damage, intensify, increase, heighten. **2 = get/grow/become worse**, take a turn for the worse, deteriorate, degenerate, retrogress, decline, sink, slip, slide, go downhill. **Opposites:** improve.

worship NOUN = **reverence**, veneration, homage, respect, honour, adoration, devotion, praise, prayer, glorification, exaltation, extolment; [formal] laudation. ▶VERB **1 = revere**, venerate, pay homage to, honour, adore, praise, pray to, glorify, exalt, extol; [formal] laud. **2 = adore**, be devoted to, cherish, treasure, admire, adulate, idolize, hero-worship, lionize; [inf] be wild about.

worth NOUN **1 = financial value**, value, price, cost. **2 = value**, use, usefulness, advantage, benefit, service, gain, profit, avail, help, assistance, aid.

worthless ADJ **1 = valueless**, of little/no financial value; [inf] rubbishy, trashy. **2 = useless**, of no use, of no benefit, to no avail, futile, ineffective, ineffectual, pointless, nugatory. **3 = good-for-nothing**, useless, despicable, contemptible,

base, low, vile, corrupt, depraved; [inf] no-good, no-account.
Opposites: valuable, useful, worthwhile.

worthwhile ADJ = **worth it**, worth the effort, valuable, of value, useful, of use, beneficial, advantageous, helpful, profitable, gainful, productive, constructive, justifiable.

worthy ADJ = **virtuous**, good, moral, upright, righteous, honest, decent, honourable, respectable, reputable, trustworthy, reliable, irreproachable, blameless, unimpeachable, admirable, praiseworthy, laudable, commendable, deserving, meritorious.
Opposites: disreputable.
■ **worthy of** = **deserving**, meriting.

wound NOUN = **injury**, lesion, cut, graze, scratch, gash, laceration, tear, puncture, slash, sore.
▶ VERB = **cut**, graze, scratch, gash, lacerate, tear, puncture, pierce, stab, slash, injure, hurt,

damage, harm.

wrap VERB 1 = **envelop**, enfold, encase, enclose, cover, swathe, bundle up, swaddle. 2 = **wrap up**, parcel up, package, do up, tie up, gift-wrap.
▶ NOUN = **shawl**, stole, cloak, cape, mantle.

wrath NOUN = **anger**, rage, fury, annoyance, exasperation, high dudgeon, bad temper, ill humour, irritation, crossness, displeasure, irascibility; [poetic/ literary] ire.
Opposites: happiness.

wreathe VERB 1 = **cover**, envelop, festoon, garland, adorn, decorate. 2 = **twist**, wind, coil, twine, entwine, curl, spiral, wrap.

wreck NOUN 1 = **shipwreck**, sunken ship/vessel, derelict. 2 = **wrecking**, wreckage, destruction, devastation, ruination, ruin, demolition, smashing, shattering, disruption, disintegration, undoing.
▶ VERB 1 = **smash**, demolish, ruin, damage; [inf] write

w

off. **2 = destroy**, devastate, ruin, demolish, smash, shatter, disrupt, undo, spoil, mar, play havoc with.
3 = shipwreck, sink, capsize, run aground.

wreckage NOUN **= wreck**, debris, ruins, remains, remnants, fragments.

wrench VERB **= twist**, pull, tug, yank, wrest, jerk, tear, force.

wrest VERB **= twist**, wrench, pull, snatch, take away, remove.

wretch NOUN **1 = poor creature/soul/thing**, miserable creature, unfortunate, poor devil.
2 = scoundrel, villain, ruffian, rogue, rascal, reprobate, criminal, delinquent, miscreant; [inf] creep, jerk, louse, rat, swine, skunk; [inf, dated] rotter; [archaic] blackguard.

wretched ADJ
1 = miserable, unhappy, sad, broken-hearted, sorrowful, sorry, distressed, disconsolate, downcast, down, downhearted, dejected, crestfallen, cheerless, depressed, melancholy, gloomy, doleful, forlorn, woebegone, abject.
2 = poor, bad, substandard, low-quality, inferior, pathetic, worthless.
Opposites: cheerful, excellent.

wriggle VERB **= twist**, squirm, writhe, jiggle, wiggle, snake, crawl, slink.

wring VERB **1 = twist**, squeeze. **2 = extract**, force, coerce, exact, extort, wrest, wrench, screw.

wrinkle NOUN **= crease**, fold, pucker, gather, furrow, ridge, line, corrugation, crinkle, crumple, rumple.
▸VERB **= crease**, pucker, gather, furrow, line, corrugate, crumple, rumple.

write VERB **1 = write down**, put in writing, put in black and white, commit to paper, jot down, note, set down, take down, record, register, list, inscribe, scribble, scrawl.
2 = compose, draft,

create, pen, dash off.
- **write off** 1 = **forget about**, disregard, give up for lost, cancel, annul, nullify, wipe out, cross out, score out.
2 = **damage beyond repair**, wreck, smash, crash, destroy, demolish; [N. Amer. inf] total.

writer NOUN = **author**, wordsmith, penman, novelist, essayist, biographer, journalist, columnist, scriptwriter; [inf] scribbler, pen-pusher.

writhe VERB = **twist about**, twist and turn, roll about, squirm, wriggle, jerk, thrash, flail, toss, struggle.

writing NOUN
1 = **handwriting**, hand, penmanship, script, print, calligraphy, scribble, scrawl. 2 = **work**, opus, book, volume, publication, composition.

wrong ADJ 1 = **incorrect**, inaccurate, in error, erroneous, wide of the mark, mistaken, inexact, imprecise, unsound, faulty, false; [inf] off beam, barking up the wrong tree, off target.
2 = **unsuitable**, inappropriate, inapt, inapposite, undesirable, infelicitous. 3 = **immoral**, bad, wicked, evil, unlawful, illegal, illicit, lawless, criminal, delinquent, felonious, dishonest, dishonourable, corrupt, unethical, sinful, iniquitous, blameworthy, culpable; [inf] crooked.
4 = **amiss**, awry, out of order, not right, faulty, defective.
Opposites: right.
▶ NOUN 1 = **badness**, immorality, sin, sinfulness, wickedness, evil, iniquity, unlawfulness, crime, dishonesty, dishonour, injustice, transgression, abuse; [inf] crookedness.
2 = **misdeed**, offence, injury, crime, infringement, infraction, injustice, grievance, outrage, atrocity.
Opposites: right.
▶ VERB 1 = **abuse**, mistreat, maltreat, harm, hurt, do injury to.

w

2 = **misrepresent**, malign, dishonour, impugn, vilify, defame, slander, libel, denigrate, insult; [inf] bad-mouth.

wrongdoer NOUN
= **lawbreaker**, criminal, delinquent, culprit, offender, felon, villain, miscreant, evil-doer, sinner, transgressor, malefactor; [inf] wrong 'un.

wrongful ADJ = **unfair**, unjust, improper, unjustified, unwarranted, unlawful, illegal, illegitimate, illicit.

wry ADJ 1 = **twisted**, distorted, contorted, crooked, lopsided, askew.
2 = **ironic**, sardonic, mocking, sarcastic, dry, droll, witty, humorous.

W

Yy

yank VERB = **pull**, tug, jerk, wrench.
▶ NOUN = **pull**, jerk, wrench.

yardstick NOUN = **measure**, standard, gauge, scale, guide, guideline, touchstone, criterion, benchmark, model, pattern.

yarn NOUN 1 = **thread**, fibre, strand. 2 = **story**, tale, anecdote, fable, traveller's tale; [inf] tall tale/story, cock and bull story.

yawning ADJ = **wide**, wide open, gaping, cavernous.

yearly ADJ = **annual**, once a year, every year.

yearn VERB = **long**, pine, have a longing, crave, desire, want, wish for, hanker after, covet, fancy, hunger for, thirst for; [inf] have a yen for.

yell VERB = **shout**, cry out, howl, scream, shriek, screech, squeal, roar, bawl, whoop; [inf] holler.

yes ADV = **all right**, of course, by all means, sure, certainly, in the affirmative; [inf] yeah, yah, yep, uh-huh; [Brit. inf] righto.
Opposites: no.

yield VERB 1 = **give**, return, bring in, fetch, earn, net, produce, supply, provide, generate, furnish. 2 = **give up**, surrender, relinquish, part with, deliver up, turn over, give over, remit, cede, renounce, resign, abdicate, forgo. 3 = **admit/concede defeat**, surrender, capitulate, submit, lay down one's arms, give in, give up the struggle, succumb, raise/show the white flag, throw in the towel/

sponge, cave in.
Opposites: withhold, resist.

yoke NOUN **1 = harness**, collar, coupling.
2 = oppression, tyranny, enslavement, slavery, servitude, bondage, thrall.

yokel NOUN **= rustic**, countryman, countrywoman, peasant, country bumpkin, provincial; [N. Amer. inf] hayseed, hillbilly.

young ADJ **1 = youthful**, juvenile, junior, adolescent, in the springtime of life, in one's salad days. **2 = new**, recent, undeveloped, fledgling, in the making.

Opposites: old.

youngster NOUN **= young adult/person**, youth, juvenile, teenager, adolescent, lad, boy, young man/woman, girl; [Scottish & N. English] lass; [inf] kid, shaver, young 'un.

youth NOUN **1 = young days**, early years, teens, early life, adolescence, boyhood, girlhood.
2 = boy, young man, lad, youngster, juvenile, teenager, adolescent; [inf] kid.

youthful ADJ **= young**, active, vigorous, spry, sprightly.
Opposites: old.

y

Zz

zany ADJ = **eccentric**, peculiar, odd, ridiculous, absurd, comic, clownish, madcap, funny, amusing, weird; [inf] screwy, wacky; [Brit. inf] daft; [N. Amer. inf] kooky.
Opposites: conventional.

zeal NOUN 1 = **ardour**, fervour, fervency, passion, fire, devotion, vehemence, intensity, enthusiasm, eagerness, keenness, earnestness, vigour, energy, verve, gusto, zest, fanaticism; [inf] zing. 2 = **zealotry**, fanaticism, extremism.
Opposites: apathy.

zealot NOUN = **enthusiast**, fanatic, extremist, radical, militant, bigot.

zealous ADJ = **ardent**, fervent, fervid, passionate, impassioned, devoted, intense, enthusiastic, eager, keen, earnest, vigorous, energetic, zestful, fanatical.
Opposites: apathetic.

zenith NOUN = **highest/high point**, crowning point, height, top, acme, peak, pinnacle, climax, prime, meridian, apex, apogee, vertex.
Opposites: nadir.

zero NOUN 1 = **nought**, nothing, cipher.
2 = **nothing**, naught, nil; [inf] zilch, not a sausage.
■ **zero in on** = **focus on**, centre on, concentrate on, home in on, pinpoint.

zest NOUN 1 = **relish**, gusto, enthusiasm, eagerness, zeal, vigour, liveliness, energy, enjoyment, joy, delectation, appetite; [inf] zing, oomph.
2 = **piquancy**, spice,

pungency, flavour, relish, tang, savour, interest.

zone NOUN = **area**, sector, section, belt, district, region, province.

zoom VERB = **fly**, buzz, rush, dash, pelt, race, tear, shoot, scurry, speed, hurry, hasten, whizz, hare, zip, zap.

Collective names for animals and birds

Many of these are fanciful or humorous terms which probably never had any real currency but were popularized by antiquarian writers, notably Joseph Strutt in *Sports and Pastimes of England* (1801).

a shrewdness of **apes**
a herd or pace of **asses**
a troop of **baboons**
a cete of **badgers**
a sloth of **bears**
a swarm, drift, hive, or erst of **bees**
a flock, flight, or pod of **birds**
a herd, gang, or obstinacy of **buffalo**
a bellowing of **bullfinches**
a drove of **bullocks**
a clowder or glaring of **cats**
an army of **caterpillars**
a herd or drove of **cattle**
a brood, clutch, or peep of **chickens**
a chattering of **choughs**
a rag or rake of **colts**
a covert of **coots**
a herd of **cranes**
a bask of **crocodiles**
a murder of **crows**
a litter of **cubs**
a herd of **curlew**
a herd or mob of **deer**
a pack or kennel of **dogs**

a school of **dolphins**

a trip of **dotterel** (a type of bird)

a flight, dole, or piteousness of **doves**

a paddling of **ducks** (on water)

a safe of **ducks** (on land)

a fling of **dunlin**

a herd or parade of **elephants**

a herd or gang of **elk**

a busyness of **ferrets**

a charm of **finches**

a shoal or run of **fish**

a swarm or cloud of **flies**

a skulk of **foxes**

a gaggle of **geese** (on land)

a skein, team, or wedge of **geese** (in flight)

a herd of **giraffe**

a cloud of **gnats**

a flock, herd, or trip of **goats**

a band of **gorillas**

a pack or covey of **grouse**

a down, mute, or husk of **hares**

a cast of **hawks**

a siege of **herons**

a bloat of **hippopotami**

a drove, string, stud, or team of **horses**

a pack, cry, or kennel of **hounds**

a flight or swarm of **insects**

a fluther or smack of **jellyfish**

a mob or troop of **kangaroos**

a litter or kindle of **kittens**

a desert of **lapwings**

a bevy or exaltation of **larks**

a leap of **leopards**

a pride or sawt of **lions**
a tiding of **magpies**
a sord or suit of **mallard**
a stud of **mares**
a richesse of **martens**
a labour of **moles**
a troop of **monkeys**
a span or barren of **mules**
a watch of **nightingales**
a parliament or stare of **owls**
a yoke of **oxen**
a pandemonium of **parrots**
a covey of **partridges**
a muster of **peacocks**
a muster, parcel, or rookery of **penguins**
a bevy or head of **pheasants**
a kit of **pigeons** (in flight)
a litter or herd of **pigs**
a congregation, stand, or wing of **plovers**
a rush or flight of **pochards**
a pod, school, herd, or turmoil of **porpoises**
a covey of **ptarmigan**
a litter of **pups**
a bevy or drift of **quail**
a bury of **rabbits**
a string of **racehorses**
an unkindness of **ravens**
a crash of **rhinoceros**
a bevy of roe **deer**
a parliament, building, or rookery of **rooks**
a hill of **ruffs**
a pod, herd, or rookery of **seals**
a flock, herd, trip, or mob of **sheep**

a dopping of **sheldrake**
a wisp or walk of **snipe**
a host of **sparrows**
a murmuration of **starlings**
a flight of **swallows**
a game or herd of **swans** (on land)
a wedge of **swans** (in flight)
a drift, herd, or sounder of **swine**
a spring of **teal**
a knot of **toads**
a hover of **trout**
a rafter of **turkeys**
a bale or turn of **turtles**
a bunch or knob of **waterfowl**
a school, herd, pod, or gam of **whales**
a company or trip of **wigeon**
a sounder of **wild boar**
a dout or destruction of **wild cats**
a team of **wild ducks** (in flight)
a bunch, trip, plump, or knob of **wildfowl**
a pack or rout of **wolves**
a fall of **woodcock**
a descent of **woodpeckers**
a herd of **wrens**
a zeal of **zebras**

Games and puzzles wordbuilder

These words can be particularly useful to players of word games. Proper names are excluded, as are abbreviations that are not pronounced as they are spelt, such as *Dr* and *Mr*, since they are not allowed in most games.

Two-letter words

aa: rough lava containing cinders

ab: an abdominal muscle

ad: an advertisement

ag: [S. African] expressing various emotions, e.g. irritation, grief, or pleasure

ah: expressing surprise, sympathy, pleasure, etc.

ai: the three-toed sloth

am: the present tense of *be*

an: a form of the indefinite article

as: used to refer to extent or amount

at: expressing location or time

aw: expressing mild protest, entreaty, etc.

ba: (in Egyptian mythology) the soul

be: exist

bi: bisexual

bo: a kind of fig tree

by: beside

da: your father

DJ: a disc jockey

do: perform (an action)

dy: a type of sediment

eh: seeking explanation or agreement

El: an elevated railway or section of railway

em: a measuring unit in printing

en: a measuring unit in printing

er: expressing doubt or hesitation

ex: a former spouse or partner

fa: a musical note

Ga: a member of a people living in Ghana

GI: a soldier in the US army

go: move or travel

ha: expressing surprise, triumph, etc.

he: a male person or animal previously mentioned

hi: used as a greeting

ho: expressing surprise, triumph, etc.

id: a part of the mind

if: introducing a conditional clause

in: within

io: a North American moth

is: the present tense of *be*

it: a thing previously mentioned

ja: [S. African] yes

jo: [Scottish, archaic] a sweetheart

Ju: a kind of Chinese pottery

ka: (in Egyptian mythology) the spirit

ki: a plant of the lily family

KO: a knockout in a boxing match

la: a musical note

li: a Chinese unit of distance

Io: [archaic] used to draw attention to something

ma: your mother

MD: [Brit.] a managing director

me: myself

mi: a musical note

mo: a moment

MP: a Member of Parliament

mu: the 12th letter of the Greek alphabet

my: belonging to me

no: not any

nu: the 13th letter of the Greek alphabet

ob: a type of gene

od: a power once thought to pervade the natural world

of: belonging to

og: [Austral., archaic] a shilling

oh: expressing surprise, anger, disappointment, etc.

oi: used to attract attention

OK: used to express assent, agreement, etc.

om: a mystic syllable which constitutes a sacred mantra

on: supported by or covering

op: an operation

or: used to link alternatives

os: a bone

ou: a Hawaiian bird

ow: expressing pain

ox: a cow or bull

oy: = oi

Oz: Australia

pa: your father

pi: the 16th letter of the Greek alphabet

po: a chamber pot

qi: (in Chinese philosophy) the life force

ra: (in Norway and Sweden) a moraine

re: a musical note

ri: a Japanese unit of length

se: a Chinese musical instrument

si: = te

so: therefore

ta: thank you

te: a musical note

ti: = te

TV: television

uh: expressing hesitation

um: expressing hesitation

up: towards a higher position

us: myself and others

Wa: a member of a people living on the borders of China and Burma

we: myself and others

Wu: a dialect of Chinese

xi: the 14th letter of the Greek alphabet

xu: a unit of money in Vietnam

ye: [archaic] the plural form of *thou*

Yi: a people living in parts of China

yo: used as a greeting

yu: an ancient Chinese wine container

Words containing *q* not followed by *u*

qadi: a Muslim judge

qanat: an irrigation tunnel

qasida: an Arabic or Persian poem

qawwal: a qawwali singer

qawwali: Muslim devotional music

qi: (in Chinese philosophy) the life force

qibla: the direction towards Mecca

qigong: a Chinese system of physical exercises

qin: a Chinese musical instrument

qintar: a unit of money in Albania

qiviut: wool from the musk ox

qwerty: the standard layout of typewriters and keyboards

tariqa: the Sufi method of spiritual learning

Words beginning with x

xanthan: a polysaccharide

xanthate: a chemical compound

xanthene: a chemical compound

xanthic: yellowish

xanthin: a yellow colouring matter

xanthine: a biochemical compound

xanthoma: a yellow patch on the skin

xebec: a sailing ship

xeme: a fork-tailed gull

xenia: gifts to a guest or guests

xenial: relating to hospitality

xenon: a gas

xeric: very dry

xeroma: abnormal dryness of a body part

xerox: to photocopy

Xhosa: a South African people or their language

xi: the 14th letter of the Greek alphabet

xiphoid: sword-shaped

Xmas: Christmas

xoanon: a wooden image of a god

xography: a photographic process

xu: a unit of money in Vietnam

xylan: a compound found in wood

xylary: of or relating to xylem

xylem: plant tissue

xylene: a liquid hydrocarbon

xylite: a volatile liquid

xylol: = xylene

xylose: a plant sugar

xyrid: a sedge-like herb
xyster: a surgical instrument
xyston: an ancient Greek spear

xystus: an ancient Greek portico

Wedding anniversaries

Year	Name		Year	Name
1st	Paper		13th	Lace
2nd	Cotton		14th	Ivory
3rd	Leather		15th	Crystal
4th	Linen (Silk)		20th	China
5th	Wood		25th	Silver
6th	Iron		30th	Pearl
7th	Wool (Copper)		35th	Coral (Jade)
8th	Bronze		40th	Ruby
9th	Pottery (China)		45th	Sapphire
10th	Tin (Aluminium)		50th	Gold
11th	Steel		55th	Emerald
12th	Silk		60th	Diamond

Symbols and punctuation marks

,	comma	−	minus; negative
.	full stop; point	×	multiplication sign; by (in measurements)
;	semi-colon	÷	division sign
:	colon	=	equals
'	apostrophe	:	ratio
' '	single quotation marks	>	greater than
" "	double quotation marks	<	less than
		⩾	greater than or equal to
!	exclamation mark	⩽	less than or equal to
?	question mark	≠	is not equal to
( )	brackets; parentheses	≈	is approximately equal to
[ ]	square brackets		
{ }	braces	√	square root
/	solidus; oblique; slash	°	degree
\	backslash	∞	infinity
#	hash; number (N. Amer.)	'	prime; minute(s) of arc; foot/feet
%	percent	"	double prime; second(s) of arc; inch(es)
∴	therefore		
∵	because	£	pound sterling
"	ditto	$	dollar
&	ampersand	€	euro
&c.	et cetera	©	copyright
@	at or per	♂	male
§	section	♀	female
~	swung dash	○	new moon
...	ellipsis	☽	moon, first quarter
¶	paragraph	●	full moon
+	plus; positive	☾	moon, last quarter

Roman numerals

1	I	15	XV	100	C
2	II	16	XVI	101	CI
3	III	17	XVII	144	CXLIV
4	IV	18	XVIII	200	CC
5	V	19	XIX	400	CD (or CCCC)
6	VI	20	XX	500	D
7	VII	21	XXI	900	CM (or DCCCC)
8	VIII	30	XXX	1000	M
9	IX	40	XL	1900	MCM (or MDCCCC)
10	X	50	L	1995	MCMXCV
11	XI	60	LX	1999	MCMXCIX
12	XII	70	LXX	2000	MM
13	XIII	80	LXXX	2001	MMI
14	XIV	90	XC	2002	MMII

The phonetic alphabet

This alphabet was devised by NATO in the mid 1950s, and represents a development of earlier systems in use in the British and American armed forces. Approved by aviation and telecommunications bodies, it is now in widespread use in the English-speaking world.

A	Alpha	H	Hotel	O	Oscar	V	Victor
B	Bravo	I	India	P	Papa	W	Whisky
C	Charlie	J	Juliet	Q	Quebec	X	X-ray
D	Delta	K	Kilo	R	Romeo	Y	Yankee
E	Echo	L	Lima	S	Sierra	Z	Zulu
F	Foxtrot	M	Mike	T	Tango		
G	Golf	N	November	U	Uniform